Financial Aid
for Hispanic Americans
2006-2008

RSP FINANCIAL AID DIRECTORIES
OF INTEREST TO MINORITIES

College Student's Guide to Merit and Other No-Need Funding, 2005-2007
Selected as one of the "Outstanding Titles of the Year" by *Choice,* this directory describes 1,300 no-need funding opportunities for college students. 464 pages. ISBN 1-58841-102-8. $32.50, plus $6 shipping.

Directory of Financial Aids for Women, 2005-2007
Nearly 1,500 funding programs set aside for women are described in this biennial directory, which *School Library Journal* calls "the cream of the crop." 528 pages. ISBN 1-58841-131-1. $45, plus $6 shipping.

Financial Aid for African Americans, 2006-2008
Nearly 1,400 scholarships, fellowships, grants, and internships open to African Americans are described in this award-winning directory. 542 pages. ISBN 1-58841-133-8. $40, plus $6 shipping.

Financial Aid for Asian Americans, 2006-2008
This is the source to use if you are looking for financial aid for Asian Americans; more than 1,000 funding opportunities are described. 402 pages. ISBN 1-58841-134-6. $37.50, plus $6 shipping.

Financial Aid for Hispanic Americans, 2006-2008
More than 1,200 funding programs open to Americans of Mexican, Puerto Rican, Central American, or other Latin American heritage are described here. 484 pages. ISBN 1-58841-135-4. $40, plus $6 shipping.

Financial Aid for Native Americans, 2006-2008
Detailed information is provided on 1,400 funding opportunities open to American Indians, Native Alaskans, and Native Pacific Islanders. 562 pages. ISBN 1-58841-136-2. $42.50, plus $6 shipping.

Financial Aid for Research and Creative Activities Abroad, 2005-2007
Described here are 1,000 scholarships, fellowships, grants, etc. available to support research, professional, or creative activities abroad. 278 pages. ISBN 1-58841-107-9. $45, plus $6 shipping.

Financial Aid for Study and Training Abroad, 2005-2007
This directory, which *Children's Bookwatch* calls "invaluable," describes nearly 1,000 financial aid opportunities available to support study abroad. 358 pages. ISBN 1-58841-094-3. $39.50, plus $5 shipping.

Financial Aid for the Disabled and Their Families, 2006-2008
Named one of the "Best Reference Books of the Year" by *Library Journal,* this directory describes in detail more than 1,200 funding opportunities. 502 pages. ISBN 1-58841-148-6. $40, plus $6 shipping.

Financial Aid for Veterans, Military Personnel, and Their Dependents, 2006-2008
According to *Reference Book Review,* this directory (with its 1,100 entries) is "the most comprehensive guide available on the subject." 443 pages. ISBN 1-58841-143-5. $40, plus $6 shipping.

High School Senior's Guide to Merit and Other No-Need Funding, 2005-2007
Here's your guide to 1,100 funding programs that *never* look at income level when making awards to college-bound high school seniors. 416 pages. ISBN 1-58841-100-1. $29.95, plus $5 shipping.

How to Pay for Your Degree in Education & Related Fields, 2006-2008
Here's hundreds of funding opportunities to support undergraduate and graduate students preparing for a career in teaching, guidance, etc. 222 pages. ISBN 1-58841-146-X. $30, plus $6 shipping.

Money for Christian College Students, 2005-2007
This is the only directory to describe nearly 800 funding opportunities available to support Christian students working on an undergraduate or graduate degree (secular or religious). 238 pages. ISBN 1-58841-118-4. $30, plus $6 shipping.

Money for Graduate Students in the Social & Behavioral Sciences, 2005-2007
Described here are the 1,100 biggest and best funding opportunities available to students working on a graduate degree in the social or behavioral sciences. 332 pages. ISBN 1-58841-141-9. $42.50, plus $6 shipping.

RSP Funding for Nursing Students, 2006-2008
You'll find 500+ scholarships, fellowships, loans, grants, and awards here that can be used for study, research, professional, or other nursing activities. 198 pages. ISBN 1-58841-157-5. $30, plus $6 shipping.

Financial Aid for Hispanic Americans 2006-2008

Gail Ann Schlachter
R. David Weber

A List of Scholarships, Fellowships, Loans, Grants, Awards, and Internships Open Primarily or Exclusively to Hispanic Americans and a Set of Six Indexes (Program Title, Sponsoring Organizations, Residency, Tenability, Subject, and Deadline Date)

Reference Service Press
El Dorado Hills, California
2006

ISBN: 1-58841-135-4

10 9 8 7 6 5 4 3 2 1

Reference Service Press (RSP) began in 1977 with a single financial aid publication *(The Directory of Financial Aids for Women)* and now specializes in the development of financial aid resources in multiple formats, including books, large print books, disks, CD-ROMs, print-on-demand reports, eBooks, and online sources. Long recognized as a leader in the field, RSP has been called, by the *Simba Report on Directory Publishing,* "a true success in the world of independent directory publishers." Both Kaplan Educational Centers and Military.com have hailed RSP as "the leading authority on scholarships."

Reference Service Press
El Dorado Hills Business Park
5000 Windplay Drive, Suite 4
El Dorado Hills, CA 95762
　　(916) 939-9620
　　Fax: (916) 939-9626
　　E-mail: info@rspfunding.com
Visit our web site: www.rspfunding.com

Manufactured in the United States of America
Price: $40.00, plus $6 shipping.

ACADEMIC INSTITUTIONS, LIBRARIES, ORGANIZATIONS AND OTHER QUANTITY BUYERS:
Discounts on this book are available for bulk purchases. Write or call for information on our discount programs.

Contents

Introduction

PURPOSE OF THE DIRECTORY

Despite the recent steps taken to curtail affirmative action and equal opportunity programs, the financial aid picture for minorities has never looked brighter. Currently, billions of dollars are set aside specifically for Hispanic Americans and other minorities. This funding is open to applicants at any level (high school through postdoctoral and professional) for study, research, travel, training, career development, or innovative effort.

While numerous directories have been prepared to identify and describe general financial aid programs (those open to all segments of society), they have never covered more than a small portion of the programs designed primarily or exclusively for minorities. Before *Financial Aid for Hispanic Americans* and its predecessor (*Directory of Financial Aids for Minorities*) were published, many advisors, librarians, scholars, researchers, and students were unaware of the extensive funding opportunities available to Hispanic Americans and other minorities. Now, with the ongoing publication of *Financial Aid for Hispanic Americans,* up-to-date and detailed information is available in a single volume about the special resources set aside for members of this group.

Financial Aid for Hispanic Americans is prepared biennially as part of Reference Service Press' four-volume *Minority Funding Set* (the other volumes cover funding for African Americans, Asian Americans, and Native Americans). Each of the volumes in this set is sold separately, or the complete set can be purchased at a discounted price (for more information contact Reference Service Press's marketing department).

No other source, in print or online, offers the coverage provided by these titles. That's why the Grantsmanship Center labeled the set "a must for every organization serving minorities" and *Reference Books Bulletin* selected each of the volumes in the *Minority Funding Set* as the "Editor's Choice." *Financial Aid for Hispanic Americans,* itself, has also received rave reviews. The National Chicano Council on Higher Education called it "a most necessary publication," it was chosen as a "Recommended Resource" by the Ventures Scholars Program, and *Vista: The Hispanic Magazine* pronounced it a "very comprehensive work." Perhaps *Reference Books Bulletin* sums up the critical reaction best: "accurate, comprehensive financial aid information in an easy to use, well arranged format."

EXTENT OF UPDATING IN THE 2006-2008 EDITION

The preparation of each new edition of *Financial Aid for Hispanic Americans* involves extensive updating and revision. To insure that the information included in the 2006-2008 edition of the directory is both reliable and current, the editors at Reference Service Press 1) reviewed and updated all relevant programs covered in the previous edition of the directory, 2) collected information on all programs open to Hispanic Americans that were added to Reference Service Press' funding database since the last edition of the directory, and then 3) searched extensively for new program leads in a variety of sources, including printed directories, news reports, journals, newsletters, house organs, annual reports, and sites on the Internet. Since all program descriptions included in the directory are written directly from information supplied by the sponsoring organizations (no information is ever taken from secondary sources), we contacted all sponsoring organizations identified in this process up to four times in writing and, if necessary, up to 3 times by telephone. Unfortunately, despite our best efforts, some sponsoring organizations failed to respond to our data requests; consequently, their programs are not included in this edition of the directory.

The 2006-2008 edition of *Financial Aid for Hispanic Americans* completely revises and updates the previous edition. Programs that have ceased operations have been dropped from the listing. Profiles of continuing programs have been rewritten to reflect operations in 2006-2008; more than 85 percent of the continuing programs reported substantive changes in their locations, requirements (particularly application deadline), benefits, or eligibility requirements since 2003. In addition, more than 375 new entries have been added to the program section of the directory. The resulting listing describes more than 1,200 scholarships, fellowships, loans, grants, awards, and internships.

WHAT MAKES THIS DIRECTORY UNIQUE?

The 2006-2008 edition of *Financial Aid for Hispanic Americans* will help Hispanic Americans (persons whose origins are from Mexico, Central America, Puerto Rico, Cuba, or other Latin American countries) tap into the billions of dollars available to them, as minorities, to support study, research, creative activities, past accomplishments, future projects, professional development, work experience, and many other activities. The listings cover every major subject area, are sponsored by more than 900 different private and public agencies and organizations, and are open to Hispanic Americans at any level, from college-bound high school students through professionals and postdoctorates.

In addition to its extensive and focused coverage, *Financial Aid for Hispanic Americans* offers several other unique features. Covered here are hundreds of funding opportunities not listed in any other source (so even if you have checked other directories, you will want to look through the listings here). Unlike other funding directories, which generally follow a straight alphabetical arrangement, this one groups entries by type (scholarships, grants, awards, etc.), making it easy to search for appropriate programs. The same convenience is offered in the indexes, where title, organization, geographic, subject, and deadline date entries are each subdivided by type of funding. Finally, we have tried to anticipate all the ways you might wish to search for funding. The volume is organized so you can identify programs not only by type, but by specific subject, sponsoring organization, program title, residency requirements, where the money can be spent, and even deadline date. Plus, we've included all the information you'll need to decide if a program is right for you: purpose, eligibility requirements, financial data, duration, special features, limitations, number awarded, and application date. You even get fax numbers, toll-free numbers, e-mail addresses, and web sites (when available), along with complete contact information.

ARRANGEMENT OF THE DIRECTORY

Financial Aid for Hispanic Americans is divided into two sections: 1) a descriptive list of funding opportunities open to Hispanic Americans and 2) a set of six indexes.

Financial Aid Programs Open to Hispanic Americans. The first section of the directory describes 1,210 funding opportunities open to Hispanic Americans. The programs described here are sponsored by more than 900 different government agencies, professional organizations, corporations, sororities and fraternities, foundations, religious groups, educational associations, and military/veterans organizations. All areas of the sciences, social sciences, and humanities are covered.

Entries in this section are grouped into the following six categories, to help you in your search for a specific kind of financial assistance (e.g., a scholarship for undergraduate study, a grant for independent research, an award for outstanding literary achievement):

> *Scholarships:* Programs that support studies at the undergraduate level in the United States. Usually no return of service or repayment is required. For information on funding for research on the undergraduate level, see the Grants category below.

> *Fellowships:* Programs that support studies at the graduate level in the United States, including work on a master's degree, doctorate, professional degree (e.g., law, medicine), or specialist's cer-

tificate. Usually no return of service or repayment is required. For information on funding for research on the graduate level, see the Grants category below.

Loans: Programs that provide money that eventually must be repaid—in cash or in service and with or without interest. Forgivable loans (along with scholarship/loans and loans-for-service) are also described in this part of the directory.

Grants: Programs that provide funds to support Hispanic Americans' innovative efforts, travel, projects, creative activities, or research on any level (from undergraduate to postdoctorate, professional, or other). In some cases, proposals must be submitted by institutions or organizations only; in others, individual minority group members may submit proposals directly.

Awards: Competitions, prizes, and honoraria granted in recognition of Hispanic Americans' personal accomplishments, professional contributions, or public service. Prizes received solely as the result of entering contests are excluded.

Internships: Work experience programs for Hispanic American undergraduates, graduate students, and recent graduates. Only salaried positions are described.

Programs that supply more than one type of assistance are listed in all relevant subsections. For example, both undergraduate and graduate students may apply for the Association of Cuban Engineers Scholarships, so the program is described in both the scholarship and the fellowship subsections.

Entries in each subsection are arranged alphabetically by program title. Each program entry (see the sample entry on page 7) has been designed to provide a concise profile that includes information (when available) on program title, organization address and telephone numbers (including toll-free and fax numbers), e-mail addresses, web site, purpose, eligibility, money awarded, duration, special features, limitations, number of awards, and application deadline. The information reported for each of the programs in this section was supplied in response to research inquiries distributed through the first quarter of 2006. While this listing is intended to be as comprehensive as possible, some sponsoring organizations did not respond to our research requests and, consequently, are not included in this edition of the directory.

The focus of the directory is on "portable" (noninstitution-specific) programs open primarily or exclusively to Hispanic Americans or to minority pools that specifically include Hispanic Americans. Excluded from this listing are:

Awards for which American citizens would be ineligible: Programs open only to nationals from other countries (e.g., South American nations) are not covered.

Awards tenable only outside the United States: Since there are comprehensive and up-to-date directories that describe available funding for study and research abroad (see the list of Reference Service Press titles opposite the directory's title page), only programs that fund activities in the United States are covered here.

Minority programs that specifically exclude Hispanic Americans: Programs that are open to specific minority groups, but not to Hispanic Americans (e.g., programs only for Asian Americans), are excluded.

Programs that are open equally to all segments of the population: Only funding opportunities set aside primarily of exclusively for Hispanic Americans are included here.

Programs that offer small monetary awards: The emphasis here is on programs that offer significant compensation. If the maximum a program offers is less than the equivalent of $500 per year, it is not included in this listing.

Programs open to residents in a restricted geographic location: In general, programs are excluded if they are open only to the residents of a limited geographic area (anything below the state level).

Programs administered by individual academic institutions solely for their own students: The directory identifies "portable" programs—ones that can be used at any number of schools. Financial aid administered by individual schools specifically for their currently-enrolled students is not covered. Write directly to the schools you are considering to get information on their offerings.

Indexes. The six indexes included in *Financial Aid for Hispanic Americans* will help you target appropriate financial aid opportunities. Program Title, Sponsoring Organization, Residency, Tenability, Subject, and Calendar Indexes each follow a word-by-word alphabetical arrangement and pinpoint the entry numbers (not page numbers) that you should check.

Program Title Index. If you know the name of a particular funding program and want to find out where it is covered in the directory, use the Program Title Index. To assist you in your search, every program is listed by all its known names, former names, and abbreviations. Since one program can be included in several subsections (e.g., a program providing assistance to both undergraduate and graduate students is described in both the scholarships and the fellowships subsections), each entry number in the index has been coded to indicate program type (e.g., "F" = Fellowships; "A" = Awards). By using this coding system, you can avoid duplicate entries and turn directly to the programs that match your financial interests.

Sponsoring Organization Index. This index makes it easy to identify agencies that offer funding primarily or exclusively to Hispanic Americans. More than 900 organizations are indexed here. As in the Program Title Index, we've used a code to help you determine which organizations offer scholarships, fellowships, loans, grants, awards, and/or internships.

Residency Index. Some programs listed in this book are restricted to Hispanic Americans in a particular state or region. Others are open to Hispanic Americans wherever they live. This index helps you identify programs available only to residents in your area as well as programs that have no residency requirements. Further, to assist you in your search, we've also indicated the type of funding offered to residents in each of the areas listed in the index.

Tenability Index. This index identifies the geographic locations where the funding described in *Financial Aid for Hispanic Americans* may be used. Index entries (city, county, state, province, region, country, continent) are arranged alphabetically (word by word) and subdivided by program type. Use this index when you are looking for money to support your activities in a particular geographic area.

Subject Index. This index allows you to identify the subject focus of each of the financial aid opportunities described in *Financial Aid for Hispanic Americans*. More than 250 different subject terms are listed. Extensive "see" and "see also" references, as well as type-of-program subdivisions, will help you locate appropriate funding opportunities.

Calendar Index. Since most financial aid programs have specific deadline dates, some may have closed by the time you begin to look for funding. You can use the Calendar Index to determine which programs are still open. This index is arranged by program type (e.g., scholarship, loan, internship) and subdivided by month during which the deadline falls. Filing dates can and quite often do vary from year to year; consequently, this index should be used only as a guide for deadlines beyond 2008.

TIPS ON HOW TO USE THE DIRECTORY

To Locate Programs Offering a Particular Type of Assistance. If you are looking for programs offering a particular type of financial aid (e.g., a scholarship for undergraduate courses, a grant for independent research, an award for outstanding literary achievement), turn first to the definitions of the various program types on pages 4-5 in the Introduction and then browse through the entries in each of the appropriate categories in the first section of the directory (scholarships, fellowships, loans, grants, awards, or internships). Keep in mind that more than one of these subsections may contain funding leads for you. For example, if you are a graduate student looking for money to help you pay for the educational and research costs associated with your master's degree, you will not want to overlook the opportunities described in the fellowships, loans, grants, and even awards subsections. Note: since programs with multiple purposes are listed in every appropriate location, each of these subsections

SAMPLE ENTRY

(1) **[118]**

(2) **EL NUEVO CONSTRUCTOR SCHOLARSHIP PROGRAM**

(3) Hispanic College Fund
Attn: National Director
1717 Pennsylvania Avenue, N.W., Suite 460
Washington, D.C. 20006
(202) 296-5400   Toll-free: (800) 644-4223
Fax: (202) 296-3774
E-mail: hispaniccollegefund@earthlink.net
Web: www.hispanicfund.org

(4) **Purpose** To provide financial assistance to Hispanic American undergraduate students who are interested in preparing for a career in the construction industry.

(5) **Eligibility** This program is open to U.S. citizens of Hispanic background (at least 1 grandparent must be 100% Hispanic) who are entering their freshman, sophomore, junior, or senior year of college. Applicants must be working on a bachelor's or associate degree in a field related to construction and have a cumulative GPA of 3.0 or higher. They must be applying to or enrolled in a college or university in the 50 states or Puerto Rico as a full-time student. Financial need is considered in the selection process.

(6) **Financial data** Stipends range from $500 to $5,000, depending on the need of the recipient, and average approximately $3,000. Funds are paid directly to the recipient's college or university to help cover tuition and fees.

(7) **Duration** 1 year; recipients may reapply.

(8) **Additional information** This program is sponsored by *El Nuevo Constructor,* a Hanley Wood LLC publication. All applications must be submitted online; no paper applications are available.

(9) **Number awarded** Varies each year.

(10) **Deadline** April of each year.

DEFINITION

(1) **Entry number:** Consecutive number assigned to the funding profiles and used to index the entry.

(2) **Program title:** Title of scholarship, fellowship, loan, grant, award, or internship.

(3) **Sponsoring organization:** Name, address, and telephone number, toll-free number, fax number, e-mail address, and/or web site (when information was available) for organization sponsoring the program.

(4) **Purpose:** Identifies the major program requirements; read the rest of the entry for additional detail.

(5) **Eligibility:** Qualifications required of applicants, plus information on application procedure and selection process.

(6) **Financial data:** Financial details of the program, including fixed sum, average amount, or range of funds offered, expenses for which funds may and may not be applied, and cash-related benefits supplied (e.g., room and board).

(7) **Duration:** Period for which support is provided; renewal prospects.

(8) **Additional information:** Any unusual (generally nonmonetary) benefits, features, restrictions, or limitations associated with the program.

(9) **Number awarded:** Total number of recipients each year or other specified period.

(10) **Deadline:** The month by which applications must be submitted.

functions as a self-contained entity. As a result, you can browse through any of the subsections in the directory without first consulting an index.

To Locate a Particular Financial Aid Program.   If you know the name of a particular financial aid program, and the type of assistance offered by the program (scholarship, fellowship, grant, etc.), then go directly to the appropriate category in the first section of the directory, where you will find the program profiles arranged alphabetically by title. But be careful: program titles can be misleading. For example, the Bureau of Land Management Award is actually a scholarship, not an award, and the Reforma Scholarship is really a fellowship rather than a scholarship. So, if you are looking for a specific program and do not find it in the subsection you have checked, be sure to refer to the Program Title Index to see if it is covered elsewhere in the directory. To save time, always check the Program Title Index first if you know the name of a specific award but are not sure under which subsection it has been listed. Since we index each program by all its known names and abbreviations, you'll also be able to track down a program there when you only know the popular rather than official name.

To Locate Programs Sponsored by a Particular Organization.   The Sponsoring Organization Index makes it easy to identify agencies that provide financial assistance to Hispanic Americans or to identify specific financial aid programs offered by a particular organization. Each entry number in the index is coded to identify program type, so that you can easily target appropriate entries.

To Browse Quickly Through the Listings.   Turn to the type of funding that interests you (scholarships, fellowships, awards, etc.) and read the "Purpose" paragraph in each entry. In seconds, you'll know if this is an opportunity that you might want to pursue. If it is, be sure to read the rest of the information in the entry, to make sure you meet all of the program requirements before writing or going on the Internet for an application form. Please, save your time and energy. Don't apply if you don't qualify!

To Locate Funding Available to Hispanic Americans from or Tenable in a Particular City, County, or State.   The Residency Index identifies financial aid programs open to Hispanic Americans in a particular state, region, etc. The Tenability Index shows where the money can be spent. In both indexes, "see" and "see also" references are used liberally, and index entries for a particular geographic area are subdivided by type of program (scholarships, fellowships, loans, grants, awards, internships) to help you identify the funding that's right for you. When using these indexes, always check the listings under the term "United States," since the programs indexed there have no geographic restrictions and can be used in any area.

To Locate Financial Aid Programs Open to Hispanic Americans in a Particular Subject Area.   Turn to the Subject Index first if you are interested in identifying financial aid programs for Hispanic Americans in a particular subject area (more than 250 different subject fields are listed there). To facilitate your search, the type of funding available (scholarships, fellowships, loans, grants, awards, internships) is clearly labeled. Extensive cross-references are provided. As part of your search, be sure to check the listings in the index under the heading "General Programs;" those programs provide funding in any subject area (although they may be restricted in other ways).

To Locate Financial Aid Programs for Hispanic Americans by Deadline Date.   If you are working with specific time constraints and want to weed out the financial aid programs whose filing dates you won't be able to meet, turn first to the Calendar Index and check the program references listed under the appropriate program type and month. Keep in mind: not all sponsoring organizations supplied deadline information, so not all programs are indexed in this section. To identify every relevant financial aid program, regardless of filing date, read through all the entries in each of the program categories (scholarships, fellowships, etc.) that apply.

To Locate Financial Aid Programs Open to All Segments of the Population.   Only programs available to Hispanic Americans are listed in this publication. However, there are thousands of other programs that are open equally to all segments of the population. To identify these programs, talk to your local librarian, check with your financial aid office on campus, or use a computerized scholarship or grant search service.

PLANS TO UPDATE THE DIRECTORY

This volume, covering 2006-2008, is the fifth edition of *Financial Aid for Hispanic Americans.* The next biennial edition will cover the years 2008-2010 and will be issued in mid-2008.

OTHER RELATED PUBLICATIONS

In addition to *Financial Aid for Hispanic Americans,* Reference Service Press publishes several other titles dealing with fundseeking, including the award-winning *Directory of Financial Aids for Women; Financial Aid for the Disabled and Their Families;* and *Financial Aid for Veterans, Military Personnel, and Their Dependents.* Since each of these titles focuses on a separate population group, there is very little duplication in the listings. For more information on Reference Service Press' award-winning publications, write to the company at 5000 Windplay Drive, Suite 4, El Dorado Hills, CA 95762, give us a call at (916) 939-9620, fax us at (916) 939-9626, send us an e-mail at info@rspfunding.com, or visit our expanded web site: www.rspfunding.com.

ACKNOWLEDGEMENTS

A debt of gratitude is owed all the organizations that contributed information to the 2006-2008 edition of *Financial Aid for Hispanic Americans.* Their generous cooperation has helped to make this publication a current and comprehensive survey of awards.

ABOUT THE AUTHORS

Dr. Gail Ann Schlachter has worked for more than three decades as a library administrator, a library educator, and an administrator of library-related publishing companies. Among the reference books to her credit are the biennially-issued *Directory of Financial Aids for Women* and two award-winning bibliographic guides: *Minorities and Women: A Guide to Reference Literature in the Social Sciences* (which was chosen as an "outstanding reference book of the year" by *Choice)* and *Reference Sources in Library and Information Services* (which won the first Knowledge Industry Publications "Award for Library Literature"). She was the reference book review editor for *RQ* (now *Reference and User Services Quarterly)* for 10 years, is a past president of the American Library Association's Reference and User Services Association, is the former editor-in-chief of the *Reference and User Services Association Quarterly,* and is currently serving her third term on the American Library Association's governing council. In recognition of her outstanding contributions to reference service, Dr. Schlachter has been awarded both the Isadore Gilbert Mudge Citation and the Louis Shores/Oryx Press Award.

Dr. R. David Weber teaches economics and history at East Los Angeles College (Wilmington, California), where he directed the Honors Program for many years. He has written a number of critically-acclaimed reference works, including *Dissertations in Urban History* and the three-volume *Energy Information Guide.* With Gail Schlachter, he is the author of Reference Service Press' *Financial Aid for the Disabled and Their Families,* which was selected by *Library Journal* as one of the "best reference books of the year," and a number of other financial aid titles, including the *College Student's Guide to Merit and Other No-Need Funding,* which was chosen as one of the "outstanding reference books of the year" by *Choice.*

Financial Aid Programs
Open to Hispanic Americans

Scholarships ●
Fellowships ●
Loans ●
Grants ●
Awards ●
Internships ●

Scholarships

Described here are 389 funding programs open to Hispanic Americans that are available to fund studies on the undergraduate level in the United States. Usually no return of service or repayment is required. Note: other funding opportunities for Hispanic American undergraduates are also described in the Loans, Grants, Awards, and Internships sections. So, if you are looking for a particular program and don't find it in this section, be sure to check the Program Title Index to see if it is covered elsewhere in the directory.

[1]
ABC HISPANIC SCHOLARSHIP FUNDS

American Baptist Churches USA
Attn: National Ministries
P.O. Box 851
Valley Forge, PA 19482-0851
(610) 768-2067   Toll-free: (800) ABC-3USA, ext. 2067
Fax: (610) 768-2453
E-mail: karen.drummond@abc-usa.org
Web: www.nationalministries.org

Purpose To provide financial assistance to Hispanic Americans who are interested in preparing for or furthering a church career in the American Baptist Church (ABC).

Eligibility This program is open to Hispanic American members of the church or its recognized institutions who demonstrate financial need. They must be enrolled on at least a two-thirds basis in an accredited institution, working on an undergraduate degree or first professional degree in a seminary. Applicants must be currently serving or planning to serve in a vocation with the church or with its recognized institutions. They must be U.S. citizens who have been a member of an American Baptist Church for at least 1 year.

Financial data The stipends range from $500 to $3,000 per year.

Duration 1 year; may be renewed.

Deadline May of each year.

[2]
ACCOUNTANCY BOARD OF OHIO EDUCATION ASSISTANCE PROGRAM

Accountancy Board of Ohio
77 South High Street, 18th Floor
Columbus, OH 43215-6128
(614) 466-4135   Fax: (614) 466-2628
Web: acc.ohio.gov/edrule.html

Purpose To provide financial assistance to minority and financially disadvantaged students enrolled in an accounting education program at Ohio academic institutions approved by the Accountancy Board of Ohio.

Eligibility This program is open to minority and financially disadvantaged Ohio residents enrolled full time as sophomores, juniors, or seniors in an accounting program at an accredited college or university in the state. Students who remain in good standing at their institutions and who enter a qualified fifth-year program are also eligible, if funds are available. Minority is defined as people with significant ancestry from Africa (excluding the Middle East), Asia (excluding the Middle East), Central America and the Caribbean islands, South America, and the islands of the Pacific Ocean. Financial disadvantage is defined according to information provided on the Free Application for Federal Student Aid (FAFSA). U.S. citizenship or permanent resident status is required.

Financial data The amount of the stipend is determined annually but does not exceed the in-state tuition at Ohio public universities.

Duration 1 year; nonrenewable.

Number awarded Several each year.

Deadline May or November of each year.

[3]
¡ADELANTE! FUND SCHOLARSHIP PROGRAM

¡Adelante! U.S. Education Leadership Fund
8415 Datapoint Drive, Suite 400
San Antonio, TX 78229
(210) 692-1971   Fax: (210) 692-1951
Toll-free: (877) 692-1971
E-mail: info@adelantefund.org
Web: www.adelantefund.org

Purpose To provide financial aid, internships, and leadership training to upper-division Hispanic students enrolled in Hispanic Serving Institutions (HSIs).

Eligibility This program is open to Hispanic students currently enrolled in HSIs. Applicants must have a GPA of 3.0 or higher, be eligible to receive financial aid, be juniors or seniors in college, agree to attend the Adelante Leadership Institute, be eligible to participate in a summer internship, exhibit leadership, and provide 2 letters of recommendation. Most recipients are the first in their families to complete a college education.

Financial data The maximum stipend is $3,000 per year.

Duration 1 year.

Additional information This fund was established by the Hispanic Association of Colleges and Universities in 1997 and became a separate organization in 1999. Recipients must participate in a summer internship and the Adelante Leadership Institute.

Number awarded Varies each year; recently, 22 students received scholarships.

[4]
ADOBE SYSTEMS/HENAAC SCHOLARS PROGRAM

Hispanic Engineer National Achievement Awards
   Conference
3900 Whiteside Street
Los Angeles, CA 90063
(323) 262-0997   Fax: (323) 262-0946
E-mail: info@henaac.org
Web: www.henaac.org/scholarships.htm

Purpose To provide financial assistance to Hispanic undergraduate students majoring in computer science.

Eligibility This program is open to Hispanic undergraduate students who are enrolled full time in computer science. Applicants must be entering their junior or senior year and have a GPA of 3.0 or higher. Academic achievement and campus community activities are considered in the selection process. U.S. citizenship is required.

Financial data Stipends range from $1,000 to $5,000.

Duration 1 year; recipients may reapply.

Additional information This program is sponsored by Adobe Systems as part of its effort to support the mission of the Hispanic Engineer National Achievement Awards Conference (HENAAC) to promote technical excellence and leadership in the Hispanic community.

Number awarded 1 or more each year.

Deadline April of each year.

[5]
ADVANCING HISPANIC EXCELLENCE IN TECHNOLOGY, ENGINEERING, MATH, AND SCIENCE (AHETEMS) SCHOLARSHIP PROGRAM

Society of Hispanic Professional Engineers
5400 East Olympic Boulevard, Suite 210
Los Angeles, CA 90022
(323) 725-3970   Fax: (323) 725-0316
Web: www.shpe.org.

Purpose To provide financial assistance to Hispanic undergraduate and graduate students preparing for a career in science, technology, engineering, mathematics, or a related field.

Eligibility This program is open to members of the Society of Hispanic Professional Engineers (SHPE) who are accepted into or attending an accredited 2-year or 4-year college or university in the United States or Puerto Rico. Applicants must be enrolled full time with a major in science, technology, engineering, mathematics, or a related field. High school seniors and undergraduates must have a GPA of 2.5 or higher; graduate students must have a GPA of 3.25 or higher. Along with their application, they must submit a 1-page personal statement covering their family background, community involvement, leadership roles, achievements, and short-term and long-term goals and aspirations. Both merit-based and need-based scholarships are available. U.S. citizenship or permanent resident status is required.

Financial data Stipends range from $1,000 to $3,000.

Duration 1 year.

Additional information Information is also available from the AHETEMS Scholarship Program, 5012 Monarda Way, Fort Worth, TX 76123, (817) 361-8670, E-mail: rschwan@shpe.org.

Number awarded 1 or more each year.

Deadline March of each year.

[6]
AEA TECHNOLOGY SCHOLARSHIP PROGRAM

Oregon University System
Attn: Chancellor's Office, Industry Affairs Division
Capital Center, Suite 1065
18640 N.W. Walker Road
Beaverton, OR 97006-8966
(503) 725-2918   Fax: (503) 775-2921
E-mail: aeaschol@ous.edu
Web: www.ous.edu/ecs/scholarships.html

Purpose To provide financial assistance to Oregon high school seniors (especially underrepresented minorities and women) interested in studying designated computer and engineering fields at selected public universities in the state.

Eligibility This program is open to seniors graduating from high schools in Oregon who plan to attend Eastern Oregon University, Oregon Institute of Technology, Oregon State University, Portland State University, Southern Oregon University, Western Oregon University, or the University of Oregon. Applicants must be planning to major in biochemistry, chemical engineering, chemistry, computer engineering, computer science, electrical engineering, electronic engineering, engineering technology, industrial engineering, mathematics, mechanical engineering, or physics (not all majors are available at each institution). Women and ethnic minorities underrepresented in the technology industry (Black Americans, Hispanic Americans, and Native Americans) are strongly encouraged to apply. Selection is based on academic performance; college entrance examination scores; mathematics, science, and technology course work; achievements; leadership; civic participation; interests; employment; insight into and commitment to a career in technology; and communication skill.

Financial data The stipend is $2,500 per year.

Duration 1 year; may be renewed up to 3 additional years if the recipient maintains a GPA of 3.0 or higher.

Additional information This program was established in 1999 by Intel, which offered it to the Oregon Council of the AeA (formerly American Electronics Association) in the following year. Currently, Intel and other Oregon AeA member companies (such as Xerox and Hewlett Packard) provide ongoing support.

Number awarded Varies each year; recently, this program awarded 25 new scholarships.

Deadline March of each year.

[7]
AETNA/NCEMNA SCHOLARS PROGRAM

National Coalition of Ethnic Minority Nurse Associations
c/o Dr. Betty Smith Williams, President
6101 West Centinela Avenue, Suite 378
Culver City, CA 90230
(310) 258-9515   Fax: (310) 258-9513
E-mail: bwilliams@ncemna.org
Web: www.ncemna.org/scholarships.html

Purpose To provide financial assistance to nursing students who are members of constituent organizations of the National Coalition of Ethnic Minority Nurse Associations (NCEMNA) working on a 4-year or master's degree.

Eligibility This program is open to members of the 5 associations that comprise NCEMNA: the Asian American/Pacific Islander Nurses Association, Inc. (AAPINA), the National Alaska Native American Indian Nurses Association, Inc. (NANAINA), the National Association of Hispanic Nurses, Inc. (NAHN), the National Black Nurses Association, Inc. (NBNA), and the Philippine Nurses Association of America, Inc. (PNAA). Applicants must be currently attending or applying to a 4-year or master's degree program in nursing. Along with their application, they must submit a letter of reference, demonstration of leadership and involvement in the ethnic community, and statement of career goals.

Financial data The stipend is $2,000.

Duration 1 year.

Additional information This program was established in 2004 with a grant from the Aetna Foundation.

Number awarded 5 each year: 1 nominee from each of the constituent associations.

[8]
AFSCME/UNCF UNION SCHOLARS PROGRAM

United Negro College Fund
Attn: Corporate Scholars Program
P.O. Box 1435
Alexandria, VA 22313-9998
Toll-free: (866) 671-7237   E-mail: internship@uncf.org
Web: www.uncf.org/internships/index.asp

Purpose To provide financial assistance to students of color who are interested in working during the summer on an organizing campaign for the American Federation of State, County and Municipal Employees (AFSCME).

Eligibility This program is open to students of color, including African Americans, Hispanic Americans, Asian/Pacific Islander Americans, and American Indians/Alaskan Natives. Applicants must be second semester sophomores or juniors and majoring in ethnic studies, women's studies, labor studies, American studies, sociology, anthropology, history, political science, psychology, social work, or economics. They must have a GPA of 2.5 or higher and be interested in working on a union organizing campaign at 1 of several locations in the United States.

Financial data The program provides a stipend of $4,000, on-site housing at their location, a week-long orientation and training, and (based on successful performance during the organizing campaign) a $5,000 scholarship.

Duration 10 weeks for the organizing assignment; 1 year for the scholarship.

Number awarded Varies each year.

Deadline February of each year.

[9]
AIA/AAF MINORITY/DISADVANTAGED SCHOLARSHIP PROGRAM

American Institute of Architects
Attn: American Architectural Foundation
1735 New York Avenue, N.W.
Washington, DC 20006-5292
(202) 626-7511   Fax: (202) 626-7420
E-mail: info@archfoundation.org
Web: www.archfoundation.org

Purpose To provide financial assistance to high school and college students from minority and/or disadvantaged backgrounds who are interested in studying architecture in college.

Eligibility This program is open to students from minority and/or disadvantaged backgrounds who are high school seniors, students in a community college or technical school transferring to an accredited architectural program, or college freshmen entering a professional degree program at an accredited program of architecture. Students who have completed 1 or more years of a 4-year college curriculum are not eligible. Initially, candidates must be nominated by 1 of the following organizations or persons: an individual architect or firm, a chapter of the American Institute of Architects (AIA), a community design center, a guidance counselor or teacher, the dean or professor at an accredited school of architecture, or the director of a community or civic organization. Nominees are reviewed and eligible candidates are invited to complete an application form in which they write an essay describing the reasons they are interested in becoming an architect and provide documentation of academic excellence and financial need. Selection is based primarily on financial need.

Financial data Awards range from $500 to $2,500 per year, depending upon individual need. Students must apply for supplementary funds from other sources.

Duration 9 months; may be renewed for up to 2 additional years.

Additional information This program is offered jointly by the American Architectural Foundation (AAF) and the AIA.

Number awarded Up to 20 each year.

Deadline Nominations are due by December of each year; final applications must be submitted in January.

[10]
AIMMS EXCELLENCE SCHOLARSHIPS

Maryland State Department of Education
Attn: Achievement Initiative for Maryland's Minority
   Students Council
200 West Baltimore Street
Baltimore, MD 21201
(410) 887-2446
Web: www.msde.state.md.us

Purpose To provide financial assistance for college to Maryland high school seniors who have demonstrated leadership in addressing diversity.

Eligibility This program is open to seniors in high schools in Maryland who plan to attend a community college, university, college, or technical/vocational school. Applicants must have a GPA of 3.0 or higher. They must submit an essay about their leadership in 1 or more of the following areas: 1) academic, school, or community support for diverse students; 2) promotion of positive intergroup relations and understanding; or 3) performance of services to increase success among diverse groups of students. Diverse groups include race/ethnicity, gender, age, disability, or poverty. Selection is based on academic success and contributions to better understanding and appreciation among diverse groups.

Financial data Stipends are $1,000 or $500.

Duration 1 year.

Additional information This program began in 1999. The scholarship for $1,000 is designated the Barbara Dezmon Scholarship

Number awarded 11 each year: 1 at $1,000 and 10 at $500.

Deadline July of each year.

[11]
AIR FORCE ENHANCED ROTC HISPANIC SERVING INSTITUTION SCHOLARSHIP PROGRAM

U.S. Air Force
Attn: Headquarters AFROTC/RRUC
551 East Maxwell Boulevard
Maxwell AFB, AL 36112-5917
(334) 953-2091   Toll-free: (866) 423-7682
Fax: (334) 953-6167
Web: www.afrotc.com

Purpose To provide financial assistance to students at designated Hispanic Serving Institutions (HSIs) who are willing to join Air Force ROTC in college and serve as Air Force officers following completion of their bachelor's degree.

Eligibility This program is open to U.S. citizens who are at least 17 years of age and currently enrolled at 1 of 8 designated HSIs that have an Air Force ROTC unit on campus. Applicants must have a cumulative GPA of 2.5 or higher. At the time of commissioning, they may be no more than 31 years of age. They must be able to pass the Air Force Officer Qualifying Test (AFOQT) and the Air Force ROTC Physical Fitness Test. Currently, the program is accepting applications from students with any major.

Financial data Awards are type 2 AFROTC scholarships that provide for payment of tuition and fees, to a maximum of $15,000 per year, plus an annual book allowance of $600. Recipients are also awarded a tax-free subsistence allowance for 10 months of each year that is $300 per month during the sophomore year, $350 during the junior year, and $400 during the senior year.

Duration Up to 3 and a half years (beginning as early as the spring semester of the freshman year).

Additional information The designated universities are California State University at Fresno, California State University at San Bernardino, New Mexico State University, the University of Miami, the University of New Mexico, the University of Puerto Rico at Rio Piedras, the University of Puerto Rico at Mayaguez, and the University of Texas at San Antonio. While scholarship recipients can major in any subject, they must complete 4 years of aerospace studies courses. They must also attend a 4-week summer training camp at an Air Force base, usually between their sophomore and junior years; 2-year scholarship awardees attend in the summer after their junior year. Current military personnel are eligible for early release from active duty in order to enter the Air Force ROTC program. Following completion of their bachelor's degree, scholarship recipients earn a commission as a second lieutenant in the Air Force and serve at least 4 years.

Number awarded Up to 120 each year: 15 at each of the participating AFROTC units.

Deadline Applications may be submitted at any time.

[12]
AIR FORCE REGULAR ROTC HISPANIC SERVING INSTITUTION SCHOLARSHIP PROGRAM

U.S. Air Force
Attn: Headquarters AFROTC/RRUC
551 East Maxwell Boulevard
Maxwell AFB, AL 36112-5917
(334) 953-2091   Toll-free: (866) 423-7682
Fax: (334) 953-6167
Web: www.afrotc.com

Purpose To provide financial assistance to students at Hispanic Serving Institutions (HSIs) who are willing to join Air Force ROTC in college and serve as Air Force officers following completion of their bachelor's degree.

Eligibility This program is open to U.S. citizens at least 17 years of age who are currently enrolled at 1 of the 42 HSIs that have an Air Force ROTC unit on campus or that have a cross-enrollment agreement with another school that hosts a unit. Applicants do not need to be Hispanic as long as they are attending an HSI and have a cumulative GPA of 2.5 or higher. At the time of commissioning, they may be no more than 31 years of age. They must be able to pass the Air Force Officer Qualifying Test (AFOQT) and the Air

Force ROTC Physical Fitness Test. Currently, the program is accepting applications from students with any major.

Financial data Awards are type 2 AFROTC scholarships that provide for payment of tuition and fees, to a maximum of $15,000 per year, plus an annual book allowance of $600. Recipients are also awarded a tax-free subsistence allowance for 10 months of each year that is $300 per month during the sophomore year, $350 during the junior year, and $400 during the senior year.

Duration 2 to 3 years, beginning during the current term.

Additional information While scholarship recipients can major in any subject, they must complete 4 years of aerospace studies courses. They must also attend a 4-week summer training camp at an Air Force base, usually between their sophomore and junior years; 2-year scholarship awardees attend in the summer after their junior year. Current military personnel are eligible for early release from active duty in order to enter the Air Force ROTC program. Following completion of their bachelor's degree, scholarship recipients earn a commission as a second lieutenant in the Air Force and serve at least 4 years.

Number awarded Varies each year. AFROTC units at every HSI may nominate an unlimited number of cadets to receive these scholarships.

Deadline Applications may be submitted at any time.

[13]
AIR PRODUCTS AND CHEMICALS SCHOLARSHIP FOR DIVERSITY IN ENGINEERING

Association of Independent Colleges and Universities
    of Pennsylvania
101 North Front Street
Harrisburg, PA 17101-1405
(717) 232-8649   Fax: (717) 233-8574
E-mail: info@aicup.org
Web: www.aicup.org

Purpose To provide financial assistance to women and minority students at member institutions of the Association of Independent Colleges and Universities of Pennsylvania (AICUP) who are majoring in designated fields of engineering.

Eligibility This program is open to full-time undergraduate students at designated AICUP colleges and universities who are women and/or members of the following minority groups: American Indians, Alaska Natives, Asians, Blacks/African Americans, Hispanics/Latinos, Native Hawaiians, or Pacific Islanders. Applicants must be juniors majoring in chemical or mechanical engineering with a GPA of 2.7 or higher. Along with their application, they must submit an essay on their characteristics, accomplishments, primary interests, plans, and goals, and what sets them apart.

Financial data The stipend is $7,500 per year.

Duration 1 year; may be renewed 1 additional year if the recipient maintains appropriate academic standards.

Additional information This program, sponsored by Air Products and Chemicals, Inc., is available at the following AICUP colleges and universities: Bucknell University, Carnegie Mellon University, Drexel University, Gannon University, Geneva College, Grove City College, Lafayette College, Lehigh University, Messiah College, Swarthmore College, Villanova University, Widener University, and Wilkes University.

Number awarded 2 each year.
Deadline April of each year.

[14]
ALABAMA HISPANIC ASSOCIATION UNDERGRADUATE SCHOLARSHIPS

Alabama Hispanic Association
Attn: Scholarships Committee
1595 Slaughter Road, Suite A
Madison, AL 35758
(256) 325-4AHA
E-mail: aha@alabamahispanicassociation.org
Web: www.alabamahispanicassociation.org

Purpose To provide financial assistance to Hispanic undergraduate students from Alabama.

Eligibility This program is open to Hispanic residents of Alabama who are enrolled or planning to enroll as an undergraduate student. Applicants must have a GPA of 2.5 or higher. Selection is based on academic excellence and financial need.

Financial data Stipends range from $1,000 to $2,000. Funds may be used for tuition, books, or room and board.

Duration 1 year.

Number awarded 1 or more each year.

[15]
ALLISON TRANSMISSION AND INDIANAPOLIS METAL CENTER SCHOLARSHIPS

National FFA Organization
Attn: Scholarship Office
6060 FFA Drive
P.O. Box 68960
Indianapolis, IN 46268-0960
(317) 802-4321   Fax: (317) 802-5321
E-mail: scholarships@ffa.org
Web: www.ffa.org

Purpose To provide financial assistance for college to FFA members who are from an ethnic minority group and interested in majoring in selected fields.

Eligibility This program is open to members who are graduating high school seniors planning to enroll full time in college. Applicants must be members of ethnic minority groups and interested in working on a 4-year degree in the following areas of agriculture: management, finance, science, engineering, and related specialties, although non-agricultural majors are also eligible. They must have a GPA of 3.0 or higher and be able to demonstrate financial need. Selection is based on academic achievement (10 points for GPA, 10 points for SAT or ACT score, 10 points for class rank), leadership in FFA activities (30 points), leadership in community activities (10 points), and participation in the Supervised Agricultural Experience (SAE) program (30 points). U.S. citizenship is required.

Financial data The stipend is $5,000 per year. Funds are paid directly to the recipient.

Duration 1 year; nonrenewable.

Additional information Funding for these scholarships is provided by the Allison Transmission and Indianapolis Metal Center of General Motors Corporation.

Number awarded 2 each year.

Deadline February of each year.

[16]
ALMA EXLEY SCHOLARSHIP

New Britain Foundation for Public Giving
Attn: Donor Relations Manager
29 Russell Street
New Britain, CT 06052-1312
(860) 229-6018   Fax: (860) 229-2011
E-mail: cfarmer@nbfoundation.org
Web: www.nbfoundation.org

Purpose To provide financial assistance to minority college students in Connecticut who are interested in preparing for a teaching career.

Eligibility This program is open to students of color in Connecticut who have passed the Praxis examination and have been admitted to a certified teacher preparation program at an accredited 4-year college or university in the state.

Financial data A stipend is awarded (amount not specified).

Duration 1 year.

Number awarded 1 each year.

[17]
ALPFA LOS ANGELES CHAPTER SCHOLARSHIPS

Association of Latino Professionals in Finance and
   Accounting-Los Angeles Chapter
c/o Jose Manzano, Treasurer
Manzano and Associates
2162 Tulane Avenue
Long Beach, CA 90815
(562) 547-5990   E-mail: joselmanzano@aol.com

Purpose To provide financial assistance to Hispanic undergraduate accounting students from any state attending school in southern California.

Eligibility This program is open to undergraduate students at colleges and universities in southern California who have demonstrated an interest in accounting. Applicants must be of Hispanic descent and have completed or be enrolled in an intermediate accounting course. Selection is based on academic achievement, financial need, and community involvement.

Financial data Stipends range from $1,250 to $2,500.

Duration 1 year.

Number awarded Varies each year; recently, 9 of these scholarships were awarded.

[18]
AMD/HENAAC SCHOLARS PROGRAM

Hispanic Engineer National Achievement Awards
   Conference
3900 Whiteside Street
Los Angeles, CA 90063
(323) 262-0997   Fax: (323) 262-0946
E-mail: info@henaac.org
Web: www.henaac.org

Purpose To provide financial assistance to Hispanic undergraduate students majoring in computer and electrical engineering.

Eligibility This program is open to Hispanic undergraduate students who are enrolled full time in computer or electrical engineering. Applicants must have a GPA of 3.5 or higher. Academic achievement and campus community activities are considered in the selection process. U.S. citizenship is required.

Financial data Stipends range from $1,000 to $5,000.

Duration 1 year; recipients may reapply.

Additional information This program is sponsored by AMD (Advanced Micro Devices, Inc.) as part of its effort to support the mission of the Hispanic Engineer National Achievement Awards Conference (HENAAC): to promote technical excellence and leadership in the Hispanic community.

Number awarded 1 or more each year.

Deadline April of each year.

[19]
AMELIA KEMP MEMORIAL SCHOLARSHIP

Women of the Evangelical Lutheran Church in America
Attn: Scholarships
8765 West Higgins Road
Chicago, IL 60631-4189
(773) 380-2730   Toll-free: (800) 638-3522, ext. 2730
Fax: (773) 380-2419   E-mail: womenelca@elca.org
Web: www.womenoftheelca.org

Purpose To provide financial assistance to lay women of color who are members of Evangelical Lutheran Church of America (ELCA) congregations and who wish to study on the undergraduate, graduate, professional, or vocational school level.

Eligibility These scholarships are available to ELCA lay women of color who are at least 21 years of age and have experienced an interruption of at least 2 years in their education since high school. Applicants must have been admitted to an educational institution to prepare for a career in other than a church-certified profession. U.S. citizenship is required.

Financial data The amount of the award varies, depending on the availability of funds.

Duration Up to 2 years.

Number awarded Varies each year, depending upon the funds available.

Deadline February of each year.

[20]
AMERADA HESS/HENAAC SCHOLARS PROGRAM

Hispanic Engineer National Achievement Awards
    Conference
3900 Whiteside Street
Los Angeles, CA 90063
(323) 262-0997   Fax: (323) 262-0946
E-mail: info@henaac.org
Web: www.henaac.org/scholarships.htm

Purpose To provide financial assistance to Hispanic undergraduate students majoring in engineering and related fields.

Eligibility This program is open to Hispanic undergraduate students who are enrolled full time in computer science, engineering, material science, mathematics, or applied science. Applicants must have a GPA of 3.0 or higher. There is no citizenship requirement. Academic achievement and campus community activities are considered in the selection process.

Financial data Stipends range from $1,000 to $5,000.

Duration 1 year; recipients may reapply.

Additional information This program is sponsored by the Amerada Hess Foundation as part of its effort to support the mission of the Hispanic Engineer National Achievement Awards Conference (HENAAC): to promote technical excellence and leadership in the Hispanic community.

Number awarded 1 or more each year.

Deadline April of each year.

[21]
AMERICAN ASSOCIATION OF BLACKS IN ENERGY SCHOLARSHIP

American Association of Blacks in Energy
Attn: Scholarship Committee
927 15th Street, N.W., Suite 200
Washington, DC 20005
(202) 371-9530   Fax: (202) 371-9218
E-mail: aabe@aabe.org
Web: www.aabe.org/mission/scholarships.html

Purpose To provide financial assistance to underrepresented minority high school seniors who are interested in majoring in engineering, mathematics, or physical science in college.

Eligibility This program is open to members of minority groups underrepresented in the energy industry (African Americans, Hispanics, and Native Americans) who are graduating high school seniors. Applicants must have a "B" academic average overall and a "B" average in mathematics and science courses. They must be planning to attend an accredited college or university to major in engineering, mathematics, or the physical sciences. Along with their application, they must submit a 350-word essay covering why they should receive this scholarship, their professional career objectives, and any other pertinent information. Financial need is also considered in the selection process. The applicant who demonstrates the most outstanding achievement and promise is presented with the Premier Award. All applications must be submitted to the local office of the sponsoring organization in the student's state. For a list of local offices, contact the scholarship committee at the national office.

Financial data The stipends are $1,500. The Premier Award is an additional $3,000. All funds are paid directly to the students upon proof of enrollment at an accredited college or university.

Duration 1 year; nonrenewable.

Number awarded 6 each year (1 in each of the organization's regions); of those 6 winners, 1 is chosen to receive the Premier Award.

Deadline February of each year.

[22]
AMERICAN CHEMICAL SOCIETY SCHOLARS PROGRAM

American Chemical Society
Attn: Department of Diversity Programs
1155 16th Street, N.W.
Washington, DC 20036
(202) 872-6250   Toll-free: (800) 227-5558, ext. 6250
Fax: (202) 776-8003   E-mail: scholars@acs.org
Web: www.chemistry.org/scholars

Purpose To provide financial assistance to underrepresented minority students with a strong interest in chemistry and a desire to prepare for a career in a chemically-related science.

Eligibility This program is open to 1) college-bound high school seniors; 2) college freshmen, sophomores, and juniors enrolled full time at an accredited college or university; 3) community college graduates and transfer students who plan to study for a bachelor's degree; and 4) community college freshmen. Applicants must be African American, Hispanic/Latino, or American Indian. They must be majoring or planning to major in chemistry, biochemistry, chemical engineering, or other chemically-related fields, such as environmental science, materials science, or toxicology, and planning to prepare for a career in the chemical sciences or chemical technology. Students planning careers in medicine or pharmacy are not eligible. U.S. citizenship or permanent resident status is required. Selection is based on academic merit (GPA of 3.0 or higher) and financial need.

Financial data The maximum stipend is $2,500 for the freshman year in college or $3,000 per year for sophomores, juniors, and seniors.

Duration 1 year; may be renewed.

Additional information This program was established in 1994.

Number awarded Approximately 100 new awards are granted each year.

Deadline February of each year.

[23]
AMERICAN DENTAL HYGIENISTS' ASSOCIATION INSTITUTE MINORITY SCHOLARSHIPS

American Dental Hygienists' Association
Attn: Institute for Oral Health
444 North Michigan Avenue, Suite 3400
Chicago, IL 60611
(312) 440-8918   Toll-free: (800) 735-4916
Fax: (312) 440-8929   E-mail: institute@adha.net
Web: www.adha.org/institute/Scholarship/index.htm

Purpose To provide financial assistance to minority students and males of any race enrolled in undergraduate programs in dental hygiene.

Eligibility This program is open to members of groups currently underrepresented in the dental hygiene profession (Native Americans, African Americans, Hispanics, Asians, and males) who are active members of the Student American Dental Hygienists' Association (SADHA) or the American Dental Hygienists' Association (ADHA). Applicants must have a GPA of 3.0 or higher, be able to document financial need of at least $1,500, and have completed at least 1 year of full-time enrollment in an accredited dental hygiene program in the United States. Along with their application, they

must submit a statement that covers their long-term career goals, their intended contribution to the dental hygiene profession, their professional interests, and the manner in which their degree will enhance their professional capacity.

Financial data Stipends range from $1,000 to $2,000.

Duration 1 year; nonrenewable.

Number awarded 2 each year.

Deadline April of each year.

[24]
AMERICAN DIETETIC ASSOCIATION BACCALAUREATE (DIDACTIC OR COORDINATED PROGRAM) SCHOLARSHIPS

American Dietetic Association
Attn: Accreditation, Education Programs, and Student Operations
120 South Riverside Plaza, Suite 2000
Chicago, IL 60606-6995
(312) 899-0040   Toll-free: (800) 877-1600, ext. 5400
Fax: (312) 899-4817   E-mail: education@eatright.org
Web: www.eatright.org

Purpose To provide financial assistance to undergraduate student members of the American Dietetic Association (ADA).

Eligibility This program is open to ADA members enrolled at a CADE-accredited/approved college or university program for at least junior status in the dietetics program. Applicants must be U.S. citizens or permanent residents and show promise of being a valuable, contributing member of the profession. Some scholarships require membership in a specific dietetic practice group, residency in a specific state, or underrepresented minority group status. The same application form can be used for all categories.

Financial data Stipends range from $500 to $4,500.

Duration 1 year.

Number awarded Varies each year, depending upon the funds available. Recently, the sponsoring organization awarded 144 scholarships for all its programs.

Deadline February of each year.

[25]
AMERICAN METEOROLOGICAL SOCIETY UNDERGRADUATE SCHOLARSHIPS

American Meteorological Society
Attn: Fellowship/Scholarship Program
45 Beacon Street
Boston, MA 02108-3693
(617) 227-2426, ext. 246   Fax: (617) 742-8718
E-mail: scholar@ametsoc.org
Web: www.ametsoc.org

Purpose To provide financial assistance to undergraduates (minorities are particularly encouraged) majoring in meteorology or an aspect of atmospheric sciences.

Eligibility This program is open to full-time students entering their final year of undergraduate study and majoring in meteorology or an aspect of the atmospheric or related oceanic and hydrologic sciences. Applicants must intend to make atmospheric or related sciences their career. They must be U.S. citizens or permanent residents enrolled at a U.S. institution and have a cumulative GPA of 3.25 or higher. Along with their application, they must submit 200-

word essays on 1) their most important achievements that qualify them for this scholarship, and 2) their career goals in the atmospheric or related oceanic or hydrologic fields. Selection is based on academic excellence and achievement; financial need is not considered. The sponsor specifically encourages applications from women, minorities, and students with disabilities who are traditionally underrepresented in the atmospheric and related oceanic sciences.

Financial data Stipends range from $700 to $5,000 per year.

Duration 1 year.

Additional information This program includes the following named scholarships: the Howard H. Hanks, Jr. Scholarship in Meteorology ($700), the AMS 75th Anniversary Endowed Scholarship ($2,000), the Om and Saraswati (Sara) Bahethi Scholarship ($2,000), the Howard T. Orville Endowed Scholarship in Meteorology ($5,000), the George S. Benton Scholarship ($3,500), the Carl W. Kreitzberg Endowed Scholarship ($2,000), the Dr. Pedro Grau Undergraduate Scholarship ($2,500), the Guillermo Salazar Rodriguez Scholarship ($2,500), the John R. Hope Endowed Scholarship in Atmospheric Science ($2,500), the Richard and Helen Hagemeyer Scholarship ($3,000), and the Werner A. Baum Endowed Scholarship ($5,000). Requests for an application must be accompanied by a self-addressed stamped envelope.

Number awarded 11 each year.

Deadline February of each year.

[26]
AMERICAN PHILOLOGICAL ASSOCIATION MINORITY SCHOLARSHIP

American Philological Association
Attn: Executive Director
University of Pennsylvania
291 Logan Hall
249 South 36th Street
Philadelphia, PA 19104-6304
(215) 898-4975   Fax: (215) 573-7874
E-mail: apaclassics@sas.upenn.edu
Web: www.apaclassics.org

Purpose To prepare minority undergraduates during the summer for advanced work in the classics.

Eligibility Eligible to apply are minority (African American, Hispanic American, Asian American, and Native American) undergraduate students who wish to engage in summer study as preparation for graduate work in the classics. Applicants may propose participation in summer programs in Italy, Greece, Egypt, or other classical centers; language training at institutions in the United States or Canada; or other relevant courses of study. Selection is based on academic qualifications, especially in classics; demonstrated ability in at least 1 classical language; quality of the proposal for study with respect to preparation for a career in classics; and financial need. Applications must be endorsed by a member of the American Philological Association (APA).

Financial data The maximum award is $3,000.

Duration 1 summer.

Number awarded 1 each year.

Deadline February of each year.

[27]
ANA MULTICULTURAL EXCELLENCE SCHOLARSHIP FUND

American Association of Advertising Agencies
Attn: Manager of Diversity Programs
405 Lexington Avenue, 18th Floor
New York, NY 10174-1801
(212) 682-2500   Toll-free: (800) 676-9333
Fax: (212) 682-8391   E-mail: tiffany@aaaa.org
Web: www.aaaa.org/diversity/foundation/funds.htm

Purpose To provide financial assistance to multicultural students who are working on an undergraduate degree in advertising.

Eligibility This program is open to undergraduate students who are U.S. citizens of proven multicultural heritage and have at least 1 grandparent of multicultural heritage. Final selection of recipients is made by advertising agencies that are chosen as winners of Multicultural Excellence Awards by the Association of National Advertisers (ANA). For that competition, advertising firms submit samples of their campaigns that ran for at least 3 months and were directed at multicultural markets. Entries are submitted in 5 categories: African American, Asian, Hispanic, General (e.g., Native American, Russian, Polish), or Campaign with Significant Results. Winners of those awards select recipients of these scholarships on the basis of demonstrated academic ability.

Financial data A stipend is awarded (amount not specified).

Duration 1 year.

Additional information This program was established by ANA in 2001. The American Association of Advertising Agencies (AAAA) assumed administration in 2003.

Number awarded 5 each year.

[28]
ANHEUSER-BUSCH FOUNDATION SCHOLARSHIPS

Chicago Urban League
Attn: Education Department
4510 South Michigan Avenue
Chicago, IL 60653-3898
(773) 451-3565   Fax: (773) 285-7772
E-mail: info@cul-chicago.org
Web: www.cul-chicago.org

Purpose To provide financial assistance to Illinois residents of color interested in full-time study at a 4-year college or university.

Eligibility This program is open to minority residents of Illinois who will be full-time freshmen at a 4-year college or university. Applicants must have a GPA of 2.5 or higher and be able to demonstrate financial need. An interview is required.

Financial data The stipend is $2,500 per year.

Duration 4 years.

Additional information This program is supported by the Anheuser-Busch Foundation, which makes the final decision on selection of recipients.

Number awarded Varies each year.

Deadline May of each year.

[29]
ANNE FORD SCHOLARSHIP

National Center for Learning Disabilities
Attn: Scholarship
381 Park Avenue South, Suite 1401
New York, NY 10016-8806
(212) 545-7510   Fax: (212) 545-9665
E-mail: AFScholarship@ncld.org
Web: www.ld.org

Purpose To provide financial assistance for college to high school seniors (particularly minorities and women) with learning disabilities.

Eligibility This program is open to high school seniors with learning disabilities who plan to work on a university degree. Applicants must submit an essay (750 to 1,000 words in length) describing their learning disability and how it has affected their life, including scholastic development, relationships with family and friends, community involvement, and future aspirations. They should specify their positive and negative experiences with a learning disability, and elaborate on how they have coped with the negative aspects. Their essay should demonstrate how they meet the program's goal of supporting "a person who has faced the challenges of having a learning disability and who, through hard work and perseverance, has created a life of purpose and achievement." If they prefer, they may submit a video or audio tape (up to 15 minutes in length) with accompanying script or outline that describes their experiences with a learning disability. Other required submissions include high school transcripts, portfolios (if applicable), 3 letters of recommendation, a financial statement (financial need is strongly considered in the selection process), and SAT and/or ACT scores. U.S. citizenship is required. Minorities and women are specifically encouraged to apply.

Financial data The stipend is $2,500 per year.

Duration 4 years, provided the recipient submits annual reports (written or in video format) detailing their progress in school and describing their insights about their personal growth.

Additional information This program was established in 2002.

Number awarded 1 each year.

Deadline December of each year.

[30]
APPRAISAL INSTITUTE MINORITIES AND WOMEN EDUCATIONAL SCHOLARSHIP PROGRAM

Appraisal Institute
Attn: Minorities and Women Scholarship Fund
550 West Van Buren Street, Suite 1000
Chicago, IL 60607
(312) 335-4121   Fax: (312) 335-4118
E-mail: sbarnes@appraisalinstitute.org
Web: www.appraisalinstitute.org

Purpose To provide financial assistance to women and minority undergraduate students majoring in real estate or allied fields.

Eligibility This program is open to members of groups underrepresented in the real estate appraisal profession. Those groups include women, American Indians, Alaska Natives, Asians, Black or African Americans, Hispanics or Latinos, and Native Hawaiians or other Pacific Islanders. Applicants must be full- or part-time students enrolled in real estate courses within a degree-granting college, university, or junior college. They must submit evidence of demonstrated financial need and a GPA of 2.5 or higher. U.S. citizenship is required.

Financial data The stipend is $1,000 per year. Funds are paid directly to the recipient's institution to be used for tuition and fees.

Duration 1 year.

Number awarded At least 1 each year.

Deadline April of each year.

[31]
APS SCHOLARSHIPS FOR MINORITY UNDERGRADUATE STUDENTS WHO MAJOR IN PHYSICS

American Physical Society
Attn: Committee on Minorities
One Physics Ellipse
College Park, MD 20740-3844
(301) 209-3232   Fax: (301) 209-0865
Web: www.aps.org/educ/com/scholars/index.cfm

Purpose To provide financial assistance to underrepresented minority students interested in studying physics on the undergraduate level.

Eligibility Any African American, Hispanic American, or Native American who plans to major in physics and who is a high school senior or college freshman or sophomore may apply. U.S. citizenship or permanent resident status is required. The selection committee especially encourages applications from students who are attending or planning to attend institutions with historically or predominantly Black, Hispanic, or Native American enrollment. Selection is based on commitment to the study of physics and plans to work on a physics baccalaureate degree.

Financial data Stipends are $2,000 per year in the first year or $3,000 in the second year; funds must be used for tuition, room, and board. In addition, $500 is awarded to the host department.

Duration 1 year; renewable for 1 additional year with the approval of the APS selection committee.

Additional information APS conducts this program, which began in 1980 as the Corporate-Sponsored Scholarships for Minority Undergraduate Students Who Major in Physics, in conjunction with the Corporate Associates of the American Institute of Physics. Each scholarship is sponsored by a corporation, which is normally designated as the sponsor. A corporation generally sponsors from 1 to 10 scholarships, depending upon its size and utilization of physics in the business.

Number awarded Usually, 20 to 25 of these scholarships are awarded each year.

Deadline January of each year.

[32]
ARKANSAS CONFERENCE ETHNIC LOCAL CHURCH CONCERNS SCHOLARSHIPS

United Methodist Church-Arkansas Conference
Attn: Ethnic Local Church Concerns
Two Trudie Kibbe Reed Drive
Little Rock, AR 72202-3770
(501) 324-8000   Toll-free: (877) 646-1816
Fax: (501) 324-8018   E-mail: mallen@arumc.org
Web: www.arumc.org

Purpose To provide financial assistance for college to ethnic minority Methodist students from Arkansas.

Eligibility This program is open to ethnic minority undergraduate students who are active members of local congregations affiliated with the Arkansas Conference of the United Methodist Church. Applicants must be currently enrolled in an institution of higher education. Along with their application, they must submit a transcript and documentation of participation in local church activities.

Financial data The stipend is $1,000.

Duration 1 year; may be renewed.

Number awarded 1 or more each year.

Deadline September of each year.

[33]
ARKANSAS GAME AND FISH SCHOLARSHIP

Arkansas Game and Fish Commission
Two Natural Resources Drive
Little Rock, AR 72205
(501) 223-6300   Toll-free: (800) 364-4263
Web: www.agfc.com

Purpose To provide financial assistance to high school seniors and undergraduates (particularly minorities) from Arkansas interested in preparing for a career in fish and wildlife management.

Eligibility Applicants must be high school seniors or college undergraduates interested in preparing for a career in the field of natural resource conservation and/or wildlife law enforcement, including fishery management, environmental education and interpretation, and related fields. They must be Arkansas residents, have at least a 2.5 GPA, and intend to attend school on a full-time basis. Selection is based on merit. Minorities are particularly encouraged to apply. Full-time employees of the Arkansas Game and Fish Commission, their spouses, and their children are not eligible for these scholarships.

Financial data The stipend is $1,000 per year. Funds are to be used for tuition, books, fees, and lodging.

Duration 1 year; may be awarded for up to 4 additional years.

Additional information Applicants must not have received a full scholarship from another source. They must attend or be accepted for admission at an accredited 4-year college or university in the state.

Number awarded 25 each year.

Deadline October of each year.

[34]
ASCE MAINE SECTION SCHOLARSHIP

American Society of Civil Engineers-Maine Section
c/o Holly Anderson, P.E.
Maine Department of Transportation
Urban and Arterial Highway Program
16 State House Section
Augusta, ME 04333-0016
(207) 624-3349   E-mail: holly.anderson@state.me.us

Purpose To provide financial assistance to high school seniors (particularly minorities and women) in Maine who are interested in studying civil engineering in college.

Eligibility This program is open to graduating high school seniors who are Maine residents and who intend to study civil engineering in college. Women and minorities are especially encouraged to apply. Applicants must submit a 200-word statement describing why they have chosen civil engineering as a career and what they hope to accomplish by being a civil engineer. Selection is based on the statement, academic performance, extracurricular activities, and letters of recommendation.

Financial data The stipend is $2,000.

Duration 1 year; nonrenewable.

Number awarded 1 each year.

Deadline January of each year.

[35]
ASOCIATION BORICUA DE DALLAS SCHOLARSHIPS

Asociatión Boricua de Dallas, Inc.
Attn: Scholarship Committee
P.O. Box 740784
Dallas, TX 75374-0784
Fax: (972) 488-2990
Web: www.boricuadallas.org/english/scholarship.htm

Purpose To provide financial assistance for college to Hispanic residents of Texas, particularly the Dallas area.

Eligibility This program is open to Hispanic residents of Texas (particularly Collin, Denton, Dallas, and Tarrant counties). Applicants must be planning to start college as a full-time student to work on an academic, technical, or vocational degree. They must have a GPA of 2.8 or higher and an ACT score of 21 or higher (or the equivalent on the SAT). Along with their application, they must submit documentation of financial need and an essay on why an education is important to them, including their educational plans, career choice, and future goals.

Financial data A stipend is awarded (amount not specified).

Duration 1 year.

Number awarded Varies each year; recently, 15 of these scholarships were awarded.

Deadline May of each year.

[36]
ASSOCIATED COLLEGES OF ILLINOIS SCHOLARSHIP PROGRAM

Associated Colleges of Illinois
Attn: Executive Director
20 North Wacker Drive, Suite 1456
Chicago, IL 60606
(312) 263-2391, ext. 23   Fax: (312) 263-3424
E-mail: aci@acifund.org
Web: www.acifund.org

Purpose To provide financial assistance to minority and other students attending or planning to attend an academic institution affiliated with the Associated Colleges of Illinois (ACI).

Eligibility Eligible to apply are students entering or currently enrolled at the 24 private colleges and universities that are members of ACI. The program includes 5 categories of awards: 1) first-generation and minority scholarships, to support students who are the first in their family to attend college and encourage minority achievement and graduation; 2) college-to-work scholarships, to attract more students to specific fields of study and career paths; 3) basic needs scholarships, to address students' unmet financial needs; 4) emergency assistance scholarships, to direct critical financial support to students experiencing personal or family emergencies; and 5) academic merit scholarships, to reward the best and the brightest students.

Financial data Awards depend on the availability of funds and the need of the recipient.

Duration 1 year; may be renewed.

Additional information Members of ACI are Augustana College, Aurora University, Concordia University, Dominican University, Elmhurst College, Eureka College, Greenville College, Illinois College, Illinois Wesleyan University, Knox College, Lake Forest College, Lewis University, McKendree College, Millikin University, Monmouth College, North Central College, North Park University, Olivet Nazarene University, Principia College, Quincy University, Rockford College, Saint Xavier University, Trinity Christian College, and University of St. Francis. This program includes the following named scholarships: the A. Montgomery Ward Scholarship, the Betty A. DeVries Memorial Fund, the Carole B. Whitcomb Endowed Scholarship, the Fifth Third Bank Scholarship Award, the Grover Hermann Foundation Scholarship, HSBC Scholars, the James S. Copley Foundation Scholarship, MB Financial Bank Scholarship, the McGraw Foundation Emergency Award, the Michelle and Peter Willmott Fund for Minority Leadership, the Motorola Scholarship, the Motorola Minority Scholarship, the Nick Amatangelo Scholarship, the Paul Hucko Memorial Scholarship, the Pepper Family Scholarship, the Polk Brothers Minority Scholarship, the UPS Scholarship, the Vulcan Materials Scholarship, and the Ward Scholarship.

Number awarded Varies each year; since 1990, this program has awarded more than $2 million in financial aid to 1,600 students.

[37]
ASSOCIATED FOOD DEALERS OF MICHIGAN MINORITY SCHOLARSHIPS

Associated Food Dealers of Michigan
Attn: AFD Foundation
18470 West Ten Mile Road
Southfield, MI 48075
(248) 557-9600   Toll-free: (800) 666-6233
Fax: (248) 557-9610   E-mail: info@afdom.org
Web: www.afdom.org

Purpose To provide financial assistance to minority high school seniors and currently-enrolled college students in Michigan.

Eligibility This program is open to high school seniors as well as college freshmen, sophomores, and juniors. Applicants must be members of at least 1 of the following minority groups: African American, Hispanic Americans, Asian American, Native American, or Arab/Chaldean American. Preferential consideration is given to applicants who are either employed by a company (for at least 6 months) or whose parent is employed by a company (for at least 1 year) that is an AFD member; however, membership is not required. Selection is based on academic performance, leadership, and participation in school and community activities.

Financial data The stipend is $1,000.

Duration 1 year; recipients may reapply.

Additional information This program is administered by Scholarship Program Administrators, Inc., 1201 Eighth Avenue South, P.O. Box 23737, Nashville, TN 27202-3737, (615) 320-3149, Fax: (615) 320-3151, E-mail: info@spaprog.com. Recipients must attend college on a full-time basis.

Number awarded At least 10 each year.

Deadline March of each year.

[38]
ASSOCIATION FOR WOMEN GEOSCIENTISTS MINORITY SCHOLARSHIP

Association for Women Geoscientists
Attn: AWG Foundation
P.O. Box 30645
Lincoln, NE 68503-0645
E-mail: awgscholarship@yahoo.com
Web: www.awg.org/eas/minority.html

Purpose To provide financial assistance to underrepresented minority women who are interested in working on an undergraduate degree in the geosciences.

Eligibility This program is open to women who are African American, Hispanic, or Native American (including Eskimo, Hawaiian, Samoan, or American Indian). Applicants must be full-time students working on, or planning to work on, an undergraduate degree in the geosciences (including geology, geophysics, geochemistry, hydrology, meteorology, physical oceanography, planetary geology, or earth science education). They must submit a 500-word essay on why they have chosen to major in the geosciences and their career goals, 2 letters of recommendation, high school and/or college transcripts, and SAT or ACT scores. Financial need is not considered in the selection process.

Financial data A total of $5,000 is available for this program each year.

Duration 1 year; may be renewed.

Additional information This program, first offered in 2004, is supported by ExxonMobil Foundation.
Number awarded 1 or more each year.
Deadline May of each year.

[39]
ASSOCIATION OF CUBAN ENGINEERS SCHOLARSHIPS

Association of Cuban Engineers
Attn: Selection Committee
P.O. Box 557575
Miami, FL 33255-7575
(305) 649-7429
Web: www.a-i-c.org

Purpose To provide financial assistance to undergraduate and graduate students of Cuban American heritage who are interested in preparing for a career in engineering.
Eligibility This program is open to U.S. citizens and legal residents who have completed at least 30 units of college work in the United States and are majoring or planning to major in some aspect of engineering. Applicants must be attending an ABET-accredited college or university within the United States or Puerto Rico as a full-time student with a GPA of 3.0 or higher. They must be of Cuban or other Hispanic heritage (at least 1 grandparent Cuban or other Hispanic nationality). Along with their application, they must submit brief essays on their family history, professional goals, extracurricular activities, work experience, and how they will help other Cuban and Hispanic engineering students in the future. Financial need is not considered in the selection process.
Financial data Stipends range from $500 to $1,000.
Duration 1 year.
Additional information This program includes the Luciano Goicochea Award (for the top-rated Cuban American student at the University of Miami) and the Noel Betancourt Award (for the top-rated Cuban American student at Florida International University).
Number awarded Up to 20 each year.
Deadline November of each year.

[40]
ASSOCIATION OF LATINO PROFESSIONALS IN FINANCE AND ACCOUNTING SCHOLARSHIPS

Association of Latino Professionals in Finance and
    Accounting
Attn: Scholarships
510 West Sixth Street, Suite 400
Los Angeles, CA 90017
(213) 243-0004   Fax: (213) 243-0006
E-mail: scholarships@national.alpfa.org
Web: www.alpfa.org

Purpose To provide financial assistance to undergraduate and graduate students of Hispanic descent who are preparing for a career in a field related to finance or accounting.
Eligibility This program is open to full-time undergraduate and graduate students who have completed at least 15 undergraduate units at a college or university in the United States or Puerto Rico with a GPA of 3.0 or higher. Applicants must be of Hispanic heritage, defined as having 1 parent fully Hispanic or both parents half Hispanic. They must

be working on a degree in accounting, finance, information technology, or a related field. Along with their application, they must submit a 2-page personal statement that addresses their Hispanic heritage and family background, personal and academic achievements, academic plans and career goals, efforts and plans for making a difference in their community, and financial need. U.S. citizenship or permanent resident status is required.
Financial data Stipends range from $1,000 to $5,000.
Duration 1 year.
Additional information The sponsoring organization was formerly named the American Association of Hispanic Certified Public Accountants. This program is administered by the Hispanic College Fund, 1717 Pennsylvania Avenue, Suite 460, Washington, DC 20006, (202) 296-5400, (800) 644-4223, Fax: (202) 296-3774.
Number awarded Varies each year; recently, 78 of these scholarships, worth $195,000, were awarded.
Deadline April of each year.

[41]
AVON GRANT SCHOLARSHIPS

Chicago Urban League
Attn: Education Department
4510 South Michigan Avenue
Chicago, IL 60653-3898
(773) 451-3565   Fax: (773) 285-7772
E-mail: info@cul-chicago.org
Web: www.cul-chicago.org

Purpose To provide financial assistance to Illinois residents who are women of color interested in full-time study at a 4-year college or university.
Eligibility This program is open to minority women residents of Illinois who will be full-time freshmen at a 4-year college or university. Applicants must have a GPA of 2.5 or higher, be a head of household, and be able to demonstrate financial need. An interview is required.
Financial data The stipend is $1,000 per year.
Duration 1 year.
Number awarded 2 each year.
Deadline May of each year.

[42]
AWIS SEATTLE SCHOLARSHIPS

Association for Women in Science-Seattle Chapter
c/o Fran Solomon, Scholarship Committee Chair
5805 16th Avenue, N.E.
Seattle, WA 98105
(206) 522-6441   E-mail: fran.solomon@metrokc.gov
Web: www.scn.org

Purpose To provide financial assistance to women undergraduates from any state majoring in science, mathematics, or engineering at colleges and universities in western Washington.
Eligibility This program is open to women from any state entering their junior or senior year at a 4-year college or university in western Washington. Applicants must have a declared major in science (e.g., biological sciences, environmental science, biochemistry, chemistry, pharmacy, geology, computer science, physics), mathematics, or engineering. Along with their application, they must submit

essays on the events that led to their choice of a major, their current career plans and long-term goals, and their volunteer and community activities. Financial need is considered in the selection process. At least 1 scholarship is reserved for a woman from a group that is underrepresented in science, mathematics, and engineering careers, including Native American Indians and Alaska Natives, Black/African Americans, Mexican Americans/Chicanas/Latinas, Native Pacific Islanders (Polynesians, Melanesians, and Micronesians), and women with disabilities.

Financial data Stipends range from $1,000 to $1,500.

Duration 1 year.

Additional information This program includes the following named awards: the Virginia Badger Scholarship, the Angela Paez Memorial Scholarship, and the Fran Solomon Scholarship. Support for the program is provided by several sponsors, including the American Chemical Society, Iota Sigma Pi, Rosetta Inpharmatics, and ZymoGenetics, Inc.

Number awarded Varies each year; recently, 11 of these scholarships were awarded.

Deadline March of each year.

[43]
BAKER FAMILY FOUNDATION SCHOLARSHIP

Baker Family Foundation
17 Gelnnon Farm Lane
Lebanon, NJ 08833
E-mail: info@bakerfamilyfoundation.org
Web: www.baakerfamilyfoundation.org

Purpose To provide financial assistance to high school students (especially minorities) facing obstacles when trying to attend college.

Eligibility Open to high school seniors interested in attending college. While the foundation does not target any specific ethnic group, the majority of the recipients come from urban minority groups. The first step in the application process is to find a sponsor, who will then submit part 1 of the preliminary application. If selected for the next stage, students submit part 2 of the application, as well as financial, academic, and any other necessary documentation. References are contacted and the candidates are interviewed. From this group, finalists are selected. Selection is based on financial need, desire to achieve, and academic performance (generally a GPA of 3.0 or higher).

Financial data The amount awarded varies, depending upon several factors: personal and family resources, the applicant's financial aid package, other outside scholarships, and any unusual circumstances that might have financial impact. The foundation attempts to "fill the gap" between the true costs of attending school and all other sources of financial aid. Funds may be used for tuition, room and board, transportation, day care expenses, family assistance, computer training, and college prep classes.

Duration 1 year; may be renewed if the recipient maintains at least a "B" average, continues to demonstrate financial need, and remains a student in good standing.

Number awarded Varies each year.

Deadline While applications may be submitted at any time, students are encouraged to submit their applications as soon after the first of the new year as possible.

[44]
BARBARA JORDAN MEMORIAL SCHOLARSHIP

Association of Texas Professional Educators
Attn: Scholarships
305 East Huntland Drive, Suite 300
Austin, TX 78752-3792
(512) 467-0071   Toll-free: (800) 777-ATPE
Fax: (512) 467-2203
Web: www.atpe.org/Awards/index.html

Purpose To provide financial assistance to undergraduate and graduate students enrolled in educator preparation programs at predominantly ethnic minority institutions in Texas.

Eligibility This program is open to juniors, seniors, and graduate students enrolled in educator preparation programs at predominantly ethnic minority institutions in Texas. Applicants must submit a 2-page essay on their personal philosophy toward education, why they want to become an educator, who influenced them the most in making their career decision, and why they are applying for the scholarship. Financial need is not considered in the selection process.

Financial data The stipend is $1,500 per year.

Duration 1 year.

Additional information The qualifying institutions are Huston-Tillotson College, Jarvis Christian College, Our Lady of the Lake University, Paul Quinn College, Prairie View A&M University, St. Mary's University of San Antonio, Sul Ross State University, Sul Ross State University Rio Grande College, Texas A&M International University, Texas A&M University at Kingsville, Texas Southern University, University of Houston, University of Houston-Downtown, University of St. Thomas, University of Texas at Brownsville and Texas Southmost College, University of Texas at El Paso, University of Texas at San Antonio, University of Texas-Pan American, University of the Incarnate Word, and Wiley College.

Number awarded Up to 6 each year.

Deadline May of each year.

[45]
BASF AGRICULTURAL PRODUCTS SCHOLARSHIPS

National FFA Organization
Attn: Scholarship Office
6060 FFA Drive
P.O. Box 68960
Indianapolis, IN 46268-0960
(317) 802-4321   Fax: (317) 802-5321
E-mail: scholarships@ffa.org
Web: www.ffa.org

Purpose To provide financial assistance to women and minority FFA members who are interested in studying specified agribusiness fields in college.

Eligibility This program is open to members who are either graduating high school seniors planning to enroll in college or students already enrolled in college. Applicants must 1) be interested in working full time on a 4-year degree in agricultural marketing, merchandising, or sales; 2) be women or members of a minority group; 3) have a GPA of 3.0 or higher; 4) have participated in community service; and 5) be able to demonstrate strong leadership skills and financial need. Selection is based on academic achievement (10 points for GPA, 10 points for SAT or ACT score, 10 points for class rank), leadership in FFA activities (30 points), leadership in community activities (10 points), and participation in the Supervised Agricultural Experience (SAE) program (30 points). U.S. citizenship is required.

Financial data The stipend is $1,000. Funds are paid directly to the recipient.

Duration 1 year; nonrenewable.

Additional information Funding for these scholarships is provided by BASF Agricultural Products.

Number awarded 7 each year.

Deadline February of each year.

[46]
BILOXI SUN HERALD MINORITY SCHOLARSHIP PROGRAM

Biloxi Sun Herald
Attn: Scholarship Committee
P.O. Box 4567
Biloxi, MS 39535-4567
(228) 896-2365   Fax: (228) 896-2151
Web: www.sunherald.com

Purpose To provide financial assistance to minority high school students in Mississippi who are interested in attending college to prepare for a career in the newspaper industry.

Eligibility This program is open to minority high school seniors graduating from high schools in Mississippi. They must be interested in attending college to prepare for a career in the news or business aspects of the newspaper industry. Along with their application, they must submit a 500-word essay on why they want to prepare for a career in the newspaper industry. Selection is based on the essay, 2 letters of recommendation, a transcript of grades (including SAT/ACT scores), journalism or business experience, and extracurricular activities.

Financial data The stipend is $1,000.

Duration 1 year.

Additional information The recipients of these scholarships are automatically entered into competition for the Knight Ridder Minority Scholarship Program of $40,000 over 4 years.

Number awarded 1 each year.

Deadline January of each year.

[47]
BLUE CROSS BLUE SHIELD OF WISCONSIN NURSING SCHOLARSHIPS

Wisconsin League for Nursing
2121 East Newport Avenue
Milwaukee, WI 53211-2952
(414) 332-6271
Web: www.cuw.edu/wln/scholarship.htm

Purpose To provide financial assistance to residents (especially minorities) of Wisconsin attending a school of nursing in the state.

Eligibility This program is open to residents of Wisconsin who working on an undergraduate degree at an accredited school of nursing in the state. Applicants must have completed at least half the credits needed for graduation. They may obtain applications only from their school of nursing; no applications are sent from the sponsor's office. Ethnic minority students are especially encouraged to apply. Selection is based on scholastic ability, professional abilities and/or community service, understanding of the nursing profession, goals upon graduation, and financial need.

Financial data Stipends range from $500 to $1,000.

Duration 1 year.

Additional information Information is also available from Mary Ann Tanner, P.O. Box 107, Long Lake, WI 53542-0107. This program is sponsored by Blue Cross Blue Shield of Wisconsin.

Number awarded Varies each year. Recently, 5 of these scholarships were awarded.

Deadline July of each year.

[48]
BNSF SCHOLARSHIP PROGRAM

Hispanic College Fund
Attn: National Director
1717 Pennsylvania Avenue, N.W., Suite 460
Washington, D.C. 20006
(202) 296-5400   Toll-free: (800) 644-4223
Fax: (202) 296-3774
E-mail: hcf-info@hispanicfund.org
Web: www.hispanicfund.org

Purpose To provide financial assistance to Hispanic American undergraduate students from designated states who are interested in preparing for a career in a business-related field.

Eligibility This program is open to U.S. citizens of Hispanic background (at least 1 grandparent must be 100% Hispanic) who are entering their freshman, sophomore, junior, or senior year of college. Applicants must be residents of Arizona, California, Colorado, Illinois, Kansas, Missouri, New Mexico, or Texas. They must be working on a bachelor's degree in accounting, economics, engineering, finance, information systems, marketing, or a related major and have a cumulative GPA of 3.0 or higher. They must be applying to or enrolled in a college or university in the 50 states or Puerto Rico as a full-time student. Financial need is considered in the selection process.

Financial data Stipends range from $500 to $5,000, depending on the need of the recipient, and average approximately $3,000. Funds are paid directly to the recipient's college or university to help cover tuition and fees.

Duration 1 year; recipients may reapply.

Additional information This program is sponsored by the Burlington Northern Santa Fe (BNSF) Foundation and administered by the Hispanic College Fund (HCF). All applications must be submitted online; no paper applications are available.

Number awarded Varies each year.

Deadline April of each year.

[49]
BOB GLAHN SCHOLARSHIP IN STATISTICAL METEOROLOGY

American Meteorological Society
Attn: Fellowship/Scholarship Program
45 Beacon Street
Boston, MA 02108-3693
(617) 227-2426, ext. 246   Fax: (617) 742-8718
E-mail: scholar@ametsoc.org
Web: www.ametsoc.org

Purpose To provide financial assistance to undergraduates (especially underrepresented minorities, women, and persons with disabilities) majoring in meteorology or an aspect of atmospheric sciences with an interest in statistical meteorology.

Eligibility This program is open to full-time students entering their final year of undergraduate study and majoring in meteorology or an aspect of the atmospheric or related oceanic and hydrologic sciences. Applicants must intend to make atmospheric or related sciences their career, with preference given to students who have demonstrated a strong interest in statistical meteorology. They must be U.S. citizens or permanent residents enrolled at a U.S. institution and have a cumulative GPA of 3.25 or higher. Along with their application, they must submit 200-word essays on 1) their most important achievements that qualify them for this scholarship, and 2) their career goals in the atmospheric or related oceanic or hydrologic fields. Selection is based on academic excellence and achievement; financial need is not considered. The sponsor specifically encourages applications from women, minorities, and students with disabilities who are traditionally underrepresented in the atmospheric and related oceanic sciences.

Financial data The stipend is $2,500 per year.

Duration 1 year.

Additional information Requests for an application must be accompanied by a self-addressed stamped envelope.

Number awarded 1 each year.

Deadline February of each year.

[50]
BOB STANLEY AND AL COMPTON MINORITY AND INTERNATIONAL SCHOLARSHIP

Baptist Communicators Association
Attn: Scholarship Committee
1715-K South Rutherford Boulevard, Suite 295
Murfreesboro, TN 37130
(615) 904-0152   E-mail: bca.office@comcast.net
Web: www.baptistcommunicators.org/scholar.htm

Purpose To provide financial assistance to minority and international students who are working on an undergraduate degree to prepare for a career in Baptist communications.

Eligibility This program is open to undergraduate students of minority ethnic or international origin. Applicants must be majoring in communications, English, journalism, or public relations with a GPA of 2.5 or higher. Their vocational objective must be in Baptist communications. Along with their application, they must submit a statement explaining why they desire to receive this scholarship.

Financial data The stipend is $1,000.

Duration 1 year; recipients may reapply.

Additional information This program was established in 1996.

Number awarded 1 each year.

Deadline January of each year.

[51]
BOOKER T. WASHINGTON SCHOLARSHIPS

National FFA Organization
Attn: Scholarship Office
6060 FFA Drive
P.O. Box 68960
Indianapolis, IN 46268-0960
(317) 802-4321   Fax: (317) 802-5321
E-mail: scholarships@ffa.org
Web: www.ffa.org

Purpose To provide financial assistance to minority FFA members who are interested in studying agriculture in college.

Eligibility This program is open to members who are graduating high school seniors planning to enroll full time in college. Applicants must be members of a minority ethnic group (African American, Asian American, Pacific Islander, Hispanic, Alaska Native, or American Indian) planning to work on a 4-year degree in agriculture. Selection is based on academic achievement (10 points for GPA, 10 points for SAT or ACT score, 10 points for class rank), leadership in FFA activities (30 points), leadership in community activities (10 points), and participation in the Supervised Agricultural Experience (SAE) program (30 points). U.S. citizenship is required.

Financial data Scholarships are either $10,000 or $5,000. Funds are paid directly to the recipient.

Duration 1 year; nonrenewable.

Number awarded 4 each year: 1 at $10,000 and 3 at $5,000.

Deadline February of each year.

[52]
BREAKTHROUGH TO NURSING SCHOLARSHIPS FOR RACIAL/ETHNIC MINORITIES

National Student Nurses' Association
Attn: NSNA Foundation
45 Main Street, Suite 606
Brooklyn, NY 11201
(718) 210-0705   Fax: (718) 210-0710
E-mail: nsna@nsna.org
Web: www.nsna.org

Purpose To provide financial assistance to disadvantaged minority undergraduate and graduate students who wish to prepare for careers in nursing.

Eligibility This program is open to students currently enrolled in state-approved schools of nursing or pre-nursing associate degree, baccalaureate, diploma, generic doctorate, or generic master's programs. Graduating high school seniors are not eligible. Support for graduate education is provided only for a first degree in nursing. Applicants must be able to demonstrate that they are from a disadvantaged background, including membership in a racial or ethnic minority underrepresented among registered nurses (American Indian or Alaska Native, Hispanic or Latino, Native

Hawaiian or other Pacific Islander, Black or African American, or Asian). Selection is based on academic achievement, financial need, and involvement in student nursing organizations and community health activities.

Financial data Stipends range from $1,000 to $2,500. A total of $120,000 is awarded each year by the foundation for all its scholarship programs.

Duration 1 year.

Additional information Applications must be accompanied by a $10 processing fee.

Number awarded Varies each year. Approximately 14 of these scholarships were awarded recently.

Deadline January of each year.

[53]
BROWN AND CALDWELL MINORITY SCHOLARSHIP

Brown and Caldwell
Attn: Scholarship Program
201 North Civic Drive, Suite 115
P.O. Box 8045
Walnut Creek, CA 94596
(925) 937-9010　　　　　　　　　Fax: (925) 937-9026
E-mail: scholarships@brwncald.com
Web: www.brownandcaldwell.com

Purpose To provide financial assistance to minority students working on an undergraduate degree in an environmental or engineering field.

Eligibility This program is open to members of minority groups (African Americans, Hispanics, Asians, Pacific Islanders, Native Americans, and Alaska Natives) who are full-time students in their junior year at an accredited 4-year college or university. Applicants must have a GPA of 3.0 or higher with a declared major in civil, chemical, or environmental engineering or an environmental science (e.g., biology, ecology, geology, hydrogeology, industrial hygiene, toxicology). Along with their application, they must submit an essay (up to 250 words) on why they chose to major in an environmental discipline. They must be U.S. citizens or permanent resident and available to participate in a summer internship at a Brown and Caldwell office. Financial need is not considered in the selection process.

Financial data The stipend is $3,000.

Duration 1 year.

Additional information As part of the paid summer internship at a Brown and Caldwell office at 1 of more than 40 cities in the country, the program provides a mentor to guide the intern through the company's information and communications resources.

Number awarded 1 each year.

Deadline February of each year.

[54]
BROWN FOUNDATION COLLEGE SCHOLARSHIPS

Brown Foundation for Educational Equity, Excellence
　and Research
1515 S.E. Monroe
Topeka, KS 66612
(785) 235-3939　　　　　　　　　Fax: (785) 235-1001
E-mail: brownfound@juno.com
Web: brownvboard.org/foundatn/sclrbroc.htm

Purpose To provide financial assistance to currently-enrolled college juniors of color who are interested in preparing for a teaching career.

Eligibility To be eligible for this scholarship, applicants must meet the following requirements: be a minority; be a college junior; be admitted to a teacher education program; be enrolled in an institution of higher education with an accredited program in education; have at least a 3.0 GPA; be enrolled at least half time; and submit 2 recommendations (from a teacher, counselor, or other school official and from a person familiar with the applicant). Selection is based on GPA, extracurricular activities, career plans, essays, and recommendations.

Financial data The stipend is $500 per year.

Duration 2 years (junior and senior years).

Additional information The first Brown Foundation Scholarships were awarded in 1989.

Number awarded 1 each year.

Deadline March of each year.

[55]
BUFFETT FOUNDATION SCHOLARSHIP PROGRAM

Buffett Foundation
Attn: Scholarship Office
P.O. Box 4508
Decatur, IL 62525
(402) 451-6011　　　　　　　E-mail: buffettfound@aol.com
Web: www.BuffettScholarships.org

Purpose To provide financial assistance to entering or currently-enrolled college students (preference given to minorities) in Nebraska.

Eligibility This program is open to U.S. citizens who are Nebraska residents. Applicants must be entering or currently enrolled in a state school, community college, or trade school in Nebraska. They must be in financial need, be the only family member presently receiving a grant from the foundation, have at least a 2.5 GPA, and have applied for federal financial aid. Selection is based on academic performance and financial need. Preference is given to minority students, students with disabilities, and married or unmarried students with dependents.

Financial data The maximum stipend is $2,500 per semester. Funds are sent directly to the recipient's school and must be used to pay tuition and fees; they may not be used to pay for books or other expenses.

Duration Up to 5 years for a 4-year college, or up to 3 years for a 2-year school. Students on scholarship may not drop out for a period of time and be reinstated as a scholarship recipient; they must reapply along with first-time students.

Additional information Students on a 12-month program or the quarter system may use the scholarship for summer tuition; students on the semester system may not use funds for summer school. Students who are not working must enroll in at least 12 credit hours; students who are working must enroll in at least 9 credit hours.

Deadline   April of each year.

[56]
BUREAU OF LAND MANAGEMENT AWARD

Hispanic Association of Colleges and Universities
Attn: National Scholarship Program
One Dupont Circle, N.W. Suite 605
Washington, DC 20036
(202) 467-0893   Fax: (202) 496-9177
TTY: (800) 855-2880   E-mail: scholarships@hacu.net
Web: scholarships.hacu.net/applications/applicants

Purpose   To provide financial assistance to undergraduate students who are majoring in fields related to natural resources at institutions that are members of the Hispanic Association of Colleges and Universities (HACU).

Eligibility   This program is open to full-time undergraduate students at HACU member and partner colleges and universities who are majoring in natural resource management or a related field. Applicants must submit an essay of 200 to 250 words that describes their academic and/or career goals, where they expect to be and what they expect to be doing 10 years from now, and what skills they can bring to an employer. They must be able to demonstrate financial need and a GPA of 3.2 or higher.

Financial data   The stipend is $3,000 per year.

Duration   1 year; nonrenewable.

Additional information   This program is sponsored by the U.S. Bureau of Land Management and administered by HACU.

Number awarded   1 or more each year.

Deadline   May of each year.

[57]
BUSINESS REPORTING INTERN PROGRAM FOR MINORITY COLLEGE SOPHOMORES AND JUNIORS

Dow Jones Newspaper Fund
P.O. Box 300
Princeton, NJ 08543-0300
(609) 452-2820   Fax: (609) 520-5804
E-mail: newsfund@wsj.dowjones.com
Web: DJNewspaperFund.dowjones.com

Purpose   To provide work experience and financial assistance to minority college students who are interested in careers in journalism.

Eligibility   This program is open to college sophomores and juniors who are U.S. citizens interested in careers in journalism and participating in a summer internship at a daily newspaper as a business reporter. Applicants must be members of a minority group (African American, Hispanic, Asian American, Pacific Islander, American Indian, or Alaskan Native) enrolled as full-time students. They must submit a resume, 3 to 5 recently-published clips, an list of courses with grades, and a 500-word essay.

Financial data   Interns receive a salary of $350 per week during the summer and a $1,000 scholarship at the successful completion of the program.

Duration   10 weeks for the summer internship; 1 year for the scholarship.

Number awarded   Up to 12 each year.

Deadline   October of each year.

[58]
CALIFORNIA REAL ESTATE ENDOWMENT FUND SCHOLARSHIP PROGRAM

California Community Colleges
Attn: Student Financial Assistance Programs
1102 Q Street
Sacramento, CA 95814-6511
(916) 324-0925   E-mail: rquintan@cccco.edu
Web: www.cccco.edu

Purpose   To provide financial assistance to disadvantaged California community college students who are studying real estate.

Eligibility   This program is open to students at community colleges in California who are majoring in real estate or (if their college does not offer a real estate major) business administration with a concentration in real estate. Applicants must have completed at least a 3-unit college course in real estate with a grade of "C" or better and must be enrolled in at least 6 semester units of real estate for the semester of the scholarship. Students must meet 1 of the following financial need criteria: 1) have completed the Free Application for Federal Student Aid (FAFSA) and been determined by their college to have financial need; 2) come from a family with an income less than $12,885 for 1 person, $17,415 for 2 persons, $21,945 for 3 persons, $26,475 for 4 persons, or an additional $4,530 for each additional family member; or 3) come from a family with an income less than $50,000 and be from a disadvantaged group (have low economic status and/or have been denied opportunities in society for reasons of gender, race, ethnicity, economics, language, education, physical disabilities, or other mitigating factors). Scholarships are awarded on a first-come, first-served basis.

Financial data   Awards up to $400 per semester are available.

Duration   1 semester; may be renewed if the student remains enrolled in at least 6 units of real estate with a GPA of 2.0 or higher.

Additional information   Students apply to their community college, not to the sponsoring organization.

Number awarded   From 75 to 90 each year; approximately $60,000 per year is available for this program.

Deadline   April of each year.

[59]
CALIFORNIA STRAWBERRY SCHOLARSHIP PROGRAM

California Strawberry Commission
180 Westridge Drive, Suite 101
P.O. Box 269
Watsonville, CA 95076-0269
(831) 724-1301   Fax: (831) 724-5973
Web: www.calstrawberry.com

Purpose   To provide financial assistance for college to high school seniors whose parents are farm workers in California's major strawberry-growing regions.

Eligibility   This program is open to high school seniors and the children of farm workers who have been employed (for at least the last 2 consecutive seasons) in the California strawberry harvest in these regions of the state, including Watsonville/Salinas, Santa Maria, Oxnard, Orange County/San Diego, and Fresno. Applicants must be applying for full-time enrollment at a 4-year college or university, junior college, or accredited trade school. They must be sponsored by a California strawberry grower. Along with their application, they must submit an essay (up to 2 pages) describing their career goals, a current high school transcript, and 2 letters of recommendation. Selection is based on merit. Application material is available in both English and Spanish.

Financial data Stipends range from $500 to $1,500 per year.

Duration 1 year. The nonprofit California Strawberry Growers Scholarship Fund, established in 1995, supports students who have received this scholarship in their high school senior year; all recipients may reapply each year for continued funding for their second, third, and fourth year of college and first year of graduate school.

Additional information This program was established in 1994. Recipients may major in any field.

Number awarded Varies each year; recently, 25 new recipients received a total of $18,700 in support and 64 continuing recipients received $46,650.

[60]
CALIFORNIA TABLE GRAPE WORKERS' SCHOLARSHIP PROGRAM

California Table Grape Commission
Attn: Scholarship Committee
392 West Fallbrook, Suite 101
Fresno, CA 93711-6150
(559) 447-8350   Toll-free: (800) 813-8478
Fax: (559) 447-9184
E-mail: info@freshcaliforniagrapes.com
Web: www.tablegrape.com

Purpose To provide financial assistance to the children of California table grape field workers who are interested in attending a branch of the California State University system.

Eligibility This program is open to high school graduates or seniors graduating in June. They, or their parents, must have worked in either of the 2 previous California table grape harvests. Farmers and their families, raisin and wine grape workers, students currently enrolled in college, permanent staff and members of the California Table Grape Commission and their families, and commission suppliers are not eligible. All applicants must intend to attend a 4-year college or university in California. Selection is based on academic performance, financial need, obstacles overcome, leadership ability and/or community service, and ability to succeed.

Financial data The stipend is $4,000 per year.

Duration 4 years, provided the recipient maintains a GPA of 2.0 or higher. Recipients must attend a branch of the California State University on a full-time basis.

Number awarded 3 each year.

Deadline March of each year.

[61]
CAMINO AL EXITO SCHOLARSHIP PROGRAM

Hispanic Scholarship Fund
Attn: Selection Committee
55 Second Street, Suite 1500
San Francisco, CA 94105
(415) 808-2350   Toll-free: (877) HSF-INFO
Fax: (415) 808-2302   E-mail: highschool@hsf.net
Web: www.hsf.net/scholarship/programs/camino.php

Purpose To provide financial assistance for college or graduate school to Hispanic residents of selected cities throughout the United States and children of Telemundo employees.

Eligibility This program is open to U.S. citizens, permanent residents, and visitors with a passport stamped I-551 who are of Hispanic heritage. Applicants must be 1) children of Telemundo employees, or 2) residents of the target Telemundo markets of Chicago, Los Angeles, Miami, or New York. They must have a GPA of 3.0 or higher and be graduating high school seniors or full-time undergraduate or graduate students at an accredited college or university in the United States, Puerto Rico, or the U.S. Virgin Islands. Along with their application, they must submit 600-word essays on 1) how their Hispanic heritage, family upbringing, and/or role models have influenced their personal long-term goals; 2) how they contribute to their community and what they have learned from their experiences; and 3) an academic challenge they have faced and how they have overcome it. Selection is based on academic achievement, personal strengths, leadership, and financial need.

Financial data Stipends range from $2,500 to $5,000 per year.

Duration 1 year.

Number awarded 1 or more each year.

Deadline December of each year.

[62]
CAMP SCHOLARSHIPS

College Assistance Migrant Program
Attn: Alumni Association
202 Sixth Avenue
Lewiston, ID 83501
(208) 792-2101   Fax: (208) 792-2550
E-mail: ggalindo@campaa.org
Web: campaa.org/Scholarships.html

Purpose To provide financial assistance for college to high school seniors from migrant or seasonal farmworker families.

Eligibility This program is open to migrant and seasonal farmworkers and their families working in agricultural activities directly related to the production of crops, dairy products, poultry, or livestock; the cultivation or harvesting of trees; or fish farms. Applicants may verify eligibility in 1 of 3 ways: 1) participation during high school or eligibility to participate in a Title 1 Migrant Education Program; 2) participation or eligibility to participate in the Workforce Investment Act (WIA); or 3) verification that they or their parents have spent at least 75 days during the past 24 months as a migrant and/or seasonal (not year-round) farmworker as their primary employment. They must also plan to enroll as a freshman at a 4-year college or university that participates in the College Assistance Migrant Program (CAMP) of the

U.S. Department of Education to complete a bachelor's degree, be a U.S. citizen or permanent resident, and be able to document financial need.

Financial data The stipends depend on the need of the recipients and the school they attend.

Duration 1 year.

Additional information Currently, 45 colleges and universities participate in the CAMP program, including schools in Arkansas, California, Colorado, Florida, Georgia, Idaho, Kansas, Michigan, Mississippi, Missouri, New Mexico, New York, Ohio, Oregon, Pennsylvania, Puerto Rico, Texas, Washington, and Wisconsin.

Number awarded Approximately 2,400 each year.

Deadline February of each year.

[63]
CANFIT PROGRAM SCHOLARSHIPS

California Adolescent Nutrition, Physical Education, and
  Culinary Arts Scholarships
2140 Shattuck Avenue, Suite 610
Berkeley, CA 94704
(510) 644-1533   Toll-free: (800) 200-3131
Fax: (510) 644-1535   E-mail: info@canfit.org
Web: www.canfit.org/scholarships.html

Purpose To provide financial assistance to minority undergraduate and graduate students who are studying nutrition, physical education, or culinary arts in California.

Eligibility Eligible to apply are American Indians/Alaska Natives, African Americans, Asians/Pacific Islanders, and Latinos/Hispanics who are enrolled in either: 1) an approved master's or doctoral graduate program in nutrition, public health nutrition, or physical education or in a preprofessional practice program approved by the American Dietetic Association at an accredited university in California; or, 2) an approved bachelor's or professional certificate program in culinary arts, nutrition, or physical education at an accredited university or college in California. Graduate student applicants must have completed at least 12 units of graduate course work and have a cumulative GPA of 3.0 or higher; undergraduate applicants must have completed 50 semester units or the equivalent of college credits and have a cumulative GPA of 2.5 or higher. Selection is based on financial need, academic goals, and community nutrition or physical education activities.

Financial data Graduate stipends are $1,000 each and undergraduate stipends are $500 per year.

Additional information A goal of the California Adolescent Nutrition and Fitness (CANFit) program is to improve the nutritional status and physical fitness of California's low-income multi-ethnic youth aged 10 to 14. By offering these scholarships, the program hopes to encourage more students to consider careers in adolescent nutrition and fitness.

Number awarded 5 graduate scholarships and 10 undergraduate scholarships are available each year.

Deadline March of each year.

[64]
CARL A. SCOTT BOOK SCHOLARSHIPS

Council on Social Work Education
Attn: Chair, Carl A. Scott Memorial Fund
1725 Duke Street, Suite 500
Alexandria, VA 22314-3457
(703) 683-8080   Fax: (703) 683-8099
E-mail: eafrancis@cswe.org
Web: www.cswe.org

Purpose To provide financial assistance to ethnic minority social work students in their last year of study for a baccalaureate or master's degree.

Eligibility This program is open to students from ethnic groups of color (African American, Asian American, Mexican American, Puerto Rican, and American Indian) who are in the last year of study for a social work degree in an accredited baccalaureate or master's degree program. Applicants must have a cumulative GPA of 3.0 or higher and be enrolled full time. They must demonstrate a commitment to work for equity and social justice in social work.

Financial data The award is $500.

Duration This is a 1-time award.

Number awarded 2 each year.

Deadline May of each year.

[65]
CAROLE SIMPSON SCHOLARSHIP

Radio and Television News Directors Foundation
1600 K Street, N.W., Suite 700
Washington, DC 20006-2838
(202) 467-5218   Fax: (202) 223-4007
E-mail: karenb@rtndf.org
Web: www.rtndf.org

Purpose To provide financial assistance to outstanding undergraduate students, especially minorities, who are interested in preparing for a career in electronic journalism.

Eligibility Eligible are sophomore or more advanced undergraduate students enrolled in an electronic journalism sequence at an accredited or nationally-recognized college or university. Applicants must submit 1 to 3 examples of reporting or producing skills on audio or video cassette tapes (no more than 15 minutes total), a description of their role on each story and a list of who worked on each story and what they did, a statement explaining why they are seeking a career in broadcast or cable journalism, and a letter of endorsement from a faculty sponsor that verifies the applicant has at least 1 year of school remaining. Preference is given to undergraduate students of color.

Financial data The stipend is $2,000, paid in semiannual installments of $1,000 each.

Duration 1 year.

Additional information The Radio and Television News Directors Foundation (RTNDF) also provides an all-expense paid trip to the Radio-Television News Directors Association (RTNDA) annual international conference. It defines electronic journalism to include radio, television, cable, and online news. Previous winners of any RTNDF scholarship or internship are not eligible.

Number awarded 1 each year.

Deadline April of each year.

[66]
CAROLINA RICE/UNIVISION RADIO SCHOLARSHIPS

Riviana Foods Inc.
Attn: The Carolina Scholarship
75-22 37th Avenue, Suite 224
Jackson Heights, NY 11327
Web: www.carolinarice.com/scholarship

Purpose To recognize and reward, with college scholarships, Hispanic and other high school seniors in the New York/New Jersey metropolitan areas who submit outstanding essays.

Eligibility This competition is open to seniors graduating from high schools in the greater New York/New Jersey metropolitan area. Applicants must submit an essay, up to 250 words in length, on the topic "How does my education affect my family." Essays may be written in Spanish or in English. Selection is based on conciseness, originality, grammar, and spelling. Finalists are interviewed.

Financial data The award is a $2,000 college scholarship.

Duration The competition is held annually.

Additional information This program, which began in 1987, is jointly sponsored by Riviana Foods Inc. of Houston, Texas and Univision Communications Inc., the premier Spanish- language media company in the United States. Information is also available from Barbara Miller, Hispanic Broadcasting Corporation, 485 Madison Avenue, New York, NY 10022, (212) 310-6077.

Number awarded 5 each year.

Deadline February of each year.

[67]
CASA OF OREGON SCHOLARSHIP

Hispanic Metropolitan Chamber
Attn: Scholarship Committee
P.O. Box 1837
Portland, OR 97207
(503) 222-0280
Web: www.hmccoregon.com

Purpose To provide financial assistance for college and graduate school to Hispanic residents of Oregon and Clark County, Washington who are from a farmworker household.

Eligibility This program is open to residents of Oregon and Clark County, Washington who are of Hispanic ancestry. Applicants must be from a farmworker family and be enrolled or planning to enroll in an accredited community college, 4-year university, or graduate school. Along with their application, they must submit 250-word essays on what being a Latino student means to them, their life as a member of a farmworker family and the obstacles they have had to overcome, why they should be selected to receive another scholarship from this sponsor (if they are applying for a renewal), and/or what they intend to do with their degree in 10 years (if they are a first-time applicant). If they wish to be considered for a scholarship for low-income families, they may also submit documentation of financial need.

Financial data The stipend is $2,500.

Duration 1 year; may be renewed.

Number awarded Varies each year; recently, 3 of these scholarships were awarded.

Deadline February of each year.

[68]
CATERPILLAR SCHOLARS AWARD

Society of Manufacturing Engineers
Attn: SME Education Foundation
One SME Drive
P.O. Box 930
Dearborn, MI 48121-0930
(313) 425-3304   Toll-free: (800) 733-4763, ext. 3304
Fax: (313) 425-3411   E-mail: foundation@sme.org
Web: www.sme.org

Purpose To provide financial assistance to undergraduates (special attention given to minorities) enrolled in a degree program in manufacturing engineering or manufacturing engineering technology.

Eligibility Applicants must be full-time students attending a degree-granting institution in North America and preparing for a career in manufacturing engineering. They must have completed at least 30 units in a manufacturing engineering or manufacturing engineering technology curriculum with a minimum GPA of 3.0. Minority applicants may apply as incoming freshmen. Need is not considered in awarding scholarships (unless 2 or more applicants have equal qualifications).

Financial data The stipend is $2,000.

Duration 1 year; may be renewed.

Additional information This program is sponsored by Caterpillar, Inc.

Number awarded 5 each year.

Deadline January of each year.

[69]
CELEBRATING DIVERSITY SCHOLARS PROGRAM

McDonald's Family Restaurants of Greater Washington, D.C.
c/o GolinHarris
2200 Clarendon Boulevard, Suite 1100
Arlington, VA 22201
(703) 741-7500   E-mail: molear@golinharris.com
Web: www.mcdonaldsexpo.com

Purpose To provide financial assistance for college to high school seniors in the greater Washington, D.C. area who have helped to develop an appreciation for cultural diversity.

Eligibility This program is open to college-bound seniors graduating from high schools in Washington, D.C. and designated counties or cities in Maryland, Virginia, and West Virginia. Applicants must be able to demonstrate academic achievement (GPA of 3.0 or higher), leadership, character, and community service. Along with their application, they must submit 200-word essays on 1) how education is important in developing an appreciation for cultural diversity, and 2) the best lessons they have learned from their community service experiences.

Financial data The stipend is $1,500. Funds are paid directly to the recipient's college or university.

Duration 1 year.

Additional information A goal of this program is to honor diversity and award scholarships across ethnic groups. It is available to residents of the District of Columbia; the Maryland counties of Alleghany, Calvert, Carroll, Charles, Cumberland, Frederick, Garrett, Montgomery, Prince George's, St. Mary's, and Washington; the Virginia counties of Arlington, Clarke, Culpeper, Fairfax, Fauquier, Frederick, King George, Loudoun, Page, Prince William, Rappahannock, Shenandoah, Spotsylvania, Stafford, Warren, and Westmoreland; the independent Virginia cities of Alexandria, Fairfax, Falls Church, Fredericksburg, Manassas, Manassas Park, and Winchester; and the West Virginia counties of Berkeley, Grant, Hampshire, Hardy, Jefferson, Mineral, and Morgan.

Number awarded At least 50 each year.

Deadline February of each year.

[70]
CHARLOTTE OBSERVER MINORITY SCHOLARSHIPS

Charlotte Observer
Attn: Zaira Goodman
600 South Tryon Street
P.O. Box 30308
Charlotte, NC 28230-3038
(704) 358-5715   Fax: (704) 358-5707
E-mail: zgoodman@charlotteobserver.com
Web: www.charlotteobserver.com

Purpose To provide financial assistance to minority high school seniors in North and South Carolina who are interested in preparing for a career in the newspaper field.

Eligibility This program is open to minority seniors at high schools in the service area of the *Charlotte Observer* (North and South Carolina). Applicants must be planning to attend college to study advertising, finance, human resources, information/Internet technology, marketing, or other field related to journalism and business communications. They must submit an original essay explaining why they want to prepare for a career in journalism or business communications, what they know about Knight Ridder and how they see themselves contributing to the company in the future, 2 letters of recommendation, a transcript, SAT/ACT scores, and up to 3 samples of work with bylines. Selection is based primarily on GPA and involvement in school publications.

Financial data The stipend is $1,000 per year.

Duration 1 year.

Additional information The recipients of these scholarships are automatically entered into competition for the Knight Ridder Minority Scholarship Program of $40,000 over 4 years.

Number awarded 2 each year.

Deadline November of each year.

[71]
CHEN SCHOLARSHIP

Coors Hispanic Employee Network
Attn: Grace Valdez
P.O. Box 1454
Golden, CO 80401
(303) 277-5258   Fax: (303) 277-5568

Purpose To provide financial assistance for college to high school seniors in Colorado who are of Hispanic descent.

Eligibility Applicants must be U.S. citizens, be Colorado residents, be of Hispanic heritage, be high school seniors, have a GPA of 2.5 or higher, and be planning to attend col-

lege after graduation. Selection is based on academic record, financial need, and educational plans. To apply, students must submit a signed application, a personal statement, a transcript, and 2 letters of recommendation.

Financial data The stipend is $1,000 per year.

Duration 1 year.

Additional information This program was established in 1991.

Number awarded 10 each year.

Deadline February of each year.

[72]
CHERYL TORRENCE-CAMPBELL SCHOLARSHIPS

National Institutes of Health Black Scientists
   Association
Attn: Scholarship Committee
P.O. Box 2262
Kensington, MD 20891-2262
Web: bsa.od.nih.gov

Purpose To provide financial assistance to underrepresented minority high school seniors from Washington, D.C. who plan to study science in college.

Eligibility This program is open to seniors graduating from public and private high schools in the District of Columbia who are members of ethnic or racial groups underrepresented in the field of biomedical research. Applicants must have been accepted into an accredited college or university to major in the sciences. They must submit a 1-page essay on why they have chosen to major in science in college. Preference is given to students who are financially disadvantaged.

Financial data The stipend is $1,000.

Duration 1 year.

Number awarded 2 each year.

Deadline May of each year.

[73]
CHEVROLET EXCELLENCE IN EDUCATION AWARD FOR HISPANIC STUDENTS

General Motors Corporation
Chevrolet Motor Division
Attn: GM Scholarship Administration Center
700 West Fifth Avenue
Mail Code 2001
Naperville, IL 60563
Toll-free: (888) 377-5233
E-mail: scholarshipinfo@gmsac.com

Purpose To provide financial assistance for college to Hispanic American high school seniors.

Eligibility This program is open to Hispanic students currently completing the senior year of high school with sufficient credits to graduate in the spring term with a GPA of 3.2 or higher. Applicants must be planning to enrolled in an accredited 2-year or 4-year college or university in the following fall. They must be able to demonstrate both academic excellence and community service (e.g., activities, volunteerism, work experience) and be a U.S. citizen or have eligibility to work in the United States. Along with their application, they must include a letter of recommendation from a high school teacher or administrator, official transcripts from their high school, and a personal statement (500 to 750 words) about how their high school experiences (academics, extracurricular activities, outside activities, work experience) have prepared them for college and why they should be considered for this scholarship. Selection is based on that statement, academic performance, leadership and participation in school and community activities, work experience, and career and educational aspirations. Financial need is not considered.

Financial data The stipend is $1,000 per year.

Duration 1 year.

Additional information This program was established by the Chevrolet Motor Division of General Motors Corporation.

Number awarded Varies each year.

Deadline April of each year.

[74]
CHICANA/LATINA FOUNDATION SCHOLARSHIPS

Chicana/Latina Foundation
Attn: Scholarship Program
1419 Burlingame Avenue, Suite N
Burlingame, CA 94010
(650) 373-1084　　　　　　　Fax: (650) 373-1090
E-mail: info@chicanalatina.org
Web: www.chicanalatina.org/scholarship.html

Purpose To provide financial assistance for higher education to Latina women who live in or come from any state and attend school in the San Francisco Bay area.

Eligibility This program is open to Latina women who either have resided for at least 2 years in or are currently enrolled in accredited colleges, universities, or community colleges in the following California counties: Alameda, Contra Costa, Marin, Monterey, Napa, San Francisco, San Mateo, Santa Clara, Santa Cruz, Solano, or Sonoma. Undergraduate students must have completed at least 15 college units, must be enrolled as full-time students, must have a GPA of 2.5 or higher, and must complete 3 essays (on their family background, their community activities, and their career goals). Graduate students must verify acceptance to a graduate school and complete a supplementary application that requires 3 essays: on an issue affecting the Latina community in the Bay area, on their personal background, and on their leadership of their younger Chicana/Latina sisters so they stay in school and graduate. Selection is based on commitment to Latina women's progress and development, demonstrated leadership qualities, involvement within the Latino community, clarity of direction and goals, academic achievement, and letters of recommendation. Students who received a scholarship from the foundation within the past 4 years are not eligible.

Financial data The stipend is $1,500 per year.

Duration 1 year.

Additional information The foundation was formerly known as the Chicana Foundation of Northern California. Recipients must agree to volunteer at least 5 hours in the following year in support of the Chicana/Latina Foundation.

Number awarded Varies each year; recently, 18 of these scholarships were awarded.

Deadline March of each year.

[75]
CHIPS QUINN SCHOLARS PROGRAM

Freedom Forum
Attn: Chips Quinn Scholars Program
1101 Wilson Boulevard
Arlington, VA 22209
(703) 284-3934　　　　　　　Fax: (703) 284-3543
E-mail: kcatone@freedomforum.org
Web: www.chipsquinn.org

Purpose To provide work experience, career mentoring, and scholarship support to minority college students and recent graduates who are majoring in journalism.

Eligibility This program is open to students of color who are college juniors, seniors, or recent graduates with journalism majors or career goals in newspapers. Candidates must be nominated or endorsed by journalism faculty, campus media advisers, editors of newspapers, or leaders of minority journalism associations. They must be enrolled at an Historically Black College or University (HBCU) or a college or university that has significant numbers of students who are members of ethnic or racial minority groups. Along with their application, they must submit a resume, transcripts, work samples, 2 letters of recommendation, and an essay on why they believe they should be selected for this program. They must have a car and be available to work as a full-time intern during the spring or summer. U.S. citizenship or permanent resident status is required. Campus newspaper experience is strongly encouraged.

Financial data Students chosen for this program receive a travel stipend to attend a workshop at the Freedom Forum in Arlington, Virginia prior to reporting for their internship. Upon completion of the internship, they receive a $1,000 scholarship.

Duration Internships are for 10 to 12 weeks; the scholarship is for 1 year.

Additional information This program was established in 1991 in memory of the late John D. Quinn Jr., managing editor of the *Poughkeepsie Journal*. Funding is provided by the Freedom Forum, formerly the Gannett Foundation. After graduating from college and obtaining employment with a newspaper, alumni of this program are eligible to apply for fellowship support to attend professional journalism development activities.

Number awarded Varies each year. Recently, 94 scholarships were awarded, including 23 who completed their internships in spring and 71 whose internships were in the summer. Since the program began, 828 scholars have been selected.

Deadline October of each year.

[76]
CHOOSENURSING.COM SCHOLARSHIP PROGRAM

Coalition for Nursing Careers in California
Attn: chooseNursing.com
1950 Franklin Street, Ninth Floor
Oakland, CA 94612
(510) 987-2279　　　　　　　Fax: (510) 987-1299
Web: www.choosenursing.com

Purpose To provide financial assistance to underrepresented and financially disadvantaged students at nursing schools in California.

Eligibility This program is open to students enrolled in an accredited associate or bachelor's nursing degree program in California. Applicants must come from an underrepresented and financially disadvantaged (family income may not exceed $50,000 per family member) group. They must have a GPA of 2.5 or higher and may not yet have a R.N. license. Along with their application, they must submit a 500-word essay on what led them to choose a career in nursing, the obstacles or challenges they have faced and overcome to get where they are today, and their professional goals or aspirations for their nursing career. Selection is based on financial need, academic achievement, health care involvement, and enthusiasm or passion for nursing.

Financial data The stipend is $2,000.

Duration 1 year.

Additional information This program, first offered in 2002, is sponsored by *NurseWeek* magazine, chooseNursing.com, and the Coalition for Nursing Careers in California.

Number awarded 5 each year.

Deadline October of each year.

[77]
CLEVELAND ADVERTISING ASSOCIATION EDUCATION FOUNDATION SCHOLARSHIPS

Cleveland Advertising Association
Attn: Education Foundation
20325 Center Ridge Road, Suite 670
Cleveland, OH 44116
(440) 673-0020   Fax: (440) 673-0025
E-mail: adassoc@clevead.com
Web: www.clevead.com/education/scholarships.php

Purpose To provide financial assistance to undergraduate students (especially minorities) who are residents of Ohio majoring in a field related to advertising at a college or university in the state.

Eligibility This program is open to residents of Ohio who are full-time seniors, juniors, or second-semester sophomores at colleges and universities in the state. Applicants must be majoring in advertising or a related communications/marketing field and have a GPA of 3.0 or higher. They must submit transcripts, 2 letters of recommendation, and an essay describing their career goals. Financial need is not considered in the selection process. Some of the scholarships are set aside for U.S. citizens of African, Asian, Hispanic, Native American, or Pacific Island descent.

Financial data Stipends range from $1,000 to $2,500.

Duration 1 year.

Additional information This program includes the following named scholarships: the Arras Group Minority Scholarship, the Wyse Advertising Scholarship, the Thomas Brennan Memorial Scholarship, the Hitchcock Fleming and Associates Scholarship, the Innis Maggiore Scholarship, the Marcus Thomas Scholarship, the Laurie Mitchell and Company Scholarship, and the Plain Dealer Bob Hagley Scholarship.

Number awarded Varies each year. Recently, this program awarded 11 scholarships: 2 at $2,500, 1 at $2,000, 3 at $1,500, and 5 at $1,000.

Deadline October of each year.

[78]
COCA-COLA ADVANCING TO UNIVERSITIES SCHOLARSHIP PROGRAM

Hispanic Scholarship Fund
Attn: Selection Committee
55 Second Street, Suite 1500
San Francisco, CA 94105
(415) 808-2350   Toll-free: (877) HSF-INFO
Fax: (415) 808-2302   E-mail: cctransfer@hsf.net
Web: www.hsf.net

Purpose To provide financial assistance to Hispanic American students who are attending selected community colleges and interested in transferring to a 4-year institution.

Eligibility This program is open to U.S. citizens, permanent residents, and visitors with a passport stamped I-551. Applicants must be of Hispanic heritage and enrolled part time or full time at designated community colleges with a GPA of 3.0 or higher. They must be planning to transfer and enroll full time at an accredited 4-year college or university in the United States. Along with their application, they must submit 600-word essays on 1) how their Hispanic heritage, family upbringing, and/or role models have influenced their personal long-term goals; 2) how they contribute to their community and what they have learned from their experiences; and 3) an academic challenge they have faced and how they have overcome it. Selection is based on academic achievement, personal strengths, leadership, and financial need.

Financial data Stipends range from $1,000 to $2,000 per year.

Duration 1 year.

Additional information The designated community colleges include those in the Atlanta area (Atlanta Metropolitan College, Dalton College, Darton College, Gainesville College, Georgia Perimeter College); California (East Los Angeles College, Los Angeles City College, Los Angeles Mission College, Los Angeles Pierce College, Chabot College, Ohlone College, San Jose City College); Chicago (Harold Washington College, Richard J. Daley College, Wilbur Wright College); Florida (Broward Community College, Miami-Dade Community College, Daytona Beach Community College, Southern College, Valencia Community College, Hillsborough Community College, St. Petersburg Junior College); New York (Borough of Manhattan Community College, Bronx Community College, La Guardia Community College, Queensborough Community College); and Texas (El Paso Community College, El Centro College, Eastfield College, Richland College, Houston Community College). This program is sponsored by the Hispanic Scholarship Fund (HSF) in partnership with the Coca-Cola Foundation.

Number awarded 1 or more each year.

Deadline January of each year.

[79]
COLGATE "BRIGHT SMILES, BRIGHT FUTURES" MINORITY SCHOLARSHIPS

American Dental Hygienists' Association
Attn: Institute for Oral Health
444 North Michigan Avenue, Suite 3400
Chicago, IL 60611
(312) 440-8918   Toll-free: (800) 735-4916
Fax: (312) 440-8929   E-mail: institute@adha.net
Web: www.adha.org/institute/Scholarship/index.htm

Purpose To provide financial assistance to minority students and males of any race enrolled in undergraduate programs in dental hygiene.

Eligibility This program is open to members of groups currently underrepresented in the dental hygiene profession (Native Americans, African Americans, Hispanics, Asians, and males) who are active members of the Student American Dental Hygienists' Association (SADHA) or the American Dental Hygienists' Association (ADHA). Applicants must have a GPA of 3.0 or higher, be able to document financial need of at least $1,500, and have completed at least 1 year of full-time enrollment in an accredited dental hygiene program in the United States. Along with their application, they must submit a statement that covers their long-term career goals, their intended contribution to the dental hygiene profession, their professional interests, and the manner in which their degree will enhance their professional capacity.

Financial data Stipends range from $1,000 to $2,000.

Duration 1 year; nonrenewable.

Additional information These scholarships are sponsored by the Colgate-Palmolive Company.

Number awarded 2 each year.

Deadline April of each year.

[80]
COLLEGE SCHOLARSHIP PROGRAM OF THE HISPANIC SCHOLARSHIP FUND

Hispanic Scholarship Fund
Attn: Selection Committee
55 Second Street, Suite 1500
San Francisco, CA 94105
(415) 808-2350   Toll-free: (877) HSF-INFO
Fax: (415) 808-2302   E-mail: college1@hsf.net
Web: www.hsf.net/scholarship/programs/college.php

Purpose To provide financial assistance for college or graduate school to Hispanic American students.

Eligibility This program is open to U.S. citizens, permanent residents, and visitors with a passport stamped I-551. Applicants must be of Hispanic heritage and enrolled full time in a degree program at an accredited community college, 4-year university, or graduate school in the United States, Puerto Rico, or the U.S. Virgin Islands. They must have completed at least 12 undergraduate units with a GPA of 3.0 or higher and have applied for federal financial aid. Along with their application, they must submit 600-word essays on 1) how their Hispanic heritage, family upbringing, and/or role models have influenced their personal long-term goals; 2) how they contribute to their community and what they have learned from their experiences; and 3) an academic challenge they have faced and how they have overcome it. Selection is based on academic achievement, personal strengths, leadership, and financial need.

Financial data Stipends normally range from $1,000 to $3,000 per year.

Duration 1 year; recipients may reapply.

Additional information Since this program began in 1975, more than $144 million has been awarded to more than 68,000 Hispanic students.

Number awarded More than 4,000 each year.

Deadline October of each year.

[81]
COLLEGE STUDENT PRE-COMMISSIONING INITIATIVE

U.S. Coast Guard
Attn: Coast Guard Recruiting
4200 Wilson Boulevard, Suite 450
Arlington, VA 22203
Toll-free: (877) NOW-USCG, ext. 2115
Web: www.gocoastguard.com/scholarships.html

Purpose To provide financial assistance to college students at minority institutions willing to serve in the Coast Guard following graduation.

Eligibility This program is open to students enrolled as sophomores or juniors at approved 4-year Historically Black Colleges and Universities (HBCUs), Hispanic Serving Institutions (HSIs), and other approved minority institutions of higher learning. Applicants must be U.S. citizens; have a GPA of 2.5 or higher; have scores of 1000 or higher on the SAT, 1100 or higher on the SAT I, 23 or higher on the ACT, or 110 or higher on the ASVAB GT; be between 21 and 26 years of age at the time of college graduation; and meet all physical requirements for a Coast Guard commission. They must agree to attend the Coast Guard Officer Candidate School following graduation and serve on active duty as an officer for at least 3 years.

Financial data Those selected to participate receive full payment of tuition, books, and fees; monthly housing and food allowances; medical and life insurance; special training in leadership, management, law enforcement, navigation, and marine science; 30 days paid vacation per year; and a monthly salary of up to $2,200.

Duration 2 years.

Number awarded Varies each year.

Deadline February of each year.

[82]
COLORADO SOCIETY OF CPAS ETHNIC DIVERSITY SCHOLARSHIPS FOR HIGH SCHOOL STUDENTS

Colorado Society of Certified Public Accountants
Attn: CSCPA Educational Foundation
7979 East Tufts Avenue, Suite 500
Denver, CO 80237-2845
(303) 741-8613   Toll-free: (800) 523-9082 (within CO)
Fax: (303) 773-6344   E-mail: gmantz@cocpa.org
Web: www.cocpa.org

Purpose To provide financial assistance to minority high school seniors in Colorado who plan to study accounting in college.

Eligibility This program is open to African American, Hispanic, Asian American, American Indian, and Pacific Islander high school seniors in Colorado planning to major in accounting at a college or university in the state. Applicants must have a GPA of 3.0 or higher. Selection is based primarily on scholastic achievement.

Financial data The stipend is $1,000.

Duration 1 year; nonrenewable.

Number awarded 3 each year.

Deadline February of each year.

[83]
COMMUNITY COLLEGE TRANSFER PROGRAM OF THE HISPANIC SCHOLARSHIP FUND

Hispanic Scholarship Fund
Attn: Selection Committee
55 Second Street, Suite 1500
San Francisco, CA 94105
(415) 808-2350   Toll-free: (877) HSF-INFO
Fax: (415) 808-2302   E-mail: cctransfer@hsf.net
Web: www.hsf.net

Purpose To provide financial assistance to Hispanic American students who are attending a community college and interested in transferring to a 4-year institution.

Eligibility This program is open to U.S. citizens, permanent residents, and visitors with a passport stamped I-551. Applicants must be of Hispanic heritage and part-time or full-time community college students with a GPA of 3.0 or higher. They must be planning to transfer and enroll full time at an accredited 4-year college or university in the United States, Puerto Rico, or the U.S. Virgin Islands and have applied for federal financial aid. Along with their application, they must submit 600-word essays on 1) how their Hispanic heritage, family upbringing, and/or role models have influenced their personal long-term goals; 2) how they contribute to their community and what they have learned from their experiences; and 3) an academic challenge they have faced and how they have overcome it. Selection is based on academic achievement, personal strengths, leadership, and financial need.

Financial data Stipends range from $1,000 to $2,500 per year.

Duration 1 year; may reapply.

Number awarded At least 600 each year.

Deadline January of each year.

[84]
CONGRESSIONAL HISPANIC CAUCUS INSTITUTE SCHOLARSHIP AWARDS

Congressional Hispanic Caucus Institute, Inc.
911 Second Street, N.E.
Washington, DC 20002
(202) 543-1771   Toll-free: (800) EXCEL-DC
Fax: (202) 546-2143   E-mail: chci@chci.org
Web: www.chciyouth.org

Purpose To provide financial assistance for college or graduate school to students of Hispanic descent.

Eligibility This program is open to U.S. citizens and permanent residents who are Hispanic as defined by the U.S. Census Bureau (individuals of Mexican, Puerto Rican, Cuban, Central and South American, and other Spanish and Latin American descent). Applicants must be attending or planning to attend an accredited community college, 4-year university, or professional or graduate program as a full-

time student. They must submit evidence of financial need, consistent active participation in public and/or community service activities, good writing skills, and 1-page essays on 1) how effective the public education system has been in addressing the needs of the Latino community and what policy recommendations they suggest to improve the system; and 2) the field of study they plan to pursue and how the Latino community will benefit.

Financial data The stipend is $2,500 at 4-year and graduate institutions or $1,000 at 2-year community colleges.

Duration 1 year.

Number awarded Varies each year. Recently, 63 of these scholarships were awarded: 5 to community college students, 40 to undergraduates, and 18 to graduate students.

Deadline April of each year.

[85]
CONNECTICUT ASSOCIATION OF LATINOS IN HIGHER EDUCATION SCHOLARSHIPS

Connecticut Association of Latinos in Higher
   Education, Inc.
950 Main Street, Suite 1104
Hartford, CT 06103-1207
(860) 906-5234
E-mail: ca-CALAHE@ccc.commnet.edu
Web: www.calahe.org

Purpose To provide financial assistance for college to Latino residents of Connecticut.

Eligibility This program is open to graduating high school seniors and current college students who have been residents of Connecticut during the preceding 12 months. Applicants must come from a Latino background and have a GPA of 3.0 or higher. U.S. citizenship or permanent resident status is required. Selection is based on academic achievement, financial need, community service, and an essay on "How do you feel education is going to impact your ability to continue assisting others to pursue an education?"

Financial data A stipend is awarded (amount not specified).

Duration 1 year.

Additional information Further information on this program is available from Dr. Wilson Luna, Gateway Community College, Dean of Student Services, 60 Sargent Drive, New Haven, CT 06511, (203) 285-2210, Fax: (203) 285-2142, E-mail: wluna@gwcc.commnet.edu, and from the Hartford Foundation for Public Giving, 85 Gillett Street, Hartford, CT 06105, (860) 548-1888, Fax: (860) 524-8346, E-mail: hfpg2@hfpg.org. The program includes the John Soto Scholarship, the Marta Vallin Memorial Scholarship, and the Thomas M. Blake Memorial Scholarship (limited to students from the Hartford Public Schools).

Number awarded Varies each year; recently, 7 of these scholarships were awarded.

Deadline April of each year.

[86]
CONNECTICUT EDUCATION FOUNDATION SCHOLARSHIPS FOR MINORITY COLLEGE STUDENTS

Connecticut Education Foundation, Inc.
c/o Connecticut Education Association
21 Oak Street, Suite 500
Hartford, CT 06106-8001
(860) 525-5641   Toll-free: (800) 842-4316
Fax: (860) 725-6388   E-mail: phila@cea.org
Web: www.cea.org/cef/minguidelines.html

Purpose To provide financial assistance to minority college students in Connecticut who are interested in preparing for a teaching career.

Eligibility This program is open to minority students (Blacks, Native Americans or Alaskan Natives, Asian or Pacific Islanders, and Hispanics or Latinos) who have been accepted into a teacher preparation program at an accredited college or university in Connecticut. Applicants must have earned a GPA of 2.75 or higher. Finalists may be interviewed. Financial need is considered in the selection process.

Financial data The stipend is $750.

Duration 1 year; may be renewed.

Number awarded At least 1 each year.

Deadline April of each year.

[87]
CONNECTICUT EDUCATION FOUNDATION SCHOLARSHIPS FOR MINORITY HIGH SCHOOL STUDENTS

Connecticut Education Foundation, Inc.
c/o Connecticut Education Association
21 Oak Street, Suite 500
Hartford, CT 06106-8001
(860) 525-5641   Toll-free: (800) 842-4316
Fax: (860) 725-6388   E-mail: phila@cea.org
Web: www.cea.org/cef/minguidelines.html

Purpose To provide financial assistance to minority high school students in Connecticut who are interested in preparing for a teaching career.

Eligibility This program is open to minority students (Blacks, Native Americans or Alaskan Natives, Asian or Pacific Islanders, and Hispanics or Latinos) who have been accepted at an accredited 2- or 4-year college or university in Connecticut. Applicants must intend to enter the teaching profession. They must have earned a GPA of 2.75 or higher. Finalists may be interviewed. Financial need is considered in the selection process.

Financial data The stipend is $500.

Duration 1 year; may be renewed.

Number awarded At least 1 each year.

Deadline April of each year.

[88]
CONNECTICUT MINORITY TEACHER INCENTIVE PROGRAM

Connecticut Department of Higher Education
Attn: Office of Student Financial Aid
61 Woodland Street
Hartford, CT 06105-2326
(860) 947-1855   Fax: (860) 947-1838
E-mail: mtip@ctdhe.org
Web: www.ctdhe.org/SFA/sfa.htm

Purpose To provide financial assistance and loan repayment to minority upper-division college students in Connecticut who are interested in teaching at public schools in the state.

Eligibility This program is open to minority juniors and seniors enrolled full time in Connecticut college and university teacher preparation programs. Students must be nominated by the education dean at their institution.

Financial data The maximum stipend is $5,000 per year. In addition, if recipients complete a credential and teach at a public school in Connecticut, they may receive up to $2,500 per year, for up to 4 years, to help pay off college loans.

Duration Up to 2 years.

Number awarded Varies each year.

Deadline September of each year.

[89]
CONNECTICUT SPECIAL EDUCATION TEACHER INCENTIVE GRANT

Connecticut Department of Higher Education
Attn: Education and Employment Information Center
61 Woodland Street
Hartford, CT 06105-2326
(860) 947-1846   Toll-free: (800) 842-0229 (within CT)
Fax: (860) 947-1311   E-mail: setig@ctdhe.org
Web: www.ctdhe.org/SFA/sfa.htm

Purpose To provide financial assistance to undergraduate and graduate students (particularly underrepresented minorities) in Connecticut who are preparing for a career as a special education teacher.

Eligibility This program is open to full-time juniors and seniors and full- or part-time graduate students who are residents of Connecticut. Applicants must be enrolled in 1) special education teacher preparation programs at selected universities in Connecticut; or 2) out-of-state teacher preparation programs seeking cross-endorsement for teaching "low-incidence student" areas. They must be nominated by the dean of education at their school and have a stated intent to teach in a Connecticut public school, an approved private special education facility, or a Regional Educational Service Center. Priority is given to minority (African American, Hispanic/Latino, Asian American, and Native American) and bilingual students and to Connecticut residents enrolled in an approved out-of-state program.

Financial data The stipend is $5,000 per year for full-time study or $2,000 per year for part-time graduate study.

Duration 1 year.

Additional information The approved in-state programs are at Central Connecticut State University, Fairfield University, Saint Joseph College, Southern Connecticut State University, University of Connecticut, and University of Hartford. The programs for students seeking cross-endorsement certification for teaching students who are blind and partially-sighted or visually impaired are at Hunter College of CUNY (New York, New York), Dominican College (Orangeburg, New York), Teachers College of Columbia University (New York, New York), and University of Northern Colorado (Greeley, Colorado). The programs for students seeking cross-endorsement certification for teaching students who are deaf or hearing-impaired are at Hunter College, Teachers College, Clarke School for the Deaf at Smith College (Northampton, Massachusetts), and Boston University (Boston, Massachusetts).

Number awarded Varies each year.

Deadline August of each year.

[90]
CONNTESOL SCHOLARSHIPS

Connecticut Teachers of English to Speakers of Other
  Languages
c/o Sue Goldstein
42 Crosswinds Drive
Noank, CT 06340
E-mail: goldstei@galaxyinternet.net

Purpose To provide financial assistance for college to Connecticut high school seniors whose native language is not English.

Eligibility This program is open to seniors graduating from high schools in Connecticut whose first language is not English. Selection is based on academic achievement, community service, an essay, and financial need.

Financial data The stipend is at least $250 for students at 2-year colleges or $500 for students at 4-year colleges and universities.

Duration 1 year.

Number awarded 2 each year.

Deadline May of each year.

[91]
COORS LIGHT ACADEMIC SUCCESS IN EDUCATION (CLASE) SCHOLARSHIP AWARD

Hispanic Association of Colleges and Universities
Attn: National Scholarship Program
One Dupont Circle, N.W. Suite 605
Washington, DC 20036
(202) 467-0893   Fax: (202) 496-9177
TTY: (800) 855-2880   E-mail: scholarships@hacu.net
Web: scholarships.hacu.net/applications/applicants

Purpose To provide financial assistance to undergraduate and graduate students studying business or pharmacy at institutions in California that belong to the Hispanic Association of Colleges and Universities (HACU).

Eligibility This program is open to full-time undergraduate and graduate students at 4-year HACU member and partner colleges in California. Applicants must have a declared major in pharmacy or business and a GPA of 3.0 or higher. They must be able to demonstrate financial need. Along with their application, they must submit an essay of 200 to 250 words that describes their academic and/or career goals, where they expect to be and what they expect to be doing 10 years from now, and what skills they can bring to an employer.

Financial data The stipend is $1,000 per year.

Duration 1 year; nonrenewable.

Additional information This program is sponsored by the Coors Brewing Company and administered by HACU. Recently, the sponsor provided additional funding in conjunction with the concert tour of the musical group *Maná Revolución de Amor*. For every concert ticket sold, the group donated $0.50 and Coors matched with an additional $0.50, to a combined maximum contribution of $200,000.

Number awarded Varies each year.

Deadline May of each year.

[92]
COX NEWSPAPER DIVISION MINORITY JOURNALISM SCHOLARSHIP

Cox Newspapers, Inc.
Attn: Scholarship Administrator
6205 Peachtree Dunwoody Road
P.O. Box 105720
Atlanta, GA 30348
(678) 645-0000
Web: www.coxnews.com

Purpose To provide work experience and financial assistance to minority undergraduate and graduate students from areas served by selected Cox Enterprises newspapers who are preparing for a career in the newspaper industry.

Eligibility This program is open to minority (African American, Hispanic, Asian American, Native American) undergraduate and graduate students interested in newspaper careers. Applicants must be interested in continuing their program of study as well as working as an intern at a participating Cox newspaper. Cox employees and their families are eligible. Each newspaper establishes its own criteria regarding GPA requirements, supporting documentation, and essay requirements. In general, applicants must have demonstrated an interest in the department (newsroom, online, advertising, accounting, marketing, or information technology) in which they would like to intern and be able to demonstrate experience with campus publications and/or daily deadlines.

Financial data All educational expenses are paid for 4 years of college, including room, board, books, and tuition. The approximate total value of the award is $40,000.

Duration The scholarship is awarded for 4 years. The recipient is expected to intern at the newspaper during the summer and holiday breaks throughout the 4 years of college.

Additional information The scholarship is administered by major newspapers owned by the sponsor: the *Atlanta Journal and Constitution, Austin American-Statesman,* and *Palm Beach Post.* Applications are available from the Cox Newspapers headquarters in Atlanta, the offices of the various Cox-owned newspapers, and from guidance offices of high schools in the city selected for the scholarship for that year.

Number awarded 1 each year.

Deadline April of each year.

[93]
CSCPA ETHNIC DIVERSITY SCHOLARSHIPS FOR COLLEGE STUDENTS

Colorado Society of Certified Public Accountants
Attn: CSCPA Educational Foundation
7979 East Tufts Avenue, Suite 500
Denver, CO 80237-2845
(303) 741-8613   Toll-free: (800) 523-9082 (within CO)
Fax: (303) 773-6344   E-mail: gmantz@cocpa.org
Web: www.cocpa.org

Purpose To provide financial assistance to minority undergraduate or graduate students in Colorado who are studying accounting.

Eligibility This program is open to African Americans, Hispanics, Asian Americans, American Indians, and Pacific Islanders studying at a college or university in Colorado at the associate, baccalaureate, or graduate level. Applicants must have completed at least 1 intermediate accounting class, be declared accounting majors, have completed at least 8 semester hours of accounting classes, and have a GPA of at least 3.0. Selection is based first on scholastic achievement and second on financial need.

Financial data The stipend is $1,000. Funds are paid directly to the recipient's school to be used for books, tuition, room, board, fees, and expenses.

Duration 1 year; recipients may reapply.

Number awarded 2 each year.

Deadline June of each year.

[94]
C.T. LANG JOURNALISM MINORITY SCHOLARSHIP AND INTERNSHIP

Albuquerque Journal
Attn: Scholarship Committee
7777 Jefferson Street, N.E.
P.O. Drawer J
Albuquerque, NM 87103
(505) 823-7777

Purpose To provide financial assistance and work experience to minority upper-division students in journalism programs at universities in New Mexico.

Eligibility This program is open to minority students majoring or minoring in journalism at a New Mexico university in their junior year with a GPA of 2.5 or higher. Applicants must be enrolled full time. They must be planning a career in newswriting, photography, design, copy editing, or online. Selection is based on clips of published stories, a short autobiography that explains the applicant's interest in the field, a grade transcript, and a letter of recommendation.

Financial data The scholarship is $1,000 per semester; the recipient also receives a paid internship and moving expenses.

Duration The scholarship is for 2 semesters (fall and spring). The internship is for 1 semester.

Additional information This program is funded by the *Albuquerque Journal,* where the internship takes place.

Number awarded 1 each year.

Deadline December of each year.

[95]
DAIMLERCHRYSLER/HENAAC SCHOLARS PROGRAM

Hispanic Engineer National Achievement Awards
    Conference
3900 Whiteside Street
Los Angeles, CA 90063
(323) 262-0997   Fax: (323) 262-0946
E-mail: info@henaac.org
Web: www.henaac.org

Purpose To provide financial assistance to Hispanic undergraduate students majoring in electrical or mechanical engineering.

Eligibility This program is open to Hispanic undergraduate students who are enrolled full time in electrical or mechanical engineering. Applicants must have a GPA of 3.0 or higher and be able to work in the United States. Academic achievement and campus community activities are considered in the selection process. U.S. citizenship is required.

Financial data Stipends range from $1,000 to $5,000.

Duration 1 year; recipients may reapply.

Additional information This program is sponsored by DaimlerChrysler as part of its effort to support the mission of the Hispanic Engineer National Achievement Awards Conference (HENAAC): to promote technical excellence and leadership in the Hispanic community.

Number awarded 1 or more each year.

Deadline April of each year.

[96]
DAMON P. MOORE SCHOLARSHIP

Indiana State Teachers Association
Attn: Scholarships
150 West Market Street, Suite 900
Indianapolis, IN 46204
(317) 263-3400   Toll-free: (800) 382-4037
Fax: (317) 655-3700   E-mail: kmcallen@ista-in.org
Web: www.ista-in.org

Purpose To provide financial assistance to ethnic minority high school seniors in Indiana who are interested in studying education in college.

Eligibility This program is open to ethnic minority public high school seniors in Indiana who are interested in studying education in college. Selection is based on academic achievement, leadership ability as expressed through co-curricular activities and community involvement, recommendations, and a 300-word essay on their educational goals and how they plan to use this scholarship.

Financial data The stipend is $1,000.

Duration 1 year; may be renewed for 2 additional years if the recipient maintains at least a "C+" GPA.

Additional information This program was established in 1987.

Number awarded 1 each year.

Deadline February of each year.

[97]
DCNNOA/GENERAL DYNAMICS SCHOLARSHIP

National Naval Officers Association-Washington, D.C.
    Chapter
Attn: Scholarship Program
9805 Fox Run Drive
Clinton, MD 20735-3087
(202) 874-4994   E-mail: willie.evans@occ.treas.gov
Web: www.dcnnoa.org

Purpose To provide financial assistance to minority high school seniors from the Washington, D.C. area who are interested in majoring in engineering in college.

Eligibility This program is open to minority seniors at high schools in the Washington, D.C. metropolitan area who plan to enroll full time in an engineering program at an accredited 2-year or 4-year college or university. Applicants must have a GPA of 3.0 or higher and be U.S. citizens or permanent residents. Selection is based on academic achievement, community involvement, and financial need.

Financial data The stipend is $5,000 per year.

Duration 1 year; nonrenewable.

Additional information Recipients are not required to join or affiliate with the military in any way. This program is sponsored by General Dynamics.

Number awarded 1 each year.

Deadline March of each year.

[98]
DELL/UNCF CORPORATE SCHOLARS PROGRAM

United Negro College Fund
Attn: Corporate Scholars Program
P.O. Box 1435
Alexandria, VA 22313-9998
Toll-free: (866) 671-7237   E-mail: internship@uncf.org
Web: www.uncf.org/internships/index.asp

Purpose To provide financial assistance and work experience to undergraduate and graduate students, especially minorities, majoring in designated fields and interested in an internship at Dell Computer Corporation's corporate headquarters near Austin, Texas.

Eligibility This program is open to rising juniors and graduate students who are enrolled full time at institutions that are members of the United Negro College Fund (UNCF) or at any other 4-year college or university. Applicants must be majoring in business administration, computer science, engineering (computer, electrical, or mechanical), finance, human resources, management information systems, marketing, or supply chain management with a GPA of 3.0 or higher. Along with their application, they must submit a 1-page essay about themselves and their career goals, including information about their personal background and any particular challenges they have faced. Finalists are interviewed by a team of representatives from Dell, the program's sponsor.

Financial data The program provides a paid summer internship, housing accommodations in Austin, round-trip transportation to and from Austin, and (based on financial need and successful internship performance) a $10,000 scholarship.

Duration 10 to 12 weeks for the internship; 1 year for the scholarship.

Number awarded Varies each year.

Deadline January of each year.

[99]
DENNY'S SCHOLARSHIP PROGRAM

Hispanic College Fund
Attn: National Director
1717 Pennsylvania Avenue, N.W., Suite 460
Washington, D.C. 20006
(202) 296-5400   Toll-free: (800) 644-4223
Fax: (202) 296-3774
E-mail: hispaniccollegefund@earthlink.net
Web: www.hispanicfund.org

Purpose To provide financial assistance to Hispanic American undergraduate students who are interested in preparing for a career in business, computer science, or engineering.

Eligibility This program is open to U.S. citizens of Hispanic background (at least 1 grandparent must be 100% Hispanic) who are entering their freshman, sophomore, junior, or senior year of college. Applicants must be working on a bachelor's degree in business, computer science, engineering, or a business-related major and have a cumulative GPA of 3.0 or higher. They must be applying to or enrolled in a college or university in the 50 states or Puerto Rico as a full-time student. Financial need is considered in the selection process.

Financial data Stipends range from $500 to $5,000, depending on the need of the recipient, and average approximately $3,000. Funds are paid directly to the recipient's college or university to help cover tuition and fees.

Duration 1 year; recipients may reapply.

Additional information This program, which began in 1996, is sponsored by Denny's. All applications must be submitted online; no paper applications are available.

Number awarded Varies each year.

Deadline April of each year.

[100]
DESGC UNDERGRADUATE TUITION SCHOLARSHIPS

Delaware Space Grant Consortium
c/o University of Delaware
Bartol Research Institute
104 Center Mall, #217
Newark, DE 19716-4793
(302) 831-1094   Fax: (302) 831-1843
E-mail: desgc@bartol.udel.edu
Web: www.delspace.org

Purpose To provide financial support to undergraduate students (particularly minorities, women, and persons with disabilities) in Delaware and Pennsylvania involved in space-related studies.

Eligibility This program is open to undergraduate students in aerospace engineering and space science-related fields studying at institutions belonging to the Delaware Valley Space Grant College (DVSGC) Consortium. U.S. citizenship is required. As a component of the U.S. National Aeronautics and Space Administration (NASA) Space Grant program, this program encourages applications from women, minorities, and persons with disabilities.

Financial data This program provides tuition assistance up to $4,000 per year.

Duration 1 year; may be renewed.

Additional information This program, established in 1996, is funded by NASA. Members of the consortium include Delaware State University (Dover, Delaware), Delaware Technical and Community College (Dover, Georgetown, Newark, and Wilmington, Delaware), Franklin and Marshall College (Lancaster, Pennsylvania), Gettysburg College (Gettysburg, Pennsylvania), Lehigh University (Bethlehem, Pennsylvania), Swarthmore College (Swarthmore, Pennsylvania), University of Delaware (Newark, Delaware), Villanova University (Villanova, Pennsylvania), and Wilmington College (New Castle, Delaware).

Number awarded Varies each year; recently, 8 of these scholarships were awarded.

Deadline February of each year.

[101]
DIETETIC TECHNICIAN PROGRAM SCHOLARSHIPS

American Dietetic Association
Attn: Accreditation, Education Programs, and Student
   Operations
120 South Riverside Plaza, Suite 2000
Chicago, IL 60606-6995
(312) 899-0040   Toll-free: (800) 877-1600, ext. 5400
Fax: (312) 899-4817   E-mail: education@eatright.org
Web: www.eatright.org

Purpose To provide financial assistance to student members of the American Dietetic Association (ADA) who are in the first year of a dietetic technician program.

Eligibility This program is open to ADA student members in the first year of study in a CADE-approved or accredited dietetic technician program. Applicants must be U.S. citizens or permanent residents and show promise of being a valuable, contributing member of the profession. Some scholarships require membership in a specific dietetic practice group, residency in a specific state, or underrepresented minority group status. The same application form can be used for all categories.

Financial data Stipends range from $500 to $4,500.

Duration 1 year.

Additional information Funds must be used for the second year of study.

Number awarded Varies each year, depending upon the funds available. Recently, the sponsoring organization awarded 144 scholarships for all its programs.

Deadline February of each year.

[102]
DON SAHLI–KATHY WOODALL MINORITY STUDENT SCHOLARSHIPS

Tennessee Education Association
801 Second Avenue North
Nashville, TN 37201-1099
(615) 242-8392   Toll-free: (800) 342-8267
Fax: (615) 259-4581
Web: www.teateachers.org

Purpose To provide financial assistance to minority high school seniors in Tennessee who are interested in majoring in education.

Eligibility This program is open to minority high school seniors in Tennessee who are planning to major in education. Application must be made by either a Future Teachers of America chapter affiliated with the Tennessee Education Association (TEA) or by the student with the recommendation of an active TEA member. Selection is based on academic record, leadership ability, economic need, and demonstrated interest in becoming a teacher.

Financial data The stipend is $1,000.

Duration 1 year.

Number awarded 1 each year.

Deadline February of each year.

[103]
DONALD AND ITASKER THORNTON MEMORIAL SCHOLARSHIP

Thornton Sisters Foundation
P.O. Box 21
Atlantic Highlands, NJ 07716
(732) 872-1353   E-mail: tsfoundation2001@yahoo.com
Web: www.thorntonsisters.com/ttsf.htm

Purpose To provide financial assistance for college to women of color in New Jersey.

Eligibility This program is open to women of color (defined as African Americans, Latino Americans, Caribbean Americans, and Native Americans) who are graduating from high schools in New Jersey. Applicants must have a GPA of "C+" or higher and be able to document financial need. They must be planning to attend an accredited 4-year college or university. Along with their application, they must submit a 500-word essay describing their family background, personal and/or economic disadvantages, honors or academic distinctions, and community involvement and activities.

Financial data A stipend is awarded (amount not specified). Funds are to be used for tuition and/or books.

Duration 1 year; nonrenewable.

Number awarded 1 or more each year.

Deadline May of each year.

[104]
DOUVAS MEMORIAL SCHOLARSHIP

Wyoming Department of Education
Attn: Director, Programs Unit
2300 Capitol Avenue
Cheyenne, WY 82002-0050
(307) 777-7168   Fax: (307) 777-6234

Purpose To provide financial assistance to high school seniors or students in Wyoming who are first-generation Americans.

Eligibility This program is open to first-generation youth in Wyoming who demonstrate need and are motivated to attend college. First-generation Americans are those born in the United States but whose parents were not born here. Applicants must be high school seniors or between the ages of 18 and 22. They must be Wyoming residents and be willing to use the scholarship at Wyoming's community colleges or the University of Wyoming.

Financial data The stipend is $500, payable in 2 equal installments. Funds are paid directly to the recipient's school.

Duration 1 year.
Additional information This scholarship was first awarded in 1995.
Number awarded 1 each year.
Deadline April of each year.

[105]
DR. HILDEGARD E. PEPLAU SCHOLARSHIP

American Psychiatric Nurses Association
Attn: APN Foundation
1555 Wilson Boulevard, Suite 515
Arlington, VA 22209
(703) 243-2443　　　　　　Fax: (703) 243-3390
E-mail: inform@apna.org
Web: www.apna.org/foundation/scholarships.html

Purpose To provide financial assistance to students and registered nurses (especially minorities) working on a degree in nursing.
Eligibility This program is open to students and registered nurses enrolled in an NLN-accredited program in nursing. Applicants must submit 3 essays (each up to 500 words) on the following topics: 1) their career goals, how education will enhance those goals, and their contribution to the profession; 2) their professional activities, involvement, continuing education, and scholarly contributions; and 3) their voluntary community activities. Financial need is not considered in the selection process. Minorities are especially encouraged to apply.
Financial data The stipend is $1,000.
Duration 1 year.
Number awarded 1 or more each year.
Deadline January of each year.

[106]
DR. JUAN ANDRADE, JR. SCHOLARSHIP FOR YOUNG HISPANIC LEADERS

United States Hispanic Leadership Institute
431 South Dearborn Street, Suite 1203
Chicago, IL 60605
(312) 427-8683　　　　　　Fax: (312) 427-5183
E-mail: ushli@aol.com
Web: quepasa.osu.edu/MHSLCscholarship.doc

Purpose To provide financial assistance for college to Hispanic students in the United States.
Eligibility This program is open to U.S. citizens and permanent residents who are enrolled or accepted for enrollment as full-time students at a 4-year college or university or a 2-year school in the United States. Applicants must have at least 1 parent of Hispanic ancestry. They must be able to demonstrate financial need. Along with their application, they must submit 1) a 250- to 500-word essay on their family history, life and/or work experiences that have influenced them, pertinent extracurricular and community involvement activities, and a self-description; 2) a 500- to 750-word essay on the future of Hispanics in America, the kind of leadership needed, and any role they hope to play in providing such leadership; 3) a transcript; and 4) 3 letters of reference.
Financial data The stipend is $1,000 for students attending a 4-year institution and $500 for students attending a 2-year school.

Duration 1 year.
Additional information This program began in 1994. Recipients are expected to pay for their own travel expenses to Chicago to attend a luncheon of the sponsor where they are introduced. Expenses for lodging and meals are covered by the sponsor.
Number awarded 1 or more each year.
Deadline September of each year.

[107]
DR. JUAN D. VILLARREAL-HDA FOUNDATION SCHOLARSHIPS

Hispanic Dental Association
Attn: HDA Foundation
188 West Randolph Street, Suite 415
Chicago, IL 60601
(312) 577-4013　　　　　　Toll-free: (800) 852-7921
Fax: (312) 577-0052
E-mail: HispanicDental@hdassoc.org
Web: www.hdassoc.org

Purpose To provide financial assistance to Hispanic dental hygiene and dental students at institutions in Texas.
Eligibility This program is open to Hispanic dental hygiene and dental students. Applicants must have been accepted or be currently enrolled at an accredited dental school in Texas as a full-time student. Along with their application, they must submit an essay on their career goals, especially their contribution to the Hispanic community. Selection is based on commitment and dedication to improving health in the Hispanic community, leadership skills, scholastic achievement, and community service.
Financial data Stipends are $1,000 or $500.
Duration 1 year.
Additional information This program began in 1995.
Number awarded 1 or more each year.
Deadline June of each year for dental students; July of each year for dental hygiene students.

[108]
DR. SCHOLL FOUNDATION SCHOLARSHIPS

Chicago Urban League
Attn: Education Department
4510 South Michigan Avenue
Chicago, IL 60653-3898
(773) 451-3565　　　　　　Fax: (773) 285-7772
E-mail: info@cul-chicago.org
Web: www.cul-chicago.org

Purpose To provide financial assistance to Illinois residents of color enrolled at a 4-year college or university.
Eligibility This program is open to Illinois residents of color who are full-time undergraduate students at a 4-year college or university with at least a 2.5 GPA. Applicants may be majoring in any field. They must be able to demonstrate financial need.
Financial data The stipend is $2,000 per year.
Duration 1 year.
Additional information This program is offered as part of the Chicago Urban League's Whitney M. Young, Jr. Memorial Scholarship Fund, established in 1970. It is sponsored by the Dr. Scholl Foundation.
Number awarded Varies each year.

Deadline   May of each year.

[109]
EAST OHIO CONFERENCE BOARD OF ORDAINED MINISTRY ETHNIC MINORITY GRANTS

United Methodist Church-East Ohio Conference
Attn: Board of Ordained Ministry
8800 Cleveland Avenue, N.W.
P.O. Box 2800
North Canton, OH 44720
(330) 499-3972   Toll-free: (800) 831-3972
Fax: (330) 499-3279
Web: www.eocumc.com

Purpose   To provide financial assistance to ethnic minority undergraduate and graduate students who are preparing for ordained ministry in the East Ohio Conference.

Eligibility   This program is open to ethnic minority college and graduate students who are preparing for ordained ministry in the East Ohio Conference. Students must be recommended to receive this aid either by their District Superintendent or by the District Committee on Ordained Ministry where they hold their relationship. Applicants must attend a college or seminary that is fully accredited by the University Senate. They do not need to be certified candidates. Ethnic minority undergraduate pre-theological students are also eligible.

Financial data   The stipend is $500 per year.

Duration   1 year.

Additional information   Information is also available from Preston Forbes, Seminary Scholarships and Grants Secretary, 9071 Inverrary Drive, Warren, OH 44484, (330) 856-2631, E-mail: forbes@onecom.com.

Number awarded   1 or more each year.

Deadline   September of each year.

[110]
EATON MULTICULTURAL SCHOLARS PROGRAM

Eaton Corporation
Attn: EMSP
1111 Superior Avenue
Cleveland, OH 44114-2584
(216) 523-4354   E-mail: mildredneumann@eaton.com
Web: www.eatonjobs.com/career/career_choices.asp

Purpose   To provide financial assistance and work experience to minority college students interested in a career as an engineer.

Eligibility   This program is open to full-time minority students who are U.S. citizens or permanent residents. Applicants must have completed 1 year in an accredited program and have 3 remaining years of course work before completing a bachelor's degree. They must be majoring in computer science/data processing, electrical engineering, or mechanical engineering. Selection is based on academic performance, the student's school recommendation, and an expressed interest in pursuing challenging and rewarding internship assignments.

Financial data   Stipends range from $500 to $3,000 per year. Funds are paid directly to the recipient's university to cover the cost of tuition, books, supplies, equipment, and fees.

Duration   3 years.

Additional information   In addition to the scholarships, recipients are offered paid summer internships at company headquarters in Cleveland. The target schools participating in this program recently were Cornell, Detroit-Mercy, Florida A&M, Georgia Tech, Illinois at Chicago, Illinois at Urbana-Champaign, Lawrence Technological, Marquette, Massachusetts Institute of Technology, Michigan at Ann Arbor, Michigan at Dearborn, Michigan State, Milwaukee School of Engineering, Minnesota, Morehouse College, North Carolina A&T State, North Carolina State, Northwestern, Notre Dame, Ohio State, Purdue, Southern, Tennessee, Western Michigan, and Wisconsin at Madison. This program was established in 1994. Until 2002, it was known as the Eaton Minority Engineering Scholars Program.

Number awarded   Varies each year.

Deadline   December of each year.

[111]
ECHHO SCHOLARSHIP

Educators in College Helping Hispanics Onward
c/o Maggie McClendon
1 University Plaza
Youngstown, OH 44555-0001
Web: www.echho.org/aid.html

Purpose   To provide financial assistance for college to Hispanic Americans.

Eligibility   Open to Hispanic Americans who are U.S. citizens or permanent residents, have a high school or college GPA of at least 2.5, and have applied to, have been accepted at, or are currently enrolled at a postsecondary institution that is a member of Educators in College Helping Hispanics Onward (E.C.H.H.O.). Applicants must be 1 of the following: a graduating high school senior, a GED recipient, a nontraditional student (23 years of age or older), or a currently-enrolled undergraduate student.

Financial data   The stipend is at least $500.

Duration   1 year.

Deadline   March of each year.

[112]
ED BRADLEY SCHOLARSHIP

Radio and Television News Directors Foundation
1600 K Street, N.W., Suite 700
Washington, DC 20006-2838
(202) 467-5218   Fax: (202) 223-4007
E-mail: karenb@rtndf.org
Web: www.rtndf.org

Purpose   To provide financial assistance to outstanding undergraduate students, especially minorities, who are preparing for a career in electronic journalism.

Eligibility   Eligible are sophomore or more advanced undergraduate students enrolled in an electronic journalism sequence at an accredited or nationally-recognized college or university. Applicants must submit 1 to 3 examples of reporting or producing skills on audio or video cassette tapes (no more than 15 minutes total), a statement explaining why they are interested in a career in broadcast or cable journalism, and a letter of endorsement from a faculty sponsor that verifies the applicant has at least 1 year of school remaining. Preference is given to undergraduate students of color.

Financial data The stipend is $10,000, paid in semiannual installments of $5,000 each.
Duration 1 year.
Additional information The Radio and Television News Directors Foundation (RTNDF) also provides an all-expense paid trip to the Radio-Television News Directors Association (RTNDA) annual international conference. It defines electronic journalism to include radio, television, cable, and online news. Previous winners of any RTNDF scholarship or internship are not eligible.
Number awarded 1 each year.
Deadline April of each year.

[113]
EDUCATIONAL ADVANCEMENT BSN SCHOLARSHIPS

American Association of Critical-Care Nurses
Attn: Educational Advancement Scholarships
101 Columbia
Aliso Viejo, CA 92656-4109
(949) 362-2000, ext. 338
Toll-free: (800) 899-AACN, ext. 338
Fax: (949) 362-2020   E-mail: info@aacn.org
Web: www.aacn.org

Purpose To provide financial assistance to members of the American Association of Critical-Care Nurses (AACN) who are working on a B.S.N. degree in nursing.
Eligibility This program is open to registered nurses who are current members of the association and enrolled in an accredited B.S.N. degree program. Applicants must be nurses who hold an active R.N. license and are currently working in critical care or have 1 year's experience in the last 3 years. They must have a cumulative GPA of 3.0 or higher and plan to hold junior or upper-division status in the fall semester. Along with their application, they must submit narratives on 1) how they see their nursing practice changing as a result of their baccalaureate degree; and 2) their contributions to critical care nursing, including work, community, and profession-related activities. Financial need is not considered in the selection process. Qualified ethnic minority candidates receive at least 20% of these awards.
Financial data The stipend is $1,500 per year. The funds are sent directly to the recipient's college or university and may be used only for tuition, fees, books, and supplies.
Duration 1 year; recipients may reapply.
Number awarded Varies each year; recently, 5 of these scholarships were awarded.
Deadline March of each year.

[114]
EDWARD D. STONE, JR. AND ASSOCIATES MINORITY SCHOLARSHIP

Landscape Architecture Foundation
Attn: Scholarship Program
818 18th Street, N.W., Suite 810
Washington, DC 20006-3520
(202) 331-7070   Fax: (202) 331-7079
E-mail: rfigura@lafoundation.org
Web: www.laprofession.org

Purpose To provide financial assistance to minority college students who wish to study landscape architecture.

Eligibility This program is open to African American, Hispanic, Native American, and minority college students of other cultural and ethnic backgrounds, if they are entering their final 2 years of undergraduate study in landscape architecture. Applicants must submit a 500-word essay on a design or research effort they wish to pursue (explaining how it will contribute to the advancement of the profession and to their ethnic heritage), 4 to 8 35mm color slides or black-and-white photographs of their best work, and 2 letters of recommendation. Selection is based on professional experience, community involvement, extracurricular activities, and financial need.
Financial data The stipend is $1,000.
Duration 1 year.
Number awarded 2 each year.
Deadline April of each year.

[115]
EDWARD DAVIS SCHOLARSHIP FUND

Edward Davis Education Foundation
585 East Larned Street, Suite 100
Detroit, MI 48226
(313) 963-2209   Toll-free: (877) 847-9060
Web: www.automag.com/EDEFoundation/default.asp

Purpose To provide financial assistance to minority students interested in preparing for a career in an automotive-related profession.
Eligibility Applicants must be minority high school seniors or currently-enrolled college students who are interested in preparing for a career in the automotive industry. High school students must have a GPA of 3.0 or higher; college students must have at least a 2.5. To apply, students must complete an application; provide proof of acceptance or enrollment in an accredited college, university, vocational institute, or technical school; and submit an essay (up to 200 words) on "The Importance of Diversity in the Automobile Industry."
Financial data A stipend is awarded (amount not specified). Since its inception, the program has awarded more than $200,000 in stipends.
Duration 1 year.
Additional information This scholarship, established in 1998, honors the first African American to own a new car dealership.
Deadline November of each year.

[116]
EDWARD S. ROTH MANUFACTURING ENGINEERING SCHOLARSHIP

Society of Manufacturing Engineers
Attn: SME Education Foundation
One SME Drive
P.O. Box 930
Dearborn, MI 48121-0930
(313) 425-3304   Toll-free: (800) 733-4763, ext. 3304
Fax: (313) 425-3411   E-mail: foundation@sme.org
Web: www.sme.org

Purpose To provide financial assistance to students (especially minorities) enrolled or planning to enroll in a degree program in manufacturing engineering at selected universities.

Eligibility This program is open to U.S. citizens who are graduating high school seniors or currently-enrolled undergraduate or graduate students. Applicants must be enrolled or planning to enroll as a full-time student at 1 of 13 selected 4-year universities to work on a bachelor's or master's degree in manufacturing engineering. They must have a GPA of 3.0 or higher. Preference is given to 1) students demonstrating financial need, 2) minority students, and 3) students participating in a co-op program. Some preference may also be given to graduating high school seniors and graduate students.

Financial data The stipend is $2,500.

Duration 1 year; may be renewed.

Additional information The eligible institutions are California Polytechnic State University at San Luis Obispo, California State Polytechnic State University at Pomona, University of Miami (Florida), Bradley University, Central State University (Ohio), Miami University (Ohio), Boston University, Worcester Polytechnic Institute, University of Massachusetts, St. Cloud State University, University of Texas-Pan American, Brigham Young University, and Utah State University.

Number awarded 1 each year.

Deadline January of each year.

[117]
EISENHOWER HISPANIC-SERVING INSTITUTIONS FELLOWSHIPS

Department of Transportation
Federal Highway Administration
Attn: National Highway Institute, HNHI-20
4600 North Fairfax Drive, Suite 800
Arlington, VA 22203-1553
(703) 235-0538   Fax: (703) 235-0593
E-mail: transportationedu@fhwa.dot.gov
Web: www.nhi.fhwa.dot.gov/ddetfp.asp

Purpose To provide financial assistance for undergraduate study in transportation-related fields to students at Hispanic Serving Institutions.

Eligibility These fellowships are intended for students who are enrolled at federally-designated 4-year Hispanic-Serving Institutions (HSIs) and who are working on a degree in a transportation-related field (i.e., engineering, accounting, business, architecture, environmental sciences, etc.). Applicants must have entered their junior year, have at least a 3.0 GPA, and have a faculty sponsor.

Financial data The stipend covers the fellow's full cost of education, including tuition and fees.

Duration 1 year.

Number awarded Varies each year; recently, 18 students received support from this program.

Deadline February of each year.

[118]
EL NUEVO CONSTRUCTOR SCHOLARSHIP PROGRAM

Hispanic College Fund
Attn: National Director
1717 Pennsylvania Avenue, N.W., Suite 460
Washington, D.C. 20006
(202) 296-5400   Toll-free: (800) 644-4223
Fax: (202) 296-3774
E-mail: hispaniccollegefund@earthlink.net
Web: www.hispanicfund.org

Purpose To provide financial assistance to Hispanic American undergraduate students who are interested in preparing for a career in the construction industry.

Eligibility This program is open to U.S. citizens of Hispanic background (at least 1 grandparent must be 100% Hispanic) who are entering their freshman, sophomore, junior, or senior year of college. Applicants must be working on a bachelor's or associate degree in a field related to construction and have a cumulative GPA of 3.0 or higher. They must be applying to or enrolled in a college or university in the 50 states or Puerto Rico as a full-time student. Financial need is considered in the selection process.

Financial data Stipends range from $500 to $5,000, depending on the need of the recipient, and average approximately $3,000. Funds are paid directly to the recipient's college or university to help cover tuition and fees.

Duration 1 year; recipients may reapply.

Additional information This program is sponsored by *El Nuevo Constructor,* a Hanley Wood LLC publication. All applications must be submitted online; no paper applications are available.

Number awarded Varies each year.

Deadline April of each year.

[119]
ELLEN AND FEDERICO JIMENEZ SCHOLARSHIP PROGRAM

Mexican American Legal Defense and Educational
 Fund
634 South Spring Street, 11th Floor
Los Angeles, CA 90014-1974
(213) 629-2512   Fax: (213) 629-0266
E-mail: undergradfund@maldef.org
Web: www.maldef.org/education/jimenez.htm

Purpose To provide financial assistance to Latino students who are attending or planning to attend a community college or state university in California or Texas.

Eligibility This program is open to Latino high school seniors and current college students who are ineligible to receive federal and/or state financial aid. Applicants must have a demonstrated commitment to serving the Latino community in the United States and have been accepted to a community college or state university in California or Texas as a full-time student. Along with their application, they must submit a 750-word personal statement on their reasons for pursuing higher education, their interest in a particular career field, their professional objectives, and their past involvement in activities that they believe to have served or benefited the Latino community and how those activities relate to their decision to pursue higher education. A Social Security number is not required. Selection is based on demonstrated involvement in and commitment to serve the Latino community, academic achievement, and financial need.

Financial data The stipend is $2,000 per year.
Duration 1 year.
Number awarded 25 each year.
Deadline September of each year.

[120]
ELLEN MASIN PERSINA SCHOLARSHIP

National Press Club
Attn: General Manager's Office
529 14th Street, N.W.
Washington, DC 20045
(202) 662-7532   E-mail: jbooze@press.org
Web: www.press.org/programs/aboutscholarship.cfm

Purpose To provide funding to minority high school seniors interested in preparing for a journalism career in college.

Eligibility This program is open to minority high school seniors who have been accepted to college and plan to prepare for a career in journalism. Applicants must 1) demonstrate an ongoing interest in journalism through work in high school and/or other media; 2) submit a 1-page essay on why they want to prepare for a career in journalism; and 3) have a GPA of 2.75 or higher in high school. Financial need is considered in the selection process.

Financial data The stipend is $5,000 per year.
Duration 4 years.
Additional information The program began in 1991. In the past, the Press Club has drawn on the Washington Association of Black Journalists and Youth Connections (a nationwide organization that produces free papers written by high school students).
Number awarded 1 or more each year.
Deadline February of each year.

[121]
ENCOURAGE MINORITY PARTICIPATION IN OCCUPATIONS WITH EMPHASIS ON REHABILITATION

Courage Center
Attn: EMPOWER Scholarship Program
3915 Golden Valley Road
Minneapolis, MN 55422
(763) 520-0214   Toll-free: (888) 8-INTAKE
Fax: (763) 520-0392   TTY: (763) 520-0245
E-mail: suep@courage.org
Web: www.courage.org

Purpose To provide financial assistance to students of color interested in preparing for a career in the medical rehabilitation field.

Eligibility This program is open to ethnically diverse students accepted at or enrolled in an institution of higher learning. Applicants must demonstrate a career interest in the medical rehabilitation field by completing at least 200 hours of career-related volunteer service. They must have a GPA of 2.0 or higher. Selection is based on career intentions and achievements, not academic rank.

Financial data The stipend is $1,500.
Duration 1 year.

Additional information This program is also identified by its acronym as the EMPOWER Scholarship Award.
Number awarded 2 each year.
Deadline April of each year.

[122]
ENVIRONMENTAL EDUCATIONAL SCHOLARSHIP PROGRAM

Missouri Department of Natural Resources
Attn: Environmental Educational Scholarship Program
P.O. Box 176
Jefferson City, MO 65102
(573) 526-8411   Toll-free: (800) 334-6946
TDD: (800) 379-2419
E-mail: daspec@dnr.state.mo.us
Web: www.dnr.state.mo.us/eesp

Purpose To provide financial assistance to underrepresented and minority students from Missouri who are or will be working on a bachelor's or master's degree in an environmental field.

Eligibility This program is open to minority and underrepresented residents of Missouri who have graduated from an accredited high school with a GPA of 3.0 or higher. Students who are already enrolled in college must have a GPA of 2.5 or higher and must be full-time undergraduate or graduate students. Applicants may be 1) engineering students in civil, chemical, environmental, mechanical, or agricultural engineering; 2) environmental students in geology, biology, wildlife management, planning, natural resources, or a closely-related course of study; 3) chemistry students in the field of environmental chemistry; or 4) law enforcement students in environmental law enforcement. They must submit a 1-page essay on their environmental education career goals. Selection is based on the essay, GPA and test scores, school and community activities, leadership, and character.

Financial data A stipend is $2,000 per year.
Duration 1 year; may be renewed if the recipient maintains a GPA of 2.5 or higher and full-time enrollment.
Number awarded Varies each year.
Deadline June of each year.

[123]
ENVIRONMENTAL MANAGEMENT SCHOLARSHIP

Hispanic Scholarship Fund Institute
1001 Connecticut Avenue, N.W., Suite 632
Washington, DC 20036
(202) 296-0009   Fax: (202) 296-3633
E-mail: info@hsfi.org
Web: www.hsfi.org/scholarships/energy.asp

Purpose To provide financial assistance to Hispanic undergraduate students majoring in designated business, engineering, and science fields related to the U.S. Department of Energy (DOE) goals of environmental restoration and waste management.

Eligibility This program is open to U.S. citizens and permanent residents of Hispanic background who have completed at least 12 undergraduate credits with a GPA of 3.0 or higher. Applicants must be interested in preparing for a career supportive of the DOE goals of environmental restoration and waste management. Eligible academic majors are in the fields of business (management and system analysis), engineering (agricultural, chemical, civil, electrical, environmental, industrial, mechanical, metallurgical, nuclear, and petroleum), and science (applied math or physics, chemistry, computer science, ecology, environmental, epidemiology, geology, health physics, hydrology, radiochemistry, radio-ecology, and toxicology). Along with their application, they must submit a 2-page essay on 1) how their academic major, interests, and career goals correspond to environmental restoration and waste management issues; and 2) how their Hispanic background and family upbringing have influenced their academic and personal goals. Selection is based on the essay, academic record, academic plans and career goals, financial need, commitment to DOE's goal of environmental restoration and waste management, and a letter of recommendation.

Financial data The stipend is $3,000 per year for 4-year university students or $2,000 per year for community college students.

Duration 1 year.

Additional information This program, which began in 1990, is sponsored by DOE's Office of Environmental Management. Recipients must enroll full time at a college or university in the United States.

Number awarded Varies each year.

Deadline March of each year.

[124]
ERNST & YOUNG LLP MINORITY LEADERSHIP AWARDS

New Jersey Society of Certified Public Accountants
Attn: Student Programs Coordinator
425 Eagle Rock Avenue, Suite 100
Roseland, NJ 07068-1723
(973) 226-4494, ext. 209   Fax: (973) 226-7425
E-mail: njscpa@njscpa.org
Web: www.njscpa.org

Purpose To provide financial assistance to minority undergraduates in New Jersey who are preparing for a career as a certified public accountant.

Eligibility This program is open to African American, Asian, Hispanic, and Native American residents of New Jersey who are attending a college or university in the state. Applicants must be sophomores who are majoring or concentrating in accounting and have completed at least 3 credits in accounting courses. Along with their application, they must submit a letter of recommendation from an accounting professor, an official transcript indicating a GPA of 3.2 or higher, a resume, and an essay of 250 to 500 words on what motivated them to choose accounting as a career choice.

Financial data The stipend is $5,000.

Duration 1 year.

Additional information This program is sponsored by Ernst & Young.

Number awarded 2 each year.

Deadline January of each year.

[125]
ERNST & YOUNG SCHOLARSHIP PROGRAM

Hispanic College Fund
Attn: National Director
1717 Pennsylvania Avenue, N.W., Suite 460
Washington, D.C. 20006
(202) 296-5400   Toll-free: (800) 644-4223
Fax: (202) 296-3774
E-mail: hispaniccollegefund@earthlink.net
Web: www.hispanicfund.org

Purpose To provide financial assistance to Hispanic American undergraduate students who are interested in preparing for a career in accounting.

Eligibility This program is open to U.S. citizens of Hispanic background (at least 1 grandparent must be 100% Hispanic) who are entering their sophomore or junior year of college. Applicants must be working on a bachelor's degree in accounting or a related field and have a cumulative GPA of 3.0 or higher. They must be enrolled in a college or university in the 50 states or Puerto Rico as a full-time student. Financial need is considered in the selection process.

Financial data Stipends range from $500 to $5,000, depending on the need of the recipient, and average approximately $3,000. Funds are paid directly to the recipient's college or university to help cover tuition and fees.

Duration 1 year; recipients may reapply.

Additional information This program is sponsored by Ernst & Young. All applications must be submitted online; no paper applications are available.

Number awarded Varies each year.

Deadline April of each year.

[126]
ESTER BOONE MEMORIAL SCHOLARSHIPS

National Naval Officers Association-Washington, D.C.
   Chapter
Attn: Scholarship Program
9805 Fox Run Drive
Clinton, MD 20735-3087
(202) 874-4994   E-mail: willie.evans@occ.treas.gov
Web: www.dcnnoa.org

Purpose To provide financial assistance to minority high school seniors from the Washington, D.C. area.

Eligibility This program is open to minority seniors at high schools in the Washington, D.C. metropolitan area who plan to enroll full time at an accredited 2-year or 4-year college or university. Applicants must have a GPA of 2.5 or higher. Selection is based on academic achievement, community involvement, and financial need.

Financial data The stipend is $1,000 per year.

Duration 1 year. This program includes the Ester Boone Memorial Sustaining Scholarship, which is renewable.

Additional information Recipients are not required to join or affiliate with the military in any way.

Number awarded 11 each year: 10 nonrenewable scholarships and 1 that is renewable.

Deadline March of each year.

[127]
ETHAN AND ALLAN MURPHY ENDOWED MEMORIAL SCHOLARSHIP

American Meteorological Society
Attn: Fellowship/Scholarship Program
45 Beacon Street
Boston, MA 02108-3693
(617) 227-2426, ext. 246   Fax: (617) 742-8718
E-mail: scholar@ametsoc.org
Web: www.ametsoc.org

Purpose To provide financial assistance to undergraduates (particularly underrepresented minorities, women, and persons with disabilities) majoring in meteorology or an aspect of atmospheric sciences with an interest in weather forecasting.

Eligibility This program is open to full-time students entering their final year of undergraduate study and majoring in meteorology or an aspect of the atmospheric or related oceanic and hydrologic sciences. Applicants must intend to make atmospheric or related sciences their career and be able to demonstrate, through curricular or extracurricular activities, an interest in weather forecasting or in the value and utilization of forecasts. They must be U.S. citizens or permanent residents enrolled at a U.S. institution and have a cumulative GPA of 3.25 or higher. Along with their application, they must submit 200-word essays on 1) their most important achievements that qualify them for this scholarship, and 2) their career goals in the atmospheric or related oceanic or hydrologic fields. Selection is based on academic excellence and achievement; financial need is not considered. The sponsor specifically encourages applications from women, minorities, and students with disabilities who are traditionally underrepresented in the atmospheric and related oceanic sciences.

Financial data The stipend is $2,000 per year.

Duration 1 year.

Additional information Requests for an application must be accompanied by a self-addressed stamped envelope.

Number awarded 1 each year.

Deadline February of each year.

[128]
ETHNIC AWARENESS COMMITTEE SCHOLARSHIP

Washington Financial Aid Association
c/o James D. Flowers, Scholarship Committee
University of Washington
105 Schmitz, Box 355880
Seattle, WA 98195-5880
(206) 616-2309   E-mail: jflowers@washington.edu
Web: www.wfaa.org/ethnicawareness.html

Purpose To provide financial assistance for college to high school seniors or currently-enrolled college students of color in Washington.

Eligibility Open to graduating high school seniors or currently-enrolled college students of color who are or will be attending a college or university belonging to the Washington Financial Aid Association. Applicants must be able to demonstrate leadership abilities, have at least a 3.0 GPA, have financial need, and enroll or plan to enroll at least half time at an eligible private or public community college, technical school, college, or university. To apply, they must

submit a typed personal statement, 2 letters of recommendation, and an official college and/or high school transcript.

Financial data Stipends range up to $1,000.

Duration 1 year.

Number awarded 1 or more each year.

Deadline June of each year.

[129]
ETHNIC MINORITY BACHELOR'S SCHOLARSHIPS IN ONCOLOGY NURSING

Oncology Nursing Society
Attn: ONS Foundation
125 Enterprise Drive
Pittsburgh, PA 15275-1214
(412) 859-6100, ext. 8503   Toll-free: (866) 257-4ONS
Fax: (412) 859-6160   E-mail: foundation@ons.org
Web: www.ons.org

Purpose To provide financial assistance to ethnic minorities interested in working on undergraduate studies in oncology nursing.

Eligibility The candidate must 1) demonstrate an interest in and commitment to cancer nursing; 2) be enrolled in an undergraduate nursing degree program at an NLN- or CCNE-accredited school of nursing (the program must have application to oncology nursing); 3) have a current license to practice as a registered nurse or a practical (vocational) nurse; 4) not have previously received a bachelor's scholarship from this sponsor; and 5) be a member of an ethnic minority group (Native American, African American, Asian American, Pacific Islander, Hispanic/Latino, or other ethnic minority background). Applicants must submit an essay of 250 words or less on their role in caring for persons with cancer and a statement of their professional goals and their relationship to the advancement of oncology nursing. Financial need is not considered in the selection process.

Financial data The stipend is $2,000.

Duration 1 year.

Additional information This program includes a mentoring component with an individual in the applicant's area of clinical interest. When appropriate, efforts are made to match the applicant and mentor by ethnicity. At the end of each year of scholarship participation, recipients must submit a summary describing their educational activities. Applications must be accompanied by a $5 fee.

Number awarded 3 each year.

Deadline January of each year.

[130]
ETHNIC MISSIONS SCHOLARSHIP PROGRAM

Baptist General Convention of Texas
Attn: Ethnic Missions
333 North Washington
Dallas, TX 75246-1798
(214) 828-5342   Toll-free: (800) 352-5342
Fax: (214) 828-5284   E-mail: porraz@bgct.org
Web: www.bgct.org/ethnic_missions

Purpose To provide financial assistance for college or seminary education to ethnic and deaf students in Texas who are members of Texas Baptist ethnic congregations.

Eligibility This program is open to members of Texas Baptist congregations who are Asian, Hispanic, or deaf and have a "sense of call" as a lay person or minister. Applicants must be U.S. citizens or permanent residents, have resided in Texas for at least 1 year, demonstrate financial need, and plan to attend or be attending a Texas Baptist university or the Southwestern Baptist Theological Seminary. Students still in high school must have a GPA of at least 3.0; students previously enrolled in a college or seminary must have at least a 2.0 GPA. Applicants must submit brief essays on what they, as a Baptist, believe about God, Jesus, sin, salvation, church membership, and baptism. They must also explain how they became a Christian, why they are seeking a Christian university education, and what they plan to do following graduation.

Financial data The grant for full-time students is $800 per year or $400 per semester. Part-time students receive $27 per credit hour.

Duration 1 year; may be renewed.

Additional information The scholarships are funded through the Week of Prayer and the Mary Hill Davis Offering for state missions sponsored annually by Women's Missionary Union of Texas.

[131]
FALU FOUNDATION SCHOLARSHIP

Falú Foundation
c/o Universal Business and Media School
220 East 106th Street
New York, NY 10029
(212) 828-6699   Fax: (212) 360-1231
E-mail: falu@falufoundation.org
Web: www.falufoundation.org/scolarform.htm

Purpose To provide funding to Hispanic students interested in preparing for a career in technology.

Eligibility This program is open to Hispanic students who are interested in preparing for a career in computer technology or information technology. Applicants must be enrolled in or admitted to an accredited business school, college, or university.

Financial data The stipend is $1,000.

Number awarded 1 or more each year.

[132]
FANTA U SCHOLARSHIP PROGRAM

Hispanic Scholarship Fund
Attn: Selection Committee
55 Second Street, Suite 1500
San Francisco, CA 94105
(415) 808-2350   Toll-free: (877) HSF-INFO
Fax: (415) 808-2302   E-mail: highschool@hsf.net
Web: www.hsf.net/support/campaigns/fantaU.php

Purpose To provide financial assistance to Hispanic American high school seniors from designated areas of Texas, New Mexico, and Oklahoma who are interested in attending college.

Eligibility This program is open to U.S. citizens, permanent residents, and visitors with a passport stamped I-551 who are of Hispanic heritage. Applicants must have applied for federal financial aid and be seniors at high schools in designated counties in Texas, New Mexico, or Oklahoma. They must have a GPA of 3.0 or higher and plans to enroll full time at an accredited college or university in the United

States, Puerto Rico, or the U.S. Virgin Islands for the following fall. Along with their application, they must submit 600-word essays on 1) how their Hispanic heritage, family upbringing, and/or role models have influenced their personal long-term goals; 2) how they contribute to their community and what they have learned from their experiences; and 3) an academic challenge they have faced and how they have overcome it. Selection is based on academic achievement, personal strengths, leadership, and financial need.

Financial data The stipend is $1,000.

Duration 1 year.

Additional information This program is sponsored by the Coca-Cola Bottling Company of West Texas, the Coca-Cola Bottling Company of Southwest Texas, and the Coca-Cola Bottling Company of East Texas as part of the high school scholarship program of the Hispanic Scholarship Fund (HSF). It is available in 131 counties in Texas (for a list, contact HSF) plus Dona Ana, Quay, and Union counties in New Mexico and Alfalfa, Beaver, Beckham, Custer, Dewey, Ellis, Harper, Major, Roger Mills, Texas, Washita, Woods, and Woodward counties in Oklahoma

Number awarded 150 each year.

Deadline February of each year.

[133]
FIRST DATA WESTERN UNION FOUNDATION SCHOLARSHIP

First Data Western Union Foundation
Attn: Scholarship Program
6200 South Québec Street, Suite 370 AU
Greenwood Village, CO 80111
(303) 967-6606
Web: www.firstdatawesternunion.org

Purpose To provide financial assistance to immigrant students so they can realize their educational dreams.

Eligibility This program is open to immigrant students, from high school seniors to currently-enrolled college students. Applicants must have a high school diploma or GED and live within the United States or Puerto Rico. Selection is based on personal challenges overcome, initiative, commitment to learning and working hard, and financial need. Special consideration is given to applicants who "show academic promise and a strong desire for advancing their educational and career goals."

Financial data Stipends range from $500 to $3,000. Funds must be used for tuition, fees, or books and must be used within 1 year of the award date.

Duration Both 1-time and renewable scholarships (up to 4 years) are offered.

Additional information Recipients must attend school on a full-time basis.

Deadline February, May, or November of each year.

[134]
FISHER BROADCASTING SCHOLARSHIPS FOR MINORITIES

Fisher Communications
Attn: Minority Scholarship
100 Fourth Avenue North, Suite 510
Seattle, WA 98109
(206) 404-7000   Fax: (206) 404-6037
E-mail: Info@fsci.com
Web: www.fsci.com/x100.xml

Purpose To provide financial assistance to minority college students in selected states who are interested in preparing for a career in broadcasting, marketing, or journalism.

Eligibility This program is open to students of non-white origin who are U.S. citizens, have a GPA of 2.5 or higher, and are at least sophomores enrolled in 1) a broadcasting, marketing, or journalism curriculum leading to a bachelor's degree at an accredited 4-year college or university; 2) a broadcast curriculum at an accredited community college, transferable to a 4-year baccalaureate degree program; or 3) a broadcast curriculum at an accredited vocational/technical school. Applicants must be either 1) residents of Washington, Oregon, Idaho, or Montana; or 2) attending a school in those states. They must submit an essay that explains their financial need, education and career goals, and school activities; a copy of their college transcript; and 2 letters of recommendation. Selection is based on need, academic achievement, and personal qualities.

Financial data A stipend is awarded (amount not specified).

Duration 1 year; recipients may reapply.

Additional information This program began in 1987.

Number awarded Varies; a total of $10,000 is available for this program each year.

Deadline April of each year.

[135]
FLEMING/BLASZCAK SCHOLARSHIP

Society of Plastics Engineers
Attn: SPE Foundation
14 Fairfield Drive
Brookfield, CT 06804-0403
(203) 740-5447   Fax: (203) 775-1157
E-mail: foundation@4spe.org
Web: www.4spe.org/foundation/scholarships.php

Purpose To provide financial assistance to Mexican American undergraduate and graduate students who have a career interest in the plastics industry.

Eligibility This program is open to full-time undergraduate and graduate students of Mexican descent who are enrolled in a 4-year college or university. Applicants must be U.S. citizens or legal residents. They must 1) have a demonstrated or expressed interest in the plastics industry; 2) be majoring in or taking courses that would be beneficial to a career in the plastics or polymer industry (e.g., plastics engineering, polymer sciences, chemistry, physics, chemical engineering, mechanical engineering, or industrial engineering); 3) be in good academic standing at their school; and 4) be able to document financial need. Along with their application, they must submit 3 letters of recommendation; a high school and/or college transcript; a 1- to 2-page state-

ment telling why they are interested in the scholarship, their qualifications, and their educational and career goals in the plastics industry; and documentation of their Mexican heritage.

Financial data The stipend is $2,000 per year. Funds are paid directly to the recipient's school.

Duration 1 year.

Additional information This program is sponsored by Cal Mold Inc. and Formula Plastics.

Number awarded 1 each year.

Deadline January of each year.

[136]
FLORIDA SOCIETY OF NEWSPAPER EDITORS MINORITY SCHOLARSHIP PROGRAM

Florida Society of Newspaper Editors
c/o Florida Press Association
2636 Mitcham Drive
Tallahassee, FL 32308
(850) 222-5790   Fax: (850) 224-6012
E-mail: info@fsne.org
Web: www.fsne.org/minorityscholar.html

Purpose To provide financial assistance and summer work experience to minority upper-division students majoring in journalism at a college or university in Florida.

Eligibility This program is open to minority students in accredited journalism or mass communication programs at Florida 4-year colleges and universities. Applicants must be full-time students in their junior year, have at least a 3.0 GPA, and be willing to participate in a paid summer internship at a Florida newspaper. Along with their application, they must submit a 300-word autobiographical essay explaining why they want to prepare for a career in print journalism and provide a standard resume, references, and clips or examples of relevant classroom work.

Financial data Winners are given a paid summer internship at a participating newspaper between their junior and senior year. Upon successfully completing the internship, the students are awarded a $3,000 scholarship (paid in 2 equal installments) to be used during their senior year.

Duration 1 summer for the internship; 1 academic year for the scholarship.

Additional information Information is also available from Rosemary Armao, FSNE Scholarship Committee, c/o The Sarasota Herald Tribune, 801 South Tamiami Trail, Sarasota, FL 34230.

Number awarded 1 each year.

Deadline March of each year.

[137]
FLORIDA YES TEACH! SCHOLARSHIP PROGRAM

Florida Independent College Fund
929 North Spring Garden Avenue, Suite 165
DeLand, FL 32720-0981
(386) 734-2745   Fax: (386) 734-0839
E-mail: yesteach@ficf.org
Web: www.ficf.org/yesteach

Purpose To provide financial assistance to college graduates (particularly minorities) who have degrees in fields other than education and wish to become teachers by returning to school at designated private colleges and universities in Florida to obtain professional certification.

Eligibility This program is open to people in Florida who have a college degree in a field other than education and wish to become a teacher. Applicants must be interested in enrolling in 1 of 27 designated independent colleges or universities in Florida that offer alternative teacher certification training, continuing education courses, advanced degrees, online course offerings, and online support services. They must register with the Yes Teach! web site. Priority is given to the first 200 people who complete the "1st Class Tutorial" and get teaching jobs in Florida. Selection is based on 5 factors: 1) did the participant get a job as a Florida teacher; 2) is the participant working on a professional certificate; 3) is the new teacher employed in a targeted high-need school; 4) is this new teacher teaching a high-need subject; and 5) is this teacher from an underrepresented population.

Financial data The stipend depends on the 5 selection factors. The largest awards go to teachers who qualify on all 5 factors.

Duration 1 year.

Additional information This program is cosponsored by the Florida Department of Education and the Florida Independent College Fund (FICF). For a list of the 27 eligible institutions, contact the FICF.

Number awarded Varies each year.

[138]
FORD MOTOR COMPANY/HENAAC SCHOLARS PROGRAM

Hispanic Engineer National Achievement Awards
  Conference
3900 Whiteside Street
Los Angeles, CA 90063
(323) 262-0997   Fax: (323) 262-0946
E-mail: info@henaac.org
Web: www.henaac.org

Purpose To provide financial assistance to Hispanic undergraduate students majoring in engineering and related fields.

Eligibility This program is open to Hispanic undergraduate students who are majoring in computer science or the following engineering fields: aeronautical, electrical, industrial, and mechanical. Applicants must have a GPA of 3.0 or higher. Academic achievement and campus community activities are considered in the selection process. U.S. citizenship is required.

Financial data The stipend ranges from $1,000 to $5,000.

Duration 1 year.

Additional information This program is sponsored by Ford Motor Company as part of its effort to support the mission of the Hispanic Engineer National Achievement Awards Conference (HENAAC): to promote technical excellence and leadership in the Hispanic community.

Number awarded 5 each year.

Deadline April of each year.

[139]
FORE DIVERSITY SCHOLARSHIPS

American Health Information Management Association
Attn: Foundation of Research and Education
233 North Michigan Avenue, Suite 2150
Chicago, IL 60601-5806
(312) 233-1168   Fax: (312) 233-1090
E-mail: fore@ahima.org
Web: www.ahima.org/fore/programs.cfm

Purpose To provide financial assistance to minority members of the American Health Information Management Association (AHIMA) who are interested in working on an undergraduate or graduate degree in health information administration or technology.

Eligibility This program is open to AHIMA members who are enrolled in a health information administration or health information technology program accredited by the Commission on Accreditation of Allied Health Education Programs. Applicants must be minorities, be working on an undergraduate or graduate degree on at least a half-time basis, and have a GPA of 3.0 or higher. U.S. citizenship is required. Selection is based (in order of importance) on GPA and academic achievement, volunteer and work experience, commitment to the health information management profession, suitability to the health information management profession, quality and suitability of references provided, and clarity of application.

Financial data Stipends range from $1,000 to $5,000.

Duration 1 year; nonrenewable.

Number awarded Varies each year. Recently, 5 of these scholarships were awarded: 4 to undergraduates and 1 to a graduate student.

Deadline May of each year.

[140]
FORTUNE BRANDS SCHOLARS PROGRAM

United Negro College Fund
Attn: Corporate Scholars Program
P.O. Box 1435
Alexandria, VA 22313-9998
Toll-free: (866) 671-7237   E-mail: internship@uncf.org
Web: www.uncf.org/internships/index.asp

Purpose To provide financial assistance and work experience to minorities who are either juniors majoring in fields related to business or law students interested in an internship at corporate headquarters of Fortune Brands.

Eligibility This program is open to juniors and first- and second-year law students who are members of minority groups. Applicants must have a GPA of 3.0 or higher and an undergraduate major in accounting, finance, human resources, information systems, information technology, or marketing. They must be attending a designated college, university, or law school and be interested in an internship at Fortune Brands corporate headquarters in Lincolnshire, Illinois. Along with their application, they must submit a resume, 2 letters of recommendation, and official transcripts.

Financial data The program provides a paid internship and (based on successful internship performance) a $7,500 scholarship.

Duration 8 to 10 weeks for the internship; 1 year for the scholarship.

Additional information Eligible undergraduate institutions are Florida A&M University, Florida State University, Hampton University, Howard University, Morehouse College, North Carolina A&T State University, Northwestern University, Spelman College, University of Chicago, and University of Wisconsin. Participating law schools are those at Howard University, Northwestern University, University of Chicago, and University of Wisconsin.

Number awarded Varies each year.

Deadline February of each year.

[141]
FORUM FOR CONCERNS OF MINORITIES SCHOLARSHIPS

American Society for Clinical Laboratory Science
Attn: Forum for Concerns of Minorities
6701 Democracy Boulevard, Suite 300
Bethesda, MD 20817
(301) 657-2768   Fax: (301) 657-2909
E-mail: ascls@ascls.org
Web: www.ascls.org/leadership/awards/fcm.asp

Purpose To provide financial assistance to minority students in clinical laboratory scientist and clinical laboratory technician programs.

Eligibility This program is open to minority students who are enrolled in a program in clinical laboratory science, including clinical laboratory science/medical technology (CLS/MT) and clinical laboratory technician/medical laboratory technician (CLT/MLT). Applicants must be able to demonstrate financial need. Membership in the American Society for Clinical Laboratory Science is encouraged but not required.

Financial data Stipends depend on the need of the recipients and the availability of funds.

Duration 1 year.

Number awarded 2 each year: 1 to a CLS/MT student and 1 to a CLT/MLT student.

Deadline March of each year.

[142]
FOUNDERS SCHOLARSHIP

Society of Mexican American Engineers and Scientists
Attn: Scholarships
711 West Bay Area Boulevard, Suite 206
Webster, TX 77598-3677
(281) 557-3677   Fax: (281) 557-3757
E-mail: scholarships@maes-natl.org
Web: www.maes-natl.org

Purpose To provide financial assistance to undergraduate and graduate student members of the Society of Mexican American Engineers and Scientists (MAES).

Eligibility This program is open to MAES student members who are full-time undergraduate or graduate students at a college or university in the United States. Community college students must be enrolled in majors that can transfer to a 4-year institution offering a baccalaureate degree. All applicants must be majoring in a field of science or engineering. U.S. citizenship or permanent resident status is required. Selection is based on financial need; academic achievement; personal qualities, strengths, and leadership

abilities; and timeliness and completeness of the application.

Financial data The stipend is $2,500.

Duration 1 year.

Additional information Recipients must attend the MAES International Symposium's Medalla de Oro Banquet in October.

Number awarded 1 each year.

Deadline October of each year.

[143]
FRANK KAZMIERCZAK MEMORIAL MIGRANT SCHOLARSHIP

Geneseo Migrant Center
27 Lackawanna Avenue
Mount Morris, NY 14510-1096
(585) 658-7960   Toll-free: (800) 245-5681
Fax: (585) 658-7969   E-mail: info@migrant.net
Web: www.migrant.net/sch_kazmierczak.htm

Purpose To provide financial assistance for college to migrant farmworker youth interested in preparing for a career in teaching.

Eligibility This program is open to migrant farmworkers and their children who are interested in preparing for a career as a teacher. Priority is given to applicants who have experienced mobility within the past 3 years. They must submit a personal essay of 300 to 500 words on their reasons for wanting to become a teacher, 2 letters of recommendation, and an official school transcript. Selection is based on financial need, academic achievement, and history of migration for agricultural employment.

Financial data The stipend is $1,000.

Duration 1 year.

Number awarded 1 each year.

Deadline January of each year.

[144]
FREESCALE/HENAAC SCHOLARS PROGRAM

Hispanic Engineer National Achievement Awards
    Conference
3900 Whiteside Street
Los Angeles, CA 90063
(323) 262-0997   Fax: (323) 262-0946
E-mail: info@henaac.org
Web: www.henaac.org/scholarships.htm

Purpose To provide financial assistance to Hispanic undergraduate students majoring in computer science or designated fields of engineering.

Eligibility This program is open to Hispanic undergraduate students who are enrolled full time in computer science or electrical or computer engineering. Applicants must be entering their sophomore, junior, or senior year and have a GPA of 3.0 or higher. Academic achievement and campus community activities are considered in the selection process. U.S. citizenship is required.

Financial data The stipend is $5,000.

Duration 1 year; recipients may reapply.

Additional information This program is sponsored by Freescale Semiconductor as part of its effort to support the mission of the Hispanic Engineer National Achievement Awards Conference (HENAAC): to promote technical excellence and leadership in the Hispanic community. The recipient is required to accept a summer internship (where and when available) with Freescale Semiconductor.

Number awarded 1 or more each year.

Deadline April of each year.

[145]
FULFILLING OUR DREAMS SCHOLARSHIP PROGRAM

Salvadoran American Leadership and Educational Fund
Attn: Education and Youth Programs Manager
1625 West Olympic Boulevard, Suite 718
Los Angeles, CA 90015
(213) 480-1052   Fax: (213) 487-2530
E-mail: info@salef.org
Web: salef.org/Scholarships.html

Purpose To provide financial assistance for college and graduate school to Salvadoran Americans and other Americans of Hispanic descent.

Eligibility This program is open to high school seniors and graduates who have been accepted at a 4-year university, undergraduates in 2- and 4-year colleges and universities, and graduate students. Applicants do not need to provide proof of documented immigrant status, but they must be of Salvadoran, Central American, or other Latino background. Along with their application, they must submit a 750-word statement on their goals, aspirations, and ambitions; ways to give back to the community; leadership involvement; why they chose their field of study; and short- and long-term goals and how they plan to contribute to the community after graduation. They must be able to demonstrate financial need, have a GPA of at least 2.5, and have a history of community service and involvement. An interview may be required.

Financial data Stipends range from $500 to $2,500.

Duration 1 year.

Additional information This program began in 1998. Recipients are paired with a professional in their field of study who serves as a mentor, providing moral support and direction. Funding for this program comes from the Bank of America Foundation and the Los Angeles Department of Water and Power.

Number awarded 50 or more each year.

Deadline June of each year.

[146]
FUTURE ELECTRONICS/HENAAC SCHOLARS PROGRAM

Hispanic Engineer National Achievement Awards
    Conference
3900 Whiteside Street
Los Angeles, CA 90063
(323) 262-0997   Fax: (323) 262-0946
E-mail: info@henaac.org
Web: www.henaac.org/scholarships.htm

Purpose To provide financial assistance to Hispanic undergraduate students majoring in engineering and related fields.

Eligibility This program is open to Hispanic undergraduate students who are enrolled full time in computer science, engineering, material science, mathematics, or applied sci-

ence. Applicants must have a GPA of 3.0 or higher. There is no citizenship requirement. Academic achievement and campus community activities are considered in the selection process.

Financial data Stipends range from $1,000 to $5,000.

Duration 1 year; recipients may reapply.

Additional information This program is sponsored by the Future Electronics as part of its effort to support the mission of the Hispanic Engineer National Achievement Awards Conference (HENAAC): to promote technical excellence and leadership in the Hispanic community.

Number awarded 1 or more each year.

Deadline April of each year.

[147]
GATES MILLENNIUM UNDERGRADUATE SCHOLARS PROGRAM

Bill and Melinda Gates Foundation
P.O. Box 10500
Fairfax, VA 22031-8044
Toll-free: (877) 690-GMSP
Web: www.gmsp.org

Purpose To provide financial assistance to outstanding low-income minority students, particularly those interested in majoring in specific fields in college.

Eligibility This program is open to African Americans, Alaska Natives, American Indians, Hispanic Americans, and Asian Pacific Islander Americans who are graduating high school seniors with a GPA of 3.3 or higher. Principals, teachers, guidance counselors, tribal higher education representatives, and other professional educators are invited to nominate students with outstanding academic qualifications, especially those likely to succeed in the fields of mathematics, science, engineering, education, or library science. Nominees should have significant financial need and demonstrated leadership abilities through participation in community service, extracurricular, or other activities. U.S. citizenship or permanent resident status is required. Nominees must be planning to enter an accredited college or university as a full-time, degree-seeking freshman in the following fall.

Financial data The program covers the cost of tuition, fees, books, and living expenses not paid for by grants and scholarships already committed as part of the recipient's financial aid package.

Duration 4 years or the completion of the undergraduate degree, if the recipient maintains at least a 3.0 GPA.

Additional information This program, established in 1999, is funded by the Bill and Melinda Gates Foundation and administered by the United Negro College Fund with support from the American Indian Graduate Center, the Hispanic Scholarship Fund, and the Organization of Chinese Americans.

Number awarded Under the Gates Millennium Scholars Program, a total of 4,000 students receive support each year.

Deadline January of each year.

[148]
GENERAL MOTORS ENGINEERING EXCELLENCE AWARD

Hispanic Association of Colleges and Universities
Attn: National Scholarship Program
One Dupont Circle, N.W. Suite 605
Washington, DC 20036
(202) 467-0893   Fax: (202) 496-9177
TTY: (800) 855-2880   E-mail: scholarships@hacu.net
Web: scholarships.hacu.net/applications/applicants

Purpose To provide financial assistance to undergraduate and graduate engineering students at institutions that are members of the Hispanic Association of Colleges and Universities (HACU).

Eligibility This program is open to full-time undergraduate and graduate students at 4-year HACU member and partner colleges and universities who are working on an engineering degree. Applicants must submit an essay of 200 to 250 words that describes their academic and/or career goals, where they expect to be and what they expect to be doing 10 years from now, and what skills they can bring to an employer. They must be able to demonstrate financial need and a GPA of 3.2 or higher.

Financial data The stipend is $2,000 per year.

Duration 1 year; may be renewed.

Additional information This program is sponsored by General Motors and administered by HACU.

Number awarded 1 or more each year.

Deadline May of each year.

[149]
GENERAL MOTORS SCHOLARSHIP PROGRAM OF THE HISPANIC SCHOLARSHIP FUND

Hispanic Scholarship Fund
Attn: Selection Committee
55 Second Street, Suite 1500
San Francisco, CA 94105
(415) 808-2350   Toll-free: (877) HSF-INFO
Fax: (415) 808-2302   E-mail: highschool@hsf.net
Web: www.hsf.net/scholarship/programs/gm.php

Purpose To provide financial assistance to Hispanic Americans who are interested in attending college to major in engineering or business.

Eligibility This program is open to U.S. citizens, permanent residents, and visitors with a passport stamped I-551 who are of Hispanic heritage. Applicants must have a GPA of 3.0 or higher and be enrolled or planning to enroll full time at an accredited 4-year college or university in the United States, Puerto Rico, or the U.S. Virgin Islands to major in business or engineering. Along with their application, they must submit 600-word essays on 1) how their Hispanic heritage, family upbringing, and/or role models have influenced their personal long-term goals; 2) how they contribute to their community and what they have learned from their experiences; and 3) an academic challenge they have faced and how they have overcome it. Selection is based on academic achievement, personal strengths, leadership, and financial need.

Financial data The stipend is $2,500 per year.

Duration 1 year.

Additional information This program is jointly sponsored by General Motors and the Hispanic Scholarship Fund (HSF).

Number awarded 1 or more each year.

Deadline June of each year.

[150]
GEORGE M. BROOKER COLLEGIATE SCHOLARSHIP FOR MINORITIES

Institute of Real Estate Management Foundation
Attn: Foundation Coordinator
430 North Michigan Avenue
Chicago, IL 60611-4090
(312) 329-6008   Toll-free: (800) 837-0706, ext. 6008
Fax: (312) 410-7908   E-mail: kholmes@irem.org
Web: www.irem.org

Purpose To provide financial assistance to minorities interested in preparing (on the undergraduate or graduate school level) for a career in the real estate management industry.

Eligibility This program is open to junior, senior, and graduate minority (non-Caucasian) students majoring in real estate, preferably with an emphasis on management, asset management, or related fields. Applicants must be interested in beginning a career in real estate management upon graduation. They must have earned a GPA of 3.0 or higher in their major, have completed at least 2 college courses in real estate, and write an essay (up to 500 words) on why they want to follow a career in real estate management. U.S. citizenship is required. Selection is based on academic success and a demonstrated commitment to a career in real estate management.

Financial data Stipends are $1,000 for undergraduates or $2,500 for graduate students. Funds are disbursed to the institution the student attends to be used only for tuition expenses.

Duration 1 year; nonrenewable.

Number awarded 3 each year: 2 undergraduate awards and 1 graduate award.

Deadline March of each year.

[151]
GEORGIA SPACE GRANT CONSORTIUM FELLOWSHIPS

Georgia Space Grant Consortium
c/o Georgia Institute of Technology
Aerospace Engineering
Paul Weber Space Science and Technology Building, Room 210
Atlanta, GA 30332-0150
(404) 894-0521   Fax: (404) 894-9313
E-mail: wanda.pierson@aerospace.gatech.edu
Web: www.ae.gatech.edu/research/gsgc

Purpose To provide financial assistance for undergraduate and graduate study of space-related fields to students (particularly minorities, women, and students with disabilities) at member institutions of the Georgia Space Grant Consortium (GSGC).

Eligibility This program is open to U.S. citizens who are undergraduate and graduate students at member institutions of the GSGC. Applicants must be working on a degree in mathematics, science, engineering, computer science, or a technical discipline related to space. Selection is based on transcripts, 3 letters of reference, and an essay of 100 to 500 words on the applicant's professional interests and objectives and their relationship to the field of aerospace. Awards are provided as part of the Space Grant program of the U.S. National Aeronautics and Space Administration, which encourages participation by women, minorities, and people with disabilities.

Financial data A stipend is awarded (amount not specified).

Additional information Institutions that are members of the GSGC include Albany State University, Clark Atlanta University, Columbus State University, Fort Valley State University, Georgia Institute of Technology, Kennesaw State University, Mercer University, Morehouse College, Spelman College, State University of West Georgia, and the University of Georgia. This program is funded by NASA.

Number awarded 1 each year.

[152]
GERRY VANDAVEER SCHOLARSHIP

Kansas Association of Migrant Directors
c/o Cynthia Adcock
USD 305
P.O. Box 797
Salina, KS 67402
(785) 309-4718   E-mail: Cynthia.Adcock@ksde.org

Purpose To provide financial assistance for college to current or former migrants graduating from high schools in Kansas.

Eligibility This program is open to seniors graduating from high schools in Kansas and GED recipients who are current or former migrants. Applicants must be planning to attend a college or university in Kansas as a full-time student. Along with their application, they must submit a paragraph about their educational goals, explaining why they want to go to college and describing their plans after graduation. Selection is based on the essay, GPA, school performance, and financial need.

Financial data The stipend is $250 per semester ($500 per year).

Duration 4 semesters (2 years).

Number awarded Varies each year; recently, 2 of these scholarships were awarded.

Deadline March of each year.

[153]
GILBERT MARTINEZ DIVERSITY SCHOLARSHIPS

Colorado Educational Services and Development
  Association
P.O. Box 40214
Denver, CO 80204
Web: www.cesda.org

Purpose To provide financial assistance for college to high school seniors in Colorado who are first-generation college students and/or members of underrepresented ethnic or racial minorities.

Eligibility This program is open to seniors graduating from high schools in Colorado who are 1) the first member of their family to attend college; 2) members of an underre-

presented ethnic or racial minority (African American, Asian-Pacific Islander, American Indian, Hispanic/Chicano/Latino); and/or 1) able to demonstrate financial need. Applicants must have a GPA of 2.8 or higher and be planning to enroll at a 2- or 4-year college or university in Colorado. U.S. citizenship or permanent resident status is required. Selection is based on leadership and community service (particularly within minority communities), past academic performance, personal and professional accomplishments, personal attributes, special abilities, academic goals, and financial need.

Financial data The stipend is $1,000.

Duration 1 year; nonrenewable.

Additional information Information is also available from Marianna Bagge, Scholarship Committee, P.O. Box 621146, Littleton, CO 80162, (303) 225-8576, (800) 888-2787, ext. 8576.

Number awarded 6 each year.

Deadline February of each year.

[154]
GILLETTE/NATIONAL URBAN LEAGUE SCHOLARSHIP FOR MINORITY STUDENTS

National Urban League
Attn: Scholarship Coordinator
120 Wall Street
New York, NY 10005
(212) 558-5300   Toll-free: (888) 839-0467
Fax: (212) 344-5332   E-mail: info@nul.org
Web: www.nul.org

Purpose To provide financial assistance to minority students who are interested in completing their college education in designated areas of business and engineering.

Eligibility Eligible to apply are minority students who are pursuing full-time studies leading to a bachelor's degree at an accredited institution of higher learning. They must be juniors or third-year students at the time the scholarship award begins, have a GPA of 3.0 or higher, be U.S. citizens or permanent residents or have a student visa, be able to demonstrate financial need, and be majoring in business-related fields (e.g., accounting, business administration, economics, engineering, finance, human resource management, ITS, manufacturing operations, marketing, MIS, public relations). Applications must be endorsed by an Urban League affiliate.

Financial data The stipend is $2,500 per year. Funds must be used for tuition, room, board, and the purchase of required educational materials and books.

Duration 2 years.

Number awarded Approximately 5 each year.

Deadline January of each year.

[155]
GLORIA AND JOSEPH MATTERA NATIONAL SCHOLARSHIP FUND FOR MIGRANT CHILDREN

Geneseo Migrant Center
27 Lackawanna Avenue
Mount Morris, NY 14510-1096
(585) 658-7960   Toll-free: (800) 245-5681
Fax: (585) 658-7969   E-mail: info@migrant.net
Web: www.migrant.net/sch_mattera.htm

Purpose To provide financial assistance for college to migrant farmworker youth.

Eligibility This program is open to migrant farmworker youth with a recent history of movement for agricultural employment. Priority is given to current interstate migrant youth. Applicants must be 1) enrolled in or accepted at an accredited public or private college, technical school, or vocational school, or 2) a dropout or a potential dropout from high school who shows promise of ability to continue schooling. They must submit a personal essay telling about their background, career and personal goals, and why they should receive this assistance. Selection is based on the essay, background in migrant farmwork, academic potential, and financial need.

Financial data The amount varies, depending upon the financial need and potential of the recipient. Generally, awards range from $150 to $500 per year.

Duration 1 year; may be renewed.

Number awarded Approximately 100 each year.

Deadline Applications may be submitted at any time.

[156]
GORDON STAFFORD SCHOLARSHIP IN ARCHITECTURE

Stafford King Wiese Architects
Attn: Scholarship Selection Committee
622 20th Street
Sacramento, CA 95814
(916) 443-4829   Fax: (916) 443-0719
E-mail: connie_van_berkel@skwaia.com
Web: www.skwaia.com

Purpose To provide financial assistance to members of minority groups interested in studying architecture in college.

Eligibility This program is open to students accepted by an accredited school of architecture as first-year or transfer students. Applicants must be U.S. citizens or permanent residents who are ethnic persons of color (defined as Black, Hispanic, Native American, Pacific-Asian, or Asian-Indian). They must submit a 500-word statement expressing their desire to study architecture. Finalists are interviewed and must travel to Sacramento, California at their own expense.

Financial data The stipend is $2,000 per year. That includes $1,000 deposited in the recipient's school account and $1,000 paid to the recipient's directly.

Duration 1 year; may be renewed up to 4 additional years.

Additional information This program was established in 1995 to celebrate the 50th anniversary of the architectural firm that sponsors it.

Number awarded Up to 5 of these scholarships may be active at a time.

Deadline June of each year.

[157]
GRACE BYRNE UNDERGRADUATE SCHOLARSHIP

Women's Transportation Seminar-Puget Sound Chapter
c/o Lorelei Mesic, Scholarship Co-Chair
W&H Pacific
3350 Monte Villa Parkway
Bothell, WA 98021-8972
(425) 951-4872   Fax: (425) 951-4808
E-mail: lmesic@whpacific.com
Web: www.wtspugetsound.org/nscholarships.html

Purpose To provide financial assistance to women (particularly women of color) undergraduate students from Washington working on a degree related to transportation.

Eligibility This program is open to women who are residents of Washington, studying at a college in the state, or working as an intern in the state. Applicants must be currently enrolled in an undergraduate degree program in a transportation-related field, such as engineering, planning, finance, or logistics. They must have a GPA of 3.0 or higher and plans to prepare for a career in a transportation-related field. Minority candidates are encouraged to apply. Along with their application, they must submit a 500-word statement about their career goals after graduation and why they think they should receive this scholarship award. Selection is based on that statement, academic record, and transportation-related activities or job skills. Financial need is not considered.

Financial data The stipend is $1,500.

Duration 1 year.

Additional information The winner is also nominated for scholarships offered by the national organization of the Women's Transportation Seminar.

Number awarded 1 each year.

Deadline October of each year.

[158]
HACE CAREER ACHIEVEMENT AWARDS

Hispanic Alliance for Career Enhancement
Attn: College Programs
25 East Washington Street, Suite 1500
Chicago, IL 60602
(312) 435-0498   Fax: (312) 435-1494
E-mail: haceorg@hace-usa.org
Web: www.hace-usa.org/collegepage.htm

Purpose To provide financial assistance to Hispanic students working on an undergraduate degree at selected universities.

Eligibility This program is open to U.S. citizens and permanent residents who are enrolled or planning to enroll in a partner university of the sponsoring organization. Applicants must have a GPA of 2.5 or higher and at least 1 parent of Hispanic or Latino heritage. Along with their application, they must submit 300-word essays on 1) their autobiography, including their Hispanic background, where they grew up, and their immediate family; and 2) their career plans for the next 5 to 10 years.

Financial data The stipend is $1,000.

Duration 1 year; nonrenewable.

Additional information The partner institutions are DePaul University, the University of Illinois at Chicago, the University of Texas at Austin, Rice University, the University of Houston, Texas A&M University, Columbia University, Cornell University, New York University, and Rutgers University.

Number awarded Varies each year; recently, 7 of these scholarships were awarded.

Deadline February of each year.

[159]
HACE SCHOLARSHIPS

Hispanic Alliance for Career Enhancement
Attn: College Programs
25 East Washington Street, Suite 1500
Chicago, IL 60602
(312) 435-0498   Fax: (312) 435-1494
E-mail: haceorg@hace-usa.org
Web: www.hace-usa.org/collegepage.htm

Purpose To provide financial assistance to Hispanic students working on an undergraduate degree.

Eligibility This program is open to U.S. citizens and permanent residents who are enrolled or planning to enroll in a college or university in the United States (other than a partner institution of the sponsoring organization). Applicants must have a GPA of 2.5 or higher and at least 1 parent of Hispanic or Latino heritage. Along with their application, they must submit 300-word essays on 1) their autobiography, including their Hispanic background, where they grew up, and their immediate family; and 2) their career plans for the next 5 to 10 years.

Financial data The stipend is $1,000.

Duration 1 year; nonrenewable.

Additional information The partner institutions are DePaul University, the University of Illinois at Chicago, the University of Texas at Austin, Rice University, the University of Houston, Texas A&M University, Columbia University, Cornell University, New York University, and Rutgers University.

Number awarded Varies each year; recently, 9 of these scholarships were awarded.

Deadline February of each year.

[160]
HANA SCHOLARSHIPS

United Methodist Church
Attn: General Board of Higher Education and Ministry
Office of Loans and Scholarships
1001 19th Avenue South
P.O. Box 340007
Nashville, TN 37203-0007
(615) 340-7344   Fax: (615) 340-7367
E-mail: umscholar@gbhem.org
Web: www.gbhem.org

Purpose To provide financial assistance to upper-division and graduate Methodist students who are of Hispanic, Asian, Native American, Alaska Native, or Pacific Islander ancestry.

Eligibility This program is open to full-time juniors, seniors, and graduate students at accredited colleges and universities in the United States who have been active, full

members of a United Methodist Church for at least 1 year prior to applying. Applicants must have at least 1 parent who is Hispanic, Asian, Native American, Alaska Native, or Pacific Islander. They must be able to demonstrate involvement in their Hispanic, Asian, or Native American (HANA) community. Selection is based on that involvement, academic ability, and financial need. U.S. citizenship or permanent resident status is required.

Financial data The stipend is $1,000 for undergraduates or $3,000 for graduate students.

Duration 1 year; recipients may reapply.

Number awarded 50 each year.

Deadline March of each year.

[161]
HENAAC STUDENT LEADERSHIP AWARDS

Hispanic Engineer National Achievement Awards
   Conference
3900 Whiteside Street
Los Angeles, CA 90063
(323) 262-0997   Fax: (323) 262-0946
E-mail: info@henaac.org
Web: www.henaac.org

Purpose To provide financial assistance to Hispanic undergraduate and graduate students majoring in engineering and related fields.

Eligibility This program is open to Hispanic undergraduate and graduate students who are majoring in computer science, engineering, material science, or mathematics. Applicants must have a GPA of 3.0 or higher. Academic achievement and campus community activities are considered in the selection process. U.S. citizenship is required.

Financial data The stipend ranges from $1,000 to $5,000.

Duration 1 year.

Additional information This program is sponsored by the Hispanic Engineer National Achievement Awards Conference (HENAAC): to promote technical excellence and leadership in the Hispanic community.

Number awarded 2 each year: 1 undergraduate and 1 graduate student.

Deadline April of each year.

[162]
HIGH SCHOOL SCHOLARSHIP PROGRAM OF THE HISPANIC SCHOLARSHIP FUND

Hispanic Scholarship Fund
Attn: Selection Committee
55 Second Street, Suite 1500
San Francisco, CA 94105
(415) 808-2350   Toll-free: (877) HSF-INFO
Fax: (415) 808-2302   E-mail: highschool@hsf.net
Web: www.hsf.net/scholarship/programs/hs.php

Purpose To provide financial assistance to Hispanic American high school seniors who are interested in attending college.

Eligibility This program is open to U.S. citizens, permanent residents, and visitors with a passport stamped I-551. Applicants must be high school seniors of Hispanic heritage and have applied for federal financial aid. They must have a GPA of 3.0 or higher and concrete plans to enroll full time at an accredited 2-year or 4-year college or university in the

United States, Puerto Rico, or the U.S. Virgin Islands for the following fall. Along with their application, they must submit 600-word essays on 1) how their Hispanic heritage, family upbringing, and/or role models have influenced their personal long-term goals; 2) how they contribute to their community and what they have learned from their experiences; and 3) an academic challenge they have faced and how they have overcome it. Selection is based on academic achievement, personal strengths, leadership, and financial need.

Financial data Stipends range from $1,000 to $2,500 per year.

Duration 1 year.

Additional information Since this program began in 1975, more than $144 million has been awarded to more than 68,000 Hispanic students.

Number awarded Varies each year.

Deadline December of each year.

[163]
H.I.S. PROGRAM

Hispanic College Fund
Attn: National Director
1717 Pennsylvania Avenue, N.W., Suite 460
Washington, D.C. 20006
(202) 296-5400   Toll-free: (800) 644-4223
Fax: (202) 296-3774
E-mail: hispaniccollegefund@earthlink.net
Web: www.hispanicfund.org

Purpose To provide financial assistance and summer work experience to Hispanic American undergraduate students who are interested in preparing for a career in telecommunications.

Eligibility This program is open to U.S. citizens of Hispanic background (at least 1 grandparent must be 100% Hispanic) who are entering their freshman, sophomore, junior, or senior year of college. Applicants must be working on a bachelor's degree in accounting, business administration, computer science, economics, engineering specialties, finance, information systems, management, or other relevant technology or business fields. They must have an interest in telecommunications, have a cumulative GPA of 3.0 or higher, and be available to complete at least 2 consecutive summer internships before graduating from college. Financial need is considered in the selection process.

Financial data Stipends range from $500 to $5,000, depending on need and academic achievement. Funds are paid directly to the recipient's college or university to help cover tuition and fees.

Duration 1 year; recipients may reapply.

Additional information This program is a joint venture of the Hispanic College Fund (which provides scholarships), INROADS (which provides monthly coaching, leadership development, community service, and mentorship), and Sprint (which provides 10- to 12-week paid summer internships). All applications must be submitted online; no paper applications are available.

Number awarded Varies each year.

Deadline April of each year.

[164]
HISPANIC CHURCH MULTIPLICATION TEAM SCHOLARSHIPS

Southern Baptist Convention
North American Mission Board
Attn: Church Multiplication Team
4200 North Point Parkway
Alpharetta, GA 30022-4176
(770) 410-6235   Fax: (770) 410-6012
E-mail: jdoyle@namb.net
Web: www.namb.net

Purpose To provide financial assistance to Hispanic American Baptists interested in religious vocations.

Eligibility This program is open to Hispanic Americans who are U.S. citizens involved in some type of approved Baptist ministry. Applicants must be able to demonstrate financial need. Only students in accredited institutions working toward a basic college (bachelor's) or seminary (M.Div.) degree are eligible. As part of the selection process, applicants must submit an essay describing their interest in and commitment to a Christian vocation.

Financial data The maximum grants are $500 per year for students attending accredited colleges, $600 per year for students in non-Southern Baptist Convention seminaries, and $850 per year for students at 1 of the 6 Southern Baptist Convention seminaries.

Duration 1 year; renewable.

Additional information The 6 Southern Baptist seminaries are Golden Gate Baptist Theological Seminary (Mill Valley, California), Midwestern Baptist Theological Seminary (Kansas City, Missouri), New Orleans Baptist Theological Seminary (New Orleans, Louisiana), Southeastern Baptist Theological Seminary (Wake Forest, North Carolina), Southern Baptist Theological Seminary (Louisville, Kentucky), and Southwestern Baptist Theological Seminary (Fort Worth, Texas).

Number awarded Varies each year.

Deadline Applications may be submitted at any time, but they must be received at least 1 month (preferably sooner) before the student enrolls in a school.

[165]
HISPANIC COLLEGE FUND SCHOLARSHIPS

Hispanic College Fund
Attn: National Director
1717 Pennsylvania Avenue, N.W., Suite 460
Washington, D.C. 20006
(202) 296-5400   Toll-free: (800) 644-4223
Fax: (202) 296-3774
E-mail: hispaniccollegefund@earthlink.net
Web: www.hispanicfund.org

Purpose To provide financial assistance to Hispanic American undergraduate students.

Eligibility This program is open to U.S. citizens of Hispanic background (at least 1 grandparent must be 100% Hispanic) who are entering their freshman, sophomore, junior, or senior year of college. Applicants must be working on a bachelor's or associate degree and have a cumulative GPA of 3.0 or higher. They must be applying to or enrolled in a college or university in the 50 states or Puerto Rico as a full-time student. Financial need is considered in the selection process.

Financial data Stipends range from $500 to $5,000, depending on the need of the recipient, and average approximately $3,000. Funds are paid directly to the recipient's college or university to help cover tuition and fees.

Duration 1 year; recipients may reapply.

Additional information All applications must be submitted online; no paper applications are available.

Number awarded Varies each year; recently, 208 students were supported by this program, including 70 freshmen, 57 sophomores, 47 juniors, and 34 seniors.

Deadline April of each year.

[166]
HISPANIC CONTRACTORS OF COLORADO SCHOLARSHIPS

Hispanic Contractors of Colorado
1114 West Seventh Avenue, Suite 210
Denver, CO 80204
(303) 893-3893   Fax: (303) 893-2877
Web: www.hispanic-contractors.org

Purpose To provide financial assistance for college to Hispanic residents of Colorado who are interested in preparing for a career in the construction industry.

Eligibility This program is open to residents of Colorado of Hispanic heritage who have been accepted at or are attending an accredited college, university, or technical school. Applicants must have a cumulative GPA of 2.5 or higher and a declared major or certificate interest in a construction-related field (e.g., architecture, construction management, construction technology, engineering, HVAC certificate). Students in a 4-year college or university program must be juniors or above. Selection is based on a statement on career goals and why the applicant has chosen a career in construction, academic achievement, 2 letters of recommendation, community service and/or extracurricular activities, and financial need.

Financial data A stipend is awarded (amount not specified).

Duration 1 year.

Number awarded 1 or more each year.

Deadline March of each year.

[167]
HISPANIC HERITAGE YOUTH AWARDS

Hispanic Heritage Awards Foundation
2600 Virginia Avenue, N.W., Suite 406
Washington, DC 20037
(202) 861-9797   Toll-free: (866) 665-2112
Fax: (202) 861-9799
E-mail: contact@hispanicheritageawards.org
Web: www.hispanicheritageawards.org

Purpose To recognize and reward, with college scholarships, Hispanic high school seniors from selected metropolitan areas throughout the country who have excelled in various areas of activity.

Eligibility This program is open to high school seniors who are U.S. citizens or permanent residents and of Hispanic heritage (at least 1 parent must be of able to trace family origins to Spain, Latin America, or the Spanish-speaking Caribbean). Awards were recently presented to students in 12 metropolitan regions: Chicago, Dallas, Houston, Los Angeles, Miami, New York City, Philadelphia, Phoenix, San Antonio, San Diego, northern California, and Washington, D.C. Applicants competed for awards in the following 6 categories: community service, engineering and mathematics, academic excellence, journalism, sports, or health care. They must have a GPA of 2.75 or higher. Along with their application, they must submit an essay that describes their personal qualities and strengths, dedication to community service and the impact it has had on their life, future career goals, areas of interest, and significance of heritage and/or family in their life. Selection criteria include, but are not limited to, the following: academic achievement, compelling essay responses, meritorious achievements in the applicant's chosen category, contribution to the community, overall character as a role model, and letters of recommendation.

Financial data In each category and each city, gold regional winners receive $3,000 and silver regional winners receive $2,000. Awards are in the form of educational grants that recipients may use for any aspect of their college career (tuition, books, room, and board). The gold regional winners then advance to a national competition. National winners receive an additional $5,000 educational grant, a state-of-the-art laptop computer, an all-expense paid trip to Miami for the winner and a parent to attend the award announcement event, and an all-expense paid trip to Washington, D.C. for the winner and a parent to attend the awards ceremony at the John F. Kennedy Center for the Performing Arts.

Duration The awards are presented annually.

Additional information This program began in 1998 with sponsorship by the Fannie Mae Foundation for 5 cities and 1 category. More sponsors have resulted in the addition of more categories and cities. Recent sponsors have included Dr Pepper for community service, ExxonMobil for engineering and mathematics, Chase Manhattan Bank and MasterCard for academic excellence, NBC and Telemundo for journalism, Subway for sports, and GlaxoSmithKline for health care. Awardees must attend, at their own expense, a local awards ceremony for the region they have selected.

Number awarded Recently, 144 regional winners were selected: a gold and a silver in each of the 6 categories from each of the 12 cities. From those, 6 national winners were chosen: 1 in each of the categories.

Deadline February of each year.

[168]
HISPANIC METROPOLITAN CHAMBER SCHOLARSHIPS

Hispanic Metropolitan Chamber
Attn: Scholarship Committee
P.O. Box 1837
Portland, OR 97207
(503) 222-0280
Web: www.hmccoregon.com

Purpose To provide financial assistance for college and graduate school to Hispanic residents of Oregon and Clark County, Washington.

Eligibility This program is open to residents of Oregon and Clark County, Washington who are of Hispanic ancestry. Applicants must have a GPA of 2.75 or higher and be enrolled or planning to enroll in an accredited community college, 4-year university, or graduate school. Along with their application, they must submit 250-word essays on what being a Latino student means to them, why they should be selected to receive another scholarship from this sponsor (if they are applying for a renewal), and/or what they intend to do with their degree in 10 years (if they are a first-time applicant). If they wish to be considered for a scholarship for low-income families, they may also submit documentation of financial need.

Financial data Stipends range from $1,000 to $5,000.

Duration 1 year; may be renewed.

Number awarded Varies each year; recently, 45 of these scholarships were awarded.

Deadline February of each year.

[169]
HISPANIC PUBLIC RELATIONS ASSOCIATION SCHOLARSHIP PROGRAM

Hispanic Public Relations Association
Attn: Scholarship Committee Chair
660 South Figueroa Street, Suite 1140
Los Angeles, CA 90017
(310) 244-6467
E-mail: karen_barragan@spe.sony.com
Web: www.hprala.org/scholarship.html

Purpose To provide financial assistance to Hispanic undergraduate students from any state attending college in southern California who are preparing for a career in public relations.

Eligibility This program is open to Hispanic students entering the junior or senior year at 4-year colleges and universities in southern California. Applicants must have a GPA of 2.7 or higher cumulatively and 3.0 or higher in their major subject. Preference is given to students majoring in public relations, but students in communication studies, journalism, advertising, and/or marketing are also eligible. Students majoring in other disciplines but planning to work in the public relations industry may also apply. Along with their application, they must submit a letter of recommendation, official university transcripts, a 1- to 2-page personal statement explaining their career and educational aspirations as well as their involvement in the Hispanic community, a 1-page resume, and writing samples. Any materials submitted in Spanish must include an English translation.

Financial data A stipend is awarded (amount not specified).

Duration 1 year.

Additional information Recipients are expected to attend the sponsor's Premio Awards dinner in October.

Number awarded 1 or more each year.

Deadline May of each year.

[170]
HORACE AND SUSIE REVELS CAYTON SCHOLARSHIP

Public Relations Society of America-Puget Sound
  Chapter
c/o Diane Beins
1006 Industry Drive
Seattle, WA 98188-4801
(206) 623-8632
E-mail: prsascholarship@asi-seattle.net
Web: www.prsapugetsound.org/cayton

Purpose To provide financial assistance to minority upper-classmen from Washington who are interested in preparing for a career in public relations.

Eligibility This program is open to U.S. citizens who are members of minority groups, defined as African Americans, Asian Americans, Hispanic/Latino Americans, Native Americans, and Pacific Islanders. Applicants must be juniors or seniors attending a college in Washington or Washington students (who graduated from a Washington high school or whose parents live in the state year-round) attending college elsewhere. They must be able to demonstrate aptitude in public relations and related courses, activities, and/or internships. Along with their application, they must submit a description of their career goals and the skills that are most important in general to a public relations career (15 points in the selection process); a description of their activities in communications in class, on campus, in the community, or during internships, including 3 samples of their work (15 points); a statement on the value of public relations to an organization (10 points); a description of any barriers, financial or otherwise, they have encountered in pursuing their academic or personal goals and how they have addressed them (15 points); a discussion of their heritage, and how their cultural background and/or the discrimination they may have experienced has impacted them (15 points); a certified transcript (15 points); and 2 or more letters of recommendation (15 points).

Financial data The stipend is $2,500.

Duration 1 year.

Additional information This program was established in 1992.

Number awarded 1 each year.

Deadline March of each year.

[171]
HORISONS SCHOLARSHIPS

Pueblo Hispanic Education Foundation
Administration Building, Room 325
2200 Bonforte Boulevard
Pueblo, CO 81001
(719) 546-2563   Fax: (719) 546-0504
E-mail: pphef@aol.com
Web: www.phef.net

Purpose To provide financial assistance to Hispanic undergraduate students from Colorado.

Eligibility This program is open to full-time undergraduate students of Hispanic descent who are residents of Colorado. Applicants must submit an essay on their career and educational goals, school activities and awards, interests, community service and volunteer work, and work experience. Selection is based on financial need, proven ability,

GPA, community and volunteer service, and educational desire. Preference is given to students of low to moderate income, continuing students, and single parents.

Financial data Stipends are generally $1,000 per year.

Duration 1 year. Recipients may reapply if they maintain a cumulative GPA of 2.0 or higher as first-time freshmen and 2.5 or higher as continuing students.

Additional information The title of this program stands for "Hispanic Outreach In Search of New Scholars." This is the largest scholarship program in southern Colorado. Funds are not available for summer school. Recipients are required to perform 40 hours of community service at a non-profit agency.

Number awarded Varies each year; recently, 63 of these scholarships were awarded.

Deadline February of each year.

[172]
HP SCHOLAR PROGRAM

Hewlett-Packard Company
Attn: Scholar Program Manager
8000 Foothills Boulevard
MS 5214
Roseville, CA 95747
(916) 785-3809　　　　E-mail: hpscholars@hp.com
Web: www.hp.com/go/hpscholars

Purpose To provide financial assistance and summer work experience to underrepresented minority high school seniors and community college transfer students who are interested in studying computer engineering, electrical engineering, or computer science at designated universities.

Eligibility This program is open to graduating high school seniors and community college students who are members of an underrepresented minority group (African American, Latino, or American Indian). Applicants must be planning to major in electrical engineering, computer engineering, or computer science at the University of California at Los Angeles, San Jose State University, North Carolina A&T University, the University of Washington, or Morgan State University. They must be interested in working during the summer at a major Hewlett-Packard (HP) location in California, Colorado, Idaho, Oregon, Texas, or Washington. Selection is based on academic achievement, financial need, family's educational history (priority is given to first-generation students), letters of recommendation, a personal statement (communication skills, personal and professional qualities, community involvement), connections to HP Philanthropy and Education Partnerships, and demonstrated interest in math, science, and engineering.

Financial data The stipend is $3,000 per year. In addition, students receive a salary when they work at HP facilities during the summer. They also receive an HP laptop, printer, and PDA. The total value of the award exceeds $40,000 per student.

Duration 4 years of university study plus 3 summers of internships.

Additional information Applications must be submitted to the school the student wishes to attend.

Number awarded Approximately 120 each year.

Deadline March of each year.

[173]
HSF/CITIGROUP FELLOWS PROGRAM

Hispanic Scholarship Fund
Attn: Selection Committee
55 Second Street, Suite 1500
San Francisco, CA 94105
(415) 808-2350　　　　Toll-free: (877) HSF-INFO
Fax: (415) 808-2302　　　E-mail: college1@hsf.net
Web: www.hsf.net

Purpose To provide financial assistance to Hispanic upper-division students working on a degree related to business at designated universities.

Eligibility This program is open to U.S. citizens, permanent residents, and visitors with a passport stamped I-551 who are of Hispanic heritage. Applicants must be 1) residents of or enrolled full time at a 4-year college or university in the New York City metropolitan area, the Miami/Fort Lauderdale area, Tampa, Dallas, Los Angeles, or the San Francisco Bay area; or 2) enrolled full time at Columbia University, Cornell University, Dartmouth University, Duke University, Georgetown University, Harvard University, New York University, Northwestern University, Princeton University, Rutgers University, Stanford University, University of California at Los Angeles, University of Chicago, University of Pennsylvania, University of Virginia, University of Texas at Austin, or Yale University. They must be entering their junior year with a GPA of 3.2 or higher and a major in business, economics, finance, or business administration. Along with their application, they must submit 600-word essays on 1) how their Hispanic heritage, family upbringing, and/or role models have influenced their personal long-term goals; 2) how they contribute to their community and what they have learned from their experiences; and 3) an academic challenge they have faced and how they have overcome it. Selection is based on academic achievement, personal strengths, leadership, and financial need.

Financial data The stipend is $5,000 per year.

Duration 2 years (the junior and senior years of college).

Additional information This program is funded by the Citigroup Foundation, which also arranges for a Citigroup employee to be paired with each student recipient as a mentor. Students are also invited to a professional development conference in the fall of their junior and senior years, with all expenses paid by the foundation.

Number awarded 1 or more each year.

Deadline April of each year.

[174]
HYATT HOTEL FUND FOR MINORITY LODGING MANAGEMENT STUDENTS

American Hotel & Lodging Educational Foundation
Attn: Manager of Foundation Programs
1201 New York Avenue, N.W., Suite 600
Washington, DC 20005-3931
(202) 289-3188　　　　Fax: (202) 289-3199
E-mail: ahlef@ahlef.org
Web: www.ahlf.org/scholarships

Purpose To provide financial assistance to minority college students working on a degree in hotel management.

Eligibility Applicants must be attending a 4-year college or university that is a member of the Council on Hotel, Restaurant and Institutional Education. They must be minorities and majoring in hotel management. Each member university may nominate 1 student. The most outstanding students receive this scholarship.

Financial data The stipend is $2,000.

Duration 1 year.

Additional information Funding for this program is provided by Hyatt Hotels & Resorts.

Number awarded Varies each year; recently, 18 of these scholarships were awarded.

Deadline March of each year.

[175]
ICI EDUCATIONAL FOUNDATION SCHOLARSHIP PROGRAM

Hispanic College Fund
Attn: National Director
1717 Pennsylvania Avenue, N.W., Suite 460
Washington, D.C. 20006
(202) 296-5400   Toll-free: (800) 644-4223
Fax: (202) 296-3774
E-mail: hispaniccollegefund@earthlink.net
Web: www.hispanicfund.org

Purpose To provide financial assistance to Hispanic American undergraduate students who are interested in preparing for a career in business, computer science, or engineering.

Eligibility This program is open to U.S. citizens of Hispanic background (at least 1 grandparent must be 100% Hispanic) who are entering their freshman, sophomore, junior, or senior year of college. Applicants must be working on a bachelor's or associate degree in business, computer science, engineering or a business-related major and have a cumulative GPA of 3.0 or higher. They must be applying to or enrolled in a college or university in the 50 states or Puerto Rico as a full-time student. Financial need is considered in the selection process.

Financial data Stipends range from $500 to $5,000, depending on the need of the recipient, and average approximately $3,000. Funds are paid directly to the recipient's college or university to help cover tuition and fees.

Duration 1 year; recipients may reapply.

Additional information This program is sponsored by the ICI Educational Foundation. All applications must be submitted online; no paper applications are available.

Number awarded Varies each year.

Deadline April of each year.

[176]
IDAHO MIGRANT COUNCIL HISPANIC SCHOLARSHIP FUND

Idaho Migrant Council, Inc.
Attn: Employment and Training Grants Specialist
317 Happy Day Boulevard, Suite 250
Caldwell, ID 83607
(208) 454-1652   Fax: (208) 459-0448

Purpose To provide financial assistance for college to Hispanic high school seniors in Idaho.

Eligibility This program is open to residents of Idaho who are of Hispanic origin. Applicants must be planning to enter college in Idaho as freshmen in the following fall. They must have a GPA of 2.5 or higher. Selection is based on a 1-page

statement on educational goals, high school transcripts, 3 letters of recommendation, and financial need.

Financial data The stipend is $1,000.

Duration 1 year; nonrenewable.

Additional information Recipients are expected to attend the sponsor's annual meeting in September to accept their award.

Number awarded 5 or 6 each year.

Deadline April of each year.

[177]
IDAHO MINORITY AND "AT RISK" STUDENT SCHOLARSHIP

Idaho State Board of Education
Len B. Jordan Office Building
650 West State Street, Room 307
P.O. Box 83720
Boise, ID 83720-0037
(208) 332-1574   Fax: (208) 334-2632
E-mail: board@osbe.state.id.us
Web: www.idahoboardofed.org

Purpose To provide financial assistance for college to disabled and other "at risk" high school seniors in Idaho.

Eligibility This program focuses on talented students who may be at risk of failing to meet their goals because of physical, economic, or cultural limitations. Applicants must be high school graduates, be Idaho residents, and meet at least 3 of the following 5 requirements: 1) have a disability; 2) be a member of an ethnic minority group historically underrepresented in higher education in Idaho; 3) have substantial financial need; 4) be a first-generation college student; 5) be a migrant farm worker or a dependent of a farm worker.

Financial data The maximum stipend is $3,000 per year.

Duration 1 year; may be renewed for up to 3 additional years.

Additional information This program was established in 1991 by the Idaho state legislature. Information is also available from high school counselors and financial aid offices of colleges and universities in Idaho. Recipients must plan to attend or be attending 1 of 8 participating colleges and universities in the state on a full-time basis. For a list of those schools, write to the State of Idaho Board of Education.

Number awarded Approximately 40 each year.

[178]
IDAHO SPACE GRANT CONSORTIUM SCHOLARSHIP PROGRAM

Idaho Space Grant Consortium
c/o University of Idaho
College of Engineering
P.O. Box 441011
Moscow, ID 83844-1011
(208) 885-6438   Fax: (208) 885-6645
E-mail: isgc@uidaho.edu
Web: isgc.uidaho.edu

Purpose To provide financial assistance for study in space-related fields to undergraduate students (especially underrepresented minorities, women, and persons with disabilities) at institutions belonging to the Idaho Space Grant Consortium (ISGC).

Eligibility This program is open to undergraduate students at ISGC member institutions. Applicants must be majoring in engineering, mathematics, science, or science/math education and have a cumulative GPA of 3.0 or higher. They should be planning to work on a 4-year degree in a space-related field. Along with their application, they must submit a 500-word essay on their future career and educational goals and why they believe the U.S. National Aeronautics and Space Administration (NASA) should support their education. U.S. citizenship is required. As a component of the NASA Space Grant program, the ISGC encourages participation by women, underrepresented minorities, and persons with disabilities.

Financial data The stipend is up to $1,000 per year. Funds are to be used to pay for registration at colleges in the consortium.

Duration 1 year; may be renewed.

Additional information Members of the consortium include Albertson College of Idaho, Boise State University, College of Southern Idaho, Idaho State University, Lewis Clark State College, North Idaho College, Northwest Nazarene College, Brigham Young University of Idaho, and the University of Idaho. This program is funded by NASA.

Number awarded Varies each year.

Deadline February of each year.

[179]
IDAHO STATE BROADCASTERS ASSOCIATION SCHOLARSHIPS

Idaho State Broadcasters Association
270 North 27th Street, Suite B
Boise, ID 83702-4741
(208) 345-3072   Fax: (208) 343-8946
E-mail: isba@rmci.net
Web: www.idahobroadcasters.org/scholarships.aspx

Purpose To provide financial assistance to students at Idaho colleges and universities who are preparing for a career in the broadcasting field.

Eligibility This program is open to full-time students at Idaho schools who are preparing for a career in broadcasting, including business administration, sales, journalism, and engineering. Applicants must have a GPA of at least 2.0 for the first 2 years of school or 2.5 for the last 2 years. Along with their application, they must submit a letter of recommendation from the general manager of a broadcasting state that is a member of the Idaho State Broadcasters Association and a 1-page essay describing their career plans and why they want the scholarship. Applications are encouraged from a wide and diverse student population. The Wayne C. Cornils Scholarship is reserved for a less advantaged applicant.

Financial data The stipend for the general scholarships is $1,000. The amount of the Wayne C. Cornils Scholarship depends on the need of the recipient.

Duration 1 year.

Number awarded 3 each year: 2 general scholarships and the Cornils Scholarship.

Deadline March of each year.

[180]
ILLINOIS MIGRANT COUNCIL SCHOLARSHIPS

Illinois Migrant Council
Attn: Youth Program Coordinator
28 East Jackson Boulevard, Suite 1600
Chicago, IL 60604
(312) 663-1522, ext. 210   Fax: (312) 663-1994
E-mail: evelasquez@illinoismigrant.org
Web: www.illinoismigrant.org/schol.html

Purpose To provide financial assistance for college to Hispanic and other minority migrant and seasonal farmworkers and their children in Illinois.

Eligibility This program is open to Illinois residents who are Hispanic and other minority migrant or seasonal farmworkers and their descendants. Applicants must be high school seniors who have been accepted by an Illinois vocational institute or 2-year or 4-year college or university. They must have a GPA of at least "C+" and be able to meet low income guidelines.

Financial data A stipend is awarded (amount not specified).

Duration 1 year.

Number awarded Varies each year.

Deadline July of each year.

[181]
ILLINOIS MINORITY REAL ESTATE SCHOLARSHIP

Illinois Association of Realtors
Attn: Illinois Real Estate Educational Foundation
3180 Adloff Lane, Suite 400
P.O. Box 19451
Springfield, IL 62794-9451
(217) 529-2600   E-mail: IARaccess@iar.org
Web: www.illinoisrealtor.org/iar/about/minority.htm

Purpose To provide financial assistance to Illinois residents who are members of minority groups and preparing for a career in real estate.

Eligibility This program is open to residents of Illinois who are African American, Hispanic or Latino, Native American, or Asian. Applicants must be interested in preparing for a career in real estate by pursuing: 1) courses to meet Illinois salesperson license requirement; 2) course work to meet Illinois broker license requirement; 3) course work required for Illinois appraisal licensing/certification; 4) professional development unrelated to obtaining license/certification; or 5) an undergraduate or graduate program of study. Along with their application, they must submit information on their employment history, transcripts, evidence of financial need, and an essay that describes their career goals and explains why they believe they should receive scholarship assistance through this program.

Financial data The maximum stipend is $500.

Duration Funds must be used within 24 months of the award date.

Deadline Applications may be submitted at any time, but they must be received at least 12 weeks prior to the beginning of the school term for which financial assistance is requested.

[182]
IMAGE DE SEATTLE SCHOLARSHIPS

Image de Seattle
Attn: Scholarship Committee
P.O. Box 21247
Seattle, WA 98111
(206) 443-3800

Purpose To provide financial assistance to Hispanic American students from the state of Washington who are interested in working on an undergraduate or graduate degree.

Eligibility This program is open to high school seniors, undergraduates, and graduate school students who are Hispanic Americans and have been residents of the state of Washington for at least the past 12 months. Applicants must submit a 1-page statement on their goals and plans for the future, their chosen field of study, and a brief biography that includes their identification with the Hispanic community. Financial need is not considered in the selection process.

Financial data The stipend is $500.

Duration 1 year.

Additional information Recipients must agree to provide 25 hours of community service within 1 year of selection.

Number awarded 3 each year.

Deadline May of each year.

[183]
INDUSTRY MINORITY SCHOLARSHIPS

American Meteorological Society
Attn: Fellowship/Scholarship Program
45 Beacon Street
Boston, MA 02108-3693
(617) 227-2426, ext. 246   Fax: (617) 742-8718
E-mail: scholar@ametsoc.org
Web: www.ametsoc.org

Purpose To provide financial assistance to underrepresented minority students entering college and planning to major in meteorology or an aspect of atmospheric sciences.

Eligibility This program is open to members of minority groups traditionally underrepresented in the sciences (Hispanics, Native Americans, and Black/African Americans) who are entering their freshman year at a college or university and planning to work on a degree in the atmospheric or related oceanic and hydrologic sciences. Applicants must submit an official high school transcript showing grades from the past 3 years, a letter of recommendation from a high school teacher or guidance counselor, a copy of scores from an SAT or similar national entrance exam, and a 500-word essay on how they would use their college education in atmospheric sciences (or a closely-related field) to make their community a better place in which to live. Selection is based on the essay and academic performance in high school.

Financial data The stipend is $3,000 per year.

Duration 1 year; may be renewed for the second year of college study.

Additional information This program is funded by grants from industry and by donations to the American Meteorological Society (AMS) 21st Century Campaign.

Requests for an application must be accompanied by a self-addressed stamped envelope.

Number awarded Varies each year; recently, 10 of these scholarships were awarded.

Deadline February of each year.

[184]
INDUSTRY UNDERGRADUATE SCHOLARSHIPS

American Meteorological Society
Attn: Fellowship/Scholarship Coordinator
45 Beacon Street
Boston, MA 02108-3693
(617) 227-2426, ext. 246   Fax: (617) 742-8718
E-mail: scholar@ametsoc.org
Web: www.ametsoc.org

Purpose To provide financial assistance to undergraduate students (particularly minorities, women, and students with disabilities) preparing for a career in the atmospheric and related oceanic and hydrologic sciences.

Eligibility This program is open to full-time students entering their junior year who are either 1) enrolled or planning to enroll in a course of study leading to a bachelor's degree in the atmospheric or related oceanic or hydrologic sciences, or 2) enrolled in a program leading to a bachelor's degree in science or engineering who have demonstrated a clear intent to prepare for a career in the atmospheric or related oceanic or hydrologic sciences following completion of appropriate specialized education at the graduate level. Applicants must have a GPA of 3.25 or higher and be U.S. citizens or permanent residents. Along with their application, they must submit 200-word essays on 1) their most important achievements that qualify them for this scholarship, and 2) their career goals in the atmospheric or related oceanic or hydrologic fields. Selection is based on academic performance and recommendations. The sponsor specifically encourages applications from women, minorities, and students with disabilities who are traditionally underrepresented in the atmospheric and related oceanic sciences.

Financial data The stipend is $2,000 per academic year.

Duration 1 year; may be renewed for the final year of college study.

Additional information Requests for an application must be accompanied by a self-addressed stamped envelope.

Number awarded Varies each year; recently, 12 of these scholarships were awarded.

Deadline February of each year.

[185]
INTERNATIONAL COMMUNICATIONS INDUSTRIES ASSOCIATION COLLEGE SCHOLARSHIPS

International Communications Industries Association, Inc.
Attn: Director of Strategic Initiatives
11242 Waples Mill Road, Suite 200
Fairfax, VA 22030
(703) 273-7200   Toll-free: (800) 659-7469
Fax: (703) 278-8082   E-mail: dwilbert@infocomm.org
Web: www.infocomm.org

Purpose To provide financial assistance to college students and entering graduate students (especially minorities and women) who are interested in preparing for a career in the audiovisual industry.

Eligibility This program is open to 1) college juniors completing their bachelor's degree in the following year; 2) college seniors who plan to enter graduate school; and 3) students in their final year of study for an associate degree. Applicants must have a GPA of 2.75 or higher in a program of audio, visual, audiovisual, electronics, telecommunications, technical theater, data networking, software development, or information technology. Students in other programs, such as journalism, may be eligible if they can demonstrate a relationship to career goals in the audiovisual industry. Along with their application, they must submit essays on why they are applying for this scholarship, why they are interested in the audiovisual industry, and their professional plans following graduation. Minority and women candidates are especially encouraged to apply. Selection is based on the essays, presentation of the application, GPA, work experience, and letters of recommendation.

Financial data The stipend is $2,500.

Duration 1 year.

Additional information Recipients are required to work during the summer as paid interns with a manufacturer, dealer, designer, or other firm that is a member of the International Communications Industries Association.

Number awarded Varies each year; recently, 7 of these scholarships were awarded.

Deadline April of each year.

[186]
INTERNATIONAL COMMUNICATIONS INDUSTRIES ASSOCIATION HIGH SCHOOL SCHOLARSHIPS

International Communications Industries Association, Inc.
Attn: Director of Strategic Initiatives
11242 Waples Mill Road, Suite 200
Fairfax, VA 22030
(703) 273-7200   Toll-free: (800) 659-7469
Fax: (703) 278-8082   E-mail: dwilbert@infocomm.org
Web: www.infocomm.org

Purpose To provide financial assistance for college to high school seniors (especially minorities and women) interested in preparing for a career in the audiovisual industry.

Eligibility This program is open to graduating high school seniors who have a GPA of 2.75 or higher. Applicants must have been accepted by an accredited postsecondary institution to work on a certificate or degree in audio, visual, audiovisual, electronics, telecommunications, technical theater, data networking, software development, or information

technology. Students in other programs, such as journalism, may be eligible if they can demonstrate a relationship to career goals in the audiovisual industry. Along with their application, they must submit 1) an essay of 150 to 200 words on the career path they see themselves pursuing in the next 5 years and why, and 2) an essay of 250 to 300 words on the experience or person that most influenced them in selecting the audiovisual industry as their career of choice. Minority and women candidates are especially encouraged to apply. Selection is based on the essays, presentation of the application, GPA, work experience, and letters of recommendation.

Financial data The stipend is $500.

Duration 1 year.

Additional information Recipients are also offered a paid internship with a manufacturer, dealer, designer, or other firm that is a member of the International Communications Industries Association.

Number awarded Varies each year; recently, 9 of these scholarships were awarded.

Deadline April of each year.

[187]
JACKIE ROBINSON SCHOLARSHIPS

Jackie Robinson Foundation
Attn: Education and Leadership Development Program
3 West 35th Street, 11th Floor
New York, NY 10001-2204
(212) 290-8600   Fax: (212) 290-8081
E-mail: general@jackierobinson.org
Web: www.jackierobinson.org

Purpose To provide financial assistance for college to minority high school seniors.

Eligibility This program is open to members of an ethnic minority group who are high school seniors accepted at a 4-year college or university. Applicants must be able to demonstrate high academic achievement (ACT score of 21 or higher or the equivalent on the SAT), financial need, and leadership potential. U.S. citizenship is required.

Financial data The stipend is $6,000 per year.

Duration 4 years.

Additional information The program also offers personal and career counseling on a year-round basis, a week of interaction with other scholarship students from around the country, and assistance in obtaining summer jobs and permanent employment after graduation. It was established in 1973 by a grant from Chesebrough-Pond.

Number awarded 100 or more each year.

Deadline March of each year.

[188]
JAMES CARLSON MEMORIAL SCHOLARSHIP

Oregon Student Assistance Commission
Attn: Grants and Scholarships Division
1500 Valley River Drive, Suite 100
Eugene, OR 97401-2146
(541) 687-7395   Toll-free: (800) 452-8807, ext. 7395
Fax: (541) 687-7419
E-mail: awardinfo@mercury.osac.state.or.us
Web: www.osac.state.or.us

Purpose To provide financial assistance to Oregon residents (particularly minorities) majoring in education on the undergraduate or graduate school level.

Eligibility This program is open to residents of Oregon who are U.S. citizens or permanent residents. Applicants must be either 1) college seniors or fifth-year students majoring in elementary or secondary education or 2) graduate students working on an elementary or secondary certificate. Full-time enrollment and financial need are required. Priority is given to 1) members of African American, Asian American, Hispanic, or Native American ethnic groups; 2) dependents of members of the Oregon Education Association; and 3) applicants committed to teaching autistic children.

Financial data Stipend amounts vary; recently, they were at least $1,300.

Duration 1 year.

Additional information This program is administered by the Oregon Student Assistance Commission (OSAC) with funds provided by the Oregon Community Foundation, 1221 S.W. Yamhill, Suite 100, Portland, OR 97205, (503) 227-6846, Fax: (503) 274-7771.

Number awarded Varies each year; recently, 3 of these scholarships were awarded.

Deadline February of each year.

[189]
JAMES ECHOLS SCHOLARSHIP

California Association for Health, Physical Education,
    Recreation and Dance
Attn: Chair, Scholarship Committee
1501 El Camino Avenue, Suite 3
Sacramento, CA 95815-2748
(916) 922-3596   Toll-free: (800) 499-3596 (within CA)
Fax: (916) 922-0133   E-mail: cahperd@cahperd.org
Web: www.cahperd.org

Purpose To provide financial assistance to minority student members of the California Association for Health, Physical Education, Recreation and Dance.

Eligibility This program is open to California residents who have been members of the association for at least 60 days and are attending a 2-year or 4-year college or university in California. Applicants must be undergraduate or graduate students majoring in health, physical education, recreation, or dance and have completed at least 60 semester hours of college work. Selection is based on scholastic proficiency (a GPA of 3.0 or higher); leadership ability in school, community, and professional activities; and personal qualities of enthusiasm, cooperativeness, responsibility, initiative, and ability to work with others. This scholarship is awarded to the highest-ranked minority (Asian, African American, Latino, or Native American) applicant.

Financial data The stipend is $750.

Duration 1 year.

Additional information Information is also available from Nicolas Fraire, CAHPERD Scholarship Chair, 3792 Willowpark Drive, San Jose, CA 95118.

Number awarded 1 each year.

Deadline December of each year.

[190]
JAMES J. WYCHOR SCHOLARSHIPS

Minnesota Broadcasters Association
Attn: Scholarship Program
3033 Excelsior Boulevard, Suite 301
Minneapolis, MN 55416
(612) 926-8123   Toll-free: (800) 245-5838
Fax: (612) 926-9761
E-mail: meischen@minnesotabroadcasters.com
Web: www.minnesotabroadcasters.com

Purpose To provide financial assistance to Minnesota residents interested in studying broadcasting in college.

Eligibility This program is open to residents of Minnesota who are accepted or enrolled at an accredited postsecondary institution offering a broadcast-related curriculum. Applicants must have a high school or college GPA of 2.5 or higher and must submit a 200-word essay on why they wish to prepare for a career in broadcasting or electronic media. Employment in the broadcasting industry is not required, but students who are employed must include a letter from their general manager describing the duties they have performed as a radio or television station employee and evaluating their potential for success in the industry. Financial need is not considered in the selection process. Some of the scholarships are awarded only to minority and women candidates.

Financial data The stipend is $1,500.

Duration 1 year; recipients who are college seniors may reapply for an additional 1-year renewal.

Number awarded 10 each year, distributed as follows: 3 within the 7-county metro area, 5 allocated geographically throughout the state (northeast, northwest, central, southeast, southwest), and 2 reserved specifically for women and minority applicants.

Deadline May of each year.

[191]
JEAN MARSHALL MINORITY SCHOLARSHIPS

New Jersey State Nurses Association
Attn: Institute for Nursing
1479 Pennington Road
Trenton, NJ 08618-2661
(609) 883-5335, ext. 15
Toll-free: (888) UR-NJSNA, ext. 15
Fax: (609) 883-5343   E-mail: vickie@njsna.org
Web: www.njsna.org/institute/institute.htm

Purpose To provide financial assistance to minority undergraduates in New Jersey who are preparing for a career as a nurse.

Eligibility All applicants must be New Jersey residents currently enrolled in an associate degree, baccalaureate, or diploma nursing program located in New Jersey. They must be members of 1 of the following groups: African American,

Hispanic, American Indian or Alaskan Native, Asian, or Pacific Islander. Applicants who are R.N.s must be members of the New Jersey State Nurses Association (a copy of their membership card must be submitted with their application). Selection is based on financial need, academic achievement, and leadership potential.

Financial data A stipend is awarded (amount not specified).

Duration 1 year.

Number awarded Varies each year; recently, 1 of these scholarships was awarded.

Deadline November of each year.

[192]
JERE W. THOMPSON, JR. SCHOLARSHIP

Dallas Foundation
Attn: Scholarship Administrator
900 Jackson Street, Suite 150
Dallas, TX 75202
(214) 741-9898   Fax: (214) 741-9848
E-mail: cmcnally@dallasfoundation.org
Web: www.dallasfoundation.org

Purpose To provide financial assistance and work experience to disadvantaged students who are majoring in civil engineering at public universities in Texas.

Eligibility This program is open to disadvantaged students in civil engineering or construction engineering at public colleges and universities in Texas; special consideration is given to residents of counties in the service area of the North Texas Tollway Authority: Collin, Dallas, Denton, or Tarrant. At the time of application, students must be full-time sophomores. Finalists may be interviewed. Financial need is considered in the selection process.

Financial data Stipends range up to $2,000 per semester, beginning in the recipient's junior year; the maximum award is $8,000 over 4 semesters.

Duration 1 semester; may be renewed for up to 3 additional semesters, provided the recipient remains a full-time student, maintains at least a 2.5 GPA, and submits a grade report within 45 days after the end of each semester.

Additional information Recipients of the Thompson Scholarship are given an opportunity for a paid internship in the Dallas area during the summer between their junior and senior year. Assignments are available at the scholarship's sponsors: North Texas Tollway Authority, Brown and Root Services, Carter & Burgess, Inc., and HNTB Companies.

Number awarded 1 each year.

Deadline March of each year.

[193]
JIMMY A. YOUNG MEMORIAL EDUCATION RECOGNITION AWARD

American Association for Respiratory Care
Attn: American Respiratory Care Foundation
9425 North MacArthur Boulevard, Suite 100
Irving, TX 75063-4706
(972) 243-2272   Fax: (972) 484-2720
E-mail: info@aarc.org
Web: www.aarc.org/awards/young.html

Purpose To provide financial assistance to college students, especially minorities, interested in becoming respiratory therapists.

Eligibility Candidates must be enrolled in an accredited respiratory therapy program, have completed at least 1 semester/quarter of the program, and have a GPA of 3.0 or higher. Preference is given to nominees of minority origin. Applications must include 6 copies of an original referenced paper on some aspect of respiratory care and letters of recommendation. The foundation prefers that the candidates be nominated by a school or program, but any student may initiate a request for sponsorship by a school (in order that a deserving candidate is not denied the opportunity to compete simply because the school does not initiate the application).

Financial data The stipend is $1,000. The award also provides airfare, 1 night's lodging, and registration for the association's international congress.

Duration 1 year.

Number awarded 1 each year.

Deadline June of each year.

[194]
JOANNA BISTANY MEMORIAL SCHOLARSHIP PROGRAM

National Association of Hispanic Journalists
Attn: Scholarship Committee
1000 National Press Building
529 14th Street, N.W.
Washington, DC 20045-2001
(202) 662-7145   Toll-free: (888) 346-NAHJ
Fax: (202) 662-7144   E-mail: nahj@nahj.org
Web: www.nahj.org

Purpose To provide financial assistance to Hispanic American students interested in preparing for a career in English-language television news.

Eligibility This program is open to college students who are interested in preparing for a career as a reporter or producer in the field of English-language television news. Selection is based on commitment to the field of journalism, academic achievement, awareness of the Latino community, and financial need.

Financial data A stipend is awarded (amount not specified).

Duration 1 year.

Additional information This program, which began in 2003, is sponsored by ABC News and administered by the National Association of Hispanic Journalists (NAHJ) as part of its Rubén Salazar Scholarship Fund.

Number awarded 1 each year.

Deadline January of each year.

[195]
JOEL GARCIA MEMORIAL SCHOLARSHIPS

California Chicano News Media Association
c/o University of Southern California
Annenberg School of Journalism
300 South Grand Avenue, Suite 3950
Los Angeles, CA 90071
(213) 437-4408   Fax: (213) 437-4423
E-mail: ccnmainfo@ccnma.org
Web: www.ccnma.org

Purpose To provide financial assistance to Latino students in California interested in preparing for a career in journalism.

Eligibility This program is open to high school seniors and college students of Latino descent who are California residents or students from other states attending a college or university in California. Applicants may major in any field, but they must enroll full time and be able to prove a sincere interest in preparing for a career in journalism. They must submit 1) an essay of 300 to 500 words explaining their family background, including any hardships they have experienced, and what they believe is the role of Latino journalists in the news media; 2) samples of their journalism-related work (e.g., newspaper articles, photographs, or TV or radio audition tapes); 3) transcripts; and 4) letters of reference. Finalists are interviewed. Selection is based on academic achievement, commitment to the journalism field, awareness of the community in which they live, and financial need.

Financial data Stipends range from $500 to $2,000.

Duration 1 year.

Additional information This program includes the Los Angeles Times/Frank del Olmo Scholarships.

Number awarded Varies each year; recently, 13 of these scholarships were awarded.

Deadline March of each year.

[196]
JOSE MARTI SCHOLARSHIP CHALLENGE GRANT FUND

Florida Department of Education
Attn: Office of Student Financial Assistance
1940 North Monroe Street, Suite 70
Tallahassee, FL 32303-4759
(850) 410-5200   Toll-free: (888) 827-2004
Fax: (850) 487-1809   E-mail: osfa@fldoe.org
Web: www.FloridaStudentFinancialAid.org

Purpose To provide financial assistance to Hispanic American high school seniors and graduate students in Florida.

Eligibility This program is open to Florida residents of Spanish culture who were born in, or whose natural parent was born in, Mexico, Spain, or a Hispanic country of the Caribbean, Central America, or South America. Applicants must be citizens or eligible noncitizens of the United States, be enrolled or planning to enroll as full-time undergraduate or graduate students at an eligible postsecondary school in Florida, be able to demonstrate financial need as determined by a nationally-recognized needs analysis service, and have earned a cumulative GPA of 3.0 or higher in high school or, if a graduate school applicant, in undergraduate course work.

Financial data The grant is $2,000 per academic year. Available funds are contingent upon matching contributions from private sources.

Duration 1 year; may be renewed if the student maintains full-time enrollment and a GPA of 3.0 or higher and continues to demonstrate financial need.

Number awarded Varies each year; recently, this program presented 98 awards.

Deadline March of each year.

[197]
JPMORGANCHASE SCHOLARSHIP PROGRAM OF THE HISPANIC SCHOLARSHIP FUND

Hispanic Scholarship Fund
Attn: Selection Committee
55 Second Street, Suite 1500
San Francisco, CA 94105
(415) 808-2350   Toll-free: (877) HSF-INFO
Fax: (415) 808-2302   E-mail: college1@hsf.net
Web: www.hsf.net

Purpose To provide financial assistance to Hispanic upper-division students working on a degree in a field related to business.

Eligibility This program is open to U.S. citizens, permanent residents, and visitors with a passport stamped I-551 who are of Hispanic heritage. Applicants must be currently enrolled full time as a sophomore or junior at an accredited 4-year college or university in the United States, Puerto Rico, or the U.S. Virgin Islands. They must be majoring in business administration, finance, or economics with a GPA of 3.0 or higher. Along with their application, they must submit 600-word essays on 1) how their Hispanic heritage, family upbringing, and/or role models have influenced their personal long-term goals; 2) how they contribute to their community and what they have learned from their experiences; and 3) an academic challenge they have faced and how they have overcome it. Selection is based on academic achievement, personal strengths, leadership, and financial need.

Financial data The stipend is $2,500.

Duration 1 year.

Additional information This program is jointly sponsored by JPMorganChase and the Hispanic Scholarship Fund (HSF).

Number awarded 1 or more each year.

Deadline November of each year.

[198]
KANSAS ESOL/BILINGUAL EDUCATION SCHOLARSHIP

Kansas Association of Migrant Directors
c/o Cynthia Adcock
USD 305
P.O. Box 797
Salina, KS 67402
(785) 309-4718   E-mail: Cynthia.Adcock@ksde.org

Purpose To provide financial assistance for college to seniors graduating from high schools in Kansas who have been enrolled in a bilingual or English for Speakers of Other Languages (ESOL) program.

Eligibility This program is open to seniors graduating from high schools in Kansas who are currently in a bilingual or ESOL program. Applicants must be planning to attend a college or university in Kansas as a full-time student. Along with their application, they must submit a paragraph about their educational goals, explaining why they want to go to college and describing their plans after graduation. Selection is based on the essay, GPA, school performance, and financial need.

Financial data The stipend is $250 per semester ($500 per year).

Duration 4 semesters (2 years).

Number awarded Varies each year; recently, 3 of these scholarships were awarded.

Deadline March of each year.

[199]
KANSAS ETHNIC MINORITY SCHOLARSHIP PROGRAM

Kansas Board of Regents
Attn: Student Financial Aid
1000 S.W. Jackson Street, Suite 520
Topeka, KS 66612-1368
(785) 296-3518   Fax: (785) 296-0983
E-mail: dlindeman@ksbor.org
Web: www.kansasregents.com

Purpose To provide financial assistance to minority students in Kansas who are interested in attending college in the state.

Eligibility Eligible to apply are Kansas residents who fall into 1 of these minority groups: American Indian, Alaskan Native, African American, Asian, Pacific Islander, or Hispanic. Applicants may be current college students (enrolled in community colleges, colleges, or universities in Kansas), but high school seniors graduating in the current year receive priority consideration. Minimum academic requirements include 1 of the following: 1) ACT score of 21 or higher or SAT equivalent; 2) cumulative GPA of 3.0 or higher; 3) high school rank in upper 33%; 4) completion of the Kansas Scholars Curriculum (4 years of English, 3 years of mathematics, 3 years of science, 3 years of social studies, and 2 years of foreign language); 5) selection by the National Merit Corporation in any category; or 6) selection by the College Board as a Hispanic Scholar.

Financial data A stipend of up to $1,850 is provided, depending on financial need and availability of state funds.

Duration 1 year; may be renewed for up to 3 additional years (4 additional years for designated 5-year programs) if the recipient maintains a 2.0 cumulative GPA and has financial need.

Additional information There is a $10 application fee.

Number awarded Approximately 200 each year.

Deadline April of each year.

[200]
KATU THOMAS R. DARGAN MINORITY SCHOLARSHIP

KATU-TV
Attn: Human Resources
2153 N.E. Sandy Boulevard
P.O. Box 2
Portland, OR 97207-0002
(503) 231-4222
Web: www.katu.com/insidekatu/scholarship.asp

Purpose To provide financial assistance and work experience to minority students from Oregon and Washington who are studying broadcasting or communications in college.

Eligibility This program is open to Native Americans, African Americans, Hispanic Americans, or Asian Americans who are U.S. citizens, currently enrolled in the first, second, or third year at a 4-year college or university or an accredited community college in Oregon or Washington, or, if a resident of Oregon or Washington, at a school in any state. Applicants must be majoring in broadcasting or communications and have a GPA of 3.0 or higher. Community college students must be enrolled in a broadcast curriculum that is transferable to a 4-year accredited university. Finalists will be interviewed. Selection is based on financial need, academic achievement, and an essay on personal and professional goals.

Financial data The stipend is $4,000. Funds are sent directly to the recipient's school.

Duration 1 year; recipients may reapply if they have maintained a GPA of 3.0 or higher.

Additional information Winners are also eligible for a paid internship in selected departments at Fisher Broadcasting/KATU in Portland, Oregon.

Number awarded 1 each year.

Deadline April of each year.

[201]
KEN KASHIWAHARA SCHOLARSHIP

Radio and Television News Directors Foundation
1600 K Street, N.W., Suite 700
Washington, DC 20006-2838
(202) 467-5218   Fax: (202) 223-4007
E-mail: karenb@rtndf.org
Web: www.rtndf.org

Purpose To provide financial assistance to outstanding undergraduate students, especially minorities, who are interested in preparing for a career in electronic journalism.

Eligibility Eligible are sophomore or more advanced undergraduate students enrolled in an electronic journalism sequence at an accredited or nationally-recognized college or university. Applicants must submit 1 to 3 examples of reporting or producing skills on audio or video cassette tapes (no more than 15 minutes total), a description of their role on each story and a list of who worked on each story and what they did, a statement explaining why they are seeking a career in broadcast or cable journalism, and a letter of endorsement from a faculty sponsor that verifies the applicant has at least 1 year of school remaining. Preference is given to undergraduate students of color.

Financial data The stipend is $2,500, paid in semiannual installments of $1,250 each.

Duration 1 year.

Additional information The Radio and Television News Directors Foundation (RTNDF) also provides an all-expense paid trip to the Radio-Television News Directors Association (RTNDA) annual international conference. It defines electronic journalism to include radio, television, cable, and online news. Previous winners of any RTNDF scholarship or internship are not eligible.

Number awarded 1 each year.

Deadline April of each year.

[202]
KENTUCKY ANNUAL CONFERENCE ETHNIC SCHOLARSHIPS

United Methodist Church-Kentucky Annual Conference
Attn: Commission on Higher Education and Campus
  Ministry
7400 Floydsburg Road
Crestwood, KY 40014-8202
(502) 425-3884   Toll-free: (800) 530-7236
Fax: (502) 426-5181
Web: www.kyumc.org

Purpose To provide financial assistance for college to ethnic minority residents of Kentucky who are members of the United Methodist Church.

Eligibility This program is open to ethnic minority residents of Kentucky who are members of the United Methodist Church and attending or planning to attend a college or university. Candidates must be nominated by their pastor, Wesley Foundation director, and/or chair of their local church higher education and campus ministry work area. Each church may nominate only 1 person. The letter of nomination must include information on the candidate's academic achievements, local church involvement, community involvement, goals and plans, and financial need.

Financial data The stipend is $500.

Duration 1 year.

Additional information Recipients must attend the Annual Conference session to receive the award.

Number awarded 2 each year.

Deadline April of each year.

[203]
KNIGHT RIDDER MINORITY SCHOLARS PROGRAM

Knight Ridder, Inc.
Attn: Office of Diversity
50 West San Fernando Street, Suite 1200
San Jose, CA 95113
(408) 938-7734   Fax: (408) 938-7755
Web: www.knightridderscholars.com

Purpose To provide financial assistance and work experience to minority high school seniors who are interested in going to college to prepare for a career in journalism.

Eligibility This program is open to minority seniors graduating from high schools in areas served by Knight Ridder. Applicants must be interested in attending college to prepare for a career in the newspaper industry. They first apply to their local Knight Ridder newspaper and compete for local scholarships; selected winners are then nominated for this award. Both "news" and "business" students are eligible.

Financial data The stipend is $5,000 per year for the freshman and sophomore year and $15,000 per year for the junior and senior year.

Duration 1 year; may be renewed for up to 3 additional years, if the recipient maintains a GPA of 3.0 or higher and satisfactory performance on internships.

Additional information Recipients are offered an internship opportunity at a Knight Ridder newspaper during the summer. News scholars work in the newsroom, writing and editing stories, taking photographs, crafting illustrations, and designing news pages. Business scholars complete internships in advertising, marketing, information technology, circulation, and other areas essential to the industry. At the end of the sophomore year, recipients must agree to work at a Knight Ridder newspaper for 1 year after graduation.

Number awarded Up to 5 each year: 2 for news, 2 for business, and 1 for either.

[204]
LA ESTRELLA LATINA DE CARL'S JR. SCHOLARSHIP PROGRAM

Carl's Jr.
Attn: Cheryl Beamer
6307 Carpinteria Avenue, Suite A
Carpinteria, CA 93013
(805) 745-7663   Toll-free: (800) 422-4141
E-mail: cbeamer@ckr.com
Web: www.carlsjr.com/news/14

Purpose To provide financial assistance to students (primarily Hispanics) in designated states who can demonstrate that they have been "A Star" in their community.

Eligibility This program is open to seniors graduating from high schools in Arizona, California, Nevada, New Mexico, and Texas. Applicants must be high school seniors or graduates younger than 21 years of age and planning to enroll for the first time as a full-time undergraduate student at an accredited 2-year or 4-year college, university, or vocational school. Along with their application, they must submit an essay describing how they have been "A Star" in their community. Selection is based on academic record, school and community leadership and participation, work experience, future goals, financial need, and other family circumstances.

Financial data The stipend is $1,000.

Duration 1 year; nonrenewable.

Additional information This program began in 1999. Applications are available at participating Carl's Jr. restaurants. The program is administered by Scholarship Management Services of Scholarship America, One Scholarship Way, P.O. Box 297, St. Peter, MN 56082, (507) 931-1682, (800) 537-4180, Fax: (507) 931-9168, E-mail: smsinfo@csfa.org.

Number awarded 60 each year.

Deadline January of each year.

[205]
LA UNIDAD LATINA SCHOLARSHIPS

La Unidad Latina Foundation, Inc.
359 Prospect Avenue
Brooklyn, NY 11215
E-mail: foundation@launidadlatina.org
Web: foundation.launidadlatina.org

Purpose To provide financial assistance to Hispanic students who are working on a bachelor's or master's degree.

Eligibility This program is open to students of Hispanic background who have completed at least 1 semester of higher education. Applicants must be enrolled full time at an accredited 4-year college or university in the United States. Along with their application, they must submit brief essays on the courses in which they are enrolled in the current semester, their financial need, their academic plans and career goals, an instance in which someone has left an indelible mark in their life and why, their extracurricular activities, any honors or awards they have received, and their special interests or hobbies.

Financial data Stipends range from $250 to $1,000.

Duration 1 year.

Number awarded Varies each year; recently, 24 of these scholarships (18 in fall, 6 in spring) were awarded.

Deadline February of each year for spring semester; October of each year for fall semester.

[206]
LAGRANT FOUNDATION SCHOLARSHIPS

LAGRANT FOUNDATION
555 South Flower Street, Suite 700
Los Angeles, CA 90071-2423
(323) 469-8680   Fax: (323) 469-8683
Web: www.lagrantfoundation.org

Purpose To provide financial assistance to minority high school seniors or college students who are interested in majoring in advertising, public relations, or marketing.

Eligibility This program is open to African Americans, Asian Pacific Americans, Hispanics, or Native Americans who are full-time students at a 4-year accredited institution or high school seniors planning to attend a 4-year accredited institution on a full-time basis. Applicants must have a GPA of 2.5 or higher and be majoring or planning to major in advertising, marketing, or public relations. They must submit 1) a 1- to 2-page essay outlining their career goals; what steps they will take to increase ethnic representation in the fields of advertising, marketing, and public relations; and the role of an advertising, marketing, or public relations practitioner; 2) a paragraph explaining how they are financing or planning to finance their education and why they need financial assistance; 3) a paragraph explaining the high school, college, and/or community activities in which they are involved; 4) a brief paragraph describing any honors and awards they have received; 5) if they are currently employed, a paragraph indicating the hours worked each week, responsibilities, and if the job will be kept while attending school; 6) a resume; and 7) an official transcript. Applicants majoring in public relations must write an essay on the importance and relevance of the Arthur W. Page Society Principles.

Financial data The stipend is $5,000 per year.

Duration 1 year.

Number awarded 10 each year.

Deadline March of each year.

[207]
LANDMARK SCHOLARS PROGRAM

Landmark Publishing Group
c/o Rich Martin, Managing Editor
The Roanoke Times
201 West Campbell Avenue
Roanoke, VA 24011
(540) 981-3211   Toll-free: (800) 346-1234
E-mail: rich.martin@roanoke.com
Web: www.landmarkcommunications.com

Purpose To provide work experience and financial aid to minority undergraduates who are interested in preparing for a career in journalism.

Eligibility This program is open to minority college sophomores, preferably those with ties to the mid-Atlantic states (Delaware, Maryland, North Carolina, South Carolina, Virginia, and Washington, D.C.). Applicants must be full-time students with a GPA of 2.5 or higher. They must be interested in preparing for a career in print journalism and in an internship as a reporter, photographer, graphic artist, sports writer, copy editor, or page designer.

Financial data The stipend is $5,000 per year. During the summers following their sophomore and junior years, recipients are provided with paid internships. Following graduation, they are offered a 1-year internship with full benefits and the possibility of continued employment.

Duration 2 years (the junior and senior years of college).

Additional information The internships are offered at the *News & Record* in Greensboro, North Carolina, the *Virginian-Pilot* in Norfolk, Virginia, or the *Roanoke Times* in Roanoke, Virginia.

Number awarded 1 or more each year.

Deadline November of each year.

[208]
LATIN AMERICAN EDUCATIONAL FOUNDATION SCHOLARSHIPS

Latin American Educational Foundation
Attn: Scholarship Selection Committee
924 West Colfax Avenue, Suite 103
Denver, CO 80204
(303) 446-0541   Fax: (303) 446-0526
E-mail: carmen@laef.org
Web: www.laef.org

Purpose To provide financial aid to Hispanic American undergraduate students in Colorado.

Eligibility This program is open to Colorado residents who are of Hispanic heritage and/or actively involved in the Hispanic community. Applicants must have been accepted at an accredited college, university, or vocational school and must have a cumulative GPA of 3.0 or higher. Along with their application, they must submit a 1-page essay on their interests and career goals, how they anticipate achieving their goals, and what has motivated them to pursue higher education. Selection is based on the essay, community involvement, academic achievement, letters of recommendation, an interview, and financial need.

Financial data The amount of the award depends on the need of the recipient, ranging from $500 to $3,000. Scholarships may be used at Colorado colleges and universities or at out-of-state institutions. Most colleges and universities within Colorado participate in the Colorado Higher Education Partnership; member institutions provide additional funds to match the award granted by this foundation.

Duration 1 year; recipients may reapply.

Additional information This program was established in 1949. Sponsors include Hewlett Packard, American Family Insurance, CH2MHill, Coors Brewing Company, State Farm Insurance, Lucent Technologies, and Wells Fargo Bank. Recipients are required to perform 10 hours of community service during the academic year.

Number awarded Varies each year; recently, 221 of these scholarships were awarded.

Deadline February of each year.

[209]
LATINA LEADERSHIP NETWORK STUDENT SCHOLARSHIPS

Latina Leadership Network
c/o Maria E. Ramirez, Vice President North
Ohlone College Counseling Department
43600 Mission Boulevard
Fremont, CA 94539-0390
(510) 659-6126
Web: www.latina-leadership-network.org/awards.php

Purpose To provide financial assistance to Latina students attending community colleges in California.

Eligibility This program is open to Latina students (one parent fully Latino or each parent half Latino) enrolled at community colleges in California. Applicants must have completed at least 24 units of college work with a GPA of 2.0 or higher. Along with their application, they must submit a 1-page essay on the impact of their college experience on their personal life, what they expect to be doing 5 years from now, and their personal commitment to Latina leadership. Selection is based on the essay, academic achievement, community involvement, and 2 letters of recommendation.

Financial data The stipend is $500.

Duration 1 year.

Number awarded 5 each year.

Deadline February of each year.

[210]
LATINO COLLEGE EXPO SCHOLARSHIP AWARDS

Latino College Expo, Inc.
Attn: Scholarship Committee
511 Avenue of the Americas
PMB 192
New York, NY 10011
(212) 677-1108, ext. 156
E-mail: LatinoExpo@aol.com
Web: www.latinocollegeexpo.org

Purpose To provide financial assistance for college to Latino high school seniors in New York, New Jersey, and Connecticut.

Eligibility This program is open to Latino seniors at high schools in the New York tri-state area of New York, New Jersey, and Connecticut. Applicants must be U.S. citizens or permanent residents planning to attend a college or university as a full-time student in the following fall. They must submit high school transcripts (with a 4-year high school average of 85% or higher), SAT score, a list of academic accomplishments and honors (including any advanced placement courses completed with grades), 2 teacher recommendations, and a 250-word essay.

Financial data The stipend is $500.

Duration 1 year.

Number awarded 4 each year.

Deadline March of each year.

[211]
LAWRENCE R. FOSTER MEMORIAL SCHOLARSHIP

Oregon Student Assistance Commission
Attn: Grants and Scholarships Division
1500 Valley River Drive, Suite 100
Eugene, OR 97401-2146
(541) 687-7395   Toll-free: (800) 452-8807, ext. 7395
Fax: (541) 687-7419
E-mail: awardinfo@mercury.osac.state.or.us
Web: www.osac.state.or.us

Purpose To provide financial assistance for college or graduate school to residents of Oregon (particularly minorities) who are interested in preparing for a public health career.

Eligibility This program is open to residents of Oregon who are attending a 4-year college or university in any state to prepare for a career in public health (not private practice). First preference is given to applicants who are either working in public health or enrolled as graduate students in that field. Second preference is given to undergraduates entering the junior or senior year of a health program, including nursing, medical technology, and physician assistant. A general preference is given to applicants from diverse cultures. Along with their application, they must submit a 1- to 2-page essay on their interest, experience, and future plans for a public health career

Financial data Stipend amounts vary; recently, they were at least $4,167.

Duration 1 year.

Additional information This program is administered by the Oregon Student Assistance Commission (OSAC) with funds provided by the Oregon Community Foundation, 1221 S.W. Yamhill, Suite 100, Portland, OR 97205, (503) 227-6846, Fax: (503) 274-7771.

Number awarded Varies each year; recently, 6 of these scholarships were awarded.

Deadline February of each year.

[212]
LEADERSHIP FOR DIVERSITY SCHOLARSHIP

California School Library Association
717 K Street, Suite 515
Sacramento, CA 95814-3477
(916) 447-2684   Fax: (916) 447-2695
E-mail: csla@pacbell.net
Web: www.schoolibrary.org

Purpose To encourage underrepresented minority students to get a credential as a library media teacher in California.

Eligibility This program is open to students who are members of a traditionally underrepresented group enrolled in a college or university library media teacher credential program in California. Applicants must intend to work as a library media teacher in a California school library media center for a minimum of 3 years. Along with their application, they must submit a 250-word statement on their school library media career interests and goals, why they should be considered, what they can contribute, their commitment to serving the needs of our multicultural and multilingual students, and their financial situation.

Financial data The stipend is $1,000.

Duration 1 year.

Number awarded 1 each year.

Deadline June of each year.

[213]
LEON C. HART MEMORIAL SCHOLARSHIP

Gravure Association of America
Attn: Gravure Education Foundation
1200-A Scottsville Road
Rochester, NY 14624
(585) 436-2150   Fax: (585) 436-7689
E-mail: lwshatch@gaa.org
Web: www.gaa.org/GEF/scholarships.htm

Purpose To provide financial assistance to college students, especially those from diverse ethnic backgrounds, who are interested in a career in printing.

Eligibility This program is open to students who are enrolled full time in a field related to printing at a designated learning resource center supported by the Gravure Education Foundation (GEF) of the Gravure Association of America. Applicants must have a GPA of 3.0 or higher. Along with their application, they must submit a 250-word essay on "How Involvement in my Community/School Has Made a Difference." Selection is based on the essay, financial need, transcripts, and either extracurricular involvement in school activities or community involvement. Preference is given to students of diverse ethnic backgrounds and to students who show an interest in printing education as a career path.

Financial data The stipend is $1,000.

Duration 1 year.

Additional information GEF learning resource centers are located at the following universities: Rochester Institute of Technology, Western Michigan University, California Polytechnic State University at San Luis Obispo, Arizona State University, Clemson University, Murray State University, and the University of Wisconsin at Stout. This program is named in honor of a former executive director of the GEF who began his career as a printer for the Afro-American Newspaper in Baltimore, Maryland.

Number awarded 1 each year.

Deadline May of each year.

[214]
LEONARD M. PERRYMAN COMMUNICATIONS SCHOLARSHIP FOR ETHNIC MINORITY STUDENTS

United Methodist Communications
Attn: Communications Resourcing Team
810 12th Avenue South
P.O. Box 320
Nashville, TN 37202-0320
(615) 742-5481   Toll-free: (888) CRT-4UMC
Fax: (615) 742-5485
E-mail: scholarships@umcom.org
Web: www.umcom.org

Purpose To provide financial assistance to minority United Methodist college students who are interested in careers in religious communications.

Eligibility This program is open to United Methodist ethnic minority students enrolled in accredited institutions of higher education as juniors or seniors. Applicants must be interested in preparing for a career in religious communications. For the purposes of this program, "communications" is meant to cover audiovisual, electronic, and print journalism. Selection is based on Christian commitment and involvement in the life of the United Methodist church, academic achievement, journalistic experience, clarity of purpose, and professional potential as a religious journalist.

Financial data The stipend is $2,500 per year.

Duration 1 year.

Additional information The scholarship may be used at any accredited institution of higher education.

Number awarded 1 each year.

Deadline March of each year.

[215]
LOCKHEED MARTIN SCHOLARSHIP PROGRAM

Hispanic College Fund
Attn: National Director
1717 Pennsylvania Avenue, N.W., Suite 460
Washington, D.C. 20006
(202) 296-5400   Toll-free: (800) 644-4223
Fax: (202) 296-3774
E-mail: hispaniccollegefund@earthlink.net
Web: www.hispanicfund.org

Purpose To provide financial assistance to Hispanic American undergraduate students who are interested in preparing for a career in computer science or engineering.

Eligibility This program is open to U.S. citizens of Hispanic background (at least 1 grandparent must be 100% Hispanic) who are entering their freshman, sophomore, junior, or senior year of college. Applicants must be working on a bachelor's degree in engineering, computer science, or a related major and have a cumulative GPA of 3.0 or higher. They must be applying to or enrolled in a college or university in the 50 states or Puerto Rico as a full-time student. Financial need is considered in the selection process.

Financial data Stipends range from $500 to $5,000, depending on the need of the recipient, and average approximately $3,000. Funds are paid directly to the recipient's college or university to help cover tuition and fees.

Duration 1 year; recipients may reapply.

Additional information This program is sponsored by the Lockheed Martin Corporation. All applications must be submitted online; no paper applications are available.

Number awarded Varies each year.

Deadline April of each year.

[216]
LOREN W. CROW MEMORIAL SCHOLARSHIP

American Meteorological Society
Attn: Fellowship/Scholarship Program
45 Beacon Street
Boston, MA 02108-3693
(617) 227-2426, ext. 246   Fax: (617) 742-8718
E-mail: scholar@ametsoc.org
Web: www.ametsoc.org

Purpose To provide financial assistance to undergraduates (particularly minorities, women, and students with disabilities) majoring in meteorology or an aspect of atmospheric sciences with an interest in applied meteorology.

Eligibility This program is open to full-time students entering their final year of undergraduate study and majoring in meteorology or an aspect of the atmospheric or related oceanic and hydrologic sciences. Applicants must intend to make atmospheric or related sciences their career, with preference given to students who have demonstrated a strong interest in applied meteorology. They must be U.S. citizens or permanent residents enrolled at a U.S. institution and have a cumulative GPA of 3.25 or higher. Along with their application, they must submit 200-word essays on 1) their most important achievements that qualify them for this scholarship, and 2) their career goals in the atmospheric or related oceanic or hydrologic fields. Selection is based on academic excellence and achievement; financial need is not considered. The sponsor specifically encourages applications from women, minorities, and students with disabilities who are traditionally underrepresented in the atmospheric and related oceanic sciences.

Financial data The stipend is $2,000 per year.

Duration 1 year.

Additional information Requests for an application must be accompanied by a self-addressed stamped envelope.

Number awarded 1 each year.

Deadline February of each year.

[217]
LOUIS B. RUSSELL, JR. MEMORIAL SCHOLARSHIP

Indiana State Teachers Association
Attn: Scholarships
150 West Market Street, Suite 900
Indianapolis, IN 46204
(317) 263-3400   Toll-free: (800) 382-4037
Fax: (317) 655-3700   E-mail: kmcallen@ista-in.org
Web: www.ista-in.org

Purpose To provide financial assistance to ethnic minority high school seniors in Indiana who are interested in pursuing vocational education.

Eligibility This program is open to ethnic minority high school seniors in Indiana who are interested in continuing their education in the area of industrial arts, vocational education, or technical preparation at an accredited postsecondary institution. Selection is based on academic achievement, leadership ability as expressed through co-curricular

activities and community involvement, recommendations, and a 300-word essay on their educational goals and how they plan to use this scholarship.

Financial data The stipend is $1,000.

Duration 1 year; may be renewed for 1 additional year.

Number awarded 1 each year.

Deadline February of each year.

[218]
LOUISE MORITZ MOLITORIS LEADERSHIP AWARD

Women's Transportation Seminar
Attn: National Headquarters
1666 K Street, N.W., Suite 1100
Washington, DC 20006
(202) 496-4340   Fax: (202) 496-4349
E-mail: wts@wtsnational.org
Web: www.wtsnational.org

Purpose To provide financial assistance to undergraduate women (particularly women of color) interested in a career in transportation.

Eligibility This program is open to women who are working on an undergraduate degree in transportation or a transportation-related field (e.g., transportation engineering, planning, finance, or logistics). Applicants must have a GPA of 3.0 or higher. They must submit a 500-word statement about their career goals after graduation and why they think they should receive the scholarship award; their statement should specifically address the issue of leadership. Applications must be submitted first to a local chapter; the chapters forward selected applications for consideration on the national level. Minority candidates are encouraged to apply. Selection is based on transportation involvement and goals, job skills, academic record, and leadership potential; financial need is not considered.

Financial data The stipend is $3,000.

Duration 1 year.

Additional information Local chapters may also award additional funding to winners for their area.

Number awarded 1 each year.

Deadline Applications must be submitted by November to a local WTS chapter.

[219]
LOWRIDER MAGAZINE SCHOLARSHIP FUND

Lowrider Magazine
Attn: Scholarship Fund
2400 East Katella Avenue, 11th Floor
Anaheim, CA 92806
(714) 939-2400   Fax: (714) 978-6390
Web: www.lowridermagazine.com

Purpose To provide financial assistance for college to Chicano/Latino students.

Eligibility Applicants must be of Latino descent, have a GPA of 3.0 or higher, and be currently enrolled as college sophomores, juniors, or seniors. They must submit an official transcript, 2 letters of recommendation, a 1-page essay outlining their financial situation, and a 2-page essay on 1 of 3 topics that change annually. Recently, the topics were 1) "What does calling yourself Chicano or Chicana mean to you?" 2) "How can you use your education/degree to help the Chicano community?" or 3) "Has Affirmative Action served a good purpose and should institutes of higher learning continue to use this policy?"

Financial data Stipends range from $100 to $1,000.

Duration 1 year.

Additional information This program started in 1990. No phone calls are accepted. Requests for applications must be accompanied by a self-addressed stamped envelope.

Number awarded Varies each year.

Deadline May of each year.

[220]
MAES GENERAL SCHOLARSHIPS

Society of Mexican American Engineers and Scientists
Attn: Scholarships
711 West Bay Area Boulevard, Suite 206
Webster, TX 77598-3677
(281) 557-3677   Fax: (281) 557-3757
E-mail: scholarships@maes-natl.org
Web: www.maes-natl.org

Purpose To provide financial assistance to undergraduate and graduate student members of the Society of Mexican American Engineers and Scientists (MAES).

Eligibility This program is open to MAES student members who are full-time undergraduate or graduate students at a college or university in the United States. Community college students must be enrolled in majors that can transfer to a 4-year institution offering a baccalaureate degree. All applicants must be majoring in a field of science or engineering. U.S. citizenship or permanent resident status is required. Selection is based on financial need; academic achievement; personal qualities, strengths, and leadership abilities; and timeliness and completeness of the application.

Financial data The stipend is $1,000.

Duration 1 year.

Additional information Recipients must attend the MAES International Symposium's Medalla de Oro Banquet in October.

Number awarded 1 or more each year.

Deadline October of each year.

[221]
MARIA ELENA SALINAS SCHOLARSHIP PROGRAM

National Association of Hispanic Journalists
Attn: Scholarship Committee
1000 National Press Building
529 14th Street, N.W.
Washington, DC 20045-2001
(202) 662-7145   Toll-free: (888) 346-NAHJ
Fax: (202) 662-7144   E-mail: nahj@nahj.org
Web: www.nahj.org

Purpose To provide financial assistance and work experience to Hispanic American students interested in preparing for a career as a journalist in Spanish-language radio or television.

Eligibility This program is open to high school seniors, undergraduates, and first-year graduate students. Applicants must demonstrate a sincere desire to prepare for a career as a journalist in Spanish-language television or radio. They must submit 1) an essay in Spanish that explains why they are interested in a career as a Spanish-language

journalist, and 2) work samples that are in Spanish. Selection is based on commitment to the field of journalism, academic achievement, awareness of the Latino community, and financial need.

Financial data The stipend is $5,000 per year; the program also provides funding for an internship during the summer

Duration 2 years.

Additional information This program, which began in 2002, is sponsored by the Univision network and administered by the National Association of Hispanic Journalists (NAHJ) as part of its Rubén Salazar Scholarship Fund. The recipient participates in a summer internship with either the news division of the Univision network or with a Univision affiliate near them.

Number awarded 2 each year.

Deadline January of each year.

[222]
MARK J. SCHROEDER ENDOWED SCHOLARSHIP IN METEOROLOGY

American Meteorological Society
Attn: Fellowship/Scholarship Program
45 Beacon Street
Boston, MA 02108-3693
(617) 227-2426, ext. 246   Fax: (617) 742-8718
E-mail: scholar@ametsoc.org
Web: www.ametsoc.org

Purpose To provide financial assistance to students (particularly minorities, women, and students with disabilities) who are majoring in meteorology or some aspect of atmospheric sciences who demonstrate financial need.

Eligibility This program is open to full-time students entering their final year of undergraduate study and majoring in meteorology or an aspect of the atmospheric or related oceanic and hydrologic sciences. Applicants must intend to make atmospheric or related sciences their career. They must be U.S. citizens or permanent residents enrolled at a U.S. institution and have a cumulative GPA of 3.25 or higher. Along with their application, they must submit 200-word essays on 1) their most important achievements that qualify them for this scholarship, and 2) their career goals in the atmospheric or related oceanic or hydrologic fields. Selection is based on academic excellence and achievement and financial need. The sponsor specifically encourages applications from women, minorities, and students with disabilities who are traditionally underrepresented in the atmospheric and related oceanic sciences.

Financial data The stipend is $5,000.

Duration 1 year.

Additional information This scholarship was established in 1995. Requests for an application must be accompanied by a self-addressed stamped envelope.

Number awarded 1 each year.

Deadline February of each year.

[223]
MARTIN LUTHER KING, JR. MEMORIAL SCHOLARSHIP FUND

California Teachers Association
Attn: Human Rights Department
P.O. Box 921
Burlingame, CA 94011-0921
(650) 552-5370   E-mail: scholarships@cta.org
Web: www.cta.org

Purpose To provide financial assistance for college or graduate school to racial and ethnic minorities in California who are members of the California Teachers Association (CTA), children of members, or members of the Student CTA.

Eligibility This program is open to members of a racial or ethnic minority group who are 1) active CTA members; 2) dependent children of active, retired-life, or deceased CTA members; or 3) members of Student CTA. Applicants must be interested in preparing for a teaching career in public education or already engaged in such a career.

Financial data Stipends vary each year, depending upon the amount of contributions received and the financial need of individual recipients.

Duration 1 year.

Number awarded Varies each year. Recently, 23 of these scholarships were awarded: 10 to CTA members, 8 to children of CTA members, and 5 to Student CTA members.

Deadline March of each year.

[224]
MARTIN LUTHER KING, JR. SCHOLARSHIP

North Carolina Association of Educators, Inc.
Attn: Minority Affairs Commission
700 South Salisbury Street
P.O. Box 27347
Raleigh, NC 27611-7347
(919) 832-3000, ext. 211
Toll-free: (800) 662-7924, ext. 211
Fax: (919) 839-8229
Web: www.ncae.org

Purpose To provide financial assistance for college to minority and other high school seniors in North Carolina.

Eligibility Applicants must be North Carolina residents enrolled as seniors in high school. They must be planning to continue their education upon graduation. Applications are considered and judged by members of the association's Minority Affairs Commission. Selection is based on character, personality, and scholastic achievement.

Financial data The amount of the stipend depends on the availability of funding.

Duration 1 year.

Number awarded 1 each year.

Deadline January of each year.

[225]
MARYLAND SPACE SCHOLARS PROGRAM

Maryland Space Grant Consortium
c/o Johns Hopkins University
203 Bloomberg Center for Physics and Astronomy
3400 North Charles Street
Baltimore, MD 21218-2686
(410) 516-7351   Fax: (410) 516-4109
E-mail: info@mdspacegrant.org
Web: www.mdspacegrant.org/scholars_about.html

Purpose To provide financial assistance to undergraduates (particularly underrepresented minorities, women, and students with disabilities) who are interested in studying space-related fields at selected universities in Maryland that are members of the Maryland Space Grant Consortium.

Eligibility This program is open to residents of Maryland and graduates of Maryland high schools who are enrolled full time at a member institution. Applicants must be interested in preparing for a career in mathematics, science, engineering, technology, or a space-related field. They must be majoring in a relevant field, including (but not limited to) astronomy, the biological and life sciences, chemistry, computer science, engineering, geological sciences, or physics. U.S. citizenship is required. Along with their application, they must submit an essay of 200 to 500 words on how this scholarship will help them meet their educational and financial goals. This program is a component of the U.S. National Aeronautics and Space Administration (NASA) Space Grant program, which encourages participation by women, underrepresented minorities, and persons with disabilities.

Financial data Scholars receive partial payment of tuition at the participating university they attend.

Duration 1 year; may be renewed if the recipient maintains a GPA of 3.0 or higher.

Additional information The participating universities are Hagerstown Community College, Johns Hopkins University, Morgan State University, Towson University, the University of Maryland at College Park, and Washington College. Funding for this program is provided by NASA.

Number awarded Varies each year; recently 16 of these scholarships were awarded (2 at Johns Hopkins University, 5 at Morgan State University, 2 at Hagerstown Community College, 2 at Towson University, and 5 at the University of Maryland at College Park).

Deadline August of each year.

[226]
MASTERFOODS USA UNDERGRADUATE MENTORED SCHOLARSHIPS FOR COLLEGE STUDENTS

Institute of Food Technologists
Attn: Scholarship Department
525 West Van Buren, Suite 1000
Chicago, IL 60607
(312) 782-8424   Fax: (312) 782-8348
E-mail: info@ift.org
Web: www.ift.org

Purpose To provide financial assistance to minority undergraduates interested in studying food science or food technology.

Eligibility This program is open to members of minority groups (African Americans, Native Indians, Hispanic Americans, and Asian Americans) who are entering the junior year of a food science or food technology program at an educational institution in the United States. Applicants may be transferring from another program in a 4-year college or from a 2-year junior college. Along with their application, they must submit an essay on their career aspirations; a list of awards, honors, and scholarships they have received; a list of extracurricular activities and/or hobbies; and a summary of their work experience. Financial need is not considered in the selection process.

Financial data   The stipend is $4,000 per year. Recipients are also invited to attend the annual meeting of the Institute of Food Technologists (IFT); travel expenses up to $550 are reimbursed.

Duration   1 year; may be renewed if the recipient maintains a GPA of 3.0 or higher and participates in a mentoring program.

Additional information   Completed applications must be submitted to the department head of the educational institution the applicant is attending. The department forwards the application to IFT along with a plan for mentoring the student if a scholarship is awarded.

Number awarded   5 each year.

Deadline   January of each year.

[227]
MASTERFOODS USA UNDERGRADUATE MENTORED SCHOLARSHIPS FOR HIGH SCHOOL SENIORS

Institute of Food Technologists
Attn: Scholarship Department
525 West Van Buren, Suite 1000
Chicago, IL 60607
(312) 782-8424   Fax: (312) 782-8348
E-mail: info@ift.org
Web: www.ift.org

Purpose   To provide financial assistance to minority high school seniors interested in studying food science or food technology in college.

Eligibility   This program is open to high school seniors planning to enroll in a food science or food technology program at an educational institution in the United States. Applicants must be members of minority groups (African American, Native Indian, Hispanic American, or Asian American) with a GPA of 3.0 or higher and scores of at least 25 on the ACT or the equivalent on the SAT. Along with their application, they must submit a brief biographical sketch and a statement on why they would like to become a food technologist. Financial need is not considered in the selection process.

Financial data   The stipend is $4,000 per year. Recipients are also invited to attend the annual meeting of the Institute of Food Technologists (IFT); travel expenses up to $550 are reimbursed.

Duration   1 year; may be renewed if the recipient maintains a GPA of 3.0 or higher and participates in a mentoring program.

Additional information   Completed applications must be submitted to the department head of the educational institution the applicant is attending. The department forwards the application to IFT along with a plan for mentoring the student if a scholarship is awarded.

Number awarded   2 each year.

Deadline   May of each year.

[228]
MAUREEN L. AND HOWARD N. BLITMAN, P.E. SCHOLARSHIP TO PROMOTE DIVERSITY IN ENGINEERING

National Society of Professional Engineers
Attn: Education Services
1420 King Street
Alexandria, VA 22314-2794
(703) 684-2833   Fax: (703) 836-4875
E-mail: jiglesias@nspe.org
Web: www.nspe.org/scholarships/sc1-hs.asp

Purpose   To provide financial assistance for college to members of underrepresented ethnic minority groups interested in preparing for a career in engineering.

Eligibility   This program is open to members of underrepresented ethnic minorities (African Americans, Hispanics, or Native Americans) who are high school seniors accepted into an ABET-accredited engineering program at a 4-year college or university. Applicants must have a GPA of 3.5 or higher and strong SAT or ACT scores. They must submit brief essays on an experience they consider significant to their interest in engineering, how their study of engineering will contribute to their long-term career plans, how their ethnic background has influenced their personal development and perceptions, and anything special about them that they would like the selection committee to know. Financial need is not considered in the selection process. U.S. citizenship is required.

Financial data   The stipend is $5,000 per year; funds are paid directly to the recipient's institution.

Duration   1 year; nonrenewable.

Number awarded   1 each year.

Deadline   February of each year.

[229]
MEFUSA SCHOLARSHIPS FOR LATINO/AS

Minority Educational Foundation of the United States of America
Attn: Scholarship Program
3160 Wedgewood Court
Reno, NV 89509-7103

Purpose   To provide financial assistance to Latino/a high school seniors who are interested in attending a community college.

Eligibility   This program is open to Latino/as graduating from high schools anywhere in the United States. Applicants must be planning to attend a community college on a full-time basis. As part of the selection process, they must submit a 1,000-word essay on their educational and career goals, how a community college education will help them to achieve those goals, and how they plan to serve the Latino community after completing their education. Selection is based on the essay, high school GPA (2.5 or higher), SAT or ACT scores, involvement in the Latino community, and financial need.

Financial data   The stipend is $5,000 per year.

Duration 1 year; may be renewed 1 additional year if the recipient maintains full-time enrollment and a GPA of 2.5 or higher.

Additional information The Minority Educational Foundation of the United States of America (MEFUSA) was established in 2001 to meet the needs of minority students who "show a determination to get a college degree," but who, for financial or other personal reasons, are not able to attend a 4-year college or university. Requests for applications should be accompanied by a self-addressed stamped envelope, the student's e-mail address, and the source where they found the scholarship information.

Number awarded Up to 100 each year.

Deadline April of each year.

[230]
MENTOR GRAPHICS SCHOLARSHIPS

Oregon Student Assistance Commission
Attn: Grants and Scholarships Division
1500 Valley River Drive, Suite 100
Eugene, OR 97401-2146
(541) 687-7395   Toll-free: (800) 452-8807, ext. 7395
Fax: (541) 687-7419
E-mail: awardinfo@mercury.osac.state.or.us
Web: www.osac.state.or.us

Purpose To provide financial assistance to Oregon residents (especially underrepresented minorities and women) who are working on a college degree in computer science or engineering.

Eligibility This program is open to residents of Oregon who are U.S. citizens or permanent residents. Applicants must be full-time students in their junior or senior year of college and majoring in electrical engineering or computer science/engineering. Preference is given to female, African American, Native American, or Hispanic applicants. Financial need must be demonstrated.

Financial data The stipend is at least $2,000.

Duration 1 year.

Number awarded Varies each year; recently, 4 of these scholarships were awarded.

Deadline February of each year.

[231]
MERCEDES-BENZ SCHOLARSHIPS

Chicago Urban League
Attn: Education Department
4510 South Michigan Avenue
Chicago, IL 60653-3898
(773) 451-3565   Fax: (773) 285-7772
E-mail: info@cul-chicago.org
Web: www.cul-chicago.org

Purpose To provide financial assistance to Illinois residents of color interested in studying a field related to automotive technology in college.

Eligibility This program is open to Illinois residents of color who are graduating high school seniors with a GPA of 2.5 or higher and planning to enroll as full-time undergraduate students at a 4-year college or university, Triton College, or 1 of the City Colleges of Chicago. Applicants must be planning to major in automotive technology or a field related to the automotive industry (e.g., engineering,

computer science, business, or accounting). They must be able to demonstrate financial need.

Financial data The stipend is $1,000 per year.

Duration 4 years.

Additional information This program is offered as part of the Chicago Urban League's Whitney M. Young, Jr. Memorial Scholarship Fund, established in 1970.

Number awarded 4 each year.

Deadline May of each year.

[232]
MEXICAN AMERICAN ENGINEERS AND SCIENTISTS PRESIDENTIAL SCHOLARSHIP

Society of Mexican American Engineers and Scientists
Attn: Scholarships
711 West Bay Area Boulevard, Suite 206
Webster, TX 77598-3677
(281) 557-3677   Fax: (281) 557-3757
E-mail: scholarships@maes-natl.org
Web: www.maes-natl.org

Purpose To provide financial assistance to undergraduate and graduate student members of the Society of Mexican American Engineers and Scientists (MAES).

Eligibility This program is open to MAES student members who are full-time undergraduate or graduate students at a college or university in the United States. Community college students must be enrolled in majors that can transfer to a 4-year institution offering a baccalaureate degree. All applicants must be majoring in a field of science or engineering. U.S. citizenship or permanent resident status is required. Selection is based on financial need; academic achievement; personal qualities, strengths, and leadership abilities; and timeliness and completeness of the application.

Financial data The stipend is $2,000.

Duration 1 year.

Additional information Recipients must attend the MAES International Symposium's Medalla de Oro Banquet in October.

Number awarded 1 each year.

Deadline October of each year.

[233]
MEXICAN FIESTA SCHOLARSHIPS

Wisconsin Hispanic Scholarship Foundation, Inc.
1220 West Windlake Avenue
Milwaukee, WI 53215
(414) 383-7066   Fax: (414) 383-6677
E-mail: fiestamilw@aol.com
Web: www.mexicanfiesta.org/whsf/index.html

Purpose To provide financial assistance to Hispanic American students in Wisconsin who are interested in attending college or graduate school.

Eligibility Applicants must be at least 50% Hispanic, be high school seniors or full-time undergraduate or graduate students, have earned a GPA of 2.75 or higher, be Wisconsin residents, and be bilingual in Spanish and English.

Financial data The amount of the stipend depends on the number of students selected.

Duration 1 year; recipients may reapply.

Additional information Recipients can attend college in any state. Funds for this program are raised each year at the Mexican Fiesta, held in Milwaukee for 3 days each August. Recipients must perform 20 hours of volunteer work in the Hispanic community.

Number awarded Varies; a total of $20,000 is awarded in scholarships each year.

Deadline March of each year.

[234]
MICHAEL BAKER CORPORATION SCHOLARSHIP PROGRAM FOR DIVERSITY IN ENGINEERING

Association of Independent Colleges and Universities
  of Pennsylvania
101 North Front Street
Harrisburg, PA 17101-1405
(717) 232-8649   Fax: (717) 233-8574
E-mail: info@aicup.org
Web: www.aicup.org

Purpose To provide financial assistance to women and minority students at member institutions of the Association of Independent Colleges and Universities of Pennsylvania (AICUP) who are majoring in designated fields of engineering.

Eligibility This program is open to full-time undergraduate students at designated AICUP colleges and universities who are women and/or members of the following minority groups: American Indians, Alaska Natives, Asians, Blacks/African Americans, Hispanics/Latinos, Native Hawaiians, or Pacific Islanders. Applicants must be juniors majoring in architectural, civil, or environmental engineering with a GPA of 3.0 or higher. Along with their application, they must submit an essay on what they believe will be the greatest challenge facing the engineering profession over the next decade, and why.

Financial data The stipend is $1,000 per year.

Duration 1 year; may be renewed 1 additional year if the recipient maintains appropriate academic standards.

Additional information This program, sponsored by the Michael Baker Corporation, is available at the following AICUP colleges and universities: Bucknell University, Carnegie Mellon University, Drexel University, Gannon University, Geneva College, Grove City College, Lafayette College, Lehigh University, Messiah College, Swarthmore College, Villanova University, Widener University, and Wilkes University.

Number awarded 1 each year.

Deadline April of each year.

[235]
MICROSOFT NATIONAL SCHOLARSHIPS

Microsoft Corporation
Attn: National Minority Technical Scholarship
One Microsoft Way
Redmond, WA 98052-8303
(425) 882-8080   TTY: (800) 892-9811
E-mail: scholars@microsoft.com
Web: www.microsoft.com/college/ss_overview.mspx

Purpose To provide financial assistance and summer work experience to undergraduate students, especially underrepresented minorities and women, interested in pre-

paring for a career in computer science or other related technical fields.

Eligibility This program is open to students who are enrolled full time and making satisfactory progress toward an undergraduate degree in computer science, computer engineering, or a related technical discipline (such as math or physics) with a demonstrated interest in computer science. Applicants must be enrolled in their sophomore or junior year and have earned a GPA of 3.0 or higher. Although all students who meet the eligibility criteria may apply, a large majority of scholarships are awarded to female and underrepresented minority (African American, Hispanic, and Native American) students. Along with their application, students must submit an essay that describes the following 4 items: 1) how they demonstrate their passion for technology outside the classroom; 2) the toughest technical problem they have worked on, how they addressed the problem, their role in reaching the outcome if it was team-based, and the final outcome; 3) a situation that demonstrates initiative and their willingness to go above and beyond; and 4) how they are currently funding their college education.

Financial data Scholarships cover 100% of the tuition as posted by the financial aid office of the university or college the recipient designates. Scholarships are made through that school and are not transferable to other academic institutions. Funds may be used for tuition only and may not be used for other costs on the recipient's bursar bill.

Duration 1 year.

Additional information Selected recipients are offered a paid summer internship where they will have a chance to develop Microsoft products.

Number awarded Varies. A total of $540,000 is available for this program each year.

Deadline January of each year.

[236]
MIGRANT FARMWORKER BACCALAUREATE SCHOLARSHIP

Geneseo Migrant Center
27 Lackawanna Avenue
Mount Morris, NY 14510-1096
(585) 658-7960   Toll-free: (800) 245-5681
Fax: (585) 658-7969   E-mail: info@migrant.net
Web: www.migrant.net/sch_mfb.htm

Purpose To provide financial assistance to migrant farmworkers who are currently enrolled in college.

Eligibility This program is open to migrant farmworker students with a history of migrating for employment in agriculture. Applicants must have completed at least 1 year of college. Along with their application, they must submit a personal essay of at least 500 words on their background, career and personal goals, and why they should receive this assistance; 3 letters of recommendation; a college transcript; and documentation of financial need.

Financial data The stipend is $2,000 per year. These funds are intended to be in addition to any that the student receives through federal, state, or other scholarship assistance as an undergraduate. The same annual amount is available for graduate study or loan repayment.

Duration 1 year; may be renewed for an additional 2 years of undergraduate study. Recipients also have the option of an additional 2 years of graduate support or 3 years of loan repayment.

Additional information Following completion of their baccalaureate degree, recipients may apply for additional support as a graduate student or for assistance in repayment of educational loans.

Number awarded 1 each year.

Deadline June of each year.

[237]
MINNESOTA SPACE GRANT CONSORTIUM SCHOLARSHIPS AND FELLOWSHIPS

Minnesota Space Grant Consortium
c/o University of Minnesota
Department of Aerospace Engineering and Mechanics
107 Akerman Hall
110 Union Street S.E.
Minneapolis, MN 55455
(612) 626-9295   Fax: (612) 626-1558
E-mail: mnsgc@aem.umn.edu
Web: www.aem.umn.edu

Purpose To provide financial assistance for space-related studies to undergraduate and graduate students (particularly underrepresented minorities, women, and persons with disabilities) in Minnesota.

Eligibility This program is open to graduate and undergraduate full-time students at institutions that are affiliates of the Minnesota Space Grant Consortium. U.S. citizenship and a GPA of 3.2 or higher are required. Eligible fields of study include the physical sciences (astronomy, astrophysics, chemistry, computer science, mathematics, physics, planetary geoscience, and planetary science), life sciences (biology, biochemistry, botany, health science/nutrition, medicine, molecular/cellular biology, and zoology), social sciences (anthropology, architecture, art, economics, education, history, philosophy, political science/public policy, and psychology), earth sciences (atmospheric science, climatology/meteorology, environmental science, geography, geology, geophysics, and oceanography), and engineering (agricultural, aeronautical, aerospace, architectural, bioengineering, chemical, civil, computer, electrical, electronic, environmental, industrial, materials science, mechanical, mining, nuclear, petroleum, engineering science, and engineering mechanics). The Minnesota Space Grant Consortium is a component of the U.S. National Aeronautics and Space Administration (NASA) Space Grant program, which encourages participation by women, underrepresented minorities, and persons with disabilities.

Financial data This program awards approximately $125,000 in undergraduate scholarships and $25,000 in graduate fellowships each year. The amounts of the awards are set by each of the participating institutions, which augment funding from this program with institutional resources.

Duration 1 year; renewable.

Additional information This program is funded by NASA. The member institutions are: Augsburg College, Bethel College, Bemidji State University, College of St. Catherine, Carleton College, Concordia College, Fond du Lac Community College, Itasca Community College, Leech Lake Tribal College, Macalaster College, Normandale Community College, Southwest State University, University of Minnesota at Duluth, University of Minnesota at Twin Cities, and University of St. Thomas.

Number awarded 8 to 12 undergraduate scholarships and 2 to 3 graduate fellowships are awarded each year.

Deadline March of each year.

[238]
MINORITIES IN GOVERNMENT FINANCE SCHOLARSHIP

Government Finance Officers Association
Attn: Scholarship Committee
203 North LaSalle Street, Suite 2700
Chicago, IL 60601-1210
(312) 977-9700   Fax: (312) 977-4806
Web: www.gfoa.org/services/scholarships.shtml

Purpose To provide financial assistance to minority upper-division and graduate students who are preparing for a career in state and local government finance.

Eligibility This program is open to upper-division and graduate students who are preparing for a career in public finance with a major in public administration, accounting, finance, political science, economics, or business administration (with a specific focus on government or nonprofit management). Applicants must be members of a minority group, citizens or permanent residents of the United States or Canada, and able to provide a letter of recommendation from a representative of their school. Selection is based on career plans, academic record, plan of study, letters of recommendation, and GPA. Financial need is not considered.

Financial data The stipend is $5,000.

Duration 1 year.

Additional information Funding for this program is provided by Fidelity Investments Tax-Exempt Services Company.

Number awarded 1 or more each year.

Deadline February of each year.

[239]
MINORITY COMMUNITY COLLEGE TRANSFER SCHOLARSHIPS

State University System of Florida
Attn: Office of Academic and Student Affairs
325 West Gaines Street, Suite 1501
Tallahassee, FL 32399-1950
(850) 245-0467   Fax: (850) 245-9667
E-mail: we're.listening@fldoe.org
Web: www.fldoe.org

Purpose To provide financial assistance to minority community college students in Florida who are interested in transferring to a school within the State University System of Florida (SUS).

Eligibility This program is open to minority community college students who complete A.A. or A.S. degrees from an accredited Florida community college between December and August of the current year. Applicants must have been admitted as degree-seeking junior-level students at an SUS institution. All recipients must have participated in, received a waiver for, or passed the College-Level Academic Skills Test program. In addition, male applicants must have complied with the Selective Service System registration requirements. Students may apply for need awards, merit/need awards, or merit awards. The minimum cumulative GPA on postsecondary credits is 2.0 for need-based applicants or 3.0 for merit/need and merit applicants.

Financial data A stipend is awarded (amount not specified); funds are paid in 2 equal installments.

Duration Up to 6 semesters, provided the need recipient maintains at least a 2.0 GPA and the need/merit or merit recipient maintains at least a 3.0 average.

Additional information This program is administered by the equal opportunity program at each of the 11 SUS 4-year institutions. Contact that office for further information.

Number awarded Several each year.

Deadline May of each year.

[240]
MINORITY GEOSCIENCE STUDENT SCHOLARSHIPS

American Geological Institute
Attn: Minority Participation Program
4220 King Street
Alexandria, VA 22302-1502
(703) 379-2480, ext. 227   Fax: (703) 379-7563
E-mail: cmm@agiweb.org
Web: www.agiweb.org/mpp/index.html

Purpose To provide financial assistance to underrepresented minority undergraduate and graduate students interested in working on a degree in the geosciences.

Eligibility This program is open to members of ethnic minority groups underrepresented in the geosciences (Blacks, Hispanics, American Indians, Eskimos, Hawaiians, and Samoans). U.S. citizenship or permanent resident status is required. Applicants must be full-time students enrolled in an accredited institution working on an undergraduate or graduate degree in the geosciences, including geology, geophysics, hydrology, meteorology, physical oceanography, planetary geology, and earth science education; students in other natural sciences, mathematics, or engineering are not eligible. Selection is based on a 250-word essay on career goals and why the applicant has chosen a geoscience as a major, work experience, recommendations, honors and awards, extracurricular activities, and financial need.

Financial data Stipends range from $500 to $3,000 per year.

Duration 1 academic year; renewable if the recipient maintains satisfactory performance.

Additional information Funding for this program is provided by ExxonMobil Corporation, ConocoPhillips, ChevronTexaco Corporation, Marathon Corporation, and the Seismological Society of America.

Number awarded Varies each year; recently, 19 of these scholarships were awarded.

Deadline March of each year.

[241]
MINORITY NURSE MAGAZINE SCHOLARSHIP PROGRAM

Minority Nurse Magazine
Attn: Career Recruitment Media
211 West Wacker Drive, Suite 900
Chicago, IL 60606
(312) 525-3095   Fax: (312) 429-3336
E-mail: pam.chwedyk@careermedia.com
Web: www.minoritynurse.com

Purpose To provide financial assistance to members of minority groups who are working on a bachelor's degree in nursing.

Eligibility This program is open to minority nursing students currently enrolled in 1) the third or fourth year of an accredited B.S.N. program; 2) an accelerated program leading to a B.S.N. degree (e.g., R.N. to B.S.N., B.A. to B.S.N.); or 3) an accelerated master's entry nursing program (e.g., R.N. to M.S.N., B.S. to M.S.N.) Selection is based on academic excellence (GPA of 3.0 or higher), demonstrated commitment of service to the student's minority community, and financial need. U.S. citizenship of permanent resident status is required.

Financial data The stipends are $1,000 or $500.

Duration 1 year.

Additional information These scholarships were first offered in 2000. Winners are announced in the fall issue of *Minority Nurse* magazine

Number awarded 4 each year: 2 at $1,000 and 2 at $500.

Deadline June of each year.

[242]
MINORITY SCHOLARSHIP AWARD IN PHYSICAL THERAPY

American Physical Therapy Association
Attn: Department of Minority/International Affairs
1111 North Fairfax Street
Alexandria, VA 22314-1488
(703) 706-3144   Toll-free: (800) 999-APTA, ext. 3144
Fax: (703) 706-8519   TDD: (703) 683-6748
E-mail: min-intl@apta.org
Web: www.apta.org

Purpose To provide financial assistance to minority students who are interested in becoming a physical therapist or physical therapy assistant.

Eligibility This program is open to minority students who are in the final year of a professional physical therapy or physical therapy assistant education program. Applicants must submit an essay outlining their professional goals and minority service. U.S. citizenship or permanent resident status is required. Selection is based on 1) demonstrated evidence of contributions in the area of minority affairs and services with an emphasis on contributions made while enrolled in a physical therapy program; 2) potential to contribute to the profession of physical therapy; and 3) scholastic achievement.

Financial data The stipend varies; recently, minimum awards were $1,500 for physical therapy students or $750 for physical therapy assistant students.

Duration 1 year.

Number awarded Varies each year; recently, 6 of these awards were granted to physical therapy students and 4 to physical therapy assistant students.

Deadline November of each year.

[243]
MINORITY SCHOLARSHIP AWARDS FOR COLLEGE STUDENTS IN CHEMICAL ENGINEERING

American Institute of Chemical Engineers
Attn: Awards Administrator
Three Park Avenue
New York, NY 10016-5991
(212) 591-7107   Fax: (212) 591-8890
E-mail: awards@aiche.org
Web: www.aiche.org/awards

Purpose To provide financial assistance for study in chemical engineering to underrepresented minority college student members of the American Institute of Chemical Engineers (AIChE).

Eligibility This program is open to undergraduate student AIChE members who are also members of a minority group that is underrepresented in chemical engineering (African Americans, Hispanics, Native Americans, and Alaskan Natives). Each AIChE chapter may nominate 1 member. Selection is based on academic record (including a GPA of 3.0 or higher), participation in AIChE student and professional activities, a 300-word letter on career objectives and plans, and financial need.

Financial data The stipend is $1,000.

Duration 1 year; nonrenewable.

Number awarded Approximately 10 each year.

Deadline Nominations must be submitted by May of each year.

[244]
MINORITY SCHOLARSHIP AWARDS FOR INCOMING COLLEGE FRESHMEN IN CHEMICAL ENGINEERING

American Institute of Chemical Engineers
Attn: Awards Administrator
Three Park Avenue
New York, NY 10016-5991
(212) 591-7107   Fax: (212) 591-8890
E-mail: awards@aiche.org
Web: www.aiche.org/awards

Purpose To provide financial assistance for study in science or engineering to incoming minority freshmen.

Eligibility Eligible are members of a minority group that is underrepresented in chemical engineering (African Americans, Hispanics, Native Americans, and Alaskan Natives). Applicants must be graduating high school seniors planning to enroll in a 4-year university with a major in science or engineering. They must be nominated by an American Institute of Chemical Engineers (AIChE) local section. Selection is based on academic record (including a GPA of 3.0 or higher), participation in school and work activities, a 300-word letter outlining the reasons for choosing science or engineering, and financial need.

Financial data The stipend is $1,000.

Duration 1 year; nonrenewable.

Number awarded Approximately 10 each year.

Deadline Nominations must be submitted by May of each year.

[245]
MNACC STUDENT OF COLOR SCHOLARSHIP

Minnesota Association of Counselors of Color
Attn: Rudy Hernandez, Scholarship Co-Chair
University of Minnesota
128 Pleasant Street, S.E.
Minneapolis, MN 55455
(612) 626-1513   Toll-free: (800) 752-1000
E-mail: r-hern@umn.edu
Web: www.mnacc.org

Purpose To provide financial assistance to high school seniors of color in Minnesota who plan to attend college in the area.

Eligibility This program is open to seniors graduating from public and private high schools in Minnesota who are U.S. citizens or permanent residents of ethnic minority (African American/Black, American Indian or Alaskan Native, Asian or Pacific Islander, Hispanic/Chicano-Latino) descent. Applicants must be planning to attend a 4-year college or university, a 2-year college, or a trade or technical college that is a member of the Minnesota Association of Counselors of Color (MnACC). Along with their application, they must submit an essay, up to 500 words in length, on 1 of the following topics: 1 of their most meaningful achievements, their future goals, or their involvement within their community.

Financial data The stipend is $500.

Duration 1 year; nonrenewable.

Additional information These scholarships may be used at approximately 45 MnACC colleges, universities, and technical schools in Minnesota, Michigan Technological University (Houghton), North Dakota State College of Science (Wahpeton), North Dakota State University (Fargo), the University of North Dakota (Grand Forks), the University of Wisconsin at River Falls, or the University of Wisconsin at Superior.

Number awarded Varies each year.

Deadline March of each year.

[246]
MODELO MUNDIAL-WORLD MODEL COMPETITION

JCPenney Company, Inc.
Attn: Modelo Mundial
P.O. Box 100001
Dallas, TX 75301-8112
(972) 431-4655   E-mail: cbsmith@jcpenney.com
Web: www.jcpenneymodelomundial.com

Purpose To recognize and reward outstanding Hispanic models.

Eligibility This program is open to men and women of Hispanic descent who are between the ages of 16 and 21, reside in the vicinity of a participating JCPenney store, are currently enrolled in high school or an accredited institution of higher education, and have a GPA of 3.0 or higher. Applicants may not be professional models or currently affiliated with a modeling agency. They must submit a 1-page essay describing their academic achievements, extracurricular achievements, and community involvement. Essays are judged on writing skills, flair for self-expression, and leadership skills. Men and women compete separately at the regional level, and the winners advance to the national competition in Miami, Florida in June.

Financial data Regional winners receive round-trip airfare to Miami and hotel accommodations for 5 days. National winners receive a $10,000 scholarship and a $1,000 JCPenney gift card. National runners-up receive a $5,000 scholarship and a $500 JCPenney gift care.

Duration The competition is held annually.

Additional information This competition has been sponsored by JCPenney since 1990. Through 2002, it was known as the Hispanic Designers Model Search. Its current sponsors include the Havanera Company, Mudd, Reebok, and The Original Arizona Jean Company. Scholarships are provided by Univision, a Spanish language television network in the United States. The participating JCPenney stores operate in Albuquerque, Chicago, Dallas/Fort Worth, Denver, El Paso, Houston, Las Vegas, Los Angeles/San Diego, Miami, McAllen/Harlingen/Brownsville (Texas), New Jersey/New York, Orlando, Phoenix/Tucson, Sacramento/Fresno, Salt Lake City, San Antonio, San Francisco/San Jose, Tampa, Washington, D.C., Puerto Rico, and (in Mexico) Monterrey, Mexico City, and Leon.

Number awarded 46 regional winners (1 man and 1 woman from each of the 23 markets), 2 national grand winners (1 man and 1 woman), and 2 runners-up (also 1 man and 1 woman).

Deadline May of each year.

[247]
MONSIGNOR PHILIP KENNEY SCHOLARSHIP FUND

New Hampshire Charitable Foundation
37 Pleasant Street
Concord, NH 03301-4005
(603) 225-6641   Toll-free: (800) 464-6641
Fax: (603) 225-1700   E-mail: info@nhcf.org
Web: www.nhcf.org

Purpose To provide financial assistance for college to minority and other students from New Hampshire.

Eligibility This program is open to New Hampshire students who are economically disadvantaged, with a preference for Hispanics and other minorities who are enrolled in undergraduate study. Nontraditional students, both full and part time, are encouraged to apply. At least 1 scholarship is designated for a minority student from Merrimack County.

Financial data The scholarship designated for a minority student from Merrimack has a stipend of $1,000. Other stipends vary.

Duration 1 year; recipients may reapply.

Number awarded Varies; in addition to the 1 scholarship for a minority student from Merrimack County, a total of $10,000 is available each year.

Deadline April of each year.

[248]
MONTANA SPACE GRANT CONSORTIUM UNDERGRADUATE SCHOLARSHIPS

Montana Space Grant Consortium
c/o Montana State University
416 Cobleigh Hall
P.O. Box 173835
Bozeman, MT 59717-3835
(406) 994-4223   Fax: (406) 994-4452
E-mail: msgc@montana.edu
Web: spacegrant.montana.edu

Purpose To provide financial assistance to students (particularly underrepresented minorities, women, and students with disabilities) in Montana who are interested in working on an undergraduate degree in the space sciences and/or engineering.

Eligibility This program is open to full-time undergraduate students at member institutions of the Montana Space Grant Consortium (MSGC) majoring in fields related to space sciences and engineering. Those fields include, but are not limited to, astronomy, biological and life sciences, chemical engineering, chemistry, civil engineering, computer sciences, electrical engineering, geological sciences, mechanical engineering, and physics. Priority is given to students who have been involved in aerospace-related research. U.S. citizenship is required. The MSGC is a component of the U.S. National Aeronautics and Space Administration (NASA) Space Grant program, which encourages participation by women, underrepresented minorities, and persons with disabilities. Financial need is not considered in the selection process.

Financial data The stipend is $1,000 per year.

Duration 1 year; may be renewed.

Additional information The MSGC member institutions are Blackfeet Community College, Carroll College, Chief Dull Knife College, Fort Belknap College, Fort Peck Community College, Little Big Horn College, Montana State University at Billings, Montana State University at Bozeman, Montana State University-Northern, Montana Tech, Rocky Mountain College, Salish Kootenai College, Stone Child College, the University of Montana, and the University of Montana-Western. Funding for this program is provided by NASA.

Number awarded Varies each year; recently, 26 of these scholarships were awarded.

Deadline March of each year.

[249]
MORRIS SCHOLARSHIP

Morris Scholarship Fund
Attn: Scholarship Selection Committee
525 S.W. Fifth Street, Suite A
Des Moines, IA 50309-4501
(515) 282-8192   Fax: (515) 282-9117
E-mail: morris@assoc-mgmt.com
Web: www.morrisscholarship.org

Purpose To provide financial assistance to minority undergraduate, graduate, and law students in Iowa.

Eligibility This program is open to minority students (African Americans, Asian/Pacific Islanders, Hispanics, or Native Americans) who are interested in studying at a college, graduate school, or law school. Applicants must be either

Iowa residents and high school graduates who are attending a college or university anywhere in the United States or non-Iowa residents who are attending a college or university in Iowa; preference is given to native Iowans who are attending an Iowa college or university. Along with their application, they must submit an essay of 250 to 500 words on why they are applying for this scholarship, activities or organizations in which they are involved, and their future plans. Selection is based on the essay, academic achievement (GPA of 2.5 or higher), community service, and financial need.

Financial data The stipend is $1,500 per year.

Duration 1 year; may be renewed.

Additional information This fund was established in 1978 in honor of the J.B. Morris family, who founded the Iowa branch of the National Association for the Advancement of Colored People and published the *Iowa Bystander* newspaper.

Number awarded Varies each year; recently, 11 of these scholarships were awarded.

Deadline January of each year.

[250]
MOTOROLA/HENAAC SCHOLARS PROGRAM

Hispanic Engineer National Achievement Awards
   Conference
3900 Whiteside Street
Los Angeles, CA 90063
(323) 262-0997   Fax: (323) 262-0946
E-mail: info@henaac.org
Web: www.henaac.org

Purpose To provide financial assistance to Hispanic undergraduate students majoring in electrical engineering.

Eligibility This program is open to Hispanic undergraduate students who are enrolled full time in electrical engineering. Academic achievement and campus community activities are considered in the selection process. U.S. citizenship is required.

Financial data Stipends range from $1,000 to $5,000.

Duration 1 year; recipients may reapply.

Additional information This program is sponsored by Motorola as part of its effort to support the mission of the Hispanic Engineer National Achievement Awards Conference (HENAAC): to promote technical excellence and leadership in the Hispanic community.

Number awarded 1 or more each year.

Deadline April of each year.

[251]
M&T BANK SCHOLARSHIP PROGRAM

Hispanic College Fund
Attn: National Director
1717 Pennsylvania Avenue, N.W., Suite 460
Washington, D.C. 20006
(202) 296-5400   Toll-free: (800) 644-4223
Fax: (202) 296-3774
E-mail: hcf-info@hispanicfund.org
Web: www.hispanicfund.org

Purpose To provide financial assistance to Hispanic American undergraduate students from Maryland, New York, Virginia, and Pennsylvania who are interested in pre-

paring for a career in business, computer science, or engineering.

Eligibility This program is open to U.S. citizens of Hispanic background (at least 1 grandparent must be 100% Hispanic) who are entering their freshman, sophomore, junior, or senior year of college. Applicants must be residents of Maryland, New York, Virginia, or Pennsylvania. They must be working on a bachelor's degree in business, computer science, engineering, or a business-related major and have a cumulative GPA of 3.0 or higher. They must be applying to or enrolled in a college or university in the 50 states or Puerto Rico as a full-time student. Financial need is considered in the selection process.

Financial data Stipends range from $500 to $5,000, depending on the need of the recipient, and average approximately $3,000. Funds are paid directly to the recipient's college or university to help cover tuition and fees.

Duration 1 year; recipients may reapply.

Additional information This program is sponsored by M&T Bank and administered by the Hispanic College Fund (HCF). All applications must be submitted online; no paper applications are available.

Number awarded Varies each year.

Deadline April of each year.

[252]
MVSNA STUDENT SCHOLARSHIP

Missouri Vocational Special Need Association
c/o Shawn Brice
Missouri Department of Elementary and Secondary
   Education
Division of Career Education–Special Needs
205 Jefferson Street
P.O. Box 480
Jefferson City, MO 65102-0480
(573) 522-1775   Fax: (573) 526-4261
E-mail: Shawn.Brice@dese.mo.us
Web: dese.mo.gov

Purpose To provide financial assistance to vocational/technical students in Missouri who are members of designated special populations.

Eligibility This program is open to Missouri vocational/technical students who are members of special populations, defined as individuals who are academically or economically disadvantaged, have limited English proficiency, or are nontraditional, disabled, pregnant teenagers, single/teen parents, or foster children. Applicants must submit brief essays on their professional or career goals; the challenges they have had to overcome to reach their educational goals; how they have received help from their school, teachers, or community; and how the award will help them in pursuing continued education. Selection is based on realism of career goal, financial need, unusual circumstances, and personal references.

Financial data A stipend is awarded (amount not specified).

Duration 1 year.

Additional information Information is also available from Cindy Grizzell, MVSNA Awards Chair, Waynesville Technical Academy, 810 Roosevelt, Waynesville, MO 65583, (573) 774-6106, E-mail: cgrizzell@waynesville.k12.mo.us.

Number awarded 1 each year.

Deadline April of each year.

[253]
NAHJ GENERAL SCHOLARSHIPS

National Association of Hispanic Journalists
Attn: Scholarship Committee
1000 National Press Building
529 14th Street, N.W.
Washington, DC 20045-2001
(202) 662-7145   Toll-free: (888) 346-NAHJ
Fax: (202) 662-7144   E-mail: nahj@nahj.org
Web: www.nahj.org

Purpose To provide financial assistance to Hispanic American undergraduate and graduate students interested in preparing for careers in the media.

Eligibility This program is open to Hispanic American high school seniors, undergraduates, and graduate students who are interested in preparing for a career in English- or Spanish-language print, broadcast (radio or television), online, or photojournalism; students majoring in other fields must be able to demonstrate a strong interest in preparing for a career in journalism. Applicants must submit an official transcript; a 1-page resume with their educational background, work history, awards, internships, other scholarships, language proficiency, and any work done for their school newspaper, radio, and/or television station; samples of their work; 2 reference letters; a 500-word autobiography in the form of a news story; and documentation of financial need. Selection is based on commitment to the field of journalism, academic achievement, awareness of the Latino community, and financial need.

Financial data Stipends range from $1,000 to $2,000.

Duration 1 year.

Additional information This program is administered by the National Association of Hispanic Journalists (NAHJ) as a component of its Rubén Salazar Scholarship Fund.

Number awarded Varies each year; recently 20 of these scholarships were awarded.

Deadline January of each year.

[254]
NASA HISPANIC EXPLORERS SCHOLARSHIP PROGRAM

Hispanic College Fund
Attn: National Director
1717 Pennsylvania Avenue, N.W., Suite 460
Washington, D.C. 20006
(202) 296-5400   Toll-free: (800) 644-4223
Fax: (202) 296-3774
E-mail: hispaniccollegefund@earthlink.net
Web: www.hispanicfund.org

Purpose To provide financial assistance to Hispanic American undergraduate students who are interested in preparing for a career in a field of interest to the U.S. National Aeronautics and Space Administration (NASA).

Eligibility This program is open to U.S. citizens of Hispanic background (at least 1 grandparent must be 100% Hispanic) who are entering their freshman, sophomore, junior, or senior year of college. Applicants must be working on a bachelor's degree in science, computer science, engineering, or a NASA-related major and have a cumulative GPA of 3.0 or higher. They must be applying to or enrolled in a college or university in the 50 states or Puerto Rico as a full-time student. Financial need is considered in the selection process.

Financial data Stipends range from $500 to $5,000, depending on the need of the recipient, and average approximately $3,000. Funds are paid directly to the recipient's college or university to help cover tuition and fees.

Duration 1 year; recipients may reapply.

Additional information This program is sponsored by NASA. All applications must be submitted online; no paper applications are available.

Number awarded Varies each year.

Deadline April of each year.

[255]
NASCAR/WENDELL SCOTT AWARD

Hispanic Association of Colleges and Universities
Attn: National Scholarship Program
One Dupont Circle, N.W. Suite 605
Washington, DC 20036
(202) 467-0893   Fax: (202) 496-9177
TTY: (800) 855-2880   E-mail: scholarships@hacu.net
Web: scholarships.hacu.net/applications/applicants

Purpose To provide financial assistance to undergraduate and graduate students majoring in any field at member institutions of the Hispanic Association of Colleges and Universities (HACU) who are interested in the motorsports industry.

Eligibility This program is open to undergraduate and graduate students at HACU member and partner colleges and universities. Applicants may be majoring in any field, but they must be able to demonstrate a recreational or professional interest in the motorsports industry. Undergraduates must be enrolled full time, have a GPA of 3.0 or higher, and be able to use the scholarship during their junior or senior year. Graduate students must be enrolled at least part time and have a GPA of 3.2 or higher. Applicants must submit an essay of 200 to 250 words that describes their academic and/or career goals, where they expect to be and what they expect to be doing 10 years from now, and what skills they can bring to an employer. Financial need is considered in the selection process.

Financial data The stipend is $1,500 for undergraduates or $2,000 for graduate students.

Duration 1 year.

Additional information This program is sponsored by NASCAR and administered by HACU.

Number awarded 1 or more each year.

Deadline May of each year.

[256]
NATIONAL ASSOCIATION OF HISPANIC FEDERAL EXECUTIVES SCHOLARSHIP

National Association of Hispanic Federal Executives
Attn: NAHFE Scholarship Foundation Inc.
P.O. Box 469
Herndon, VA 20172-0469
(703) 787-0291   Fax: (703) 787-4675
E-mail: NAHFE@cs.com
Web: www.nahfe.org/scholars.htm

Purpose To provide financial assistance for college to Hispanic American high school seniors.

Eligibility Eligible to apply are graduating high school seniors of Hispanic American descent. Scholarships are awarded in 3 categories: 1) deserving Hispanic high school seniors on the basis of outstanding academic achievement (GPA of 3.5 or higher), community service, and financial need; 2) deserving Hispanic high school seniors on the basis of satisfactory academic achievement (GPA from 2.8 to 3.5), community involvement, and financial need; and 3) deserving Hispanic high school seniors on the basis of academic merit only (GPA of 3.5 or higher). As part of the application process, students must submit a completed application form, a copy of their high school transcript, 2 letters of recommendation, and a 300-word essay describing their professional or career goals. For scholarships in the first 2 categories listed above, students must also provide proof of financial need (e.g., a copy of the most recent income tax return).

Financial data A stipend is awarded (generally, at least $1,000).

Duration Up to 4 years.

Additional information This program was established in 1999. Information is also available from Bill Rodriguez, 5717 Marble Arch Way, Alexandria, VA 22315, (703) 971-3204, E-mail: BillRodriguez@compuserve.com.

Deadline May of each year.

[257]
NATIONAL ASSOCIATION OF HISPANIC NURSES SCHOLARSHIPS

National Association of Hispanic Nurses
Attn: National Awards and Scholarship Committee
    Chair
1501 16th Street, N.W.
Washington, DC 20036
(202) 387-2477   Fax: (202) 483-7183
E-mail: thehispanicnurses@earthlink.net
Web: www.thehispanicnurses.org

Purpose To provide financial assistance for nursing education to members of the National Association of Hispanic Nurses (NAHN).

Eligibility Eligible are members of the association enrolled in associate, diploma, baccalaureate, graduate, or practical/vocational nursing programs at NLN-accredited schools of nursing. Applicants must submit a 1-page essay that reflects their qualifications and potential for leadership in nursing for the Hispanic community. U.S. citizenship or permanent resident status is required. Selection is based on academic excellence (preferably a GPA of 3.0 or higher), potential for leadership in nursing, and financial need.

Financial data The stipend is $1,000.

Duration 1 year.

Number awarded Varies each year, depending on the availability of funds.

Deadline April of each year.

[258]
NATIONAL CAUCUS OF HISPANIC SCHOOL BOARD MEMBERS SCHOLARSHIPS

National School Boards Association
Attn: National Caucus of Hispanic School Board
    Members
1680 Duke Street
Alexandria, VA 22314-3493
(703) 838-6157   Fax: (703) 683-7590
E-mail: info@nsba.org
Web: www.nsba.org/caucus

Purpose To provide financial assistance for college to Hispanic high school seniors.

Eligibility This program is open to high school seniors of Hispanic origin who have been accepted to an accredited 4-year college or university. Applicants must have a GPA of 3.0 or higher and be able to demonstrate financial need. Along with their application, they must submit an autobiographical statement that includes a paragraph about their financial need.

Financial data The stipend is $1,000.

Duration 1 year.

Additional information This program was established in 1999. Funding is provided by Washington Mutual Bank and the Philip Morris Corporation.

Number awarded 5 each year.

Deadline March of each year.

[259]
NATIONAL LATINA ALLIANCE SCHOLARSHIPS

National Latina Alliance
633 West Fifth Street, Suite 1150
Los Angeles, CA 90071
(323) 980-7992 E-mail: info@nationallatinaalliance.org
Web: www.nationallatinaalliance.org/ScholProg.htm

Purpose To provide financial assistance for college or other career education to Latinas.

Eligibility This program is open to Latinas who are 1) graduating high school seniors; 2) currently enrolled in a college or university; 3) returning to school after an absence of at least 2 years; or 4) preparing for a nontraditional career (e.g., chef, artist, entrepreneur, nurse). Applicants must have a GPA of 2.5 or higher and be able to document financial need. They must submit a 1-page essay on the question, "As a Latina, what do you think is important for the success of the community?" Reentry applicants must also provide a 1-page essay discussing their reason for withdrawing from school. Nontraditional career students must provide documentation regarding their career.

Financial data Stipends range from $500 to $1,000, depending on the need of the recipient.

Duration 1 year.

Additional information Information is also available from Gloria Michel, Education Committee Chair, c/o Guerra & Associates, 1100 South Flower Street, Suite 2100, Los Angeles, CA 90015.

Number awarded Varies each year; recently, 17 of these scholarships were awarded.

Deadline March of each year.

[260]
NAVESNP/PINEY MOUNTAIN PRESS STUDENT AWARD

National Association of Vocational Education Special
    Needs Personnel
c/o Marjorie Eckman, Awards Chair
719 Gulf Lab Road
Cheswick, PA 15024
(412) 323-3970   E-mail: ME50@aol.com
Web: www.specialpopulations.org/award.htm

Purpose To provide financial assistance to vocational/technical students who are members of a special population.

Eligibility This program is open to vocational/technical students who are members of a special population, defined to include those who are academically or economically disadvantaged, limited English proficient, nontraditional, disabled, pregnant teenagers, single/teen parents, or foster children. Applicants must demonstrate how they have overcome barriers to achieve their highest potential for success. Selection is based on their choice of a realistic career goal, financial need, unusual circumstances, and letters of reference.

Financial data The stipend is $1,000.

Duration 1 year.

Additional information Piney Mountain Press supports half the stipend.

Number awarded 1 each year.

Deadline October of each year.

[261]
NEBRASKA SPACE GRANT STATEWIDE SCHOLARSHIP COMPETITION

Nebraska Space Grant Consortium
c/o University of Nebraska at Omaha
Engineering, No. 116
6001 Dodge Street
Omaha, NE 68182-0406
(402) 554-3772
Toll-free: (800) 858-8648, ext. 4-3772 (within NE)
Fax: (402) 554-3781   E-mail: nasa@unomaha.edu
Web: www.unomaha.edu/~nasa/funding/ssc.html

Purpose To provide financial assistance to undergraduate and graduate students (particularly minorities, women, and students with disabilities) in Nebraska interested in aerospace-related study or research.

Eligibility This program is open to undergraduate and graduate students at schools that are members of the Nebraska Space Grant Consortium. Applicants must be U.S. citizens participating in approved aviation or aerospace-related research or course work. Selection is based primarily on past academic performance in the classroom. Special attention is given to applications submitted by women, underrepresented minorities, and persons with disabilities.

Financial data Maximum awards are $500 per semester for undergraduate or graduate course work, $750 per

semester for undergraduate research, or $2,500 per semester for graduate research.

Duration 1 semester; may be renewed if the recipient maintains a GPA of 3.0 or higher.

Additional information The following schools are members of the Nebraska Space Grant Consortium: University of Nebraska at Omaha, University of Nebraska at Lincoln, University of Nebraska at Kearney, University of Nebraska Medical Center, Creighton University, Western Nebraska Community College, Chadron State College, College of St. Mary, Metropolitan Community College, Grace University, Hastings College, Little Priest Tribal College, and Nebraska Indian Community College. Funding for this program is provided by the National Aeronautics and Space Administration.

Deadline April of each year.

[262]
NELLIE STONE JOHNSON SCHOLARSHIP

Minnesota State University Student Association
Attn: Scholarship
108 Como Avenue
St. Paul, MN 55103-1820
(651) 224-1518   Fax: (651) 224-9753
E-mail: nsj@msusa.net
Web: www.msusa.net/nellie_stjo.html

Purpose To provide financial assistance to racial minority union members and their families who are interested in working on an undergraduate or graduate degree at a Minnesota state college or university.

Eligibility This program is open to students in 2-year, undergraduate, and graduate programs at a Minnesota state university, community college, or consolidated campus. Applicants must be a minority (Asian, American Indian, Alaska Native, Black/African American, Hispanic/Latino, Native Hawaiian, or Pacific Islander) union member or the child, grandchild, or spouse of a minority union member. They must submit a 2-page statement about their background, educational goals, career goals, and other activities that may impact the cause of human or civil rights. Awards may be reserved for women. Preference is given to Minnesota residents. A personal or telephone interview may be required.

Financial data Stipends range from $500 to $2,000.

Duration 1 year; may be renewed up to 3 additional years for student working on a bachelor's degree, 1 additional year for students working on a master's degree, or 1 additional year for students in a community or technical college program.

Number awarded 1 or more each year. If multiple awards are made, at least 1 recipient must be female.

Deadline March of each year.

[263]
NEW HORIZONS SCHOLARSHIPS

New Horizons Scholars Program
55 Second Street, 15th Floor
San Francisco, CA 94105-3491
Toll-free: (866) 3-HORIZON
Web: www.hsf.net

Purpose To provide financial assistance for college to Hispanic and African American high school seniors who are infected with Hepatitis C or who are dependents of someone with Hepatitis C.

Eligibility This program is open to high school seniors planning to enroll full time at a 4-year college or university in the following fall. Applicants must be of African American heritage or of Hispanic heritage (each parent half Hispanic or 1 parent fully Hispanic) and have a high school GPA of 3.0 or higher. Along with their application, they must submit 1) verification by a physician that they have Hepatitis C or are the dependent of a person with Hepatitis C; 2) transcripts; 3) a letter of recommendation; 4) documentation of financial need; and 5) a personal statement that addresses the following topics: heritage and family background, personal and academic achievements, academic plans and career goals, efforts toward making a difference in the community, and financial need.

Financial data The stipend is $2,500 per year.

Duration 4 years.

Additional information This program began in 2003 as the result of a partnership of the Thurgood Marshall Scholarship Fund and the Hispanic Scholarship Fund, with support from the Roche Foundation.

Number awarded 1 or more each year.

Deadline February of each year.

[264]
NEW YORK STATE MIGRANT STUDENT SCHOLARSHIP

Geneseo Migrant Center
27 Lackawanna Avenue
Mount Morris, NY 14510-1096
(585) 658-7960   Toll-free: (800) 245-5681
Fax: (585) 658-7969   E-mail: info@migrant.net
Web: www.migrant.net/sch_nys.htm

Purpose To provide financial assistance for college to migrant farmworker high school seniors from New York.

Eligibility This program is open to migrant farmworker students with a history of migration to and/or within New York state. Applicants must have senior status in high school and plans to attend a postsecondary institution or other advanced training. Along with their application, they must submit a statement of at least 250 words on their background and interest in higher education, at least 1 letter of recommendation, and a copy of their current Migrant Certificate of Eligibility (COE). Selection is based on demonstrated commitment to educational goals, participation in school and Migrant Education Outreach Program (MEOP) activities, participation in community and/or non-school activities, citizenship, evidence of high mobility (interstate or intrastate), record of overcoming unusual obstacles, and financial need.

Financial data The stipend is $500 or $250.

Duration 1 year.

Number awarded 1 at $500 or 2 at $250 each year.

Deadline April of each year.

[265]
NEWHOUSE SCHOLARSHIP PROGRAM

National Association of Hispanic Journalists
Attn: Scholarship Committee
1000 National Press Building
529 14th Street, N.W.
Washington, DC 20045-2001
(202) 662-7145   Toll-free: (888) 346-NAHJ
Fax: (202) 662-7144   E-mail: nahj@nahj.org
Web: www.nahj.org

Purpose To provide financial assistance and summer work experience to Hispanic American undergraduate students interested in preparing for careers in the media.

Eligibility This program is open to college juniors and seniors who are of Hispanic descent and interested in preparing for a career in English-language journalism as a reporter, editor, photographer, or graphic artist. Applicants must submit an official transcript; a 1-page resume with their educational background, work history, awards, internships, other scholarships, language proficiency, and any work done for their school newspaper, radio, and/or television station; samples of their work; 2 reference letters; a 500-word autobiography written as a news story; and documentation of financial need. Selection is based on commitment to the field of journalism, academic achievement, awareness of the Latino community, and financial need.

Financial data The stipend is $5,000 per year; the program also provides funding to attend the association's convention and an internship during the summer between the junior and senior year.

Duration 2 years.

Additional information This program, which began in 1994, is sponsored by the Newhouse Foundation and administered by the National Association of Hispanic Journalists (NAHJ) as part of its Rubén Salazar Scholarship Fund. The recipient participates in a summer internship at a Newhouse Newspaper.

Number awarded 2 each year.

Deadline January of each year.

[266]
NEWSROOM DIVERSITY SCHOLARSHIP

Society of Professional Journalists-Kansas Professional Chapter
c/o Lori O'Toole Buselt, Scholarship Chair
The Wichita Eagle
P.O. Box 820
Wichita, KS 67201-0820
(316) 268-6327   Fax: (316) 268-6627
E-mail: kansas@spj.org
Web: www.spj.org/kansas/scholarship.htm

Purpose To provide financial assistance to minority students at colleges and universities in Kansas who are interested in a career in journalism.

Eligibility This program is open to members of racial minority groups who are juniors and seniors at colleges and universities in Kansas. Sophomores may apply, designating the award for their junior year. Applicants do not have to be journalism or communication majors, but they must demonstrate a strong and sincere interest in print journalism, broadcast journalism, or photojournalism. They must have a GPA of 2.5 or higher and participate in outside journalism-related activities demonstrated by involvement in student or trade organizations and/or student or other news organizations or publications. Along with their application, they must submit 4 to 6 examples of their best work (clips or stories, copies of photographs, tapes or transcripts of broadcasts). Selection is based on the quality of work submitted, academic standing, references, and financial need.

Financial data The stipend is $1,000.

Duration 1 year.

Number awarded 1 each year.

Deadline March of each year.

[267]
NEXT GENERATION OF PUBLIC SERVANTS SCHOLARSHIP

Hispanic Scholarship Fund Institute
1001 Connecticut Avenue, N.W., Suite 632
Washington, DC 20036
(202) 296-0009   Fax: (202) 296-3633
E-mail: info@hsfi.org
Web: www.hsfi.org/scholarships/generation.asp

Purpose To provide financial assistance to Hispanic and other students majoring in designated business, engineering, social science, and science fields who are interested in employment with the U.S. Department of Energy (DOE).

Eligibility This program is open to U.S. citizens enrolled full time as sophomores with a GPA of 2.8 or higher. Applicants must be interested in preparing for a career with the DOE in an energy-related field. Eligible academic majors are in the fields of business (accounting, business administration, finance, and management), engineering (biomedical, chemical, civil, computer, electrical, environmental, industrial, materials, mechanical, metallurgical, nuclear, and petroleum), social science (economics, organizational psychology, political science, and sociology), and science (biological sciences, computer science, geology, information technology, mathematics, microbiology, and physics). They must be willing to participate in co-ops with the DOE. Along with their application, they must submit a 2-page essay on why a career in public service interests them, how their academic major connects with their stated DOE career goal, why the DOE should invest in them through this program, and how they believe the DOE will benefit from this investment. Selection is based on academic achievement, financial need, demonstrated commitment to public service, and interest in federal employment with the DOE.

Financial data The stipend is $3,000 per year.

Duration 1 year; may be renewed up to 2 additional years if the recipient maintains full-time enrollment and a GPA of 2.8 or higher.

Additional information This program, sponsored by DOE's Office of Economic Impact and Diversity, is administered by the Hispanic Scholarship Fund Institute as part of its effort to increase Hispanic participation in federal service.

Number awarded Varies each year.

Deadline February of each year.

[268]
NMJGSA SCHOLARSHIPS

National Minority Junior Golf Scholarship Association
Attn: Scholarship Committee
4950 East Thomas Road
Phoenix, AZ 85018
(602) 258-7851   Fax: (602) 258-3412
E-mail: sdean@nmjgsa.org
Web: www.nmjgsa.org/scholarships.html

Purpose To provide financial assistance to minority high school seniors and undergraduate students who excel at golf.

Eligibility This program is open to minority high school seniors and undergraduate students already enrolled in college. Applicants are asked to write a 500-word essay on this question: "One of the principal goals of education and golf is fostering ways for people to respect and get along with individuals who think, dress, look, and act differently. How might you make this goal a reality?" Selection is based on academic achievement; personal recommendations; participation in golf, school, and community activities; and financial need.

Financial data Stipends range from 1-time awards of $1,000 to 4-year awards of $6,000 per year. Funds are paid directly to the recipient's college.

Duration 1 year or longer.

Additional information This program was established in 1984. Support is provided by the Jackie Robinson Foundation, PGA of America, Anheuser-Busch, the Tiger Woods Foundation, and other cooperating organizations.

Number awarded Varies; generally 80 or more each year.

Deadline April of each year.

[269]
NNOA/BOOZ-ALLEN & HAMILTON SCHOLARSHIP

National Naval Officers Association-Washington, D.C.
    Chapter
Attn: Scholarship Program
9805 Fox Run Drive
Clinton, MD 20735-3087
(202) 874-4994   E-mail: willie.evans@occ.treas.gov
Web: www.dcnnoa.org

Purpose To provide financial assistance to minority high school seniors from the Washington, D.C. area who are interested in majoring in computer sciences in college.

Eligibility This program is open to minority seniors at high schools in the Washington, D.C. metropolitan area who plan to enroll full time in a computer science program at an accredited 2-year or 4-year college or university. Applicants must have a GPA of 3.0 or higher and be U.S. citizens or permanent residents. Selection is based on academic achievement, community involvement, interpersonal and leadership skills, creativity, drive, and maturity.

Financial data The stipend is $5,000 per year.

Duration 1 year; nonrenewable.

Additional information Recipients are not required to join or affiliate with the military in any way. This program is sponsored by Booz-Allen & Hamilton, and recipients have an option to work with the firm as a summer intern.

Number awarded 1 each year.

Deadline March of each year.

[270]
NORTH CAROLINA HISPANIC COLLEGE FUND

North Carolina Society of Hispanic Professionals
P.O. Box 1557
Apex, NC 27502-3557
(919) 654-4516   Fax: (919) 654-4524
E-mail: mailbox@theNCSHP.org
Web: www.theNCSHP.org/NCHCF/NCHCF.htm

Purpose To provide financial assistance for college to Hispanic students from North Carolina.

Eligibility This program is open to seniors and recent graduates from North Carolina high schools who are of Hispanic/Latino background. Applicants must be enrolled or planning to enroll at a community college or a 2- or 4-year college or university and be committed to public service and community development. They must have a high school GPA of 2.5 or higher. Along with their application, they must submit a 500-word essay on their Hispanic parentage and family background, personal and academic achievements, academic plans and career goals, and past and current efforts (as well as future plans) towards making a difference in their community. Semi-finalists are asked to have a personal interview. Preference is given to full-time students (although part-time students are encouraged to apply) and to foreign-born applicants and the native-born children of foreign-born parents. Previous involvement in a club or community organization is encouraged. Financial need is not considered in the selection process.

Financial data Stipends range from $500 to $2,500. Funds are paid directly to the college or university. Scholarships under $1,000 are paid in the fall semester. For scholarships over $1,000, half is paid in the fall and half in the spring. Funds are designated for tuition, room, and board.

Duration 1 year; may be renewed up to 3 additional years.

Number awarded Varies each year.

Deadline January of each year.

[271]
NORTHROP GRUMMAN/HENAAC SCHOLARS PROGRAM

Hispanic Engineer National Achievement Awards
   Conference
3900 Whiteside Street
Los Angeles, CA 90063
(323) 262-0997   Fax: (323) 262-0946
E-mail: info@henaac.org
Web: www.henaac.org

Purpose To provide financial assistance to Hispanic undergraduate students majoring in engineering and related fields.

Eligibility This program is open to Hispanic undergraduate students who are majoring in the following engineering fields: aerospace, chemical, civil, computer, electrical, industrial, manufacturing, marine, mechanical, ocean, or structural. Students majoring in computer science, information science, mathematics, naval architecture, and physics are also eligible. Applicants must have a GPA of 3.0 or higher. U.S. citizenship is required.

Financial data The stipend ranges from $1,000 to $5,000.

Duration 1 year.

Additional information This program is sponsored by Northrop Grumman as part of its effort to support the mission of the Hispanic Engineer National Achievement Awards Conference (HENAAC): to promote technical excellence and leadership in the Hispanic community.

Number awarded 5 each year.

Deadline April of each year.

[272]
NORTHWEST JOURNALISTS OF COLOR SCHOLARSHIP AWARDS

Northwest Journalists of Color
c/o Michael Ko
The Seattle Times
1120 John Street
Seattle, WA 98109
(206) 515-5653   E-mail: mko@aajaseattle.org
Web: www.aajaseattle.org

Purpose To provide financial assistance to minority students from Washington state who are interested in careers in journalism.

Eligibility These scholarships are open to minority (Asian American, African American, Native American, and Latino) students from Washington state who are planning a career in broadcast, photo, or print journalism. Applicants may be high school seniors or college undergraduates who are residents of Washington state, although they may attend college anywhere in the country. Along with their application, they must submit 1) a brief essay about themselves, including why they want to be a journalist, challenges they foresee, how they think they can contribute to the profession, and the influence their ethnic heritage might have on their perspective as a working journalist; 2) the kinds of experience they are seeking from this fellowship and why they are a good candidate for it; 3) up to 3 work samples; 4) reference letters; and 5) documentation of financial need.

Financial data Stipends range up to $1,000.

Duration 1 year; may be renewed.

Additional information This program, established in 1986, is sponsored by the Seattle chapters of the Asian American Journalists Association, the Native American Journalists Association, the National Association of Black Journalists, and the Latino Media Association. It includes the Walt and Milly Woodward Memorial Scholarship donated by the Western Washington Chapter of the Society of Professional Journalists. Other funding is provided by KING/5 Television, the *Seattle Post-Intelligencer,* and the *Seattle Times.*

Number awarded Varies each year; recently, 11 of these scholarships were awarded.

Deadline April of each year.

[273]
NSBE/SHPE/SWE MEMBERS SCHOLARSHIP

Morgan Stanley
c/o Joyce Arencibia, IT College Recruiting
750 Seventh Avenue, 30th Floor
New York, NY 10019
(212) 762-4000
E-mail: diversityrecruiting@morganstanley.com
Web: www.morganstanley.com

Purpose To provide financial assistance and work experience to members of the National Society of Black Engineers (NSBE), Society of Hispanic Professional Engineers (SHPE), and Society of Women Engineers (SWE) who are working on an undergraduate degree in computer science or engineering.

Eligibility This program is open to active members of NSBE, SHPE, and SWE who are enrolled in their sophomore or junior year of college (or the third or fourth year of a 5-year program). Applicants must be enrolled full time and have a GPA of 3.0 or higher. They must be willing to commit to a paid summer internship in the Morgan Stanley Information Technology Division. All majors and disciplines are eligible, but preference is given to students preparing for a career in computer science or engineering. Along with their application, they must submit 1-page essays on 1) why they are applying for this scholarship and why they should be selected as a recipient; 2) a technical project on which they worked, either through a university course or previous work experience, their role in the project, and how they contributed to the end result; and 3) a software, hardware, or new innovative application of existing technology that they would create if they could and the impact it would have. Financial need is not considered in the selection process.

Financial data Students who receive a scholarship as juniors (or fourth-year students in a 5-year program) receive $10,000 for their final year of college. Students who receive a scholarship as sophomores (or third-year students in a 5-year program) receive $5,000 for their junior year (or fourth year of a 5-year program).

Duration 1 year; may be renewed for the final year for students who receive a scholarship as sophomores (or third-year students in a 5-year program).

Additional information The program includes a paid summer internship in the Morgan Stanley Information Technology Division in the summer following the time of application.

Number awarded 1 or more each year.

Deadline February of each year.

[274]
NVIDIA CORPORATION/HENAAC SCHOLARS PROGRAM

Hispanic Engineer National Achievement Awards
   Conference
3900 Whiteside Street
Los Angeles, CA 90063
(323) 262-0997   Fax: (323) 262-0946
E-mail: info@henaac.org
Web: www.henaac.org/scholarships.htm

Purpose To provide financial assistance to Hispanic undergraduate students majoring in engineering and related fields.

Eligibility This program is open to Hispanic undergraduate students who are enrolled full time in computer science, engineering, material science, mathematics, or applied science. Applicants must have a GPA of 3.0 or higher. There is no citizenship requirement. Academic achievement and campus community activities are considered in the selection process.

Financial data Stipends range from $1,000 to $5,000.

Duration 1 year; recipients may reapply.

Additional information This program is sponsored by the NVIDIA Corporation as part of its effort to support the mission of the Hispanic Engineer National Achievement Awards Conference (HENAAC): to promote technical excellence and leadership in the Hispanic community.

Number awarded 1 or more each year.

Deadline April of each year.

[275]
OHIO NEWSPAPERS FOUNDATION MINORITY SCHOLARSHIPS

Ohio Newspapers Foundation
1335 Dublin Road, Suite 216-B
Columbus, OH 43215-7038
(614) 486-6677   Fax: (614) 486-4940
E-mail: kpouliot@ohionews.org
Web: www.ohionews.org/scholarships.html

Purpose To provide financial assistance for college to minority high school seniors in Ohio planning to prepare for a career in journalism.

Eligibility This program is open to high school seniors in Ohio who are members of minority groups (African American, Hispanic, Asian American, or American Indian) and planning to prepare for a career in newspaper journalism. Applicants must have a high school GPA of 2.5 or higher and demonstrate writing ability in an autobiography of 750 to 1,000 words that describes their academic and career interests, awards, extracurricular activities, and journalism-related activities.

Financial data The stipend is $1,500.

Duration 1 year; nonrenewable.

Additional information This program was established in 1990.

Number awarded 3 each year.

Deadline March of each year.

[276]
OHIO SPACE GRANT CONSORTIUM COMMUNITY COLLEGE SCHOLARSHIP

Ohio Space Grant Consortium
c/o Ohio Aerospace Institute
22800 Cedar Point Road
Cleveland, OH 44142
(440) 962-3032   Toll-free: (800) 828-OSGC
Fax: (440) 962-3057   E-mail: osgc@oai.org
Web: www.osgc.org/Scholarship.html

Purpose To provide financial assistance to minority and other students at selected community colleges in Ohio who are interested in continuing their studies at a 4-year university in the state that is a member of the Ohio Space Grant Consortium (OSGC).

Eligibility This program is open to U.S. citizens who are students at designated community colleges in Ohio, normally enrolled full time in their freshman year (although applications are accepted from part-time students demonstrating academic merit and from students at any stage of their college career). Applicants must be enrolled in a program that includes course work related to an understanding of or interest in technological fields supporting aerospace, e.g. associate degrees related to mathematics, science, and such advanced technology fields as engineering, computers, electronics, and industrial technology. They must also have a GPA of 3.0 or higher and plans to continue their education in a 4-year program at an OSGC-member university. Along with their application, they must submit college transcripts, 2 letters of recommendation, and a brief resume of their education, significant accomplishments, work experience, educational and professional goals, and any other relevant information. Women, underrepresented minorities, and persons with disabilities are particularly encouraged to apply.

Financial data The stipend is $1,000.

Duration 1 year; nonrenewable.

Additional information These scholarships are funded through the National Space Grant College and Fellowship Program administered by the National Aeronautics and Space Administration (NASA), with matching funds provided by the member colleges, the Ohio Aerospace Institute, and private industry. The participating institutions include Columbus State Community College, Cuyahoga Community College, Lorain County Community College, Owens Community College, Lakeland Community College, and Terra Community College. OSGC member institutions include the University of Akron, Case Western Reserve University, Cedarville University, Central State University, University of Cincinnati, Cleveland State University, University of Dayton, Marietta College (petroleum engineering), Miami University (manufacturing engineering), Ohio Northern University, Ohio State University, Ohio University, University of Toledo, Wilberforce University, Wright State University, and Youngstown State University.

Number awarded 1 or more each year.

[277]
OHIO SPACE GRANT CONSORTIUM JUNIOR SCHOLARSHIPS

Ohio Space Grant Consortium
c/o Ohio Aerospace Institute
22800 Cedar Point Road
Cleveland, OH 44142
(440) 962-3032   Toll-free: (800) 828-OSGC
Fax: (440) 962-3057   E-mail: osgc@oai.org
Web: www.osgc.org/Scholarship.html

Purpose To provide financial assistance to minority and other students in their junior year at selected universities in Ohio who wish to work on a bachelor's degree in an aerospace-related field.

Eligibility These scholarships are available to U.S. citizens who expect to complete within 2 years the requirements for a bachelor of science degree in an aerospace-related discipline (aeronautical engineering, aerospace engineering, astronomy, biology, chemical engineering, chemistry, civil engineering, computer engineering and sci-

ence, control engineering, electrical engineering, engineering mechanics, geography, geology, industrial engineering, manufacturing engineering, materials science and engineering, mathematics, mechanical engineering, petroleum engineering, physics, and systems engineering). Applicants must be attending 1 of the participating universities in Ohio. They must propose and initiate a research project on campus under the guidance of a faculty member. Women, underrepresented minorities, and physically challenged persons are particularly encouraged to apply. Selection is based on academic record, recommendations, and a personal statement of career goals, anticipated benefits from the Space Grant program, and plans for their research laboratory experience.

Financial data The stipend is $2,000.

Duration 1 year; recipients may apply for a senior scholarship if they maintain satisfactory academic performance and good progress on their research project.

Additional information These scholarships are funded through the National Space Grant College and Fellowship Program administered by the National Aeronautics and Space Administration (NASA), with matching funds provided by the member universities, the Ohio Aerospace Institute, and private industry. The participating institutions include the University of Akron, Case Western Reserve University, Cedarville University, Central State University, University of Cincinnati, Cleveland State University, University of Dayton, Marietta College (petroleum engineering), Miami University (manufacturing engineering), Ohio Northern University, Ohio State University, Ohio University, University of Toledo, Wilberforce University, Wright State University, and Youngstown State University.

Number awarded Varies each year; recently, 20 of these scholarships were awarded.

Deadline February of each year.

[278]
OREGON SPACE GRANT UNDERGRADUATE SCHOLARSHIP PROGRAM

Oregon NASA Space Grant Consortium
c/o Oregon State University
B092 Kerr Administration Building
Corvallis, OR 97331-2103
(541) 737-2414   Fax: (541) 737-9946
E-mail: spacegrant@oregonstate.edu
Web: www.oregonspacegrant.orst.edu

Purpose To provide financial assistance for study in space-related fields to minority and other undergraduate students at colleges and universities that are members of the Oregon Space Grant (OSG).

Eligibility This program is open to undergraduate students at member institutions who are enrolled full time in science and engineering fields related to the mission of the U.S. National Aeronautics and Space Administration (NASA). U.S. citizenship is required. Selection is based on scholastic achievement, career goals, a 500-word essay on a space-related topic, and 2 letters of recommendation. Applications are especially encouraged from women, underrepresented minorities, and people with disabilities.

Financial data The stipend is $1,000.

Duration 1 year.

Additional information Institutions that are members of OSG include Oregon State University, Portland State University, the University of Oregon, Southern Oregon University, Eastern Oregon University, and Oregon Institute of Technology. This program is funded by NASA.

Number awarded 10 each year.

Deadline November of each year.

[279]
ORNELAS ASSOCIATES MINORITY SCHOLARSHIP FUND

American Association of Advertising Agencies
Attn: Manager of Diversity Programs
405 Lexington Avenue, 18th Floor
New York, NY 10174-1801
(212) 682-2500   Toll-free: (800) 676-9333
Fax: (212) 682-8391   E-mail: tiffany@aaaa.org
Web: www.aaaa.org/diversity/foundation/funds.htm

Purpose To provide financial assistance to Latino students who are working on an undergraduate or graduate degree in advertising.

Eligibility This program is open to undergraduate and graduate students who are U.S. citizens of proven Latino heritage or at least 1 parent of Latino heritage. Applicants must have participated in the Multicultural Advertising Intern Program of the American Association of Advertising Agencies. Along with their application, they must submit an essay of 250 to 500 words on the topic: "As a Latino, I value ganas (passion), adelante (progress), Latino pride, and diversity by..." Selection is based on the essay, academic ability, and community involvement.

Financial data The stipend is $5,000.

Duration 1 year.

Additional information This program was established in 2001.

Number awarded 1 each year.

Deadline June of each year.

[280]
OSGC EDUCATION PROGRAM

Oklahoma NASA Space Grant Consortium
c/o University of Oklahoma
College of Geosciences
Ditmars House, Suite 5
1623 Cross Center Drive
Norman, Oklahoma 73069
(405) 325-6559   Fax: (405) 325-5537
E-mail: vduca@ou.edu
Web: 129.15.32.115/scholarships/index.html

Purpose To provide financial assistance to underrepresented minority and other students in Oklahoma who are enrolled in aerospace-related studies at the undergraduate and graduate level.

Eligibility This program is open to undergraduate and graduate students at member and affiliate institutions of the Oklahoma Space Grant Consortium (OSGC). U.S. citizenship is required. The OSGC is a component of the U.S. National Aeronautics and Space Administration (NASA) Space Grant program, which encourages participation by women, underrepresented minorities, and persons with disabilities.

Financial data Financing depends on the availability of funds.

Additional information Members of OSGC are Oklahoma State University, the University of Oklahoma, Cameron University, and Langston University. Write to the sponsor for information on the program at each participating university. This program is funded by NASA.

[281]
PACIFICARE LATINO HEALTH SCHOLARS PROGRAM

PacifiCare Foundation
3100 Lake Center Drive
P.O. Box 25186
Santa Ana, CA 92799
(714) 825-5233
Web: www.pacificare.com

Purpose To provide financial assistance to Latino high school seniors in designated states planning to major in a health care field in college.

Eligibility This program is open to seniors graduating from high schools in Arizona, California, Colorado, Nevada, Oklahoma, Oregon, Texas, and Washington. Applicants must have a GPA of 3.0 or higher, be fluent in Spanish, and have been accepted as a full-time student at a university, community college, or accredited technical college. Their proposed field of study must relate to health care, including (but not limited to) nursing, medical interpretation, health claims examiner, health information technology programs, pharmacy technician, public health, psychology, or pre-medical studies. Along with their application, they must submit a 2-page essay (in both English and Spanish) on their personal and academic accomplishments, community involvement, volunteer and leadership activities, academic plans, and the reason they want a career in the health care field.

Financial data The stipend is $2,000.

Duration 1 year.

Additional information This program was established in 2003.

Number awarded Approximately 50 each year.

Deadline June of each year.

[282]
PAGE EDUCATION FOUNDATION GRANTS

Page Education Foundation
P.O. Box 581254
Minneapolis, MN 55458-1254
(612) 332-0406   E-mail: info@page-ed.org
Web: www.page-ed.org

Purpose To provide funding for college to students of color in Minnesota.

Eligibility This program is open to students of color who are graduating from high school in Minnesota and planning to attend a postsecondary school in the state. Applicants must submit an essay of 400 to 500 words that deals with why they believe education is important, their plans for the future, and the service-to-children project they would like to complete in the coming school year. Selection is based on the essay, 3 letters of recommendation, and financial need.

Financial data Stipends range from $900 to $2,500 per year.

Duration 1 year; may be renewed up to 3 additional years.

Additional information This program was founded in 1988 by Alan Page, a former football player for the Minnesota Vikings. While attending college, the Page Scholars fulfill a service-to-children contract that brings them into contact with K-8 grade school students of color.

Number awarded Varies each year; recently, 570 Page Scholars were enrolled, of whom 61% were African American, 27% Asian American, 11% Chicano/Latino, and 1% American Indian.

Deadline April of each year.

[283]
PALH SCHOLARSHIPS

American Academy of Physician Assistants
Attn: Physician Assistants of Latino Heritage
950 North Washington Street
Alexandria, VA 22314-1552
Toll-free: (800) 596-7494   Fax: (703) 684-1924
E-mail: palh@aapa.org
Web: www.aapa.org/spec/PALH_Scholarship.html

Purpose To provide financial assistance to student members of the Physician Assistants for Latino Health (PALH) within the American Academy of Physician Assistants (AAPA).

Eligibility Applicants for these scholarships must be members of both the AAPA and its PALH caucus and enrolled in a physician assistant program. Their application must include a statement on their personal background, pertinent experiences working with underserved Latino communities, future goals and expectations upon completing their physician assistant program, and why they should be considered for a PALH scholarship. Financial need is not considered in the selection process.

Financial data The stipend is $500 per year.

Duration 1 year.

Number awarded 2 each year.

Deadline March of each year.

[284]
PDEF MICKEY WILLIAMS MINORITY STUDENT SCHOLARSHIP

Society of Nuclear Medicine
Attn: Committee on Awards
1850 Samuel Morse Drive
Reston, VA 20190-5316
(703) 708-9000, ext. 1255   Fax: (703) 708-9020
E-mail: grantinfo@snm.org
Web: www.snm.org

Purpose To provide financial support to minority students working on an associate or bachelor's degree in nuclear medicine technology.

Eligibility This program is open to students accepted or enrolled in a baccalaureate or associate degree program in nuclear medicine technology. Applicants must be members of a minority group: African American, Native American (including American Indian, Eskimo, Hawaiian, and Samoan), Hispanic American, Asian American, or Pacific Islander. They must have a cumulative GPA of 2.5 or higher and be able to demonstrate financial need. U.S. citizenship or permanent resident status is required.

Financial data The stipend is $5,000.

Duration 1 year; may be renewed for 1 additional year.

Additional information This program is supported by corporate sponsors of the Professional Development and Education Fund (PDEF) of the Society of Nuclear Medicine Technologist Section

Number awarded 1 each year.

Deadline October of each year.

[285]
PENNSYLVANIA SPACE GRANT CONSORTIUM SCHOLARSHIPS

Pennsylvania Space Grant Consortium
c/o Pennsylvania State University
2217 Earth-Engineering Sciences Building
University Park, PA 16802
(814) 863-7687   Fax: (814) 863-8286
E-mail: spacegrant@psu.edu
Web: www.psu.edu/spacegrant/highered/scholar.html

Purpose To provide financial assistance for space-related study to minority and other undergraduate students at universities affiliated with the Pennsylvania Space Grant Consortium.

Eligibility This program is open to full-time undergraduate students at participating universities. Applicants must be studying a field that does, or can, promote the understanding, assessment, and utilization of space, including aerospace, earth science, or space science. U.S. citizenship is required. Students from underrepresented groups (women, minorities, rural populations, and those with disabilities) are especially encouraged to apply.

Financial data The stipend is set by each participating university. At Pennsylvania State University, for instance, it is $4,000 per year.

Duration 1 year.

Additional information Participating institutions include Carnegie Mellon University, Clarion University, Pennsylvania State University, University of Pittsburgh, Susquehanna University, Lincoln University, Temple University, West Chester University, and Pennsylvania State University at Abington. At Pennsylvania State University, the award is designated as the Sylvia Stein Memorial Space Grant Scholarship. This program is sponsored by the U.S. National Aeronautics and Space Administration (NASA).

Number awarded Varies each year.

Deadline Each participating university sets its own deadline.

[286]
PFIZER/UNCF CORPORATE SCHOLARS PROGRAM

United Negro College Fund
Attn: Corporate Scholars Program
P.O. Box 1435
Alexandria, VA 22313-9998
Toll-free: (866) 671-7237   E-mail: internship@uncf.org
Web: www.uncf.org/internships/index.asp

Purpose To provide financial assistance and work experience to minority undergraduate and graduate students majoring in designated fields and interested in an internship at a Pfizer facility.

Eligibility This program is open to sophomores, juniors, graduate students, and first-year law students who are African American, Hispanic American, Asian/Pacific Islander American, or American Indian/Alaskan Native. Applicants must have a GPA of 3.0 or higher and be enrolled at an institution that is a member of the United Negro College Fund (UNCF) or at another targeted college or university. They must be working on 1) a bachelor's degree in animal science, business, chemistry (organic or analytical), human resources, logistics, microbiology, organizational development, operations management, pre-veterinary medicine, or supply chain management; 2) a master's degree in chemistry (organic or analytical), finance, human resources, or organizational development; or 3) a law degree. Eligibility is limited to U.S. citizens, permanent residents, asylees, refugees, and lawful temporary residents. Along with their application, they must submit a 1-page essay about themselves and their career goals, including information about their interest in Pfizer (the program's sponsor), their personal background, and any particular challenges they have faced.

Financial data The program provides an internship stipend of up to $5,000, housing accommodations near Pfizer Corporate facilities, and (based on successful internship performance) a $15,000 scholarship.

Duration 8 to 10 weeks for the internship; 1 year for the scholarship.

Additional information Opportunities for first-year law students include the summer internship only.

Number awarded Varies each year.

Deadline January of each year.

[287]
PHILLIP ARREOLA RETURNING STUDENT SCHOLARSHIPS

Hispanic Chamber of Commerce-Wisconsin
Attn: Scholarship Committee
816 West National Avenue
Milwaukee, WI 53204
(414) 643-6963   Fax: (414) 643-6994
E-mail: eagosto@hccw.org
Web: www.hccw.org

Purpose To provide financial assistance to Hispanic students at colleges and universities in Wisconsin.

Eligibility This program is open to Hispanic students currently enrolled full time at a college or university in Wisconsin or who have experienced at least a 1-year lapse in their undergraduate education. Applicants must be residents of Wisconsin, have a high school diploma or GED, and be U.S. citizens or permanent residents. Selection is based on academic achievement, participation in school activities, involvement in community activities, and financial need.

Financial data The stipend is $1,000.

Duration 1 year; nonrenewable.

Number awarded Varies each year; recently, 2 of these scholarships were awarded.

Deadline March of each year.

[288]
PHILLIP ARREOLA SCHOLARSHIPS

Hispanic Chamber of Commerce-Wisconsin
Attn: Scholarship Committee
816 West National Avenue
Milwaukee, WI 53204
(414) 643-6963   Fax: (414) 643-6994
E-mail: eagosto@hccw.org
Web: www.hccw.org

Purpose To provide financial assistance for college to Hispanic high school seniors in Wisconsin.

Eligibility This program is open to Hispanic students graduating from high school in Wisconsin and planning to attend an accredited college or university in the state. Applicants must be residents of Wisconsin; have a history of academic achievement, participation in school activities, and involvement in community activities; be able to demonstrate financial need; and be U.S. citizens or permanent residents.

Financial data The stipend is $2,500 per year.

Duration 4 years, provided the recipient remains enrolled full time with a GPA of 2.5 or higher.

Additional information Recipients are required to volunteer for 20 hours of community service annually.

Number awarded Varies each year; recently, 3 of these scholarships were awarded.

Deadline March of each year.

[289]
PIPELINE SCHOLARSHIPS

Society of Mexican American Engineers and Scientists
Attn: Scholarships
711 West Bay Area Boulevard, Suite 206
Webster, TX 77598-3677
(281) 557-3677   Fax: (281) 557-3757
E-mail: scholarships@maes-natl.org
Web: www.maes-natl.org

Purpose To provide financial assistance to undergraduate and graduate student members of the Society of Mexican American Engineers and Scientists (MAES).

Eligibility This program is open to MAES student members who are full-time undergraduate or graduate students at a college or university in the United States. Community college students must be enrolled in majors that can transfer to a 4-year institution offering a baccalaureate degree. All applicants must be majoring in a field of science or engineering. U.S. citizenship or permanent resident status is required. Selection is based on financial need; academic achievement; personal qualities, strengths, and leadership abilities; and timeliness and completeness of the application.

Financial data The stipend is $4,000.

Duration 1 year.

Additional information Recipients must attend the MAES International Symposium's Medalla de Oro Banquet in October.

Number awarded 1 or more each year.

Deadline October of each year.

[290]
PLAN COLLEGE SCHOLARSHIPS

Professional Latino Association Northwest
c/o Elena Guevara
Box 355845
Seattle, WA 98195
(206) 616-1085
Web: ourseattle.com/plan/sch.php

Purpose To provide financial assistance to Latino residents of Washington who are attending college.

Eligibility This program is open to residents of Washington who are enrolled full time in a 2- or 4-year undergraduate college or university with a GPA of 2.75 or higher. Applicants must be of Latino or Hispanic descent and able to demonstrate financial need. Along with their application, they must submit a letter of recommendation (from a faculty member, adviser, academic personnel, or community leader), a copy of their college transcript, and an essay that describes their personal and educational background, academic and career goals, involvement in school and/or community organizations, financial need, and how their career will enhance their community.

Financial data A stipend is awarded (amount not specified).

Duration 1 year.

Number awarded Varies each year; recently, the Professional Latino Association Northwest (PLAN) awarded a total of $25,000 in scholarships.

Deadline March of each year.

[291]
PLAN HIGH SCHOOL SCHOLARSHIPS

Professional Latino Association Northwest
c/o Maria M. Ivarra
2600 S.W. Thistle Street
Seattle, WA 98126
(206) 252-8603
Web: ourseattle.com/plan/sch.php

Purpose To provide financial assistance for college to Latino high school seniors in Washington.

Eligibility This program is open to seniors graduating from high schools in Washington who are of Latino or Hispanic descent. Applicants must be planning to attend an accredited undergraduate college, university, or vocational institute. They must be able to demonstrate financial need. Along with their application, they must submit 2 letters of recommendation (from a teacher, counselor, or community leader): a copy of their high school transcript: and answers to 3 questions on their school and community activities, honors and awards, and unusual or serious economic hardships.

Financial data A stipend is awarded (amount not specified).

Duration 1 year.

Number awarded Varies each year; recently, the Professional Latino Association Northwest (PLAN) awarded a total of $25,000 in scholarships.

Deadline March of each year.

[292]
PLANNING & THE BLACK COMMUNITY DIVISION SCHOLARSHIP

American Planning Association
Attn: Member Services Department
122 South Michigan Avenue, Suite 1600
Chicago, IL 60603-6107
(312) 431-9100   Fax: (312) 431-9985
E-mail: pbcd@pbcd.freeservers.com
Web: www.pbcdplanning.freeservers.com

Purpose To provide financial assistance to underrepresented minority undergraduate students interested in majoring in planning or a related field.

Eligibility This program is open to African American, Hispanic, and Native American undergraduate students in their second, third, or fourth year of study. Applicants must be majoring in planning or a related field (e.g., community development, environmental sciences, public administration, transportation, or urban studies). They must submit a 2- to 5-page personal and background statement describing how their education will be applied to career goals and why they chose planning or a related field as a career. U.S. citizenship is required. Selection is based on academic ability, financial need, and commitment to the profession.

Financial data The stipend is $2,500.

Duration 1 year.

Number awarded 1 each year.

Deadline May of each year.

[293]
P.O. PISTILLI SCHOLARSHIPS

Design Automation Conference
c/o Cherrice Traver
Union College
ECE Department
Schenectady, NY 12308
(518) 388-6326   Fax: (518) 388-6789
E-mail: traverc@union.edu
Web: doc.union.edu/acsee.html

Purpose To provide financial assistance to female, minority, or disabled high school seniors who are interested in preparing for a career in computer science or electrical engineering.

Eligibility Eligible to apply are "underrepresented" high school seniors: women, African Americans, Hispanic Americans, Native Americans, and persons with disabilities. Applicants must be interested in preparing for a career in electrical engineering, computer engineering, or computer science. They must have at least a 3.0 GPA, have demonstrated high achievements in math and science courses, and be able to demonstrate significant financial need. U.S. citizenship is not required, but applicants must be U.S. residents when they apply and must plan to attend an accredited U.S. college or university. They must submit a completed application form, 3 letters of recommendation, official transcripts, ACT/SAT and/or PSAT scores, a personal statement outlining future goals, a copy of their latest income tax return, and a copy of the FAFSA form they submitted.

Financial data Stipends are $4,000 per year. Awards are paid each year in 2 equal installments.

Duration 1 year; renewable for up to 4 additional years.

Additional information This program is funded by the Design Automation Conference and the IEEE Circuits and System Society. It is directed by the Association for Computing Machinery's Special Interest Group on Design Automation.

Number awarded 2 to 7 each year.

Deadline January of each year.

[294]
PORTLAND PRESS HERALD/MAINE SUNDAY TELEGRAM SCHOLARSHIP FUND

Maine Community Foundation
Attn: Program Director
245 Main Street
Ellsworth, ME 04605
(207) 667-9735   Toll-free: (877) 700-6800
Fax: (207) 667-0447   E-mail: info@mainecf.org
Web: www.mainecf.org/scholar.html

Purpose To provide financial assistance to students of color who are interested in studying journalism at a college or university in Maine.

Eligibility This program is open to students of color from anywhere in the United States who are interested in majoring in journalism, media studies, or related majors. First priority is given to students at the University of Southern Maine, but if no qualifying candidates apply from that school, students attending other 4-year postsecondary educational institutions in Maine are considered. Preference is given to applicants entering or currently enrolled as full-time students preparing for a career in print journalism. Selection is based on academic potential, financial need, and a demonstrated interest in and aptitude for print journalism.

Financial data A stipend is paid (amount not specified).

Duration 1 year; may be renewed.

Additional information This program was established in 2000.

Number awarded 1 or more each year.

Deadline May of each year.

[295]
PRIVATE COLLEGES & UNIVERSITIES MAGAZINE MULTICULTURAL SCHOLARSHIP

Private Colleges & Universities, Inc.
Attn: *PC&U* Multicultural Edition Scholarship Program
2 LAN Drive, Suite 100
P.O. Box 349
Westford, MA 01886
(978) 692-5092
E-mail: mc.scholar@privatecolleges.com
Web: www.privatecolleges.com

Purpose To provide financial assistance to high school seniors and graduates of color who are planning to enroll as a freshman in a private college or university.

Eligibility All students of color who are currently residents of the United States or its territories and who plan to enroll in a baccalaureate degree program at a participating private college or university (for a list, write to the sponsor) are eligible. Applicants must submit a 1,000-word statement about their community service activities, a high school transcript, and a recommendation by someone in their community (not a family member). Selection is based on academic

merit (transcripts, class rank, and GPA) and on service to the community.

Financial data The stipend is $2,000.

Duration 1 year; nonrenewable.

Number awarded 5 each year.

Deadline December of each year.

[296]
PROCTER & GAMBLE ORAL CARE–HDA FOUNDATION SCHOLARSHIPS

Hispanic Dental Association
Attn: HDA Foundation
188 West Randolph Street, Suite 415
Chicago, IL 60601
(312) 577-4013   Toll-free: (800) 852-7921
Fax: (312) 577-0052
E-mail: HispanicDental@hdassoc.org
Web: www.hdassoc.org

Purpose To provide financial assistance to Hispanic students interested in preparing for a career in a dental profession.

Eligibility This program is open to Hispanics who are entering as first-year students into an accredited dental, dental hygiene, dental assisting, or dental technician program. Applicants must have a GPA of 3.0 or higher. Along with their application, they must submit an essay on their career goals. Selection is based on scholastic achievement, community service, leadership skill, and commitment to improving health in the Hispanic community.

Financial data Stipends are $1,000 or $500.

Duration 1 year.

Additional information This program, which began in 1994, is sponsored by Procter & Gamble Company.

Number awarded Numerous scholarships are awarded each year.

Deadline June of each year for dental students; July of each year for hygiene, assisting, and laboratory technician students.

[297]
PROJECT SEED SCHOLARSHIPS

American Chemical Society
Attn: Education Division
1155 16th Street, N.W.
Washington, DC 20036
(202) 872-4380   Toll-free: (800) 227-5558, ext. 4380
E-mail: r_rasheed@acs.org
Web: www.chemistry.org/education/SEED.html

Purpose To provide financial assistance for college to high school students who participated in the American Chemical Society's Project SEED: Summer Education Experience for the Disadvantaged.

Eligibility Applicants for Project SEED must have completed the junior or senior year in high school, live within commuting distance of a sponsoring institution, have completed a course in high school chemistry, and come from an economically disadvantaged family. The standards for economic disadvantage follow federal poverty guidelines for family size, but the maximum family income is $32,000 except in cases where other factors are present that may deter a student from considering a career in science; family income may be up to $44,000 if the student is a member of an ethnic group underrepresented in the sciences (African American, Hispanic, American Indian), if the parents have not attended college, or if the family is single-parent or very large. Participants in the Project SEED program are eligible to apply for these scholarships during their senior year in high school if they plan to major in college in a chemical science or engineering field, such as chemistry, chemical engineering, biochemistry, materials science, or another closely-related field.

Financial data Stipends up to $5,000 per year are available.

Duration 1 year; nonrenewable.

Number awarded Varies each year; recently, 35 of these scholarships were awarded.

Deadline February of each year.

[298]
PUBLIC RELATIONS STUDENT SOCIETY OF AMERICA MULTICULTURAL AFFAIRS SCHOLARSHIPS

Public Relations Student Society of America
Attn: Director of Education
33 Irving Place, Third Floor
New York, NY 10003-2376
(212) 460-1474   Fax: (212) 995-0757
E-mail: prssa@prsa.org
Web: www.prssa.org

Purpose To provide financial assistance to minority college students who are interested in preparing for a career in public relations.

Eligibility This program is open to minority (African American/Black, Hispanic/Latino, Asian, Native American, Alaskan Native, or Pacific Islander) students who are at least juniors at an accredited 4-year college or university. Applicants must be attending full time, be able to demonstrate financial need, and have earned a GPA of 3.0 or higher. Membership in the Public Relations Student Society of America is preferred but not required. A major or minor in public relations is preferred; students who attend a school that does not offer a public relations degree or program must be enrolled in a communications degree program (e.g., journalism, mass communications).

Financial data The stipend is $1,500.

Duration 1 year.

Additional information This program was established in 1989.

Number awarded 2 each year.

Deadline April of each year.

[299]
PWC MINORITY SCHOLARS PROGRAM

PricewaterhouseCoopers LLP
Attn: Office of Diversity & WorkLife Quality
1177 Avenue of the Americas
New York, NY 10036
(646) 471-4000   Fax: (646) 471-3188
Web: www.pwcglobal.com

Purpose To provide financial assistance to underrepresented minority undergraduate students interested in preparing for a career in public accounting.

Eligibility This program is open to African American, Native American, and Hispanic American students entering their sophomore or junior year of college. Applicants must have a GPA of 3.3 or higher, be able to demonstrate interpersonal skills and leadership ability, and intend to prepare for a career in public accounting (audit, tax, or forensic accounting). They must be attending 1 of the 31 colleges and universities that are part of the PricewaterhouseCoopers (PwC) Priority School Network and must be legally authorized to work in the United States. Finalists are interviewed in person by a PwC partner, manager or recruiter.

Financial data The stipend is $3,000 per year.

Duration 1 year; may be renewed if the recipient maintains a GPA of 3.3 or higher.

Additional information Recipients also participate in the annual Minorities in Business Leadership Conference (held in New York City), are considered for an internship position with PwC, and engage in a mentoring program. This program began in 1990.

Number awarded 60 each year.

Deadline January of each year.

[300]
RACIAL ETHNIC EDUCATIONAL SCHOLARSHIPS

Synod of the Trinity
Attn: Scholarships
3040 Market Street
Camp Hill, PA 17011-4599
(717) 737-0421, ext. 232
Toll-free: (800) 242-0534, ext. 232
Fax: (717) 737-8211   E-mail: Pnash@syntrinity.org
Web: www.syntrinity.org

Purpose To provide financial assistance for college to ethnic minority students in Pennsylvania, West Virginia, and designated counties in Ohio.

Eligibility This program is open to members of a racial minority group (African American, Asian, Hispanic, Latino, Middle Eastern, or Native American) who are attending or planning to attend an accredited college or vocational school as a full-time student. Applicants may be of any religious denomination, but they must be residents of the Presbyterian Church (USA) Synod of the Trinity, which covers all of Pennsylvania; West Virginia except for the counties of Berkeley, Grant, Hampshire, Hardy, Jefferson, Mineral, Morgan, and Pendleton; and the Ohio counties of Belmont, Harrison, Jefferson, Monroe, and the southern sector of Columbiana. They must be able to demonstrate financial need and U.S. citizenship or permanent resident status.

Financial data Awards range from $100 to $1,000 per year, depending on the need of the recipient.

Duration 1 year; may be renewed up to 3 additional years, provided that the recipient maintains a GPA of 1.75 or higher for the second year and 2.0 or higher for the third and fourth years.

Number awarded Varies each year.

Deadline April of each year.

[301]
RALPH BUNCHE SUMMER INSTITUTE

American Political Science Association
Attn: Ralph Bunch Summer Institute
1527 New Hampshire Avenue, N.W.
Washington, DC 20036-1206
(202) 483-2512   Fax: (202) 483-2657
E-mail: minority@apsanet.org
Web: www.apsanet.org/section_397.cfm

Purpose To introduce underrepresented minority undergraduate students to the world of graduate study and to encourage their eventual application to a Ph.D. program in political science.

Eligibility Applications are invited from African American, Latino(a), and Native American college students completing their junior year. They must be interested in attending graduate school and working on a degree in a field related to political science. U.S. citizenship is required.

Financial data Participants receive a stipend of $200 per week plus full support of tuition, transportation, room, board, books, and instructional materials.

Duration 5 weeks during the summer.

Additional information The institute includes 2 transferable credit courses (1 in quantitative analysis and the other on race and American politics). In addition, guest lecturers and recruiters from Ph.D. programs visit the students. Classes are held on the campus of Duke University. Most students who attend the institute excel in their senior year and go on to graduate school, many with full graduate fellowships and teaching assistantships.

Number awarded 20 each year.

Deadline February of each year.

[302]
RAYMOND H. TROTT SCHOLARSHIP FOR BANKING

Rhode Island Foundation
Attn: Scholarship Coordinator
One Union Station
Providence, RI 02903
(401) 274-4564   Fax: (401) 751-7983
E-mail: libbym@rifoundation.org
Web: www.rifoundation.org

Purpose To provide financial assistance to Rhode Island undergraduates of color interested in preparing for a career in banking.

Eligibility This program is open to minority residents of Rhode Island who are entering their senior year in college. Applicants must plan to prepare for a career in banking and be able to demonstrate financial need. Along with their application, they must submit an essay (up to 300 words) on the impact they would like to have on the banking industry.

Financial data The stipend is $1,000.

Duration 1 year; nonrenewable.

Additional information This program was established in 1980.

Number awarded 1 each year.

Deadline June of each year.

[303]
RCA ETHNIC SCHOLARSHIP FUND

Reformed Church in America
Attn: Policy, Planning, and Administration Services
475 Riverside Drive, Room 1814
New York, NY 10115
(212) 870-3243   Toll-free: (800) 722-9977, ext. 3243
Fax: (212) 870-2499   E-mail: kbradsell@rca.org
Web: www.rca.org/aboutus/councils/scholarships.php

Purpose To provide assistance to minority student members of the Reformed Church in America (RCA) who are interested in working on an undergraduate degree.

Eligibility Applicants must be a member of a minority group (American Indian, African American, Hispanic, or Pacific or Asian American), be admitted to a college or other institution of higher learning, and be a member of an RCA congregation or be admitted to an RCA college. Priority is given to applicants who will enter colleges or universities and students enrolled in occupational training programs. Selection is based primarily on financial need.

Financial data The stipend depends on the need of the recipient, but is at least $500.

Duration 1 academic year; may be renewed until completion of an academic program.

Number awarded Several each year.

Deadline April of each year.

[304]
RDW GROUP, INC. MINORITY SCHOLARSHIP FOR COMMUNICATIONS

Rhode Island Foundation
Attn: Scholarship Coordinator
One Union Station
Providence, RI 02903
(401) 274-4564   Fax: (401) 751-7983
E-mail: libbym@rifoundation.org
Web: www.rifoundation.org

Purpose To provide financial assistance to Rhode Island students of color interested in preparing for a career in communications.

Eligibility This program is open to minority undergraduate and graduate students who are Rhode Island residents. Applicants must intend to major in communications (including computer graphics, art, cinematography, or other fields that would prepare them for a career in advertising). They must be able to demonstrate financial need and a commitment to a career in communications. Along with their application, they must submit an essay (up to 300 words) on the impact they would like to have on the communications field.

Financial data The stipend is $2,000.

Duration 1 year; nonrenewable.

Additional information This program is sponsored by the RDW Group, Inc.

Number awarded 1 each year.

Deadline April of each year.

[305]
RENE MATOS SCHOLARSHIP

National Hispanic Coalition of Federal Aviation
  Employees
Attn: Scholarship Selection Committee
P.O. Box 735
Pomona, NJ 08240
(609) 485-6910   E-mail: president@nhcfae.org
Web: www.nhcfae.com/scholarship.htm

Purpose To provide financial assistance to minority and women students who are working on an undergraduate or graduate degree.

Eligibility This program is open to minority and women students who are accepted to or attending an accredited college, university, or vocational/trade school. Applicants may be graduating high school seniors, current undergraduates, or graduate students. Selection is based on academic achievement, community involvement, financial need, honors and awards, leadership, personal qualities and strengths, and student activities.

Financial data A stipend is awarded (amount not specified).

Duration 1 year; may be renewed.

Additional information The National Hispanic Coalition of Federal Aviation Employees, established in 1978, is a nonprofit organization comprised mainly of Hispanics who are employed at the Federal Aviation Administration. Requests for applications must be accompanied by a self-addressed stamped envelope. Phone calls and faxed applications are not accepted.

Number awarded 1 or more each year.

Deadline April of each year.

[306]
RICHARD B. FISHER SCHOLARSHIP

Morgan Stanley
c/o Joyce Arencibia, IT College Recruiting
750 Seventh Avenue, 30th Floor
New York, NY 10019
(212) 762-4000
E-mail: diversityrecruiting@morganstanley.com
Web: www.morganstanley.com

Purpose To provide financial assistance and work experience to members of minority groups who are preparing for a career in technology within the financial services industry.

Eligibility This program is open to members of minority groups who are enrolled in their sophomore or junior year of college (or the third or fourth year of a 5-year program). Applicants must be enrolled full time and have a GPA of 3.0 or higher. They must be willing to commit to a paid summer internship in the Morgan Stanley Information Technology Division. All majors and disciplines are eligible, but preference is given to students preparing for a career in technology within the financial services industry. Along with their application, they must submit 1-page essays on 1) why they are applying for this scholarship and why they should be selected as a recipient; 2) a technical project on which they worked, either through a university course or previous work experience, their role in the project, and how they contributed to the end result; and 3) a software, hardware, or new innovative application of existing technology that they

would create if they could and the impact it would have. Financial need is not considered in the selection process.

Financial data The stipend is $5,000.

Duration 1 year.

Additional information The program includes a paid summer internship in the Morgan Stanley Information Technology Division in the summer following the time of application.

Number awarded 1 or more each year.

Deadline February of each year.

[307]
RICHARD S. SMITH SCHOLARSHIP

United Methodist Church
Attn: Division on Ministries with Young People
P.O. Box 340003
Nashville, TN 37203-0003
(615) 340-7184   Toll-free: (877) 899-2780, ext. 7184
Fax: (615) 340-1764   E-mail: umyouthorg@gbod.org
Web: www.umyouth.org/scholarships.html

Purpose To provide financial assistance to minority high school seniors who wish to prepare for a Methodist church-related career.

Eligibility This program is open to graduating high school seniors who are members of racial/ethnic minority groups and have been active members of a United Methodist church for at least 1 year. Applicants must have been admitted to an accredited college or university to prepare for a church-related career. They must have maintained at least a "C" average throughout high school and be able to demonstrate financial need. Along with their application, they must submit brief essays on their participation in church projects and activities, a leadership experience, the role their faith plays in their life, the church-related vocation to which God is calling them, and their extracurricular interests and activities. U.S. citizenship or permanent resident status is required.

Financial data The stipend is $1,000.

Duration 1 year; nonrenewable.

Additional information This scholarship was first awarded in 1997. Recipients must enroll full time in their first year of undergraduate study.

Number awarded 2 each year.

Deadline May of each year.

[308]
ROCKWELL AUTOMATION SCHOLARSHIPS

Society of Women Engineers
230 East Ohio Street, Suite 400
Chicago, IL 60611-3265
(312) 596-5223   Fax: (312) 644-8557
E-mail: hq@swe.org
Web: www.societyofwomenengineers.org

Purpose To provide financial assistance to upper-division women (particularly minority women) majoring in computer science or designated engineering specialties.

Eligibility This program is open to women who are entering their junior year at an ABET-accredited college or university. Applicants must be majoring in computer science or computer, electrical, industrial, mechanical, or software engineering and have at GPA of 3.5 or higher. Along with their application, they must submit a 1-page essay on why they want to be an engineer, how they believe they will make a difference as an engineer, and what influenced them to study engineering. Selection is based on merit and leadership potential. Preference is given to members of underrepresented minority groups.

Financial data The stipend is $3,000.

Duration 1 year.

Additional information This program, established in 1991, is supported by Rockwell Automation, Inc.

Number awarded 2 each year.

Deadline January of each year.

[309]
RONALD H. BROWN MEMORIAL SCHOLARSHIP

Travel Industry Association of America
Attn: TIA Foundation
1100 New York Avenue, N.W., Suite 450
Washington, DC 20005-3934
(202) 408-8422   Fax: (202) 408-1255
Web: www.tia.org

Purpose To provide financial assistance to minority undergraduate students interested in studying travel and tourism.

Eligibility This program is open to minorities who are interested in working on an undergraduate degree in the travel and tourism field. Candidates must first be nominated by a department head at a 4-year college or university that has a travel and tourism program. Nominees are then contacted by the foundation and invited to complete an application, including an essay on what segment of the tourism industry interests them and why.

Financial data The stipend is $3,000 per year.

Duration 1 year.

Number awarded 1 each year.

[310]
ROSEWOOD FAMILY SCHOLARSHIP FUND

Florida Department of Education
Attn: Office of Student Financial Assistance
1940 North Monroe Street, Suite 70
Tallahassee, FL 32303-4759
(850) 410-5200   Toll-free: (888) 827-2004
Fax: (850) 487-1809   E-mail: osfa@fldoe.org
Web: www.FloridaStudentFinancialAid.org

Purpose To provide financial assistance for undergraduate education to needy minority students who wish to study in Florida.

Eligibility This program is open to residents of any state who wish to attend state universities, public community colleges, or public postsecondary vocational/technical schools in Florida. Applicants must be a minority, defined as Black but not of Hispanic origin, Asian, Pacific Islander, Hispanic, American Indian, or Alaskan Native. Preference is given to descendants of African American Rosewood families (whose members were killed by a mob in January 1923). Other minority undergraduate students are considered if funds remain available after awarding Rosewood descendants. Financial need must be demonstrated.

Financial data Awards cover the actual costs of tuition and fees, up to $4,000 per year.

Duration 1 year; may be renewed up to 3 additional years provided the student maintains full-time enrollment and a GPA of 2.0 or higher.

Number awarded 25 each year.

Deadline March of each year.

[311]
ROYCE OSBORN MINORITY STUDENT SCHOLARSHIPS

American Society of Radiologic Technologists
Attn: ASRT Education and Research Foundation
15000 Central Avenue, S.E.
Albuquerque, NM 87123-3917
(505) 298-4500   Toll-free: (800) 444-2778, ext. 2541
Fax: (505) 298-5063   E-mail: foundation@asrt.org
Web: www.asrt.org

Purpose To provide financial assistance to minority students enrolled in entry-level radiologic sciences programs.

Eligibility This program is open to African Americans, Native Americans (including American Indians, Eskimos, Hawaiians, and Samoans), Hispanic Americans, Asian Americans, and Pacific Islanders who are enrolled in an entry-level radiologic sciences program. Applicants must have a GPA in radiologic sciences core courses of 3.0 or higher and be able to demonstrate financial need. They may not have a previous degree or certificate in the radiologic sciences. Along with their application, they must submit an essay of 450 to 500 words on their reason for entering the radiologic sciences, career goals, and financial need. Only U.S. citizens, nationals, and permanent residents are eligible.

Financial data The stipend is $4,000.

Duration 1 year; may be renewed for 1 additional year.

Number awarded 5 each year.

Deadline January of each year.

[312]
SALLIE MAE FUND FIRST IN MY FAMILY SCHOLARSHIP PROGRAM

Hispanic College Fund
Attn: National Director
1717 Pennsylvania Avenue, N.W., Suite 460
Washington, D.C. 20006
(202) 296-5400   Toll-free: (800) 644-4223
Fax: (202) 296-3774
E-mail: hispaniccollegefund@earthlink.net
Web: www.hispanicfund.org

Purpose To provide financial assistance to Hispanic American undergraduate students who are the first in their family to attend college and are majoring in business, computer science, or engineering.

Eligibility This program is open to U.S. citizens of Hispanic background (at least 1 grandparent must be 100% Hispanic) who are entering their freshman, sophomore, junior, or senior year of college and are the first member of their family to attend college. Applicants must be working on a bachelor's degree in business, computer science, engineering, or a business-related major and have a cumulative GPA of 3.0 or higher. They must be applying to or enrolled in a college or university in the 50 states or Puerto Rico as a full-time student. Financial need is considered in the selection process.

Financial data Stipends range from $1,000 to $5,000, depending on the need of the recipient. Funds are paid directly to the recipient's college or university to help cover tuition and fees.

Duration 1 year; recipients may reapply.

Additional information This program is sponsored by the Sallie Mae Community Foundation for the National Capital Region and the Sallie Mae Fund. All applications must be submitted online; no paper applications are available.

Number awarded Varies each year; recently, 155 of these scholarships were awarded.

Deadline April of each year.

[313]
SCHOLARSHIPS FOR DEPENDENTS OF ICIA MEMBERS

International Communications Industries Association, Inc.
Attn: Director of Strategic Initiatives
11242 Waples Mill Road, Suite 200
Fairfax, VA 22030
(703) 273-7200   Toll-free: (800) 659-7469
Fax: (703) 278-8082   E-mail: dwilbert@infocomm.org
Web: www.infocomm.org/Foundation/Scholarships

Purpose To provide financial assistance for college to dependents of minority and other members of the International Communications Industries Association (ICIA) interested in preparing for a career in the audiovisual industry.

Eligibility This program is open to graduating high school seniors and current college students who are the children, stepchildren, and spouses of employees at ICIA member companies. Applicants must have a GPA of 2.75 or higher and be majoring or planning to major in audio, visual, audiovisual, electronics, telecommunications, technical theater, data networking, software development, or information technology. Students in other programs, such as journalism, may be eligible if they can demonstrate a relationship to career goals in the audiovisual industry. Along with their application, they must submit 1) an essay of 150 to 200 words on the career path they see themselves pursuing in the next 5 years and why, and 2) an essay of 250 to 300 words on the experience or person that most influenced them in selecting the audiovisual industry as their career of choice. Minority and women candidates are especially encouraged to apply. Selection is based on the essays, presentation of the application, GPA, work experience, and letters of recommendation.

Financial data The stipend is $1,500.

Duration 1 year.

Number awarded Varies each year; recently, 3 of these scholarships were awarded.

Deadline April of each year.

[314]
SCHOLARSHIPS FOR MINORITY ACCOUNTING STUDENTS

American Institute of Certified Public Accountants
Attn: Academic and Career Development Division
1211 Avenue of the Americas
New York, NY 10036-8775
(212) 596-6223   Fax: (212) 596-6292
E-mail: educat@aicpa.org
Web: www.aicpa.org

Purpose To provide financial assistance to underrepresented minorities interested in studying accounting at the undergraduate or graduate school level.

Eligibility Undergraduate applicants must be minority students who are enrolled full time, have completed at least 30 semester hours of college work (including at least 6 semester hours in accounting), be majoring in accounting with an overall GPA of 3.3 or higher, and be U.S. citizens or permanent residents. Minority students who are interested in a graduate degree must be 1) in the final year of a 5-year accounting program; 2) an undergraduate accounting major currently accepted or enrolled in a master's-level accounting, business administration, finance, or taxation program; or 3) any undergraduate major currently accepted in a master's-level accounting program. Selection is based primarily on merit (academic and personal achievement); financial need is evaluated as a secondary criteria. For purposes of this program, the American Institute of Certified Public Accountants (AICPA) considers minority students to be those of Black, Native American/Alaskan Native, Pacific Island, or Hispanic ethnic origin.

Financial data The maximum stipend is $5,000 per year.

Duration 1 year; may be renewed, if recipients are making satisfactory progress toward graduation.

Additional information These scholarships are granted by the institute's Minority Educational Initiatives Committee.

Number awarded Varies each year; recently, 157 students received funding through this program.

Deadline May of each year.

[315]
SCIENCE TEACHER PREPARATION PROGRAM

Alabama Alliance for Science, Engineering, Mathematics, and Science Education
Attn: Project Director
University of Alabama at Birmingham
Campbell Hall, Room 401
1300 University Boulevard
Birmingham, AL 35294-1170
(205) 934-8762   Fax: (205) 934-1650
E-mail: LDale@uab.edu
Web: www.uab.edu/istp/alabama.html

Purpose To provide financial assistance to underrepresented minority students at designated institutions in Alabama who are interested in preparing for a career as a science teacher.

Eligibility This program is open to members of underrepresented minority groups who have been unconditionally admitted to a participating Alabama college or university. Applicants may 1) be entering freshmen or junior college transfer students who intend to major in science education and become certified to teach in elementary, middle, or high school; 2) have earned a degree in mathematics, science, or education and are seeking to become certified to teach; or 3) have earned a degree in mathematics, science, or education and are enrolled in a fifth-year education program leading to a master's degree and certification.

Financial data   The stipend is $1,000 per year.

Duration   1 year; may be renewed.

Additional information   Support for this program is provided by the National Science Foundation. The participating institutions are Alabama A&M University, Alabama State University, Auburn University, Miles College, Stillman College, Talladega College, Tuskegee University, University of Alabama at Birmingham, and University of Alabama in Huntsville.

Number awarded   Varies each year.

[316]
SCOTTS COMPANY SCHOLARS PROGRAM

Golf Course Superintendents Association of America
Attn: Scholarship and Student Programs Manager
1421 Research Park Drive
Lawrence, KS 66049-3859
(785) 832-3678   Toll-free: (800) 472-7878, ext. 3678
E-mail: psmith@gcsaa.org
Web: www.gcsaa.org

Purpose   To provide financial assistance and summer work experience to high school seniors and college students, particularly those from diverse backgrounds, who are preparing for a career in golf management.

Eligibility   This program is open to high school seniors and college students (freshmen, sophomores, and juniors) who are interested in preparing for a career in golf management (the "green industry"). Applicants should come from diverse ethnic, cultural, and socioeconomic backgrounds, defined to include women, minorities, and people with disabilities. Selection is based on cultural diversity, academic achievement, extracurricular activities, leadership, employment potential, essay responses, and letters of recommendation. Financial need is not considered. Finalists are selected for summer internships and then compete for scholarships.

Financial data   Each intern receives a $500 award. Scholarship stipends are $2,500.

Duration   1 year.

Additional information   The program is funded by a permanent endowment established by Scotts Company. Finalists are responsible for securing their own internships.

Number awarded   5 interns and 2 scholarship winners are selected each year.

Deadline   February of each year.

[317]
SERVICE LEAGUE MINORITY NURSING SCHOLARSHIP

Akron General Medical Center
Attn: Human Resources Department, Nurse Recruitment
400 Wabash Avenue
Akron, OH 44307
(330) 344-6867   E-mail: rkovalchik@agmc.org
Web: www.agmc.org/scholar.asp

Purpose   To provide financial assistance to minority nursing students from Ohio who are working on a baccalaureate degree.

Eligibility   This program is open to graduates of high schools in Ohio who have been accepted by an accredited baccalaureate nursing program in the state. Employees of Akron General Medical Center and their children and spouses are also eligible. Applicants must have a GPA of 2.8 or higher and be a member of a racial or ethnic minority group (African American, Hispanic, Asian/Pacific Islander, American Indian/Alaskan Native). They must submit a short essay on the reason they chose nursing as a career and why they believe they have the qualities and skills necessary to be a successful nurse. Selection is based on academic achievement and financial need.

Financial data   A stipend is awarded (amount not specified).

Duration   1 year.

Number awarded   1 or more each year.

Deadline   February of each year.

[318]
SHARON D. BANKS MEMORIAL UNDERGRADUATE SCHOLARSHIP

Women's Transportation Seminar
Attn: National Headquarters
1666 K Street, N.W., Suite 1100
Washington, DC 20006
(202) 496-4340   Fax: (202) 496-4349
E-mail: wts@wtsnational.org
Web: www.wtsnational.org

Purpose   To provide financial assistance to minority and other undergraduate women interested in a career in transportation.

Eligibility   This program is open to women who are working on an undergraduate degree in transportation or a transportation-related field (e.g., transportation engineering, planning, finance, or logistics). Applicants must have at least a 3.0 GPA and be interested in a career in transportation. They must submit a 500-word statement about their career goals after graduation and why they think they should receive the scholarship award. Applications must be submitted first to a local chapter; the chapters forward selected applications for consideration on the national level. Minority candidates are encouraged to apply. Selection is based on transportation involvement and goals, job skills, and academic record; financial need is not considered.

Financial data   The stipend is $3,000.

Duration   1 year.

Additional information   This program was established in 1992. Local chapters may also award additional funding to winners for their area.

ment, personal strengths, leadership, and financial need.

Number awarded 1 each year.
Deadline Applications must be submitted by November to a local WTS chapter.

[319]
SHAW INDUSTRIES/HENAAC SCHOLARS PROGRAM

Hispanic Engineer National Achievement Awards
  Conference
3900 Whiteside Street
Los Angeles, CA 90063
(323) 262-0997   Fax: (323) 262-0946
E-mail: info@henaac.org
Web: www.henaac.org/scholarships.htm

Purpose To provide financial assistance to Hispanic undergraduate students majoring in designated fields of engineering at universities in the Southeast.
Eligibility This program is open to Hispanic undergraduate students who are enrolled full time in chemical, electrical, industrial, mechanical, or textile engineering. Applicants must be entering their junior or senior year at a university in the southeastern United States and have a GPA of 3.0 or higher. Academic achievement and campus community activities are considered in the selection process. U.S. citizenship is required.
Financial data Stipends range from $1,000 to $5,000.
Duration 1 year; recipients may reapply.
Additional information This program is sponsored by Shaw Industries as part of its effort to support the mission of the Hispanic Engineer National Achievement Awards Conference (HENAAC): to promote technical excellence and leadership in the Hispanic community.
Number awarded 1 or more each year.
Deadline April of each year.

[320]
SOCIETY OF ACTUARIES SCHOLARSHIPS FOR MINORITY STUDENTS

Society of Actuaries
Attn: Minority Scholarship Coordinator
475 North Martingale Road, Suite 800
Schaumburg, IL 60173-2226
(847) 706-3509   Fax: (847) 706-3599
E-mail: cleathe@soa.org
Web: www.beanactuary.org/minority/scholarship.cfm

Purpose To provide financial assistance to underrepresented minority undergraduate students who are interested in preparing for an actuarial career.
Eligibility This program is open to African Americans, Hispanics, and Native North Americans who are Canadian or U.S. citizens or have a permanent resident visa. Before applying for this program, students should have taken either the SAT or the ACT. Applicants must be admitted to a college or university offering either a program in actuarial science or courses that will prepare them for an actuarial career. Selection is based on financial need, academic achievement, demonstrated mathematical ability, and understanding of and interest in an actuarial career.
Financial data The amount of the award depends on the need and merit of the recipient. There is no limit to the size

of the scholarship. Recipients are awarded an additional $500 for each actuarial examination they have passed.
Duration 1 year; may be renewed.
Additional information This program is jointly sponsored by the Society of Actuaries and the Casualty Actuarial Society.
Number awarded There is no limit to the number of scholarships awarded.
Deadline April of each year.

[321]
SOCIETY OF HISPANIC PROFESSIONAL ENGINEERS SCHOLARSHIP PROGRAM

Hispanic Scholarship Fund
Attn: Selection Committee
55 Second Street, Suite 1500
San Francisco, CA 94105
(415) 808-2350   Toll-free: (877) HSF-INFO
Fax: (415) 808-2302   E-mail: highschool@hsf.net
Web: www.hsf.net/scholarship/programs/shpe.php

Purpose To provide financial assistance for college to Hispanic Americans who are interested in majoring in designated fields of science.
Eligibility This program is open to U.S. citizens, permanent residents, and visitors with a passport stamped I-551 who are of Hispanic heritage. Applicants may be graduating high school seniors, community college students transferring to a 4-year institution, or continuing college students as long as they have a GPA of 3.0 or higher. They must be enrolled or planning to enroll full time at an accredited college or university in the United States to major in computer science, physical science, applied science, mathematics, or engineering. Along with their application, they must submit 600-word essays on 1) how their Hispanic heritage, family upbringing, and/or role models have influenced their personal long-term goals; 2) how they contribute to their community and what they have learned from their experiences; and 3) an academic challenge they have faced and how they have overcome it. Selection is based on academic achievement, personal strengths, leadership, and financial need.
Financial data Stipends range from $1,250 to $2,500 per year.
Duration 1 year.
Additional information This program is jointly sponsored by the Society of Hispanic Professional Engineers (SHPE) and the Hispanic Scholarship Fund (HSF).
Number awarded Varies each year; recently, 69 of these scholarships were awarded: 7 at $1,250, 2 at $1,307, and 60 at $2,500.
Deadline June of each year.

[322]
SOCIETY OF HISPANIC PROFESSIONAL ENGINEERS SCHOLARSHIPS

Society of Hispanic Professional Engineers Foundation
Attn: Director, Educational Programs
3900 Whiteside Street
Los Angeles, CA 90063
(323) 415-9600   Fax: (323) 415-7038
E-mail: kathy@shpefoundation.org
Web: www.shpefoundation.org

Purpose To provide undergraduate or graduate scholarships to deserving Hispanic American students preparing for a career in engineering or science.

Eligibility This program is open to Hispanic students enrolled or planning to enroll full time in an undergraduate or graduate degree program to prepare for a career in science or engineering. Applicants must submit an essay on how this scholarship would assist them in reaching their long-term goals. Selection is based on the essay, academic achievement, commitment to a college education, involvement in school and community activities, counselor recommendations, and financial need.

Financial data The stipends range from $500 to $7,000 per year.

Duration 1 academic year; renewal is possible.

Additional information These scholarships were first awarded in 1979.

Number awarded Varies each year. Recently, 375 of these scholarships, worth $275,000, were awarded.

Deadline May of each year.

[323]
SPANISH BAPTIST CONVENTION OF NEW MEXICO SCHOLARSHIP

Baptist Convention of New Mexico
Attn: Director, Language Missions
5325 Wyoming Boulevard, N.E.
P.O. Box 94485
Albuquerque, NM 87199-4485
(505) 924-2345   Fax: (505) 924-2320
E-mail: gsuarez@bcnm.com
Web: www.bcnm.com

Purpose To provide financial assistance for college or seminary to Hispanic Baptist students from New Mexico.

Eligibility This program is open to college and seminary students who are active members of churches affiliated with the Baptist Convention of New Mexico. Applicants must be of Hispanic background and committed to full-time Christian service.

Financial data A stipend is awarded (amount not specified).

Duration 1 year; may be renewed.

Number awarded 1 or more each year.

Deadline April of each year.

[324]
SPRINT SCHOLARSHIP PROGRAM

North Carolina Community College System
Attn: Student Development Services
200 West Jones Street
5016 Mail Service Center
Raleigh, NC 27699-5016
(919) 807-7106   Fax: (919) 807-7164
E-mail: littlep@ncccs.cc.nc.us
Web: www.ncccs.cc.nc.us

Purpose To provide financial assistance to North Carolina residents (particularly minorities) studying at publicly-supported technical or vocational schools in the state.

Eligibility This program is open to North Carolina residents enrolled full time in the 34 community colleges in Sprint's local service areas in the state. Applicants must be enrolled or planning to enroll in a course of study leading to an associate of applied science degree or vocational diploma. Priority is given to women, "displaced workers," and minorities (defined by Sprint as African Americans, Hispanics, American Indians/Native Alaskans, Pacific Islanders, and Asians). Selection is based on scholastic achievements, individual financial need, participation in outside activities, and demonstrated interest in a technical or vocational career.

Financial data The stipend is $700 per year.

Duration 1 year; may be renewed 1 additional year if the recipient maintains a GPA at or above the level required for graduation

Additional information Recipients are encouraged to seek employment with Sprint (the program's sponsor) after graduation. There are no special application forms for the scholarship. Students apply to their local community college, not to the system office. Each eligible school selects its own recipients from applicants meeting the above criteria.

Number awarded 34 each year: 1 at each participating community college.

[325]
STAN BECK FELLOWSHIP

Entomological Society of America
Attn: Entomological Foundation
9332 Annapolis Road, Suite 210
Lanham, MD 20706-3150
(301) 459-9082   Fax: (301) 459-9084
E-mail: melodie@entfdn.org
Web: www.entfdn.org/beck.html

Purpose To assist "needy" students working on an undergraduate or graduate degree in science who are nominated by members of the Entomological Society of America (ESA).

Eligibility This program is open to students working on an undergraduate or graduate degree in entomology at a college or university in Canada, Mexico, or the United States. Candidates must be nominated by members of the society. They must be "needy" students; for the purposes of this program, need may be based on physical limitations, or economic, minority, or environmental conditions.

Financial data The stipend is $2,000 per year.

Duration 1 year; may be renewed up to 3 additional years.

Additional information Recipients are expected to be present at the society's annual meeting, where the award will be presented.
Number awarded 1 or more each year.
Deadline June of each year.

[326]
STANLEY E. JACKSON SCHOLARSHIP AWARD FOR ETHNIC MINORITY GIFTED/TALENTED STUDENTS WITH DISABILITIES

Council for Exceptional Children
Attn: Yes I Can! Foundation for Exceptional Children
1110 North Glebe Road, Suite 300
Arlington, VA 22201-5704
(703) 620-3660   Toll-free: (800) 224-6830, ext. 462
Fax: (703) 264-9494   TTY: (866) 915-5000
E-mail: yesican@cec.sped.org
Web: yesican.sped.org/scholarship/index.html

Purpose To provide financial assistance for college to gifted minority students with disabilities.
Eligibility Applicants must be gifted or talented in 1 or more of the following categories: general intellectual ability, specific academic aptitude, creativity, leadership, or visual or performing arts. They must be disabled, financially needy, ready to begin college, and a member of an ethnic minority group (e.g., Asian, African American, Hispanic, or Native American). Candidates must submit a 200-word statement of philosophical, educational, and occupational goals as part of the application process. Selection is based on academic achievement, ability, promise, and financial need. U.S. citizenship is required.
Financial data The stipend is $500.
Duration 1 year; nonrenewable.
Additional information Scholarships may be used for 2- or 4-year college programs or for vocational, technical, or fine arts training programs. Recipients must enroll full time.
Number awarded 1 or more each year.
Deadline January of each year.

[327]
STANLEY E. JACKSON SCHOLARSHIP AWARD FOR ETHNIC MINORITY STUDENTS WITH DISABILITIES

Council for Exceptional Children
Attn: Yes I Can! Foundation for Exceptional Children
1110 North Glebe Road, Suite 300
Arlington, VA 22201-5704
(703) 620-3660   Toll-free: (800) 224-6830, ext. 462
Fax: (703) 264-9494   TTY: (866) 915-5000
E-mail: yesican@cec.sped.org
Web: yesican.sped.org/scholarship/index.html

Purpose To provide financial assistance for college to minority students with disabilities.
Eligibility Applicants must be students with disabilities who intend to enroll for the first time on a full-time basis in a college, university, vocational/technical school, or fine arts institute and are able to document financial need. Only minority (African American, Asian, Native American, or Hispanic) students are eligible for the award. Candidates must submit a 200-word statement of philosophical, educational, and occupational goals as part of the application process.

Selection is based on academic achievement, ability, promise, and financial need. U.S. citizenship is required.
Financial data The stipend is $500.
Duration 1 year; nonrenewable.
Additional information Scholarships may be used for 2- or 4-year college programs or for vocational, technical, or fine arts training programs. Recipients must enroll full time.
Number awarded 1 or more each year.
Deadline January of each year.

[328]
THE STATE NEWSPAPER AND KNIGHT RIDDER MINORITY SCHOLARSHIP PROGRAM

The State Newspaper
Attn: Tanya Fogg Young
1401 Shop Road
P.O. Box 1333
Columbia, SC 29202-1333
(803) 771-8659   Fax: (803) 540-3041
E-mail: tfyoung@thestate.com
Web: www.thestate.com

Purpose To provide financial assistance to minority high school seniors in South Carolina interested in attending college to prepare for a newspaper career.
Eligibility This program is open to minority seniors graduating from high schools in South Carolina. Applicants must be interested in attending college to prepare for a career in journalism or business communications. Along with their application, they must submit a transcript with grades and SAT/ACT scores, 2 letters of recommendation, up to 5 samples of work (for journalism students), a list of any journalism or business experience, a description of extracurricular activities, and an essay on why they want to prepare for a career in journalism or business communications.
Financial data The stipend is $500.
Duration 1 year.
Additional information The recipients of these scholarships are entered into competition for the Knight Ridder Minority Scholarship Program of $40,000 over 4 years.
Number awarded 1 each year.
Deadline January of each year.

[329]
STUDENT OPPORTUNITY SCHOLARSHIPS FOR ETHNIC MINORITY GROUPS

Presbyterian Church (USA)
Attn: Office of Financial Aid for Studies
100 Witherspoon Street, Room M-052
Louisville, KY 40202-1396
(502) 569-5745   Toll-free: (888) 728-7228, ext. 5745
Fax: (502) 569-8766   E-mail: KSmith@ctr.pcusa.org
Web: www.pcusa.org

Purpose To provide financial assistance for college to high school seniors of racial/ethnic minority heritage who are Presbyterians.
Eligibility This program is open to members of the Presbyterian Church (USA) who are from racial/ethnic minority groups (Asian American, African American, Hispanic American, Native American, Alaska Native). Applicants must be able to demonstrate financial need, be high school seniors entering college as full-time students, and be U.S. citizens

or permanent residents. They must submit a recommendation from their high school guidance counselor, a high school transcript, and an essay (up to 500 words in length) on their career goals and how they plan to achieve them.

Financial data Stipends range from $100 to $1,000 per year, depending upon the financial need of the recipient.

Duration 1 year; may be renewed for up to 3 additional years if the recipient continues to need financial assistance and demonstrates satisfactory academic progress.

Number awarded Varies each year.

Deadline April of each year.

[330]
SUMMER WORKSHOPS WRITING COMPETITION FOR MINORITY HIGH SCHOOL STUDENTS

Dow Jones Newspaper Fund
P.O. Box 300
Princeton, NJ 08543-0300
(609) 452-2820   Fax: (609) 520-5804
E-mail: newsfund@wsf.dowjones.com
Web: DJNewspaperFund.dowjones.com

Purpose To recognize and reward (with college scholarships) outstanding participants in journalism workshops for minority high school students.

Eligibility Each summer, workshops on college campuses around the country allow minority high school students to experience work on a professional-quality publication. Students are taught to write, report, design, and layout a newspaper on topics relevant to youth. The director of each workshop nominates 1 student who submits an article from the workshop newspaper and an essay on why he/she wants to pursue journalism as a career. The students whose articles and essay are judged most outstanding receive these college scholarships.

Financial data The award is a college scholarship of $1,000.

Duration Workshops normally last 2 weeks during the summer. Scholarships are for 1 year and may be renewed for 1 additional year if the recipient maintains a GPA of 2.5 or higher and an interest in journalism.

Additional information Recently, workshops were held on college campuses in Alabama, Arizona, Arkansas, California, Florida, Illinois, Kentucky, Massachusetts, Minnesota, Mississippi, Missouri, New Jersey, New York, Ohio, Oklahoma, Pennsylvania, South Dakota, Texas, Virginia, Washington, and Wisconsin. For the name and address of the director of each workshop, contact the Newspaper Fund.

Number awarded 8 each year.

[331]
SYNOD OF THE COVENANT ETHNIC STUDENT SCHOLARSHIPS

Synod of the Covenant
Attn: CECA Ethnic Scholarship Committee
1911 Indianwood Circle, Suite B
Maumee, OH 43537-4063
(419) 754-4050
Toll-free: (800) 848-1030 (within MI and OH)
Web: www.synodofthecovenant.org

Purpose To provide financial assistance to ethnic students working on an undergraduate degree (with priority given to Presbyterian applicants from Ohio and Michigan).

Eligibility This program is open to ethnic minority students working full or part time on a baccalaureate degree or certification at a college, university, or vocational school. Applicants must have a GPA of 3.0 or higher and be able to demonstrate participation in a Presbyterian church. Priority is given to Presbyterian applicants from the states of Michigan and Ohio. Financial need is considered in the selection process.

Financial data The maximum amount allowed within a calendar year is $600 (for full-time students in their first year), $800 (for renewals to full-time students), or $400 (for part-time students). Funds are made payable to the session for distribution.

Duration Students are eligible to receive scholarships 1 time per year, up to a maximum of 5 years. Renewals are granted provided 1) the completed application is received before the deadline date, 2) the recipient earned at least a 2.0 GPA last year, and 3) the application contains evidence of Presbyterian church participation and continued spiritual development.

Number awarded Varies each year.

Deadline September of each year for fall semester; February of each year for spring semester.

[332]
SYSCO SCHOLARSHIP AWARD

Hispanic Association of Colleges and Universities
Attn: National Scholarship Program
One Dupont Circle, N.W. Suite 605
Washington, DC 20036
(202) 467-0893   Fax: (202) 496-9177
TTY: (800) 855-2880   E-mail: scholarships@hacu.net
Web: scholarships.hacu.net/applications/applicants

Purpose To provide financial assistance to undergraduate students at member institutions of the Hispanic Association of Colleges and Universities (HACU) who are majoring in food service or business.

Eligibility This program is open to undergraduate students at HACU member and partner colleges and universities who have a declared major in either food service and hospitality or business with an emphasis on distribution and sales. Applicants must have a GPA of 3.0 or higher and be able to demonstrate financial need. They must submit an essay of 200 to 250 words that describes their academic and/or career goals, where they expect to be and what they expect to be doing 10 years from now, and what skills they can bring to an employer.

Financial data The stipend is $2,000.

Duration 1 year.

Additional information This program is sponsored by SYSCO and administered by HACU.

Number awarded 1 or more each year.

Deadline May of each year.

[333]
TAYLOR MICHAELS SCHOLARSHIP PROGRAM

Magic Johnson Foundation
9100 Wilshire Boulevard
East Tower, Suite 700
Beverly Hills, CA 90212
(310) 246-4400   Toll-free: (888) MAGIC-05
Web: www.magicjohnson.org/taylor_michaels_mjf.htm

Purpose To provide financial assistance to high school seniors from designated inner-city areas who are interested in attending a 4-year university.

Eligibility This program is open to seniors at high schools in inner-city areas of Atlanta, Cleveland, Houston, Los Angeles, and New York who are planning to attend a 4-year college or university as a full-time student. Applicants must have a GPA of 2.5 or higher and a record of involvement in extracurricular or community service activities. They must agree to participate in various activities of the sponsor, including a mentoring program, life and practical skills classes conducted by the foundation staff and guest presenters, and "A Midsummer Night's Magic" scholarship award ceremony.

Financial data Stipends range from $1,000 to full tuition.

Duration 4 years.

Additional information This program was established in 1998. During their 4 years in college, scholars continue to participate in activities arranged by the sponsor: mentorship for incoming scholarship recipients, community service, support of sponsor events as volunteers, seminars that assist students applying for graduate school, and seminars that assist students in making the transition from college to the workplace.

Number awarded Varies each year. Since its establishment, 150 students have received support.

[334]
TEACHERS FOR TOMORROW SCHOLARSHIP PROGRAM

Edison International
Attn: Educational Relations
P.O. Box 800
Rosemead, CA 91770
(626) 302-3382   Fax: (626) 302-3007
Web: www.edison.com

Purpose To provide financial assistance to minority and other students at designated campuses of the California State University (CSU) system who are working on their teaching credential.

Eligibility This program is open to students enrolled as a full-time CSU student in a teacher preparation program (single subject, multiple subject, or special education credential) at designated campuses in southern California. Applicants must have a cumulative GPA of 3.0 or higher and be able to demonstrate financial need. Preference is given to applicants who are economically and educationally disadvantaged. Selection is based on 2 letters of reference, a

2-page essay describing reasons for entering the teaching profession, and a 1-page statement that reflects a commitment to education and service to the community.

Financial data The stipend is $5,000 per year.

Duration 1 year.

Additional information The eligible CSU campuses are those at Dominguez Hills, Fullerton, Long Beach, Los Angeles, Northridge, Pomona, and San Bernardino. This program was established in 1999.

Number awarded 25 each year.

Deadline Students must apply to the financial aid office of their university by January of each year; each financial aid officer must submit the nominations from that institution by February of each year.

[335]
TEXAS SPACE GRANT CONSORTIUM UNDERGRADUATE SCHOLARSHIPS

Texas Space Grant Consortium
Attn: Administrative Assistant
3925 West Braker Lane, Suite 200
Austin, TX 78759
(512) 471-3583   Toll-free: (800) 248-8742
Fax: (512) 471-3585 E-mail: jurgens@tsgc.utexas.edu
Web: www.tsgc.utexas.edu/grants

Purpose To provide financial assistance to underrepresented minority and other undergraduate students at Texas universities working on degrees in the fields of space science and engineering.

Eligibility Applicants must be U.S. citizens, eligible for financial assistance, and registered for full-time study as juniors or seniors in an undergraduate program at 1 of the participating universities. Students apply to their university representative; each representative then submits up to 3 candidates into the statewide selection process. Fields of study have included aerospace engineering, biology, chemical engineering, chemistry, electrical engineering, geology, industrial engineering, mathematics, mechanical engineering, and physics. The program encourages participation by members of groups underrepresented in science and engineering (persons with disabilities, women, African Americans, Hispanic Americans, Native Americans, and Pacific Islanders). Scholarships are awarded competitively, on the basis of above-average performance in academics, participation in space education projects, participation in research projects, and exhibited leadership qualities.

Financial data The stipend is $1,000.

Duration 1 year; nonrenewable.

Additional information The participating universities are Baylor University, Lamar University, Prairie View A&M University, Rice University, San Jacinto College, Southern Methodist University, Sul Ross State University, Texas A&M University (including Kingsville and Corpus Christi campuses), Texas Christian University, Texas Southern University, Texas Tech University, Trinity University, University of Houston (including Clear Lake and Downtown campuses), University of Texas at Arlington, University of Texas at Austin, University of Texas at Dallas, University of Texas at El Paso, University of Texas at San Antonio, and University of Texas/Pan American. This program is funded by the National Aeronautics and Space Administration (NASA).

Number awarded Varies each year; recently, 29 of these scholarships were awarded.

Deadline March of each year.

[336]
THIRD WAVE FOUNDATION WOODLAKE SCHOLARSHIPS

Third Wave Foundation
511 West 25th Street, Suite 301
New York, NY 10002
(212) 675-0700   Fax: (212) 255-6653
E-mail: info@thirdwavefoundation.org
Web: www.thirdwavefoundation.org

Purpose To provide educational assistance to undergraduate and graduate women of color who have been involved as social change activists.

Eligibility This program is open to full-time and part-time students under 30 years of age who are enrolled in, or have been accepted to, an accredited university, college, vocational/technical school, community college, or graduate school. Applicants must be women of color who place greater emphasis on social justice and the struggle for justice and equality over academic performance and who integrate social justice into all areas of their lives. They must submit 500-word essays on 1) their current social change involvement and how it relates to their educational and life goals; and 2) if they would describe themselves as a feminist and why. Graduate students and students planning to study abroad through a U.S. university program are also eligible. Selection is based on financial need and commitment to social justice work.

Financial data Stipends are $3,000 or $1,000 per year.

Duration 1 year.

Number awarded Varies each year. Recently, 8 of these scholarships were awarded: 6 at $3,000 and 2 at $1,000.

Deadline March or September of each year.

[337]
TILLIE GOLUB-SCHWARTZ MEMORIAL SCHOLARSHIP FOR MINORITIES

Golub Foundation
c/o Price Chopper Scholarship Office, Mailbox 60
501 Duanesburg Road
P.O. Box 1074
Schenectady, NY 12301
(518) 356-9450   Toll-free: (877) 877-0870
Web: www.pricechopper.com

Purpose To provide financial assistance for college to minority high school seniors in selected areas of several states: Connecticut, Massachusetts, New Hampshire, New York, Pennsylvania, and Vermont.

Eligibility This program is open to high school seniors in areas of Connecticut, Massachusetts, New Hampshire, New York, Pennsylvania, and Vermont served by Price Chopper Supermarkets who plan to attend an accredited 2-year or 4-year college or university in those states. Applicants must be Alaskan Native, American Indian, Asian, Pacific Islander, Black (not of Hispanic origin), Puerto Rican, Mexican American, or other Hispanic. Along with their application, they must submit information on their educational history, including grades, Regents marks (if applicable), rank in

class, and SAT and/or ACT scores; honors and awards; participation in school, extracurricular, civic, and/or leadership activities; 3 reference letters; and a 1,000-word essay on how they have demonstrated a commitment to humanity through their involvement in community, church, and/or school activities.

Financial data The stipend is $2,000 per year.

Duration 4 years.

Additional information The Golub Corporation is the parent company of Price Chopper Supermarkets, which operates in the following counties: in Connecticut, Litchfield, New Haven, and Windham; in Massachusetts, Berkshire, Hampden, Hampshire, Middlesex, and Worcester; in New Hampshire, Cheshire, Grafton, and Sullivan; in New York, Albany, Broome, Cayuga, Chenango, Clinton, Columbia, Cortland, Delaware, Dutchess, Essex, Franklin, Fulton, Greene, Hamilton, Herkimer, Jefferson, Lewis, Madison, Montgomery, Oneida, Onondaga, Orange, Oswego, Otsego, Rensselaer, St. Lawrence, Saratoga, Schenectady, Sullivan, Schoharie, Tioga, Tompkins, Ulster, Warren, and Washington; in Pennsylvania, Lackawanna, Luzerne, Susquehanna, Wayne, and Wyoming; in Vermont, Addison, Bennington, Caledonia, Chittenden, Essex, Franklin, Grand Isle, Lamoille, Orange, Orleans, Rutland, Washington, Windham, and Windsor.

Number awarded 1 each year.

Deadline March of each year.

[338]
TIME WARNER SCHOLARSHIP AWARD

Hispanic Association of Colleges and Universities
Attn: National Scholarship Program
One Dupont Circle, N.W. Suite 605
Washington, DC 20036
(202) 467-0893   Fax: (202) 496-9177
TTY: (800) 855-2880   E-mail: scholarships@hacu.net
Web: scholarships.hacu.net/applications/applicants

Purpose To provide financial assistance to undergraduate students at member institutions of the Hispanic Association of Colleges and Universities (HACU) who are majoring in fields related to the news industry.

Eligibility This program is open to undergraduate students at 4-year HACU member and partner colleges and universities who have completed at least 12 units. Applicants may be majoring in any field, but they must have an interest in the entertainment, news, media, or telecommunications industries. They must have a GPA of 3.0 or higher and be able to demonstrate financial need. Along with their application, they must submit an essay of 200 to 250 words that describes their academic and/or career goals, where they expect to be and what they expect to be doing 10 years from now, and what skills they can bring to an employer.

Financial data The stipend is $2,000.

Duration 1 year; may be renewed.

Additional information This program is sponsored by Time Warner and administered by HACU. Recipients may be considered for paid summer internships at Time Warner through its "STARS" program.

Number awarded 1 or more each year.

Deadline May of each year.

[339]
TRIDENT–HDA FOUNDATION SCHOLARSHIPS

Hispanic Dental Association
Attn: HDA Foundation
188 West Randolph Street, Suite 415
Chicago, IL 60601
(312) 577-4013   Toll-free: (800) 852-7921
Fax: (312) 577-0052
E-mail: HispanicDental@hdassoc.org
Web: www.hdassoc.org

Purpose To provide financial assistance to Hispanic students interested in preparing for a career in a dental profession.

Eligibility This program is open to Hispanics who are entering or enrolled in an accredited dental or dental hygiene program. Applicants must have a GPA of 3.0 or higher. Along with their application, they must submit an essay on their career goals. Selection is based on scholastic achievement, community service, leadership skill, and commitment to improving health in the Hispanic community.

Financial data The stipend is $1,500.

Duration 1 year.

Additional information This program, which began in 2004, is sponsored by Cadbury Adams, maker of Trident Sugarfree Chewing Gum.

Number awarded 1 or more each year.

Deadline June of each year for dental students; July of each year for dental hygiene students.

[340]
UNCF/HOUSEHOLD CORPORATE SCHOLARS PROGRAM

United Negro College Fund
Attn: Corporate Scholars Program
P.O. Box 1435
Alexandria, VA 22313-9998
Toll-free: (866) 671-7237   E-mail: internship@uncf.org
Web: www.uncf.org/internships/index.asp

Purpose To provide financial assistance and work experience to minority and other students majoring in fields related to business.

Eligibility This program is open to rising juniors majoring in accounting, business, computer science, finance, human resources, or marketing with a GPA of 3.0 or higher. Applicants must be interested in an internship with Household International, the program's sponsor, at 1 of the following sites: Bridgewater, New Jersey; Charlotte, North Carolina; Chesapeake, Virginia; Chicago, Illinois; Dallas, Texas; Indianapolis, Indiana; Jacksonville, Florida; Monterey, California; New Castle, Delaware; San Diego, California; or Tampa, Florida. Preference is given to applicants who reside in those areas, but students who live in other areas are also considered. African Americans, Hispanic Americans, American Indians, and Asian Americans are encouraged to apply. Along with their application, students must submit an essay on their personal and career goals and objectives, a letter of recommendation, and an official transcript.

Financial data This program provides a stipend of up to $10,000 per year and a paid internship.

Duration 8 to 10 weeks for the internships; 1 year for the scholarships, which may be renewed.

Number awarded Varies each year.

Deadline February of each year.

[341]
UNCF/SPRINT SCHOLARS PROGRAM

United Negro College Fund
Attn: Corporate Scholars Program
P.O. Box 1435
Alexandria, VA 22313-9998
Toll-free: (866) 671-7237   E-mail: internship@uncf.org
Web: www.uncf.org/internships/index.asp

Purpose To provide financial assistance and work experience to minority students who are majoring in selected business and science fields.

Eligibility This program is open to members of minority groups who are enrolled full time as juniors or seniors at a 4-year college or university in the United States. Applicants must have a GPA of 3.0 or higher and be majoring in accounting, business, computer engineering, computer information systems, computer science, economics, electrical engineering, finance, industrial engineering, journalism, marketing, management information systems, public relations, or statistics. They must be interested in a summer internship at Sprint. Along with their application, they must submit a 1-page personal statement describing their career interests and goals, a current resume, a letter of recommendation, official transcripts, and a financial need statement.

Financial data This program provides a paid internship and (upon successful completion of the internship) a need-based stipend of up to $7,500.

Duration 10 to 12 weeks for the internships; 1 year for the scholarships.

Additional information This program is sponsored by Sprint. Recipients may attend any of the 39 member institutions of the United Negro College Fund (UNCF), other Historically Black Colleges and Universities (HBCUs), or an accredited majority 4-year college or university.

Number awarded Varies each year.

Deadline October of each year.

[342]
UNITED METHODIST ETHNIC MINORITY SCHOLARSHIPS

United Methodist Church
Attn: General Board of Higher Education and Ministry
Office of Loans and Scholarships
1001 19th Avenue South
P.O. Box 340007
Nashville, TN 37203-0007
(615) 340-7344   Fax: (615) 340-7367
E-mail: umscholar@gbhem.org
Web: www.gbhem.org

Purpose To provide financial assistance to undergraduate Methodist students who are of ethnic minority ancestry.

Eligibility This program is open to full-time undergraduate students at accredited colleges and universities in the United States who have been active, full members of a United Methodist Church for at least 1 year prior to applying. Applicants must have at least 1 parent who is African American, Hispanic, Asian, Native American, Alaska Native, or Pacific Islander. They must have a GPA of 2.5 or higher and be able to demonstrate financial need. U.S. citizenship, permanent resident status, or membership in a central conference of the United Methodist Church is required.

Financial data A stipend is awarded (amount not specified).

Duration 1 year; recipients may reapply.

Number awarded Varies each year.

Deadline April of each year.

[343]
UNITED METHODIST SCHOLARSHIP PROGRAM

United Methodist Church
Attn: General Board of Higher Education and Ministry
Office of Loans and Scholarships
1001 19th Avenue South
P.O. Box 340007
Nashville, TN 37203-0007
(615) 340-7344   Fax: (615) 340-7367
E-mail: umscholar@gbhem.org
Web: www.gbhem.org

Purpose To provide financial assistance to undergraduate and graduate students attending schools affiliated with the United Methodist Church.

Eligibility This program is open to U.S. citizens and permanent residents who have been active, full members of a United Methodist Church for at least 1 year prior to applying; members of the A.M.E., A.M.E. Zion, and other "Methodist" denominations are not eligible. Undergraduates must have been admitted to a full-time degree program at a United Methodist-related college or university and have a GPA of 2.5 or above. Most graduate scholarships are designated for persons working on a degree in theological studies (M.Div., D.Min., Ph.D.) or higher education administration, or for older adults changing their careers. Some scholarships are designated for racial ethnic undergraduate or graduate students. Applications are available from the financial aid office of the United Methodist school the applicant attends or from the chair of their annual conference Board of Higher Education and Campus Ministry.

Financial data The funding is intended to supplement the students' own resources.

Duration 1 year; renewal policies are set by participating universities.

Number awarded Varies each year.

[344]
UNITED PARCEL SERVICE SCHOLARSHIP FOR MINORITY STUDENTS

Institute of Industrial Engineers
Attn: Chapter Operations Department
3577 Parkway Lane, Suite 200
Norcross, GA 30092
(770) 449-0461, ext. 118   Toll-free: (800) 494-0460
Fax: (770) 263-8532   E-mail: srichards@iienet.org
Web: www.iienet.org

Purpose To provide financial assistance to minority undergraduates who are studying industrial engineering at a school in the United States, Canada, or Mexico.

Eligibility Eligible to be nominated are minority undergraduate students enrolled in any school in the United States and its territories, Canada, or Mexico, provided the school's engineering program is accredited by an agency recognized by the Institute of Industrial Engineers (IIE) and the student is pursuing a full-time course of study in industrial engineering with a GPA of at least 3.4. They must have at least 5 full quarters or 3 full semesters remaining until graduation. Students may not apply directly for these awards; they must be nominated by the head of their industrial engineering department. Nominees must be IIE members. Selection is based on scholastic ability, character, leadership, potential service to the industrial engineering profession, and need for financial assistance.

Financial data The stipend is $4,000.

Duration 1 year.

Additional information Funding for this program is provided by the UPS Foundation.

Number awarded 1 each year.

Deadline November of each year.

[345]
UNIVERSITY OF NORTH CAROLINA CAMPUS SCHOLARSHIPS-PART I

North Carolina State Education Assistance Authority
Attn: Scholarship and Grant Services
10 Alexander Drive
P.O. Box 14103
Research Triangle Park, NC 27709-4103
(919) 549-8614   Toll-free: (800) 700-1775
Fax: (919) 549-8481   E-mail: information@ncseaa.edu
Web: www.ncseaa.edu

Purpose To provide financial assistance to students at University of North Carolina (UNC) constituent institutions whose enrollment contributes to the diversity of the undergraduate population.

Eligibility This program is open to undergraduate students who are enrolled or planning to enroll full time at 1 of the 16 UNC institutions. Applicants must have graduated in the top 40% of their high school class, have a weighted GPA of 3.0 or higher, have an SAT score higher than the SAT score of the previous freshman class, and have a record of positive involvement in extracurricular activities. They must be able to demonstrate "exceptional financial need." Their enrollment must "contribute to the intellectual experiences and diversity of the undergraduate population."

Financial data The amount of the award depends upon the financial need of the recipient and the availability of funds.

Duration 1 year; may be renewed. Students must submit applications to the constituent institution's financial aid office rather than directly to the North Carolina State Education Assistance Authority.

Additional information This program was established in 2003 as a replacement for the former North Carolina Minority Presence Grants, North Carolina Freshmen Scholars Program, North Carolina Incentive Scholarship Program, and the North Carolina Legislative College Opportunity Program.

Number awarded Varies each year; recently, a total of 3,076 UNC Campus Scholarships, with a total value of $5,648,874, were awarded.

Deadline Deadline dates vary; check with the appropriate constituent institution.

[346]
UPS DIVERSITY SCHOLARSHIPS

American Society of Safety Engineers
Attn: ASSE Foundation
1800 East Oakton Street
Des Plaines, IL 60018
(847) 768-3441   Fax: (847) 296-9220
E-mail: mrosario@asse.org
Web: www.asse.org

Purpose To provide financial assistance to minority undergraduate student members of the American Society of Safety Engineers (ASSE).

Eligibility This program is open to ASSE student members who are enrolled in a 4-year degree program in occupational safety and health or a closely-related field (e.g., safety engineering, safety management, systems safety, environmental science, industrial hygiene, ergonomics, fire science). Applicants must be U.S. citizens and members of a minority ethnic or racial group. They must be full-time students who have completed at least 60 semester hours with a GPA of 3.0 or higher. As part of the selection process, they must submit 2 essays of 300 words or less: 1) why they are seeking a degree in safety, a brief description of their current activities, and how those relate to their career goals and objectives; and 2) why they should be awarded this scholarship (including career goals and financial need).

Financial data Stipends range from $4,000 to $6,000 per year.

Duration 1 year; nonrenewable.

Additional information Funding for this program is provided by the UPS Foundation.

Number awarded Varies each year; recently, 2 of these scholarships at $5,250 each were awarded.

Deadline November of each year.

[347]
USA FUNDS ACCESS TO EDUCATION SCHOLARSHIPS

Scholarship America
Attn: Scholarship Management Services
One Scholarship Way
P.O. Box 297
St. Peter, MN 56082
(507) 931-1682   Toll-free: (800) 537-4180
Fax: (507) 931-9168
E-mail: scholarship@usafunds.org
Web: www.usafunds.org

Purpose To provide financial assistance to undergraduate and graduate students, especially those who are members of ethnic minority groups or have physical disabilities.

Eligibility This program is open to high school seniors and graduates who plan to enroll or are already enrolled in full-time undergraduate or graduate course work at an accredited 2- or 4-year college, university, or vocational/technical school. Half-time undergraduate students are also eligible. Up to 50% of the awards are targeted at students who have a documented physical disability or are a member of an ethnic minority group, including but not limited to Native Hawaiian, Alaskan Native, Black/African American, Asian, Pacific Islander, American Indian, or Hispanic/Latino. Residents of 49 states (residents of Hawaii are eligible for a separate program), the District of Columbia,

Puerto Rico, Guam, the U.S. Virgin Islands, and all U.S. territories and commonwealths are eligible. Preference is given to applicants from the following states: Arizona, Indiana, Kansas, Maryland, Mississippi, Nevada, and Wyoming. Applicants must also be U.S. citizens or eligible noncitizens and come from a family with an annual adjusted gross income of $35,000 or less. In addition to financial need, selection is based on past academic performance and future potential, leadership and participation in school and community activities, work experience, career and educational aspirations, and goals.

Financial data The stipend is $1,500 per year for full-time undergraduate or graduate students or $750 per year for half-time undergraduate students. Funds are paid jointly to the student and the school.

Duration 1 year; may be renewed until the student receives a final degree or certificate or until the total award to a student reaches $6,000, whichever comes first. Renewal requires the recipient to maintain a GPA of 2.5 or higher.

Additional information This program, established in 2000, is sponsored by USA Funds, which serves as the education loan guarantor and administrator in the 7 states where the program gives preference.

Number awarded Varies each year; recently, a total of $2.85 million was available for this program.

Deadline March of each year.

[348]
USA FUNDS HAWAII SILVER ANNIVERSARY SCHOLARSHIPS

Scholarship America
Attn: Scholarship Management Services
One Scholarship Way
P.O. Box 297
St. Peter, MN 56082
(507) 931-1682   Toll-free: (800) 537-4180
Fax: (507) 931-9168
E-mail: scholarship@usafunds.org
Web: www.usafunds.org

Purpose To provide financial assistance to undergraduate and graduate students from Hawaii, especially those who are members of ethnic minority groups or have physical disabilities.

Eligibility This program is open to high school seniors and graduates who are residents of Hawaii planning to enroll or already enrolled in full-time undergraduate or graduate course work at an accredited 2- or 4-year college, university, or vocational/technical school. Half-time undergraduate students are also eligible. Up to 50% of the awards are targeted at students who have a documented physical disability or are a member of an ethnic minority group, including but not limited to Native Hawaiian, Alaskan Native, Black/African American, Asian, Pacific Islander, American Indian, or Hispanic/Latino. Applicants must also be U.S. citizens or eligible noncitizens and come from a family with an annual adjusted gross income of $50,000 or less. In addition to financial need, selection is based on past academic performance and future potential, leadership and participation in school and community activities, work experience, career and educational aspirations, and goals.

Financial data The stipend is $1,500 per year for full-time undergraduate or graduate students or $750 per year for half-time undergraduate students. Funds are paid jointly to the student and the school.

Duration 1 year; may be renewed until the student receives a final degree or certificate or until the total award to a student reaches $6,000, whichever comes first. Renewal requires the recipient to maintain a GPA of 2.5 or higher.

Additional information This program, first offered in 2004, is sponsored by SMS Hawaii, the USA Funds affiliate that serves as the education loan guarantor and administrator in Hawaii and 7 other states. Information is also available from SMS Hawaii, 1314 South King Street, Suite 861, Honolulu, HI 96814, (808) 593-2262, (866) 497-USAF, ext. 7573, Fax: (808) 593-8268, E-mail: lteniya@usafunds.org.

Number awarded Varies each year; recently, a total of $300,000 was available for this program.

Deadline March of each year.

[349]
VATE MINORITY SCHOLARSHIP AWARD

Virginia Association of Teachers of English
Attn: Chuck Miller, Executive Secretary
1417 Birchwood Drive
Crozet, VA 22932
(434) 823-1483   E-mail: CMillerCrz@adelphia.net
Web: www.seva.net/~vate/Recognition.html

Purpose To provide financial assistance to minority students at colleges and universities in Virginia who are preparing for a career as a teacher of English language arts.

Eligibility This program is open to minority students enrolled in a teacher preparation program at a Virginia college or university. Applicants must be preparing to teach English language arts on the elementary or secondary level. Membership in the Virginia Association of Teachers of English (VATE) is required. Along with their application, they must submit a resume, 2 professional recommendations, and a statement (from 100 to 500 words) on what they will contribute in the classroom.

Financial data A stipend is awarded (amount not specified).

Duration 1 year.

Additional information Information is also available from Robert Williams, Radford University, Department of English, P.O. Box 6935, Radford, VA 24142, (540) 831-6700, E-mail: rohwilli@radford.edu.

Number awarded 1 each year.

Deadline August of each year.

[350]
VERIZON WORKFORCE RESPONSE SCHOLARSHIPS

Independent Colleges of Washington
600 Stewart Street, Suite 600
Seattle, WA 98101
(206) 623-4494   Fax: (206) 625-9621
E-mail: info@icwashington.org
Web: www.icwashington.org

Purpose To provide financial assistance to minority students preparing for a career in teaching or nursing at col-

leges and universities that are members of Independent Colleges of Washington (ICW).

Eligibility This program is open to students completing their junior year at ICW-member colleges and universities. Applicants must be members of underserved or minority populations. They must be majoring in education or nursing. Along with their application, they must submit a 1-page essay on why they chose to prepare for a career in teaching and/or nursing. Preference is given to community college graduates. Financial need is considered in the selection process.

Financial data The stipend is $2,500.

Duration 1 year; nonrenewable.

Additional information The ICW-member institutions are Gonzaga University, Heritage College, Pacific Lutheran University, Saint Martin's College, Seattle Pacific University, Seattle University, University of Puget Sound, Walla Walla College, Whitman College, and Whitworth College.

Number awarded 4 each year.

Deadline October of each year.

[351]
VERMONT SPACE GRANT UNDERGRADUATE SCHOLARSHIPS

Vermont Space Grant Consortium
c/o University of Vermont
College of Engineering and Mathematics
Votey Building, Room 209
12 Colchester Avenue
Burlington, VT 05405-0156
(802) 656-1429   Fax: (802) 656-8802
E-mail: zeno@emba.uvm.edu
Web: www.emba.uvm.edu/VSGC/scholarship.html

Purpose To provide financial assistance for undergraduate study in space-related fields to minority and other students in Vermont.

Eligibility This program is open to Vermont residents who are 1) enrolled in an undergraduate degree program at a Vermont institution of higher education with a GPA of 3.0 or higher or 2) seniors graduating from a high school in Vermont. Applicants must be planning to pursue a professional career that has direct relevance to the U.S. aerospace industry and the goal of the National Aeronautics and Space Administration (NASA) in such fields as astronomy, biology, engineering, mathematics, physics, and other basic sciences (including earth sciences and medicine). They must submit an essay, up to 3 pages in length, on their career plans and the relationship of those plans to areas of interest to NASA. U.S. citizenship is required. Selection is based on academic standing, letters of recommendation, and the essay. The Vermont Space Grant Consortium (VSGC) is a component of the NASA Space Grant program, which encourages participation by women, underrepresented minorities, and persons with disabilities.

Financial data The stipend is $1,500 per year.

Duration 1 year; may be renewed upon reapplication.

Additional information This program is funded by NASA. Participating institutions are the College of Engineering and Mathematics at the University of Vermont, St. Michael's College, Norwich University, Vermont Technical College, the Vermont State Mathematics Coalition, and Burlington Aviation Technology School/Burlington Technical Center.

Number awarded Up to 10 each year.

Deadline February of each year.

[352]
VIKKI CARR SCHOLARSHIP AWARDS

Vikki Carr Scholarship Foundation
P.O. Box 780968
San Antonio, TX 78278
(210) 699-0205 Fax: (210) 699-0611
E-mail: info@vcsf.net
Web: www.vcsf.net

Purpose To provide financial assistance for college to Latino residents of Texas.

Eligibility This program is open to students of Latino heritage who are between 17 and 22 years of age, legal U.S. residents, and residents of Texas. Applicants must submit a short autobiography (up to 500 words) on their special interests, career goals, and reasons for pursuing a higher education. Selection is based on the essay, academic achievement, financial need, and community involvement.

Financial data The stipend ranges from $500 to $3,000.

Duration 1 year; renewable.

Additional information This program was established in 1971. More than half a million dollars in scholarships has been awarded since then.

Number awarded Varies each year.

Deadline March of each year.

[353]
VINSON & ELKINS L.L.P. SCHOLARSHIP

Vinson & Elkins L.L.P.
Attn: Scholarship Foundation
2300 First City Tower
1001 Fannin Street
Houston, TX 77002-6760
(713) 758-2222 Fax: (713) 758-2346
E-mail: lhughes@velaw.com
Web: www.velaw.com

Purpose To provide financial assistance to high school seniors of African American or Hispanic origins from low-income families in selected large urban areas in Texas who are interested in eventually preparing for a career in law.

Eligibility Eligible to apply for this support are students who are graduating seniors at selected public high schools in the greater Austin, Dallas, or Houston area who have been accepted to a university of college located somewhere in the United States. Applicants must be interested in preparing for a career in law, have financial need, be in the top 20% of their class, have an excellent SAT score, be U.S. citizens or residents of the 3 cities for at least the past 6 years, have a valid Social Security card, and be of African American or Hispanic origins. Selection is based on career interest, financial need, academic performance, scores on standardized tests, recommendations, and indication of leadership potential.

Financial data The stipend is $2,500 per year. Funds must be used for tuition, fees, books, supplies, and/or equipment.

Duration 1 year; may be renewed for up to 3 additional years.

Additional information Upon completion of each academic year of study, recipients must submit a final report to the scholarship foundation.

Deadline March of each year.

[354]
VIRGINIA HIGHER EDUCATION TEACHER ASSISTANCE PROGRAM

State Council of Higher Education for Virginia
Attn: Financial Aid Office
James Monroe Building
101 North 14th Street, Ninth Floor
Richmond, VA 23219-3659
(804) 225-2600 Toll-free: (877) 515-0138
Fax: (804) 225-2604 TDD: (804) 371-8017
E-mail: fainfo@schev.edu
Web: www.schev.edu

Purpose To provide financial assistance to minority and other residents of Virginia who are enrolled or interested in enrolling in a K-12 teacher preparation program in college.

Eligibility This program is open to residents of Virginia who are enrolled, or intend to enroll, full time in an eligible K-12 teacher preparation program at a public or private Virginia college or university. Applicants must 1) be U.S. citizens or eligible noncitizens; 2) demonstrate financial need; 3) have a cumulative college GPA of 2.5 or higher; and 4) be nominated by a faculty member. Preference is given to applicants enrolled in a teacher shortage content area (recently including special education, mathematics, chemistry, physics, earth and space sciences, foreign languages, and technology education), minority students enrolled in any content area for teacher preparation, and males enrolled in any approved elementary or middle school teacher preparation program.

Financial data Stipends are $2,000 per year for students at 4-year institutions or $1,000 per year for students at 2-year institutions.

Duration 1 year; may be renewed if funds are available and the recipient maintains satisfactory academic progress.

Additional information Applications and further information are available at the financial aid office of colleges and universities in Virginia. This program, established in 2000, is funded in part with federal funds from the Special Leveraging Educational Assistance Partnership (SLEAP) program.

Number awarded Varies each year.

[355]
VIRGINIA SOCIETY OF CERTIFIED PUBLIC ACCOUNTANTS MINORITY UNDERGRADUATE SCHOLARSHIP

Virginia Society of Certified Public Accountants
   Education Foundation
Attn: Educational Foundation
4309 Cox Road
P.O. Box 4620
Glen Allen, VA 23058-4620
(804) 270-5344   Toll-free: (800) 733-8272
Fax: (804) 273-1741   E-mail: vscpa@vscpa.com
Web: www.vscpa.com

Purpose To provide financial assistance to minority students enrolled in an undergraduate accounting program in Virginia.

Eligibility Applicants must be minority students (African Americans, Hispanic Americans, Native American Indians, or Asian Pacific Americans) currently enrolled in a Virginia college or university undergraduate accounting program. They must be U.S. citizens, be majoring in accounting, have completed at least 6 hours of accounting, be currently registered for 3 more credit hours of accounting, and have a GPA of 3.0 or higher. Along with their applications, they must submit a 1-page essay on how they are financing their education, how they plan to use their accounting education, and why they should be awarded this scholarship. Selection is based on the essay (50%), an official undergraduate transcript (15%), a current resume, (25%), and a faculty letter of recommendation (10%).

Financial data A stipend is awarded (amount not specified). A total of $10,000 is available for this program each year.

Duration 1 year.

Number awarded Varies each year; recently, 3 of these scholarships were awarded.

Deadline April of each year.

[356]
VIRGINIA SPACE GRANT COMMUNITY COLLEGE SCHOLARSHIP PROGRAM

Virginia Space Grant Consortium
Attn: Fellowship Coordinator
Old Dominion University Peninsula Center
600 Butler Farm Road
Hampton, VA 23666
(757) 766-5210   Fax: (757) 766-5205
E-mail: vsgc@odu.edu
Web: www.vsgc.odu.edu/html/fellowships.htm

Purpose To provide financial assistance to underrepresented minority and other students who are interested in pursuing space-related studies at community colleges in Virginia.

Eligibility This program is open to students currently enrolled in a Virginia community college who are U.S. citizens and have completed at least the first semester of their program with a GPA of 3.0 or higher. Awards are generally made to full-time students, but part-time students demonstrating academic merit are also eligible. Applicants can be enrolled in any program that includes course work related to an understanding of or interest in technological fields supporting aerospace; that includes (but is not limited to)

computers, electronics, engineering, industrial technology, and mathematics. Since a particular goal of the program is to increase the participation of underrepresented minorities, women, and persons with disabilities in aerospace-related, high technology careers, the sponsor especially encourages applications from those students.

Financial data The maximum stipend is $1,500.

Duration 1 year; nonrenewable.

Additional information This program is funded by the U.S. National Aeronautics and Space Administration (NASA).

Number awarded Approximately 10 each year.

Deadline February of each year.

[357]
VIRGINIA SPACE GRANT TEACHER EDUCATION SCHOLARSHIP PROGRAM

Virginia Space Grant Consortium
Attn: Fellowship Coordinator
Old Dominion University Peninsula Center
600 Butler Farm Road
Hampton, VA 23666
(757) 766-5210   Fax: (757) 766-5205
E-mail: vsgc@odu.edu
Web: www.vsgc.odu.edu/html/fellowships.htm

Purpose To provide financial assistance for college to underrepresented minority and other students in Virginia planning a career as science, mathematics, or technology educators.

Eligibility This program is open to full-time undergraduate students at the Virginia Space Grant Consortium (VSGC) colleges and universities in a track that will qualify them to teach in a pre-college setting. Priority is given to those majoring in technology education, mathematics, or science, particularly earth, space, or environmental science. Applicants may apply while seniors in high school or sophomores in a community college, with the award contingent on their enrollment at a VSGC college and entrance into a teacher certification program. They must submit a statement of academic goals and plan of study, explaining their reasons for desiring to enter the teaching profession, specifically the fields of science, mathematics, or technology education. Students currently enrolled in a VSGC college can apply when they declare their intent to enter the teacher certification program. Students enrolled in a master of education degree program leading to teacher certification in eligible fields are also eligible to apply. Applicants must be U.S. citizens with a GPA of 3.0 or higher. Since an important purpose of this program is to increase the participation of underrepresented minorities, women, and persons with disabilities in science, mathematics, and technology education, the VSGC especially encourages applications from those students.

Financial data The maximum stipend is $1,000.

Duration 1 year; nonrenewable.

Additional information The VSGC institutions are College of William and Mary, Hampton University, Old Dominion University, the University of Virginia, and Virginia Polytechnic Institute and State University. This program is funded by the U.S. National Aeronautics and Space Administration (NASA).

Number awarded Approximately 10 each year.

Deadline   February of each year.

[358]
WAL-MART ACHIEVERS AWARD

Hispanic Association of Colleges and Universities
Attn: National Scholarship Program
One Dupont Circle, N.W. Suite 605
Washington, DC 20036
(202) 467-0893   Fax: (202) 496-9177
TTY: (800) 855-2880   E-mail: scholarships@hacu.net
Web: scholarships.hacu.net/applications/applicants

Purpose   To provide financial assistance to undergraduate business students at institutions that are members of the Hispanic Association of Colleges and Universities (HACU).

Eligibility   This program is open to full-time undergraduate students at HACU member and partner colleges and universities who are enrolled in their sophomore or junior year with a major in business administration, general management, food merchandising, marketing, or retail management. Applicants must submit an essay of 200 to 250 words that describes their academic and/or career goals, where they expect to be and what they expect to be doing 10 years from now, and what skills they can bring to an employer. They must be able to demonstrate financial need and a GPA of 3.0 or higher. Preference is given to applicants who are working while attending school and have an interest in retail management.

Financial data   The stipend is $1,000 per year.

Duration   1 year; nonrenewable.

Additional information   This program is sponsored by Wal-Mart and administered by HACU.

Number awarded   1 or more each year.

Deadline   May of each year.

[359]
WARNER NORCROSS & JUDD PARALEGAL ASSISTANT STUDIES SCHOLARSHIP

Grand Rapids Community Foundation
Attn: Scholarship Coordinator
209-C Waters Building
161 Ottawa Avenue N.W., 209-C
Grand Rapids, MI 49503-2757
(616) 454-1751, ext. 103   Fax: (616) 454-6455
E-mail: rbishop@grfoundation.org
Web: www.grfoundation.org

Purpose   To provide financial assistance to minority residents of Michigan who are interested in working on a paralegal degree at an institution in the state.

Eligibility   This program is open to minority students currently residing in Michigan. Applicants must be accepted at or enrolled in an accredited public or private 2- or 4-year college or university with a declared major in paralegal/legal assistant studies. The institution must also be in Michigan.

Financial data   The stipend is $2,000.

Duration   1 year.

Additional information   Funding for this program is provided by the law firm Warner Norcross & Judd LLP.

Number awarded   1 each year.

Deadline   April of each year.

[360]
WARNER NORCROSS & JUDD SECRETARIAL STUDIES SCHOLARSHIP

Grand Rapids Community Foundation
Attn: Scholarship Coordinator
209-C Waters Building
161 Ottawa Avenue N.W., 209-C
Grand Rapids, MI 49503-2757
(616) 454-1751, ext. 103   Fax: (616) 454-6455
E-mail: rbishop@grfoundation.org
Web: www.grfoundation.org

Purpose   To provide financial assistance to minority residents of Michigan who are interested in enrolling in a legal assistant/secretarial program at an institution in the state.

Eligibility   This program is open to minority students currently residing in Michigan. Applicants must be accepted at or enrolled in an accredited public or private 2- or 4-year college, university, vocational school, or business school with a declared major in legal assistant/legal secretarial studies. The institution must also be in Michigan.

Financial data   The stipend is $1,000.

Duration   1 year.

Additional information   Funding for this program is provided by the law firm Warner Norcross & Judd LLP.

Number awarded   1 each year.

Deadline   April of each year.

[361]
WARREN G. MAGNUSON EDUCATIONAL SUPPORT PERSONNEL SCHOLARSHIP GRANT

Washington Education Association
32032 Weyerhaeuser Way South
P.O. Box 9100
Federal Way, WA 98063-9100
(253) 765-7029   Toll-free: (800) 622-3393, ext. 7029
E-mail: cmartinez@washingtonea.org
Web: www.washingtonea.org

Purpose   To provide funding to Educational Support Personnel (ESP) members of the Washington Education Association (WEA), particularly minority members, who are interested in taking classes to obtain an initial teaching certificate.

Eligibility   This program is open to WEA/ESP members who are engaged in course work related to obtaining an initial teaching certificate. Applicants must submit a plan for obtaining an initial certificate, a letter describing their passion to become a teacher, evidence of activities and/or leadership in the association, and 3 to 5 letters of reference. Minority members of the association are especially encouraged to apply; 1 of the scholarships is reserved for them.

Financial data   The stipend is $1,000.

Duration   These are 1-time grants.

Number awarded   3 each year, including 1 reserved for a minority member.

Deadline   February of each year.

[362]
WASA/PEMCO 21ST CENTURY EDUCATOR SCHOLARSHIP

Washington Association of School Administrators
825 Fifth Avenue, S.E.
Olympia, WA 98501
(360) 943-5717   Toll-free: (800) 859-9272
Fax: (360) 352-2043   E-mail: selder@wasa-oly.org
Web: www.wasa-oly.org

Purpose To provide financial assistance to minority and other high school seniors in the state of Washington who are interested in majoring in education in college.

Eligibility This program is open to high school seniors who are enrolled in a Washington public or accredited private school, have a GPA of 3.0 or higher, and intend to major and prepare for a career in K-12 education. Applicants must submit a completed application form, a criteria essay, a goals essay, 3 reference letters, and an official grades transcript. They compete in 3 applicant pools: eastern Washington, western Washington, and minorities. Selection is based on leadership, community service, honors and awards, student activities, and educational goals.

Financial data The stipend is $1,000 per year.

Duration 4 years.

Additional information This program is sponsored jointly by the Washington Association of School Administrators (WASA) and the PEMCO Foundation. Faxed applications will not be accepted.

Number awarded 3 each year: 1 to a minority student, 1 to a student from eastern Washington, and 1 to a student from western Washington.

Deadline March of each year.

[363]
WASHINGTON BUREAU MINORITY SCHOLARSHIPS

Knight Ridder Newspapers-Washington Bureau
Attn: Anthony Pugh
700 12th Street, N.W., Suite 1000
Washington, DC 20005-3994
(202) 383-6013   Fax: (202) 383-3738
E-mail: tpugh@krwashington.com
Web: www.krwashington.com

Purpose To provide financial assistance to minority high school seniors from the Washington, D.C. area who are interested in attending college to prepare for a career in the newspaper industry.

Eligibility This program is open to minority seniors graduating from high schools in the metropolitan area of Washington, D.C. Applicants must be able to demonstrate an interest in journalism, but they are not required to have been school newspaper reporters or editors. They may be photographers, graphic artists, computer experts, delivery workers with an interest in circulation, or business and advertising staff members. Along with their application, they must submit a transcript of grades (with a GPA of 3.0 or higher), SAT/ACT scores, 2 letters of recommendation, a list of journalism or business experience, information on extracurricular activities, up to 5 samples of work with bylines (for journalism applicants), and a 500-word essay on why they want to prepare for a career in journalism or communication business.

Financial data The stipend is $1,000.

Duration 1 year.

Additional information The recipients of these scholarships are entered into competition for the Knight Ridder Minority Scholarship Program of $40,000 over 4 years.

Number awarded 2 each year.

Deadline January of each year.

[364]
WASHINGTON DENTAL SERVICE FOUNDATION SCHOLARSHIPS

Washington Dental Service Foundation
Attn: Grant Administrator
P.O. Box 75688
Seattle, WA 98125
(206) 528-2337   Toll-free: (800) 572-7835, ext. 2337
Fax: (206) 528-7373
E-mail: Foundation@DeltaDentalWA.com
Web: www.DeltaDentalWA.com

Purpose To provide financial assistance to members of underrepresented minority groups in Washington who are interested in preparing for a career as a dental hygienist, dental assistant, or laboratory technician.

Eligibility This program is open to residents of Washington who are African or Black Americans, Native Americans, Alaskan Natives, Hispanics/Latinos, or Pacific Islanders. Applicants must be planning to enroll in an eligible program in dental hygiene, dental assisting, or laboratory technology at a community or technical college in the state. They must be able to demonstrate financial need. Along with their application, they must submit essays of 100 to 300 words on 1) why they are interested in becoming a dental professional; 2) their career goals, how they decided upon those goals, and how completion of their proposed program will help them reach those goals; 3) how they have prepared themselves academically for those chosen program of study; 4) a leadership experience they have had in school, work, athletics, family, church, community, or other area of their life; and 5) how they help or serve others in their family and/or community.

Financial data Stipends range from $1,000 to $4,000 per year, depending on the need of the recipient.

Duration 1 year.

Number awarded 1 or more each year.

Deadline September of each year.

[365]
WASHINGTON MUTUAL MINORITY TEACHER SCHOLARSHIP

Independent Colleges of Washington
600 Stewart Street, Suite 600
Seattle, WA 98101
(206) 623-4494   Fax: (206) 625-9621
E-mail: info@icwashington.org
Web: www.icwashington.org

Purpose To provide financial assistance to minority students preparing for a career in teaching at colleges and universities that are members of Independent Colleges of Washington (ICW).

Eligibility This program is open to minority students at ICW-member colleges and universities. Applicants must be able to demonstrate financial need and a commitment to preparing for a career as a teacher (through either selection of a major or course load). They must submit a 1-page essay on why they are interested in a career in teaching. Selection criteria include education courses taken, activities, and community service.

Financial data The stipend is $3,000.

Duration 1 year; nonrenewable.

Additional information The ICW-member institutions are Gonzaga University, Heritage College, Pacific Lutheran University, Saint Martin's College, Seattle Pacific University, Seattle University, University of Puget Sound, Walla Walla College, Whitman College, and Whitworth College.

Number awarded Multiple scholarships are awarded each year.

Deadline April of each year.

[366]
WASHINGTON NASA SPACE GRANT CONSORTIUM UNDERGRADUATE SCHOLARSHIPS

Washington NASA Space Grant Consortium
c/o University of Washington
401A Johnson Hall
Box 351310
Seattle, WA 98195-1310
(206) 543-1943   Toll-free: (800) 659-1943
Fax: (206) 543-0179
Web: www.waspacegrant.org/undergr.html

Purpose To provide financial assistance for college to minority and other students in Washington who wish to study science, engineering, or mathematics with an emphasis on space.

Eligibility This program is open to residents of Washington who are attending or planning to attend institutions that are members of the Washington NASA Space Grant Consortium. Applicants must be interested in majoring in space-related aspects of science, engineering, or mathematics. U.S. citizenship is required. The program values diversity and strongly encourages women and minorities to apply.

Financial data Each participating college or university determines its awards.

Duration 1 year; may be renewed.

Additional information This program is funded by the U.S. National Aeronautics and Space Administration (NASA). Members of the consortium include Northwest Indian College, Seattle Central Community College, the University of Washington, and Washington State University.

Number awarded Varies each year.

Deadline Each participating college or university establishes its own deadline.

[367]
WASHINGTON POST YOUNG JOURNALISTS DEVELOPMENT PROGRAM

Washington Post
Attn: Public Relations Department
1150 15th Street, N.W.
Washington, DC 20071
(202) 334-7969
Web: washpost.com

Purpose To provide financial assistance to minority and other high school seniors in the Washington, D.C. area who are interested in preparing for a career in newspaper journalism.

Eligibility This program is open to high school seniors in 19 designated public school systems in the Washington, D.C. area. Applicants must have an interest in a print journalism career and a command of the English language. All students are eligible, but special emphasis is placed on participation by minority students. From the original applicants, a group is selected to participate in a program of 4 Saturday seminars at *The Washington Post*. During those seminars, conducted by the newspaper's reporters and editors, students produce a newspaper or magazine story. Scholarship winners are selected on the basis of those stories, attendance and participation in the seminars, and financial need.

Financial data The stipend is $2,500.

Duration 1 year; nonrenewable.

Additional information The eligible public school systems are those in Washington, D.C.; the counties of Anne Arundel, Calvert, Charles, Frederick, Howard, Montgomery, Prince George's, and St. Mary's in Maryland; the cities of Alexandria, Falls Church, Manassas, and Manassas Park in Virginia; and the counties of Arlington, Fairfax, Fauquier, Loudoun, Prince William, and Stafford in Virginia. This program, which began in 1997, is offered in collaboration with the National Association of Hispanic Journalists and the Asian American Journalists Association

Number awarded Recently, 19 students were selected to participate in the seminar. From among those, 2 were chosen to receive scholarships.

Deadline February of each year.

[368]
WASHINGTON STATE GEAR UP SCHOLARSHIP PROGRAM

Washington Higher Education Coordinating Board
917 Lakeridge Way
P.O. Box 43430
Olympia, WA 98504-3430
(360) 753-7833   Fax: (360) 753-7808
TDD: (360) 753-7809   E-mail: johnmcl@hecb.wa.gov
Web: www.hecb.wa.gov/CollegePrep/gu/guindex.asp

Purpose To provide financial and other assistance for college to low-income, disadvantaged middle and high school students in selected areas throughout Washington.

Eligibility This program is open to students in grades 7-12 in Washington communities who are low income and at risk. Participants receive tutoring and academic and career counseling, visit college campuses, perform community service, meet regularly with mentors, and attend informational seminars on such topics as financial aid, admissions, career planning, and student success strategies. During their junior and senior years, they get help preparing for college entrance examinations and completing admissions and financial aid applications.

Financial data Participants receive stipends and scholarships for college.

Duration Up to 4 years, provided the recipient remains drug-, crime-, and alcohol-free; maintains a GPA of 2.0 or higher; and participates in community service projects.

Additional information The communities currently participating in this program are Aberdeen, Elma, Hoquiam, Inchelium, Quincy, Seattle, Spokane, Tacoma, Taholah,

Wapato, White Swan, and Yakima. GEAR UP is a federal program that stands for Gaining Early Awareness and Readiness for Undergraduate Programs. In Washington, it operates as a partnership among the Higher Education Coordinating Board, the Office of the Governor, and the University of Washington. It began operating in 1999 as the successor to the National Early Intervention Scholarship and Partnership Program.

Number awarded Currently, 1,200 students in grades 7-12 are participating.

[369]
WASHINGTON STATE HISPANIC CHAMBER OF COMMERCE SCHOLARSHIPS

Washington State Hispanic Chamber of Commerce
Attn: WSHCC Scholarship Trust Fund
P.O. Box 21925
Seattle, WA 98111-3925
(206) 441-8894   E-mail: information@wshcc.com
Web: www.wshcc.com/ScholarshipFund/index.htm

Purpose To provide financial assistance for college to Hispanic residents of Washington.

Eligibility This program is open to Hispanic residents of Washington who are attending or planning to attend a college or university in the state. Applicants are not required to be U.S. citizens or permanent resident aliens, but they must have a Social Security number or tax identification number. Selection is based on GPA (30%), an essay (30%), and community involvement (40%). Financial need is not considered.

Financial data Stipends are $3,000 or $2,500.

Duration 1 year.

Number awarded Varies each year. Recently, 5 of these scholarships were awarded: 1 at $3,000 and 4 at $2,500.

[370]
WASHINGTON STATE NEED GRANT

Washington Higher Education Coordinating Board
917 Lakeridge Way
P.O. Box 43430
Olympia, WA 98504-3430
(360) 753-7851   Fax: (360) 753-7808
TDD: (360) 753-7809   E-mail: info@hecb.wa.gov
Web: www.hecb.wa.gov

Purpose To provide financial assistance for undergraduate study to Washington residents who come from a low-income or disadvantaged family.

Eligibility This program is open to residents of Washington whose family income is equal to or less than 55% of the state median (currently defined as $18,000 for a family of 1 ranging to $48,000 for a family of 8) or who are disadvantaged (defined to mean a student who by reasons of adverse cultural, educational, environmental, experiential, or familial circumstance is unlikely to aspire to, or enroll in, higher education). Applicants must be enrolled or planning to enroll at least half time in an eligible certificate, bachelor's degree, or first associate degree program. They may not be working on a degree in theology.

Financial data The stipend depends on the type of institution the recipient attends. Recently, it was $1,908 per year at community, technical, and private career colleges; $3,026 at public comprehensive universities (Central Washington University, Eastern Washington University, The Evergreen State College, and Western Washington University); $3,798 at public research universities (University of Washington and Washington State University); or $4,032 at independent universities.

Duration 1 academic year; renewal is possible for up to 3 additional years.

Additional information Consideration is automatic with the institution's receipt of the student's completed financial aid application. This program began in 1969.

Number awarded Varies each year; recently, more than 49,000 students received about $106 million in benefits from this program.

Deadline Varies according to the participating institution; generally in October of each year.

[371]
WEAC SCHOLARSHIPS

Wisconsin Education Association Council
33 Nob Hill Drive
P.O. Box 8003
Madison, WI 53708-8003
(608) 276-7711   Toll-free: (800) 362-8034
Web: www.weac.org/AboutWEA/scholarship.htm

Purpose To provide financial assistance for college to high school seniors whose parent is a member of the Wisconsin Education Association Council (WEAC) and who plan to study education in college.

Eligibility This program is open to high school seniors whose parent is an active WEAC member, an active retired member, or a parent who died while holding a WEAC membership. Applicants must rank in the top 25% of their graduating class or have a GPA of 3.0 or higher, plan to major or minor in education in college, and intend to teach in Wisconsin. Selection is based primarily on GPA, a 300-word essay, letters of recommendation, and school and community activities. Secondary consideration may be given to other factors, including financial need. The Kathy Mann Memorial Scholarship is reserved for a minority student.

Financial data The stipend is $1,450 per year.

Duration 4 years, provided the recipient remains eligible.

Number awarded 4 each year. If no minority student applies, the Kathy Mann Memorial Scholarship is awarded to a fourth non-minority applicant.

Deadline February of each year.

[372]

WEST VIRGINIA SPACE GRANT CONSORTIUM UNDERGRADUATE NASA SPACE GRANT FELLOWSHIPS

West Virginia Space Grant Consortium
c/o West Virginia University
College of Engineering and Mineral Resources
G-68 Engineering Sciences Building
P.O. Box 6070
Morgantown, WV 26506-6070
(304) 293-4099, ext. 3737   Fax: (304) 293-4970
E-mail: nasa@cemr.wvu.edu
Web: www.nasa.wvu.edu/scholarships.htm

Purpose To provide financial assistance to minority and other high school seniors who wish to attend academic institutions affiliated with the West Virginia Space Grant Consortium to prepare for a career in space-related science or engineering.

Eligibility This program is open to high school seniors in West Virginia who are planning to attend a college or university that is a member of the West Virginia Space Grant Consortium. U.S. citizenship is required. Selection is based on academic record and desire to prepare for a career in science or engineering. The consortium is a component of the Space Grant program of the U.S. National Aeronautics and Space Administration (NASA). Women and minorities are strongly encouraged to apply.

Financial data The program provides payment of full tuition, fees, room, and board.

Duration 4 years.

Additional information Funding for this program is provided by NASA. During the summers, some recipients work at a NASA center on a project under the supervision of a NASA advisor; others work with researchers at their respective colleges. The consortium includes Bethany College, Fairmont State College, Marshall University, Salem International University, Shepherd College, West Liberty State College, West Virginia Institute of Technology, West Virginia State College, West Virginia University, West Virginia Wesleyan College, and Wheeling-Jesuit University.

Number awarded Varies each year.

Deadline Each participating college or university establishes its own deadline.

[373]

WEST VIRGINIA SPACE GRANT CONSORTIUM UNDERGRADUATE SCHOLARSHIP PROGRAM

West Virginia Space Grant Consortium
c/o West Virginia University
College of Engineering and Mineral Resources
G-68 Engineering Sciences Building
P.O. Box 6070
Morgantown, WV 26506-6070
(304) 293-4099, ext. 3737   Fax: (304) 293-4970
E-mail: nasa@cemr.wvu.edu
Web: www.nasa.wvu.edu/scholarships.htm

Purpose To provide financial assistance to minority and other undergraduates at academic institutions affiliated with the West Virginia Space Grant Consortium who wish to prepare for a career in space-related science or engineering.

Eligibility This program is open to undergraduates at member institutions of the consortium. Applicants must be U.S. citizens and West Virginia residents. Selection is based on academic record and desire to prepare for a career in science or engineering. The consortium is a component of the Space Grant program of the U.S. National Aeronautics and Space Administration (NASA). Women and minorities are strongly encouraged to apply.

Financial data Stipends are either $2,000 or $1,000.

Duration 1 year.

Additional information Funding for this program is provided by NASA. In addition to their class work, recipients either work with faculty members in their major department on a research project or participate in the Consortium Challenge Program by working with elementary students on their science projects. The consortium members are Bethany College, Fairmont State College, Marshall University, Salem International University, Shepherd College, West Liberty State College, West Virginia Institute of Technology, West Virginia State College, West Virginia University, West Virginia Wesleyan College, and Wheeling-Jesuit University.

Number awarded Varies each year.

Deadline Each participating college or university establishes its own deadline.

[374]

WESTERN REGION SCHOLARSHIPS

Society of Mexican American Engineers and Scientists-
   Western Region
c/o Phillip Diaz
Northrop Grumman-Mission Systems
DH4-2936
1815 Glenn Curtiss Street
Carson, CA 90746
(310) 764-3157
Web: www.maeslongbeach.org/conference

Purpose To provide financial assistance for college to undergraduate members of the Society of Mexican American Engineers and Scientists (MAES) enrolled at colleges and universities in selected western states.

Eligibility This program is open to Hispanic Americans who have completed at least 1 semester as a full-time undergraduate at a college or university in Arizona, California, Idaho, Montana, Nevada, Oregon, Utah, Washington, or Wyoming. Applicants must be U.S. citizens or permanent residents, members of MAES, and majoring in science or engineering. Community college applicants must be enrolled in majors that can transfer to a 4-year institution offering a baccalaureate degree. Along with their application, they must submit a 1- to 2-page personal statement covering their family background, involvement in school and community activities, leadership roles and activities, achievements, current higher education status, career goals, and financial need.

Financial data Stipends range from $200 to $1,000.

Duration 1 year.

Additional information Recipients are required to attend the scholarship awards banquet.

Number awarded 1 or more each year.

Deadline February of each year.

[375]
WHO'S WHO AMONG AMERICAN HIGH SCHOOL STUDENTS SCHOLARSHIPS

National FFA Organization
Attn: Scholarship Office
6060 FFA Drive
P.O. Box 68960
Indianapolis, IN 46268-0960
(317) 802-4321   Fax: (317) 802-5321
E-mail: scholarships@ffa.org
Web: www.ffa.org

Purpose To provide financial assistance to FFA members from inner-city locations who are interested in working on a college degree.

Eligibility This program is open to members who are graduating high school seniors from inner-city schools who are planning to enroll full time in college. Applicants must be interested in working on a degree (any major) at a 2-year or 4-year institution. Selection is based on academic achievement (10 points for GPA, 10 points for SAT or ACT score, 10 points for class rank), leadership in FFA activities (30 points), leadership in community activities (10 points), and participation in the Supervised Agricultural Experience (SAE) program (30 points). Financial need is also considered. U.S. citizenship is required.

Financial data Stipends are $1,500. Funds are paid directly to the recipient.

Duration 1 year; nonrenewable.

Additional information This program is funded by the ECI Scholarship Foundation of Educational Communications Inc., publisher of *Who's Who Among American High School Students.*

Number awarded 1 each year.

Deadline February of each year.

[376]
WILLIAM RUCKER GREENWOOD SCHOLARSHIP

Association for Women Geoscientists
Attn: AWG Foundation
P.O. Box 30645
Lincoln, NE 68503-0645
E-mail: awgscholarship@yahoo.com
Web: www.awg.org/members/po_scholarships.html

Purpose To provide financial assistance to minority women working on an undergraduate or graduate degree in the geosciences in the Potomac Bay region.

Eligibility This program is open to minority women who are currently enrolled as full-time undergraduate or graduate geoscience majors in an accredited, degree-granting college or university in Delaware, the District of Columbia, Maryland, Virginia, or West Virginia. Selection is based on the applicant's 1) awareness of the importance of community outreach as demonstrated by participation in geoscience or earth science educational activities, and 2) potential for leadership as a future geoscience professional.

Financial data The stipend is $1,000. The recipient also is granted a 1-year membership in the Association for Women Geoscientists (AWG).

Duration 1 year.

Additional information This program is sponsored by the AWG Potomac Area Chapter. Information is also avail-

able from Laurel M. Bybell, U.S. Geological Survey, 926 National Center, Reston, VA 20192.

Number awarded 1 each year.

Deadline April of each year.

[377]
WISCONSIN INSTITUTE OF CERTIFIED PUBLIC ACCOUNTANTS MINORITY SCHOLARSHIPS

Wisconsin Institute of Certified Public Accountants
Attn: WICPA Educational Foundation
235 North Executive Drive, Suite 200
P.O. Box 1010
Brookfield, WI 53008-1010
(414) 785-0445
Toll-free: (800) 772-6939 (within WI and MN)
Fax: (414) 785-0838   E-mail: Tammy@wicpa.org
Web: www.wicpa.org

Purpose To provide financial assistance to minority high school seniors in Wisconsin who are interested in majoring in accounting.

Eligibility This program is open to high school seniors who are residents of Wisconsin and African American, Hispanic, Native American, Indian, or Asian. Applicants must have earned a GPA of 3.0 or higher, be planning to attend a Wisconsin college or university, and be planning to begin academic work leading to an accounting major and a bachelor's degree.

Financial data The stipend is $375 per academic semester for the first 2 years, $500 per semester during the third year, and $750 per semester during the fourth year. The total award is $4,000 over 4 years. Funds may be used only for tuition and books.

Duration 4 years.

Number awarded Varies each year; recently, 2 of these scholarships were awarded.

Deadline February of each year.

[378]
WISCONSIN MINORITY UNDERGRADUATE RETENTION GRANTS

Wisconsin Higher Educational Aids Board
131 West Wilson Street, Room 902
P.O. Box 7885
Madison, WI 53707-7885
(608) 267-2212   Fax: (608) 267-2808
E-mail: mary.kuzdas@heab.state.wi.us
Web: heab.state.wi.us/programs.html

Purpose To provide financial assistance to minorities in Wisconsin who are currently enrolled in college.

Eligibility African Americans, Hispanic Americans, and American Indians in Wisconsin are eligible to apply if they are enrolled as sophomores, juniors, seniors, or fifth-year undergraduates in a 4-year nonprofit institution or as second-year students in a 2-year program at a public vocational institution in the state. Grants are also available to students who were admitted to the United States after December 31, 1975 and who are a former citizen of Laos, Vietnam, or Cambodia or whose ancestor was a citizen of 1 of those countries. They must be nominated by their institution and be able to demonstrate financial need.

Financial data Stipends range from $250 to $2,500 per year.

Duration Up to 4 years.

Additional information The Wisconsin Higher Educational Aids Board administers this program for students in private nonprofit institutions and public vocational institutions. The University of Wisconsin has a similar program for students attending any of the branches of that system. Eligible students should apply through their school's financial aid office.

Number awarded Varies each year.

Deadline Deadline dates vary by institution; check with your school's financial aid office.

[379]
WISCONSIN SPACE GRANT CONSORTIUM UNDERGRADUATE SCHOLARSHIPS

Wisconsin Space Grant Consortium
c/o University of Wisconsin at Green Bay
Natural and Applied Sciences
2420 Nicolet Drive
Green Bay, WI 54311-7001
(920) 465-2108   Fax: (920) 465-2376
E-mail: wsgc@uwgb.edu
Web: www.uwgb.edu/wsgc/students/us.asp

Purpose To provide financial support to underrepresented minority and other undergraduate students at universities participating in the Wisconsin Space Grant Consortium (WSGC).

Eligibility This program is open to undergraduate students enrolled at 1 of the universities participating in the WSGC. Applicants must be U.S. citizens; be working full time on a bachelor's degree in space science, aerospace, or interdisciplinary space studies (including, but not limited to, engineering, the sciences, architecture, law, business, and medicine); and have a GPA of 3.0 or higher. The consortium especially encourages applications from underrepresented minorities, women, and students with disabilities. Selection is based on academic performance and potential for success.

Financial data Stipends up to $1,500 per year are available.

Duration 1 academic year.

Additional information Funding for this program is provided by the U.S. National Aeronautics and Space Administration. The schools participating in the consortium include the University of Wisconsin campuses at Green Bay, La Crosse, Madison, Milwaukee, Oshkosh, Parkside, and Whitewater; College of the Menominee Nation; Marquette University; Carroll College; Lawrence University; Milwaukee School of Engineering; Ripon College; and Medical College of Wisconsin.

Number awarded Varies each year; recently, 21 of these scholarships were awarded.

Deadline February of each year.

[380]
WISCONSIN TALENT INCENTIVE PROGRAM (TIP) GRANTS

Wisconsin Higher Educational Aids Board
131 West Wilson Street, Room 902
P.O. Box 7885
Madison, WI 53707-7885
(608) 266-1665   Fax: (608) 267-2808
E-mail: john.whitt@heab.state.wi.us
Web: heab.state.wi.us/programs.html

Purpose To provide financial assistance for college to needy and educationally disadvantaged students in Wisconsin.

Eligibility This program is open to residents of Wisconsin entering a college or university in the state who meet requirements of both financial need and educational disadvantage. Financial need qualifications include 1) family contribution (a dependent student whose expected parent contribution is $200 or less, an independent student with dependents whose academic year contribution is $200 or less, or an independent student with no dependents whose maximum contribution is $1,200 or less); 2) AFDC benefits (a dependent student whose family is receiving AFDC benefits or an independent student who is receiving AFDC benefits); or 3) unemployment (a dependent student whose parents are ineligible for unemployment compensation and have no current income from employment, or an independent student and spouse, if married, who are ineligible for unemployment compensation and have no current income from employment). Educational disadvantage qualifications include students who are 1) minorities (African American, Native American, Hispanic, or southeast Asian); 2) enrolled in a special academic support program due to insufficient academic preparation; 3) a first-generation college student (neither parent graduated from a 4-year college or university); 4) disabled according to the Department of Workforce Development, Division of Vocational Rehabilitation; 5) currently or formerly incarcerated in a correctional institution; or 6) from an environmental and academic background that deters the pursuit of educational plans. Students already in college are not eligible.

Financial data Grants range up to $1,800 per year.

Duration 1 year; may be renewed up to 4 additional years provided the recipient continues to be a Wisconsin resident enrolled at least half time in a degree or certificate program, makes satisfactory academic progress, demonstrates financial need, and remains enrolled continuously from semester to semester and from year to year. If recipients withdraw from school or cease to attend classes for any reason (other than medical necessity), they may not reapply.

Number awarded Varies each year.

[381]
WISCONSIN UNITED METHODIST HISPANIC SCHOLARSHIP

Wisconsin United Methodist Foundation
Attn: Director
750 Windsor Street, Suite 305
P.O. Box 620
Sun Prairie, WI 53590-0620
(608) 837-9582   Toll-free: (888) 903-9863
Fax: (608) 837-2492   E-mail: wumf@wumf.org
Web: www.wisconsinumc.org/wumf/Grants.htm

Purpose To provide financial assistance for college to Hispanic members of United Methodist churches in Wisconsin.

Eligibility This program is open to United Methodist Hispanic students from Wisconsin who are enrolled or planning to enroll in college or vocational/technical school. Selection is based on GPA, financial need, work experience (including volunteer work), school and community activities and awards, and a letter of recommendation from their United Methodist pastor.

Financial data The stipend is $500.

Duration 1 year.

Number awarded 1 or more each year.

Deadline April of each year.

[382]
WORLDSTUDIO FOUNDATION SCHOLARSHIPS

Worldstudio Foundation
200 Varick Street, Suite 507
New York, NY 10014
(212) 366-1317, ext. 18   Fax: (212) 807-0024
E-mail: scholarshipcoordinator@worldstudio.org
Web: www.worldstudio.org/schol/index.html

Purpose To provide financial assistance to undergraduate and graduate students, especially minorities, who wish to study fine or commercial arts, design, or architecture.

Eligibility This program is open to undergraduate and graduate students who are currently enrolled or planning to enroll at an accredited college or university and major in 1 of the following areas: advertising (art direction only), architecture, crafts, environmental graphics, fashion design, film/video (direction or cinematography only), film/theater design (including set, lighting, and costume design), fine arts, furniture design, graphic design, industrial/product design, interior design, landscape architecture, new media, photography, surface/textile design, or urban planning. Although not required, minority status is a significant factor in the selection process. International students may apply if they are enrolled at a U.S. college or university. Applicants must have a GPA of 2.0 or higher. Along with their application, they must submit a 600-word statement of purpose that includes a brief autobiography, an explanation of how their experiences have influenced their creative work and/or their career plans, and how they see themselves contributing to the community at large in the future. Selection is based on that statement, the quality of submitted work, financial need, minority status, and academic record.

Financial data Basic scholarships range from $1,000 to $2,000, but awards between $3,000 and $5,000 are also presented at the discretion of the jury. Honorable mentions are $100. Funds are paid directly to the recipient's school.

Duration 1 academic year. Recipients may reapply.

Additional information The foundation encourages the scholarship recipients to focus on ways that their work can address issues of social and environmental responsibility. This program includes the following named awards: the Sherry and Gary Baker Award, the Bobolink Foundation Award, the Bombay Sapphire Awards, the Richard and Jean Coyne Family Foundation Awards, the David A. Dechman Foundation Awards, the Philip and Edina Jennison Award, the Kraus Family Foundation Awards, the Dena McKelvey Award. the New York Design Center Award, the Rudin Foundation Awards, the Starr Foundation Awards, and the John F. Wright III Award.

Number awarded Varies each year; recently, 24 scholarships and 7 honorable mentions were awarded.

Deadline March of each year.

[383]
WORLDSTUDIO FOUNDATION SPECIAL ANIMATION AND ILLUSTRATION SCHOLARSHIPS

Worldstudio Foundation
200 Varick Street, Suite 507
New York, NY 10014
(212) 366-1317, ext. 18   Fax: (212) 807-0024
E-mail: scholarshipcoordinator@worldstudio.org
Web: www.worldstudio.org/schol/specawards.html

Purpose To provide financial assistance to members of disadvantaged and ethnic minority groups who wish to study illustration, animation, or cartooning in college.

Eligibility This program is open to members of disadvantaged or minority groups who are currently enrolled or planning to enroll in an accredited college or university in the United States. Applicants must be majoring or planning to major in illustration, animation, or cartooning. They must submit their most recent college or high school transcripts, documentation of financial need, a portfolio of their work, and a 600-word statement of purpose that includes a brief autobiography and how they plan to contribute to the community. International students are also eligible. Selection is based on the quality of submitted work, the strength of the written statement of purpose, financial need, and academic record.

Financial data The stipend is $1,500. Funds are paid directly to the recipient's school.

Duration 1 academic year. Recipients may reapply.

Additional information This program was established in 2002 with funding from the W.K. Kellogg Foundation.

Number awarded 25 each year.

Deadline March of each year.

[384]
WPS RESOURCES FOUNDATION BUSINESS AND TECHNOLOGY SCHOLARSHIPS

Wisconsin Public Service Corporation
Attn: WPS Resources Foundation, Inc.
c/o Scholarship Assessment Service
P.O. Box 5189
Appleton, WI 54912-5189
(920) 832-8322
Web: www.wpsr.com/community/minoritybus.asp

Purpose To provide financial assistance to women and minority upper-division students who are majoring in business or engineering at selected universities.

Eligibility This program is open to women and African American, Native American, Asian American, and Hispanic students who are enrolled full time as a junior or senior at a participating university with a GPA of 2.8 or higher. They must be majoring in business or engineering (chemical, civil, computer, electrical, environmental, industrial, or mechanical). Along with their application, they must submit 1) a 250-word essay on why they chose their current major and what career they hope to enter after graduation, and 2) a 350-word essay on a selection of topics that relate to challenges facing the energy industry.

Financial data The stipend is $1,500.

Duration 1 year; may be renewed if the recipient remains in good academic standing.

Additional information The participating universities are Marquette University, Michigan Technological University, Milwaukee School of Engineering, University of Wisconsin at Green Bay, University of Wisconsin at Platteville, University of Wisconsin at Madison, University of Minnesota, Iowa State University, St. Norbert College, Notre Dame University, and University of Michigan at Ann Arbor.

Number awarded Varies each year; recently, 15 of these scholarships were awarded.

Deadline January of each year.

[385]
WTS PUGET SOUND CHAPTER SCHOLARSHIP

Women's Transportation Seminar-Puget Sound Chapter
c/o Lorelei Mesic, Scholarship Co-Chair
W&H Pacific
3350 Monte Villa Parkway
Bothell, WA 98021-8972
(425) 951-4872   Fax: (425) 951-4808
E-mail: lmesic@whpacific.com
Web: www.wtspugetsound.org/nscholarships.html

Purpose To provide financial assistance to women undergraduate and graduate students, particularly minority women, from Washington who are working on a degree related to transportation and have financial need.

Eligibility This program is open to women who are residents of Washington, studying at a college in the state, or working as an intern in the state. Applicants must be currently enrolled in an undergraduate or graduate degree program in a transportation-related field, such as engineering, planning, finance, or logistics. They must have a GPA of 3.0 or higher and plans to prepare for a career in a transportation-related field. Minority candidates are encouraged to apply. Along with their application, they must submit a 500-word statement about their career goals after graduation,

their financial need, and why they think they should receive this scholarship award. Selection is based on transportation goals, academic record, transportation-related activities or job skills, and financial need.

Financial data The stipend is $1,500.

Duration 1 year.

Additional information The winner is also nominated for scholarships offered by the national organization of the Women's Transportation Seminar.

Number awarded 1 each year.

Deadline October of each year.

[386]
WTS/ITS WASHINGTON INTELLIGENT TRANSPORTATION SYSTEMS SCHOLARSHIP

Women's Transportation Seminar-Puget Sound Chapter
c/o Lorelei Mesic, Scholarship Co-Chair
W&H Pacific
3350 Monte Villa Parkway
Bothell, WA 98021-8972
(425) 951-4872   Fax: (425) 951-4808
E-mail: lmesic@whpacific.com
Web: www.wtspugetsound.org/nscholarships.html

Purpose To provide financial assistance to minority and other undergraduate and graduate students from Washington working on a degree related to intelligent transportation systems (ITS).

Eligibility This program is open to students who are residents of Washington, studying at a college in the state, or working as an intern in the state. Applicants must be currently enrolled in an undergraduate or graduate degree program related to the design, implementation, operation, and maintenance of ITS technologies. They must be majoring in transportation or a related field, including transportation engineering, systems engineering, electrical engineering, planning, finance, or logistics, and be taking courses in such ITS-related fields of study as computer science, electronics, and digital communications. In addition, they must have a GPA of 3.0 or higher and plans to prepare for a career in a transportation-related field. Minority candidates are encouraged to apply. Along with their application, they must submit a 500-word statement about their career goals after graduation, how those relate to ITS, and why they think they should receive this scholarship award. Selection is based on that statement, academic record, and transportation-related activities or job skills. Financial need is not considered.

Financial data The stipend is $1,500.

Duration 1 year.

Additional information This program is co-sponsored by ITS Washington.

Number awarded 1 each year.

Deadline October of each year.

[387]
XEROX TECHNICAL MINORITY SCHOLARSHIP PROGRAM

Xerox Corporation
Attn: Technical Minority Scholarship Program
150 State Street, Fourth Floor
Rochester, NY 14614
(585) 422-7689   E-mail: xtmsp@imcouncil.com
Web: www.xerox.com

Purpose To provide financial assistance to minorities interested in undergraduate or graduate education in the sciences and/or engineering.

Eligibility This program is open to minorities (people of African American, Asian, Pacific Islander, Native American, Native Alaskan, or Hispanic descent) working full time on an undergraduate or graduate degree in chemistry, computing and software systems, engineering (chemical, computer, electrical, imaging, manufacturing, mechanical, optical, or software), information management, laser optics, material science, physics, or printing management science. Applicants must be U.S. citizens or permanent residents with a GPA of 3.0 or higher and attending, or planning to attend, a 4-year college or university.

Financial data The maximum stipend is $1,000 per year.

Duration 1 year.

Number awarded Approximately 150 each year.

Deadline September of each year.

[388]
YALE NEW HAVEN HOSPITAL MINORITY NURSING AND ALLIED HEALTH SCHOLARSHIPS

Yale New Haven Hospital
Attn: Human Resources
20 York Street
New Haven, CT 06510-3202
(203) 688-5226   Fax: (203) 688-6670
E-mail: lacamera@ynhh.org
Web: www.ynhh.org/ynhch/ch_comm.html#career

Purpose To provide financial assistance to minority high school seniors in Connecticut interested in studying nursing or allied health fields in college.

Eligibility This program is open to graduating seniors at high schools in Connecticut who are members of minority groups. Applicants must be interested in attending a 4-year college or university with an accredited program in nursing, respiratory therapy, medical technology, pharmacy, or radiation therapy. Selection is based on academic record, teacher evaluations, an essay, and extracurricular activities.

Financial data The stipend is $1,500 per year.

Duration 1 year.

Number awarded 4 each year.

Deadline February of each year.

[389]
YOF SCHOLARSHIPS

Youth Opportunities Foundation
8820 South Sepulveda Boulevard, Suite 208
P.O. Box 45762
Los Angeles, CA 90045
(310) 670-7664   Fax: (310) 670-5238
Web: www.yoflatinoscholars.com

Purpose To provide financial assistance for college to Hispanic American high school seniors in California.

Eligibility This program is open to seniors graduating from high schools in California who have at least 1 parent of Latin American origin. Applicants must have a strong SAT score and a demonstrated record of leadership activities. Non-citizens are eligible. Preference is given to applicants who demonstrate the greatest financial need.

Financial data Stipends range from $100 to $500.

Duration 1 year; nonrenewable.

Number awarded Varies each year.

Deadline March of each year.

Fellowships

Described here are 289 funding programs open to Hispanic Americans that are to be used to fund studies on the graduate (for a master's degree, doctorate, professional degree, or specialist's certificate) or postgraduate level in the United States. Usually no return of service or repayment is required. Note: other funding opportunities for Hispanic Americans on the graduate or postgraduate level are also described in the Loans, Grants, Awards, and Internships sections. So, if you are looking for a particular program and don't find it in this section, be sure to check the Program Title Index to see if it is covered elsewhere in the directory.

[390]
AAUW CAREER DEVELOPMENT GRANTS

American Association of University Women
Attn: AAUW Educational Foundation
301 ACT Drive, Department 177
P.O. Box 4030
Iowa City, IA 52243-4030
(319) 337-1716   Fax: (319) 337-1204
E-mail: aauw@act.org
Web: www.aauw.org

Purpose To provide financial assistance to women (particularly women of color) who are seeking career advancement, career change, or reentry into the work force.

Eligibility This program is open to women who are U.S. citizens or permanent residents, have earned a bachelor's degree, received their most recent degree more than 4 years ago, and plan to work toward a master's degree, second bachelor's degree, or specialized training in technical or professional fields. Applicants must be planning to undertake course work at an accredited 2- or 4-year college or university (or a technical school that is licensed, accredited, or approved by the U.S. Department of Education). Special consideration is given to qualified members of the American Association of University Women (AAUW), women of color, women working on their first advanced degree, and women working on degrees in nontraditional fields. Doctoral students and candidates eligible for other fellowship programs of the AAUW may not apply for these grants.

Financial data The awards range from $2,000 to $8,000. The funds are to be used for tuition, fees, books, supplies, local transportation, and dependent care.

Duration 1 year, beginning in July; nonrenewable.

Number awarded Approximately 60 each year.

Deadline December of each year.

[391]
ABC HISPANIC SCHOLARSHIP FUNDS

American Baptist Churches USA
Attn: National Ministries
P.O. Box 851
Valley Forge, PA 19482-0851
(610) 768-2067   Toll-free: (800) ABC-3USA, ext. 2067
Fax: (610) 768-2453
E-mail: karen.drummond@abc-usa.org
Web: www.nationalministries.org

Purpose To provide financial assistance to Hispanic Americans who are interested in preparing for or furthering a church career in the American Baptist Church (ABC).

Eligibility This program is open to Hispanic American members of the church or its recognized institutions who demonstrate financial need. They must be enrolled on at least a two-thirds basis in an accredited institution, working on an undergraduate degree or first professional degree in a seminary. Applicants must be currently serving or planning to serve in a vocation with the church or with its recognized institutions. They must be U.S. citizens who have been a member of an American Baptist Church for at least 1 year.

Financial data The stipends range from $500 to $3,000 per year.

Duration 1 year; may be renewed.

Deadline May of each year.

[392]
ACCOUNTANCY BOARD OF OHIO EDUCATION ASSISTANCE PROGRAM

Accountancy Board of Ohio
77 South High Street, 18th Floor
Columbus, OH 43215-6128
(614) 466-4135   Fax: (614) 466-2628
Web: acc.ohio.gov/edrule.html

Purpose To provide financial assistance to minority and financially disadvantaged students enrolled in an accounting education program at Ohio academic institutions approved by the Accountancy Board of Ohio.

Eligibility This program is open to minority and financially disadvantaged Ohio residents enrolled full time as sophomores, juniors, or seniors in an accounting program at an accredited college or university in the state. Students who remain in good standing at their institutions and who enter a qualified fifth-year program are also eligible, if funds are available. Minority is defined as people with significant ancestry from Africa (excluding the Middle East), Asia (excluding the Middle East), Central America and the Caribbean islands, South America, and the islands of the Pacific Ocean. Financial disadvantage is defined according to information provided on the Free Application for Federal Student Aid (FAFSA). U.S. citizenship or permanent resident status is required.

Financial data The amount of the stipend is determined annually but does not exceed the in-state tuition at Ohio public universities.

Duration 1 year; nonrenewable.

Number awarded Several each year.

Deadline May or November of each year.

[393]
ACOUSTICAL SOCIETY OF AMERICA GRADUATE FELLOWSHIP FOR MINORITIES

Acoustical Society of America
Attn: Office Manager
2 Huntington Quadrangle, Suite 1NO1
Melville, NY 11747-4502
(516) 576-2360   Fax: (516) 576-2377
E-mail: asa@aip.org
Web: www.acoustics.org/education.html

Purpose To provide financial assistance to underrepresented minorities who are working on a graduate degree in acoustics.

Eligibility This program is open to U.S. and Canadian citizens and permanent residents who are members of a minority group that is underrepresented in the sciences (Hispanic, African American, or Native American). Applicants must be enrolled in or accepted to a graduate degree program as a full-time student. Their program of study may be in a field of pure and applied science and engineering directly related to acoustics, including acoustical oceanography, architectural acoustics, animal bioacoustics, biomedical ultrasound and bioresponse to vibration, engineering acoustics, musical acoustics, noise, physical acoustics, psychological acoustics, physiological acoustics, signal processing in acoustics, speech communication, structural acoustics and vibration, and underwater acoustics. Along with their application, they must submit a statement on why they are enrolled in their present academic program, including how they intend to use their graduate education to develop a career and how the study of acoustics is relevant to their career objectives.

Financial data The stipend is $15,000 per year. The sponsor strongly encourages the host educational institution to waive all tuition costs and assessed fees. Fellows also receive $1,000 for travel to attend a national meeting of the sponsor.

Duration 1 year; may be renewed for 1 additional year if the recipient is making normal progress toward a degree and is enrolled full time

Additional information This program was established in 1992.

Number awarded 1 or more each year.

Deadline March of each year.

---

[394]
ADRIENNE M. AND CHARLES SHELBY ROOKS FELLOWSHIP FOR RACIAL AND ETHNIC THEOLOGICAL STUDENTS

United Church of Christ
Attn: Local Church Ministries
700 Prospect Avenue East
Cleveland, OH 44115-1100
(216) 736-3865   Fax: (216) 736-3783
E-mail: lcm@ucc.org
Web: www.ucc.org/education/scholarships

Purpose To provide financial assistance to minority students who are either enrolled at an accredited seminary preparing for a career of service in the United Church of Christ or working on a doctoral degree in the field of religion.

Eligibility This program is open to members of a congregation of the United Church of Christ who are from an underrepresented ethnic group (African American, Hispanic American, Asian American, Native American Indian, or Pacific Islander). Applicants must be either 1) enrolled in an accredited school of theology in the United States or Canada with the intent to become a pastor or teacher within the United Church of Christ, or 2) doctoral (Ph.D., Th.D., or Ed.D.) students within a field related to religious studies. Seminary students must have a GPA in all postsecondary work of 3.0 or higher and must have begun the in-care process; preference is given to students who have demonstrated leadership through a history of service to the church and scholarship through exceptional academic performance. For doctoral students, preference is given to applicants who have demonstrated academic excellence, teaching effectiveness, and commitment to the United Church of Christ and who intend to become professors in colleges, seminaries, or graduate schools.

Financial data Grants range from $500 to $5,000 per year.

Duration 1 year; may be renewed.

Number awarded Varies each year; recently, 21 of these scholarships, worth $97,000, were awarded.

Deadline February of each year.

---

[395]
ADVANCING HISPANIC EXCELLENCE IN TECHNOLOGY, ENGINEERING, MATH, AND SCIENCE (AHETEMS) SCHOLARSHIP PROGRAM

Society of Hispanic Professional Engineers
5400 East Olympic Boulevard, Suite 210
Los Angeles, CA 90022
(323) 725-3970   Fax: (323) 725-0316
Web: www.shpe.org.

Purpose To provide financial assistance to Hispanic undergraduate and graduate students preparing for a career in science, technology, engineering, mathematics, or a related field.

Eligibility This program is open to members of the Society of Hispanic Professional Engineers (SHPE) who are accepted into or attending an accredited 2-year or 4-year college or university in the United States or Puerto Rico. Applicants must be enrolled full time with a major in science, technology, engineering, mathematics, or a related field. High school seniors and undergraduates must have a GPA of 2.5 or higher; graduate students must have a GPA of 3.25 or higher. Along with their application, they must submit a 1-page personal statement covering their family background, community involvement, leadership roles, achievements, and short-term and long-term goals and aspirations. Both merit-based and need-based scholarships are available. U.S. citizenship or permanent resident status is required.

Financial data Stipends range from $1,000 to $3,000.

Duration 1 year.

Additional information Information is also available from the AHETEMS Scholarship Program, 5012 Monarda Way, Fort Worth, TX 76123, (817) 361-8670, E-mail: rschwan@shpe.org.

Number awarded 1 or more each year.

Deadline March of each year.

---

[396]
AETNA/NCEMNA SCHOLARS PROGRAM

National Coalition of Ethnic Minority Nurse Associations
c/o Dr. Betty Smith Williams, President
6101 West Centinela Avenue, Suite 378
Culver City, CA 90230
(310) 258-9515   Fax: (310) 258-9513
E-mail: bwilliams@ncemna.org
Web: www.ncemna.org/scholarships.html

Purpose To provide financial assistance to nursing students who are members of constituent organizations of the National Coalition of Ethnic Minority Nurse Associations (NCEMNA) working on a 4-year or master's degree.

Eligibility This program is open to members of the 5 associations that comprise NCEMNA: the Asian American/Pacific Islander Nurses Association, Inc. (AAPINA), the National Alaska Native American Indian Nurses Association, Inc. (NANAINA), the National Association of Hispanic Nurses, Inc. (NAHN), the National Black Nurses Association, Inc. (NBNA), and the Philippine Nurses Association of America, Inc. (PNAA). Applicants must be currently attending or applying to a 4-year or master's degree program in nursing. Along with their application, they must submit a letter of reference, demonstration of leadership and involvement in the ethnic community, and statement of career goals.

Financial data The stipend is $2,000.

Duration 1 year.

Additional information This program was established in 2004 with a grant from the Aetna Foundation.

Number awarded 5 each year: 1 nominee from each of the constituent associations.

[397]
AICPA FELLOWSHIPS FOR MINORITY DOCTORAL STUDENTS

American Institute of Certified Public Accountants
Attn: Academic and Career Development Division
1211 Avenue of the Americas
New York, NY 10036-8775
(212) 596-6270   Fax: (212) 596-6292
E-mail: educat@aicpa.org
Web: www.aicpa.org

Purpose To provide financial assistance to minority doctoral students who wish to prepare for a career teaching accounting at the college level.

Eligibility This program is open to minority students who have applied to and/or been accepted into a doctoral program with a concentration in accounting; have earned a master's degree or completed a minimum of 3 years of full-time work in accounting, are attending or planning to attend school full time; and agree not to work full time in a paid position, teach more than 1 course as a teaching assistant, or work more than 25% as a research assistant. U.S. citizenship is required. Preference is given to applicants who have attained a C.P.A. designation. For purposes of this program, the American Institute of Certified Public Accountants (AICPA) considers minority students as those of Black, Native American, or Pacific Island races, or of Hispanic ethnic origin.

Financial data Awards range up to $12,000 per year (although most are about $8,000).

Duration 1 year; may be renewed up to 4 additional years.

Number awarded Varies each year; recently, 18 of these fellowships were awarded.

Deadline March of each year.

[398]
ALBERT W. DENT STUDENT SCHOLARSHIP

American College of Healthcare Executives
One North Franklin Street, Suite 1700
Chicago, IL 60606-3529
(312) 424-2800   Fax: (312) 424-0023
E-mail: ache@ache.org
Web: www.ache.org

Purpose To provide financial assistance to minority graduate student members of the American College of Healthcare Executives.

Eligibility This program is open to student associates of the organization in good standing. Applicants must be minority students enrolled full time in a health care management graduate program, able to demonstrate financial need, and a U.S. or Canadian citizen.

Financial data The stipend is $3,500.

Duration 1 year.

Additional information The program was established and named in honor of Dr. Albert W. Dent, the foundation's first Black fellow and president emeritus of Dillard University.

Number awarded Varies each year.

Deadline March of each year.

[399]
AMELIA KEMP MEMORIAL SCHOLARSHIP

Women of the Evangelical Lutheran Church in America
Attn: Scholarships
8765 West Higgins Road
Chicago, IL 60631-4189
(773) 380-2730   Toll-free: (800) 638-3522, ext. 2730
Fax: (773) 380-2419   E-mail: womenelca@elca.org
Web: www.womenoftheelca.org

Purpose To provide financial assistance to lay women of color who are members of Evangelical Lutheran Church of America (ELCA) congregations and who wish to study on the undergraduate, graduate, professional, or vocational school level.

Eligibility These scholarships are available to ELCA lay women of color who are at least 21 years of age and have experienced an interruption of at least 2 years in their education since high school. Applicants must have been admitted to an educational institution to prepare for a career in other than a church-certified profession. U.S. citizenship is required.

Financial data The amount of the award varies, depending on the availability of funds.

Duration Up to 2 years.

Number awarded Varies each year, depending upon the funds available.

Deadline February of each year.

[400]
AMERICAN ASSOCIATION OF OBSTETRICIANS AND GYNECOLOGISTS FOUNDATION SCHOLARSHIPS

American Association of Obstetricians and
    Gynecologists Foundation
Attn: Administrative Director
409 12th Street, S.W.
Washington, DC 20024-2188
(202) 863-1647   Fax: (202) 554-0453
E-mail: ejones@acog.org
Web: www.agosonline.org

Purpose To provide funding to physicians (particularly minorities and women) interested in a program of research training in obstetrics and gynecology.

Eligibility Applicants must have an M.D. degree and be eligible for the certification process of the American Board of Obstetrics and Gynecology (ABOG). They must document departmental planning for a significant research training experience to be conducted by 1 or more faculty mentors. There is no formal application form, but departments must supply a description of the candidate's qualifications, including a curriculum vitae, bibliography, prior training, past research experience, and evidence of completion of residency training in obstetrics and gynecology; a comprehensive description of the proposed training program; a description of departmental resources appropriate to the training; a list of other research grants, training grants, or scholarships previously or currently held by the applicant; and a budget. Applicants for the scholarship sponsored by ABOG must verify that 90% of their time and effort will be dedicated to the research training and conduct of research. Applicants for the scholarship sponsored by the Society for Maternal-Fetal Medicine (SMFM) must also have completed MFM subspecialty training or be in the second or third year of an ABOG-approved MFM training program at the time of applying. Candidates for that scholarship must also be members or associate members of the SMFM. Preference for both awards is given to training in areas currently under-represented in obstetrics and gynecology. A personal interview may be requested. Priority is given to individuals who have not previously received extramural funding for research training. Women and minority candidates are strongly encouraged to apply. Selection is based on the scholarly, clinical, and research qualifications of the candidate; evidence of the candidate's commitment to an investigative career in academic obstetrics and gynecology in the United States or Canada; qualifications of the sponsoring department and mentor; and quality of the research project.

Financial data The grant is $100,000 per year, of which at least $5,000 but not more than $15,000 must be used for employee benefits. In addition, sufficient funds to support travel to the annual fellows' retreat must be set aside. The balance of the funds may be used for salary, technical support, and supplies. The grant co-sponsored by the SMFM must be matched by an institutional commitment of at least $30,000 per year.

Duration 1 year; may be renewed for 2 additional years, based on satisfactory progress of the scholar.

Number awarded 2 each year: 1 co-sponsored by ABOG and 1 co-sponsored by SMFM.

Deadline August of each year.

[401]
AMERICAN BAR ASSOCIATION LEGAL OPPORTUNITY SCHOLARSHIP

American Bar Association
Attn: Fund for Justice and Education
321 North Clark Street
Chicago, IL 60610
(312) 988-5415   Fax: (312) 988-6392
E-mail: fje@staff.abanet.org
Web: www.abanet.org/fje/losfpage.html

Purpose To provide financial assistance to racial and ethnic minority students who are interested in attending law school.

Eligibility This program is open to racial and ethnic minority college graduates who are interested in attending an ABA-accredited law school. Only students beginning law school may apply; students who have completed 1 or more semesters of law school are not eligible. Applicants must have a cumulative GPA of 2.5 or higher and be citizens or permanent residents of the United States. Financial need must be demonstrated.

Financial data The stipend is $5,000 per year.

Duration 1 year; may be renewed for 2 additional years if satisfactory performance in law school has been achieved.

Additional information This program began in the 2000-01 academic year.

Number awarded Approximately 20 each year.

Deadline February of each year.

[402]
AMERICAN COLLEGE OF SPORTS MEDICINE GRADUATE SCHOLARSHIPS FOR MINORITIES AND WOMEN

American College of Sports Medicine
Attn: Research Review Committee
401 West Michigan Street
P.O. Box 1440
Indianapolis, IN 46206-1440
(317) 637-9200   Fax: (317) 637-7817
E-mail: mwayne@acsm.org
Web: www.acsm.org/grants/scholarships.htm

Purpose To provide financial assistance to minority and women graduate students who are interested in preparing for a career in sports medicine or exercise science.

Eligibility This program is open to minorities and women who have been accepted in a full-time master's, Ph.D., M.D., or equivalent degree program in sports medicine, exercise science, or other related field. Minorities are defined as American Indians, Alaskan Natives, Asians, Pacific Islanders, Blacks, and Hispanics. Applicants must submit 3 letters of professional recommendation (including at least 1 from a current member of the American College of Sports Medicine), evidence of participation in sports medicine or exercise science (including documentation of research and scholarly activities), transcripts, GRE or MCAT scores, and a 300-word description of short- and long-term career goals.

Financial data The stipend is $1,500 per year. Funds are to be used to cover tuition and/or fees.

Duration 1 year; may be renewed for up to 3 additional years.

Additional information Recipients are given a 1 year's free membership in the American College of Sports Medicine.

Deadline April of each year.

[403]
AMERICAN DIETETIC ASSOCIATION GRADUATE SCHOLARSHIPS

American Dietetic Association
Attn: Accreditation, Education Programs, and Student Operations
120 South Riverside Plaza, Suite 2000
Chicago, IL 60606-6995
(312) 899-0040   Toll-free: (800) 877-1600, ext. 5400
Fax: (312) 899-4817   E-mail: education@eatright.org
Web: www.eatright.org

Purpose To provide financial assistance to graduate student members of the American Dietetic Association (ADA).

Eligibility This program is open to ADA members who are enrolled or planning to enroll in a master's or doctoral degree program in dietetics. Applicants who are currently completing a dietetic internship or preprofessional practice program that is combined with a graduate program may also apply. The graduate scholarships are available only to U.S. citizens and permanent residents. Applicants should intend to practice in the field of dietetics. Some scholarships require specific areas of study (e.g., public health nutrition, food service administration) and status as a registered dietitian. Others may require membership in a specific dietetic practice group, residency in a specific state, or underrepresented minority group status. The same application form can be used for all categories.

Financial data Stipends range from $500 to $4,500.

Duration 1 year.

Number awarded Varies each year, depending upon the funds available. Recently, the sponsoring organization awarded 144 scholarships for all its programs.

Deadline February of each year.

[404]
AMERICAN POLITICAL SCIENCE ASSOCIATION MINORITY FELLOWS PROGRAM

American Political Science Association
Attn: APSA Minority Fellows Program
1527 New Hampshire Avenue, N.W.
Washington, DC 20036-1206
(202) 483-2512   Fax: (202) 483-2657
E-mail: apsa@apsanet.org
Web: www.apsanet.org/section_427.cfm

Purpose To provide financial assistance to underrepresented minorities interested in working on a doctoral degree in political science.

Eligibility This program is open to African Americans, Latino(a)s, and Native Americans who are in their senior year at a college or university or currently enrolled in a master's degree program. Applicants must be planning to enroll in a doctoral program in the following academic year for the first time. They must be U.S. citizens and able to demonstrate financial need.

Financial data The stipend is $2,000 per year.

Duration 2 years.

Additional information In addition to the fellows who receive stipends from this program, fellows without stipend are recommended for admission and financial support to every doctoral political science program in the country. This program was established in 1969.

Number awarded 6 each year.

Deadline October of each year.

[405]
AMERICAN SOCIETY OF CRIMINOLOGY GRADUATE FELLOWSHIPS FOR ETHNIC MINORITIES

American Society of Criminology
Attn: Awards Committee
1314 Kinnear Road, Suite 212
Columbus, OH 43212-1156
(614) 292-9207   Fax: (614) 292-6767
E-mail: asc41@infinet.com
Web: www.asc41.com/minorfel.htm

Purpose To provide financial assistance to ethnic minority doctoral students in criminology and criminal justice.

Eligibility This program is open to African American, Asian American, Latino, and Native American doctoral students planning to enter the field of criminology and criminal justice. Applicants must submit an up-to-date curriculum vitae; an indication of race or ethnicity; copies of undergraduate and graduate transcripts; a statement of need and prospects for other financial assistance; a letter describing career plans, salient experiences, and nature of interest in criminology and criminal justice; and 3 letters of reference.

Financial data Stipends up to $6,000 are available.

Duration 1 year.

Additional information This fellowship was first awarded in 1989.

Number awarded 3 each year.

Deadline February of each year.

[406]
AMERICAN SPEECH-LANGUAGE-HEARING FOUNDATION SCHOLARSHIP FOR MINORITY STUDENTS

American Speech-Language-Hearing Foundation
Attn: Graduate Student Scholarship Competition
10801 Rockville Pike
Rockville, MD 20852-3279
(301) 897-5700   Toll-free: (800) 498-2071
Fax: (301) 571-0457   TTY: (800) 498-2071
E-mail: foundation@asha.org
Web: www.ashfoundation.org

Purpose To provide financial assistance to minority graduate students in communication sciences and disorders programs.

Eligibility This program is open to full-time graduate students who are enrolled in communication sciences and disorders programs, with preference given to U.S. citizens who are members of a racial or ethnic minority group. Selection is based on academic promise and outstanding academic achievement. Master's (but not doctoral) candidates must be enrolled in an ASHA Educational Standards Board (ESB) accredited program.

Financial data The stipend ranges from $2,000 to $4,000. Funds must be used for educational support (e.g., tuition, books, school living expenses), not for personal or conference travel.

Duration 1 year.

Number awarded 1 each year.

Deadline June of each year.

[407]
APA PLANNING FELLOWSHIPS

American Planning Association
Attn: Member Services Department
122 South Michigan Avenue, Suite 1600
Chicago, IL 60603-6107
(312) 431-9100   Fax: (312) 431-9985
E-mail: fellowship@planning.org
Web: www.planning.org/institutions/scholarship.htm

Purpose To support underrepresented minority students enrolled in master's degree programs at recognized planning schools.

Eligibility This program is open to first- and second-year graduate students in urban and regional planning who are members of the following minority groups: African American, Hispanic American, or Native American. Applicants must be citizens of the United States and able to document financial need. They must submit a 2- to 5-page personal statement describing how their graduate education will be applied to career goals and why they chose planning as a career path, 2 letters of recommendation, and official transcripts. Selection is based on the personal statement and letters of recommendation, academic performance and/or improvement during the past 2 years, and financial need.

Financial data Awards range from $1,000 to $5,000 per year. The money may be applied to tuition and living expenses only. Payment is made to the recipient's university and divided by terms in the school year.

Duration 1 year; recipients may reapply.

Additional information The fellowship program started in 1970 as a Ford Foundation Minority Fellowship Program.

Number awarded Varies each year.

Deadline April of each year.

[408]
ARL INITIATIVE TO RECRUIT A DIVERSE WORKFORCE

Association of Research Libraries
Attn: Program Officer for Training & Diversity
21 Dupont Circle, N.W., Suite 800
Washington, DC 20036
(202) 296-2296   Fax: (202) 872-0884
E-mail: arlhq@arl.org
Web: www.arl.org/diversity/init

Purpose To provide financial assistance to members of underrepresented racial and ethnic groups who are interested in preparing for a career as an academic or research librarian.

Eligibility This program is open to members of racial and ethnic minority groups that are underrepresented as professionals in academic and research libraries. Applicants must be interested in working on an M.L.S. degree in an ALA-accredited program. Along with their application, they must submit a 350-word essay on what attracts them to a career in a research library. The essays are judged on clarity and content of form, clear goals and benefits, enthusiasm, potential growth perceived, and professional goals.

Financial data The stipend is $5,000 per year.

Duration 2 years.

Additional information This program began in 2000. Recipients must agree to work for at least 2 years in a library that is a member of the Association of Research Libraries (ARL) after completing their degree.

Number awarded The program's goal is to award up to 15 of these scholarships each year.

Deadline July of each year.

[409]
ASCA FOUNDATION SCHOLARSHIPS

American School Counselor Association
Attn: ASCA Foundation
1101 King Street, Suite 625
Alexandria, VA 22314
(703) 683-ASCA   Toll-free: (800) 306-4722
Fax: (703) 683-1619
E-mail: asca@schoolcounselor.org
Web: www.schoolcounselor.org

Purpose To provide financial assistance for graduate school to members of the American School Counselor Association (ASCA), especially males and minorities.

Eligibility This program is open to ASCA members working on a master's degree in school counseling. Applicants must submit a 2-page essay on how school counselors should be held accountable for fulfilling their duties and responsibilities. Males and minorities are especially encouraged to apply.

Financial data The stipend is $1,000.

Duration 1 year.

Additional information Support for this program is provided by Anheuser-Busch.

Number awarded Up to 10 each year.

Deadline October of each year.

[410]
ASSOCIATION OF CUBAN ENGINEERS SCHOLARSHIPS

Association of Cuban Engineers
Attn: Selection Committee
P.O. Box 557575
Miami, FL 33255-7575
(305) 649-7429
Web: www.a-i-c.org

Purpose To provide financial assistance to undergraduate and graduate students of Cuban American heritage who are interested in preparing for a career in engineering.

Eligibility This program is open to U.S. citizens and legal residents who have completed at least 30 units of college work in the United States and are majoring or planning to major in some aspect of engineering. Applicants must be attending an ABET-accredited college or university within the United States or Puerto Rico as a full-time student with a GPA of 3.0 or higher. They must be of Cuban or other Hispanic heritage (at least 1 grandparent Cuban or other Hispanic nationality). Along with their application, they must submit brief essays on their family history, professional goals, extracurricular activities, work experience, and how they will help other Cuban and Hispanic engineering students in the future. Financial need is not considered in the selection process.

Financial data Stipends range from $500 to $1,000.

Duration 1 year.

Additional information This program includes the Luciano Goicochea Award (for the top-rated Cuban American student at the University of Miami) and the Noel Betancourt Award (for the top-rated Cuban American student at Florida International University).

Number awarded Up to 20 each year.

Deadline November of each year.

[411]
ASSOCIATION OF LATINO PROFESSIONALS IN FINANCE AND ACCOUNTING SCHOLARSHIPS

Association of Latino Professionals in Finance and
  Accounting
Attn: Scholarships
510 West Sixth Street, Suite 400
Los Angeles, CA 90017
(213) 243-0004   Fax: (213) 243-0006
E-mail: scholarships@national.alpfa.org
Web: www.alpfa.org

Purpose To provide financial assistance to undergraduate and graduate students of Hispanic descent who are preparing for a career in a field related to finance or accounting.

Eligibility This program is open to full-time undergraduate and graduate students who have completed at least 15 undergraduate units at a college or university in the United States or Puerto Rico with a GPA of 3.0 or higher. Applicants must be of Hispanic heritage, defined as having 1 parent fully Hispanic or both parents half Hispanic. They must be working on a degree in accounting, finance, information technology, or a related field. Along with their application, they must submit a 2-page personal statement that addresses their Hispanic heritage and family background, personal and academic achievements, academic plans and career goals, efforts and plans for making a difference in their community, and financial need. U.S. citizenship or permanent resident status is required.

Financial data Stipends range from $1,000 to $5,000.

Duration 1 year.

Additional information The sponsoring organization was formerly named the American Association of Hispanic Certified Public Accountants. This program is administered by the Hispanic College Fund, 1717 Pennsylvania Avenue, Suite 460, Washington, DC 20006, (202) 296-5400, (800) 644-4223, Fax: (202) 296-3774.

Number awarded Varies each year; recently, 78 of these scholarships, worth $195,000, were awarded.

Deadline April of each year.

[412]
ASTRAZENECA FELLOWSHIP/FACULTY TRANSITION AWARDS

Foundation for Digestive Health and Nutrition
Attn: Research Awards Coordinator
4930 Del Ray Avenue
Bethesda, MD 20814-2512
(301) 222-4005   Fax: (301) 222-4010
E-mail: info@fdhn.org
Web: www.fdhn.org

Purpose To provide funding to physicians (especially those who are minority group members or women) for research training in an area of gastrointestinal, liver function, or related diseases.

Eligibility This program is open to trainee members of the American Gastroenterological Association (AGA) who are M.D.s or M.D./Ph.D.s currently holding a gastroenterology-related fellowship at an accredited North American institution. Applicants must be committed to an academic career; have completed 2 years of research training at the start of this award; be sponsored by an AGA member who directs a gastroenterology-related unit that is engaged in research training in a North American medical school, affiliated teaching hospital, or research institute; and be cosponsored by the director of a basic research laboratory (or other comparable laboratory) who is committed to the training and development of the applicant. Minorities and women investigators are strongly encouraged to apply. Selection is based on novelty, feasibility, and significance of the proposal; attributes of the candidate; record and commitment of the sponsors; and the institutional and laboratory environment.

Financial data The stipend is $40,000 per year. Funds are to be used as salary support for the recipient. Indirect costs are not allowed.

Duration 2 years.

Additional information This award is administered by the Foundation for Digestive Health and Nutrition (FDHN) and sponsored by the AGA with support from AstraZeneca Pharmaceuticals, L.P. Finalists for the award are interviewed. Although the host institution may supplement the award, the applicant may not concurrently have a similar training award or grant from another organization. All publications coming from work funded by this program must acknowledge the support of the award.

Number awarded Up to 4 each year.

Deadline September of each year.

[413]
AT&T LABORATORIES FELLOWSHIP PROGRAM

AT&T Laboratories
Attn: Fellowship Administrator
180 Park Avenue, Room C103
P.O. Box 971
Florham Park, NJ 07932-0971
(973) 360-8109   Fax: (973) 360-8881
E-mail: recruiting@research.att.com
Web: www.research.att.com/academic/alfp.html

Purpose To provide financial assistance and work experience to underrepresented minority and women students who are working on a doctoral degree in computer and communications-related fields.

Eligibility This program is open to minorities underrepresented in the sciences (Blacks, Hispanics, and Native Americans) and to women. Applicants must be U.S. citizens or permanent residents beginning full-time Ph.D. study in a discipline relevant to the business of AT&T; currently, those include communications, computer science, electrical engineering, human computer interaction, industrial engineering, information science, mathematics, operations research, and statistics. Along with their application, they must submit a personal statement on why they are enrolled in their present academic program and how they intend to use their technical training, official transcripts, 3 academic references, and GRE scores. Selection is based on potential for success in scientific research.

Financial data This program covers all educational expenses during the school year, including tuition, books, fees, and approved travel expenses; education expenses for summer study or university research; a stipend for living expenses of $2,380 per month (paid for 10 months of the year); and support for attending approved scientific conferences.

Duration 1 year; may be renewed for up to 2 additional years, as long as the fellow continues making satisfactory progress toward the Ph.D.

Additional information The AT&T Laboratories Fellowship Program (ALFP) provides a mentor who is a staff member at AT&T Labs as well as a summer research internship within AT&T Laboratories during the first summer. The ALFP replaces the Graduate Research Program for Women (GRPW) and the Cooperative Research Fellowship Program (CRFP) run by the former AT&T Bell Laboratories. If recipients accept other support, the tuition payment and stipend received from that fellowship will replace that provided by this program. The other provisions of this fellowship will remain in force and the stipend will be replaced by an annual grant of $2,000.

Number awarded Approximately 8 each year.

Deadline January of each year.

[414]
BALFOUR PHI DELTA PHI MINORITY SCHOLARSHIP PROGRAM

Phi Delta Phi International Legal Fraternity
1426 21st Street, N.W., First Floor
Washington, DC 20036
(202) 223-6801   Toll-free: (800) 368-5606
Fax: (202) 223-6808   E-mail: info@phideltaphi.org
Web: www.phideltaphi.org

Purpose To provide financial assistance to minorities who are members of Phi Delta Phi International Legal Fraternity.

Eligibility All ethnic minority members of the legal fraternity are eligible to apply for this scholarship. Selection is based on participation, ethics, and scholastics.

Financial data The stipend is $3,000 per year.

Duration 1 year.

Additional information This scholarship was established in 1997. Funding for this scholarship comes from the Lloyd G. Balfour Foundation.

Number awarded 1 each year.

Deadline October of each year.

[415]
BARBARA JORDAN MEMORIAL SCHOLARSHIP

Association of Texas Professional Educators
Attn: Scholarships
305 East Huntland Drive, Suite 300
Austin, TX 78752-3792
(512) 467-0071   Toll-free: (800) 777-ATPE
Fax: (512) 467-2203
Web: www.atpe.org/Awards/index.html

Purpose To provide financial assistance to undergraduate and graduate students enrolled in educator preparation programs at predominantly ethnic minority institutions in Texas.

Eligibility This program is open to juniors, seniors, and graduate students enrolled in educator preparation programs at predominantly ethnic minority institutions in Texas. Applicants must submit a 2-page essay on their personal philosophy toward education, why they want to become an educator, who influenced them the most in making their career decision, and why they are applying for the

scholarship. Financial need is not considered in the selection process.

Financial data The stipend is $1,500 per year.

Duration 1 year.

Additional information The qualifying institutions are Huston-Tillotson College, Jarvis Christian College, Our Lady of the Lake University, Paul Quinn College, Prairie View A&M University, St. Mary's University of San Antonio, Sul Ross State University, Sul Ross State University Rio Grande College, Texas A&M International University, Texas A&M University at Kingsville, Texas Southern University, University of Houston, University of Houston-Downtown, University of St. Thomas, University of Texas at Brownsville and Texas Southmost College, University of Texas at El Paso, University of Texas at San Antonio, University of Texas-Pan American, University of the Incarnate Word, and Wiley College.

Number awarded Up to 6 each year.

Deadline May of each year.

[416]
BEHAVIORAL SCIENCES POSTDOCTORAL FELLOWSHIPS IN EPILEPSY

Epilepsy Foundation
Attn: Research Department
4351 Garden City Drive
Landover, MD 20785-7223
(301) 459-3700   Toll-free: (800) EFA-1000
Fax: (301) 577-2684   TDD: (800) 332-2070
E-mail: grants@efa.org
Web: www.epilepsyfoundation.org

Purpose To provide funding to postdoctorates (especially minorities, women, and persons with disabilities) in the behavioral sciences who wish to pursue research training in an area related to epilepsy.

Eligibility Individuals who have received their doctoral degree in a behavioral science field by the time the fellowship begins and desire additional postdoctoral research experience in epilepsy may apply. Academic faculty holding the rank of instructor or above are not eligible, nor are graduate or medical students, medical residents, permanent government employees, or employees of private industry. Appropriate fields of study in the behavioral sciences include sociology, social work, anthropology, nursing, economics, and others relevant to epilepsy research and practice. Because these fellowships are designed as training opportunities, the quality of the training plans and environment are considered in the selection process. Other selection criteria include the scientific quality of the proposed research, a statement regarding the relevance of the research to epilepsy, the applicant's qualifications, and the preceptor's qualifications. Applications from women, members of minority groups, and people with disabilities are especially encouraged. U.S. citizenship is not required, but the research must be conducted in the United States.

Financial data Grants up to $30,000 per year are available.

Duration 1 year.

Number awarded Varies each year; recently, 2 of these fellowships were awarded.

Deadline February of each year.

[417]
BELL LABS GRADUATE RESEARCH FELLOWSHIP PROGRAM

Lucent Technologies
Attn: Fellowship Programs Manager
283 King George Road, Room B1-D26
Warren, NJ 07059
(732) 559-6971   E-mail: coopgraduate@lucent.com
Web: www.lucent.com/news/foundation/blgrfp

Purpose To provide financial assistance and work experience to women and underrepresented minorities who wish to work on a doctoral degree in designated fields of science and engineering.

Eligibility This program is open to women and underrepresented minorities who plan to work full-time on a doctoral degree in chemical engineering, chemistry, communications science, computer science and engineering, electrical engineering, information science, materials science, mathematics, mechanical engineering, operations research, physics, or statistics. Applicants usually are graduating college seniors, but first-year graduate students are also considered. U.S. citizenship or permanent resident status is required. Selection is based on scholastic attainment and evidence of ability and potential as a research scientist.

Financial data Fellowships provide full tuition and university fees, an annual stipend of $17,000, a book allowance of $250 per semester, and an annual grant of $1,000 for travel to conferences.

Duration 1 year; may be renewed for up to 3 additional years if the fellow makes satisfactory progress toward the doctoral degree.

Additional information Bell Laboratories established the Cooperative Research Fellowship Program (CRFP) for underrepresented minorities in 1972. A parallel program, the Graduate Research Program for Women (GRPW), was established in 1974. In 2003, at the direction of the Lucent Foundation, those programs were merged under the current name. During their first summer in the program, fellows are expected to working with a mentor at Bell Labs on a research project in their area of interest. Fellows are encouraged to continue their association with their mentors during the following academic year and throughout their graduate studies. Information is also available from Scholarship America, Attn: Scholarship Management Services, One Scholarship Way, P.O. Box 297, St. Peter, MN 56082, (507) 931-1682, (800) 537-4180, Fax: (507) 931-9168, E-mail: smsinfo@csfa.org.

Number awarded Approximately 10 each year.

Deadline January of each year.

[418]
BILL BERNBACH MINORITY SCHOLARSHIP FUND

American Association of Advertising Agencies
Attn: Manager of Diversity Programs
405 Lexington Avenue, 18th Floor
New York, NY 10174-1801
(212) 682-2500   Toll-free: (800) 676-9333
Fax: (212) 682-8391   E-mail: tiffany@aaaa.org
Web: www.aaaa.org/diversity/foundation/funds.htm

Purpose To provide financial assistance to multicultural students interested in working on a graduate degree in advertising.

Eligibility This program is open to African Americans, Asian Americans, Hispanic Americans, and Native Americans who are interested in studying the advertising creative arts at designated institutions. Applicants must have already received an undergraduate degree and be able to demonstrate financial need. As part of the selection process, they must submit 10 samples of creative work in their respective field of expertise.

Financial data The stipend is $5,000.

Duration Most awards are for 2 years.

Additional information This program began in 1997 and currently provides scholarships to students at the Adcenter at Virginia Commonwealth University, the Creative Circus and the Portfolio Center in Atlanta, and the Miami Ad School.

Number awarded 4 each year.

[419]
BOARD OF GOVERNORS MEDICAL SCHOLARSHIP PROGRAM

North Carolina State Education Assistance Authority
Attn: Scholarship and Grant Services
10 T.W. Alexander Drive
P.O. Box 14103
Research Triangle Park, NC 27709-4103
(919) 549-8614   Toll-free: (800) 700-1775
Fax: (919) 549-8481   E-mail: information@ncseaa.edu
Web: www.ncseaa.edu

Purpose To provide financial assistance to residents (especially minorities) of North Carolina who have been admitted to a medical school in the state.

Eligibility Students must be nominated for this program. Nominees must be residents of North Carolina, be able to demonstrate financial need, express an intent to practice medicine in North Carolina, and have been accepted for admission to 1 of the 4 medical schools in North Carolina: Bowman Gray School of Medicine at Wake Forest University, Duke University School of Medicine, East Carolina University School of Medicine, and the University of North Carolina at Chapel Hill School of Medicine. Minorities are especially encouraged to apply.

Financial data Each scholarship provides a stipend of $5,000 a year, plus tuition and mandatory fees.

Duration 1 year; renewable up to 3 additional years, provided the recipient makes satisfactory academic progress, continues to have financial need, and remains interested in medical practice in North Carolina.

Number awarded 20 new awards are granted each year. Recently, a total of 81 students were receiving $1,637,085 in support through this program

Deadline April of each year.

[420]
BOSTON CHAPTER MINORITY SCHOLARSHIP

Special Libraries Association-Boston Chapter
Attn: Danielle Green Barney, Co-Chair, Affirmative
   Action Committee
6 Warren Road
Framingham, MA 01702
(617) 495-8306   Fax: (617) 496-3811
E-mail: dbarney@hbs.edu
Web: www.sla.org/chapter/cbos/awards.htm

Purpose To provide financial assistance for library education to minority graduate students from New England.

Eligibility This program is open to members of minority groups (African Americans, Hispanics, Asian Americans, Pacific Islanders, Native Hawaiians, American Indians, and Alaskan Natives) who are enrolled or planning to enroll in an accredited graduate library science program. Applicants must be residents of New England or attending school in the region. They must submit an essay (500 to 750 words) on their interest and experience in special libraries. Financial need is not considered in the selection process.

Financial data The stipend is $2,000.

Duration 1 year.

Number awarded 1 each year.

Deadline April of each year.

[421]
C. CLYDE FERGUSON LAW SCHOLARSHIP

New Jersey Commission on Higher Education
Attn: Educational Opportunity Fund
20 West State Street, Seventh Floor
P.O. Box 542
Trenton, NJ 08625-0542
(609) 984-2709   Fax: (609) 292-7225
E-mail: nj_che@che.state.nj.us
Web: www.state.nj.us

Purpose To provide financial assistance to disadvantaged and minority students who want to study law in New Jersey.

Eligibility Applicants must be disadvantaged students or members of an ethnic minority group that has been historically underrepresented in the legal profession. They must have been New Jersey residents for at least 12 months before receiving the award. They must plan to enroll full time in the Minority Student Program at law schools in New Jersey (Rutgers University School of Law at Newark, Rutgers University School of Law at Camden, or Seton Hall Law School). Applicants may be former or current undergraduate recipients of the New Jersey Educational Opportunity Fund (EOF) grant or students who would have met the undergraduate EOF grant eligibility requirements. Financial need must be demonstrated.

Financial data Awards are based on financial need. In no case, however, can awards exceed the maximum amount of tuition, fees, room, and board charged at Rutgers University School of Law at Newark.

Duration 1 year; may be renewed.

[422]
CALIFORNIA SPACE GRANT GRADUATE STUDENT PROGRAM

California Space Grant Consortium
c/o University of California at San Diego
California Space Institute
9500 Gilman Drive, Department 0524
La Jolla, CA 92093-0524
(858) 822-1597   Fax: (858) 534-7840
E-mail: spacegrant@ucsd.edu
Web: calspace.ucsd.edu/casgc/scholarships.html

Purpose To provide financial assistance (particularly to underrepresented minorities, women, and persons with disabilities) for graduate study and research in space-related science, engineering, or technology at the branches of the University of California.

Eligibility This program is open to graduate students in space-related science, engineering, and technology at the campuses of the UC system. Most programs include research components. U.S. citizenship is required. As the California element of the Space Grant program of the U.S. National Aeronautics and Space Administration (NASA), this program encourages applications from underrepresented ethnic or gender groups and by persons with disabilities.

Financial data Each campus sets its own stipend.

Duration 1 year.

Additional information This program is funded by NASA.

Number awarded Varies each year.

Deadline Each of the participating UC campuses sets its own deadline.

[423]
CALIFORNIA STATE PSYCHOLOGICAL ASSOCIATION FOUNDATION MINORITY SCHOLARSHIP PROGRAM

California State Psychological Association Foundation
Attn: Scholarship Coordinator
3835 North Freeway Boulevard, Suite 240
Sacramento, CA 95834-1955
(916) 286-7979   Fax: (916) 325-9790
Web: fdncenter.org

Purpose To provide financial assistance to minority students interested in working on a doctoral degree in psychology in California.

Eligibility Applicants must be full-time graduate students who are enrolled or accepted in a doctoral-level psychology program at an accredited California school. Applicants must belong to 1 of the following ethnic groups: Black/African American, Hispanic/Latino, Asian/Asian American, American Indian/Alaskan Native, or Pacific Islander. Along with their application, they must submit 3 to 5 letters of recommendation, an official transcript, and documentation of financial need. Selection is based on potential for completing doctoral-level work in psychology. No distinction or preference is made for practitioner versus academic programs. Priority is given to applicants with demonstrated community involvement or leadership, whose graduate program focuses on ethnic minority cultural issues, and who plan to work with direct delivery of services to a culturally diverse population in either private or public settings.

Financial data The stipend is $2,000.

Duration 1 year; nonrenewable.

Additional information This program was established in 1991.

Number awarded 3 each year: 1 each to a first-, second-, and third-year doctoral student.

Deadline October of each year.

[424]
CAMINO AL EXITO SCHOLARSHIP PROGRAM

Hispanic Scholarship Fund
Attn: Selection Committee
55 Second Street, Suite 1500
San Francisco, CA 94105
(415) 808-2350   Toll-free: (877) HSF-INFO
Fax: (415) 808-2302   E-mail: highschool@hsf.net
Web: www.hsf.net/scholarship/programs/camino.php

Purpose To provide financial assistance for college or graduate school to Hispanic residents of selected cities throughout the United States and children of Telemundo employees.

Eligibility This program is open to U.S. citizens, permanent residents, and visitors with a passport stamped I-551 who are of Hispanic heritage. Applicants must be 1) children of Telemundo employees, or 2) residents of the target Telemundo markets of Chicago, Los Angeles, Miami, or New York. They must have a GPA of 3.0 or higher and be graduating high school seniors or full-time undergraduate or graduate students at an accredited college or university in the United States, Puerto Rico, or the U.S. Virgin Islands. Along with their application, they must submit 600-word essays on 1) how their Hispanic heritage, family upbringing, and/or role models have influenced their personal long-term goals; 2) how they contribute to their community and what they have learned from their experiences; and 3) an academic challenge they have faced and how they have overcome it. Selection is based on academic achievement, personal strengths, leadership, and financial need.

Financial data Stipends range from $2,500 to $5,000 per year.

Duration 1 year.

Number awarded 1 or more each year.

Deadline December of each year.

[425]
CANFIT PROGRAM SCHOLARSHIPS

California Adolescent Nutrition, Physical Education, and
   Culinary Arts Scholarships
2140 Shattuck Avenue, Suite 610
Berkeley, CA 94704
(510) 644-1533   Toll-free: (800) 200-3131
Fax: (510) 644-1535   E-mail: info@canfit.org
Web: www.canfit.org/scholarships.html

Purpose To provide financial assistance to minority undergraduate and graduate students who are studying nutrition, physical education, or culinary arts in California.

Eligibility Eligible to apply are American Indians/Alaska Natives, African Americans, Asians/Pacific Islanders, and Latinos/Hispanics who are enrolled in either: 1) an approved master's or doctoral graduate program in nutrition, public health nutrition, or physical education or in a preprofessional practice program approved by the American Dietetic

Association at an accredited university in California; or, 2) an approved bachelor's or professional certificate program in culinary arts, nutrition, or physical education at an accredited university or college in California. Graduate student applicants must have completed at least 12 units of graduate course work and have a cumulative GPA of 3.0 or higher; undergraduate applicants must have completed 50 semester units or the equivalent of college credits and have a cumulative GPA of 2.5 or higher. Selection is based on financial need, academic goals, and community nutrition or physical education activities.

Financial data Graduate stipends are $1,000 each and undergraduate stipends are $500 per year.

Additional information A goal of the California Adolescent Nutrition and Fitness (CANFit) program is to improve the nutritional status and physical fitness of California's low-income multi-ethnic youth aged 10 to 14. By offering these scholarships, the program hopes to encourage more students to consider careers in adolescent nutrition and fitness.

Number awarded 5 graduate scholarships and 10 undergraduate scholarships are available each year.

Deadline March of each year.

[426]
CARL A. SCOTT BOOK SCHOLARSHIPS

Council on Social Work Education
Attn: Chair, Carl A. Scott Memorial Fund
1725 Duke Street, Suite 500
Alexandria, VA 22314-3457
(703) 683-8080   Fax: (703) 683-8099
E-mail: eafrancis@cswe.org
Web: www.cswe.org

Purpose To provide financial assistance to ethnic minority social work students in their last year of study for a baccalaureate or master's degree.

Eligibility This program is open to students from ethnic groups of color (African American, Asian American, Mexican American, Puerto Rican, and American Indian) who are in the last year of study for a social work degree in an accredited baccalaureate or master's degree program. Applicants must have a cumulative GPA of 3.0 or higher and be enrolled full time. They must demonstrate a commitment to work for equity and social justice in social work.

Financial data The award is $500.

Duration This is a 1-time award.

Number awarded 2 each year.

Deadline May of each year.

[427]
CASA OF OREGON SCHOLARSHIP

Hispanic Metropolitan Chamber
Attn: Scholarship Committee
P.O. Box 1837
Portland, OR 97207
(503) 222-0280
Web: www.hmccoregon.com

Purpose To provide financial assistance for college and graduate school to Hispanic residents of Oregon and Clark County, Washington who are from a farmworker household.

Eligibility This program is open to residents of Oregon and Clark County, Washington who are of Hispanic ancestry. Applicants must be from a farmworker family and be enrolled or planning to enroll in an accredited community college, 4-year university, or graduate school. Along with their application, they must submit 250-word essays on what being a Latino student means to them, their life as a member of a farmworker family and the obstacles they have had to overcome, why they should be selected to receive another scholarship from this sponsor (if they are applying for a renewal), and/or what they intend to do with their degree in 10 years (if they are a first-time applicant). If they wish to be considered for a scholarship for low-income families, they may also submit documentation of financial need.

Financial data The stipend is $2,500.

Duration 1 year; may be renewed.

Number awarded Varies each year; recently, 3 of these scholarships were awarded.

Deadline February of each year.

[428]
CATHY L. BROCK MEMORIAL SCHOLARSHIP

Institute for Diversity in Health Management
Attn: Education Program Coordinator
One North Franklin Street, 28th Floor
Chicago, IL 60606
Toll-free: (800) 233-0996   Fax: (312) 422-4566
E-mail: clopez@aha.org
Web: www.diversityconnection.com

Purpose To provide financial assistance to minorities who are entering or continuing graduate students in health care management or business management.

Eligibility This program is open to members of ethnic minority groups who are either accepted to graduate school or first- or second-year graduate students. Applicants must be accepted or enrolled in an accredited program in health care management or business management and have a GPA of 3.0 or higher. They must demonstrate commitment to a career in health services administration, financial need, solid extracurricular and community service activities, and a strong interest and experience in finance. U.S. citizenship or permanent resident status is required.

Financial data The stipend is $1,000.

Duration 1 year.

Number awarded 1 or more each year, depending on the availability of funds.

Deadline October of each year.

[429]
CAVE MEMORIAL AWARD

National Optometric Association
c/o Dr. Charles Comer, Association Manager
3723 Main Street
P.O. Box F
East Chicago, IL 46312
Toll-free: (877) 394-2020   Fax: (219) 398-1077
E-mail: ccomer2@aol.com
Web: www.natoptassoc.org

Purpose To provide financial assistance to members (particularly members who are minorities) of the National Optometric Student Association (NOSA).

Eligibility This program is open to NOSA members enrolled in a school or college of optometry. Applicants must have a GPA of 2.5 or higher and be able to demonstrate community involvement. Along with their application, they must submit a 2-page statement on their career goals, community and college involvement, and how they feel they can affect minority communities in a positive way. Financial need is considered in the selection process.

Financial data The stipend is $500.

Duration 1 year.

Additional information The National Optometric Association was founded in 1969 with the goal of recruiting minority students for schools and colleges of optometry. It remains committed to improving the quality and accessibility of eye care in minority and other historically underserved communities.

Number awarded 1 each year.

Deadline April of each year.

[430]
CENTOCOR EXCELLENCE IN IBD CLINICAL RESEARCH AWARDS

Foundation for Digestive Health and Nutrition
Attn: Research Awards Coordinator
4930 Del Ray Avenue
Bethesda, MD 20814-2512
(301) 222-4005   Fax: (301) 222-4010
E-mail: info@fdhn.org
Web: www.fdhn.org

Purpose To provide funding to senior gastroenterology fellows (especially minorities and women) interested in preparing for a research career in inflammatory bowel diseases (IBD).

Eligibility This program is open to trainee members of the American Gastroenterological Association (AGA) who have an M.D. or equivalent degree. Applicants must be currently enrolled in an accredited gastroenterology-related fellowship at a U.S. institution and committed to an academic career. They must be interested in additional full-time research training in IBD clinical science to acquire modern laboratory skills. Their sponsor must be an AGA member engaged in research training at an academic gastroenterology-related unit of a medical school, affiliated teaching hospital, or research institute. A co-sponsor must be the director of a clinical or other comparable laboratory who is committed to the training and development of the applicant. The institution must provide them with at least 75% protected time. Women and minority investigators are strongly encouraged to apply. Selection is based on novelty, feasibility, and significance of the proposal; attributes of the candidate; record and commitment of the sponsors; and the institutional and laboratory environment.

Financial data The grant is $70,000 per year. No institutional indirect costs are allowed.

Duration 1 year; nonrenewable.

Additional information This program is administered by the Foundation for Digestive Health and Nutrition (FDHN) with support from Centocor, Inc. and the AGA.

Number awarded 5 each year.

Deadline January of each year.

[431]
CHICANA/LATINA FOUNDATION SCHOLARSHIPS

Chicana/Latina Foundation
Attn: Scholarship Program
1419 Burlingame Avenue, Suite N
Burlingame, CA 94010
(650) 373-1084   Fax: (650) 373-1090
E-mail: info@chicanalatina.org
Web: www.chicanalatina.org/scholarship.html

Purpose To provide financial assistance for higher education to Latina women who live in or come from any state and attend school in the San Francisco Bay area.

Eligibility This program is open to Latina women who either have resided for at least 2 years in or are currently enrolled in accredited colleges, universities, or community colleges in the following California counties: Alameda, Contra Costa, Marin, Monterey, Napa, San Francisco, San Mateo, Santa Clara, Santa Cruz, Solano, or Sonoma. Undergraduate students must have completed at least 15 college units, must be enrolled as full-time students, must have a GPA of 2.5 or higher, and must complete 3 essays (on their family background, their community activities, and their career goals). Graduate students must verify acceptance to a graduate school and complete a supplementary application that requires 3 essays: on an issue affecting the Latina community in the Bay area, on their personal background, and on their leadership of their younger Chicana/Latina sisters so they stay in school and graduate. Selection is based on commitment to Latina women's progress and development, demonstrated leadership qualities, involvement within the Latino community, clarity of direction and goals, academic achievement, and letters of recommendation. Students who received a scholarship from the foundation within the past 4 years are not eligible.

Financial data The stipend is $1,500 per year.

Duration 1 year.

Additional information The foundation was formerly known as the Chicana Foundation of Northern California. Recipients must agree to volunteer at least 5 hours in the following year in support of the Chicana/Latina Foundation.

Number awarded Varies each year; recently, 18 of these scholarships were awarded.

Deadline March of each year.

[432]
CLA SCHOLARSHIP FOR MINORITY STUDENTS IN MEMORY OF EDNA YELLAND

California Library Association
717 20th Street, Suite 200
Sacramento, CA 95814
(916) 447-8541   Fax: (916) 447-8394
E-mail: info@cla-net.org
Web: www.cla-net.org/awards/ednayelland.php

Purpose To provide financial assistance to students of ethnic minority origin in California who are interested in preparing for a career in library or information science.

Eligibility This program is open to California residents who are members of ethnic minority groups (American Indian, African American/Black, Mexican American/Chicano, Latino/Hispanic, Asian American, Pacific Islander, or Filipino). Applicants must be enrolled or accepted for enrollment in a master's program at an accredited graduate library school in California. Evidence of financial need and U.S. citizenship or permanent resident status must be submitted. Finalists are interviewed.

Financial data The stipend is $2,500.

Duration 1 academic year.

Additional information This fellowship is named for the executive secretary of the California Library Association from 1947 to 1963 who worked to promote the goals of the California Library Association and the profession. Until 1985, it was named the Edna Yelland Memorial Scholarship.

Number awarded 3 each year.

Deadline May of each year.

[433]
CLINICAL RESEARCH POST-DOCTORAL FELLOWSHIP PROGRAM

American Nurses Association
Attn: Ethnic Minority Fellowship Programs
600 Maryland Avenue, S.W., Suite 100 West
Washington, DC 20024-2571
(202) 651-7244   Fax: (202) 651-7007
E-mail: emfp@ana.org
Web: www.nursingworld.org

Purpose To provide funding to postdoctoral minority nurses interested in a program of research and study on psychiatric, mental health, and substance abuse issues that impact the lives of ethnic minority people.

Eligibility This program is open to doctoral-prepared nurses who are members of an ethnic or racial minority group, including but not limited to Blacks or African Americans, Hispanics or Latinos, American Indians and Alaska Natives, Asians and Asian Americans, and Native Hawaiians and other Pacific Islanders. Applicants must be able to demonstrate a commitment to a research career in nursing and psychiatric/mental health issues affecting ethnic minority populations. They must be interested in a program of full-time postdoctoral study, with a research focus on such issues of concern to minority populations as child abuse, violence in intimate relationships, mental health disorders, substance abuse, mental health service utilization, and stigma as a barrier to mental health care and personal resilience. U.S. citizenship or permanent resident status and membership in the American Nurses Association are required.

Financial data The stipend is $28,260 per year.

Duration Up to 2 years.

Additional information Funds for this program are provided by the Substance Abuse and Mental Health Services Administration.

Number awarded 1 or more each year.

[434]
CLINICAL RESEARCH PRE-DOCTORAL FELLOWSHIP PROGRAM

American Nurses Association
Attn: Ethnic Minority Fellowship Programs
600 Maryland Avenue, S.W., Suite 100 West
Washington, DC 20024-2571
(202) 651-7244   Fax: (202) 651-7007
E-mail: emfp@ana.org
Web: www.nursingworld.org

Purpose To provide financial assistance to minority nurses who are doctoral candidates interested in psychiatric, mental health, and substance abuse issues that impact the lives of ethnic minority people.

Eligibility This program is open to nurses who have a master's degree and are members of an ethnic or racial minority group, including but not limited to Blacks or African Americans, Hispanics or Latinos, American Indians and Alaska Natives, Asians and Asian Americans, and Native Hawaiians and other Pacific Islanders. Applicants must be able to demonstrate a commitment to a research career in nursing and psychiatric/mental health issues affecting ethnic minority populations. They must be interested in a program of full-time doctoral study, with a research focus on such issues of concern to minority populations as child abuse, violence in intimate relationships, mental health disorders, substance abuse, mental health service utilization, and stigma as a barrier to mental health care and personal resilience. U.S. citizenship or permanent resident status and membership in the American Nurses Association are required. Selection is based on research potential, scholarship, writing ability, knowledge of broad issues in mental health nursing, and professional commitment to ethnic minority concerns.

Financial data Fellows receive a stipend of $20,772 per year and $5,000 in tuition assistance.

Duration 3 to 5 years.

Additional information Funds for this program are provided by the Substance Abuse and Mental Health Services Administration.

Number awarded 1 or more each year.

Deadline February of each year.

[435]
COLLEGE SCHOLARSHIP PROGRAM OF THE HISPANIC SCHOLARSHIP FUND

Hispanic Scholarship Fund
Attn: Selection Committee
55 Second Street, Suite 1500
San Francisco, CA 94105
(415) 808-2350   Toll-free: (877) HSF-INFO
Fax: (415) 808-2302   E-mail: college1@hsf.net
Web: www.hsf.net/scholarship/programs/college.php

Purpose To provide financial assistance for college or graduate school to Hispanic American students.

Eligibility This program is open to U.S. citizens, permanent residents, and visitors with a passport stamped I-551. Applicants must be of Hispanic heritage and enrolled full time in a degree program at an accredited community college, 4-year university, or graduate school in the United States, Puerto Rico, or the U.S. Virgin Islands. They must have completed at least 12 undergraduate units with a GPA of 3.0 or higher and have applied for federal financial aid. Along with their application, they must submit 600-word essays on 1) how their Hispanic heritage, family upbringing, and/or role models have influenced their personal long-term goals; 2) how they contribute to their community and what they have learned from their experiences; and 3) an academic challenge they have faced and how they have overcome it. Selection is based on academic achievement, personal strengths, leadership, and financial need.

Financial data Stipends normally range from $1,000 to $3,000 per year.

Duration 1 year; recipients may reapply.

Additional information Since this program began in 1975, more than $144 million has been awarded to more than 68,000 Hispanic students.

Number awarded More than 4,000 each year.

Deadline October of each year.

[436]
CONGRESSIONAL HISPANIC CAUCUS INSTITUTE SCHOLARSHIP AWARDS

Congressional Hispanic Caucus Institute, Inc.
911 Second Street, N.E.
Washington, DC 20002
(202) 543-1771   Toll-free: (800) EXCEL-DC
Fax: (202) 546-2143   E-mail: chci@chci.org
Web: www.chciyouth.org

Purpose To provide financial assistance for college or graduate school to students of Hispanic descent.

Eligibility This program is open to U.S. citizens and permanent residents who are Hispanic as defined by the U.S. Census Bureau (individuals of Mexican, Puerto Rican, Cuban, Central and South American, and other Spanish and Latin American descent). Applicants must be attending or planning to attend an accredited community college, 4-year university, or professional or graduate program as a full-time student. They must submit evidence of financial need, consistent active participation in public and/or community service activities, good writing skills, and 1-page essays on 1) how effective the public education system has been in addressing the needs of the Latino community and what policy recommendations they suggest to improve the system; and 2) the field of study they plan to pursue and how the Latino community will benefit.

Financial data The stipend is $2,500 at 4-year and graduate institutions or $1,000 at 2-year community colleges.

Duration 1 year.

Number awarded Varies each year. Recently, 63 of these scholarships were awarded: 5 to community college students, 40 to undergraduates, and 18 to graduate students.

Deadline April of each year.

[437]
CONNECTICUT COMMUNITY COLLEGE MINORITY TEACHING FELLOWSHIPS

Connecticut Community College System
Attn: System Officer for Diversity Awareness
61 Woodland Street
Hartford, CT 06105-9949
(860) 244-7606   Fax: (860) 566-6624
E-mail: karmstrong@commnet.edu
Web: www.commnet.edu/minority_fellowship.asp

Purpose To provide financial assistance and work experience to graduate students, especially minorities, in Connecticut who are interested in preparing for a career in community college teaching or administration.

Eligibility This program is open to graduate students who have completed at least 6 credits of graduate work and have indicated an interest in a career in community colleges. Applicants must be willing to commit to at least 1 year of employment in the Connecticut Community College System. Although all qualified graduate students are eligible, the program encourages applicants to register who strengthen the racial and cultural diversity of the minority fellow registry. That includes, in particular, making all possible efforts to recruit from historically underrepresented people (Asians, Blacks, and Hispanics).

Financial data Fellows receive a stipend of $3,500 per semester.

Duration 1 year; may be renewed.

Additional information Fellows are expected to dedicate 9 hours per week to the program. They spend 6 hours per week in teaching-related activities under the supervision of a mentor. During the second semester, they assist the mentor in teaching a course. The remaining time is spent on program and campus orientation activities, attendance at relevant faculty or staff meetings, and participation in other college meetings or professional development activities.

Number awarded Up to 13 each year: 1 at each of the 12 colleges in the system and 1 in the chancellor's office.

[438]
CONNECTICUT SPECIAL EDUCATION TEACHER INCENTIVE GRANT

Connecticut Department of Higher Education
Attn: Education and Employment Information Center
61 Woodland Street
Hartford, CT 06105-2326
(860) 947-1846   Toll-free: (800) 842-0229 (within CT)
Fax: (860) 947-1311   E-mail: setig@ctdhe.org
Web: www.ctdhe.org/SFA/sfa.htm

Purpose To provide financial assistance to undergraduate and graduate students (particularly underrepresented minorities) in Connecticut who are preparing for a career as a special education teacher.

Eligibility This program is open to full-time juniors and seniors and full- or part-time graduate students who are residents of Connecticut. Applicants must be enrolled in 1) special education teacher preparation programs at selected universities in Connecticut; or 2) out-of-state teacher preparation programs seeking cross-endorsement for teaching "low-incidence student" areas. They must be nominated by the dean of education at their school and have a stated intent to teach in a Connecticut public school, an approved private special education facility, or a Regional Educational Service Center. Priority is given to minority (African American, Hispanic/Latino, Asian American, and Native American) and bilingual students and to Connecticut residents enrolled in an approved out-of-state program.

Financial data The stipend is $5,000 per year for full-time study or $2,000 per year for part-time graduate study.

Duration 1 year.

Additional information The approved in-state programs are at Central Connecticut State University, Fairfield University, Saint Joseph College, Southern Connecticut State University, University of Connecticut, and University of Hartford. The programs for students seeking cross-endorsement certification for teaching students who are blind and partially-sighted or visually impaired are at Hunter College of CUNY (New York, New York), Dominican College (Orangeburg, New York), Teachers College of Columbia University (New York, New York), and University of Northern Colorado (Greeley, Colorado). The programs for students seeking cross-endorsement certification for teaching students who are deaf or hearing-impaired are at Hunter College, Teachers College, Clarke School for the Deaf at Smith College (Northampton, Massachusetts), and Boston University (Boston, Massachusetts).

Number awarded Varies each year.

Deadline August of each year.

[439]
CONSORTIUM FOR GRADUATE STUDY IN MANAGEMENT FELLOWSHIPS

Consortium for Graduate Study in Management
5585 Pershing Avenue, Suite 240
St. Louis, MO 63112
(314) 877-5500   Toll-free: (888) 658-6814
Fax: (314) 877-5505   E-mail: frontdesk@cgsm.org
Web: www.cgsm.org

Purpose To provide financial assistance and work experience to underrepresented racial minorities interested in preparing for a management career in business.

Eligibility Eligible to apply are African Americans, Hispanic Americans (Chicanos, Cubans, Dominicans, and Puerto Ricans), and Native Americans who have graduated from college and are interested in a career in business. An undergraduate degree in business or economics is not required. Applicants must be U.S. citizens and planning to work on an M.B.A. degree at 1 of the consortium's 13 schools. Preference is given to applicants under 31 years of age.

Financial data The fellowship pays full tuition and required fees. Summer internships with the consortium's cooperative sponsors, providing paid practical experience, are also offered.

Duration Up to 4 semesters. The participating schools are Carnegie Mellon University, Dartmouth College, Emory University, Indiana University, University of Michigan, New York University, University of North Carolina at Chapel Hill, University of Rochester, University of Southern California, University of Texas at Austin, University of Virginia, Washington University, and University of Wisconsin at Madison.

Additional information Fellowships are tenable at member schools only.

Number awarded Varies; up to 400 each year.

Deadline The early deadline is the end of November of each year. The final deadline is in January of each year.

[440]
CONSUELO W. GOSNELL MEMORIAL SCHOLARSHIPS

National Association of Social Workers
Attn: NASW Foundation
750 First Street, N.E., Suite 700
Washington, DC 20002-4241
(202) 408-8600, ext. 298   Fax: (202) 336-8313
E-mail: naswfoundation@naswdc.org
Web: www.naswfoundation.org/gosnell.asp

Purpose To provide financial assistance to Native American, Hispanic American, and other students interested in working on a master's degree in social work.

Eligibility This program is open to students who have applied to or been accepted into an accredited M.S.W. program. Applicants must have demonstrated a commitment to working with, or have a special affinity with, American Indian, Alaska Native, or Hispanic/Latino populations in the United States. They must be members of the National Association of Social Workers (NASW), have the potential for completing an M.S.W. program, and have a GPA of 3.0 or higher. Applicants who have demonstrated a commitment to working with public or voluntary nonprofit agencies or with local grassroots groups in the United States are also eligible.

Financial data The stipends range from $1,000 to $4,000 per year.

Duration Up to 1 year; may be renewed for 1 additional year.

Number awarded Up to 10 each year.

Deadline March of each year.

[441]
COORS LIGHT ACADEMIC SUCCESS IN EDUCATION (CLASE) SCHOLARSHIP AWARD

Hispanic Association of Colleges and Universities
Attn: National Scholarship Program
One Dupont Circle, N.W. Suite 605
Washington, DC 20036
(202) 467-0893   Fax: (202) 496-9177
TTY: (800) 855-2880   E-mail: scholarships@hacu.net
Web: scholarships.hacu.net/applications/applicants

Purpose To provide financial assistance to undergraduate and graduate students studying business or pharmacy at institutions in California that belong to the Hispanic Association of Colleges and Universities (HACU).

Eligibility This program is open to full-time undergraduate and graduate students at 4-year HACU member and partner colleges in California. Applicants must have a declared major in pharmacy or business and a GPA of 3.0 or higher. They must be able to demonstrate financial need. Along with their application, they must submit an essay of 200 to 250 words that describes their academic and/or career goals, where they expect to be and what they expect to be doing 10 years from now, and what skills they can bring to an employer.

Financial data The stipend is $1,000 per year.

Duration 1 year; nonrenewable.

Additional information This program is sponsored by the Coors Brewing Company and administered by HACU. Recently, the sponsor provided additional funding in conjunction with the concert tour of the musical group *Maná Revolución de Amor*. For every concert ticket sold, the group donated $0.50 and Coors matched with an additional $0.50, to a combined maximum contribution of $200,000.

Number awarded Varies each year.

Deadline May of each year.

[442]
CROWELL & MORING DIVERSITY IN THE LEGAL PROFESSION SCHOLARSHIPS

Crowell & Moring LLP
Attn: Diversity in the Legal Profession Scholarship
1001 Pennsylvania Avenue, N.W.
Washington, DC 20004-2595
(202) 624-2849   Fax: (202) 628-5116
E-mail: scholarship@crowell.com
Web: www.crowell.com/diversityscholarship

Purpose To provide financial assistance to minority students from any state attending a law school in the District of Columbia.

Eligibility This program is open to students of racial or ethnic minority origin (American Indian/Alaskan Native, Black/African American or African, Hispanic/Latino, or Asian/Pacific Islander). Applicants must be enrolled in the first year (or second year for students in a part-time or joint degree program) at an accredited law school in the District of Columbia. They must submit a personal statement of 1,000 words or less on 1) significant obstacles, disadvantages, and/or challenges that they have overcome in pursuit of a legal education; and 2) how they plan to use their legal education upon completion of law school and how they foresee this scholarship assisting in that regard. Selection is based on academic performance, leadership skills, work experience, community service, special accomplishments and honors, and financial need.

Financial data Stipends are $10,000 or $7,500.

Duration 1 year.

Additional information This program was established in 2005.

Number awarded 3 each year: 1 at $10,000 and 2 at $7,500.

Deadline April of each year.

[443]
CSCPA ETHNIC DIVERSITY SCHOLARSHIPS FOR COLLEGE STUDENTS

Colorado Society of Certified Public Accountants
Attn: CSCPA Educational Foundation
7979 East Tufts Avenue, Suite 500
Denver, CO 80237-2845
(303) 741-8613   Toll-free: (800) 523-9082 (within CO)
Fax: (303) 773-6344   E-mail: gmantz@cocpa.org
Web: www.cocpa.org

Purpose To provide financial assistance to minority undergraduate or graduate students in Colorado who are studying accounting.

Eligibility This program is open to African Americans, Hispanics, Asian Americans, American Indians, and Pacific Islanders studying at a college or university in Colorado at the associate, baccalaureate, or graduate level. Applicants must have completed at least 1 intermediate accounting class, be declared accounting majors, have completed at least 8 semester hours of accounting classes, and have a GPA of at least 3.0. Selection is based first on scholastic achievement and second on financial need.

Financial data The stipend is $1,000. Funds are paid directly to the recipient's school to be used for books, tuition, room, board, fees, and expenses.

Duration 1 year; recipients may reapply.

Number awarded 2 each year.

Deadline June of each year.

[444]
D. AUGUSTUS STRAKER SCHOLARSHIP

D. Augustus Straker Bar Association
Attn: Foundation Board
P.O. Box 1898
Troy, MI 48099-1898
Web: www.michbar.org/localbars/straker/home.html

Purpose To provide financial assistance to minority students at law schools in Michigan.

Eligibility This program is open to minority students enrolled in a certified law school program within the state of Michigan. Applicants must demonstrate scholarly dedication, involvement in school and community activities, and the ability to articulate a vision that indicates prospects for long-term success in the practice of law, especially as it relates to representing minority viewpoints within the system of jurisprudence.

Financial data The stipend is $2,500.

Duration 1 year.

Additional information The D. Augustus Straker Bar Association was founded in 1990 as a proactive organization for African American attorneys. It was named in honor of the first African American attorney to argue a case before the Michigan Supreme Court (in 1890).

Number awarded 2 each year.

Deadline March of each year.

[445]
DAVIS WRIGHT TREMAINE 1L DIVERSITY SCHOLARSHIP PROGRAM

Davis Wright Tremaine LLP
Attn: Recruiting Administrator
2600 Century Square
1501 Fourth Avenue
Seattle, WA 98101-1688
(206) 622-3150   Fax: (206) 628-7699
E-mail: seattle@dwt.com
Web: www.dwt.com/recruit/diversity.htm

Purpose To provide financial assistance and summer work experience to law students of color.

Eligibility This program is open to first-year law students of color and others of diverse background. Applicants must possess a strong academic record as an undergraduate and in first year of law school, an interest in participating in community and civic opportunities, and a willingness to commit

to working in the sponsor's Seattle or Portland office during the summer between their first and second year of law school. They must submit a current resume, a complete undergraduate transcript, grades from the first semester of law school, a short personal essay indicating their interest in the scholarship, a legal writing sample, and 2 or 3 references. Although demonstrated need may be taken into account, applicants need not disclose their financial circumstances.

Financial data The award consists of a $7,500 stipend for second-year tuition and expenses and a paid summer clerkship.

Duration 1 academic year and summer.

Number awarded 3 each year: 2 in the Seattle office and 1 in the Portland office.

Deadline January of each year.

[446]
DELL/UNCF CORPORATE SCHOLARS PROGRAM

United Negro College Fund
Attn: Corporate Scholars Program
P.O. Box 1435
Alexandria, VA 22313-9998
Toll-free: (866) 671-7237 E-mail: internship@uncf.org
Web: www.uncf.org/internships/index.asp

Purpose To provide financial assistance and work experience to undergraduate and graduate students, especially minorities, majoring in designated fields and interested in an internship at Dell Computer Corporation's corporate headquarters near Austin, Texas.

Eligibility This program is open to rising juniors and graduate students who are enrolled full time at institutions that are members of the United Negro College Fund (UNCF) or at any other 4-year college or university. Applicants must be majoring in business administration, computer science, engineering (computer, electrical, or mechanical), finance, human resources, management information systems, marketing, or supply chain management with a GPA of 3.0 or higher. Along with their application, they must submit a 1-page essay about themselves and their career goals, including information about their personal background and any particular challenges they have faced. Finalists are interviewed by a team of representatives from Dell, the program's sponsor.

Financial data The program provides a paid summer internship, housing accommodations in Austin, round-trip transportation to and from Austin, and (based on financial need and successful internship performance) a $10,000 scholarship.

Duration 10 to 12 weeks for the internship; 1 year for the scholarship.

Number awarded Varies each year.

Deadline January of each year.

[447]
DELORES A. AUZENNE FELLOWSHIP FOR GRADUATE STUDY

State University System of Florida
Attn: Office of Academic and Student Affairs
325 West Gaines Street, Suite 1501
Tallahassee, FL 32399-1950
(850) 245-0467   Fax: (850) 245-9667
E-mail: we're.listening@fldoe.org
Web: www.fldoe.org

Purpose To provide financial assistance to minority students in Florida working on a graduate degree in an underrepresented discipline.

Eligibility Eligible to be nominated are minority students working on a graduate degree at a public university in Florida. Nominees must be enrolled in full-time studies in a discipline in which there is an underrepresentation of the minority group to which they belong. A GPA of 3.0 or higher and U.S. citizenship or permanent resident status are required.

Financial data The stipend is $5,000 per year.

Duration 1 year; may be renewed if the recipient maintains full-time enrollment and at least a 3.0 GPA.

Additional information This program is administered by the equal opportunity program at each of the 11 State University System of Florida 4-year institutions. Contact that office for further information.

Number awarded 5 each year.

[448]
DOMINICAN BAR ASSOCIATION LAW SCHOOL SCHOLARSHIPS

Dominican Bar Association
Attn: Law School Scholarship Program
P.O. Box 203
New York, NY 10013
(917) 898-0DBA
Web: www.dominicanbarassociation.org

Purpose To provide financial assistance to law students who are committed to serving the Latino community.

Eligibility This program is open to students currently enrolled in their first, second, or third year of law school. Applicants must submit a 750-word personal statement on their reasons for studying law, interest in a particular field, professional objectives, plans after law school, and past involvement in activities that they believe have served or benefited the Latino community and how those activities relate to their decision to prepare for a career in the legal profession. Selection is based on academic and personal achievement, financial need, and demonstrated involvement in and commitment to serve the Latino community through the legal profession.

Financial data Stipends range from $500 to $7,000.

Duration 1 year.

Number awarded 1 or more each year.

Deadline March of each year.

[449]
DR. HILDEGARD E. PEPLAU SCHOLARSHIP

American Psychiatric Nurses Association
Attn: APN Foundation
1555 Wilson Boulevard, Suite 515
Arlington, VA 22209
(703) 243-2443   Fax: (703) 243-3390
E-mail: inform@apna.org
Web: www.apna.org/foundation/scholarships.html

Purpose To provide financial assistance to students and registered nurses (especially minorities) working on a degree in nursing.

Eligibility This program is open to students and registered nurses enrolled in an NLN-accredited program in nursing. Applicants must submit 3 essays (each up to 500 words) on the following topics: 1) their career goals, how education will enhance those goals, and their contribution to the profession; 2) their professional activities, involvement, continuing education, and scholarly contributions; and 3) their voluntary community activities. Financial need is not considered in the selection process. Minorities are especially encouraged to apply.

Financial data The stipend is $1,000.

Duration 1 year.

Number awarded 1 or more each year.

Deadline January of each year.

[450]
DR. JOHN HOWLETTE AND C. CLAYTON POWELL STUDENT FOUNDERS AWARD

National Optometric Association
c/o Dr. Charles Comer, Association Manager
3723 Main Street
P.O. Box F
East Chicago, IL 46312
Toll-free: (877) 394-2020   Fax: (219) 398-1077
E-mail: ccomer2@aol.com
Web: www.natoptassoc.org

Purpose To provide financial assistance to members of the National Optometric Student Association (NOSA).

Eligibility This program is open to NOSA members enrolled in the first, second, or third year at a school or college of optometry. Applicants must have a GPA of 3.0 or higher and be able to demonstrate leadership within the profession and community. Along with their application, they must submit a 2-page statement on their career goals, community and college involvement, and how they feel they can affect minority communities in a positive way. Financial need is considered in the selection process.

Financial data The stipend is $500.

Duration 1 year.

Additional information The National Optometric Association was founded in 1969 with the goal of recruiting minority students for schools and colleges of optometry. It remains committed to improving the quality and accessibility of eye care in minority and other historically underserved communities.

Number awarded 1 each year.

Deadline April of each year.

[451]
DR. JUAN D. VILLARREAL–HDA FOUNDATION SCHOLARSHIPS

Hispanic Dental Association
Attn: HDA Foundation
188 West Randolph Street, Suite 415
Chicago, IL 60601
(312) 577-4013   Toll-free: (800) 852-7921
Fax: (312) 577-0052
E-mail: HispanicDental@hdassoc.org
Web: www.hdassoc.org

Purpose To provide financial assistance to Hispanic dental hygiene and dental students at institutions in Texas.

Eligibility This program is open to Hispanic dental hygiene and dental students. Applicants must have been accepted or be currently enrolled at an accredited dental school in Texas as a full-time student. Along with their application, they must submit an essay on their career goals, especially their contribution to the Hispanic community. Selection is based on commitment and dedication to improving health in the Hispanic community, leadership skills, scholastic achievement, and community service.

Financial data Stipends are $1,000 or $500.

Duration 1 year.

Additional information This program began in 1995.

Number awarded 1 or more each year.

Deadline June of each year for dental students; July of each year for dental hygiene students.

[452]
DR. NANCY FOSTER SCHOLARSHIP PROGRAM

National Oceanic and Atmospheric Administration
Attn: National Ocean Service
Office of the Assistant Administrator
1305 East-West Highway, 13th Floor
Silver Spring, MD 20910-3281
(301) 713-3074   E-mail: fosterscholars@noaa.gov
Web: fosterscholars.noaa.gov

Purpose To provide financial assistance to graduate students, especially minorities and women, who are interested in working on a degree in fields related to marine sciences.

Eligibility This program is open to U.S. citizens, particularly women and members of minority groups, currently working on or intending to work on a master's or doctoral degree in oceanography, marine biology, or maritime archaeology, including the curation, preservation, and display of maritime artifacts. Selection is based on academic record, recommendations, financial need, career goals and objectives, and the applicant's potential for success in a graduate study program.

Financial data The program provides a stipend of $20,000 per year and a tuition allowance of up to $12,000 per year.

Duration Up to 2 years for master's degree students or up to 4 years for doctoral students.

Additional information These scholarships were first awarded in 2001.

Number awarded 4 each year.

Deadline April of each year.

[453]
DRI LAW STUDENT DIVERSITY SCHOLARSHIP

DRI-The Voice of the Defense Bar
Attn: Diversity Scholarship Committee
150 North Michigan Avenue, Suite 300
Chicago, IL 60601
(312) 795-1101   Fax: (312) 795-0747
E-mail: dri@dri.org
Web: www.dir.org/dir/about/diversityawards.cfm

Purpose To provide financial assistance to minority and women law students.

Eligibility This program is open to students entering their second year of law school who are African American, Hispanic, Asian, Pan Asian, Native American, or female. Applicants must submit an essay, up to 1,000 words, on the topic "With the Continuing Decline in the Number of Civil Trials, What Methods Can Defense Lawyers Adopt to Preserve the Civil Jury System?" Selection is based on that essay, demonstrated academic excellence, service to the profession, service to the community, and service to the cause of diversity. Students affiliated with the Association of Trial Lawyers of America as members, student members, or employees are not eligible. Finalists are invited to participate in personal interviews.

Financial data The stipend is $10,000 per year.

Duration 1 year.

Additional information This program was established in 2004.

Number awarded 2 each year.

Deadline September of each year.

[454]
EAST OHIO CONFERENCE BOARD OF ORDAINED MINISTRY ETHNIC MINORITY GRANTS

United Methodist Church-East Ohio Conference
Attn: Board of Ordained Ministry
8800 Cleveland Avenue, N.W.
P.O. Box 2800
North Canton, OH 44720
(330) 499-3972   Toll-free: (800) 831-3972
Fax: (330) 499-3279
Web: www.eocumc.com

Purpose To provide financial assistance to ethnic minority undergraduate and graduate students who are preparing for ordained ministry in the East Ohio Conference.

Eligibility This program is open to ethnic minority college and graduate students who are preparing for ordained ministry in the East Ohio Conference. Students must be recommended to receive this aid either by their District Superintendent or by the District Committee on Ordained Ministry where they hold their relationship. Applicants must attend a college or seminary that is fully accredited by the University Senate. They do not need to be certified candidates. Ethnic minority undergraduate pre-theological students are also eligible.

Financial data The stipend is $500 per year.

Duration 1 year.

Additional information Information is also available from Preston Forbes, Seminary Scholarships and Grants Secretary, 9071 Inverrary Drive, Warren, OH 44484, (330) 856-2631, E-mail: forbes@onecom.com.

Number awarded 1 or more each year.

Deadline September of each year.

[455]
EDUCATIONAL ADVANCEMENT GRADUATE SCHOLARSHIPS

American Association of Critical-Care Nurses
Attn: Educational Advancement Scholarships
101 Columbia
Aliso Viejo, CA 92656-4109
(949) 362-2000, ext. 338
Toll-free: (800) 899-AACN, ext. 338
Fax: (949) 362-2020   E-mail: info@aacn.org
Web: www.aacn.org

Purpose To assist members of the American Association of Critical-Care Nurses (AACN) who are working on a graduate degree in nursing.

Eligibility This program is open to registered nurses who are current members of the association and enrolled in an accredited master's or doctoral degree program in nursing. Applicants must hold an active R.N. license and be currently working in critical care or have 1 year's experience in the last 3 years. They must have a cumulative GPA of 3.0 or higher. Along with their application, they must submit 1) a 1-page essay on how they see their nursing practice changing as a result of their graduate degree; and 2) a 2-page exemplar (an essay describing a situation in which their intervention made a difference in a patient's outcome). Financial need is not considered in the selection process. Qualified ethnic minority candidates receive at least 20% of these awards.

Financial data The stipend is $1,500. The funds are sent directly to the recipient's college or university and may be used only for tuition, fees, books, and supplies.

Duration 1 year; recipients may reapply.

Number awarded Varies each year; recently, 72 of these scholarships were awarded.

Deadline March of each year.

[456]
EDWARD S. ROTH MANUFACTURING ENGINEERING SCHOLARSHIP

Society of Manufacturing Engineers
Attn: SME Education Foundation
One SME Drive
P.O. Box 930
Dearborn, MI 48121-0930
(313) 425-3304   Toll-free: (800) 733-4763, ext. 3304
Fax: (313) 425-3411   E-mail: foundation@sme.org
Web: www.sme.org

Purpose To provide financial assistance to students (especially minorities) enrolled or planning to enroll in a degree program in manufacturing engineering at selected universities.

Eligibility This program is open to U.S. citizens who are graduating high school seniors or currently-enrolled undergraduate or graduate students. Applicants must be enrolled or planning to enroll as a full-time student at 1 of 13 selected 4-year universities to work on a bachelor's or master's degree in manufacturing engineering. They must have a GPA of 3.0 or higher. Preference is given to 1) students demonstrating financial need, 2) minority students, and 3)

students participating in a co-op program. Some preference may also be given to graduating high school seniors and graduate students.

Financial data The stipend is $2,500.

Duration 1 year; may be renewed.

Additional information The eligible institutions are California Polytechnic State University at San Luis Obispo, California State Polytechnic State University at Pomona, University of Miami (Florida), Bradley University, Central State University (Ohio), Miami University (Ohio), Boston University, Worcester Polytechnic Institute, University of Massachusetts, St. Cloud State University, University of Texas-Pan American, Brigham Young University, and Utah State University.

Number awarded 1 each year.

Deadline January of each year.

[457]
EISENHOWER GRADUATE TRANSPORTATION FELLOWSHIPS

Department of Transportation
Federal Highway Administration
Attn: National Highway Institute, HNHI-20
4600 North Fairfax Drive, Suite 800
Arlington, VA 22203-1553
(703) 235-0538   Fax: (703) 235-0593
E-mail: transportationedu@fhwa.dot.gov
Web: www.nhi.fhwa.dot.gov/ddetfp.asp

Purpose To provide financial assistance to graduate students (especially minorities) working on a master's or doctoral degree in transportation-related fields.

Eligibility This program is open to 1) university seniors planning to work on a master's degree; and 2) students in their final year of master's degree study or research planning to work on a Ph.D. or equivalent doctoral degree. Applicants must be interested in working on a research-based graduate engineering degree and entering the transportation profession after completing their higher level education. The institution they plan to attend must be known for its academic reputation in transportation, have ongoing research in 1 or more areas of transportation, and offer advanced degrees in fields of study that are directly related to transportation. Selection is based on academic records (class standing, GPA, and official transcripts), transportation work experience (including employer's endorsement), and recommendations. U.S. citizenship is required. Students at Historically Black Colleges and Universities (HBCUs), Hispanic Serving Institutions (HSIs), and Tribal Colleges (TCs) are especially encouraged to apply.

Financial data Fellows receive tuition and fees (to a maximum of $10,000 per year), monthly stipends of $1,700 for master's degree students or $2,000 for doctoral students, and a 1-time allowance of up to $1,500 for travel to an annual meeting of the Transportation Research Board to present the findings of their research.

Duration For master's degree students, 24 months, and the degree must be completed within 3 years; for doctoral students, 36 months, and the degree must be completed within 5 years.

Number awarded Approximately 100 to 120 each year.

Deadline February of each year.

[458]
ELLIOTT C. ROBERTS, SR. SCHOLARSHIP

Institute for Diversity in Health Management
Attn: Education Program Coordinator
One North Franklin Street, 28th Floor
Chicago, IL 60606
Toll-free: (800) 233-0996   Fax: (312) 422-4566
E-mail: clopez@aha.org
Web: www.diversityconnection.com

Purpose To provide financial assistance to minority graduate students in health care management or business management.

Eligibility This program is open to members of ethnic minority groups who are second-year graduate students. Applicants must be accepted or enrolled in an accredited program in health care management or business management and have a GPA of 3.0 or higher. They must demonstrate commitment to a career in health services administration, financial need, solid extracurricular activities, and a commitment to community service. U.S. citizenship or permanent resident status is required.

Financial data The stipend is $1,000.

Duration 1 year.

Number awarded 1 or more each year, depending on the availability of funds.

Deadline October of each year.

[459]
EMAF FELLOWSHIP PROGRAM

Society for Human Resource Management
Attn: Employment Management Association Foundation
1800 Duke Street
Alexandria, VA 22314-3499
(703) 548-3440   Toll-free: (800) 283-SHRM
Fax: (703) 535-6490   TDD: (703) 548-6999
E-mail: wflowers@shrm.org
Web: www.shrm.org/emaf/fellow.asp

Purpose To provide financial assistance to students enrolled or planning to enroll in a graduate program in the human resources field.

Eligibility Students are eligible to apply if they are 1) full-time college seniors who intend to prepare for a career in human resources in a generalist or employment/staffing capacity and have been accepted into an accredited graduate program; 2) full-time graduate students currently working on a degree that will lead them to a career in human resources in a generalist or employment/staffing capacity who have a GPA of 3.0 or higher; or 3) experienced degree holders who are returning to school for the purpose of re-careering or career advancement and have been accepted in an accredited graduate program related to the human resources generalist or employment/staffing field. U.S. citizenship is required. Selection is based on demonstrated scholastic achievement, leadership ability, work experience, and commitment to a career in a human resources field. At least 1 of the awards is designated for a qualified applicant from an ethnic or racial group underrepresented in the profession.

Financial data The stipend is $5,000, payable in 2 equal installments. Funds are made payable jointly to the recipient and the recipient's school.

Duration 1 year; recipients may reapply but may receive only 1 additional award.

Additional information This program includes 1 fellowship designated as the Richard Gast Fellowship. Funding for this program is provided by the Employment Management Association Foundation; the program is administered by Scholarship America, One Scholarship Way, P.O. Box 297, St. Peter, MN 56082, (507) 931-1682, (800) 537-4180, Fax: (507) 931-9168, E-mail: smsinfo@csfa.org.

Number awarded Up to 5 each year.

Deadline January of each year.

[460]
ENVIRONMENTAL EDUCATIONAL SCHOLARSHIP PROGRAM

Missouri Department of Natural Resources
Attn: Environmental Educational Scholarship Program
P.O. Box 176
Jefferson City, MO 65102
(573) 526-8411   Toll-free: (800) 334-6946
TDD: (800) 379-2419
E-mail: daspec@dnr.state.mo.us
Web: www.dnr.state.mo.us/eesp

Purpose To provide financial assistance to underrepresented and minority students from Missouri who are or will be working on a bachelor's or master's degree in an environmental field.

Eligibility This program is open to minority and underrepresented residents of Missouri who have graduated from an accredited high school with a GPA of 3.0 or higher. Students who are already enrolled in college must have a GPA of 2.5 or higher and must be full-time undergraduate or graduate students. Applicants may be 1) engineering students in civil, chemical, environmental, mechanical, or agricultural engineering; 2) environmental students in geology, biology, wildlife management, planning, natural resources, or a closely-related course of study; 3) chemistry students in the field of environmental chemistry; or 4) law enforcement students in environmental law enforcement. They must submit a 1-page essay on their environmental education career goals. Selection is based on the essay, GPA and test scores, school and community activities, leadership, and character.

Financial data A stipend is $2,000 per year.

Duration 1 year; may be renewed if the recipient maintains a GPA of 2.5 or higher and full-time enrollment.

Number awarded Varies each year.

Deadline June of each year.

[461]
ETHNIC IN-SERVICE TRAINING FUND

United Methodist Church
General Board of Higher Education and Ministry
Attn: Section of Chaplains and Related Ministries
1001 19th Avenue South
P.O. Box 340007
Nashville, TN 37203-0007
(615) 340-7392   Fax: (615) 340-7395
E-mail: sespino@gbhem.org
Web: www.gbhem.org/chaplains/mistscholarship.html

Purpose To provide funding to Methodists who are members of racial and ethnic minority groups involved in Clinical Pastoral Education (CPE) for pastoral counseling or hospital chaplaincy.

Eligibility This program is open to racial and ethnic minorities who have been active in a local United Methodist Church. Applicants must have been accepted into an accredited CPE program for pastoral counseling or hospital chaplaincy. They must submit a 2-page paper on their call to the ordained ministry and a 1-page paper on how CPE will enhance their ministry.

Financial data The stipend depends on the need of the recipient, the cost of the program, and the availability of funds.

Number awarded Varies each year.

Deadline March or August of each year.

[462]
ETHNIC MINORITY MASTER'S SCHOLARSHIPS IN ONCOLOGY NURSING

Oncology Nursing Society
Attn: ONS Foundation
125 Enterprise Drive
Pittsburgh, PA 15275-1214
(412) 859-6100, ext. 8503   Toll-free: (866) 257-4ONS
Fax: (412) 859-6160   E-mail: foundation@ons.org
Web: www.ons.org

Purpose To provide financial assistance to ethnic minorities interested in working on a master's degree in oncology nursing.

Eligibility The candidate must 1) demonstrate an interest in and commitment to oncology nursing; 2) be enrolled in a graduate nursing degree program at an NLN- or CCNE-accredited school of nursing (the program must have application to oncology nursing); 3) not have previously received a master's scholarship from this sponsor; 4) have a current license to practice as a registered nurse; and 5) be a member of an ethnic minority group (Native American, African American, Asian American, Pacific Islander, Hispanic/Latino, or other ethnic minority background). Applicants must submit an essay of 250 words or less on their role in caring for persons with cancer and a statement of their professional goals and their relationship to the advancement of oncology nursing. Financial need is not considered in the selection process.

Financial data The stipend is $3,000.

Duration 1 year.

Additional information Recipients may attend school on a part-time or full-time basis. This program includes a mentoring component with an individual in the applicant's area of clinical interest. When appropriate, efforts are made to match the applicant and mentor by ethnicity. At the end of each year of scholarship participation, recipients must submit a summary describing their educational activities.

Number awarded 2 each year.

Deadline January of each year.

[463]
EURASIA PREDISSERTATION TRAINING FELLOWSHIPS

Social Science Research Council
Attn: Eurasia Program
810 Seventh Avenue
New York, NY 10019
(212) 377-2700   Fax: (212) 377-2727
E-mail: eurasia@ssrc.org
Web: www.ssrc.org

Purpose To provide funding to graduate students (especially minorities and women) interested in being trained to conduct research related to Eurasia area studies.

Eligibility This program is open to graduate students enrolled in a discipline of the social sciences or humanities that deals with the new states of Eurasia, the Soviet Union, and/or the Russian empire. Research related to the non-Russian states, regions, and peoples is particularly encouraged. Regions and countries currently supported by the program include Armenia, Azerbaijan, Belarus, Georgia, Kazakhstan, Kyrgyzstan, Moldova, Russian Federation, Tajikistan, Turkmenistan, Ukraine, and Uzbekistan; funding is not presently available for research on the Baltic states. Applicants must be in the early stages of their graduate career (preference is given to those in their first or second years) and should not yet have submitted a dissertation prospectus or proposal to their department. They must be interested in the following types of training: language learning at a recognized program in the United States or abroad; formal training away from their home institution to acquire analytical or methodological skills normally unavailable to them; or well-defined exploratory research expressly leading to the formulation of a dissertation proposal. U.S. citizenship or permanent resident status is required. Minorities and women are particularly encouraged to apply.

Financial data Grants range from $3,000 to $7,000. Funds may not be used for tuition or support at the student's home institution.

Duration Awards may be disbursed over a 9-month period, but most grants are from 3 months to 1 semester. No more than 4 months may be spent outside the United States.

Additional information Funding for this program is provided by the U.S. Department of State under the Program for Research and Training on Eastern Europe and the Independent States of the Former Soviet Union (Title VIII).

Number awarded Varies each year; recently, 5 of these fellowships were awarded.

Deadline November of each year.

[464]
FARELLA BRAUN + MARTEL DIVERSITY SCHOLARSHIPS

Farella Braun + Martel LLP
Attn: Henry Fong
235 Montgomery Street
San Francisco, CA 94104
(415) 954-4452   Fax: (415) 954-4480
Web: www.fbm.com

Purpose To provide financial assistance to students from any state who are enrolled at selected law schools in northern California and come from socially and ethnically diverse backgrounds.

Eligibility This program is open to full-time, first-year law students at the University of California's Boalt Hall, the University of California Hastings College of the Law, the University of California at Davis King Hall, Santa Clara University, Golden Gate University, the University of San Francisco, and Stanford University. Applicants must come from socially and ethnically diverse backgrounds. Selection is based on academic accomplishments, ability to balance school with other activities, demonstrated commitment to serving both the legal profession and the community, and financial need. Preference is given to applicants who demonstrate a commitment to working and living in the San Francisco Bay area.

Financial data The stipend is $4,000.

Duration 1 year.

Additional information This program began in 2001.

Number awarded 3 each year.

Deadline April of each year.

[465]
FATHER JOSEPH P. FITZPATRICK SCHOLARSHIPS

Puerto Rican Legal Defense and Education Fund
Attn: Education Division
99 Hudson Street, 14th Floor
New York, NY 10013-2815
(212) 739-7497   Toll-free: (800) 328-2322
Fax: (212) 431-4276   E-mail: sonji_patrick@prldef.org
Web: www.prldef.org/Scholarship.htm

Purpose To provide financial assistance to Puerto Rican and other Latino law students interested in public interest work.

Eligibility This program is open to Puerto Rican or other Latino students who are currently enrolled in an ABA-accredited law school (first- and second-year students or third-year evening students). Applicants must submit a personal essay discussing their career goals, school and community activities, and any activities demonstrating their commitment to public interest work. Selection is based on academic standing, financial need, and demonstrated interest and involvement in the Latino community.

Financial data The stipend is $1,500.

Duration 1 year.

Additional information This award was established in 1995.

Number awarded 4 each year.

Deadline January of each year.

[466]
FELLOWSHIP PROGRAM IN AIDS CARE

National Medical Fellowships, Inc.
Attn: Scholarship Program
5 Hanover Square, 15th Floor
New York, NY 10004
(212) 483-8880   Fax: (212) 483-8897
E-mail: info@nmfonline.org
Web: www.nmf-online.org

Purpose To provide funding to underrepresented minority medical students who wish to receive specialized training in treating AIDS.

Eligibility This program is open to African American, Native Hawaiian, Alaskan Native, American Indian, Mexican American, and mainland Puerto Rican students enrolled in the second or third year of medical school. Candidates must be interested in participating in a multidisciplinary training program in HIV/AIDS clinical care and research at the University of California at San Francisco's AIDS Research Institute. Along with their application, they must submit a personal statement on their reasons for applying for this fellowship and what they expect to gain from the experience, including career plans over the next 10 years. Selection is based on academic achievement, leadership potential, and potential for distinguished contributions to medicine.

Financial data The stipend of $7,000 is intended to cover room, board, travel, and other related expenses.

Duration 4 weeks, during October of the participants' third or fourth year.

Additional information This program is a joint initiative of the University of California at San Francisco's Aids Research Institute and National Medical Fellowships, Inc. Funding is provided by Kaiser Permanente, the California HealthCare Foundation, and Aetna Foundation, Inc.

Number awarded Up to 8 each year.

Deadline June of each year.

[467]
FERMILAB DOCTORAL FELLOWSHIP PROGRAM FOR MINORITY STUDENTS IN PHYSICS

Fermi National Accelerator Laboratory
Attn: Manager, Equal Opportunity Office
MS 117
P.O. Box 500
Batavia, IL 60510-0500
(630) 840-4633   Fax: (630) 840-5207
E-mail: engram@fnal.gov
Web: www.fnal.gov

Purpose To provide financial assistance for doctoral study in physics to underrepresented minority students at universities that are members of the Universities Research Association, Inc. (URA).

Eligibility This program is open to doctoral students who are members of minority groups historically underrepresented in physics (Hispanics, African Americans, and Native Americans). Applicants must be enrolled at any of the 81 universities in the United States that are URA members. They must be U.S. citizens or permanent residents. Along with their application, they must submit a statement on why they want to participate in this program, why they are considering physics as their course of study in graduate school, how they intend to use their physics training after they complete their education, and whether they plan to work or do postdoctoral study after completing their education. Selection is based on that statement, financial need, university transcripts, and a progress letter from the thesis advisor.

Financial data   The stipend depends on the availability of funds and the needs of the student.

Duration   1 year; may be renewed up to 6 additional years.

Additional information   Fermilab scientists are assigned to all recipients as advisors to aid their progress in graduate school. In addition, students are encouraged to work summers at Fermilab under the supervision of a staff physicist. Funding support for this program is provided by the U.S. Department of Energy.

Number awarded   Varies each year.

Deadline   July of each year.

[468]
FINNEGAN HENDERSON DIVERSITY SCHOLARSHIP

Finnegan, Henderson, Farabow, Garrett & Dunner, LLP
Attn: Director of Professional Recruitment and
    Development
1300 I Street, N.W.
Washington, D.C. 20005-3315
(202) 408-4034   Fax: (202) 408-4400
E-mail: suzanne.gentes@finnegan.com
Web: www.finnegan.com

Purpose   To provide financial assistance and work experience to minority law students interested in a career in intellectual property law.

Eligibility   This program is open to law students from underrepresented minority groups who have demonstrated a commitment to a career in intellectual property law and are currently enrolled either as a first-year full-time student or second-year part-time student. The sponsor defines underrepresented minorities to include American Indians/Alaskan Natives, Blacks/African Americans, Asian Americans/Pacific Islanders, and Hispanics/Latinos. Applicants must have earned an undergraduate degree in life sciences, engineering, or computer science, or have substantial prior trademark experience. Selection is based on academic performance at the undergraduate, graduate (if applicable), and law school level; relevant work experience; community service; leadership skills; and special accomplishments.

Financial data   The stipend is $12,000 per year.

Duration   1 year; may be renewed 1 additional year as long as the recipient completes a summer associateship with the sponsor and maintains of GPA of 3.0 or higher.

Additional information   The sponsor, the world's largest intellectual property law firm, established this scholarship in 2003. Summer associateships are available at its offices in Washington, D.C.; Atlanta, Georgia; Cambridge, Massachusetts; Palo Alto, California; or Reston, Virginia.

Number awarded   1 each year.

Deadline   May of each year.

[469]
FLORIDA LIBRARY ASSOCIATION MINORITY SCHOLARSHIPS

Florida Library Association
Attn: Chair, Scholarship Committee
1133 West Morse Boulevard, Suite 201
Winter Park, FL 32789-3788
(407) 647-8839   Fax: (407) 629-2502
E-mail: mjs@crowsegal.com
Web: www.flalib.org/library/fla/schol.htm

Purpose   To provide financial assistance to minority students working on a graduate degree in library and information science in Florida.

Eligibility   This program is open to residents of Florida who are working on a graduate degree in library and information science at schools in the state. Applicants must be members of a minority group: Black/African American, American Indian/Alaska Native, Asian/Pacific Islander, or Hispanic/Latino. They must have some experience in a Florida library and must commit to working in a Florida library for at least 1 year after graduation. Along with their application, they must submit 1) a list of activities, honors, awards, and/or offices held during college and outside college; and 2) a statement of their reasons for entering librarianship and their career goals with respect to Florida libraries.

Financial data   The stipend is $2,000 per year.

Duration   1 year.

Number awarded   1 each year.

Deadline   January of each year.

[470]
FLORIDA SPACE GRANT CONSORTIUM FELLOWSHIP PROGRAM

Florida Space Grant Consortium
c/o Center for Space Education
Building M6-306, Room 7010
Mail Stop: FSGC
Kennedy Space Center, FL 32899
(321) 452-4301   Fax: (321) 449-0739
E-mail: fsgc@mail.ufl.edu
Web: fsgc.engr.ucf.edu

Purpose   To provide financial assistance to graduate students (particularly minorities, women, and persons with disabilities) in space studies at universities participating in the Florida Space Grant Consortium (FSGC).

Eligibility   Eligible to be nominated for this program are U.S. citizens who are enrolled full time in master's or doctoral programs at universities participating in the consortium. Nominees must be enrolled in a space-related field of study, broadly defined to include aeronautics, astronautics, remote sensing, atmospheric sciences, and other fundamental sciences and technologies relying on and/or directly impacting space technological resources. Included within that definition are space science; earth observing science; space life sciences; space medicine; space policy, law, and engineering; astronomy and astrophysics; space facilities and applications; and space education. Their undergraduate GPA should be at least 3.5. The program particularly solicits nominations of women, minorities, and students with disabilities.

Financial data The maximum stipend is $20,000 per year for doctoral candidates or $12,000 per year for master's degree students.

Duration 1 year; may be renewed up to 2 additional years for doctoral candidates or 1 additional year for master's degree students, provided the recipient maintains a GPA of 3.5 or higher.

Additional information This program is funded by the U.S. National Aeronautics and Space Administration (NASA). The consortium member universities are Bethune-Cookman College, Eckerd College, Embry-Riddle Aeronautical University, Florida A&M University, Florida Atlantic University, Florida Community Colleges, Florida Gulf Coast University, Florida Institute of Technology, Florida International University, Florida Southern College, Florida State University, University of Central Florida, University of Florida, University of Miami, University of North Florida, University of South Florida, and University of West Florida.

Number awarded 3 or 4 each year.

Deadline Notices of intent must be submitted by January of each year. Completed proposals are due in April.

[471]
FLOYD H. SKINNER LAW SCHOLARSHIPS

Floyd H. Skinner Bar Association
c/o President, Angela T. Ross
Smith Haughley Rice and Roegge
200 Calder Plaza Building
250 Monroe Avenue, N.W.
Grand Rapids, MI 49503-2251
(616) 774-8000   Fax: (616) 774-2461
E-mail: atross@shrr.com

Purpose To provide financial assistance for law school to minorities with a tie to Michigan.

Eligibility This program is open to minority law students who 1) are residents of western Michigan; 2) attend a Michigan law school; or 3) have previously participated in the Grand Rapids Minority Clerkship program. Applicants must be admitted to or currently attending law school full time. Selection is based on academic achievement, demonstrated leadership ability, community activism, and financial need.

Financial data The stipend is $1,000.

Duration 1 year.

Additional information Most members of the Floyd H. Skinner Bar Association are African American attorneys. Information is also available from the Scholarship Committee Chair, James L. Hopewell, Meijer, Inc., Fredrick Meijer Building 985/4, 2929 Walker Avenue, N.W., Grand Rapids, MI 49544, (616) 453-6711.

Number awarded 1 or more each year, depending on the number of qualified applicants and availability of funds.

Deadline October of each year.

[472]
FOLEY & LARDNER MINORITY SCHOLARSHIP

Foley & Lardner, Attorneys at Law
Attn: Diversity Partner
777 East Wisconsin Avenue
Milwaukee, WI 53202-5367
(414) 297-5520   Fax: (414) 297-4900
E-mail: mmcsweeney@foley.com
Web: www.foley.com

Purpose To provide scholarships to first-year minority students attending selected law schools.

Eligibility Minority students in the first year of law school are eligible to apply if they are attending the following schools: Duke, Florida, Georgetown, Michigan, Northwestern, Stanford, UCLA, or Wisconsin. First-year law students include both summer starters and fall starters. Selection is based on interest in or ties to a city in which the sponsor practices, involvement in community activities and minority student organizations, undergraduate record, and work or personal achievements. Financial need is not a consideration.

Financial data The stipend is $5,000; funds are paid at the beginning of the recipient's second semester in law school and must be applied to tuition, books, fees, and other expenses incident to law school attendance.

Duration 1 semester (the second semester of the first year in law school).

Additional information The U.S. cities in which the sponsor has offices are Chicago, Detroit, Los Angeles, Sacramento, San Diego, Palo Alto, San Francisco, Jacksonville, New York, Orlando, Tallahassee, Tampa, West Palm Beach, Madison, Milwaukee, and Washington, D.C.

Number awarded 8 each year (1 at each of the participating schools).

Deadline September of each year.

[473]
FORE DIVERSITY SCHOLARSHIPS

American Health Information Management Association
Attn: Foundation of Research and Education
233 North Michigan Avenue, Suite 2150
Chicago, IL 60601-5806
(312) 233-1168   Fax: (312) 233-1090
E-mail: fore@ahima.org
Web: www.ahima.org/fore/programs.cfm

Purpose To provide financial assistance to minority members of the American Health Information Management Association (AHIMA) who are interested in working on an undergraduate or graduate degree in health information administration or technology.

Eligibility This program is open to AHIMA members who are enrolled in a health information administration or health information technology program accredited by the Commission on Accreditation of Allied Health Education Programs. Applicants must be minorities, be working on an undergraduate or graduate degree on at least a half-time basis, and have a GPA of 3.0 or higher. U.S. citizenship is required. Selection is based (in order of importance) on GPA and academic achievement, volunteer and work experience, commitment to the health information management profession, suitability to the health information management profession, quality and suitability of references provided, and clarity of application.

Financial data Stipends range from $1,000 to $5,000.

Duration 1 year; nonrenewable.

Number awarded Varies each year. Recently, 5 of these scholarships were awarded: 4 to undergraduates and 1 to a graduate student.

Deadline May of each year.

[474]
FORTUNE BRANDS SCHOLARS PROGRAM

United Negro College Fund
Attn: Corporate Scholars Program
P.O. Box 1435
Alexandria, VA 22313-9998
Toll-free: (866) 671-7237   E-mail: internship@uncf.org
Web: www.uncf.org/internships/index.asp

Purpose To provide financial assistance and work experience to minorities who are either juniors majoring in fields related to business or law students interested in an internship at corporate headquarters of Fortune Brands.

Eligibility This program is open to juniors and first- and second-year law students who are members of minority groups. Applicants must have a GPA of 3.0 or higher and an undergraduate major in accounting, finance, human resources, information systems, information technology, or marketing. They must be attending a designated college, university, or law school and be interested in an internship at Fortune Brands corporate headquarters in Lincolnshire, Illinois. Along with their application, they must submit a resume, 2 letters of recommendation, and official transcripts.

Financial data The program provides a paid internship and (based on successful internship performance) a $7,500 scholarship.

Duration 8 to 10 weeks for the internship; 1 year for the scholarship.

Additional information Eligible undergraduate institutions are Florida A&M University, Florida State University, Hampton University, Howard University, Morehouse College, North Carolina A&T State University, Northwestern University, Spelman College, University of Chicago, and University of Wisconsin. Participating law schools are those at Howard University, Northwestern University, University of Chicago, and University of Wisconsin.

Number awarded Varies each year.

Deadline February of each year.

[475]
FOUNDERS SCHOLARSHIP

Society of Mexican American Engineers and Scientists
Attn: Scholarships
711 West Bay Area Boulevard, Suite 206
Webster, TX 77598-3677
(281) 557-3677   Fax: (281) 557-3757
E-mail: scholarships@maes-natl.org
Web: www.maes-natl.org

Purpose To provide financial assistance to undergraduate and graduate student members of the Society of Mexican American Engineers and Scientists (MAES).

Eligibility This program is open to MAES student members who are full-time undergraduate or graduate students at a college or university in the United States. Community college students must be enrolled in majors that can transfer to a 4-year institution offering a baccalaureate degree. All applicants must be majoring in a field of science or engineering. U.S. citizenship or permanent resident status is required. Selection is based on financial need; academic achievement; personal qualities, strengths, and leadership abilities; and timeliness and completeness of the application.

Financial data The stipend is $2,500.

Duration 1 year.

Additional information Recipients must attend the MAES International Symposium's Medalla de Oro Banquet in October.

Number awarded 1 each year.

Deadline October of each year.

[476]
FREDRIKSON & BYRON FOUNDATION MINORITY SCHOLARSHIPS

Fredrikson & Byron Foundation
4000 Pillsbury Center
200 South Sixth Street
Minneapolis, MN 55402-1425
(612) 492-7117   Fax: (612) 492-7077
Web: www.fredlaw.com/firm/scholarship.htm

Purpose To provide financial assistance and summer work experience to minority law students from any state who will be practicing in the Twin Cities area of Minnesota.

Eligibility This program is open to African American, Asian American, Pacific Islander, Hispanic, Native American, and Alaska Native students enrolled in their first year of law school. Applicants must be interested in practicing law in the Minneapolis-St. Paul area. Along with their application, they must submit 2 recommendations, a writing sample from their first-year legal writing course, transcripts from undergraduate and law school, and a resume. Financial need is not considered.

Financial data The fellowship stipend is $5,000. The internship portion of the program provides a $1,000 weekly stipend.

Duration 1 year.

Additional information The scholarship is jointly sponsored by Fredrikson & Byron, P.A. and the Fredrikson & Byron Foundation. Fellows are also eligible to participate in an internship at the firm's offices in Minneapolis.

Number awarded Up to 2 each year.

Deadline March of each year.

[477]
FULFILLING OUR DREAMS SCHOLARSHIP PROGRAM

Salvadoran American Leadership and Educational Fund
Attn: Education and Youth Programs Manager
1625 West Olympic Boulevard, Suite 718
Los Angeles, CA 90015
(213) 480-1052   Fax: (213) 487-2530
E-mail: info@salef.org
Web: salef.org/Scholarships.html

Purpose To provide financial assistance for college and graduate school to Salvadoran Americans and other Americans of Hispanic descent.

Eligibility This program is open to high school seniors and graduates who have been accepted at a 4-year university, undergraduates in 2- and 4-year colleges and universities, and graduate students. Applicants do not need to provide proof of documented immigrant status, but they must be of Salvadoran, Central American, or other Latino background. Along with their application, they must submit a 750-word statement on their goals, aspirations, and ambitions; ways to give back to the community; leadership involvement; why they chose their field of study; and short- and long-term goals and how they plan to contribute to the community after graduation. They must be able to demonstrate financial need, have a GPA of at least 2.5, and have a history of community service and involvement. An interview may be required.

Financial data Stipends range from $500 to $2,500.

Duration 1 year.

Additional information This program began in 1998. Recipients are paired with a professional in their field of study who serves as a mentor, providing moral support and direction. Funding for this program comes from the Bank of America Foundation and the Los Angeles Department of Water and Power.

Number awarded 50 or more each year.

Deadline June of each year.

[478]
GATES MILLENNIUM GRADUATE SCHOLARS PROGRAM

Bill and Melinda Gates Foundation
P.O. Box 10500
Fairfax, VA 22031-8044
Toll-free: (877) 690-GMSP
Web: www.gmsp.org

Purpose To provide financial assistance for graduate studies in selected subject areas to outstanding low-income minority students.

Eligibility This program is open to low-income African Americans, Native Alaskans, American Indians, Hispanic Americans, and Asian Pacific Islander Americans who are nominated by a professional educator. Nominees must be U.S. citizens who are enrolled or about to enroll in graduate school to work on a graduate degree in engineering, mathematics, science, education, or library science. They must have a GPA of 3.3 or higher, be able to demonstrate significant financial need, and have demonstrated leadership commitment through participation in community service (i.e., mentoring/tutoring, volunteer work in social service organizations, and involvement in church initiatives), extra-

curricular activities (student government and athletics), or other activities that reflect leadership abilities.

Financial data The program covers the full cost of graduate study: tuition, fees, books, and living expenses not paid for by grants and scholarships already committed as part of the recipient's financial aid package.

Duration Up to 4 years (up to and including the doctorate), if the recipient maintains at least a 3.0 GPA.

Additional information This program, established in 1999, is funded by the Bill and Melinda Gates Foundation and administered by the United Negro College Fund with support from the American Indian Graduate Center, the Hispanic Scholarship Fund, and the Organization of Chinese Americans.

Number awarded Under the Gates Millennium Scholars Program, a total of 4,000 students receive support each year.

Deadline January of each year.

[479]
GEM M.S. ENGINEERING FELLOWSHIP PROGRAM

National Consortium for Graduate Degrees for
    Minorities in Engineering and Science (GEM)
P.O. Box 537
Notre Dame, IN 46556
(574) 631-7771   Fax: (574) 287-1486
E-mail: gem.1@nd.edu
Web: www.gemfellowship.org

Purpose To provide financial assistance and summer work experience to underrepresented minority graduate students in engineering.

Eligibility This program is open to U.S. citizens who are members of ethnic groups underrepresented in engineering: American Indians, African Americans, Mexican Americans, Puerto Ricans, and other Hispanic Americans. Applicants must be enrolled as at least a junior in an accredited engineering discipline with an academic record that indicates the ability to pursue graduate studies in engineering (including a GPA of 2.8 or higher). Recipients must attend 1 of the 88 GEM member universities that offer a master's degree.

Financial data The fellowship pays tuition, fees, and a stipend of $10,000 over its lifetime. In addition, each participant receives a salary during the summer work assignment as a GEM Summer Intern, making the value of the total award between $30,000 and $60,000. Employer members reimburse GEM participants for travel expenses to and from the summer work site.

Duration Up to 3 semesters or 4 quarters, plus a summer work internship lasting 10 to 14 weeks for up to 3 summers, depending on whether the student applies as a junior, senior, or college graduate; recipients begin their internship upon acceptance into the program and work each summer until completion of their master's degree.

Additional information During the summer internship, each fellow is assigned an engineering project in a research setting. Each project is based on the fellow's interest and background and is carried out under the supervision of an experienced engineer. At the conclusion of the internship, each fellow writes a project report. Recipients must work on a master's degree in the same engineering discipline as their baccalaureate degree.

Number awarded Varies each year; recently, 327 of these fellowships were awarded.

Deadline October of each year.

[480]
GEM PH.D. ENGINEERING FELLOWSHIP PROGRAM

National Consortium for Graduate Degrees for
   Minorities in Engineering and Science (GEM)
P.O. Box 537
Notre Dame, IN 46556
(574) 631-7771   Fax: (574) 287-1486
E-mail: gem.1@nd.edu
Web: www.gemfellowship.org

Purpose To provide financial assistance and summer work experience to underrepresented minority students interested in obtaining a Ph.D. degree in engineering.

Eligibility This program is open to U.S. citizens who are members of ethnic groups underrepresented in engineering: American Indians, African Americans, Mexican Americans, Puerto Ricans, and other Hispanic Americans. Applicants must have attained or be in the process of attaining a master's degree in engineering with an academic record that indicates the ability to work on a doctoral degree in engineering (including a GPA of 3.0 or higher).

Financial data The stipend is $14,000 per year, plus tuition and fees; the total value of the award is between $60,000 and $100,000.

Duration 3 to 5 years for the fellowship; 12 weeks during at least 1 summer for the internship.

Additional information This program is valid only at 1 of 88 participating GEM member universities; write to GEM for a list. The fellowship award is designed to support the student in the first year of the doctoral program without working. Subsequent years are subsidized by the respective universities and will usually include either a teaching or research assistantship. Recipients must participate in the GEM summer internship; failure to agree to accept the internship cancels the fellowship.

Number awarded Varies each year; recently, 49 of these fellowships were awarded.

Deadline October of each year.

[481]
GEM PH.D. SCIENCE FELLOWSHIP PROGRAM

National Consortium for Graduate Degrees for
   Minorities in Engineering and Science (GEM)
P.O. Box 537
Notre Dame, IN 46556
(574) 631-7771   Fax: (574) 287-1486
E-mail: gem.1@nd.edu
Web: www.gemfellowship.org

Purpose To provide financial assistance and summer work experience to underrepresented minority students interested in obtaining a Ph.D. degree in the natural sciences.

Eligibility This program is open to U.S. citizens who are members of ethnic groups underrepresented in the natural sciences: American Indians, African Americans, Mexican Americans, Puerto Ricans, and other Hispanic Americans. Applicants must be juniors, seniors, or recent baccalaureate

graduates in the natural sciences (biological sciences, chemistry, computer science, earth sciences, mathematics, and physics) with an academic record that indicates the ability to pursue doctoral studies in the natural sciences (including a GPA of 3.0 or higher).

Financial data The stipend is $14,000 per year, plus tuition and fees. In addition, there is a summer internship program that provides a salary and reimbursement for travel expenses to and from the summer work site. The total value of the award is between $60,000 and $100,000, depending upon academic status at the time of application, summer employer, and graduate school attended.

Duration 3 to 5 years for the fellowship; 12 weeks during at least 1 summer for the internship. Fellows selected as juniors or seniors intern each summer until entrance to graduate school; fellows selected after college graduation intern at least 1 summer.

Additional information This program is valid only at 1 of 88 participating GEM member universities; write to GEM for a list. The fellowship award is designed to support the student in the first year of the doctoral program without working. Subsequent years are subsidized by the respective university and will usually include either a teaching or research assistantship. Recipients must participate in the GEM summer internship; failure to agree to accept the internship cancels the fellowship. Recipients must enroll in the same scientific discipline as their undergraduate major.

Number awarded Varies each year; recently, 40 of these fellowships were awarded.

Deadline October of each year.

[482]
GENERAL MOTORS ENGINEERING EXCELLENCE AWARD

Hispanic Association of Colleges and Universities
Attn: National Scholarship Program
One Dupont Circle, N.W. Suite 605
Washington, DC 20036
(202) 467-0893   Fax: (202) 496-9177
TTY: (800) 855-2880   E-mail: scholarships@hacu.net
Web: scholarships.hacu.net/applications/applicants

Purpose To provide financial assistance to undergraduate and graduate engineering students at institutions that are members of the Hispanic Association of Colleges and Universities (HACU).

Eligibility This program is open to full-time undergraduate and graduate students at 4-year HACU member and partner colleges and universities who are working on an engineering degree. Applicants must submit an essay of 200 to 250 words that describes their academic and/or career goals, where they expect to be and what they expect to be doing 10 years from now, and what skills they can bring to an employer. They must be able to demonstrate financial need and a GPA of 3.2 or higher.

Financial data The stipend is $2,000 per year.

Duration 1 year; may be renewed.

Additional information This program is sponsored by General Motors and administered by HACU.

Number awarded 1 or more each year.

Deadline May of each year.

[483]
GEORGE A. STRAIT MINORITY STIPEND

American Association of Law Libraries
Attn: Membership Coordinator
53 West Jackson Boulevard, Suite 940
Chicago, IL 60604
(312) 939-4764   Fax: (312) 431-1097
E-mail: membership@aall.org
Web: www.aallnet.org/services/sch_strait.asp

Purpose To provide financial assistance to minority college seniors or college graduates who are interested in becoming law librarians.

Eligibility This program is open to college graduates with meaningful law library experience who are members of minority groups and intend to have a career in law librarianship. Applicants must be degree candidates at an ALA-accredited library school or an ABA-accredited law school. Along with their application, they must submit a personal statement that discusses their interest in law librarianship, reason for applying for this scholarship, career goals as a law librarian, and other pertinent information.

Financial data The stipend is $3,500.

Duration 1 year.

Additional information This program, established in 1990, is currently supported by Thomson West.

Number awarded 1 each year.

Deadline March of each year.

[484]
GEORGE M. BROOKER COLLEGIATE SCHOLARSHIP FOR MINORITIES

Institute of Real Estate Management Foundation
Attn: Foundation Coordinator
430 North Michigan Avenue
Chicago, IL 60611-4090
(312) 329-6008   Toll-free: (800) 837-0706, ext. 6008
Fax: (312) 410-7908   E-mail: kholmes@irem.org
Web: www.irem.org

Purpose To provide financial assistance to minorities interested in preparing (on the undergraduate or graduate school level) for a career in the real estate management industry.

Eligibility This program is open to junior, senior, and graduate minority (non-Caucasian) students majoring in real estate, preferably with an emphasis on management, asset management, or related fields. Applicants must be interested in beginning a career in real estate management upon graduation. They must have earned a GPA of 3.0 or higher in their major, have completed at least 2 college courses in real estate, and write an essay (up to 500 words) on why they want to follow a career in real estate management. U.S. citizenship is required. Selection is based on academic success and a demonstrated commitment to a career in real estate management.

Financial data Stipends are $1,000 for undergraduates or $2,500 for graduate students. Funds are disbursed to the institution the student attends to be used only for tuition expenses.

Duration 1 year; nonrenewable.

Number awarded 3 each year: 2 undergraduate awards and 1 graduate award.

Deadline March of each year.

[485]
GEORGE V. POWELL DIVERSITY SCHOLARSHIP

Lane Powell Spears Lubersky LLP
Attn: Administrator of Attorney Recruiting
1420 Fifth Avenue, Suite 4100
Seattle, WA 98101-2338
(206) 223-6123   Fax: (206) 223-7107
E-mail: rodenl@lanepowell.com
Web: www.lanepowell.com

Purpose To provide financial assistance and work experience to law students who will contribute to the diversity of the legal community

Eligibility This program is open to second-year students in good standing at an ABA-accredited law school. Applicants must be able to contribute meaningfully to the diversity of the legal community and have a demonstrated desire to work, live, and eventually practice law in Seattle or Portland. They must submit a cover letter including a statement indicating eligibility to participate in the program, resume, current copy of law school transcript, legal writing sample, and list of 2 or 3 professional or academic references. Selection is based on academic achievement and record of leadership abilities, community service, and involvement in community issues.

Financial data The program provides a stipend of $6,000 for the third year of law school and a paid summer associate clerkship.

Duration 1 year, including the summer.

Additional information This program was established in 2005. Clerkships are provided at the offices of the sponsor in Seattle or Portland.

Number awarded 1 each year.

Deadline October of each year.

[486]
GEORGIA SPACE GRANT CONSORTIUM FELLOWSHIPS

Georgia Space Grant Consortium
c/o Georgia Institute of Technology
Aerospace Engineering
Paul Weber Space Science and Technology Building, Room 210
Atlanta, GA 30332-0150
(404) 894-0521   Fax: (404) 894-9313
E-mail: wanda.pierson@aerospace.gatech.edu
Web: www.ae.gatech.edu/research/gsgc

Purpose To provide financial assistance for undergraduate and graduate study of space-related fields to students (particularly minorities, women, and students with disabilities) at member institutions of the Georgia Space Grant Consortium (GSGC).

Eligibility This program is open to U.S. citizens who are undergraduate and graduate students at member institutions of the GSGC. Applicants must be working on a degree in mathematics, science, engineering, computer science, or a technical discipline related to space. Selection is based on transcripts, 3 letters of reference, and an essay of 100 to 500 words on the applicant's professional interests and objectives and their relationship to the field of aerospace. Awards are provided as part of the Space Grant program of the U.S. National Aeronautics and Space Administration, which encourages participation by women, minorities, and people with disabilities.

Financial data A stipend is awarded (amount not specified).

Additional information Institutions that are members of the GSGC include Albany State University, Clark Atlanta University, Columbus State University, Fort Valley State University, Georgia Institute of Technology, Kennesaw State University, Mercer University, Morehouse College, Spelman College, State University of West Georgia, and the University of Georgia. This program is funded by NASA.

Number awarded 1 each year.

[487]
GERALDINE R. DODGE FOUNDATION FELLOWSHIP

College Art Association of America
Attn: Fellowship Program
275 Seventh Avenue
New York, NY 10001-6798
(212) 691-1051, ext. 242   Fax: (212) 627-2381
E-mail: fellowship@collegeart.org
Web: www.collegeart.org/caa/career/fellowship.html

Purpose To provide financial assistance and work experience to art historians from culturally diverse backgrounds who are completing graduate degrees and are interested in working in New Jersey.

Eligibility This program is open to art historians who have been underrepresented in the field because of their race, religion, gender, age, national origin, sexual orientation, disability, or history of economic disadvantage. Applicants must be U.S. citizens or permanent residents and able to demonstrate financial need. They must expect to receive the M.F.A. or Ph.D. degree in the year following application and then be interested in working at a cultural institution in New Jersey.

Financial data The stipend is $5,000.

Duration 1 year: the final year of the degree program.

Additional information In addition to providing a stipend for the terminal year of their degree program, the College Art Association (CAA) helps fellows search for employment at a museum, art center, college, or university in New Jersey. Upon securing a position, CAA provides a $10,000 subsidy to the employer as part of the fellow's salary. Participating organizations must match this 2:1. In addition to administrative and/or teaching responsibilities, all fellows' positions must include a curatorial or public service component. Salary or stipend, position description, and term of employment will vary and are determined in consultation with individual fellows and their potential employers. This program began in 1993. Funding is provided by the Milton & Sally Avery Arts Foundation, Geraldine R. Dodge Foundation, National Endowment for the Arts, National Endowment for the Humanities, and Terra Foundation for the Arts.

Number awarded 1 each year.

Deadline January of each year.

[488]
GRAD SCHOLARSHIPS

Pueblo Hispanic Education Foundation
Administration Building, Room 325
2200 Bonforte Boulevard
Pueblo, CO 81001
(719) 546-2563   Fax: (719) 546-0504
E-mail: pphef@aol.com
Web: www.phef.net

Purpose To provide financial assistance to Hispanic graduate students from Colorado.

Eligibility This program is open to full-time Hispanic graduate students who are residents of Colorado. Applicants must submit an essay on their career and educational goals, school activities and awards, interests, community service and volunteer work, and work experience. Selection is based on financial need, proven ability, GPA, community and volunteer service, and educational desire. Preference is given to students of low to moderate income, continuing students, and single parents.

Financial data Stipends are generally $2,000 per year.

Duration 1 year. Recipients may reapply if they maintain a cumulative GPA of 2.5 or higher.

Additional information The title of this program stands for "Grooming Role Models for Advanced Degrees." It was established in 1993 and is sponsored by the Temple Buell Foundation and the Pueblo Hispanic Education Foundation. Funds are not available for summer school. Recipients are required to perform 40 hours of community service at a nonprofit agency.

Number awarded Varies each year; recently, 4 of these scholarships were awarded.

Deadline March of each year.

[489]
GRADUATE FELLOWSHIP IN PHILANTHROPY AND HUMAN RIGHTS

Higher Education Consortium for Urban Affairs
Attn: Graduate Fellowship Coordinator
2233 University Avenue West, Suite 210
St. Paul, MN 55114-1698
(651) 646-8831   Toll-free: (800) 554-1089
E-mail: mshiozawa@hecua.org
Web: www.hecua.org

Purpose To provide financial assistance and work experience to graduate students of color in Minnesota who are interested in working in the fields of philanthropy and human rights.

Eligibility This program is open to graduate students at universities in Minnesota who are members of ethnic or cultural groups historically underrepresented in higher education. Applicants may be studying any academic discipline, but they must be interested in working part time at the Otto Bremer Foundation while they are engaged in study for their graduate degree. Their work for the foundation involves philanthropy and human rights, including social and economic justice, shelter and housing, civic engagement, health disparities and resources, civic engagement, or organizational effectiveness within nonprofits. They must be able to collaborate their academic work with research for nonprofit organizations in Minnesota, Wisconsin, North Dakota, or Montana. Along with their application, they must submit a resume or curriculum vitae, 3 letters of reference, official academic transcripts, and a 1,500-word essay about themselves, their interest and involvement in human rights and social change, and their current research interest in their academic program. Selection is based on how the applicants think, analyze, and write; their definition and commitment to human rights; experiences that predict their potential in human rights, nonprofits, and fulfilling the objectives of the fellowship; current research interest and program; academic merit; and evidence of support from their academic institution.

Financial data Fellows receive $12,000, either as a scholarship (paid directly to them) or as a stipend (paid to their university for tuition).

Duration 1 year.

Additional information This program, established in 2003, is funded by the Otto Bremer Foundation.

Number awarded 3 each year.

Deadline February of each year.

[490]
HANA SCHOLARSHIPS

United Methodist Church
Attn: General Board of Higher Education and Ministry
Office of Loans and Scholarships
1001 19th Avenue South
P.O. Box 340007
Nashville, TN 37203-0007
(615) 340-7344   Fax: (615) 340-7367
E-mail: umscholar@gbhem.org
Web: www.gbhem.org

Purpose To provide financial assistance to upper-division and graduate Methodist students who are of Hispanic, Asian, Native American, Alaska Native, or Pacific Islander ancestry.

Eligibility This program is open to full-time juniors, seniors, and graduate students at accredited colleges and universities in the United States who have been active, full members of a United Methodist Church for at least 1 year prior to applying. Applicants must have at least 1 parent who is Hispanic, Asian, Native American, Alaska Native, or Pacific Islander. They must be able to demonstrate involvement in their Hispanic, Asian, or Native American (HANA) community. Selection is based on that involvement, academic ability, and financial need. U.S. citizenship or permanent resident status is required.

Financial data The stipend is $1,000 for undergraduates or $3,000 for graduate students.

Duration 1 year; recipients may reapply.

Number awarded 50 each year.

Deadline March of each year.

[491]
HAROLD AMOS MEDICAL FACULTY DEVELOPMENT PROGRAM

Amos Medical Faculty Development Program
Attn: Director
8701 Georgia Avenue, Suite 411
Silver Spring, MD 20910
(301) 565-4080   Fax: (301) 565-4088
E-mail: amfdp@starpower.net
Web: www.amfdp.org/applicat.htm

Purpose To provide financial support and research training to minority physicians who are interested in academic careers in biomedical research, clinical investigation, or health services research.

Eligibility African American, Mexican American, Native American, and mainland Puerto Rican physicians residing in the United States are eligible to apply if they have completed or will have completed formal clinical training. Applicants must be U.S. citizens or permanent residents with outstanding academic backgrounds and a commitment to academic medicine. Preference is given to physicians who have recently completed their clinical training and are seeking advanced research training. An interview is required.

Financial data The stipend is $65,000 per year; an additional $26,350 per year is provided as a research allowance.

Duration 2 years; renewable for an additional 2 years.

Additional information Fellows study and conduct research under the supervision of a senior faculty member located at any academic center in the United States that is noted for the training of young faculty and that offers research opportunities of interest to the fellow. Previously, this program was known as the Robert Wood Johnson Foundation's Minority Medical Faculty Development Program. The name was changed in 2004 to honor Dr. Harold Amos. the first African-American to chair a department, now the Department of Microbiology and Medical Genetics, of the Harvard Medical School, a founding member of the National Advisory Committee of the Robert Wood Johnson Foundation's Minority Medical Faculty Development Program, and the program's National Program Director between 1989 and 1993.

Number awarded Up to 12 each year.

Deadline March of each year.

[492]
HELENE M. OVERLY MEMORIAL GRADUATE SCHOLARSHIP

Women's Transportation Seminar
Attn: National Headquarters
1666 K Street, N.W., Suite 1100
Washington, DC 20006
(202) 496-4340   Fax: (202) 496-4349
E-mail: wts@wtsnational.org
Web: www.wtsnational.org

Purpose To provide financial assistance to women (particularly minority women) graduate students interested in preparing for a career in transportation.

Eligibility This program is open to women who are enrolled in a graduate degree program in a transportation-related field (e.g., transportation engineering, planning, finance, or logistics). Applicants must have at least a 3.0 GPA and be interested in a career in transportation. They must submit a 750-word statement about their career goals after graduation and why they think they should receive the scholarship award. Applications must be submitted first to a local chapter; the chapters forward selected applications for consideration on the national level. Minority women are particularly encouraged to apply. Selection is based on transportation involvement and goals, job skills, and academic record.

Financial data The stipend is $6,000.

Duration 1 year.

Additional information This program was established in 1981. Local chapters may also award additional funding to winners for their area.

Number awarded 1 each year.

Deadline Applications must be submitted by November to a local WTS chapter.

[493]
HELLER EHRMAN DIVERSITY FELLOWSHIPS

Heller Ehrman White & McAuliffe LLP
Attn: Ethnic Diversity Task Force
275 Middlefield Road
Menlo Park, CA 94025-3506
(650) 324-7171   Fax: (650) 324-0638
E-mail: lkite@hewm.com
Web: www.hewm.com

Purpose To provide financial assistance and work experience to law students who can contribute to the diversity of the legal community.

Eligibility This program is open to first-year law students who show promise of contributing to the diversity of the law student and legal community. Applicants must possess a record of academic, employment, community, and/or other achievement indicating potential for success in law school and in the legal profession. Along with their application, they must submit a statement, up to 500 words, on their interest in the fellowship and how they would contribute to the diversity of the legal profession.

Financial data The program provides a stipend of $7,500 for law school and a paid summer associate clerkship.

Duration 1 year, including the summer.

Additional information This program was established in 2004. Clerkships are provided at offices of the sponsor in each of its 4 regions: Bay Area (San Francisco and Silicon Valley), east coast (New York and Washington, D.C.), northwest (Seattle), and southern California (Los Angeles and San Diego).

Number awarded 4 each year: 1 in each of the firm's regions.

Deadline January of each year.

[494]
HENAAC STUDENT LEADERSHIP AWARDS

Hispanic Engineer National Achievement Awards
   Conference
3900 Whiteside Street
Los Angeles, CA 90063
(323) 262-0997   Fax: (323) 262-0946
E-mail: info@henaac.org
Web: www.henaac.org

Purpose To provide financial assistance to Hispanic undergraduate and graduate students majoring in engineering and related fields.

Eligibility This program is open to Hispanic undergraduate and graduate students who are majoring in computer science, engineering, material science, or mathematics. Applicants must have a GPA of 3.0 or higher. Academic achievement and campus community activities are considered in the selection process. U.S. citizenship is required.

Financial data The stipend ranges from $1,000 to $5,000.

Duration 1 year.

Additional information This program is sponsored by the Hispanic Engineer National Achievement Awards Conference (HENAAC): to promote technical excellence and leadership in the Hispanic community.

Number awarded 2 each year: 1 undergraduate and 1 graduate student.

Deadline April of each year.

[495]
HERBERT W. NICKENS MEDICAL STUDENT SCHOLARSHIPS

Association of American Medical Colleges
Attn: Division of Diversity Policy and Programs
2450 N Street, N.W.
Washington, DC 20037-1127
(202) 828-0570   Fax: (202) 828-1125
E-mail: nickensawards@aamc.org
Web: www.aamc.org

Purpose To provide financial assistance to medical students who have demonstrated efforts to address the healthcare needs of minorities.

Eligibility This program is open to U.S. citizens and permanent residents entering their third year of study at a U.S. allopathic medical school. Each medical school may nominate 1 student for these awards. The letter must describe the nominee's 1) academic achievement through the first and second year, including special awards and honors, clerkships or special research projects, and extracurricular activities in which the student has shown leadership abilities; 2) leadership efforts to eliminate inequities in medical education and health care; and 3) demonstrated leadership efforts in addressing the educational, societal, and healthcare needs of minorities. Nominees must submit a curriculum vitae and a 250-word essay that discusses their motivation to pursue a medical career and how they anticipate working to improve the health and health care of minorities.

Financial data The stipend is $5,000.

Duration 1 year.

Number awarded 5 each year.

Deadline March of each year.

[496]
HHMI-NIH RESEARCH SCHOLARS PROGRAM

Howard Hughes Medical Institute
One Cloister Court, Building 60
Bethesda, MD 20814-1460
(301) 951-6770   Toll-free: (800) 424-9924
Fax: (301) 951-6776   E-mail: gpub@hhmi.org
Web: www.hhmi.org/cloister

Purpose To give outstanding students (particularly under-represented minorities and women) at U.S. medical or dental schools the opportunity to receive educational funding and research training at the National Institutes of Health (NIH), in Bethesda, Maryland.

Eligibility To apply, students must be in good standing at a medical or dental school in the United States or Puerto Rico. There are no citizenship requirements, but applicants must be authorized to work in the United States. Those who are enrolled in an M.D./Ph.D. program or who already have an M.D. or a Ph.D. in a natural science are not eligible. After the conclusion of the program year, a small number of outstanding Research Scholars are selected to receive continued support for up to 2 years while completing studies toward the M.D. degree. To be eligible for this support, Research Scholars must be returning directly to medical school at the conclusion of their participation in the Research Scholars Program, and they may not be enrolled in an M.D./Ph.D., Ph.D., or Sc.D. degree program. These awards are based on demonstrated research abilities, potential for future achievement in biomedical research, and career intentions (including any plans for additional research training upon completion of medical school). Students' financial indebtedness resulting from school loans may also be considered as a secondary factor. Women and members of underrepresented minority groups are encouraged to apply.

Financial data Research Scholars receive an annual salary of $25,000 for rent, food, and other living expenses. Scholars are also eligible for medical, life, and accidental death and dismemberment insurance. Students are reimbursed for round-trip moving expenses for personal belongings (not furniture) for themselves and their dependents from and back to medical school. In addition, tuition is paid for Research Scholars who wish to take courses from the Foundation for Advanced Education in the Sciences (FAES). They also receive allowances for the purchase of textbooks and scientific journals related to their area of research and for travel to scientific meetings. Research Scholars who are chosen to receive support to complete their studies toward the M.D. degree are given an annual stipend of $16,000 and a $15,000 annual allowance toward tuition and other education-related expenses.

Duration 1 year, beginning in July or August; may be extended for 2 additional years.

Additional information Research Scholars work as part of a research team in a laboratory at the NIH's main campus in Bethesda, conducting basic research under the mentorship of an NIH senior investigator or preceptor. They learn the latest laboratory techniques and experience the creative thinking involved in at least 1 of the following biomedical areas: biochemistry, biophysics, biostatistics, cell biology, developmental biology, epidemiology, genetics, immunology, mathematical and computational biology, microbiology, molecular biology, neuroscience, pharmacology, phys-iology, structural biology, and virology. This program is unique in that it does not require students to propose a research project or select a laboratory at the NIH as part of the application process. Instead, Research Scholars are encouraged to take their first couple of weeks in the program to interview investigators and explore different laboratories at the NIH before making a selection. This program is jointly sponsored by the Howard Hughes Medical Institute and the National Institutes of Health—the largest private and public biomedical research institutions in the United States. It complements the HHMI Research Training Fellowships for Medical Students Program; students may not apply to both programs in the same year. Applicants must apply online using the sponsor's web-based application system.

Number awarded 40 or more each year.

Deadline January of each year.

[497]
HISPANIC CHURCH MULTIPLICATION TEAM SCHOLARSHIPS

Southern Baptist Convention
North American Mission Board
Attn: Church Multiplication Team
4200 North Point Parkway
Alpharetta, GA 30022-4176
(770) 410-6235   Fax: (770) 410-6012
E-mail: jdoyle@namb.net
Web: www.namb.net

Purpose To provide financial assistance to Hispanic American Baptists interested in religious vocations.

Eligibility This program is open to Hispanic Americans who are U.S. citizens involved in some type of approved Baptist ministry. Applicants must be able to demonstrate financial need. Only students in accredited institutions working toward a basic college (bachelor's) or seminary (M.Div.) degree are eligible. As part of the selection process, applicants must submit an essay describing their interest in and commitment to a Christian vocation.

Financial data The maximum grants are $500 per year for students attending accredited colleges, $600 per year for students in non-Southern Baptist Convention seminaries, and $850 per year for students at 1 of the 6 Southern Baptist Convention seminaries.

Duration 1 year; renewable.

Additional information The 6 Southern Baptist seminaries are Golden Gate Baptist Theological Seminary (Mill Valley, California), Midwestern Baptist Theological Seminary (Kansas City, Missouri), New Orleans Baptist Theological Seminary (New Orleans, Louisiana), Southeastern Baptist Theological Seminary (Wake Forest, North Carolina), Southern Baptist Theological Seminary (Louisville, Kentucky), and Southwestern Baptist Theological Seminary (Fort Worth, Texas).

Number awarded Varies each year.

Deadline Applications may be submitted at any time, but they must be received at least 1 month (preferably sooner) before the student enrolls in a school.

[498]
HISPANIC HIGHER EDUCATION SCHOLARSHIP FUND

New Jersey Mental Health Institute
Attn: Henry Acosta, Project Director
The Neuman Building
3575 Quakerbridge Road, Suite 102
Mercerville, NJ 08619
(609) 838-5488, ext. 205   Fax: (609) 838-5480
Web: www.njmhi.org/higherscholarship.htm

Purpose   To provide financial assistance to Hispanic students working on a master's degree in social work at New Jersey universities.

Eligibility   This program is open to U.S. citizens and permanent residents of Hispanic background who have a baccalaureate degree. Applicants must be interested in working on a master's degree in social work at a university in New Jersey. They must be bilingual (English and Spanish) in both their verbal and written communications. Along with their application, they must submit a brief personal statement explaining why they believe they should receive this scholarship and a 1-page essay on why they are entering the field of social work and how they plan to contribute to the field. Selection is based on information in the application, a personal interview, and an in-person written and verbal communications skills test.

Financial data   A stipend is awarded (amount not specified).

Duration   1 year.

Additional information   This program was established in 2002.

Number awarded   1 each year.

Deadline   April of each year.

[499]
HISPANIC LAWYERS SCHOLARSHIP FUND

Hispanic Lawyers Association of Illinois
c/o Jesse H. Ruiz
Gardner, Carton & Douglas LLC
191 North Wacker Drive, Suite 3700
Chicago, IL 60606-1698
(312) 569-1135   Fax: (312) 569-3135
E-mail: jruiz@gcd.com
Web: www.hlai.org/scholarship.htm

Purpose   To provide financial assistance to first-year Latino law students in Illinois.

Eligibility   This program is open to first-year Latino students who either attend an Illinois law school or are Illinois residents attending law school in another state. Applicants must submit a 2-page statement on why their background and experience illustrate a commitment to the legal and social needs of the Latino community. Selection is based on academic achievement, financial need, and contributions to the Latino community.

Financial data   The stipend is $2,500 per year.

Duration   1 year; nonrenewable.

Number awarded   4 or 5 each year.

Deadline   March of each year.

[500]
HISPANIC METROPOLITAN CHAMBER SCHOLARSHIPS

Hispanic Metropolitan Chamber
Attn: Scholarship Committee
P.O. Box 1837
Portland, OR 97207
(503) 222-0280
Web: www.hmccoregon.com

Purpose   To provide financial assistance for college and graduate school to Hispanic residents of Oregon and Clark County, Washington.

Eligibility   This program is open to residents of Oregon and Clark County, Washington who are of Hispanic ancestry. Applicants must have a GPA of 2.75 or higher and be enrolled or planning to enroll in an accredited community college, 4-year university, or graduate school. Along with their application, they must submit 250-word essays on what being a Latino student means to them, why they should be selected to receive another scholarship from this sponsor (if they are applying for a renewal), and/or what they intend to do with their degree in 10 years (if they are a first-time applicant). If they wish to be considered for a scholarship for low-income families, they may also submit documentation of financial need.

Financial data   Stipends range from $1,000 to $5,000.

Duration   1 year; may be renewed.

Number awarded   Varies each year; recently, 45 of these scholarships were awarded.

Deadline   February of each year.

[501]
HISPANIC SCHOLARSHIP TRUST FUND

Episcopal Church Center
Attn: Office of Hispanic Ministry
815 Second Avenue
New York, NY 10017-4594
(212) 922-5394   Toll-free: (800) 334-7626, ext. 5394
Fax: (212) 867-7652

Purpose   To provide financial assistance to Hispanic Americans interested in theological education within the Episcopal Church in the United States of America (ECUSA).

Eligibility   Applicants must be students of Hispanic descent seeking to complete courses in theological education at an accredited institution in order to fulfill the requirements for ordination in the ECUSA.

Financial data   The amount of the award depends on the needs of the recipient and the availability of funds.

Number awarded   Varies each year; recently, 4 candidates for ordination received support from this fund.

Deadline   April of each year.

[502]

HISPANIC THEOLOGICAL INITIATIVE DOCTORAL GRANTS

Hispanic Theological Initiative
12 Library Place
Princeton, NJ 08540
(609) 252-1721   Toll-free: (800) 575-5522
Fax: (609) 252-1738   E-mail: hti@ptsem.edu
Web: www.htiprogram.org/scholarships/doctoral.htm

Purpose To provide financial assistance to Latino/a doctoral students who are interested in a career of scholarly service to a faith community.

Eligibility This program is open to full-time doctoral students (Ph.D., Ed.D., Th.D., or equivalent only) who are Latinos/as from the United States or Puerto Rico. Applicants must be U.S. citizens or permanent residents committed to serving the Latino faith community. Selection is based on the scholarly promise of the applicant as indicated by GPA and GRE scores, academic quality of written work submitted by the applicant, recommendations by professors giving witness to the applicant's potential to contribute to the academic community as a scholar, and recommendations by Latino church/community leaders giving witness to the applicant's commitment to and leadership in the Latino community.

Financial data The grant is $15,000 for the first year or $13,000 for the second year. The program requires that the institution provide a tuition scholarship.

Duration Up to 2 years. Scholars who apply during the first year of doctoral course work initially receive support for 1 year only; they must reapply for the second year. The award may not be used during the year the students undergo their doctoral examinations and are not taking courses.

Additional information The program, funded by Pew Charitable Trusts, also provides the awardees with a Latino/a faculty member to serve as a mentor to monitor and encourage their progress.

Number awarded Varies each year; recently, 4 first-year and 6 second-year scholarships were awarded.

Deadline November of each year for first-year awards; December of each year for renewals.

[503]

HIV/AIDS RESEARCH FELLOWSHIPS

American Psychological Association
Attn: Minority Fellowship Program
750 First Street, N.E.
Washington, DC 20002-4242
(202) 336-6127   Fax: (202) 336-6012
TDD: (202) 336-6123   E-mail: mfp@apa.org
Web: www.apa.org/mfp/hprogram.html

Purpose To provide financial assistance to psychology doctoral students (especially minorities) who are preparing for a career involving research on HIV/AIDS issues and ethnic minority populations.

Eligibility This program is open to full-time doctoral students who can demonstrate a strong commitment to a career in HIV/AIDS research related to ethnic minorities. Students from the complete range of psychology disciplines are encouraged to apply if their training and research interests are related to mental health and HIV/AIDS. Clinical, counseling, and school psychology students must demonstrate that they will receive substantial training in research and the delivery of services to people with HIV/AIDS. Members of minority groups (African Americans, Alaskan Natives, American Indians, Asian Americans, Hispanics/Latinos, Native Hawaiians, and Pacific Islanders) are especially encouraged to apply. U.S. citizenship or permanent resident status is required. Selection is based on commitment to a career in research that focuses on HIV/AIDS in ethnic minority communities, knowledge of ethnic minority psychology or HIV/AIDS issues, the fit between career goals and training environment selected, potential for a research career demonstrated through accomplishments and goals, scholarship and grades, and letters of recommendation.

Financial data The stipend is that established by the National Institutes of Health for predoctoral students, currently $20,772 per year.

Duration 1 year; may be renewed for up to 2 additional years.

Additional information Funding is provided by the U.S. National Institute of Mental Health. Students who receive a federally-funded grant from another source may not also accept funds from this program.

Number awarded Varies each year.

Deadline January of each year.

[504]

HOLLY A. CORNELL SCHOLARSHIP

American Water Works Association
Attn: Scholarship Coordinator
6666 West Quincy Avenue
Denver, CO 80235-3098
(303) 347-6206   Fax: (303) 795-7603
E-mail: ncole@awwa.org
Web: www.awwa.org/About/scholars

Purpose To provide financial assistance to outstanding minority and female students interested in pursuing advanced training in the field of water supply and treatment.

Eligibility Minority and female students who anticipate completing the requirements for a master's degree in engineering no sooner than December of the following year are eligible. Students who have been accepted into graduate school but have not yet begun graduate study are encouraged to apply. Recipients of the Larson Aquatic Research Support (LARS) M.S. Scholarship are not eligible for this program. Selection is based on the quality of the applicant's academic record and the potential to provide leadership in the field of water supply and treatment.

Financial data The stipend is $5,000.

Duration 1 year.

Additional information Funding for this program comes from the consulting firm CH2M Hill. The association reserves the right not to make an award for any year in which an outstanding candidate is not identified.

Number awarded 1 each year.

Deadline January of each year.

[505]
HOWARD HUGHES MEDICAL INSTITUTE RESEARCH TRAINING FELLOWSHIPS FOR MEDICAL STUDENTS

Howard Hughes Medical Institute
Attn: Office of Grants and Special Programs
4000 Jones Bridge Road
Chevy Chase, MD 20815-6789
(301) 215-8883   Fax: (301) 215-8888
E-mail: fellows@hhmi.org
Web: www.hhmi.org/medfellowships

Purpose To provide financial assistance to minority and other medical students interested in pursuing research training.

Eligibility Applicants must be enrolled in a medical school in the United States, although they may be citizens of any country. They must describe a proposed research project to be conducted at an academic or nonprofit research institution in the United States, other than a facility of the National Institutes of Health in Bethesda, Maryland. Research proposals should reflect the interests of the Howard Hughes Medical Institute (HHMI), especially in biochemistry, bioinformatics, biophysics, biostatistics, cell biology, developmental biology, epidemiology, genetics, immunology, mathematical and computational biology, microbiology, molecular biology, neuroscience, pharmacology, physiology, structural biology, and virology. Applications from women and minorities underrepresented in the sciences (Blacks, Hispanics, Native Americans, Native Alaskans, and Native Pacific Islanders) are especially encouraged. Students enrolled in M.D./Ph.D., Ph.D., or Sc.D. programs and those who have completed a Ph.D. or Sc.D. in a laboratory-based science are not eligible. Selection is based on letters of reference, the research plan, and a mentor's plans for training the student.

Financial data Fellows receive a stipend of $25,000 per year; their institution receives an institutional allowance of $5,500 and a research allowance of $5,500. Research Training Fellows who are chosen to receive support to complete their studies toward the M.D. degree are given an annual stipend of $21,000 and a $16,000 annual allowance toward tuition and other education-related expenses.

Duration 1 year; may be renewed for a second year of research. A small number of fellows may be allowed to return to medical school and continue receiving support for 2 additional years.

Additional information This program complements the HHMI-NIH Research Scholars Program; students may not apply to both programs in the same year. Fellows may not be enrolled in an M.D./Ph.D. program. Applicants must apply online using the sponsor's web-based application system.

Number awarded Up to 60 each year.

Deadline January of each year.

[506]
HOWARD MAYER BROWN FELLOWSHIP

American Musicological Society
201 South 34th Street
Philadelphia, PA 19104-6313
(215) 898-8698   Toll-free: (888) 611-4AMS
Fax: (215) 573-3673   E-mail: ams@sas.upenn.edu
Web: www.ams-net.org/hmb.html

Purpose To provide financial assistance to minority students who are working on a doctoral degree in the field of musicology.

Eligibility This program is open to members of minority groups historically underrepresented in the field of musicology. In the United States, that includes African Americans, Native Americans, Hispanic Americans, and Asian Americans. In Canada, it refers to visible minorities. Applicants must have completed at least 1 year of academic work at an institution with a graduate program in musicology and be planning to complete a Ph.D. degree in the field. There are no restrictions on research area, age, or sex. Candidates must submit a personal statement summarizing their musical and academic background and stating why they wish to work on an advanced degree in musicology, letters of support from 3 faculty members, a curriculum vitae, and samples of their work (such as term papers or published material). U.S. or Canadian citizenship is required.

Financial data The stipend is $14,000 per year.

Duration 1 year; nonrenewable.

Additional information Information is also available from Ellen T. Harris, Massachusetts Institute of Technology, 4-246, 77 Massachusetts Avenue, Cambridge, MA 02139-4301, E-mail: eharris@mit.edu.

Number awarded 1 each year.

Deadline January of each year.

[507]
HSF/PFIZER INC. FELLOWSHIP PROGRAM

Hispanic Scholarship Fund
Attn: Selection Committee
55 Second Street, Suite 1500
San Francisco, CA 94105
(415) 808-2350   Toll-free: (877) HSF-INFO
Fax: (415) 808-2302   E-mail: college1@hsf.net
Web: www.hsf.net/scholarship/programs/pfizer.php

Purpose To provide financial assistance and work experience to Hispanic students working on a graduate degree in selected science-related fields at designated universities.

Eligibility This program is open to U.S. citizens, permanent residents, and visitors with a passport stamped I-551 who are of Hispanic heritage. Applicants must be enrolled full time at Carnegie Mellon University, Columbia University, Cornell University, Harvard University, Massachusetts Institute of Technology, New York University, Northwestern University, Stanford University, University of California at Berkeley, University of California at Los Angeles, University of Chicago, University of Pennsylvania, University of Texas at Austin, or University of Virginia. They must have a GPA of 3.0 or higher in a degree program in biostatistics, business administration, computer engineering, computer information systems, economics, electrical engineering, epidemiology, health administration, medicine, or public health. Along with their application, they must submit 600-word essays on 1) how their Hispanic heritage, family upbringing, and/or role models have influenced their personal long-term goals; 2) how they contribute to their community and what they have learned from their experiences; and 3) an academic challenge they have faced and how they have overcome it. Selection is based on academic achievement, personal strengths, leadership, and financial need. A mandatory summer internship is included in the program.

Financial data The fellowship stipend is $10,000 per year. A salary is paid for the internship.

Duration 2 years (the second year is contingent on successful completion of the 12-week summer internship).

Additional information This program is jointly sponsored by the Hispanic Scholarship Fund (HSF) and Pfizer Inc.

Number awarded 1 or more each year.

Deadline June of each year.

[508]
HUGH J. ANDERSEN MEMORIAL SCHOLARSHIPS

National Medical Fellowships, Inc.
Attn: Scholarship Program
5 Hanover Square, 15th Floor
New York, NY 10004
(212) 483-8880   Fax: (212) 483-8897
E-mail: info@nmfonline.org
Web: www.nmf-online.org

Purpose To provide financial assistance to underrepresented minority medical students who reside or attend school in Minnesota.

Eligibility This program is open to African Americans, Mexican Americans, Native Hawaiians, Alaska Natives, American Indians, and mainland Puerto Ricans who have completed at least 1 year of medical school. Applicants must be Minnesota residents enrolled in an accredited U.S. medical school or students from any state attending Minnesota medical schools. Selection is based on leadership, community service, and financial need. Direct applications are not accepted; candidates must be nominated by medical school deans.

Financial data The award is $2,500.

Duration 1 year.

Additional information This award was established in 1982.

Number awarded Up to 5 each year.

Deadline Nominations must be submitted by September of each year.

[509]
IBM PHD FELLOWSHIP PROGRAM

IBM Corporation
Attn: University Relations
1133 Westchester Avenue
White Plains, NY 10604
Toll-free: (800) IBM-4YOU   TTY: (800) IBM-3383
E-mail: phdfellow@us.ibm.com
Web: www-306.ibm.com

Purpose To provide financial assistance and work experience to students (particularly minorities and women) working on a Ph.D. in a research area of broad interest to IBM.

Eligibility Students nominated for this fellowship should be enrolled full time in an accredited U.S. or Canadian college or university and should have completed at least 1 year of graduate study in the following fields: business, chemistry, computer science, electrical engineering, materials sciences, mathematics, mechanical engineering, physics, or related disciplines. They should be planning a career in research. Nominations must be made by a faculty member and endorsed by the department head. IBM values diversity and encourages nominations of women, minorities, and others who contribute to that diversity. Selection is based on the applicants' potential for research excellence, the degree to which their technical interests align with those of IBM, and academic progress to date.

Financial data Fellows receive tuition, fees, and a stipend of $17,500 per year.

Duration 1 year; may be renewed up to 3 additional years, provided the recipient is renominated, interacts with IBM's technical community, and demonstrates continued progress and achievement.

Additional information Recipients are offered an internship at 1 of the IBM Research Division laboratories and are given an IBM ThinkPad.

Number awarded Varies each year.

Deadline December of each year.

[510]
ILLINOIS MINORITY REAL ESTATE SCHOLARSHIP

Illinois Association of Realtors
Attn: Illinois Real Estate Educational Foundation
3180 Adloff Lane, Suite 400
P.O. Box 19451
Springfield, IL 62794-9451
(217) 529-2600   E-mail: IARaccess@iar.org
Web: www.illinoisrealtor.org/iar/about/minority.htm

Purpose To provide financial assistance to Illinois residents who are members of minority groups and preparing for a career in real estate.

Eligibility This program is open to residents of Illinois who are African American, Hispanic or Latino, Native American, or Asian. Applicants must be interested in preparing for a career in real estate by pursuing: 1) courses to meet Illinois salesperson license requirement; 2) course work to meet Illinois broker license requirement; 3) course work required for Illinois appraisal licensing/certification; 4) professional development unrelated to obtaining license/certification; or 5) an undergraduate or graduate program of study. Along with their application, they must submit information on their employment history, transcripts, evidence of financial need, and an essay that describes their career goals and explains why they believe they should receive scholarship assistance through this program.

Financial data The maximum stipend is $500.

Duration Funds must be used within 24 months of the award date.

Deadline Applications may be submitted at any time, but they must be received at least 12 weeks prior to the beginning of the school term for which financial assistance is requested.

[511]
IMAGE DE SEATTLE SCHOLARSHIPS

Image de Seattle
Attn: Scholarship Committee
P.O. Box 21247
Seattle, WA 98111
(206) 443-3800

Purpose To provide financial assistance to Hispanic American students from the state of Washington who are interested in working on an undergraduate or graduate degree.

Eligibility This program is open to high school seniors, undergraduates, and graduate school students who are Hispanic Americans and have been residents of the state of Washington for at least the past 12 months. Applicants must submit a 1-page statement on their goals and plans for the future, their chosen field of study, and a brief biography that includes their identification with the Hispanic community. Financial need is not considered in the selection process.

Financial data The stipend is $500.

Duration 1 year.

Additional information Recipients must agree to provide 25 hours of community service within 1 year of selection.

Number awarded 3 each year.

Deadline May of each year.

[512]
INDUSTRY/GOVERNMENT GRADUATE FELLOWSHIPS

American Meteorological Society
Attn: Fellowship/Scholarship Coordinator
45 Beacon Street
Boston, MA 02108-3693
(617) 227-2426, ext. 246　　　Fax: (617) 742-8718
E-mail: scholar@ametsoc.org
Web: www.ametsoc.org

Purpose To encourage students (particularly minorities, women, and students with disabilities) entering their first year of graduate school to work on an advanced degree in the atmospheric and related oceanic and hydrologic sciences.

Eligibility This program is open to students entering their first year of graduate study who wish to pursue advanced degrees in the atmospheric or related oceanic or hydrologic sciences. Applicants must be U.S. citizens or permanent residents and have a GPA of 3.25 or higher. Along with their application, they must submit 200-word essays on 1) their most important achievements that qualify them for this scholarship, and 2) their career goals in the atmospheric or related oceanic or hydrologic fields. Selection is based on academic record as an undergraduate. The sponsor specifically encourages applications from women, minorities, and students with disabilities who are traditionally underrepresented in the atmospheric and related oceanic sciences.

Financial data The stipend is $22,000 per academic year.

Duration 9 months.

Additional information This program was initiated in 1991. It is funded by high-technology firms and government agencies. Requests for an application must be accompanied by a self-addressed stamped envelope.

Number awarded Varies each year; recently, 15 of these scholarships were awarded.

Deadline February of each year.

[513]
INTERNATIONAL COMMUNICATIONS INDUSTRIES ASSOCIATION COLLEGE SCHOLARSHIPS

International Communications Industries Association, Inc.
Attn: Director of Strategic Initiatives
11242 Waples Mill Road, Suite 200
Fairfax, VA 22030
(703) 273-7200　　　Toll-free: (800) 659-7469
Fax: (703) 278-8082　　E-mail: dwilbert@infocomm.org
Web: www.infocomm.org

Purpose To provide financial assistance to college students and entering graduate students (especially minorities and women) who are interested in preparing for a career in the audiovisual industry.

Eligibility This program is open to 1) college juniors completing their bachelor's degree in the following year; 2) college seniors who plan to enter graduate school; and 3) students in their final year of study for an associate degree. Applicants must have a GPA of 2.75 or higher in a program of audio, visual, audiovisual, electronics, telecommunications, technical theater, data networking, software development, or information technology. Students in other programs, such as journalism, may be eligible if they can demonstrate a relationship to career goals in the audiovisual industry. Along with their application, they must submit essays on why they are applying for this scholarship, why they are interested in the audiovisual industry, and their professional plans following graduation. Minority and women candidates are especially encouraged to apply. Selection is based on the essays, presentation of the application, GPA, work experience, and letters of recommendation.

Financial data The stipend is $2,500.

Duration 1 year.

Additional information Recipients are required to work during the summer as paid interns with a manufacturer, dealer, designer, or other firm that is a member of the International Communications Industries Association.

Number awarded Varies each year; recently, 7 of these scholarships were awarded.

Deadline April of each year.

[514]
IOWA CONFERENCE ETHNIC MINORITY SCHOLARSHIP

United Methodist Church-Iowa Conference
Attn: Board of Ordained Ministry
500 East Court Avenue, Suite C
Des Moines, IA 50309
(515) 283-1991　　　Fax: (515) 288-1906
Web: www.iaumc.org

Purpose To provide financial assistance to minority students preparing for ordained ministry under the Iowa Conference of the United Methodist Church.

Eligibility This program is open to certified candidates for ministry who are 1) African Americans, Asian Americans, Hispanic Americans, or Native Americans, and 2) in good standing with their district Committee on Ordained Ministry of the Iowa Conference of the United Methodist Church. Applicants must be enrolled in a graduate school listed by the University Senate and intending to complete a master's degree (either an M.Div. or a master's degree in specialized ministry), be ordained as a deacon or elder, and serve in ministry in the Iowa Conference.

Financial data The stipend is $500 per year. Grants are intended as supplements to the Automatic Grants Program that provides $2,000 per year.

Duration 1 year; may be renewed for up to 2 additional years.

Additional information Information is also available from the Rev. Mike Morgan, 1298 Seventh Avenue, Marion, IA 52302, (319) 377-4856, Fax: (319) 377-5392, E-mail: mike@fumcmarion.org.

Number awarded 1 or more each year.

Deadline May or November of each year.

[515]
J. ROBERT GLADDEN SOCIETY RESIDENT SCHOLARSHIPS

J. Robert Gladden Society
6300 North River Road, Suite 727
Rosemont, IL 60018
(847) 698-1633   Fax: (847) 823-4921
E-mail: swift@aaos.org
Web: www.gladdensociety.org/scholarships/pgy5.htm

Purpose To provide funding to underrepresented minority orthopedic residents who are studying for their qualifying examinations.

Eligibility This program is open to members of underrepresented minority groups who are PGY 5 residents in accredited orthopedic programs. Applicants must be members of the J. Robert Gladden Society (JRGS) or recommended by a member. They must be interested in participating in a review course in preparation for their certifying examinations.

Financial data The grant is $1,000.

Duration Grants are awarded annually.

Number awarded 10 each year.

Deadline February of each year.

[516]
JAMES CARLSON MEMORIAL SCHOLARSHIP

Oregon Student Assistance Commission
Attn: Grants and Scholarships Division
1500 Valley River Drive, Suite 100
Eugene, OR 97401-2146
(541) 687-7395   Toll-free: (800) 452-8807, ext. 7395
Fax: (541) 687-7419
E-mail: awardinfo@mercury.osac.state.or.us
Web: www.osac.state.or.us

Purpose To provide financial assistance to Oregon residents (particularly minorities) majoring in education on the undergraduate or graduate school level.

Eligibility This program is open to residents of Oregon who are U.S. citizens or permanent residents. Applicants must be either 1) college seniors or fifth-year students majoring in elementary or secondary education or 2) graduate students working on an elementary or secondary certifi-

cate. Full-time enrollment and financial need are required. Priority is given to 1) members of African American, Asian American, Hispanic, or Native American ethnic groups; 2) dependents of members of the Oregon Education Association; and 3) applicants committed to teaching autistic children.

Financial data Stipend amounts vary; recently, they were at least $1,300.

Duration 1 year.

Additional information This program is administered by the Oregon Student Assistance Commission (OSAC) with funds provided by the Oregon Community Foundation, 1221 S.W. Yamhill, Suite 100, Portland, OR 97205, (503) 227-6846, Fax: (503) 274-7771.

Number awarded Varies each year; recently, 3 of these scholarships were awarded.

Deadline February of each year.

[517]
JAMES ECHOLS SCHOLARSHIP

California Association for Health, Physical Education, Recreation and Dance
Attn: Chair, Scholarship Committee
1501 El Camino Avenue, Suite 3
Sacramento, CA 95815-2748
(916) 922-3596   Toll-free: (800) 499-3596 (within CA)
Fax: (916) 922-0133   E-mail: cahperd@cahperd.org
Web: www.cahperd.org

Purpose To provide financial assistance to minority student members of the California Association for Health, Physical Education, Recreation and Dance.

Eligibility This program is open to California residents who have been members of the association for at least 60 days and are attending a 2-year or 4-year college or university in California. Applicants must be undergraduate or graduate students majoring in health, physical education, recreation, or dance and have completed at least 60 semester hours of college work. Selection is based on scholastic proficiency (a GPA of 3.0 or higher); leadership ability in school, community, and professional activities; and personal qualities of enthusiasm, cooperativeness, responsibility, initiative, and ability to work with others. This scholarship is awarded to the highest-ranked minority (Asian, African American, Latino, or Native American) applicant.

Financial data The stipend is $750.

Duration 1 year.

Additional information Information is also available from Nicolas Fraire, CAHPERD Scholarship Chair, 3792 Willowpark Drive, San Jose, CA 95118.

Number awarded 1 each year.

Deadline December of each year.

[518]

JOHN MCLENDON MEMORIAL MINORITY POSTGRADUATE SCHOLARSHIP AWARD

National Association of Collegiate Directors of Athletics
Attn: NACDA Foundation
24651 Detroit Road
P.O. Box 16428
Cleveland, OH 44116
(440) 892-4000   Fax: (440) 892-4007
E-mail: bhorning@nacda.com
Web: nacda.collegesports.com

Purpose To provide financial assistance and work experience to minority college seniors who are interested in working on a graduate degree in athletics administration.

Eligibility This program is open to minority college students who are seniors, are attending school on a full-time basis, have a GPA of 3.0 or higher, intend to attend graduate school to earn a degree in athletics administration, and are involved on the college or community level. Candidates are not required to be student athletes. Current graduate students are not eligible.

Financial data The stipend is $10,000. In addition, 1 recipient each year is offered the opportunity to serve a 9-month internship in the office of the National Association of Collegiate Directors of Athletics (NACDA).

Duration 1 year.

Additional information Recipients must maintain full-time status during the senior year to retain their eligibility. They must attend NACDA-member institutions.

Number awarded 5 each year.

Deadline January of each year.

[519]

JOHN STANFORD MEMORIAL WLMA SCHOLARSHIP

Washington Library Media Association
P.O. Box 50194
Bellevue, WA 98015-0194
E-mail: wlma@earthlink.net
Web: www.wlma.org/Association/scholar.htm

Purpose To provide financial assistance to ethnic minorities in Washington who are interested in preparing for a library media career.

Eligibility This program is open to residents of Washington who are working toward a library media endorsement or graduate degree in the field. Applicants must be members of an ethnic minority group. They must be working or planning to work in a school library. Along with their application, they must submit documentation of financial need and a description of themselves that includes their plans for the future, interest in librarianship, and plans for further education.

Financial data The stipend is $1,000.

Duration 1 year.

Additional information Information is also available from Camille Hefty, Scholarship Chair, 2728 Webber Court, Steilacoom, WA 98388-2849, (253) 589-3223, E-mail: camille_hefty@fp.k12.wa.us.

Number awarded 1 each year.

Deadline April of each year.

[520]

JOSE MARTI SCHOLARSHIP CHALLENGE GRANT FUND

Florida Department of Education
Attn: Office of Student Financial Assistance
1940 North Monroe Street, Suite 70
Tallahassee, FL 32303-4759
(850) 410-5200   Toll-free: (888) 827-2004
Fax: (850) 487-1809   E-mail: osfa@fldoe.org
Web: www.FloridaStudentFinancialAid.org

Purpose To provide financial assistance to Hispanic American high school seniors and graduate students in Florida.

Eligibility This program is open to Florida residents of Spanish culture who were born in, or whose natural parent was born in, Mexico, Spain, or a Hispanic country of the Caribbean, Central America, or South America. Applicants must be citizens or eligible noncitizens of the United States, be enrolled or planning to enroll as full-time undergraduate or graduate students at an eligible postsecondary school in Florida, be able to demonstrate financial need as determined by a nationally-recognized needs analysis service, and have earned a cumulative GPA of 3.0 or higher in high school or, if a graduate school applicant, in undergraduate course work.

Financial data The grant is $2,000 per academic year. Available funds are contingent upon matching contributions from private sources.

Duration 1 year; may be renewed if the student maintains full-time enrollment and a GPA of 3.0 or higher and continues to demonstrate financial need.

Number awarded Varies each year; recently, this program presented 98 awards.

Deadline March of each year.

[521]

JUANITA ROBLES-LOPEZ/PAMPERS PARENTING INSTITUTE AND PROCTER & GAMBLE SCHOLARSHIP

National Association of Hispanic Nurses
Attn: National Awards and Scholarship Committee Chair
1501 16th Street, N.W.
Washington, DC 20036
(202) 387-2477   Fax: (202) 483-7183
E-mail: thehispanicnurses@earthlink.net
Web: www.thehispanicnurses.org

Purpose To provide financial assistance to members of the National Association of Hispanic Nurses (NAHN) interested in a master's degree in maternal-child nursing.

Eligibility Eligible are members of the association enrolled in a master's degree program in a maternal-child nursing program. Applicants must submit an statement outlining the maternal child needs affecting Hispanic communities and their potential leadership in that area. U.S. citizenship or permanent resident status is required. Selection is based on academic excellence (preferably a GPA of 3.0 or higher), potential for leadership in nursing, and financial need.

Financial data The stipend is $2,000.

Duration 1 year.

Additional information Funding for this scholarship is provided by Procter & Gamble Company and Pampers Parenting Institute.

Number awarded 1 each year.

Deadline April of each year.

[522]
JUSTICE ALLEN E. BROUSSARD SCHOLARSHIPS

Justice Allen E. Broussard Scholarship Foundation
c/o Jill Dessalines
McKesson Corporation Law Department
One Post Street, 34th Floor
San Francisco, CA 94104-5296
(415) 983-7680
E-mail: scholarship@broussard-scholarship.org
Web: www.broussard-scholarship.org

Purpose To provide financial assistance to minority students from any state enrolled in law schools in the San Francisco Bay area.

Eligibility This program is open to minority students, preferably those entering their first year, at law schools in the Bay area. Applicants must submit a 250-word essay on why they should be awarded this scholarship. Selection is based on the essay, academic record, extracurricular activities (with emphasis on service-oriented extracurricular activities directed toward the enhancement of opportunities for minorities), letters of recommendation, and financial need.

Financial data The stipend is $5,000.

Duration 1 year.

Additional information This program was originally established in 1996.

Number awarded 3 each year.

Deadline March of each year.

[523]
KALA SINGH MEMORIAL SCHOLARSHIP

American Speech-Language-Hearing Foundation
Attn: Graduate Student Scholarship Competition
10801 Rockville Pike
Rockville, MD 20852-3279
(301) 897-5700   Toll-free: (800) 498-2071
Fax: (301) 571-0457   TTY: (800) 498-2071
E-mail: foundation@asha.org
Web: www.ashfoundation.org

Purpose To provide financial assistance to international or minority students who are interested in working on a graduate degree in communication sciences and disorders.

Eligibility Applicants must be college graduates who are accepted for graduate study in the United States in a communication sciences and disorders program or enrolled as a full-time graduate student. The fund gives priority to foreign or minority (American Indian, Alaskan Native, Asian, Pacific Islander, Black, Hispanic) students. Students who previously received a scholarship from the American Speech-Language-Hearing Foundation are not eligible.

Financial data The stipend ranges from $2,000 to $4,000. Funds must be used for educational support (e.g., tuition, books, school living expenses), not for personal or conference travel.

Duration The award is granted annually.

Number awarded 1 each year.

Deadline June of each year.

[524]
KPMG MINORITY ACCOUNTING DOCTORAL SCHOLARSHIPS

KPMG Foundation
Attn: Scholarship Administrator
Three Chestnut Ridge Road
Montvale, NJ 07645-0435
(201) 307-7932   Fax: (201) 307-7093
E-mail: fionarose@kpmg.com
Web: kpmgfoundation.org/foundinit.asp#min

Purpose To provide funding to underrepresented minority students working on a doctoral degree in accounting.

Eligibility Applicants must be African Americans, Hispanic Americans, or Native Americans. They must be U.S. citizens or permanent residents and accepted or enrolled in a full-time accounting doctoral program. Along with their application, they must submit a brief letter explaining their reason for working on a Ph.D. in accounting.

Financial data The stipend is $10,000 per year.

Duration 1 year; may be renewed up to 4 additional years.

Additional information These funds are not intended to replace funds normally made available by the recipient's institution. The foundation recommends that the recipient's institution also award, to the recipient, a $5,000 annual stipend, a teaching or research assistantship, and a waiver of tuition and fees.

Number awarded Varies each year; recently, 14 new scholarships were awarded and another 65 were renewed.

Deadline April of each year.

[525]
LA UNIDAD LATINA SCHOLARSHIPS

La Unidad Latina Foundation, Inc.
359 Prospect Avenue
Brooklyn, NY 11215
E-mail: foundation@launidadlatina.org
Web: foundation.launidadlatina.org

Purpose To provide financial assistance to Hispanic students who are working on a bachelor's or master's degree.

Eligibility This program is open to students of Hispanic background who have completed at least 1 semester of higher education. Applicants must be enrolled full time at an accredited 4-year college or university in the United States. Along with their application, they must submit brief essays on the courses in which they are enrolled in the current semester, their financial need, their academic plans and career goals, an instance in which someone has left an indelible mark in their life and why, their extracurricular activities, any honors or awards they have received, and their special interests or hobbies.

Financial data Stipends range from $250 to $1,000.

Duration 1 year.

Number awarded Varies each year; recently, 24 of these scholarships (18 in fall, 6 in spring) were awarded.

Deadline February of each year for spring semester; October of each year for fall semester.

[526]
LASPACE GRADUATE FELLOWSHIPS

Louisiana Space Consortium
c/o Louisiana State University
Department of Physics and Astronomy
371 Nicholson Hall
Baton Rouge, LA 70803-4001
(225) 578-8697   Fax: (225) 578-1222
E-mail: laspace@lsu.edu
Web: laspace.lsu.edu

Purpose To provide financial assistance to students (particularly minorities, women, and persons with disabilities) working on a graduate degree in an aerospace-related discipline at a college or university belonging to the Louisiana Space Consortium (LaSPACE).

Eligibility This program is open to U.S. citizens working on a master's or doctoral degree in a space- or aerospace-related field as a full-time student at 1 of the LaSPACE member schools. Applicants should have a GPA of 3.0 or higher and GRE scores in excess of 1000. Members of groups underrepresented in science, mathematics, and engineering (women, minorities, and persons with disabilities) are strongly encouraged to apply. Selection is based on scholastic accomplishment, research experience and productivity, leadership and recognitions, intellectual abilities and character, and relevance of the proposed graduate work to space and aerospace fields or programs.

Financial data The stipend is $17,500 per year for students working on a master's degree or $20,000 per year for students working on a doctorate.

Duration 1 year; renewable for up to 2 additional years for master's degree students and up to 4 additional years for Ph.D. students.

Additional information Fellows work with an established aerospace researcher at 1 of the LaSPACE member institutions: Dillard University, Grambling State University, L.S.U. Agricultural Center, Louisiana State University and A&M College, Louisiana Tech University, Loyola University, McNeese State University, Nicholls State University, Northwestern State University of Louisiana, Southeastern Louisiana University, Southern University and A&M College, Southern University at New Orleans, Southern University at Shreveport-Bossier City, Tulane University, University of New Orleans, University of Louisiana at Lafayette, University of Louisiana at Monroe, and Xavier University of Louisiana. Funding for this program is provided by the U.S. National Aeronautics and Space Administration (NASA). Fellows are expected to describe the work in a yearly written report and in seminars presented to various audiences.

Number awarded 1 to 3 each year.

Deadline October of each year.

[527]
LAWRENCE R. FOSTER MEMORIAL SCHOLARSHIP

Oregon Student Assistance Commission
Attn: Grants and Scholarships Division
1500 Valley River Drive, Suite 100
Eugene, OR 97401-2146
(541) 687-7395   Toll-free: (800) 452-8807, ext. 7395
Fax: (541) 687-7419
E-mail: awardinfo@mercury.osac.state.or.us
Web: www.osac.state.or.us

Purpose To provide financial assistance for college or graduate school to residents of Oregon (particularly minorities) who are interested in preparing for a public health career.

Eligibility This program is open to residents of Oregon who are attending a 4-year college or university in any state to prepare for a career in public health (not private practice). First preference is given to applicants who are either working in public health or enrolled as graduate students in that field. Second preference is given to undergraduates entering the junior or senior year of a health program, including nursing, medical technology, and physician assistant. A general preference is given to applicants from diverse cultures. Along with their application, they must submit a 1- to 2-page essay on their interest, experience, and future plans for a public health career

Financial data Stipend amounts vary; recently, they were at least $4,167.

Duration 1 year.

Additional information This program is administered by the Oregon Student Assistance Commission (OSAC) with funds provided by the Oregon Community Foundation, 1221 S.W. Yamhill, Suite 100, Portland, OR 97205, (503) 227-6846, Fax: (503) 274-7771.

Number awarded Varies each year; recently, 6 of these scholarships were awarded.

Deadline February of each year.

[528]
LEADERSHIP FOR DIVERSITY SCHOLARSHIP

California School Library Association
717 K Street, Suite 515
Sacramento, CA 95814-3477
(916) 447-2684   Fax: (916) 447-2695
E-mail: csla@pacbell.net
Web: www.schoollibrary.org

Purpose To encourage underrepresented minority students to get a credential as a library media teacher in California.

Eligibility This program is open to students who are members of a traditionally underrepresented group enrolled in a college or university library media teacher credential program in California. Applicants must intend to work as a library media teacher in a California school library media center for a minimum of 3 years. Along with their application, they must submit a 250-word statement on their school library media career interests and goals, why they should be considered, what they can contribute, their commitment to serving the needs of our multicultural and multilingual students, and their financial situation.

Financial data The stipend is $1,000.

Duration 1 year.

Number awarded 1 each year.
Deadline June of each year.

[529]
LIBRARY AND INFORMATION TECHNOLOGY ASSOCIATION/OCLC MINORITY SCHOLARSHIP

American Library Association
Attn: Library and Information Technology Association
50 East Huron Street
Chicago, IL 60611-2795
(312) 280-4270   Toll-free: (800) 545-2433, ext. 4270
Fax: (312) 280-3257   TDD: (312) 944-7298
TDD: (888) 814-7692   E-mail: lita@ala.org
Web: www.lita.org

Purpose To provide financial assistance to minority graduate students interested in preparing for a career in library automation.

Eligibility Applicants must be American or Canadian citizens, interested in working on a master's degree in library/information science (with a focus on library automation), and a member of 1 of the following ethnic groups: American Indian, Alaskan Native, Asian, Pacific Islander, African American, or Hispanic. The award is based on academic excellence, leadership potential, evidence of a commitment to a career in library automation and information technology, and prior activity and experience in those fields. Economic need is considered when all other criteria are equal.

Financial data The stipend is $3,000.

Duration 1 year.

Additional information This scholarship, first awarded in 1991, is funded by Online Computer Library Center (OCLC) and administered by the Library and Information Technology Association (LITA) of the American Library Association.

Number awarded 1 each year.
Deadline February of each year.

[530]
LIONEL C. BARROWS MINORITY DOCTORAL STUDENT SCHOLARSHIP

Association for Education in Journalism and Mass Communication
Attn: Communication Theory and Methodology Division
234 Outlet Pointe Boulevard, Suite A
Columbia, SC 29210-5667
(803) 798-0271   Fax: (803) 772-3509
E-mail: aejmc@aejmc.org
Web: www.aejmc.org

Purpose To provide financial assistance to minorities who are interested in working on a doctorate in mass communication.

Eligibility This program is open to minority students enrolled in a Ph.D. program in journalism and mass communication. Applicants must submit 2 letters of recommendation, a resume, and a brief letter outlining their research interests and career plans. Membership in the association is not required, but applicants must be U.S. citizens or permanent residents. Selection is based on the likelihood that the applicant's work will contribute to communication theory and/or methodology.

Financial data The stipend is $1,400.

Duration 1 year.

Additional information This program began in 1972. Information is also available from Michael S. Shapiro, Cornell University, Department of Communication, 319 Kennedy Hall, Ithaca, NY 14853, (607) 255-6356, E-mail: mas29@cornell.edu.

Number awarded 1 each year.
Deadline June of each year.

[531]
LITA/LSSI MINORITY SCHOLARSHIP

American Library Association
Attn: Library and Information Technology Association
50 East Huron Street
Chicago, IL 60611-2795
(312) 280-4270   Toll-free: (800) 545-2433, ext. 4270
Fax: (312) 280-3257   TDD: (312) 944-7298
TDD: (888) 814-7692   E-mail: lita@ala.org
Web: www.lita.org

Purpose To provide financial assistance to minority graduate students interested in preparing for a career in library automation.

Eligibility Applicants must be American or Canadian citizens, interested in working on a master's degree in library/information science (with a focus on library automation), and a member of 1 of the following ethnic groups: American Indian, Alaskan Native, Asian, Pacific Islander, African American, or Hispanic. The award is based on academic excellence, leadership potential, evidence of a commitment to a career in library automation and information technology, and prior activity and experience in those fields. Economic need is considered only when all other criteria are equal.

Financial data The stipend is $2,500.

Duration 1 year.

Additional information This scholarship, first awarded in 1995, is funded by Library Systems & Services, Inc. (LSSI) and administered by the Library and Information Technology Association (LITA) of the American Library Association.

Number awarded 1 each year.
Deadline February of each year.

[532]
MAES GENERAL SCHOLARSHIPS

Society of Mexican American Engineers and Scientists
Attn: Scholarships
711 West Bay Area Boulevard, Suite 206
Webster, TX 77598-3677
(281) 557-3677   Fax: (281) 557-3757
E-mail: scholarships@maes-natl.org
Web: www.maes-natl.org

Purpose To provide financial assistance to undergraduate and graduate student members of the Society of Mexican American Engineers and Scientists (MAES).

Eligibility This program is open to MAES student members who are full-time undergraduate or graduate students at a college or university in the United States. Community college students must be enrolled in majors that can transfer to a 4-year institution offering a baccalaureate degree. All applicants must be majoring in a field of science or engineering. U.S. citizenship or permanent resident status is required. Selection is based on financial need; academic achievement; personal qualities, strengths, and leadership abilities; and timeliness and completeness of the application.

Financial data The stipend is $1,000.

Duration 1 year.

Additional information Recipients must attend the MAES International Symposium's Medalla de Oro Banquet in October.

Number awarded 1 or more each year.

Deadline October of each year.

[533]
MALDEF LAW SCHOOL SCHOLARSHIP PROGRAM

Mexican American Legal Defense and Educational
   Fund
634 South Spring Street, 11th Floor
Los Angeles, CA 90014-1974
(213) 629-2512   Fax: (213) 629-0266
Web: www.maldef.org/education/scholarships.htm

Purpose To provide financial assistance to Latino students who are attending or interested in attending law school.

Eligibility Any person of Latino descent who is presently enrolled or will be enrolled during the year of application as a full-time law student is eligible to apply. Selection is based upon academic achievement, demonstrated involvement in and commitment to serving the Latino community through the legal profession, potential for successful completion of a graduate or law degree, and financial need.

Financial data Stipends range from $3,000 to $7,000 per year.

Duration 1 year.

Number awarded Varies each year; recently, 8 of these scholarships were awarded.

Deadline September of each year.

[534]
MARRIAGE AND FAMILY THERAPY MINORITY FELLOWSHIP PROGRAM

American Association for Marriage and Family Therapy
Attn: Awards Committee
112 South Alfred Street
Alexandria, VA 22314
(703) 838-9808   Fax: (703) 838-9805
Web: www.aamft.org

Purpose To provide financial assistance to minority students enrolled in graduate and post-degree training programs in marriage and family therapy.

Eligibility Eligible to apply are minority students (including African Americans, Hispanics, Native Americans, Asian Americans, and Pacific Islanders) enrolled in university graduate education programs or post-degree institutes that provide training in marriage and family therapy. They must be citizens of the United States or Canada and show promise in and commitment to a career in marital and family therapy education, research, or practice. Along with their application, they must submit a personal statement explaining how their racial or ethnic background has had an impact on them and their career decision; the statement should

include their professional interests, goals, and commitment to the field of marriage and family therapy.

Financial data The stipend is $1,000. Awardees also receive a plaque and funding to attend the association's annual conference.

Duration 1 year.

Additional information This program began in 1986.

Number awarded Up to 3 each year.

Deadline January of each year.

[535]
MARTIN LUTHER KING, JR. MEMORIAL SCHOLARSHIP FUND

California Teachers Association
Attn: Human Rights Department
P.O. Box 921
Burlingame, CA 94011-0921
(650) 552-5370   E-mail: scholarships@cta.org
Web: www.cta.org

Purpose To provide financial assistance for college or graduate school to racial and ethnic minorities in California who are members of the California Teachers Association (CTA), children of members, or members of the Student CTA.

Eligibility This program is open to members of a racial or ethnic minority group who are 1) active CTA members; 2) dependent children of active, retired-life, or deceased CTA members; or 3) members of Student CTA. Applicants must be interested in preparing for a teaching career in public education or already engaged in such a career.

Financial data Stipends vary each year, depending upon the amount of contributions received and the financial need of individual recipients.

Duration 1 year.

Number awarded Varies each year. Recently, 23 of these scholarships were awarded: 10 to CTA members, 8 to children of CTA members, and 5 to Student CTA members.

Deadline March of each year.

[536]
MATTHEWS AND BRANSCOMB LAW SCHOLARSHIP FUND

San Antonio Area Foundation
110 Broadway, Suite 230
San Antonio, TX 78205
(210) 225-2243   Fax: (210) 225-1980
E-mail: info@saafdn.org
Web: www.saafdn.org

Purpose To provide financial assistance to Hispanic and African American students at law schools in Texas who are residents of the state.

Eligibility This program is open to residents of Texas who are enrolled in their first year at a law school in the state. Applicants must be Hispanics or African Americans interested in practicing law in San Antonio or Corpus Christi. They must have LSAT scores in the 80th percentile or higher and be able to demonstrate special scholastic, athletic, extracurricular, or community service achievement.

Financial data The stipend is at least $1,500.

Duration 1 year; may be renewed.

Number awarded 1 or 2 each year.
Deadline February of each year.

[537]
MENTAL HEALTH AND SUBSTANCE ABUSE SERVICES FELLOWSHIP

American Psychological Association
Attn: Minority Fellowship Program
750 First Street, N.E.
Washington, DC 20002-4242
(202) 336-6127   Fax: (202) 336-6012
TDD: (202) 336-6123   E-mail: mfp@apa.org
Web: www.apa.org/mfp/cprogram.html

Purpose To provide financial assistance to doctoral students committed to providing mental health and substance abuse services to ethnic minority populations.

Eligibility Applicants must be U.S. citizens or permanent residents, enrolled full time in an accredited doctoral program, and committed to a career in psychology related to ethnic minority mental health and substance abuse services. Members of ethnic minority groups (African Americans, Hispanics/Latinos, American Indians, Alaskan Natives, Asian Americans, Native Hawaiians, and other Pacific Islanders) are especially encouraged to apply. Preference is given to students specializing in clinical, school, and counseling psychology. Students of any other specialty will be considered if they plan careers in which their training will lead to delivery of mental health or substance abuse services to ethnic minority populations. Selection is based on commitment to ethnic minority health and substance abuse services, knowledge of ethnic minority psychology or mental health issues, the fit between career goals and training environment selected, potential to become a culturally competent mental health service provider demonstrated through accomplishments and goals, scholarship and grades, and letters of recommendation.

Financial data The stipend is the amount established by the National Institutes of Health for predoctoral students, currently $20,772 per year.

Duration 1 academic or calendar year; may be renewed for up to 2 additional years.

Additional information Funding is provided by the U.S. Substance Abuse and Mental Health Services Administration.

Number awarded Varies each year.
Deadline January of each year.

[538]
MENTAL HEALTH RESEARCH FELLOWSHIP

American Psychological Association
Attn: Minority Fellowship Program
750 First Street, N.E.
Washington, DC 20002-4242
(202) 336-6127   Fax: (202) 336-6012
TDD: (202) 336-6123   E-mail: mfp@apa.org
Web: www.apa.org/mfp/rprogram.html

Purpose To provide financial assistance to doctoral students interested in preparing for a career in mental health or psychological research as it relates to ethnic minority populations.

Eligibility Applicants must be U.S. citizens or permanent residents, enrolled full time in an accredited doctoral program, and committed to a career as a researcher specializing in mental health issues of concern to ethnic minority populations. African American Hispanic/Latino, American Indian, Asian American, Alaskan Native, Native Hawaiian, and other Pacific Islander students are especially encouraged to apply. Students specializing in all disciplines of psychology are eligible as long as their training and research interests are related to mental health. Selection is based on commitment to a career in research that focuses on ethnic minority mental health, knowledge of ethnic minority psychology or mental health issues, fit between career goals and training environment selected, potential for a research career as demonstrated through accomplishments and productivity, scholarship and grades, and letters of recommendation.

Financial data The stipend is the amount established by the National Institutes of Health for predoctoral students, currently $20,772 per year.

Duration 1 academic or calendar year; may be renewed for up to 2 additional years.

Additional information Funding is provided by the U.S. National Institute of Mental Health, a component of the National Institutes of Health.

Number awarded Varies each year; recently, 22 of these fellowships were awarded.

Deadline January of each year.

[539]
METROPOLITAN LIFE FOUNDATION AWARDS PROGRAM FOR ACADEMIC EXCELLENCE IN MEDICINE

National Medical Fellowships, Inc.
Attn: Scholarship Program
5 Hanover Square, 15th Floor
New York, NY 10004
(212) 483-8880   Fax: (212) 483-8897
E-mail: info@nmfonline.org
Web: www.nmf-online.org

Purpose To provide financial assistance to underrepresented minority medical students who reside or attend school in designated cities throughout the country.

Eligibility This program is open to African American, mainland Puerto Rican, Mexican American, Native Hawaiian, Alaska Native, or American Indian medical students in their second through fourth year who are nominated by their dean. Nominees must be enrolled in medical schools located in (or residents of) the following cities: Phoenix, Arizona; San Francisco/Oakland/Bay area, California; Los Angeles, California; Denver, Colorado; Miami, Florida; Tampa/St. Petersburg, Florida; Atlanta, Georgia; Aurora/Chicago, Illinois; Boston, Massachusetts; St. Louis, Missouri; Albany, New York; metropolitan New York area (including New York City, southern New York, Long Island, central and northern New Jersey, and southern Connecticut); Rensselaer, New York; Utica, New York; Dayton, Ohio; Tulsa, Oklahoma; Philadelphia, Pennsylvania; Pittsburgh, Pennsylvania; Scranton, Pennsylvania; Warwick/Providence, Rhode Island; Greenville, South Carolina; Austin, Texas; Dallas/Fort Worth, Texas; or Houston, Texas. Selection is based on demonstrated financial need, outstanding academic achievement, leadership, and potential for distinguished contributions to medicine.

Financial data   The stipend is $4,000.

Duration   1 year; nonrenewable.

Additional information   Funding for this program, established in 1987, is provided by the Metropolitan Life Foundation of New York, New York.

Number awarded   17 each year.

Deadline   November of each year.

[540]
MEXICAN AMERICAN BAR ASSOCIATION SCHOLARSHIPS

Mexican American Bar Association
634 South Spring Street, Suite 918
Los Angeles, CA 90014
(213) 622-8890   Fax: (213) 622-8842
E-mail: administrator@mabalawyers.org
Web: www.mabalawyers.org/foundation.htm

Purpose   To provide financial assistance to students of Latino heritage from any state who are enrolled at law schools in southern California.

Eligibility   This program is open to students at law schools in southern California. Applicants must be of Latino heritage.

Financial data   The stipend is $2,500.

Duration   1 year.

Additional information   Information is also available from Tomás Olmos, (323) 653-6530.

Number awarded   Varies each year; recently, 12 of these scholarships were awarded.

[541]
MEXICAN AMERICAN ENGINEERS AND SCIENTISTS PRESIDENTIAL SCHOLARSHIP

Society of Mexican American Engineers and Scientists
Attn: Scholarships
711 West Bay Area Boulevard, Suite 206
Webster, TX 77598-3677
(281) 557-3677   Fax: (281) 557-3757
E-mail: scholarships@maes-natl.org
Web: www.maes-natl.org

Purpose   To provide financial assistance to undergraduate and graduate student members of the Society of Mexican American Engineers and Scientists (MAES).

Eligibility   This program is open to MAES student members who are full-time undergraduate or graduate students at a college or university in the United States. Community college students must be enrolled in majors that can transfer to a 4-year institution offering a baccalaureate degree. All applicants must be majoring in a field of science or engineering. U.S. citizenship or permanent resident status is required. Selection is based on financial need; academic achievement; personal qualities, strengths, and leadership abilities; and timeliness and completeness of the application.

Financial data   The stipend is $2,000.

Duration   1 year.

Additional information   Recipients must attend the MAES International Symposium's Medalla de Oro Banquet in October.

Number awarded   1 each year.

Deadline   October of each year.

[542]
MEXICAN FIESTA SCHOLARSHIPS

Wisconsin Hispanic Scholarship Foundation, Inc.
1220 West Windlake Avenue
Milwaukee, WI 53215
(414) 383-7066   Fax: (414) 383-6677
E-mail: fiestamilw@aol.com
Web: www.mexicanfiesta.org/whsf/index.html

Purpose   To provide financial assistance to Hispanic American students in Wisconsin who are interested in attending college or graduate school.

Eligibility   Applicants must be at least 50% Hispanic, be high school seniors or full-time undergraduate or graduate students, have earned a GPA of 2.75 or higher, be Wisconsin residents, and be bilingual in Spanish and English.

Financial data   The amount of the stipend depends on the number of students selected.

Duration   1 year; recipients may reapply.

Additional information   Recipients can attend college in any state. Funds for this program are raised each year at the Mexican Fiesta, held in Milwaukee for 3 days each August. Recipients must perform 20 hours of volunteer work in the Hispanic community.

Number awarded   Varies; a total of $20,000 is awarded in scholarships each year.

Deadline   March of each year.

[543]
MFT MINORITY SUPERVISION STIPEND PROGRAM

American Association for Marriage and Family Therapy
Attn: Awards Committee
112 South Alfred Street
Alexandria, VA 22314
(703) 838-9808   Fax: (703) 838-9805
Web: www.aamft.org

Purpose   To support the recruitment, training, and retention of minorities as supervisors in the field of marriage and family therapy.

Eligibility   Eligible to apply are minority individuals (including African Americans, Hispanics, Native Americans, Asian Americans, and Pacific Islanders) enrolled in a program to become marriage and family therapy supervisors approved by the American Association for Marriage and Family Therapy (AAMFT). Applicants must be U.S. or Canadian citizens or permanent visa residents and hold a graduate degree in marriage and family therapy or a related discipline. Information on financial need is not required but is a significant factor considered in the review process.

Financial data   Awardees receive up to $750 to offset the cost of supervision, waiver of the supervision application processing fee, and waiver of the registration fee to attend the AAMFT conference.

Duration   1 year.

Additional information   This program began in 1990.

Number awarded   Up to 2 each year.

Deadline January of each year.

[544]
MICHELE CLARK FELLOWSHIP

Radio and Television News Directors Foundation
1600 K Street, N.W., Suite 700
Washington, DC 20006-2838
(202) 467-5218   Fax: (202) 223-4007
E-mail: karenb@rtndf.org
Web: www.rtndf.org/asfi/fellowships/minority.html

Purpose To provide financial assistance for professional development to minority journalists employed in electronic news.

Eligibility This program is open to minority journalists employed in television or radio news who have 10 years or less of full-time experience. Applications must include samples of the journalist's work done as the member of a news staff, with a script and tape (audio or video) up to 15 minutes.

Financial data The grant is $1,000 plus an all-expense paid trip to the international convention of the Radio-Television News Directors Association held that year.

Duration The grant is presented annually.

Additional information The grant, named for CBS journalist Michele Clark, may be used in any way to improve the craft and enhance the excellence of the recipient's news operation.

Number awarded 1 each year.

Deadline April of each year.

[545]
MILDRED COLODNY SCHOLARSHIP FOR GRADUATE STUDY IN HISTORIC PRESERVATION

National Trust for Historic Preservation
Attn: Scholarship Coordinator
1785 Massachusetts Avenue, N.W.
Washington, DC 20036-2117
(202) 588-6124   Toll-free: (800) 944-NTHP, ext. 6124
Fax: (202) 588-6059   E-mail: david_field@nthp.org
Web: www.nthp.org/help/colodny.html

Purpose To provide financial assistance and summer work experience to graduate students (particularly minority students) interested in working on a degree in a field related to historic preservation.

Eligibility Eligible to apply are students in their final year of undergraduate study intending to enroll in a graduate program in historic preservation and graduate students enrolled in or intending to enroll in historic preservation programs; these programs may be in a department of history, architecture, American studies, urban planning, museum studies, or a related field with a primary emphasis on historic preservation. Applicants must submit an essay in which they discuss their career goals and how their pursuit of a graduate preservation degree relates to those goals, including evidence of their interest in, commitment to, and/or potential for leadership in the field of preservation. Selection is based on the essay, a resume, 2 letters of recommendation, academic transcripts, and financial need. Applications are especially encouraged from people of diverse racial, ethnic, cultural, and economic backgrounds.

Financial data The program provides a stipend of up to $15,000 towards graduate school tuition, a stipend of $5,000 for a summer internship with the sponsor following the student's first year of study, and up to $1,500 towards the student's attendance at a National Preservation Conference.

Duration 1 year; nonrenewable.

Additional information Internships may be completed at 1) the sponsor's Washington, D.C. office; 2) a regional office or historic museum site; or 3) the offices of 1 of the sponsor's partner organizations.

Number awarded 1 each year.

Deadline February of each year.

[546]
MINNESOTA SPACE GRANT CONSORTIUM SCHOLARSHIPS AND FELLOWSHIPS

Minnesota Space Grant Consortium
c/o University of Minnesota
Department of Aerospace Engineering and Mechanics
107 Akerman Hall
110 Union Street S.E.
Minneapolis, MN 55455
(612) 626-9295   Fax: (612) 626-1558
E-mail: mnsgc@aem.umn.edu
Web: www.aem.umn.edu

Purpose To provide financial assistance for space-related studies to undergraduate and graduate students (particularly underrepresented minorities, women, and persons with disabilities) in Minnesota.

Eligibility This program is open to graduate and undergraduate full-time students at institutions that are affiliates of the Minnesota Space Grant Consortium. U.S. citizenship and a GPA of 3.2 or higher are required. Eligible fields of study include the physical sciences (astronomy, astrophysics, chemistry, computer science, mathematics, physics, planetary geoscience, and planetary science), life sciences (biology, biochemistry, botany, health science/nutrition, medicine, molecular/cellular biology, and zoology), social sciences (anthropology, architecture, art, economics, education, history, philosophy, political science/public policy, and psychology), earth sciences (atmospheric science, climatology/meteorology, environmental science, geography, geology, geophysics, and oceanography), and engineering (agricultural, aeronautical, aerospace, architectural, bioengineering, chemical, civil, computer, electrical, electronic, environmental, industrial, materials science, mechanical, mining, nuclear, petroleum, engineering science, and engineering mechanics). The Minnesota Space Grant Consortium is a component of the U.S. National Aeronautics and Space Administration (NASA) Space Grant program, which encourages participation by women, underrepresented minorities, and persons with disabilities.

Financial data This program awards approximately $125,000 in undergraduate scholarships and $25,000 in graduate fellowships each year. The amounts of the awards are set by each of the participating institutions, which augment funding from this program with institutional resources.

Duration 1 year; renewable.

Additional information This program is funded by NASA. The member institutions are: Augsburg College, Bethel College, Bemidji State University, College of St.

Catherine, Carleton College, Concordia College, Fond du Lac Community College, Itasca Community College, Leech Lake Tribal College, Macalaster College, Normandale Community College, Southwest State University, University of Minnesota at Duluth, University of Minnesota at Twin Cities, and University of St. Thomas.

Number awarded 8 to 12 undergraduate scholarships and 2 to 3 graduate fellowships are awarded each year.

Deadline March of each year.

[547]
MINORITIES IN GOVERNMENT FINANCE SCHOLARSHIP

Government Finance Officers Association
Attn: Scholarship Committee
203 North LaSalle Street, Suite 2700
Chicago, IL 60601-1210
(312) 977-9700   Fax: (312) 977-4806
Web: www.gfoa.org/services/scholarships.shtml

Purpose To provide financial assistance to minority upper-division and graduate students who are preparing for a career in state and local government finance.

Eligibility This program is open to upper-division and graduate students who are preparing for a career in public finance with a major in public administration, accounting, finance, political science, economics, or business administration (with a specific focus on government or nonprofit management). Applicants must be members of a minority group, citizens or permanent residents of the United States or Canada, and able to provide a letter of recommendation from a representative of their school. Selection is based on career plans, academic record, plan of study, letters of recommendation, and GPA. Financial need is not considered.

Financial data The stipend is $5,000.

Duration 1 year.

Additional information Funding for this program is provided by Fidelity Investments Tax-Exempt Services Company.

Number awarded 1 or more each year.

Deadline February of each year.

[548]
MINORITY ACCESS TO RESEARCH CAREERS (MARC) FACULTY PREDOCTORAL FELLOWSHIPS

National Institute of General Medical Sciences
Attn: Division of Minority Opportunities in Research
45 Center Drive, Suite 2AS37
Bethesda, MD 20892-6200
(301) 594-3900   Fax: (301) 480-2753
E-mail: at21z@nih.gov
Web: www.nih.gov/nigms

Purpose To enable faculty at minority and minority-serving institutions to complete a Ph.D. degree in the biomedical sciences.

Eligibility This program is open to full-time faculty in a biomedical or behavioral science department (including mathematics) at minority and minority-serving institutions who lack a Ph.D. degree. The institution must be a college or university where the candidate has been employed for at least 3 years and that has substantial enrollments of students in biomedical and related sciences from minority

groups underrepresented in those sciences. The candidate must have been accepted into the doctoral program at a research university, institution, or center with active biomedical and behavioral science research faculties. They must be sponsored by their home institution, which must have granted them a study leave and where they are expected to return after completing their doctoral degree. Only U.S. citizens, nationals, and permanent residents are eligible.

Financial data The fellowships provide a stipend of $32,820 per year and a supplement that offsets the cost of tuition, fees, and health insurance at a rate of 100% up to $3,000 and 60% of costs above $3,000. An institutional allowance of $2,750 per year is also provided.

Duration Up to 5 years.

Deadline April or December of each year.

[549]
MINORITY DENTAL STUDENT SCHOLARSHIP

American Dental Association
Attn: ADA Foundation
211 East Chicago Avenue
Chicago, IL 60611
(312) 440-2547   Fax: (312) 440-3526
E-mail: adaf@ada.org
Web: www.ada.org

Purpose To provide financial assistance to underrepresented minorities who wish to enter the field of dentistry.

Eligibility This program is open to U.S. citizens from a minority group that is currently underrepresented in the dental profession: Native American, African Americans, or Hispanics. Applicants must have a GPA of 3.0 or higher and be entering second-year students at a dental school in the United States accredited by the Commission on Dental Accreditation. Selection is based upon academic achievement, a written summary of personal and professional goals, letters of reference, and demonstrated financial need.

Financial data The maximum stipend is $2,500. Funds are sent directly to the student's financial aid office to be used to cover tuition, fees, books, supplies, and living expenses.

Duration 1 year.

Additional information This program, established in 1991, is supported by the Harry J. Bosworth Company, John O. Butler Company, Colgate-Palmolive, Oral-B Laboratories, and Procter & Gamble Company. Students receiving a full scholarship from any other source are ineligible to receive this scholarship.

Number awarded 25 each year.

Deadline July of each year.

[550]
MINORITY FACULTY DEVELOPMENT SCHOLARSHIP AWARD IN PHYSICAL THERAPY

American Physical Therapy Association
Attn: Department of Minority/International Affairs
1111 North Fairfax Street
Alexandria, VA 22314-1488
(703) 706-3144   Toll-free: (800) 999-APTA, ext. 3144
Fax: (703) 706-8519   TDD: (703) 683-6748
E-mail: min-intl@apta.org
Web: www.apta.org

Purpose To provide financial assistance to minority faculty members in physical therapy who are interested in working on a doctoral degree.

Eligibility This program is open to U.S. citizens and permanent residents who are members of the following minority groups: African American or Black, Asian, Native Hawaiian or other Pacific Islander, American Indian or Alaska Native, or Hispanic/Latino. Applicants must be full-time faculty members, teaching in an accredited or developing professional physical therapist education program, who will have completed the equivalent of 2 full semesters of post-professional doctoral course work. They must possess a license to practice physical therapy in a U.S. jurisdiction and be enrolled as a student in an accredited post-professional doctoral program whose content has a demonstrated relationship to physical therapy. Along with their application, they must submit transcripts of all post-professional doctoral course work, a curriculum vitae, and a plan of study for attaining the doctoral degree. Selection is based on 1) demonstrated evidence of contributions in the area of minority affairs and services; 2) contributions to the profession of physical therapy; and 3) scholastic achievement.

Financial data A stipend is awarded (amount not specified).

Duration 1 year.

Additional information This program was established in 1999.

Number awarded 1 or more each year.

Deadline November of each year.

[551]
MINORITY FELLOWSHIP PROGRAM IN MENTAL HEALTH

American Sociological Association
Attn: Minority Affairs Program
1307 New York Avenue, N.W., Suite 700
Washington, DC 20005-4701
(202) 383-9005, ext. 322   Fax: (202) 638-0882
TDD: (202) 872-0486
E-mail: minority.affairs@asanet.org
Web: www.asanet.org

Purpose To provide financial assistance to minority doctoral candidates in sociology who are interested in preparing to conduct research on mental health issues relating to minority groups.

Eligibility These fellowships are available to U.S. citizens or permanent residents who are Blacks/African Americans, Latinos (e.g., Chicanos, Puerto Ricans, Cubans), American Indians or Alaskan Natives, Asian Americans (e.g., southeast Asian, Japanese, Chinese, Korean), or Pacific Islanders (e.g., Filipino, Samoan, Hawaiian, Guamanian). The competition is open to students beginning or continuing study in sociology at the doctoral level. Selection is based on commitment to research in mental health and mental illness, scholarship, writing ability, research potential, and financial need.

Financial data The stipend is $20,772 per year.

Duration 1 year; renewable for 3 additional years.

Additional information This program is funded by a grant from the U.S. National Institute of Mental Health, a component of the National Institutes of Health. Upon completion of their studies, recipients are expected to engage in mental health and mental illness research and/or teaching for a period equal to the period of support beyond 12 months.

Number awarded 10 to 12 each year.

Deadline January of each year.

[552]
MINORITY GEOSCIENCE STUDENT SCHOLARSHIPS

American Geological Institute
Attn: Minority Participation Program
4220 King Street
Alexandria, VA 22302-1502
(703) 379-2480, ext. 227   Fax: (703) 379-7563
E-mail: cmm@agiweb.org
Web: www.agiweb.org/mpp/index.html

Purpose To provide financial assistance to underrepresented minority undergraduate and graduate students interested in working on a degree in the geosciences.

Eligibility This program is open to members of ethnic minority groups underrepresented in the geosciences (Blacks, Hispanics, American Indians, Eskimos, Hawaiians, and Samoans). U.S. citizenship or permanent resident status is required. Applicants must be full-time students enrolled in an accredited institution working on an undergraduate or graduate degree in the geosciences, including geology, geophysics, hydrology, meteorology, physical oceanography, planetary geology, and earth science education; students in other natural sciences, mathematics, or engineering are not eligible. Selection is based on a 250-word essay on career goals and why the applicant has chosen a geoscience as a major, work experience, recommendations, honors and awards, extracurricular activities, and financial need.

Financial data Stipends range from $500 to $3,000 per year.

Duration 1 academic year; renewable if the recipient maintains satisfactory performance.

Additional information Funding for this program is provided by ExxonMobil Corporation, ConocoPhillips, ChevronTexaco Corporation, Marathon Corporation, and the Seismological Society of America.

Number awarded Varies each year; recently, 19 of these scholarships were awarded.

Deadline March of each year.

[553]
MINORITY NEUROSCIENCE POSTDOCTORAL FELLOWSHIP PROGRAM

Society for Neuroscience
Attn: Education Department
11 Dupont Circle, N.W., Suite 500
Washington, DC 20036
(202) 462-6688   Fax: (202) 462-9740
E-mail: info@sfn.org
Web: apu.sfn.org

Purpose To provide funding to minority postdoctoral fellows participating in mental health related neuroscience research and training programs.

Eligibility This program is open to postdoctoral fellows in neuroscience who are members of traditionally underrepresented racial and ethnic minority groups (African Americans, Hispanics, Native Americans, Alaskan Natives, Asians, and Pacific Islanders). Applicants must be U.S. citizens or permanent residents enrolled in a program of research and training to prepare for a career in neuroscience research laboratories. Along with their application, they must submit 2 academic letters of recommendation, a 1- to 2-page essay describing their area of interest and research goals in neuroscience, a 1- to 2-page essay describing how their career goals are consistent with the goals of the program to increase diversity in neuroscience, undergraduate and graduate transcripts, a current resume or curriculum vitae, copies of papers and abstracts they have authored or co-authored, a 1-page summary of their dissertation, and a biosketch of the home institution advisor (if available).

Financial data Fellows receive a stipend that is based on number of years of postdoctoral experience, in accordance with standard National Research Service Award guidelines (currently, ranging from $35,568 per year for no experience to $51,036 for 7 or more years). Other benefits include travel assistance and registration to attend the annual meeting of the Society for Neuroscience (SfN), enrichment programs that include funds to participate in activities outside the fellow's home laboratory, and mentoring opportunities with a mentor chosen from the SfN membership.

Duration 2 years, contingent upon adequate research progress and academic standing.

Additional information This program, established in 1991, is sponsored largely by the National Institute of Mental Health with additional support from the National Institute of Neurological Disorders and Stroke. Information is also available from Joanne Berger-Sweeney, Wellesley College, Department of Biological Sciences, 106 Central Street, Wellesley, MA 02481-8203, (781) 283-3503, Fax: (781) 283-3704, E-mail: mnfp@wellesley.edu.

Number awarded 5 each year.

Deadline March, August, or December of each year.

[554]
MINORITY NEUROSCIENCE PREDOCTORAL FELLOWSHIP PROGRAM

Society for Neuroscience
Attn: Education Department
11 Dupont Circle, N.W., Suite 500
Washington, DC 20036
(202) 462-6688   Fax: (202) 462-9740
E-mail: info@sfn.org
Web: apu.sfn.org

Purpose To provide funding to minority graduate students participating in mental health related neuroscience research and training programs.

Eligibility This program is open to doctoral students in neuroscience who are members of traditionally underrepresented racial and ethnic minority groups (African Americans, Hispanics, Native Americans, Alaskan Natives, Asians, and Pacific Islanders). Applicants must be U.S. citizens or permanent residents enrolled in a program of research and training to prepare for a career in neuroscience research laboratories. Along with their application, they must submit 2 academic letters of recommendation, a 1- to 2-page essay describing their area of interest and research goals in neuroscience, a 1- to 2-page essay describing how their career goals are consistent with the goals of the program to increase diversity in neuroscience, undergraduate and graduate transcripts, a current resume or curriculum vitae, copies of papers and abstracts they have authored or co-authored, and a biosketch of the home institution advisor (if available).

Financial data Fellows receive a stipend in accordance with standard National Research Service Award guidelines (currently, $20,772 per year). Other benefits include travel assistance and registration to attend the annual meeting of the Society for Neuroscience (SfN), enrichment programs that include funds to participate in activities outside the fellow's home laboratory, and mentoring opportunities with a mentor chosen from the SfN membership.

Duration 3 years, contingent upon adequate research progress and academic standing.

Additional information This program, established in 1991, is sponsored largely by the National Institute of Mental Health with additional support from the National Institute of Neurological Disorders and Stroke. Information is also available from Joanne Berger-Sweeney, Wellesley College, Department of Biological Sciences, 106 Central Street, Wellesley, MA 02481-8203, (781) 283-3503, Fax: (781) 283-3704, E-mail: mnfp@wellesley.edu.

Number awarded 12 each year.

Deadline August of each year.

[555]
MINORITY POSTDOCTORAL RESEARCH FELLOWSHIPS

National Science Foundation
Directorate for Biological Sciences
Attn: Division of Biological Infrastructure
4201 Wilson Boulevard, Room 615
Arlington, VA 22230
(703) 292-8470   TDD: (703) 292-5090
E-mail: ckimsey@nsf.gov
Web: www.nsf.gov/bio

Purpose To provide financial assistance for postdoctoral research training in the United States or abroad to underrepresented minority scientists in the biological, social, economic, and behavioral sciences.

Eligibility This program is open to U.S. citizens and permanent residents who will complete their doctorate within a year or have completed it within the previous 4 years but have not completed more than 2 years of postdoctoral support. Applicants must be a member of an ethnic group that is significantly underrepresented at advanced levels of science and engineering in the United States, including Native Americans (Alaska Natives and American Indians), African Americans, Hispanics, and Native Pacific Islanders. They must be proposing research training that falls within the program areas of the National Science Foundation (NSF) Directorate for Biological Sciences or the Directorate for Social, Behavioral, and Economic Sciences to be conducted at any appropriate nonprofit U.S. or foreign institution (government laboratory, institution of higher education, national laboratory, or public or private research institute), but not at the same institution where the doctorate was obtained.

Financial data The program provides a stipend of $36,000 per year, an institutional allowance of $5,000 for partial reimbursement of indirect research costs (space, equipment, general purpose supplies, and fringe benefits), and a special allowance of $9,000 for direct research costs (materials and supplies, subscription fees, and recovery costs for databases, travel, and publication expenses).

Duration 2 years; applicants who propose to spend their 2-year tenure at a foreign institution may apply for a third year of support at an appropriate U.S. institution.

Additional information Information on the programs from the Directorate for Social, Behavioral, and Economic Sciences is available at (703) 292-8763, E-mail: jperhoni@nsf.gov.

Number awarded Approximately 12 each year.

Deadline November of each year.

[556]
MISSOURI SPACE GRANT CONSORTIUM GRADUATE FELLOWSHIPS

Missouri Space Grant Consortium
c/o University of Missouri at Rolla
229 Mechanical Engineering Building
1870 Miner Circle
Rolla, MO 65409-0050
(573) 341-4699   Fax: (573) 341-4607
E-mail: finaish@umr.edu
Web: www.umr.edu/~spaceg

Purpose To provide financial assistance to graduate students (particularly minorities and women) in Missouri who are working on a degree in an aerospace field.

Eligibility This program is open to graduate students working on a degree in an aerospace field at member institutions of the Missouri Space Grant Consortium. Selection is based on academic records, recommendation letters from sponsoring faculty, student publications and academic achievements, and a statement of interest. U.S. citizenship is required. The Missouri Space Grant Consortium is a component of the U.S. National Aeronautics and Space Administration (NASA), which encourages participation by women and underrepresented minorities.

Financial data The maximum stipend is $13,000 per year.

Duration 1 year.

Additional information The consortium members are Southwest Missouri State University, University of Missouri at Columbia, University of Missouri at Rolla, University of Missouri at St. Louis, and Washington University. This program is funded by NASA.

Number awarded Varies each year; recently, $65,000 was available for this program.

[557]
MLA SCHOLARSHIP FOR MINORITY STUDENTS

Medical Library Association
Attn: Professional Development Department
65 East Wacker Place, Suite 1900
Chicago, IL 60601-7298
(312) 419-9094, ext. 28   Fax: (312) 419-8950
E-mail: mlapd2@mlahq.org
Web: www.mlanet.org/awards/grants/minstud.html

Purpose To assist minority students interested in preparing for a career in medical librarianship.

Eligibility This program is open to racial minority students (Asians, African Americans, Hispanics, Native Americans, or Pacific Islander Americans) who are entering a graduate program in librarianship or who have completed less than half of their academic requirements for the master's degree in library science. They must be interested in preparing for a career in medical librarianship. Selection is based on academic record, letters of reference, professional potential, and the applicant's statement of career objectives. U.S. or Canadian citizenship or permanent resident status is required.

Financial data The stipend is $5,000.

Duration 1 year.

Additional information This scholarship was first awarded in 1973.

Number awarded 1 each year.

Deadline November of each year.

[558]
MLA/ARL LEADERSHIP AND CAREER DEVELOPMENT PROGRAM

Medical Library Association
Attn: Professional Development Department
65 East Wacker Place, Suite 1900
Chicago, IL 60601-7298
(312) 419-9094, ext. 28   Fax: (312) 419-8950
E-mail: mlapd2@mlahq.org
Web: www.mlanet.org

Purpose To provide an opportunity for minority mid-career librarians to engage in leadership and career development activities.

Eligibility This program is open to mid-career professionals at academic and research libraries. Applicants must be members of minority ethnic groups (African Americans, Hispanics, Asians, Native Americans, or Pacific Islanders). They must be interested in taking advantage of advancement and leadership opportunities.

Financial data The stipend is $6,000.

Duration 1 year.

Additional information This program is jointly managed by the Medical Library Association (MLA) and the Association of Research Libraries (ARL) with funding from the National Library of Medicine.

Number awarded 2 each year.

[559]
MONTANA SPACE GRANT CONSORTIUM GRADUATE FELLOWSHIPS

Montana Space Grant Consortium
c/o Montana State University
416 Cobleigh Hall
P.O. Box 173835
Bozeman, MT 59717-3835
(406) 994-4223   Fax: (406) 994-4452
E-mail: msgc@montana.edu
Web: spacegrant.montana.edu

Purpose To provide financial assistance to students (particularly minorities, women, and students with disabilities) in Montana who are interested in working on a graduate degree in the space sciences and/or engineering.

Eligibility This program is open to full-time graduate students in Montana working on degrees in fields related to space sciences and engineering; those fields include, but are not limited to, astronomy, biological and life sciences, chemical engineering, chemistry, civil engineering, computer sciences, electrical engineering, geological sciences, mechanical engineering, and physics. Priority is given to students who have been involved in aerospace-related research. U.S. citizenship is required. The Montana Space Grant Consortium is a component of the U.S. National Aeronautics and Space Administration (NASA) Space Grant program, which encourages participation by women, underrepresented minorities, and persons with disabilities. Financial need is not considered in the selection process.

Financial data The fellowships provide payment of tuition and fees plus a stipend of $15,000 per year.

Duration 1 year; may be renewed.

Additional information Funding for this program is provided by NASA.

Number awarded Varies each year; recently, 5 of these fellowships were awarded.

Deadline March of each year.

[560]
MORRIS SCHOLARSHIP

Morris Scholarship Fund
Attn: Scholarship Selection Committee
525 S.W. Fifth Street, Suite A
Des Moines, IA 50309-4501
(515) 282-8192   Fax: (515) 282-9117
E-mail: morris@assoc-mgmt.com
Web: www.morrisscholarship.org

Purpose To provide financial assistance to minority undergraduate, graduate, and law students in Iowa.

Eligibility This program is open to minority students (African Americans, Asian/Pacific Islanders, Hispanics, or Native Americans) who are interested in studying at a college, graduate school, or law school. Applicants must be either Iowa residents and high school graduates who are attending a college or university anywhere in the United States or non-Iowa residents who are attending a college or university in Iowa; preference is given to native Iowans who are attending an Iowa college or university. Along with their application, they must submit an essay of 250 to 500 words on why they are applying for this scholarship, activities or organizations in which they are involved, and their future plans. Selection is based on the essay, academic achievement (GPA of 2.5 or higher), community service, and financial need.

Financial data The stipend is $1,500 per year.

Duration 1 year; may be renewed.

Additional information This fund was established in 1978 in honor of the J.B. Morris family, who founded the Iowa branch of the National Association for the Advancement of Colored People and published the *Iowa Bystander* newspaper.

Number awarded Varies each year; recently, 11 of these scholarships were awarded.

Deadline January of each year.

[561]
NAHJ GENERAL SCHOLARSHIPS

National Association of Hispanic Journalists
Attn: Scholarship Committee
1000 National Press Building
529 14th Street, N.W.
Washington, DC 20045-2001
(202) 662-7145   Toll-free: (888) 346-NAHJ
Fax: (202) 662-7144   E-mail: nahj@nahj.org
Web: www.nahj.org

Purpose To provide financial assistance to Hispanic American undergraduate and graduate students interested in preparing for careers in the media.

Eligibility This program is open to Hispanic American high school seniors, undergraduates, and graduate students who are interested in preparing for a career in English- or Spanish-language print, broadcast (radio or television), online, or photojournalism; students majoring in other fields must be able to demonstrate a strong interest in preparing for a career in journalism. Applicants must submit an official transcript; a 1-page resume with their educational background, work history, awards, internships, other scholarships, language proficiency, and any work done for their school newspaper, radio, and/or television station; samples of their work; 2 reference letters; a 500-word autobiography in the form of a news story; and documentation of financial need. Selection is based on commitment to the field of journalism, academic achievement, awareness of the Latino community, and financial need.

Financial data Stipends range from $1,000 to $2,000.

Duration 1 year.

Additional information This program is administered by the National Association of Hispanic Journalists (NAHJ) as a component of its Rubén Salazar Scholarship Fund.

Number awarded Varies each year; recently 20 of these scholarships were awarded.

Deadline January of each year.

[562]
NASA-DESGC GRADUATE STUDENT FELLOWSHIPS

Delaware Space Grant Consortium
c/o University of Delaware
Bartol Research Institute
104 Center Mall, #217
Newark, DE 19716-4793
(302) 831-1094   Fax: (302) 831-1843
E-mail: desgc@bartol.udel.edu
Web: www.delspace.org

Purpose To provide financial support to graduate students (particularly minority, women, and disabled students) in Delaware and Pennsylvania involved in space-related studies.

Eligibility This program is open to graduate students at member institutions of the Delaware Space Grant Consortium (DESGC) embarking on or involved in aerospace-related research, technology, or design. Fields of interest have included astronomy, chemical engineering, geography, marine studies, materials science, mechanical engineering, and physics. U.S. citizenship is required. The DESGC is a component of the U.S. National Aeronautics and Space Administration (NASA) Space Grant program, which encourages applications from women, minorities, and persons with disabilities.

Financial data This program covers tuition and provides stipends.

Duration 1 year; may be renewed.

Additional information This program, established in 1991, is funded by NASA. Members of the consortium include Delaware State University (Dover, Delaware), Delaware Technical and Community College (Dover, Georgetown, Newark, and Wilmington, Delaware), Franklin and Marshall College (Lancaster, Pennsylvania), Gettysburg College (Gettysburg, Pennsylvania), Lehigh University (Bethlehem, Pennsylvania), Swarthmore College (Swarthmore, Pennsylvania), University of Delaware (Newark, Delaware), Villanova University (Villanova, Pennsylvania), and Wilmington College (New Castle, Delaware).

Number awarded Varies each year; since this program was established, it has awarded 45 fellowships to 27 graduate students.

Deadline February of each year.

[563]
NASCAR/WENDELL SCOTT AWARD

Hispanic Association of Colleges and Universities
Attn: National Scholarship Program
One Dupont Circle, N.W. Suite 605
Washington, DC 20036
(202) 467-0893   Fax: (202) 496-9177
TTY: (800) 855-2880   E-mail: scholarships@hacu.net
Web: scholarships.hacu.net/applications/applicants

Purpose To provide financial assistance to undergraduate and graduate students majoring in any field at member institutions of the Hispanic Association of Colleges and Universities (HACU) who are interested in the motorsports industry.

Eligibility This program is open to undergraduate and graduate students at HACU member and partner colleges and universities. Applicants may be majoring in any field, but they must be able to demonstrate a recreational or professional interest in the motorsports industry. Undergraduates must be enrolled full time, have a GPA of 3.0 or higher, and be able to use the scholarship during their junior or senior year. Graduate students must be enrolled at least part time and have a GPA of 3.2 or higher. Applicants must submit an essay of 200 to 250 words that describes their academic and/or career goals, where they expect to be and what they expect to be doing 10 years from now, and what skills they can bring to an employer. Financial need is considered in the selection process.

Financial data The stipend is $1,500 for undergraduates or $2,000 for graduate students.

Duration 1 year.

Additional information This program is sponsored by NASCAR and administered by HACU.

Number awarded 1 or more each year.

Deadline May of each year.

[564]
NASP MINORITY SCHOLARSHIP

National Association of School Psychologists
Attn: Education and Research Trust
4340 East-West Highway, Suite 402
Bethesda, MD 20814
(301) 657-0270, ext. 234   Fax: (301) 657-0275
TTY: (301) 657-4155   E-mail: kbritton@naspweb.org
Web: www.nasponline.org/about_nasp/minority.html

Purpose To provide financial assistance to minority graduate students enrolled in a school psychology program.

Eligibility This program is open to minority students who are U.S. citizens enrolled in a regionally-accredited school psychology program in the United States. Applicants must have a GPA of 3.0 or higher. Doctoral candidates are not eligible. Applications must be accompanied by 1) a resume that includes undergraduate and/or graduate schools attended, awards and honors, student and professional activities, work and volunteer experiences, research and publications, workshops or other presentations, and any special skills, training, or experience, such as bilingualism, teaching experience, or mental health experience; 2) a statement, up to 1,000 words, of professional goals; 3) at least 2 letters of recommendation, including at least 1 from a faculty member from their undergraduate or graduate studies (if a first-year student) or at least 1 from a faculty member of their school psychology program (if a second- or third-year student); 4) a completed financial statement; 5) an official transcript of all graduate course work (first-year students may submit an official undergraduate transcript); 6) other personal accomplishments that the applicant wishes to be considered; and 7) a letter of acceptance from a school psychology program for first-year applicants.

Financial data   The stipend is $5,000.

Duration   1 year; may be renewed up to 2 additional years.

Number awarded   1 each year.

Deadline   January of each year.

[565]
NATIONAL ASSOCIATION OF HISPANIC NURSES SCHOLARSHIPS

National Association of Hispanic Nurses
Attn: National Awards and Scholarship Committee
  Chair
1501 16th Street, N.W.
Washington, DC 20036
(202) 387-2477   Fax: (202) 483-7183
E-mail: thehispanicnurses@earthlink.net
Web: www.thehispanicnurses.org

Purpose   To provide financial assistance for nursing education to members of the National Association of Hispanic Nurses (NAHN).

Eligibility   Eligible are members of the association enrolled in associate, diploma, baccalaureate, graduate, or practical/vocational nursing programs at NLN-accredited schools of nursing. Applicants must submit a 1-page essay that reflects their qualifications and potential for leadership in nursing for the Hispanic community. U.S. citizenship or permanent resident status is required. Selection is based on academic excellence (preferably a GPA of 3.0 or higher), potential for leadership in nursing, and financial need.

Financial data   The stipend is $1,000.

Duration   1 year.

Number awarded   Varies each year, depending on the availability of funds.

Deadline   April of each year.

[566]
NATIONAL CRUSADE SCHOLARSHIP PROGRAM

United Methodist Church
Attn: General Board of Global Ministries
475 Riverside Drive, Room 1351
New York, NY 10115
(212) 870-3787   Toll-free: (800) 654-5929
E-mail: Scholars@gbgm-umc.org
Web: www.gbgm-umc.org

Purpose   To provide financial assistance to minority students who are interested in attending graduate school to prepare for leadership within the United Methodist Church.

Eligibility   This program is open to U.S. citizens and permanent residents who are ethnic and racial minority graduate students (African Americans, Hispanic Americans, Pacific/Asian Americans, and Native Americans). They must be working on their first graduate degree (M.Div., M.A., Ph.D., D.D.S., M.D., M.Ed., M.B.A., or other graduate degree). Preference is given to members of the United Methodist Church

and to persons entering Christian vocations. Applicants should be committed to preparing themselves for leadership in mission to church and society and serving for at least 10 years. Financial need must be demonstrated.

Financial data   The amount awarded varies, depending upon the availability of funds and the need of the recipient. Recently, stipends ranged from $1,000 to $2,500.

Duration   Up to 3 years, but only to complete 1 degree.

Additional information   These awards are funded by the World Communion Offering received in United Methodist churches on the first Sunday in October.

Number awarded   Varies each year; recently, 23 of these scholarships were awarded.

Deadline   January of each year.

[567]
NATIONAL DEFENSE SCIENCE AND ENGINEERING GRADUATE FELLOWSHIP PROGRAM

American Society for Engineering Education
Attn: NDSEG Fellowship Program
1818 N Street, N.W., Suite 600
Washington, DC 20036-2479
(202) 331-3516   Fax: (202) 265-8504
E-mail: ndseg@asee.org
Web: www.asee.org/ndseg

Purpose   To provide financial assistance to doctoral students (particularly minorities, women, and students with disabilities) in the areas of science and engineering that are of military importance.

Eligibility   Graduate students in the following specialties are eligible: aeronautical and astronautical engineering; biosciences, including toxicology; chemical engineering; chemistry; civil engineering; cognitive, neural, and behavioral sciences; computer and computational sciences; electrical engineering; geosciences, including terrain, water, and air; materials science and engineering; mathematics; mechanical engineering; naval architecture and ocean engineering; oceanography; and physics, including optics. Applicants must be U.S. citizens or nationals in the final year of undergraduate study or the first year of graduate study and planning to work on a doctoral degree in 1 of the indicated specialties. Applications are particularly encouraged from women, members of ethnic minority groups (American Indians, African Americans, Hispanics or Latinos, Native Hawaiians, Alaska Natives, Asians, and Pacific Islanders), and persons with disabilities. Selection is based on all available evidence of ability, including academic records, letters of recommendation, and GRE scores.

Financial data   The annual stipend is $30,500 for the first year, $31,000 for the second year; and $31,500 for the third year; the program also pays the recipient's institution full tuition and required fees (not to include room and board). An additional allowance may be considered for a student with a disability.

Duration   3 years, as long as satisfactory academic progress is maintained.

Additional information   This program is sponsored by the Army Research Office, the Air Force Office of Scientific Research, and the Office of Naval Research. Recipients do not incur any military or other service obligation. They must attend school on a full-time basis.

Number awarded   Approximately 180 each year.

Deadline January of each year.

[568]
NATIONAL HEART, LUNG, AND BLOOD INSTITUTE MENTORED CAREER AWARD FOR FACULTY AT MINORITY INSTITUTIONS

National Heart, Lung, and Blood Institute
Attn: Division of Extramural Affairs
6701 Rockledge Drive, Room 10135
Bethesda, MD 20892-7950
(301) 435-0222   Fax: (301) 480-1060
E-mail: tm280y@nih.gov
Web: www.nhlbi.nih.gov

Purpose To provide funding to faculty investigators at minority schools interested in receiving further research training in areas relevant to cardiovascular, pulmonary, and hematologic diseases.

Eligibility Candidates for this award must be faculty members who are U.S. citizens, nationals, or permanent residents at the time of application; have a doctoral degree or equivalent in a biomedical or behavioral science; wish to receive specialized training in cardiovascular, pulmonary, hematologic, or sleep disorders research; have the background and potential to benefit from the training; and are committed to providing research opportunities and cultivating an interest in research for students from disadvantaged backgrounds at their institution. They must be teaching at a college or university with student enrollment drawn substantially from minority ethnic groups (including African Americans/Blacks, Hispanics, American Indians, Alaska Native, and non-Asian Pacific Islanders). Candidates must identify and complete arrangements with a mentor (at the same institution or at a collaborating research center) who is recognized as an accomplished investigator in the research area proposed and who will provide guidance for their development and research plans. They are also encouraged to recruit at least 1 and up to 2 students from disadvantaged backgrounds, including racial and ethnic minorities at their institution, to serve as research assistants.

Financial data The awardee receives salary support of up to $75,000 per year plus fringe benefits. Student research assistants receive up to $10 per hour. Support for up to 5% of the mentor's salary during the summer experience may also be awarded. In addition, up to $36,000 per year may be provided for research project requirements and related support (e.g., technical personnel costs, supplies, equipment, candidate travel, telephone charges, publication costs, and tuition for necessary courses). Facilities and administrative costs may be reimbursed at the rate of 8% of total direct costs.

Duration Academic years and summers for 3 to 5 years.

Additional information Awardees must commit 100% of their effort during summer and/or off-quarter periods and at least 25% of their effort during the academic year.

Number awarded Varies each year.

Deadline Letters of intent must be submitted by May of each year; final applications are due in June.

[569]
NATIONAL HISPANIC FOUNDATION FOR THE ARTS ENTERTAINMENT INDUSTRY SCHOLARSHIP PROGRAM

Hispanic Scholarship Fund
Attn: Selection Committee
55 Second Street, Suite 1500
San Francisco, CA 94105
(415) 808-2350   Toll-free: (877) HSF-INFO
Fax: (415) 808-2302   E-mail: college1@hsf.net
Web: www.hsf.net/scholarship/programs/nhfa.php

Purpose To provide financial assistance to Hispanic students working on a graduate degree in the arts at designated universities.

Eligibility This program is open to U.S. citizens, permanent residents, and visitors with a passport stamped I-551 who are of Hispanic heritage. Applicants must be enrolled full time at Columbia University, Harvard University, New York University, Northwestern University, University of California at Los Angeles, University of Southern California, or Yale University. They must have a GPA of 3.0 or higher in a degree program in drama/theater, music, set design, costume design, lighting design, film (writing, directing, production), broadcast communications, entertainment law, or business administration with an emphasis on entertainment management. Along with their application, they must submit 600-word essays on 1) how their Hispanic heritage, family upbringing, and/or role models have influenced their personal long-term goals; 2) how they contribute to their community and what they have learned from their experiences; and 3) an academic challenge they have faced and how they have overcome it. Selection is based on academic achievement, personal strengths, leadership, and financial need.

Financial data The stipend is $2,500.

Duration 1 year.

Additional information This program is presented by the National Hispanic Foundation for the Arts in partnership with the Hispanic Scholarship Fund (HSF).

Number awarded 1 or more each year.

Deadline June of each year.

[570]
NATIONAL PHYSICAL SCIENCE CONSORTIUM GRADUATE FELLOWSHIPS

National Physical Science Consortium
c/o University of Southern California
3716 South Hope Street, Suite 348
Los Angeles, CA 90007-4344
(213) 743-2409   Toll-free: (800) 854-NPSC
Fax: (213) 743-2407   E-mail: npschq@npsc.org
Web: www.npsc.org

Purpose To provide financial assistance and summer work experience to underrepresented minorities and women interested in working on a Ph.D. in designated science and engineering fields.

Eligibility This program is open to U.S. citizens who are seniors graduating from college with a GPA of 3.0 or higher, enrolled in the first or second year of a doctoral program, completing a terminal master's degree, or returning from the work force and holding no more than a master's degree. Students currently in the third or subsequent year of a Ph.D. program or who already have a doctoral degree in any field

(Ph.D., M.D., J.D., Ed.D.) are ineligible. Applicants must be interested in working on a Ph.D. in the physical sciences or related fields of science or engineering. The program welcomes applications from all qualified students and continues to emphasize the recruitment of underrepresented minority (African American, Hispanic, Native American Indian, Eskimo, Aleut, and Pacific Islander) and women physical science and engineering students. Fellowships are provided to students at the 117 universities that are members of the consortium. Selection is based on academic standing (GPA), course work taken in preparation for graduate school, university and/or industry research experience, letters of recommendation, and GRE scores.

Financial data The fellowship pays tuition and fees plus an annual stipend of $16,000. It also provides on-site paid summer employment to enhance technical experience. The exact value of the fellowship depends on academic standing, summer employment, and graduate school attended, but exceeds $200,000.

Duration Support is initially provided for 2 or 3 years, depending on the employer-sponsor. If the fellow makes satisfactory progress and continues to meet the conditions of the award, support may continue for a total of up to 6 years or completion of the Ph.D., whichever comes first.

Additional information This program began in 1989. Tuition and fees are provided by the participating universities. Stipends and summer internships are provided by sponsoring organizations. Students must submit separate applications for internships, which may have additional eligibility requirements. Internships are currently available at Amgen Inc. in Thousand Oaks, California (biochemistry, chemistry, organic chemistry, and life sciences); HRL Laboratories in Malibu, California (chemistry, computer science, materials science, and physics); Lawrence Livermore National Laboratory in Livermore, California (astronomy, chemistry, computer science, geology, materials science, mathematics, and physics); Los Alamos National Laboratory in Los Alamos, New Mexico (computer science, engineering, mathematics, and physics); National Security Agency in Fort Meade, Maryland (astronomy, chemistry, computer science, geology, materials science, mathematics, and physics); Sandia National Laboratory in Livermore, California (biology, chemistry, computer science, environmental science, geology, materials science, mathematics, and physics); and Sandia National Laboratory in Albuquerque, New Mexico (chemical engineering, chemistry, computer science, materials science, mathematics, mechanical engineering, and physics). Fellows must submit a separate application for dissertation support in the year prior to the beginning of their dissertation research program, but not until they can describe their intended research in general terms.

Number awarded Varies each year; recently, 13 of these fellowships were awarded.

Deadline November of each year.

[571]
NATIONAL SOCIETY OF HISPANIC MBAS SCHOLARSHIP PROGRAM

National Society of Hispanic MBAs
Attn: Education Specialist
1303 Walnut Hill Lane, Suite 300
Irving, TX 75038
(214) 596-9338, ext. 228   Toll-free: (877) 467-4622
Fax: (214) 596-9325
E-mail: scholarships@nshmba.org
Web: www.nshmba.org/scholarships.asp

Purpose To provide financial assistance to Hispanic American graduate students interested in working on a master's degree in business administration.

Eligibility Eligible to apply are full-time or part-time graduate students who are interested in working on a master's degree in management or business. Applicants may be currently enrolled in graduate school or planning to attend. They must be U.S. citizens or permanent residents and be of Hispanic background (1 parent must be fully Hispanic or both parents must be half Hispanic). Selection is based on academic achievement (GPA of 3.0 or higher), participation in community development or service, letters of recommendation, financial need, and a 1-page essay on issues affecting Hispanics in the United States (recently, applicants were asked to assume that they were the admissions director of a university and to describe how they would increase Hispanic representation in the graduate management and business program).

Financial data Stipends generally range from $2,500 to $5,000 for full-time students and up to $1,500 for part-time students.

Duration 1 year; recipients may reapply.

Additional information This program is administered by Scholarship America.

Number awarded Varies each year. Recently, this program awarded $617,000 in scholarships.

Deadline April of each year.

[572]
NATIONAL URBAN FELLOWS PROGRAM

National Urban Fellows, Inc.
Attn: Program Director
59 John Street, Suite 310
New York, NY 10038
(212) 349-6200   Fax: (212) 349-7478
E-mail: lbenitez@nuf.org
Web: www.nuf.org

Purpose To provide mid-career minority and women public sector professionals with an opportunity to strengthen leadership skills through an academic program coupled with a mentorship.

Eligibility This program is open to minorities and women who are U.S. citizens, have a bachelor's degree, have at least 3 years of administrative or managerial experience, have demonstrated exceptional ability and leadership potential, meet academic admission requirements, have a high standard of integrity and work ethic, and are committed to the solution of urban problems. Applicants must a 1,000-word autobiographical statement and a 1,000-word statement on their career goals. Semifinalists are interviewed.

Financial data The stipend is $25,000. The program also provides full payment of tuition, a relocation allowance of $500, a book allowance of $500, and reimbursement for program-related travel.

Duration 14 months.

Additional information The program begins with a summer semester of study at Bernard M. Baruch College of the City University of New York. Following this, fellows spend 9 months in mentorship assignments with a senior administrator in a government agency, a major nonprofit, or a foundation. The final summer is spent in another semester of study at Baruch College. Fellows who successfully complete all requirements are granted a master's of public administration from that college. A $35 processing fee must accompany each application.

Number awarded Varies; approximately 20 each year.

Deadline February of each year.

[573]
NCAA ETHNIC MINORITY POSTGRADUATE SCHOLARSHIP PROGRAM

National Collegiate Athletic Association
Attn: Leadership Advisory Board
700 West Washington Avenue
P.O. Box 6222
Indianapolis, IN 46206-6222
(317) 917-6477   Fax: (317) 917-6888
Web: www.ncaa.org

Purpose To provide funding to ethnic minority graduate students who are interested in preparing for a career in intercollegiate athletics.

Eligibility This program is open to members of minority groups who have been accepted into a program at a National Collegiate Athletic Association (NCAA) member institution that will prepare them for a career in intercollegiate athletics (athletics administrator, coach, athletic trainer, or other career that provides a direct service to intercollegiate athletics). Applicants must be U.S. citizens, have performed with distinction as a student body member at their respective undergraduate institution, and be entering the first semester or term of their postgraduate studies. Selection is based on the applicant's involvement in extracurricular activities, course work, commitment to preparing for a career in intercollegiate athletics, and promise for success in that career. Financial need is not considered.

Financial data The stipend is $6,000; funds are paid to the college or university of the recipient's choice.

Duration 1 year; nonrenewable.

Number awarded 16 each year; 3 of the scholarships are reserved for applicants who completed undergraduate study at an NCAA Division III institution.

Deadline February of each year.

[574]
NEBRASKA SPACE GRANT STATEWIDE SCHOLARSHIP COMPETITION

Nebraska Space Grant Consortium
c/o University of Nebraska at Omaha
Engineering, No. 116
6001 Dodge Street
Omaha, NE 68182-0406
(402) 554-3772
Toll-free: (800) 858-8648, ext. 4-3772 (within NE)
Fax: (402) 554-3781   E-mail: nasa@unomaha.edu
Web: www.unomaha.edu/~nasa/funding/ssc.html

Purpose To provide financial assistance to undergraduate and graduate students (particularly minorities, women, and students with disabilities) in Nebraska interested in aerospace-related study or research.

Eligibility This program is open to undergraduate and graduate students at schools that are members of the Nebraska Space Grant Consortium. Applicants must be U.S. citizens participating in approved aviation or aerospace-related research or course work. Selection is based primarily on past academic performance in the classroom. Special attention is given to applications submitted by women, underrepresented minorities, and persons with disabilities.

Financial data Maximum awards are $500 per semester for undergraduate or graduate course work, $750 per semester for undergraduate research, or $2,500 per semester for graduate research.

Duration 1 semester; may be renewed if the recipient maintains a GPA of 3.0 or higher.

Additional information The following schools are members of the Nebraska Space Grant Consortium: University of Nebraska at Omaha, University of Nebraska at Lincoln, University of Nebraska at Kearney, University of Nebraska Medical Center, Creighton University, Western Nebraska Community College, Chadron State College, College of St. Mary, Metropolitan Community College, Grace University, Hastings College, Little Priest Tribal College, and Nebraska Indian Community College. Funding for this program is provided by the National Aeronautics and Space Administration.

Deadline April of each year.

[575]
NELLIE STONE JOHNSON SCHOLARSHIP

Minnesota State University Student Association
Attn: Scholarship
108 Como Avenue
St. Paul, MN 55103-1820
(651) 224-1518   Fax: (651) 224-9753
E-mail: nsj@msusa.net
Web: www.msusa.net/nellie_stjo.html

Purpose To provide financial assistance to racial minority union members and their families who are interested in working on an undergraduate or graduate degree at a Minnesota state college or university.

Eligibility This program is open to students in 2-year, undergraduate, and graduate programs at a Minnesota state university, community college, or consolidated campus. Applicants must be a minority (Asian, American Indian, Alaska Native, Black/African American, Hispanic/Latino, Native Hawaiian, or Pacific Islander) union member or the child, grandchild, or spouse of a minority union member. They must submit a 2-page statement about their background, educational goals, career goals, and other activities that may impact the cause of human or civil rights. Awards may be reserved for women. Preference is given to Minnesota residents. A personal or telephone interview may be required.

Financial data Stipends range from $500 to $2,000.

Duration 1 year; may be renewed up to 3 additional years for student working on a bachelor's degree, 1 additional year for students working on a master's degree, or 1 additional year for students in a community or technical college program.

Number awarded 1 or more each year. If multiple awards are made, at least 1 recipient must be female.

Deadline March of each year.

[576]
NEW JERSEY HISPANIC BAR FOUNDATION SCHOLARSHIP

New Jersey Hispanic Bar Foundation, Inc.
P.O. Box 2325
Princeton, NJ 08543
Web: www.njhbf.org/scholarship.htm

Purpose To provide financial assistance to Hispanic law students from New Jersey.

Eligibility This program is open to students who have completed at least 1 year at an ABA-approved law school in the United States and have been residents of New Jersey for at least 3 years prior to enrolling in law school. Applicants must be of Hispanic ancestry (at least 1 parent of Hispanic descent) with a GPA of 2.0 or higher. They must submit a statement describing their recent community and/or law school activities and how, after they graduate as a lawyer, they intend to contribute to the advancement of the community and the legal profession. Financial need is considered in the selection process.

Financial data A stipend is awarded (amount not specified).

Duration 1 year; may be renewed.

Number awarded 1 or more each year.

Deadline August of each year.

[577]
NEW MEXICO GRADUATE SCHOLARSHIP PROGRAM

New Mexico Commission on Higher Education
Attn: Financial Aid and Student Services
1068 Cerrillos Road
P.O. Box 15910
Santa Fe, NM 87506-5910
(505) 827-1217   Toll-free: (800) 279-9777
Fax: (505) 827-7392
E-mail: highered@che.state.nm.us
Web: www.nmche.org/collegefinance/gradshol.asp

Purpose To provide financial assistance for graduate education to underrepresented groups in New Mexico.

Eligibility Applicants for this program must be New Mexico residents who are members of underrepresented groups, particularly minorities and women. Preference is given to 1) students enrolled in business, engineering, com-

puter science, mathematics, or agriculture and 2) American Indian students enrolled in any graduate program. All applicants must be U.S. citizens or permanent residents enrolled in graduate programs at public institutions of higher education in New Mexico.

Financial data The maximum stipend is $7,500 per year.

Duration 1 year; may be renewed.

Additional information Information is available from the dean of graduate studies at the participating New Mexico public institution. Recipients must serve 10 hours per week in an unpaid internship or assistantship.

Number awarded Varies each year, depending on the availability of funds.

Deadline Deadlines are established by the participating institutions.

[578]
NEW YORK SPACE GRANT CONSORTIUM GRADUATE FELLOWSHIPS

New York Space Grant Consortium
c/o Cornell University
517 Space Sciences Building
Ithaca, NY 14853-6801
(607) 255-2710   Fax: (607) 255-1767
E-mail: spacegrant@astro.cornell.edu
Web: astro.cornell.edu/SpaceGrant/grads.html

Purpose To provide financial assistance for graduate study in space-related fields at designated universities in New York.

Eligibility This program is open to graduate students at selected universities that belong to the New York Space Grant Consortium. Applicants must be studying space-related fields, including aerospace engineering, astronomy, electrical engineering, geological sciences, or mechanical engineering. U.S. citizenship is required. The New York Space Grant Consortium is a component of the U.S. National Aeronautics and Space Administration (NASA) Space Grant program, which encourages participation by women, underrepresented minorities, and persons with disabilities.

Financial data Each participating institution establishes its own stipend level.

Duration 1 year.

Additional information The participating universities are Cornell University, City College of the City University of New York, Clarkson University, Columbia University, SUNY Buffalo, Polytechnic University, and Rensselaer Polytechnic Institute. This program is funded by NASA.

Number awarded Varies each year.

[579]
NINR MENTORED RESEARCH SCIENTIST DEVELOPMENT AWARD FOR MINORITY INVESTIGATORS

National Institute of Nursing Research
Attn: Division of Extramural Research
6701 Democracy Boulevard, Room 710
Bethesda, MD 20892-4870
(301) 594-6152   Fax: (301) 480-8260
E-mail: janice.phillips@nih.gov
Web: www.nih.gov/ninr

Purpose To provide funding for research career development to postdoctoral nursing investigators who are members of underrepresented minority groups.

Eligibility This program is open to full-time nursing faculty members at Traditionally Minority Based Institutions (TMBIs) as well as other universities, colleges, hospitals, and laboratories. Candidates must be U.S. citizens, nationals, or permanent residents from ethnic/racial groups determined by their institution to be underrepresented in biomedical or behavioral nursing research. They must have a research or health-professional doctorate (e.g., Ph.D., D.N.Sc.) or its equivalent; have demonstrated the capacity or potential for a productive independent research career; have a Registered Nurse license; and have secured the commitment of an appropriate research mentor actively involved in research relevant to the mission of the National Institute of Nursing Research (NINR). Proposals must include both a research plan and a research career development plan that will develop knowledge and research skills relevant to the candidate's career goals. The TMBI or majority academic institution must demonstrate a firm commitment to the development of the applicant as a productive, independent investigator in nursing research and to the pursuit of the research career development plan. The candidate should describe a career development program that will maximize use of relevant research and educational resources available in the TMBI or majority academic institution and in the mentor's institution.

Financial data The grant provides up to $50,000 per year for salary and fringe benefits plus an additional $20,000 per year for such other expenses as tuition, fees, and books related to career development; research expenses, such as supplies, equipment, and technical personnel; travel to research meetings or trainings; and statistical services, including personnel, research, and computer time. Facilities and administrative costs are allowed at 8% of total direct costs.

Duration 3 years.

Additional information These grants have been awarded annually since 1998. Grantees are expected to spend at least 75% of their professional effort time to the program and the other 25% devoted to other research-related and/or teaching or clinical pursuits consistent with the objectives of the award.

Number awarded 3 to 4 new grants are awarded each year.

Deadline October of each year.

[580]
NMF NEED-BASED SCHOLARSHIP PROGRAM

National Medical Fellowships, Inc.
Attn: Scholarship Program
5 Hanover Square, 15th Floor
New York, NY 10004
(212) 483-8880   Fax: (212) 483-8897
E-mail: info@nmfonline.org
Web: www.nmf-online.org

Purpose To provide financial assistance to underrepresented minority medical students.

Eligibility This program is open to U.S. citizens enrolled in the first or second year of an accredited M.D. or D.O. degree-granting program in the United States. Applicants must be African American, Mexican American, Native Hawaiian, Alaska Native, American Indian, or mainland Puerto Rican. They must submit an essay of 500 to 1,000 words on their motivation for a career in medicine and their personal and professional goals over the next 10 years. Selection is based primarily on financial need.

Financial data The amount of the award depends on the student's total resources (including parental and spousal support), cost of education, and receipt of additional scholarships; recently, individual awards ranged from $500 to $10,000 per year.

Duration 1 year for first-year students; may be renewed for the second year only.

Number awarded Varies each year; recently, more than 300 students received support from this program.

Deadline June of each year.

[581]
NORTH AMERICAN DOCTORAL FELLOWSHIPS

The Fund for Theological Education, Inc.
825 Houston Mill Road, Suite 250
Atlanta, GA 30329
(404) 727-1450   Fax: (404) 727-1490
E-mail: fte@thefund.org
Web: www.thefund.org

Purpose To provide financial assistance to underrepresented racial and ethnic minority students enrolled in a doctoral program in religious or theological studies.

Eligibility This program is open to continuing students enrolled full time in a Ph.D. or Th.D. program in religious or theological studies. Applicants must be citizens or permanent residents of the United States or Canada who are racial or ethnic minority students traditionally underrepresented in graduate education. D.Min. students are ineligible. Preference is given to students nearing completion of their degree. Selection is based on commitment to teaching and scholarship, academic achievement, capacity for leadership in theological scholarship, and financial need.

Financial data Stipends range from $5,000 to $10,000 per year, depending on financial need.

Duration 1 year; may be renewed up to 2 additional years.

Additional information Funding for this program is provided by the National Council of Churches, proceeds from the book *Stony the Road We Trod: African American Biblical Interpretation,* an endowment from the Hearst Foundation, and the previously established FTE Black Doctoral Program supported by Lilly Endowment, Inc.

Number awarded Varies each year; recently, 8 of these scholarships were awarded.

Deadline February of each year.

[582]
NSCA MINORITY SCHOLARSHIPS

National Strength and Conditioning Association
Attn: Foundation
1955 North Union Boulevard
P.O. Box 9908
Colorado Springs, CO 80932-0908
(719) 632-6722   Toll-free: (800) 815-6826
Fax: (719) 632-6367   E-mail: foundation@nsca-lift.org
Web: www.nsca-lift.org/foundation

Purpose To provide financial assistance to members of the National Strength and Conditioning Association (NSCA) who are minorities interested in preparing for a career in strength training and conditioning.

Eligibility This program is open to members who are minorities and have been accepted into an accredited postsecondary institution to work on a graduate degree in the strength and conditioning field. They must submit a 500-word essay describing their course of study, career goals, and financial need.

Financial data The stipend is $1,000.

Duration 1 year.

Additional information The NSCA is a nonprofit organization of strength and conditioning professionals, including coaches, athletic trainers, physical therapists, educators, researchers, and physicians. This program was first offered in 2003.

Number awarded 2 each year.

Deadline March of each year.

[583]
NSF GRADUATE RESEARCH FELLOWSHIPS

National Science Foundation
Directorate for Education and Human Resources
Attn: Division of Graduate Education
4201 Wilson Boulevard, Room 907N
Arlington, VA 22230
(703) 292-8694   Fax: (703) 292-9048
E-mail: grfp@nsf.gov
Web: www.ehr.nsf.gov/dge/programs/grf

Purpose To provide financial assistance to women, minorities, persons with disabilities, and others interested in working on a master's or doctoral degree in fields supported by the National Science Foundation (NSF).

Eligibility This program is open to U.S. citizens, nationals, and permanent residents who wish to work on research-based master's or doctoral degrees in science, mathematics, or engineering. Awards are also made for work toward a research-based Ph.D. in science education that requires a science competence comparable to that for Ph.D. candidates in scientific disciplines. Research in bioengineering is also eligible if it involves 1) diagnosis or treatment-related goals that apply engineering principles to problems in biology and medicine while advancing engineering knowledge, or 2) aiding persons with disabilities. Other work in medical, dental, law, public health, or practice-oriented professional degree programs, or in joint sci-

ence-professional degree programs, such as M.D./Ph.D. and J.D./Ph.D. programs, is not eligible. Other categories of ineligible support include 1) clinical, counseling, business, or management fields; 2) other education programs; 3) history (except in history of science) or social work; 4) clinical research or research with disease-related goals, including work on the etiology, diagnosis, or treatment of physical or mental disease, abnormality, or malfunction in human beings or animals; 5) research involving animal models of research with disease-related goals; and 6) testing of drugs or other procedures for disease-related goals. Applications normally should be submitted during the senior year in college or in the first year of graduate study; eligibility is limited to those who have completed no more than 12 months of graduate study since completion of a baccalaureate degree. Applicants who have already earned an advanced degree in science, engineering, or medicine (including an M.D., D.D.S., or D.V.M.) are ineligible. Selection is based on intellectual merit and broader impacts. Intellectual merit includes intellectual ability and other accepted requisites for scholarly scientific study, such as the ability to work as a member of a team as well as independently, to interpret and communicate research findings, and to plan and conduct research. The broader impacts criterion includes contributions that 1) encourage diversity, broaden opportunities, and enable the participation of all citizens (including women and men, underrepresented minorities, and persons with disabilities) in science and engineering; 2) enhance scientific and technical understanding; and 3) benefit society.

Financial data The stipend is $30,000 per year, plus a $10,500 cost-of-education allowance given to the recipient's institution. If a fellow affiliates with a foreign institution, tuition and fees are reimbursed to the fellow up to a maximum of $10,500 per tenure year.

Duration Up to 3 years, usable over a 5-year period.

Additional information Fellows may choose as their fellowship institution any appropriate nonprofit U.S. or foreign institution of higher education.

Number awarded Approximately 1,000 each year.

Deadline November of each year for applications in life sciences, chemistry, computer and information science and engineering, social science, and physics and astronomy; December of each year for applications in mathematical sciences, geosciences, psychology, and engineering.

[584]
OHIO SPACE GRANT CONSORTIUM DOCTORAL FELLOWSHIP

Ohio Space Grant Consortium
c/o Ohio Aerospace Institute
22800 Cedar Point Road
Cleveland, OH 44142
(440) 962-3032   Toll-free: (800) 828-OSGC
Fax: (440) 962-3057   E-mail: osgc@oai.org
Web: www.osgc.org/Fellowship.html

Purpose To provide financial assistance to minority and other graduate students working on a doctoral degree in an aerospace-related discipline at major universities in Ohio.

Eligibility These fellowships are available to U.S. citizens enrolled full time in a doctoral program in an aerospace-related discipline (aeronautical engineering, aerospace engineering, astronomy, biology, chemical engineering, chemistry, civil engineering, computer engineering and science, control engineering, electrical engineering, engineering mechanics, geology, industrial engineering, manufacturing engineering, materials science and engineering, mathematics, mechanical engineering, petroleum engineering, physics, and systems engineering) at 1 of the participating universities in Ohio. Applicants must have completed a master's degree or 2 years of graduate study. Women, underrepresented minorities, and physically challenged persons are particularly encouraged to apply. Selection is based on academic achievement, recommendations, academic background, and the relevance of the applicant's research interests and experience.

Financial data The stipend is $18,000 per year plus tuition at the university attended.

Duration Up to 3 years.

Additional information These fellowships are funded through the National Space Grant College and Fellowship Program administered by the National Aeronautics and Space Administration (NASA), with matching funds provided by the member universities, the Ohio Aerospace Institute, and private industry. The participating universities include: Air Force Institute of Technology, University of Akron, Case Western Reserve University, University of Cincinnati, Cleveland State University, University of Dayton, Ohio State University, Ohio University, University of Toledo, Wright State University, and Youngstown State University. Recipients are required to conduct a significant portion of their doctoral research in residence at NASA Glenn Research Center/Ohio Aerospace Institute or at another approved NASA center.

Number awarded 2 each year.

Deadline February of each year.

[585]
OHIO SPACE GRANT CONSORTIUM MASTER'S FELLOWSHIP

Ohio Space Grant Consortium
c/o Ohio Aerospace Institute
22800 Cedar Point Road
Cleveland, OH 44142
(440) 962-3032   Toll-free: (800) 828-OSGC
Fax: (440) 962-3057   E-mail: osgc@oai.org
Web: www.osgc.org/Fellowship.html

Purpose To provide financial assistance to minority and other graduate students who wish to work on a master's degree in an aerospace-related discipline at major universities in Ohio.

Eligibility These fellowships are available to U.S. citizens enrolled full time in a master's degree program in an aerospace-related discipline (aeronautical engineering, aerospace engineering, astronomy, biology, chemical engineering, chemistry, civil engineering, computer engineering and science, control engineering, electrical engineering, engineering mechanics, geology, industrial engineering, manufacturing engineering, materials science and engineering, mathematics, mechanical engineering, petroleum engineering, physics, and systems engineering) at 1 of the participating universities in Ohio. Women, underrepresented minorities, and physically challenged persons are particularly encouraged to apply. Selection is based on academic achievement, recommendations, academic background,

and the relevance of the applicant's research interests and experience.

Financial data The stipend is $14,000 per academic year plus tuition at the university attended.

Duration Up to 18 months; may be renewed for an additional 12 months.

Additional information These fellowships are funded through the National Space Grant College and Fellowship Program administered by the National Aeronautics and Space Administration (NASA), with matching funds provided by the member universities, the Ohio Aerospace Institute, and private industry. The participating universities include: Air Force Institute of Technology, University of Akron, Case Western Reserve University, University of Cincinnati, Cleveland State University, University of Dayton, Ohio State University, Ohio University, University of Toledo, Wright State University, and Youngstown State University.

Number awarded 4 each year.

Deadline February of each year.

[586]
ONE-YEAR-ON-CAMPUS PROGRAM

Sandia National Laboratories
Attn: Staffing Department 3535
MS-1023
P.O. Box 5800
Albuquerque, NM 87185-1023
(505) 844-3441   Fax: (505) 844-6636
E-mail: pacover@sandia.gov
Web: www.sandia.gov/employment/index.html

Purpose To enable minority students to obtain a master's degree in engineering or computer science and also work at Sandia National Laboratories.

Eligibility This program is open to minority students with a bachelor's degree in engineering or computer science and a GPA of 3.2 or higher. Participants must apply to 3 schools jointly selected by the program and themselves. They must be prepared to obtain a master's degree within 1 year. The fields of study (not all fields are available at all participating universities) include computer science, electrical engineering, mechanical engineering, civil engineering, chemical engineering, nuclear engineering, materials sciences, and petroleum engineering. Applicants must be interested in working at the sponsor's laboratories during the summer between graduation from college and the beginning of their graduate program, and then following completion of their master's degree.

Financial data Participants receive a competitive salary while working at the laboratories on a full-time basis and a stipend while attending school.

Duration 1 year.

Additional information During their summer assignment, participants work at the laboratories, either in Albuquerque, New Mexico or in Livermore, California. Upon successful completion of the program, they return to Sandia's hiring organization as a full-time member of the technical staff. This program began in 1968. Application to schools where students received their undergraduate degree is not recommended. After the schools accept an applicant, the choice of a school is made jointly by the laboratories and the participant.

Number awarded　Varies each year; since the program began, more than 350 engineers and computer scientists have gone to work at Sandia with master's degrees.

[587]
OPERATION JUMP START II SCHOLARSHIPS

American Association of Advertising Agencies
Attn: Manager of Diversity Programs
405 Lexington Avenue, 18th Floor
New York, NY 10174-1801
(212) 682-2500　　　　Toll-free: (800) 676-9333
Fax: (212) 682-8391　　　E-mail: tiffany@aaaa.org
Web: www.aaaa.org/diversity/foundation/funds.htm

Purpose　To provide financial assistance to multicultural art directors and copywriters interested in working on a graduate degree in advertising.

Eligibility　This program is open to African Americans, Asian Americans, Hispanic Americans, and Native Americans who are interested in studying the advertising creative arts at designated institutions. Applicants must have already received an undergraduate degree and be able to demonstrate financial need. As part of the selection process, they must submit 10 samples of creative work in their respective field of expertise.

Financial data　The stipend is $10,000.

Duration　Most awards are for 2 years.

Additional information　This program began in 2002 and currently provides scholarships to students at the Adcenter at Virginia Commonwealth University, the Creative Circus and the Portfolio Center in Atlanta, the Miami Ad School, the University of Texas at Austin, Pratt Institute, the Minneapolis College of Art and Design, and the Art Center College of Design at Pasadena.

Number awarded　20 each year.

[588]
ORGANIC CHEMISTRY GRADUATE STUDENT FELLOWSHIPS

American Chemical Society
Division of Organic Chemistry
1155 16th Street, N.W.
Washington, DC 20036
(202) 872-4408　　　　Toll-free: (800) 227-5558
E-mail: divisions@acs.org
Web: www.organicdivision.org/fellowships.html

Purpose　To provide financial assistance to advanced doctoral students (particularly minorities and women) in organic chemistry.

Eligibility　This program is open to students working toward a Ph.D. degree in organic chemistry who have completed the second year of graduate study by the time the fellowship period begins. Applicants must submit 3 letters of recommendation, a resume, and a short essay on a research area of their choice. U.S. citizenship or permanent resident status is required. Selection is based primarily on evidence of research accomplishment. Applications from women and minorities are especially encouraged.

Financial data　The stipend is $20,000. Fellows also receive travel support to present a poster of their work at the National Organic Symposium.

Duration　1 year.

Additional information　This program was established in 1982. It includes the Emmanuil Troyansky Fellowship. Information is also available from Scott Rychnovsky, University of California at Irvine, School of Physical Sciences, 3038A FRH, Mail Code 2025, Irvine, CA 92697, (949) 824-8292, Fax: (949) 824-6369, E-mail: srychnov@uci.edu.

Number awarded　Varies each year; recently, 14 of these fellowships were awarded.

Deadline　May of each year.

[589]
ORNELAS ASSOCIATES MINORITY SCHOLARSHIP FUND

American Association of Advertising Agencies
Attn: Manager of Diversity Programs
405 Lexington Avenue, 18th Floor
New York, NY 10174-1801
(212) 682-2500　　　　Toll-free: (800) 676-9333
Fax: (212) 682-8391　　　E-mail: tiffany@aaaa.org
Web: www.aaaa.org/diversity/foundation/funds.htm

Purpose　To provide financial assistance to Latino students who are working on an undergraduate or graduate degree in advertising.

Eligibility　This program is open to undergraduate and graduate students who are U.S. citizens of proven Latino heritage or at least 1 parent of Latino heritage. Applicants must have participated in the Multicultural Advertising Intern Program of the American Association of Advertising Agencies. Along with their application, they must submit an essay of 250 to 500 words on the topic: "As a Latino, I value ganas (passion), adelante (progress), Latino pride, and diversity by..." Selection is based on the essay, academic ability, and community involvement.

Financial data　The stipend is $5,000.

Duration　1 year.

Additional information　This program was established in 2001.

Number awarded　1 each year.

Deadline　June of each year.

[590]
OSB SCHOLARSHIPS

Oregon State Bar
Attn: Affirmative Action Program
5200 S.W. Meadows Road
P.O. Box 1689
Lake Oswego, OR 97035-0889
(503) 431-6338
Toll-free: (800) 452-8260, ext. 338 (within OR)
Fax: (503) 598-6938　　　E-mail: dgigoux@osbar.org
Web: www.osbar.org

Purpose　To provide financial assistance to minority students in Oregon who are currently attending law school.

Eligibility　This program is open to minority (African American, Asian, Hispanic, Native American) students who are entering or attending an Oregon law school and planning to practice law in Oregon upon graduation. Along with their application, they must submit 1) a personal statement on their history of disadvantage or barriers to educational advancement, personal experiences of discrimination, extraordinary financial obligations, composition of immediate family, extraordinary health or medical needs, and languages in which they are fluent; and 2) a state bar statement in which they describe their intention to practice law in Oregon and how they will improve the quality of legal service or increase access to justice in Oregon. Selection is based on financial need (30%), the personal statement (25%), the state bar statement (25%), community activities (10%), and employment history (10%).

Financial data The stipend is $1,000 per semester. Funds are credited to the recipient's law school tuition account.

Duration 1 year; recipients may reapply.

Additional information Recipients are encouraged to contribute monetarily to the Oregon State Bar's affirmative action program once they become employed.

Number awarded 8 each year.

Deadline February of each year.

[591]
OSGC EDUCATION PROGRAM

Oklahoma NASA Space Grant Consortium
c/o University of Oklahoma
College of Geosciences
Ditmars House, Suite 5
1623 Cross Center Drive
Norman, Oklahoma 73069
(405) 325-6559   Fax: (405) 325-5537
E-mail: vduca@ou.edu
Web: 129.15.32.115/scholarships/index.html

Purpose To provide financial assistance to underrepresented minority and other students in Oklahoma who are enrolled in aerospace-related studies at the undergraduate and graduate level.

Eligibility This program is open to undergraduate and graduate students at member and affiliate institutions of the Oklahoma Space Grant Consortium (OSGC). U.S. citizenship is required. The OSGC is a component of the U.S. National Aeronautics and Space Administration (NASA) Space Grant program, which encourages participation by women, underrepresented minorities, and persons with disabilities.

Financial data Financing depends on the availability of funds.

Additional information Members of OSGC are Oklahoma State University, the University of Oklahoma, Cameron University, and Langston University. Write to the sponsor for information on the program at each participating university. This program is funded by NASA.

[592]
PAUL D. WHITE SCHOLARSHIP

Baker & Hostetler LLP
Attn: Kathleen Ferdico
3200 National City Center
1900 East Ninth Street
Cleveland, OH 44114-3485
(216) 861-7092   Fax: (216) 696-0740
Web: www.bakerlaw.com

Purpose To provide financial assistance and summer work experience to minority students at selected law schools.

Eligibility This program is open to first- and second-year law students of African American, Hispanic, Asian American, or American Indian descent. Applicants must be attending 1 of the following schools that currently participate in the program: Case Western Reserve School of Law, Cleveland-Marshall School of Law, Howard University School of Law, Ohio State University Moritz School of Law, University of Michigan School of Law, the University of Texas School of Law, University of California at Los Angeles School of Law, University of Cincinnati College of Law, University of Denver College of Law, University of Florida Levin College of Law, and University of Colorado School of Law.

Financial data The program provides a stipend of $5,000 and a paid summer clerkship with the sponsoring firm.

Duration 1 year, including the following summer.

Number awarded 1 each year.

[593]
PEDIATRIC/VISION THERAPY AWARD

National Optometric Association
c/o Dr. Charles Comer, Association Manager
3723 Main Street
P.O. Box F
East Chicago, IL 46312
Toll-free: (877) 394-2020   Fax: (219) 398-1077
E-mail: ccomer2@aol.com
Web: www.natoptassoc.org

Purpose To provide financial assistance to members of the National Optometric Student Association (NOSA).

Eligibility This program is open to NOSA members enrolled in the third or fourth year at a school or college of optometry. Applicants must have a GPA of 2.5 or higher and be able to demonstrate community involvement. Along with their application, they must submit a 300-word essay demonstrating their aspirations as an optometrist and commitment to serve their community related to pediatric optometry or vision therapy. Financial need is considered in the selection process.

Financial data The stipend is $500.

Duration 1 year.

Additional information The National Optometric Association was founded in 1969 with the goal of recruiting minority students for schools and colleges of optometry. It remains committed to improving the quality and accessibility of eye care in minority and other historically underserved communities.

Number awarded 1 each year.

Deadline April of each year.

[594]
PENNSYLVANIA SPACE GRANT CONSORTIUM FELLOWSHIPS

Pennsylvania Space Grant Consortium
c/o Pennsylvania State University
2217 Earth-Engineering Sciences Building
University Park, PA 16802
(814) 863-7687   Fax: (814) 863-8286
E-mail: spacegrant@psu.edu
Web: www.psu.edu/spacegrant/highered/scholar.html

Purpose To provide financial assistance for space-related study to minority and other graduate students at universities affiliated with the Pennsylvania Space Grant Consortium.

Eligibility This program is open to graduate students at participating universities. Applicants must be studying a field that does, or can, promote the understanding, assessment, and utilization of space, including aerospace, earth science, or space science. U.S. citizenship is required. Students from underrepresented groups (women, minorities, rural populations, and those with disabilities) are especially encouraged to apply.

Financial data The stipend is $5,000 per year.

Duration 2 years.

Additional information Participating institutions include Pennsylvania State University, Carnegie-Mellon University, Temple University, and the University of Pittsburgh. This program is sponsored by the U.S. National Aeronautics and Space Administration (NASA).

Number awarded Varies each year.

Deadline February of each year.

[595]
PFIZER/UNCF CORPORATE SCHOLARS PROGRAM

United Negro College Fund
Attn: Corporate Scholars Program
P.O. Box 1435
Alexandria, VA 22313-9998
Toll-free: (866) 671-7237   E-mail: internship@uncf.org
Web: www.uncf.org/internships/index.asp

Purpose To provide financial assistance and work experience to minority undergraduate and graduate students majoring in designated fields and interested in an internship at a Pfizer facility.

Eligibility This program is open to sophomores, juniors, graduate students, and first-year law students who are African American, Hispanic American, Asian/Pacific Islander American, or American Indian/Alaskan Native. Applicants must have a GPA of 3.0 or higher and be enrolled at an institution that is a member of the United Negro College Fund (UNCF) or at another targeted college or university. They must be working on 1) a bachelor's degree in animal science, business, chemistry (organic or analytical), human resources, logistics, microbiology, organizational development, operations management, pre-veterinary medicine, or supply chain management; 2) a master's degree in chemistry (organic or analytical), finance, human resources, or organizational development; or 3) a law degree. Eligibility is limited to U.S. citizens, permanent residents, asylees, refugees, and lawful temporary residents. Along with their application, they must submit a 1-page essay about themselves and their career goals, including information about their interest in Pfizer (the program's sponsor), their personal background, and any particular challenges they have faced.

Financial data The program provides an internship stipend of up to $5,000, housing accommodations near Pfizer Corporate facilities, and (based on successful internship performance) a $15,000 scholarship.

Duration 8 to 10 weeks for the internship; 1 year for the scholarship.

Additional information Opportunities for first-year law students include the summer internship only.

Number awarded Varies each year.

Deadline January of each year.

[596]
PIPELINE SCHOLARSHIPS

Society of Mexican American Engineers and Scientists
Attn: Scholarships
711 West Bay Area Boulevard, Suite 206
Webster, TX 77598-3677
(281) 557-3677   Fax: (281) 557-3757
E-mail: scholarships@maes-natl.org
Web: www.maes-natl.org

Purpose To provide financial assistance to undergraduate and graduate student members of the Society of Mexican American Engineers and Scientists (MAES).

Eligibility This program is open to MAES student members who are full-time undergraduate or graduate students at a college or university in the United States. Community college students must be enrolled in majors that can transfer to a 4-year institution offering a baccalaureate degree. All applicants must be majoring in a field of science or engineering. U.S. citizenship or permanent resident status is required. Selection is based on financial need; academic achievement; personal qualities, strengths, and leadership abilities; and timeliness and completeness of the application.

Financial data The stipend is $4,000.

Duration 1 year.

Additional information Recipients must attend the MAES International Symposium's Medalla de Oro Banquet in October.

Number awarded 1 or more each year.

Deadline October of each year.

[597]
POSTDOCTORAL FELLOWSHIP IN BEHAVIORAL NEUROSCIENCE

Texas Consortium in Behavioral Neuroscience
c/o University of Texas
Department of Psychology
1 University Station A8000
Austin, TX 78712
(512) 471-1068   Fax: (512) 471-1073
E-mail: gonzalez-lima@psy.utexas.edu
Web: homepage.psy.utexas.edu

Purpose To provide an opportunity for underrepresented minority postdoctorates to obtain research training at selected universities in Texas.

Eligibility This program is open to members of underrepresented minority groups who have a doctoral degree in neuroscience, psychology, biomedical or natural sciences, or engineering. Applicants must be interested in a program of research training at the University of Texas at Austin, the University of Texas at San Antonio, the University of Texas Health Science Center at San Antonio, Texas A&M University, or Texas A&M University System Health Science Center. U.S. citizenship or permanent resident status is required.

Financial data The program provides $3,090 for health insurance, $1,200 in travel funds, and a stipend of $35,568 in the first year and $37,476 in the second year.

Duration 2 years.

Additional information This program is sponsored by 3 components of the National Institutes of Health: the National Institute of Mental Health, the National Institute on

Drug Abuse, and the National Institute of Neurological Disorders and Stroke. The training program covers brain metabolic mapping of behavioral functions, neuropharmacology, electrophysiology, and molecular neurobiology.

Number awarded 5 each year.

Deadline Applications may be submitted at any time.

[598]
POSTDOCTORAL FELLOWSHIP IN MENTAL HEALTH AND SUBSTANCE ABUSE SERVICES

American Psychological Association
Attn: Minority Fellowship Program
750 First Street, N.E.
Washington, DC 20002-4242
(202) 336-6127   Fax: (202) 336-6012
TDD: (202) 336-6123   E-mail: mfp@apa.org
Web: www.apa.org/mfp/postdocpsych.html

Purpose To provide financial assistance to minority and other postdoctoral scholars interested in a program of research training related to providing mental health and substance abuse services to ethnic minority populations.

Eligibility This program is open to U.S. citizens and permanent residents who received a doctoral degree in psychology in the last 5 years. Applicants must be interested in participating in a program of training under a qualified sponsor for research, delivery of services, or policy related to substance abuse and its relationship to the mental health or psychological well-being of ethnic minorities. Members of ethnic minority groups (African Americans, Hispanics/Latinos, American Indians, Alaskan Natives, Asian Americans, Native Hawaiians, and other Pacific Islanders) are especially encouraged to apply. Selection is based on commitment to a career in ethnic minority mental health service delivery, research, or policy; qualifications of the sponsor; the fit between career goals and training environment selected; merit of the training proposal; potential demonstrated through accomplishments and goals; and appropriateness to goals of the program.

Financial data The stipend depends on the number of years of research experience and is equivalent to the standard postdoctoral stipend level of the National Institutes of Health (currently ranging from $35,568 for no years of experience to $51,036 for 7 or more years of experience).

Duration 1 academic or calendar year; may be renewed for up to 2 additional years.

Additional information Funding is provided by the U.S. Substance Abuse and Mental Health Services Administration.

Number awarded Varies each year.

Deadline January of each year.

[599]
POSTDOCTORAL FELLOWSHIPS IN THE NEUROSCIENCES

American Psychological Association
Attn: Minority Fellowship Program
750 First Street, N.E.
Washington, DC 20002-4242
(202) 336-6127   Fax: (202) 336-6012
TDD: (202) 336-6123   E-mail: mfp@apa.org
Web: www.apa.org/mfp/pdprogram.html

Purpose To provide funding to minority postdoctorates who are interested in pursuing research training in neuroscience.

Eligibility This program is open to all U.S. citizens and permanent residents who have a Ph.D. or M.D. degree with appropriate research experience in neuroscience or an applied discipline, such as cell or molecular biology or immunology. Applicants must have career goals that are consistent with those of the program: 1) to increase ethnic and racial diversity among neuroscience researchers with a special emphasis on increasing the numbers of underrepresented ethnic minorities; and 2) to increase numbers of neuroscientists whose work is related to the federal initiative to eliminate health disparities. They must be interested in engaging in postdoctoral research training in behavioral neuroscience, cellular neurobiology, cognitive neuroscience, computational neuroscience, developmental neurobiology, membrane biophysics, molecular neurobiology, neuroanatomy, neurobiology of aging, neurobiology of disease, neurochemistry, neurogenetics, neuroimmunology, neuropathology, neuropharmacology, neurophysiology, neurotoxicology, or systems neuroscience. Students identified as underrepresented ethnic minorities in the neurosciences (African Americans, Native Americans, Hispanic Americans, and Pacific Islanders) are especially encouraged to apply. Selection is based on scholarship, research experience and potential, a research proposal, the suitability of the proposed laboratory and mentor, commitment to a research career in neuroscience, writing ability, and appropriateness to program goal.

Financial data The stipend depends on the number of years of research experience and is equivalent to the standard postdoctoral stipend level of the National Institutes of Health (currently ranging from $35,568 for no years of experience to $51,036 for 7 or more years of experience). The fellowship also provides travel funds to attend the annual meeting of the Society for Neuroscience.

Duration 1 year; may be renewed for up to 1 additional year.

Additional information The program was established in 1987. It is funded by the U.S. National Institute of Mental Health of the National Institutes of Health and administered by the American Psychological Association.

Number awarded Varies each year.

Deadline January of each year.

[600]
POSTDOCTORAL RESEARCH FELLOWSHIPS IN EPILEPSY

Epilepsy Foundation
Attn: Research Department
4351 Garden City Drive
Landover, MD 20785-7223
(301) 459-3700   Toll-free: (800) EFA-1000
Fax: (301) 577-2684   TDD: (800) 332-2070
E-mail: grants@efa.org
Web: www.epilepsyfoundation.org

Purpose To provide funding for a program of postdoctoral training to minority and other physicians and scientists committed to epilepsy research.

Eligibility Applicants must have a doctoral degree (M.D., Ph.D., or equivalent) and be a resident or postdoctoral fellow at a university, medical school, research institution, or medical center. They must be interested in participating in a training experience and research project that has potential significance for understanding the causes, treatment, or consequences of epilepsy. The program is geared toward applicants who will be trained in research in epilepsy rather than those who use epilepsy as a tool for research in other fields. Equal consideration is given to applicants interested in acquiring experience either in basic laboratory research or in the conduct of human clinical studies. Academic faculty holding the rank of instructor or higher are not eligible, nor are graduate or medical students, medical residents, permanent government employees, or employees of private industry. Applications from women, members of minority groups, and people with disabilities are especially encouraged. Selection is based on scientific quality of the proposed research, a statement regarding its relevance to epilepsy, the applicant's qualifications, the preceptor's qualifications, and the adequacy of facility and related epilepsy programs at the institution.

Financial data The grant is $40,000. No indirect costs are covered.

Duration 1 year.

Additional information Support for this program is provided by many individuals, families, and corporations, especially the American Epilepsy Society, Abbott Laboratories, Ortho-McNeil Pharmaceutical, and Pfizer Inc. The fellowship must be carried out at a facility in the United States where there is an ongoing epilepsy research program.

Number awarded Varies each year; recently, 13 of these fellowships were awarded.

Deadline August of each year.

[601]
PREDOCTORAL FELLOWSHIP AWARDS FOR MINORITY STUDENTS

National Institutes of Health
Division of Extramural Outreach and Information
    Resources
Attn: Grants Information
6701 Rockledge Drive, Suite 6095
Bethesda, MD 20892-7910
(301) 435-0714   Fax: (301) 480-0525
E-mail: GrantsInfo@nih.gov
Web: www.nih.gov

Purpose To provide financial assistance to students from underrepresented minority groups who are working on or planning to work on advanced degrees in the biomedical and behavioral sciences.

Eligibility Applicants must be citizens, nationals, or permanent residents of the United States who are working on a Ph.D. or equivalent research degree, a combined M.D./Ph.D. degree, or other combined professional doctorate/research Ph.D. degrees in the biomedical or behavioral sciences. Support is not available for individuals enrolled in medical or other professional schools unless they are enrolled in a combined professional doctorate/Ph.D. degree program in biomedical or behavioral research. Applicants must be underrepresented minority students, defined as individuals belonging to a particular ethnic or racial group that has been determined by the applicant's graduate institution to be underrepresented in biomedical or behavioral research in the United States; the program gives priority consideration to applications from African Americans, Hispanics, Native Americans, Alaskan Natives, and Pacific Islanders.

Financial data The fellowship provides an annual stipend of $20,772, a tuition and fee allowance of 100% of all costs up to $3,000 and 60% of costs above $3,000, and an institutional allowance of $2,750 for travel to scientific meetings and for laboratory and other training expenses. Additional funds may be requested to make changes or adjustments in the academic or research environment to make it possible for the individual to perform the work necessary to meet the requirements of the degree program.

Duration Up to 5 years.

Additional information These fellowships are offered by most components of the National Institutes of Health (NIH). For a list of names and telephone numbers of responsible officers at each component, contact the Division of Extramural Outreach and Information Resources.

Number awarded Varies each year.

Deadline April or November of each year.

[602]
PREDOCTORAL FELLOWSHIP IN BEHAVIORAL NEUROSCIENCE

Texas Consortium in Behavioral Neuroscience
c/o University of Texas
Department of Psychology
1 University Station A8000
Austin, TX 78712
(512) 471-1068   Fax: (512) 471-1073
E-mail: gonzalez-lima@psy.utexas.edu
Web: homepage.psy.utexas.edu

Purpose To provide an opportunity for underrepresented minority doctoral candidates to obtain research training in neuroscience at selected universities in Texas.

Eligibility This program is open to members of underrepresented minority groups who have a bachelor's degree and plan to work on a doctoral degree in neuroscience. Applicants must be interested in a program of research training at the University of Texas at Austin, the University of Texas at San Antonio, the University of Texas Health Science Center at San Antonio, Texas A&M University, or Texas A&M University System Health Science Center. U.S. citizenship or permanent resident status is required.

Financial data The program provides a total of $25,705 each year, including $6,349 for tuition, fees, and health insurance, $1,200 in travel funds, and a stipend of $20,772.

Duration 3 years.

Additional information This program is sponsored by 3 components of the National Institutes of Health: the National Institute of Mental Health, the National Institute on Drug Abuse, and the National Institute of Neurological Disorders and Stroke. The training program covers brain metabolic mapping of behavioral functions, neuropharmacology, electrophysiology, and molecular neurobiology. Trainees are required to complete courses covering the brain and behavior, scientific ethics, experimental design, and statistical analysis.

Number awarded 10 each year.

Deadline Applications may be submitted at any time.

[603]
PREDOCTORAL FELLOWSHIPS IN THE NEUROSCIENCES

American Psychological Association
Attn: Minority Fellowship Program
750 First Street, N.E.
Washington, DC 20002-4242
(202) 336-6127   Fax: (202) 336-6012
TDD: (202) 336-6123   E-mail: mfp@apa.org
Web: www.apa.org/mfp/prprogram.html

Purpose To provide financial assistance to minority and other students who are interested in completing a doctorate in neuroscience.

Eligibility This program is open to all U.S. citizens and permanent residents who are enrolled full time in a Ph.D. program. Applicants must have career goals that are consistent with those of the program: 1) to increase ethnic and racial diversity among neuroscience researchers, with a special emphasis on increasing the numbers of underrepresented ethnic minorities; and 2) to increase numbers of neuroscientists whose work is related to the federal initiative to eliminate health disparities. They must be interested in engaging in predoctoral research training in behavioral neuroscience, cellular neurobiology, cognitive neuroscience, computational neuroscience, developmental neurobiology, membrane biophysics, molecular neurobiology, neuroanatomy, neurobiology of aging, neurobiology of disease, neurochemistry, neurogenetics, neuroimmunology, neuropathology, neuropharmacology, neurophysiology, neurotoxicology, or systems neuroscience. Students identified as underrepresented ethnic minorities in the neurosciences (African Americans, Native Americans, Hispanic Americans, and Pacific Islanders) are especially encouraged to apply. Students working on a doctoral degree with a primarily clinical focus (e.g., M.D. or Psy.D) are not eligible. Selection is based on commitment to a research career in neuroscience, potential demonstrated through accomplishments and goals, fit between career goals and training environment selected, scholarship and grades, and letters of recommendation.

Financial data The stipend is the amount established by the National Institutes of Health for predoctoral students, currently $20,772 per year. The fellowship also provides travel funds to visit universities being considered for graduate training, travel funds to attend the annual meeting of the Society for Neuroscience, and a program of summer training at the Marine Biological Laboratory in Woods Hole, Massachusetts.

Duration 1 year; may be renewed for up to 2 additional years.

Additional information The program was established in 1987. It is funded by the U.S. National Institute of Mental Health of the National Institutes of Health and administered by the American Psychological Association.

Number awarded Varies each year.

Deadline January of each year.

[604]
PREDOCTORAL FELLOWSHIPS OF THE FORD FOUNDATION DIVERSITY FELLOWSHIP PROGRAM

National Research Council
Attn: Fellowship Office, GR 346A
500 Fifth Street, N.W.
Washington, DC 20001
(202) 334-2872   Fax: (202) 334-3419
E-mail: infofell@nas.edu
Web: www7.nationalacademies.org

Purpose To provide funding for predoctoral research to graduate students whose success will increase the racial and ethnic diversity of U.S. colleges and universities.

Eligibility This program is open to citizens and nationals of the United States who are enrolled or planning to enroll full time in a Ph.D. or Sc.D. degree program and are committed to a career in teaching and research at the college or university level. Applicants may be undergraduates in their senior year, individuals who have completed undergraduate study or some graduate study, or current Ph.D. or Sc.D. students who can demonstrate that they can fully utilize a 3-year fellowship award. The following are considered as positive factors in the selection process: evidence of superior academic achievement; promise of continuing achievement as scholars and teachers; membership in a group whose underrepresentation in the American professoriate has been severe and longstanding, including Black/African

Americans, Puerto Ricans, Mexican Americans/Chicanos/Chicanas, Native American Indians, Alaska Natives (Eskimos or Aleuts), and Native Pacific Islanders (Micronesians or Polynesians); capacity to respond in pedagogically productive ways to the learning needs of students from diverse backgrounds; sustained personal engagement with communities that are underrepresented in the academy and an ability to bring this asset to learning, teaching, and scholarship at the college and university level; and likelihood of using the diversity of human experience as an educational resource in teaching and scholarship. Applicants must be working on or planning to work on a degree in the following fields: anthropology, archaeology, art history, astronomy, chemistry, communications, computer science, earth sciences, economics, education, engineering, ethnomusicology, geography, history, international relations, language, life sciences, linguistics, literature, mathematics, performance study, philosophy, physics, political science, psychology, religion, sociology, and urban planning. Awards are not made for such practice-oriented areas as administration and management, audiology, business, educational administration and leadership, filmmaking, fine arts, guidance, home economics, library and information science, nursing, occupational health, performing arts, personnel, physical education, social welfare, social work, or speech pathology. Ineligibility also includes students working on a terminal master's degree; the Ed.D. degree; the degrees of Doctor of Fine Arts (D.F.A.) or Doctor of Psychology (Psy.D.); professional degrees in such areas as medicine, law, and public health; or such joint degrees as M.D./Ph.D., J.D./Ph.D., and M.F.A./Ph.D.

Financial data The program provides a stipend to the student of $17,000 per year and an award to the host institution of $5,000 per year in lieu of tuition and fees.

Duration 3 years of support is provided, to be used within a 5-year period.

Additional information The competition for this program is conducted by the National Research Council on behalf of the Ford Foundation. Applicants who merit receiving the fellowship but to whom awards cannot be made because of insufficient funds are given Honorable Mentions; this recognition does not carry with it a monetary award but honors applicants who have demonstrated substantial academic achievement. The National Research Council publishes a list of those Honorable Mentions who wish their names publicized. Fellows may not accept remuneration from another fellowship or similar external award while on this program; however, supplementation from institutional funds, educational benefits from the Department of Veterans Affairs, or educational incentive funds may be received concurrently with Ford Foundation support. Predoctoral fellows are required to submit an interim progress report 6 months after the start of the fellowship and a final report at the end of the 12 month tenure.

Number awarded Approximately 60 each year.

Deadline November of each year.

[605]
PRESBYTERIAN CHURCH CONTINUING EDUCATION GRANT AND LOAN PROGRAM

Presbyterian Church (USA)
Attn: Office of Financial Aid for Studies
100 Witherspoon Street, Room M-052
Louisville, KY 40202-1396
(502) 569-5735   Toll-free: (888) 728-7228, ext. 5735
Fax: (502) 569-8766   E-mail: LBryan@ctr.pcusa.org
Web: www.pcusa.org

Purpose To provide financial assistance for continuing education, in the form of educational grants and loans, to minority and other professional church workers of the Presbyterian Church (USA) and doctoral candidates who are church members.

Eligibility This program is open to 1) PC(USA) ministers and lay professionals who have served a congregation of 150 or fewer members for at least 3 years; and 2) PC(USA) church members enrolled in a D.Min, Ph.D., or equivalent program in religious studies. Ministers and lay professionals must be planning to attend a program of study that will lead to certification, course work at an accredited institution, or a national event sponsored by PC(USA). The study, course work, or event must be approved by a church session, presbytery, or synod. Events must be at least 3 days in duration. For church members working on a Ph.D. degree, preference is given to women and racial ethnic applicants attending PC(USA) theological institutions, colleges, or universities. U.S. citizenship or permanent resident status is required.

Financial data For ministers and lay professionals, grants for events range from $100 to $500 and grants for study or course work range from $100 to $1,000. For doctoral candidates, grants range from $500 to $1,000. The maximum loan is $2,000 per year.

Duration 1 year. Ministers and lay professionals at small churches are eligible for unlimited renewal of grants. Candidates for a D.Min. degree may renew their grants for a total of 3 years. Candidates for a Ph.D. or equivalent degree may renew their grants for a total of 4 years. Loans may be renewed to a maximum of $6,000.

Number awarded Varies each year.

Deadline November of each year.

[606]
PROCTER & GAMBLE ORAL CARE–HDA FOUNDATION SCHOLARSHIPS

Hispanic Dental Association
Attn: HDA Foundation
188 West Randolph Street, Suite 415
Chicago, IL 60601
(312) 577-4013   Toll-free: (800) 852-7921
Fax: (312) 577-0052
E-mail: HispanicDental@hdassoc.org
Web: www.hdassoc.org

Purpose To provide financial assistance to Hispanic students interested in preparing for a career in a dental profession.

Eligibility This program is open to Hispanics who are entering as first-year students into an accredited dental, dental hygiene, dental assisting, or dental technician program. Applicants must have a GPA of 3.0 or higher. Along with their application, they must submit an essay on their career goals. Selection is based on scholastic achievement, community service, leadership skill, and commitment to improving health in the Hispanic community.

Financial data Stipends are $1,000 or $500.

Duration 1 year.

Additional information This program, which began in 1994, is sponsored by Procter & Gamble Company.

Number awarded Numerous scholarships are awarded each year.

Deadline June of each year for dental students; July of each year for hygiene, assisting, and laboratory technician students.

[607]
PROCTER & GAMBLE SCHOLARSHIP

Franklin Pierce Law Center
Attn: Assistant Dean for Admissions
Two White Street
Concord, NH 03301
(603) 228-9217   E-mail: kmcdonald@piercelaw.edu
Web: www.piercelaw.edu/finan/GambleSchol.htm

Purpose To provide an opportunity for law students, especially women and minorities, to study patent and intellectual property law as a visiting scholar at Franklin Pierce Law Center in Concord, New Hampshire.

Eligibility This program is open to full-time second- and third-year students at law schools in the United States and Canada. Applicants must be interested in a program of study in patent and intellectual property law at the center. They must have sufficient undergraduate scientific and/or technical education to be admitted to the patent bar, including work in biology, biochemistry, botany, electronics technology, engineering (all types, especially civil, computer, and industrial), food technology, general chemistry, marine technology, microbiology, molecular biology, organic chemistry, pharmacology, physics, and textile technology. Their home school must agree to apply a year's credits earned at another school toward the J.D. degree. Preference is given to members of groups underrepresented among lawyers practicing patent law, including women and minorities.

Financial data The stipend is $5,000. Scholars must pay the tuition charged either by the Franklin Pierce Law Center or their home school, whichever is less.

Duration 1 academic year.

Additional information This program is sponsored by the Procter & Gamble Company.

Number awarded 1 each year.

Deadline April of each year.

[608]
PROFESSIONAL DEVELOPMENT FELLOWSHIPS FOR DOCTORAL CANDIDATES IN ART HISTORY

College Art Association of America
Attn: Fellowship Program
275 Seventh Avenue
New York, NY 10001-6798
(212) 691-1051, ext. 248   Fax: (212) 627-2381
E-mail: fellowship@collegeart.org
Web: www.collegeart.org/caa/career/fellowship.html

Purpose To provide financial assistance to doctoral candidates from socially and economically diverse backgrounds who are completing a Ph.D. degree in art history.

Eligibility This program is open to Ph.D. candidates in art history who have been underrepresented in the field because of their race, religion, gender, age, national origin, sexual orientation, disability, or financial status. Applicants must be U.S. citizens or permanent residents and able to demonstrate financial need. They must expect to receive the Ph.D. degree in the year following application.

Financial data The stipend is $5,000.

Duration 1 year: the final year of the degree program.

Additional information In addition to providing a stipend for the terminal year of their degree program, the College Art Association (CAA) helps fellows search for employment at a museum, art center, college, or university. Upon securing a position, CAA provides a $10,000 subsidy to the employer as part of the fellow's salary. Participating organizations must match this 2:1. In addition to administrative and/or teaching responsibilities, all fellows' positions must include a curatorial or public service component. Salary or stipend, position description, and term of employment will vary and are determined in consultation with individual fellows and their potential employers. This program began in 1993. Funding is provided by the Milton & Sally Avery Arts Foundation, Geraldine R. Dodge Foundation, National Endowment for the Arts, National Endowment for the Humanities, and Terra Foundation for the Arts.

Number awarded 1 each year.

Deadline January of each year.

[609]
PROFESSIONAL DEVELOPMENT FELLOWSHIPS FOR MASTER OF FINE ARTS CANDIDATES

College Art Association of America
Attn: Fellowship Program
275 Seventh Avenue
New York, NY 10001-6798
(212) 691-1051, ext. 248   Fax: (212) 627-2381
E-mail: fellowship@collegeart.org
Web: www.collegeart.org/caa/career/fellowship.html

Purpose To provide financial assistance to graduate students from socially and economically diverse backgrounds who are completing an M.F.A. degree in art history.

Eligibility This program is open to M.F.A. candidates in art history who have been underrepresented in the field because of their race, religion, gender, age, national origin, sexual orientation, disability, or financial status. Applicants must be U.S. citizens or permanent residents and able to demonstrate financial need. They must expect to receive the M.F.A. degree in the year following application.

Financial data The stipend is $5,000.

Duration 1 year: the final year of the degree program.

Additional information In addition to providing a stipend for the terminal year of their degree program, the College Art Association (CAA) helps fellows search for employment at a museum, art center, college, or university. Upon securing a position, CAA provides a $10,000 subsidy to the employer as part of the fellow's salary. Participating organizations must match this 2:1. In addition to administrative and/or teaching responsibilities, all fellows' positions must include a curatorial or public service component. Salary or stipend, position description, and term of employment will vary and are determined in consultation with individual fellows and their potential employers. This program began in 1993. Funding is provided by the Milton & Sally Avery Arts Foundation, Geraldine R. Dodge Foundation, National Endowment for the Arts, National Endowment for the Humanities, and Terra Foundation for the Arts.

Number awarded 1 each year.

Deadline January of each year.

[610]
PROGRAM FOR MINORITY RESEARCH TRAINING IN PSYCHIATRY

American Psychiatric Association
Attn: American Psychiatric Institute for Research and
    Education
1000 Wilson Boulevard, Suite 1825
Arlington, VA 22209-3901
(703) 907-8622   Toll-free: (800) 852-1390
Fax: (703) 907-1085   E-mail: eguerra@psych.org
Web: www.psych.org

Purpose To provide financial assistance to underrepresented minority medical students and residents interested in psychiatric research training.

Eligibility This program is open to underrepresented minorities (American Indians, Blacks/African Americans, Hispanics, and Pacific Islanders) at 3 levels: medical students, residents, and graduates of residency programs. All candidates must be interested in training at research-intensive departments of psychiatry in major U.S. medical schools. Training sites with excellent research facilities and resources, funded research record, research faculty (including minority researchers), and training history are preferred.

Financial data Annual stipends are $19,968 for medical students, from $44,364 to $46.404 for residents, and up to $50,808 for post-residency fellows. Other benefits include travel funds to attend the annual meeting of the American Psychiatric Association (APA) or the American College of Neuropsychopharmacology and limited tuition assistance for full-time trainees to attend specific courses that are required as part of their training.

Duration Medical students can receive support 2 to 6 months or as a summer experience. Residents may engage in full-year research training during the last year of psychiatric residency or in "year off" research training. Graduates of residency programs can undertake full-time research training for 2 years, although a third year is possible if appropriate to a trainee's career development.

Additional information This program is funded by the National Institute of Mental Health and administered by the APA's American Psychiatric Institute for Research and Education.

Number awarded Varies each year.

Deadline Medical students and residents seeking less than 1 year of training may apply at any time, but applications must be received at least 3 months before the proposed training is to begin; medical students seeking summer training should apply by March of each year; residents seeking a year or more of training and post-residency fellows should apply by November of each year.

[611]
PUBLIC POLICY AND INTERNATIONAL AFFAIRS FELLOWSHIPS

Public Policy and International Affairs Fellowship
    Program
c/o Association for Public Policy Analysis and
    Management
2100 M Street, N.W., Suite 610
P.O. Box 18766
Washington, DC 20037
(202) 496-0130   Fax: (202) 496-0134
E-mail: ppia@ppiaprogram.org
Web: www.ppiaprogram.org/programs/eligibility.php

Purpose To provide financial assistance to minority undergraduate students who are interested in preparing for graduate study in the fields of public policy and/or international affairs.

Eligibility This program is open to people of color historically underrepresented in public policy and international affairs, including African Americans, Asian Americans, Pacific Islanders, Hispanic Americans, Alaska Natives, and Native Americans. In most cases, most persons enter the program when they apply to participate in a summer institute following the junior year of college. Applicants must be U.S. citizens or permanent residents interested in a summer institute in public policy and international affairs. They must first apply directly to the summer institute. Following participation in that institute, they apply for graduate study in fields of their choice at more than 30 designated universities. For a list of participating institutions, contact the sponsor.

Financial data During the summer institute portion of the program, participants receive transportation to and from the institute site, room and board, and a $1,000 stipend. More than 30 graduate programs in public policy and/or international affairs have agreed to waive application fees and grant fellowships of at least $5,000 to students who have participated in the summer institutes.

Duration 1 summer and 1 academic year.

Additional information This program was established in 1981 when the Alfred P. Sloan Foundation provided a grant to the Association for Public Policy Analysis and Management (APPAM). From 1981 through 1988, participants were known as Sloan Fellows. From 1989 through 1995, the program was supported by the Ford Foundation and administered by the Woodrow Wilson National Fellowship Administration, so participants were known as Woodrow Wilson Fellows in Public Policy and International Affairs. Beginning in 1995, the program's name was shortened to the Public Policy and International Affairs Fellowship Program (PPIA) and its administration was moved to the Academy for Educational Development. To complement APPAM's role, the Association of Professional Schools of International Affairs (APSIA) also became an institutional sponsor. In 1999, the Ford Foundation ended its support for PPIA effective with the student cohort that participated in summer institutes in 1999. The APPAM and APSIA incorporated PPIA as an independent organization and operated the summer institutes in 2000. In 2001, the National Association of Schools of Public Affairs and Administration (NASPAA) also became a sponsor of PPIA. Beginning in summer of that year, summer institutes have been held at 4 universities: the Summer Program in Public Policy and International Affairs at the Gerald

R. Ford School of Public Policy at the University of Michigan, the Maryland Leadership Institute at the School of Public Affairs at the University of Maryland, the UCPPIA Summer Institute at the Richard & Rhoda Goldman School of Public Policy at the University of California at Berkeley, and the Junior Summer Institute at the Woodrow Wilson School of Public and International Affairs at Princeton University. For information on those institutes, contact the respective school.

Number awarded Varies each year.

[612]
PUERTO RICAN BAR ASSOCIATION SCHOLARSHIP AWARD

Puerto Rican Legal Defense and Education Fund
Attn: Education Division
99 Hudson Street, 14th Floor
New York, NY 10013-2815
(212) 739-7497   Toll-free: (800) 328-2322
Fax: (212) 431-4276   E-mail: sonji_patrick@prldef.org
Web: www.prldef.org/Scholarship.htm

Purpose To provide financial assistance to Puerto Rican and other Latino law students interested in public interest work.

Eligibility This program is open to Puerto Rican and other Latino students planning to enroll or currently enrolled in law school. Applicants may be first- or second-year students or third-year evening students. They must submit a personal essay discussing their career goals, school and community activities, and any activities demonstrating their commitment to public interest work. Candidates for an LL.M. degree are not eligible. Selection is based on financial need and academic promise.

Financial data The stipend is $2,000 per year.

Duration 1 year.

Additional information The Puerto Rican Legal Defense and Education Fund provides the candidates for selection by the Puerto Rican Bar Association, located in New York City.

Number awarded 1 or more each year.

Deadline February of each year.

[613]
PUGET SOUND CHAPTER HELENE M. OVERLY MEMORIAL SCHOLARSHIP

Women's Transportation Seminar-Puget Sound Chapter
c/o Lorelei Mesic, Scholarship Co-Chair
W&H Pacific
3350 Monte Villa Parkway
Bothell, WA 98021-8972
(425) 951-4872   Fax: (425) 951-4808
E-mail: lmesic@whpacific.com
Web: www.wtspugetsound.org/nscholarships.html

Purpose To provide financial assistance to women graduate students, particularly minority women, from Washington who are working on a degree related to transportation.

Eligibility This program is open to women who are residents of Washington, studying at a college in the state, or working as an intern in the state. Applicants must be currently enrolled in a graduate degree program in a transportation-related field, such as engineering, planning, finance,

or logistics. They must have a GPA of 3.0 or higher and plans to prepare for a career in a transportation-related field. Minority candidates are encouraged to apply. Along with their application, they must submit a 750-word statement about their career goals after graduation and why they think they should receive this scholarship award. Selection is based on that statement, academic record, and transportation-related activities or job skills. Financial need is not considered.

Financial data The stipend is $1,700.

Duration 1 year.

Additional information The winner is also nominated for scholarships offered by the national organization of the Women's Transportation Seminar.

Number awarded 1 each year.

Deadline October of each year.

[614]
RACIAL ETHNIC SUPPLEMENTAL GRANTS

Presbyterian Church (USA)
Attn: Office of Financial Aid for Studies
100 Witherspoon Street, Room M-052
Louisville, KY 40202-1396
(502) 569-5735   Toll-free: (888) 728-7228, ext. 5735
Fax: (502) 569-8766   E-mail: LBryan@ctr.pcusa.org
Web: www.pcusa.org

Purpose To provide financial assistance to minority graduate students who are Presbyterian Church (USA) members interested in preparing for church occupations.

Eligibility This program is open to racial/ethnic graduate students (Asian American, African American, Hispanic American, Native American, or Alaska Native) who are enrolled full time at a PC(USA) seminary or accredited theological institution approved by their Committee on Preparation for Ministry. Applicants must be working on 1) an M.Div. degree and enrolled as an inquirer or candidate by a PC(USA) presbytery, or 2) an M.A.C.E. degree and preparing for a church occupation. They must be PC(USA) members, U.S. citizens or permanent residents, able to demonstrate financial need, and recommended by the financial aid officer at their theological institution.

Financial data Stipends range from $500 to $1,000 per year. Funds are intended as supplements to students who have been awarded a Presbyterian Study Grant but still demonstrate remaining financial need.

Duration 1 year; may be renewed up to 2 additional years.

Number awarded Varies each year.

Deadline September of each year.

[615]
RACIAL ETHNIC THEOLOGICAL EDUCATION SCHOLARSHIP FUND

Synod of Southern California and Hawaii
Attn: Racial Ethnic Pastoral Leadership Work Group
1501 Wilshire Boulevard
Los Angeles, CA 90017-2205
(213) 483-3840, ext. 255   Fax: (213) 483-4275
E-mail: LeonFanniel@synod.org
Web: www.synod.org/REPL/schol.html

Purpose To provide financial assistance to members of racial minority groups in the Presbyterian Church (USA) Synod of Southern California and Hawaii who are preparing for a career as a pastor or other church vocation.

Eligibility Applicants must be under care of a presbytery within the Synod of Southern California and Hawaii. They must be members of racial ethnic groups interested in becoming a Presbyterian pastor or other church worker (e.g., commissioned lay pastor, certified Christian educator) and serving in a racial ethnic ministry within the PC(USA). Racial ethnic persons who already have an M.Div. degree and are from another denomination in correspondence with the PC(USA) and are seeking to meet PC(USA) requirements for ordination or transfer may also be eligible if they plan to serve in a racial ethnic congregation or an approved specialized ministry. Applicants must submit documentation of financial need, recommendations from the appropriate presbytery committee or session, a current transcript, and essays on their goals and objectives.

Financial data The stipend is $2,000 per year.

Duration 1 year; may be renewed.

Additional information These scholarships were first awarded in 1984.

Number awarded Varies each year.

Deadline April of each year.

[616]
RALPH W. SHRADER DIVERSITY SCHOLARSHIPS

Armed Forces Communications and Electronics
    Association
Attn: AFCEA Educational Foundation
4400 Fair Lakes Court
Fairfax, VA 22033-3899
(703) 631-6149   Toll-free: (800) 336-4583, ext. 6149
Fax: (703) 631-4693   E-mail: scholarship@afcea.org
Web: www.afcea.org

Purpose To provide financial assistance to master's degree students in fields related to communications and electronics.

Eligibility This program is open to students working on a master's degree who are U.S. citizens attending an accredited college or university in the United States. Applicants must be enrolled full time and studying electronics, engineering (aerospace, chemical, electrical, computer, communications, or systems), physics, communications technology, mathematics, computer science or technology, or information management systems. At least 1 of these scholarships is set aside for a woman or a minority.

Financial data The stipend is $3,000. Funds are paid directly to the recipient.

Duration 1 year.

Number awarded 5 each year, at least 1 of which is for a woman or minority candidate.

Deadline January of each year.

[617]
RDW GROUP, INC. MINORITY SCHOLARSHIP FOR COMMUNICATIONS

Rhode Island Foundation
Attn: Scholarship Coordinator
One Union Station
Providence, RI 02903
(401) 274-4564   Fax: (401) 751-7983
E-mail: libbym@rifoundation.org
Web: www.rifoundation.org

Purpose To provide financial assistance to Rhode Island students of color interested in preparing for a career in communications.

Eligibility This program is open to minority undergraduate and graduate students who are Rhode Island residents. Applicants must intend to major in communications (including computer graphics, art, cinematography, or other fields that would prepare them for a career in advertising). They must be able to demonstrate financial need and a commitment to a career in communications. Along with their application, they must submit an essay (up to 300 words) on the impact they would like to have on the communications field.

Financial data The stipend is $2,000.

Duration 1 year; nonrenewable.

Additional information This program is sponsored by the RDW Group, Inc.

Number awarded 1 each year.

Deadline April of each year.

[618]
REFORMA SCHOLARSHIP

REFORMA (National Association to Promote Library
    Services to the Spanish Speaking)
P.O. Box 25963
Scottsdale, AZ 85255-0116
(480) 471-7452   Fax: (480) 471-7442
E-mail: REFORMAoffice@riosbalderrama.com
Web: www.reforma.org/schinfo.html

Purpose To encourage and enable qualified Spanish-speaking students to prepare for a career in library or information science.

Eligibility The program is open to citizens and permanent residents of the United States who are Spanish-speaking college seniors. While eligibility is not restricted by age, sex, creed, national origin, or minority group/association membership, it is required that those who apply have a definite interest in service to the Spanish-speaking. Applicants must show evidence of commitment to a career in librarianship and the potential for high academic achievement. They should be able to demonstrate an understanding of, aptitude for, and desire to serve the Spanish-speaking community. Applicants are also judged on the basis of character and leadership potential.

Financial data The stipend is at least $1,500.

Duration 1 year.

Additional information The scholarship must be used within the academic year following notification of the award.

The recipient must enter an accredited M.L.S. or Ph.D. degree program.

Number awarded Varies each year; recently, 5 were awarded.

Deadline March of each year.

[619]
RENE MATOS SCHOLARSHIP

National Hispanic Coalition of Federal Aviation
    Employees
Attn: Scholarship Selection Committee
P.O. Box 735
Pomona, NJ 08240
(609) 485-6910   E-mail: president@nhcfae.org
Web: www.nhcfae.com/scholarship.htm

Purpose To provide financial assistance to minority and women students who are working on an undergraduate or graduate degree.

Eligibility This program is open to minority and women students who are accepted to or attending an accredited college, university, or vocational/trade school. Applicants may be graduating high school seniors, current undergraduates, or graduate students. Selection is based on academic achievement, community involvement, financial need, honors and awards, leadership, personal qualities and strengths, and student activities.

Financial data A stipend is awarded (amount not specified).

Duration 1 year; may be renewed.

Additional information The National Hispanic Coalition of Federal Aviation Employees, established in 1978, is a nonprofit organization comprised mainly of Hispanics who are employed at the Federal Aviation Administration. Requests for applications must be accompanied by a self-addressed stamped envelope. Phone calls and faxed applications are not accepted.

Number awarded 1 or more each year.

Deadline April of each year.

[620]
RESEARCH AND TRAINING FELLOWSHIPS IN EPILEPSY FOR CLINICIANS

Epilepsy Foundation
Attn: Research Department
4351 Garden City Drive
Landover, MD 20785-7223
(301) 459-3700   Toll-free: (800) EFA-1000
Fax: (301) 577-2684   TDD: (800) 332-2070
E-mail: clinical_postdocs@efa.org
Web: www.epilepsyfoundation.org

Purpose To provide funding to minority and other clinically trained professionals interested in gaining additional training in order to develop an epilepsy research program.

Eligibility Applicants must have an M.D., D.O., Ph.D., D.S., or equivalent degree and be a clinical or postdoctoral fellow at a university, medical school, or other appropriate research institution. Holders of other doctoral-level degrees (e.g., Pharm.D., D.S.N.) may also be eligible. Candidates must be interested in a program of research training that may include mechanisms of epilepsy, novel therapeutic approaches, clinical trials, development of new technolo-

gies, or behavioral and psychosocial impact of epilepsy. The training program may consist of both didactic training and a supervised research experience that is designed to develop the necessary knowledge and skills in the chosen area of research and foster the career goals of the candidate. Academic faculty holding the rank of instructor or higher are not eligible, nor are graduate or medical students, medical residents, permanent government employees, or employees of private industry. Applications from women, members of minority groups, and people with disabilities are especially encouraged. Selection is based on the quality of the proposed research training program, the applicant's qualifications, the preceptor's qualifications, and the adequacy of clinical training, research facilities, and other epilepsy-related programs at the institution.

Financial data The grant is $40,000. No indirect costs are provided.

Duration 1 year.

Additional information Support for this program is provided by many individuals, families, and corporations, especially the American Epilepsy Society, Abbott Laboratories, Ortho-McNeil Pharmaceutical, and Pfizer Inc. Grantees are expected to spend at least 50% of their time dedicated to research training and conducting research.

Number awarded Varies each year; recently, 5 of these fellowships were awarded.

Deadline October of each year.

[621]
RICHARD AND HELEN BROWN COREM SCHOLARSHIPS

United Church of Christ
Parish Life and Leadership Ministry Team
Attn: Minister for Grants, Scholarships, and Resources
700 Prospect Avenue East
Cleveland, OH 44115-1100
(216) 736-3839   Fax: (216) 736-3783
E-mail: jeffersv@ucc.org
Web: www.ucc.org/education/scholarships

Purpose To provide financial assistance to minority seminary students who are interested in becoming a pastor in the United Church of Christ (UCC).

Eligibility This program is open to students at accredited seminaries who have been members of a UCC congregation for at least 1 year. Applicants must work through 1 of the member bodies of the Council for Racial and Ethnic Ministries (COREM): United Black Christians (UBC), Council of Hispanic Ministries (CHM), Pacific Islander and Asian American Ministries (PAAM), or Council for American Indian Ministries (CAIM). They must 1) have a GPA of 3.0 or higher, 2) be enrolled in a course of study leading to ordained ministry, 3) be in care of an association or conference at the time of application, and 4) demonstrate leadership ability through participation in their local church, association, conference, or academic environment.

Financial data Stipends are approximately $10,000 per year.

Duration 1 year.

Additional information Information on the UBC is available from the Minister for African American Relations, (216) 736-2189. Information on the CHM is available from the Minister for Hispanic Relations, (216) 736-2193. Information on the PAAM is available from the Minister for Pacific Islander and Asian American Relations, (216) 736-2195. Information on the CAIM is available from the Minister for Native American Relations, (216) 736-2194.

Number awarded   Varies each year; recently, 5 scholarships were awarded by UBC, 5 by CHM, 3 by PAAM, and 1 by CAIM.

[622]
RICHARD D. HAILEY LAW STUDENT SCHOLARSHIPS

Association of Trial Lawyers of America
Attn: Minority Caucus
1050 31st Street, N.W.
Washington, DC 20007
(202) 944-2827   Toll-free: (800) 424-2725
Fax: (202) 298-6849   E-mail: info@astlahq.org
Web: www.atla.org/members/lawstud/Hailey.aspx

Purpose   To provide financial assistance for law school to minority student members of the Association of Trial Lawyers of America (ATLA).

Eligibility   This program is open to African American, Hispanic, Asian American, Native American, and biracial members of the association who are enrolled in the first or second year of law school. Selection is based on commitment to the association, involvement in student chapter activities, desire to represent victims, interest and proficiency of skills in trial advocacy, and financial need. Applicants must submit a 500-word essay on how they meet those criteria and 3 letters of recommendation.

Financial data   The stipend is $1,000.

Duration   1 year.

Number awarded   Up to 6 each year.

Deadline   May of each year.

[623]
RISK AND DEVELOPMENT FIELD RESEARCH GRANTS

Social Science Research Council
Attn: Program in Applied Economics
810 Seventh Avenue
New York, NY 10019
(212) 377-2700   Fax: (212) 377-2727
E-mail: pae@ssrc.org
Web: www.ssrc.org/pae

Purpose   To provide funding to minority and other doctoral students and postdoctoral scholars interested in conducting research on risk and uncertainty in economics.

Eligibility   This program is open to 1) full-time graduate students enrolled in economics and related Ph.D. programs (e.g., development studies or agricultural economics) at U.S. universities; and 2) scholars who have completed a Ph.D. in economics and related fields within the past 5 years and have a current position at a U.S. academic or nonprofit research institution. There are no citizenship, nationality, or (for graduate students) residency requirements. Applicants must be interested in conducting field research into questions of risk and uncertainty in the context of developing economies. Preference is given to proposals that include interdisciplinary and novel approaches, with an aim to create a better understanding of the way that individuals,

institutions, and policymakers perceive and respond to situations of risk and uncertainty. Minorities and women are particularly encouraged to apply.

Financial data   The stipend is $5,000 for graduate students or $15,000 for postdoctoral scholars. Funds must be used for field research, not general support or dissertation write-up.

Duration   1 year.

Additional information   This program, established in 1997 as the Program in Applied Economics, is administered by the Social Science Research Council with funds provided by the John D. and Catherine T. MacArthur Foundation.

Number awarded   Varies each year; recently, 17 graduate student and 4 postdoctoral fellowships were awarded.

Deadline   January of each year.

[624]
ROBERT AND MARTHA ATHERTON SCHOLARSHIP

Unitarian Universalist Association
Attn: Office of Ministerial Credentialing
25 Beacon Street
Boston, MA 02108-2800
(617) 948-6403   Fax: (617) 742-2875
E-mail: cmay@uua.org
Web: www.uua.org/awards/me.html

Purpose   To provide financial assistance to underrepresented minority and other seminary students preparing for the Unitarian Universalist (UU) ministry.

Eligibility   This program is open to second- or third-year seminary students currently enrolled full time in a UU ministerial training program with Candidate status. First priority is given to Meadville-Lombard students. Preference is also given to 1) African American, Hispanic, and Native American students, and 2) foreign students who intend to spread the faith in their native countries. Applicants must have proven their ability and dedication to the UU faith and to helping mankind.

Financial data   The stipend is at least $2,500 per year.

Duration   1 year.

Number awarded   2 each year.

Deadline   April of each year.

[625]
ROBERT TOIGO FOUNDATION FELLOWSHIPS

Robert Toigo Foundation
Attn: Fellowship Program Administrator
1230 Preservation Park Way
Oakland, CA 94612
(510) 763-5771   Fax: (510) 763-5778
E-mail: info@toigofoundation.org
Web: www.toigofoundation.org

Purpose   To provide financial assistance to minority students working on a master's degree in business administration or related field.

Eligibility   This program is open to members of minority groups (of African American, Hispanic, Native American/Alaskan Native, or Asian/Pacific Islander descent) who have been accepted to an M.B.A. program as a full-time student. Applicants must be preparing for a career in finance, including (but not limited to) investment management, investment banking, corporate finance, real estate, private equity, venture capital, sales and trading, research, or financial services consulting.

Financial data The stipend is $5,000 per year.

Duration 2 years.

Number awarded Approximately 50 each year.

Deadline February of each year.

[626]
RUTH L. KIRSCHSTEIN NRSA PROGRAM FOR NIGMS MARC PREDOCTORAL FELLOWSHIPS

National Institute of General Medical Sciences
Attn: Division of Minority Opportunities in Research
45 Center Drive, Suite 2AS37
Bethesda, MD 20892-6200
(301) 594-3900   Fax: (301) 480-2753
E-mail: at21z@nih.gov
Web: www.nih.gov/nigms

Purpose To provide financial assistance to minority doctoral students who are interested in preparing for a research career in the biomedical sciences.

Eligibility This program is open to students from minority groups underrepresented in the behavioral and biomedical sciences who are currently enrolled in a Ph.D. or equivalent research degree program, a combined M.D./Ph.D. program, or other combined professional and Ph.D. degree program in the behavioral or biomedical sciences, including mathematics. Support is not available to individuals enrolled in medical or other professional schools unless they are working on a degree combined with a Ph.D. Applicants must have graduated from an undergraduate program supported by the Minority Access to Research Careers (MARC) Branch of the National Institute of General Medical Sciences (NIGMS). Only U.S. citizens, nationals, and permanent residents are eligible.

Financial data The fellowships provide a stipend of $20,772 per year and a supplement that offsets the cost of tuition, fees, and health insurance at a rate of 100% up to $3,000 and 60% of costs above $3,000. An institutional allowance of $2,750 per year is also provided.

Duration Up to 5 years.

Additional information This program is part of the National Research Service Award program of the National Institutes of Health (NIH), named in honor of Ruth L. Kirschstein in 2002.

Deadline April or December of each year.

[627]
SABBATICALS FOR LONG-TIME ACTIVISTS OF COLOR

Alston/Bannerman Fellowship Program
1627 Lancaster Street
Baltimore, MD 21231
(410) 327-6220   Fax: (501) 421-5862
E-mail: info@AlstonBannerman.org
Web: www.AlstonBannerman.org

Purpose To finance a sabbatical for people of color who have been community activists for at least 10 years.

Eligibility This program is open to persons of color (people of African, Latino, Asian, Pacific Islander, Native American, or Arab descent) who are U.S. residents and have at least 10 years of experience as community activists. Appli-

cants must be committed to continuing to work for social change. Preference is given to applicants whose work attacks root causes of injustice by organizing those affected to take collective action; challenges the systems that perpetrate injustice and effects institutional change; builds their community's capacity for self-determination and develops grassroots leadership; acknowledges the cultural values of the community; creates accountable participatory structures in which community members have decision-making power; and contributes to building a movement for social change by making connections between issues, developing alliances with other constituencies, and collaborating with other organizations. Individuals are ineligible if they only provide services (such as substance abuse counseling, after-school programs, HIV-AIDS outreach, or shelter for the homeless) or if they advocate on behalf of a community without directly involving the members of that community in asserting their own interests and choosing their own leadership. An equal number of men and women are selected.

Financial data The stipend is $15,000.

Duration The sabbaticals are to be 3 months or longer.

Additional information Fellows are encouraged to use their sabbaticals to engage in activities that are substantially different from their normal routine. Activities during the sabbatical must strengthen the recipient's ability to contribute to social change in the future. This program was established in 1987 as the Bannerman Fellowship Program. Its name was changed in 2002. Sabbaticals must be taken within 1 year of receipt of the award. Fellows must submit a report on their sabbatical.

Number awarded At least 10 each year. Since 1988, more than 140 fellowships have been awarded.

Deadline November of each year.

[628]
SACNAS GENOME SCHOLARS PROGRAM

Society for Advancement of Chicanos and Native
   Americans in Science
333 Front Street, Suite 104
P.O. Box 8526
Santa Cruz, CA 95061-8526
(831) 459-0170   Fax: (831) 459-0194
E-mail: info@sacnas.org
Web: www.sacnas.org/genomicopportunity.html

Purpose To provide financial assistance for graduate study in genomics or bioinformatics.

Eligibility This program is open to Chicano/Latino and Native American senior undergraduate students who are members of the sponsoring organization and have accepted an offer to enter graduate school or demonstrate a commitment to enter graduate school. Applicants must be planning to work on a research degree (M.S. or Ph.D.) in genomics or bioinformatics. Selection is based on GRE scores, education and work experience, planned graduate program references, proposed plan of research, and academic record.

Financial data The stipend is $25,000.

Duration 1 year; nonrenewable.

Additional information Scholars must present research at the sponsor's annual conference.

Number awarded 1 or more each year.

Deadline January of each year.

[629]
SCHOLARSHIPS FOR MINORITY ACCOUNTING STUDENTS

American Institute of Certified Public Accountants
Attn: Academic and Career Development Division
1211 Avenue of the Americas
New York, NY 10036-8775
(212) 596-6223   Fax: (212) 596-6292
E-mail: educat@aicpa.org
Web: www.aicpa.org

Purpose To provide financial assistance to underrepresented minorities interested in studying accounting at the undergraduate or graduate school level.

Eligibility Undergraduate applicants must be minority students who are enrolled full time, have completed at least 30 semester hours of college work (including at least 6 semester hours in accounting), be majoring in accounting with an overall GPA of 3.3 or higher, and be U.S. citizens or permanent residents. Minority students who are interested in a graduate degree must be 1) in the final year of a 5-year accounting program; 2) an undergraduate accounting major currently accepted or enrolled in a master's-level accounting, business administration, finance, or taxation program; or 3) any undergraduate major currently accepted in a master's-level accounting program. Selection is based primarily on merit (academic and personal achievement); financial need is evaluated as a secondary criteria. For purposes of this program, the American Institute of Certified Public Accountants (AICPA) considers minority students to be those of Black, Native American/Alaskan Native, Pacific Island, or Hispanic ethnic origin.

Financial data The maximum stipend is $5,000 per year.

Duration 1 year; may be renewed, if recipients are making satisfactory progress toward graduation.

Additional information These scholarships are granted by the institute's Minority Educational Initiatives Committee.

Number awarded Varies each year; recently, 157 students received funding through this program.

Deadline May of each year.

[630]
SCIENCE TEACHER PREPARATION PROGRAM

Alabama Alliance for Science, Engineering,
    Mathematics, and Science Education
Attn: Project Director
University of Alabama at Birmingham
Campbell Hall, Room 401
1300 University Boulevard
Birmingham, AL 35294-1170
(205) 934-8762   Fax: (205) 934-1650
E-mail: LDale@uab.edu
Web: www.uab.edu/istp/alabama.html

Purpose To provide financial assistance to underrepresented minority students at designated institutions in Alabama who are interested in preparing for a career as a science teacher.

Eligibility This program is open to members of underrepresented minority groups who have been unconditionally admitted to a participating Alabama college or university. Applicants may 1) be entering freshmen or junior college transfer students who intend to major in science education and become certified to teach in elementary, middle, or high

school; 2) have earned a degree in mathematics, science, or education and are seeking to become certified to teach; or 3) have earned a degree in mathematics, science, or education and are enrolled in a fifth-year education program leading to a master's degree and certification.

Financial data The stipend is $1,000 per year.

Duration 1 year; may be renewed.

Additional information Support for this program is provided by the National Science Foundation. The participating institutions are Alabama A&M University, Alabama State University, Auburn University, Miles College, Stillman College, Talladega College, Tuskegee University, University of Alabama at Birmingham, and University of Alabama in Huntsville.

Number awarded Varies each year.

[631]
SELECTED PROFESSIONS FELLOWSHIPS FOR WOMEN OF COLOR

American Association of University Women
Attn: AAUW Educational Foundation
301 ACT Drive, Department 177
P.O. Box 4030
Iowa City, IA 52243-4030
(319) 337-1716   Fax: (319) 337-1204
E-mail: aauw@act.org
Web: www.aauw.org

Purpose To aid women of color who are in their final year of graduate training in the fields of business administration, law, or medicine.

Eligibility This program is open to women of color who are entering their final year of graduate study in these historically underrepresented fields: business administration (M.B.A., E.M.B.A.), law (J.D.), and medicine (M.D., D.O.). Women in medical programs may apply for either their third or final year of study. U.S. citizenship or permanent resident status is required. Special consideration is given to applicants who demonstrate professional promise in innovative or neglected areas of research and/or practice in public interest concerns.

Financial data Stipends range from $5,000 to $12,000 for the academic year.

Duration 1 academic year, beginning in September.

Deadline January of each year.

[632]
SEMICONDUCTOR RESEARCH CORPORATION MASTER'S SCHOLARSHIP PROGRAM

Semiconductor Research Corporation
Attn: Graduate Fellowship Program
Brighton Hall, Suite 120
1101 Slater Road
P.O. Box 12053
Research Triangle Park, NC 27709-2053
(919) 941-9400   Fax: (919) 941-9450
E-mail: students@src.org
Web: www.src.org/member/about/aboutmas.asp

Purpose To provide financial assistance to minorities and women interested in working on a master's degree in a field of microelectronics relevant to the interests of the Semiconductor Research Corporation (SRC).

Eligibility This program is open to women and members of underrepresented minority groups (African Americans, Hispanics, and Native Americans). Applicants must be U.S. or Canadian citizens or permanent residents admitted to an SRC participating university to pursue a master's degree in a field relevant to microelectronics under the guidance of an SRC-sponsored faculty member and under an SRC-funded contract.

Financial data The fellowship provides full tuition and fee support, a monthly stipend of $1,900, an annual grant of $2,000 to the university department with which the student recipient is associated, and travel expenses to the Graduate Fellowship Program Annual Conference.

Duration Up to 2 years.

Additional information This program was established in 1997 for underrepresented minorities and expanded to include women in 1999.

Number awarded Varies each year; recently 14 new scholars were appointed to this program.

Deadline January of each year.

[633]
SHERRY R. ARNSTEIN MINORITY STUDENT SCHOLARSHIP

American Association of Colleges of Osteopathic Medicine
Attn: Communications and Member Services
5550 Friendship Boulevard, Suite 310
Chevy Chase, MD 20815-7231
(301) 968-4174   Fax: (301) 968-4101
Web: www.aacom.org

Purpose To provide financial assistance to underrepresented minority students already enrolled in osteopathic medical school.

Eligibility This program is open to Black, Hispanic, and Native American students currently enrolled in good standing in their first, second, or third year of osteopathic medical school. Applicants must submit a 750-word essay on what osteopathic medical schools can do to recruit and retain more underrepresented minority students, what they personally plan to do as a student and as a future D.O. to help increase minority student enrollment at a college of osteopathic medicine, and how and why they were drawn to osteopathic medicine.

Financial data Stipends up to $1,000 are available.

Duration 1 year; nonrenewable.

Deadline April of each year.

[634]
SHERRY R. ARNSTEIN NEW STUDENT MINORITY SCHOLARSHIP

American Association of Colleges of Osteopathic Medicine
Attn: Communications and Member Services
5550 Friendship Boulevard, Suite 310
Chevy Chase, MD 20815-7231
(301) 968-4174   Fax: (301) 968-4101
Web: www.aacom.org

Purpose To provide financial assistance to underrepresented minority students planning to enroll at an osteopathic medical school.

Eligibility This program is open to Black, Hispanic, and Native American students who have been accepted and are planning to enroll at any of the 20 colleges of osteopathic medicine that are members of the American Association of Colleges of Osteopathic Medicine (AACOM). Applicants must submit a 750-word essay on what osteopathic medical schools can and should do to recruit and retain more underrepresented minority students and how and why they were drawn to osteopathic medicine.

Financial data Stipends up to $1,000 are available.

Duration 1 year; nonrenewable.

Deadline April of each year.

[635]
SIDNEY B. WILLIAMS, JR. INTELLECTUAL PROPERTY LAW SCHOOL SCHOLARSHIPS

American Intellectual Property Law Association
Attn: American Intellectual Property Law Education Foundation
485 Kinderkamack Road
Oradell, NY 07649
(201) 634-1870   Fax: (201) 634-1871
E-mail: admin@aiplef.org
Web: www.aiplef.org/scholarships/sidney_b_williams

Purpose To provide financial assistance to minority law school students who are interested in preparing for a career in intellectual property law.

Eligibility This program is open to members of minority groups currently enrolled in or accepted to an ABA-accredited law school. Applicants must be U.S. citizens with a demonstrated intent to engage in the full-time practice of intellectual property law. Along with their application, they must submit a 250-word essay on how this scholarship will make a difference to them in meeting their goal of engaging in the full-time practice of intellectual property law and why they intend to do so. Selection is based on 1) demonstrated commitment to developing a career in intellectual property law; 2) academic performance at the undergraduate, graduate, and law school levels (as applicable); 3) general factors, such as leadership skills, community activities, or special accomplishments; and 4) financial need.

Financial data The stipend is $10,000 per year. Funds may be used for tuition, fees, books, supplies, room, board, and a patent bar review course.

Duration 1 year; may be renewed if the recipient maintains a GPA of 2.0 or higher.

Additional information This program, which began in 2002, is administered by the Thurgood Marshall Scholarship Fund, 90 William Street, Suite 1203, New York, NY 10038, (212) 573-8888, Fax: (212) 573-8497, E-mail: pallen@tmsf.org Additional funding is provided by the American Intellectual Property Law Association, the American Bar Association's Section of Intellectual Property Law, and the Minority Corporate Counsel Association. The first class of recipients included a Chinese American, an Asian Pacific American, Mexican Americans, and African Americans. Recipients are required to join and maintain membership in the American Intellectual Property Law Association.

Number awarded Varies each year; recently, 9 of these scholarships were awarded.

Deadline February of each year.

[636]

SLA AFFIRMATIVE ACTION SCHOLARSHIP

Special Libraries Association
Attn: Scholarships
331 South Patrick Street
Alexandria, VA 22314-3501
(703 647-4900   Fax: (703) 647-4901
E-mail: sla@sla.org
Web: www.sla.org

Purpose To provide financial assistance to minority group members who are interested in preparing for a career in the fields of library or information science in the United States or Canada.

Eligibility To be eligible, applicants must be U.S. citizens or permanent residents; members of a racial minority group (Black, Hispanic, Asian, Pacific Islander, American Indian, or Alaskan Native); enrolled or accepted for enrollment in a recognized school of library or information science; and in financial need. Preference is given to members of the Special Libraries Association and to persons who have worked in and for special libraries.

Financial data The stipend is $6,000.

Duration 3 quarters or 2 semesters.

Number awarded 1 each year.

Deadline October of each year.

[637]

SLOAN MINORITY PH.D. PROGRAM

National Action Council for Minorities in Engineering
350 Fifth Avenue, Suite 2212
New York, NY 10118-2299
(212) 279-2626   Fax: (212) 629-5178
E-mail: dwalden_sloanphd@nacme.org
Web: www.nacme.org/sloan

Purpose To provide financial assistance to underrepresented minority students interested in working on a Ph.D. in mathematics, science, or engineering.

Eligibility This program is open to African Americans, Hispanic Americans, and Native Americans who are U.S. citizens or permanent residents. Applicants must be interested in pursuing a Ph.D. degree in 1 of the following fields: aeronautics and astronautics engineering, animal sciences, applied mathematics, biochemistry, bioengineering, biological sciences, chemical engineering, chemistry, civil engineering, computer engineering, computer science, electrical engineering, engineering management, environmental engineering, environmental science, industrial engineering, geoscience, materials engineering, materials science, mechanical engineering, meteorology, natural resources science, neurosciences, nuclear engineering, oceanography, optical sciences, pharmacology, physics and applied physics, plant physiology, statistics, and systems and operational engineering. Students must apply to and be accepted at a university that is participating in this program. Once they have been accepted, the faculty member with whom they will be working recommends them for support as a Sloan Scholar. Selection of Sloan Scholars is based on their application, faculty recommendation, appropriate field of study, and financial need.

Financial data Each Sloan Scholar receives a scholarship grant of up to $30,000. Scholars may draw on that money at any time during their tenure in the Ph.D. program to cover the cost of tuition, stipend, books, summer support while working toward the Ph.D., travel to professional meetings, or other approved purposes. Scholars are encouraged to discuss with their faculty and others involved with their financial support when and for what purposes they should draw upon their scholarship grant.

Duration The scholarship is a 1-time grant which scholars may utilize throughout their doctoral program.

Additional information This program, which was established in 1995, is administered by the National Action Council for Minorities in Education (NACME) and funded by the Alfred P. Sloan Foundation, 630 Fifth Avenue, Suite 2550, New York, NY 10111-0242, (212) 649-1645, Fax: (212) 757-5117, E-mail: greenwood@sloan.org. Currently, selected faculty at 38 universities are participating. For a list of those faculty members, and the fields of study that are available at each university, contact NACME.

Number awarded Varies each year. Since the program was established, it has supported more than 200 students.

Deadline Applications are accepted on a rolling basis.

[638]

SOCIETY OF HISPANIC PROFESSIONAL ENGINEERS SCHOLARSHIPS

Society of Hispanic Professional Engineers Foundation
Attn: Director, Educational Programs
3900 Whiteside Street
Los Angeles, CA 90063
(323) 415-9600   Fax: (323) 415-7038
E-mail: kathy@shpefoundation.org
Web: www.shpefoundation.org

Purpose To provide undergraduate or graduate scholarships to deserving Hispanic American students preparing for a career in engineering or science.

Eligibility This program is open to Hispanic students enrolled or planning to enroll full time in an undergraduate or graduate degree program to prepare for a career in science or engineering. Applicants must submit an essay on how this scholarship would assist them in reaching their long-term goals. Selection is based on the essay, academic achievement, commitment to a college education, involvement in school and community activities, counselor recommendations, and financial need.

Financial data The stipends range from $500 to $7,000 per year.

Duration 1 academic year; renewal is possible.

Additional information These scholarships were first awarded in 1979.

Number awarded Varies each year. Recently, 375 of these scholarships, worth $275,000, were awarded.

Deadline May of each year.

[639]
SOCIETY OF MEXICAN AMERICAN ENGINEERS AND SCIENTISTS GRADUATE STUDENT SCHOLARSHIPS

Society of Mexican American Engineers and Scientists
Attn: Scholarships
711 West Bay Area Boulevard, Suite 206
Webster, TX 77598-3677
(281) 557-3677   Fax: (281) 557-3757
E-mail: scholarships@maes-natl.org
Web: www.maes-natl.org

Purpose To provide financial assistance to graduate student members of the Society of Mexican American Engineers and Scientists (MAES).

Eligibility This program is open to MAES student members who are full-time graduate students at a college or university in the United States majoring in a field of science or engineering. U.S. citizenship or permanent resident status is required. Selection is based on financial need; academic achievement; personal qualities, strengths, and leadership abilities; and timeliness and completeness of the application.

Financial data The stipend is $3,000.

Duration 1 year.

Additional information Recipients must attend the MAES International Symposium's Medalla de Oro Banquet in October.

Number awarded 1 or more each year.

Deadline October of each year.

[640]
SOUTH CAROLINA SPACE GRANT CONSORTIUM GRADUATE FELLOWSHIPS

South Carolina Space Grant Consortium
c/o College of Charleston
Department of Geology
58 Coming Street, Room 341B
Charleston, SC 29424
(843) 953-7171   Fax: (843) 953-5446
E-mail: colganm@cofc.edu
Web: www.cofc.edu/~scsgrant

Purpose To provide financial assistance for space-related study to underrepresented minority and other graduate students in South Carolina.

Eligibility This program is open to graduate students at member institutions of the South Carolina Space Grant Consortium. Applicants must be interested in space-related studies, although the program has accepted students with interests ranging from remote sensing and engineering to astrophysics. U.S. citizenship is required. Selection is based on academic qualifications of the applicant; 2 letters of recommendation; a description of past activities, current interests, and future plans concerning an aerospace-related field; and faculty sponsorship. The South Carolina Space Grant Consortium is a component of the U.S. National Aeronautics and Space Administration (NASA) Space Grant program, which encourages the participation of women, underrepresented minorities, and persons with disabilities.

Financial data A maximum of $10,000 will be awarded, which must be matched 1:1 by the student's host institution.

Duration 1 year.

Additional information Members of the consortium are Benedict College, The Citadel, College of Charleston, Clemson University, Coastal Carolina University, Furman University, University of South Carolina, Wofford College, South Carolina State University, The Medical University of South Carolina, and University of the Virgin Islands. This program is funded by NASA.

Number awarded Varies each year.

Deadline February of each year.

[641]
SOUTHEAST EUROPEAN LANGUAGE TRAINING GRANTS FOR INDIVIDUALS

American Council of Learned Societies
Attn: Office of Fellowships and Grants
633 Third Avenue, 8C
New York, NY 10017-6795
(212) 697-1505   Fax: (212) 949-8058
E-mail: grants@acls.org
Web: www.acls.org/eeguide.htm

Purpose To provide financial support to graduate students and others (particularly minorities and women) interested in studying southeastern European languages during the summer.

Eligibility Applicants must have completed at least a 4-year college degree. They must be interested in a program of training, primarily in intensive courses offered by institutions of higher education in the United States, in the languages of southeastern Europe, including Albanian, Bosnian-Croatian-Serbian, Bulgarian, Macedonian, or Romanian. The language course may be at the beginning, intermediate, or advanced level. The awards are intended for people who will use those languages in academic research or teaching. Preference is given to applicants who 1) cannot study their chosen language at their home institution, 2) will be continuing the study of that language in the following year, and 3) have been or are beginning language study early in their academic career. Applications are particularly encouraged from women and members of minority groups.

Financial data Grants up to $2,000 are available.

Duration Summer months.

Additional information This program, reinstituted in 2002, is supported by the U.S. Department of State under the Research and Training for Eastern Europe and the Independent States of the Former Soviet Union Act of 1983 (Title VIII).

Number awarded Approximately 10 each year.

Deadline January of each year.

[642]
SPANISH BAPTIST CONVENTION OF NEW MEXICO SCHOLARSHIP

Baptist Convention of New Mexico
Attn: Director, Language Missions
5325 Wyoming Boulevard, N.E.
P.O. Box 94485
Albuquerque, NM 87199-4485
(505) 924-2345   Fax: (505) 924-2320
E-mail: gsuarez@bcnm.com
Web: www.bcnm.com

Purpose To provide financial assistance for college or seminary to Hispanic Baptist students from New Mexico.

Eligibility This program is open to college and seminary students who are active members of churches affiliated with the Baptist Convention of New Mexico. Applicants must be of Hispanic background and committed to full-time Christian service.

Financial data A stipend is awarded (amount not specified).

Duration 1 year; may be renewed.

Number awarded 1 or more each year.

Deadline April of each year.

[643]
SPECTRUM INITIATIVE SCHOLARSHIPS

American Library Association
Attn: Office for Diversity
50 East Huron Street
Chicago, IL 60611-2795
(312) 280-4276   Toll-free: (800) 545-2433, ext. 4276
Fax: (312) 280-3256   TDD: (312) 944-7298
TDD: (888) 814-7692   E-mail: diversity@ala.org
Web: www.ala.org

Purpose To provide financial assistance to minority students interested in working on a degree in librarianship.

Eligibility This program is open to ethnic minority students (African American or Black, Asian, Native Hawaiian or Pacific Islander, Latino or Hispanic, and American Indian or Alaska Native). Applicants must be U.S. or Canadian citizens or permanent residents who are planning to attend an accredited school of library science. Selection is based on academic leadership, outstanding service, commitment to a career in librarianship, statements indicating the nature of the applicant's library and other work experience, letters of reference, and personal presentation.

Financial data The stipend is $5,000 per year.

Duration 1 year; nonrenewable.

Additional information This program began in 1998. It is administered by a joint committee of the American Library Association (ALA). Funding is provided by outside contributions and returns from the ALA Future Fund and the Giles and Leo Albert Funds.

Number awarded 50 each year.

Deadline February of each year.

[644]
SREB DOCTORAL SCHOLARS PROGRAM

Southern Regional Education Board
592 10th Street N.W.
Atlanta, GA 30318-5790
(404) 875-9211, ext. 273   Fax: (404) 872-1477
E-mail: doctoral.scholars@sreb.org
Web: www.sreb.org/programs/dsp/dspindex.asp

Purpose To provide financial assistance to minority students who wish to work on a doctoral degree in the sciences at designated universities in the southern states.

Eligibility This program is open to U.S. citizens who are members of racial/ethnic minority groups (Native Americans, Hispanic Americans, Asian Americans, and African Americans) and hold or will receive a bachelor's degree from an accredited college or university. Applicants must intend to work on a Ph.D. in science, mathematics, engineering, or science or mathematics education at a participating institution. They must indicate an interest in becoming a college professor at an institution in the South. Students who are already enrolled in a doctoral program are not eligible. Study for professional degrees, such as the M.D., D.D.S., J.D., or D.V.M., as well as graduate study in education leading to an Ed.D., does not qualify.

Financial data Scholars receive waiver of tuition and fees (in or out of state) for up to 5 years, an annual stipend of $15,000 for 3 years, an annual allowance for professional development activities, and reimbursement of travel expenses to attend the Doctoral Scholars annual meeting.

Duration Up to 5 years.

Number awarded Varies each year; recently, the program was supporting 208 scholars at 54 institutions in 22 states.

Deadline March of each year.

[645]
STAN BECK FELLOWSHIP

Entomological Society of America
Attn: Entomological Foundation
9332 Annapolis Road, Suite 210
Lanham, MD 20706-3150
(301) 459-9082   Fax: (301) 459-9084
E-mail: melodie@entfdn.org
Web: www.entfdn.org/beck.html

Purpose To assist "needy" students working on an undergraduate or graduate degree in science who are nominated by members of the Entomological Society of America (ESA).

Eligibility This program is open to students working on an undergraduate or graduate degree in entomology at a college or university in Canada, Mexico, or the United States. Candidates must be nominated by members of the society. They must be "needy" students; for the purposes of this program, need may be based on physical limitations, or economic, minority, or environmental conditions.

Financial data The stipend is $2,000 per year.

Duration 1 year; may be renewed up to 3 additional years.

Additional information Recipients are expected to be present at the society's annual meeting, where the award will be presented.

Number awarded 1 or more each year.

Deadline June of each year.

[646]
SUBSTANCE ABUSE RESEARCH FELLOWSHIPS

American Psychological Association
Attn: Minority Fellowship Program
750 First Street, N.E.
Washington, DC 20002-4242
(202) 336-6127   Fax: (202) 336-6012
TDD: (202) 336-6123   E-mail: mfp@apa.org
Web: www.apa.org/mfp/sarprogram.html

Purpose To provide financial assistance to psychology doctoral students (especially minorities) who are preparing for a career involving research on substance abuse issues and ethnic minority populations.

Eligibility This program is open to full-time doctoral students who can demonstrate a strong commitment to a career in substance abuse research and the mental health or psychological well-being of ethnic minorities. Students from all psychology disciplines are encouraged to apply if their training and research interests are related to mental health and substance abuse. Clinical, counseling, and school psychology students may be eligible if they intend to specialize in substance abuse treatment and research. Members of minority groups (African Americans, Alaskan Natives, American Indians, Asian Americans, Hispanics/Latinos, Native Hawaiians, and Pacific Islanders) are especially encouraged to apply. U.S. citizenship or permanent resident status is required. Selection is based on commitment to a career in research that focuses on substance abuse in ethnic minority communities, knowledge of ethnic minority psychology or mental health issues, the fit between career goals and training environment selected, potential for a research career demonstrated through accomplishments and goals, scholarship and grades, and letters of recommendation.

Financial data The stipend is the amount established by the National Institutes of Health for predoctoral students, currently $20,772 per year.

Duration 1 year; may be renewed for up to 2 additional years.

Additional information Funding is provided by the U.S. National Institute of Mental Health. Students who receive a federally-funded grant from another source may not also accept funds from this program.

Number awarded Varies each year.

Deadline January of each year.

[647]
SUNY UNDERREPRESENTED GRADUATE MINORITY FELLOWSHIP

State University of New York
Attn: Assistant Vice Chancellor
Diversity and Affirmative Action
SUNY Plaza
Albany, NY 12246
(518) 443-5676   Fax: (518) 443-5103

Purpose To provide financial assistance for graduate study at any of the campuses of the State University of New York (SUNY) to underrepresented minority students.

Eligibility This program is open to African Americans, Hispanic Americans, and Native Americans who are U.S. citizens or permanent residents and full-time graduate or professional students at any of the participating SUNY colleges.

Financial data Awards range from $7,500 to $10,000.

Duration 1 year; renewable.

Additional information The participating institutions include the University Centers at Albany, Binghamton, Buffalo, and Stony Brook; the Health Science Centers at Brooklyn and Syracuse; the University Colleges of Arts and Sciences at Brockport, Buffalo, Cortland, Fredonia, Geneseo, New Paltz, Oneonta, Oswego, Plattsburgh, Potsdam, and Purchase; Empire State College; the College of Ceramics at Alfred University; the Institute of Technology at Utica/Rome; the College of Optometry; the Maritime College; the College of Environmental Science and Forestry; and the College of Agriculture and Life Sciences, the College of Human Ecology, the School of Industrial and Labor Relations, and the College of Veterinary Medicine at Cornell University.

Number awarded 500 each year.

Deadline November of each year.

[648]
SYNOD OF LAKES AND PRAIRIES RACIAL ETHNIC SCHOLARSHIPS

Synod of Lakes and Prairies
Attn: Committee on Racial Ethnic Ministry
8012 Cedar Avenue, South
Bloomington, MN 55425-1210
(952) 854-0144   Fax: (952) 854-6690
E-mail: office@lakesandprairies.org
Web: www.lakesandprairies.org

Purpose To provide financial assistance to minority residents of the Presbyterian Church (USA) Synod of Lakes and Prairies who are studying for the ministry.

Eligibility This program is open to members of Presbyterian churches within the Synod of Lakes and Prairies (Iowa, Minnesota, Nebraska, North Dakota, South Dakota, and Wisconsin). Applicants must be members of ethnic minority groups studying for the ministry.

Financial data Stipends range from $850 to $3,500.

Duration 1 year.

Number awarded Varies each year; recently, 9 of these scholarships were awarded.

Deadline September of each year.

[649]
SYNOD OF THE COVENANT ETHNIC THEOLOGICAL SCHOLARSHIPS

Synod of the Covenant
Attn: CECA Ethnic Scholarship Committee
1911 Indianwood Circle, Suite B
Maumee, OH 43537-4063
(419) 754-4050
Toll-free: (800) 848-1030 (within MI and OH)
Web: www.synodofthecovenant.org

Purpose To provide financial assistance to ethnic students working on a degree at an approved Presbyterian theological institution (with priority given to Presbyterian applicants from Ohio and Michigan).

Eligibility This program is open to ethnic individuals enrolled in church vocations at approved Presbyterian theological institutions. Priority is given to Presbyterian applicants from the states of Michigan and Ohio. Financial need is considered in the selection process.

Financial data Students may be awarded a maximum of $1,500 on initial application. They may receive up to $2,000 on subsequent applications with evidence of continuing progress. Funds are made payable to the session for distribution.

Duration Students are eligible to receive scholarships 1 time per year, up to a maximum of 5 years.

Number awarded Varies each year.

Deadline September of each year for fall semester; February of each year for spring semester.

[650]
TED SCRIPPS FELLOWSHIPS IN ENVIRONMENTAL JOURNALISM

University of Colorado at Boulder
Attn: Center for Environmental Journalism
1511 University Avenue
Campus Box 478
Boulder, CO 80309-0478
(303) 492-4114   E-mail: cej@colorado.edu
Web: www.colorado.edu/journalism/cej

Purpose To provide minority and other journalists with an opportunity to gain more knowledge about environmental issues at the University of Colorado at Boulder.

Eligibility This program is open to full-time U.S. print and broadcast journalists who have at least 5 years' professional experience and have completed an undergraduate degree. Applicants may be general assignment reporters, editors, producers, environmental reporters, or full-time freelancers. Prior experience in covering the environment is not required. Professionals in such related fields as teaching, public relations, or advertising are not eligible. Applicants must be interested in a program at the university that includes classes, weekly seminars, and field trips. They also must engage in independent study expected to lead to a significant piece of journalistic work. Applications are especially encouraged from women, ethnic minorities, disabled persons, and veterans (particularly veterans of the Vietnam era).

Financial data The program covers tuition and fees and pays a $44,000 stipend. Employers are strongly encouraged to continue benefits, including health insurance.

Duration 9 months.

Additional information This program, established in 1992 at the University of Michigan and transferred to the University of Colorado in 1997, is supported by the Scripps Howard Foundation. This is a non-degree program. Fellows must obtain a leave of absence from their regular employment and must return to their job following the fellowship.

Number awarded 5 each year.

Deadline February of each year.

[651]
TEXAS ASSOCIATION OF CHICANOS IN HIGHER EDUCATION GRADUATE FELLOWSHIP AWARDS

Texas Association of Chicanos in Higher Education
P.O. Box 986
Austin, TX 78767-0986
Web: www.tache.org/pdfs/award_fellow.pdf

Purpose To provide financial assistance to Hispanic residents of Texas who are enrolled in a graduate program to prepare for a career in higher education.

Eligibility This program is open to residents of Texas who are of Chicano/Latino heritage (1 parent fully Hispanic or both parents half Hispanic). Applicants must be enrolled full time in a Texas graduate or professional school in a degree program to prepare for a career in higher education or administration. They must have a cumulative GPA of 3.0 or higher. Along with their application, they must submit a personal statement of 500 to 600 words that describes their Hispanic heritage and family background; past, current, and future efforts toward making a difference in the Hispanic community; personal and academic achievements, including honors and awards; educational and career goals; and financial need.

Financial data The stipend is $1,000 per year.

Duration 1 year.

Additional information Information is also available from Julio Llanas, Fellowship Selection Committee Chair, Texas Tech University, Box 41073, Lubbock, TX 79424, (806) 742-3627, Fax: (806) 742-2592, E-mail: Julio.llanas@ttu.edu. Recipients are required to become members of the Texas Association of Chicanos in Higher Education.

Number awarded 2 each year.

Deadline December of each year.

[652]
TEXAS LIBRARY ASSOCIATION SPECTRUM SCHOLARSHIP

Texas Library Association
Attn: Director of Administration
3355 Bee Cave Road, Suite 401
Austin, TX 78746-6763
(512) 328-1518   Toll-free: (800) 580-2TLA
Fax: (512) 328-8852   E-mail: tla@txla.org
Web: www.txla.org

Purpose To provide additional funding to students at schools of library and information studies in Texas who have received a Spectrum Scholarship for minorities from the American Library Association (ALA).

Eligibility This program is open to recipients of ALA Spectrum Scholarships who are enrolled in a master's degree program in library and information studies at a Texas university. Applicants must be African American, Latino or Hispanic, Asian or Pacific Islander, or Native American. They must be members of the Texas Library Association (TLA) and agree to work for 2 years in a Texas library following completion of their master's degree requirements.

Financial data The stipend is $2,000.

Duration 1 year.

Number awarded 1 or more each year.

[653]
TEXAS MEDICAL ASSOCIATION MINORITY SCHOLARSHIP PROGRAM

Texas Medical Association
Attn: Minority Scholarship Program
401 West 15th Street
Austin, TX 78701-1680
(512) 370-1375   Toll-free: (800) 880-2828, ext. 1375
Fax: (512) 370-1635
E-mail: marcia.collins@texmed.org
Web: www.texmed.org

Purpose To provide financial assistance to members of underrepresented minority groups who are interested in attending medical school in Texas.

Eligibility This program is open to members of minority groups that are underrepresented in the medical profession. Applicants must have been accepted at a medical school in Texas.

Financial data The stipend is $5,000.

Duration 1 year; renewable.

Additional information This program began in 1999.

Number awarded Varies each year; recently, 4 of these scholarships were awarded.

[654]
TEXAS SPACE GRANT CONSORTIUM GRADUATE FELLOWSHIPS

Texas Space Grant Consortium
Attn: Administrative Assistant
3925 West Braker Lane, Suite 200
Austin, TX 78759
(512) 471-3583   Toll-free: (800) 248-8742
Fax: (512) 471-3585   E-mail: jurgens@tsgc.utexas.edu
Web: www.tsgc.utexas.edu/grants

Purpose To provide financial assistance to underrepresented and other graduate students at Texas universities working on degrees in the fields of space science and engineering.

Eligibility Applicants must be U.S. citizens, eligible for financial assistance, and registered for full-time study in a graduate program at 1 of the participating universities. Students apply to their respective university representative; each representative then submits up to 3 candidates into the statewide selection process. Fields of study have included aerospace engineering, astronomy, biology, computer science and engineering, electrical engineering, materials science and engineering, medicine, physics, and physiology. Applications from women and underrepresented students (persons with disabilities, African Americans, Hispanic Americans, Native Americans, and Pacific Islanders) are encouraged. Fellowships are awarded competitively, on the basis of GPA, Graduate Record Examination scores, interest in space, and recommendations from the applicant's university.

Financial data The stipend is $5,000 per year, to be used to supplement half-time graduate support (or a fellowship) offered by the home institution.

Duration 1 year; may be renewed for up to a maximum of 3 years, provided the recipient spends no more than 2 of those years as a master's degree candidate.

Additional information The participating universities are Baylor University, Lamar University, Prairie View A&M University, Rice University, San Jacinto College, Southern Methodist University, Sul Ross State University, Texas A&M University (including Kingsville and Corpus Christi campuses), Texas Christian University, Texas Southern University, Texas Tech University, Trinity University, University of Houston (including Clear Lake and Downtown campuses), University of Texas at Arlington, University of Texas at Austin, University of Texas at Dallas, University of Texas at El Paso, University of Texas at San Antonio, University of Texas Health Science Center at Houston, University of Texas Health Science Center at San Antonio, University of Texas Medical Branch at Galveston, University of Texas/Pan American, and University of Texas Southwestern Medical Center. This program is funded by the National Aeronautics and Space Administration (NASA).

Number awarded Varies each year; recently, 20 of these fellowships were awarded.

Deadline February of each year.

[655]
TEXAS YOUNG LAWYERS ASSOCIATION MINORITY SCHOLARSHIP PROGRAM

Texas Young Lawyers Association
Attn: Minority Involvement Committee
1414 Colorado, Suite 400-B
P.O. Box 12487
Austin, TX 78711-2487
(512) 463-1463, ext. 6429
Toll-free: (800) 204-2222, ext. 6429
Fax: (512) 463-1503
Web: www.tyla.org

Purpose To provide financial assistance to minorities and women attending law school in Texas.

Eligibility This program is open to members of recognized minority groups, including but not limited to women, African Americans, Hispanics, Asian Americans, and Native Americans. Applicants must be attending an ABA-accredited law school in Texas. Selection is based on participation in extracurricular activities inside and outside law school and financial need.

Financial data The stipend is $1,000.

Duration 1 year.

Number awarded 1 at each accredited law school in Texas.

Deadline October of each year.

[656]
THIRD WAVE FOUNDATION WOODLAKE SCHOLARSHIPS

Third Wave Foundation
511 West 25th Street, Suite 301
New York, NY 10002
(212) 675-0700   Fax: (212) 255-6653
E-mail: info@thirdwavefoundation.org
Web: www.thirdwavefoundation.org

Purpose To provide educational assistance to undergraduate and graduate women of color who have been involved as social change activists.

Eligibility This program is open to full-time and part-time students under 30 years of age who are enrolled in, or have been accepted to, an accredited university, college, vocational/technical school, community college, or graduate school. Applicants must be women of color who place greater emphasis on social justice and the struggle for justice and equality over academic performance and who integrate social justice into all areas of their lives. They must submit 500-word essays on 1) their current social change involvement and how it relates to their educational and life goals; and 2) if they would describe themselves as a feminist and why. Graduate students and students planning to study abroad through a U.S. university program are also eligible. Selection is based on financial need and commitment to social justice work.

Financial data Stipends are $3,000 or $1,000 per year.

Duration 1 year.

Number awarded Varies each year. Recently, 8 of these scholarships were awarded: 6 at $3,000 and 2 at $1,000.

Deadline March or September of each year.

[657]
TRANSPORTATION FELLOWSHIP PROGRAM

North Central Texas Council of Governments
Attn: Transportation Department
616 Six Flags Drive, Centerpoint Two
P.O. Box 5888
Arlington, TX 76005-5888
(817) 608-2325   Fax: (817) 640-7806
E-mail: lucile@dwfinfo.com
Web: www.dfwinfo.com/trans/fellowship

Purpose To provide financial assistance and work experience to ethnic minorities, women, and economically disadvantaged persons who are interested in obtaining a master's degree in Texas in preparation for a career in the field of transportation.

Eligibility This program is open to ethnic minorities (African Americans, Hispanics, American Indians, Alaskan Natives, Asians, and Pacific Islanders), women, and those who are economically disadvantaged. Only U.S. citizens or permanent residents may apply. Applicants must be interested in obtaining a master's degree at a participating university in Texas as preparation for a career in transportation. They must be pursuing a degree in an approved program of study (transportation planning, urban and regional planning, urban or spatial geography, transportation/environmental sciences, logistics, transportation or civil engineering, transportation law, transportation management, or geographic information systems). Full-time enrollment is required. Selection is based on 1) financial need; 2) interest in, and commitment to, a professional career in transportation; and 3) the applicant's ability to complete the academic and work placement responsibilities of the program.

Financial data Fellowships in the amount of $2,000 each will be awarded on a yearly basis. One-half of each award will be distributed in each of the fall and spring semesters. Funds are to be used for tuition, fees, books, and/or educational supplies.

Duration 1 year; may be renewed if the recipient maintains a GPA of 3.0 or higher.

Additional information The Federal Highway Administration, Federal Transit Administration, and the Texas Department of Transportation fund this program through the sponsor's Unified Planning Work Program for Regional Transportation Planning. Fellows are assigned to an internship in a local government in that area. Universities currently participating in the program are the University of North Texas, the University of Texas at Arlington, and the University of Texas at Dallas. Fellows are required to agree to make a good-faith effort to obtain employment in community-building fields for at least 2 consecutive years after graduation.

Deadline July of each year.

[658]
TRIDENT–HDA FOUNDATION SCHOLARSHIPS

Hispanic Dental Association
Attn: HDA Foundation
188 West Randolph Street, Suite 415
Chicago, IL 60601
(312) 577-4013   Toll-free: (800) 852-7921
Fax: (312) 577-0052
E-mail: HispanicDental@hdassoc.org
Web: www.hdassoc.org

Purpose To provide financial assistance to Hispanic students interested in preparing for a career in a dental profession.

Eligibility This program is open to Hispanics who are entering or enrolled in an accredited dental or dental hygiene program. Applicants must have a GPA of 3.0 or higher. Along with their application, they must submit an essay on their career goals. Selection is based on scholastic achievement, community service, leadership skill, and commitment to improving health in the Hispanic community.

Financial data The stipend is $1,500.

Duration 1 year.

Additional information This program, which began in 2004, is sponsored by Cadbury Adams, maker of Trident Sugarfree Chewing Gum.

Number awarded 1 or more each year.

Deadline June of each year for dental students; July of each year for dental hygiene students.

[659]
UNDERREPRESENTED MENTAL HEALTH MINORITY RESEARCH FELLOWSHIP PROGRAM

Council on Social Work Education
Attn: Minority Fellowship Program
1725 Duke Street, Suite 500
Alexandria, VA 22314-3457
(703) 683-8080, ext. 217   Fax: (703) 683-8099
E-mail: mfp@cswe.org
Web: www.cswe.org

Purpose To provide funding to racial minority members interested in preparing for a career in mental health research.

Eligibility This program is open to U.S. citizens and permanent residents who have been underrepresented in the field of social work. These include but are not limited to the following groups: American Indians/Alaskan Natives, Asian/Pacific Islanders (e.g., Chinese, East Indians, South Asians, Filipinos, Hawaiians, Japanese, Koreans, and Samoans), Blacks, and Hispanics (e.g., Mexicans/Chicanos, Puerto Ricans, Cubans, Central or South Americans). Applicants must be interested in enrolling in a doctoral-level social work program that provides strong research courses and research training in mental health. They must be interested in working on a doctoral degree as a full-time student.

Financial data Awards provide a stipend of $16,500 per year and tuition support at the rate of 100% of the first $3,000 and 60% of the remaining tuition.

Duration 1 academic year; renewable for 2 additional years if funds are available and the recipient makes satisfactory progress toward the degree objectives.

Additional information This program has been funded since 1974 by the National Institute of Mental Health of the National Institutes of Health.

Deadline February of each year.

[660]
UNITARIAN UNIVERSALIST ASSOCIATION INCENTIVE GRANTS

Unitarian Universalist Association
Attn: Office of Ministerial Credentialing
25 Beacon Street
Boston, MA 02108-2800
(617) 948-6403   Fax: (617) 742-2875
E-mail: cmay@uua.org
Web: www.uua.org

Purpose To provide financial aid to persons of color who the Unitarian Universalist Association is interested in attracting to the ministry.

Eligibility These grants are offered to persons of color who the association is particularly interested in attracting to Unitarian Universalist ministry to promote racial, cultural, or class diversity. Applicants must be in their first year of study. Decisions regarding potential recipients are made in consultation with the schools. Selection is based on merit.

Financial data A stipend is awarded (amount not specified).

Duration 1 year; nonrenewable.

Additional information In subsequent years, recipients may apply for the association's General Financial Aid Grants.

Number awarded Varies each year.

Deadline April of each year.

[661]
UNITED METHODIST SCHOLARSHIP PROGRAM

United Methodist Church
Attn: General Board of Higher Education and Ministry
Office of Loans and Scholarships
1001 19th Avenue South
P.O. Box 340007
Nashville, TN 37203-0007
(615) 340-7344   Fax: (615) 340-7367
E-mail: umscholar@gbhem.org
Web: www.gbhem.org

Purpose To provide financial assistance to undergraduate and graduate students attending schools affiliated with the United Methodist Church.

Eligibility This program is open to U.S. citizens and permanent residents who have been active, full members of a United Methodist Church for at least 1 year prior to applying; members of the A.M.E., A.M.E. Zion, and other "Methodist" denominations are not eligible. Undergraduates must

have been admitted to a full-time degree program at a United Methodist-related college or university and have a GPA of 2.5 or above. Most graduate scholarships are designated for persons working on a degree in theological studies (M.Div., D.Min., Ph.D.) or higher education administration, or for older adults changing their careers. Some scholarships are designated for racial ethnic undergraduate or graduate students. Applications are available from the financial aid office of the United Methodist school the applicant attends or from the chair of their annual conference Board of Higher Education and Campus Ministry.

Financial data The funding is intended to supplement the students' own resources.

Duration 1 year; renewal policies are set by participating universities.

Number awarded Varies each year.

[662]
UNITED METHODIST WOMEN OF COLOR SCHOLARS PROGRAM

United Methodist Church
Attn: General Board of Higher Education and Ministry
Office of Loans and Scholarships
1001 19th Avenue South
P.O. Box 340007
Nashville, TN 37203-0007
(615) 340-7344   Fax: (615) 340-7367
E-mail: umscholar@gbhem.org
Web: www.gbhem.org

Purpose To provide financial assistance to Methodist women of color who are working on a doctoral degree.

Eligibility This program is open to women of color (have at least 1 parent who is African American, Hispanic, Asian, Native American, Alaska Native, or Pacific Islander) who have a M.Div. degree. Applicants must have been active, full members of a United Methodist Church for at least 3 years prior to applying. They must be enrolled full time in a degree program at the Ph.D. or Th.D. level to prepare for a career teaching at a United Methodist seminary.

Financial data The maximum stipend is $10,000.

Duration 1 year.

Number awarded Varies each year; recently, 10 of these scholarships were awarded.

Deadline January of each year.

[663]
USA FUNDS ACCESS TO EDUCATION SCHOLARSHIPS

Scholarship America
Attn: Scholarship Management Services
One Scholarship Way
P.O. Box 297
St. Peter, MN 56082
(507) 931-1682   Toll-free: (800) 537-4180
Fax: (507) 931-9168
E-mail: scholarship@usafunds.org
Web: www.usafunds.org

Purpose To provide financial assistance to undergraduate and graduate students, especially those who are members of ethnic minority groups or have physical disabilities.

Eligibility This program is open to high school seniors and graduates who plan to enroll or are already enrolled in full-time undergraduate or graduate course work at an accredited 2- or 4-year college, university, or vocational/technical school. Half-time undergraduate students are also eligible. Up to 50% of the awards are targeted at students who have a documented physical disability or are a member of an ethnic minority group, including but not limited to Native Hawaiian, Alaskan Native, Black/African American, Asian, Pacific Islander, American Indian, or Hispanic/Latino. Residents of 49 states (residents of Hawaii are eligible for a separate program), the District of Columbia, Puerto Rico, Guam, the U.S. Virgin Islands, and all U.S. territories and commonwealths are eligible. Preference is given to applicants from the following states: Arizona, Indiana, Kansas, Maryland, Mississippi, Nevada, and Wyoming. Applicants must also be U.S. citizens or eligible noncitizens and come from a family with an annual adjusted gross income of $35,000 or less. In addition to financial need, selection is based on past academic performance and future potential, leadership and participation in school and community activities, work experience, career and educational aspirations, and goals.

Financial data The stipend is $1,500 per year for full-time undergraduate or graduate students or $750 per year for half-time undergraduate students. Funds are paid jointly to the student and the school.

Duration 1 year; may be renewed until the student receives a final degree or certificate or until the total award to a student reaches $6,000, whichever comes first. Renewal requires the recipient to maintain a GPA of 2.5 or higher.

Additional information This program, established in 2000, is sponsored by USA Funds, which serves as the education loan guarantor and administrator in the 7 states where the program gives preference.

Number awarded Varies each year; recently, a total of $2.85 million was available for this program.

Deadline March of each year.

[664]
USA FUNDS HAWAII SILVER ANNIVERSARY SCHOLARSHIPS

Scholarship America
Attn: Scholarship Management Services
One Scholarship Way
P.O. Box 297
St. Peter, MN 56082
(507) 931-1682   Toll-free: (800) 537-4180
Fax: (507) 931-9168
E-mail: scholarship@usafunds.org
Web: www.usafunds.org

Purpose To provide financial assistance to undergraduate and graduate students from Hawaii, especially those who are members of ethnic minority groups or have physical disabilities.

Eligibility This program is open to high school seniors and graduates who are residents of Hawaii planning to enroll or already enrolled in full-time undergraduate or graduate course work at an accredited 2- or 4-year college, university, or vocational/technical school. Half-time undergraduate students are also eligible. Up to 50% of the awards are

targeted at students who have a documented physical disability or are a member of an ethnic minority group, including but not limited to Native Hawaiian, Alaskan Native, Black/African American, Asian, Pacific Islander, American Indian, or Hispanic/Latino. Applicants must also be U.S. citizens or eligible noncitizens and come from a family with an annual adjusted gross income of $50,000 or less. In addition to financial need, selection is based on past academic performance and future potential, leadership and participation in school and community activities, work experience, career and educational aspirations, and goals.

Financial data The stipend is $1,500 per year for full-time undergraduate or graduate students or $750 per year for half-time undergraduate students. Funds are paid jointly to the student and the school.

Duration 1 year; may be renewed until the student receives a final degree or certificate or until the total award to a student reaches $6,000, whichever comes first. Renewal requires the recipient to maintain a GPA of 2.5 or higher.

Additional information This program, first offered in 2004, is sponsored by SMS Hawaii, the USA Funds affiliate that serves as the education loan guarantor and administrator in Hawaii and 7 other states. Information is also available from SMS Hawaii, 1314 South King Street, Suite 861, Honolulu, HI 96814, (808) 593-2262, (866) 497-USAF, ext. 7573, Fax: (808) 593-8268, E-mail: lteniya@usafunds.org.

Number awarded Varies each year; recently, a total of $300,000 was available for this program.

Deadline March of each year.

[665]
VIRGIL HAWKINS FELLOWSHIP PROGRAM

State University System of Florida
Attn: Office of Academic and Student Affairs
325 West Gaines Street, Suite 1501
Tallahassee, FL 32399-1950
(850) 245-0467   Fax: (850) 245-9667
E-mail: we're.listening@fldoe.org
Web: www.fldoe.org

Purpose To provide financial assistance to minorities in Florida who are interested in legal careers.

Eligibility First-year minority students who are attending law schools at accredited state universities in Florida are eligible to apply.

Financial data The stipend is $14,000 per year.

Duration 1 year; renewable up to 2 additional years.

Additional information This program is administered by the equal opportunity program at each of the public institutions in Florida that have a law school. Contact that office for further information.

Number awarded Varies each year; recently, more than $200,000 was available for this program.

[666]

VIRGINIA SPACE GRANT TEACHER EDUCATION SCHOLARSHIP PROGRAM

Virginia Space Grant Consortium
Attn: Fellowship Coordinator
Old Dominion University Peninsula Center
600 Butler Farm Road
Hampton, VA 23666
(757) 766-5210   Fax: (757) 766-5205
E-mail: vsgc@odu.edu
Web: www.vsgc.odu.edu/html/fellowships.htm

Purpose To provide financial assistance for college to underrepresented minority and other students in Virginia planning a career as science, mathematics, or technology educators.

Eligibility This program is open to full-time undergraduate students at the Virginia Space Grant Consortium (VSGC) colleges and universities in a track that will qualify them to teach in a pre-college setting. Priority is given to those majoring in technology education, mathematics, or science, particularly earth, space, or environmental science. Applicants may apply while seniors in high school or sophomores in a community college, with the award contingent on their enrollment at a VSGC college and entrance into a teacher certification program. They must submit a statement of academic goals and plan of study, explaining their reasons for desiring to enter the teaching profession, specifically the fields of science, mathematics, or technology education. Students currently enrolled in a VSGC college can apply when they declare their intent to enter the teacher certification program. Students enrolled in a master of education degree program leading to teacher certification in eligible fields are also eligible to apply. Applicants must be U.S. citizens with a GPA of 3.0 or higher. Since an important purpose of this program is to increase the participation of underrepresented minorities, women, and persons with disabilities in science, mathematics, and technology education, the VSGC especially encourages applications from those students.

Financial data The maximum stipend is $1,000.

Duration 1 year; nonrenewable.

Additional information The VSGC institutions are College of William and Mary, Hampton University, Old Dominion University, the University of Virginia, and Virginia Polytechnic Institute and State University. This program is funded by the U.S. National Aeronautics and Space Administration (NASA).

Number awarded Approximately 10 each year.

Deadline February of each year.

[667]

WARNER NORCROSS & JUDD LAW SCHOOL STUDIES SCHOLARSHIP

Grand Rapids Community Foundation
Attn: Scholarship Coordinator
209-C Waters Building
161 Ottawa Avenue N.W., 209-C
Grand Rapids, MI 49503-2757
(616) 454-1751, ext. 103   Fax: (616) 454-6455
E-mail: rbishop@grfoundation.org
Web: www.grfoundation.org

Purpose To provide financial assistance for law school to minorities with a residential connection to Michigan.

Eligibility This program is open to minority students entering, accepted at, or currently attending an accredited law school within the United States. Applicants must be residents of Michigan or have a connection to the state (e.g., family members reside in the state, student previously resided in the state, student attended a school in the state).

Financial data The stipend is $5,000.

Duration 1 year.

Additional information Funding for this program is provided by the law firm Warner Norcross & Judd LLP.

Number awarded 1 each year.

Deadline April of each year.

[668]

WELLSTONE FELLOWSHIP

Families USA
Attn: Wellstone Fellowship
1334 G Street, N.W.
Washington, DC 20005
(202) 628-3030   Fax: (202) 347-2417
E-mail: wellstonefellowship@familiesusa.org
Web: www.familiesusa.org

Purpose To provide social justice activists of color with an opportunity to learn more about health care advocacy work at Families USA in Washington, D.C.

Eligibility This program is open to social justice advocates from underrepresented racial and ethnic minority groups, particularly from the Black/African American, Latino, and American Indian communities. Applicants must be able to demonstrate interest in both health care and grassroots organizing and a commitment to contributing to social justice following the fellowship. Preference is given to applicants who have experience with, or demonstrate a strong interest in, working with communities of color. Although they may come from any academic discipline, a college degree is preferred. Along with their application, they must submit a 750-word essay on how their personal background has influenced their view of social justice, including their experience with or interest in grassroots organizing and how it can be used as a tool for obtaining social justice, their views on how improving access to health coverage contributes to social justice, and their commitment to working towards social justice in the future. Selection is based on merit, including relevant experience and written communication skills.

Financial data The stipend is approximately $35,000.

Duration 1 year, beginning in August.

Additional information This program was established in 2004 to honor Paul Wellstone, the United States Senator from Minnesota who died in an airplane crash in 2002. Fellows have an opportunity to learn about Medicare, Medicaid, efforts to achieve universal coverage, and other important health policy issues. At the same time, they learn about conducting health care campaigns through communication and collaboration with the network of state grassroots advocates and organizations affiliated with Families USA.

Number awarded   1 each year.

Deadline   January of each year.

[669]
WILEY MANUEL LAW FOUNDATION SCHOLARSHIPS

Wiley Manuel Law Foundation
c/o Law Offices of George Holland
1970 Broadway, Suite 900
Oakland, CA 94612
(510) 465-4100

Purpose   To provide financial assistance to minority students from any state enrolled in law schools in northern California.

Eligibility   This program is open to minority students entering their third year at law schools in northern California. Applicants should exemplify the qualities of the late Justice Wiley Manuel. Selection is based on financial need, scholarship, commitment, and community service.

Financial data   The stipend is approximately $1,500.

Duration   1 year.

Number awarded   Varies each year; recently, 7 of these scholarships were awarded.

Deadline   March of each year.

[670]
WILLIAM G. ANDERSON, D.O. SCHOLARSHIP FOR MINORITY STUDENTS

American Osteopathic Foundation
Attn: Program Manager
142 East Ontario Street
Chicago, IL 60611-2864
(312) 202-8232   Toll-free: (800) 621-1773
Fax: (312) 202-8216
E-mail: vheck@aof-foundation.org
Web: www.aof-foundation.org

Purpose   To provide financial assistance to minority students enrolled in colleges of osteopathic medicine.

Eligibility   This program is open to minority (African American, Native American, Asian American, Pacific Islander, or Hispanic) students entering their second, third, or fourth year at an accredited college of osteopathic medicine. Applicants must demonstrate academic achievement and outstanding leadership qualities.

Financial data   The stipend is $5,000.

Duration   1 year.

Additional information   This program was established in 1998.

Number awarded   1 each year.

[671]
WILLIAM RUCKER GREENWOOD SCHOLARSHIP

Association for Women Geoscientists
Attn: AWG Foundation
P.O. Box 30645
Lincoln, NE 68503-0645
E-mail: awgscholarship@yahoo.com
Web: www.awg.org/members/po_scholarships.html

Purpose   To provide financial assistance to minority women working on an undergraduate or graduate degree in the geosciences in the Potomac Bay region.

Eligibility   This program is open to minority women who are currently enrolled as full-time undergraduate or graduate geoscience majors in an accredited, degree-granting college or university in Delaware, the District of Columbia, Maryland, Virginia, or West Virginia. Selection is based on the applicant's 1) awareness of the importance of community outreach as demonstrated by participation in geoscience or earth science educational activities, and 2) potential for leadership as a future geoscience professional.

Financial data   The stipend is $1,000. The recipient also is granted a 1-year membership in the Association for Women Geoscientists (AWG).

Duration   1 year.

Additional information   This program is sponsored by the AWG Potomac Area Chapter. Information is also available from Laurel M. Bybell, U.S. Geological Survey, 926 National Center, Reston, VA 20192.

Number awarded   1 each year.

Deadline   April of each year.

[672]
WILLIAM T. PORTER MINORITY FELLOWSHIPS IN PHYSIOLOGY

American Physiological Society
Attn: Education Office
9650 Rockville Pike, Room 3111
Bethesda, MD 20814-3991
(301) 634-7132   Fax: (301) 634-7098
E-mail: education@the-aps.org
Web: www.the-aps.org

Purpose   To provide financial assistance to underrepresented minorities interested in working on a doctoral degree in physiology.

Eligibility   This program is open to U.S. citizens and permanent residents who are members of underrepresented ethnic minority groups (African Americans, Hispanics, Native Americans, Native Alaskans, and Native Pacific Islanders). Applicants must be currently enrolled in or accepted to a doctoral program in physiology at a North American university as full-time students. Selection is based on academic records, proposed study and training goals, research plans, letters of recommendation, and progress in training if already engaged.

Financial data   The stipend is $18,000. No provision is made for a dependency allowance or tuition and fees.

Duration   1 year; may be renewed for 1 additional year and, in exceptional cases, for a third year.

Additional information   This program is supported by the William Townsend Porter Foundation (formerly the Harvard Apparatus Foundation). The first Porter Fellowship was awarded in 1920. In 1966 and 1967, the American Physiological Society established the Porter Physiology Development Committee to award fellowships to minority students engaged in graduate study in physiology.

Number awarded Varies each year; recently, 8 of these fellowships were awarded.

Deadline January or June of each year.

[673]
W.K. KELLOGG FOUNDATION FELLOWSHIP PROGRAM IN HEALTH RESEARCH

National Medical Fellowships, Inc.
Attn: Scholarship Program
5 Hanover Square, 15th Floor
New York, NY 10004
(212) 483-8880   Fax: (212) 483-8897
E-mail: info@nmfonline.org
Web: www.nmf-online.org

Purpose To provide financial assistance to minorities enrolled in a doctoral program in health policy research who are committed to working with underserved populations.

Eligibility This program is open to members of minority groups (African Americans, Native Americans, Asians, and Hispanics) enrolled in doctoral programs in public health, social policy, or health policy (Ph.D., Dr.P.H., or Sc.D.). Applicants must demonstrate a willingness to complete relevant dissertation research and a commitment to work with underserved populations upon completion of the doctorate. They must include an essay of 500 to 1,000 words discussing their reasons for applying for a fellowship, their qualifications, how it will support their career plans, and which of 4 areas of focus (health policy, men's health, mental health, substance abuse) most interests them and why.

Financial data Fellowships cover tuition, fees, and a partial living stipend.

Duration Up to 5 years: 2 years to do the necessary course work and 3 years to complete the dissertation.

Additional information The program was created in 1998 with grant support from the W.K. Kellogg Foundation. Recently, it operated at 8 institutions: the RAND Graduate School, the Heller Graduate School at Brandeis University, the Joseph L. Mailman School of Public Health at Columbia University, the Harvard School of Public Health, the Johns Hopkins School of Hygiene and Public Health, the UCLA School of Public Health, the University of Michigan School of Public Health, and the University of Pennsylvania. Information is also available from the sponsor's Washington office at 1627 K Street, N.W., Suite 1200, Washington, DC 20006-1702, (202) 296-4431, Fax: (202) 293-1990.

Number awarded 5 each year.

Deadline June of each year.

[674]
WOLVERINE BAR FOUNDATION SCHOLARSHIP

Wolverine Bar Association
Attn: Wolverine Bar Foundation
645 Griswold, Suite 961
Detroit, MI 48226
(313) 962-0250   Fax: (313) 962-5906
Web: www.michbar.org/localbars/wolverine/web.html

Purpose To provide financial assistance for law school to Michigan minority students.

Eligibility This program is open to minority law students who are either currently enrolled in a Michigan law school or are Michigan residents enrolled in an out-of-state law school. Applicants must be in at least their second year of law school. Selection is based on financial need, merit, and an interview.

Financial data The stipend is at least $1,000.

Duration 1 year; nonrenewable.

Additional information The Wolverine Bar Association was established by a number of African American attorneys during the 1930s. It was the successor to the Harlan Law Club, founded in 1919 by attorneys in the Detroit area who were excluded from other local bar associations in Michigan. Information is also available from the Scholarship Committee co-chairs, Kimberly D. Stevens, (313) 235-7711, E-mail: kds0183@hotmail.com, or Vanessa Peterson Williams, (313) 877-7000, E-mail: vpwilliams@mbpia.com.

Number awarded 1 or more each year.

Deadline January of each year.

[675]
WORLDSTUDIO FOUNDATION SCHOLARSHIPS

Worldstudio Foundation
200 Varick Street, Suite 507
New York, NY 10014
(212) 366-1317, ext. 18   Fax: (212) 807-0024
E-mail: scholarshipcoordinator@worldstudio.org
Web: www.worldstudio.org/schol/index.html

Purpose To provide financial assistance to undergraduate and graduate students, especially minorities, who wish to study fine or commercial arts, design, or architecture.

Eligibility This program is open to undergraduate and graduate students who are currently enrolled or planning to enroll at an accredited college or university and major in 1 of the following areas: advertising (art direction only), architecture, crafts, environmental graphics, fashion design, film/video (direction or cinematography only), film/theater design (including set, lighting, and costume design), fine arts, furniture design, graphic design, industrial/product design, interior design, landscape architecture, new media, photography, surface/textile design, or urban planning. Although not required, minority status is a significant factor in the selection process. International students may apply if they are enrolled at a U.S. college or university. Applicants must have a GPA of 2.0 or higher. Along with their application, they must submit a 600-word statement of purpose that includes a brief autobiography, an explanation of how their experiences have influenced their creative work and/or their career plans, and how they see themselves contributing to the community at large in the future. Selection is based on that statement, the quality of submitted work, financial need, minority status, and academic record.

Financial data Basic scholarships range from $1,000 to $2,000, but awards between $3,000 and $5,000 are also presented at the discretion of the jury. Honorable mentions are $100. Funds are paid directly to the recipient's school.

Duration 1 academic year. Recipients may reapply.

Additional information The foundation encourages the scholarship recipients to focus on ways that their work can address issues of social and environmental responsibility. This program includes the following named awards: the Sherry and Gary Baker Award, the Bobolink Foundation

Award, the Bombay Sapphire Awards, the Richard and Jean Coyne Family Foundation Awards, the David A. Dechman Foundation Awards, the Philip and Edina Jennison Award, the Kraus Family Foundation Awards, the Dena McKelvey Award. the New York Design Center Award, the Rudin Foundation Awards, the Starr Foundation Awards, and the John F. Wright III Award.

Number awarded Varies each year; recently, 24 scholarships and 7 honorable mentions were awarded.

Deadline March of each year.

[676]
WTS PUGET SOUND CHAPTER SCHOLARSHIP

Women's Transportation Seminar-Puget Sound Chapter
c/o Lorelei Mesic, Scholarship Co-Chair
W&H Pacific
3350 Monte Villa Parkway
Bothell, WA 98021-8972
(425) 951-4872   Fax: (425) 951-4808
E-mail: lmesic@whpacific.com
Web: www.wtspugetsound.org/nscholarships.html

Purpose To provide financial assistance to women undergraduate and graduate students, particularly minority women, from Washington who are working on a degree related to transportation and have financial need.

Eligibility This program is open to women who are residents of Washington, studying at a college in the state, or working as an intern in the state. Applicants must be currently enrolled in an undergraduate or graduate degree program in a transportation-related field, such as engineering, planning, finance, or logistics. They must have a GPA of 3.0 or higher and plans to prepare for a career in a transportation-related field. Minority candidates are encouraged to apply. Along with their application, they must submit a 500-word statement about their career goals after graduation, their financial need, and why they think they should receive this scholarship award. Selection is based on transportation goals, academic record, transportation-related activities or job skills, and financial need.

Financial data The stipend is $1,500.

Duration 1 year.

Additional information The winner is also nominated for scholarships offered by the national organization of the Women's Transportation Seminar.

Number awarded 1 each year.

Deadline October of each year.

[677]
WTS/ITS WASHINGTON INTELLIGENT TRANSPORTATION SYSTEMS SCHOLARSHIP

Women's Transportation Seminar-Puget Sound Chapter
c/o Lorelei Mesic, Scholarship Co-Chair
W&H Pacific
3350 Monte Villa Parkway
Bothell, WA 98021-8972
(425) 951-4872   Fax: (425) 951-4808
E-mail: lmesic@whpacific.com
Web: www.wtspugetsound.org/nscholarships.html

Purpose To provide financial assistance to minority and other undergraduate and graduate students from Washing-

ton working on a degree related to intelligent transportation systems (ITS).

Eligibility This program is open to students who are residents of Washington, studying at a college in the state, or working as an intern in the state. Applicants must be currently enrolled in an undergraduate or graduate degree program related to the design, implementation, operation, and maintenance of ITS technologies. They must be majoring in transportation or a related field, including transportation engineering, systems engineering, electrical engineering, planning, finance, or logistics, and be taking courses in such ITS-related fields of study as computer science, electronics, and digital communications. In addition, they must have a GPA of 3.0 or higher and plans to prepare for a career in a transportation-related field. Minority candidates are encouraged to apply. Along with their application, they must submit a 500-word statement about their career goals after graduation, how those relate to ITS, and why they think they should receive this scholarship award. Selection is based on that statement, academic record, and transportation-related activities or job skills. Financial need is not considered.

Financial data The stipend is $1,500.

Duration 1 year.

Additional information This program is co-sponsored by ITS Washington.

Number awarded 1 each year.

Deadline October of each year.

[678]
XEROX TECHNICAL MINORITY SCHOLARSHIP PROGRAM

Xerox Corporation
Attn: Technical Minority Scholarship Program
150 State Street, Fourth Floor
Rochester, NY 14614
(585) 422-7689   E-mail: xtmsp@imcouncil.com
Web: www.xerox.com

Purpose To provide financial assistance to minorities interested in undergraduate or graduate education in the sciences and/or engineering.

Eligibility This program is open to minorities (people of African American, Asian, Pacific Islander, Native American, Native Alaskan, or Hispanic descent) working full time on an undergraduate or graduate degree in chemistry, computing and software systems, engineering (chemical, computer, electrical, imaging, manufacturing, mechanical, optical, or software), information management, laser optics, material science, physics, or printing management science. Applicants must be U.S. citizens or permanent residents with a GPA of 3.0 or higher and attending, or planning to attend, a 4-year college or university.

Financial data The maximum stipend is $1,000 per year.

Duration 1 year.

Number awarded Approximately 150 each year.

Deadline September of each year.

Loans

Described here are 40 programs open to Hispanic Americans that provide money which must eventually be repaid—in cash or in service and with or without interest. Included here are traditional loans, loans-for-service, and forgivable loans. If you are looking for a particular program and don't find it in this section, be sure to check the Program Title Index to see if it is covered elsewhere in the directory.

[679]
ARKANSAS MINORITY MASTERS FELLOWS PROGRAM

Arkansas Department of Higher Education
Attn: Financial Aid Division
114 East Capitol Avenue
Little Rock, AR 72201-3818
(501) 371-2050   Toll-free: (800) 54-STUDY
Fax: (501) 371-2001   E-mail: finaid@adhe.arknet.edu
Web: www.arkansashighered.com/mmasters.html

Purpose To provide fellowship/loans to minority graduate students in Arkansas who want to become teachers in selected subject areas.

Eligibility Applicants must be minority (African American, Hispanic, Native American, or Asian American) residents of Arkansas who are U.S. citizens and enrolled as full-time master's degree students at an Arkansas public or independent institution with a cumulative GPA of 2.75 or higher. Also eligible are minority students in the fifth year of a 5-year teacher certification program. Recipients must be willing to teach in an Arkansas public school or public institution of higher education for at least 2 years after completion of their education. Preference is given to applicants who completed their baccalaureate degrees within the previous 2 years.

Financial data The stipend is up to $7,500 per year for full-time students (or up to $2,500 per summer for part-time summer students). This is a fellowship/loan program. The loan will be forgiven at the rate of 50% for each year the recipient teaches full time in an Arkansas public school or public institution of higher education. If the recipient does not attend college on a full-time basis, withdraws from an approved teacher education program, or does not fulfill the required teaching obligation, the loan must be repaid in full with interest at a rate up to 5 percentage points above the Federal Reserve discount rate.

Duration 1 year; may be renewed if the recipient remains a full-time student with a GPA of 3.0 or higher.

Number awarded Varies each year; recently, 25 of these fellowship/loans were approved.

Deadline May of each year.

[680]
ARKANSAS MINORITY TEACHER SCHOLARS PROGRAM

Arkansas Department of Higher Education
Attn: Financial Aid Division
114 East Capitol Avenue
Little Rock, AR 72201-3818
(501) 371-2050   Toll-free: (800) 54-STUDY
Fax: (501) 371-2001   E-mail: finaid@adhe.arknet.edu
Web: www.arkansashighered.com/mteachers.html

Purpose To provide scholarship/loans to minority undergraduates in Arkansas who want to become teachers.

Eligibility Applicants must be minority (African American, Native American, Hispanic, or Asian American) residents of Arkansas who are U.S. citizens and enrolled as full-time juniors or seniors in an approved teacher certification program at an Arkansas public or independent 4-year institution. They must have a cumulative GPA of 2.5 or higher and be willing to teach in an Arkansas public school for at least 5 years after completion of their teaching certificate (3 years

if the teaching is in 1 of the 42 counties of Arkansas designated as the Delta Region; or if the teaching is in mathematics, science, or foreign language; or if the recipient is an African American male and teaches at the elementary level; or if the service is as a guidance counselor).

Financial data Awards up to $5,000 per year are available. This is a scholarship/loan program. The loan will be forgiven at the rate of 20% for each year the recipient teaches full time in an Arkansas public school (or 33% per year if the obligation is fulfilled in 3 years as described above). If the loan is not forgiven by service, it must be repaid with interest at a rate up to 5% points above the Federal Reserve discount rate.

Duration 1 year; may be renewed for 1 additional year if the recipient remains a full-time student with a GPA of 2.5 or higher.

Number awarded Varies each year; recently, 97 of these scholarship/loans were approved.

Deadline May of each year.

[681]
CALIFORNIA STATE UNIVERSITY FORGIVABLE LOAN/DOCTORAL INCENTIVE PROGRAM

California State University
Office of the Chancellor
Attn: Human Resources
401 Golden Shore, Fourth Floor
Long Beach, CA 90802-4210
(562) 951-4426   Fax: (562) 951-4954
E-mail: forgivableloan@calstate.edu
Web: www.calstate.edu/HR/FLP/index.shtml

Purpose To provide forgivable loans to graduate students who can help increase the diversity of persons qualified to compete for instructional faculty positions at campuses of the California State University (CSU) system.

Eligibility This program is open to new and continuing full-time students enrolled in a doctoral program anywhere in the United States, whether affiliated with a CSU campus or not. Applicants must present a plan of support from a full-time CSU faculty sponsor who will agree to advise and support the candidate throughout doctoral study. Selection is based on the applicant's academic record; professional qualifications; and relevant background, experience, and motivation to educate a diverse student body in the CSU system. The elements considered include unconditional acceptance into a specific doctoral program, quality of the proposed doctoral program, and other experiences or skills that enhance the potential of the candidate to educate a diverse student body; those experiences and characteristics may include experience working with persons who have a wide range of backgrounds and perspectives, research interests related to educating an increasingly diverse student body, a history of successfully overcoming economic disadvantage and adversity, experience in a variety of cultural environments, and being a first-generation college student. Special consideration is given to candidates whose proposed area of study falls where CSU campuses anticipate the greatest difficulty in filling instructional faculty positions.

Financial data Participants receive up to $10,000 per year or a maximum of $30,000 over 5 years. The loans are converted to fellowships at the rate of 20% of the total loan

amount for each postdoctoral year that the program participant teaches, for up to 5 years. Thus, the entire loan will be
forgiven after the recipient has taught full time for 5 years
on a CSU campus. Recipients who do not teach on a CSU
campus or who discontinue full-time studies will be required
to repay the total loan amount within a 15-year period at the
rate established for other student loans. The minimum
repayment required for a $30,000 loan is approximately
$287 per month to amortize the 8% per annum loan over
a 15-year period. Waiver of loan obligations can be made
in those exceptional cases where graduate work was dis-
continued for valid reasons and where repayment of the
loan would cause an unnecessary or undue hardship.
Duration Up to 5 years.
Additional information This program began in 1987. It
has loaned $32.4 million to 1,385 doctoral students enrolled
in universities throughout the nation and abroad.
Number awarded Varies each year.
Deadline The deadline varies at different CSU campuses
but typically falls in February of each year.

[682]
CENTRAL INTELLIGENCE AGENCY UNDERGRADUATE SCHOLARSHIP PROGRAM

Central Intelligence Agency
Attn: Recruitment Center
P.O. Box 4090
Reston, VA 20195
Toll-free: (800) 368-3886
Web: www.cia.gov/employment/student.html

Purpose To provide scholarship/loans and work experience to high school seniors and college sophomores, especially minorities and people with disabilities, who are interested in working for the Central Intelligence Agency (CIA)
after graduation from college.
Eligibility This program is open to U.S. citizens who are
either high school seniors or college sophomores. Seniors
must be at least 18 years of age by April of the year they
apply and have minimum scores of 21 on the ACT (or the
equivalent on the SAT). College sophomores must have a
GPA of 3.0 or higher. All applicants must be able to demonstrate financial need (household income of $70,000 or less
for a family of 4 or $80,000 or less for a family of 5 or more)
and be able to meet the same employment standards as
permanent employees of the CIA. An explicit goal of the
program is to attract minorities and students with disabilities to a career with the CIA.
Financial data Scholars are provided a salary and up to
$18,000 per year for tuition, fees, books, and supplies. They
must agree to continue employment with the CIA after college graduation for a period 1.5 times the length of their college support.
Duration 1 year; may be renewed if the student maintains
a GPA of 3.0 or higher and full-time enrollment in a 4- or
5-year college program.
Additional information Scholars work each summer at
a CIA facility. In addition to a salary, they receive the cost
of transportation between school and the Washington, D.C.
area and a housing allowance.
Number awarded Varies each year.
Deadline October of each year.

[683]
CENTRAL VALLEY NURSING SCHOLARSHIP PROGRAM

Health Professions Education Foundation
Attn: Program Administrator
818 K Street, Suite 210
Sacramento, CA 95814
(916) 324-6500   Toll-free: (800) 773-1669
Fax: (916) 324-6585
Web: www.healthprofessions.ca.gov

Purpose To provide scholarship/loans to underrepresented residents of California who plan to work on an associate, baccalaureate, or master's degree in nursing at an
institution in the state's Central Valley and then provide
direct patient care in a medically underserved area in the
region.
Eligibility This program is open to California residents
who are enrolled or accepted for enrollment in an associate,
baccalaureate, or master's degree nursing program in 6
counties of the Central Valley (Fresno, Kern, Kings, Madera,
Merced, or Tulare). Applicants must quality as underrepresented and/or economically disadvantaged. They must
agree to begin a 2-year service obligation immediately following graduation by practicing full-time nursing in direct
patient care in a medically underserved area within the
6-county region. U.S. citizenship or permanent resident status is required.
Financial data Stipends range from $8,000 to $12,000
per year. Recipients who fail to meet the service obligation
must repay all funds received.
Duration 1 year; may be renewed provided the recipient
maintains at least half-time enrollment and a GPA of 2.0 or
higher.
Additional information This program, established in
2002, is funded by a grant from the California Endowment.
Number awarded Varies each year; recently, 44 of these
scholarships (worth $402,000) were awarded, including 27
for associate degree students, 14 for baccalaureate degree
students, and 3 for master's degree students.
Deadline Applications are accepted biennially, in May or
October of even-numbered years.

[684]
DEFENSE INTELLIGENCE AGENCY UNDERGRADUATE TRAINING ASSISTANCE PROGRAM

Defense Intelligence Agency
Attn: DAH-2
Bolling Air Force Base
Building 6000
Washington, DC 20340-5100
(202) 231-4713   Fax: (202) 231-4889
TTY: (202) 231-5002
Web: www.dia.mil/Careers/Programs/utap.html

Purpose To provide loans-for-service and work experience to women, minority, and disabled high school seniors
interested in majoring in specified fields and working for the
U.S. Defense Intelligence Agency (DIA).
Eligibility This program is open to women, minorities,
and individuals with disabilities who are graduating high
school seniors and interested in majoring in 1 of the following fields in college: geography, foreign area studies, inter-

national relations, or political science. Applicants must have a high school GPA of 3.0 or higher, have an ACT score of 21 or higher (or the equivalent SAT score), be able to demonstrate financial need (household income ceiling of $65,000 for a family of 4 or $80,000 for a family of 5 or more), be U.S. citizens and from a family of U.S. citizens, and demonstrate leadership abilities through extracurricular activities, civic involvement, volunteer work, or part-time employment.

Financial data Students accepted into this program receive tuition (up to $18,000 per year) at an accredited college or university selected by the student and endorsed by the sponsor; reimbursement for books and needed supplies; an annual salary to cover college room and board expenses and for summer employment; and a position at the sponsoring agency after graduation. Recipients must work for DIA after college graduation for at least 1 and a half times the length of study. For participants who leave DIA earlier than scheduled, the agency arranges for payments to reimburse DIA for the total cost of education (including the employee's pay and allowances).

Duration 4 years.

Additional information Recipients are provided a challenging summer internship and guaranteed a job at the agency in their field of study upon graduation. Recipients must attend school on a full-time basis.

Number awarded Only a few are awarded each year.

Deadline November of each year.

[685]
DIRECT FARM LOANS FOR SOCIALLY DISADVANTAGED PERSONS

Department of Agriculture
Farm Service Agency
Attn: Office of Minority and Socially Disadvantaged
   Farmers Assistance
1400 Independence Avenue, S.W.
Washington, DC 20250-0568
(202) 720-1584   Toll-free: (866) 538-2610
Fax: (202) 720-5398   Fax: (866) 480-2824
E-mail: msda@wdc.usda.gov
Web: www.fsa.usda.gov

Purpose To lend money to eligible members of socially disadvantaged groups for the purchase or operation of family-size farms or ranches.

Eligibility For the purposes of this program, a "socially disadvantaged group" is 1 whose members "have been subjected to racial, ethnic, or gender prejudice because of their identity as members of a group without regard to their individual qualities." Those groups are women, African Americans, American Indians, Alaskan Natives, Hispanics, Asian Americans, and Pacific Islanders. Applicants may be seeking either farm ownership loans (to purchase or enlarge a farm or ranch, purchase easements or rights of way needed in the farm's operation, erect or improve buildings such as a dwelling or barn, promote soil and water conservation, or pay closing costs) or farm operating loans (to purchase livestock, poultry, farm and home equipment, feed, seed, fertilizer, chemicals, hail and other crop insurance, food, clothing, medical care, and hired labor). Loans are made to individuals, partnerships, joint operations, corporations, and cooperatives primarily and directly engaged in

farming and ranching on family-size operations; a family-size farm is defined as a farm that a family can operate and manage itself. In addition to belonging to a "socially disadvantaged group," borrowers must have a satisfactory history of meeting credit obligations, have 3 years of experience in operating a farm or ranch for an ownership loan or 1 year's experience within the last 5 years for an operating loan, be a U.S. citizen or legal resident, possess the legal capacity to incur the obligations of a loan or credit sale, and be unable to obtain sufficient credit elsewhere at reasonable rates.

Financial data The maximum loan is $200,000. Interest rates are set periodically according to the federal government's cost of borrowing.

Duration Repayment terms are generally up to 40 years for ownership loans or 1 to 7 years for operating loans.

Deadline Applications may be submitted at any time.

[686]
DIVERSIFYING HIGHER EDUCATION FACULTY IN ILLINOIS

Southern Illinois University at Carbondale
Attn: DFI Administrative Office
900 South Normal
Woody Hall C-224
Carbondale, IL 62901-4723
(618) 453-4558   E-mail: fellows@siu.edu
Web: www.dfi.siu.edu

Purpose To provide fellowship/loans to minority students interested in enrolling in graduate school programs in Illinois to prepare for a career in higher education.

Eligibility This program is open to 1) residents of Illinois who have received a high school diploma or postsecondary degree from an educational institution in the state; and 2) registered voters in Illinois with 3 or more years of residency in the state. Applicants must be members of a minority group traditionally underrepresented in graduate school enrollment in Illinois (African Americans, Hispanic Americans, Native Americans, or Asian Americans) and have been admitted to a graduate program in the state to work on a doctoral or master's degree and prepare for a career in teaching or administration at an Illinois postsecondary institution or Illinois higher education governing board. They must have a GPA of 2.75 or higher in the last 60 hours of undergraduate work or 3.2 or higher in at least 9 hours of graduate study and be able to demonstrate financial need. Along with their application, they must submit statements on their educational and career goals (including their rationale for selecting their major field of study, the relationship between the selected major and future plans, and their research interest and academic preparation) and on their underrepresented status (including how their underrepresented status influenced their personal and academic development and why they should be awarded a fellowship designated specifically for underrepresented groups in higher education).

Financial data Stipends range between $12,500 and $16,000 per year for full-time enrollment. Some participating institutions also provide a tuition waiver or scholarship. This is a fellowship/loan program. Recipients must agree to accept a position, in teaching or administration, at an Illinois postsecondary educational institution, on an Illinois higher education governing or coordinating board, or at a state agency in an education-related position. Recipients failing to fulfill the conditions of the award are required to repay 20% of the total award.

Duration Up to 2 years for master's degree students; up to 4 years for doctoral students.

Additional information The Illinois General Assembly established this program in 2004 as a successor to 2 earlier programs (both established in 1985); the Illinois Consortium for Educational Opportunity Program (ICEOP) and the Illinois Minority Graduate Incentive Program (IMGIP).

Deadline February of each year.

[687]
FACULTY LOAN REPAYMENT PROGRAM

Health Resources and Services Administration
Bureau of Health Professions
Parklawn Building, Room 8-34
5600 Fishers Lane
Rockville, MD 20857
(301) 443-1700   Toll-free: (888) 275-4772
Fax: (301) 443-0846   E-mail: flrpinfo@hrsa.gov
Web: bhpr.hrsa.gov/dsa/flrp

Purpose To repay the educational loans of faculty from disadvantaged backgrounds in health professions schools.

Eligibility Applicants for this assistance must be from a disadvantaged background, defined as individuals who either 1) come from an environment that has inhibited them from obtaining the knowledge, skill, and abilities required to enroll in and graduate from a health professions school or from a program providing education or training in an allied health profession; or 2) come from a family with an annual income below a level based on low income thresholds according to family size published by the U.S. Bureau of Census. They must 1) have a degree from a school of medicine, osteopathic medicine, dentistry, nursing, or another health profession; 2) be enrolled in an approved graduate training program in those health professions; or 3) be enrolled as a full-time student in the final year of training, leading to a degree from an eligible school.

Financial data This program repays, for each year of service, as much as $20,000 of the outstanding principal and interest on the recipient's educational loans. The employing school must agree to pay a sum (in addition to faculty salary) equal to that paid by this program.

Duration Service must be for a minimum of 2 years.

Additional information Recipients must agree to serve as a faculty member at a school of medicine, osteopathic medicine, dentistry, veterinary medicine, optometry, podiatric medicine, pharmacy, public health, allied health (including baccalaureate or graduate degree programs in dental hygiene, medical laboratory technology, occupational therapy, physical therapy, radiologic technology, speech pathology, audiology, and medical nutrition therapy), nursing, or graduate program in behavioral and mental health (including clinical psychology, clinical social work, professional counseling, and marriage and family therapy).

Number awarded Approximately 25 each year.

Deadline May of each year.

[688]
GOLDEN APPLE SCHOLARS OF ILLINOIS

Golden Apple Foundation
Attn: Director of Scholars, Recruitment and Placement
8 South Michigan Avenue, Suite 700
Chicago, IL 60603-3463
(312) 407-0433, ext. 105   Fax: (312) 407-0344
E-mail: kilduff@goldenapple.org
Web: www.goldenapple.org/scholars.htm

Purpose To provide scholarship/loans to high school seniors (particularly minorities) in Illinois who wish to study education at an Illinois college and teach in the state.

Eligibility This program is open to high school seniors at schools in Illinois. Students must be nominated by a teacher, principal, guidance counselor, or other non-family adult; self-nominations are also accepted. Nominees must be committed to teaching as a profession and must be interested in attending 1 of 53 designated colleges and universities in Illinois. A limited number of openings are also available to sophomores at those designated Illinois institutions. The program strongly encourages nomination of prospective teachers for which there is currently a shortage, especially minority and bilingual teachers.

Financial data Scholars receive a scholarship/loan of $2,500 per year to apply toward their educational expenses and a stipend of $2,000 per year for participating in a summer teaching internship. If they complete a bachelor's degree and teach for 5 years in an Illinois school of need, the loan is forgiven. Schools of need are defined as those either having Chapter I status by the U.S. Department of Education or having mediocre to poor PSAE or ISAT scores.

Duration 4 years, provided the recipient maintains a GPA of 2.0 or higher during the freshman year and 2.5 or higher in subsequent years. Students who enter the program as sophomores receive 2 years of support.

Additional information During the annual summer institutes, scholars participate in teaching internships and seminars on the art and craft of teaching. This program was established in 1988.

Number awarded Up to 100 each year.

Deadline Nominations must be submitted by November of each year.

[689]
GUARANTEED FARM LOANS FOR SOCIALLY DISADVANTAGED PERSONS

Department of Agriculture
Farm Service Agency
Attn: Office of Minority and Socially Disadvantaged
    Farmers Assistance
1400 Independence Avenue, S.W.
Washington, DC 20250-0568
(202) 720-1584   Toll-free: (866) 538-2610
Fax: (202) 720-5398   Fax: (866) 480-2824
E-mail: msda@wdc.usda.gov
Web: www.fsa.usda.gov

Purpose To guarantee loans to eligible members of socially disadvantaged groups for the purchase or operation of family-size farms or ranches.

Eligibility For the purposes of this program, a "socially disadvantaged group" is 1 whose members "have been subjected to racial, ethnic, or gender prejudice because of their identity as members of a group without regard to their individual qualities." Those groups are women, African Americans, American Indians, Alaskan Natives, Hispanic Americans, Asian Americans, and Pacific Islanders. Applicants may be seeking guarantees of loans either for farm ownership (to purchase or enlarge a farm or ranch, purchase easements or rights of way needed in the farm's operation, erect or improve buildings such as a dwelling or barn, promote soil and water conservation, or pay closing costs) or farm operation (to purchase livestock, poultry, farm and home equipment, feed, seed, fertilizer, chemicals, hail and other crop insurance, food, clothing, medical care, and hired labor). Guarantees are provided on loans by lending institutions subject to federal or state supervision. Loans are made to individuals, partnerships, joint operations, corporations, and cooperatives primarily and directly engaged in farming and ranching on family-size operations; a family-size farm is defined as a farm that a family can operate and manage itself. In addition to belonging to a "socially disadvantaged group," borrowers must have a satisfactory history of meeting credit obligations, have 3 years of experience in operating a farm or ranch for an ownership loan or 1 year's experience within the last 5 years for an operating loan, be a U.S. citizen or legal resident, possess the legal capacity to incur the obligations of a loan or credit sale, and be unable to obtain sufficient credit elsewhere at reasonable rates.

Financial data   The size of the loan is agreed upon by the borrower and the lender, but the maximum indebtedness of loans guaranteed by the Farm Service Agency (FSA) may not exceed $762,000. Interest rates can be fixed or variable, as agreed upon by the borrower and the lender, but may not exceed the rate the lender charges its average farm customer. FSA guarantees up to 95% of the loan principal and interest against loss.

Duration   Repayment terms are generally up to 40 years for ownership loans or 1 to 7 years for operating loans.

Deadline   Applications may be submitted at any time.

[690]
ILLINOIS FUTURE TEACHER CORPS PROGRAM

Illinois Student Assistance Commission
Attn: Scholarship and Grant Services
1755 Lake Cook Road
Deerfield, IL 60015-5209
(847) 948-8550   Toll-free: (800) 899-ISAC
Fax: (847) 831-8549   TDD: (847) 831-8326, ext. 2822
E-mail: collegezone@isac.org
Web: www.collegezone.com

Purpose   To provide scholarship/loans to minority and other college students in Illinois who are interested in training or retraining for a teaching career in academic shortage areas.

Eligibility   This program is open to Illinois residents who are enrolled at the junior level or higher at an institution of higher education in the state. Applicants must be planning to prepare for a career as a preschool, elementary, or secondary school teacher. Priority is given to students working on a degree in designated teacher shortage disciplines, making a commitment to teach at a hard-to-staff school, and/or planning to teach minority students. Recently, the teacher shortage disciplines included behavior disordered, bilingual teacher (K-12), cross categorical (seeking certifica-

tion in 2 or more areas of special education), general special education (including blind and deaf specialties and early childhood special education), learning disabled, mathematics (K-12), music (K-12), physical education (K-12), reading and English language arts (K-12), and speech and language impaired. Priority is given to renewal applicants. Selection is based on cumulative GPA, expected family contribution, and minority student status.

Financial data   This program pays tuition and fees, room and board, or a commuter allowance at academic institutions in Illinois. The maximum award is $5,000 or $10,000 (and may even be increased by an additional $5,000), depending on the teaching commitment the recipient makes. Funds are paid directly to the school. This is a scholarship/loan program. Recipients must agree to teach in an Illinois public, private, or parochial preschool, elementary school, or secondary school for 1 year for each full year of assistance received. The teaching obligation must be completed within 5 years of completion of the degree or certificate program for which the scholarship was awarded. That time period may be extended if the recipient serves in the U.S. armed forces, enrolls full time in a graduate program related to teaching, becomes temporarily disabled, is unable to find employment as a teacher, or takes additional courses on at least a half-time basis to teach in a specialized teacher shortage discipline. Recipients who fail to honor this work obligation must repay the award with interest.

Duration   1 year; may be renewed.

Additional information   This program was formerly known as the David A. DeBolt Teacher Shortage Scholarship Program.

Number awarded   Varies each year, depending on the availability of funds.

Deadline   Priority consideration is given to applications submitted by February of each year.

[691]
ILLINOIS PODIATRIC MEDICAL STUDENT SCHOLARSHIPS

Illinois Department of Public Health
Attn: Center for Rural Health
535 West Jefferson Street
Springfield, IL 62761
(217) 782-4977   Fax: (217) 782-3987
TTY: (800) 547-0466   E-mail: mailus@idph.state.il.us
Web: www.idph.state.il.us

Purpose   To provide scholarship/loans to Illinois residents (particularly minorities) who are interested in working on a degree in podiatry at an institution in the state.

Eligibility   This program is open to Illinois residents who are studying podiatric medicine, or have been accepted for enrollment, in a podiatry school in the state. Selection is based, in order, on the following factors: interest in pursuing podiatric medicine, previous experience with medically underserved populations, previous experience in the health care delivery system (with preference given to those whose experience has involved a primary care specialty area), academic capability as reported by the applicant's podiatric medical school, financial need, years of podiatric medical school remaining, interest in providing podiatric care to Illinois residents in designated shortage areas, and length of residence in Illinois. U.S. citizenship is required. Preference is given to minority students.

Financial data Funding is provided to cover the cost of tuition and matriculation fees. This is a scholarship/loan program. Within 30 days after Illinois licensure to practice podiatric medicine, the recipient must provide primary health care in a designated shortage area of Illinois for 1 year per academic year of scholarship support. The service must be a full-time, office-based practice providing direct patient care. Scholarship recipients who fail to fulfill their obligation to practice in designated shortage areas must pay a sum equal to 3 times the amount of the annual scholarship grant for each year the recipient fails to fulfill the obligation.

Duration Up to 2 years.

Number awarded Varies each year.

Deadline May of each year.

[692]
INDIANA MINORITY TEACHER/SPECIAL EDUCATION SERVICES SCHOLARSHIP

State Student Assistance Commission of Indiana
Attn: Grant Division
150 West Market Street, Suite 500
Indianapolis, IN 46204-2811
(317) 232-2350   Toll-free: (888) 528-4719 (within IN)
Fax: (317) 232-3260 E-mail: special@ssaci.state.in.us
Web: www.in.gov/ssaci/programs/m-teach.html

Purpose To provide scholarship/loans to Black and Hispanic undergraduate students in Indiana interested in preparing for a teaching career and to other residents of the state preparing for a career in special education, occupational therapy, or physical therapy.

Eligibility This program is open to 1) Black and Hispanic students seeking teacher certification; 2) students seeking special education teaching certification; or 3) students seeking occupational or physical therapy certification. Applicants must be Indiana residents and U.S. citizens who are enrolled or accepted for enrollment as full-time students at an academic institution in Indiana. Students who are already enrolled in college must have a GPA of 2.0 or higher. Applicants must be preparing to teach in an accredited elementary or secondary school in Indiana or to work as an occupational or physical therapist at a school or rehabilitation facility. Financial need may be considered, but it is not a requirement. Preference is given to minorities and to students enrolling in college for the first time.

Financial data Up to $1,000 annually; if students demonstrate financial need, they may receive up to $4,000 annually. For 3 out of the 5 years following graduation, recipients must teach full time in an elementary or secondary school in Indiana or practice as an occupational or physical therapist at a school or rehabilitation facility in the state.. If they fail to meet that service requirement, they are required to reimburse the state of Indiana for all funds received.

Duration 1 year; may be renewed up to 3 additional years if recipients maintain a 2.0 GPA. They may, however, take up to 6 years to complete the program from the start of receiving the first scholarship.

Additional information This program was established in 1988 to address the critical shortage of Black and Hispanic teachers in Indiana. An amendment in 1990 added the field of special education, and in 1991 the fields of occupational and physical therapy were added. Participating colleges in Indiana select the recipients. Students must submit their application to the financial aid office of the college they plan to attend (not to the State Student Assistance Commission of Indiana).

Number awarded Varies each year.

Deadline Each participating college or university establishes its filing deadline for this program.

[693]
KANSAS TEACHER SERVICE SCHOLARSHIPS

Kansas Board of Regents
Attn: Student Financial Aid
1000 S.W. Jackson Street, Suite 520
Topeka, KS 66612-1368
(785) 296-3518   Fax: (785) 296-0983
E-mail: dlindeman@ksbor.org
Web: www.kansasregents.com

Purpose To provide scholarship/loans to high school seniors, high school graduates, and selected undergraduates (particularly minorities) who are interested in preparing for a career as a teacher in Kansas.

Eligibility This program is open to Kansas residents who plan to enter the teaching profession in specific curriculum areas; recently, those included special education, mathematics, and science. Applicants must submit evidence of completion of the Kansas Scholars Curriculum (4 years of English, 4 years of mathematics, 3 years of science, 3 years of social studies, 2 years of foreign language, and 1 year of computer technology), ACT or SAT scores, high school GPA, high school class rank, and (if relevant) college transcripts and letters of recommendation from a college or university official. First priority goes to applicants who are in the final 2 years of study in teacher education and have submitted a college transcript and 1 letter of recommendation from a college official. Special consideration is given to minority applicants (academic performance being similar), because minorities continue to be underrepresented in the teaching profession in Kansas schools. Second priority goes to students who have completed the Kansas Scholars Curriculum and have competitive GPAs, ACT scores, and class rank.

Financial data Participants receive $5,000 per year. This is a scholarship/loan program. Recipients must teach in Kansas 1 year for every year of funding received, or they must repay the amount received with interest at 5% over the federal PLUS rate. The teaching must be in the specific curriculum area or in an underserved geographic area (recently including Wichita, Leavenworth, Garden City, and Kansas City).

Duration 1 year; may be renewed for up to 3 additional years or up to 4 additional years for designated 5-year courses of study requiring graduate work.

Additional information There is a $10 application fee.

Number awarded Approximately 100 each year.

Deadline March of each year.

[694]
KENTUCKY MINORITY EDUCATOR RECRUITMENT AND RETENTION SCHOLARSHIPS

Kentucky Department of Education
Attn: Division of Minority Educator Recruitment and
    Retention
500 Mero Street, 17th Floor
Frankfort, KY 40601
(502) 564-1479   Fax: (502) 564-6952
E-mail: bpelphre@kde.state.ky.us
Web: www.education.ky.gov

Purpose To provide forgivable loans to minority undergraduate and graduate students enrolled in Kentucky public institutions who want to become teachers.

Eligibility This program is open to residents of Kentucky who are undergraduate or graduate students pursuing initial teacher certification at a public university or community college in the state. Applicants must have a GPA of 2.5 or higher and either maintain full-time enrollment or be a part-time student within 18 semester hours of receiving a teacher education degree. U.S. citizenship is required.

Financial data Awards up to $5,000 per year are available. This is a scholarship/loan program. Recipients are required to teach 1 semester in Kentucky for each semester or summer term the scholarship is received. If they fail to fulfill that requirement, the scholarship converts to a loan at 12% interest.

Duration 1 year; may be renewed.

Additional information The Kentucky General Assembly established this program in 1992.

Number awarded Varies each year.

Deadline Each state college of teacher education sets its own deadline.

[695]
MENTAL HEALTH SUBSTANCE ABUSE CLINICAL FELLOWSHIP PROGRAM

Council on Social Work Education
Attn: Minority Fellowship Program
1725 Duke Street, Suite 500
Alexandria, VA 22314-3457
(703) 683-8080, ext. 217   Fax: (703) 683-8099
E-mail: mfp@cswe.org
Web: www.cswe.org

Purpose To provide forgivable loans to racial minority members interested in preparing for a clinical career in the mental health fields.

Eligibility This program is open to U.S. citizens and permanent residents who have been underrepresented in the field of social work. These include but are not limited to the following groups: American Indians/Alaskan Natives, Asian/Pacific Islanders (e.g., Chinese, East Indians, South Asians, Filipinos, Hawaiians, Japanese, Koreans, and Samoans), Blacks, and Hispanics (e.g., Mexicans/Chicanos, Puerto Ricans, Cubans, Central or South Americans). Applicants must be interested in and committed to a career in mental health and/or substance abuse with specialization in the delivery of services of ethnic and racial minority groups. They must have a master's degree in social work and be accepted to or enrolled in a full-time doctoral degree program.

Financial data Awards provide a stipend of $16,500 per year and tuition support to a maximum of $3,000.

Duration 1 academic year; renewable for 2 additional years if funds are available and the recipient makes satisfactory progress toward the degree objectives.

Additional information This program has been funded since 1978 by the Center for Mental Health Services of the Substance Abuse and Mental Health Services Administration.

Deadline February of each year.

[696]
MINORITY TEACHERS OF ILLINOIS SCHOLARSHIP PROGRAM

Illinois Student Assistance Commission
Attn: Scholarship and Grant Services
1755 Lake Cook Road
Deerfield, IL 60015-5209
(847) 948-8550   Toll-free: (800) 899-ISAC
Fax: (847) 831-8549   TDD: (847) 831-8326, ext. 2822
E-mail: collegezone@isac.org
Web: www.collegezone.com

Purpose To provide scholarship/loans to minority students in Illinois who plan to become teachers at the preschool, elementary, or secondary level.

Eligibility Applicants must be Illinois residents, U.S. citizens or eligible noncitizens, members of a minority group (African American/Black, Hispanic American, Asian American, or Native American), and high school graduates or holders of a General Educational Development (GED) certificate. They must be enrolled in college full time at the sophomore level or above, have a GPA of 2.5 or higher, not be in default on any student loan, and be enrolled or accepted for enrollment in a teacher education program.

Financial data Grants up to $5,000 per year are awarded. This is a scholarship/loan program. Recipients must agree to teach full time 1 year for each year of support received. The teaching agreement may be fulfilled at a public, private, or parochial preschool, elementary school, or secondary school in Illinois; at least 30% of the student body at those schools must be minority. It must be fulfilled within the 5-year period following the completion of the undergraduate program for which the scholarship was awarded. The time period may be extended if the recipient serves in the U.S. armed forces, enrolls full time in a graduate program related to teaching, becomes temporarily disabled, is unable to find employment as a teacher at a qualifying school, or takes additional courses on at least a half-time basis to obtain certification as a teacher in Illinois. Recipients who fail to honor this work obligation must repay the award with 5% interest.

Duration 1 year.

Number awarded Varies each year.

Deadline Priority consideration is given to applications received by February of each year.

[697]
MISSOURI MINORITY TEACHER EDUCATION SCHOLARSHIP PROGRAM

Missouri Department of Elementary and Secondary
Education
Attn: Teacher Quality and Urban Education
205 Jefferson Street
P.O. Box 480
Jefferson City, MO 65102-0480
(573) 751-1668   Fax: (573) 526-3580
E-mail: lharriso@mail.dese.state.mo.us
Web: www.dese.state.mo.us

Purpose To provide scholarship/loans to minority high school seniors, high school graduates, and college students in Missouri who are interested in preparing for a teaching career in mathematics or science.

Eligibility This program is open to Missouri residents who are African American, Asian American, Hispanic American, or Native American. Applicants must be 1) high school seniors, college students, or returning adults (without a degree) who ranked in the top 25% of their high school class and scored at or above the 75th percentile on the ACT or SAT examination; 2) individuals who have completed 30 college hours with a cumulative GPA of 3.0 or better; or 3) baccalaureate degree-holders who are returning to an approved mathematics or science program. All applicants must attend an approved teacher education program at a community college, 4-year college, or university in Missouri. Selection is based on academic performance, the quantity and quality of school and community activities, range of interests and activities, leadership abilities, interpersonal skills, and desire to enter the field of education.

Financial data The stipend is $3,000 per year. This is a scholarship/loan program. Recipients must commit to teaching in a Missouri public elementary or secondary school for 5 years following graduation. If they fail to fulfill that obligation, they must repay the state portion of the scholarship.

Duration Up to 4 years.

Number awarded 100 each year.

Deadline February of each year.

[698]
MISSOURI PROFESSIONAL AND PRACTICAL NURSING STUDENT LOAN PROGRAM

Missouri Department of Health and Senior Services
Attn: Primary Care and Rural Health
P.O. Box 570
Jefferson City, MO 65102-0570
(573) 751-6400   Toll-free: (800) 891-7415
Fax: (573) 751-6041
Web: www.dhss.state.mo.us

Purpose To provide scholarship/loans to nursing students (particularly minorities) in Missouri who agree to work in an "area of need" in the state.

Eligibility This program is open to residents of Missouri who have lived for 1 or more years in the state for purposes other than attending an educational institution. Applicants must have applied for acceptance into a full-time course of study leading to an associate degree, a diploma, a bachelor of science, or a master of science degree in nursing, or leading to the completion of educational requirements for a licensed practical nurse. The educational institution must have a Missouri program approved by the State Board of Nursing for participation in this program. Priority is given to residents of underserved areas, minority persons, and previous recipients of these loans.

Financial data The maximum loan is $5,000 per year for professional nursing education or $2,500 per year for practical nursing education. This is a scholarship/loan program. Loans are forgiven at the rate of 25% per year for qualifying employment in an area of defined need (a geographic area or a nursing specialty that is experiencing a shortage of nurses in Missouri). If the loan is not forgiven by service, it must be repaid at 9.5% interest.

Duration 1 year; may be renewed as long as the recipient is enrolled in an approved program.

Number awarded Varies each year.

Deadline June or December of each year.

[699]
NATIONAL INSTITUTES OF HEALTH UNDERGRADUATE SCHOLARSHIP PROGRAM

National Institutes of Health
Attn: Office of Loan Repayment and Scholarship
2 Center Drive, Room 2E24
Bethesda, MD 20892-0230
Toll-free: (800) 528-7689   Fax: (301) 480-5481
TTY: (888) 352-3001   E-mail: ugsp@nih.gov
Web: ugsp.info.nih.gov

Purpose To provide loans-for-service for undergraduate education in the life sciences to students from disadvantaged backgrounds.

Eligibility This program is open to U.S. citizens, nationals, and permanent residents who are enrolled or accepted for enrollment as full-time students at accredited institutions of higher education and committed to careers in biomedical, behavioral, and social science health-related research. Applicants must come from a family that meets federal standards of low income, currently defined as a family with an annual income below $18,620 for a 1-person family, ranging to below $63,140 for families of 8 or more. They must have a GPA of 3.5 or higher or be in the top 5% of their class. Selection is based on commitment to a career in biomedical, behavioral, or social science health-related research as an employee of the National Institutes of Health (NIH); academic achievements; recommendations and evaluations of skills, abilities, and goals; and relevant extracurricular activities. Applicants are ranked according to the following priorities: first, juniors and seniors who have completed 2 years of undergraduate course work including 4 core science courses in biology, chemistry, physics, and calculus; second, other undergraduates who have completed those 4 core science courses; third, freshmen and sophomores at accredited undergraduate institutions; and fourth, high school seniors who have been accepted for enrollment as full-time students at accredited undergraduate institutions. The sponsor especially encourages applications from underrepresented minorities, women, and individuals with disabilities.

Financial data Stipends are available up to $20,000 per year, to be used for tuition, educational expenses (such as books and lab fees), and qualified living expenses while attending a college or university. Recipients incur a service obligation to work as an employee of the NIH in Bethesda, Maryland for 10 consecutive weeks (during the summer) during the sponsored year and, upon graduation, for 52 weeks for each academic year of scholarship support. The NIH 52-week employment obligation may be deferred if the recipient goes to graduate or medical school.

Duration 1 year; may be renewed for up to 3 additional years.

Number awarded 15 each year.

Deadline February of each year.

[700]
NEW MEXICO MINORITY DOCTORAL ASSISTANCE LOAN-FOR-SERVICE PROGRAM

New Mexico Commission on Higher Education
Attn: Financial Aid and Student Services
1068 Cerrillos Road
P.O. Box 15910
Santa Fe, NM 87506-5910
(505) 827-1217   Toll-free: (800) 279-9777
Fax: (505) 827-7392
E-mail: highered@che.state.nm.us
Web: www.nmche.org/collegefinance/minoritydoc.asp

Purpose To provide loans-for-service to underrepresented minorities and women who reside in New Mexico and are interested in working on a graduate degree in selected fields.

Eligibility Eligible to apply for this program are ethnic minorities and women who have received a baccalaureate and/or master's degree from a state-supported 4-year higher education institution in New Mexico; wish to work on a doctoral degree at an eligible sponsoring New Mexico institution in mathematics, engineering, the physical or life sciences, or any other academic discipline in which ethnic minorities and women are demonstrably underrepresented in New Mexico colleges and universities; and are willing after obtaining their degree to teach at an institution of higher education in the state. Applicants must be U.S. citizens and New Mexico residents.

Financial data This is a loan-for-service program in which the amount of the loan (up to $25,000 per year) may be wholly or partially forgiven upon completion of service as a college instructor in New Mexico.

Duration 1 year; may be renewed for up to 2 additional years for students who enter with a master's degree or up to 3 additional years for students who begin with a baccalaureate degree.

Additional information Sponsoring institutions nominate candidates to the Commission on Higher Education for these awards. Recipients must agree to teach at the college/university level in New Mexico upon completion of their doctoral degree. If the sponsoring institution where the recipient completes the degree is unable to provide a tenure-track position, it must arrange placement at another alternate and mutually-acceptable New Mexico public postsecondary institution.

Number awarded Up to 12 each year.

Deadline March of each year.

[701]
NEW YORK CITY DEPARTMENT OF EDUCATION GRADUATE SCHOLARSHIP PROGRAM

New York City Department of Education
Division of Human Resources
Attn: Office of Incentive Programs
65 Court Street, Room 102
Brooklyn, NY 11201
(718) 935-2449

Purpose To provide scholarship/loans to bilingual and other college graduates who are interested in working on a master's degree in a designated critical shortage area and subsequently working in that field in the New York City public schools.

Eligibility This program is open to college graduates who have a bachelor's degree with a GPA of 3.0 or higher. Applicants must be interested in working on a master's degree in 1 of the following areas: monolingual and bilingual deaf and hard of hearing, bilingual special education, monolingual and bilingual speech language pathology/audiology, monolingual and bilingual visually impaired, bilingual school counseling, bilingual school psychology, and bilingual school social work. For the bilingual programs, applicants must be able to speak Spanish, Russian, Haitian Creole, or Chinese (Mandarin/Cantonese). U.S. citizenship or permanent resident status is required. Each critical subject shortage area designates specified colleges or universities in the New York City region where the degree may be obtained.

Financial data This is a scholarship/loan program. Recipients are reimbursed for the full cost of tuition for their approved master's degree. They must serve as New York State certified professionals for the New York City public schools in the area in which they earn a master's degree for as many years (no less than 2 or more than 5) as they receive financial assistance through this program.

Duration Up to 5 years.

Additional information Applications must be filed in person. There is a nonrefundable $15 application fee. Recipients must complete at least 12 credits per year with a grade of "C" or better.

Number awarded Varies each year.

Deadline July of each year.

[702]
NEW YORK STATE REGENTS HEALTH CARE SCHOLARSHIPS FOR MEDICINE AND DENTISTRY

New York State Education Department
Office of K-16 Initiatives and Access Programs
Attn: Scholarships and Grants Administration Unit
Education Building Addition, Room 1078
Albany, NY 12234
(518) 486-1319   E-mail: kiap@mail.nysed.gov
Web: www.highered.nysed.gov

Purpose To provide fellowship/loans to minority or educationally disadvantaged students in New York who are entering or already enrolled in an approved program in medicine or dentistry.

Eligibility This program is open to U.S. citizens or permanent residents who are residents of New York. Applicants must be interested in studying full time at an approved New York State medical or dental school. The law requires that awards be made to eligible candidates in the following order: first priority is given to candidates who are economically disadvantaged and a minority group member historically underrepresented in the professions; second priority is given to candidates who are a minority group member historically underrepresented in the professions; and third priority is given to any candidate who is enrolled in or a graduate of 1 of these state-supported opportunity programs: Search for Education, Elevation and Knowledge (SEEK) or College Discovery at City University; Educational Opportunity Program (EOP) in the State University system; or Higher Education Opportunity Program (HEOP) at an independent college. For purposes of this program, underrepresented minorities include African Americans, Hispanics, Native Americans, and Alaskan Natives. Students are considered economically disadvantaged if they are a member of 1) a household supported by 1 parent if dependent, by the student or by a spouse if independent, whose total annual income is less than specified levels that range from $13,700 for a family of 1 to $41,650 for a family of 7: 2) a household supported by more than 1 worker (parent if dependent, student and spouse if independent) in which the total annual income does not exceed the specified levels by more than $4,800; 3) a household supported by 1 worker (parent if dependent, student if independent) who is the sole support of a 1-parent family in which the total annual income does not exceed the specified levels by more than $4,800; or 4) a household supported by 1 worker (parent if dependent, student if independent) who is working 2 or more jobs at the same time in which the total annual income does not exceed the specified levels by more than $1,800.

Financial data Scholarship holders receive from $1,000 to $10,000 per year, depending on income. No award can exceed the actual cost of attendance. After completion of their professional studies, scholarship holders are required to practice 12 months for each annual payment received, including at least 24 months in a designated physician-shortage area in New York. If they fail to comply with the service commitment requirements, they must repay the full amount of the scholarship plus interest within 5 years.

Duration Up to 4 years.

Additional information Information is also available from the New York State Higher Education Services Corporation, 99 Washington Avenue, Albany, NY 12255, (518) 473-1574, (888) NYS-HESC, Fax: (518) 473-3749, TDD: (800) 445-5234, E-mail: webmail@hesc.com.

Number awarded Approximately 100 each year: 80 to medical students and 20 to dental students.

Deadline April of each year.

[703]
NEW YORK STATE REGENTS PROFESSIONAL OPPORTUNITY SCHOLARSHIPS

New York State Education Department
Office of K-16 Initiatives and Access Programs
Attn: Scholarships and Grants Administration Unit
Education Building Addition, Room 1078
Albany, NY 12234
(518) 486-1319   E-mail: kiap@mail.nysed.gov
Web: www.highered.nysed.gov

Purpose To provide forgivable loans to underrepresented minority and economically disadvantaged students in New York who are interested in preparing for selected professional careers.

Eligibility Candidates must be U.S. citizens or permanent residents and legal residents of New York for 1 year prior to application. The law requires that awards be made to eligible candidates in the following order: first priority is given to candidates who are economically disadvantaged and a minority group member historically underrepresented in the professions; second priority is given to candidates who are a minority group member historically underrepresented in the professions; and third priority is given to candidates who are enrolled in or a graduate of 1 of these state-supported opportunity programs: Search for Education, Elevation and Knowledge (SEEK) or College Discovery at City University; Educational Opportunity Program (EOP) in the State University system; or Higher Education Opportunity Program (HEOP) at an independent college. Scholarships are available for study in the following areas at the associate degree level: dental hygiene, dietetics and nutrition, massage therapy, occupational therapy assistant, ophthalmic dispensing, physical therapy assistant, registered physician assistant, respiratory therapy, or veterinary technician; at the baccalaureate degree level: certified public accountancy, architecture, athletic trainer, dietetics and nutrition, professional engineering, interior design, landscape architecture, registered nurse, occupational therapy, pharmacy, physical therapy, registered physician assistant, or veterinary technician; at the master's degree level: acupuncture, architecture, audiology, landscape architecture, midwifery, nurse practitioner, occupational therapy, physical therapy, registered physician assistant, social work, or speech language pathology; at the doctoral degree level: chiropractic, optometry, pharmacy, podiatry, psychology, or veterinary medicine; or at the J.D. level: law. For purposes of this program, underrepresented minorities include African Americans, Hispanics, Native Americans, and Alaskan Natives. Students are considered economically disadvantaged if they are a member of 1) a household supported by 1 parent if dependent, by the student or by a spouse if independent, whose total annual income is less than specified levels that range from $13,700 for a family of 1 to $41,650 for a family of 7: 2) a household supported by more than 1 worker (parent if dependent, student and spouse if independent) in which the total annual income does not exceed the specified levels by more than $4,800; 3) a household supported by 1 worker (parent if dependent, student if independent) who is the sole support of a 1-parent family in which the total annual income does not exceed the specified levels by more than $4,800; or 4) a household supported by 1 worker (parent if dependent, student if independent) who is working 2 or more jobs at the same time in which the total annual income does not exceed the specified levels by more than $1,800.

Financial data The stipends range from $1,000 to $5,000 per year, depending on income. No award can exceed the actual cost of attendance. After completion of their professional studies, scholarship holders are required to practice in New York for 12 months for each annual payment received. If they do not comply with the service commitment requirements, they must repay the full amount of the scholarship monies plus penalty and interest within 5 years.

Duration Up to 4 years (or 5 years for certain programs), within a 7-year period.

Additional information Information is also available from the New York State Higher Education Services Corporation, 99 Washington Avenue, Albany, NY 12255, (518) 473-1574, (888) NYS-HESC, Fax: (518) 473-3749, TDD: (800) 445-5234, E-mail: webmail@hesc.com.

Number awarded Varies each year; recently, 220 of these scholarships were available.

Deadline April of each year.

[704]
NORTH CAROLINA PRINCIPAL FELLOWS PROGRAM

North Carolina Principal Fellows Commission
Attn: Director
P.O. Box 4440
Chapel Hill, NC 27515-4440
(919) 962-4575   Fax: (919) 962-0488
E-mail: mupdike@northcarolina.edu
Web: www.ga.unc.edu/Principal_Fellows

Purpose To provide scholarship/loans to minority and other students in North Carolina who are interested in working on a master's degree in educational administration.

Eligibility This program is open to residents of North Carolina who have at least 4 years of successful teaching or other relevant experience. Applicants must have been admitted as a full-time first-year student in a master's degree program in educational administration at 1 of the following institutions: Appalachian State University, East Carolina University, Fayetteville State University, North Carolina A&T State University, North Carolina Central University, North Carolina State University, University of North Carolina at Chapel Hill, University of North Carolina at Charlotte, University of North Carolina at Greensboro, University of North Carolina at Wilmington, or Western Carolina University. They must be willing to complete the school administrator program supported by the scholarship, pass the school administration certification examination within 24 months following graduation, and provide 4 years of full-time service as a school administrator in North Carolina within 6 months. U.S. citizenship is required. The sponsor specifically encourages women and minorities to apply. Selection is based on undergraduate academic record (GPA of 3.2 or higher), leadership and management potential, communication skills, and moral and ethical standards.

Financial data These scholarship/loans are $20,000 per year for full-time study. Funds are to be used to pay for tuition, fees, and living expenses while in the program. Should the recipient not complete the educational program or not serve in an eligible school administration position in North Carolina for 4 years within 6 years of completing the program, the funds must be repaid at an interest rate of 10%.

Duration 2 years: the first year is devoted to full-time academic study at 1 of the participating schools in North Carolina and the second year is spent as an intern at a public school in the state.

Additional information This program was established by the North Carolina General Assembly in 1993 and became effective for the 1994-95 academic year. It is now cosponsored by the North Carolina Principal Fellows Commission and the North Carolina State Education Assistance Authority. Recipients may not be employed full time during

the 2-year period. To satisfy the requirements of this scholarship/loan program, recipients must seek, obtain, and maintain employment as an assistant principal or principal in a public school or a U.S. government school in North Carolina for 4 years after graduation.

Number awarded Up to 200 each year.

Deadline January of each year.

[705]
NORTH CAROLINA TEACHING FELLOWS SCHOLARSHIP PROGRAM

North Carolina Teaching Fellows Commission
Koger Center, Cumberland Building
3739 National Drive, Suite 210
Raleigh, NC 27612
(919) 781-6833   Fax: (919) 781-6527
E-mail: tfellows@ncforum.org
Web: www.teachingfellows.org

Purpose To provide scholarship/loans to minority and other high school seniors in North Carolina who wish to prepare for a career in teaching.

Eligibility This program is open to seniors at high schools in North Carolina who are interested in preparing for a career as a teacher and have been accepted for enrollment at a participating school in the state. Applicants must demonstrate superior achievement on the basis of high school grades, class standing, SAT scores, a writing sample, community service, extracurricular activities, and references from teachers and members of the community. U.S. citizenship is required. A particular goal of the program is to recruit and retain greater numbers of male and minority teacher education candidates in North Carolina.

Financial data The maximum stipend is $6,500 per year. This is a scholarship/loan program; recipients must teach in a North Carolina public school 1 year for each year of support received. If they cannot fulfill the service requirement, they must repay the loan with 10% interest.

Duration 1 year; renewable for up to 3 additional years if the recipient maintains full-time enrollment and a GPA of 2.25 or higher for the freshman year and 2.50 or higher in the sophomore year.

Additional information The participating schools are Appalachian State University, East Carolina University, Elon College, Meredith College, North Carolina A&T State University, University of North Carolina at Asheville, North Carolina Central University, North Carolina State University, University of North Carolina at Pembroke, University of North Carolina at Chapel Hill, University of North Carolina at Charlotte, University of North Carolina at Greensboro, University of North Carolina at Wilmington, and Western Carolina University. This program was established in 1986 and the first fellows were named in 1987.

Number awarded Up to 400 each year. Approximately 20% of the program's recipients are minority and 30% are male.

Deadline October of each year.

[706]
NORTH CAROLINA UNDERGRADUATE NURSE SCHOLARS PROGRAM

North Carolina State Education Assistance Authority
Attn: Scholarship and Grant Services
10 T.W. Alexander Drive
P.O. Box 14103
Research Triangle Park, NC 27709-4103
(919) 549-8614   Toll-free: (800) 700-1775
Fax: (919) 549-8481   E-mail: information@ncseaa.edu
Web: www.ncseaa.edu

Purpose   To provide scholarship/loans to minority and other students in North Carolina who wish to prepare for a career in nursing.

Eligibility   Applicants must be high school seniors, high school graduates, or currently-enrolled college students who are U.S. citizens, North Carolina residents, and interested in becoming a nurse. Students must plan to enter a North Carolina college, university, or hospital that prepares students for licensure as a registered nurse. Applications are encouraged from nontraditional students, including older individuals, ethnic minorities, males, and individuals with previous careers and/or degrees who are pursuing nursing studies. U.S. citizenship and full-time enrollment are required. Selection is based on academic achievement, leadership potential, and the promise of service as a registered nurse in North Carolina; financial need is not considered.

Financial data   Annual stipends are $3,000 for candidates for an associate degree, $3,000 for candidates for a diploma in nursing, or $5,000 or $3,000 for students in a B.S.N. program. This is a scholarship/loan program; 1 year of full-time work as a nurse in North Carolina cancels 1 year of support under this program. Recipients who fail to honor the work obligation must repay the balance plus 10% interest.

Duration   1 year; may be renewed 1 additional year by candidates for an associate degree, registered nurses completing a B.S.N. degree, and community college transfer students and juniors in a B.S.N. program, or for 3 additional years by freshmen and nontraditional students in a B.S.N. program.

Additional information   The North Carolina General Assembly created this program in 1989; the first recipients were funded for the 1990-91 academic year.

Number awarded   Varies; generally, up to 450 new undergraduate degree awards are made each year. Recently, a total of 834 students were receiving $3,414,500 through this program.

Deadline   February of each year for B.S.N. programs; May of each year for A.D.N. and diploma students.

[707]
PRESBYTERIAN CHURCH CONTINUING EDUCATION GRANT AND LOAN PROGRAM

Presbyterian Church (USA)
Attn: Office of Financial Aid for Studies
100 Witherspoon Street, Room M-052
Louisville, KY 40202-1396
(502) 569-5735   Toll-free: (888) 728-7228, ext. 5735
Fax: (502) 569-8766   E-mail: LBryan@ctr.pcusa.org
Web: www.pcusa.org

Purpose   To provide financial assistance for continuing education, in the form of educational grants and loans, to minority and other professional church workers of the Presbyterian Church (USA) and doctoral candidates who are church members.

Eligibility   This program is open to 1) PC(USA) ministers and lay professionals who have served a congregation of 150 or fewer members for at least 3 years; and 2) PC(USA) church members enrolled in a D.Min, Ph.D., or equivalent program in religious studies. Ministers and lay professionals must be planning to attend a program of study that will lead to certification, course work at an accredited institution, or a national event sponsored by PC(USA). The study, course work, or event must be approved by a church session, presbytery, or synod. Events must be at least 3 days in duration. For church members working on a Ph.D. degree, preference is given to women and racial ethnic applicants attending PC(USA) theological institutions, colleges, or universities. U.S. citizenship or permanent resident status is required.

Financial data   For ministers and lay professionals, grants for events range from $100 to $500 and grants for study or course work range from $100 to $1,000. For doctoral candidates, grants range from $500 to $1,000. The maximum loan is $2,000 per year.

Duration   1 year. Ministers and lay professionals at small churches are eligible for unlimited renewal of grants. Candidates for a D.Min. degree may renew their grants for a total of 3 years. Candidates for a Ph.D. or equivalent degree may renew their grants for a total of 4 years. Loans may be renewed to a maximum of $6,000.

Number awarded   Varies each year.

Deadline   November of each year.

[708]
PRIMARY CARE RESOURCE INITIATIVE FOR MISSOURI

Missouri Department of Health and Senior Services
Attn: Primary Care and Rural Health
P.O. Box 570
Jefferson City, MO 65102-0570
(573) 751-6400   Toll-free: (800) 891-7415
Fax: (573) 751-6041
Web: www.dhss.state.mo.us

Purpose   To provide scholarship/loans to minority and other residents of Missouri who are interested in working as a health care professional in an underserved area of the state following graduation.

Eligibility   This program is open to residents of Missouri who have lived for 1 or more years in the state for purposes other than attending an educational institution. Applicants must have been accepted by or currently be attending a Missouri school offering a course of study leading to a degree as 1) a doctor of allopathic (M.D.) or osteopathic (D.O.) medicine; 2) a doctor of dentistry (D.D.S.); 3) a bachelor of science (B.S.) in a field leading to acceptance into a school of medicine or into a master of science (M.S.N.) degree program leading to certification as a primary care advanced practice nurse; or 4) a bachelor of science (B.S.) in dental hygiene. Physicians and dentists in primary care residency programs are also eligible. Priority is given to residents of medically underserved areas in Missouri, minority group members, and previous recipients.

Financial data For undergraduate students enrolled in an accredited bachelor of science degree in dental hygiene, nursing, or a pre-medicine or pre-dental program, the maximum loan is $5,000 per year for full-time enrollment. Medical (M.D. or D.O.) students are eligible for loans in the amount of tuition, to a maximum of $25,000 per year. Students in 6-year medical programs may receive $10,000 per year for the first 2 years and up to $25,000 per year for the last 4 years. Physicians and dentists in primary care residency programs are eligible for loans of $10,000 per year. This is a scholarship/loan program. Loans of 5 years or more are forgiven at the rate of 20% per year for qualifying employment in an area of defined need (a geographic area or a population that is experiencing a shortage of primary health care providers in Missouri). Loans for less than 5 years are forgiven on a year-for-year basis. If the loan is not forgiven by service, it must be repaid within 48 months at 9.5% interest.

Duration Full-time undergraduate students may receive up to 4 loans. part-time Medical students may receive loans for up to 4 or 6 years, depending on the length of their program. Physicians and dentists in primary care residency programs may receive up to 3 years of loans.

Additional information This program is also known as the PRIMO Loan Program.

Number awarded Varies each year.

Deadline June or December of each year.

[709]
STOKES EDUCATIONAL SCHOLARSHIP PROGRAM

National Security Agency
Office of Recruitment and Staffing (Stokes)
9800 Savage Road, Suite 6779
P.O. Box 1661, Suite 6779
Fort Meade, MD 20755-6779
Toll-free: (866) 672-4473
Web: www.nsa.gov/programs/employ/utp.cfm

Purpose To provide minority and other high school seniors with scholarship/loans and work experience at the National Security Agency (NSA).

Eligibility This program is open to graduating high school seniors, particularly minorities, who 1) are planning a college major in electrical or computer engineering, computer science, mathematics, or foreign languages (recent language interests included Amharic, Arabic, Chinese, Dari, modern Greek, Hindi, Japanese, Korean, Pashto, Persian/Farsi, Somali, Swahili, Turkish, and Urdu/Punjabi); 2) have minimum scores of 25 on the ACT (or the equivalent on the SAT); 3) have a GPA of 3.0 or higher; 4) are U.S. citizens; and 5) demonstrate leadership abilities. Also eligible are college sophomores who are U.S. citizens, have a GPA of 3.0 or higher, and have completed 6 credits in 1 of the

core languages. Applicants must include a 1-page essay on why they want to have a career with the NSA.

Financial data Participants receive college tuition for 4 years, reimbursement for books and certain fees, a year-round salary, and a housing allowance and travel reimbursement during summer employment if the distance between the agency and school exceeds 75 miles. Following graduation, participants must work for the agency for 1 and a half times their length of study, usually 5 years. Students who leave agency employment earlier must repay the tuition cost.

Duration 4 years, followed by employment at the agency for 5 years.

Additional information Participants must attend classes full time and work at the agency during the summer in jobs tailored to their course of study. They must maintain at least a 3.0 GPA. This program, established in 1986, was formerly known as the National Security Agency Undergraduate Training Program.

Number awarded Varies each year.

Deadline November of each year.

[710]
TENNESSEE MINORITY TEACHING FELLOWS PROGRAM

Tennessee Student Assistance Corporation
Parkway Towers
404 James Robertson Parkway, Suite 1950
Nashville, TN 37243-0820
(615) 741-1346   Toll-free: (800) 342-1663
Fax: (615) 741-6101   E-mail: tsac@mail.state.tn.us
Web: www.tnscholardollars.com

Purpose To provide scholarship/loans to minority Tennesseans who wish to enter the teaching field.

Eligibility This program is open to minority residents of Tennessee who are either high school seniors planning to attend a college or university in the state or continuing college students at a Tennessee college or university. High school seniors must have a GPA of 2.75 or higher and either have an ACT score of at least 18 (or its SAT equivalent) or rank in the top 25% of their high school class. Continuing college students must have a college GPA of 2.5 or higher. All applicants must agree to teach at the K-12 level in a Tennessee public school following graduation from college.

Financial data The scholarship/loan is $5,000 per year. Recipients incur an obligation to teach at the K-12 level in a Tennessee public school 1 year for each year the award is received.

Duration 1 year; may be renewed for up to 3 additional years.

Additional information This program was established in 1989.

Number awarded 20 new awards are granted each year.

Deadline April of each year.

[711]
TEXAS DEPARTMENT OF TRANSPORTATION CONDITIONAL GRANT PROGRAM

Texas Department of Transportation
Attn: Employment Opportunities Section
125 East 11th Street
Austin, TX 78701-2483
(512) 416-4976
Web: www.dot.state.tx.us/employment/recruiting.htm

Purpose To provide scholarship/loans to minorities and women in Texas who are interested in majoring in designated areas and then working for the Texas Department of Transportation.

Eligibility This program is open to minorities (Black, Hispanic, American Indian, Asian, Pacific Islander) and women who are residents of Texas. High school applicants must have a GPA of 3.0 or higher or at least 21 on the ACT (or the equivalent on the SAT); plan to attend an accredited 4-year public college or university in Texas as a full-time student; plan to major in civil engineering; be willing to work for the Texas Department of Transportation for at least 2 years after graduation; and not be more than 30 days delinquent on any child support obligation. College or university applicants must have a GPA of 2.5 or higher; be attending a 4-year public college or university in Texas; be taking at least 12 hours per semester; have declared a major in civil engineering; be willing to work for the Texas Department of Transportation for at least 2 years after graduation; not be in repayment status for a previously-awarded Conditional Grant; and be no more than 30 days delinquent on any child support obligation.

Financial data The grant covers tuition, fees and a stipend, up to a maximum of $3,000 per semester or $6,000 per year. The exact amount awarded is based on the recipient's documented financial need. This is a scholarship/loan program. Recipients must repay the full amount of the grant if they fail to graduate, or maintain a cumulative GPA of 2.5 or higher, or stay in school, or stay in an approved major, or work for the Texas Department of Transportation for the required period of time.

Duration 1 year; may be renewed.

Additional information Recipients must attend school on a full-time basis (at least 12 hours per semester), maintain a GPA of 2.5 or higher, graduate in an approved major, and work for the Texas Department of Transportation for at least 2 years.

Number awarded Varies each year.

Deadline February of each year.

[712]
VERMONT LOAN FORGIVENESS FOR CULTURALLY DIVERSE EDUCATION STUDENTS

Vermont Teacher Diversity Scholarship Program
Attn: Director
P.O. Box 359
Waterbury, VT 05676-0359
(802) 241-3379   Fax: (802) 241-3369
E-mail: phyl.newbeck@vsc.edu
Web: templeton.vsc.edu/teacherdiversity

Purpose To forgive the educational loans of students from diverse racial and ethnic backgrounds at colleges in Vermont who wish to become public school teachers in the state.

Eligibility This program is open to students enrolled or planning to enroll at designated colleges and universities in Vermont to prepare for licensure as a public school teacher. Applicants must come from diverse racial and ethnic backgrounds and be willing to become teachers in the Vermont public school system. As part of their application, they must submit brief essays on why they believe it is important for children in grades K-12 to be exposed to teachers from diverse backgrounds, why they believe their particular background is appropriate for them to be considered for this program, why they want to be a teacher, the experiences they have had that have prepared them for the challenge of teaching, and the challenges they expect to experience as a person whose background may differ from the majority culture. Selection is based on racial and ethnic diversity, leadership qualities, experience working with children, employment history (if applicable), educational history, commitment to teaching in Vermont, understanding of diversity and issues related to power and privilege in the United States, and academic potential. Preference is given to residents of Vermont, but students from all states are encouraged to apply.

Financial data If participants in this program are hired as public school teachers in Vermont, $4,000 of their college loans are forgiven for each year they teach.

Duration Participants may receive up to 3 years of loan forgiveness (for a total of $12,000).

Additional information This program, formerly known as Coming Home, operates in partnership with several organizations in the state (including the Vermont Student Assistance Corporation, the Vermont Department of Education, and Vermont-NEA) and with 16 designated colleges and universities in the states. Participants in this program are not required to attend those schools, but they are encouraged to investigate them.

Number awarded Varies each year; recently, 10 of the program's scholars were working on a degree in education at a participating Vermont college or university.

Deadline March or October of each year.

[713]
VIRGINIA MEDICAL SCHOLARSHIP PROGRAM

Virginia Department of Health
Attn: Center for Primary Care and Rural Health
1500 East Main Street, Suite 227
Richmond, VA 23219
(804) 786-4891   Fax: (804) 371-0116
Web: www.vdh.state.va.us

Purpose To provide loans-for-service to minority and other medical students who are willing to practice as primary care physicians in Virginia.

Eligibility This program is open to medical students pursuing primary care medical education at designated schools in Virginia and Tennessee. Graduate medical students in the first year of a primary care residency are also eligible. Primary care specialties include family practice, general internal medicine, pediatrics, and obstetrics/gynecology. Applicants must intend to practice in underserved areas within Virginia. Preference is given to residents of Virginia, residents from rural and medically underserved areas, and minority students.

Financial data The maximum assistance is $10,000 per year. Repayment begins after completion of a 3-year residency (or 4 years for obstetrics/gynecology). Repayment is made through practice as a primary care physician in Virginia Medically Underserved Areas (VMUAs) designated by the Board of Health.

Duration 1 year; may be renewed for up to 4 additional years, for a total loan of $50,000.

Additional information The designated schools are Eastern Virginia Medical School of the Medical College of Hampton Roads (Norfolk, Virginia), the University of Virginia School of Medicine (Charlottesville, Virginia), the Medical College of Virginia of the Virginia Commonwealth University (Richmond, Virginia), James H. Quillen College of Medicine of East Tennessee State University (Johnson City, Tennessee), and Pikeville College School of Osteopathic Medicine (Pikeville, Kentucky).

Number awarded Varies each year; 4 scholarships are set aside for East Tennessee State University and the number assigned to the 3 Virginia schools is determined by the funding provided by the Virginia General Assembly.

Deadline Deadlines are established by the directors of financial aid at the participating medical schools.

[714]
VIRGINIA NURSE PRACTITIONER/NURSE MIDWIFE SCHOLARSHIP PROGRAM

Virginia Department of Health
Attn: Office of Health Policy and Planning
109 Governor Street, 1016 East Office
P.O. Box 2448
Richmond, VA 23218
(804) 864-7433   Fax: (804) 864-7440
E-mail: Margie.Thomas@vdh.virginia.gov
Web: www.vdh.state.va.us

Purpose To provide forgivable loans to minority and other nursing students in Virginia who are willing to work as nurse practitioners and/or midwives in the state following graduation.

Eligibility This program is open to residents of Virginia who are enrolled or accepted for enrollment full time at a nurse practitioner program in the state or a nurse midwifery program in a nearby state. Applicants must have a cumulative GPA of at least 3.0 in undergraduate and/or graduate courses. Preference is given to 1) residents of designated medically underserved areas of Virginia; 2) students enrolled in family practice, obstetrics and gynecology, pediatric, adult health, and geriatric nurse practitioner programs; and 3) minority students. Selection is based on scholastic achievement, character, and stated commitment to postgraduate employment in a medically underserved area of Virginia.

Financial data The amount of the award depends on the availability of funds. Recipients must agree to serve in a designated medically underserved area of Virginia for a period of years equal to the number of years of scholarship support received. The required service must begin within 2 years of the recipient's graduation and must be in a facility that provides services to persons who are unable to pay for the service and that participates in all government-

sponsored insurance programs designed to assure full access to medical care service for covered persons. If the recipient fails to complete the course of study, or pass the licensing examination, or provide the required service, all scholarship funds received must be repaid with interest.

Duration 1 year; may be renewed for 1 additional year.

Number awarded Varies each year.

Deadline June of each year.

[715]
VIRGINIA TEACHING SCHOLARSHIP LOAN PROGRAM

Virginia Department of Education
Attn: Division of Teacher Education and Licensure
P.O. Box 2120
Richmond, VA 23218-2120
(804) 371-2475   Toll-free: (800) 292-3820
Fax: (804) 786-6759
Web: www.pen.k12.va.us

Purpose To provide scholarship/loans to upper-division and graduate students in Virginia who are interested in a career in teaching.

Eligibility This program is open to Virginia residents who are enrolled full or part time as a junior, senior, or graduate student in a state-approved teacher preparation program in Virginia with a GPA of 2.7 or higher. Applicants must agree to engage in full-time teaching in designated teacher shortage areas within Virginia following graduation. Males interested in teaching at the elementary and middle school levels and people of color in all teaching areas also qualify.

Financial data The scholarship/loan is $3,720 per year. Loans are forgiven at the rate of $2,000 for each year the recipient teaches in designated teacher shortage areas. If the recipient fails to fulfill the teaching service requirement, the loan must be repaid with interest.

Duration 1 year; may be renewed 1 additional year.

Additional information Critical shortage teaching areas in Virginia are currently identified as foreign languages, science (including, in order of priority preference, physics, earth science, chemistry, and biology), all areas of special education (severe emotional disturbances, hearing disabilities, learning disabilities, mental retardation, severe disabilities, visual disabilities, early childhood special education, and speech-language pathology), career and technical education (including technology education, trade and industrial education, business education, and family and consumer sciences), mathematics, English as a second language, middle grades 6-8, library media K-12, art preK-12, and reading specialist.

Number awarded Varies each year. Recently, 163 of these scholarship/loans were granted, including 47 in special education, 20 in science, 4 in foreign language, 2 in technology education, 24 in mathematics, 4 in English as a second language, 1 in library media, 3 for reading specialists, 1 in agricultural education, 22 for males in elementary or middle grades, and 35 for people of color.

[716]
WELLS FARGO LATINO BUSINESS LOAN PROGRAM

Wells Fargo Bank
Attn: National Business Banking Center
P.O. Box 340214
Sacramento, CA 95834-0214
Toll-free: (800) 35-WELLS, ext. 350
Web: www.wellsfargo.com

Purpose To loan money to Latino-owned businesses.

Eligibility To qualify for a loan, Latino business owners must have a satisfactory personal and business credit history, have been in business for at least 3 years, have a profitable business with sufficient cash flow to meet their new and current financial obligations, and have not declared bankruptcy in the past 10 years. Applicants may be interested in 1) an unsecured, revolving line of credit; 2) financing for new and used machinery, equipment, and vehicles; or 3) equity loans or lines of credit secured by commercial real estate.

Financial data This program offers unsecured, revolving lines of credit up to $100,000, equipment loans up to $50,000, and equity loans from $25,000 to $250,000. Interest rates are variable.

Number awarded Varies each year. This program, established in 1997 in conjunction with the United States Hispanic Chamber of Commerce, has a goal of lending $3 billion over 10 years to Latino small business owners.

Deadline Applications may be requested at any time.

[717]
WISCONSIN MINORITY BUSINESS DEVELOPMENT LOAN PROGRAM

Wisconsin Department of Commerce
Attn: Bureau of Minority Business Development
201 West Washington Avenue
P.O. Box 7970
Madison, WI 53707-7970
(608) 267-9550   Fax: (608) 267-2829
E-mail: MBD@commerce.state.wi.us
Web: www.commerce.state.wi.us

Purpose To provide low-interest loans to businesses owned by minorities in Wisconsin.

Eligibility This program is open to businesses in Wisconsin that have completed a comprehensive business plan and that are at least 51% owned by a Black, Hispanic, American Indian, Eskimo, Asian Pacific, Asian Indian, Aleut, or Native Hawaiian. Applicants must be interested in a loan for land, construction, acquisition of an existing business, purchase of equipment, or working capital. Factors considered in loan approval include whether the applicant has at least 2 years of relevant work experience, if the applicant's education and/or training is relevant to the proposed business venture, if the applicant has cash reserves (equity) necessary to invest in the proposed business, if a local bank and/or other local organization has made a funding commitment to the project, if the business will have a positive economic impact upon the local community, the number of jobs that will be created or retained, if the proposed business will have a negative impact upon other local businesses, and if the proposed business will be located in a target area.

Financial data Loan amounts vary. Ideally, this loan should provide 25% of total investment; other financing should include 5% from personal equity, 45% from a bank loan, and 25% from a development corporation. Interest rates are fixed at levels below market rates, typically 4%.

Duration Real estate loans are for 10 to 15 years, equipment loans for 5 to 10 years, and working capital loans for 5 to 7 years.

Number awarded Varies each year.

Deadline Applications may be submitted at any time.

[718]
WISCONSIN MINORITY TEACHER LOANS

Wisconsin Higher Educational Aids Board
131 West Wilson Street, Room 902
P.O. Box 7885
Madison, WI 53707-7885
(608) 267-2212   Fax: (608) 267-2808
E-mail: mary.kuzdas@heab.state.wi.us
Web: heab.state.wi.us/programs.html

Purpose To provide scholarship/loans to minorities in Wisconsin who are interested in teaching in Wisconsin school districts with large minority enrollments.

Eligibility African Americans, Hispanic Americans, and American Indians in Wisconsin are eligible to apply if they are enrolled full time as juniors or seniors in an independent or public institution in the state. The program also includes students who were admitted to the United States after December 31, 1975 and who are a former citizen of Laos, Vietnam, or Cambodia or whose ancestor was a citizen of 1 of those countries. Applicants must be enrolled in a program leading to teaching licensure and must agree to teach in a Wisconsin school district in which minority students constitute at least 29% of total enrollment or in a school district participating in the inter-district pupil transfer program.

Financial data Scholarship/loans are provided up to $2,500 per year. For each year the student teaches in an eligible school district, 25% of the loan is forgiven; if the student does not teach in an eligible district, the loan must be repaid at an interest rate of 5%.

Duration 1 year; may be renewed 1 additional year.

Additional information Eligible students should apply through their school's financial aid office.

Number awarded Varies each year.

Deadline Deadline dates vary by institution; check with your school's financial aid office.

Grants

Described here are 240 programs that provide funds to Hispanic Americans for innovative efforts, travel, projects, creative activities, or research on any level (from undergraduate to postdoctorate and professional). In some cases, proposals may be submitted by institutions or organizations only; in others, individual Hispanic Americans may submit proposals directly. If you are looking for a particular program and don't find it in this section, be sure to check the Program Title Index to see if it is covered elsewhere in the directory.

[719]
ABC TALENT DEVELOPMENT SCHOLARSHIP-GRANT PROGRAM

ABC Entertainment
Attn: Talent Development Programs
500 South Buena Vista Street
Burbank, CA 91521-4390
(818) 460-7770   E-mail: abc.fellowships@abc.com
Web: www.abctalendevelopment.com

Purpose   To provide funding to emerging artists (including high school, college, and graduate students) from diverse backgrounds in selected cities throughout the United States who are interested in completing a creative project.

Eligibility   This program is open to high school, college, and graduate students from Chicago, Houston, Los Angeles, Minneapolis, New York, Raleigh-Durham, and Washington, D.C. Applications must be submitted through participating sponsors (high schools, colleges, universities, or civic, social service, or professional organizations) in those communities. Emerging artists who are members of sponsoring organizations are also eligible to apply. Many of the designated sponsors focus on service to minorities and students with disabilities, because a goal of the program is to discover, develop, and encourage creative talent from diverse backgrounds. Applicants must be proposing to complete an existing creative project. They must submit a work resume, personal bio, essay of 500 to 800 words on their career goals and interest in the field, and samples of the proposed project. If the project involves a screenplay or television script, submissions must include a treatment, 10 pages of proposed story idea, and a detailed budget. If the project involves a video, submissions must include a sample reel of a previously completed film or video project, a proposal, and a detailed budget. Material that may not be submitted in support of an application includes published material (e.g., short stories), scripts adapted from other material not indicative of writing for television or film, sequels to motion pictures, plays, magazine articles, drawings, projects that have been fully executed creatively (i.e., polished scripts or videos needing post production only), or projects that have been previously entered into a competition or festival.

Financial data   Individuals receive grants of $20,000 to help finance the development of their project. Sponsoring organizations with winning submissions receive $10,000 grants to further develop their creative programs.

Duration   1 year.

Additional information   Selected participants are paired with a mentor at Walt Disney Studios or ABC Entertainment. The program concludes with a 3-day workshop in Los Angeles. Recently, the sponsoring organizations included the International Latino Cultural Center of Chicago, the Mille Lacs Band of Ojibwe, American Indian Artists, Inc, the International Agency for Minority Artist Affairs, National Hispanic Foundation for the Arts, National Asian American Telecommunications Association, National Association for the Advancement of Colored People, and the Media Access Office of the California Governor's Committee on Employment of People with Disabilities. This program began in 2001.

Number awarded   Varies each year; recently, 16 of these grants were awarded.

Deadline   December of each year.

[720]
ABE FELLOWSHIP PROGRAM

Social Science Research Council
Attn: Japan Program
810 Seventh Avenue
New York, NY 10019
(212) 377-2700   Fax: (212) 377-2727
E-mail: abe@ssrc.org
Web: www.ssrc.org/fellowships/abe

Purpose   To provide funding to postdoctoral scholars (particularly minorities and women) interested in conducting research on contemporary policy-relevant affairs in Japan.

Eligibility   This program is open to American and Japanese research professionals who have doctorate-equivalent or professional experience (other nationals affiliated with an American or Japanese institution are also eligible to apply). Applicants should be interested in conducting multidisciplinary research on topics of pressing global concern. Currently, research must focus on the 3 themes of global issues, problems common to industrial and industrializing societies, and issues that pertain to U.S.-Japan relations. Within those 3 themes, research may address issues related to technology and society; consumption, labor, and markets; human security; civil society; bioethics; aging societies and other life-span issues; transnational economic relations; sustainable development and global environmental issues; and foreign assistance. Previous language training is not a prerequisite for this fellowship. Minorities and women are particularly encouraged to apply.

Financial data   The terms of the fellowship include a base award and funds to pay supplementary research and travel expenses as necessary for completion of the research project.

Duration   The program provides support for 3 to 12 months over a 24-month period.

Additional information   Fellows are expected to affiliate with an American or Japanese institution appropriate to their research aims. In addition to receiving fellowship awards, fellows attend annual Abe Fellows Conferences, which promote the development of an international network of scholars concerned with research on contemporary policy issues. Funds are provided by the Japan Foundation's Center for Global Partnership. Fellows should plan to spend at least one third of their tenure abroad in Japan or the United States.

Deadline   August of each year.

[721]
ABF POSTDOCTORAL FELLOWSHIPS IN LAW AND SOCIAL SCIENCE

American Bar Foundation
Attn: Assistant Director
750 North Lake Shore Drive
Chicago, IL 60611
(312) 988-6500   Fax: (312) 988-6579
E-mail: fellowships@abfn.org
Web: www.abf-sociolegal.org/Fellowship/index.html

Purpose   To provide funding to postdoctoral scholars (particularly minorities) who wish to conduct research on law, the legal profession, and legal institutions.

Eligibility   Applications are invited from junior scholars who completed all requirements for their Ph.D. within the past 2 years; in exceptional circumstances, candidates with a J.D. who have substantial social science training may also be considered. Proposed research must be in the general area of sociolegal studies or in social scientific approaches to law, the legal profession, or legal institutions and legal processes. Applications must include 1) a sample of written work; 2) 2 letters of recommendation; 3) a curriculum vitae; and 4) a statement describing research interests and achievements to date and plans for the fellowship period. Minority candidates are especially encouraged to apply.

Financial data The stipend is $30,000 per year; fringe benefits are also provided. Fellows may request up to $3,500 each fellowship year for research support. Relocation expenses of up to $1,000 may be reimbursed on application.

Duration 1 year; may be renewed for 1 additional year.

Additional information Fellows are offered access to the computing and word processing facilities of the American Bar Foundation and the libraries of Northwestern University and the University of Chicago. This program was established in 1996. Fellowships must be held in residence at the American Bar Foundation. Appointments to the fellowship are full time; fellows are not permitted to undertake other work.

Number awarded 2 each year.

Deadline January of each year.

[722]
ACADEMIC RESEARCH ENHANCEMENT AWARD

National Institutes of Health
Division of Extramural Outreach and Information
  Resources
Attn: Grants Information
6701 Rockledge Drive, Suite 6095
Bethesda, MD 20892-7910
(301) 435-0714   Fax: (301) 480-0525
E-mail: GrantsInfo@nih.gov
Web: www.nih.gov

Purpose To stimulate research in educational institutions (particularly minority and women's institutions) that provide baccalaureate training for a significant number of American research scientists but that have not been major participants in National Institutes of Health (NIH) programs.

Eligibility This grant program is offered to researchers at domestic institutions that award baccalaureate or advanced degrees in the sciences related to health, except those that have received research grants and cooperative agreements from the National Institutes of Health (NIH) totaling more than $3 million per year in each of 4 or more of the preceding 7 years. Health professional schools (e.g., schools of medicine, dentistry, nursing, osteopathy, pharmacy, veterinary medicine, public health, allied health, optometry, chiropractic, podiatry, naturopath) are eligible, as are officially discrete campuses of a university. Investigators eligible for the program are those who will not have active research grant support from the NIH at the time of application. Members of underrepresented racial and ethnic groups and individuals with disabilities are always encouraged to apply for NIH programs. Scientists working in eligible minority and women's educational institutions are particularly encouraged to submit an application for this program.

Financial data Grants provide up to $150,000 in direct costs, plus applicable facilities and administrative costs, for a 36-month period. Allowable direct costs include salaries for the principal investigator and other research personnel (including students), supplies, equipment, travel, and other items specifically associated with the proposed research project.

Duration Up to 36 months.

Additional information Investigators applying for this program may not submit a separate grant application for essentially the same project to the NIH. Principal investigators are expected to conduct the majority of their research at their own institution, although limited access to special facilities or equipment at another institution is permitted.

Number awarded Varies each year; recently, 214 of these grants, with funding of $31,055,000 were awarded.

Deadline January, May, or September of each year.

[723]
ACLS FELLOWSHIPS

American Council of Learned Societies
Attn: Office of Fellowships and Grants
633 Third Avenue, 8C
New York, NY 10017-6795
(212) 697-1505   Fax: (212) 949-8058
E-mail: grants@acls.org
Web: www.acls.org/felguide.htm

Purpose To provide research funding to scholars (particularly minorities and women) in all disciplines of the humanities and the humanities-related social sciences.

Eligibility This program is open to scholars at all stages of their careers who received a Ph.D. degree at least 2 years previously. Established scholars who can demonstrate the equivalent of the Ph.D. in publications and professional experience may also qualify. Applicants must be U.S. citizens or permanent residents who have not held supported leave time for at least 3 years prior to the start of the proposed research. Appropriate fields of specialization include, but are not limited to, anthropology, archaeology, art history, economics, film, geography, history, languages and literatures, law, linguistics, musicology, philosophy, political science, psychology, religion, rhetoric and communication, and sociology. Proposals in those fields of the social sciences are eligible only if they employ predominantly humanistic approaches (e.g., economic history, law and literature, political philosophy). Proposals in interdisciplinary and cross-disciplinary studies are welcome, as are proposals focused on any geographic region or on any cultural or linguistic group. Awards are available at 3 academic levels: full professor, associate professor, and assistant professor. Applications are particularly invited from women and members of minority groups.

Financial data The maximum grant is $50,000 for full professors and equivalent, $40,000 for associate professors and equivalent, or $30,000 for assistant professors and equivalent. Normally, fellowships are intended as salary replacement and may be held concurrently with other fellowships, grants, and sabbatical pay, up to an amount equal to the candidate's current academic year salary.

Duration 6 to 12 months.

Additional information This program is supported in part by funding from the Ford Foundation, the Andrew W.

Mellon Foundation, the National Endowment for the Humanities, the William and Flora Hewlett Foundation, and the Rockefeller Foundation.

Number awarded Varies each year. Recently, 68 of these fellowships were awarded: 17 to full professors, 16 to associate professors, 34 to assistant professors (including 27 designated as ACLS/Andrew W. Mellon Foundation Junior Faculty Fellowships and 1 designated as an ACLS/Oscar Handlin Fellowship), and 1 independent scholar.

Deadline September of each year.

[724]
ACLS/SSRC/NEH INTERNATIONAL AND AREA STUDIES FELLOWSHIPS

American Council of Learned Societies
Attn: Office of Fellowships and Grants
633 Third Avenue, 8C
New York, NY 10017-6795
(212) 697-1505   Fax: (212) 949-8058
E-mail: grants@acls.org
Web: www.acls.org/felguide.htm

Purpose To provide funding to postdoctoral scholars (particularly minorities and women) interested in conducting humanities-related research on the societies and cultures of Asia, Africa, the Near and Middle East, Latin America and the Caribbean, eastern Europe, and the former Soviet Union.

Eligibility This program is open to U.S. citizens and residents who have lived in the United States for at least 3 years. Applicants must have a Ph.D. degree and not have received supported research leave time for at least 3 years prior to the start of the proposed research. They must be interested in conducting humanities and humanities-related social science research on the societies and cultures of Asia, Africa, the Middle East, Latin America and the Caribbean, east Europe, or the former Soviet Union. Selection is based on the intellectual merit of the proposed research and the likelihood that it will produce significant and innovative scholarship. Applications are particularly invited from women and members of minority groups.

Financial data The maximum grant is $50,000 for full professors and equivalent, $40,000 for associate professors and equivalent, or $30,000 for assistant professors and equivalent. These fellowships may not be held concurrently with another major fellowship.

Duration 6 to 12 months.

Additional information This program is jointly supported by the American Council of Learned Societies (ACLS) and the Social Science Research Council (SSRC), with funding provided by the National Endowment for the Humanities (NEH).

Number awarded Approximately 10 each year.

Deadline September of each year.

[725]
ADVANCE FELLOWS AWARDS

National Science Foundation
Attn: ADVANCE Program
4201 Wilson Boulevard
Arlington, VA 22230
(703) 292-5111   TDD: (703) 292-5090
E-mail: ahogan@nsf.gov
Web: www.nsf.gov/home/crssprgm/advance

Purpose To provide funding to women scholars, particularly minority women, who are entering or reentering an academic career and wish to undertake research and other projects in science and engineering fields supported by the National Science Foundation (NSF).

Eligibility This program is open to women who are affiliated or plan to affiliate with an institution of higher learning in the United States, its territories or possessions, or the Commonwealth of Puerto Rico. Applicants must have a Ph.D. in a field of science or engineering supported by NSF; be a U.S. citizen, national, or permanent resident; and be establishing a full-time independent academic research and education career. They must 1) have received their first doctoral degree in science or engineering from 1 to 4 years previously, be in a postdoctoral or equivalent status, have never held a tenure-track or tenured position, and have not served as a principal investigator on any NSF award with the exception of doctoral dissertation, postdoctoral fellowship, or research-planning grants; or 2) be out of the full-time science and engineering workforce and have been out of that workforce for 2 to 8 years to attend to family responsibilities; or 3) either have resigned from a full-time academic science or engineering appointment because of relocation of a spouse in the preceding 24 months and not have a tenure-track or tenured position or be planning to leave a full-time academic science or engineering appointment because of relocation of a spouse to occur in the 12 months following the proposal due date. All applications must include a career development component that describes plans for career-enhancing research and education activities. Applicants who already have an academic affiliation must describe the facilities at their institution that are available for them to carry out their career development plan; applicants who are not currently affiliated must identify the institutional resources necessary for the proposed activities and describe plans for affiliating with a host institution. Members of underrepresented minority groups and individuals with disabilities are especially encouraged to apply.

Financial data Awards provide annual salary support of up to $60,000 plus applicable fringe benefits and a career development allotment of up to $25,000 per year (to be used for activities directly related to the proposed research and education activities in the fellow's career development plan, such as computing, travel to professional workshops, materials and supplies, publication charges, technical support, student support, and related needs). Indirect costs may be included at the host or home institution's standard rate.

Duration Up to 3 years.

Additional information Information is available from coordinators in each of the NSF directorates; for a list of their names and telephone numbers, contact the sponsor. If the recipient does not currently have an academic appointment, the award will commence only when she affiliates with a host institution that agrees to provide the resources necessary to support the proposed career-development plan.

Number awarded 20 to 40 each year.

Deadline June of each year.

[726]
ADVANCED FOSSIL RESOURCE CONVERSION AND UTILIZATION RESEARCH BY HISTORICALLY BLACK COLLEGES AND UNIVERSITIES AND OTHER MINORITY INSTITUTIONS

Department of Energy
Attn: National Energy Technology Laboratory
626 Cochrans Mill Road
P.O. Box 10940 (MS 921-107)
Pittsburgh, PA 15236-0940
(412) 386-5425   Toll-free: (800) 553-7681
Fax: (412) 386-6137
E-mail: Michael.DeStefano@netl.doe.gov
Web: www.netl.doe.gov

Purpose To provide support to researchers at Historically Black Colleges and Universities (HBCUs) and other minority institutions for research projects on advanced coal, oil, and natural gas concepts.

Eligibility Applications are solicited from federally-recognized HBCUs and other minority institutions to conduct research projects on fossil energy. Proposals must involve collaboration with an industrial partner, and each research team must include a teaching professor and at least 30% of personnel time must be to pay for student assistance. The proposed research must relate to 1 of the following technical topics: 1) advanced environmental control technologies for coal; 2) advanced coal utilization; 3) clean fuels technology; 4) oil shale and oil (tar) sands processing, environmental factors, and geology; 5) horizontal coil tubing and high speed drilling systems for tubing drill rigs; 6) natural gas exploration, production, and storage; 7) fuel cells; and 8) faculty/student exploratory research training grants.

Financial data Maximum funding for technical projects is $80,000 for 1-year grants, $140,000 for 2-year grants, or $200,000 for 3-year grants. Maximum funding for faculty/student research training grants is $20,000. Total annual funding for this program is approximately $950,000.

Duration Up to 3 years for technical projects; 1 year for faculty/student exploratory research training grants.

Additional information This program is supported by the Office of Fossil Energy within the U.S. Department of Energy.

Number awarded Approximately 4 to 5 grants on technical topics and 2 to 3 faculty/student exploratory research training grants are awarded each year.

Deadline January of each year.

[727]
AGA FOUNDATION OUTCOMES RESEARCH AWARDS

Foundation for Digestive Health and Nutrition
Attn: Research Awards Coordinator
4930 Del Ray Avenue
Bethesda, MD 20814-2512
(301) 222-4005   Fax: (301) 222-4010
E-mail: info@fdhn.org
Web: www.fdhn.org

Purpose To provide funding to young investigators (particularly women and minorities) interested in conducting outcomes research related to gastroenterology or hepatology.

Eligibility Applicants must hold faculty positions at accredited North American academic institutions at the time of application. They should be early in their careers (established investigators are not eligible). Candidates with an M.D. degree must have completed clinical training within the past 5 years and those with a Ph.D. must have received their degree within the past 5 years. Membership in the American Gastroenterological Association (AGA) is required. Selection is based on feasibility, scientific and technical significance, merit, originality, the anticipated contribution of the proposed research, and the availability of adequate facilities, personnel, and resources. Priority for 2 of the grants is given for the study of acid-peptic disease. Women and minority investigators are strongly encouraged to apply.

Financial data The grant is $35,000. Funds are to be used for project costs, including salary, supplies, and equipment but excluding travel. Indirect costs are not allowed.

Duration 1 year.

Additional information This award is administered by the Foundation for Digestive Health and Nutrition (FDHN) and sponsored by the AGA. Funding is provided by TAP Pharmaceuticals, Inc.

Number awarded 4 each year.

Deadline September of each year.

[728]
AGA RESEARCH SCHOLAR AWARDS

Foundation for Digestive Health and Nutrition
Attn: Research Awards Coordinator
4930 Del Ray Avenue
Bethesda, MD 20814-2512
(301) 222-4005   Fax: (301) 222-4010
E-mail: info@fdhn.org
Web: www.fdhn.org

Purpose To provide salary support for minority and other young investigators developing an independent career in an area of gastroenterology, hepatology, or related fields.

Eligibility Applicants must hold full-time faculty positions at North American universities or professional institutes at the time of application. They should be early in their careers (fellows and established investigators are not appropriate candidates). Candidates with an M.D. degree must have completed clinical training within the past 5 years and those with a Ph.D. must have received their degree within the past 5 years. Membership in the American Gastroenterological Association (AGA) is required. Selection is based on novelty, feasibility, and significance of the proposal; attributes of the candidate, including potential for independence; evidence of institutional commitment; and the research environment. Special consideration is given to applications with a focus on nutrition or geriatrics. Women and minority investigators are strongly encouraged to apply. To increase the number of underrepresented minority scientists participating in gastroenterology research, the association has reserved 1 of these awards specifically for an applicant who is African American, Mexican American, Mainland Puerto Rican, or Native American (Alaska Native, American Indian, or Native Hawaiian).

Financial data   The award is $65,000 per year. Funds are to be used for project costs, including salary, supplies, and equipment but excluding travel. Indirect costs are not allowed.

Duration   3 years.

Additional information   This award is administered by the Foundation for Digestive Health and Nutrition (FDHN) and sponsored by the AGA. Funding is provided by TAP Pharmaceuticals, Inc., AstraZeneca Pharmaceuticals, L.P., Janssen Pharmaceutica Products, L.P., Johnson & Johnson/Merck Consumer Pharmaceuticals, Roche Pharmaceuticals, and Wyeth-Ayerst Laboratories. At least 70% of the recipient's research effort should relate to the gastrointestinal tract or liver. Recipients cannot hold or have held a R01, R29, K121, K08, VA Research Award, or any award with similar objectives from nonfederal sources.

Number awarded   Varies each year. Recently, 8 of the awards were granted, including 2 designated as Roche Research Scholar Awards in Liver Diseases.

Deadline   September of each year.

[729]
AGA STUDENT RESEARCH FELLOWSHIP AWARDS

Foundation for Digestive Health and Nutrition
Attn: Research Awards Coordinator
4930 Del Ray Avenue
Bethesda, MD 20814-2512
(301) 222-4005   Fax: (301) 222-4010
E-mail: info@fdhn.org
Web: www.fdhn.org

Purpose   To provide funding for research on digestive diseases or nutrition to students (particularly minorities and women) at any level.

Eligibility   This program is open to high school, college, graduate, and medical students at accredited institutions in North America who are not yet engaged in thesis research. They must be interested in conducting research on digestive diseases or nutrition. Candidates must not hold similar salary support awards from other agencies (e.g., American Liver Foundation, Crohn's and Colitis Foundation). Women and underrepresented minority students are strongly encouraged to apply. Research must be conducted under the supervision of a preceptor who is a full-time faculty member at a North American institution, directing a research project in a gastroenterology-related area, and a member of the American Gastroenterological Association (AGA). Selection is based on novelty, feasibility, and significance of the proposal; attributes of the candidate; the record of the preceptor; evidence of institutional commit-

ment; and the laboratory environment. Applicants are grouped and evaluated according to educational level.

Financial data   Grants range from $2,000 to $3,000. No indirect costs are allowed. The award is paid directly to the student and is to be used as a stipend or for thesis research.

Duration   At least 10 weeks. The work may take place at any time during the year.

Additional information   In an effort to attract and encourage minorities, 7 of the awards are set aside specifically for underrepresented minority students, defined as African Americans, Mexican Americans, Mainland Puerto Ricans, and Native Americans (Alaskan Natives, American Indians, and Native Hawaiians). This award is administered by the Foundation for Digestive Health and Nutrition (FDHN) and sponsored by the AGA. Funds may not be used to support thesis research.

Number awarded   Varies each year. Recently, 21 of these awards were granted, including several set aside specifically for underrepresented minorities (African Americans, American Indians, Alaska and Hawaiian Natives, Mexican Americans, and Mainland Puerto Ricans).

Deadline   March of each year.

[730]
AMERICAN ANTHROPOLOGICAL ASSOCIATION MINORITY DISSERTATION FELLOWSHIP PROGRAM

American Anthropological Association
Attn: Department of Academic Relations
2200 Wilson Boulevard, Suite 600
Arlington, VA 22201-3357
(703) 528-1902   Fax: (703) 528-3546
E-mail: academic@aaanet.org
Web: www.aaanet.org

Purpose   To provide funding to minorities who are working on a Ph.D. dissertation in anthropology.

Eligibility   Native American, African American, Latino(a), and Asian American doctoral students who have been admitted to degree candidacy in anthropology are invited to apply. Applicants must be U.S. citizens, enrolled in a full-time academic program leading to a doctoral degree in anthropology, and members of the American Anthropological Association. They must have a record of outstanding academic success, have had their dissertation proposal approved by their dissertation committee prior to application, be writing a dissertation in an area of anthropological research, and need funding to complete the dissertation. To apply, students must submit an application form, a cover letter, a research plan summary, a curriculum vitae, a statement regarding employment, a disclosure statement providing information about other sources of available and pending financial support, 3 letters of recommendation, and an official transcript from their doctoral program. Selection is based on the quality of the submitted information and the judged likelihood that the applicant will have a good chance at completing the dissertation. Consideration is also given to the implications of the applicant's research to issues and concerns of the U.S. historically disadvantaged populations, relevant service to the community, and future plans.

Financial data The stipend is $10,000. Funds are sent in 2 installments (in September and in January) to the recipient's institution.
Duration 1 year; nonrenewable.
Number awarded 1 each year.
Deadline February of each year.

[731]
AMERICAN ASSOCIATION OF OBSTETRICIANS AND GYNECOLOGISTS FOUNDATION SCHOLARSHIPS

American Association of Obstetricians and
  Gynecologists Foundation
Attn: Administrative Director
409 12th Street, S.W.
Washington, DC 20024-2188
(202) 863-1647   Fax: (202) 554-0453
E-mail: ejones@acog.org
Web: www.agosonline.org

Purpose To provide funding to physicians (particularly minorities and women) interested in a program of research training in obstetrics and gynecology.
Eligibility Applicants must have an M.D. degree and be eligible for the certification process of the American Board of Obstetrics and Gynecology (ABOG). They must document departmental planning for a significant research training experience to be conducted by 1 or more faculty mentors. There is no formal application form, but departments must supply a description of the candidate's qualifications, including a curriculum vitae, bibliography, prior training, past research experience, and evidence of completion of residency training in obstetrics and gynecology; a comprehensive description of the proposed training program; a description of departmental resources appropriate to the training; a list of other research grants, training grants, or scholarships previously or currently held by the applicant; and a budget. Applicants for the scholarship sponsored by ABOG must verify that 90% of their time and effort will be dedicated to the research training and conduct of research. Applicants for the scholarship sponsored by the Society for Maternal-Fetal Medicine (SMFM) must also have completed MFM subspecialty training or be in the second or third year of an ABOG-approved MFM training program at the time of applying. Candidates for that scholarship must also be members or associate members of the SMFM. Preference for both awards is given to training in areas currently underrepresented in obstetrics and gynecology. A personal interview may be requested. Priority is given to individuals who have not previously received extramural funding for research training. Women and minority candidates are strongly encouraged to apply. Selection is based on the scholarly, clinical, and research qualifications of the candidate; evidence of the candidate's commitment to an investigative career in academic obstetrics and gynecology in the United States or Canada; qualifications of the sponsoring department and mentor; and quality of the research project.
Financial data The grant is $100,000 per year, of which at least $5,000 but not more than $15,000 must be used for employee benefits. In addition, sufficient funds to support travel to the annual fellows' retreat must be set aside. The balance of the funds may be used for salary, technical support, and supplies. The grant co-sponsored by the SMFM

must be matched by an institutional commitment of at least $30,000 per year.
Duration 1 year; may be renewed for 2 additional years, based on satisfactory progress of the scholar.
Number awarded 2 each year: 1 co-sponsored by ABOG and 1 co-sponsored by SMFM.
Deadline August of each year.

[732]
AMERICAN ASSOCIATION OF UNIVERSITY WOMEN POSTDOCTORAL RESEARCH LEAVE FELLOWSHIPS

American Association of University Women
Attn: AAUW Educational Foundation
301 ACT Drive, Department 177
P.O. Box 4030
Iowa City, IA 52243-4030
(319) 337-1716   Fax: (319) 337-1204
E-mail: aauw@act.org
Web: www.aauw.org

Purpose To enable American women scholars who have achieved distinction or promise of distinction in their fields of scholarly work to engage in additional research.
Eligibility Women of outstanding scholarly achievement who are working on postdoctoral research in any field and are U.S. citizens or permanent residents are eligible to apply; 1 award is set aside specifically for an underrepresented minority woman. Applicants must have earned the doctorate by the time the application is submitted. Support is not available for revision of a doctoral dissertation. Selection is based on scholarly excellence, experience in teaching or mentoring female students, and active commitment to helping women and girls through service in community, profession, or field of research.
Financial data The stipend is $30,000.
Duration 1 year, beginning in July.
Additional information Postdoctoral fellowships normally will not be awarded to women who have received the doctorate within the past 3 years or for revision of the dissertation. Recipients are expected to spend the fellowship year in full-time research. The award may be not be used to cover the costs of research equipment, research assistants, publication, travel to professional meetings or seminars, tuition for additional course work, or repayment of loans or other personal obligations. Applications should be made 1 year in advance of the academic year for which funding is sought.
Number awarded 20 each year in 3 fields: the arts and humanities, the social sciences, and the natural sciences. The fellowship reserved for an underrepresented minority woman is available to an applicant in any field.
Deadline November of each year.

[733]
AMERICAN EDUCATIONAL RESEARCH ASSOCIATION MINORITY FELLOWSHIP PROGRAM

American Educational Research Association
1230 17th Street, N.W.
Washington, DC 20036-3078
(202) 223-9485   Fax: (202) 775-1824
Web: www.aera.net/programs/minority

Purpose   To provide funding to minority doctoral students writing their dissertation on educational research.

Eligibility   This program is open to U.S. citizens and native residents of a U.S. possession who have advanced to candidacy and successfully defended their Ph.D./Ed.D. dissertation research proposal. Applicants must plan to work full time on their dissertation in educational research. This program is targeted for members of groups historically underrepresented in higher education (African Americans, American Indians, Alaskan Natives, Filipino Americans, Native Pacific Islanders, Mexican Americans, and Puerto Ricans). Selection is based on scholarly achievements and publications, letters of recommendation, quality and significance of the proposed research, and commitment of the applicant's faculty mentor to the goals of the program.

Financial data   The grant is $12,000 per year; nonrenewable. Also, up to $1,000 is provided to pay for travel to the sponsor's annual conference.

Duration   1 year; may be renewed for 1 additional year upon demonstration of satisfactory progress.

Additional information   The association also sponsors a number of other funding programs that give special attention to applications submitted by minorities, including the AERA/IES Dissertation Grants Program, AERA/IES Postdoctoral Fellowship Program, AERA/IES Research Grants Program, American Educational Research Association Dissertation Grants Program, American Educational Research Association Fellows Program, American Educational Research Association Postdoctoral Fellows Program, American Educational Research Association Research Fellows Program, American Educational Research Association Research Grants Program.

Number awarded   2 each year.

Deadline   February of each year.

[734]
AMERICAN METEOROLOGICAL SOCIETY GRADUATE FELLOWSHIP IN THE HISTORY OF SCIENCE

American Meteorological Society
Attn: Fellowship/Scholarship Program
45 Beacon Street
Boston, MA 02108-3693
(617) 227-2426, ext. 246   Fax: (617) 742-8718
E-mail: scholar@ametsoc.org
Web: www.ametsoc.org

Purpose   To provide financial assistance to graduate students (minorities are particularly encouraged) interested in conducting dissertation research on the history of meteorology.

Eligibility   This program is open to graduate students who are planning to complete a dissertation on the history of the atmospheric or related oceanic or hydrologic sciences. Fellowships may be used to support research at a location

away from the student's institution, provided the plan is approved by the student's thesis advisor. In such an instance, an effort is made to place the student into a mentoring relationship with a member of the society at an appropriate institution. The sponsor specifically encourages applications from women, minorities, and students with disabilities who are traditionally underrepresented in the atmospheric and related oceanic sciences.

Financial data   The stipend is $15,000 per year.

Duration   1 year.

Number awarded   1 each year.

Deadline   February of each year.

[735]
AMERICAN SOCIETY FOR CELL BIOLOGY MINORITIES AFFAIRS COMMITTEE VISITING PROFESSOR AWARDS

American Society for Cell Biology
Attn: Minority Affairs Committee
8120 Woodmont Avenue, Suite 750
Bethesda, MD 20814-2762
(301) 347-9300   Fax: (301) 347-9310
E-mail: mac@ascb.org
Web: www.ascb.org/committees/mac/visprof.cfm

Purpose   To provide funding for research to faculty members at primarily teaching institutions that serve minority students and scientists.

Eligibility   Eligible to apply for this support are professors at primarily teaching institutions. They must be interested in working in the laboratories of members of the American Society for Cell Biology during the summer. Hosts and visitor scientists are asked to submit their applications together as a proposed team. Minority professors and professors in colleges and universities with a high minority enrollment are especially encouraged to apply for this award. Minorities are defined as U.S. citizens of Black, Native American, Chicano/Hispanic, or Pacific Islands background.

Financial data   The stipend for the summer is $12,000 plus $700 for travel expenses and $2,000 to the host institution for supplies.

Duration   From 8 to 10 weeks during the summer.

Additional information   Funds for this program, established in 1997, are provided by the Minorities Access to Research Careers (MARC) program of the National Institutes of Health.

Number awarded   Varies each year; recently, 3 of these grants were awarded.

Deadline   March of each year.

[736]
AMERICAN SOCIETY OF CRIMINOLOGY UNDERGRADUATE STUDENT MINORITY SCHOLAR/MENTOR RESEARCH GRANTS

American Society of Criminology
Attn: Awards Committee
1314 Kinnear Road, Suite 212
Columbus, OH 43212-1156
(614) 292-9207   Fax: (614) 292-6767
E-mail: asc41@infinet.com
Web: www.asc41.com/uminorfel.htm

Purpose   To provide financial assistance to ethnic minority undergraduate students interested in conducting a research project in criminology and criminal justice.

Eligibility   This program is open to undergraduate students who are members of historically disadvantaged and underrepresented ethnic and racial groups. Applicants must be entering their junior year in a program in criminology and criminal justice. They must be interested in conducting a research project under the mentorship of a faculty member, who must act as a co-applicant for the funding. Along with the application, students must provide a personal statement on their career goals in criminology and another statement on how the grant would enable them to focus more time on their academic work and better achieve their career goals. Faculty members must provide 1) a written recommendation for why the student has the academic potential and career aspirations to complete graduate student in criminology successfully and prepare for an academic career; 2) student transcripts and other supporting materials; 3) a description of the proposed collaborative research project that will result in a presentation at the annual meeting of the American Society of Criminology (ASC) in the student's senior years; and 4) a description of other mentoring activities and proposed contact with the student during the junior and senior years. Selection is based on the student's potential for completing doctoral work in criminology and the quality of the proposed mentoring relationship.

Financial data   The grant provides $5,000 per year for research support and a $1,500 travel grant to attend the ASC annual meetings.

Duration   2 years (the junior and senior year of college).

Additional information   This program began in 2004. Information is also available from Todd R. Clear, Minority Scholar/Mentor Committee Chair, John Jay College of Criminal Justice, 899 Tenth Avenue, New York, NY 10019, (212) 237-8470.

Number awarded   Varies each year; recently, 4 of these grants were awarded.

Deadline   April of each year.

[737]
ANDREW W. MELLON FOUNDATION EARLY CAREER FELLOWSHIP IN ECONOMIC STUDIES

Brookings Institution
Attn: Mellon Fellows Program
1775 Massachusetts Avenue, N.W.
Washington, DC 20036-2188
(202) 797-6104   Fax: (202) 797-6181
E-mail: erobinson@brookings.edu
Web: www.brookings.edu/admin/eswebmellon.htm

Purpose   To provide funding to economists (particularly minorities and women) who are interested in conducting an independent research project in residence at the Brookings Institution.

Eligibility   This program is open to economists, especially junior faculty members who have between 2 and 6 years of teaching experience. Applicants should have a Ph.D. or equivalent and an expressed interest in analyzing applied and policy issues and empirical research. They must submit a curriculum vitae, a 500-word research proposal, 2 letters of recommendation, and copies of up to 5 significant publications and working papers. The institution particularly encourages applications from women and members of minority groups.

Financial data   Fellows receive a salary and partial support for staff and research assistance.

Duration   1 year.

Additional information   Fellows participate in workshops and conferences at the institution. Funding for this program is provided by the Andrew W. Mellon Foundation. Fellows are expected to pursue their research at the Brookings Institution.

Number awarded   1 or more each year.

Deadline   November of each year.

[738]
APA MINORITY MEDICAL STUDENT SUMMER MENTORING PROGRAM

American Psychiatric Association
Attn: Department of Minority and National Affairs
1000 Wilson Boulevard, Suite 1825
Arlington, VA 22209-3901
(703) 907-8653   Toll-free: (888) 35-PSYCH
Fax: (703) 907-7852   E-mail: mking@psych.org
Web: www.psych.org

Purpose   To provide funding to minority medical students who are interested in working on a summer project with a psychiatrist mentor.

Eligibility   This program is open to minority medical students who are interested in psychiatric issues. Minorities include American Indians, Alaska Natives, Native Hawaiians, Asian Americans, Hispanic/Latinos, and African Americans. Applicants must be interested in working with a psychiatrist mentor, primarily on clinical work with underserved minority populations and mental health care disparities. Work settings may be in a research, academic, or clinical environment. Most of them are inner-city or rural, preferably those dealing with psychiatric subspecialties, particularly substance abuse and geriatrics. Selection is based on interest of the medical student and the specialty of the mentor, practice setting, and geographic proximity of the mentor to the student.

Financial data Fellowships provide $1,500 for living expenses and up to another $1,500 for out-of-pocket expenses directly related to the conduct of the fellowship.
Duration Summer months.
Number awarded Varies each year.
Deadline February of each year.

[739]
ARCTIC RESEARCH OPPORTUNITIES
National Science Foundation
Attn: Office of Polar Programs
4201 Wilson Boulevard, Room 755S
Arlington, VA 22230
(703) 292-8029　　　　　　　　Fax: (703) 292-9082
TDD: (703) 292-5090
Web: www.nsf.gov/od/opp
Purpose To provide funding (particularly to minorities, women, and persons with disabilities) for research related to the Arctic.
Eligibility This program is open to investigators affiliated with U.S. universities, research institutions, or other organizations, including local or state governments. Applicants must be proposing to conduct research in the 3 program areas of Arctic Natural Sciences (including atmospheric sciences, biological sciences, earth sciences, glaciology, and ocean sciences); Arctic Social Sciences (including anthropology, archaeology, economics, geography, linguistics, political science, psychology, science and technology studies, sociology, traditional knowledge, and related subjects); and Arctic System Science (encompassing 3 components: 1) how do human activities interact with changes in the Arctic to affect the sustainability of ecosystems and societies? 2) what are the limits of Arctic system predictability? and 3) how will changes in Arctic cycles and feedbacks affect Arctic and global systems?). Proposals should involve field studies in the Arctic, although projects outside the Arctic but directly related to Arctic science and engineering are also considered, as are related laboratory and theoretical studies. The program particularly encourages proposals from women, minorities, and persons with disabilities.
Financial data The amounts of the awards depend on the nature of the proposal and the availability of funds.
Number awarded Varies each year. Recently, this program awarded 130 to 160 grants worth approximately $66 million.
Deadline August or February of each year.

[740]
ARKANSAS SPACE GRANT CONSORTIUM RESEARCH INFRASTRUCTURE GRANTS
Arkansas Space Grant Consortium
c/o University of Arkansas at Little Rock
Graduate Institute of Technology
2801 South University Avenue
Little Rock, AR 72204
(501) 569-8212　　　　　　　　Fax: (501) 569-8039
E-mail: asgc@ualr.edu
Web: asgc.ualr.edu/spacegrant
Purpose To provide research funding to faculty (particularly minorities, women, and persons with disabilities) at

member universities of the Arkansas Space Grant Consortium (ASGC).
Eligibility This program is open to faculty at institutions that are members of the ASGC. Applicants must be seeking research starter grants for projects that seem likely to receive support from the U.S. National Aeronautics and Space Administration (NASA) and be willing to mentor student scholarship and fellowship research. Fields of study include astronomy, biochemistry, biology, chemistry, computer science, earth science, engineering, engineering technology, instrumentation, materials science, mathematics, physics, psychology, and space medicine. The consortium is a component of NASA's Space Grant program, which encourages participation by underrepresented minorities, women, and persons with disabilities.
Financial data The funding depends on the nature of the proposal.
Duration Up to 3 years.
Additional information ASGC member institutions are Arkansas State University, University, Arkansas Tech University, Harding University, Henderson State University, Hendrix College, Lyon College, Ouachita Baptist University, University of Central Arkansas, University of Arkansas at Fayetteville, University of Arkansas at Little Rock, University of Arkansas at Montecito, University of Arkansas at Pine Bluff, University of Arkansas for Medical Sciences, and University of the Ozarks. This program is funded by NASA.
Number awarded Varies each year; since this program began in 1990, it has awarded approximately 300 of these grants.

[741]
ASA/NSF/BLS SENIOR RESEARCH FELLOW PROGRAM
American Statistical Association
Attn: Fellowship Program
1429 Duke Street, Suite 200
Alexandria, VA 22314-3415
(703) 684-1221　　　　　　　　Toll-free: (888) 231-3473
Fax: (703) 684-2037　　　E-mail: asainfo@amstat.org
Web: www.amstat.org/research_grants
Purpose To provide funding to senior researchers (particularly minorities and women) interested in conducting research in residence at the Bureau of Labor Statistics (BLS).
Eligibility This program is open to scholars interested in conducting research in the broad field of labor economics and statistics that is of interest to the BLS. Applicants must be planning to work in residence, using BLS data and facilities, and interacting with BLS staff. They should have a recognized research record and considerable expertise in their area of proposed research. Selection is based on the applicability of the proposed research to BLS programs, the value of the proposed research to science, and the quality of the applicant's research record. Qualified women and members of minority groups are especially encouraged to apply.
Financial data The stipends paid to senior research fellows are commensurate with their qualifications and experience. Fellows also receive fringe benefits and a travel allowance.

Duration The usual term is 6 to 12 months, although the duration is flexible.

Additional information Fellows are given an opportunity to conduct their research in residence and interact with staff. Funding for this program is provided by the National Science Foundation (NSF). Information is also available from the Office of Survey Methods Research, Attn: Stephen Cohen, 2 Massachusetts Avenue, N.E., Room 4915, Washington, DC 20212, (202) 691-7400, E-mail: Cohen.Steve@bls.gov, and the Office of Employment Research and Program Development, Attn: James Spletzer, 2 Massachusetts Avenue, N.E., Room 4945, Washington, DC 20212, (202) 691-7393, E-mail: Spletzer.Jim@bls.gov.

Number awarded Varies each year.

Deadline December of each year.

[742]
ASTRAZENECA FELLOWSHIP/FACULTY TRANSITION AWARDS

Foundation for Digestive Health and Nutrition
Attn: Research Awards Coordinator
4930 Del Ray Avenue
Bethesda, MD 20814-2512
(301) 222-4005   Fax: (301) 222-4010
E-mail: info@fdhn.org
Web: www.fdhn.org

Purpose To provide funding to physicians (especially those who are minority group members or women) for research training in an area of gastrointestinal, liver function, or related diseases.

Eligibility This program is open to trainee members of the American Gastroenterological Association (AGA) who are M.D.s or M.D./Ph.D.s currently holding a gastroenterology-related fellowship at an accredited North American institution. Applicants must be committed to an academic career; have completed 2 years of research training at the start of this award; be sponsored by an AGA member who directs a gastroenterology-related unit that is engaged in research training in a North American medical school, affiliated teaching hospital, or research institute; and be cosponsored by the director of a basic research laboratory (or other comparable laboratory) who is committed to the training and development of the applicant. Minorities and women investigators are strongly encouraged to apply. Selection is based on novelty, feasibility, and significance of the proposal; attributes of the candidate; record and commitment of the sponsors; and the institutional and laboratory environment.

Financial data The stipend is $40,000 per year. Funds are to be used as salary support for the recipient. Indirect costs are not allowed.

Duration 2 years.

Additional information This award is administered by the Foundation for Digestive Health and Nutrition (FDHN) and sponsored by the AGA with support from AstraZeneca Pharmaceuticals, L.P. Finalists for the award are interviewed. Although the host institution may supplement the award, the applicant may not concurrently have a similar training award or grant from another organization. All publications coming from work funded by this program must acknowledge the support of the award.

Number awarded Up to 4 each year.

Deadline September of each year.

[743]
BAY AREA COMMUNITY SERVICE SCHOLARSHIPS

National Medical Fellowships, Inc.
Attn: Scholarship Program
5 Hanover Square, 15th Floor
New York, NY 10004
(212) 483-8880   Fax: (212) 483-8897
E-mail: info@nmfonline.org
Web: www.nmf-online.org

Purpose To provide financial assistance and clinical experiences to underrepresented minority medical students at designated schools in California.

Eligibility This program is open to third- or fourth-year medical students who are African Americans, mainland Puerto Ricans, Mexican Americans, Native Hawaiians, Alaska Natives, and American Indians. Applicants must be California residents enrolled at the University of California at Davis School of Medicine, the University of California at San Francisco School of Medicine, or Stanford University School of Medicine. They must be interested in either 1) a clinical rotation at an approved community health center in the San Francisco Bay area dedicated to medically underserved populations, or 2) a basic science or clinical science research project in an area of critical need (e.g., HIV/AIDS care and research, hypertension, tuberculosis, cardiovascular disease, diabetes, asthma, substance abuse, women's health research). Selection is based on demonstrated commitment to practice in California, interest in community-based primary care or research, academic performance, financial need, and leadership.

Financial data The stipend is $7,500 for 6-week clinical rotations or 8-week research projects, or $15,000 for 12-week clinical rotations or research projects.

Duration Clinical rotations may be either 6 weeks or 12 weeks. Research projects may extend either 8 weeks or 12 weeks.

Additional information This program was established in 2002 with support from the San Francisco Foundation and the California Endowment. Information is also available from the administrator's California Regional Office, The Chancery Building, 564 Market Street, Suite 209, San Francisco, CA 94104, (415) 397-2526, Fax: (415) 397-2556. Students who choose a 12-week clinical rotation must plan and implement a clinical project at their site. Projects may involve qualitative or quantitative research, health education, or another area of relevance to the site.

Number awarded 6 each year.

Deadline December of each year.

[744]
BEHAVIORAL SCIENCES POSTDOCTORAL FELLOWSHIPS IN EPILEPSY

Epilepsy Foundation
Attn: Research Department
4351 Garden City Drive
Landover, MD 20785-7223
(301) 459-3700   Toll-free: (800) EFA-1000
Fax: (301) 577-2684   TDD: (800) 332-2070
E-mail: grants@efa.org
Web: www.epilepsyfoundation.org

Purpose To provide funding to postdoctorates (especially minorities, women, and persons with disabilities) in the behavioral sciences who wish to pursue research training in an area related to epilepsy.

Eligibility Individuals who have received their doctoral degree in a behavioral science field by the time the fellowship begins and desire additional postdoctoral research experience in epilepsy may apply. Academic faculty holding the rank of instructor or above are not eligible, nor are graduate or medical students, medical residents, permanent government employees, or employees of private industry. Appropriate fields of study in the behavioral sciences include sociology, social work, anthropology, nursing, economics, and others relevant to epilepsy research and practice. Because these fellowships are designed as training opportunities, the quality of the training plans and environment are considered in the selection process. Other selection criteria include the scientific quality of the proposed research, a statement regarding the relevance of the research to epilepsy, the applicant's qualifications, and the preceptor's qualifications. Applications from women, members of minority groups, and people with disabilities are especially encouraged. U.S. citizenship is not required, but the research must be conducted in the United States.

Financial data Grants up to $30,000 per year are available.

Duration 1 year.

Number awarded Varies each year; recently, 2 of these fellowships were awarded.

Deadline February of each year.

[745]
BEHAVIORAL SCIENCES STUDENT FELLOWSHIPS IN EPILEPSY

Epilepsy Foundation
Attn: Research Department
4351 Garden City Drive
Landover, MD 20785-7223
(301) 459-3700   Toll-free: (800) EFA-1000
Fax: (301) 577-2684   TDD: (800) 332-2070
E-mail: grants@efa.org
Web: www.epilepsyfoundation.org

Purpose To provide funding to undergraduate and graduate students (minorities, women, and persons with disabilities) interested in working on a summer research training project in a field relevant to epilepsy.

Eligibility This program is open to undergraduate and graduate students in a behavioral science program relevant to epilepsy research or clinical care, including, but not limited to, sociology, social work, psychology, anthropology, nursing, economics, vocational rehabilitation, counseling, and political science. Applicants must be interested in working on an epilepsy research project under the supervision of a qualified mentor. Because the program is designed as a training opportunity, the quality of the training plans and environment are considered in the selection process. Other selection criteria include the quality of the proposed project, the relevance of the proposed work to epilepsy, the applicant's interest in the field of epilepsy, the applicant's qualifications, and the mentor's qualifications, including his or her commitment to the student and the project. U.S. citizenship is not required, but the project must be conducted in the United States. Applications from women, members of minority groups, and people with disabilities are especially encouraged. The program is not intended for students working on a dissertation research project.

Financial data The grant is $3,000.

Duration 3 months during the summer.

Additional information This program is supported by the American Epilepsy Society, Abbott Laboratories, Ortho-McNeil Pharmaceutical Corporation, and Pfizer Inc.

Number awarded Varies each year; recently, 4 of these fellowships were awarded.

Deadline March of each year.

[746]
BERNARD L. MAJEWSKI FELLOWSHIP

University of Wyoming
Attn: American Heritage Center
P.O. Box 3924
Laramie, WY 82071-3924
(307) 766-4114   Fax: (307) 766-5511
E-mail: ahc@uwyo.edu
Web: ahc.uwyo.edu

Purpose To provide funding to scholars (especially minorities) who are interested in using the resources at the University of Wyoming's American Heritage Center to conduct research in economic geology.

Eligibility This program is open to scholars who are interested in conducting research at the center in the history of economic geology. For purposes of the fellowship, economic geology is defined as the activities of exploration and development of petroleum and base, precious, and industrial minerals, including basic geological research. Acceptable related fields include history; oral history; historical archaeology pertaining to economic geology, environmental, and natural resources history; and business or economic history related to economic geology. Applicants must be recognized scholars in 1 of those fields of research. They should have a record of publication in the field or show significant potential for publication. Young scholars, minorities, and multi-disciplinary researchers are encouraged to apply.

Financial data The grant is $2,500, paid in 2 installments: $500 upon the applicant's acceptance of the fellowship and $2,000 upon completion of the first research session at the American Heritage Center.

Duration 1 calendar year.

Additional information This program began in 1998.

Number awarded 1 each year.

Deadline February of each year.

[747]
BERRIEN FRAGOS THORN ARTS SCHOLARSHIPS FOR MIGRANT FARMWORKERS
Geneseo Migrant Center
27 Lackawanna Avenue
Mount Morris, NY 14510-1096
(585) 658-7960   Toll-free: (800) 245-5681
Fax: (585) 658-7969   E-mail: info@migrant.net
Web: www.migrant.net/sch_thorn.htm

Purpose To provide financial assistance to migrant farmworkers who are interested in developing their talents in the arts.

Eligibility This program is open to students with a "history of migration to obtain work in agriculture." Applicants must be at least 16 years of age, but they do not need to be enrolled in school. They must be interested in pursuing further development of their talents in 1 of the following disciplines: visual arts (e.g., painting, sculpture, photography); performing arts (e.g., dance, theater, music); media (e.g., film, video, animation, computer graphics); literature (e.g., poetry, short stories); or crafts (e.g., traditional folk arts, furniture, weaving, pottery). Students may submit either a complete application that includes a budget and portfolio or samples of work, or only a partial form providing basic personal information and letters of recommendation.

Financial data The maximum grant is $2,500 for students who utilize the complete application or $500 for those who submit only partial forms.

Duration These are 1-time grants.

Number awarded Varies each year.

Deadline Complete applications must be submitted by May or October of each year. Partial forms may be submitted at any time.

[748]
BYRD FELLOWSHIP PROGRAM
Ohio State University
Byrd Polar Research Center
Attn: Fellowship Committee
Scott Hall Room 108
1090 Carmack Road
Columbus, OH 43210-1002
(614) 292-6531   Fax: (614) 292-4697
Web: www-bprc.mps.ohio-state.edu

Purpose To provide funding to postdoctorates (particularly minorities and other special groups) interested in conducting research on the Arctic or Antarctic areas at Ohio State University.

Eligibility This program is open to postdoctorates of superior academic background who are interested in conducting advanced research on either Arctic or Antarctic problems at the Byrd Polar Research Center at Ohio State University. Applicants must have received their doctorates within the past 5 years. Each application should include a statement of general research interest, a description of the specific research to be conducted during the fellowship, and a curriculum vitae. Women, minorities, Vietnam-era veterans, disabled veterans, and individuals with disabilities are particularly encouraged to apply.

Financial data The stipend is $35,000 per year; an allowance of $3,000 for research and travel is also provided.

Duration 18 months.

Additional information This program was established by a major gift from the Byrd Foundation in memory of Rear Admiral Richard Evelyn Byrd and Marie Ames Byrd, his wife. Except for field work or other research activities requiring absence from campus, fellows are expected to be in residence at the university for the duration of the program.

Deadline April of each year.

[749]
BYRON HANKE FELLOWSHIP FOR GRADUATE RESEARCH ON COMMUNITY ASSOCIATIONS
Community Associations Institute
Attn: Foundation for Community Association Research
225 Reinekers Lane, Suite 300
Alexandria, VA 22314-2875
(703) 548-8600, ext. 340   Fax: (703) 684-1581
E-mail: smclaughlin@caionline.org
Web: www.cairf.org/schol/hanke.html

Purpose To provide funding to graduate students (particularly minorities) interested in working on research related to community associations.

Eligibility Applicants must be enrolled in an accredited master's, doctoral, or law program. They may be working in any subject area, but their proposed research must relate to community associations (organizations that govern common-interest communities of any kind—condominiums, cooperatives, townhouse developments, planned unit developments, and other developments where homeowners support an association with mandatory financial assessments and are subject to use and aesthetic restrictions). The proposed research may deal with management, institutions, organization and administration, public policy, architecture, as well as political, economic, social, and intellectual trends in community association housing. Academic disciplines include law, economics, sociology, and urban planning. The foundation is especially interested in substantive papers from the social sciences which place community association housing within political or economic organizational models. Minority applicants are particularly encouraged to apply. Selection is based on academic achievement, faculty recommendations, demonstrated research and writing ability, and nature of the proposed topic and its benefit to the study and understanding of community associations.

Financial data Grants range from $2,000 to $4,000. Funds are paid in 2 equal installments and may be used for tuition, books, or other educational expenses.

Duration 1 year.

Additional information The foundation may publish the final project. Recipients must provide the foundation with a copy of their final project.

Deadline Applications may be submitted at any time.

[750]
CALDER SUMMER UNDERGRADUATE RESEARCH PROGRAM

Fordham University
Attn: Louis Calder Center Biological Field Station
53 Whippoorwill Road
P.O. Box 887
Armonk, NY 10504
(914) 273-3078, ext. 10   Fax: (914) 273-2167
E-mail: wehr@fordham.edu
Web: www.fordham.edu

Purpose To provide an opportunity for undergraduates (especially minorities and women) to pursue summer research activities in biology at Fordham University's Louis Calder Center Biological Field Station.

Eligibility This program is open to undergraduates interested in conducting a summer research project of their own design at the center. Fields of interest must relate to the activities of staff who will serve as mentors on the projects; those include forest ecology, limnology, wildlife ecology, microbial ecology, Lyme disease, insect-plant interactions, evolutionary ecology, and the effects of urbanization on ecosystem processes. Applications from underrepresented minorities and women are especially encouraged.

Financial data The program provides a stipend of $3,600, housing on the site, and support for research supplies and local travel.

Duration 12 weeks during the summer.

Additional information This program has operated since 1967,

Number awarded Up to 8 each year.

Deadline February of each year.

[751]
CALIFORNIA SPACE GRANT GRADUATE STUDENT PROGRAM

California Space Grant Consortium
c/o University of California at San Diego
California Space Institute
9500 Gilman Drive, Department 0524
La Jolla, CA 92093-0524
(858) 822-1597   Fax: (858) 534-7840
E-mail: spacegrant@ucsd.edu
Web: calspace.ucsd.edu/casgc/scholarships.html

Purpose To provide financial assistance (particularly to underrepresented minorities, women, and persons with disabilities) for graduate study and research in space-related science, engineering, or technology at the branches of the University of California.

Eligibility This program is open to graduate students in space-related science, engineering, and technology at the campuses of the UC system. Most programs include research components. U.S. citizenship is required. As the California element of the Space Grant program of the U.S. National Aeronautics and Space Administration (NASA), this program encourages applications from underrepresented ethnic or gender groups and by persons with disabilities.

Financial data Each campus sets its own stipend.

Duration 1 year.

Additional information This program is funded by NASA.

Number awarded Varies each year.

Deadline Each of the participating UC campuses sets its own deadline.

[752]
CAREER DEVELOPMENT AWARD FOR MINORITY SCHOLARS IN NEUROSCIENCE

National Institute of Neurological Disorders and Stroke
Attn: Office of Minority Health and Research
Neuro Science Center
6001 Executive Boulevard, Suite 2149
Bethesda, MD 20892-9535
(301) 496-3102   Fax: (301) 594-5929
E-mail: dj140o@nih.gov
Web: www.ninds.nih.gov

Purpose To provide funding for career development to neurological research scientists who are members of underrepresented minority groups.

Eligibility This program is open to full-time faculty members at universities, colleges, hospitals, and medical, dental, or nursing schools or other institutions of higher education involved in neurological research. Candidates must be non-tenured full-time faculty with a doctoral degree who belong to a particular ethnic or racial group that has been determined by their institution to be underrepresented in biomedical or behavioral research. They must be interested in a program of research training, under the direction of a mentor, that will enable them to achieve independent investigator status. Only U.S. citizens, nationals, and permanent residents are eligible.

Financial data Grants provide an annual award of up to $85,000 for salary and fringe benefits and an annual research allowance of up to $50,000 for direct research costs. The institution may apply for up to 8% of direct costs for facilities and administrative costs.

Duration 3 to 5 years.

Number awarded Varies each year.

Deadline January, May, or September of each year.

[753]
CARNEGIE INSTITUTION OF WASHINGTON POSTDOCTORAL FELLOWSHIPS

Carnegie Institution of Washington
1530 P Street, N.W.
Washington, DC 20005-1910
(202) 387-6400   Fax: (202) 387-8092
Web: www.carnegieinstitution.org

Purpose To encourage the development of researchers (particularly minorities and women) in the fields of astronomy, geophysics, physics and related subjects, plant biology, and embryology.

Eligibility Qualified scientists who have obtained the doctoral degree are eligible. Candidates are evaluated on the basis of academic record, recommendations of professors and associates, and growth potential. Special efforts are made to recruit qualified minorities and women.

Financial data Stipends average approximately $15,000 each year; in addition to financial support, fellows receive the use of the institution's laboratory and observational facilities, including special equipment when needed. Some travel funds are provided.

Duration 1 to 2 years.

Additional information Facilities of the Carnegie Institution include the Department of Embryology in Baltimore, Maryland, the Department of Plant Biology and the Department of Global Ecology in Stanford, California, the Geophysical Laboratory and the Department of Terrestrial Magnetism in Washington, D.C., and the Observatories in Pasadena, California and Las Campanas, Chile. Fellowships are tenable at the institution's facilities only.

Number awarded More than 200 postdoctoral fellows are in residence each year.

Deadline Applications should be submitted at least 1 year in advance.

[754]
CARNEGIE INSTITUTION OF WASHINGTON PREDOCTORAL FELLOWSHIPS

Carnegie Institution of Washington
1530 P Street, N.W.
Washington, DC 20005-1910
(202) 387-6400   Fax: (202) 387-8092
Web: www.carnegieinstitution.org

Purpose To provide funding to doctoral candidates (particularly minorities and women) conducting thesis research in the sciences.

Eligibility Doctoral students from universities situated near Carnegie departments or other major universities may apply for funding to carry out their thesis research using Carnegie Institution facilities if they are working in the following areas: embryology, global ecology, plant biology, or astronomy. Special consideration is given to applications submitted by women and minorities.

Financial data The amount awarded varies, depending upon the scope of the funded research.

Duration 1 academic year, generally starting in July.

Additional information The relevant Carnegie facilities are the Department of Embryology on the grounds of The Johns Hopkins University (Baltimore, Maryland), the Departments of Plant Biology and Global Ecology on the Stanford University campus (Stanford, California), and the Observatories situated near the California Institute of Technology (Pasadena, California).

Number awarded Varies each year.

Deadline December of each year.

[755]
CAROLINA POSTDOCTORAL PROGRAM FOR FACULTY DIVERSITY

University of North Carolina at Chapel Hill
Attn: Office of the Vice Chancellor for Research and
   Economic Development
312 South Building
CB 4000
Chapel Hill, NC 27599-4000
(919) 962-1319   Fax: (919) 962-1476
E-mail: twaldrop@mail.unc.edu
Web: research.unc.edu/red/postdoc.php

Purpose To support minority scholars who are interested in teaching and conducting research at the University of North Carolina (UNC).

Eligibility This program is open to scholars from underrepresented groups who have completed their doctoral degree within the past 4 years. Applicants must be interested in teaching and conducting research at UNC. Preference is given to U.S. citizens and permanent residents. Selection is based on the evidence of scholarship potential and ability to compete for tenure track appointments at UNC and other research universities.

Financial data Fellows receive $35,625 per year, plus an allowance for research and travel. Health benefits are also available.

Duration Up to 2 years.

Additional information Fellows must be in residence at the Chapel Hill campus for the duration of the program. They teach 1 course per year and spend the rest of the time in research. This program began in 1983.

Number awarded 5 or 6 each year.

Deadline January of each year.

[756]
CDC/PRC MINORITY FELLOWSHIPS

Association of Schools of Public Health
Attn: Atlanta Office
2872 Woodcock Boulevard, Suite 211
Atlanta, GA 30341
(770) 455-6898   E-mail: hward@asph.org
Web: www.asph.org

Purpose To provide an opportunity for minority doctoral students to conduct research at Prevention Research Centers (PRCs) funded by the U.S. Centers for Disease Control and Prevention (CDC).

Eligibility This program is open to minority (African American/Black American, Hispanic/Latino, American Indian/Alaska Native, and Asian/Pacific Islander) students working on a doctoral degree at a school of public health with a CDC-funded PRC. Applicants must be proposing to conduct a research project that is related to the PRC activities and is endorsed by the PRC director. Along with their application, they must submit an essay (2 pages or less) on why they are interested in this fellowship, including specific ideas regarding their interest in the opportunity, benefits they expect to receive from the fellowship experience, how the experience will shape their future career plans, and how the proposed project will advance the field of public health prevention research. Selection is based on the essay (30 points), strength of credentials (20 points), and the project proposal (50 points). U.S. citizenship or permanent resident status is required.

Financial data The stipend is $22,500 per year. Fellows are also reimbursed up to $2,500 per year for health-related expenses, project-related travel, tuition, journal subscriptions, and association dues.

Duration 2 years.

Additional information Currently, PRCs are funded at 28 universities: University of Alabama at Birmingham, University of Albany, University of Arizona, Boston University, University of California at Berkeley, University of California at Los Angeles, University of Colorado, Columbia University, Harvard University, University of Illinois at Chicago, University of Iowa, Johns Hopkins University, University of Kentucky, University of Michigan, University of Minnesota, Morehouse School of Medicine, University of New Mexico,

University of North Carolina at Chapel Hill, University of Oklahoma, University of Pittsburgh, St. Louis University, University of South Carolina, University of South Florida, University of Texas at Houston, Tulane University, University of Washington, West Virginia University, and Yale University.

Number awarded Varies each year; recently, 4 of these fellowships were awarded.

Deadline January of each year.

[757]
CENTOCOR EXCELLENCE IN IBD CLINICAL RESEARCH AWARDS

Foundation for Digestive Health and Nutrition
Attn: Research Awards Coordinator
4930 Del Ray Avenue
Bethesda, MD 20814-2512
(301) 222-4005   Fax: (301) 222-4010
E-mail: info@fdhn.org
Web: www.fdhn.org

Purpose To provide funding to senior gastroenterology fellows (especially minorities and women) interested in preparing for a research career in inflammatory bowel diseases (IBD).

Eligibility This program is open to trainee members of the American Gastroenterological Association (AGA) who have an M.D. or equivalent degree. Applicants must be currently enrolled in an accredited gastroenterology-related fellowship at a U.S. institution and committed to an academic career. They must be interested in additional full-time research training in IBD clinical science to acquire modern laboratory skills. Their sponsor must be an AGA member engaged in research training at an academic gastroenterology-related unit of a medical school, affiliated teaching hospital, or research institute. A co-sponsor must be the director of a clinical or other comparable laboratory who is committed to the training and development of the applicant. The institution must provide them with at least 75% protected time. Women and minority investigators are strongly encouraged to apply. Selection is based on novelty, feasibility, and significance of the proposal; attributes of the candidate; record and commitment of the sponsors; and the institutional and laboratory environment.

Financial data The grant is $70,000 per year. No institutional indirect costs are allowed.

Duration 1 year; nonrenewable.

Additional information This program is administered by the Foundation for Digestive Health and Nutrition (FDHN) with support from Centocor, Inc. and the AGA.

Number awarded 5 each year.

Deadline January of each year.

[758]
CESAR E. CHAVEZ DISSERTATION FELLOWSHIP FOR U.S. LATINA/O SCHOLARS

Dartmouth College
Attn: Office of Graduate Studies
6062 Wentworth Hall, Room 304
Hanover, NH 03755-3526
(603) 646-6578
Web: www.dartmouth.edu

Purpose To provide funding to Latino/a and other doctoral students who are interested in working on their dissertation at Dartmouth College.

Eligibility This program is open to doctoral candidates who have completed all requirements for the Ph.D. except the dissertation and are planning a career in higher education. Applicants must be Latina/os or other graduate students with a demonstrated commitment and ability to advance educational diversity. They must be interested in working on their dissertation at Dartmouth College. All academic fields that are taught in the Dartmouth undergraduate Arts and Sciences curriculum are eligible.

Financial data The stipend is $25,000. In addition, fellows receive office space, library privileges, and a $2,500 research allowance.

Duration 1 year, beginning in September.

Additional information The fellows are affiliated with a department or program at Dartmouth College. Fellows are expected to be in residence at Dartmouth College for the duration of the program and to complete their dissertation during that time. They are also expected to teach a course, either as the primary instructor or as part of a team.

Number awarded 1 each year.

Deadline February of each year.

[759]
CHANCELLOR'S POSTDOCTORAL FELLOWSHIPS FOR ACADEMIC DIVERSITY

University of California at Berkeley
Attn: Office of the Chancellor
Office for Faculty Equity
200 California Hall
Berkeley, CA 94720-1500
(510) 642-1935   E-mail: admin.ofe@berkeley.edu
Web: facultyequity.chance.berkeley.edu

Purpose To increase the number of ethnic minority faculty members at the University of California at Berkeley.

Eligibility This program is open to U.S. citizens and permanent residents who received a doctorate within 3 years of the start of the fellowship. The program particularly solicits applications from individuals who are members of ethnic minority groups that are underrepresented in American universities. Special consideration is given to applicants committed to careers in university research and teaching and whose life experience, research, or employment background will contribute significantly to academic diversity and excellence at the Berkeley campus. An application form is not required. Interested applicants should submit a curriculum vitae, a statement of proposed research (up to 5 pages), sample publications, and 1 dissertation chapter. In addition, 3 letters of recommendation are required (1 must be from the dissertation advisor).

Financial data The stipend is $37,000 per year (11 months, plus 1 month vacation). Costs associated with 1-way transportation to Berkeley for the fellow and immediate family members and removal expenses are reimbursable, up to $2,000. In addition, up to $500 is available each year for supplies and related expenses, $3,000 for research-related expenses, and $1,000 for health insurance.

Duration 2 years.

Additional information Research opportunities, mentoring, and guidance are provided as part of the program.

Deadline November of each year.

[760]
CHARLES A. RYSKAMP RESEARCH FELLOWSHIPS

American Council of Learned Societies
Attn: Office of Fellowships and Grants
633 Third Avenue, 8C
New York, NY 10017-6795
(212) 697-1505   Fax: (212) 949-8058
E-mail: grants@acls.org
Web: www.acls.org/rysguide.htm

Purpose To provide financial assistance to advanced assistant professors (particularly minorities and women) in all disciplines of the humanities and the humanities-related social sciences.

Eligibility This program is open to tenure-track faculty members at the advanced assistant professor level and untenured associate professors in the humanities and related social sciences. Applicants must have successfully completed their institution's last reappointment review before tenure review. They must have a Ph.D. or equivalent degree and be employed at an academic institution in the United States. Appropriate fields of specialization include, but are not limited to, anthropology, archaeology, art history, economics, film, geography, history, languages and literatures, law, linguistics, musicology, philosophy, political science, psychology, religion, rhetoric and communication, and sociology. Proposals in the social sciences are eligible only if they employ predominantly humanistic approaches (e.g., law and literature, political philosophy). Proposals in interdisciplinary and cross-disciplinary studies are welcome, as are proposals focused on any geographic region or on any cultural or linguistic group. Applicants are encouraged to spend substantial periods of their leaves in residential interdisciplinary centers, research libraries, or other scholarly archives in the United States or abroad. Applications are particularly invited from women and members of minority groups.

Financial data Fellows receive a stipend of $60,000, a fund of $2,500 for research and travel, and the possibility of an additional summer's support, if justified by a persuasive case.

Duration 1 academic year (9 months) plus an additional summer's research (2 months) if justified.

Additional information This program, first available for the 2002-03 academic year, is supported by funding from the Andrew W. Mellon Foundation.

Number awarded Up to 12 each year.

Deadline September of each year.

[761]
CHICANA STUDIES DISSERTATION FELLOWSHIP

University of California at Santa Barbara
Attn: Department of Chicana and Chicano Studies
1713 South Hall
Santa Barbara, CA 93106-4120
(805) 893-5546   Fax: (805) 893-4076
Web: www.chicst.ucsb.edu

Purpose To assist promising Chicana scholars in completing their dissertations, preparing for university teaching and/or research, and achieving increased professional recognition.

Eligibility Candidates must be Ph.D. candidates working on a dissertation in the humanities, social sciences, or interdisciplinary studies whose research focuses on Chicana studies. Interested women should submit a letter of application describing progress toward the Ph.D., a dissertation proposal, a curriculum vitae, and a writing sample. They must be interested in completing their dissertation while in residence at the University of California at Santa Barbara.

Financial data The value of the award is $20,000 plus benefits.

Duration 9 months.

Additional information Fellows are expected to work on their dissertation and teach an undergraduate course during the fellowship period. Recipients must be in residence at the University of California at Santa Barbara for the entire fellowship period.

Number awarded 2 each year.

Deadline March of each year.

[762]
CHICANA/LATINA DISSERTATION FELLOWSHIP

University of California at Davis
Attn: Chicana/Latina Research Center
2223 Social Sciences and Humanities
One Shields Avenue
Davis, CA 95616
(530) 752-8882   Fax: (530) 754-8622
E-mail: clrc@ucdavis.edu
Web: cougar.ucdavis.edu/chi/clrc/index.html

Purpose To provide funding to women interested in conducting dissertation research in Chicana/Latina studies in residence at the University of California at Davis (UCD).

Eligibility This program is open to women who are engaged in dissertation research on issues of concern to Chicanas/Latinas at universities other than UCD. Comparative studies of Chicanas/Latinas and indigenous women are also eligible. Applicants must have been advanced to candidacy by the fellowship period, have completed their dissertation prospectus, and have made substantial progress on their dissertation.

Financial data The fellowship provides a stipend of $21,000 plus an allowance of $1,500 for research support and conference travel.

Duration 1 academic year.

Additional information In addition to conducting research, fellows are given the opportunity to deliver 1 public lecture and participate in the activities of the Chicana/Latina Research Center. Fellows must be in residence on the Davis campus.

Number awarded 1 each year.

Deadline June of each year.

[763]
CHICANO STUDIES POSTDOCTORAL AND VISITING SCHOLARS FELLOWSHIP PROGRAM

University of California at Los Angeles
Chicano Studies Research Center
Attn: IAC Coordinator
193 Haines Hall
P.O. Box 951544
Los Angeles, CA 90095-1544
(310) 825-2363
Web: www.gdnet.ucla.edu/iacweb/pstweber.htm

Purpose To provide funding to scholars interested in conducting research in Chicano studies at UCLA's Chicano Studies Research Center.

Eligibility Applicants must have completed a doctoral degree in Chicano or related studies. They must be interested in teaching or conducting research at UCLA's Chicano Studies Research Center. UCLA faculty, students, and staff are not eligible. U.S. citizenship or permanent resident status is required.

Financial data Fellows receive a stipend of $30,000 to $35,000 (depending on rank, experience, and date of completion of the Ph.D.), health benefits, and up to $4,000 in research support.

Duration 1 academic year; may be renewed.

Additional information Fellows must teach or do research in the programs of the center. The award is offered in conjunction with UCLA's Institute of American Cultures (IAC).

Number awarded 1 each year.

Deadline January of each year.

[764]
CINTAS FOUNDATION FELLOWSHIPS

Institute of International Education
Attn: Student Programs Division
809 United Nations Plaza
New York, NY 10017-3580
(212) 984-5565   Fax: (212) 984-5325
E-mail: cintas@iie.org
Web: www.iie.org/fulbright/cintas

Purpose To enable creative artists of Cuban birth or lineage to pursue their artistic endeavors anywhere outside of Cuba.

Eligibility Eligible are creative artists of Cuban citizenship or lineage living outside of Cuba who desire to pursue their artistic activities in the United States or other countries. Applications are accepted from visual artists (including painting, sculpture, installation art, design, video art, and photography) annually and from artists in other fields on a rotational basis (literature and architecture in 2006, music composition in 2007, filmmaking in 2008). Only professionals who have completed their training may apply.

Financial data Grants are $10,000.

Duration 1 year.

Additional information These fellowships are funded by the Cintas Foundation, established in memory of Oscar B. Cintas, former Cuban Ambassador to the United States. Fel-

lowships are not awarded for academic study, research, or writing; performing artists are not eligible.

Number awarded Up to 10 each year.

Deadline February of each year.

[765]
CIRES VISITING FACULTY, POSTDOCTORAL, AND SABBATICAL FELLOWSHIPS

University of Colorado at Boulder
Attn: Cooperative Institute for Research in
    Environmental Sciences
Campus Box 216
Boulder, CO 80309-0216
(303) 492-8773   Fax: (303) 492-1149
E-mail: cires@cires.colorado.edu
Web: cires.colorado.edu/cires.vf.html

Purpose To provide an opportunity for scholars (particularly minorities) to conduct research in the sciences at the Cooperative Institute for Research in Environmental Sciences (CIRES) at the University of Colorado.

Eligibility This program is open to Ph.D. scientists at all levels and to faculty planning sabbatical leave. Recent Ph.D. recipients and those affiliated with minority institutions are especially encouraged to apply. Scientists from all countries are eligible. Applicants must be interested in conducting research at CIRES in the following areas: advanced observing and modeling systems, climate system variability, geodynamics, planetary metabolism, and regional processes. Selection is based on the likelihood of interactions between the visiting fellows and the scientists at CIRES and the degree to which both parties will benefit from the exchange of new ideas.

Financial data The salary is commensurate with qualifications, current salary, and cost of living considerations.

Duration 1 year; the program may begin at anytime during the year.

Additional information This program is sponsored jointly by the University of Colorado and the National Oceanic and Atmospheric Administration (with support from other public and private sources).

Number awarded Up to 6 each year.

Deadline December of each year.

[766]
CLINICAL RESEARCH POST-DOCTORAL FELLOWSHIP PROGRAM

American Nurses Association
Attn: Ethnic Minority Fellowship Programs
600 Maryland Avenue, S.W., Suite 100 West
Washington, DC 20024-2571
(202) 651-7244   Fax: (202) 651-7007
E-mail: emfp@ana.org
Web: www.nursingworld.org

Purpose To provide funding to postdoctoral minority nurses interested in a program of research and study on psychiatric, mental health, and substance abuse issues that impact the lives of ethnic minority people.

Eligibility This program is open to doctoral-prepared nurses who are members of an ethnic or racial minority group, including but not limited to Blacks or African Americans, Hispanics or Latinos, American Indians and Alaska

Natives, Asians and Asian Americans, and Native Hawaiians and other Pacific Islanders. Applicants must be able to demonstrate a commitment to a research career in nursing and psychiatric/mental health issues affecting ethnic minority populations. They must be interested in a program of full-time postdoctoral study, with a research focus on such issues of concern to minority populations as child abuse, violence in intimate relationships, mental health disorders, substance abuse, mental health service utilization, and stigma as a barrier to mental health care and personal resilience. U.S. citizenship or permanent resident status and membership in the American Nurses Association are required.

Financial data   The stipend is $28,260 per year.

Duration   Up to 2 years.

Additional information   Funds for this program are provided by the Substance Abuse and Mental Health Services Administration.

Number awarded   1 or more each year.

[767]
CLINICAL RESEARCH PRE-DOCTORAL FELLOWSHIP PROGRAM

American Nurses Association
Attn: Ethnic Minority Fellowship Programs
600 Maryland Avenue, S.W., Suite 100 West
Washington, DC 20024-2571
(202) 651-7244   Fax: (202) 651-7007
E-mail: emfp@ana.org
Web: www.nursingworld.org

Purpose   To provide financial assistance to minority nurses who are doctoral candidates interested in psychiatric, mental health, and substance abuse issues that impact the lives of ethnic minority people.

Eligibility   This program is open to nurses who have a master's degree and are members of an ethnic or racial minority group, including but not limited to Blacks or African Americans, Hispanics or Latinos, American Indians and Alaska Natives, Asians and Asian Americans, and Native Hawaiians and other Pacific Islanders. Applicants must be able to demonstrate a commitment to a research career in nursing and psychiatric/mental health issues affecting ethnic minority populations. They must be interested in a program of full-time doctoral study, with a research focus on such issues of concern to minority populations as child abuse, violence in intimate relationships, mental health disorders, substance abuse, mental health service utilization, and stigma as a barrier to mental health care and personal resilience. U.S. citizenship or permanent resident status and membership in the American Nurses Association are required. Selection is based on research potential, scholarship, writing ability, knowledge of broad issues in mental health nursing, and professional commitment to ethnic minority concerns.

Financial data   Fellows receive a stipend of $20,772 per year and $5,000 in tuition assistance.

Duration   3 to 5 years.

Additional information   Funds for this program are provided by the Substance Abuse and Mental Health Services Administration.

Number awarded   1 or more each year.

Deadline   February of each year.

[768]
CMS DISSERTATION FELLOWSHIPS

Centers for Medicare & Medicaid Services
Attn: Acquisition and Grants Group
C2-21-15
7500 Security Boulevard
Baltimore, MD 21244-1850
(410) 786-5701   Toll-free: (877) 267-2323
TTY: (410) 786-0727   TTY: (866) 226-1819
Web: cms.hhs.gov/researchers/priorities/grants.asp

Purpose   To provide financial assistance to doctoral candidates (particularly minorities and women) writing dissertations in various social science disciplines that focus on health care financing and delivery issues.

Eligibility   Students enrolled in an accredited doctoral degree program in social, management, or health sciences may apply for these research grants if they are sponsored by their universities and conducting or intending to conduct research on issues related to the delivery or financing of health care services. Topics of special interest to the Centers for Medicare & Medicaid Services (CMS) include monitoring and evaluating CMS programs; improving managed care payment and delivery; improving fee-for-service payment and delivery; future trends influencing our programs; strengthening Medicaid, State Children's Health Insurance Program (SCHIP), and state programs; meeting the needs of vulnerable populations; outcomes, quality, and performance; and building research capacity. Applicants must have completed all course work and academic requirements for the doctoral degree, other than the research and dissertation. Applications from minority and women researchers are specifically encouraged. Selection is based on topic significance (25 points), research design (50 points), support structure (15 points), and budgetary appropriateness (10 points).

Financial data   The budget for direct costs (investigator's salary, travel, data processing, and supplies) may be up to $30,000; the sponsoring university may receive indirect costs of up to 8% of direct costs.

Additional information   Until 2001, the Centers for Medicare & Medicaid Services was known as the Health Care Financing Administration. Applications must be submitted jointly by the student and the university, but funds are dispensed only to the university.

Number awarded   Varies each year; recently, 9 of these grants were awarded.

Deadline   October of each year.

[769]
CMS HISPANIC HEALTH SERVICES RESEARCH GRANT PROGRAM

Centers for Medicare & Medicaid Services
Attn: Acquisition and Grants Group
C2-21-15
7500 Security Boulevard
Baltimore, MD 21244-1850
(410) 786-7250   Toll-free: (877) 267-2323
TTY: (410) 786-0727   TTY: (866) 226-1819
E-mail: RBragg@cms.hhs.gov
Web: cms.hhs.gov/researchers/priorities/grants.asp

Purpose   To provide funding to Hispanic scholars interested in carrying out Hispanic American health services research activities.

Eligibility Applicants must be 1) faculty members at a Hispanic Serving Institution (HSI) that offers a Ph.D. or master's degree in administration, management, allied health, nursing, pharmacology, public health, public policy, finance, gerontology, marketing, health care administration, or social work; 2) a member of Hispanic Serving Health Professions; 3) a member of the Inter-University Program for Latino Research; or 4) a member of another Hispanic association with a health services research component. They must be interested in conducting small research projects that examine health services research issues related to the Hispanic population.

Financial data Grants range from $100,000 to $125,000 per year.

Duration Up to 2 years.

Additional information Until 2001, the Centers for Medicare & Medicaid Services was known as the Health Care Financing Administration.

Number awarded Varies each year; recently, 3 of these grants were awarded.

Deadline June of each year.

[770]
COLIN L. POWELL MINORITY POSTDOCTORAL FELLOWSHIP IN TROPICAL DISEASE RESEARCH

National Foundation for Infectious Diseases
Attn: Grants Manager
4733 Bethesda Avenue, Suite 750
Bethesda, MD 20814-5278
(301) 656-0003   Fax: (301) 907-0878
E-mail: info@nfid.org
Web: www.nfid.org

Purpose To provide research funding to underrepresented minorities who wish to become specialists and researchers in the field of tropical diseases.

Eligibility This program is open to members of minority groups underrepresented in the biomedical sciences who have a doctorate from a recognized university and are citizens or permanent residents of the United States. Applicants must have arranged with an American or foreign laboratory where they can conduct their research. The laboratory should be supervised by a recognized leader in tropical disease research. Researchers who have received a fellowship, research grant, or traineeship in excess of the amount of this award from the federal government or another foundation are ineligible. Selection is based on the applicant's scholarship performance and professional qualifications, scientific merit of the proposed research project, validity of the research rationale, and adequacy of the facilities available to the applicant, host department, and host institution.

Financial data The grant is $30,000, of which $3,000 may be used for travel and supplies (at the discretion of the fellow).

Duration 1 year.

Additional information This program is sponsored by the National Foundation for Infectious Diseases and GlaxoSmithKline. It is also available from the Infectious Diseases Society of America, 66 Canal Center Plaza, Suite 600, Alexandria, VA 22314, (703) 299-0200, Fax: (703) 299-0204.

Number awarded 1 each year.

Deadline January of each year.

[771]
COLLABORATIVE ARTHRITIS AND MUSCULOSKELETAL AND SKIN DISEASES SCIENCE AWARD

National Institute of Arthritis and Musculoskeletal and Skin Diseases
Attn: Program Director for Health Disparities and Women's Health Research
6701 Democracy Boulevard, Suite 800
Bethesda, MD 20892-4872
(301) 451-6514   Fax: (301) 480-4543
E-mail: cl225r@nih.gov
Web: www.nih.gov/niams

Purpose To provide support to faculty members at minority institutions to allow them to collaborate with principal investigators of active regular research grants funded by the National Institute of Arthritis and Musculoskeletal and Skin Diseases (NIAMS).

Eligibility This program is open to full-time faculty members at minority-serving institutions (defined as public or private nonprofit institutions with substantial minority enrollment) who have the skills, knowledge, and resources necessary to develop and implement a research career in arthritis, musculoskeletal diseases, or skin diseases. Applicants must have a doctoral degree in a basic or clinical science and have completed 1 or more years of postdoctoral research training. They must apply in collaboration with a senior investigator at a research-intensive institution who has current research support from NIAMS. Proposals must involve an investigator-initiated research project in which the applicant and a collaborating scientist work in a clearly-defined area of mutual research interest related to arthritis, musculoskeletal diseases, or skin diseases. The applicant investigator must be a U.S. citizen, national, or permanent resident who intends to develop a career in relevant research. Members of racial and ethnic minority groups, women, and persons with disabilities are especially encouraged to apply as investigators and to serve as collaborators.

Financial data Grants range up to $200,000 per year in direct costs.

Duration Up to 5 years.

Deadline January, May, or September of each year.

[772]
COLLABORATIVE NEUROLOGICAL SCIENCES AWARD

National Institute of Neurological Disorders and Stroke
Attn: Office of Minority Health and Research
6001 Executive Boulevard, Suite 2149
Bethesda, MD 20892-5929
(301) 496-3102   Fax: (301) 594-5929
E-mail: ag38x@nih.gov
Web: www.ninds.nih.gov

Purpose To provide funding for neurological science research to scientists at predominantly minority institutions.

Eligibility This program is open to an applicant investigator, who holds a doctoral degree in a basic or clinical science area and is a full-time employee of a predominantly minority institution in the United States, and a collaborating investigator, who is a grantee from a research-intensive institution and who has current support from the National Institutes of Health (NIH) to conduct neurological science research. The applicant investigator must document the potential for excellence in research and teaching and provide evidence of the intent to develop a career in neurological science research. The collaborating investigator must be an individual holding a senior academic position, such as an associate or full professor, and must have demonstrated research competency by competing successfully for current NIH research grant support. The applicant investigator must also be a U.S. citizen, national, or permanent resident. The proposal must involve joint research efforts, specialized training in research techniques, and participation in research seminars. Minority institutions are defined as universities and colleges that offer the Ph.D., M.D., and/or equivalent health professional degrees and where more than 50% of the students enrolled are from racial or ethnic minority groups

Financial data Awards range up to $200,000 per year in direct costs, including up to $75,000 for the collaborator.

Duration Up to 5 years.

Additional information This program is offered jointly by the National Institute of Neurological Disorders and Stroke (NINDS), the National Institute on Deafness and Other Communication Disorders (NIDCD), and the National Institute on Drug Abuse (NIDA).

Number awarded Varies each year.

[773]
COMMUNITY ACTION GRANTS

American Association of University Women
Attn: AAUW Educational Foundation
301 ACT Drive, Department 177
P.O. Box 4030
Iowa City, IA 52243-4030
(319) 337-1716   Fax: (319) 337-1204
E-mail: aauw@act.org
Web: www.aauw.org

Purpose To provide seed money to branches or divisions of the American Association of University Women (AAUW) or to individual women (particularly women of color) for projects or nondegree research that promotes education and equity for women and girls.

Eligibility This program is open to individual women who are U.S. citizens or permanent residents, AAUW branches, AAUW state organizations, and local community-based nonprofit organizations. Applicants must be proposing projects that have direct public impact, are nonpartisan, and take place within the United States or its territories. They must focus on K-12 and community college girls' and women's achievements in mathematics, science, or technology; the proposal must involve planning activities and coalition building during the first year and implementation and evaluation the following year. Special consideration is given to AAUW branch and state applicants who seek partners for collaborative projects; collaborators can include local schools or school districts, businesses, and other community-based organizations. Applications from women of color and underrepresented groups as well as applica-

tions for projects that meet the needs of underserved populations are especially encouraged.

Financial data Grants range from $5,000 to $10,000. Funds are to be used for such project-related expenses as office space and mailing, promotional materials, honoraria, and transportation. Funds cannot cover salaries for project directors or regular, ongoing overhead costs for any organization.

Duration 2 years.

Number awarded Varies each year.

Deadline January of each year.

[774]
CONNECTICUT SPACE GRANT COLLEGE CONSORTIUM GRADUATE STUDENT FELLOWSHIPS

Connecticut Space Grant College Consortium
c/o University of Hartford
UT 219
200 Bloomfield Avenue
West Hartford, CT 06117-1599
(860) 768-4813   Fax: (860) 768-5073
E-mail: ctspgrant@hartford.edu
Web: uhaweb.hartford.edu/ctspgrant

Purpose To provide funding to graduate students (particularly underrepresented minorities, women, and persons with disabilities) at member institutions of the Connecticut Space Grant College Consortium interested in working on space-related projects under the guidance of a faculty member.

Eligibility This program is open to full-time graduate students at member institutions of the Connecticut Space Grant College Consortium. Applicants must be proposing to conduct research in aerospace science and engineering in areas normally funded by the U.S. National Aeronautics and Space Administration (NASA). U.S. citizenship is required. The program actively encourages women, underrepresented minorities, and those with disabilities to apply.

Financial data The grant is $6,250.

Duration 1 semester or 1 year.

Additional information Member institutions are the University of Connecticut, University of Hartford, University of New Haven, and Trinity College. This program is funded by NASA.

Number awarded 4 each year.

Deadline October or May of each year.

[775]
CONNECTICUT SPACE GRANT COLLEGE CONSORTIUM STUDENT PROJECT GRANTS

Connecticut Space Grant College Consortium
c/o University of Hartford
UT 219
200 Bloomfield Avenue
West Hartford, CT 06117-1599
(860) 768-4813   Fax: (860) 768-5073
E-mail: ctspgrant@hartford.edu
Web: uhaweb.hartford.edu/ctspgrant

Purpose To provide funding to undergraduate students (particularly underrepresented minorities, women, and persons with disabilities) at member institutions of the Connecticut Space Grant College Consortium who need to purchase supplies or equipment for space-related projects.

Eligibility This program is open to undergraduate students at member institutions of the Connecticut Space Grant College Consortium. Applicants must be proposing to conduct a project in aerospace science and engineering in areas normally funded by the U.S. National Aeronautics and Space Administration (NASA). U.S. citizenship is required. A faculty member must agree to serve as project advisor. The program actively encourages women, underrepresented minorities, and those with disabilities to apply.

Financial data The maximum grant is $500. Funds may be used for supplies and materials only, not for travel, entertainment, entry fees, tuition, salaries, fringe benefits, or indirect costs.

Duration 1 semester or 1 year.

Additional information Member institutions are the University of Connecticut, University of Hartford, University of New Haven, and Trinity College. This program is funded by NASA.

Number awarded 1 or more each year.

Deadline October or May of each year.

[776]
CONNECTICUT SPACE GRANT COLLEGE CONSORTIUM UNDERGRADUATE STUDENT FELLOWSHIPS

Connecticut Space Grant College Consortium
c/o University of Hartford
UT 219
200 Bloomfield Avenue
West Hartford, CT 06117-1599
(860) 768-4813   Fax: (860) 768-5073
E-mail: ctspgrant@hartford.edu
Web: uhaweb.hartford.edu/ctspgrant

Purpose To enable undergraduate students (particularly underrepresented minorities, women, and persons with disabilities) at member institutions of the Connecticut Space Grant College Consortium to work on space-related projects under the guidance of a faculty member.

Eligibility This program is open to full-time undergraduate students at member institutions of the Connecticut Space Grant College Consortium. Applicants must be proposing to conduct a senior project, honors research, or other educational project in aerospace science and engineering in areas normally funded by the U.S. National Aeronautics and Space Administration (NASA). U.S. citizenship is required. The program actively encourages women, underrepresented minorities, and those with disabilities to apply.

Financial data Grants are $2,500.

Duration 1 semester or 1 year.

Additional information Member institutions are the University of Connecticut, University of Hartford, University of New Haven, and Trinity College. This program is funded by NASA.

Number awarded 10 each year.

Deadline October or May of each year.

[777]
CONTEMPLATIVE PRACTICE FELLOWSHIPS

American Council of Learned Societies
Attn: Office of Fellowships and Grants
633 Third Avenue, 8C
New York, NY 10017-6795
(212) 697-1505   Fax: (212) 949-8058
E-mail: grants@acls.org
Web: www.acls.org/conprac.htm

Purpose To provide funding to college faculty members (particularly minorities and women) interested in conducting research leading to the development of courses and teaching materials that integrate contemplative practices into courses.

Eligibility This program is open to full-time faculty members at accredited academic institutions in the arts, humanities, and humanities-related sciences and social sciences. There are no citizenship requirements. Applicants must be interested in conducting individual or collaborative research to advance scholarship in the field of contemplative practices and to encourage innovative pedagogy and course design. Methodologies that include practical and experiential approaches to the subject matter are especially welcome. Proposals of particular interest are those in which classroom contemplative practices are related clearly to the content of the course itself. Applications are particularly invited from women and members of minority groups.

Financial data The maximum grant is $10,000.

Duration 1 semester or 1 summer.

Additional information This program is sponsored by the Center for Contemplative Mind in Society and funded by the Fetzer Institute.

Number awarded Approximately 6 each year.

Deadline November of each year.

[778]
COVAD BROADBAND ENTREPRENEUR AWARD

Association for Enterprise Opportunity
1601 North Kent Street, Suite 1101
Arlington, VA 22209
(703) 841-7760   Fax: (703) 841-7748
E-mail: aeo@assoceo.org
Web: www.microenterpriseworks.org/projects/covad

Purpose To provide funding to entrepreneurs (especially women, minorities, and people with disabilities) who are interested in obtaining broadband access to the Internet.

Eligibility This program is open to low- and moderate-income entrepreneurs who have 5 or fewer employees, $35,000 or less cash on hand, and no access to traditional bank loans. Preference is given to entrepreneurs who are women, minorities, or people with disabilities. Applicants must be based in and/or serve clients within the service area of Covad Communications Group, Inc. in the following states: Arizona, California, Illinois, Massachusetts, Michigan, New Mexico, Pennsylvania, or Tennessee. They must own or have regular access to a computer and be able to implement installation of broadband within 30 days of the grant award. It is not necessary that entrepreneurs have existing access to the Internet or an e-mail address as long as they intend to use the grant funds to set up Internet and e-mail service. They must submit a cover letter and business plan that demonstrate how broadband access will improve and strengthen their business.

Financial data Grants provide a $500 cash award (which may be used for purchase of a new computer) and free Covad broadband installation and service for 1 year. The total value of the grant is more than $2,500.

Duration These are 1-time grants.

Additional information Covad Communications Group, Inc. established this program in 2003 and selected the Association for Enterprise Opportunity (AEO) to administer it. Information is available from 10 local partners selected by AEO to process and forward applications. Those 10 local organizations are CHARO Community Development Corporation of Los Angeles, Community Business Network of Boston, Detroit Entrepreneurship Institute, Inc. of Detroit, New Mexico Community Development Loan Fund of Albuquerque, Renaissance Entrepreneurship Center of San Francisco, Self-Employment Loan Fund of Phoenix, Start Up of East Palo Alto, California, The Abilities Fund of Centerville, Iowa, Women's Opportunities Resource Center of Philadelphia, and Women's Self-Employment Project of Chicago.

Number awarded Up to 144 each year.

Deadline Each of the 10 local partners sets its own deadline date.

[779]
CULTURAL ANTHROPOLOGY GRANTS FOR HIGH RISK EXPLORATORY RESEARCH

National Science Foundation
Directorate for Social, Behavioral, and Economic
  Sciences
Attn: Division of Behavioral and Cognitive Sciences
4201 Wilson Boulevard, Room 995
Arlington, VA 22230
(703) 292-8758   TDD: (703) 292-9068
E-mail: splattne@nsf.gov
Web: www.nsf.gov/sbe/bcs/anthro/highrisk.htm

Purpose To provide funding to scholars (particularly minorities, women, and persons with disabilities) interested in conducting high-risk research in cultural anthropology.

Eligibility This program is open to scholars interested in conducting research projects in anthropology that might be considered too risky for normal review procedures. A project is considered risky if the data may not be obtainable in spite of all reasonable preparation on the researcher's part. Proposals for extremely urgent research where access to the data may not be available in the normal review schedule, even with all reasonable preparation by the researcher, are also appropriate for this program. Graduate students are not eligible to apply. Women, minorities, and persons with disabilities are strongly encouraged to participate in this program.

Financial data Grants up to $25,000, including indirect costs, are available.

Number awarded Varies each year, depending on the availability of funds.

Deadline Applications may be submitted at any time.

[780]
CULTURAL ANTHROPOLOGY RESEARCH EXPERIENCE FOR GRADUATES SUPPLEMENTS

National Science Foundation
Directorate for Social, Behavioral, and Economic
  Sciences
Attn: Division of Behavioral and Cognitive Sciences
4201 Wilson Boulevard, Room 995
Arlington, VA 22230
(703) 292-8758   TDD: (703) 292-9068
E-mail: splattne@nsf.gov
Web: www.nsf.gov/sbe/sber/anthro

Purpose To provide funding to graduate students (particularly minorities, women, and persons with disabilities) interested in conducting dissertation research in cultural anthropology.

Eligibility Applications may be submitted through regular university channels by dissertation advisors on behalf of graduate students in cultural anthropology. The faculty member must be a principal investigator on a research grant from the National Science Foundation. The application must be for supplemental funds for a doctoral student's closely mentored but independent research experience. The student's research should be a creative project, not a clerk or assistant's task. Selection is based on the appropriateness and value of the educational experience for the student participant, particularly the independence and theoretical significance of the student's activities and the quality of the supervision. Each principal investigator normally may seek funding for only 1 graduate student; exceptions are considered for training additional qualified students who are members of underrepresented groups. Women, minorities, and persons with disabilities are strongly encouraged to participate in this program.

Financial data Supplemental grants up to $5,000 are available. Institutions are encouraged to treat these supplements like dissertation research grants (which incur no indirect costs).

Duration 1 year.

Number awarded Varies each year, depending on the availability of funds.

Deadline January of each year.

[781]
DEFENSE POLICY FELLOWSHIPS

American Association for the Advancement of Science
Attn: Science and Technology Policy Fellowship
  Programs
1200 New York Avenue, N.W.
Washington, DC 20005-3920
(202) 326-6700   Fax: (202) 289-4950
E-mail: fellowships@aaas.org
Web: fellowships.aaas.org/defense

Purpose To provide postdoctoral and mid-career scientists and engineers (particularly underrepresented minorities and persons with disabilities) with an opportunity to supply current technical knowledge to U.S. Department of Defense (DoD) programs.

Eligibility Prospective fellows must have a Ph.D. or equivalent doctoral-level degree in a physical, biological, or social science, any field of engineering, or any relevant interdisciplinary field; persons with a master's degree in engineering and at least 3 years of post-degree experience are also eligible. Candidates must demonstrate exceptional competence in some area of science or engineering; communicate and work effectively with decision-makers and others outside of the scientific and engineering community; exhibit willingness and flexibility to tackle problems in a number of non-scientific areas; demonstrate sensitivity toward political, economic, and technological issues; and have some experience and/or strong interest in integrating modern science, technology, and business practices in the area of defense. Applicants must be U.S. citizens and must obtain a security clearance; federal employees are not eligible. Underrepresented minorities and persons with disabilities are especially encouraged to apply.

Financial data The stipend is $60,000 plus allowances for health insurance and professional travel.

Duration 1 year, beginning in September; may be renewed for 1 additional year.

Additional information Fellows work in 1 of the following offices: the Office of the Under Secretary of Defense for Acquisition, Technology and Logistics; the Missile Defense Agency; the Office of Naval Research; the U.S. Army's Research Office; or the Defense Threat Reduction Agency. Assignments may involve significant interagency, Congressional, or international activity. The program includes a 2-week orientation on international affairs and executive branch and Congressional operations.

Number awarded 3 or more each year.

Deadline January of each year.

[782]
DEFENSE UNIVERSITY RESEARCH INSTRUMENTATION PROGRAM

Army Research Office
Attn: AMSRL-RO-RI
4300 South Miami Boulevard
P.O. Box 12211
Research Triangle Park, NC 27709-2211
(919) 549-4207   Fax: (919) 549-4248
Web: www.aro.army.mil/research/index.htm

Purpose To provide funding to researchers at colleges and universities in designated states, especially those at Historically Black Colleges and Universities (HBCUs) and other Minority Institutions (MIs), for the purchase of equipment.

Eligibility This program is open to researchers at colleges and universities in the United States with degree-granting programs in science, mathematics, and/or engineering. Applicants must be seeking funding for the acquisition of major equipment to augment current or to develop new research capabilities to support research in technical areas of interest to the Department of Defense. Proposals are encouraged from researchers at HBCUs and MIs.

Financial data Grants range from $50,000 to $1,000,000; recently, they averaged $207,000.

Duration Grants are typically 1 year in length.

Additional information Information about this program is also available from the Air Force Office of Scientific Research, 4015 Wilson Boulevard, Room 713, Arlington, VA 22203-1954, (703) 696-7315, Fax: (703) 696-7320, E-mail: info@afosr.af.mil; and the Office of Naval Research, 875

North Randolph Street, Suite 1425, Arlington, VA 22203-1995, (703) 696-4111, Fax: (703) 588-1013.

Number awarded Varies; a total of approximately $41 million in new awards is available through the participating Department of Defense agencies each year.

Deadline August of each year.

[783]
DESGC SUMMER SCHOLARSHIPS

Delaware Space Grant Consortium
c/o University of Delaware
Bartol Research Institute
104 Center Mall, #217
Newark, DE 19716-4793
(302) 831-1094   Fax: (302) 831-1843
E-mail: desgc@bartol.udel.edu
Web: www.delspace.org

Purpose To provide funding to undergraduate students (particularly minorities, women, and persons with disabilities) in Delaware and Pennsylvania for summer research on space-related subjects.

Eligibility This program is open to undergraduate students at member or affiliate colleges and universities of the Delaware Space Grant Consortium (DESGC). Applicants must have a proven interest and aptitude for space-related studies and be proposing a summer research project. U.S. citizenship is required. The DESGC is a component of the U.S. National Aeronautics and Space Administration (NASA) Space Grant program, which encourages applications from women, minorities, and persons with disabilities.

Financial data A stipend is provided (amount not specified).

Duration Summer months.

Additional information This program, established in 1994, is funded by NASA. Members of the consortium include Delaware State University (Dover, Delaware), Delaware Technical and Community College (Dover, Georgetown, Newark, and Wilmington, Delaware), Franklin and Marshall College (Lancaster, Pennsylvania), Gettysburg College (Gettysburg, Pennsylvania), Lehigh University (Bethlehem, Pennsylvania), Swarthmore College (Swarthmore, Pennsylvania), University of Delaware (Newark, Delaware), Villanova University (Villanova, Pennsylvania), and Wilmington College (New Castle, Delaware).

Number awarded Varies each year; recently, 10 of these scholarships were awarded.

Deadline February of each year.

[784]
DIPLOMACY FELLOWSHIPS

American Association for the Advancement of Science
Attn: Science and Technology Policy Fellowship
  Programs
1200 New York Avenue, N.W.
Washington, DC 20005-3920
(202) 326-6700   Fax: (202) 289-4950
E-mail: fellowships@aaas.org
Web: fellowships.aaas.org/diplomacy

Purpose To provide postdoctoral and mid-career scientists and engineers (particularly underrepresented minorities and persons with disabilities) with an opportunity to work with various federal agencies in areas that involve international affairs, foreign policy, or international development.

Eligibility Prospective fellows must have a Ph.D. or equivalent doctoral-level degree in a physical, biological, or social science, any field of engineering, or any relevant interdisciplinary field; persons with a master's degree in engineering and at least 3 years of post-degree experience are also eligible. Candidates must demonstrate exceptional competence in some area of science or engineering; be cognizant of the ways in which science and technology affect a broad range of international development and foreign policy issues; communicate and work effectively with decision-makers and others outside of the scientific and engineering communities; exhibit willingness and flexibility to tackle problems in a number of nonscientific areas; demonstrate sensitivity toward political, economic, and social issues; and have some experience and/or strong interest in applying knowledge toward the solution of problems in the area of foreign affairs or international development. Applicants must be U.S. citizens and must obtain a security clearance; federal employees are not eligible. Underrepresented minorities and persons with disabilities are especially encouraged to apply.

Financial data The stipend ranges from $60,000 to $75,000 plus allowances for health insurance and professional travel.

Duration 1 year, beginning in September; may be renewed for 1 additional year.

Additional information Assignments are available at: 1) the U.S. Agency for International Development (USAID), where fellows work on matters related to sustainable development, especially in economic growth, the environment, population and health, democratization, humanitarian assistance, and education; 2) the Department of State where fellows may be assigned to the Bureau of Oceans and International Environmental and Scientific Affairs; the Bureau of Democracy, Human Rights and Labor; the Bureau of Economic and Business Affairs; any of the 4 bureaus that report to the Under Secretary for Arms Control and International Security Affairs; or any of the 6 regional bureaus of State; or 3) the Fogarty International Center of the National Institutes of Health (NIH) where they work with a community of researchers, administrators, and policymakers to advance medical research through international cooperation. All and Extension Service of the U.S. Department of Agriculture (USDA), where they work with program specialists and national program leaders to help develop activities that support international project objectives in Armenia. All fellowship assignments provide international travel opportunities. At the State Department, that program is known as the Parker-Gentry Fellowship. At NIH, the program is designated the Sheldon M. Wolff, M.D. Fellowship on International Health.

Number awarded 15 or more each year: 10 or more at USAID, 1 or more at the State Department, and 1 at NIH.

Deadline January of each year.

[785]
DISSERTATION FELLOWSHIPS IN EAST EUROPEAN STUDIES

American Council of Learned Societies
Attn: Office of Fellowships and Grants
633 Third Avenue, 8C
New York, NY 10017-6795
(212) 697-1505   Fax: (212) 949-8058
E-mail: grants@acls.org
Web: www.acls.org/eeguide.htm

Purpose To provide funding to doctoral candidates (particularly minorities and women) interested in conducting dissertation research in the social sciences and humanities relating to eastern Europe.

Eligibility This program is open to U.S. citizens or permanent residents who have completed all requirements for a doctorate in east European studies except the dissertation. Applicants may be working in any discipline of the humanities and the social sciences, including comparative work considering more than 1 country of eastern Europe or relating east European societies to those of other parts of the world. Most awards are for work on southeast Europe, including Albania, Bosnia and Herzegovina, Bulgaria, Croatia, Macedonia, Romania, and Serbia and Montenegro (including Kosovo). A few awards may be available for work on the Czech Republic, Estonia, Hungary, Latvia, Lithuania, Poland, Slovakia, and Slovenia. The fellowships are intended to support dissertation writing in the United States after research is complete, although short visits to the countries of eastern Europe may be proposed. Selection is based on the scholarly potential of the applicant, the quality and scholarly importance of the proposed work, and its importance to the development of east European studies. Applications are particularly invited from women and members of minority groups.

Financial data The maximum stipend is $17,000. Recipients' home universities are required (consistent with their policies and regulations) to provide or to waive normal academic year tuition payments or to provide alternative cost-sharing support.

Duration 1 year.

Additional information This program is sponsored jointly by the American Council of Learned Societies, (ACLS) and the Social Science Research Council, funded by the U.S. Department of State under the Research and Training for Eastern Europe and the Independent States of the Former Soviet Union Act of 1983 (Title VIII) but administered by ACLS.

Number awarded Approximately 10 each year.

Deadline November of each year.

[786]
DISSERTATION FELLOWSHIPS OF THE FORD FOUNDATION DIVERSITY FELLOWSHIP PROGRAM

National Research Council
Attn: Fellowship Office, GR 346A
500 Fifth Street, N.W.
Washington, DC 20001
(202) 334-2872   Fax: (202) 334-3419
E-mail: infofell@nas.edu
Web: www7.nationalacademies.org

Purpose To provide funding for dissertation research to graduate students whose success will increase the racial and ethnic diversity of U.S. colleges and universities.

Eligibility This program is open to citizens and nationals of the United States who are Ph.D. or Sc.D. degree candidates committed to a career in teaching and research at the college or university level. The following are considered as positive factors in the selection process: evidence of superior academic achievement; promise of continuing achievement as scholars and teachers; membership in a group whose underrepresentation in the American professoriate has been severe and longstanding, including Black/African Americans, Puerto Ricans, Mexican Americans or Chicanos, Native American Indians, Alaska Natives (Eskimos or Aleuts), and Native Pacific Islanders (Micronesians or Polynesians); capacity to respond in pedagogically productive ways to the learning needs of students from diverse backgrounds; sustained personal engagement with communities that are underrepresented in the academy and an ability to bring this asset to learning, teaching, and scholarship at the college and university level; and likelihood of using the diversity of human experience as an educational resource in teaching and scholarship. Applicants must be working to complete their dissertation in the following fields: anthropology, archaeology, art history, astronomy, chemistry, communications, computer science, earth sciences, economics, education, engineering, ethnomusicology, geography, history, international relations, language, life sciences, linguistics, literature, mathematics, performance study, philosophy, physics, political science, psychology, religion, sociology, and urban planning. Awards are not made for such practice-oriented areas as administration and management, audiology, business, educational administration and leadership, filmmaking, fine arts, guidance, home economics, library and information science, nursing, occupational health, performing arts, personnel, physical education, social welfare, social work, or speech pathology. Ineligibility also includes students working on a terminal master's degree; the Ed.D. degree; the degrees of Doctor of Fine Arts (D.F.A.) or Doctor of Psychology (Psy.D.); professional degrees in such areas as medicine, law, and public health; or such joint degrees as M.D./Ph.D., J.D./Ph.D., and M.F.A./Ph.D.

Financial data The stipend is $21,000 per year; stipend payments are made through fellowship institutions.

Duration 9 to 12 months.

Additional information The competition for this program is conducted by the National Research Council on behalf of the Ford Foundation. Fellows may not accept remuneration from another fellowship or similar external award while on this program; however, supplementation from institutional funds, educational benefits from the Department of Veterans Affairs, or educational incentive funds may be received concurrently with Ford Foundation support. Dissertation fellows are required to submit an interim progress report 6 months after the start of the fellowship and a final report at the end of the 12 month tenure.

Number awarded Approximately 35 each year.

Deadline November of each year.

[787]
DISSERTATION FELLOWSHIPS OF THE MINORITY SCHOLAR-IN-RESIDENCE PROGRAM

Consortium for a Strong Minority Presence at Liberal
    Arts Colleges
c/o Administrative Assistant, President's Office
Grinnell College
1121 Park Street
Grinnell, IA 50112-1690
(641) 269-3000   E-mail: cousins@grinnell.edu
Web: www.grinnell.edu/dean/csmp

Purpose To provide an opportunity for minority scholars to work on their dissertation while in residence at selected liberal arts colleges.

Eligibility This program is open to African American, Asian American, Hispanic American, and Native American doctoral candidates who have completed all the requirements for the Ph.D. or M.F.A. except the dissertation. Applicants must be interested in a residency at a member institution of the Consortium for a Strong Minority Presence at Liberal Arts Colleges during which they will complete their dissertation.

Financial data Dissertation fellows receive a stipend based on the average salary paid to instructors at the participating college. Modest funds are made available to finance the fellow's proposed research, subject to the usual institutional procedures.

Duration 1 year.

Additional information The following schools are participating in the program: Bowdoin College, Bryn Mawr College, Carleton College, Claremont McKenna College, Coe College, College of Wooster, Colorado College, Denison University, DePauw University, Dickinson College, Gettysburg College, Grinnell College, Hamilton College, Haverford College, Hope College, Juniata College, Lewis and Clark College, Luther College, Macalester College, Mount Holyoke College, Oberlin College, Occidental College, Pitzer College, Pomona College, Rhodes College, St. Olaf College, Skidmore College, Southwestern University, Swarthmore College, Trinity University, University of the South, Vassar College, Wellesley College, Wheaton College, Whitman College, and Willamette University. Fellows are expected to teach at least 1 course, participate in departmental seminars, and interact with students.

Number awarded Varies each year.

Deadline November of each year.

[788]

DISSERTATION-YEAR FELLOWSHIPS FOR U.S. MINORITIES IN HUMANITIES, SOCIAL SCIENCES, BUSINESS AND OTHER FIELDS

Northeast Consortium for Dissertation Scholars-in-Residence
Attn: Dean Donnie Perkins
Northeastern University
360 Huntington Avenue 424CP
Boston, MA 02115
(617) 373-2133   E-mail: d.perkins@neu.edu

Purpose To provide an opportunity for doctoral candidates from underrepresented minority groups to complete their dissertation while in residence at participating colleges and universities in the Northeast.

Eligibility This program is open to members of underrepresented minority groups who are at the dissertation writing stage of their doctoral program in the humanities or social sciences. Applicants may be working at a university anywhere in the country but must be interested in completing their dissertation at a college or university in the Northeast. They must be able to demonstrate that they can complete the dissertation while at the host campus. Along with their application, they must submit a curriculum vitae, a statement of scholarship and teaching goals, 3 letters of recommendation (including 1 from the dissertation advisor at their home campus), a copy of the dissertation prospectus, and a graduate school transcript. U.S. citizenship is required.

Financial data The stipend ranges from $25,000 to $30,000 per year. The host campus will provide computer and library privileges as well as office space for each of its scholars.

Duration 12 months.

Additional information This program began in 2001. Recently, the host campuses were Northeastern University, Allegheny College, Colgate University, Middlebury College, Rensselaer Polytechnic Institute, Stonehill College, and the University of Vermont. Although the scholars have no formal teaching assignment, they are expected to present their work-in-progress at 2 or 3 campus-wide or department-wide forums during the year and to meet with undergraduates to discuss succeeding in graduate school.

Number awarded Varies each year. Each participating college or university hosts 1 or more dissertation scholars.

Deadline January of each year.

[789]

DOCTORAL DISSERTATION FELLOWSHIPS IN LAW AND SOCIAL SCIENCE

American Bar Foundation
Attn: Assistant Director
750 North Lake Shore Drive
Chicago, IL 60611
(312) 988-6500   Fax: (312) 988-6579
E-mail: fellowships@abfn.org
Web: www.abf-sociolegal.org/Fellowship/pre.html

Purpose To provide funding to doctoral candidates (particularly minorities) who wish to conduct research on law, the legal profession, and legal institutions.

Eligibility Applications are invited from outstanding students who are candidates for a Ph.D. degree in the social sciences. They must have completed all doctoral requirements except the dissertation. Proposed research must be in the general area of sociolegal studies or in social scientific approaches to law, the legal profession, or legal institutions. The dissertation must address critical issues in the field and show promise of making a major contribution to social scientific understanding of law and legal processes. Applications must include 1) transcripts of graduate work; 2) 2 letters of recommendation; 3) a curriculum vitae; and 4) a dissertation prospectus or proposal with an outline of the substance and methodology of the intended research. Minority students are especially encouraged to apply.

Financial data The stipend is $15,000 per year. Fellows also may request up to $1,000 each fellowship year to reimburse expenses associated with dissertation research, travel to meet with dissertation advisors, and travel to conferences at which papers are presented. Moving expenses of up to $1,000 may be reimbursed on application.

Duration 1 year; may be renewed for 1 additional year.

Additional information Fellows are offered access to the computing and word processing facilities of the American Bar Foundation and the libraries of Northwestern University and the University of Chicago. This program was established in 1987. Fellowships must be held in residence at the American Bar Foundation. Appointments to the fellowship are full time; fellows are not permitted to undertake other work.

Number awarded 2 each year.

Deadline January of each year.

[790]

DR. SUZANNE LEGO RESEARCH GRANT

American Psychiatric Nurses Association
Attn: APN Foundation
1555 Wilson Boulevard, Suite 515
Arlington, VA 22209
(703) 243-2443   Fax: (703) 243-3390
E-mail: inform@apna.org
Web: www.apna.org/foundation/scholarships.html

Purpose To provide funding to graduate students and registered nurses (especially minorities) interested in conducting a research project in the field of psychiatric nursing.

Eligibility This program is open to registered nurses with at least a master's degree in psychiatric mental health nursing or a related field. Students completing a master's thesis or doctoral dissertation may also apply if their thesis or dissertation committee approves. Applicants must be proposing to conduct a research project on psychotherapeutic interventions in nursing. Selection is based on the scientific merit of the proposal and its potential for knowledge development of psychotherapeutic interventions relevant to the practice of psychiatric nursing. Minorities are especially encouraged to apply.

Financial data The grant is $1,000. Funds are not provided for principal or co-investigator's salary, educational assistance such as tuition or textbooks, travel, presenting a paper or attending a conference, or purchase of personal computers or other equipment.

Duration 1 year.

Number awarded 1 or more each year.

Deadline January of each year.

[791]
EDUCATIONAL TESTING SERVICE POSTDOCTORAL FELLOWSHIP AWARD PROGRAM

Educational Testing Service
Attn: Fellowships
Rosedale Road
MS 09-R
Princeton, NJ 08541-0001
(609) 734-1806　　　　　E-mail: fellowships@ets.org
Web: www.ets.org/research/fellowships.html

Purpose To provide financial assistance to postdoctorates (especially minorities and women) who wish to conduct independent research at the Educational Testing Service (ETS).

Eligibility Applicants must have a doctorate in a relevant discipline and be able to provide evidence of prior research. They must be interested in conducting research at ETS in 1 of the following areas: computer science, education, learning, literacy, minority issues, policy research, psychology, statistics, teaching, educational technology, or testing issues (including alternate forms of assessment for special populations and new forms of assessment). Selection is based on the scholarship and importance of the proposed research. An explicit goal of the program is to increase the number of women and minority professionals in educational measurement and related fields.

Financial data The stipend is $50,000 per year; fellows and their families also receive limited reimbursement for relocation expenses.

Duration 1 year, normally beginning in September.

Additional information Fellows work with senior staff at the Educational Testing Service in Princeton, New Jersey.

Number awarded Up to 3 each year.

Deadline January of each year.

[792]
EDUCATIONAL TESTING SERVICE VISITING SCHOLAR PROGRAM

Educational Testing Service
Attn: Visiting Scholar Program
Rosedale Road
MS 18-N
Princeton, NJ 08541-0001
(609) 683-2473　　　　　Fax: (609) 683-2800
E-mail: egilmore@ets.org
Web: www.ets.org/research/fellowships.html

Purpose To provide funding to postdoctoral scholars or color who wish to learn more about issues related to minorities at the Educational Testing Service (ETS).

Eligibility This program is open to members of underrepresented groups who are experienced liberal arts community college or university teachers or administrators. Applicants must be interested in spending time at the ETS campus studying issues related to test design and development and learning to write and review test questions and related materials for a variety of testing programs, including elementary and secondary education tests, college admission and placement tests, graduate admission tests, professional assessments for teachers and administrators, and international assessments.

Financial data The stipend is set in relation to compensation at the home institution. Scholars and their families also receive reimbursement for relocation expenses.

Duration 4 weeks during the summer.

Additional information Fellows work with senior staff at ETS in Princeton, New Jersey and have access to senior research staff. This program was established in 2000.

Number awarded Several each year.

Deadline January of each year.

[793]
EISENHOWER GRANTS FOR RESEARCH FELLOWSHIPS

Department of Transportation
Federal Highway Administration
Attn: National Highway Institute, HNHI-20
4600 North Fairfax Drive, Suite 800
Arlington, VA 22203-1553
(703) 235-0538　　　　　Fax: (703) 235-0593
E-mail: transportationedu@fhwa.dot.gov
Web: www.nhi.fhwa.dot.gov/ddetfp.asp

Purpose To enable students (especially minorities) to participate in research activities at facilities of the U.S. Department of Transportation (DOT) Federal Highway Administration in the Washington, D.C. area.

Eligibility This program is open to 1) students in their junior year of a baccalaureate program who will complete their junior year before being awarded a fellowship; 2) students in their senior year of a baccalaureate program; and 3) students who have completed their baccalaureate degree and are enrolled in a program leading to a master's, Ph.D., or equivalent degree. Applicants must be U.S. citizens enrolled in an accredited U.S. institution of higher education working on a degree full time and planning to enter the transportation profession after completing their higher education. They select 1 or more projects from a current list of research projects underway at various DOT facilities; the research will be conducted with academic supervision provided by a faculty advisor from their home university (which grants academic credit for the research project) and with technical direction provided by the DOT staff. Specific requirements for the target projects vary; most require engineering backgrounds, but others involve transportation planning, information management, public administration, physics, materials science, statistical analysis, operations research, chemistry, economics, technology transfer, urban studies, geography, and urban and regional planning. The DOT encourages students at Historically Black Colleges and Universities (HBCUs) and Hispanic Serving Institutions (HSIs) to apply for these grants. Selection is based on: match of the student's qualifications with the proposed research project (including the student's ability to accomplish the project in the available time), recommendation letters regarding the nominee's qualifications to conduct the research, academic records (including class standing, GPA, and transcripts), and transportation work experience (if any) including the employer's endorsement.

Financial data Fellows receive full tuition and fees that relate to the academic credits for the approved research project and a monthly stipend of $1,450 for college seniors, $1,700 for master's students, or $2,000 for doctoral students. An allowance for travel to and from the DOT facility where the research is conducted is also provided, but selectees are responsible for their own housing accommodations. Faculty advisors are allowed 1 site review on projects over 6 months and 2 site reviews on projects over 9 months; travel and per diem are provided for those site reviews.

Duration Tenure is normally 3, 6, 9, or 12 months.

Number awarded Varies each year; recently, 9 students participated in this program.

Deadline February of each year.

[794]
ELSEVIER RESEARCH INITIATIVE AWARD

Foundation for Digestive Health and Nutrition
Attn: Research Awards Coordinator
4930 Del Ray Avenue
Bethesda, MD 20814-2512
(301) 222-4005   Fax: (301) 222-4010
E-mail: info@fdhn.org
Web: www.fdhn.org

Purpose To provide funding to new or established investigators (especially minorities and women) for pilot research projects in areas related to gastroenterology or hepatology.

Eligibility Applicants must have an M.D. or Ph.D. degree (or the equivalent) and a faculty position at an accredited North American institution. They may not hold grants for projects on a similar topic from other agencies. Individual membership in the American Gastroenterology Association (AGA) is required. Women and minority investigators are strongly encouraged to apply. Selection is based on novelty, importance, feasibility, environment, commitment of the institution, and overall likelihood that the project will lead to more substantial grant applications.

Financial data The grant is $25,000 per year. Funds may be used for salary, supplies, or equipment. Indirect costs are not allowed.

Duration 1 year.

Additional information This award is administered by the Foundation for Digestive Health and Nutrition and sponsored by the AGA and Elsevier Science Publishing Company.

Number awarded 1 each year.

Deadline January of each year.

[795]
EPILEPSY FOUNDATION RESEARCH GRANTS PROGRAM

Epilepsy Foundation
Attn: Research Department
4351 Garden City Drive
Landover, MD 20785-7223
(301) 459-3700   Toll-free: (800) EFA-1000
Fax: (301) 577-2684   TDD: (800) 332-2070
E-mail: grants@efa.org
Web: www.epilepsyfoundation.org

Purpose To provide funding to junior investigators (particularly minorities, women, and persons with disabilities) interested in conducting research that will advance the understanding, treatment, and prevention of epilepsy.

Eligibility Applicants must have a doctoral degree and an academic appointment at the level of assistant professor in

a university or medical school (or equivalent standing at a research institution or medical center). They must be interested in conducting basic or clinical research in the biological, behavioral, or social sciences related to the causes of epilepsy. Faculty with appointments at the level of associate professor or higher are not eligible. Applications from women, members of minority groups, and people with disabilities are especially encouraged. U.S. citizenship is not required, but the research must be conducted in the United States. Selection is based on the scientific quality of the research plan, the relevance of the proposed research to epilepsy, the applicant's qualifications, and the adequacy of the institution and facility where research will be conducted.

Financial data The maximum grant is $40,000.

Duration 1 year. An additional year of support may be requested through re-application.

Additional information Support for this program is provided by many individuals, families, and corporations, especially the American Epilepsy Society, Abbott Laboratories, Ortho-McNeil Pharmaceutical, and Pfizer Inc.

Number awarded Varies each year; recently, 7 of these grants were awarded.

Deadline August of each year.

[796]
EPILEPSY RESEARCH AWARDS PROGRAM

American Epilepsy Society
342 North Main Street
West Hartford, CT 06117-2507
(860) 586-7505   Fax: (860) 586-7550
Web: www.aesnet.org

Purpose To provide funding to investigators (particularly minorities and women) anywhere in the world interested in conducting research related to epilepsy.

Eligibility This program is open to active scientists and clinicians working in all aspects of epilepsy. Candidates must be nominated by their home institution. There are no geographic restrictions; nominations from outside the United States and North America are welcome. Nominations of women and members of minority groups are especially encouraged. Selection is based on pioneering research, originality of research, quality of publications, research productivity, relationship of the candidate's work to problems in epilepsy, training activities, other contributions in epilepsy, and productivity over the next decade; all criteria are weighted equally.

Financial data The grant is $50,000. No institutional overhead is allowed.

Additional information This program, established in 1991, is funded by the Milken Family Foundation.

Number awarded 2 each year.

Deadline August of each year.

[797]
ETHNIC MINORITY RESEARCHER AND MENTORSHIP GRANT

Oncology Nursing Society
Attn: Research Team
125 Enterprise Drive
Pittsburgh, PA 15275-1214
(412) 859-6298   Toll-free: (866) 257-4ONS
Fax: (412) 859-6160   E-mail: research@ons.org
Web: www.ons.org

Purpose To provide funding to members of ethnic minority groups interested in conducting oncology nursing research.

Eligibility Principal investigators must be ethnic minority researchers (Native American, African American, Asian American, Pacific Islander, Hispanic/Latino, or other ethnic minority background). Beginning or novice researchers must utilize a research mentor for consultive services in research design and statistical analyses. Preference is given to projects that involve nurses in the design and conduct of the research activity and that promote theoretically based oncology practice. Graduate students are encouraged to apply for funding that supports work that is considered preliminary in nature or related to their thesis or dissertation.

Financial data The grant is $8,500 ($7,500 for the conduct of the research project and $1,000 for the research mentor or consultant). Funding is not provided for projects that are already completed or nearing completion, payment of tuition, or institutional indirect costs.

Duration Up to 2 years.

Additional information Every effort is made to find an ethnic minority mentor; however, the primary criteria for matching the investigator and mentor is the substantive area of the research and the expertise of the mentor. This program is supported by Ortho Biotech Products, L.P.

Number awarded 1 each year.

Deadline October of each year.

[798]
EURASIA DISSERTATION WRITE-UP FELLOWSHIPS

Social Science Research Council
Attn: Eurasia Program
810 Seventh Avenue
New York, NY 10019
(212) 377-2700   Fax: (212) 377-2727
E-mail: eurasia@ssrc.org
Web: www.ssrc.org

Purpose To provide funding to graduate students (particularly minorities and women) completing a dissertation dealing with Eurasia.

Eligibility This program is open to students who have completed field research for their doctoral dissertation and who plan to work on writing it during the next academic year. Applicants must have been conducting research in a discipline of the social sciences or humanities that deals with the Russian Empire, the Soviet Union, or the New States of Eurasia. Research related to the non-Russian states, regions, and peoples is particularly encouraged. Regions and countries currently supported by the program include Armenia, Azerbaijan, Belarus, Georgia, Kazakhstan, Kyrgyzstan, Moldova, Russian Federation, Tajikistan, Turkmenistan, Ukraine, and Uzbekistan; funding is not presently available for research on the Baltic states. U.S. citizenship or permanent resident status is required. Minorities and women are particularly encouraged to apply.

Financial data Grants up to $15,000 are available.

Duration Up to 1 year.

Additional information Funding for this program is provided by the U.S. Department of State under the Program for Research and Training on Eastern Europe and the Independent States of the Former Soviet Union (Title VIII).

Number awarded Varies each year; recently, 7 of these fellowships were awarded.

Deadline November of each year.

[799]
EURASIA POSTDOCTORAL RESEARCH FELLOWSHIPS

Social Science Research Council
Attn: Eurasia Program
810 Seventh Avenue
New York, NY 10019
(212) 377-2700   Fax: (212) 377-2727
E-mail: eurasia@ssrc.org
Web: www.ssrc.org

Purpose To provide funding to scholars (especially minorities and women) who recently received a Ph.D. in fields related to the study of Eurasia and who wish to engage in further scholarly activity.

Eligibility This program is open to junior faculty and independent scholars who are within the first 5 years of having received their Ph.D., have no more than 3 years' experience in a tenure-track position, and require release time from teaching and administrative duties for the completion of ongoing projects, substantive retooling, and/or preliminary research on new projects. Applicants must be working in a discipline of the social sciences or humanities that deals with the new states of Eurasia, the Soviet Union, and/or the Russian empire. Research related to the non-Russian states, regions, and peoples is particularly encouraged. Regions and countries currently supported by the program include Armenia, Azerbaijan, Belarus, Georgia, Kazakhstan, Kyrgyzstan, Moldova, Russian Federation, Tajikistan, Turkmenistan, Ukraine, and Uzbekistan; funding is not presently available for research on the Baltic states. U.S. citizenship or permanent resident status is required. Minorities and women are particularly encouraged to apply.

Financial data The maximum grant is $20,000. In most cases, scholars should use approximately $15,000 to release themselves from teaching and administrative obligations in their departments and $5,000 for research expenses.

Duration All funds must be expended within no more than 18 to 24 months of receiving the award.

Additional information Funding for this program is provided by the U.S. Department of State under the Program for Research and Training on Eastern Europe and the Independent States of the Former Soviet Union (Title VIII).

Number awarded Varies each year; recently, 3 of these fellowships were awarded.

Deadline November of each year.

[800]
EURASIA TEACHING FELLOWSHIPS

Social Science Research Council
Attn: Eurasia Program
810 Seventh Avenue
New York, NY 10019
(212) 377-2700   Fax: (212) 377-2727
E-mail: eurasia@ssrc.org
Web: www.ssrc.org

Purpose To provide funding to scholars (particularly minorities and women) in fields related to the study of Eurasia who wish to create course curricula.

Eligibility This program is open to faculty at all career levels in a discipline of the social sciences or humanities that deals with the New States of Eurasia, the Soviet Union, and/or the Russian empire. Applicants must be interested in creating original and creative curricula for courses that are completely new or for substantial revisions of a course previously taught. They should have a proven track record of research and teaching in their field of Eurasian studies. Proposals should have an interdisciplinary or comparative outlook, encompass a diverse range of literatures and/or source media (including audio, video, and web content), and make appropriate use of various pedagogical approaches. Proposals that target unique and important student audiences, provide a substantial addition or significantly diversify existing departmental and/or university curricula, or that otherwise fill an important niche or fulfill an instructional gap are especially encouraged. U.S. citizenship or permanent resident status is required. Minorities and women are particularly encouraged to apply.

Financial data The grant is $10,000.

Duration Awardees are expected to demonstrate departmental and institutional support for adding the proposed course to the university's list of offered courses within a 2-year period of time.

Additional information Funding for this program is provided by the U.S. Department of State under the Program for Research and Training on Eastern Europe and the Independent States of the Former Soviet Union (Title VIII).

Number awarded Varies each year.

Deadline January of each year.

[801]
FACULTY AND STUDENT TEAMS (FAST) PROGRAM

Department of Energy
Attn: Office of Science
1000 Independence Avenue, S.W.
Washington, DC 20585
(202) 586-7174   Toll-free: (800) DIAL-DOE
Fax: (202) 586-0019
E-mail: todd.clark@science.doe.gov
Web: www.scied.science.doe.gov

Purpose To provide support to faculty-student teams, especially those from institutions serving women and minorities, interested in conducting summer research at designated laboratories of the Department of Energy.

Eligibility This program is open to teams of faculty and students from colleges and universities with limited prior research capabilities and those institutions serving populations, women, and minorities underrepresented in the fields of science, engineering, and technology. Faculty applicants must be U.S. citizens or permanent residents. Students must be currently enrolled as undergraduates, have completed at least 1 semester of college work, be U.S. citizens or permanent residents, have a GPA of 2.5 or higher, and have coverage under a health insurance plan. Preference is given to faculty at community colleges; at universities and colleges that are in the 50th percentile or lower of total federal funding; and those associated with 1 of the following programs supported by the National Science Foundation (NSF): Tribal Colleges and Universities Program (TCUP), Historically Black Colleges and Universities Undergraduate Program (HBCU-UP), Louis Stokes Alliances for Minority Participation (LSAMP), Centers of Research Excellence in Science and Technology (CREST), Advanced Technology Education (ATE), Computer Science, Engineering, and Mathematics Scholarships (CSEMS), and Program for People with Disabilities.

Financial data Students receive a stipend of $4,500, allocated as 10 weekly stipends of $400 each and up to $500 for travel. Faculty members receive a stipend equal to 2/9 of their academic year salary, up to $12,000. Both student and faculty team members receive funding assistance with travel and housing. An additional grant of $1,000 is available as support for unusual travel expenses incurred by people with disabilities.

Duration 10 weeks during the summer. Students may participate in only 2 of these projects.

Additional information Teams work on specified projects at the following Department of Energy facilities: Argonne National Laboratory, Brookhaven National Laboratory, Lawrence Berkeley National Laboratory, Oak Ridge National Laboratory, or Pacific Northwest National Laboratory.

Number awarded Varies each year.

Deadline March of each year.

[802]
FACULTY AWARDS FOR RESEARCH

American Society for Engineering Education
Attn: Projects Department
1818 N Street, N.W., Suite 600
Washington, DC 20036-2479
(202) 331-3509   Fax: (202) 265-8504
E-mail: nasa@asee.org
Web: www.asee.org

Purpose To provide funding for space-related summer research to faculty at recognized minority colleges and universities.

Eligibility This program is open to full-time faculty at 1) an accredited 2-year or 4-year minority college or university with enrollment of a single underrepresented minority group or the combination of underrepresented minority groups that exceeds 50% of the total student enrollment; 2) an accredited 2-year or 4-year Hispanic-Serving Institution (HSI); 3) an accredited 2-year or 4-year Historically Black College or University (HBCU); or 4) a recognized Tribal College or University (TCU). Applicants must be U.S. citizens who have a Ph.D. in an engineering, mathematics, or science discipline applicable to research and/or technology development needs of the National Aeronautics and Space Administration (NASA). They must be interested in conducting a summer research project at a participating NASA center. Women, underrepresented minorities, and persons with disabilities are strongly encouraged to apply. Selection is based on relevance and merit of the research (40%), qualifications of the faculty applicant (40%), and overall academic benefit to the faculty applicant and his or her institution (20%).

Financial data The stipend is $1,200 per week, for a maximum of $12,000. A relocation allowance of $1,500 is available for fellows who live more than 50 miles from their assigned center and reasonable travel expenses for a round-trip are also reimbursed for fellows who receive the relocation allowance. The maximum allowance for relocation and travel is $2,000. To facilitate the participation of individuals with disabilities, NASA provides up to $1,500 in supplemental funding for special assistance and/or equipment necessary to enable the principal investigator to perform the work under the award.

Duration 10 weeks during the summer.

Additional information This program, established in 1992, is currently managed by the American Society for Engineering Education (ASEE) and the Universities Space Research Association (USRA) with funding from NASA's Minority University Research and Education Programs. Participating NASA centers are Ames Research Center (Moffett Field, California); Hugh L. Dryden Flight Research Facility (Edwards, California); Goddard Space Flight Center (Greenbelt, Maryland) and its Wallops Flight Facility (Wallops Island, Virginia) and Goddard Institute for Space Studies (New York, New York); Jet Propulsion Laboratory (Pasadena, California); Lyndon B. Johnson Space Center (Houston, Texas) and its White Sands Test Facility (Las Cruces, New Mexico); John F. Kennedy Space Center (Cape Canaveral, Florida); Langley Research Center (Hampton, Virginia); Glenn Research Center (Cleveland, Ohio); George C. Marshall Space Flight Center (Huntsville, Alabama); and John C. Stennis Space Center (Stennis Space Center, Mississippi).

Number awarded Varies each year.

[803]
FACULTY RESEARCH AWARDS FOR HISTORICALLY BLACK, HISPANIC-SERVING, AND TRIBAL COLLEGES AND UNIVERSITIES

National Endowment for the Humanities
Attn: Division of Research Programs
1100 Pennsylvania Avenue, N.W., Room 318
Washington, DC 20506
(202) 606-8466   Fax: (202) 606-8204
TDD: (866) 372-2930   E-mail: er-faculty@neh.gov
Web: www.neh.gov

Purpose To provide funding to faculty members at Historically Black Colleges and Universities (HBCUs), Hispanic Serving Institutions (HSIs), and Tribal Colleges and Universities (TCUs) who are interested in working on a research project in the humanities.

Eligibility This program is open to faculty members at HBCUs, HSIs, and TCUs who hold a full-time tenured, tenure-track, or annual contract position. Applicants must be U.S. citizens or foreign nationals who have resided in the United States or its jurisdictions for at least 3 years. The proposed project should contribute to scholarly knowledge or to the public's understanding of the humanities in the

form of publications, presentations, and classroom teaching. Grants may be awarded to individual faculty or 2 faculty collaborating on a single project. Support is not provided for graduate course work, but the proposed project may contribute to the completion of a doctoral dissertation. Grants are not provided for studying teaching methods or theories; surveying courses and programs; preparing institutional curricula; works in the creative or performing arts; projects that seek to promote a particular political, philosophical, religious, or ideological point of view; or projects that advocate a particular program of social action. Selection is based on: 1) the intellectual significance of the project to the humanities, including its contribution to knowledge and learning; 2) the quality or promise of quality of the applicant's work as an interpreter of the humanities; 3) the quality of the conception, definition, organization, and description of the project; and 4) the feasibility of the proposed plan of work and the likelihood that the applicant will complete the project.

Financial data Short-term grants are $24,000; long-term grants are $40,000.

Duration 6 to 8 months for short-term grants; 9 to 12 months for long-term grants.

Number awarded Varies each year.

Deadline April of each year.

[804]
FACULTY RESEARCH ENHANCEMENT SUPPORT PROGRAM

National Institutes of Health
National Institute of Child Health and Human
    Development
Director, Extramural Associates Program
6100 Executive Boulevard, Room 5E03
Bethesda, MD 20892-7510
(301) 435-2736   Fax: (301) 480-0393
E-mail: mk51q@nih.gov
Web: www.nih.gov

Purpose To improve opportunities for faculty at minority and women's colleges and universities to participate in a program at the National Institutes of Health (NIH) in Bethesda, Maryland during the summer.

Eligibility This program is open to faculty at 1) domestic private and public women's colleges and educational institutions with significant underrepresented minority student populations that offer programs in the biomedical or behavioral sciences; and 2) community colleges that meet those enrollment criteria and have established significant collaborative research activities or bridge programs with institutions that award at least a baccalaureate science degree. Applicants should be full-time faculty who have earned degrees in the life sciences (biomedical or behavioral sciences) or in the physical sciences (chemistry, mathematics, engineering, or physics). Academic science administrators and mid-level and senior faculty are preferable. Members of underrepresented racial and ethnic groups and individuals with disabilities are always encouraged to apply for NIH programs.

Financial data Salaries are comparable to those being received by the associate at the time of selection. Cost-sharing is required, depending on the institution's resources. Travel, housing, and subsistence expenses while at NIH, and any costs incurred that are directly related to the training, are reimbursed by the NIH. The maximum award to sponsoring institutions is $30,000 in direct costs for the first year and $50,000 annually for subsequent years; facilities and administrative costs are fixed at 8% of total direct costs.

Duration 10 weeks during the summer. Awards to institutions are up to 3 years.

Additional information During their tenure at the NIH, associates acquire a thorough knowledge of the NIH, the support mechanisms through which research is being accomplished, and the policies and procedures which govern the awarding of grants and contracts. Associates also obtain information about other federal health-related programs; grant and contract activities; legislative, budgetary and similar processes; and administrative procedures, including participation in staff meetings, review meetings, site visits, workshops, and conferences. Following completion of the program, associates return to their institutions with an Extramural Associates Research Development Award (EARDA) which provides developmental funds to the associate's institution for a period of 3 years, with a possible extension to 6 years.

Number awarded Varies each year; recently, 3 to 5 awards have been available through this program.

Deadline Letters of intent must be submitted by May of each year; completed applications are due in June.

[805]
FELLOWSHIPS FOR POSTDOCTORAL RESEARCH IN SOUTHEAST EUROPEAN STUDIES

American Council of Learned Societies
Attn: Office of Fellowships and Grants
633 Third Avenue, 8C
New York, NY 10017-6795
(212) 697-1505   Fax: (212) 949-8058
E-mail: grants@acls.org
Web: www.acls.org/eeguide.htm

Purpose To provide funding to postdoctorates (particularly minorities and women) interested in conducting original research in the social sciences and humanities relating to southeastern Europe.

Eligibility Applicants must be U.S. citizens or permanent residents who hold a Ph.D. degree or equivalent as demonstrated by professional experience and publications. Their field of study must be in the social sciences or humanities relating to Albania, Bosnia and Herzegovina, Bulgaria, Croatia, Macedonia, Romania, or Serbia and Montenegro. Comparative work considering more than 1 country of southeastern Europe or relating southeastern European societies to those of other parts of the world are also supported. All proposals should be for scholarly work, the product of which is to be disseminated in English. Fellowships may not be used for work in western Europe. Selection is based on the scholarly merit of the proposal, its importance to the development of eastern European studies, and the scholarly potential, accomplishments, and financial need of the applicant. Applications are particularly invited from women and members of minority groups.

Financial data Up to $25,000 is provided as a stipend. Funds are intended primarily as salary replacement, but

they may be used to supplement sabbatical salaries or awards from other sources.

Duration 6 to 12 consecutive months.

Additional information This program is sponsored jointly by the American Council of Learned Societies, (ACLS) and the Social Science Research Council, funded by the U.S. Department of State under the Research and Training for Eastern Europe and the Independent States of the Former Soviet Union Act of 1983 (Title VIII) but administered by ACLS.

Number awarded 4 or 5 each year.

Deadline November of each year.

[806]
FELLOWSHIPS IN ENVIRONMENTAL REGULATORY IMPLEMENTATION

Resources for the Future
Attn: Coordinator for Academic Programs
1616 P Street, N.W.
Washington, DC 20036-1400
(202) 328-5060   Fax: (202) 939-3460
E-mail: mankin@rff.org
Web: www.rff.org

Purpose To provide funding to postdoctoral researchers (especially minorities and women) who are interested in conducting research that documents the implementation and outcomes of environmental regulation.

Eligibility This program is open to scholars from universities and research organizations who have a doctoral or equivalent degree or equivalent professional research experience. Applicants must be interested in conducting research that examines environmental regulations in practice and can be used to inform regulators, industry, and others of assumptions of environmental laws and policies. The proposed research must be documentary in nature, without arguing in favor of any particular policy or result. Funding is not available for studies balancing costs and benefits or conducting other policy analyses of regulations. Interested scholars must first submit a pre-proposal that describes the project and its expected result, schedule, and budget. Women and minority candidates are strongly encouraged to apply. Preference is given to applicants who have sabbatical or other sources of support from their home institution.

Financial data Fellows receive an annual stipend commensurate with experience, research support, office facilities and limited support for relocation (if they choose to conduct the project at RFF), and funding for travel and conferences. Fellowships do not provide medical insurance or other RFF fringe benefits.

Duration 1 or 2 years.

Additional information Fellows may be in residence at RFF or remain at their current institution. They are requested to visit RFF to discuss progress on their research. This program is supported by the Andrew W. Mellon Foundation.

Number awarded 1 each year.

Deadline Pre-proposals must be submitted by January of each year. Final proposals are due in February.

[807]
FELLOWSHIPS IN SCIENCE AND INTERNATIONAL AFFAIRS

Harvard University
John F. Kennedy School of Government
Belfer Center for Science and International Affairs
Attn: Fellowship Coordinator
79 John F. Kennedy Street
Cambridge, MA 02138
(617) 495-3745   Fax: (617) 495-8963
E-mail: kathleen_siddell@harvard.edu
Web: bcsia.ksg.harvard.edu

Purpose To provide funding for research (by minority and other professionals, postdoctorates, or graduate students) in areas of interest to the Belfer Center for Science and International Affairs at Harvard University in Cambridge, Massachusetts.

Eligibility The postdoctoral fellowship is open to recent recipients of the Ph.D. or equivalent degree, university faculty members, and employees of government, military, international, humanitarian, and private research institutions who have appropriate professional experience. Applicants for predoctoral fellowships must have passed general examinations. Lawyers, economists, physical scientists, and others of diverse disciplinary backgrounds are also welcome to apply. The program especially encourages applications from women, minorities, and citizens of all countries. All applicants must be interested in conducting research in 1 of the 5 major program areas of the center: the international security program; the environment and natural resources program; the science, technology, and public policy program; the World Peace Foundation program on intrastate conflict, conflict prevention, and conflict resolution; and the Caspian Studies program. Fellowships may also be available in other specialized programs, such as science, technology, and globalization; managing the atom; domestic preparedness for terrorism; science and technology for sustainability; and energy technology innovation.

Financial data The stipend is $34,000 for postdoctoral research fellows or $20,000 for predoctoral research fellows. Health insurance is also provided.

Duration 10 months.

Number awarded A limited number each year.

Deadline January of each year.

[808]
FIELD INITIATED PROJECT GRANTS OF THE NATIONAL INSTITUTE ON DISABILITY AND REHABILITATION RESEARCH

Department of Education
Office of Special Education and Rehabilitative Services
Attn: National Institute on Disability and Rehabilitation
   Research
400 Maryland Avenue, S.W., Room 3414, MES
Washington, DC 20202-2645
(202) 205-5880   Fax: (202) 205-8515
TDD: (202) 205-4475   E-mail: donna.nangle@ed.gov
Web: www.ed.gov

Purpose To provide funding (especially to minorities) for research and related activities that involve disabilities and rehabilitation.

Eligibility This program is open to researchers at institutions of higher education, nonprofit organizations, and public or private agencies. Preference is given to researchers at Historically Black Colleges and Universities (HBCUs), Hispanic-Serving Institutions (HSIs), American Indian Tribal Colleges and Universities, and other institutions of higher education whose minority student enrollment is at least 50%. Applicants may be proposing to conduct either research or development activities. Invitational priorities are established each year; recently, those included projects that 1) improve the exit of individuals with disabilities from buildings, vehicles, and other settings in emergencies; 2) study use of the new "International Classification of Functioning, Disability and Health" systems in promoting the independence and quality of life of persons with disabilities; 3) collaborate with international assistive technology and rehabilitation engineering projects, 4) enhance the functioning of people with chronic fatigue; 5) study chronic pain and pain management strategies to enhance the functioning of individuals with disabilities; or 6) study mental health interventions related to traumatic stress of individuals with disabilities.

Financial data Maximum awards are $150,000 per year.

Duration 3 years.

Number awarded Varies each year; recently, 30 grants were available through this program.

Deadline December of each year.

[809]
FIRST BOOK GRANT PROGRAM FOR MINORITY SCHOLARS

Louisville Institute
Attn: Executive Director
1044 Alta Vista Road
Louisville, KY 40205-1798
(502) 992-5432   Fax: (502) 894-2286
E-mail: info@louisville-institute.org
Web: www.louisville-institute.org

Purpose To provide funding to scholars of color interested in completing a major research and book project that focuses on an aspect of Christianity in North America.

Eligibility This program is open to members of a racial/ethnic minority group (African Americans, Hispanics, Native Americans, Asian Americans, Arab Americans, and Pacific Islanders) who have an earned doctoral degree (normally the Ph.D. or Th.D.). Applicants must be a pre-tenured faculty member in a full-time, tenure-track position at an accredited institution of higher education (college, university, or seminary) in North America. They must be able to negotiate a full academic year free from teaching and committee responsibilities in order to engage in a scholarly research project leading to the publication of their first (or second) book focusing on an aspect of Christianity in North America. Selection is based on the intellectual quality of the research and writing project, its potential to contribute to scholarship in religion, and the potential contribution of the research to the vitality of North American Christianity.

Financial data The grant is $45,000. Awards are intended to make possible a full academic year of sabbatical research and writing by providing up to half of the grantee's salary and benefits for that year. Funds are paid directly to the grantee's institution, but no indirect costs are allowed.

Duration 1 academic year; nonrenewable.

Additional information The Louisville Institute is located at Louisville Presbyterian Theological Seminary and is supported by the Lilly Endowment. Grantees may not accept other awards that provide a stipend during the tenure of this award and must be released from all teaching and committee responsibilities during the award year.

Number awarded Up to 3 each year.

Deadline February of each year.

[810]
FIVE COLLEGE FELLOWSHIP PROGRAM FOR MINORITY SCHOLARS

Five Colleges, Incorporated
Attn: Five Colleges Fellowship Program Committee
97 Spring Street
Amherst, MA 01002-2324
(413) 256-8316   Fax: (413) 256-0249
E-mail: neckert@fivecolleges.edu
Web: www.fivecolleges.edu

Purpose To provide funding to minority graduate students who have completed all the requirements for the Ph.D. except the dissertation and are interested in teaching at selected colleges in Massachusetts.

Eligibility Fellows are chosen by the host department in each of the 5 participating campuses (Amherst, Hampshire, Mount Holyoke, Smith, and the University of Massachusetts). Applicants must be minority graduate students at an accredited school who have completed all doctoral requirements except the dissertation and are interested in devoting full time to the completion of the dissertation.

Financial data The stipend is $30,000 plus a research grant, fringe benefits, office space, library privileges, and housing assistance.

Duration 9 months, beginning in September.

Additional information Although the primary goal is completion of the dissertation, each fellow also has many opportunities to experience working with students and faculty colleagues on the host campus as well as with those at the other colleges. The fellows are also given an opportunity to teach (generally as a team teacher, in a section of a core course, or in a component within a course). Fellows meet monthly with each other to share their experiences. At Smith College, this program is named Mendenhall Fellowships for Minority Scholars.

Number awarded 5 each year: 1 at each of the participating colleges.

Deadline November of each year.

[811]
FLORIDA SPACE GRANT CONSORTIUM UNDERGRADUATE SPACE RESEARCH PARTICIPATION PROGRAM

Florida Space Grant Consortium
c/o Center for Space Education
Building M6-306, Room 7010
Mail Stop: FSGC
Kennedy Space Center, FL 32899
(321) 452-4301   Fax: (321) 449-0739
E-mail: fsgc@mail.ufl.edu
Web: fsgc.engr.ucf.edu

Purpose To provide funding to undergraduate students (particularly minorities, women, and persons with disabilities) at universities participating in the Florida Space Grant Consortium (FSGC) who wish to work on a summer research project.

Eligibility This program is open to juniors and seniors at colleges and universities that are members of the consortium. Students must be nominated by a faculty member at a consortium institution or by a researcher in a Florida industrial facility who proposes to mentor the student on a summer research project. Students are particularly encouraged to participate at an institution other than their own. Nominees must be enrolled in a space-related field of study, broadly defined to include aeronautics, astronautics, remote sensing, atmospheric sciences, and other fundamental sciences and technologies relying on and/or directly impacting space technological resources. Included within that definition are space science; earth observing science; space life sciences; space medicine; space policy, law, and engineering; space facilities and applications; and space education. The program particularly solicits nominations of women, minorities, and students with disabilities.

Financial data The grant is $3,000, to be used as a student stipend. The sponsoring university or industry may provide additional funds for the student stipend but may not charge for overhead or indirect costs.

Duration 10 weeks during the summer.

Additional information This program is funded by the U.S. National Aeronautics and Space Administration (NASA). The consortium member universities are Bethune-Cookman College, Eckerd College, Embry-Riddle Aeronautical University, Florida A&M University, Florida Atlantic University, Florida Community Colleges, Florida Gulf Coast University, Florida Institute of Technology, Florida International University, Florida Southern College, Florida State University, University of Central Florida, University of Florida, University of Miami, University of North Florida, University of South Florida, and University of West Florida.

Number awarded 15 each year.

Deadline Notices of intent must be submitted by January of each year. Completed proposals are due in March.

[812]
FOREIGN POLICY STUDIES PREDOCTORAL FELLOWSHIPS

Brookings Institution
Attn: Foreign Policy Studies
1775 Massachusetts Avenue, N.W.
Washington, DC 20036-2103
(202) 797-6043   Fax: (202) 797-2481
E-mail: syerkes@brookings.edu
Web: www.brookings.edu/admin/fellowships.htm

Purpose To support predoctoral research on U.S. foreign policy and international relations (particularly by minorities and women) at the Brookings Institution.

Eligibility This program is open to doctoral students who have completed their preliminary examinations and have selected a dissertation topic that directly relates to public policy issues and the major research issues of the Brookings Institution. Candidates cannot apply to conduct research at the institution; they must be nominated by their graduate department. They may be at any stage of their dissertation research. Selection is based on 1) relevance of the topic to contemporary U.S. foreign policy and/or post-Cold War international relations, and 2) evidence that the research will be facilitated by access to the institution's resources or to Washington-based organizations. The institution particularly encourages the nomination of women and minority candidates.

Financial data Fellows receive a stipend of $20,500 for the academic year, supplementary assistance for copying and other essential research requirements up to $750, reimbursement for transportation, health insurance, reimbursement for research-related travel up to $750, and access to computer/library facilities.

Duration 1 year, beginning in September.

Additional information Fellows participate in seminars, conferences, and meetings at the institution. Outstanding dissertations may be published by the institution. Fellows are expected to conduct their research at the Brookings Institution.

Number awarded A limited number are awarded each year.

Deadline Nominations must be submitted by mid-December and applications by mid-February.

[813]
FREDERICK BURKHARDT RESIDENTIAL FELLOWSHIPS FOR RECENTLY TENURED SCHOLARS

American Council of Learned Societies
Attn: Office of Fellowships and Grants
633 Third Avenue, 8C
New York, NY 10017-6795
(212) 697-1505   Fax: (212) 949-8058
E-mail: grants@acls.org
Web: www.acls.org/burkguid.htm

Purpose To provide funding to scholars (particularly minorities and women) in all disciplines of the humanities and the humanities-related social sciences who are interested in conducting research at designated residential centers.

Eligibility This program is open to citizens and permanent residents of the United States who achieved tenure in a humanities or humanities-related social science discipline at a U.S. institution within the past 4 years. Applicants must be interested in conducting research at 1 of 11 participating residential centers in the United States or abroad. Appropriate fields of specialization include, but are not limited to, anthropology, archaeology, art history, economics, film, geography, history, languages and literatures, law, linguistics, musicology, philosophy, political science, psychology, religion, rhetoric and communication, and sociology. Proposals in those fields of the social sciences are eligible only if they employ predominantly humanistic approaches (e.g., economic history, law and literature, political philosophy). Proposals in interdisciplinary and cross-disciplinary studies are welcome, as are proposals focused on any geographic region or on any cultural or linguistic group. Applications are particularly invited from women and members of minority groups.

Financial data The stipend is $75,000. If that stipend exceeds the fellow's normal academic year salary, the excess is available for research and travel expenses.

Duration 1 academic year.

Additional information This program, which began in 1999, is supported by funding from the Andrew W. Mellon Foundation with additional support from the Rockefeller Foundation. The participating residential research centers are the National Humanities Center (Research Triangle Park, North Carolina), the Center for Advanced Study in the Behavioral Sciences (Stanford, California), the Institute for Advanced Study, Schools of Historical Studies and Social Science (Princeton, New Jersey), the Radcliffe Institute for Advanced Study at Harvard University (Cambridge, Massachusetts), the American Antiquarian Society (Worcester, Massachusetts), the Folger Shakespeare Library (Washington, D.C.), the Newberry Library (Chicago, Illinois), the Huntington Library, Art Collections, and Botanical Gardens (San Marino, California), the American Academy in Rome, Collegium Budapest, and Villa I Tatti (Florence, Italy).

Number awarded Up to 11 each year.

Deadline September of each year.

[814]
FRONTIERS IN PHYSIOLOGY PROFESSIONAL DEVELOPMENT FELLOWSHIPS

American Physiological Society
Attn: Education Office
9650 Rockville Pike, Room 3111
Bethesda, MD 20814-3991
(301) 634-7132   Fax: (301) 634-7098
E-mail: education@the-aps.org
Web: www.the-aps.org/education/frontiers/index.htm

Purpose To provide an opportunity for middle/high school life science teachers (particularly minorities) to participate in a summer research project in physiology.

Eligibility This program is open to science teachers at middle schools (grades 6-9) and high schools (grades 9-12) who do not have recent (within 10 years) laboratory experience in physiology or the life sciences, do not have an advanced degree in laboratory science, and are not a candidate for an advanced degree in a laboratory science. Applicants do not need to have extensive mathematics skills, but they must be able to demonstrate a commitment to excellence in teaching, strong observation skills, and a desire to learn about research first-hand. Teachers who are members of minority groups underrepresented in science (African Americans, Hispanics, and Native Americans) or who teach in schools with a predominance of underrepresented minority students are especially encouraged to apply. Teachers must apply jointly with a member of the American Physiological Society (APS) at a research institution in the same geographic area as their home and school.

Financial data For the summer research experience, teachers receive a stipend of $500 per week (to a maximum of $4,000), a grant of $250 for participation in the summer forum, a grant of $250 for development and field testing of new inquiry-based laboratory or lesson, $400 for completion of online reflections and reading assignments, and $100 for completion of project evaluation activities. For the remainder of the year, they receive $2,500 for reimbursement of travel costs to attend the Science Teaching Forum, $1,000 for reimbursement of travel costs to attend the International Congress of Physiological Sciences, and $300 for materials to field-test a new inquiry-based laboratory or lesson. The maximum total value of the fellowship is $8,800.

Duration 1 year, including 7 to 8 weeks during the summer for participation in the research experience.

Additional information This program enables teachers to work on a summer research project in the laboratory of their APS sponsor, use the Internet to expand their repertory of teaching methods and their network of colleagues, and develop an inquiry-based classroom activity or laboratory, along with a corresponding web page. They also take a break from their summer research to attend a 1-week Science Teaching Forum in Washington D.C. where they work with APS staff, physiologists, and mentors to explore and practice effective teaching methods focused on how to integrate inquiry, equity, and the Internet into their classrooms. This program is supported by the National Center for Research Resources (NCRR) and the National Institute of Diabetes and Digestive and Kidney Diseases (NIDDK). both components of the National Institutes of Health (NIH).

Number awarded Varies each year; recently 16 of these fellowships were awarded.

Deadline January of each year.

[815]
GAIUS CHARLES BOLIN FELLOWSHIPS FOR MINORITY GRADUATE STUDENTS

Williams College
Attn: Dean of the Faculty
Hopkins Hall, Third Floor
800 Main Street
Williamstown, MA 01267
(413) 597-4351   E-mail: gburda@williams.edu
Web: www.williams.edu/admin-depts/deanfac

Purpose To provide financial assistance to minority doctoral students at any school who are interested in teaching courses at Williams College while working on their dissertation.

Eligibility Applicants must be minority graduate students, have completed all doctoral work except for the dissertation, be U.S. citizens, be working on degrees in the humanities or the natural, social, or behavioral sciences, and be willing to teach a course at Williams College. They must submit a full curriculum vitae, a graduate school transcript,

3 letters of recommendation, a copy of their dissertation prospectus, and a description of their teaching interests.

Financial data Fellows receive $31,000 for the academic year, plus housing assistance, office space, computer and library privileges, and a research allowance of up to $4,000.

Duration 1 academic year, beginning in September.

Additional information Bolin fellows are assigned a faculty advisor in the appropriate department. This program was established in 1985. Fellows are expected to teach a 1-semester course. They must be in residence at Williams College for the duration of the fellowship.

Number awarded 2 each year.

Deadline November of each year.

[816]
GEOLOGICAL SOCIETY OF AMERICA GENERAL RESEARCH GRANTS PROGRAM

Geological Society of America
Attn: Program Officer-Grants, Awards and Recognition
3300 Penrose Place
P.O. Box 9140
Boulder, CO 80301-9140
(303) 357-1028   Toll-free: (800) 472-1988, ext. 1028
Fax: (303) 357-1070   E-mail: awards@geosociety.org
Web: www.geosociety.org

Purpose To provide support to graduate student members (particularly minorities, women, and the disabled) of the Geological Society of America (GSA) interested in conducting research at universities in the United States, Canada, Mexico, or Central America.

Eligibility This program is open to GSA members working on a master's or doctoral degree at a university in the United States, Canada, Mexico, or Central America. Applicants must be interested in conducting research on geology. Minorities, women, and persons with disabilities are strongly encouraged to apply. Selection is based on the scientific merits of the problems, the capability of the investigator, and the reasonableness of the budget.

Financial data Grants can be used for the cost of travel, room and board in the field, materials and supplies, and other expenses directly related to the fulfillment of the research contract. Expenses requested for equipment or rental of equipment, film, some supplies, computer time, software, thin sections, and in-house charges for analytical instruments usually provided by a university must be fully justified. Funds cannot be used for the purchase of ordinary field equipment, for maintenance of the families of the grantees and their assistants, as reimbursement for work already accomplished, to attend professional meetings, for thesis preparation, to defray the costs of tuition, or for the employment of persons to conduct research. Recently, grants averaged $1,750.

Duration 1 year.

Additional information In addition to general grants, GSA awards a number of specialized grants: the Gretchen L. Blechschmidt Award for women (especially in the fields of biostratigraphy and/or paleoceanography); the John T. Dillon Alaska Research Award for earth science problems particular to Alaska; the Robert K. Fahnestock Memorial Award for the field of sediment transport or related aspects of fluvial geomorphology; the Lipman Research Award for volcanology and petrology; the Bruce L. "Biff" Reed Award for studies in the tectonic and magmatic evolution of Alaska; the Alexander Sisson Award for studies in Alaska and the Caribbean; the Harold T. Stearns Fellowship Award for work on the geology of the Pacific Islands and the circum-Pacific region; the Parke D. Snavely, Jr. Cascadia Research Fund Award for studies of the Pacific Northwest convergent margin; the Alexander and Geraldine Wanek Fund Award for studies of coal and petroleum; the Charles A. and June R.P. Ross Research Fund Award for stratigraphy; and the John Montagne Fund Award for research in the field of quaternary geology or geomorphology. Furthermore, 9 of the 14 GSA divisions (geophysics, hydrogeology, sedimentary geology, structural geology and tectonics, archaeological geology, coal geology, planetary geology, quaternary geology and geomorphology, and engineering geology) also offer divisional grants. Some of those awards are named: the Allan V. Cox Award of the Geophysics Division, the Claude C. Albritton, Jr. Scholarship of the Archaeological Geology Division, the Antoinette Lierman Medlin Scholarships of the Coal Geology Division, the J. Hoover Mackin Research Grants and the Arthur D. Howard Research Grants of the Quaternary Geology and Geomorphology Division, and the Roy J. Shlemon Scholarship Awards of the Engineering Geology Division. In addition, 4 of the 6 geographic sections (south-central, north-central, southeastern, and northeastern) offer grants to graduate students at universities within their section.

Number awarded Varies each year; recently, the society awarded 224 grants worth more than $400,000 through this and all of its specialized programs.

Deadline January of each year.

[817]
GEOLOGICAL SOCIETY OF AMERICA UNDERGRADUATE STUDENT RESEARCH GRANTS

Geological Society of America
Attn: Program Officer-Grants, Awards and Recognition
3300 Penrose Place
P.O. Box 9140
Boulder, CO 80301-9140
(303) 357-1028   Toll-free: (800) 472-1988, ext. 1028
Fax: (303) 357-1070   E-mail: awards@geosociety.org
Web: www.geosociety.org

Purpose To provide support to undergraduate student members (particularly minorities, women, and the disabled) of the Geological Society of America (GSA) interested in conducting research at universities in designated sections of the United States.

Eligibility This program is open to undergraduate students who are majoring in geology at universities in 4 GSA sections: north-central, northeastern, south-central, and southeastern. Applicants must be student associates of the GSA. Applications from women, minorities, and persons with disabilities are strongly encouraged.

Financial data Grant amounts vary.

Duration 1 year.

Additional information Within the 4 participating sections, information is available from the secretary. For the name and address of the 4 section secretaries, contact the sponsor.

Number awarded 1 or more each year in each of the 4 sections.

Deadline January of each year.

[818]
GEORGE WASHINGTON WILLIAMS FELLOWSHIPS

Independent Press Association
Attn: Executive Editor
2729 Mission Street, Suite 201
San Francisco, CA 94110
(415) 643-4401, ext. 116   Fax: (415) 643-4402
E-mail: gww@indypress.org
Web: www.indypress.org/programs/gwwfellow.html

Purpose To provide journalists of color with an opportunity to engage in public interest and socially responsible journalism.

Eligibility This program is open to journalists of color who have at least 3 years of professional reporting and writing experience. College journalism or internship experience does not qualify as professional experience. Preference is given to applicants with backgrounds in investigative or enterprise reporting. Previous reporting or other experience in the chosen subject area is desirable. The program is open only to U.S. citizens or to foreign journalists who have established relationships with U.S. publications. Applicants must be seeking support for either an individual story or investigative depth reporting. The preferred topics change periodically, but recently included the environment, health care and health care policy, new Americans, the war on terrorism, and gay and lesbian people of color.

Financial data Investigative depth reporting fellows receive $1,500 per month plus expenses to produce 1 or more stories. Individual story fellows are paid a rate equivalent to the going national commercial rate for comparable stories and assisted in placing the story.

Duration 3 to 12 months.

Additional information This program is named in honor of the African American journalist who first exposed conditions in the former Belgian Congo when he published an open letter to King Leopold II in 1890. Fellows are required to complete either a story or series of stories for publication. They may also be expected to attend special events and conferences sponsored by the program to present reports on their work to date and to discuss their own journalistic experiences with interns in the sponsor's student journalism program.

Number awarded 1 or more each year.

Deadline May or November of each year.

[819]
GERALD OSHITA MEMORIAL FELLOWSHIP

Djerassi Resident Artists Program
Attn: Admissions
2325 Bear Gulch Road
Woodside, CA 94062-4405
(650) 747-1250   Fax: (650) 747-0105
E-mail: drap@djerassi.org
Web: www.djerassi.org/oshita.html

Purpose To provide an opportunity for composers of color to participate in the Djerassi Resident Artists Program.

Eligibility This program is open to composers of color interested in utilizing a residency to compose, study, rehearse, and otherwise advance their own creative projects.

Financial data The fellow is offered housing, meals, studio space, and a stipend of $2,500.

Duration 4 to 5 weeks, from late March through mid-November.

Additional information This fellowship was established in 1994. The program is located in northern California, 45 miles south of San Francisco, on 600 acres of rangeland, redwood forests, and hiking trails.

Number awarded 1 each year.

Deadline February of each year.

[820]
GERBER FELLOWSHIP IN PEDIATRIC NUTRITION

National Medical Fellowships, Inc.
Attn: Scholarship Program
5 Hanover Square, 15th Floor
New York, NY 10004
(212) 483-8880   Fax: (212) 483-8897
E-mail: info@nmfonline.org
Web: www.nmf-online.org

Purpose To provide funding to underrepresented minority medical students and residents who are interested in conducting research on pediatric nutrition.

Eligibility This program is open to African Americans, Native Hawaiians, Alaska Natives, American Indians, Mexican Americans, and mainland Puerto Ricans who are 1) students enrolled in accredited U.S. medical schools, 2) students enrolled in U.S. colleges of osteopathic medicine, or 3) medical residents in U.S. programs. Candidates must be nominated by their deans or graduate education directors. They must be participating in ongoing research in the area of pediatric nutrition. U.S. citizenship is required. Selection is based on academic achievement and motivation to prepare for a career in pediatric nutrition research.

Financial data The grant is $3,000.

Duration 1 year; nonrenewable.

Additional information This award was established in 1997 with grant support from the Gerber Companies Foundation.

Number awarded 1 each year.

Deadline October of each year.

[821]
GERTRUDE AND MAURICE GOLDHABER DISTINGUISHED FELLOWSHIPS

Brookhaven National Laboratory
Attn: Dr. Leonard Newman
Building 815E
P.O. Box 5000
Upton, NY 11973-5000
(631) 344-4467   E-mail: newman@bnl.gov
Web: www.bnl.gov/hr/goldhaber.asp

Purpose To provide funding to postdoctoral scientists (particularly minorities and women) interested in conducting research at Brookhaven National Laboratory (BNL).

Eligibility This program is open to scholars who are no more than 3 years past receipt of the Ph.D. and are interested in working at BNL. Candidates must be interested in working in close collaboration with a member of the BNL

scientific staff and qualifying for a scientific staff position at BNL upon completion of the appointment. The sponsoring scientist must have an opening and be able to support the candidate at the standard starting salary for postdoctoral research associates. The program especially encourages applications from minorities and women.

Financial data The program provides additional funds to bring the salary to $70,000 per year.

Duration 3 years.

Additional information This program is funded by Battelle Memorial Institute and the State University of New York at Stony Brook.

Number awarded 1 or 2 each year.

[822]
GILBERT F. WHITE POSTDOCTORAL FELLOWSHIP PROGRAM

Resources for the Future
Attn: Coordinator for Academic Programs
1616 P Street, N.W.
Washington, DC 20036-1400
(202) 328-5060   Fax: (202) 939-3460
E-mail: mankin@rff.org
Web: www.rff.org

Purpose To provide funding to postdoctoral researchers (particularly minorities and women) who wish to devote a year to scholarly work at Resources for the Future (RFF) in Washington, D.C.

Eligibility This program is open to individuals in any discipline who have completed their doctoral requirements and are interested in conducting scholarly research at RFF in social or policy science areas that relate to natural resources, energy, or the environment. Teaching and/or research experience at the postdoctoral level is preferred though not essential. Individuals holding positions in government as well as at academic institutions are eligible. Women and minority candidates are strongly encouraged to apply.

Financial data Fellows receive an annual stipend (based on their academic salary) plus research support, office facilities at RFF, and an allowance of up to $1,000 for moving or living expenses. Fellowships do not provide medical insurance or other RFF fringe benefits.

Duration 11 months.

Additional information Fellows are assigned to an RFF research division—the Energy and Natural Resources division, the Quality of the Environment division or the Center for Risk, Resource, and Environmental Management. Fellows are expected to be in residence at Resources for the Future for the duration of the program.

Number awarded 1 each year.

Deadline February of each year.

[823]
GOVERNANCE STUDIES PREDOCTORAL FELLOWSHIPS

Brookings Institution
Attn: Governmental Studies
1775 Massachusetts Avenue, N.W.
Washington, DC 20036-2188
(202) 797-6090   Fax: (202) 797-6144
E-mail: sbinder@brookings.edu
Web: www.brookings.edu/admin/fellowships.htm

Purpose   To support predoctoral policy-oriented research in governmental studies (particularly by minorities and women) at the Brookings Institution.

Eligibility   This program is open to doctoral students who have completed their preliminary examinations and have selected a dissertation topic that directly relates to the study of public policy and political institutions and thus to the major interests of the Brookings Institution. Candidates cannot apply to conduct research at the institution; they must be nominated by their graduate department. The proposed research should benefit from access to the data, opportunities for interviewing, and consultation with senior staff members afforded by the institution and by residence in Washington, D.C. The institution particularly encourages the nomination of women and minority candidates.

Financial data   Fellows receive a stipend of $20,500 for the academic year, supplementary assistance for copying and other essential research requirements up to $750, reimbursement for research-related travel up to $750, health insurance, reimbursement for transportation, and access to computer/library facilities.

Duration   1 year.

Additional information   Fellows participate in seminars, conferences, and meetings at the institution. Outstanding dissertations may be published by the institution. Fellows are expected to conduct their research at the Brookings Institution.

Number awarded   A limited number are awarded each year.

Deadline   Nominations must be submitted by mid-December and applications by mid-February.

[824]
HAMBURG FELLOWSHIP PROGRAM

Stanford University
Center for International Security and Cooperation
Attn: Fellowship Program Coordinator
Encina Hall, Room E210
616 Serra Street
Stanford, CA 94305-6165
(650) 723-9626   Fax: (650) 723-0089
E-mail: barbara.platt@stanford.edu
Web: www.cisac.stanford.edu

Purpose   To provide funding to doctoral students (particularly minorities and women) who are interested in working on their dissertation at Stanford University's Center for International Security and Cooperation (which must focus on issues related to preventing deadly conflict).

Eligibility   This program is open to advanced doctoral students who have completed all of the curricular and residency requirements at their own institutions and who are engaged in the research and write-up stage of their disser-

tations in a field related to the prevention of deadly conflict. Applicants must be interested in writing their dissertation at Stanford University's Center for International Security and Cooperation. Fields of study may include anthropology, economics, history, law, political science, sociology, medicine, or the natural and physical sciences. Specific topics might include issues of policing, judiciaries, and civil-military relations; the use of sanctions and other economic tools for the prevention of conflict; early warning mechanisms, mediation processes, and other forms of third-party intervention; environmental degradation and its effects on deadly conflict; the role of non-lethal weapons and other military technologies in preventing conflict; the role of leadership in prevention of conflict. Applications from women and minorities are encouraged.

Financial data   The stipend is $20,000. Reimbursement for some travel and health insurance expenses may be available for fellows and their immediate dependents.

Duration   9 months.

Additional information   This program began in 1997. It honors Dr. David Hamburg, the retiring president of the Carnegie Corporation of New York, whose gift to the center made the program possible. Fellows join faculty, research staff, and other fellows at the center, where they have an office to ensure their integration into the full spectrum of research activities.

Number awarded   Varies each year.

Deadline   January of each year.

[825]
HAROLD AMOS MEDICAL FACULTY DEVELOPMENT PROGRAM

Amos Medical Faculty Development Program
Attn: Director
8701 Georgia Avenue, Suite 411
Silver Spring, MD 20910
(301) 565-4080   Fax: (301) 565-4088
E-mail: amfdp@starpower.net
Web: www.amfdp.org/applicat.htm

Purpose   To provide financial support and research training to minority physicians who are interested in academic careers in biomedical research, clinical investigation, or health services research.

Eligibility   African American, Mexican American, Native American, and mainland Puerto Rican physicians residing in the United States are eligible to apply if they have completed or will have completed formal clinical training. Applicants must be U.S. citizens or permanent residents with outstanding academic backgrounds and a commitment to academic medicine. Preference is given to physicians who have recently completed their clinical training and are seeking advanced research training. An interview is required.

Financial data   The stipend is $65,000 per year; an additional $26,350 per year is provided as a research allowance.

Duration   2 years; renewable for an additional 2 years.

Additional information   Fellows study and conduct research under the supervision of a senior faculty member located at any academic center in the United States that is noted for the training of young faculty and that offers research opportunities of interest to the fellow. Previously, this program was known as the Robert Wood Johnson Foundation's Minority Medical Faculty Development Program. The name was changed in 2004 to honor Dr. Harold Amos. the first African-American to chair a department, now the Department of Microbiology and Medical Genetics, of the Harvard Medical School, a founding member of the National Advisory Committee of the Robert Wood Johnson Foundation's Minority Medical Faculty Development Program, and the program's National Program Director between 1989 and 1993.

Number awarded Up to 12 each year.

Deadline March of each year.

[826]
HEALTH SCIENCES STUDENT FELLOWSHIPS IN EPILEPSY

Epilepsy Foundation
Attn: Research Department
4351 Garden City Drive
Landover, MD 20785-7223
(301) 459-3700   Toll-free: (800) EFA-1000
Fax: (301) 577-2684   TDD: (800) 332-2070
E-mail: grants@efa.org
Web: www.epilepsyfoundation.org

Purpose To provide financial assistance to medical and health science graduate students (particularly minorities, women, and students with disabilities) interested in working on an epilepsy project during the summer.

Eligibility This program is open to students enrolled, or accepted for enrollment, in a medical school, a doctoral program, or other graduate program. Applicants must have a defined epilepsy-related study or research plan to be carried out under the supervision of a qualified mentor. Because the program is designed as a training opportunity, the quality of the training plans and environment are considered in the selection process. Other selection criteria include the quality of the proposed project, the relevance of the proposed work to epilepsy, the applicant's interest in the field of epilepsy, the applicant's qualifications, and the mentor's qualifications, including his or her commitment to the student and the project. U.S. citizenship is not required, but the project must be conducted in the United States. Applications from women, members of minority groups, and people with disabilities are especially encouraged. The program is not intended for students working on a dissertation research project.

Financial data Stipends are $3,000.

Duration 3 months during the summer.

Additional information Support for this program is provided by many individuals, families, and corporations, especially the American Epilepsy Society, Abbott Laboratories, Ortho-McNeil Pharmaceutical, and Pfizer Inc.

Number awarded Varies each year; recently, 1 of these fellowships was awarded.

Deadline March of each year.

[827]
HENRY LUCE FOUNDATION/ACLS DISSERTATION FELLOWSHIPS IN AMERICAN ART

American Council of Learned Societies
Attn: Office of Fellowships and Grants
633 Third Avenue, 8C
New York, NY 10017-6795
(212) 697-1505   Fax: (212) 949-8058
E-mail: grants@acls.org
Web: www.acls.org/luceguid.htm

Purpose To provide financial assistance to doctoral students (especially minorities and women) interested in conducting dissertation research anywhere in the world on the history of American art.

Eligibility This program is open to Ph.D. candidates in departments of art history whose dissertations are focused on the history of the visual arts in the United States and are object-oriented. Applicants must be proposing to conduct research at their home institution, abroad, or at another appropriate site. U.S. citizenship or permanent resident status is required. Students preparing theses for a Master of Fine Arts degree are not eligible. Applications are particularly invited from women and members of minority groups.

Financial data The grant is $20,000. Fellowship funds may not be used to pay tuition costs.

Duration 1 year; nonrenewable.

Additional information This program is funded by the Henry Luce Foundation and administered by the American Council of Learned Societies (ACLS).

Number awarded 10 each year.

Deadline November of each year.

[828]
HHMI-NIH RESEARCH SCHOLARS PROGRAM

Howard Hughes Medical Institute
One Cloister Court, Building 60
Bethesda, MD 20814-1460
(301) 951-6770   Toll-free: (800) 424-9924
Fax: (301) 951-6776   E-mail: gpub@hhmi.org
Web: www.hhmi.org/cloister

Purpose To give outstanding students (particularly underrepresented minorities and women) at U.S. medical or dental schools the opportunity to receive educational funding and research training at the National Institutes of Health (NIH), in Bethesda, Maryland.

Eligibility To apply, students must be in good standing at a medical or dental school in the United States or Puerto Rico. There are no citizenship requirements, but applicants must be authorized to work in the United States. Those who are enrolled in an M.D./Ph.D. program or who already have an M.D. or a Ph.D. in a natural science are not eligible. After the conclusion of the program year, a small number of outstanding Research Scholars are selected to receive continued support for up to 2 years while completing studies toward the M.D. degree. To be eligible for this support, Research Scholars must be returning directly to medical school at the conclusion of their participation in the Research Scholars Program, and they may not be enrolled in an M.D./Ph.D., Ph.D., or Sc.D. degree program. These awards are based on demonstrated research abilities, potential for future achievement in biomedical research, and career intentions (including any plans for additional research training upon completion of medical school). Students' financial indebtedness resulting from school loans may also be considered as a secondary factor. Women and members of underrepresented minority groups are encouraged to apply.

Financial data Research Scholars receive an annual salary of $25,000 for rent, food, and other living expenses. Scholars are also eligible for medical, life, and accidental death and dismemberment insurance. Students are reimbursed for round-trip moving expenses for personal belongings (not furniture) for themselves and their dependents from and back to medical school. In addition, tuition is paid for Research Scholars who wish to take courses from the Foundation for Advanced Education in the Sciences (FAES). They also receive allowances for the purchase of textbooks and scientific journals related to their area of research and for travel to scientific meetings. Research Scholars who are chosen to receive support to complete their studies toward the M.D. degree are given an annual stipend of $16,000 and a $15,000 annual allowance toward tuition and other education-related expenses.

Duration 1 year, beginning in July or August; may be extended for 2 additional years.

Additional information Research Scholars work as part of a research team in a laboratory at the NIH's main campus in Bethesda, conducting basic research under the mentorship of an NIH senior investigator or preceptor. They learn the latest laboratory techniques and experience the creative thinking involved in at least 1 of the following biomedical areas: biochemistry, biophysics, biostatistics, cell biology, developmental biology, epidemiology, genetics, immunology, mathematical and computational biology, microbiology, molecular biology, neuroscience, pharmacology, physiology, structural biology, and virology. This program is unique in that it does not require students to propose a research project or select a laboratory at the NIH as part of the application process. Instead, Research Scholars are encouraged to take their first couple of weeks in the program to interview investigators and explore different laboratories at the NIH before making a selection. This program is jointly sponsored by the Howard Hughes Medical Institute and the National Institutes of Health—the largest private and public biomedical research institutions in the United States. It complements the HHMI Research Training Fellowships for Medical Students Program; students may not apply to both programs in the same year. Applicants must apply online using the sponsor's web-based application system.

Number awarded 40 or more each year.

Deadline January of each year.

[829]
HISPANIC THEOLOGICAL INITIATIVE DISSERTATION YEAR GRANTS

Hispanic Theological Initiative
12 Library Place
Princeton, NJ 08540
(609) 252-1721
Fax: (609) 252-1738
Toll-free: (800) 575-5522
E-mail: hti@ptsem.edu
Web: www.htiprogram.org

Purpose To provide financial assistance to Latino/a doctoral candidates who are completing a dissertation as part of their preparation for a career of scholarly service to a faith community.

Eligibility This program is open to Latinos/as who have completed all requirements for a Ph.D. or Ed.D. except the dissertation and plan to complete the dissertation at the end of the award year. Applicants must be U.S. citizens or permanent residents committed to serving the Latino faith community in the United States or Puerto Rico. Candidates who plan to study in Latin America or Europe are not eligible. Selection is based on recommendations by professors giving witness to the applicant's potential to contribute to the academic community as a scholar, recommendations by Latino church or community leaders giving witness to the applicant's commitment and leadership to the Latino community, potential of the applicant to contribute to the academic community as demonstrated by the dissertation proposal, and ability of the applicant to articulate the relevance of the research to the Latino community.

Financial data The grant is $16,000.

Duration 1 year; nonrenewable.

Additional information The program, funded by Pew Charitable Trusts, also provides the awardees with 1) skilled editorial support to facilitate a timely completion of the dissertation; 2) a mid-year workshop to monitor and encourage the writing process, to provide a time for discussion of the dissertation, and to provide collegial support.

Number awarded 6 each year.

Deadline December of each year.

[830]
HISPANIC THEOLOGICAL INITIATIVE SPECIAL MENTORING AWARDS

Hispanic Theological Initiative
12 Library Place
Princeton, NJ 08540
(609) 252-1721
Fax: (609) 252-1738
Web: www.htiprogram.org
Toll-free: (800) 575-5522
E-mail: hti@ptsem.edu

Purpose To provide funding for networking activities to Latino/a doctoral candidates in theology.

Eligibility This program is open to Latinos/as who have 1) finished all of their Ph.D. course work and are preparing for exams, or 2) been awarded a stipend that will be withdrawn or diminished if the student receives other funds. Applicants must be U.S. citizens or permanent residents committed to serving the Latino faith community in the United States or Puerto Rico. They must be seeking networking funds to keep them connected with the Hispanic Theological Initiative and its benefits.

Financial data The grant is $1,000.

Duration 1 year; nonrenewable.

Additional information The program, funded by Pew Charitable Trusts, also provides the awardees with a mentor to help them pass their doctoral examinations.

Number awarded 6 each year.

Deadline January of each year.

[831]
HORIZONS/FRAMELINE FILM AND VIDEO COMPLETION FUND

Frameline
Attn: Film and Video Completion Fund
145 Ninth Street, Suite 300
San Francisco, CA 94103
(415) 703-8650   Fax: (415) 861-1404
E-mail: info@frameline.org
Web: www.frameline.org/fund

Purpose To provide funding to lesbian and gay film/video artists.

Eligibility This program is open to lesbian and gay artists (particularly people of color and women) who are in the last stages of the production of documentary, educational, animated, or experimental projects about or of interest to lesbians, gay men, bisexuals, and transgender people and their communities. Applicants may be independent artists, students, producers, or nonprofit corporations. They must be interested in completion or post-production work, including subtitling or conversion from video to film (or vice versa). In particular, women and people of color are encouraged to apply. Selection is based on financial need, the contribution the grant will make to completing the project, assurances that the project will be completed, and the statement the project makes about lesbian, gay, bisexual, and transgender people and/or issues of concern to them and their communities. Grants are not awarded for script development, research, pre-production, or production work.

Financial data Grants range from $3,000 to $5,000.

Number awarded Varies each year; recently, 4 of these grants were awarded.

Deadline October of each year.

[832]
HOWARD HUGHES MEDICAL INSTITUTE RESEARCH TRAINING FELLOWSHIPS FOR MEDICAL STUDENTS

Howard Hughes Medical Institute
Attn: Office of Grants and Special Programs
4000 Jones Bridge Road
Chevy Chase, MD 20815-6789
(301) 215-8883   Fax: (301) 215-8888
E-mail: fellows@hhmi.org
Web: www.hhmi.org/medfellowships

Purpose To provide financial assistance to minority and other medical students interested in pursuing research training.

Eligibility Applicants must be enrolled in a medical school in the United States, although they may be citizens of any country. They must describe a proposed research project to be conducted at an academic or nonprofit research institution in the United States, other than a facility of the National Institutes of Health in Bethesda, Maryland. Research proposals should reflect the interests of the Howard Hughes Medical Institute (HHMI), especially in biochemistry, bioinformatics, biophysics, biostatistics, cell biology, developmental biology, epidemiology, genetics, immunology, mathematical and computational biology, microbiology, molecular biology, neuroscience, pharmacology, physiology, structural biology, and virology. Applications from women and minorities underrepresented in the sciences

(Blacks, Hispanics, Native Americans, Native Alaskans, and Native Pacific Islanders) are especially encouraged. Students enrolled in M.D./Ph.D., Ph.D., or Sc.D. programs and those who have completed a Ph.D. or Sc.D. in a laboratory-based science are not eligible. Selection is based on letters of reference, the research plan, and a mentor's plans for training the student.

Financial data Fellows receive a stipend of $25,000 per year; their institution receives an institutional allowance of $5,500 and a research allowance of $5,500. Research Training Fellows who are chosen to receive support to complete their studies toward the M.D. degree are given an annual stipend of $21,000 and a $16,000 annual allowance toward tuition and other education-related expenses.

Duration 1 year; may be renewed for a second year of research. A small number of fellows may be allowed to return to medical school and continue receiving support for 2 additional years.

Additional information This program complements the HHMI-NIH Research Scholars Program; students may not apply to both programs in the same year. Fellows may not be enrolled in an M.D./Ph.D. program. Applicants must apply online using the sponsor's web-based application system.

Number awarded Up to 60 each year.

Deadline January of each year.

[833]
HUD DOCTORAL DISSERTATION RESEARCH GRANT PROGRAM

Department of Housing and Urban Development
Attn: Office of University Partnerships
451 Seventh Street, S.W., Room 8106
Washington, DC 20410
(800) 245-2691, est. 3181   Fax: (301) 519-5767
E-mail: oup@oup.org
Web: www.oup.org/about/ddrg.html

Purpose To provide funding to doctoral candidates (especially minorities and women) interested in conducting dissertation research related to housing and urban development issues.

Eligibility This program is open to currently-enrolled doctoral candidates in an academic discipline that provides policy-relevant insight on issues in housing and urban development. Applicants must have fully-developed and approved dissertation proposals that can be completed within 2 years and must have completed all written and oral Ph.D. requirements. Funded fields of study have included anthropology, architecture, economics, history, planning, political science, public policy, social work, and sociology. Research must relate to the empowerment principles of the Department of Housing and Urban Development (HUD): a commitment to 1) socially and economically viable communities, 2) stable and supportive families, 3) economic growth, 4) reciprocity and balancing individual rights and responsibilities, and 5) reducing the separation of communities by race and income in American life. Women and minority candidates are encouraged to apply.

Financial data The stipend is $25,000 per year. The program expects that the recipients' universities will support their research by contributing a substantial waiver of tuition and fees, office space, equipment, computer time, or similar items needed to complete the dissertation.

Duration   These are 1-time grants.

Additional information   This program was established in 1994.

Number awarded   Up to 16 each year.

Deadline   June of each year.

[834]
HUD URBAN SCHOLARS POSTDOCTORAL FELLOWSHIP PROGRAM

National Research Council
Attn: Fellowship Office, GR 346A
500 Fifth Street, N.W.
Washington, DC 20001
(202) 334-2872   Fax: (202) 334-3419
E-mail: infofell@nas.edu
Web: www7.nationalacademies.org

Purpose   To provide funding to recent postdoctorates (especially minorities and women) interested in conducting research on topics of interest to the U.S. Department of Housing and Urban Development (HUD).

Eligibility   Applicants must have received a Ph.D. degree within the past 7 years and currently have an academic appointment at an institution of higher learning. They must be interested in conducting research on 1 of HUD's strategic goals for the year; recently, those goals included topics related to providing increased homeownership and rental opportunities for low- and moderate-income persons with disabilities, the elderly, minorities, and families with limited English proficiency; improving our nation's communities; encouraging accessible design features; providing full and equal access to grass-roots faith-based and other community-based organizations; improved housing conditions for families living in colonies (rural communities located within 150 miles of the border between the United States and Mexico), Appalachia, the Mississippi Delta, and tribal areas; participation in minority-serving institutions in HUD programs; participation in the HUD Energy Star program; ending chronic homelessness; ensuring equal opportunity in housing; or embracing high standards of ethics, management, and accountability. Applicants must work with a mentor, who can be someone in their institution or elsewhere but must be a well-respected scholar in the area of the proposed research. Selection is based on appropriateness of the methodology and approach to the topic (25 points), need for the research (20 points), relevance of the research to HUD's strategic goals (15 points), applicant's capacity to do the research (15 points), commitment of the university (10 points), likelihood of timely completion of the research project (10 points), and quality of the mentoring plan (5 points).

Financial data   The maximum grant is $55,000. The following items may be included: salary for 1 summer and the last 3 months of the fellowship; graduate assistants to work on the project; up to $2,500 per course for the cost of employing a replacement for the courses if the university relieves the applicant from teaching responsibilities; computer software, survey development and administration, and the purchase of data; travel expenses to collect data or to make presentations at meetings on findings; transcription

services and compensation for interviews; and up to 8% for the university's indirect costs.

Duration   Up to 15 months.

Number awarded   Approximately 10 each year.

Deadline   December of each year.

[835]
IDAHO SPACE GRANT CONSORTIUM GRADUATE FELLOWSHIPS

Idaho Space Grant Consortium
c/o University of Idaho
College of Engineering
P.O. Box 441011
Moscow, ID 83844-1011
(208) 885-6438   Fax: (208) 885-1399
E-mail: isgc@uidaho.edu
Web: isgc.uidaho.edu

Purpose   To provide funding for research in space-related fields to graduate students (particularly underrepresented minorities and women) at institutions belonging to the Idaho Space Grant Consortium (ISGC).

Eligibility   This program is open to graduate students at ISGC member institutions. Applicants may be majoring in engineering, mathematics, science, or science/math education, but they must be interested in conducting research in an area of focus of the National Aeronautics and Space Administration (NASA). An undergraduate and current GPA of 3.0 or higher and U.S. citizenship are required. As a component of the NASA Space Grant program, ISGC encourages participation by women, underrepresented minorities, and persons with disabilities.

Financial data   The stipend is up to $6,000 per year. Funds are to be used to pay for registration fees at colleges in the consortium.

Duration   1 year; may be renewed.

Additional information   Members of the consortium include Albertson College of Idaho, Boise State University, College of Southern Idaho, Idaho State University, Lewis Clark State College, North Idaho College, Northwest Nazarene College, Brigham Young University of Idaho, and the University of Idaho. This program is funded by NASA.

Number awarded   Varies each year.

Deadline   February of each year.

[836]
IDAHO SPACE GRANT CONSORTIUM RESEARCH INITIATION GRANTS

Idaho Space Grant Consortium
c/o University of Idaho
College of Engineering
P.O. Box 441011
Moscow, ID 83844-1011
(208) 885-7303   Fax: (208) 885-6645
E-mail: isgc@uidaho.edu
Web: isgc.uidaho.edu

Purpose   To provide funding for research in space-related fields to faculty members (particularly underrepresented minorities, women, and persons with disabilities) at institutions belonging to the Idaho Space Grant Consortium (ISGC).

Eligibility This program is open to faculty members in aeronautics, space, and related fields at institutions affiliated with ISGC. Applicants must be seeking funding for research programs that will result in proposals to the U.S. National Aeronautics and Space Administration (NASA) and other federal, state, and private organizations for further funding and continued program development. Travel to a NASA center or enterprise is strongly encouraged. U.S. citizenship is required. As a component of the NASA Space Grant program, ISGC encourages participation by women, underrepresented minorities, and persons with disabilities. Selection is based on the relevance of the proposal to ISGC and NASA goals, relevance to aerospace and space sciences, collaboration plan with a NASA center or enterprise, involvement of undergraduate students in the research, technical merit, potential for continued external funding, and the proposed budget.

Financial data Grants up to $30,000 are provided (up to $15,000 per year) but require an equal matching amount from the recipient's university, college, or department. Salaries may be used as a source of the required match.

Duration Up to 2 years.

Additional information Members of the consortium include Albertson College of Idaho, Boise State University, College of Southern Idaho, Idaho State University, Lewis Clark State College, North Idaho College, Northwest Nazarene College, Brigham Young University of Idaho, and the University of Idaho. This program is funded by NASA.

Number awarded Varies each year.

Deadline February of each year.

[837]
ILLINOIS ARTS COUNCIL ETHNIC AND FOLK ARTS MASTER/APPRENTICE PROGRAM

Illinois Arts Council
100 West Randolph, Suite 10-500
Chicago, IL 60601
(312) 814-6750   Toll-free: (800) 237-6994 (within IL)
Fax: (312) 814-1471   TTY: (312) 814-4831
E-mail: info@arts.state.il.us
Web: www.state.il.us/agency/iac

Purpose To provide funding to master ethnic and folk artists in Illinois and their apprentices for a program of training in traditional art forms.

Eligibility This program is open to teams of 2 Illinois residents, 1 of whom qualifies as a master artist (an individual who is recognized within his or her community as a person who has achieved the highest possible level of a traditional or classical ethnic art form) and 1 of whom qualifies as an apprentice (an individual with some experience in a traditional or classical ethnic art form who wishes to attain mastery of that art). Ethnic and folk arts are defined as those artistic practices that have a community or family base, express that community's aesthetic heritage and tradition, and have endured through several generations; they should reflect the particular culture of the ethnic, language, regional, tribal, or nationality group from which they spring. The art form may involve traditional crafts, music, dance, or storytelling. Both the master artist and the apprentice must be U.S. citizens or permanent residents who have resided in Illinois for at least 12 months. Selection is based on the artistic quality of both master artist and apprentice as determined by community standards, traditionality of art form and master artist, evidence of apprentice's commitment to the traditional art form, content and feasibility of work planned for the period of the apprenticeship, and quality and appropriateness of the documentation submitted. Priority is given to apprenticeships that take place outside of institutional settings.

Financial data The honoraria are $2,000 for the master and $1,000 for the apprentice.

Duration Most apprenticeships should include between 80 and 120 hours of instruction.

Number awarded Varies each year.

Deadline August of each year.

[838]
INDIANA SPACE GRANT CONSORTIUM GRADUATE FELLOWSHIPS

Indiana Space Grant Consortium
c/o Purdue University
School of Industrial Engineering
1287 Grissom Hall
West Lafayette, IN 47907-1287
(765) 494-5873   Fax: (765) 496-3449
E-mail: bcaldwel@ecn.purdue.edu
Web: www.insgc.org

Purpose To provide funding to graduate students (particularly underrepresented minorities, women, and students with disabilities) at member institutions of the Indiana Space Grant Consortium (INSGC) interested in conducting research related to space.

Eligibility This program is open to graduate students enrolled full time at institutions that are members of the INSGC. Applicants must be interested in conducting research related to 1 of the strategic enterprise areas of the U.S. National Aeronautics and Space Administration (NASA): space science, earth science, biological and physical research, human exploration and development of space, and aerospace technology. U.S. citizenship is required. The program encourages representation of women, underrepresented minorities, and persons with disabilities.

Financial data The maximum grant is $5,000 per year for master's degree students or $10,000 for doctoral students.

Duration 1 year; students may not receive an award in consecutive years.

Additional information This program is funded by NASA. The academic member institutions of the INSGC are Purdue University, Ball State University, Indiana University, Indiana University-Purdue University at Indianapolis, Purdue University at Calumet, Taylor University, University of Evansville, University of Notre Dame, and Valparaiso University.

Number awarded Varies each year. Approximately $60,000 is available for undergraduate scholarships and graduate fellowships.

Deadline February of each year.

[839]
INSTITUTE FOR CIVIL SOCIETY FELLOWSHIPS
Vermont Studio Center
80 Pearl Street
P.O. Box 613
Johnson, VT 05656
(802) 635-2727   Fax: (802) 635-2730
E-mail: info@vermontstudiocenter.org
Web: www.vermontstudiocenter.org

Purpose To provide funding to minority artists from designated cities in several eastern states who are interested in a residency at the Vermont Studio Center in Johnson, Vermont.

Eligibility Eligible to apply for this support are painters, sculptors, printmakers, and photographers who are members of a minority group and residents of New Haven (Connecticut), Jersey City (New Jersey), or Baltimore (Maryland). Applicants must be interested in a residency at the center in Johnson, Vermont. Visual artists must submit up to 20 slides of their work, poets must submit up to 10 pages, and other writers must submit 10 to 15 pages. Selection is based on artistic merit and financial need.

Financial data The residency covers studio space, room, board, lectures, studio visits, and travel expenses.

Duration 4 weeks.

Additional information This program is sponsored by the Institute for Civil Society.

Number awarded 3 each year.

Deadline June of each year.

[840]
INSTITUTE FOR RESEARCH ON POVERTY VISITING SCHOLARS PROGRAM
University of Wisconsin at Madison
Attn: Institute for Research on Poverty
3412 Social Science Building
1180 Observatory Drive
Madison, WI 53706-1393
(608) 262-6358   Fax: (608) 265-3119
E-mail: evanson@ssc.wisc.edu
Web: www.irp.wisc.edu

Purpose To provide minority scholars with an opportunity to visit the Institute for Research on Poverty (IRP) at the University of Wisconsin (UW) at Madison.

Eligibility This program is open to minority scholars, especially those in the beginning years of their academic careers. They are invited to visit UW, interact with its faculty in residence, become acquainted with the staff and resources of IRP, and present lectures. Applicants should submit a letter describing their poverty research interests and experience, the proposed dates for a visit, a current curriculum vitae, and 2 examples of written material.

Financial data Monetary support is provided. Transportation, lodging, and food are covered.

Duration 1 to 2 weeks.

Additional information During their visit, scholars are invited to give a seminar, to work on their own projects, and to confer with an IRP adviser who will arrange for an interchange with other IRP affiliates.

Number awarded Up to 3 each year.

Deadline June of each year.

[841]
INTERNATIONAL SECURITY AND COOPERATION POSTDOCTORAL FELLOWSHIPS
Stanford University
Center for International Security and Cooperation
Attn: Fellowship Program Coordinator
Encina Hall, Room E210
616 Serra Street
Stanford, CA 94305-6165
(650) 723-9626   Fax: (650) 723-0089
E-mail: barbara.platt@stanford.edu
Web: www.cisac.stanford.edu

Purpose To provide funding to postdoctorates (particularly minorities and women) who are interested in conducting research on arms control and international security at Stanford University's Center for International Security and Cooperation.

Eligibility This program is open to scholars who have a Ph.D. or equivalent degree from the United States or abroad. Applicants must be interested in researching international security and arms control issues at the center. Fields of study might include anthropology, economics, history, law, political science, sociology, medicine, or the natural and physical sciences. Topics suitable for support might include the causes and prevention of terrorism; security relationships around the world; U.S.-Russian strategic relations; peacekeeping; prevention of deadly conflicts; U.S. defense and arms control policies; proliferation of nuclear, chemical, and biological weapons; security in south and east Asia; the commercialization of national defense technologies; and ethnic and civil conflict. The center is especially interested in applications from minorities and women.

Financial data The stipend is at least $33,000, depending on experience. Additional funds may be available for dependents and travel.

Duration 9 months.

Number awarded Varies; generally, 2 each year.

Deadline January of each year.

[842]
INTERNATIONAL SECURITY AND COOPERATION PREDOCTORAL FELLOWSHIPS
Stanford University
Center for International Security and Cooperation
Attn: Fellowship Program Coordinator
Encina Hall, Room E210
616 Serra Street
Stanford, CA 94305-6165
(650) 723-9626   Fax: (650) 723-0089
E-mail: barbara.platt@stanford.edu
Web: www.cisac.stanford.edu

Purpose To provide funding to doctoral students, particularly minorities and women, who are interested in writing a dissertation on the problems of arms control and international security at Stanford University's Center for International Security and Cooperation.

Eligibility Students currently enrolled in doctoral programs at academic institutions in the United States who would benefit from access to the facilities offered by the center are eligible to apply. Fields of study might include anthropology, economics, history, law, political science, sociology, medicine, or the natural and physical sciences.

Topics suitable for support might include the causes and prevention of terrorism; security relationships around the world; U.S.-Russian strategic relations; peacekeeping; prevention of deadly conflicts; U.S. defense and arms control policies; proliferation of nuclear, chemical, and biological weapons; security in south and east Asia; the commercialization of national defense technologies; and ethnic and civil conflict. The center is especially interested in receiving applications from minorities and women.

Financial data The stipend is $20,000. Additional funds may be available for dependents and travel.

Duration 9 months.

Number awarded Varies; generally, 4 each year.

Deadline January of each year.

[843]
INTERNATIONAL SECURITY AND COOPERATION PROFESSIONAL FELLOWSHIPS

Stanford University
Center for International Security and Cooperation
Attn: Fellowship Program Coordinator
Encina Hall, Room E210
616 Serra Street
Stanford, CA 94305-6165
(650) 723-9626   Fax: (650) 723-0089
E-mail: barbara.platt@stanford.edu
Web: www.cisac.stanford.edu

Purpose To provide funding to professionals (particularly minorities and women) who are interested in conducting research on arms control and international security at Stanford University's Center for International Security and Cooperation.

Eligibility This program is open to military officers or civilian members of the U.S. government, members of military or diplomatic services from other countries, and journalists interested in arms control and international security issues. Applicants must be interested in conducting research on international security and arms control issues at the center. Topics suitable for support might include the causes and prevention of terrorism; security relationships around the world; U.S.-Russian strategic relations; peacekeeping; prevention of deadly conflicts; U.S. defense and arms control policies; proliferation of nuclear, chemical, and biological weapons; security in south and east Asia; the commercialization of national defense technologies; and ethnic and civil conflict. The center is especially interested in applications from minorities and women.

Financial data The stipend depends on experience and is determined on a case-by-case basis. Additional funds may be available for dependents and travel.

Duration 9 months.

Number awarded Varies each year.

Deadline January of each year.

[844]
J. ROBERT GLADDEN SOCIETY TRAVELING FELLOWSHIPS

J. Robert Gladden Society
6300 North River Road, Suite 727
Rosemont, IL 60018
(847) 698-1633   Fax: (847) 823-4921
E-mail: swift@aaos.org
Web: www.gladdensociety.org

Purpose To provide funding to members of the J. Robert Gladden Society (JRGS) who are minorities and interested in traveling for additional study.

Eligibility This program is open to members of underrepresented minority groups who have been in practice as orthopedic surgeons for 2 to 3 years. Applicants must be interested in visiting another institution to increase their surgical skills, learn new techniques, or expand their practice interests. They must be members of the JRGS planning to visit a site or practice where another JRGS member is involved. Preference is given to applicants planning to work with a senior JRGS member.

Financial data Grants provide reimbursement of travel expenses up to $6,000.

Duration 4 weeks or more.

Additional information Grantees are expected to give a report to the JRGS annual luncheon, held in conjunction with the annual meeting of the American Academy of Orthopaedic Surgeons (AAOS).

Number awarded 1 or more each year.

Deadline November of each year.

[845]
JEFFREY CAMPBELL GRADUATE FELLOWS PROGRAM

St. Lawrence University
Attn: Human Resources/Office of Equity Programs
Jeffrey Campbell Graduate Fellowship Program
Canton, NY 13617
(315) 229-5509
Web: www.stlawu.edu

Purpose To provide funding to minority graduate students who have completed their course work and are interested in conducting research at St. Lawrence University in New York.

Eligibility This program is open to graduate students who are members of racial or ethnic groups historically underrepresented at the university and in American higher education. Applicants must have completed their course work and preliminary examinations for the Ph.D. or M.F.A. They must be interested in working on their dissertations or terminal degree projects while in residence at the University.

Financial data The stipend is $25,000 per academic year. Additional funds may be available to support travel to conferences and professional meetings. Office space and a personal computer are provided.

Duration 1 academic year.

Additional information This program is named for 1 of the university's early African American graduates. Recipients must teach 1 course a semester in a department or program at St. Lawrence University related to their research interests. In addition, they must present a research-based paper in the fellows' lecture series each semester.

Deadline February of each year.

[846]
JOHN AND ELIZABETH PHILLIPS FELLOWSHIP

Phillips Exeter Academy
Attn: Dean of Faculty
20 Main Street
Exeter, NH 03833-2460
(603) 772-3405   Fax: (603) 772-4393
E-mail: faculty@exeter.edu
Web: www.exeter.edu

Purpose To provide funding to underrepresented teachers interested in a residency at Phillips Exeter Academy in Exeter, New Hampshire.

Eligibility This program is open to scholars and teachers from groups traditionally underrepresented in the secondary school environment who might not otherwise consider teaching in a residential secondary school. Candidates may come from other educational institutions, direct from college or graduate school, or from non-academic settings.

Financial data Fellows receive a competitive salary.

Duration 1 to 3 academic years.

Additional information Fellows live in residence at Phillips Exeter Academy, where they affiliate with a specific academic department and coordinate their teaching responsibilities with a faculty mentor. They serve on important faculty committees and engage in oversight of dormitories, athletics, and extracurricular activities. This fellowship was first offered for the 1998-99 academic year.

Number awarded Up to 4 each year.

[847]
JOSEPH L. FISHER DOCTORAL DISSERTATION FELLOWSHIPS

Resources for the Future
Attn: Coordinator for Academic Programs
1616 P Street, N.W.
Washington, DC 20036-1400
(202) 328-5060   Fax: (202) 939-3460
E-mail: mankin@rff.org
Web: www.rff.org

Purpose To support doctoral dissertation research in economics (particularly by minorities and women) on issues related to the environment, natural resources, or energy.

Eligibility This program is open to graduate students in the final year of research on a dissertation related to the environment, natural resources, or energy. Applicants must submit a brief letter of application and a curriculum vitae, a graduate transcript, a 1-page abstract of the dissertation, a technical summary of the dissertation (up to 2,500 words), a letter from the student's department chair, and 2 letters of recommendation from faculty members on the student's dissertation committee. The technical summary should describe clearly the aim of the dissertation, its significance in relation to the existing literature, and the research methods to be used. Women and minority candidates are strongly encouraged to apply.

Financial data The stipend is $12,000 per year.

Duration 1 academic year.

Additional information It is expected that recipients will not hold other employment during the fellowship period.

Recipients must notify Resources for the Future of any financial assistance they receive from any other source for support of doctoral work.

Number awarded 2 or 3 each year.

Deadline February of each year.

[848]
LATINO POSTDOCTORAL FELLOWSHIPS AT THE SMITHSONIAN INSTITUTION

Smithsonian Institution
Attn: Office of Fellowships
Victor Building, Suite 9300, MRC 902
P.O. Box 37012
Washington, DC 20013-7012
(202) 275-0655   Fax: (202) 275-0489
E-mail: siofg@si.edu
Web: www.si.edu

Purpose To provide funding to Latino postdoctoral scholars interested in conducting research at the Smithsonian Institution.

Eligibility This program is open Latino/a scholars who have completed a doctoral degree less than 7 years before the application deadline. Applicants must intend to conduct research in U.S. Latino history, art, or culture at the Smithsonian Institution. Selection is based on the proposal's merit, including the significance of the study to the discipline in general and to Latino research in particular, the methodology to be used, the applicant's ability to carry out the proposed research and study, the likelihood that the research could be completed in the requested time, and the extent to which the Smithsonian, through its various resources, could contribute to the proposed research.

Financial data The stipend is $30,000 per year; also provided are a travel allowance and a research allowance of up to $4,000.

Duration From 3 to 12 months.

Additional information Fellows are expected to spend most of their tenure in residence at the Smithsonian, although up to one third of the fellowship tenure may be spent away from the Smithsonian conducting research at another institution or in the field (but not at the applicant's home institution).

Number awarded Varies each year, depending on the availability of funds.

Deadline January of each year.

[849]
LATINO PREDOCTORAL FELLOWSHIPS AT THE SMITHSONIAN INSTITUTION

Smithsonian Institution
Attn: Office of Fellowships
Victor Building, Suite 9300, MRC 902
P.O. Box 37012
Washington, DC 20013-7012
(202) 275-0655   Fax: (202) 275-0489
E-mail: siofg@si.edu
Web: www.si.edu

Purpose To provide funding to Latino doctoral students interested in conducting research at the Smithsonian Institution.

Eligibility This program is open to Latinos/as who have completed preliminary course work and examinations for the doctoral degree and are engaged in dissertation research in U.S. Latino history, art, or culture. Applicants must have the approval of their university to conduct their doctoral research at the Smithsonian Institution. Selection is based on the proposal's merit, including the significance of the study to the discipline in general and to Latino research in particular, the methodology to be used, the applicant's ability to carry out the proposed research and study, the likelihood that the research could be completed in the requested time, and the extent to which the Smithsonian, through its various resources, could contribute to the proposed research.

Financial data The stipend is $20,000 per year; also provided are a travel allowance and a research allowance of up to $4,000.

Duration From 3 to 12 months.

Additional information Fellows are expected to spend most of their tenure in residence at the Smithsonian, although up to one third of the fellowship tenure may be spent away from the Smithsonian conducting research at another institution or in the field (but not at the applicant's home institution).

Number awarded Varies each year, depending on the availability of funds.

Deadline January of each year.

[850]
LATINO SENIOR FELLOWSHIPS AT THE SMITHSONIAN INSTITUTION

Smithsonian Institution
Attn: Office of Fellowships
Victor Building, Suite 9300, MRC 902
P.O. Box 37012
Washington, DC 20013-7012
(202) 275-0655   Fax: (202) 275-0489
E-mail: siofg@si.edu
Web: www.si.edu

Purpose To provide funding to senior Latino scholars interested in conducting research at the Smithsonian Institution.

Eligibility This program is open to Latinos/as who have completed a doctoral degree more than 7 years before the application deadline. Applicants must intend to conduct research in U.S. Latino history, art, or culture at the Smithsonian Institution. Selection is based on the proposal's merit, including the significance of the study to the discipline in general and to Latino research in particular, the methodology to be used, the applicant's ability to carry out the proposed research and study, the likelihood that the research could be completed in the requested time, and the extent to which the Smithsonian, through its various resources, could contribute to the proposed research.

Financial data The stipend is $35,000 per year; also provided are a travel allowance and a research allowance of up to $4,000.

Duration From 3 to 12 months.

Additional information Fellows are expected to spend most of their tenure in residence at the Smithsonian, although up to one third of the fellowship tenure may be spent away from the Smithsonian conducting research at

another institution or in the field (but not at the applicant's home institution).

Number awarded Varies each year, depending on the availability of funds.

Deadline January of each year.

[851]
LEO GOLDBERG FELLOWSHIPS

National Optical Astronomy Observatories
Attn: Human Resources Manager
P.O. Box 26732
Tucson, AZ 85726
(520) 318-8100   Fax: (520) 318-8456
E-mail: hrnoao@noao.edu
Web: www.noao.edu/goldberg/fellows.html

Purpose To provide an opportunity for postdoctorates (particularly underrepresented minorities and women) in astronomy to conduct research at the facilities of the National Optical Astronomy Observatories (NOAO) in Arizona or Chile.

Eligibility This program is open to recent Ph.D. recipients in observational astronomy, astronomical instrumentation, or theoretical astrophysics. Applicants must be interested in conducting a research program of their own choosing or participating in a current NOAO initiative at Kitt Peak National Observatory (KPNO) near Tucson, Arizona or Cerro Tololo Inter-American Observatory (CTIO) in La Serena, Chile. Women and candidates from underrepresented minorities are particularly encouraged to apply. Selection is based on the applicant's promise for an outstanding career in astronomy, their proposed use of KPNO or CTIO facilities, the relationship of their research to an proposed interaction with NOAO programs to plan the next generation of community facilities, and the relationship of their research to programs conducted by NOAO staff.

Financial data A competitive salary is paid. Additional support is provided to fellows and their families in Chile.

Duration 5 years. The first 4 years are spent either at Kitt Peak or in La Serena; the final year is spent at an U.S. university or astronomical institute willing to host the fellow.

Additional information NOAO is supported under a contract between the National Science Foundation and the Association of Universities for Research in Astronomy, Inc. This program was formerly known as the NOAO 5-Year Science Fellowship.

Number awarded 1 each year.

Deadline November of each year.

[852]
LIBRARY OF CONGRESS FELLOWSHIPS IN INTERNATIONAL STUDIES

American Council of Learned Societies
Attn: Office of Fellowships and Grants
633 Third Avenue, 8C
New York, NY 10017-6795
(212) 697-1505   Fax: (212) 949-8058
E-mail: grants@acls.org
Web: www.acls.org/locguide.htm

Purpose To provide financial assistance to scholars (particularly minorities and women) in all disciplines of the humanities and the social sciences who are interested in using the foreign language collections of the Library of Congress.

Eligibility This program is open to U.S. citizens and permanent residents who hold a Ph.D. in a discipline of the humanities or social sciences. Proposals in multidisciplinary and cross-disciplinary studies are also welcome, as are proposals focused on single or multiple geographical areas. Research must require use of the foreign language collections of the Library of Congress. Preference is given to scholars at an early stage of their career (within 7 years of completing their doctorate). Applicants may be affiliated with any academic institution, although independent scholars are also eligible. Applications are particularly invited from women and members of minority groups.

Financial data The stipend is $3,500 per month.

Duration 4 to 9 months; fellowships may be combined with sabbatical and other fellowship funds to extend the research period up to a total of 12 months.

Additional information This program, established in 2001, is supported by funding from the Andrew W. Mellon Foundation, the Association of American Universities, and the Library of Congress. Additional support for research concerning east or southeast Asia is provided by the Henry Luce Foundation. During the fellowship period, scholars are expected to be engaged in full-time research at the Library of Congress.

Number awarded Up to 10 each year.

Deadline November of each year.

[853]
LILLA JEWEL AWARD FOR WOMEN ARTISTS

McKenzie River Gathering Foundation
Attn: Office Manager
2705 East Burnside, Suite 210
Portland, OR 97214
(503) 289-1517   Toll-free: (800) 489-6743
Fax: (503) 232-1731   E-mail: info@mrgfoundation.org
Web: www.mrgfoundation.org

Purpose To provide funding to women (particularly women of color) who are artists in Oregon.

Eligibility Eligible to apply for this funding are women artists in Oregon. The artistic category rotates on a quadriennial cycle among performing arts (2006), media arts (2007), visual arts (2008), and literary arts and music (2009). Although the award is not based on financial need, the intent is to support a woman artist who lacks traditional access to funding. Selection is based on the artistic impact of the work presented for consideration; whether the artist is a member of another traditionally underfunded group, such as women of color or lesbians; the ideas embodied in the work as represented in the written application; how the work challenges the status quo and supports the sponsor's mission of progressive social change; and the potential impact of the award on the artist at this point in her career.

Financial data The maximum grant is $4,000.

Duration 1 year.

Additional information This is the only funding available to individuals through the McKenzie River Gathering Foundation.

Number awarded 1 each year.

[854]
LYMAN T. JOHNSON POSTDOCTORAL FELLOWSHIP

University of Kentucky
Attn: Executive Vice President for Research
201 Gillis Building
Lexington, KY 40506-0033
(859) 257-5294   Fax: (859) 323-2800
E-mail: vpr@email.uky.edu
Web: www.rgs.uky.edu/students/postdocs.htm

Purpose To provide an opportunity for recent minority postdoctorates to conduct research at the University of Kentucky (UK).

Eligibility This program is open to minorities who have completed a doctoral degree within the past 2 years in a graduate or professional area in which minorities are underrepresented. Applicants must demonstrate evidence of scholarship with competitive potential for a tenure-track faculty appointment at a research university and compatibility of specific research interests with those in doctorate-granting units at the UK. They should submit a letter of application, a curriculum vitae, sample publications or dissertation chapters, a research proposal, 3 letters of recommendation, and a letter from a potential mentor at the university outlining the general research program. U.S. citizenship or permanent resident status is required.

Financial data The fellowship provides a stipend of $35,000 plus $5,000 for support of research activities.

Duration Up to 2 years.

Additional information In addition to conducting an individualized research program under the mentorship of 1 or more UK professors, fellows actively participate in research and teaching as well as service to the university, their profession, and the community. This program began in 1992.

Number awarded 1 each year.

Deadline January or July of each year.

[855]
MANY VOICES RESIDENCIES

Playwrights' Center
2301 Franklin Avenue East
Minneapolis, MN 55406-1099
(612) 332-7481   Fax: (612) 332-6037
E-mail: info@pwcenter.org
Web: www.pwcenter.org/fellowships_MV.htm

Purpose To provide funding for Minnesota playwrights of color so they can spend a year in residence at the Playwrights' Center in Minneapolis.

Eligibility This program is open to playwrights of color who have been citizens or permanent residents of the United States and residents of Minnesota for at least 1 year. Applicants must be interested in playwriting and creating theater in a supportive artists' community at the Playwrights' Center. Selection is based on the applicant's commitment, proven talent, and artistic potential.

Financial data The program provides a stipend of $1,250; a mentorship with an established playwright or theater artist of their choosing; a full scholarship to a center class; a private script workshop with professional actors, directors, and dramaturgs; a public reading with professional actors and an audience discussion; and a 1-year membership in the Playwrights' Center.

Duration 9 months, beginning in October.

Additional information Fellows must be in residence at the Playwrights' Center for the duration of the program. This program is funded by a grant from the Jerome Foundation.

Number awarded 8 each year.

Deadline July of each year.

[856]
MARTIN LUTHER KING, JR., CESAR CHAVEZ, ROSA PARKS VISITING PROFESSORS PROGRAM

University of Michigan
Attn: Office of the Associate Provost—Academic Affairs
503 Thompson Street
3084 Fleming Administration Building 1340
Ann Arbor, MI 48109-1340
(734) 764-3982   Fax: (734) 764-4546
E-mail: provost@umich.edu
Web: www.provost.umich.edu

Purpose To provide funds for minority scholars to visit and lecture/teach at the University of Michigan.

Eligibility Outstanding minority (African American, Asian American, Latino/a (Hispanic) American, and Native American) postdoctorates or scholars/practitioners are eligible to be nominated by University of Michigan department chairs or deans to visit and lecture there. Nominations that include collaborations with other universities are of high priority.

Financial data Visiting Professors receive round-trip transportation and an appropriate honorarium.

Duration Visits range from 1 to 5 days.

Additional information This program was established in 1986. Visiting Professors are expected to lecture or teach at the university, offer at least 1 event open to the general public, and meet with minority campus/community groups, including local K-12 schools.

Number awarded Varies each year.

Deadline January for the summer term; March for the fall term; August for the winter term; and November for the spring term.

[857]
MATHEMATICA SUMMER FELLOWSHIPS

Mathematica Policy Research, Inc.
Attn: Human Resources
600 Alexander Park
P.O. Box 2393
Princeton, NU 08543-2393
(609) 799-3535   Fax: (609) 799-0005
E-mail: HRNJ@mathematica-mpr.com
Web: www.mathinc.com

Purpose To provide an opportunity for graduate students (particularly minority students) in social policy fields to work on an independent summer research project at an office of Mathematica Policy Research, Inc.

Eligibility This program is open to students enrolled in a master's or Ph.D. program in public policy or a social science. Applicants must be interested in conducting independent research on a policy issue of relevance to the economic and social problems of minority groups. Traditionally, that includes those of African American, Hispanic, Asian,

and Native American ancestry, although proposals focusing on another group, such as people with disabilities, may be considered. The proposed research must relate to the work of Mathematica, but fellows do not work on Mathematica projects. Qualified minority students are encouraged to apply.

Financial data The stipend is $6,000 (or $2,000 per month). Fellows also receive $500 for project-related expenses.

Duration 3 months during the summer.

Additional information Mathematica offices are located in Princeton (New Jersey), Cambridge (Massachusetts), and Washington, D.C. Fellows may indicate their choice of location, but they are assigned to the office where the work of the research staff meshes best with their topic and interests.

Number awarded Up to 5 each year.

Deadline March of each year.

[858]
MCNAMARA FAMILY CREATIVE ARTS PROJECT GRANTS

Hispanic Scholarship Fund
Attn: Selection Committee
55 Second Street, Suite 1500
San Francisco, CA 94105
(415) 808-2350   Toll-free: (877) HSF-INFO
Fax: (415) 808-2302   E-mail: college1@hsf.net
Web: www.hsf.net

Purpose To provide funding to Hispanic undergraduate and graduate students interested in beginning and completing an art project.

Eligibility This program is open to U.S. citizens, permanent residents, and visitors with a passport stamped I-551. Applicants must be of Hispanic heritage and working full time on an undergraduate or graduate degree at an accredited college or university in the United States, Puerto Rico, or the U.S. Virgin Islands. They must have completed at least 12 undergraduate units with a GPA of 3.0 or higher and be majoring in the arts, including (but not limited to) media, film, performing arts, communications, and writing. Along with their application, they must submit a 3-page concept paper describing the art project for which they are seeking funding, a portfolio of their work, and 600-word essays on 1) how their Hispanic heritage, family upbringing, and/or role models have influenced their personal long-term goals; 2) how they contribute to their community and what they have learned from their experiences; and 3) an academic challenge they have faced and how they have overcome it. Selection is based on those submissions, academic record, plans and career goals, community service, and financial need.

Financial data Grants range from $5,000 to $20,000.

Duration These are 1-time grants.

Additional information This program is offered by the Hispanic Scholarship Fund (HSF) in partnership with the McNamara Family Foundation

Number awarded 1 or more each year.

Deadline May of each year.

[859]
MENTAL HEALTH DISSERTATION RESEARCH GRANTS TO INCREASE DIVERSITY IN THE MENTAL HEALTH RESEARCH ARENA

National Institute of Mental Health
Attn: Office for Special Populations
6001 Executive Boulevard, Room 8125
Bethesda, MD 20892-9659
(301) 443-2847   Fax: (301) 443-8022
E-mail: ms265g@nih.gov
Web: www.nimh.nih.gov

Purpose To provide financial support to underrepresented minority doctoral candidates planning to prepare for a research career in any area relevant to mental health and/or mental disorders.

Eligibility This program is open to doctoral candidates conducting dissertation research in a field related to mental health and/or mental disorders at a university, college, or professional school with an accredited doctoral degree granting program. Applicants must be members of an ethnic or racial group that has been determined by their institution to be underrepresented in biomedical or behavioral research. They must be U.S. citizens, nationals, or permanent residents.

Financial data Grants provide up to $30,000 per year in direct costs.

Duration 1 year; may be renewed 1 additional year.

Number awarded Varies each year.

Deadline April, August, or December of each year.

[860]
MENTORED CLINICAL SCIENTIST AWARD FOR UNDERREPRESENTED MINORITIES

National Cancer Institute
Attn: Comprehensive Minority Biomedical Branch
6116 Executive Boulevard, Suite 7031
Bethesda, MD 20892-8350
(301) 496-7344   Fax: (301) 402-4551
TTY: (301) 451-0088   E-mail: ba101m@nih.gov
Web: www.nci.nih.gov

Purpose To provide funding to underrepresented minorities who are interested in a program of research training in clinical oncology under the supervision of an experienced mentor.

Eligibility This program is open to U.S. citizens, nationals, and permanent residents who have a health professional doctorate and can demonstrate broad clinical training, competence in clinical activities, and a serious intent for a career in laboratory or field-based (not patient-oriented) cancer research. Candidates must be sponsored by a domestic, nonprofit or for-profit organization, public or private (such as a university, college, hospital, laboratory, unit of state or local government, or eligible agency of the federal government). They must qualify as an underrepresented minority individual, defined as members of a particular ethnic, racial, or other group determined by their institution to be underrepresented in cancer-related biomedical, behavioral, clinical, or social science research, e.g., first generation college students or graduates, socio-economically disadvantaged persons, or persons with disabilities. The mentor must 1) have extensive research experience; 2) be able to demonstrate an appreciation of the cul-

tural, socioeconomic, and research background of the individual candidate; and 3) recognize the personal attention that minority candidates often need to pursue successful research careers. If possible, women, underrepresented minority individuals, and persons with disabilities should be involved as mentors to serve as role models.

Financial data The award provides salary up to $75,000 per year plus related fringe benefits. In addition, up to $30,000 per year is provided for the following types of expenses: tuition, fees, and books related to career development; research expenses, such as supplies, equipment, and technical personnel; statistical services, including personnel and computer time; tuition, fees, and books related to career development; and travel to research meetings or for training. Facilities and administrative costs are reimbursed at 8% of modified total direct costs.

Duration Up to 5 years.

Additional information This program was established in 2002 as the successor of a program designated the Minorities in Clinical Oncology Program Grants Recipients must devote at least 75% of their full-time professional effort to cancer-related research and training activities.

Number awarded Varies each year, depending on the availability of funds.

Deadline January, May, or September of each year.

[861]
MFP DISSERTATION SUPPORT

American Nurses Association
Attn: Ethnic Minority Fellowship Programs
600 Maryland Avenue, S.W., Suite 100 West
Washington, DC 20024-2571
(202) 651-7244   Fax: (202) 651-7007
E-mail: emfp@ana.org
Web: www.nursingworld.org

Purpose To provide funding to minority nurses who are working on a dissertation on a topic of interest to the Minority Fellowship Program (MFP) of the American Nurses Association.

Eligibility This program is open to nurses who are completing a doctoral dissertation and are members of an ethnic or racial minority group, including but not limited to Blacks or African Americans, Hispanics or Latinos, American Indians and Alaska Natives, Asians and Asian Americans, and Native Hawaiians and other Pacific Islanders. Applicants must be able to demonstrate a commitment to a research career in nursing and psychiatric/mental health issues affecting ethnic minority populations. They must be working on a doctoral dissertation with a focus on such issues of concern to minority populations as child abuse, violence in intimate relationships, mental health disorders, substance abuse, mental health service utilization, and stigma as a barrier to mental health care and personal resilience. U.S. citizenship or permanent resident status and membership in the American Nurses Association are required.

Financial data Grants range from $1,000 to $5,000.

Duration These are 1-time grants.

Additional information Funds for this program are provided by the Substance Abuse and Mental Health Services Administration.

Number awarded 1 or more each year.

[862]
MICHIGAN SPACE GRANT CONSORTIUM FELLOWSHIPS

Michigan Space Grant Consortium
c/o University of Michigan
2106 Space Physics Research Laboratory
2455 Hayward Avenue
Ann Arbor, MI 48109-2143
(734) 764-9508　　　Fax: (734) 764-4585
E-mail: blbryant@umich.edu
Web: www.engin.umich.edu/dept/aero/msgc/fellow

Purpose To provide funding to students (particularly underrepresented minorities, women, and persons with disabilities) at member institutions of the Michigan Space Grant Consortium who wish to conduct space-related research.

Eligibility This program is open to undergraduate and graduate students at affiliates of the Michigan consortium who are proposing to conduct research in aerospace, space science, earth system science, and other related fields in science, engineering, or mathematics; students working on educational research topics in mathematics, science, or technology are also eligible. Applicants must identify a mentor in the faculty research, education, or public service communities with whom they intend to work and who is available to write a letter of recommendation for the student. U.S. citizenship is required. Women, underrepresented minorities, and persons with disabilities are especially encouraged to apply.

Financial data The maximum grant is $2,500 for undergraduates or $5,000 for graduate students.

Additional information The consortium consists of Eastern Michigan University, Grand Valley State University, Hope College, Michigan State University, Michigan Technological University, Oakland University, Saginaw Valley State University, University of Michigan, Wayne State University, and Western Michigan University. This program is supported by the U.S. National Aeronautics and Space Administration (NASA).

Number awarded Varies; a total of $125,000 is available for these fellowships each year.

Deadline November of each year.

[863]
MICHIGAN SPACE GRANT CONSORTIUM RESEARCH SEED GRANTS

Michigan Space Grant Consortium
c/o University of Michigan
2106 Space Physics Research Laboratory
2455 Hayward Avenue
Ann Arbor, MI 48109-2143
(734) 764-9508　　　Fax: (734) 764-4585
E-mail: blbryant@umich.edu
Web: www.umich.edu/~msgc

Purpose To provide funding to faculty (especially underrepresented minorities, women, and persons with disabilities) at member institutions of the Michigan Space Grant Consortium (MSGC) who are interested in conducting space-related research.

Eligibility This program is open to faculty (research and professorial) at affiliates of the MSGC. Applicants must be interested in conducting a research project in engineering,

science, mathematics, life sciences, or related educational areas. Preference is given to projects focusing on aerospace, space, or earth system science, although awards are not strictly limited to those topics. Initiation of a new area of research is preferred over efforts to continue an existing project or study. Women, underrepresented minorities, and persons with disabilities are encouraged to apply.

Financial data Grants up to $5,000 are available. At least 1:1 cost matching (cash contributions or in-kind support) with nonfederal funds is required.

Additional information The consortium consists of Eastern Michigan University, Grand Valley State University, Hope College, Michigan State University, Michigan Technological University, Oakland University, Saginaw Valley State University, University of Michigan, Wayne State University, and Western Michigan University. This program is supported by the U.S. National Aeronautics and Space Administration (NASA).

Number awarded Varies each year.

Deadline November of each year.

[864]
MICROBIOLOGY UNDERGRADUATE RESEARCH FELLOWSHIP

American Society for Microbiology
Attn: Education Board
1752 N Street, N.W.
Washington, DC 20036-2904
(202) 942-9283　　　Fax: (202) 942-9329
E-mail: Fellowships-CareerInformation@asmusa.org
Web: www.asm.org

Purpose To provide underrepresented minority college students with the opportunity to work on a summer research project in microbiology under the mentorship of a member of the American Society for Microbiology (ASM).

Eligibility This program is open to African Americans, Hispanic Americans, Native Americans, Alaskan Native Americans, and Native Pacific Islanders who 1) are enrolled as full-time undergraduate students; 2) have taken introductory courses in biology, chemistry, and (preferably) microbiology prior to applying; 3 have a strong interest in obtaining a Ph.D. or M.D./Ph.D. in the microbiological sciences; 4) have laboratory research experience; and 5) are U.S. citizens or permanent residents. Applicants must be interested in conducting basic science research at a host institution during the summer under an ASM mentor. Selection is based on academic achievement, achievement in previous research experiences or independent projects, career goals as a research scientist, commitment to research, personal motivation to participate in the project, willingness to conduct summer research with an ASM member located at an institution other than their own, and leadership skills.

Financial data Students receive $3,500 as a stipend, up to $850 for student lodging, up to $500 for round-trip travel to the host institution, 1-year student membership in the ASM, and travel support up to $1,000 if they present the results of the research project at the ASM general meeting the following year.

Duration 10 to 12 weeks during the summer.

Additional information Recently, placements were available at Albert Einstein College of Medicine (Bronx, New York) and Tufts University School of Medicine (Boston, Massachusetts). In addition to their research activities, fellows participate in a weekly seminar series, journal club, GRE preparatory course, graduate admission counseling, and career counseling.

Number awarded 5 to 8 students are placed at each institution.

Deadline January of each year.

[865]
MILLENDER FELLOWSHIP

Wayne State University
Attn: Associate Provost for Academic Programs
656 West Kirby
4116 Faculty/Administration Building
Detroit, MI 48202
(313) 577-2023   Fax: (313) 577-5666
Web: www.millenderfund.org/fellowship.htm

Purpose To provide professional experience in Detroit to minorities who recently earned a master's degree and are interested in preparing for a public service-oriented career.

Eligibility Prior affiliation with Wayne State University is not required. Eligibility is open to minorities who have a commitment to public service and can demonstrate a record of successful accomplishment in some graduate educational program and/or through equivalent experience. Applicants must have completed a master's degree (or have equivalent professional experience) by the start of the fellowship. Writing, research, computer, and Internet skills are important.

Financial data The stipend is $30,000 plus fringe benefits. Some funds may be available to assist with moving.

Duration 9 months; nonrenewable.

Additional information Funds for this program come from the Robert L. Millender Sr. Memorial Fund. Fellows work directly with top executives of major public or private nonprofit organizations in Detroit. Previous fellows have served in the office of the mayor of Detroit, Detroit Economic Growth Corporation, New Detroit Inc., Southeastern Michigan Council of Governments, and similar agencies. This program is modeled after the White House and Congressional Fellowship programs. Fellows must devote full time to their assignments. They must live in the Detroit metropolitan area for the duration of the program. A mid-year and a final report are required.

Number awarded 1 each year.

Deadline March of each year.

[866]
MINORITY ACCESS TO RESEARCH CAREERS (MARC) FACULTY SENIOR FELLOWSHIPS

National Institute of General Medical Sciences
Attn: Division of Minority Opportunities in Research
45 Center Drive, Suite 2AS37
Bethesda, MD 20892-6200
(301) 594-3900   Fax: (301) 480-2753
E-mail: at21z@nih.gov
Web: www.nih.gov/nigms

Purpose To provide funding for advanced research training to faculty members at academic institutions serving predominantly minority students.

Eligibility This program is open to full-time faculty at minority and minority serving institutions (such as Historically Black Colleges and Universities, Hispanic Service Institutions, and other institutions that have substantial enrollments of students from minority groups underrepresented in the biomedical sciences) that offer at least the baccalaureate degree in the biomedical and behavioral sciences, including mathematics. Applicants must have held their faculty position for at least 3 years and have received the Ph.D. or equivalent at least 7 years previously. They must be seeking additional training in a relevant science and must intend to return to their home institution after completion of their fellowship. The training may be at any nonprofit private or public institution in the United States with suitable facilities. Only U.S. citizens, nationals, and permanent residents are eligible. Support is not available to established independent investigators to receive training to increase their scientific capabilities or to postdoctoral investigators seeking to improve their research potential prior to becoming independent investigators

Financial data Annual stipends up to $51,036 are provided. An institutional allowance of up to $4,000 may also be requested to help defray costs directly related to the candidate's training.

Duration 9 to 12 months.

Number awarded Varies each year.

Deadline April or December of each year.

[867]
MINORITY DISSERTATION RESEARCH GRANTS IN AGING

National Institute on Aging
Attn: Office of Extramural Affairs
7201 Wisconsin Avenue, Room 2C-218
Bethesda, MD 20892-9205
(301) 496-9322   Fax: (301) 402-2945
E-mail: rb42h@nih.gov
Web: www.nih.gov/nia

Purpose To provide financial assistance to underrepresented minority doctoral students who wish to conduct research in the United States or abroad on aging.

Eligibility This program is open to doctoral candidates conducting research on a dissertation with an aging-related focus, including the 4 extramural programs within the National Institute on Aging (NIA): the biology of aging program, the behavioral and social research program, the neuroscience and neuropsychology of aging program, and the geriatrics and clinical gerontology program. Applicants must be members of a particular ethnic or racial group that has been determined by their institution to be underrepresented in biomedical or behavioral research, including African Americans, Hispanic Americans, Native Americans, Alaskan Natives, and Pacific Islanders. Only U.S. citizens, nationals, and permanent residents are eligible. The applicant organization must be a domestic college or university supporting doctoral training, although the performance site may be foreign or domestic.

Financial data Direct costs may not exceed $30,000 in total or $25,000 in any single year. The institution may receive up to 8% of direct costs as facilities and administrative costs per year.

Duration Up to 2 years.

Number awarded 5 or 6 each year.
Deadline March or November of each year.

[868]
MINORITY FACULTY FELLOWSHIP PROGRAM

Indiana University
Attn: Minority Faculty Fellowship Program
Memorial Hall West, Room 108
1021 East Third Street
Bloomington, IN 47405-7005
(812) 855-0542   Fax: (812) 856-5477
E-mail: mffp@indiana.edu
Web: www.indiana.edu/~mffp

Purpose To aid in recruiting outstanding underrepresented minority faculty to the Indiana University campus and to identify minority scholars who might be available for longer-term positions.
Eligibility African American, U.S. Latino(a), and Native American scholars who either are nearing completion of the doctorate or have completed the doctorate within the last 4 years are encouraged to apply for this appointment at Indiana University. The program seeks candidates who have demonstrated a strong commitment to scholarly research and creative teaching. U.S. citizenship or permanent resident status is required.
Financial data The fellowship package includes a salary equivalent to that ordinarily paid to an Indiana University faculty member of the same rank, plus a $4,000 stipend for research and living expenses.
Duration Summer months or academic year.
Additional information The program was established in 1986. Summer fellows teach 1 or 2 courses. Academic-year fellows teach in the fall and spring terms.
Number awarded Up to 10 each year.
Deadline November of each year.

[869]
MINORITY MEDICAL STUDENT SUMMER EXTERNSHIP IN ADDICTION PSYCHIATRY

American Psychiatric Association
Attn: Department of Minority and National Affairs
1000 Wilson Boulevard, Suite 1825
Arlington, VA 22209-3901
(703) 907-8653   Toll-free: (888) 35-PSYCH
Fax: (703) 907-7852   E-mail: mking@psych.org
Web: www.psych.org

Purpose To provide funding to minority medical students who are interested in working on a research project during the summer with a mentor who specializes in addiction psychiatry.
Eligibility This program is open to minority medical students who have a specific interest in services related to substance abuse treatment and prevention. Minorities include American Indians, Alaska Natives, Native Hawaiians, Asian Americans, Hispanic/Latinos, and African Americans. Applicants must be interested in working with a mentor who specializes in addiction psychiatry. Work settings provide an emphasis on working clinically with or studying underserved minority populations and issues of co-occurring disorders, substance abuse treatment, and mental health disparity. Most of them are in inner-city or rural settings.

Financial data Externships provide $1,500 for travel expenses to go to the work setting of the mentor and up to another $1,500 for out-of-pocket expenses directly related to the conduct of the externship.
Duration 1 month during the summer.
Additional information Funding for this program is provided by the Substance Abuse and Mental Health Services Administration (SAMHSA).
Number awarded 10 each year.
Deadline April of each year.

[870]
MINORITY NEUROSCIENCE POSTDOCTORAL FELLOWSHIP PROGRAM

Society for Neuroscience
Attn: Education Department
11 Dupont Circle, N.W., Suite 500
Washington, DC 20036
(202) 462-6688   Fax: (202) 462-9740
E-mail: info@sfn.org
Web: apu.sfn.org

Purpose To provide funding to minority postdoctoral fellows participating in mental health related neuroscience research and training programs.
Eligibility This program is open to postdoctoral fellows in neuroscience who are members of traditionally underrepresented racial and ethnic minority groups (African Americans, Hispanics, Native Americans, Alaskan Natives, Asians, and Pacific Islanders). Applicants must be U.S. citizens or permanent residents enrolled in a program of research and training to prepare for a career in neuroscience research laboratories. Along with their application, they must submit 2 academic letters of recommendation, a 1- to 2-page essay describing their area of interest and research goals in neuroscience, a 1- to 2-page essay describing how their career goals are consistent with the goals of the program to increase diversity in neuroscience, undergraduate and graduate transcripts, a current resume or curriculum vitae, copies of papers and abstracts they have authored or co-authored, a 1-page summary of their dissertation, and a biosketch of the home institution advisor (if available).
Financial data Fellows receive a stipend that is based on number of years of postdoctoral experience, in accordance with standard National Research Service Award guidelines (currently, ranging from $35,568 per year for no experience to $51,036 for 7 or more years). Other benefits include travel assistance and registration to attend the annual meeting of the Society for Neuroscience (SfN), enrichment programs that include funds to participate in activities outside the fellow's home laboratory, and mentoring opportunities with a mentor chosen from the SfN membership.
Duration 2 years, contingent upon adequate research progress and academic standing.
Additional information This program, established in 1991, is sponsored largely by the National Institute of Mental Health with additional support from the National Institute of Neurological Disorders and Stroke. Information is also available from Joanne Berger-Sweeney, Wellesley College, Department of Biological Sciences, 106 Central Street, Wellesley, MA 02481-8203, (781) 283-3503, Fax: (781) 283-3704, E-mail: mnfp@wellesley.edu.
Number awarded 5 each year.

Deadline March, August, or December of each year.

[871]
MINORITY NEUROSCIENCE PREDOCTORAL FELLOWSHIP PROGRAM

Society for Neuroscience
Attn: Education Department
11 Dupont Circle, N.W., Suite 500
Washington, DC 20036
(202) 462-6688   Fax: (202) 462-9740
E-mail: info@sfn.org
Web: apu.sfn.org

Purpose To provide funding to minority graduate students participating in mental health related neuroscience research and training programs.

Eligibility This program is open to doctoral students in neuroscience who are members of traditionally underrepresented racial and ethnic minority groups (African Americans, Hispanics, Native Americans, Alaskan Natives, Asians, and Pacific Islanders). Applicants must be U.S. citizens or permanent residents enrolled in a program of research and training to prepare for a career in neuroscience research laboratories. Along with their application, they must submit 2 academic letters of recommendation, a 1- to 2-page essay describing their area of interest and research goals in neuroscience, a 1- to 2-page essay describing how their career goals are consistent with the goals of the program to increase diversity in neuroscience, undergraduate and graduate transcripts, a current resume or curriculum vitae, copies of papers and abstracts they have authored or co-authored, and a biosketch of the home institution advisor (if available).

Financial data Fellows receive a stipend in accordance with standard National Research Service Award guidelines (currently, $20,772 per year). Other benefits include travel assistance and registration to attend the annual meeting of the Society for Neuroscience (SfN), enrichment programs that include funds to participate in activities outside the fellow's home laboratory, and mentoring opportunities with a mentor chosen from the SfN membership.

Duration 3 years, contingent upon adequate research progress and academic standing.

Additional information This program, established in 1991, is sponsored largely by the National Institute of Mental Health with additional support from the National Institute of Neurological Disorders and Stroke. Information is also available from Joanne Berger-Sweeney, Wellesley College, Department of Biological Sciences, 106 Central Street, Wellesley, MA 02481-8203, (781) 283-3503, Fax: (781) 283-3704, E-mail: mnfp@wellesley.edu.

Number awarded 12 each year.

Deadline August of each year.

[872]
MINORITY POSTDOCTORAL RESEARCH FELLOWSHIPS

National Science Foundation
Directorate for Biological Sciences
Attn: Division of Biological Infrastructure
4201 Wilson Boulevard, Room 615
Arlington, VA 22230
(703) 292-8470   TDD: (703) 292-5090
E-mail: ckimsey@nsf.gov
Web: www.nsf.gov/bio

Purpose To provide financial assistance for postdoctoral research training in the United States or abroad to underrepresented minority scientists in the biological, social, economic, and behavioral sciences.

Eligibility This program is open to U.S. citizens and permanent residents who will complete their doctorate within a year or have completed it within the previous 4 years but have not completed more than 2 years of postdoctoral support. Applicants must be a member of an ethnic group that is significantly underrepresented at advanced levels of science and engineering in the United States, including Native Americans (Alaska Natives and American Indians), African Americans, Hispanics, and Native Pacific Islanders. They must be proposing research training that falls within the program areas of the National Science Foundation (NSF) Directorate for Biological Sciences or the Directorate for Social, Behavioral, and Economic Sciences to be conducted at any appropriate nonprofit U.S. or foreign institution (government laboratory, institution of higher education, national laboratory, or public or private research institute), but not at the same institution where the doctorate was obtained.

Financial data The program provides a stipend of $36,000 per year, an institutional allowance of $5,000 for partial reimbursement of indirect research costs (space, equipment, general purpose supplies, and fringe benefits), and a special allowance of $9,000 for direct research costs (materials and supplies, subscription fees, and recovery costs for databases, travel, and publication expenses).

Duration 2 years; applicants who propose to spend their 2-year tenure at a foreign institution may apply for a third year of support at an appropriate U.S. institution.

Additional information Information on the programs from the Directorate for Social, Behavioral, and Economic Sciences is available at (703) 292-8763, E-mail: jperhoni@nsf.gov.

Number awarded Approximately 12 each year.

Deadline November of each year.

[873]
MISSILE DEFENSE AGENCY PILOT PROGRAM FOR SCIENCE AND TECHNOLOGY RESEARCH AT HISTORICALLY BLACK COLLEGES AND UNIVERSITIES AND MINORITY INSTITUTIONS

Missile Defense Agency
Attn: Office of the Advanced Systems (MDA/AS)
FOB 2, Navy Annex, Room 3704A
7100 Defense Pentagon
Washington, DC 20301-7100
(703) 697-3579   E-mail: external.affairs@mda.osd.mil
Web: www.mda.mil/mdalink/pdf/guide.pdf

Purpose To provide funding to investigators at Historically Black Colleges and Universities (HBCUs) and Minority Institutions (MIs) interested in conducting research related to the mission of the Missile Defense Agency (MDA).

Eligibility This program is open to investigators at HBCUs and MIs interested in conducting research in the following general areas: 1) sensing, imaging, ranging, and discrimination; 2) phenomenology studies for ballistic missile defense; 3) electronic and photonic materials and devices; 4) information processing and computing technologies; 5) directed energy and non-linear optical devices and processes; 6) miniature interceptor technology, propulsion, and kill enhancement; and 7) power generation and conditioning. Selection is based on anticipated benefits of the research effort to the MDA mission; scientific/technical quality of the research proposal and its relevance to the topic description; qualifications of the principal investigator, other key staff, and consultants; and adequacy of management planning and controls.

Financial data The maximum grant is $150,000 per year.

Duration 12 to 24 months.

Number awarded Varies each year.

Deadline December of each year.

[874]
MONTANA SPACE GRANT CONSORTIUM RESEARCH INITIATION GRANTS

Montana Space Grant Consortium
c/o Montana State University
261 EPS Building
P.O. Box 173835
Bozeman, MT 59717-3835
(406) 994-4223   Fax: (406) 994-4452
E-mail: msgc@montana.edu
Web: spacegrant.montana.edu

Purpose To provide seed money for research in Montana related to space sciences and engineering.

Eligibility This program is open to individuals in Montana (most of the awards go to full-time graduate students) who need support to conduct research related to space sciences and/or engineering. This program is part of the U.S. National Aeronautics and Space Administration (NASA) Space Grant program, which encourages participation by women, underrepresented minorities, and persons with disabilities.

Financial data These grants provide "seed money" only.

Duration 1 year; generally nonrenewable.

Additional information Awardees are required to submit a follow-on proposal to NASA for regular research funding during the year of the grant.

Number awarded Varies each year; recently, 4 of these grants were awarded.

[875]
MORE FACULTY DEVELOPMENT AWARDS

National Institute of General Medical Sciences
Attn: Division of Minority Opportunities in Research
45 Center Drive, Suite 2AS37
Bethesda, MD 20892-6200
(301) 594-3900   Fax: (301) 480-2753
E-mail: at21z@nih.gov
Web: www.nih.gov/nigms

Purpose To enable faculty at minority institutions to sharpen their research skills by spending intervals conducting full-time research in a research-intensive laboratory.

Eligibility Candidates for this program must have been full-time permanent faculty in a biomedically-related science (including behavioral science) or mathematics at the home institution for at least 3 years; have received the Ph.D. or equivalent at least 5 years before the date of the application; intend to remain at the home institution at the end of the training period; demonstrate a commitment to research and teaching in a minority institution; plan to conduct research in a science (including mathematics) related to biomedical or behavioral research; and be a citizen or permanent resident of the United States. The home institution must be a domestic private or public educational institution with a significant enrollment of underrepresented minorities, defined as African Americans, Hispanic Americans, Native Americans, and Pacific Islanders, that offers at least the baccalaureate degree in the biomedical or behavioral sciences or mathematics. The research institution is the university or other institution at which the candidate conducts full-time research and takes courses; the research institution may not be the same as the home institution.

Financial data Candidates may request a salary equal to their actual annual salary and appropriate fringe benefits prorated for the time during which they are engaged in full-time research (salary support is not provided for the time candidates are enrolled in academic courses); up to $3,000 per year for supplies, equipment, travel, and other costs directly related to their full-time research experience; and funds to pay tuition and fees for 1 course per academic term to be taken at the research institution. Any expected concurrent sabbatical or any other salary support for the proposed period in residence is taken into account. A travel allowance equivalent to round-trip coach airfare between the visiting scientist's home institution and the sponsoring institution is provided. The sponsoring institution may receive up to $3,000 as an allowance for costs of supplies, supporting services, and demonstration costs related to activities proposed for the visiting scientist.

Duration Research may be conducted at intervals over a period of 2 to 5 years.

Additional information The National Institute of General Medical Sciences, a component of the National Institutes of Health (NIH), operates this program as part of its Minority Opportunities for Research (MORE) Division.

Number awarded Varies each year.

Deadline January, May, or September of each year.

[876]
NASA FACULTY FELLOWSHIP PROGRAM

American Society for Engineering Education
Attn: Projects Department
1818 N Street, N.W., Suite 600
Washington, DC 20036-2479
(202) 331-3509   Fax: (202) 265-8504
E-mail: nasa@asee.org
Web: www.asee.org

Purpose To provide support to underrepresented minority and other faculty members in engineering and science who wish to conduct summer research at facilities of the National Aeronautics and Space Administration (NASA).

Eligibility This program is open to tenured or tenure-track faculty at 4-year institutions and full-time faculty at 2-year institutions. Applicants must be U.S. citizens who have a Ph.D. in an engineering, mathematics, or science discipline applicable to research and/or technology development needs of the National Aeronautics and Space Administration (NASA). They must be interested in conducting a summer research project at a participating NASA center. Faculty who participated in this program within the past 5 years, who have received more than $300,000 in NASA funding within the past 5 years, or who have received a NASA Faculty Awards for Research grant are not eligible. Women, underrepresented minorities, and persons with disabilities are strongly encouraged to apply. Selection is based on relevance and merit of the research (40%), qualifications of the faculty applicant (40%), and overall academic benefit to the faculty applicant and his or her institution (20%).

Financial data The stipend is $1,200 per week, for a maximum of $12,000. A relocation allowance of $1,500 is available for fellows who live more than 50 miles from their assigned center and reasonable travel expenses for a round-trip are also reimbursed for fellows who receive the relocation allowance. The maximum allowance for relocation and travel is $2,000. To facilitate the participation of individuals with disabilities, NASA provides up to $1,500 in supplemental funding for special assistance and/or equipment necessary to enable the principal investigator to perform the work under the award.

Duration 10 weeks during the summer.

Additional information Participating NASA centers are Ames Research Center (Moffett Field, California); Hugh L. Dryden Flight Research Facility (Edwards, California); Goddard Space Flight Center (Greenbelt, Maryland) and its Wallops Flight Facility (Wallops Island, Virginia) and Goddard Institute for Space Studies (New York, New York); Jet Propulsion Laboratory (Pasadena, California); Lyndon B. Johnson Space Center (Houston, Texas) and its White Sands Test Facility (Las Cruces, New Mexico); John F. Kennedy Space Center (Cape Canaveral, Florida); Langley Research Center (Hampton, Virginia); Glenn Research Center (Cleveland, Ohio); George C. Marshall Space Flight Center (Huntsville, Alabama); and John C. Stennis Space Center (Stennis Space Center, Mississippi). This program is funded by NASA and administered by the American Society for Engineering Education (ASEE) and the Universities Space Research Association (USRA).

Number awarded Varies each year.

Deadline January of each year.

[877]
NASA GRADUATE STUDENT RESEARCH PROGRAM

National Aeronautics and Space Administration
Attn: Office of Human Resources and Education
Code FE
Washington, DC 20546-0001
(202) 358-0402   Fax: (202) 358-3032
E-mail: kblanding@mail.hq.nasa.gov
Web: fellowships.hq.nasa.gov/gsrp/program

Purpose To provide funding to graduate students (particularly minorities, women, and students with disabilities) interested in conducting research in fields of interest to the U.S. National Aeronautics and Space Administration (NASA).

Eligibility This program is open to full-time students enrolled or planning to enroll in an accredited graduate program at a U.S. college or university. Applicants must be citizens of the United States, sponsored by a faculty advisor or department chair, and interested in conducting research in space sciences at their home university or at NASA field centers. Selection is based on academic qualifications, quality of the proposed research and its relevance to NASA's program, the student's proposed utilization of center research facilities (except for NASA headquarters), and ability of the student to accomplish the defined research. African Americans, Native Americans, Alaskan Natives, Mexican Americans, Puerto Ricans, Native Pacific Islanders, women, and persons with disabilities are strongly urged to apply.

Financial data The program provides a $18,000 student stipend, a $3,000 student expense allowance, and a $3,000 university allowance.

Duration 1 year; may be renewed for up to 2 additional years.

Additional information This program was established in 1980. Awards for NASA Headquarters are sponsored by the Office of Space Science (OSS), the Office of Biological and Physical Research (OBPR), and the Office of Earth Science (OES). The areas of interest include structure/evolution of the universe, origins/planetary systems, solar system exploration, sun-earth connection, information systems, microgravity science and applications, life sciences, and earth sciences. Fellows selected by NASA Headquarters conduct research at their respective universities. Other awards are distributed through NASA field centers, each of which has its own research agenda and facilities. These centers include Ames Research Center (Moffett Field, California), Dryden Flight Research Facility (Edwards, California), Goddard Space Flight Center (Greenbelt, Maryland), Jet Propulsion Laboratory (Pasadena, California), Johnson Space Center (Houston, Texas), Kennedy Space Center (Kennedy Space Center, Florida), Langley Research Center (Hampton, Virginia), Glenn Research Center (Cleveland, Ohio), Marshall Space Flight Center (Huntsville, Alabama), and Stennis Space Center (Stennis Space Center, Mississippi). Fellows spend some period of time in residence at the center, taking advantage of the unique research facilities of the installation and working with center personnel. Travel outside the United States is allowed if it is essential to the research effort and charged to a grant.

Number awarded This program supports approximately 300 graduate students each year.

Deadline　January of each year.

[878]
NATIONAL CANCER INSTITUTE TRANSITION CAREER DEVELOPMENT AWARD TO PROMOTE DIVERSITY

National Cancer Institute
Attn: Comprehensive Minority Biomedical Branch
6116 Executive Boulevard, Suite 7031
Bethesda, MD 20892-8350
(301) 496-7344　　　　　Fax: (301) 402-4551
TTY: (301) 451-0088　　　E-mail: ba101m@nih.gov
Web: www.nci.nih.gov

Purpose　To provide funding to underrepresented scientists who are transitioning from a mentored research environment to an independent research and academic career.

Eligibility　This program is open to U.S. citizens, nationals, and permanent residents who 1) have a research or a health professional doctorate or equivalent; 2) have been in or currently are in a "mentored" research postdoctoral position and have completed 2 years or more of research in that capacity; and 3) intend to conduct a research project highly relevant to cancer biology, etiology, pathogenesis, prevention, diagnosis, and treatment that has the potential for establishing an independent research program. Candidates must be sponsored by a domestic, nonprofit or for-profit organization, public or private (such as a university, college, hospital, laboratory, unit of state or local government, or eligible agency of the federal government) that can demonstrate a commitment to the development of the research careers of junior underrepresented minority research scientists in biomedical cancer research. They must qualify as an underrepresented minority individual, defined as members of a particular ethnic, racial, or other group determined by their institution to be underrepresented in biomedical, behavioral, clinical, or social sciences, e.g., first generation college students or graduates, socio-economically disadvantaged persons, or persons with disabilities.

Financial data　The award provides salary up to $75,000 per year plus related fringe benefits. In addition, up to $50,000 per year is provided for the following types of expenses: research expenses, such as supplies, equipment, and technical personnel; statistical services, including personnel and computer time; tuition, fees, and books related to career development; and travel to research meetings or for training. Facilities and administrative costs are reimbursed at 8% of modified total direct costs.

Duration　Up to 3 years.

Additional information　Recipients must devote at least 75% of their full-time professional effort to cancer-related research and peer review activities. The remaining 25% can be divided among other activities only if they are consistent with the program goals, i.e., the candidate's development into an independent investigator.

Number awarded　Approximately 10 each year.

Deadline　January, May, or September of each year.

[879]
NATIONAL CENTER FOR ATMOSPHERIC RESEARCH POSTDOCTORAL APPOINTMENTS

National Center for Atmospheric Research
Attn: Advanced Study Program
1850 Table Mesa Drive
P.O. Box 3000
Boulder, CO 80307-3000
(303) 497-1598　　　　　Fax: (303) 497-1328
E-mail: paulad@ucar.edu
Web: www.asp.ucar.edu/asp/pdann.html

Purpose　To provide funding to recent Ph.D.s (particularly minorities and women) who wish to conduct research at the National Center for Atmospheric Research (NCAR) in Boulder, Colorado.

Eligibility　This program is open to recent Ph.D.s and Sc.D.s in applied mathematics, chemistry, engineering, and physics as well as specialists in atmospheric sciences from such disciplines as biology, economics, geography, geology, and science education. Applicants must be interested in conducting research at the center in atmospheric sciences and global change. Selection is based on the applicant's scientific capability and potential, originality and independence, and ability to take advantage of the research opportunities at center. Applications from women and minorities are encouraged.

Financial data　The stipend is $46,000 in the first year and $47,000 in the second year. Fellows also receive life and health insurance, a relocation allowance (up to $1,000 for travel within the United States or up to $2,500 for travel from abroad), and scientific travel reimbursement up to $1,500 per year.

Duration　2 years.

Additional information　NCAR is operated by the University Corporation for Atmospheric Research (a consortium of 61 universities) and sponsored by the National Science Foundation.

Number awarded　Varies; currently, 7 to 10 each year.

Deadline　January of each year.

[880]
NATIONAL EDUCATIONAL ENRICHMENT PROGRAM FOR MINORITY GRADUATE STUDENTS FELLOWSHIP IN GERONTOLOGY

National Hispanic Council on Aging
2713 Ontario Road, N.W.
Washington, DC 20009
(202) 745-2521　　　　　Fax: (202) 745-2222
E-mail: nhcoa@nhcoa.org
Web: www.nhcoa.org/andrus_foundation.htm

Purpose　To provide funding to graduate students from underrepresented minority groups interested in conducting research and attending a seminar about current developments related to elderly minorities.

Eligibility　This program is open to Latino, African American, and Native American graduate students. Applicants must be interested in participating in a program that includes 1) research activities at their home academic institutions or another campus, and 2) a seminar at the sponsoring organization.

Financial data Fellows receive a $2,000 stipend, travel and per diem for the seminar, and reimbursement for books and other approved expenses.

Duration 2 months, including 1 week for the seminar in Washington, D.C.

Additional information The seminar includes study of the policy-making process, the resource allocation process in relation to minority aging, a review of research being conducted presently that addresses issues of minority elderly, the research topic of each fellow, and an examination of leadership roles that future minority gerontologists must assume to improve the quality of life for minority elderly. This program is jointly sponsored by the National Caucus and Center on Black Aged, the National Hispanic Council on Aging, and the National Indian Council on Aging. Funding is provided by the Andrus Foundation of the American Association of Retired Persons

Number awarded 9 each year: 3 selected by each sponsoring organization.

[881]
NATIONAL ESTUARINE RESEARCH RESERVE SYSTEM GRADUATE FELLOWSHIPS

National Oceanic and Atmospheric Administration
Office of Ocean and Coastal Resource Management
Attn: Estuarine Reserves Division
Silver Spring Metro Center Building 4, 11th Floor
1305 East-West Highway
Silver Spring, MD 20910
(301) 713-3155, ext. 172   Fax: (301) 713-4363
E-mail: susan.white@noaa.gov
Web: nerrs.noaa.gov/Fellowship

Purpose To provide funding to minority and other graduate students interested in conducting research within National Estuarine Research Reserves.

Eligibility This program is open to students admitted to or enrolled in a full-time master's or doctoral program at U.S. accredited universities. Applicants should have completed a majority of their course work at the beginning of their fellowship and have an approved thesis research program focused on improving coastal zone management while providing hands-on training in conducting ecological monitoring. Proposed research topics must address 1 of the following topics: 1) eutrophiation, effects of non-point source pollution and/or nutrient dynamics; 2) habitat conservation and/or restoration; 3) biodiversity and/or the effects of invasive species on estuarine ecosystems; 4) mechanisms for sustaining resources within estuarine ecosystems; or 5) economic, sociological, and/or anthropological research applicable to estuarine ecosystem management. They must be willing to conduct their research within the National Estuarine Research Reserves. Minority students are encouraged to apply.

Financial data The amount of the fellowship is $20,000; at least 30% of total project cost match is required by the applicant (i.e., $7,500 match for a total project cost of $27,000). Requested overhead costs are limited to 10% of the federal amount. Waived overhead costs may be used as match. Funds may be used for any combination of research support, salary, tuition, supplies, or other costs as needed, including overhead.

Duration 1 to 3 years.

Additional information For a list of the National Estuarine Research Reserves, with the name and address of a contact person at each, write to the sponsor. Fellows are required to work with the research coordinator or manager at the host reserve to develop a plan to participate in the reserve's research and/or monitoring program for up to 15 hours per week.

Number awarded Approximately 27 each year.

Deadline October of each year.

[882]
NCI MENTORED PATIENT-ORIENTED RESEARCH FOR UNDERREPRESENTED MINORITIES

National Cancer Institute
Attn: Comprehensive Minority Biomedical Branch
6116 Executive Boulevard, Suite 7031
Bethesda, MD 20892-8350
(301) 496-7344   Fax: (301) 402-4551
TTY: (301) 451-0088   E-mail: ba101m@nih.gov
Web: www.nci.nih.gov

Purpose To provide funding to underrepresented minorities who are interested in a program of research training in patient-oriented oncology under the supervision of an experienced mentor.

Eligibility This program is open to U.S. citizens, nationals, and permanent residents who have a health professional doctorate and are committed to a career in patient-oriented cancer research. Candidates must be sponsored by a domestic, nonprofit or for-profit organization, public or private (such as a university, college, hospital, laboratory, unit of state or local government, or eligible agency of the federal government) that can demonstrate a commitment to the development of the research careers of junior underrepresented minority research scientists in clinical oncology. They must qualify as an underrepresented minority individual, defined as members of a particular ethnic, racial, or other group determined by their institution to be underrepresented in biomedical and behavioral research, e.g., first generation college students or graduates, socio-economically disadvantaged persons, or persons with disabilities. At least 2 mentors are required: 1 who is recognized as an accomplished clinical investigator and at least 1 additional mentor or advisor who is recognized as an accomplished independent basic science investigator in the proposed research area.

Financial data The award provides salary up to $75,000 per year plus related fringe benefits. In addition, up to $30,000 per year is provided for the following types of expenses: tuition, fees, and books related to career development; research expenses, such as supplies, equipment, and technical personnel; statistical services, including personnel and computer time; tuition, fees, and books related to career development; and travel to research meetings or for training. Facilities and administrative costs are reimbursed at 8% of modified total direct costs.

Duration Up to 5 years.

Additional information Recipients must devote at least 75% of their full-time professional effort to cancer-related research and training activities.

Number awarded Varies each year.

Deadline January, May, or September of each year.

[883]
NEUROFIBROMATOSIS RESEARCH PROGRAM CLINICAL TRIAL AWARDS

U.S. Army
Medical Research and Materiel Command
Attn: MCMR-ZB-C
1077 Patchel Street (Building 1077)
Fort Detrick, MD 21702-5024
(301) 619-7079   Fax: (301) 619-7792
E-mail: cdmrp.pa@det.amedd.army.mil
Web: cdmrp.army.mil

Purpose To provide funding to minority and other scientists interested in conducting clinical research on neurofibromatosis.

Eligibility This program is open to researchers at all academic levels at universities, colleges, hospitals, laboratories, companies, and agencies of local, state, and federal governments. The sponsor is especially interested in receiving applications from Historically Black Colleges and Universities and Minority Institutions (HBCU/MI). Applicants must be interested in conducting clinical research that has the potential to improve today's approach to the treatment and/or management of neurofibromatosis and/or Schwannomatosis. Phase I clinical trials should focus on determining the safety, toxicity, tolerability, and pharmacokinetics or pharmacodynamics of new interventions, devices, or treatment schedules in humans; applicants for those trials must include a clear scientific rationale for the trial as well as adequate preclinical supplemental data to support the feasibility of their hypotheses and approaches. Phase II clinical trials should focus on defining the efficacy of new interventions or devices; applicants for those trials must include Phase I or pilot clinical trial data, adequate preclinical supplemental data to support the feasibility of their hypotheses and approaches, and a detailed plan for completion. All areas of laboratory, clinical, behavioral, and epidemiological research and eligible, including all disciplines within the basic, clinical, psychosocial, behavioral, sociocultural, and environmental sciences; nursing; occupational health; alternative therapies; public health and policy; and economics. Proposals that address the needs of minority, low-income, rural, and other underrepresented and/or medically underserved populations are especially encouraged.

Financial data The grant depends on the nature of the proposal. Approximately $2.8 million is available for this program each year. Institutions are expected to cost share.

Duration Up to 3 years for Phase I clinical trials; up to 4 years for Phase II clinical trials.

Additional information The Neurofibromatosis Research Program was established in 1996 as part of the Congressionally Directed Medical Research Programs of the U.S. Department of Defense.

Number awarded 1 or 2 each year.

Deadline February of each year.

[884]
NEUROFIBROMATOSIS RESEARCH PROGRAM CONCEPT AWARDS

U.S. Army
Medical Research and Materiel Command
Attn: MCMR-ZB-C
1077 Patchel Street (Building 1077)
Fort Detrick, MD 21702-5024
(301) 619-7079   Fax: (301) 619-7792
E-mail: cdmrp.pa@det.amedd.army.mil
Web: cdmrp.army.mil

Purpose To provide funding to minority and other scientists interested in conducting preliminary research on neurofibromatosis.

Eligibility This program is open to researchers at all academic levels at universities, colleges, hospitals, laboratories, companies, and agencies of local, state, and federal governments. The sponsor is especially interested in receiving applications from Historically Black Colleges and Universities and Minority Institutions (HBCU/MI). Applicants must be interested in conducting research that explores untested, high-risk questions relevant to neurofibromatosis and/or Schwannomatosis. Projects are not intended to support the next step in an already established research project and do not require presentation pr preliminary data. All areas of laboratory, clinical, behavioral, and epidemiological research and eligible, including all disciplines within the basic, clinical, psychosocial, behavioral, sociocultural, and environmental sciences; nursing; occupational health; alternative therapies; public health and policy; and economics. Concepts from such complementary areas of science as chemistry, biophysics, mathematics, and engineering are encouraged. Proposals that address the needs of minority, low-income, rural, and other underrepresented and/or medically underserved populations are especially welcome.

Financial data The maximum grant is $100,000, including both direct and indirect costs. Institutions are expected to cost share.

Duration 1 year.

Additional information The Neurofibromatosis Research Program was established in 1996 as part of the Congressionally Directed Medical Research Programs of the U.S. Department of Defense.

Number awarded 10 each year.

Deadline February of each year.

[885]
NEUROFIBROMATOSIS RESEARCH PROGRAM INVESTIGATOR-INITIATED RESEARCH AWARDS

U.S. Army
Medical Research and Materiel Command
Attn: MCMR-ZB-C
1077 Patchel Street (Building 1077)
Fort Detrick, MD 21702-5024
(301) 619-7079   Fax: (301) 619-7792
E-mail: cdmrp.pa@det.amedd.army.mil
Web: cdmrp.army.mil

Purpose To provide funding to minority and other established scientists interested in conducting research on neurofibromatosis.

Eligibility This program is open to independent investigators at the level of assistant professor or higher at universities, colleges, hospitals, laboratories, companies, and agencies of local, state, and federal governments. The sponsor is especially interested in receiving applications from Historically Black Colleges and Universities and Minority Institutions (HBCU/MI). Applicants must be interested in conducting basic or clinical research that will 1) provide insight into the molecular mechanisms underlying the development of neurofibromatosis and related diseases; 2) result in substantial improvement over today's approach to the diagnosis and treatment of neurofibromatosis and/or Schwannomatosis; and 3) enhance the quality of life for persons with those diseases. All areas of laboratory, clinical, behavioral, and epidemiological research and eligible, including all disciplines within the basic, clinical, psychosocial, behavioral, sociocultural, and environmental sciences; nursing; occupational health; alternative therapies; public health and policy; and economics. Proposals that address the needs of minority, low-income, rural, and other underrepresented and/or medically underserved populations are especially welcome.

Financial data The maximum grant is $2 million, including both direct and indirect costs. Institutions are expected to cost share.

Duration 4 years.

Additional information The Neurofibromatosis Research Program was established in 1996 as part of the Congressionally Directed Medical Research Programs of the U.S. Department of Defense.

Number awarded 2 or 3 each year.

Deadline February of each year.

[886]
NEUROFIBROMATOSIS RESEARCH PROGRAM NEW INVESTIGATOR AWARDS

U.S. Army
Medical Research and Materiel Command
Attn: MCMR-ZB-C
1077 Patchel Street (Building 1077)
Fort Detrick, MD 21702-5024
(301) 619-7079   Fax: (301) 619-7792
E-mail: cdmrp.pa@det.amedd.army.mil
Web: cdmrp.army.mil

Purpose To provide funding to minority and other junior scientists interested in developing their expertise in neurofibromatosis.

Eligibility This program is open to independent investigators below the level of assistant professor at universities, colleges, hospitals, laboratories, companies, and agencies of local, state, and federal governments. The sponsor is especially interested in receiving applications from Historically Black Colleges and Universities and Minority Institutions (HBCU/MI). Applicants must be interested in conducting projects that will assist them in becoming established neurofibromatosis researchers. Proposals do not require preliminary data, but they should be based on a sound scientific rationale established through a critical review and analysis of the literature and/or logical reasoning. All areas of laboratory, clinical, behavioral, and epidemiological research and eligible, including all disciplines within the basic, clinical, psychosocial, behavioral, sociocultural, and environmental sciences; nursing; occupational health; alternative therapies; public health and policy; and economics.

Proposals that address the needs of minority, low-income, rural, and other underrepresented and/or medically underserved populations are especially welcome.

Financial data The grant is $150,000 per year in direct costs. Institutions are expected to cost share.

Duration 3 years.

Additional information The Neurofibromatosis Research Program was established in 1996 as part of the Congressionally Directed Medical Research Programs of the U.S. Department of Defense.

Number awarded 2 or 3 each year.

Deadline February of each year.

[887]
NEW YORK PUBLIC LIBRARY FELLOWSHIPS

American Council of Learned Societies
Attn: Office of Fellowships and Grants
633 Third Avenue, 8C
New York, NY 10017-6795
(212) 697-1505   Fax: (212) 949-8058
E-mail: grants@acls.org
Web: www.acls.org/felguide.htm

Purpose To provide funding to postdoctorates (particularly minorities and women) interested in conducting research at the Dorothy and Lewis B. Cullman Center for Scholars and Writers of the New York Public Library.

Eligibility Applicants must be U.S. citizens or permanent residents who hold a Ph.D. degree and have not held supported research leave time for at least 3 years prior to the start of the proposed research. Applicants must be interested in conducting research in the humanities and humanities-related social sciences at the New York Public Library's Dorothy and Lewis B. Cullman Center for Scholars and Writers. Applications are particularly invited from women and members of minority groups.

Financial data Fellowships provide a maximum stipend of $50,000 and, if necessary, a housing allowance to enable the fellow to live in New York during the fellowship term.

Duration 9 months, beginning in September

Additional information This program was first offered for 1999-2000, the inaugural year of the center. Candidates must also submit a separate application that is available from the New York Public Library, Humanities and Social Sciences Library, Dorothy and Lewis B. Cullman Center for Scholars and Writers, Fifth Avenue and 42nd Street, New York, NY 10018-2788, E-mail: csw@nypl.org. Fellows are required to be in continuous residence at the center and participate actively in its activities and programs.

Number awarded Up to 5 each year.

Deadline September of each year.

[888]
NEW YORK SEA GRANT AND HUDSON RIVER NATIONAL ESTUARINE RESEARCH RESERVE COOPERATIVE RESEARCH FELLOWSHIP

New York Sea Grant
Attn: Nordica Holochuck, Extension Specialist
10 Westbrook Lane
Kingston, NY 12401-3824
(845) 340-3983   E-mail: nch8@cornell.edu
Web: www.seagrant/sunysb.edu

Purpose To provide funding for master's and doctoral candidates (particularly minorities) who are working on a thesis related to the Hudson River.

Eligibility This program is open to master's and doctoral candidates who are seeking funding for thesis research related to the Hudson River. Although they are preferred, the fellowship is not limited to students in New York state. Minority students are especially encouraged to submit applications. Although research in other areas relevant to the missions of the sponsors may be submitted, proposals that emphasize 1 or more of the following 4 areas are given priority: 1) develop evaluation techniques to measure restoration success and/or remediation techniques to restore disturbed coastal environments and habitat; 2) determine functional impacts/importance of introduced and native species on estuarine wetland ecosystem functioning and develop effective detection and control mechanisms; 3) identify and/or evaluate anthropogenic effects on estuarine wetland ecosystem functions; and 4) identify and/or evaluate relationships between wetland ecosystems and the drainage basin.

Financial data The stipend is $14,000 per year. Another $2,000 per year is provided to cover operational costs (e.g., travel costs and supplies).

Duration 2 years, beginning between June 1 and September 1 of each year.

Additional information This program is jointly sponsored by the New York Sea Grant and the Hudson River National Estuarine Research Reserve. Information is also available from Charles Nieder, Research Coordinator, Hudson River National Estuarine Research Reserve, New York State Department of Environmental Conservation, c/o Bard College Field Station, Annandale, NY 12504, (845) 758-7013, E-mail: wcnieder@gw.dec.state.ny.us. Recipients must submit a 6-month progress report and a final report. They must also make a final oral presentation and/or a poster of research results.

Number awarded 1 each year.

Deadline February of each year.

[889]
NHLBI MENTORED MINORITY FACULTY DEVELOPMENT AWARD

National Heart, Lung, and Blood Institute
Attn: Division of Epidemiology and Clinical Applications
6701 Rockledge Drive, Room 8158
Bethesda, MD 20892-7934
(301) 435-0709   Fax: (301) 480-1667
E-mail: ls32t@nih.gov
Web: www.nhlbi.nih.gov

Purpose To provide funding to underrepresented minority faculty members interested in developing into independent biomedical investigators in research areas relevant to the mission of the National Heart, Lung, and Blood Institute (NHLBI).

Eligibility This program is open to faculty members at U.S. domestic institutions (universities, colleges, hospitals, laboratories, units of state and local governments, and eligible agencies of the federal government) who have a doctoral degree or equivalent in the biomedical or behavioral sciences. Candidates must be members of a particular ethnic or racial group that their institution has determined to be underrepresented in biomedical or behavioral research, including African Americans/Blacks, Hispanics, American Indians, Alaska Natives, and non-Asian Pacific Islanders. They must 1) be U.S. citizens, nationals, or permanent residents; 2) have completed their doctoral degree at least 2 years previously; 3) have at least 1 year of documented research experience; and 4) have identified a sponsor who is an accomplished investigator in the proposed research area and has experience in developing independent investigators. The proposed research development plan must enable the candidate to become an independent investigator in cardiovascular, pulmonary, hematologic, and sleep disorders research with either a clinical or basic science emphasis.

Financial data The awardee receives salary support of up to $75,000 per year plus fringe benefits. Support for up to 5% of the sponsor's salary may also be requested. In addition, up to $30,000 per year may be provided for research project requirements and related support (e.g., technical personnel costs, supplies, equipment, candidate travel, telephone charges, publication costs, and tuition for necessary courses). Facilities and administrative costs may be reimbursed at the rate of 8% of total direct costs.

Duration 3 to 5 years.

Additional information At least 75% of the awardee's effort must be devoted to the research program. The remainder may be devoted to other clinical and teaching pursuits that are consistent with the program goals of developing the awardee into an independent biomedical scientist or the maintenance of the teaching and/or clinical skills needed for an academic research career.

Number awarded Varies each year; recently, 10 to 12 awards were available through this program with total funding of $1,200,000.

Deadline June of each year.

[890]
NINR MENTORED RESEARCH SCIENTIST DEVELOPMENT AWARD FOR MINORITY INVESTIGATORS

National Institute of Nursing Research
Attn: Division of Extramural Research
6701 Democracy Boulevard, Room 710
Bethesda, MD 20892-4870
(301) 594-6152   Fax: (301) 480-8260
E-mail: janice.phillips@nih.gov
Web: www.nih.gov/ninr

Purpose To provide funding for research career development to postdoctoral nursing investigators who are members of underrepresented minority groups.

Eligibility This program is open to full-time nursing faculty members at Traditionally Minority Based Institutions

(TMBIs) as well as other universities, colleges, hospitals, and laboratories. Candidates must be U.S. citizens, nationals, or permanent residents from ethnic/racial groups determined by their institution to be underrepresented in biomedical or behavioral nursing research. They must have a research or health-professional doctorate (e.g., Ph.D., D.N.Sc.) or its equivalent; have demonstrated the capacity or potential for a productive independent research career; have a Registered Nurse license; and have secured the commitment of an appropriate research mentor actively involved in research relevant to the mission of the National Institute of Nursing Research (NINR). Proposals must include both a research plan and a research career development plan that will develop knowledge and research skills relevant to the candidate's career goals. The TMBI or majority academic institution must demonstrate a firm commitment to the development of the applicant as a productive, independent investigator in nursing research and to the pursuit of the research career development plan. The candidate should describe a career development program that will maximize use of relevant research and educational resources available in the TMBI or majority academic institution and in the mentor's institution.

Financial data The grant provides up to $50,000 per year for salary and fringe benefits plus an additional $20,000 per year for such other expenses as tuition, fees, and books related to career development; research expenses, such as supplies, equipment, and technical personnel; travel to research meetings or trainings; and statistical services, including personnel, research, and computer time. Facilities and administrative costs are allowed at 8% of total direct costs.

Duration 3 years.

Additional information These grants have been awarded annually since 1998. Grantees are expected to spend at least 75% of their professional effort time to the program and the other 25% devoted to other research-related and/or teaching or clinical pursuits consistent with the objectives of the award.

Number awarded 3 to 4 new grants are awarded each year.

Deadline October of each year.

[891]
NMSGC K-12 EDUCATION ENHANCEMENT PROGRAM

New Mexico Space Grant Consortium
c/o New Mexico State University
Wells Hall, Bay 4
MSC SG, Box 30001
Las Cruces, NM 88003-0001
(505) 646-6414   Fax: (505) 646-7791
E-mail: nmsgc@pathfinder.nmsu.edu
Web: spacegrant.nmsu.edu

Purpose To provide support for the development of space-related academic programs to minority and other teachers and staff at K-12 schools in New Mexico.

Eligibility This program is open to teachers and staff at New Mexico public and private who are seeking funding for project-based curriculum development in the science, mathematics, and technology areas. Courses must be part of the regular academic program, such as physics, calculus,

or principles of technology. They should 1) focus on involving women, underrepresented groups, and persons with disabilities in all aspects of education, including preparing them to enter higher education institutions in programs for science, mathematics, engineering, and technical fields; 2) develop instructional technology, technology transfer, and other technological courses that use emerging technology developed by the U.S. National Aeronautics and Space Administration (NASA) in the space, aerospace, aeronautics, and launch-related areas; and 3) enhance or improve student retention and achievement. All teachers, staff, and students who receive support for this program must be U.S. citizens. The New Mexico Space Grant Consortium (NMSGC) is a component of the NASA Space Grant program, which encourages participation by women, underrepresented minorities, and persons with disabilities.

Financial data Grants range from $1,000 to $20,000. Institutions must provide 120% nonfederal matching funds.

Duration Up to 1 year.

Additional information This program is funded by NASA.

Number awarded Varies each year.

Deadline November of each year.

[892]
NMSGC RESEARCH OPPORTUNITIES AWARDS PROGRAM

New Mexico Space Grant Consortium
c/o New Mexico State University
Wells Hall, Bay 4
MSC SG, Box 30001
Las Cruces, NM 88003-0001
(505) 646-6414   Fax: (505) 646-7791
E-mail: nmsgc@pathfinder.nmsu.edu
Web: spacegrant.nmsu.edu

Purpose To provide funding for space-related research to underrepresented minority and other faculty at institutions that are members of the New Mexico Space Grant Consortium (NMSGC).

Eligibility This program is open to faculty at NMSGC institutions who do not currently have research support. Proposals may include, but are not limited to, the KC-135 Project, pre-proposal visits to a field center of the U.S. National Aeronautics and Space Administration (NASA), support for an undergraduate or graduate student to join a faculty member at a field center for part of a summer term, support to develop a new research project among scientists at several consortium campuses, and/or faculty summer support at facilities not covered by existing programs. All research must be space, aerospace, aeronautics, or launch related. All faculty, students, or staff who receive support for this program must be U.S. citizens. The NMSGC is a component of the NASA Space Grant program, which encourages participation by women, underrepresented minorities, and persons with disabilities.

Financial data Grants up to $15,000 are available.

Duration Up to 1 year.

Additional information The NMSGC institutional members are: New Mexico State University, New Mexico Institute of Mining and Technology, University of New Mexico, Doña Ana Branch Community College, and San Juan Community College. This program is funded by NASA.

Number awarded Varies each year.
Deadline November of each year.

[893]
NMSGC UNDERGRADUATE EDUCATION ENHANCEMENT PROGRAM

New Mexico Space Grant Consortium
c/o New Mexico State University
Wells Hall, Bay 4
MSC SG, Box 30001
Las Cruces, NM 88003-0001
(505) 646-6414   Fax: (505) 646-7791
E-mail: nmsgc@pathfinder.nmsu.edu
Web: spacegrant.nmsu.edu

Purpose To provide support for the development of space-related academic programs to underrepresented minority and other faculty at institutions that are members of the New Mexico Space Grant Consortium (NMSGC).

Eligibility This program is open to faculty at NMSGC institutions who are seeking funding for project-based course development, capstone courses, curriculum or course re-design, course re-design for web-based courses or distance education, and student retention and achievement programs in the undergraduate science, engineering, and technology areas. Courses must be part of the regular academic program in space, aerospace, aeronautics, and launch-related areas. They should focus on involving women, underrepresented groups, and persons with disabilities in all aspects of education, including fellowship awards, curriculum development, and degree programs in scientific, engineering, and technical fields. All faculty, staff, and students who receive support for this program must be U.S. citizens. The NMSGC is a component of the U.S. National Aeronautics and Space Administration (NASA) Space Grant program, which encourages participation by women, underrepresented minorities, and persons with disabilities.

Financial data Grants range from $1,000 to $15,000. Institutions must provide 120% nonfederal matching funds. Grants may be used to support faculty or staff release time, graduate and undergraduate student support, or travel related to the course. Funds may not be used to support tuition.

Duration Up to 1 year.

Additional information The NMSGC institutional members are: New Mexico State University, New Mexico Institute of Mining and Technology, University of New Mexico, Doña Ana Branch Community College, and San Juan Community College. This program is funded by NASA.

Number awarded Varies each year.

Deadline November of each year.

[894]
NORTH CAROLINA SPACE GRANT CONSORTIUM GRADUATE FELLOWSHIPS

North Carolina Space Grant Consortium
c/o North Carolina State University
Mechanical and Aerospace Engineering
1009 Capability Drive, Room 216E
Box 7515
Raleigh, NC 27695-7515
(919) 515-4240   Fax: (919) 515-5934
E-mail: space_grant@eos.ncsu.edu
Web: www.mae.ncsu.edu/spacegrant

Purpose To provide funding for space-related research during the summer to graduate students (especially minorities, women, and students with disabilities) at institutions affiliated with the North Carolina Space Grant Consortium (NCSGC).

Eligibility This program is open to full-time graduate students at institutions affiliated with the NCSGC. Applicants must be working on degrees in engineering or science disciplines of interest to the U.S. National Aeronautics and Space Administration (NASA) and have a GPA of 3.0 or higher. Selection is based on the quality of the research proposal (50%), relevance to space (25%), and academic achievement of the candidate (25%). U.S. citizenship or permanent resident status is required. A primary goal of this program is the recruitment and retention of underrepresented minorities, women, and the physically challenged into space-related fields.

Financial data The maximum grant is $7,500.

Duration Summer months.

Additional information The affiliated institutions are North Carolina State University, North Carolina A&T State University, Duke University, North Carolina Central University, the University of North Carolina at Charlotte, the University of North Carolina at Chapel Hill, the University of North Carolina at Pembroke, and Winston-Salem State University. This program is funded by NASA.

Number awarded At least 5 each year.

Deadline January of each year.

[895]
NORTH CAROLINA SPACE GRANT CONSORTIUM UNDERGRADUATE SCHOLARSHIPS

North Carolina Space Grant Consortium
c/o North Carolina State University
Mechanical and Aerospace Engineering
1009 Capability Drive, Room 216E
Box 7515
Raleigh, NC 27695-7515
(919) 515-4240   Fax: (919) 515-5934
E-mail: space_grant@eos.ncsu.edu
Web: www.mae.ncsu.edu/spacegrant

Purpose To provide funding for space-related research to undergraduate students (particularly minorities, women, and students with disabilities) at institutions affiliated with the North Carolina Space Grant Consortium (NCSGC).

Eligibility This program is open to full-time undergraduate students at institutions affiliated with the NCSGC. Applicants must be working on degrees in engineering or science disciplines of interest to the U.S. National Aeronautics and Space Administration (NASA) and have a GPA of 3.0 or greater. Selection is based on the quality of the research proposal (50%), relevance to space (25%), and academic achievement of the candidate (25%). U.S. citizenship or permanent resident status is required. A primary goal of this program is the recruitment and retention of underrepresented minorities, women, and the physically challenged into space-related fields.

Financial data The maximum grant is $5,000 for a summer project or $2,500 for an academic year project.

Duration 1 summer or 1 academic year.

Additional information The affiliated institutions are North Carolina State University, North Carolina A&T State University, Duke University, North Carolina Central University, the University of North Carolina at Charlotte, the University of North Carolina at Chapel Hill, the University of North Carolina at Pembroke, and Winston-Salem State University. This program is funded by NASA.

Number awarded At least 10 each year.

Deadline January of each year.

[896]
N.S. BIENSTOCK FELLOWSHIP

Radio and Television News Directors Foundation
1600 K Street, N.W., Suite 700
Washington, DC 20006-2838
(202) 467-5218							Fax: (202) 223-4007
E-mail: karenb@rtndf.org
Web: www.rtndf.org/asfi/fellowships/minority.html

Purpose To provide financial assistance for professional development to minority journalists employed in electronic news.

Eligibility This program is open to minority journalists employed in electronic news who have 10 years of less of full-time experience. Applications must include samples of the journalist's work done as the member of a news staff, with a script and tape (audio or video) up to 15 minutes.

Financial data The grant is $2,500 plus an all-expense paid trip to the international convention of the Radio-Television News Directors Association held that year.

Duration The grant is presented annually.

Additional information The grant, established in 1999, may be used in any way to improve the craft and enhance the excellence of the recipient's news operation.

Number awarded 1 each year.

Deadline April of each year.

[897]
NSF DIRECTOR'S AWARD FOR DISTINGUISHED TEACHING SCHOLARS

National Science Foundation
Directorate for Education and Human Resources
Attn: Division of Undergraduate Education
4201 Wilson Boulevard, Room 835N
Arlington, VA 22230
(703) 292-4627							Fax: (703) 292-9015
TDD: (703) 292-5090					E-mail: hlevitan@nsf.gov
Web: www.ehr.nsf.gov

Purpose To recognize and reward, with funding for additional research, minority and other scholars affiliated with institutions of higher education who have contributed to teaching of science, technology, engineering, and mathematics (STEM) at the K-12 and undergraduate level.

Eligibility This program is open to teaching-scholars affiliated with institutions of higher education who are nominated by their president, chief academic officer, or other independent researcher. Nominees should have integrated research and education and approached both education and research in a scholarly manner. They should have demonstrated leadership in their respective fields as well as innovativeness and effectiveness in facilitating K-12 and undergraduate student learning in STEM disciplines. Consideration is given to faculty who have a history of substantial impact on 1) research in a STEM discipline or on STEM educational research; or 2) the STEM education of K-16 students who have diverse interests and aspirations, including future K-12 teachers of science and mathematics, students who plan to pursue STEM careers, and those who need to understand science and mathematics in a society increasingly dependent on science and technology. Based on letters of nomination, selected scholars are invited to submit applications for support of their continuing efforts to integrate education and research. Nominations of women, underrepresented minorities, and persons with disabilities are especially encouraged.

Financial data The maximum grant is $300,000 for the life of the project.

Duration 4 years.

Number awarded Approximately 6 each year.

Deadline Preliminary proposals are due in November of each year; full applications must be submitted in February.

[898]
NUTRITION ACTION FELLOWSHIP

Center for Science in the Public Interest
Attn: Executive Director
1875 Connecticut Avenue, N.W., Suite 300
Washington, DC 20009-5728
(202) 332-9110							Fax: (202) 265-4954
E-mail: cspi@cspinet.org
Web: www.cspinet.org/job/nutrition_fellow.html

Purpose To provide funding to minority and other post-doctorates interested in serving as a nutrition advocate at the Center for Science in the Public Interest.

Eligibility This program is open to recent graduates with a Ph.D. or M.D. who are interested in serving as a nutrition advocate at the center. Applicants should have demonstrated interest in public interest advocacy and nutrition science, food safety, or health policy. They should also be able to demonstrate academic achievement and writing ability. Minorities, women, and persons with disabilities are particularly encouraged to apply.

Financial data The stipend is $35,000. A generous and comprehensive benefits package is also provided.

Duration 1 year, preferably starting in summer.

Additional information Fellows work in the center's Washington office on nutrition science policy and/or food safety issues.

Number awarded 1 each year.

Deadline Applications may be submitted at any time.

[899]
OFFICE OF NAVAL RESEARCH SABBATICAL LEAVE PROGRAM

American Society for Engineering Education
Attn: Projects Department
1818 N Street, N.W., Suite 600
Washington, DC 20036-2479
(202) 331-3525   Fax: (202) 265-8504
E-mail: projects@asee.org
Web: www.asee.org

Purpose To provide support to minority and other faculty members in engineering and science who wish to conduct research at selected Navy facilities while on sabbatical leave.

Eligibility This program is open to U.S. citizens with teaching or research appointments in engineering and science at U.S. universities or colleges. Applicants must intend to conduct research while in residence at selected facilities of the U.S. Navy. Faculty from Historically Black Colleges and Universities, Hispanic Serving Institutions, and Tribal Colleges and Universities are especially encouraged to apply.

Financial data Fellows receive a stipend equivalent to the difference between their regular salary and the sabbatical leave pay from their home institution. Fellows who must relocate their residence receive a relocation allowance and all fellows receive a travel allowance.

Duration Appointments are for a minimum of 1 semester and a maximum of 1 year.

Additional information Participating facilities include the Naval Air Warfare Center, Aircraft Division (Patuxent River, Maryland); Naval Air Warfare Center, Naval Training Systems Division (Orlando, Florida); Naval Air Warfare Center, Weapons Division (China Lake, California); Space and Naval Warfare Systems Center (San Diego, California); Naval Facilities Engineering Service Center (Port Hueneme, California); Naval Research Laboratories (Washington, D.C.; Stennis Space Center, Mississippi; and Monterey, California); Naval Surface Warfare Centers (Bethesda, Maryland; Indian Head, Maryland; Dahlgren, Virginia; and Panama City, Florida); Naval Undersea Warfare Center (Newport, Rhode Island and New London, Connecticut); Defense Equal Opportunity Management Institute (Cocoa Beach, Florida); Navy Personnel Research, Studies & Technology Department (Millington, Tennessee); Naval Dental Research Institute (Great Lakes, Illinois); Naval Aerospace Medical Research Laboratory (Pensacola, Florida); Naval Health Research Center (San Diego, California); Naval Medical Research Center (Silver Spring, Maryland); Naval Medical Research Center Detachment (Lima and Iquitos, Peru); Naval Medical Research Unit 2 (Jakarta, Indonesia); Naval Medical Research Unit 3 (Cairo, Egypt); Naval Medical Research Institute Toxicology Detachment (Wright Patterson Air Force Base, Dayton, Ohio); and Naval Submarine Medical Research Laboratory (Groton, Connecticut); This program is funded by the U.S. Navy's Office of Naval Research but administered by the American Society for Engineering Education.

Number awarded Varies each year.

Deadline Applications may be submitted at any time, but they must be received at least 6 months prior to the proposed sabbatical leave starting date.

[900]
OFFICE OF NAVAL RESEARCH SUMMER FACULTY RESEARCH PROGRAM

American Society for Engineering Education
Attn: Projects Department
1818 N Street, N.W., Suite 600
Washington, DC 20036-2479
(202) 331-3525   Fax: (202) 265-8504
E-mail: projects@asee.org
Web: www.asee.org

Purpose To provide support to minority and other faculty members in engineering and science who wish to conduct summer research at selected Navy facilities.

Eligibility This program is open to U.S. citizens with teaching or research appointments in engineering and science at U.S. universities or colleges. In addition to appointments as Summer Faculty Fellows, positions as Senior Summer Faculty Fellows are available to applicants who have at least 6 years of research experience in their field of expertise since earning a Ph.D. or equivalent degree and a substantial, significant record of research accomplishments and publications. A limited number of appointments are also available as Distinguished Summer Faculty Fellows to faculty members who are pre-eminent in their field of research, with a senior appointment at a leading research university and international recognition for their research accomplishments. Faculty from Historically Black Colleges and Universities, Hispanic Serving Institutions, and Tribal Colleges and Universities are especially encouraged to apply.

Financial data The weekly stipend is $1,400 at the Summer Faculty Fellow level, $1,650 at the Senior Summer Faculty Fellow level, and $1,900 at the Distinguished Summer Faculty Fellow level. Fellows who must relocate their residence receive a relocation allowance and all fellows receive a travel allowance.

Duration 10 weeks during the summer; fellows may reapply in subsequent years.

Additional information Participating facilities include the Naval Air Warfare Center, Aircraft Division (Patuxent River, Maryland); Naval Air Warfare Center, Naval Training Systems Division (Orlando, Florida); Naval Air Warfare Center, Weapons Division (China Lake, California); Space and Naval Warfare Systems Center (San Diego, California); Naval Facilities Engineering Service Center (Port Hueneme, California); Naval Research Laboratories (Washington, D.C.; Stennis Space Center, Mississippi; and Monterey, California); Naval Surface Warfare Centers (Bethesda, Maryland; Indian Head, Maryland; Dahlgren, Virginia; and Panama City, Florida); Naval Undersea Warfare Center (Newport, Rhode Island and New London, Connecticut); Defense Equal Opportunity Management Institute (Cocoa Beach, Florida); Navy Personnel Research, Studies & Technology Department (Millington, Tennessee); Naval Dental Research Institute (Great Lakes, Illinois); Naval Aerospace Medical Research Laboratory (Pensacola, Florida); Naval Health Research Center (San Diego, California); Naval Medical Research Center (Silver Spring, Maryland); Naval Medical Research Center Detachment (Lima and Iquitos, Peru); Naval Medical Research Unit 2 (Jakarta, Indonesia); Naval Medical Research Unit 3 (Cairo, Egypt); Naval Medical Research Institute Toxicology Detachment (Wright Patterson Air Force Base, Dayton, Ohio); and Naval Submarine Medical Research Laboratory (Groton, Connecticut); This program is funded by the U.S. Navy's Office of Naval Research but administered by the American Society for Engineering Education.

Number awarded Varies each year.

Deadline November of each year.

[901]
OHIO SPACE GRANT CONSORTIUM SENIOR SCHOLARSHIP

Ohio Space Grant Consortium
c/o Ohio Aerospace Institute
22800 Cedar Point Road
Cleveland, OH 44142
(440) 962-3032   Toll-free: (800) 828-OSGC
Fax: (440) 962-3057   E-mail: osgc@oai.org
Web: www.osgc.org/Scholarship.html

Purpose To provide financial assistance to minority and other students in their senior year at designated universities in Ohio who wish to conduct research while working on a baccalaureate degree in an aerospace-related field.

Eligibility These scholarships are available to U.S. citizens who expect to complete the requirements for a bachelor's degree in an aerospace-related discipline (aeronautical engineering, aerospace engineering, astronomy, biology, chemical engineering, chemistry, civil engineering, computer engineering and science, control engineering, electrical engineering, engineering mechanics, geography, geology, industrial engineering, manufacturing engineering, materials science and engineering, mathematics, mechanical engineering, petroleum engineering, physics, and systems engineering) within 1 year. They must be attending 1 of the participating universities in Ohio. Women, underrepresented minorities, and physically challenged persons are particularly encouraged to apply. Applicants must propose a research project to be conducted during the scholarship period in a campus laboratory. Selection is based on academic record, recommendations, the proposed research project, and a personal statement of career goals and anticipated benefits from the Space Grant program.

Financial data The grant is $3,000.

Duration 1 year.

Additional information These scholarships are funded through the National Space Grant College and Fellowship Program administered by the National Aeronautics and Space Administration (NASA), with matching funds provided by the member universities, the Ohio Aerospace Institute, and private industry. The participating institutions are the University of Akron, Case Western Reserve University, Cedarville University, Central State University, University of Cincinnati, Cleveland State University, University of Dayton, Marietta College (petroleum engineering), Miami University (Manufacturing engineering), Ohio Northern University, Ohio State University, Ohio University, University of Toledo, Wilberforce University, Wright State University, and Youngstown State University. Scholars are required to describe their research at an annual spring research symposium sponsored by the consortium.

Number awarded Varies each year; recently, 31 of these scholarships were awarded.

Deadline February of each year.

[902]
ORGANIZATIONAL LEARNING FOR HOMELAND SECURITY FELLOWSHIP PROGRAM

Stanford University
Center for International Security and Cooperation
Attn: Fellowship Program Coordinator
Encina Hall, Room E210
616 Serra Street
Stanford, CA 94305-6165
(650) 723-9626   Fax: (650) 723-0089
E-mail: barbara.platt@stanford.edu
Web: www.cisac.stanford.edu

Purpose To provide funding to scholars and professionals (particularly minorities and women) who are interested in conducting research on organizational learning and homeland security.

Eligibility This program is open to predoctoral candidates, postdoctoral scholars, scientists, engineers, and professionals (e.g., military officers or civilian members of the U.S. government, members of military or diplomatic services from other countries, and journalists interested in international security issues). Applicants must be interested in conducting research on a broad range of topics related to organizational learning and homeland security. Topics may be historical, with potential lessons for current homeland security issues. Disciplines may include anthropology, computer science, history, law, medicine, operations research, political science, or sociology. Examples of topics suitable for support include (but are not limited to) learning from military and other exercises and simulations; learning from success and failure in intelligence and forecasting; historical interactions and competitive learning between state and non-state organizations; earlier U.S. civil defense efforts, with implications for homeland security; learning from engineering failures, with lessons for homeland security; or causes and prevention of terrorism. Applications from women and minorities are encouraged.

Financial data Stipends are determined on a case-by-case basis commensurate with experience and availability of other funds. Health insurance is provided, and funds are available for travel and other research-related expenses.

Duration 9 months.

Additional information This program, established in 2004, is offered by Stanford University's Center for International Security and Cooperation (CISAC) in cooperation with the Naval Postgraduate School (NPS) in Monterey, California. Fellows must be in residence at CISAC (or split their time between CISAC and NPS) and participate in a monthly seminar held jointly between CISAC and NPS. They are expected to produce a research product (e.g., dissertation chapters, draft article or articles, book manuscript).

Number awarded Varies each year.

Deadline February of each year.

[903]
OSGC RESEARCH PROGRAM
Oklahoma NASA Space Grant Consortium
c/o University of Oklahoma
College of Geosciences
Ditmars House, Suite 5
1623 Cross Center Drive
Norman, Oklahoma 73069
(405) 325-6559   Fax: (405) 325-5537
E-mail: vduca@ou.edu
Web: 129.15.32.115/research/index.html

Purpose To provide funding to minority and other faculty and staff at member institutions of the Oklahoma Space Grant Consortium (OSGC) who are interested in conducting research related to the mission of the U.S. National Aeronautics and Space Administration (NASA).

Eligibility This program provides support for space-related research activities at member and affiliate institutions of the OSGC. Proposals may be submitted by faculty and staff of those institutions 1) to foster multi-disciplinary and multi-university research through special conferences, programs, and correspondence; and 2) to enhance the support infrastructure for faculty to facilitate the pursuit of NASA-related research, including both administrative support and marginal funds for travel and critical equipment or supplies. The OSGC is a component of the NASA Space Grant program, which encourages participation by women, minorities, and persons with disabilities.

Financial data Financing depends on the availability of funds.

Additional information Members of OSGC are Oklahoma State University, the University of Oklahoma, Cameron University, and Langston University. This program is funded by NASA.

[904]
PAUL P. VOURAS DISSERTATION RESEARCH GRANT
Association of American Geographers
Attn: Executive Assistant
1710 16th Street, N.W.
Washington, DC 20009-3198
(202) 234-1450   Fax: (202) 234-2744
E-mail: ekhater@aag.org
Web: www.aag.org

Purpose To provide financial assistance to minority and other members of the Association of American Geographers who are preparing dissertations in geography.

Eligibility Graduate students currently working on a Ph.D. in geography are eligible to apply if they have completed all of the requirements except the dissertation and have been members of the association for at least 1 year prior to submitting an application. Preference is given to minority applicants.

Financial data The amount awarded varies, up to a maximum of $500.

Duration 1 year.

Additional information Funds must be used for direct research expenses only and may not be used to cover overhead costs.

Number awarded 1 each year.

Deadline December of each year.

[905]
PEACE SCHOLAR DISSERTATION FELLOWSHIPS
United States Institute of Peace
Attn: Jennings Randolph Program for International
    Peace
1200 17th Street, N.W., Suite 200
Washington, DC 20036-3011
(202) 429-3886   Fax: (202) 429-6063
TDD: (202) 457-1719   E-mail: fellows@usip.org
Web: www.usip.org/fellows/scholars.html

Purpose To provide financial support to minority and other doctoral candidates working on dissertations that address the nature of international conflict and ways to prevent or end conflict and to sustain peace.

Eligibility This program is open to doctoral candidates, from anywhere in the world, who are enrolled in U.S. universities and conducting dissertation research on international peace and conflict management. Projects from a broad range of disciplines (political science, history, sociology, economics, anthropology, psychology, conflict resolution, and other fields within the humanities and social sciences, including interdisciplinary programs) are welcome. Priority is given to projects that contribute knowledge relevant to the formulation of policy on international peace and conflict issues. Women and members of minority groups are especially encouraged to apply. Selection is based on the candidate's record of achievement and/or leadership potential; the significance and potential of the project for making an important contribution to knowledge, practice, or public understanding; and the quality of the project design and its feasibility within the timetable proposed.

Financial data The stipend is $17,000 per year.

Duration 12 months, beginning in September.

Additional information These fellowships, first awarded in 1988, are tenable at the recipient's university or any other appropriate research site. This program is offered as part of the Jennings Randolph Program for International Peace at the United States Institute of Peace. These awards are not made for projects that constitute policymaking for a government agency or private organization; focus to any substantial degree on conflicts within U.S. domestic society; or adopt a partisan, advocacy, or activist stance.

Number awarded Varies each year; recently, 10 of these fellowships were awarded.

Deadline January of each year.

[906]
PEMBROKE CENTER POSTDOCTORAL FELLOWSHIPS
Brown University
Attn: Pembroke Center for Teaching and Research on
    Women
Box 1958
Providence, RI 02912
(401) 863-2643   Fax: (401) 863-1298
E-mail: Elizabeth_Barboza@Brown.edu
Web: www.pembrokecenter.org/RP-Postdoctoral.asp

Purpose To provide research support for minority and other scholars interested in conducting research at Brown University's Pembroke Center for Teaching and Research on Women on the cross-cultural study of gender.

Eligibility Fellowships are open to scholars in the humanities, social sciences, or life sciences who do not have a tenured position at an American college or university. Applicants must be willing to spend a year in residence at the Pembroke Center for Teaching and Research on Women and participate in a research project related to gender. The project focuses on a theme that changes annually (recently: "The Orders of Time"). The center encourages minority and Third World scholars to apply.

Financial data The stipend is $30,000.

Duration 1 academic year.

Additional information Postdoctoral fellows in residence participate in weekly seminars and present at least 2 public papers during the year, as well as conduct an individual research project. Supplementary funds are available for assistance with travel expenses from abroad. This program includes the following named fellowships: the Nancy L. Buc Postdoctoral Fellowship, the Artemis A.W. and Martha Joukowsky Postdoctoral Fellowship, and the Carol G. Lederer Postdoctoral Fellowship.

Number awarded 3 or 4 each year.

Deadline December of each year.

[907]
PICKWICK POSTDOCTORAL FELLOWSHIP IN SLEEP

National Sleep Foundation
Attn: Pickwick Club
1522 K Street, N.W., Suite 500
Washington, DC 20005
(202) 347-3471, ext. 203   Fax: (202) 347-3472
E-mail: nsf@sleepfoundation.org
Web: www.sleepfoundation.org

Purpose To enable young researchers, especially minorities, to devote the major portion of their professional effort to the study of sleep and sleep disorders.

Eligibility Applicants for this fellowship must be in recognized North American programs of study or laboratories with strong mentorship in the appropriate area. They must have an M.D., D.V.M., or D.O. degree; the degree or subsequent training must have been completed within the past 5 years. Fellowships are available for basic, applied, or clinical research. Applicants may not have a faculty position or have received an NIH grant. Minorities are specifically encouraged to apply.

Financial data The grant is $40,000 per year.

Duration 1 or 2 years.

Additional information This program was established in 1995. The Pickwick Club is named after the society described in Charles Dickens' *The Pickwick Papers;* the Pickwick Club honors those who, like Mr. Pickwick, are concerned with "a sensation of bodily weariness that in vain contends against an inability to sleep."

Deadline November of each year.

[908]
POSTDOCTORAL FELLOWSHIP IN BEHAVIORAL NEUROSCIENCE

Texas Consortium in Behavioral Neuroscience
c/o University of Texas
Department of Psychology
1 University Station A8000
Austin, TX 78712
(512) 471-1068   Fax: (512) 471-1073
E-mail: gonzalez-lima@psy.utexas.edu
Web: homepage.psy.utexas.edu

Purpose To provide an opportunity for underrepresented minority postdoctorates to obtain research training at selected universities in Texas.

Eligibility This program is open to members of underrepresented minority groups who have a doctoral degree in neuroscience, psychology, biomedical or natural sciences, or engineering. Applicants must be interested in a program of research training at the University of Texas at Austin, the University of Texas at San Antonio, the University of Texas Health Science Center at San Antonio, Texas A&M University, or Texas A&M University System Health Science Center. U.S. citizenship or permanent resident status is required.

Financial data The program provides $3,090 for health insurance, $1,200 in travel funds, and a stipend of $35,568 in the first year and $37,476 in the second year.

Duration 2 years.

Additional information This program is sponsored by 3 components of the National Institutes of Health: the National Institute of Mental Health, the National Institute on Drug Abuse, and the National Institute of Neurological Disorders and Stroke. The training program covers brain metabolic mapping of behavioral functions, neuropharmacology, electrophysiology, and molecular neurobiology.

Number awarded 5 each year.

Deadline Applications may be submitted at any time.

[909]
POSTDOCTORAL FELLOWSHIP IN MENTAL HEALTH AND SUBSTANCE ABUSE SERVICES

American Psychological Association
Attn: Minority Fellowship Program
750 First Street, N.E.
Washington, DC 20002-4242
(202) 336-6127   Fax: (202) 336-6012
TDD: (202) 336-6123   E-mail: mfp@apa.org
Web: www.apa.org/mfp/postdocpsych.html

Purpose To provide financial assistance to minority and other postdoctoral scholars interested in a program of research training related to providing mental health and substance abuse services to ethnic minority populations.

Eligibility This program is open to U.S. citizens and permanent residents who received a doctoral degree in psychology in the last 5 years. Applicants must be interested in participating in a program of training under a qualified sponsor for research, delivery of services, or policy related to substance abuse and its relationship to the mental health or psychological well-being of ethnic minorities. Members of ethnic minority groups (African Americans, Hispanics/Latinos, American Indians, Alaskan Natives, Asian Americans, Native Hawaiians, and other Pacific Islanders) are especially encouraged to apply. Selection is based on commitment to a career in ethnic minority mental health service delivery, research, or policy; qualifications of the sponsor; the fit between career goals and training environment selected; merit of the training proposal; potential demonstrated through accomplishments and goals; and appropriateness to goals of the program.

Financial data The stipend depends on the number of years of research experience and is equivalent to the standard postdoctoral stipend level of the National Institutes of Health (currently ranging from $35,568 for no years of experience to $51,036 for 7 or more years of experience).

Duration 1 academic or calendar year; may be renewed for up to 2 additional years.

Additional information Funding is provided by the U.S. Substance Abuse and Mental Health Services Administration.

Number awarded Varies each year.

Deadline January of each year.

[910]
POSTDOCTORAL FELLOWSHIPS IN THE NEUROSCIENCES

American Psychological Association
Attn: Minority Fellowship Program
750 First Street, N.E.
Washington, DC 20002-4242
(202) 336-6127　　　　　　Fax: (202) 336-6012
TDD: (202) 336-6123　　　　E-mail: mfp@apa.org
Web: www.apa.org/mfp/pdprogram.html

Purpose To provide funding to minority postdoctorates who are interested in pursuing research training in neuroscience.

Eligibility This program is open to all U.S. citizens and permanent residents who have a Ph.D. or M.D. degree with appropriate research experience in neuroscience or an applied discipline, such as cell or molecular biology or immunology. Applicants must have career goals that are consistent with those of the program: 1) to increase ethnic and racial diversity among neuroscience researchers with a special emphasis on increasing the numbers of underrepresented ethnic minorities; and 2) to increase numbers of neuroscientists whose work is related to the federal initiative to eliminate health disparities. They must be interested in engaging in postdoctoral research training in behavioral neuroscience, cellular neurobiology, cognitive neuroscience, computational neuroscience, developmental neurobiology, membrane biophysics, molecular neurobiology, neuroanatomy, neurobiology of aging, neurobiology of disease, neurochemistry, neurogenetics, neuroimmunology, neuropathology, neuropharmacology, neurophysiology, neurotoxicology, or systems neuroscience. Students identified as underrepresented ethnic minorities in the neurosciences (African Americans, Native Americans, Hispanic Americans, and Pacific Islanders) are especially encouraged to apply. Selection is based on scholarship, research experience and potential, a research proposal, the suitability of the proposed laboratory and mentor, commitment to a research career in neuroscience, writing ability, and appropriateness to program goal.

Financial data The stipend depends on the number of years of research experience and is equivalent to the stan-

dard postdoctoral stipend level of the National Institutes of Health (currently ranging from $35,568 for no years of experience to $51,036 for 7 or more years of experience). The fellowship also provides travel funds to attend the annual meeting of the Society for Neuroscience.

Duration 1 year; may be renewed for up to 1 additional year.

Additional information The program was established in 1987. It is funded by the U.S. National Institute of Mental Health of the National Institutes of Health and administered by the American Psychological Association.

Number awarded Varies each year.

Deadline January of each year.

[911]
POSTDOCTORAL FELLOWSHIPS OF THE FORD FOUNDATION DIVERSITY FELLOWSHIP PROGRAM

National Research Council
Attn: Fellowship Office, GR 346A
500 Fifth Street, N.W.
Washington, DC 20001
(202) 334-2860　　　　　　Fax: (202) 334-3419
E-mail: infofell@nas.edu
Web: www7.nationalacademies.org

Purpose To provide funding for postdoctoral research to scholars whose success will increase the racial and ethnic diversity of U.S. colleges and universities.

Eligibility This program is open to U.S. citizens and nationals who earned a Ph.D. or Sc.D. degree within the past 7 years and are committed to a career in teaching and research at the college or university level. The following are considered as positive factors in the selection process: evidence of superior academic achievement; promise of continuing achievement as scholars and teachers; membership in a group whose underrepresentation in the American professoriate has been severe and longstanding, including Black/African Americans, Puerto Ricans, Mexican Americans/Chicanos/Chicanas, Native American Indians, Alaska Natives (Eskimos or Aleuts), and Native Pacific Islanders (Micronesians or Polynesians); capacity to respond in pedagogically productive ways to the learning needs of students from diverse backgrounds; sustained personal engagement with communities that are underrepresented in the academy and an ability to bring this asset to learning, teaching, and scholarship at the college and university level; and likelihood of using the diversity of human experience as an educational resource in teaching and scholarship. Applicants must have earned their degree in 1 of the following fields: anthropology, archaeology, art history, astronomy, chemistry, communications, computer science, earth sciences, economics, education, engineering, ethnomusicology, geography, history, international relations, language, life sciences, linguistics, literature, mathematics, performance study, philosophy, physics, political science, psychology, religion, sociology, or urban planning. Awards are not made for such practice-oriented areas as administration and management, audiology, business, educational administration and leadership, filmmaking, fine arts, guidance, home economics, library and information science, nursing, occupational health, performing arts, personnel, physical education, social welfare, social work, or speech pathology. In addition, awards are not made in such areas as medicine, law, or public health. Research may be conducted at an appropriate institution of higher education in the United States (normally) or abroad, including universities, museums, libraries, government or national laboratories, privately sponsored nonprofit institutes, government chartered nonprofit research organizations, or centers for advanced study. Applicants should designate a faculty member or other scholar to serve as host at the proposed fellowship institution. They are encouraged to choose a host institution other than that where they are affiliated at the time of application.

Financial data The stipend is $40,000. Funds may be supplemented by sabbatical leave pay or other sources of support that do not carry with them teaching or other responsibilities. The employing institution receives an allowance of $1,500, paid after fellowship tenure is completed; the employing institution is expected to match the grant and to use the allowance and the match to assist with the fellow's continuing research expenditures.

Duration 9 or 12 months.

Additional information Fellows may not accept another major fellowship while they are being supported by this program.

Number awarded Approximately 20 each year.

Deadline December of each year.

[912]
POSTDOCTORAL FELLOWSHIPS OF THE MINORITY SCHOLAR-IN-RESIDENCE PROGRAM

Consortium for a Strong Minority Presence at Liberal
   Arts Colleges
c/o Administrative Assistant, President's Office
Grinnell College
1121 Park Street
Grinnell, IA 50112-1690
(641) 269-3000   E-mail: cousins@grinnell.edu
Web: www.grinnell.edu/dean/csmp

Purpose To make available the facilities of liberal arts colleges to minority scholars who recently received their doctoral/advanced degree.

Eligibility This program is open to African American, Asian American, Hispanic American, and Native American scholars in the liberal arts and engineering who received the Ph.D. or M.F.A. degree within the past 5 years. Applicants must be interested in a residency at a participating institution that is part of the Consortium for a Strong Minority Presence at Liberal Arts Colleges.

Financial data Fellows receive a stipend equivalent to the average salary paid by the host college to beginning assistant professors. Modest funds are made available to finance the fellow's proposed research, subject to the usual institutional procedures.

Duration 1 year.

Additional information The following schools are participating in the program: Bowdoin College, Bryn Mawr College, Carleton College, Claremont McKenna College, Coe College, College of Wooster, Colorado College, Denison University, DePauw University, Dickinson College, Gettysburg College, Grinnell College, Hamilton College, Haverford College, Hope College, Juniata College, Lewis and Clark College, Luther College, Macalester College, Mount Holyoke College, Oberlin College, Occidental College, Pitzer

College, Pomona College, Rhodes College, St. Olaf College, Skidmore College, Southwestern University, Swarthmore College, Trinity University, University of the South, Vassar College, Wellesley College, Wheaton College, Whitman College, and Willamette University. Fellows are expected to teach at least 1 course in each academic term of residency, participate in departmental seminars, and interact with students.

Number awarded Varies each year.

Deadline November of each year.

[913]
POSTDOCTORAL FELLOWSHIPS ON SEXUALITY AND POLICY

Social Science Research Council
Attn: Sexuality Research Fellowship Program
810 Seventh Avenue
New York, NY 10019
(212) 377-2700   Fax: (212) 377-2727
E-mail: srfp@ssrc.org
Web: www.ssrc.org/fellowships/sexuality

Purpose To provide financial support for postdoctoral research on sexuality and public policy.

Eligibility This program is open to scholars who received a Ph.D. within the past 10 years and are not already tenured (although they can occupy a tenure-track position). There are no citizenship requirements. Applicants must be interested in conducting research in sexuality that focuses on policy analysis, policy development, and/or implementation and is relevant to local, state, or national concerns. Topics may include (but are not limited to) criminal justice and incarceration; culture, race, and ethnicity; immigration and migration; institutional influences, such as religion, education, or media, on sexuality and social policy; labor, employment, and economics; marriage and family formation; militarization, war, and peacekeeping; pornography; public health, wellness, and health care issues; reproductive health and population issues; sex work and prostitution; sexual development and aging; sexuality and disability; sexual movements, sexual rights, and/or sexual politics; sexual orientation and identity; sexual violence, coercion, abuse, exploitation, and harassment; sexual education and curriculum design, implementation, and evaluation; sexuality and the law; sexuality and the media; sexually-transmitted diseases and infections; and social movements, sexual rights, and/or sexual politics. Applications are invited from a wide range of disciplines and fields, including but not limited to anthropology, demography, economics, education, history, law, linguistics, philosophy, political science, psychology, public health, public policy, and sociology, as well as such interdisciplinary programs as sociomedical sciences, jurisprudence and social policy, or American, ethnic, family, labor, media, and urban studies; applications from biomedical or other fields outside the social sciences are welcome as long as they are grounded in social science theory and methodology. Policymakers, advocates, service providers, and program administrators who conduct research in various settings (such as business, federal or state government, and community settings) are also eligible. Applicants should work in partnership with another scholar or professional who will function in the advisory capacity of research consultant. The research consultant must have a doctoral degree from a U.S. or accredited foreign university, be able to demonstrate commitment to human sexuality research through previous publication record and experience, and be able to provide substantive expertise to the applicant in specific areas of research methodology, design, and/or policy. Women and members of minority groups are especially encouraged to apply.

Financial data Grants range from $50,000 to $60,000, to cover research costs and living expenses. An additional $5,000 is awarded to the fellow's research consultant.

Duration 1 year.

Additional information Funding for this program is provided by the Ford Foundation.

Number awarded Approximately 6 each year.

Deadline December of each year.

[914]
POSTDOCTORAL RESEARCH FELLOWSHIPS IN EPILEPSY

Epilepsy Foundation
Attn: Research Department
4351 Garden City Drive
Landover, MD 20785-7223
(301) 459-3700   Toll-free: (800) EFA-1000
Fax: (301) 577-2684   TDD: (800) 332-2070
E-mail: grants@efa.org
Web: www.epilepsyfoundation.org

Purpose To provide funding for a program of postdoctoral training to minority and other physicians and scientists committed to epilepsy research.

Eligibility Applicants must have a doctoral degree (M.D., Ph.D., or equivalent) and be a resident or postdoctoral fellow at a university, medical school, research institution, or medical center. They must be interested in participating in a training experience and research project that has potential significance for understanding the causes, treatment, or consequences of epilepsy. The program is geared toward applicants who will be trained in research in epilepsy rather than those who use epilepsy as a tool for research in other fields. Equal consideration is given to applicants interested in acquiring experience either in basic laboratory research or in the conduct of human clinical studies. Academic faculty holding the rank of instructor or higher are not eligible, nor are graduate or medical students, medical residents, permanent government employees, or employees of private industry. Applications from women, members of minority groups, and people with disabilities are especially encouraged. Selection is based on scientific quality of the proposed research, a statement regarding its relevance to epilepsy, the applicant's qualifications, the preceptor's qualifications, and the adequacy of facility and related epilepsy programs at the institution.

Financial data The grant is $40,000. No indirect costs are covered.

Duration 1 year.

Additional information Support for this program is provided by many individuals, families, and corporations, especially the American Epilepsy Society, Abbott Laboratories, Ortho-McNeil Pharmaceutical, and Pfizer Inc. The fellowship must be carried out at a facility in the United States where there is an ongoing epilepsy research program.

Number awarded Varies each year; recently, 13 of these fellowships were awarded.

Deadline August of each year.

[915]
PREDOCTORAL FELLOWSHIP IN BEHAVIORAL NEUROSCIENCE

Texas Consortium in Behavioral Neuroscience
c/o University of Texas
Department of Psychology
1 University Station A8000
Austin, TX 78712
(512) 471-1068   Fax: (512) 471-1073
E-mail: gonzalez-lima@psy.utexas.edu
Web: homepage.psy.utexas.edu

Purpose To provide an opportunity for underrepresented minority doctoral candidates to obtain research training in neuroscience at selected universities in Texas.

Eligibility This program is open to members of underrepresented minority groups who have a bachelor's degree and plan to work on a doctoral degree in neuroscience. Applicants must be interested in a program of research training at the University of Texas at Austin, the University of Texas at San Antonio, the University of Texas Health Science Center at San Antonio, Texas A&M University, or Texas A&M University System Health Science Center. U.S. citizenship or permanent resident status is required.

Financial data The program provides a total of $25,705 each year, including $6,349 for tuition, fees, and health insurance, $1,200 in travel funds, and a stipend of $20,772.

Duration 3 years.

Additional information This program is sponsored by 3 components of the National Institutes of Health: the National Institute of Mental Health, the National Institute on Drug Abuse, and the National Institute of Neurological Disorders and Stroke. The training program covers brain metabolic mapping of behavioral functions, neuropharmacology, electrophysiology, and molecular neurobiology. Trainees are required to complete courses covering the brain and behavior, scientific ethics, experimental design, and statistical analysis.

Number awarded 10 each year.

Deadline Applications may be submitted at any time.

[916]
PREDOCTORAL RESEARCH TRAINING FELLOWSHIPS IN EPILEPSY

Epilepsy Foundation
Attn: Research Department
4351 Garden City Drive
Landover, MD 20785-7223
(301) 459-3700   Toll-free: (800) EFA-1000
Fax: (301) 577-2684   TDD: (800) 332-2070
E-mail: grants@efa.org
Web: www.epilepsyfoundation.org

Purpose To provide funding to minority and other doctoral candidates in designated fields for dissertation research on a topic related to epilepsy.

Eligibility This program is open to full-time graduate students working on a Ph.D. in biochemistry, genetics, neuroscience, nursing, pharmacology, pharmacy, physiology, or psychology. Applicants must be conducting dissertation research on a topic relevant to epilepsy under the guidance of a mentor with expertise in the area of epilepsy investigation. Applications from women, members of minority groups, and people with disabilities are especially encouraged. Selection is based on the relevance of the proposed work to epilepsy, the applicant's qualifications, the mentor's qualifications, the scientific quality of the proposed dissertation research, the quality of the training environment for research related to epilepsy, and the adequacy of the facility.

Financial data The grant is $20,000, consisting of $19,000 for a stipend and $1,000 to support travel to attend the annual meeting of the American Epilepsy Society.

Duration 1 year.

Additional information Support for this program, which began in 1998, is provided by many individuals, families, and corporations, especially the American Epilepsy Society, Abbott Laboratories, Ortho-McNeil Pharmaceutical, and Pfizer Inc.

Number awarded Varies each year; recently, 3 of these fellowships were awarded.

Deadline August of each year.

[917]
PROGRAM FOR MINORITY RESEARCH TRAINING IN PSYCHIATRY

American Psychiatric Association
Attn: American Psychiatric Institute for Research and
    Education
1000 Wilson Boulevard, Suite 1825
Arlington, VA 22209-3901
(703) 907-8622   Toll-free: (800) 852-1390
Fax: (703) 907-1085   E-mail: eguerra@psych.org
Web: www.psych.org

Purpose To provide financial assistance to underrepresented minority medical students and residents interested in psychiatric research training.

Eligibility This program is open to underrepresented minorities (American Indians, Blacks/African Americans, Hispanics, and Pacific Islanders) at 3 levels: medical students, residents, and graduates of residency programs. All candidates must be interested in training at research-intensive departments of psychiatry in major U.S. medical schools. Training sites with excellent research facilities and resources, funded research record, research faculty (including minority researchers), and training history are preferred.

Financial data Annual stipends are $19,968 for medical students, from $44,364 to $46.404 for residents, and up to $50,808 for post-residency fellows. Other benefits include travel funds to attend the annual meeting of the American Psychiatric Association (APA) or the American College of Neuropsychopharmacology and limited tuition assistance for full-time trainees to attend specific courses that are required as part of their training.

Duration Medical students can receive support 2 to 6 months or as a summer experience. Residents may engage in full-year research training during the last year of psychiatric residency or in "year off" research training. Graduates of residency programs can undertake full-time research training for 2 years, although a third year is possible if appropriate to a trainee's career development.

Additional information This program is funded by the National Institute of Mental Health and administered by the APA's American Psychiatric Institute for Research and Education.

Number awarded Varies each year.

Deadline Medical students and residents seeking less than 1 year of training may apply at any time, but applications must be received at least 3 months before the proposed training is to begin; medical students seeking summer training should apply by March of each year; residents seeking a year or more of training and post-residency fellows should apply by November of each year.

[918]
PROSTATE CANCER CLINICAL TRIAL AWARDS

U.S. Army
Medical Research and Materiel Command
Attn: MCMR-ZB-C
1077 Patchel Street (Building 1077)
Fort Detrick, MD 21702-5024
(301) 619-7079   Fax: (301) 619-7792
E-mail: cdmrp.pa@det.amedd.army.mil
Web: cdmrp.army.mil

Purpose To provide funding to minority and other scientists interested in conducting clinical research on prostate cancer.

Eligibility This program is open to independent investigators at any level (regardless of ethnicity, nationality, or citizenship status) at universities, colleges, hospitals, laboratories, companies, and agencies of local, state, and federal governments. The sponsor is especially interested in receiving applications from Historically Black Colleges and Universities and Minority Institutions (HBCU/MI). Applicants must be interested in conducting clinical research that has the potential to impact the treatment, diagnosis, detection, or prevention of prostate cancer. Proposals should focus on new interventions (e.g., drugs, biologics, devices). Phase I clinical trials should focus on determining the safety, toxicity, tolerability, and pharmacokinetics or pharmacodynamics of new interventions, devices, or treatment schedules in humans; applicants for those trials must include a clear scientific rationale for the trial as well as adequate preclinical supplemental data to support the feasibility of their hypotheses and approaches. Phase II clinical trials should focus on defining the efficacy of new interventions or devices; applicants for those trials must include Phase I or pilot clinical trial data, adequate preclinical supplemental data to support the feasibility of their hypotheses and approaches, and a detailed plan for completion. Phase I/II clinical trials must meet both sets of requirements.

Financial data The grant is $250,000 per year in direct costs. Institutions are expected to cost share.

Duration 3 years.

Additional information The Prostate Cancer Research Program was established in 1997 as part of the Congressionally Directed Medical Research Programs of the U.S. Department of Defense.

Number awarded Approximately 5 each year.

Deadline December of each year.

[919]
R. ROBERT & SALLY D. FUNDERBURG RESEARCH SCHOLAR AWARD IN GASTRIC BIOLOGY RELATED TO CANCER

Foundation for Digestive Health and Nutrition
Attn: Research Awards Coordinator
4930 Del Ray Avenue
Bethesda, MD 20814-2512
(301) 222-4005   Fax: (301) 222-4010
E-mail: info@fdhn.org
Web: www.fdhn.org

Purpose To provide funding to minority and other established investigators who are working on research that enhances fundamental understanding of gastric cancer pathobiology.

Eligibility This program is open to faculty at accredited North American institutions who have established themselves as independent investigators in the field of gastric biology, pursuing novel approaches to gastric mucosal cell biology, regeneration and regulation of cell growth, inflammation as precancerous lesions, genetics of gastric carcinoma, oncogenes in gastric epithelial malignancies, epidemiology of gastric cancer, etiology of gastric epithelial malignancies, or clinical research in diagnosis or treatment of gastric carcinoma. Applicants must be individual members of the American Gastroenterological Association (AGA). Women and minority investigators are strongly encouraged to apply. Selection is based on the novelty, feasibility, and significance of the proposal; attributes of the candidate; and the likelihood that support will lead to a research career in the field of gastric biology. Preference is given to novel approaches, especially for initiation of projects by young investigators or established investigators new to the field.

Financial data The award is $25,000 per year. Funds are to be used for the salary of the investigator. Indirect costs are not allowed.

Duration 2 years.

Additional information This program is administered by the Foundation for Digestive Health and Nutrition (FDHN) and sponsored by the AGA.

Number awarded 1 each year.

Deadline September of each year.

[920]
REGINALD F. LEWIS AND CHARLES HAMILTON HOUSTON FELLOWSHIPS FOR LAW TEACHING

Harvard Law School
Attn: Lewis/Houston Committee
Griswold 220
Cambridge, MA 02138
(617) 495-3100
Web: www.law.harvard.edu

Purpose To provide an opportunity for lawyers, especially minorities, to prepare for a career in law teaching by conducting a research project at Harvard Law School.

Eligibility This program is open to law school graduates who will enhance the diversity of the profession; applications from minority candidates are especially encouraged. Applicants must be interested in preparing for a career as a law professor by conducting a research project in the field in which they expect to teach. They must submit a detailed description (3 to 4 pages) of the project, a statement of their interests in teaching, a statement of the fields in which they expect to teach and pursue research, a resume, a copy of their undergraduate and law school transcripts, and 2 letters of reference.

Financial data The stipend is $25,000 per year.

Duration 1 year.

Additional information The Lewis Fellowship is named for a prominent African American graduate of the Harvard Law School; the Houston Fellowship is named for a distinguished lawyer and teacher who was the first African American to serve on the *Harvard Law Review.* Fellows must prepare a major article for publication during the fellowship period; a schedule of research and work must be established with a faculty supervisor. Although fellows may audit courses, they may not be degree candidates.

Number awarded 2 each year.

Deadline February of each year.

[921]
RESEARCH AND TRAINING FELLOWSHIPS IN EPILEPSY FOR CLINICIANS

Epilepsy Foundation
Attn: Research Department
4351 Garden City Drive
Landover, MD 20785-7223
(301) 459-3700   Toll-free: (800) EFA-1000
Fax: (301) 577-2684   TDD: (800) 332-2070
E-mail: clinical_postdocs@efa.org
Web: www.epilepsyfoundation.org

Purpose To provide funding to minority and other clinically trained professionals interested in gaining additional training in order to develop an epilepsy research program.

Eligibility Applicants must have an M.D., D.O., Ph.D., D.S., or equivalent degree and be a clinical or postdoctoral fellow at a university, medical school, or other appropriate research institution. Holders of other doctoral-level degrees (e.g., Pharm.D., D.S.N.) may also be eligible. Candidates must be interested in a program of research training that may include mechanisms of epilepsy, novel therapeutic approaches, clinical trials, development of new technologies, or behavioral and psychosocial impact of epilepsy. The training program may consist of both didactic training and a supervised research experience that is designed to develop the necessary knowledge and skills in the chosen area of research and foster the career goals of the candidate. Academic faculty holding the rank of instructor or higher are not eligible, nor are graduate or medical students, medical residents, permanent government employees, or employees of private industry. Applications from women, members of minority groups, and people with disabilities are especially encouraged. Selection is based on the quality of the proposed research training program, the applicant's qualifications, the preceptor's qualifications, and the adequacy of clinical training, research facilities, and other epilepsy-related programs at the institution.

Financial data The grant is $40,000. No indirect costs are provided.

Duration 1 year.

Additional information Support for this program is provided by many individuals, families, and corporations, especially the American Epilepsy Society, Abbott Laboratories,

Ortho-McNeil Pharmaceutical, and Pfizer Inc. Grantees are expected to spend at least 50% of their time dedicated to research training and conducting research.

Number awarded Varies each year; recently, 5 of these fellowships were awarded.

Deadline October of each year.

[922]
RESEARCH FELLOWSHIP IN PHYSICS AT BROOKHAVEN NATIONAL LABORATORY

Brookhaven National Laboratory
Attn: Human Resources, Position MK9999
Building 185
Upton, NY 11973-5000
(631) 344-2871   Fax: (631) 344-7170
E-mail: mrk@bnl.gov
Web: www.bnl.gov/physics

Purpose To provide funding for research to underrepresented groups in the physics program at Brookhaven National Laboratory (BNL).

Eligibility This program is open to U.S. citizens who have recently completed (or will complete before taking up the fellowship) a Ph.D. in the 3 major areas represented in the physics department at BNL: high energy physics, nuclear physics, and condensed matter physics. Because women and minorities remain underrepresented within the physics research community, those groups are emphasized in recruitment for these fellowships at BNL.

Financial data The program provides a competitive salary and benefits package as well as an allowance for moving expenses and transportation for the fellow and family members. Short-term on-site housing is available.

Duration 2 years.

Additional information The BNL facilities available to the fellow include the Alternating Gradient Synchrotron (AGS), the Relativistic Heavy Ion Collider (RHIC), the National Synchrotron Light Source (NSLS), and the forthcoming Center for Functional Nanomaterials (CFN).

Deadline January of each year.

[923]
RISK AND DEVELOPMENT FIELD RESEARCH GRANTS

Social Science Research Council
Attn: Program in Applied Economics
810 Seventh Avenue
New York, NY 10019
(212) 377-2700   Fax: (212) 377-2727
E-mail: pae@ssrc.org
Web: www.ssrc.org/pae

Purpose To provide funding to minority and other doctoral students and postdoctoral scholars interested in conducting research on risk and uncertainty in economics.

Eligibility This program is open to 1) full-time graduate students enrolled in economics and related Ph.D. programs (e.g., development studies or agricultural economics) at U.S. universities; and 2) scholars who have completed a Ph.D. in economics and related fields within the past 5 years and have a current position at a U.S. academic or nonprofit research institution. There are no citizenship, nationality, or (for graduate students) residency requirements. Applicants

must be interested in conducting field research into questions of risk and uncertainty in the context of developing economies. Preference is given to proposals that include interdisciplinary and novel approaches, with an aim to create a better understanding of the way that individuals, institutions, and policymakers perceive and respond to situations of risk and uncertainty. Minorities and women are particularly encouraged to apply.

Financial data The stipend is $5,000 for graduate students or $15,000 for postdoctoral scholars. Funds must be used for field research, not general support or dissertation write-up.

Duration 1 year.

Additional information This program, established in 1997 as the Program in Applied Economics, is administered by the Social Science Research Council with funds provided by the John D. and Catherine T. MacArthur Foundation.

Number awarded Varies each year; recently, 17 graduate student and 4 postdoctoral fellowships were awarded.

Deadline January of each year.

[924]
ROBERT D. WATKINS MINORITY GRADUATE FELLOWSHIP

American Society for Microbiology
Attn: Education Board
1752 N Street, N.W.
Washington, DC 20036-2904
(202) 942-9283   Fax: (202) 942-9329
E-mail: Fellowships-CareerInformation@asmusa.org
Web: www.asm.org

Purpose To provide funding for research in microbiology to underrepresented minority doctoral students who are members of the American Society for Microbiology (ASM).

Eligibility This program is open to African Americans, Hispanic Americans, Native Americans, Alaskan Native Americans, and Native Pacific Islanders enrolled as full-time graduate students who have completed their first year of doctoral study and who are members of the society. Applicants must propose a joint research plan in collaboration with a society member scientist. They must have completed all graduate course work requirements for the doctoral degree by the date of the activation of the fellowship. U.S. citizenship or permanent resident status is required. Selection is based on academic achievement, evidence of a successful research plan developed in collaboration with a research advisor/mentor, and relevant career goals in the microbiological sciences.

Financial data Students receive $19,000 per year as a stipend; funds may not be used for tuition or fees.

Duration 3 years.

Number awarded Varies each year.

Deadline April of each year.

[925]
ROBERT R. MCCORMICK TRIBUNE MINORITY FELLOWSHIP IN URBAN JOURNALISM AT THE CHICAGO REPORTER

Chicago Reporter
Attn: Senior Editor
332 South Michigan Avenue, Suite 500
Chicago, IL 60604
(312) 427-4830, ext. 3861   Fax: (312) 427-6130
Web: www.chicagoreporter.com/min_fellowship

Purpose To provide opportunities for minority journalists to work on projects at the *Chicago Reporter.*

Eligibility Experienced minority journalists with a baccalaureate degree and at least 3 years of print reporting experience are eligible to apply for this fellowship at the *Chicago Reporter.* Applicants must be able to demonstrate a strong interest in urban affairs and investigative reporting. Fluency in Spanish is a plus.

Financial data The position pays a competitive salary and benefits.

Duration 1 year, beginning in October.

Additional information Fellows work at the *Chicago Reporter,* a monthly newspaper known for its coverage of the role minorities play in newspapers. Recipients may take courses at Northwestern University's Medill School of Journalism.

Number awarded 1 each year.

Deadline August of each year.

[926]
SCIENCE POLICY AND INTERNATIONAL SECURITY FELLOWSHIP PROGRAM

Stanford University
Center for International Security and Cooperation
Attn: Fellowship Program Coordinator
Encina Hall, Room E210
616 Serra Street
Stanford, CA 94305-6165
(650) 723-9626   Fax: (650) 723-0089
E-mail: barbara.platt@stanford.edu
Web: www.cisac.stanford.edu

Purpose To provide funding to minority and other mid-career scholars who are interested in conducting research on international security or arms control issues at Stanford University's Center for International Security and Cooperation.

Eligibility This program is open to scientists and engineers who have demonstrated excellence in their specialties. Applicants should be interested in conducting interdisciplinary research at the center on such topics as policy issues regarding nuclear, biological, and chemical weapons and delivery systems; prospects for international control of weapons of mass destruction; nuclear weapons safety and security; global diffusion of information technology; assessing antiballistic missile defenses; export controls on high technology; defense conversion; environmental security; and security issues associated with energy development. Fellowships are available for both postdoctoral fellows and mid-career professionals. Scientists in academic and research institutions, government, and industry from both the United States and abroad may apply. The center is par-

ticularly interested in receiving applications from minorities or women.

Financial data Stipends are determined on a case-by-case basis commensurate with experience and availability of other funds. Health insurance is provided, and funds are available for travel and other research-related expenses.

Duration 11 months.

Additional information Science fellows pursue research, audit courses, and work with the center's faculty and research staff. They have the opportunity to interact with specialists in arms control, politics, and military affairs.

Number awarded 3 each year.

Deadline February of each year.

[927]
SCIENTIST DEVELOPMENT AWARD FOR NEW MINORITY FACULTY

National Institute of Mental Health
Attn: Office of Research Training and Career
    Development
6001 Executive Boulevard, Room 7213
Bethesda, MD 20892-9647
(301) 443-3107   Fax: (301) 443-4822
E-mail: mc49n@nih.gov
Web: www.nimh.nih.gov

Purpose To provide financial support to new minority faculty members to initiate a program of research and to help them to become outstanding independent investigators in the mental health field.

Eligibility This program is open to new non-tenured faculty members at domestic, nonprofit, public and private universities, colleges, and professional schools engaged in mental health research who are U.S. citizens, nationals, or permanent residents. Applicants must be members of minority groups, defined as individuals belonging to a particular ethnic or racial group that has been determined by the grantee institution to be underrepresented in biomedical or behavioral research. They must have earned a doctorate (Ph.D., M.D., D.Sc., etc.) by the time the award is made and must be proposing to devote at least 75% of professional time to career development activities, research, or other research-related activities relevant to their career goals in mental health.

Financial data Salary support depends on the established structure for full-time, 12-month staff appointments at the grantee institution. The awards through this program are 100% of base for salaries up to $48,000, $48,000 for base salaries of $48,001 to $64,000, or 75% of base for salaries over $64,000, to a maximum of $90,000. In addition, funds up to $50,000 per year may be requested to support research and/or career development activities. Reimbursement of facilities and administrative costs is limited to 8% of total direct costs.

Duration 3 to 5 years; nonrenewable.

Additional information Applications must designate a mentor to work with the candidate. The proposed mentor must be a recognized, well-established, active investigator in the candidate's proposed research area who has not served in this role during the candidate's pre- or postdoctoral training.

Deadline January, May, or September of each year.

[928]
SOUTH CAROLINA SPACE GRANT CONSORTIUM RESEARCH GRANTS

South Carolina Space Grant Consortium
c/o College of Charleston
Department of Geology
58 Coming Street, Room 341B
Charleston, SC 29424
(843) 953-7171   Fax: (843) 953-5446
E-mail: colganm@cofc.edu
Web: www.cofc.edu

Purpose To provide funding for space-related research to underrepresented minority and other faculty at institutional members of the South Carolina Space Grant Consortium.

Eligibility This program is open to tenured or tenure-track faculty at member institutions of the South Carolina Space Grant Consortium. Applicants must be proposing to conduct research in earth science, space science, aeronautics, or the human exploration and development of space. Priority is given to researchers who wish to conduct research at a center of the U.S. National Aeronautics and Space Administration (NASA). Selection is based on scientific merit of the proposed project, relevancy to NASA strategic plans, project personnel, and reasonableness of budget. The South Carolina Space Grant Consortium is a component of the NASA Space Grant program, which encourages the participation of women, underrepresented minorities, and persons with disabilities.

Financial data Grants range up to $30,000. Grants must be matched on a 1:1 basis with nonfederal funds.

Duration 1 year.

Additional information Members of the consortium are Benedict College, The Citadel, College of Charleston, Clemson University, Coastal Carolina University, Furman University, University of South Carolina, Wofford College, South Carolina State University, The Medical University of South Carolina, and University of the Virgin Islands. This program is funded by NASA.

Number awarded 2 or more each year.

Deadline Letters of intent must be submitted by May of each year. Final proposals are due in June.

[929]
SOUTH CAROLINA SPACE GRANT CONSORTIUM UNDERGRADUATE RESEARCH PROGRAM

South Carolina Space Grant Consortium
c/o College of Charleston
Department of Geology
58 Coming Street, Room 341B
Charleston, SC 29424
(843) 953-7171   Fax: (843) 953-5446
E-mail: colganm@cofc.edu
Web: www.cofc.edu/~scsgrant

Purpose To provide financial assistance for space-related research to minority and other undergraduate students in South Carolina.

Eligibility This program is open to undergraduate students at member institutions of the South Carolina Space Grant Consortium. Applicants should be rising juniors or seniors interested in aerospace and space-related studies, including the basic sciences, astronomy, science education, planetary science, environmental studies, engineering, fine

arts, and journalism. U.S. citizenship is required. Selection is based on academic qualifications of the applicant; 2 letters of recommendation; a description of past activities, current interests, and future plans concerning a space science or aerospace-related field; and faculty sponsorship. Women and minorities are encouraged to apply.

Financial data The stipend is $3,000. Up to $500 of the $3,000 will be available for research related expenses, not including any application fees.

Duration 1 academic year or 10 weeks during the summer.

Additional information Members of the consortium are Benedict College, The Citadel, College of Charleston, Clemson University, Coastal Carolina University, Furman University, University of South Carolina, Wofford College, South Carolina State University, The Medical University of South Carolina, and University of the Virgin Islands. This program is funded by the U.S. National Aeronautics and Space Administration

Number awarded Varies each year.

Deadline January of each year.

[930]
SOUTHERN REGIONAL EDUCATION BOARD DISSERTATION-YEAR FELLOWSHIP

Southern Regional Education Board
592 10th Street N.W.
Atlanta, GA 30318-5790
(404) 875-9211, ext. 269   Fax: (404) 872-1477
E-mail: doctoral.scholars@sreb.org
Web: www.sreb.org/programs/dsp/dspindex.asp

Purpose To provide financial assistance to minority students who wish to complete a doctoral dissertation while in residence at a university in the southern states.

Eligibility This program is open to U.S. citizens who are members of racial/ethnic minority groups (Native Americans, Hispanic Americans, Asian Americans, and African Americans) and have completed all requirements for a Ph.D. except the dissertation. Applicants must be in a position to write full time and must expect to complete the dissertation within the year of the fellowship. Eligibility is limited to individuals who plan to become full-time faculty members at a southern institution upon completion of their doctoral degree. It does not include students working on a professional degree (M.D., D.B.A., D.D.S., J.D., and D.V.M.) or doing graduate work leading to the Ed.D.

Financial data Fellows receive waiver of tuition and fees (in or out of state), a stipend of $15,000, and a small grant for research expenses.

Duration 1 year; nonrenewable.

Number awarded Varies each year.

Deadline March of each year.

[931]
STARTER RESEARCH GRANTS

National Science Foundation
Directorate for Biological Sciences
Attn: Division of Biological Infrastructure
4201 Wilson Boulevard, Room 615
Arlington, VA 22230
(703) 292-8470   TDD: (703) 292-5090
E-mail: ckimsey@nsf.gov
Web: www.nsf.gov/bio

Purpose To help underrepresented minority scientists interested in establishing an independent research program in the biological, social, economic, and behavioral sciences.

Eligibility This program is open to U.S. citizens and permanent residents who are members of an ethnic group that is significantly underrepresented at advanced levels of science and engineering in the United States, including Native Americans (Alaska Natives and American Indians), African Americans, Hispanics, and Native Pacific Islanders. They must have received a Minority Postdoctoral Research Fellowship from the National Science Foundation (NSF) and have accepted a tenure-track position at a U.S. institution. Their field of study must fall within the program areas of the NSF Directorate for Biological Sciences or Directorate for Social, Behavioral, and Economic Sciences.

Financial data Grants up to $50,000 are available; the recipient's institution must provide matching funds on a 2:1 basis.

Duration 1 year; nonrenewable.

Additional information Information on the programs from the Directorate for Social, Behavioral, and Economic Sciences is available at (703) 292-8763, E-mail: jperhoni@nsf.gov.

Number awarded Approximately 6 each year.

Deadline Applications may be submitted at any time.

[932]
SUPPLEMENTAL FUNDING FOR SUPPORT OF WOMEN, MINORITY, AND DISABLED ENGINEERING RESEARCH ASSISTANTS

National Science Foundation
Directorate for Engineering
Attn: Division of Engineering Education and Centers
4201 Wilson Boulevard, Room 585
Arlington, VA 22230
(703) 292-8380   Fax: (703) 292-9051
TDD: (703) 292-5090
Web: www.eng.nsf.gov/eec

Purpose To encourage principal investigators on projects funded by the National Science Foundation (NSF) to include in their research projects high school and/or undergraduate engineering research assistants who are members of groups underrepresented in the advanced levels of U.S. science and engineering.

Eligibility The supplemental funding is expected to support students from underrepresented groups who will contribute to the NSF project with meaningful research work under the supervision of the principal investigator. For the purposes of this program, "underrepresented groups" include 1) minority groups (i.e., Native American, African American, Hispanic, Alaskan Native, or Native Pacific Islander); 2) women; and 3) persons with disabilities. Students must be citizens or nationals of the United States at the time of proposal submission.

Financial data Supplemental funding of up to $5,000, including indirect costs, may be requested for each student to be added to the project. Funds provided by this program are limited to 2 students per grant. Up to 10% of this amount may be used for supplies and services. Additional funds in excess of $5,000 may be requested, if necessary, to provide special equipment, modify equipment, or provide other services required specifically for the participation of physically handicapped individuals.

Duration The support may be used for a summer, quarter, or academic year.

Additional information Support may be requested in 2 ways: 1) requests for supplemental funding may be included in the initial proposal submission; or 2) current grantees may request supplemental funding of existing grants to add up to 2 students to the grant. Students interested in participating in this program should contact the sponsor to obtain a list of principal investigators in their area who have research grants from the Directorate for Engineering. The students are expected to be involved in an interesting and challenging aspect of the research, and the principal investigator should be available to participate in the research experience with the student.

Number awarded Varies each year.

[933]
SYLVIA TAYLOR JOHNSON MINORITY FELLOWSHIP IN EDUCATIONAL MEASUREMENT

Educational Testing Service
Attn: Fellowships
Rosedale Road
MS 09-R
Princeton, NJ 08541-0001
(609) 734-1806   E-mail: fellowships@ets.org
Web: www.ets.org/research/fellowships/stjmfel.html

Purpose To provide funding to minority scholars who are interested in conducting independent research under the mentorship of senior researchers at the Educational Testing Service (ETS).

Eligibility This program is open to minority scholars who have earned a doctorate within the past 10 years and are U.S. citizens or permanent residents. Applicants must be prepared to conduct independent research at ETS under the mentorship of a senior researcher. They should have a commitment to education and an independent body of scholarship that signals the promise of continuing contributions to educational measurement. Studies focused on issues concerning the education of minority students are especially encouraged. Selection is based on the scholar's record of accomplishment and proposed topic of research.

Financial data The stipend is set in relation to compensation at the home institution. Scholars and their families also receive reimbursement for relocation expenses.

Duration Up to 2 years.

Number awarded 1 each year.

Deadline January of each year.

[934]
TEXAS SPACE GRANT CONSORTIUM K-12 EDUCATION PROGRAMS

Texas Space Grant Consortium
Attn: Program Manager
3925 West Braker Lane, Suite 200
Austin, TX 78759
(512) 471-3583   Toll-free: (800) 248-8742
Fax: (512) 471-3585
E-mail: proposals@tsgc.utexas.edu
Web: www.tsgc.utexas.edu/epo

Purpose To provide funding to underrepresented minority and other faculty and staff at institutional members of the Texas Space Grant Consortium (TSGC) who are interested in developing projects to help K-12 teachers learn more about the benefits of space exploration and space-based research.

Eligibility This program is open to individuals qualified to serve as principal investigators at TSGC members in good standing. Applicants must be interested in developing a project for the professional development of K-12 teachers in Texas that will assist them to learn more about the benefits of space exploration and space-based research. Principal investigators must be U.S. citizens. The program encourages the participation of principal investigators who are women, underrepresented minorities, or persons with disabilities.

Financial data Grants up to $15,000 are available. Funds may be used for salary, wages, and fringe benefits for the principal investigator, staff, graduate students, and undergraduate students; tuition costs for graduate students; domestic travel; and materials and supplies. No funding is provided for overhead or indirect costs.

Duration The project must be completed within 2 years.

Additional information The participating universities are Baylor University, Lamar University, Prairie View A&M University, Rice University, San Jacinto College, Southern Methodist University, Sul Ross State University, Texas A&M University (including Kingsville and Corpus Christi campuses), Texas Christian University, Texas Southern University, Texas Tech University, Trinity University, University of Houston (including Clear Lake and Downtown campuses), University of Texas at Arlington, University of Texas at Austin, University of Texas at Dallas, University of Texas at El Paso, University of Texas at San Antonio, and University of Texas/Pan American. This program is funded by the National Aeronautics and Space Administration (NASA).

Number awarded 4 to 7 each year.

Deadline Notices of intent must be submitted by January of each year; completed proposals are due by the end of March.

[935]
TRAVEL AWARDS FOR MINORITY GRADUATE STUDENTS

National Science Foundation
Directorate for Biological Sciences
Attn: Division of Biological Infrastructure
4201 Wilson Boulevard, Room 615
Arlington, VA 22230
(703) 292-8470   TDD: (703) 292-5090
E-mail: ckimsey@nsf.gov
Web: www.nsf.gov/bio

Purpose To enable underrepresented minority graduate students to travel in the United States or abroad to assist in the selection of a postdoctoral mentor and to apply for postdoctoral fellowships.

Eligibility This program is open to U.S. citizens and permanent residents who are members of an ethnic group that is significantly underrepresented at advanced levels of science and engineering in the United States, including Native Americans (Alaska Natives and American Indians), African Americans, Hispanics, and Native Pacific Islanders. Applicants must be within 18 months of earning their Ph.D. degrees. Their field of study must fall within the program areas of the Directorate for Biological Sciences or the Directorate for Social, Behavioral, and Economic Sciences of the National Science Foundation (NSF). Awards are intended to allow them to travel within the United States or abroad to select a postdoctoral mentor or to develop an application for an NSF Minority Postdoctoral Research Fellowship.

Financial data Awards up to $4,000 are provided for airfare and living expenses while visiting the host scientist's institution.

Duration Up to 3 visits may be supported.

Additional information Information on the programs from the Directorate for Social, Behavioral, and Economic Sciences is available at (703) 292-8763, E-mail: jperhoni@nsf.gov.

Number awarded Approximately 7 each year.

Deadline Applications may be submitted at any time, but they must be received at least 3 months prior to the planned travel.

[936]
TUBEROUS SCLEROSIS COMPLEX RESEARCH PROGRAM CONCEPT AWARDS

U.S. Army
Medical Research and Materiel Command
Attn: MCMR-PLF
1077 Patchel Street (Building 1077)
Fort Detrick, MD 21702-5024
(301) 619-7079   Fax: (301) 619-7792
E-mail: cdmrp.pa@det.amedd.army.mil
Web: cdmrp.army.mil

Purpose To provide funding to minority and other scientists interested in conducting preliminary research on Tuberous Sclerosis complex.

Eligibility This program is open to scientists at universities, colleges, hospitals, laboratories, companies, and agencies of local, state, and federal governments. The sponsor is especially interested in receiving applications from Historically Black Colleges and Universities and Minority Institutions (HBCU/MI). Applicants must be interested in conducting innovative research directed toward improved prevention, diagnosis, and/or treatment of Tuberous Sclerosis. The proposed research projects should involve the exploration of untested, high-risk questions relevant to Tuberous Sclerosis and are not intended to support the next step in an already established research project. Presentation of preliminary data is not required. Proposals that address the needs of minority, low-income, rural, and other underrepresented and/or medically underserved populations are especially encouraged.

Financial data The maximum grant is $100,000, including both direct and indirect costs. Institutions are expected to cost share.

Duration 1 year.

Additional information The Tuberous Sclerosis Complex Research Program was established in 2002 as part of the Congressionally Directed Medical Research Programs of the U.S. Department of Defense.

Number awarded Approximately 7 each year.

Deadline February of each year.

[937]
TUBEROUS SCLEROSIS COMPLEX RESEARCH PROGRAM IDEA DEVELOPMENT AWARDS

U.S. Army
Medical Research and Materiel Command
Attn: MCMR-PLF
1077 Patchel Street (Building 1077)
Fort Detrick, MD 21702-5024
(301) 619-7079　　　Fax: (301) 619-7792
E-mail: cdmrp.pa@det.amedd.army.mil
Web: cdmrp.army.mil

Purpose To provide funding to minority and other scientists interested in conducting advanced research on Tuberous Sclerosis complex.

Eligibility This program is open to independent investigators at the level of assistant professor or equivalent at universities, colleges, hospitals, laboratories, companies, and agencies of local, state, and federal governments. The sponsor is especially interested in receiving applications from Historically Black Colleges and Universities and Minority Institutions (HBCU/MI). Applicants must be interested in conducting innovative research directed toward improved prevention, diagnosis, and/or treatment of Tuberous Sclerosis. All applications must include preliminary data relevant to the proposed project. Proposals that address the needs of minority, low-income, rural, and other underrepresented and/or medically underserved populations are especially encouraged.

Financial data The maximum grant is $425,000, including both direct and indirect costs. Institutions are expected to cost share.

Duration 2 to 3 years.

Additional information The Tuberous Sclerosis Complex Research Program was established in 2002 as part of the Congressionally Directed Medical Research Programs of the U.S. Department of Defense.

Number awarded Approximately 3 each year.

Deadline February of each year.

[938]
TUBEROUS SCLEROSIS COMPLEX RESEARCH PROGRAM NATURAL HISTORY DEVELOPMENT AWARDS

U.S. Army
Medical Research and Materiel Command
Attn: MCMR-PLF
1077 Patchel Street (Building 1077)
Fort Detrick, MD 21702-5024
(301) 619-7079　　　Fax: (301) 619-7792
E-mail: cdmrp.pa@det.amedd.army.mil
Web: cdmrp.army.mil

Purpose To provide funding to minority and other scientists interested in conducting research on the natural history of Tuberous Sclerosis complex.

Eligibility This program is open to researchers at all academic levels at universities, colleges, hospitals, laboratories, companies, and agencies of local, state, and federal governments. The sponsor is especially interested in receiving applications from Historically Black Colleges and Universities and Minority Institutions (HBCU/MI). Applicants must be interested in conducting a multi-institutional natural history study that will ascertain and analyze sufficient numbers of patients with Tuberous Sclerosis to yield a substantial normative data set and provide quantitative data on related tumor growth and/or other manifestations of the disease.

Financial data The maximum grant is $150,000, including both direct and indirect costs. Institutions are expected to cost share.

Duration 18 months.

Additional information The Tuberous Sclerosis Complex Research Program was established in 2002 as part of the Congressionally Directed Medical Research Programs of the U.S. Department of Defense.

Number awarded Approximately 2 each year.

Deadline February of each year.

[939]
UNCF/PFIZER POSTDOCTORAL FELLOWSHIPS

United Negro College Fund
Attn: Pfizer Biomedical Research Initiative
8260 Willow Oaks Corporate Drive
P.O. Box 10444
Fairfax, VA 22031-4511
(703) 205-3503　　　Fax: (703) 205-3574
E-mail: uncfpfizer@uncf.org
Web: www.uncf.org/pfizer/textpage.htm

Purpose To provide financial assistance to underrepresented minority postdoctoral fellows who are interested in pursuing biomedical research.

Eligibility This program is open to members of minority groups that are underrepresented in the biomedical science research fields (African Americans, Hispanic Americans, Native Americans, Natives of the U.S. Pacific islands, and Alaskan Natives). Applicants must have been appointed as postdoctoral fellows at an academic or non-academic research institution (private industrial laboratories are excluded). They must be U.S. citizens or permanent residents who have a Ph.D. in a life or physical science and are interested in preparing for a career in biomedical science education and research.

Financial data The total award is $53,500, including up to $44,500 as a stipend for the fellow (the maximum stipend is $35,000 for any 12-month period), up to $4,000 for fringe benefits, and up to $5,000 for supplies, equipment, and travel. Funds may not be used to support institutional indirect costs or faculty and staff salaries.

Duration 12 to 24 months.

Additional information This program is funded by Pfizer Inc. Fellows are mentored by a Pfizer staff scientist.

Number awarded At least 4 each year.

Deadline April of each year.

[940]
UNITED STATES INSTITUTE OF PEACE SENIOR FELLOWSHIPS

United States Institute of Peace
Attn: Jennings Randolph Program for International
   Peace
1200 17th Street, N.W., Suite 200
Washington, DC 20036-3011
(202) 429-3886   Fax: (202) 429-6063
TDD: (202) 457-1719   E-mail: fellows@usip.org
Web: www.usip.org/fellows/srfellows.html

Purpose To provide funding to minority and other professionals who wish to conduct research at the United States Institute of Peace (USIP) in Washington, D.C.

Eligibility This program is open to candidates from a wide variety of professional backgrounds, including governmental and nongovernmental practitioners in international security, peacemaking, and public affairs; scholars and researchers; and media and communications specialists. Fellows may be at any stage of their careers and have any educational background. They should be proposing a research project related to preventive diplomacy, ethnic and regional conflicts, peacekeeping and peace operations, peace settlements, post-conflict reconstruction and reconciliation, democratization and the rule of law, cross-cultural negotiations, U.S. foreign policy in the 21st century, and related topics. Preference is given to projects that demonstrate relevance to the sources and nature of interstate or civil conflict, with ways to prevent, limit, or end violent conflict, and with post-conflict reconstruction and reconciliation. Candidates must be proposing to produce 1 or more products, such as books or monographs published by USIP Press, reports published by the institute, articles for professional or academic journals, op-eds and articles for newspapers or magazines, radio or TV media projects, demonstrations or simulations, teaching curricula, lectures or other public speaking, or workshops, seminars, or symposia, while at the institute. Applicants may be citizens of any country. Women and members of minority groups are especially encouraged to apply. Selection is based on the candidate's record of achievement and/or leadership potential; the significance and potential of the project for making an important contribution to knowledge, practice, or public understanding; and the quality of the project design and its feasibility within the timetable proposed.

Financial data The stipend is based on the fellow's earned income for the preceding year, up to a maximum of $80,000. In the case of candidates from countries with salaries greatly different from the United States, seniority is the basis for calculation. Also provided are transportation to and from Washington, D.C. for the fellow and eligible family members.

Duration Up to 10 months.

Additional information These fellowships, first awarded in 1988, are tenable at the United States Institute of Peace in Washington, D.C., where fellows interact with other fellows and Institute staff by presenting their work and participating in workshops, conferences, and other events. These awards are not made for projects that constitute policymaking for a government agency or private organization; focus to any substantial degree on conflicts within U.S. domestic society, or adopt a partisan, advocacy, or activist stance.

Number awarded Varies each year; recently, 14 of these fellowships were awarded.

Deadline September of each year.

[941]
UNIVERSITY OF CALIFORNIA PRESIDENT'S POSTDOCTORAL FELLOWSHIP PROGRAM

University of California
Attn: Office of the President
1111 Franklin Street, 11th Floor
Oakland, CA 94607-5200
(510) 987-9503   Fax: (510) 587-6077
E-mail: kim.adkinson@ucop.edu
Web: www.ucop.edu/acadadv/ppfp

Purpose To provide minority and other recent postdoctorates who are committed to careers in university teaching and research with an opportunity to conduct research at 1 of the 10 University of California campuses.

Eligibility This program is open to U.S. citizens or permanent residents who have a Ph.D. from an accredited university. Applicants must be proposing to conduct research at a branch of the university under the mentorship of a faculty or laboratory sponsor. For the humanities, arts, social sciences, and professions, preference is given to candidates whose research emphasizes such issues as diversity, multiculturalism, and communities underserved by traditional academic research. The program is particularly interested in research that considers such issues as race, ethnicity, and/or gender as they relate to traditional academic fields. That includes research in such areas as community development, social justice, educational reform, economic development, public health and safety, and the dynamics of multicultural communities. For the life sciences, physical sciences, mathematics, and engineering, preference is given to candidates who have participated in teaching, mentoring, or outreach programs that promote educational opportunities for underrepresented students in higher education. In all fields, special consideration is given to applicants who have demonstrated significant academic achievement by overcoming such barriers as economic, social, or educational disadvantage. The program is particularly interested in applicants whose family members may have experienced barriers in participation in higher education, who are bilingual or bicultural, or who have participated in teaching, mentoring, or outreach programs (e.g., MESA, Puente) that are designed to foster the participation of underrepresented students in higher education.

Financial data The stipend is $33,800 to $35,300 for fields except mathematics, engineering, and the physical sciences; in those fields, stipends range from $35,300 to

$44,000, depending upon experience. The program also offers health benefits and up to $4,000 for supplemental and research-related expenses.

Duration Appointments are for 1 academic year, with possible renewal for a second year.

Additional information Research may be conducted on any of the University of California's 10 campuses (Berkeley, Davis, Irvine, Los Angeles, Merced, Riverside, San Diego, San Francisco, Santa Barbara, or Santa Cruz). The program provides mentoring and guidance in preparing for an academic career. This program was established in 1984 to encourage applications from minority and women scholars in fields where they were severely underrepresented; it is now open to all qualified candidates who are committed to university careers in research, teaching, and service that will enhance the diversity of the academic community at the university.

Number awarded 15 to 20 each year.

Deadline November of each year.

[942]
UNIVERSITY OF WISCONSIN VISITING MINORITY SCHOLAR LECTURE PROGRAM

University of Wisconsin at Madison
Attn: Wisconsin Center for Education Research
1025 West Johnson Street, Suite 785
Madison, WI 53706
(608) 263-4200   Fax: (608) 263-6448
E-mail: uw-wcer@education.wisc.edu
Web: www.wcer.wisc.edu

Purpose To make minority scholars and their work in education more visible on the University of Wisconsin (UW) campus.

Eligibility Minority scholars on the faculty of other universities are invited to present lectures on topics related to minorities and education at the University of Wisconsin. Candidates are nominated through a solicitation process within the university's school of education.

Financial data Lecturers receive travel expenses and an honorarium.

Duration Each visit lasts 2 days.

Additional information The visiting scholar makes a general presentation open to the University of Wisconsin's community and meets with a group of minority students at the university to discuss the scholar's work. This program is cosponsored by the University of Wisconsin's School of Education and the Wisconsin Center for Education Research.

Number awarded 6 each year.

[943]
UNIVERSITY POSTDOCTORAL FELLOWSHIP PROGRAM

Ohio State University
Attn: Dean of the Graduate School
250E University Hall
230 North Oval Mall
Columbus, OH 43210-1366
(614) 292-6031   Fax: (614) 292-3656
E-mail: clark.31@osu.edu
Web: www.gradsch.ohio-state.edu

Purpose To provide an opportunity for minority and other recent postdoctorates to conduct research at Ohio State University (OSU).

Eligibility Nominations may be submitted by OSU graduate faculty members who would like to coordinate a fellow's research. Faculty sponsors can host only 1 University Postdoctoral Fellow at a time. Eligible to be nominated are individuals who have held a doctorate or M.F.A. for 5 years or less. Nomination of minority and women candidates is particularly encouraged. Certain categories of persons are ineligible to be nominated: persons with doctoral or M.F.A. degrees from OSU, persons currently on appointment at OSU (or who have held a postdoctoral appointment there), senior faculty (associate or full professors) from other institutions, individuals who received a Ph.D. or M.F.A. more than 5 years ago, and international scholars who would not qualify for a J1 visa. Selection is based on the credentials of the postdoctoral candidates, the reputation of the faculty sponsors and the quality of their research program, the project proposed by the postdoctoral candidates with the guidance of their faculty sponsors, and the extent to which the candidates will enhance the research environment at the university through interactions with faculty, researchers, and graduate students.

Financial data The monthly stipend is $2,000 plus a $500 moving allowance and a $500 travel allowance (to attend professional meetings).

Duration From 9 to 12 months; nonrenewable.

Additional information Fellows are not OSU employees so they may not conduct research required by a grant and may not be asked to teach a course.

Number awarded Approximately 6 each year.

Deadline January of each year.

[944]
VIRGINIA SPACE GRANT AEROSPACE GRADUATE RESEARCH FELLOWSHIPS

Virginia Space Grant Consortium
Attn: Fellowship Coordinator
Old Dominion University Peninsula Center
600 Butler Farm Road
Hampton, VA 23666
(757) 766-5210   Fax: (757) 766-5205
E-mail: vsgc@odu.edu
Web: www.vsgc.odu.edu/html/fellowships.htm

Purpose To provide financial assistance for research in space-related fields to minority and other graduate students in Virginia.

Eligibility This program is open to graduate students who will be enrolled in a program of full-time study in an aerospace-related discipline at 1 of the Virginia Space Grant

Consortium (VSGC) Colleges. Applicants must be U.S. citizens with a GPA of 3.0 or higher. They must submit a research proposal with a plan of study that includes its key elements, what the applicant intends to accomplish, and the aerospace application of the proposed research activity. Eligibility is not limited to science and engineering majors; students in any field of study that includes course work related to an understanding of or interest in aerospace may apply. Selection is based on the applicants' academic qualifications, the quality of their proposed research plan, and its relevance to this program. Since an important purpose of this program is to increase the participation of underrepresented minorities, females, and persons with disabilities in aerospace-related careers, the VSGC especially encourages applications from those students.

Financial data The grant is $5,000. Funds are add-on awards, designed to supplement and enhance such basic graduate research support as research assistantships, teaching assistantships, and nonfederal scholarships and fellowships.

Duration 1 year; may be renewed up to 2 additional years.

Additional information The VSGC colleges are College of William and Mary, Hampton University, Old Dominion University, the University of Virginia, and Virginia Polytechnic Institute and State University. This program is funded by the U.S. National Aeronautics and Space Administration (NASA). Awardees are required to certify through their academic department that basic research support of at least $5,000 is being provided before receipt of Space Grant funds.

Number awarded At least 5 each year.

Deadline February of each year.

[945]
VIRGINIA SPACE GRANT AEROSPACE UNDERGRADUATE RESEARCH SCHOLARSHIPS

Virginia Space Grant Consortium
Attn: Fellowship Coordinator
Old Dominion University Peninsula Center
600 Butler Farm Road
Hampton, VA 23666
(757) 766-5210   Fax: (757) 766-5205
E-mail: vsgc@odu.edu
Web: www.vsgc.odu.edu/html/fellowships.htm

Purpose To provide financial assistance for research in space-related fields to minority and other undergraduate students in Virginia.

Eligibility This program is open to undergraduate students who will be enrolled in a program of full-time study in an aerospace-related discipline at 1 of the Virginia Space Grant Consortium (VSGC) Colleges. Applicants must be U.S. citizens who have completed at least 2 years of an undergraduate program with a GPA of 3.0 or higher. They must be proposing to participate in an active, identified research activity that has aerospace applications. The research must be supervised by a faculty mentor and may be conducted on the home campus or at an industrial or government facility. It should be continuous and may be conducted any time during the academic year, summer, or both. Since an important purpose of this program is to increase the participation of underrepresented minorities, females, and persons with

disabilities in aerospace-related careers, the VSGC especially encourages applications from those students.

Financial data Grants provide a student stipend of $3,000 during the academic year and a $3,500 stipend during the summer (either before or after the academic year). Recipients may request an additional $1,000 research allocation for materials and travel to support research activities conducted during the academic year and/or a $1,000 research allocation during the summer. The maximum award per year cannot exceed $8,500.

Duration 1 year; renewable.

Additional information The VSGC colleges are College of William and Mary, Hampton University, Old Dominion University, the University of Virginia, and Virginia Polytechnic Institute and State University. This program is funded by the U.S. National Aeronautics and Space Administration (NASA). Awardees are required to participate in the VSGC annual student research conference in late March or early April.

Number awarded Varies each year.

Deadline February of each year.

[946]
WALT DISNEY STUDIOS AND ABC ENTERTAINMENT WRITING FELLOWSHIP PROGRAM

Walt Disney Studios and ABC Entertainment
Attn: Writing Fellowship Program
500 South Buena Vista Street
Burbank, CA 91521-4389
(818) 560-6894   E-mail: abc.fellowships@abc.com
Web: www.abctalendevelopment.com

Purpose To provide support to minority and other writers interested in developing their craft at Walt Disney Studios and ABC Entertainment.

Eligibility This program is open to all writers, although a goal of the program is to seek out and employ culturally and ethnically diverse new writers. Applicants must submit a writing sample; for the feature films division, that should be a completed live-action motion picture screenplay (up to 120 pages) or a full-length 2-to-3 act play; for the television division, the sample should be a full-length script appropriate for a half-hour or 1-hour television series, based on a current prime time television or cable broadcast series.

Financial data The salary is $50,000.

Duration 1 year, beginning in January.

Additional information Fellows train with creative teams either at Walt Disney Studios or ABC Entertainment. This program began in 1990.

Number awarded Up to 11 each year.

Deadline June of each year.

[947]
WASHINGTON NASA SPACE GRANT CONSORTIUM SEED GRANTS FOR FACULTY

Washington NASA Space Grant Consortium
c/o University of Washington
401A Johnson Hall
Box 351310
Seattle, WA 98195-1310
(206) 543-1943   Toll-free: (800) 659-1943
Fax: (206) 543-0179
Web: www.waspacegrant.org/faculty.html

Purpose   To provide funding to minority and other faculty at member institutions of the Washington NASA Space Grant Consortium who are interested in conducting space-related research.

Eligibility   This program is open to faculty members at institutions that are members of the consortium. Applicants must be interested in initiating research efforts in disciplines relevant to the missions of the U.S. National Aeronautics and Space Administration (NASA) on earth and in space. The program values diversity and strongly encourages women and minorities to apply.

Financial data   Grants range from $10,000 to $20,000. Matching funds must be provided.

Duration   1 year.

Additional information   This program is funded by NASA. Members of the consortium include Northwest Indian College, Seattle Central Community College, the University of Washington, and Washington State University.

Number awarded   1 each year.

[948]
W.E.B. DUBOIS FELLOWSHIP PROGRAM

Department of Justice
National Institute of Justice
Attn: W.E.B. DuBois Fellowship Program
810 Seventh Street, N.W.
Washington, DC 20531
(202) 616-3233
Web: www.ojp.usdoj.gov/nij/funding.htm

Purpose   To provide funding to minority and other junior investigators interested in conducting research on the "confluence of crime, justice, and culture in various societal contexts."

Eligibility   This program is open to investigators who have a Ph.D. or other doctoral-level degree or a legal degree of J.D. or higher. Applicants should be early in their careers. They must be interested in conducting research that relates to the following high-priority topics: law enforcement/policing; justice systems (sentencing, courts, prosecution, defense); corrections; investigative and forensic sciences, including DNA; counterterrorism and critical incidents; crime prevention and causes of crime; violence and victimization, including violent crimes; drugs, alcohol, and crime; interoperability, spatial information, and automated systems; and program evaluation. The research should emphasize crime, violence, and the administration of justice in diverse cultural contexts. Because of that focus, the sponsor strongly encourages applications from diverse racial and ethnic backgrounds.

Financial data   The grant is approximately $75,000. Funds may be used for salary, fringe benefits, reasonable

costs of relocation, travel essential to the project, and office expenses not provided by the sponsor. Indirect costs are limited to 20%.

Duration   6 to 12 months; fellows are required to be in residence at the National Institute of Justice (NIJ) for the first 2 months and may elect to spend all or part of the remainder of the fellowship period either in residence at NIJ or at their home institution.

Number awarded   1 each year.

Deadline   January of each year.

[949]
WEST VIRGINIA SPACE GRANT CONSORTIUM GRADUATE FELLOWSHIP PROGRAM

West Virginia Space Grant Consortium
c/o West Virginia University
College of Engineering and Mineral Resources
G-68 Engineering Sciences Building
P.O. Box 6070
Morgantown, WV 26506-6070
(304) 293-4099, ext. 3737   Fax: (304) 293-4970
E-mail: nasa@cemr.wvu.edu
Web: www.nasa.wvu.edu/scholarships.htm

Purpose   To provide financial assistance to minority and other graduate students at designated academic institutions affiliated with the West Virginia Space Grant Consortium who wish to conduct research on space-related science or engineering topics.

Eligibility   This program is open to graduate students at participating member institutions of the consortium. Applicants must be interested in working on a research project with a faculty member who has received a West Virginia Space Grant Consortium Research Initiation Grant. U.S. citizenship is required. The consortium is a component of the Space Grant program of the U.S. National Aeronautics and Space Administration (NASA). Women and minorities are strongly encouraged to apply.

Financial data   The amount of the award for the graduate student depends on the amount of the research grant that the faculty member has received.

Duration   1 year.

Additional information   Funding for this program is provided by NASA. The participating consortium members are Marshall University, West Virginia Institute of Technology, West Virginia University, and Wheeling-Jesuit University.

Number awarded   Varies each year.

[950]
WEST VIRGINIA SPACE GRANT CONSORTIUM RESEARCH INITIATION GRANTS

West Virginia Space Grant Consortium
c/o West Virginia University
College of Engineering and Mineral Resources
G-68 Engineering Sciences Building
P.O. Box 6070
Morgantown, WV 26506-6070
(304) 293-4099, ext. 3737   Fax: (304) 293-4970
E-mail: nasa@cemr.wvu.edu
Web: www.nasa.wvu.edu/research.htm

Purpose   To provide funding for space-related research to minority and other faculty at academic institutions affiliated with the West Virginia Space Grant Consortium.

Eligibility This program is open to faculty members at colleges and universities that are members of the West Virginia Space Grant Consortium. Applicants must be seeking to pursue research in areas of interest to the U.S. National Aeronautics and Space Administration (NASA) and to establish long-term relationships with NASA researchers. U.S. citizenship is required. Selection is based on technical and scientific merit (30 points), potential for future funding and long-term impact (20 points), soundness of approach (20 points), relevance to NASA mission and West Virginia's priorities in science and technology (20 points), and budget (10 points). The consortium is a component of NASA's Space Grant program. Women and minorities are strongly encouraged to apply.

Financial data Grants range from $5,000 to $20,000. The consortium provides two-thirds of the total budget and the researcher's institution must agree to provide the remainder on a cost-sharing basis. At least 35% of the award must be allocated for a graduate student research assistant.

Duration 1 year.

Additional information Funding for this program is provided by NASA. The consortium includes Bethany College, Fairmont State College, Marshall University, Salem International University, Shepherd College, West Liberty State College, West Virginia Institute of Technology, West Virginia State College, West Virginia University, West Virginia Wesleyan College, and Wheeling-Jesuit University.

Number awarded Varies each year; recently, 8 of these grants were awarded.

Deadline March of each year.

[951]
WISCONSIN SPACE GRANT CONSORTIUM GRADUATE FELLOWSHIPS

Wisconsin Space Grant Consortium
c/o University of Wisconsin at Green Bay
Natural and Applied Sciences
2420 Nicolet Drive
Green Bay, WI 54311-7001
(920) 465-2108   Fax: (920) 465-2376
E-mail: wsgc@uwgb.edu
Web: www.uwgb.edu/wsgc/students/gf.asp

Purpose To provide financial assistance to underrepresented minority and other graduate students at member institutions of the Wisconsin Space Grant Consortium (WSGC) who are interested in conducting aerospace, space science, or other interdisciplinary aerospace-related research.

Eligibility This program is open to graduate students enrolled at the universities participating in the WSGC. Applicants must be U.S. citizens; be enrolled full time in a master's or Ph.D. program related to space science, aerospace, or interdisciplinary aerospace studies (including, but not limited to, engineering, the sciences, architecture, law, business, and medicine); have a GPA of 3.0 or higher; and be interested in conducting space-related research. The consortium especially encourages applications from underrepresented minorities, women, persons with disabilities, and those pursuing interdisciplinary aerospace studies. Selec-

tion is based on academic performance and space-related promise.

Financial data Grants up to $5,000 per year are provided.

Duration 1 academic year.

Additional information Funding for this program is provided by the U.S. National Aeronautics and Space Administration. The schools participating in the consortium include the University of Wisconsin campuses at Green Bay, La Crosse, Madison, Milwaukee, Oshkosh, Parkside, and Whitewater; College of the Menominee Nation; Marquette University; Carroll College; Lawrence University; Milwaukee School of Engineering; Ripon College; and Medical College of Wisconsin.

Number awarded Varies each year; recently, 7 of these fellowships were awarded.

Deadline February of each year.

[952]
WISCONSIN SPACE GRANT CONSORTIUM RESEARCH INFRASTRUCTURE PROGRAM

Wisconsin Space Grant Consortium
c/o University of Wisconsin at Madison
Space Science and Engineering Center
1225 West Dayton Street, Room 251
Madison, WI 53706-1280
(608) 263-4206   Fax: (608) 263-5974
E-mail: tom.achtor@ssec.wisc.edu
Web: www.uwgb.edu/wsgc/research/ri.asp

Purpose To provide funding to underrepresented minority and other staff members at academic and industrial affiliates of the Wisconsin Space Grant Consortium (WSGC) who are interested in developing space-related research infrastructure.

Eligibility This program is open to faculty and research staff at the WSGC universities and colleges and staff at WSGC industrial affiliates. Applicants must be interested in establishing a space-related research program. Faculty and staff on university/industry teams in all areas of research are considered, but research initiatives must focus on activities related to the mission of the U.S. National Aeronautics and Space Administration (NASA). Those activities include earth and atmospheric sciences, astronautics, aeronautics, space sciences, and other space-related fields (e.g., agriculture, business, law, medicine, nursing, social and behavioral sciences, and space architecture). Grants are made in 2 categories: 1) faculty research seed grants and/or faculty proposal writing grants; and 2) other research initiatives, such as seminars, workshops, and/or travel to NASA centers. Preference is given to applications that emphasize new lines of space-related research, establishing collaborations among faculty from liberal arts colleges with faculty from research-intensive doctoral universities, linking academic and industrial affiliates, coordinated efforts with other NASA programs, increasing research capability, building research infrastructure, establishing research collaborations, and initiating research opportunities in line with the NASA Strategic Enterprises, especially by women, underrepresented minorities, and persons with disabilities. Selection is based on the proposal topic, quality, credentials of the investigator(s), and probability of success in developing space-related research infrastructure.

Financial data For faculty research seed grants and proposal writing grants, most awards range up to $5,000, although 1 grant of $10,000 is available. For other research initiatives, the maximum grant is $1,000.

Duration 1 year. Proposals for 2-year projects may be considered if they include a 2-year budget and justification of why the project requires a 2-year effort.

Additional information Funding for this program is provided by NASA. Academic members of WSGC include the University of Wisconsin campuses at Green Bay, La Crosse, Madison, Milwaukee, Oshkosh, Parkside, and Whitewater; College of the Menominee Nation; Marquette University; Carroll College; Lawrence University; Milwaukee School of Engineering; Ripon College; and Medical College of Wisconsin. Industrial affiliates include Astronautics Corporation of America, Orbital Technologies Corporation, Space Explorers, Inc., Wisconsin Association of CESA Administrators, Wisconsin Department of Public Instruction, Wisconsin Department of Transportation, and Wisconsin Space Business Roundtable.

Number awarded Varies each year; recently, 4 of these grants were awarded.

Deadline February of each year.

[953]
WISCONSIN SPACE GRANT CONSORTIUM UNDERGRADUATE RESEARCH AWARDS

Wisconsin Space Grant Consortium
c/o University of Wisconsin at Madison
Space Science and Engineering Center
1225 West Dayton Street, Room 251
Madison, WI 53706-1280
(608) 263-4206   Fax: (608) 263-5974
E-mail: tom.achtor@ssec.wisc.edu
Web: www.uwgb.edu/wsgc/research/ur.asp

Purpose To provide funding to underrepresented minority and other undergraduate students at colleges and universities participating in the Wisconsin Space Grant Consortium (WSGC) who are interested in conducting space-related research.

Eligibility This program is open to undergraduate students enrolled at 1 of the institutions participating in the WSGC. Applicants must be U.S. citizens; be enrolled full time in an undergraduate program related to space science, aerospace, or interdisciplinary space studies; and have a GPA of 3.0 or higher. They must be proposing to create and implement a small research project of their own design as academic year, summer, or part-time employment that is directly related to their interests and career objectives in space science, aerospace, or space-related studies. Students must request a faculty or research staff member on their campus to act as an advisor; the consortium locates a scientist or engineer from 1 of the research-intensive universities to serve as a second mentor for successful applicants. The consortium especially encourages applications from students pursuing interdisciplinary space studies (e.g., engineering, the sciences, architecture, law, business, and medicine), underrepresented minorities, women, and persons with disabilities. Selection is based on academic performance and space-related promise.

Financial data Stipends up to $3,500 per year or summer session are available. An additional $500 may be awarded for exceptional expenses, such as high travel costs.

Duration 1 academic year or summer.

Additional information Funding for this program is provided by the U.S. National Aeronautics and Space Administration. The schools participating in the consortium include the University of Wisconsin campuses at Green Bay, La Crosse, Madison, Milwaukee, Oshkosh, Parkside, and Whitewater; College of the Menominee Nation; Marquette University; Carroll College; Lawrence University; Milwaukee School of Engineering; Ripon College; and Medical College of Wisconsin.

Number awarded Varies each year; recently, 9 of these grants were awarded.

Deadline February of each year.

[954]
W.K. KELLOGG FOUNDATION FELLOWSHIP PROGRAM IN HEALTH RESEARCH

National Medical Fellowships, Inc.
Attn: Scholarship Program
5 Hanover Square, 15th Floor
New York, NY 10004
(212) 483-8880   Fax: (212) 483-8897
E-mail: info@nmfonline.org
Web: www.nmf-online.org

Purpose To provide financial assistance to minorities enrolled in a doctoral program in health policy research who are committed to working with underserved populations.

Eligibility This program is open to members of minority groups (African Americans, Native Americans, Asians, and Hispanics) enrolled in doctoral programs in public health, social policy, or health policy (Ph.D., Dr.P.H., or Sc.D.). Applicants must demonstrate a willingness to complete relevant dissertation research and a commitment to work with underserved populations upon completion of the doctorate. They must include an essay of 500 to 1,000 words discussing their reasons for applying for a fellowship, their qualifications, how it will support their career plans, and which of 4 areas of focus (health policy, men's health, mental health, substance abuse) most interests them and why.

Financial data Fellowships cover tuition, fees, and a partial living stipend.

Duration Up to 5 years: 2 years to do the necessary course work and 3 years to complete the dissertation.

Additional information The program was created in 1998 with grant support from the W.K. Kellogg Foundation. Recently, it operated at 8 institutions: the RAND Graduate School, the Heller Graduate School at Brandeis University, the Joseph L. Mailman School of Public Health at Columbia University, the Harvard School of Public Health, the Johns Hopkins School of Hygiene and Public Health, the UCLA School of Public Health, the University of Michigan School of Public Health, and the University of Pennsylvania. Information is also available from the sponsor's Washington office at 1627 K Street, N.W., Suite 1200, Washington, DC 20006-1702, (202) 296-4431, Fax: (202) 293-1990.

Number awarded 5 each year.

Deadline June of each year.

[955]
WOMEN'S HEALTH IN SPORTS AND EXERCISE GRANTS

National Institute of Arthritis and Musculoskeletal and Skin Diseases
Attn: Director, Orthopaedics Program
45 Center Drive, Room 5AS-37K
Bethesda, MD 20892-6500
(301) 594-5055   Fax: (301) 480-4543
E-mail: jp149d@nih.gov
Web: www.nih.gov/niams

Purpose To provide funding to underrepresented minority and other investigators interested in conducting research related to the pathophysiology of sports injuries in women.

Eligibility This program is open to investigators at eligible institutions: for-profit and nonprofit organizations, public or private institutions (colleges, universities, laboratories), units of state and local governments, eligible agencies of the federal government, domestic or foreign institutions, and faith-based organizations. Applicants must be interested in conducting basic, translational, or patient-oriented clinical research on the pathophysiology of sports injuries in women. Proposals may deal with epidemiological issues, neuromuscular issues, basic science issues, coaching/training/equipment issues, surveillance/patient-oriented research issues, or social/psychological issues. Individuals from underrepresented racial and ethnic groups as well as individuals with disabilities are encouraged to apply for NIH programs.

Financial data Applications requesting up to $250,000 per year in direct costs must be submitted in a modular grant format. Applications requesting $500,000 or more in direct costs for any year must include a cover letter identifying the NIH staff member who has agreed to accept assignment of the application.

Duration Up to 5 years.

Additional information This program is also available through the National Institute of Child Health and Human Development, Attn: National Center for Medical and Rehabilitation Research, 6100 Executive Boulevard, Room 2A03, Bethesda, MD 20892, (301) 402-2242, Fax: (301) 402-0832, E-mail: cs388r@nih.gov.

Deadline January, May, or September of each year.

[956]
WOMEN'S STUDIES IN RELIGION PROGRAM

Harvard Divinity School
Attn: Director of Women's Studies in Religion Program
45 Francis Avenue
Cambridge, MA 02138
(617) 495-5705   Fax: (617) 495-9489
E-mail: wsrp@hds.harvard.edu
Web: www.hds.harvard.edu/wsrp

Purpose To encourage and support research on the relationship between religion, gender, and culture.

Eligibility This program is open to scholars who have a Ph.D. in the field of religion. Candidates with primary competence in other humanities, social sciences, and public policy fields who have a serious interest in religion and religious professionals with equivalent achievements are also eligible. Applicants should be proposing to conduct research projects at Harvard Divinity School's Women's Studies in Religion Program (WSRP) on topics related to the history and function of gender in religious traditions, the institutionalization of roles in religious communities, or the interaction between religion and the personal, social, and cultural situations of women. Appropriate topics include feminist theology, Biblical studies, ethics, women's history, and interdisciplinary scholarship on women in world religions. Selection is based on the quality of the applicant's research prospectus, outlining objectives and methods; its fit with the program's research priorities; the significance of the contribution of the proposed research to the study of religion, gender, and culture, and to its field; and agreement to produce a publishable piece of work by the end of the appointment.

Financial data Research associates/visiting lecturers in the WSRP receive a stipend of $40,000 and benefits for a full-time appointment.

Duration 1 academic year, from September to June.

Additional information Fellows at the WSRP devote the majority of their appointments to individual research projects in preparation for publication, meeting together regularly for discussion of research in process. They also teach a semester course related to this research and consult with faculty on current school planning for integration of women's studies into the Harvard Divinity School curriculum. Recipients are required to be in full-time residence at the school while carrying out their research project.

Number awarded 5 each year. The group each year usually includes at least 1 international scholar, 1 scholar working on a non-western tradition, 1 scholar of Judaism, and 1 minority scholar.

Deadline November of each year.

[957]
WYOMING SPACE GRANT CONSORTIUM UNDERGRADUATE RESEARCH FELLOWSHIPS

Wyoming Space Grant Consortium
c/o University of Wyoming
Physical Sciences Building, Room 210
P.O. Box 3905
Laramie, WY 82071-3905
(307) 766-2862   Fax: (307) 766-2652
E-mail: wy.spacegrant@uwyo.edu
Web: wyomingspacegrant.uwyo.edu/fellug.htm

Purpose To provide funding for space-related research to underrepresented minority and other undergraduate students in Wyoming.

Eligibility This program is currently open to undergraduate students at the University of Wyoming and all community colleges in Wyoming. Applicants must be U.S. citizens who are interested in conducting a space-related research project under the mentorship of a faculty member. A major in science or engineering is not required, because the program assumes that even non-science majors broaden their educations with a research experience. The faculty mentor must have active status and/or plan to be on-site and readily available to the student. Selection is based on the scientific merit of the proposed project, the pedagogical benefits to the student as a result of the overall research experience, and the quality of the proposal and recommendations. Wyoming Space Grant is a component of the Space Grant program of the U.S. National Aeronautics and Space Administration (NASA), which encourages participation by women, underrepresented minorities, and persons with disabilities.

Financial data Grants range up to $5,000. Funds may be used only for undergraduate salary support, at the rate of $7.75 per hour. Tuition is not provided for the student's home institution, special institutes, or off-campus programs. Other expenditures not usually supported include travel, page charges, equipment, and supplies; applicants are encouraged to seek matching funds to cover those expenditures, and proposals that include matching by non-federal funds are given priority.

Duration Research may be conducted during the academic year or summer.

Additional information This program is funded by NASA. Recipients are expected to keep the program informed of their progress, submit a final report in a timely manner, participate in publications of research results, and present a colloquium on their research.

Number awarded 4 to 6 each year.

Deadline February of each year.

[958]
ZIMMER ORTHOPAEDIC CAREER DEVELOPMENT AWARDS

Orthopaedic Research and Education Foundation
Attn: Vice President, Grants
6300 North River Road, Suite 700
Rosemont, IL 60018-4261
(847) 384-4348   Fax: (847) 698-7806
E-mail: mcquire@oref.org
Web: www.oref.org/grants/grants.html

Purpose To provide funding to new orthopedic surgeons (particularly minorities and women) who are interested in additional training and/or research.

Eligibility This program is open to orthopedic surgeons who have completed formal training within the past 4 years and have a clinical or scientific interest in total joint surgery and/or trauma treatment. Applicants must be interested in a training and/or research program that may involve support for training or investigation, support for travel and furthers training or investigation, or support to provide for special resources required to advance training or investigation. Minority and female surgeons are especially encouraged to apply.

Financial data Grants up to $50,000 per year are awarded.

Duration 1 year.

Additional information Funding for minority surgeons is provided by the J. Robert Gladden Society. Funding for women surgeons is provided by the Ruth Jackson Orthopaedic Society.

Number awarded Varies each year; recently, 8 of these grants were awarded.

Deadline September of each year.

Awards

Described in this section are 43 competitions, prizes, and honoraria open to Hispanic Americans in recognition or support of creative work, personal accomplishments, professional contributions, or public service. Excluded are prizes received solely as the result of entering contests. If you are looking for a particular program and don't find it in this section, be sure to check the Program Title Index to see if it is covered elsewhere in the directory.

[959]
ANISFIELD-WOLF BOOK AWARDS

Cleveland Foundation
1422 Euclid Avenue, Suite 1300
Cleveland, OH 44115-2001
(216) 861-3810   Fax: (216) 861-1729
E-mail: asktcf@clevefdn.org
Web: www.anisfield-wolf.org

Purpose To recognize and reward recent books that have contributed to an understanding of racism or appreciation of the rich diversity of human cultures.

Eligibility Works published in English during the preceding year that "contribute to our understanding of racism or appreciation of the rich diversity of human cultures" are eligible to be considered. Entries may be either scholarly or imaginative (fiction, poetry, memoir). Plays and screenplays are not eligible, nor are works in progress. Manuscripts and self-published works are not eligible, and no grants are made for completing or publishing manuscripts.

Financial data The prize is $10,000. If more than 1 author is chosen in a given year, the prize is divided equally among the winning books.

Duration The award is presented annually.

Additional information These awards were first presented in 1936. Information is also available from Laura Scharf, 6100 Rockside Woods Boulevard, Suite 350, Cleveland, OH 44131.

Number awarded 3 each year: 1 for fiction, 1 for nonfiction, and 1 for lifetime achievement.

Deadline January of each year.

[960]
APA PRIZE IN LATIN AMERICAN THOUGHT

American Philosophical Association
Attn: Executive Director
c/o University of Delaware
31 Amstel Avenue
Newark, DE 19716-4797
(302) 831-1112   Fax: (302) 831-8690
E-mail: apaonline@udel.edu
Web: www.apa.udel.edu

Purpose To recognize and reward authors of outstanding philosophical essays on Latin American thought.

Eligibility This award is presented to the author of the best unpublished essay on Latin American thought. Applicants must submit essays of 5,000 to 7,000 words that contain original arguments and broach philosophical topics clearly related to the specific experiences of Hispanic Americans and Latinos. They must be members of the American Philosophical Association (APA).

Financial data The prize is $500.

Duration The prize is awarded annually.

Additional information This prize was established in 2004. The winning essay is published in the *APA Newsletter on Hispanic/Latino Issues in Philosophy*.

Number awarded 1 each year.

Deadline June of each year.

[961]
BEYOND MARGINS AWARD

PEN American Center
Attn: Beyond Margins Program Assistance
588 Broadway, Suite 303
New York, NY 10012
(212) 334-1660, ext. 110   Fax: (212) 334-2181
E-mail: jmartinez@pen.org
Web: www.pen.org

Purpose To recognize and reward outstanding authors of color from any country.

Eligibility This award is presented to an author of color (African, Arab, Asian, Caribbean, Latino, and Native American) whose book-length writings were published in the United States during the current calendar year. Works of fiction, literary nonfiction, biography/memoir, and other works of literary character are strongly preferred. U.S. citizenship or residency is not required. Nominations must be submitted by publishers or agents.

Financial data The prize is $1,000.

Duration The prizes are awarded annually.

Number awarded 5 each year.

Deadline December of each year.

[962]
CAROLINA RICE/UNIVISION RADIO SCHOLARSHIPS

Riviana Foods Inc.
Attn: The Carolina Scholarship
75-22 37th Avenue, Suite 224
Jackson Heights, NY 11327
Web: www.carolinarice.com/scholarship

Purpose To recognize and reward, with college scholarships, Hispanic and other high school seniors in the New York/New Jersey metropolitan areas who submit outstanding essays.

Eligibility This competition is open to seniors graduating from high schools in the greater New York/New Jersey metropolitan area. Applicants must submit an essay, up to 250 words in length, on the topic "How does my education affect my family." Essays may be written in Spanish or in English. Selection is based on conciseness, originality, grammar, and spelling. Finalists are interviewed.

Financial data The award is a $2,000 college scholarship.

Duration The competition is held annually.

Additional information This program, which began in 1987, is jointly sponsored by Riviana Foods Inc. of Houston, Texas and Univision Communications Inc., the premier Spanish-language media company in the United States. Information is also available from Barbara Miller, Hispanic Broadcasting Corporation, 485 Madison Avenue, New York, NY 10022, (212) 310-6077.

Number awarded 5 each year.

Deadline February of each year.

[963]
CASEY FAMILY SCHOLARSHIPS FOR MALE STUDENTS OF COLOR

Orphan Foundation of America
Attn: Director of Student Services
Tall Oaks Village Center
12020-D North Shore Drive
Reston, VA 20190-4977
(571) 203-0270   Toll-free: (800) 950-4673
Fax: (571) 203-0273 E-mail: scholarships@orphan.org
Web: www.orphan.org/scholarships.html

Purpose To recognize and reward minority male students who have been in foster care and are completing a vocational or undergraduate degree.

Eligibility This program is open to male minority students enrolled in their final year of a vocational program or their senior year of an undergraduate program. Applicants must have aged out of the U.S. foster care system. Along with their application, they must submit 1) verification of their foster care status; 2) documentation of their total outstanding federal loan amount; 3) documentation from their school regarding any outstanding tuition balance they currently owe; and 4) a 5-paragraph essay explaining the single most important thing their postsecondary education has taught them and how they will take that lesson and apply it to their professional and personal life to help ensure their future success. Selection is based on financial need and merit, as commendation for ambition and tenacity in pursuing a higher education.

Financial data Awards range up to $5,000.

Duration These are 1-time awards.

Additional information This program was established in 2004 by Casey Family Programs.

Number awarded Awards are presented until funds are exhausted.

[964]
CHICANO/LATINO LITERARY PRIZE

University of California at Irvine
Department of Spanish and Portuguese
Attn: Prize Coordinator
322 Humanities Hall
Irvine, CA 92715-5275
(949) 824-5443   E-mail: cllp@uci.edu
Web: www.hnet.uci.edu

Purpose To recognize and reward the outstanding writing of Chicanos/Latinos in the United States.

Eligibility Chicano/Latino writers who identify strongly with the Hispanic community are eligible to submit unpublished manuscripts of at least 90 typed pages. Applicants must be U.S. citizens or permanent residents. Each year, a different genre of unpublished writing is rewarded, rotating among drama (2006), novels (2007), short story collections (2008), and poetry collections (2009).

Financial data The first-prize winner receives $1,000 plus transportation to Irvine, California and publication of the award-winning manuscript. The second-place winner receives $500 and the third-place winner receives $250.

Duration The competition is held annually.

Additional information The manuscripts may be in English, Spanish, or both languages.

Number awarded 3 each year.

Deadline May of each year.

[965]
DONNA JAMISON LAGO MEMORIAL SCHOLARSHIP

NextGen Network, Inc.
c/o Urbanomics Consulting Group
1010 Wisconsin Avenue, Suite 430
Washington, DC 20007
(202) 298-8226   Fax: (202) 298-8074
E-mail: info@nextgennetwork.com
Web: www.nextgennetwork.com

Purpose To recognize and reward outstanding essays written by minority high school seniors who will be going on to college.

Eligibility This competition is open to ethnic minority high school seniors in good academic standing. Entrants must be U.S. citizens and intending to attend a college or university after graduation. They must submit an essay, from 500 to 1,000 words, on a topic that changes annually; recently, students were invited to write on the following topic: "You have been elected President of the United States. What three initiatives would you want to introduce? Be specific rather than general and give arguments to support your choice." The essay should demonstrate critical thinking, creativity, and strong communication skills.

Financial data Finalists receive $1,500 each; semifinalists receive $1,000 each.

Duration The competition is held annually.

Additional information This program was formerly known as the "Path to Excellence" Scholarship Award.

Number awarded 6 each year: 3 finalists and 3 semifinalists.

Deadline March of each year.

[966]
EDWARD A. BOUCHET AWARD

American Physical Society
Attn: Honors Program
One Physics Ellipse
College Park, MD 20740-3844
(301) 209-3268   Fax: (301) 209-0865
E-mail: honors@aps.org
Web: www.aps.org/praw/bouchet/index.cfm

Purpose To recognize and reward outstanding research in physics by a member of an underrepresented minority group.

Eligibility Nominees for this award must be Blacks, Hispanics, or Native Americans who have made significant contributions to physics research and are effective communicators.

Financial data The award consists of a grant of $3,500 to the recipient, a travel allowance for the recipient to visit 3 academic institutions to deliver lectures, and an allowance for travel expenses to the meeting of the American Physical Society (APS) at which the prize is presented.

Duration The award is presented annually.

Additional information This award was established in 1994 and is currently funded by a grant from the Research Corporation. As part of the award, the recipient visits 3 academic institutions where the impact of the visit on minority students will be significant. The purpose of those visits is to deliver technical lectures on the recipient's field of specialization, to visit classrooms where appropriate, to assist the institution with precollege outreach efforts where appropriate, and to talk informally with faculty and students about research and teaching careers in physics.

Number awarded 1 each year.

Deadline June of each year.

[967]
FOUNDERS DISTINGUISHED SENIOR SCHOLAR AWARD

American Association of University Women
Attn: AAUW Educational Foundation
1111 16th Street, N.W.
Washington, DC 20036-4873
(202) 785-7609   Toll-free: (800) 326-AAUW
Fax: (202) 463-7169   TDD: (202) 785-7777
E-mail: foundation@aauw.org
Web: www.aauw.org/fga/awards/fdss.cfm

Purpose To recognize and reward American women (particularly women of color) for a lifetime of scholarly excellence.

Eligibility Eligible for nomination are women scholars who can demonstrate a lifetime of outstanding research, college or university teaching, publications, and positive impact upon women in their profession and community. U.S. citizenship or permanent resident status is required. Selection is based on lifetime commitment to women's issues in the profession or in the community, significance and impact of the nominee's scholarship upon her field, demonstrated excellence in and commitment to teaching and mentoring female college students, and total impact upon her profession and the community. The sponsor strongly encourages nomination of women of color and other underrepresented groups.

Financial data The award is $1,000.

Duration The award is presented annually.

Additional information The award includes a trip to the annual AAUW convention (where the award is presented).

Number awarded 1 each year.

Deadline February of each year.

[968]
FRANKLIN C. MCLEAN AWARD

National Medical Fellowships, Inc.
Attn: Scholarship Program
5 Hanover Square, 15th Floor
New York, NY 10004
(212) 483-8880   Fax: (212) 483-8897
E-mail: info@nmfonline.org
Web: www.nmf-online.org

Purpose To recognize and reward the outstanding academic achievement, leadership, and community service of senior medical school minority students.

Eligibility This competition is open to African American, Native Hawaiian, Alaska Native, American Indian, Mexican American, and mainland Puerto Rican students enrolled in accredited U.S. medical schools or osteopathic colleges. Candidates must be nominated by their schools during the

summer preceding their senior year. Selection is based on academic achievement, leadership, and community service.

Financial data This honor includes a certificate of merit and a $3,000 award.

Duration 1 year; nonrenewable.

Additional information This award, the first award offered by the National Medical Fellowship, was established in 1968 in memory of the Chicago bone physiologist who founded the organization.

Number awarded 1 each year.

Deadline Nominations must be submitted by July of each year.

[969]
GREGORY KOLOVAKOS AWARD

PEN American Center
Attn: Literary Awards Coordinator
588 Broadway, Suite 303
New York, NY 10012
(212) 334-1660, ext. 101   Fax: (212) 334-2181
E-mail: awards@pen.org
Web: www.pen.org

Purpose To recognize and reward outstanding contributions made by translators, editors, or critics to Hispanic literature in English translation.

Eligibility Writers, critics, and translators whose work has aided the cause of Latin American and Iberian literature in English may be nominated for this award. Letters of nomination must be received from the candidate's editor or colleague, accompanied by a copy of the nominee's vitae. Self-nominations are not accepted. The award focuses on works in Spanish, but distinguished contributions from other languages of the Hispanic world are also considered.

Financial data The award is $2,000.

Duration The award is given triennially (2006, 2009, etc.).

Additional information This award was established in 1992.

Number awarded 1 every third year.

Deadline January of the year of the award.

[970]
HISPANIC HERITAGE YOUTH AWARDS

Hispanic Heritage Awards Foundation
2600 Virginia Avenue, N.W., Suite 406
Washington, DC 20037
(202) 861-9797   Toll-free: (866) 665-2112
Fax: (202) 861-9799
E-mail: contact@hispanicheritageawards.org
Web: www.hispanicheritageawards.org

Purpose To recognize and reward, with college scholarships, Hispanic high school seniors from selected metropolitan areas throughout the country who have excelled in various areas of activity.

Eligibility This program is open to high school seniors who are U.S. citizens or permanent residents and of Hispanic heritage (at least 1 parent must be of able to trace family origins to Spain, Latin America, or the Spanish-speaking Caribbean). Awards were recently presented to students in 12 metropolitan regions: Chicago, Dallas, Houston, Los Angeles, Miami, New York City, Philadelphia, Phoenix, San Antonio, San Diego, northern California, and Washington, D.C. Applicants competed for awards in the following 6 categories: community service, engineering and mathematics, academic excellence, journalism, sports, or health care. They must have a GPA of 2.75 or higher. Along with their application, they must submit an essay that describes their personal qualities and strengths, dedication to community service and the impact it has had on their life, future career goals, areas of interest, and significance of heritage and/or family in their life. Selection criteria include, but are not limited to, the following: academic achievement, compelling essay responses, meritorious achievements in the applicant's chosen category, contribution to the community, overall character as a role model, and letters of recommendation.

Financial data In each category and each city, gold regional winners receive $3,000 and silver regional winners receive $2,000. Awards are in the form of educational grants that recipients may use for any aspect of their college career (tuition, books, room, and board). The gold regional winners then advance to a national competition. National winners receive an additional $5,000 educational grant, a state-of-the-art laptop computer, an all-expense paid trip to Miami for the winner and a parent to attend the award announcement event, and an all-expense paid trip to Washington, D.C. for the winner and a parent to attend the awards ceremony at the John F. Kennedy Center for the Performing Arts.

Duration The awards are presented annually.

Additional information This program began in 1998 with sponsorship by the Fannie Mae Foundation for 5 cities and 1 category. More sponsors have resulted in the addition of more categories and cities. Recent sponsors have included Dr Pepper for community service, ExxonMobil for engineering and mathematics, Chase Manhattan Bank and Master-Card for academic excellence, NBC and Telemundo for journalism, Subway for sports, and GlaxoSmithKline for health care. Awardees must attend, at their own expense, a local awards ceremony for the region they have selected.

Number awarded Recently, 144 regional winners were selected: a gold and a silver in each of the 6 categories from each of the 12 cities. From those, 6 national winners were chosen: 1 in each of the categories.

Deadline February of each year.

[971]
HISPANIC THEOLOGICAL INITIATIVE BOOK PRIZE AND LECTURESHIP

Hispanic Theological Initiative
12 Library Place
Princeton, NJ 08540
(609) 252-1721   Toll-free: (800) 575-5522
Fax: (609) 252-1738   E-mail: hti@ptsem.edu
Web: www.htiprogram.org/awards/book-prize.htm

Purpose To recognize and reward junior Latino scholars who have published outstanding books in theology.

Eligibility This competition is open to non-tenured Latino scholars at academic institutions in the United States in the fields of religion or theology. Candidates must have written a nonfiction book in English published in the United States that is nominated by their publisher. The book must relate to the intellectual traditions of Christianity, Judaism, or Islam. Books that deal with those traditions from a sociolog-

ical, anthropological, or cultural studies perspective are also eligible. Selection is based on scholarly excellence.

Financial data A monetary award is presented.

Duration The award is presented annually.

Additional information This award, funded by Pew Charitable Trusts, is presented at a major public ceremony held at Princeton Theological Seminary.

Number awarded 1 each year.

Deadline January of each year.

[972]
HISPANICSTUDENTS.COM SCHOLARSHIP ESSAY CONTEST

Diversity City Media
225 West Third Street, Suite 203
Long Beach, CA 90802
(562) 209-0616
E-mail: scholarship@hispanicstudents.com
Web: www.hispanicstudents.com/scholarship.html

Purpose To recognize and reward outstanding essays written by Hispanics currently enrolled or intending to enroll in college.

Eligibility This competition is open to U.S. residents attending or preparing to attend a trade school, college, or university. At least 1 of their parents must be Hispanic. They must register with HispanicStudents.com and then submit (through the Internet) an essay of 800 to 1,000 words on a topic that changes with each competition; a recent topic was, "Why More Hispanics Now Than Ever are Earning College Degrees?" Selection is based on the quality, uniqueness, and creativity of the essay.

Financial data The award is $500.

Duration The competition is held annually.

Number awarded 1 each year.

Deadline January of each year.

[973]
JAMES A. RAWLEY PRIZE

Organization of American Historians
Attn: Award and Prize Coordinator
112 North Bryan Street
P.O. Box 5457
Bloomington, IN 47408-5457
(812) 855-9852   Fax: (812) 855-0696
E-mail: oahawards@oah.org
Web: www.oah.org

Purpose To recognize and reward outstanding books dealing with race relations in the United States.

Eligibility This award is presented to the author of the outstanding book on the history of race relations in America. Entries must have been published during the current calendar year.

Financial data The award is $1,000 and a certificate.

Duration The award is presented annually.

Additional information The award was established in 1990.

Number awarded 1 each year.

Deadline September of each year.

[974]
JAMES H. ROBINSON MEMORIAL PRIZE IN SURGERY

National Medical Fellowships, Inc.
Attn: Scholarship Program
5 Hanover Square, 15th Floor
New York, NY 10004
(212) 483-8880   Fax: (212) 483-8897
E-mail: info@nmfonline.org
Web: www.nmf-online.org

Purpose To recognize and reward outstanding surgical performance by underrepresented minority medical students enrolled in their senior year at accredited medical schools.

Eligibility This program is open to African American, Native Hawaiian, Alaska Native, American Indian, Mexican American, and mainland Puerto Rican students at accredited medical schools in the United States who are graduating during the current academic year. Only nominations are accepted; students may not apply directly. Awards are given for outstanding performance in the surgical disciplines and for overall good academic standing.

Financial data The award includes a certificate of merit and a $500 stipend.

Duration The awards are presented annually; they are nonrenewable.

Additional information These awards were established in 1986 to honor the memory of James H. Robinson, who was clinical professor of surgery and associate dean of student affairs at Jefferson Medical College of Thomas Jefferson University in Philadelphia.

Number awarded 1 each year.

Deadline Nominations must be submitted by February of each year.

[975]
MARIE F. PETERS ETHNIC MINORITIES OUTSTANDING ACHIEVEMENT AWARD

National Council on Family Relations
3989 Central Avenue, N.E., Suite 550
Minneapolis, MN 55421
(763) 781-9331   Toll-free: (888) 781-9331
Fax: (763) 781-9348   E-mail: info@ncfr.com
Web: www.ncfr.org/about_us/ncfr_awards.asp

Purpose To recognize and reward minorities who have made significant contributions to the area of ethnic minority families.

Eligibility Members of the National Council on Family Relations (NCFR) who have demonstrated excellence in the area of ethnic minority families are eligible for this award. Selection is based on leadership and/or mentoring, scholarship and/or service, research, publication, teaching, community service, contribution to the ethnic minorities section, and contribution to the NCFR.

Financial data The award is $1,000 and a plaque.

Duration The award is granted biennially, in odd-numbered years.

Additional information This award, which was established in 1983, is named after a prominent Black researcher and family sociologist who served in many leadership roles in NCFR. It is sponsored by the Ethnic Minorities Section of NCFR.

Number awarded 1 every other year.

Deadline April of odd-numbered years.

[976]
MINORITY AFFAIRS COMMITTEE AWARD FOR OUTSTANDING SCHOLASTIC ACHIEVEMENT

American Institute of Chemical Engineers
Attn: Awards Administrator
Three Park Avenue
New York, NY 10016-5991
(212) 591-7107   Fax: (212) 591-8890
E-mail: awards@aiche.org
Web: www.aiche.org/awards

Purpose To recognize and reward underrepresented minority students majoring in chemical engineering who serve as role models for other minority students.

Eligibility Members of the American Institute of Chemical Engineers (AIChE) may nominate any chemical engineering student who serves as a role model for minority students in that field. Nominees must be members of a minority group that is underrepresented in chemical engineering (i.e., African American, Hispanic, Native American, Alaskan Native). Selection is based on the nominee's academic and scholarship achievements, including a GPA of 3.0 or higher, scholastic awards, research contributions, and technical presentations; the nominee's exemplary outreach activities that directly benefit or encourage minority youth in their academic pursuits; a letter from the nominee describing his or her outreach activities; and extraordinary circumstances, such as job or family matters, that impose additional responsibility.

Financial data The award consists of a plaque and a $1,500 honorarium.

Duration The award is presented annually.

Additional information This award was first presented in 1996.

Number awarded 1 each year.

Deadline Nominations must be submitted by May of each year.

[977]
MISS MEXICAN FIESTA SCHOLARSHIP PAGEANT

Wisconsin Hispanic Scholarship Foundation, Inc.
1220 West Windlake Avenue
Milwaukee, WI 53215
(414) 383-7066   Fax: (414) 383-6677
E-mail: fiestamilw@aol.com
Web: www.mexicanfiesta.org/events/contest.html

Purpose To recognize and reward, with college scholarships, Hispanic women in Wisconsin who participate in the Miss Mexican Fiesta Scholarship Pageant.

Eligibility This competition is open to women residents of Wisconsin who are single and between 17 and 25 years of age. Applicants must be at least 25% Hispanic and enrolled in a college or university. Along with their application, they must submit a 750-word personal essay on their family background, education and career experience, ambitions and importance of education in their life, how education relates to being a young woman of Mexican descent preparing for the future, reasons for entering the pageant, and how they would use the title.

Financial data   Awards are $1,500 for the winner, $500 for the first runner-up, and $300 for the second runner-up.

Duration   The competition is held annually at Mexican Fiesta in Milwaukee for 3 days each August.

Additional information   Recipients must perform 20 hours of volunteer work for Mexican Fiesta.

Number awarded   3 each year: the winner and 2 runners-up.

Deadline   May of each year.

[978]
MODELO MUNDIAL-WORLD MODEL COMPETITION

JCPenney Company, Inc.
Attn: Modelo Mundial
P.O. Box 100001
Dallas, TX 75301-8112
(972) 431-4655   E-mail: cbsmith@jcpenney.com
Web: www.jcpenneymodelomundial.com

Purpose   To recognize and reward outstanding Hispanic models.

Eligibility   This program is open to men and women of Hispanic descent who are between the ages of 16 and 21, reside in the vicinity of a participating JCPenney store, are currently enrolled in high school or an accredited institution of higher education, and have a GPA of 3.0 or higher. Applicants may not be professional models or currently affiliated with a modeling agency. They must submit a 1-page essay describing their academic achievements, extracurricular achievements, and community involvement. Essays are judged on writing skills, flair for self-expression, and leadership skills. Men and women compete separately at the regional level, and the winners advance to the national competition in Miami, Florida in June.

Financial data   Regional winners receive round-trip airfare to Miami and hotel accommodations for 5 days. National winners receive a $10,000 scholarship and a $1,000 JCPenney gift card. National runners-up receive a $5,000 scholarship and a $500 JCPenney gift care.

Duration   The competition is held annually.

Additional information   This competition has been sponsored by JCPenney since 1990. Through 2002, it was known as the Hispanic Designers Model Search. Its current sponsors include the Havanera Company, Mudd, Reebok, and The Original Arizona Jean Company. Scholarships are provided by Univision, a Spanish language television network in the United States. The participating JCPenney stores operate in Albuquerque, Chicago, Dallas/Fort Worth, Denver, El Paso, Houston, Las Vegas, Los Angeles/San Diego, Miami, McAllen/Harlingen/Brownsville (Texas), New Jersey/New York, Orlando, Phoenix/Tucson, Sacramento/Fresno, Salt Lake City, San Antonio, San Francisco/San Jose, Tampa, Washington, D.C., Puerto Rico, and (in Mexico) Monterrey, Mexico City, and Leon.

Number awarded   46 regional winners (1 man and 1 woman from each of the 23 markets), 2 national grand winners (1 man and 1 woman), and 2 runners-up (also 1 man and 1 woman).

Deadline   May of each year.

[979]
MS. LATINA USA

Dawn Ramos Productions
607 South Loving Avenue
Sherman, TX 75090-6743
(903) 891-9761   E-mail: info@misslatina.com
Web: www.misslatina.com

Purpose   To recognize and reward young Latina women who compete in a national beauty pageant.

Eligibility   This program is open to women between 18 and 29 years of age who are at least 25% Hispanic. Applicants may be single, married, or divorced, and they may have children. They appear in a nationally-televised pageant where selection is based one third on an interview, one third on swimsuit appearances, and one third on evening gown appearances. Height and weight are not factors, but contestants should be proportionate. Pageant experience and fluency in Spanish are not required.

Financial data   Each year, prizes include scholarships, gifts, a cruise to the Bahamas, a trip to Las Vegas, a modeling contract, and use of an apartment in Miami. The total value is more than $100,000.

Duration   The pageant is held annually

Number awarded   1 winner and 4 runners-up are selected each year.

[980]
NATIONAL LATINO PLAYWRITING AWARD

Arizona Theatre Company
Attn: Samantha K. Wyer
40 East 14th Street
Tucson, AZ 85701
(520) 884-8210   Fax: (520) 628-9129

Purpose   To recognize and reward outstanding unpublished, unproduced plays written by Latino/Latinas in the United States or Mexico.

Eligibility   This program is open to all Hispanics currently residing in the United States, its territories, or Mexico. Applicants may submit scripts in English, Spanish and English, or solely in Spanish; scripts in Spanish must be accompanied by an English translation. Only unpublished, unproduced plays are eligible. Full-length and 1-act plays (at least 50 pages in length) are accepted.

Financial data   The prize is $1,000 and possible inclusion in the Arizona Theatre Company's GENESIS: New Play Reading Series.

Duration   The competition is held annually.

Additional information   Previously, this award was known as the National Hispanic Playwriting Contest.

Number awarded   1 each year.

Deadline   December of each year.

[981]
NEW YORK LIBRARY ASSOCIATION MULTICULTURAL AWARD

New York Library Association
Attn: Ethnic Services Round Table
252 Hudson Avenue
Albany, NY 12210-1802
(518) 432-6952   Toll-free: (800) 252-6952
Fax: (518) 427-1697   E-mail: info@nyla.org
Web: www.nyla.org

Purpose To recognize and reward members of the New York Library Association who have contributed to multicultural activities.

Eligibility This program is open to members of the association who have promoted multicultural or multiethnic activities; multilingual activities are not considered. Selection is based on achievement, advocacy and leadership in serving the community in areas of collection development, outreach services, and development of creative multicultural materials and programs.

Financial data The award consists of $500 to be used for the purchase of books published by Routledge Publishers.

Duration The award is presented annually.

Additional information Information is also available from Zahra M. Baird, Multicultural Award Chair, Chappaqua Library, 195 South Greeley Avenue, Chappaqua, NY 10514, E-mail: zbaird@westchesterlibraries.org.

Number awarded 1 each year.

Deadline July of each year.

[982]
NSF DIRECTOR'S AWARD FOR DISTINGUISHED TEACHING SCHOLARS

National Science Foundation
Directorate for Education and Human Resources
Attn: Division of Undergraduate Education
4201 Wilson Boulevard, Room 835N
Arlington, VA 22230
(703) 292-4627   Fax: (703) 292-9015
TDD: (703) 292-5090   E-mail: hlevitan@nsf.gov
Web: www.ehr.nsf.gov

Purpose To recognize and reward, with funding for additional research, minority and other scholars affiliated with institutions of higher education who have contributed to teaching of science, technology, engineering, and mathematics (STEM) at the K-12 and undergraduate level.

Eligibility This program is open to teaching-scholars affiliated with institutions of higher education who are nominated by their president, chief academic officer, or other independent researcher. Nominees should have integrated research and education and approached both education and research in a scholarly manner. They should have demonstrated leadership in their respective fields as well as innovativeness and effectiveness in facilitating K-12 and undergraduate student learning in STEM disciplines. Consideration is given to faculty who have a history of substantial impact on 1) research in a STEM discipline or on STEM educational research; or 2) the STEM education of K-16 students who have diverse interests and aspirations, including future K-12 teachers of science and mathematics, students who plan to pursue STEM careers, and those who need to understand science and mathematics in a society increas-

ingly dependent on science and technology. Based on letters of nomination, selected scholars are invited to submit applications for support of their continuing efforts to integrate education and research. Nominations of women, underrepresented minorities, and persons with disabilities are especially encouraged.

Financial data The maximum grant is $300,000 for the life of the project.

Duration 4 years.

Number awarded Approximately 6 each year.

Deadline Preliminary proposals are due in November of each year; full applications must be submitted in February.

[983]
PAVESNP LIFE/WORK CHALLENGE AWARDS

Pennsylvania Association of Vocational Education
    Special Needs Personnel
c/o Vocational Education Services in Pennsylvania
Penn State McKeesport
4000 University Drive
101 Ostermayer
McKeesport, PA 15132
(412) 675-9065
Web: www.pavesnp.org

Purpose To recognize and reward outstanding vocational education students in Pennsylvania who have special needs.

Eligibility Nominations for these awards may be submitted by professionals or paraprofessionals who are members of the Pennsylvania Association of Vocational Education Special Needs Personnel (PAVESNP). Nominees must be enrolled in an approved career and technical program in the current or previous school year and be receiving services from a special needs program (disabled, disadvantaged, or limited-English proficient). They must demonstrate evidence of a personal commitment to maximizing individual potential, social skills that enhance employability, strong personal work ethic, and occupational competence.

Financial data Awards are $500 for first place, $300 for second, and $100 for third.

Duration Awards are presented annually.

Additional information Information is also available from Marjorie Eckman, Overbrook Administrative Center, 2140 Saw Mill Run Boulevard, Pittsburgh, PA 15210.

Number awarded 3 each year.

Deadline January of each year.

[984]
PEERMUSIC LATIN SCHOLARSHIP

Broadcast Music Inc.
Attn: BMI Foundation
320 West 57th Street
New York, NY 10019-3790
(212) 830-2537   Fax: (212) 246-2163
E-mail: info@bmifoundation.org
Web: www.bmifoundation.org/pages/peermusic.asp

Purpose To recognize and reward students at colleges and universities in selected states who submit outstanding songs or instrumental works in a Latin genre.

Eligibility This competition is open to students between 16 and 24 years of age enrolled at colleges and universities in California, Florida, Illinois, Massachusetts, New York, Puerto Rico, or Texas. Applicants may not have had any musical work commercially recorded or distributed. They must submit an original song or instrumental work in a Latin genre. The entry must be submitted on audio cassette or CD, accompanied by 3 typed copies of the lyric.

Financial data The award is $5,000.

Duration The award is presented annually.

Additional information This award, first presented in 2003, is sponsored by peermusic Companies.

Number awarded 1 each year.

Deadline January of each year.

[985]
PRESIDIO LA BAHIA AWARD

Sons of the Republic of Texas
Attn: Administrative Assistant
1717 Eighth Street
Bay City, TX 77414
(979) 245-6644   Fax: (979) 244-3819
E-mail: srttexas@srttexas.org
Web: www.srttexas.org/labahia.html

Purpose To recognize and reward the most outstanding works that demonstrate the impact and influence of the Spanish colonial heritage on the laws, customs, language, religion, architecture, and art of Texas.

Eligibility The competition is open to any person interested in Spanish colonial influence on Texas culture. Eligible to be considered are books, published papers, articles published in periodicals, and non-literary projects (such as art, architecture, and archaeological discovery).

Financial data A total of $2,000 is available annually as awards. The prize for the best book is at least $1,200; the organization may award a second-place book prize. The amounts of prizes for best published paper, article published in a periodical, and non-literary project vary each year.

Duration The competition is held annually.

Additional information This award was established in 1968.

Number awarded From 1 to 5 each year.

Deadline September of each year.

[986]
PURA BELPRE BOOK AWARD

American Library Association
Attn: Association for Library Service to Children
50 East Huron Street
Chicago, IL 60611-2795
(312) 280-2163   Toll-free: (800) 545-2433, ext. 2163
Fax: (312) 944-7671   TDD: (312) 944-7298
TDD: (888) 814-7692   E-mail: alsc@ala.org
Web: www.ala.org

Purpose To recognize and reward Latino/a authors and illustrators of outstanding books for children.

Eligibility Eligible to be nominated for this award are Latino/a authors and illustrators of outstanding original children's books that portray, affirm, and celebrate the Latino/a cultural experience. The book must have been published in, and nominees must be citizens or residents of, the United States or Puerto Rico. Fiction and nonfiction books for chil-

dren published in Spanish, English, or bilingual format are eligible.

Financial data The award is $1,000 and a medal.

Duration The award is presented biennially.

Additional information This program, established in 1996, is sponsored by REFORMA (National Association to Promote Library Services to the Spanish Speaking) and the Association for Library Service to Children of the American Library Association.

Number awarded 2 each even-numbered year: 1 to an author and 1 to an illustrator.

Deadline December of odd-numbered years.

[987]
RALPH J. BUNCHE AWARD

American Political Science Association
1527 New Hampshire Avenue, N.W.
Washington, DC 20036-1206
(202) 483-2512   Fax: (202) 483-2657
E-mail: apsa@apsanet.org
Web: www.apsanet.org/section_278.cfm

Purpose To recognize and reward outstanding scholarly books on ethnic/cultural pluralism.

Eligibility Eligible to be nominated (by publishers or individuals) are scholarly political science books issued the previous year that explore issues of ethnic and/or cultural pluralism.

Financial data The award is $500.

Duration The competition is held annually.

Number awarded 1 each year.

Deadline February of each year.

[988]
RALPH W. ELLISON MEMORIAL PRIZE

National Medical Fellowships, Inc.
Attn: Scholarship Program
5 Hanover Square, 15th Floor
New York, NY 10004
(212) 483-8880   Fax: (212) 483-8897
E-mail: info@nmfonline.org
Web: www.nmf-online.org

Purpose To recognize and reward outstanding underrepresented minorities who are graduating from medical school.

Eligibility This award is open to African American, Native Hawaiian, Alaska Native, American Indian, Mexican American, and mainland Puerto Rican students enrolled in accredited U.S. medical schools. Candidates must be nominated by their medical schools during their senior year. Selection is based on academic achievement, leadership, community service, and potential to make significant contributions to medicine.

Financial data This honor includes a certificate of merit and a $500 award.

Duration 1 year; nonrenewable.

Additional information This award was established in 1994 to honor Ralph W. Ellison, the novelist and author of *The Invisible Man* who co-chaired a fundraising effort of National Medical Fellowships, Inc.

Number awarded 1 each year.

Deadline Nominations must be submitted by February of each year.

[989]
RECOGNITION AWARD FOR EMERGING SCHOLARS

American Association of University Women
Attn: AAUW Educational Foundation
1111 16th Street, N.W.
Washington, DC 20036-4873
(202) 785-7609   Toll-free: (800) 326-AAUW
Fax: (202) 463-7169   TDD: (202) 785-7777
E-mail: emergingscholar@aauw.org
Web: www.aauw.org/fga/awards/raes.cfm

Purpose To recognize and reward minority and other young women who show promise of future academic distinction.

Eligibility Eligible for nomination are nontenured women faculty members who earned a Ph.D. or equivalent within the past 5 years. They must be U.S. citizens or permanent residents. Selection is based on demonstrated excellence in teaching, a documented and active research record, and evidence of potentially significant contributions to the awardee's field of study. The sponsor strongly encourages the nomination of women of color and other underrepresented groups.

Financial data The award is $5,000.

Duration The award is presented annually.

Additional information The award includes a trip to the annual AAUW convention (where the award is presented).

Number awarded 1 each year.

Deadline Nominations must be submitted by February of each year.

[990]
SI TV PLAYWRITING AWARD

John F. Kennedy Center for the Performing Arts
Education Department
Attn: Kennedy Center American College Theater
   Festival
2700 F Street, N.W.
Washington, DC 20566
(202) 416-8857   Fax: (202) 416-8802
E-mail: skshaffer@kennedy-center.org
Web: kennedy-center.org/education/actf/actfsitv.html

Purpose To recognize and reward outstanding plays by Latino student playwrights.

Eligibility Latino students at any accredited junior or senior college in the United States are eligible to compete, provided their college agrees to participate in the Kennedy Center American College Theater Festival (KCACTF). Undergraduate students must be carrying at least 6 semester hours, graduate students must be enrolled in at least 3 semester hours, and continuing part-time students must be enrolled in a regular degree or certificate program. This award is presented to the best student-written play by a Latino.

Financial data The prize is $2,500. The winner also receives an internship to a prestigious playwriting retreat program. Dramatic Publishing Company presents the winning playwright with an offer of a contract to publish,

license, and market the winning play. A grant of $500 is made to the theater department of the college or university producing the award-winning play.

Duration The award is presented annually.

Additional information This award, first presented in 2000, is supported by Sí TV, the nation's first television programming service designed specifically for English dominant/bilingual Latino viewers. It is part of the Michael Kanin Playwriting Awards Program. The sponsoring college or university must pay a registration fee of $250 for each production.

Number awarded 1 each year.

Deadline November of each year.

[991]
SIMON BOLIVAR LECTURE AWARD

American Psychiatric Association
Attn: Department of Minority and National Affairs
1000 Wilson Boulevard, Suite 1825
Arlington, VA 22209-3901
(703) 907-8639   Toll-free: (888) 35-PSYCH
Fax: (703) 907-7852   E-mail: abondurant@psych.org
Web: www.psych.org/psych_pract/bolivar.cfm

Purpose To recognize and reward Hispanic statesmen who have helped to publicize the problems and goals of Hispanics in the United States and to sensitize the American Psychiatric Association (APA) membership to these problems and goals.

Eligibility Prominent Hispanic statesmen who have focused attention on the problems and goals of Hispanics in the United States and Puerto Rico are considered for this award.

Financial data The award provides a $500 honorarium and a plaque. The recipient delivers a lecture at the APA annual meeting. Nonmember winners also receive travel expenses.

Duration The award is presented annually.

Additional information The winner is selected by the Committee of Hispanic Psychiatrists. This program was established in 1975.

Number awarded 1 each year.

Deadline February of each year.

[992]
SOCIETY OF HISPANIC PROFESSIONAL ENGINEERS STUDENT CHAPTER DESIGN CONTEST

Society of Hispanic Professional Engineers Foundation
Attn: Director, Educational Programs
3900 Whiteside Street
Los Angeles, CA 90063
(323) 415-9600   Fax: (323) 415-7038
E-mail: kathy@shpefoundation.org
Web: www.shpefoundation.org/design-contest.html

Purpose To recognize and reward members of student chapters of the Society of Hispanic Professional Engineers (SHPE) who submit outstanding entries in an engineering design competition.

Eligibility This program is open to members of SHPE student chapters who submit designs for a commercially marketable product that is "a benefit to mankind and improves the quality of life." The design may not be a duplicate of a currently existing commercial product, but it can be an improvement to such a product. Entries must be submitted by a team of students with the assistance of 1 to 3 industry professionals. Finalists are selected to present their design, with a working model or prototype, at the National Technical and Career Conference (NTCC).

Financial data Finalists receive grants of $400 to complete the development of their formal presentation and a $500 team travel allowance to attend the NTCC. Awards are $3,000 for the first-place team, $2,500 for second, $2,000 for third, $1,500 for fourth, and $1,000 for fifth.

Duration The competition is held annually.

Number awarded 10 finalists are selected each year; 5 of those receive awards.

Deadline October of each year.

[993]
SPHINX COMPETITION AWARDS

Sphinx Organization
Attn: Screening Committee
400 Renaissance Center, Suite 2120
Detroit, MI 48243
(313) 877-9100   Fax: (313) 887-0164
E-mail: info@sphinxmusic.org
Web: ww.sphinxmusic.org

Purpose To recognize and reward outstanding junior high, high school, and college-age Black and Latino string instrumentalists.

Eligibility This competition is open to Black and Latino instrumentalists in 2 divisions: junior, for participants who are younger than 18 years of age, and senior, for participants who are at least 18 but younger than 27 years of age. All entrants must be current U.S. residents who can compete in the instrumental categories of violin, viola, cello, and double bass. Along with their applications, they must submit a preliminary audition tape that includes all of the required preliminary repertoire for their instrument category. Based on those tapes, qualifiers are invited to participate in the semifinals and finals competitions, held at sites in Detroit and Ann Arbor, Michigan.

Financial data In the senior division, the first-place winner receives a $10,000 cash prize, solo appearances with major orchestras, and a performance with the Sphinx Symphony; the second-place winner receives a $5,000 cash prize and a performance with the Sphinx Symphony; the third-place winner receives a $3,500 cash prize and a performance with the Sphinx Symphony. In the junior division, the first-place winner receives a $5,000 cash prize and 2 performances with the Sphinx Symphony; the second-place winner receives a $3,500 cash prize and a performance with the Sphinx Symphony; the third-place winner receives a $2,000 cash prize and a performance with the Sphinx Symphony. All semifinalists receive scholarships to attend a summer program at Aspen, Blossom, BU Tanglewood, Chautauqua, DSO Summer Institute, ENCORE, Interlochen, Mark O'Connor Fiddle Conference, Musicorda, National Symphony Summer Institute, National Orchestral Institute, Orchestra of the Americas, Sewanee, or Walnut Hill School. They also receive modest stipends to augment their instrumental studies from the Music Assistance Fund (MAF) of the American Symphony Orchestra League.

Duration The competition is held annually.

Additional information The sponsoring organization was incorporated in 1996 to hold this competition, first conducted in 1998. The Sphinx Symphony is an all African American and Latino orchestra that performs at Orchestra Hall in Detroit. The MAF program was established by the New York Philharmonic in 1965 and transferred to the American Symphony Orchestra League in 1994. In 2002, it partnered with the Sphinx Organization to provide scholarships to all 18 semifinalists. Additional support for MAF is provided by ABC, Inc., Foundation, the Brown Foundation, Inc. (Houston, Texas), the International Conference of Symphony and Opera Musicians and Anheuser-Busch. The MAF program also provides full tuition scholarships to Sphinx semifinalists who attend the Indiana University School of Music, Julliard School, Manhattan School of Music, or the University of Michigan School of Music. Applications must be accompanied by a $35 fee. That fee may be waived if demonstrable need is shown.

Number awarded 18 semifinalists (from both divisions and all instrumental categories) are selected each year. Of those, 3 junior and 3 senior competitors win cash prizes.

Deadline November of each year.

[994]
SUMMER WORKSHOPS WRITING COMPETITION FOR MINORITY HIGH SCHOOL STUDENTS

Dow Jones Newspaper Fund
P.O. Box 300
Princeton, NJ 08543-0300
(609) 452-2820   Fax: (609) 520-5804
E-mail: newsfund@wsf.dowjones.com
Web: DJNewspaperFund.dowjones.com

Purpose To recognize and reward (with college scholarships) outstanding participants in journalism workshops for minority high school students.

Eligibility Each summer, workshops on college campuses around the country allow minority high school students to experience work on a professional-quality publication. Students are taught to write, report, design, and layout a newspaper on topics relevant to youth. The director of each workshop nominates 1 student who submits an article from the workshop newspaper and an essay on why he/she wants to pursue journalism as a career. The students whose articles and essay are judged most outstanding receive these college scholarships.

Financial data The award is a college scholarship of $1,000.

Duration Workshops normally last 2 weeks during the summer. Scholarships are for 1 year and may be renewed for 1 additional year if the recipient maintains a GPA of 2.5 or higher and an interest in journalism.

Additional information Recently, workshops were held on college campuses in Alabama, Arizona, Arkansas, California, Florida, Illinois, Kentucky, Massachusetts, Minnesota, Mississippi, Missouri, New Jersey, New York, Ohio, Oklahoma, Pennsylvania, South Dakota, Texas, Virginia, Washington, and Wisconsin. For the name and address of the director of each workshop, contact the Newspaper Fund.

Number awarded 8 each year.

[995]
TACHE DISTINGUISHED COMMUNITY COLLEGE FACULTY AWARD

Texas Association of Chicanos in Higher Education
P.O. Box 986
Austin, TX 78767-0986
Web: www.tache.org/pdfs/award_faculty_univ.pdf

Purpose To recognize and reward outstanding community college faculty members in Texas who are members of the Texas Association of Chicanos in Higher Education (TACHE).

Eligibility Eligible to be nominated for this award are active TACHE members who have taught for at least the last 5 years at a Texas community college. Nominees must have demonstrated a consistent pattern of teaching excellence, innovation in teaching, contributions to discipline-specific scholarship, a consistent pattern of service to the community, a consistent pattern of support of Chicano/Latino programs and students, support for and promotion of postsecondary education, and a consistent pattern of mentoring other faculty and/or students. Self-nominations are accepted.

Financial data The award is $1,000.

Duration The award is presented annually.

Additional information Information is also available from Rudy Duarte, Distinguished Community College Faculty Award Chair, Del Mar College, 101 Baldwin, Corpus Christi, TX 78404.

Number awarded 1 each year.

Deadline December of each year.

[996]
TACHE DISTINGUISHED UNIVERSITY FACULTY AWARD

Texas Association of Chicanos in Higher Education
P.O. Box 986
Austin, TX 78767-0986
Web: www.tache.org/pdfs/award_faculty_univ.pdf

Purpose To recognize and reward outstanding university faculty members in Texas who are members of the Texas Association of Chicanos in Higher Education (TACHE).

Eligibility Eligible to be nominated for this award are active TACHE members who have taught for at least the last 5 years at a Texas university. Nominees must have demonstrated a consistent pattern of excellence in teaching, innovation in teaching, a record of scholarly publications or other contributions to the profession or academic discipline, a consistent pattern of service to the community, a consistent pattern of support of Chicano/Latino programs and students, support for and promotion of postsecondary and graduate education, and a consistent pattern of mentoring other faculty and/or students. Self-nominations are accepted.

Financial data The award is $1,000.

Duration The award is presented annually.

Additional information Information is also available from Gloria B. Bahamón, Distinguished University Faculty Award Chair, University of North Texas, P.O. Box 310937, Denton, TX 76203-0937.

Number awarded 1 each year.

Deadline December of each year.

[997]
TEEN LATINA USA

Dawn Ramos Productions
607 South Loving Avenue
Sherman, TX 75090-6743
(903) 891-9761   E-mail: info@misslatina.com
Web: www.misslatina.com

Purpose To recognize and reward teen-aged Latina women who compete in a national beauty pageant.

Eligibility This program is open to women between 13 and 17 years of age who are at least 25% Hispanic. Applicants must be single and they may not have children. They appear in a nationally-televised pageant where selection is based one third on an interview, one third on swimsuit appearances, and one third on evening gown appearances. Height and weight are not factors, but contestants should be proportionate. Pageant experience and fluency in Spanish are not required.

Financial data Each year, prizes include scholarships, gifts, a cruise to the Bahamas, a trip to Las Vegas, a modeling contract, and use of an apartment in Miami. The total value is more than $25,000.

Duration The pageant is held annually

Number awarded 1 winner and 4 runners-up are selected each year.

[998]
TOMAS RIVERA MEXICAN AMERICAN CHILDREN'S BOOK AWARD

Texas State University, San Marcos Campus
Attn: Department of Curriculum and Instruction
2001 Education Building
601 University Drive
San Marcos, TX 78666-4616
(512) 245-2157
Web: www.education.txstate.edu

Purpose To recognize and reward outstanding children's books that reflect the culture of Mexican Americans in the United States.

Eligibility Eligible to be nominated for this award are children's books (fiction or nonfiction) that authentically reflect Mexican American culture in the United States.

Financial data The award is $3,000.

Duration The award is presented annually, during Hispanic Heritage month at Southwest Texas State University.

Additional information The award was first presented in 1995 by the College of Education at Texas State University, San Marcos

Number awarded 1 each year.

Deadline January of each year.

[999]
WILLIAM A. HINTON RESEARCH TRAINING AWARD

American Academy of Microbiology
Attn: Committee on Awards
1752 N Street, N.W.
Washington, DC 20036-2804
(202) 942-9226   Fax: (202) 942-9353
E-mail: awards@asmusa.org
Web: www.asm.org

Purpose To recognize and reward microbiologists for their involvement in the research training of underrepresented minorities.

Eligibility Nominees for this award must have contributed to the research training of undergraduate students, graduate students, postdoctoral fellows, or health professional students. Their efforts must have led to the increased participation of underrepresented minorities in microbiology. Self-nominations are not accepted.

Financial data The award consists of a $2,000 cash prize, a commemorative piece, and travel expenses to the presentation ceremonies at the general meeting of the American Society for Microbiology (ASM).

Duration The award is presented annually.

Additional information This award, first presented in 1998, honors 1 of the first African Americans to join the ASM.

Number awarded 1 each year.

Deadline September of each year.

[1000]
WILLIAM AND CHARLOTTE CADBURY AWARD

National Medical Fellowships, Inc.
Attn: Scholarship Program
5 Hanover Square, 15th Floor
New York, NY 10004
(212) 483-8880   Fax: (212) 483-8897
E-mail: info@nmfonline.org
Web: www.nmf-online.org

Purpose To recognize and reward underrepresented minority medical school students' outstanding academic achievement, leadership, and community service.

Eligibility This award is open to minority students enrolled in their senior year at an accredited U.S. medical school. For the purposes of this program, "minority" is defined as African American, Native Hawaiian, Alaska Native, American Indian, Mexican American, and mainland Puerto Rican. Candidates must be nominated by their medical school during the summer preceding their senior year. Selection is based on academic achievement, leadership, and community service.

Financial data This honor includes a certificate of merit and a $2,000 stipend.

Duration The award is presented annually.

Additional information This award was established in 1977.

Number awarded 1 each year.

Deadline Nominations must be submitted by July of each year.

[1001]
WYETH-AYERST LABORATORIES PRIZE IN WOMEN'S HEALTH

National Medical Fellowships, Inc.
Attn: Scholarship Program
5 Hanover Square, 15th Floor
New York, NY 10004
(212) 483-8880   Fax: (212) 483-8897
E-mail: info@nmfonline.org
Web: www.nmf-online.org

Purpose To recognize and reward outstanding underrepresented minority women medical students.

Eligibility This program is open to underrepresented minority (African American, Native Hawaiian, Alaska Native, American Indian, Mexican American, and mainland Puerto Rican) women medical students in their fourth year of study. Candidates must demonstrate exceptional academic achievement, leadership, and the potential to make significant contributions in the field of women's health. Direct applications are not accepted; candidates must be nominated by their medical school dean.

Financial data This honor includes a certificate of merit and a $5,000 stipend.

Duration The award is presented annually.

Additional information Funding for this program is provided by Wyeth-Ayerst Laboratories.

Number awarded 2 each year.

Deadline Nominations must be submitted by February of each year.

Internships

Described here are 209 work experience programs open to undergraduate, graduate, or postgraduate Hispanic Americans. Only salaried positions are covered. If you are looking for a particular program and don't find it in this section, be sure to check the Program Title Index to see if it is covered elsewhere in the directory.

[1002]
AAPG SEMESTER INTERNSHIPS IN GEOSCIENCE AND PUBLIC POLICY

American Geological Institute
Attn: Government Affairs Program
4220 King Street
Alexandria, VA 22302-1502
(703) 379-2480   Fax: (703) 379-7563
E-mail: govt@agiweb.org
Web: www.agiweb.org/gap

Purpose To provide work experience to geoscience students (especially minorities and women) who have a strong interest in federal science policy.

Eligibility This program is open to geoscience students who are interested in the public policy aspects of the discipline, especially in energy and resource issues. Applicants must submit official copies of college transcripts, a resume with the names and contact information for 2 references, and a statement of their science and policy interests and what they feel they can contribute to the program. Women and minorities are especially encouraged to apply.

Financial data The stipend is $4,000.

Duration 14 weeks, during the fall or spring semester.

Additional information This program is jointly funded by the American Geological Institute (AGI) and the American Association of Petroleum Geologists (AAPG). Activities for the interns include monitoring and analyzing geoscience-related legislation in Congress, updating legislative and policy information on AGI's web site, attending House and Senate hearings and preparing summaries, responding to information requests from AGI's member societies, and attending meetings with policy-level staff members in Congress, federal agencies, and non-governmental organizations.

Number awarded 2 each semester.

Deadline April of each year for fall internships; October of each year for spring internships.

[1003]
ACT SUMMER INTERNSHIP PROGRAM

American College Testing
Attn: Human Resources Department
500 ACT Drive
P.O. Box 168
Iowa City, IA 52243-0168
(319) 337-1763   E-mail: working@act.org
Web: www.act.org/humanresources/jobs/intern.html

Purpose To provide work experience during the summer to graduate students (particularly women and minorities) interested in careers in testing and measurement.

Eligibility This program is open to graduate students enrolled in such fields as educational psychology, measurement, program evaluation, counseling psychology, educational policy, mathematical and applied statistics, industrial or organizational psychology, and counselor education. Selection is based on technical skills, previous practical or work experience, interest in careers in testing, general academic qualifications, and the match of course work and research interests with those of sponsoring mentors. The program is also intended to assist in increasing the number of women and minority professionals in measurement and related fields.

Financial data Interns receive a stipend of $5,000 and round-trip transportation between their graduate institution and Iowa City. A supplemental living allowance of $400 is provided if a spouse and/or children accompany the intern.

Duration 8 weeks during the summer.

Additional information Assignments are available in 4 categories: 1) educational and social research; 2) industrial and organizational psychology; 3) psychometrics and statistics; and 4) vocational and career psychology. Interns work with assigned mentors and participate in weekly seminars led by the professional staff of American College Testing (ACT).

Number awarded Varies each year.

Deadline February of each year.

[1004]
¡ADELANTE! FUND SCHOLARSHIP PROGRAM

¡Adelante! U.S. Education Leadership Fund
8415 Datapoint Drive, Suite 400
San Antonio, TX 78229
(210) 692-1971   Fax: (210) 692-1951
Toll-free: (877) 692-1971
E-mail: info@adelantefund.org
Web: www.adelantefund.org

Purpose To provide financial aid, internships, and leadership training to upper-division Hispanic students enrolled in Hispanic Serving Institutions (HSIs).

Eligibility This program is open to Hispanic students currently enrolled in HSIs. Applicants must have a GPA of 3.0 or higher, be eligible to receive financial aid, be juniors or seniors in college, agree to attend the Adelante Leadership Institute, be eligible to participate in a summer internship, exhibit leadership, and provide 2 letters of recommendation. Most recipients are the first in their families to complete a college education.

Financial data The maximum stipend is $3,000 per year.

Duration 1 year.

Additional information This fund was established by the Hispanic Association of Colleges and Universities in 1997 and became a separate organization in 1999. Recipients must participate in a summer internship and the Adelante Leadership Institute.

Number awarded Varies each year; recently, 22 students received scholarships.

[1005]
AFSCME/UNCF UNION SCHOLARS PROGRAM

United Negro College Fund
Attn: Corporate Scholars Program
P.O. Box 1435
Alexandria, VA 22313-9998
Toll-free: (866) 671-7237   E-mail: internship@uncf.org
Web: www.uncf.org/internships/index.asp

Purpose To provide financial assistance to students of color who are interested in working during the summer on an organizing campaign for the American Federation of State, County and Municipal Employees (AFSCME).

Eligibility This program is open to students of color, including African Americans, Hispanic Americans, Asian/Pacific Islander Americans, and American Indians/Alaskan Natives. Applicants must be second semester sophomores or juniors and majoring in ethnic studies, women's studies, labor studies, American studies, sociology, anthropology, history, political science, psychology, social work, or economics. They must have a GPA of 2.5 or higher and be interested in working on a union organizing campaign at 1 of several locations in the United States.

Financial data The program provides a stipend of $4,000, on-site housing at their location, a week-long orientation and training, and (based on successful performance during the organizing campaign) a $5,000 scholarship.

Duration 10 weeks for the organizing assignment; 1 year for the scholarship.

Number awarded Varies each year.

Deadline February of each year.

[1006]
AIPG SUMMER INTERNSHIPS IN GEOSCIENCE AND PUBLIC POLICY

American Geological Institute
Attn: Government Affairs Program
4220 King Street
Alexandria, VA 22302-1502
(703) 379-2480, ext 212　　　Fax: (703) 379-7563
E-mail: govt@agiweb.org
Web: www.agiweb.org/gap/interns/internsu.html

Purpose To provide summer work experience to geoscience students (particularly minorities and women) who have a strong interest in federal science policy.

Eligibility This program is open to geoscience students who are interested in the public policy aspects of the discipline, especially legislation pending before Congress. Applicants must submit official copies of college transcripts, a resume with the names and contact information for 2 references, and a statement of their science and policy interests and what they feel they can contribute to the program. Minorities and women are especially encouraged to apply.

Financial data The stipend is $3,500.

Duration 12 weeks during the summer.

Additional information This program is jointly funded by the American Geological Institute (AGI) and the American Institute of Professional Geologists (AIPG). Activities for the interns include monitoring and analyzing geoscience-related legislation in Congress, updating legislative and policy information on AGI's web site, attending House and Senate hearings and preparing summaries, responding to information requests from AGI's member societies, and attending meetings with policy-level staff members in Congress, federal agencies, and non-governmental organizations.

Number awarded 3 each summer.

Deadline March of each year.

[1007]
AMERICAN COLLEGE OF HEALTHCARE EXECUTIVES MINORITY INTERNSHIP

American College of Healthcare Executives
Attn: Human Resources Manager
One North Franklin Street, Suite 1700
Chicago, IL 60606-3529
(312) 424-9342　　　Fax: (312) 424-0023
E-mail: ache@ache.org
Web: www.ache.org/carsvcs/internship.cfm

Purpose To provide minority graduate students who are members of the American College of Healthcare Executives (ACHE) with an opportunity to work at the organization's headquarters.

Eligibility This program is open to ACHE student associates or affiliates who have completed 1 year of graduate study in health care management from an accredited college or university in the United States or Canada. Applicants must be a member of a minority group. They must be interested in working in all major ACHE divisions, including administration, communications, education, executive office, finance, health administration press, management information systems, membership, regional services, and research and development. Along with their application, they must submit a short statement of interest, a current curriculum vitae, an official undergraduate transcript, and a letter of recommendation.

Financial data The stipend is $16.60 per hour.

Duration 3 months during the summer.

Additional information This program was established in 1991.

Number awarded 1 each year.

Deadline November of each year.

[1008]
AMERICAN HEART ASSOCIATION UNDERGRADUATE STUDENT RESEARCH PROGRAM

American Heart Association-Western States Affiliate
Attn: Research Department
1710 Gilbreth Road
Burlingame, CA 94010-1317
(650) 259-6725　　　Fax: (650) 259-6891
E-mail: research@heart.org
Web: www.americanheart.org

Purpose To provide students (particularly minority and women students) from California, Nevada, and Utah with an opportunity to work on a cardiovascular research project during the summer.

Eligibility This program is open to college students who are enrolled full time at an accredited academic institution at the junior or senior level and interested in a career in heart or stroke research. Applicants must be residents of California, Nevada, or Utah (or attending a college or university in 1 of those states) and interested in a summer internship at a cardiovascular research laboratory in those states. They must have completed the following (or equivalent) courses: 4 semesters (or 6 quarters) of biological sciences, physics, or chemistry; and 1 quarter of calculus, statistics, computational methods, or computer science. Selection is based on an assessment of the student's application, academic record (preference is given to students with superior academic standing), and faculty recommendations. Women and minorities are particularly encouraged to apply.

Financial data Participants receive a $4,000 stipend.

Duration 10 weeks during the summer.

Additional information Participants are assigned to laboratories in California, Nevada, or Utah to work under the direction and supervision of experienced scientists.

Deadline January of each year.

[1009]
ARIZONA SPACE GRANT CONSORTIUM UNDERGRADUATE RESEARCH INTERNSHIPS

Arizona Space Grant Consortium
c/o University of Arizona
Gerard P. Kuiper Space Sciences Building, Room 345
1629 East University Boulevard
Tucson, AZ 85721
(520) 621-8556 Fax: (520) 621-4933
E-mail: sbrew@lpl.arizona.edu
Web: spacegrant.arizona.edu

Purpose To provide an opportunity for undergraduate students (particularly minorities and women) at member and affiliate institutions of the Arizona Space Grant Consortium to participate as interns in scientific research activities on campus.

Eligibility This program is open to full-time undergraduate students at member institutions (University of Arizona, Northern Arizona University, and Arizona State University) and affiliate institutions (Pima Community College) of the consortium. Applicants must be at least sophomores and U.S. citizens, but they do not need to be science or engineering majors. Applications are especially encouraged from members of underrepresented minority groups and women.

Financial data Interns are paid at the rate of $8 per hour.

Duration 1 academic year.

Additional information Interns work with faculty members and graduate students on space-related science projects. Funding for this program is provided by the U.S. National Aeronautics and Space Administration (NASA).

Number awarded Varies; recently, the program provided for 43 interns at the University of Arizona, 8 at Northern Arizona University, 30 at Arizona State University, and 1 at Pima Community College.

Deadline June of each year.

[1010]
ARKANSAS SPACE GRANT CONSORTIUM SCHOLARSHIPS AND FELLOWSHIPS

Arkansas Space Grant Consortium
c/o University of Arkansas at Little Rock
Graduate Institute of Technology
2801 South University Avenue
Little Rock, AR 72204
(501) 569-8212 Fax: (501) 569-8039
E-mail: asgc@ualr.edu
Web: asgc.ualr.edu/spacegrant

Purpose To provide funding to students (particularly minorities, women, and persons with disabilities) at designated universities in Arkansas who are interested in working on a space-related research project.

Eligibility This program is open to undergraduate and graduate students at colleges and universities that participate in the Arkansas Space Grant Consortium (ASGC). Applicants must be interested in working with a faculty mentor on a specific research project. Fields of study include astronomy, biochemistry, biology, chemistry, computer science, earth science, engineering, engineering technology, instrumentation, materials science, mathematics, physics, psychology, and space medicine. Students must be U.S. citizens. The consortium is a component of NASA's Space Grant program, which encourages participation by underrepresented minorities, women, and persons with disabilities.

Financial data The funding depends on the nature of the proposal.

Additional information ASGC member institutions are Arkansas State University, Arkansas Tech University, Harding University, Henderson State University, Hendrix College, Lyon College, Ouachita Baptist University, University of Central Arkansas, University of Arkansas at Fayetteville, University of Arkansas at Little Rock, University of Arkansas at Montecito, University of Arkansas at Pine Bluff, University of Arkansas for Medical Sciences, and University of the Ozarks. This program is funded by NASA.

Number awarded Varies each year; since this program began in 1990, it has awarded nearly 400 undergraduate scholarships and 100 graduate fellowships.

[1011]
ARMY JUDGE ADVOCATE GENERAL'S CORPS SUMMER INTERN PROGRAM

U.S. Army
Attn: Judge Advocate Recruiting Office
1777 North Kent Street, Suite 5200
Rosslyn, VA 22209-2194
(703) 696-2822 Toll-free: (866) ARMY-JAG
Fax: (703) 588-0100
Web: www.jagcnet.army.mil

Purpose To provide law students (particularly minorities and women) with an opportunity to gain work experience during the summer in Army legal offices throughout the United States and overseas.

Eligibility This program is open to full-time students enrolled in law schools accredited by the American Bar Association. Applications are accepted both from students who are completing the first year of law school and those completing the second year. Students must be interested in a summer internship with the Army Judge Advocate General's Corps (JAGC). U.S. citizenship is required. The program actively seeks applications from women and minority group members. Selection is based on academic ability and demonstrated leadership potential.

Financial data Interns who have completed the first year of law school are paid at the GS-5 scale, starting at $11.23 per hour. Interns who have completed the second year of law school are paid at the GS-7 scale, starting at $13.91 per hour.

Duration Approximately 60 days, beginning in May or June.

Additional information Interns work under the supervision of an attorney and perform legal research, write briefs and opinions, conduct investigations, interview witnesses, and otherwise assist in preparing civil or criminal cases. Positions are available at Department of the Army legal offices in Washington, D.C. and at Army installations throughout the United States and overseas. These are not military positions. No military obligation is incurred by participating in the summer intern program.

Number awarded 100 per year: 25 first-year students and 75 second-year students.

Deadline February of each year for first-year students; October of each year for second-year students.

[1012]
ART PETERS PROGRAM

Philadelphia Inquirer
Attn: Oscar Miller, Director of Recruiting
400 North Broad Street
P.O. Box 8263
Philadelphia, PA 19101
(215) 854-5102   Fax: (215) 854-2578
E-mail: inkyjobs@phillynews.com
Web: www.philly.com/mld/philly

Purpose To provide summer copy editing experience at the *Philadelphia Inquirer* to minority college students interested in careers in journalism.

Eligibility Minority college students entering their sophomore, junior, or senior year in college are eligible to apply if they are interested in the practical work of copy editing. The internship is at the *Philadelphia Inquirer.* Selection is based on experience, potential, academic record, and extracurricular activities.

Financial data The salary is $573 per week.

Duration 10 weeks beginning in June.

Additional information After 1 week of orientation, interns are given their assignments at the *Philadelphia Inquirer:* reporters cover and write stories for the city, business, sports, or features desks; copy editors write headlines and edit articles for those desks or the national/foreign copy desk.

Number awarded 7 each year: 4 in copy-editing and 3 in reporting.

Deadline November of each year.

[1013]
ARTTABLE MENTORED INTERNSHIPS

ArtTable Inc.
270 Lafayette Street, Suite 608
New York, NY 10012-3327
(212) 343-1735   Fax: (212) 343-1430
E-mail: women@arttable.org
Web: www.arttable.org

Purpose To provide an opportunity for women art students who are from diverse backgrounds to gain mentored work experience during the summer.

Eligibility This program is open to women from diverse backgrounds who are underrepresented in the visual arts field. Applicants must be 1) in the later years of their undergraduate studies, about to graduate, and contemplating a graduate education; or 2) in the early stages of a terminal degree and seeking career opportunities related to the visual arts professions. They must be interested in working during the summer with a mentor at an art museum or simi-

lar facility in New York City, Washington D.C., northern California, or southern California. U.S. citizenship or permanent resident status is required.

Financial data The stipend is $3,000. The hosting institution or mentor receives $500 for administrative and other costs.

Duration 10 weeks during the summer.

Additional information This program began in 2000.

Number awarded 4 each year: 1 in each of the participating locations.

Deadline January of each year.

[1014]
ATLANTA JOURNAL AND CONSTITUTION MINORITY INTERNSHIPS

Atlanta Journal and Constitution
Attn: Office of Community Affairs
72 Marietta Street, N.W.
Atlanta, GA 30303
(404) 577-5772   E-mail: aeintern@ajc.com
Web: www.ajc.com

Purpose To provide summer newspaper work experience in Atlanta to Georgia college students of color who are interested in preparing for a career in journalism.

Eligibility This program is open to Georgia college students of color (Asian Americans, Hispanics, African Americans, and Native Americans) interested in newspaper careers. Applicants must be interested in working at the *Atlanta Journal-Constitution* in the newsroom, online, advertising, accounting, marketing, or information technology department. They must be enrolled as a sophomore or junior at a Georgia college or university (seniors may be considered if they plan to continue on to graduate school), have a cumulative GPA of 3.0 or higher, and have demonstrated an interest in the department where they wish to work (campus publication experience and work with daily deadlines are preferable). Along with their application, they must submit a 500-word essay explaining why they want to be a journalist and how the internship will help them pursue their goals, samples of their work, a resume, and references.

Financial data Upon successful completion of the internship, participants receive a $1,000 scholarship.

Duration The internship is 10 weeks during the summer; the scholarship is a 1-year nonrenewable award.

Number awarded 3 each year.

Deadline January of each year.

[1015]
AT&T LABORATORIES FELLOWSHIP PROGRAM

AT&T Laboratories
Attn: Fellowship Administrator
180 Park Avenue, Room C103
P.O. Box 971
Florham Park, NJ 07932-0971
(973) 360-8109   Fax: (973) 360-8881
E-mail: recruiting@research.att.com
Web: www.research.att.com/academic/alfp.html

Purpose To provide financial assistance and work experience to underrepresented minority and women students who are working on a doctoral degree in computer and communications-related fields.

Eligibility This program is open to minorities underrepresented in the sciences (Blacks, Hispanics, and Native Americans) and to women. Applicants must be U.S. citizens or permanent residents beginning full-time Ph.D. study in a discipline relevant to the business of AT&T; currently, those include communications, computer science, electrical engineering, human computer interaction, industrial engineering, information science, mathematics, operations research, and statistics. Along with their application, they must submit a personal statement on why they are enrolled in their present academic program and how they intend to use their technical training, official transcripts, 3 academic references, and GRE scores. Selection is based on potential for success in scientific research.

Financial data This program covers all educational expenses during the school year, including tuition, books, fees, and approved travel expenses; education expenses for summer study or university research; a stipend for living expenses of $2,380 per month (paid for 10 months of the year); and support for attending approved scientific conferences.

Duration 1 year; may be renewed for up to 2 additional years, as long as the fellow continues making satisfactory progress toward the Ph.D.

Additional information The AT&T Laboratories Fellowship Program (ALFP) provides a mentor who is a staff member at AT&T Labs as well as a summer research internship within AT&T Laboratories during the first summer. The ALFP replaces the Graduate Research Program for Women (GRPW) and the Cooperative Research Fellowship Program (CRFP) run by the former AT&T Bell Laboratories. If recipients accept other support, the tuition payment and stipend received from that fellowship will replace that provided by this program. The other provisions of this fellowship will remain in force and the stipend will be replaced by an annual grant of $2,000.

Number awarded Approximately 8 each year.

Deadline January of each year.

[1016]
AT&T UNDERGRADUATE RESEARCH PROGRAM

AT&T Laboratories
Attn: Undergraduate Research Program Administrator
200 Laurel Avenue, Room D32-B03
Middletown, NJ 07748
(732) 420-5092   E-mail: recruiting@research.att.com
Web: www.research.att.com/academic/urp.html

Purpose To provide work experience at AT&T Laboratories during the summer to women or members of underrepresented minority groups interested in technical employment.

Eligibility This program is open to U.S. citizens and permanent residents who are undergraduate students in at least their third year but who are not graduating prior to the summer. Applicants must be women or members of a minority group that is underrepresented in the sciences (Blacks, Hispanics, or Native Americans). They must be studying communications, computer science, computer engineering, electrical engineering, human computer interaction, industrial engineering, information science, mathematics, operations research, physics, statistics, or related fields. Selection is based on academic achievement, per-

sonal motivation, and compatibility of student interests with current AT&T Laboratories activities.

Financial data Salaries are commensurate with those of regular AT&T Laboratories employees who have comparable education and work experience (approximately $500 per week). Trainees are reimbursed for their travel to and from New Jersey. Assistance in locating housing is offered.

Duration The minimum traineeship is 10 weeks during the summer.

Additional information Trainees work at AT&T Laboratories located in Crawford Hill, Holmdel, Murray Hill, Shippany, South Plainfield, Short Hills, or West Long Branch, New Jersey. This program replaces the Summer Research Program of the former AT&T Bell Laboratories.

Number awarded 60 to 100 each year.

Deadline November of each year.

[1017]
BARBARA JORDAN HEALTH POLICY SCHOLARS PROGRAM

Henry J. Kaiser Family Foundation
1330 G Street N.W.
Washington, DC 20005
(202) 347-5270   Fax: (202) 347-5274
E-mail: bischolars@howard.edu
Web: www.kff.org/docs/topics/jordanscholars.html

Purpose To provide minority college seniors and recent graduates with an opportunity to work during the summer in a Congressional office with major health policy responsibilities.

Eligibility This program is open to members of minority groups who are entering or currently enrolled in their senior year of college or who have graduated within the last 12 months from an accredited U.S. college or university. Current law, medical, and graduate students are not eligible. Applicants must demonstrate an active interest in health policy, strong leadership skills, and community commitment. Along with their applications, they must submit 400-word essays on 1) their personal background and how it led them to be interested in health policy, and 2) their views on a current health policy issue. Selection is based on the essays, academic performance, letters of recommendation, and extracurricular activities.

Financial data Scholars receive lodging at Howard University in Washington, D.C., round-trip transportation to Washington, D.C., a daily expense allowance for meals and local transportation, and a stipend of $1,500 upon completion of the program.

Duration 9 weeks during the summer.

Additional information Scholars are first provided with an orientation to the program by its sponsors: Howard University and the Henry J. Kaiser Family Foundation. They are then assigned to work for a Congressional office or committee with significant health policy involvement. This program began in 2000.

Number awarded 16 each year.

Deadline January of each year.

[1018]
BAY AREA COMMUNITY SERVICE SCHOLARSHIPS

National Medical Fellowships, Inc.
Attn: Scholarship Program
5 Hanover Square, 15th Floor
New York, NY 10004
(212) 483-8880   Fax: (212) 483-8897
E-mail: info@nmfonline.org
Web: www.nmf-online.org

Purpose To provide financial assistance and clinical experiences to underrepresented minority medical students at designated schools in California.

Eligibility This program is open to third- or fourth-year medical students who are African Americans, mainland Puerto Ricans, Mexican Americans, Native Hawaiians, Alaska Natives, and American Indians. Applicants must be California residents enrolled at the University of California at Davis School of Medicine, the University of California at San Francisco School of Medicine, or Stanford University School of Medicine. They must be interested in either 1) a clinical rotation at an approved community health center in the San Francisco Bay area dedicated to medically underserved populations, or 2) a basic science or clinical science research project in an area of critical need (e.g., HIV/AIDS care and research, hypertension, tuberculosis, cardiovascular disease, diabetes, asthma, substance abuse, women's health research). Selection is based on demonstrated commitment to practice in California, interest in community-based primary care or research, academic performance, financial need, and leadership.

Financial data The stipend is $7,500 for 6-week clinical rotations or 8-week research projects, or $15,000 for 12-week clinical rotations or research projects.

Duration Clinical rotations may be either 6 weeks or 12 weeks. Research projects may extend either 8 weeks or 12 weeks.

Additional information This program was established in 2002 with support from the San Francisco Foundation and the California Endowment. Information is also available from the administrator's California Regional Office, The Chancery Building, 564 Market Street, Suite 209, San Francisco, CA 94104, (415) 397-2526, Fax: (415) 397-2556. Students who choose a 12-week clinical rotation must plan and implement a clinical project at their site. Projects may involve qualitative or quantitative research, health education, or another area of relevance to the site.

Number awarded 6 each year.
Deadline December of each year.

[1019]
BAY AREA MINORITY SUMMER CLERKSHIP PROGRAM

Santa Clara County Bar Association
Attn: Minority Access Committee
4 North Second Street, Suite 400
San Jose, CA 95113
(408) 287-2557   Fax: (408) 287-6083
E-mail: info@sccba.com
Web: www.sccba.org

Purpose To provide summer work experience at law firms in the San Francisco Bay area to minority students at law schools in the area.

Eligibility This program is open to first-year students from any state who are enrolled at the following law schools: Golden Gate, Santa Clara, Stanford, University of San Francisco, Boalt, and Hastings. Applicants must be members of minority groups, defined to include Native Americans, Alaska Natives, Asians, Pacific Islanders, subcontinent Indians, African Americans, other Blacks, Puerto Ricans, Mexican Americans, and other Hispanics. They must be interested in summer employment with a large law firm in their choice of 3 Bay area counties: Alameda, San Francisco, and Santa Clara. Selection is based on verbal and written communication skills, leadership, integrity, resourcefulness, and other characteristics that indicate potential for success within the legal community. Grades are not emphasized; life experience, potential, contact with community, and achievement receive strong consideration.

Financial data Students are paid the standard summer clerk salary by their particular employer.

Duration Summer months.

Additional information This program, which began in 1990, is sponsored by the Santa Clara County Bar Association, the Bar Association of San Francisco, and the Alameda County Bar Association.

Number awarded Approximately 20 each year.
Deadline January of each year.

[1020]
BELL LABS GRADUATE RESEARCH FELLOWSHIP PROGRAM

Lucent Technologies
Attn: Fellowship Programs Manager
283 King George Road, Room B1-D26
Warren, NJ 07059
(732) 559-6971   E-mail: coopgraduate@lucent.com
Web: www.lucent.com/news/foundation/blgrfp

Purpose To provide financial assistance and work experience to women and underrepresented minorities who wish to work on a doctoral degree in designated fields of science and engineering.

Eligibility This program is open to women and underrepresented minorities who plan to work full-time on a doctoral degree in chemical engineering, chemistry, communications science, computer science and engineering, electrical engineering, information science, materials science, mathematics, mechanical engineering, operations research, physics, or statistics. Applicants usually are graduating college seniors, but first-year graduate students are also considered. U.S. citizenship or permanent resident status is required. Selection is based on scholastic attainment and evidence of ability and potential as a research scientist.

Financial data Fellowships provide full tuition and university fees, an annual stipend of $17,000, a book allowance of $250 per semester, and an annual grant of $1,000 for travel to conferences.

Duration 1 year; may be renewed for up to 3 additional years if the fellow makes satisfactory progress toward the doctoral degree.

Additional information Bell Laboratories established the Cooperative Research Fellowship Program (CRFP) for underrepresented minorities in 1972. A parallel program, the Graduate Research Program for Women (GRPW), was established in 1974. In 2003, at the direction of the Lucent

Foundation, those programs were merged under the current name. During their first summer in the program, fellows are expected to working with a mentor at Bell Labs on a research project in their area of interest. Fellows are encouraged to continue their association with their mentors during the following academic year and throughout their graduate studies. Information is also available from Scholarship America, Attn: Scholarship Management Services, One Scholarship Way, P.O. Box 297, St. Peter, MN 56082, (507) 931-1682, (800) 537-4180, Fax: (507) 931-9168, E-mail: smsinfo@csfa.org.

Number awarded Approximately 10 each year.

Deadline January of each year.

[1021]
BIOMEDICAL RESEARCH TRAINING PROGRAM FOR UNDERREPRESENTED GROUPS

National Heart, Lung, and Blood Institute
Attn: Office of Minority Health Affairs
6701 Rockledge Drive, Suite 8093
Bethesda, MD 20892-7913
(301) 451-5081   Fax: (301) 480-0862
E-mail: hm31y@nih.gov
Web: www.nhlbi.nih.gov

Purpose To provide training in fundamental biomedical sciences and clinical research disciplines to undergraduate and graduate students from underrepresented groups.

Eligibility This program is open to underrepresented undergraduate and graduate students (and postbaccalaureate individuals) interested in receiving training in fundamental biomedical sciences and clinical research disciplines. Underrepresented individuals include African Americans, Hispanic Americans, Native Americans, Alaskan Natives, Native Hawaiians and Pacific Islanders, individuals with disabilities, and individuals from disadvantaged backgrounds. Applicants must be U.S. citizens or permanent residents; have completed academic course work relevant to biomedical, behavioral, or statistical research; be enrolled full time or have recently completed baccalaureate work; and have a GPA of 3.3 or higher. Research experiences available include clinical research on the normal and abnormal pathophysiologic functioning of the heart, lungs, and blood and in genetically inherited diseases of those systems; basic research on normal and abnormal cellular behavior at the molecular level; and training in epidemiology, clinical trials, and biostatistics relating to the prevalence, etiology, prevention, and treatment of heart, vascular, pulmonary, and blood diseases.

Financial data Stipends are paid at the annual rate of $22,485 for sophomores, $23,214 for juniors, $23,943 for seniors, $24,671 for postbaccalaureate individuals, $24,671 for first-year graduate students, $25,192 for second-year graduate students, or $26,025 for third-year graduate students.

Duration 6 to 24 months over a 2-year period; training must be completed in increments during consecutive academic years.

Additional information Training is conducted in the laboratories of the National Heart, Lung, and Blood Institute in Bethesda, Maryland.

Number awarded Varies each year.

Deadline February of each year.

[1022]
BROOKHAVEN NATIONAL LABORATORY SCIENCE AND ENGINEERING PROGRAMS FOR WOMEN AND MINORITIES

Brookhaven National Laboratory
Attn: Diversity Office, Human Resources Division
Building 185A
P.O. Box 5000
Upton, New York 11973-5000
(631) 344-2703   Fax: (631) 344-5305
E-mail: rpalmore@bnl.gov
Web: www.bnl.gov/diversity/programs.asp

Purpose To provide on-the-job training in scientific areas at Brookhaven National Laboratory (BNL) during the summer to underrepresented minority and women students.

Eligibility This program at BNL is open to women and underrepresented minority (African American/Black, Hispanic, Native American, or Pacific Islander) students who have completed their freshman, sophomore, or junior year of college. Applicants must be U.S. citizens or permanent residents, at least 18 years of age, and majoring in applied mathematics, biology, chemistry, computer science, engineering, high and low energy particle accelerators, nuclear medicine, physics, or scientific writing. Since no transportation or housing allowance is provided, preference is given to students who reside in the BNL area.

Financial data Participants receive a competitive stipend.

Duration 10 to 12 weeks during the summer.

Additional information Students work with members of the scientific, technical, and professional staff of BNL in an educational training program developed to give research experience.

Deadline April of each year.

[1023]
BUSINESS REPORTING INTERN PROGRAM FOR MINORITY COLLEGE SOPHOMORES AND JUNIORS

Dow Jones Newspaper Fund
P.O. Box 300
Princeton, NJ 08543-0300
(609) 452-2820   Fax: (609) 520-5804
E-mail: newsfund@wsj.dowjones.com
Web: DJNewspaperFund.dowjones.com

Purpose To provide work experience and financial assistance to minority college students who are interested in careers in journalism.

Eligibility This program is open to college sophomores and juniors who are U.S. citizens interested in careers in journalism and participating in a summer internship at a daily newspaper as a business reporter. Applicants must be members of a minority group (African American, Hispanic, Asian American, Pacific Islander, American Indian, or Alaskan Native) enrolled as full-time students. They must submit a resume, 3 to 5 recently-published clips, an list of courses with grades, and a 500-word essay.

Financial data Interns receive a salary of $350 per week during the summer and a $1,000 scholarship at the successful completion of the program.

Duration 10 weeks for the summer internship; 1 year for the scholarship.

Number awarded Up to 12 each year.

Deadline October of each year.

[1024]
CAHSEE YOUNG EDUCATORS PROGRAM

The Center for the Advancement of Hispanics in
   Science and Engineering Education
Attn: Director of Fellowships and Internships
8100 Corporate Drive, Suite 401
Landover, MD 20785
(301) 918-1014   Fax: (301) 918-1087
E-mail: yep@cahsee.org
Web: www.cahsee.org/programs/yep.html

Purpose To provide an opportunity for undergraduate
and graduate students to work as instructors or teaching
assistants during the summer at the Science, Technology,
Engineering, and Mathematics (STEM) Institute of The Center for the Advancement of Hispanics in Science and Engineering Education (CAHSEE).

Eligibility This program is open to undergraduate and
graduate students interested in working at a STEM Institute,
teaching science, technology, engineering, and mathematics to Latino pre-college students. Applicants must identify
all mathematics, science, and engineering courses they
have taken and the grades they received; any leadership
positions they have held while in college; any tutoring,
teaching, or mentoring experiences they have had; and any
summer internships and/or research experiences.

Financial data Fellows receive housing, air travel, and a
stipend of $2,750 to $3,000 (depending on assignment and
educational level).

Duration The program runs for 8 weeks in the summer,
beginning with 2 weeks of seminars in Washington, D.C. on
teaching, leadership, the theory of knowledge, and the educational system, followed by 5 weeks of teaching college-
level courses to Latino high school students at a STEM
Institute, concluding with 1 week preparing a report on the
experience.

Additional information STEM Institutes meet at George
Washington University, the City University of New York, the
University of Illinois at Chicago, Merrimack College, and
yet-to-be-determined schools in Santa Clara and Los Angeles. Graduate students and advanced seniors serve as
instructors, working with undergraduates who serve as
teaching assistants. Funding for this program is provided by
the U.S. National Aeronautics and Space Administration.

Number awarded Approximately 30 each year.

[1025]
CALIFORNIA COMMUNITY SERVICE SCHOLARSHIPS

National Medical Fellowships, Inc.
Attn: Scholarship Program
5 Hanover Square, 15th Floor
New York, NY 10004
(212) 483-8880   Fax: (212) 483-8897
E-mail: info@nmfonline.org
Web: www.nmf-online.org

Purpose To provide clinical experience to underrepresented minority medical students at schools in California.

Eligibility This program is open to third- or fourth-year
medical students who are African Americans, mainland

Puerto Ricans, Mexican Americans, Native Hawaiians,
Alaska Natives, and American Indians. Applicants must be
attending an M.D.-granting institution or college of osteopathic medicine in California. They must be interested in a
clinical rotation at an approved community health center in
California dedicated to medically underserved populations.
Selection is based on demonstrated commitment to practice in California, interest in community-based primary care
or research, academic performance, financial need, and
leadership.

Financial data The stipend is $7,500.

Duration 6 weeks.

Additional information This program was established in
2002 with support from the California Endowment. Information is also available from the administrator's California
Regional Office, The Chancery Building, 564 Market Street,
Suite 209, San Francisco, CA 94104, (415) 397-2526, Fax:
(415) 397-2556.

Number awarded 10 each year.

Deadline December of each year.

[1026]
CALIFORNIA SPACE GRANT UNDERGRADUATE PROGRAM

California Space Grant Consortium
c/o University of California at San Diego
California Space Institute
9500 Gilman Drive, Department 0524
La Jolla, CA 92093-0524
(858) 822-1597   Fax: (858) 534-7840
E-mail: spacegrant@ucsd.edu
Web: calspace.ucsd.edu/casgc/scholarships.html

Purpose To provide assistance to undergraduate students (particularly to underrepresented minorities, women,
and persons with disabilities) at member institutions of the
California Space Grant Consortium who are interested in
interning on space-related projects.

Eligibility This program is open to undergraduate students at member institutions in California who are interested
in earth and space sciences projects. The nature and availability of projects varies from time to time and institution to
institution but typically involves work as a research intern
on an ongoing activity by faculty at a member institution
and/or industry affiliate. The California Space Grant Consortium is a component of the U.S. National Aeronautics and
Space Administration (NASA) Space Grant program, which
encourages participation by underrepresented minorities,
women, and persons with disabilities.

Financial data Each campus sets its own stipend.

Duration 1 semester, summer, or year.

Additional information The participating institutions
include the 8 campuses of the University of California (at
Berkeley, Davis, Irvine, Los Angeles, Riverside, San Diego,
Santa Barbara, and Santa Cruz), California State Polytech-
nic University at Pomona, California State University at Long
Beach, Palomar Community College, Pomona College, San
Diego State University, San Francisco Art Institute, San
Jose State University, Santa Clara University, Stanford Uni-
versity, and the University of San Diego. This program is
funded by NASA.

Number awarded Varies each year.

Deadline Each of the participating institutions sets its own deadline.

[1027]
CAPITOL HILL NEWS INTERNSHIPS

Radio and Television News Directors Foundation
1600 K Street, N.W., Suite 700
Washington, DC 20006-2838
(202) 467-5218   Fax: (202) 223-4007
E-mail: karenb@rtndf.org
Web: www.rtndf.org/asfi/internships/internships.html

Purpose To provide work experience to recent graduates (especially minorities) in electronic journalism who are interested in covering Congressional activities in Washington, D.C.

Eligibility Eligible are recent (within 2 years) college graduates who majored in electronic journalism; preference is given to minority students. Applicants must include an essay explaining why they are interested in this program and how it will help meet their career goals. Excellent writing skills are essential. The sponsor recognizes African Americans, Asian Americans, Hispanic Americans, and Native Americans as minorities.

Financial data The stipend is $1,000 per month. Interns are responsible for their own housing, travel, and living expenses.

Duration 3 months; the spring program begins in March and the summer program begins in June.

Additional information Interns cover newsworthy Congressional activities and help coordinate broadcast coverage of those activities; they obtain hands-on experience in the House and Senate radio-TV galleries, working side by side with the Washington press and Congressional staff to cover the political process. The sponsor defines electronic journalism to include radio, television, cable, and online news.

Number awarded 4 each year: 2 in the spring and 2 in the summer.

Deadline January of each year for the spring program; March of each year for the summer program.

[1028]
CARNEGIE INSTITUTION OF WASHINGTON INTERN PROGRAM

Carnegie Institution of Washington
Geophysical Laboratory
Attn: Summer Intern Program Coordinator
5251 Broad Branch Road, N.W.
Washington, DC 20015-1305
(202) 478-8939   Fax: (202) 478-8901
E-mail: s.gramsch@gl.ciw.edu
Web: www.gl.ciw.edu/interns

Purpose To provide an opportunity for undergraduate students (particularly minorities and women) to participate in a research internship at the Carnegie Institution of Washington's Geophysical Laboratory or Department of Terrestrial Magnetism during the summer.

Eligibility This summer program at the Carnegie Institution of Washington is open to undergraduate students working on a degree in astronomy, biology, chemistry, geoscience, materials science, physics, or a related field. Applicants must have completed at least 30 semester hours, but graduating seniors are not eligible. U.S. citizenship or permanent resident status is required. Applicants must be interested in conducting research at the laboratory under the supervision of a staff scientist. Women and minorities are particularly encouraged to apply.

Financial data The stipend is $3,600. Also provided are housing and support for travel expenses to Washington, D.C.

Duration 10 weeks during the summer.

Additional information Funding for this program is provided by a grant from the National Science Foundation's Research Experiences for Undergraduates program.

Number awarded Varies each year; recently, 16 students participated in this program.

Deadline February of each year.

[1029]
CENTER ON BUDGET AND POLICY PRIORITIES INTERNSHIPS

Center on Budget and Policy Priorities
Attn: Internship Coordinator
820 First Street, N.E., Suite 510
Washington, DC 20002
(202) 408-1095, ext. 386   Fax: (202) 408-1056
E-mail: internship@cbpp.org
Web: www.cbpp.org/internship.html

Purpose To provide work experience at the Center on Budget and Policy Priorities (CBPP) in Washington, D.C. to undergraduates, graduate students, and recent college graduates (particularly those who are minorities or women).

Eligibility This program is open to undergraduates, graduate students, and recent college graduates who are interested in public policy issues affecting low-income families and individuals. Applicants must be interested in working at CBPP in the following areas: media, federal legislation, health policy, housing policy, income security policy, international budget project, national budget and tax policy, outreach campaigns, state budget and tax policy, state low-income initiatives, and food stamps. They should have research, fact-gathering, writing, analytic, and computer skills and a willingness to do administrative as well as substantive tasks. Women and minorities are encouraged to apply.

Financial data Undergraduate students receive $7.50 per hour for a first internship and up to $8.00 per hour subsequently. Graduate students receive $9.00 per hour for a first internship and up to $9.50 per hour subsequently. Students with a master's degree receive $10.00 per hour. Recent college graduates receive $8.00 per hour for a first internship and up to $8.50 per hour subsequently.

Duration 1 semester; may be renewed.

Additional information The center specializes in research and analysis oriented toward practical policy decisions and produces analytic reports that are accessible to public officials at national, state, and local levels, to non-profit organizations, and to the media.

Number awarded Varies each semester.

Deadline February of each year for summer internships; July of each year for fall internships; November of each year for spring internships.

[1030]
CHIPS QUINN SCHOLARS PROGRAM

Freedom Forum
Attn: Chips Quinn Scholars Program
1101 Wilson Boulevard
Arlington, VA 22209
(703) 284-3934   Fax: (703) 284-3543
E-mail: kcatone@freedomforum.org
Web: www.chipsquinn.org

Purpose To provide work experience, career mentoring, and scholarship support to minority college students and recent graduates who are majoring in journalism.

Eligibility This program is open to students of color who are college juniors, seniors, or recent graduates with journalism majors or career goals in newspapers. Candidates must be nominated or endorsed by journalism faculty, campus media advisers, editors of newspapers, or leaders of minority journalism associations. They must be enrolled at an Historically Black College or University (HBCU) or a college or university that has significant numbers of students who are members of ethnic or racial minority groups. Along with their application, they must submit a resume, transcripts, work samples, 2 letters of recommendation, and an essay on why they believe they should be selected for this program. They must have a car and be available to work as a full-time intern during the spring or summer. U.S. citizenship or permanent resident status is required. Campus newspaper experience is strongly encouraged.

Financial data Students chosen for this program receive a travel stipend to attend a workshop at the Freedom Forum in Arlington, Virginia prior to reporting for their internship. Upon completion of the internship, they receive a $1,000 scholarship.

Duration Internships are for 10 to 12 weeks; the scholarship is for 1 year.

Additional information This program was established in 1991 in memory of the late John D. Quinn Jr., managing editor of the *Poughkeepsie Journal.* Funding is provided by the Freedom Forum, formerly the Gannett Foundation. After graduating from college and obtaining employment with a newspaper, alumni of this program are eligible to apply for fellowship support to attend professional journalism development activities.

Number awarded Varies each year. Recently, 94 scholarships were awarded, including 23 who completed their internships in spring and 71 whose internships were in the summer. Since the program began, 828 scholars have been selected.

Deadline October of each year.

[1031]
CIA UNDERGRADUATE INTERNSHIP PROGRAM

Central Intelligence Agency
Attn: Recruitment Center
P.O. Box 4090
Reston, VA 20195
Toll-free: (800) 368-3886
Web: www.cia.gov/employment/student.html

Purpose To provide work experience at the Central Intelligence Agency (CIA) to undergraduates, especially minorities and people with disabilities.

Eligibility This program is open to undergraduate students, particularly minorities and people with disabilities. Applicants must be U.S. citizens, have a GPA of 3.0 or higher, be available to work in metropolitan Washington, D.C. during the summer or for a semester, and meet the same employment standards as permanent CIA employees. They must be majoring in fields such as accounting, business administration, computer science, economics, engineering, finance, foreign area studies, foreign languages, geography, graphic design, human resources, international relations, logistics, mathematics, military and foreign affairs, national security studies, physical sciences, or political science.

Financial data Student positions offer salaries competitive with the private sector and the same benefits as permanent employees. Student trainees are also eligible to apply for the agency's tuition assistance program.

Duration Interns are required to work either 1) a combination of 1 semester and 1 summer, or 2) 2 90-day summer internships.

Number awarded Varies each year.

Deadline Applications may be submitted at any time, but should be completed 6 to 9 months prior to availability for the first work period and near the end of the applicant's freshman year in college.

[1032]
CLEAN THE RAIN ORGANIZING INTERNSHIPS

National Wildlife Federation
Attn: Great Lakes Field Office
213 West Liberty, Suite 200
Ann Arbor, MI 48104-1398
(734) 769-3351   Fax: (734) 769-1449
E-mail: greatlakes@nwf.org
Web: www.nwf.org/greatlakes

Purpose To provide an opportunity for recent graduates (particularly people of color and women) to work on conservation issues at the Great Lakes field office of the National Wildlife Federation.

Eligibility This program is open to college graduates who have a bachelor's degree in biology, chemistry, ecology, environmental science, environmental engineering, natural resources, or other science field. Applicants must be interested in working on organizing aspects of the Clean the Rain project nationally and mercury phaseout work in the Great Lakes states. They must have good organizational skills and excellent communication skills (both oral and written). Familiarity with standard PC word processing, spreadsheet, database, and graphics programs is essential. Some organizing/outreach experience on other campaigns is very helpful. Applications are strongly encouraged from people of diverse backgrounds, women, people of color, people of all sexual identities, and people with disabilities.

Financial data The stipend is $160 per week. No benefits are provided.

Duration 10 weeks; interns may begin at any time.

Additional information Interns work with partner organizations in deployment and maintenance at field sites; work with other staff in drafting mini-reports on mercury in precipitation in the Great Lakes; assist in planning and coordination of materials for news conferences; assist in preparation and delivery of presentations on the mercury phaseout project; assist in coordination of national advocacy work on mercury reduction legislation and rulemaking; and assist as needed with research and outreach work related to the overall Clean the Rain campaign.

Number awarded Varies each year.

Deadline Applications may be submitted at any time.

[1033]
THE CLOISTERS SUMMER INTERNSHIP FOR COLLEGE STUDENTS

Metropolitan Museum of Art
Attn: The Cloisters
Fort Tryon Park
New York, NY 10040
(212) 650-2280
E-mail: cloistersinterns@metmuseum.org
Web: www.metmuseum.org

Purpose To provide art museum work experience during the summer at The Cloisters of the Metropolitan Museum of Art to minority and other college students.

Eligibility This program is open to undergraduate students, especially freshmen and sophomores, who are interested in art and museum careers. They must enjoy working with children and be willing to intern at the Metropolitan Museum of Art. Applicants of diverse backgrounds are particularly encouraged to apply.

Financial data The internship stipend is $2,500.

Duration 9 weeks, beginning in June.

Additional information Interns are assigned to the education department of The Cloisters, the branch museum of the Metropolitan Museum of Art devoted to the art of medieval Europe. They conduct gallery workshops for New York City day campers. This program is funded in part by the Norman and Rosita Winston Foundation, Inc.

Number awarded Varies each year.

Deadline January of each year.

[1034]
COLORADO SPACE GRANT RESEARCH SUPPORT

Colorado Space Grant Consortium
c/o University of Colorado at Boulder
Engineering and Applied Science Department
Engineering Center, Room 1B-76
Campus Box 520
Boulder, CO 80309-0520
(303) 492-3141   Fax: (303) 492-5456
E-mail: elaine.hansen@colorado.edu
Web: spacegrant.colorado.edu

Purpose To provide an opportunity to participate in space-related research to undergraduate and graduate students (particularly underrepresented minorities, women, and persons with disabilities) at member institutions of the Colorado Space Grant Consortium (CSGC).

Eligibility This program is open to undergraduate and graduate students at the 14 colleges and universities affiliated with the consortium. Applicants must be interested in participating in designing, flying, building, operating, and analyzing real space engineering and science experiments. The sponsored research activities are part of the Space Grant program of the U.S. National Aeronautics and Space Administration (NASA), which encourages participation by women, underrepresented minorities, and people with disabilities.

Financial data Stipends are provided.

Additional information The members of CSGC include the University of Colorado at Boulder, the University of Colorado at Colorado Springs, Colorado State University, the United States Air Force Academy, Pikes Peak Community College, the University of Southern Colorado, Mesa State College, the University of Northern Colorado, Western State College, Adams State College, Colorado School of Mines, Fort Lewis College, Metro State College, and Front Range Community College. This program is funded by NASA.

Number awarded Varies each year.

[1035]
CONGRESSIONAL HISPANIC CAUCUS INSTITUTE CORPORATE FELLOWSHIP

Congressional Hispanic Caucus Institute, Inc.
911 Second Street, N.E.
Washington, DC 20002
(202) 543-1771   Toll-free: (800) EXCEL-DC
Fax: (202) 546-2143   E-mail: chci@chci.org
Web: www.chciyouth.org

Purpose To provide Latino graduate students and recent college graduates with the opportunity to apply their academic expertise in the area of public-private partnerships during a work experience program in Washington, D.C.

Eligibility This program is open to U.S. citizens and permanent residents of Latino background who graduated from a college or university (with a bachelor's or graduate degree) within the past year or are currently-enrolled graduate students. Applicants must be interested in gaining experience in the area of public-private partnerships. They must be able to demonstrate high academic achievement (preference is given to those with a GPA of 3.0 or higher), consistent active participation in public and/or community service activities, and superior analytical and communication skills (oral and written).

Financial data This program provides transportation to and from Washington, D.C., a monthly stipend of $2,061 (or $2,500 for fellows who already have a graduate degree), and health insurance.

Duration 9 months, beginning in September.

Additional information Fellows are placed in the public affairs office of a corporation.

Number awarded 1 or more each year.

Deadline February of each year.

[1036]
CONGRESSIONAL HISPANIC CAUCUS INSTITUTE GENERAL PUBLIC POLICY FELLOWSHIP PROGRAM

Congressional Hispanic Caucus Institute, Inc.
911 Second Street, N.E.
Washington, DC 20002
(202) 543-1771   Toll-free: (800) EXCEL-DC
Fax: (202) 546-2143   E-mail: chci@chci.org
Web: www.chciyouth.org

Purpose To provide Latino graduate students and recent college graduates with the opportunity to apply their academic expertise in the area of public policy during a work experience program in Washington, D.C.

Eligibility   This program is open to U.S. citizens and permanent residents of Latino background who graduated from a college or university (with a bachelor's or graduate degree) within the past year or are currently-enrolled graduate students. Applicants must be interested in gaining experience in the area of public policy. They must be able to demonstrate high academic achievement (preference is given to those with a GPA of 3.0 or higher), consistent active participation in public and/or community service activities, and superior analytical and communication skills (oral and written).

Financial data   This program provides transportation to and from Washington, D.C., a monthly stipend of $2,061 (or $2,500 for fellows who already have a graduate degree), and health insurance.

Duration   9 months, beginning in September.

Additional information   Placements are available in Congressional offices and federal agencies, advocacy groups, the media, and a broad range of policy-related organizations. Fellows select the placement that best matches their interests.

Number awarded   Approximately 20 each year.

Deadline   February of each year.

[1037]
CONGRESSIONAL HISPANIC CAUCUS INSTITUTE SUMMER INTERNSHIP PROGRAM

Congressional Hispanic Caucus Institute, Inc.
911 Second Street, N.E.
Washington, DC 20002
(202) 543-1771   Toll-free: (800) EXCEL-DC
Fax: (202) 546-2143   E-mail: chci@chci.org
Web: www.chciyouth.org

Purpose   To provide Hispanic Americans with an opportunity during the summer to work directly with members of Congress on their committees or as personal staff.

Eligibility   This program is open to undergraduate students who have completed at least 1 year of college and are interested in an internship on Capitol Hill. College seniors graduating before the program begins are ineligible. Applicants must be U.S. citizens or permanent residents who can demonstrate 1) high academic achievement (preference is given to those with a GPA of 3.0 or higher); 2) consistent active participation in public and/or community service activities; and 3) strong analytic and writing skills.

Financial data   The internship provides a stipend of $2,000, transportation to and from Washington, and housing in university dormitories.

Duration   8 weeks during the summer. The internship begins in June.

Additional information   In addition to their internship, participants attend seminars and lectures that offer exposure to critical components of policy making.

Number awarded   Approximately 30 each year.

Deadline   January of each year.

[1038]
CONNECTICUT COMMUNITY COLLEGE MINORITY TEACHING FELLOWSHIPS

Connecticut Community College System
Attn: System Officer for Diversity Awareness
61 Woodland Street
Hartford, CT 06105-9949
(860) 244-7606   Fax: (860) 566-6624
E-mail: karmstrong@commnet.edu
Web: www.commnet.edu/minority_fellowship.asp

Purpose   To provide financial assistance and work experience to graduate students, especially minorities, in Connecticut who are interested in preparing for a career in community college teaching or administration.

Eligibility   This program is open to graduate students who have completed at least 6 credits of graduate work and have indicated an interest in a career in community colleges. Applicants must be willing to commit to at least 1 year of employment in the Connecticut Community College System. Although all qualified graduate students are eligible, the program encourages applicants to register who strengthen the racial and cultural diversity of the minority fellow registry. That includes, in particular, making all possible efforts to recruit from historically underrepresented people (Asians, Blacks, and Hispanics).

Financial data   Fellows receive a stipend of $3,500 per semester.

Duration   1 year; may be renewed.

Additional information   Fellows are expected to dedicate 9 hours per week to the program. They spend 6 hours per week in teaching-related activities under the supervision of a mentor. During the second semester, they assist the mentor in teaching a course. The remaining time is spent on program and campus orientation activities, attendance at relevant faculty or staff meetings, and participation in other college meetings or professional development activities.

Number awarded   Up to 13 each year: 1 at each of the 12 colleges in the system and 1 in the chancellor's office.

[1039]
CONSORTIUM FOR GRADUATE STUDY IN MANAGEMENT FELLOWSHIPS

Consortium for Graduate Study in Management
5585 Pershing Avenue, Suite 240
St. Louis, MO 63112
(314) 877-5500   Toll-free: (888) 658-6814
Fax: (314) 877-5505   E-mail: frontdesk@cgsm.org
Web: www.cgsm.org

Purpose   To provide financial assistance and work experience to underrepresented racial minorities interested in preparing for a management career in business.

Eligibility   Eligible to apply are African Americans, Hispanic Americans (Chicanos, Cubans, Dominicans, and Puerto Ricans), and Native Americans who have graduated from college and are interested in a career in business. An undergraduate degree in business or economics is not required. Applicants must be U.S. citizens and planning to work on an M.B.A. degree at 1 of the consortium's 13 schools. Preference is given to applicants under 31 years of age.

Financial data The fellowship pays full tuition and required fees. Summer internships with the consortium's cooperative sponsors, providing paid practical experience, are also offered.

Duration Up to 4 semesters. The participating schools are Carnegie Mellon University, Dartmouth College, Emory University, Indiana University, University of Michigan, New York University, University of North Carolina at Chapel Hill, University of Rochester, University of Southern California, University of Texas at Austin, University of Virginia, Washington University, and University of Wisconsin at Madison.

Additional information Fellowships are tenable at member schools only.

Number awarded Varies; up to 400 each year.

Deadline The early deadline is the end of November of each year. The final deadline is in January of each year.

[1040]
COX NEWSPAPER DIVISION MINORITY JOURNALISM SCHOLARSHIP

Cox Newspapers, Inc.
Attn: Scholarship Administrator
6205 Peachtree Dunwoody Road
P.O. Box 105720
Atlanta, GA 30348
(678) 645-0000
Web: www.coxnews.com

Purpose To provide work experience and financial assistance to minority undergraduate and graduate students from areas served by selected Cox Enterprises newspapers who are preparing for a career in the newspaper industry.

Eligibility This program is open to minority (African American, Hispanic, Asian American, Native American) undergraduate and graduate students interested in newspaper careers. Applicants must be interested in continuing their program of study as well as working as an intern at a participating Cox newspaper. Cox employees and their families are eligible. Each newspaper establishes its own criteria regarding GPA requirements, supporting documentation, and essay requirements. In general, applicants must have demonstrated an interest in the department (newsroom, online, advertising, accounting, marketing, or information technology) in which they would like to intern and be able to demonstrate experience with campus publications and/or daily deadlines.

Financial data All educational expenses are paid for 4 years of college, including room, board, books, and tuition. The approximate total value of the award is $40,000.

Duration The scholarship is awarded for 4 years. The recipient is expected to intern at the newspaper during the summer and holiday breaks throughout the 4 years of college.

Additional information The scholarship is administered by major newspapers owned by the sponsor: the *Atlanta Journal and Constitution, Austin American-Statesman,* and *Palm Beach Post.* Applications are available from the Cox Newspapers headquarters in Atlanta, the offices of the various Cox-owned newspapers, and from guidance offices of high schools in the city selected for the scholarship for that year.

Number awarded 1 each year.

Deadline April of each year.

[1041]
C.T. LANG JOURNALISM MINORITY SCHOLARSHIP AND INTERNSHIP

Albuquerque Journal
Attn: Scholarship Committee
7777 Jefferson Street, N.E.
P.O. Drawer J
Albuquerque, NM 87103
(505) 823-7777

Purpose To provide financial assistance and work experience to minority upper-division students in journalism programs at universities in New Mexico.

Eligibility This program is open to minority students majoring or minoring in journalism at a New Mexico university in their junior year with a GPA of 2.5 or higher. Applicants must be enrolled full time. They must be planning a career in newswriting, photography, design, copy editing, or online. Selection is based on clips of published stories, a short autobiography that explains the applicant's interest in the field, a grade transcript, and a letter of recommendation.

Financial data The scholarship is $1,000 per semester; the recipient also receives a paid internship and moving expenses.

Duration The scholarship is for 2 semesters (fall and spring). The internship is for 1 semester.

Additional information This program is funded by the *Albuquerque Journal,* where the internship takes place.

Number awarded 1 each year.

Deadline December of each year.

[1042]
CULTURAL RESOURCES DIVERSITY INTERN PROGRAM

Student Conservation Association, Inc.
Attn: Diversity Internships
1800 North Kent Street, Suite 102
Arlington, VA 22209
(703) 524-2441   Fax: (603) 543-1828
E-mail: diversity@thesca.org
Web: www.thesca.org/ci_diversity.cfm

Purpose To provide work experience to ethnically diverse college students and students with disabilities at facilities of the U.S. National Park Service (NPS).

Eligibility This program is open to currently-enrolled students at the sophomore or higher level. Applicants must be U.S. citizens or permanent residents with a GPA of 3.0 or higher. The program is designed to give ethnically diverse students and students with disabilities the opportunity to experience the diversity of careers in the federal sector. Applicants are assigned to a position within the NPS. Possible placements include archaeology and anthropology; historic building preservation; journalism and graphic design; civil and environmental engineering; project management and research; costumed interpretation and living history; landscape architecture; museum studies and library relations; web site design; public relations and outreach; and Native American studies.

Financial data The weekly stipend ranges from $50 to $520, depending on the program and the intern's academic level. Other benefits include a pre-term orientation, transportation to the orientation and the work site, worker's compensation, and accident insurance.

Duration 10 weeks in the summer (beginning in June), 15 weeks in the fall (beginning in September), or 15 weeks in the spring (beginning in January).

Additional information While participating in the internship, students engage in tri-weekly evening career and professional development events, ongoing career counseling, mentoring, and personal and career development services.

Number awarded Approximately 18 each year.

Deadline February of each year for summer; June of each year for fall; November of each year for spring.

[1043]
DALMAS A. TAYLOR MEMORIAL SUMMER MINORITY POLICY FELLOWSHIP

Society for the Psychological Study of Social Issues
208 I Street, N.E.
Washington, DC 20002-4340
(202) 675-6956   Fax: (202) 675-6902
E-mail: awards@spssi.org
Web: www.spssi.org/Taylor_flyer.html

Purpose To enable graduate students of color to be involved in the public policy activities of the American Psychological Association (APA) during the summer.

Eligibility This program is open to graduate students who are members of an ethnic minority group (including, but not limited to, African American, Alaskan Native, American Indian, Asian American, Hispanic, and Pacific Islander) and/or have demonstrated a commitment to a career in psychology or a related field with a focus on ethnic minority issues. Applicants must be interested in spending a summer in Washington, D.C. to work on public policy issues in conjunction with the Minority Fellowship Program of the APA. Their application must indicate why they are interested in the fellowship, their previous research experience and current interest, their interest and involvement in ethnic minority psychological issues, and how the fellowship would contribute to their career goals.

Financial data The stipend is $3,000. Housing and travel funds are also provided.

Duration Summer months.

Additional information This program was established in 2000.

Number awarded 1 each year.

Deadline January of each year.

[1044]
DAN BRADLEY FELLOWSHIP PROGRAM

Legal Aid Association of California
c/o Public Interest Clearinghouse
47 Kearney Street, Suite 705
San Francisco, CA 94108
(415) 834-0100, ext. 306   Fax: (415) 834-0202
E-mail: laac@pic.org
Web: www.pic.org/laac/laacpage.htm

Purpose To provide funding to law students (particularly students of color) interested in a summer internship with legal services programs that are members of the Legal Aid Association of California (LAAC).

Eligibility This program is open to law students who have a strong interest in working to defend and expand the legal rights of the poor and the disadvantaged. Applicants must

be interested in a summer internship with a legal aid services agency that is an LAAC member and that agrees to supervise the student on a major litigation or "impact" advocacy project. Applications must be submitted jointly by the student and a representative of an eligible legal services program. Students must include a personal statement describing their interest in pursuing the fellowship. People of color and students from low-income or working class backgrounds are particularly encouraged to apply.

Financial data The stipend is at least $2,500. The LAAC contributes $2,000 and the program selected to receive the fellow is expected to provide at least an additional $500.

Duration 8 weeks during the summer.

Additional information This program began in 1991.

Number awarded 1 or more each year.

Deadline April of each year.

[1045]
DAVIS WRIGHT TREMAINE 1L DIVERSITY SCHOLARSHIP PROGRAM

Davis Wright Tremaine LLP
Attn: Recruiting Administrator
2600 Century Square
1501 Fourth Avenue
Seattle, WA 98101-1688
(206) 622-3150   Fax: (206) 628-7699
E-mail: seattle@dwt.com
Web: www.dwt.com/recruit/diversity.htm

Purpose To provide financial assistance and summer work experience to law students of color.

Eligibility This program is open to first-year law students of color and others of diverse background. Applicants must possess a strong academic record as an undergraduate and in first year of law school, an interest in participating in community and civic opportunities, and a willingness to commit to working in the sponsor's Seattle or Portland office during the summer between their first and second year of law school. They must submit a current resume, a complete undergraduate transcript, grades from the first semester of law school, a short personal essay indicating their interest in the scholarship, a legal writing sample, and 2 or 3 references. Although demonstrated need may be taken into account, applicants need not disclose their financial circumstances.

Financial data The award consists of a $7,500 stipend for second-year tuition and expenses and a paid summer clerkship.

Duration 1 academic year and summer.

Number awarded 3 each year: 2 in the Seattle office and 1 in the Portland office.

Deadline January of each year.

[1046]
DELL/UNCF CORPORATE SCHOLARS PROGRAM

United Negro College Fund
Attn: Corporate Scholars Program
P.O. Box 1435
Alexandria, VA 22313-9998
Toll-free: (866) 671-7237   E-mail: internship@uncf.org
Web: www.uncf.org/internships/index.asp

Purpose To provide financial assistance and work experience to undergraduate and graduate students, especially minorities, majoring in designated fields and interested in an internship at Dell Computer Corporation's corporate headquarters near Austin, Texas.

Eligibility This program is open to rising juniors and graduate students who are enrolled full time at institutions that are members of the United Negro College Fund (UNCF) or at any other 4-year college or university. Applicants must be majoring in business administration, computer science, engineering (computer, electrical, or mechanical), finance, human resources, management information systems, marketing, or supply chain management with a GPA of 3.0 or higher. Along with their application, they must submit a 1-page essay about themselves and their career goals, including information about their personal background and any particular challenges they have faced. Finalists are interviewed by a team of representatives from Dell, the program's sponsor.

Financial data The program provides a paid summer internship, housing accommodations in Austin, round-trip transportation to and from Austin, and (based on financial need and successful internship performance) a $10,000 scholarship.

Duration 10 to 12 weeks for the internship; 1 year for the scholarship.

Number awarded Varies each year.

Deadline January of each year.

[1047]
DENVER BOTANIC GARDENS COLLEGE INTERNSHIPS IN APPLIED HORTICULTURE

Denver Botanic Gardens
Attn: Human Resources
909 York Street
Denver, CO 80206-3799
(720) 865-3531   Fax: (720) 865-3722
E-mail: HR@botanicgardens.org
Web: www.botanicgardens.org

Purpose To provide summer work experience in horticulture to students (especially minorities) at the Denver Botanic Gardens.

Eligibility This internship at the Denver Botanic Gardens is open to graduate students and undergraduates from any state who have completed their sophomore year and have a GPA of 2.5 or higher. Both traditional and nontraditional students, including those making career changes into the field of horticulture, are eligible. Minorities are specifically encouraged to apply.

Financial data A stipend is paid (amount not specified).

Duration 10 weeks during the summer.

Additional information Work assignments include planting, pruning, weeding, and watering on the outside grounds; seeding, transplanting, and propagation in the green-

houses; and tropical display and maintenance in the conservatory and lobby court areas. In addition, educational field trips and special projects help to round-out the program, which highlights gardening in the Front Range of the Colorado Rockies. Participants maintain a plant notebook throughout their internship.

Number awarded Approximately 6 each year.

Deadline February of each year.

[1048]
DEPARTMENT OF STATE STUDENT INTERN PROGRAM

Department of State
Attn: Recruitment Division, SA-1
Intern Coordinator
2401 E Street, N.W., Room H518
Washington, DC 20522-0108
(202) 261-8888   Toll-free: (800) JOB-OVERSEAS
Fax: (202) 261-8841
Web: www.careers.state.gov/student/prog_intrn.html

Purpose To provide a work/study opportunity to undergraduate and graduate students (particularly minorities and women) interested in foreign service.

Eligibility This program is open to full- and part-time continuing college and university juniors, seniors, and graduate students. Applications are encouraged from students with a broad range of majors, such as business or public administration, social work, economics, information management, journalism, and the biological and physical sciences, as well as those majors more traditionally identified with international affairs. U.S. citizenship is required. The State Department particularly encourages eligible women and minority students with an interest in foreign affairs to apply.

Financial data Most internships are unpaid. A few paid internships are granted to applicants who can demonstrate financial need. If they qualify for a paid internship, college juniors are placed at the GS-4 level with an annual salary of $20,952; college seniors and first-year graduate students are placed at the GS-5 level with an annual salary of $23,442; second-year graduate students are placed at the GS-7 level with an annual salary of $29,037. Interns placed abroad may also receive housing, medical insurance, a travel allowance, and a dependents' allowance.

Duration Paid internships are available only for 10 weeks during the summer. Unpaid internships are available for 1 semester or quarter during the academic year, or for 10 weeks during the summer.

Additional information About half of all internships are in Washington, D.C., or occasionally in other large cities in the United States. The remaining internships are at embassies and consulates abroad. Depending upon the needs of the department, interns are assigned junior-level professional duties, which may include research, preparing reports, drafting replies to correspondence, working in computer science, analyzing international issues, financial management, intelligence, security, or assisting in cases related to domestic and international law. Interns must agree to return to their schooling immediately upon completion of their internship.

Number awarded Approximately 800 internships are offered each year, but only about 5% of those are paid positions.

Deadline   February of each year for fall internships; June of each year for spring internships; October of each year for a summer internships.

[1049]
DIETETIC INTERNSHIP SCHOLARSHIPS

American Dietetic Association
Attn: Accreditation, Education Programs, and Student Operations
120 South Riverside Plaza, Suite 2000
Chicago, IL 60606-6995
(312) 899-0040   Toll-free: (800) 877-1600, ext. 5400
Fax: (312) 899-4817   E-mail: education@eatright.org
Web: www.eatright.org

Purpose   To provide financial assistance to student members of the American Dietetic Association (ADA) who have applied for a dietetic internship.

Eligibility   This program is open to student members who have applied for a CADE-accredited dietetic internship. Applicants must be participating in the computer-matching process, be U.S. citizens or permanent residents, and show promise of being a valuable, contributing member of the profession. Some scholarships require membership in a specific dietetic practice group, residency in a specific state, or underrepresented minority group status. The same application form can be used for all categories. Students who are currently completing the internship component of a combined graduate/dietetic internship should apply for the American Dietetic Association's Graduate Scholarship.

Financial data   Stipends range from $500 to $4,500.

Duration   1 year.

Number awarded   Varies each year, depending upon the funds available. Recently, the sponsoring organization awarded 144 scholarships for all its programs.

Deadline   February of each year.

[1050]
DOI DIVERSITY INTERN PROGRAM

Student Conservation Association, Inc.
Attn: Diversity Internships
1800 North Kent Street, Suite 102
Arlington, VA 22209
(703) 524-2441   Fax: (603) 543-1828
E-mail: diversity@thesca.org
Web: www.thesca.org/ci_diversity.cfm

Purpose   To provide work experience to ethnically diverse college and graduate students and students with disabilities at federal agencies involved with natural and cultural resources.

Eligibility   This program is open to currently-enrolled students at the sophomore or higher level. Applicants must be U.S. citizens or permanent residents with a GPA of 3.0 or higher. The program is designed to give ethnically diverse students and students with disabilities the opportunity to experience the diversity of careers in the federal sector. Applicants are assigned to a position within the U.S. Department of the Interior (DOI). Possible placements include archaeology and anthropology; wildlife and fisheries biology; business administration, accounting, and finance; civil and environmental engineering; computer science, especially GIS applications; human resources; mining and petro-

leum engineering; communications and public relations; web site and database design; environmental and realty law; geology, hydrology, and geography; Native American studies; interpretation and environmental education; natural resource and range management; public policy and administration; and surveying and mapping.

Financial data   The weekly stipend ranges from $50 to $520, depending on the program and the intern's academic level. Other benefits include a pre-term orientation, transportation to the orientation and the work site, worker's compensation, and accident insurance.

Duration   10 weeks in the summer (beginning in June) or 15 weeks in the fall (beginning in September) or spring (beginning in January).

Additional information   While participating in the internship, students engage in tri-weekly evening career and professional development events, ongoing career counseling, mentoring, and personal and career development services.

Number awarded   Approximately 20 each year.

Deadline   February of each year for summer; June of each year for fall; November of each year for spring.

[1051]
EATON MULTICULTURAL SCHOLARS PROGRAM

Eaton Corporation
Attn: EMSP
1111 Superior Avenue
Cleveland, OH 44114-2584
(216) 523-4354   E-mail: mildredneumann@eaton.com
Web: www.eatonjobs.com/career/career_choices.asp

Purpose   To provide financial assistance and work experience to minority college students interested in a career as an engineer.

Eligibility   This program is open to full-time minority students who are U.S. citizens or permanent residents. Applicants must have completed 1 year in an accredited program and have 3 remaining years of course work before completing a bachelor's degree. They must be majoring in computer science/data processing, electrical engineering, or mechanical engineering. Selection is based on academic performance, the student's school recommendation, and an expressed interest in pursuing challenging and rewarding internship assignments.

Financial data   Stipends range from $500 to $3,000 per year. Funds are paid directly to the recipient's university to cover the cost of tuition, books, supplies, equipment, and fees.

Duration   3 years.

Additional information   In addition to the scholarships, recipients are offered paid summer internships at company headquarters in Cleveland. The target schools participating in this program recently were Cornell, Detroit-Mercy, Florida A&M, Georgia Tech, Illinois at Chicago, Illinois at Urbana-Champaign, Lawrence Technological, Marquette, Massachusetts Institute of Technology, Michigan at Ann Arbor, Michigan at Dearborn, Michigan State, Milwaukee School of Engineering, Minnesota, Morehouse College, North Carolina A&T State, North Carolina State, Northwestern, Notre Dame, Ohio State, Purdue, Southern, Tennessee, Western Michigan, and Wisconsin at Madison. This program was established in 1994. Until 2002, it was known as the Eaton Minority Engineering Scholars Program.

Number awarded Varies each year.

Deadline December of each year.

[1052]
EDUCATIONAL TESTING SERVICE SUMMER PROGRAM IN RESEARCH FOR GRADUATE STUDENTS

Educational Testing Service
Attn: Internships
Rosedale Road
MS 07-R
Princeton, NJ 08541-0001
(609) 734-5949   E-mail: internships@ets.org
Web: www.ets.org/research/fellowships.html

Purpose To provide work experience at the Educational Testing Service (ETS) during the summer to minority, women, and other graduate students in educational measurement and related fields.

Eligibility This internship at ETS is open to graduate students who are currently enrolled full time in a doctoral program and have completed at least 1 year of study. Applicants must be working on a doctoral degree in the following areas: computer science, education, learning, linguistics, literacy, minority issues, policy research, psychology, psycholinguistics, psychometrics, statistics, teaching, educational technology, or testing issues (including alternate forms of assessment for special populations and new forms of assessment). Selection is based on academic record and the match of applicant interests with participating ETS researchers. An explicit goal of the program is to attract women and minority graduate students to the field of educational measurement and related disciplines.

Financial data The stipend is $5,000. In addition, participants and their families are reimbursed for travel expenses from their universities to ETS (in Princeton) and back.

Duration 2 months, beginning in June.

Additional information Participants work under the supervision of ETS staff members.

Number awarded Up to 16 each year.

Deadline January of each year.

[1053]
EDWARD R. ROYBAL PUBLIC HEALTH FELLOWSHIP

Congressional Hispanic Caucus Institute, Inc.
911 Second Street, N.E.
Washington, DC 20002
(202) 543-1771   Toll-free: (800) EXCEL-DC
Fax: (202) 546-2143   E-mail: chci@chci.org
Web: www.chciyouth.org

Purpose To provide Latino recent college graduates with the opportunity to apply their academic expertise in the area of public health policy during a work experience program in Washington, D.C.

Eligibility This program is open to U.S. citizens and permanent residents of Latino background who graduated from a college or university (with a bachelor's or graduate degree) within the past year. Applicants must be interested in gaining experience in the area of public health policy. They must be able to demonstrate high academic achievement (preference is given to those with a GPA of 3.0 or

higher), consistent active participation in public and/or community service activities, and superior analytical and communication skills (oral and written).

Financial data This program provides transportation to and from Washington, D.C., a monthly stipend of $2,500, and health insurance.

Duration 9 months, beginning in September.

Additional information Placements are available in Congressional offices and federal agencies, advocacy groups, the media, and a broad range of policy-related organizations, but must focus on health issues.

Number awarded 1 each year.

Deadline February of each year.

[1054]
EISENHOWER GRANTS FOR RESEARCH FELLOWSHIPS

Department of Transportation
Federal Highway Administration
Attn: National Highway Institute, HNHI-20
4600 North Fairfax Drive, Suite 800
Arlington, VA 22203-1553
(703) 235-0538   Fax: (703) 235-0593
E-mail: transportationedu@fhwa.dot.gov
Web: www.nhi.fhwa.dot.gov/ddetfp.asp

Purpose To enable students (especially minorities) to participate in research activities at facilities of the U.S. Department of Transportation (DOT) Federal Highway Administration in the Washington, D.C. area.

Eligibility This program is open to 1) students in their junior year of a baccalaureate program who will complete their junior year before being awarded a fellowship; 2) students in their senior year of a baccalaureate program; and 3) students who have completed their baccalaureate degree and are enrolled in a program leading to a master's, Ph.D., or equivalent degree. Applicants must be U.S. citizens enrolled in an accredited U.S. institution of higher education working on a degree full time and planning to enter the transportation profession after completing their higher education. They select 1 or more projects from a current list of research projects underway at various DOT facilities; the research will be conducted with academic supervision provided by a faculty advisor from their home university (which grants academic credit for the research project) and with technical direction provided by the DOT staff. Specific requirements for the target projects vary; most require engineering backgrounds, but others involve transportation planning, information management, public administration, physics, materials science, statistical analysis, operations research, chemistry, economics, technology transfer, urban studies, geography, and urban and regional planning. The DOT encourages students at Historically Black Colleges and Universities (HBCUs) and Hispanic Serving Institutions (HSIs) to apply for these grants. Selection is based on: match of the student's qualifications with the proposed research project (including the student's ability to accomplish the project in the available time), recommendation letters regarding the nominee's qualifications to conduct the research, academic records (including class standing, GPA, and transcripts), and transportation work experience (if any) including the employer's endorsement.

Financial data   Fellows receive full tuition and fees that relate to the academic credits for the approved research project and a monthly stipend of $1,450 for college seniors, $1,700 for master's students, or $2,000 for doctoral students. An allowance for travel to and from the DOT facility where the research is conducted is also provided, but selectees are responsible for their own housing accommodations. Faculty advisors are allowed 1 site review on projects over 6 months and 2 site reviews on projects over 9 months; travel and per diem are provided for those site reviews.

Duration   Tenure is normally 3, 6, 9, or 12 months.

Number awarded   Varies each year; recently, 9 students participated in this program.

Deadline   February of each year.

[1055]
EMMA L. BOWEN FOUNDATION INTERNSHIPS

Emma L. Bowen Foundation
Attn: Vice President, Eastern Region
524 West 57th Street
New York, NY 10019
(212) 975-2545   Fax: (212) 975-5884
E-mail: sdrice@cbs.com
Web: www.emmabowenfoundation.com

Purpose   To provide minority students with an opportunity to gain work experience during the summer at participating media companies.

Eligibility   This program is open to minority students who apply as early as their junior year in high school. Applicants must be interested in working at a media company during the summer and school breaks until they graduate from college. They must have a GPA of 3.0 or higher, plans to attend an accredited 4-year college or university, and an interest in the media industry as a career. Along with their application, they must submit an essay of 500 to 1,000 words on how the media industry helps to create the images that influence our decisions and perceptions on a daily basis.

Financial data   Interns receive a stipend of approximately $2,250 and matching compensation of $2,250 to help pay for college tuition and other expenses.

Duration   1 summer; may be renewed until the intern graduates from college if he or she maintains a GPA of 3.0 or higher.

Additional information   The sponsoring companies have included ABC, Inc., Adelphia Communications, Broadcast Music Inc., CBS Incorporated, Comcast Foundation, C-SPAN, Fox Television Stations, Inc., Gannett Television, NBC, Paxson Communications, Turner Entertainment Networks, and the Weather Channel. Students in eastern states should use the address of the Vice President, Eastern Region. Students in western states should contact the Vice President, Western Region, CBS Studio Center, Administration Building, Suite 300, 4024 Radford Avenue, Studio City, CA 91604, (818) 655-5708, Fax: (818) 655-8358, E-mail: r.turner@mptp.com.

Number awarded   Varies each year; recently, 50 new interns were selected.

[1056]
EVERETT PUBLIC SERVICE INTERNSHIPS

Everett Public Internship Program
c/o Co-op America
1612 K Street, N.W., Suite 600
Washington, DC 20006
(202) 872-5335   Fax: (202) 331-8166
E-mail: info@everettinternships.org
Web: www.everettinternships.org

Purpose   To provide work experience at public interest organizations during the summer to undergraduate and graduate students (especially minorities) who are interested in preparing for a career in public service.

Eligibility   This program is open to undergraduate and graduate students who have completed at least 2 semesters of college and are interested in working in areas of public service at 55 nonprofit organizations throughout the country. Applicants can be majoring in any field as long as they are committed to public interest work. Members of all racial and ethnic groups are eligible, but many of the participating organizations serve predominantly minority communities.

Financial data   The salary is $230 per week.

Duration   10 weeks during the summer.

Additional information   Most participating organizations are located New York City (including Brooklyn and the Bronx) or Washington, D.C., but others are in Anchorage (Alaska), Boston, Boulder (Colorado), and Brookline (Massachusetts). Applications are submitted directly to the organization where the student wishes to intern. For the addresses and telephone numbers of all the participating organizations, write to the address above.

Number awarded   More than 150 each year.

Deadline   April of each year.

[1057]
FAYETTEVILLE OBSERVER INTERNSHIPS

Fayetteville Observer
Attn: Managing Editor
458 Whitfield Street
P.O. Box 849
Fayetteville, NC 28302
(910) 486-3558   Toll-free: (800) 722-0457
Web: www.fayettevillenc.com

Purpose   To provide work experience during the summer at the *Fayetteville Observer* in North Carolina to college students (particularly minorities) interested in careers in journalism.

Eligibility   This program at the *Observer* is open to students from any state, with preference given to sophomores, juniors, and seniors. Applicants must be planning to prepare for a career in news reporting, sports reporting, feature writing, or photography. Minorities are especially encouraged to apply.

Financial data   The salary is $300 per week. No other benefits are provided. Interns must provide their own lodging and transportation.

Duration   12 weeks during the summer.

Number awarded   4 each year: 1 each in news reporting, feature writing, sports reporting, and photography.

Deadline   February of each year.

[1058]
FELLOWSHIP PROGRAM IN ACADEMIC MEDICINE FOR MINORITY STUDENTS

National Medical Fellowships, Inc.
Attn: Scholarship Program
5 Hanover Square, 15th Floor
New York, NY 10004
(212) 483-8880   Fax: (212) 483-8897
E-mail: info@nmfonline.org
Web: www.nmf-online.org

Purpose To provide an opportunity for underrepresented minority medical school students to gain research experience in biomedical research and academic medicine.

Eligibility This program is open to U.S. citizens who are members of 1 of the following underrepresented minority groups: African American, Alaska Native, American Indian, Native Hawaiian, Mexican American, or mainland Puerto Rican. Applicants must be first- through third-year students attending accredited medical schools or osteopathic colleges in the United States. M.D./Ph.D. candidates are eligible but do not receive first consideration. Applicants must submit a statement discussing their career goals over the next 10 years and how the fellowship would be instrumental in reaching those goals. Selection is based on academic achievement, potential for playing a responsible role in academic medicine, leadership ability, the clarity of the project description, the definition of the project objectives, a clear demonstration of the student's grasp of the project objectives, and evidence of a clear relationship between the student and a mentor.

Financial data The grant is $6,000, up to $2,000 of which is available to the mentor to offset expenses during the research period.

Duration 8 to 12 weeks, either during the summer or as an elective rotation during the academic year.

Additional information Interns work in a major research laboratory under the tutelage of a well-known biomedical scientist. The program was created in 1983 with grant support from The Commonwealth Fund of New York to foster mentor relationships between students and prominent scientists. The Bristol-Myers Squibb Foundation joined as a cosponsor in 1990 and assumed sole sponsorship in 1993.

Number awarded Up to 35 each year.

Deadline November of each year.

[1059]
FEMINIST MAJORITY FOUNDATION INTERNSHIP PROGRAM

Feminist Majority
Attn: Internship Coordinator
1600 Wilson Boulevard, Suite 801
Arlington, VA 22209
(703) 522-2214   Fax: (703) 522-2219
E-mail: shasannagy@feminist.org
Web: www.feminist.org

Purpose To provide work experience at the Feminist Majority to students (particularly minorities) who aspire to become leaders in the feminist movement.

Eligibility This program is open to feminist undergraduate students of any major. Preference is given to applicants who have prior experience working on women's issues on campus, in their communities, or through a previous intern-

ship or job. Applications are especially encouraged from people of color and mathematics and science majors.

Financial data Interns may perform up to 10 hours a week of administrative work at $8 per hour.

Duration 2 months or longer. Full-time internships are available during the summer and full- or part-time internships are offered during the spring and fall.

Additional information Assignments at the Feminist Majority are available in the following project areas: Feminist Majority Leadership Alliance Program, Feminist Majority Foundation Online, Global Feminism, *Ms.* Magazine, National Center for Women and Policing, Women's Health Research, Education Equity Program, and Rock for Choice. Interns work in the Washington, D.C. area (see the contact address) or in the Los Angeles office (433 South Beverly Drive, Beverly Hills, CA 90212, (310) 556-2500, Fax: (310) 556-2509, E-mail: trunning@feminist.org.

Number awarded Varies each year.

Deadline Applications may be submitted at any time; internships begin in September, January, and June of each year.

[1060]
FERMILAB SUMMER INTERNSHIPS IN SCIENCE AND TECHNOLOGY FOR MINORITY STUDENTS

Fermi National Accelerator Laboratory
Attn: Manager, Equal Opportunity Office
MS 117
P.O. Box 500
Batavia, IL 60510-0500
(630) 840-4633   Fax: (630) 840-8365
E-mail: sist@fnal.gov
Web: sist.fnal.gov

Purpose To provide summer research experience at Fermi National Accelerator Laboratory (Fermilab) to college students, especially underrepresented minorities.

Eligibility This program is open to students who have completed at least 1 year at a 4-year college in the United States with a GPA of 3.0 or higher. Applicants must be interested in working on a summer research project at Fermilab in physics, engineering, or computer science. Strong preference is given to members of minority groups that have historically been underrepresented in science and technology (Hispanics, African Americans, and Native Americans). As part of the application process, they must submit an essay on the technical courses and projects that have interested them, the scientific or engineering project that gave them the most enjoyment and why, and how this relates to what they want to do.

Financial data Weekly stipends are $554 for freshmen, $588 for sophomores, $620 for juniors, or $654 for seniors. In addition, the program provides round-trip airfare to the laboratory, housing at partial cost to the interns, and transportation between housing and the laboratory.

Duration 12 weeks, beginning in late May.

Additional information Interns join selected staff members on research projects, attend academic lectures, and prepare a final report. This program began in 1971.

Number awarded Approximately 15 each year.

Deadline February of each year.

[1061]
FINNEGAN HENDERSON DIVERSITY SCHOLARSHIP

Finnegan, Henderson, Farabow, Garrett & Dunner, LLP
Attn: Director of Professional Recruitment and
   Development
1300 I Street, N.W.
Washington, D.C. 20005-3315
(202) 408-4034   Fax: (202) 408-4400
E-mail: suzanne.gentes@finnegan.com
Web: www.finnegan.com

Purpose To provide financial assistance and work experience to minority law students interested in a career in intellectual property law.

Eligibility This program is open to law students from underrepresented minority groups who have demonstrated a commitment to a career in intellectual property law and are currently enrolled either as a first-year full-time student or second-year part-time student. The sponsor defines underrepresented minorities to include American Indians/Alaskan Natives, Blacks/African Americans, Asian Americans/Pacific Islanders, and Hispanics/Latinos. Applicants must have earned an undergraduate degree in life sciences, engineering, or computer science, or have substantial prior trademark experience. Selection is based on academic performance at the undergraduate, graduate (if applicable), and law school level; relevant work experience; community service; leadership skills; and special accomplishments.

Financial data The stipend is $12,000 per year.

Duration 1 year; may be renewed 1 additional year as long as the recipient completes a summer associateship with the sponsor and maintains of GPA of 3.0 or higher.

Additional information The sponsor, the world's largest intellectual property law firm, established this scholarship in 2003. Summer associateships are available at its offices in Washington, D.C.; Atlanta, Georgia; Cambridge, Massachusetts; Palo Alto, California; or Reston, Virginia.

Number awarded 1 each year.

Deadline May of each year.

[1062]
FLORIDA BAR FOUNDATION LEGAL SERVICES SUMMER FELLOWSHIP PROGRAM

Florida Bar Foundation
109 East Church Street, Suite 405
P.O. Box 1553
Orlando, FL 32802-1553
(407) 843-0045   Toll-free: (800) 541-2195
Fax: (407) 839-0287 E-mail: cstawicki@flabarfndn.org
Web: www.flabarfndn.org

Purpose To provide summer work experience at Florida legal assistance providers to students (particularly minority students) from law schools in the state.

Eligibility This program is open to first- and second-year students at accredited Florida law schools. Applicants must be interested in working during the summer at a legal aid and legal services provider funded by Florida's Interest on Trust Accounts (IOTA) program. Minority students are specifically encouraged to apply. Selection is based on experience in working with the low-income community, academic achievement, writing skills, and previous contact with and

long-term commitment and interest in public service/pro bono work.

Financial data The stipend is $4,000 for first-year students or $5,000 for second-year students.

Duration 11 weeks during the summer.

Additional information This program was initiated in 1995.

Number awarded 20 each year. Since the program began, 159 students have participated.

Deadline January of each year.

[1063]
FLORIDA SOCIETY OF NEWSPAPER EDITORS MINORITY SCHOLARSHIP PROGRAM

Florida Society of Newspaper Editors
c/o Florida Press Association
2636 Mitcham Drive
Tallahassee, FL 32308
(850) 222-5790   Fax: (850) 224-6012
E-mail: info@fsne.org
Web: www.fsne.org/minorityscholar.html

Purpose To provide financial assistance and summer work experience to minority upper-division students majoring in journalism at a college or university in Florida.

Eligibility This program is open to minority students in accredited journalism or mass communication programs at Florida 4-year colleges and universities. Applicants must be full-time students in their junior year, have at least a 3.0 GPA, and be willing to participate in a paid summer internship at a Florida newspaper. Along with their application, they must submit a 300-word autobiographical essay explaining why they want to prepare for a career in print journalism and provide a standard resume, references, and clips or examples of relevant classroom work.

Financial data Winners are given a paid summer internship at a participating newspaper between their junior and senior year. Upon successfully completing the internship, the students are awarded a $3,000 scholarship (paid in 2 equal installments) to be used during their senior year.

Duration 1 summer for the internship; 1 academic year for the scholarship.

Additional information Information is also available from Rosemary Armao, FSNE Scholarship Committee, c/o The Sarasota Herald Tribune, 801 South Tamiami Trail, Sarasota, FL 34230.

Number awarded 1 each year.

Deadline March of each year.

[1064]
FORD MOTOR COMPANY FELLOWS PROGRAM

National Association of Latino Elected and Appointed
   Officials
Attn: NALEO Educational Fund
1122 West Washington Boulevard, Third Floor
Los Angeles, CA 90015
(213) 747-7606, ext. 127   Fax: (213) 747-7664
E-mail: info@naleo.org
Web: www.naleo.org

Purpose To provide Latino graduate students and recent graduates from selected states with an opportunity to gain summer work experience on the staff of a member of the U.S. House of Representatives.

Eligibility This program is open to Latino residents of California, Florida, Illinois, Michigan, Texas, or Puerto Rico (although they may be attending college or graduate school in any state). Applicants must be a recent graduate of an accredited 4-year institution, a graduating college senior, or a current graduate student. They must be at least 21 years of age, demonstrate leadership potential, and possess a sense of commitment to the Latino community. Along with their application, they must submit a 1,500-word personal statement on the family, work, educational, and community experience that led them to apply to this program. U.S. citizenship or permanent resident status is required.

Financial data Interns receive transportation, meals, and housing to participate in the annual conference; transportation and housing during their orientation in Washington, D.C.; and a $1,500 stipend for the internship.

Duration 6 weeks during the summer, beginning in June.

Additional information Interns attend the annual conference of the National Association of Latino Elected and Appointed Officials (NALEO) where they meet and network with Latinos who are involved in leadership positions at the municipal, state, federal, and nonprofit levels; experience a 1-week orientation in Washington D.C. where they meet with Latino elected and appointed officials, White House staff, and Congressional staffers; and spend the rest of the time working as a Congressional intern with a member of the U.S. House of Representatives. Funding for this program is provided by the Ford Motor Company.

Number awarded 10 each year: 1 from each of the 8 designated states plus 2 selected from a national pool of applicants.

Deadline March of each year.

[1065]
FORTUNE BRANDS SCHOLARS PROGRAM

United Negro College Fund
Attn: Corporate Scholars Program
P.O. Box 1435
Alexandria, VA 22313-9998
Toll-free: (866) 671-7237   E-mail: internship@uncf.org
Web: www.uncf.org/internships/index.asp

Purpose To provide financial assistance and work experience to minorities who are either juniors majoring in fields related to business or law students interested in an internship at corporate headquarters of Fortune Brands.

Eligibility This program is open to juniors and first- and second-year law students who are members of minority groups. Applicants must have a GPA of 3.0 or higher and an undergraduate major in accounting, finance, human resources, information systems, information technology, or marketing. They must be attending a designated college, university, or law school and be interested in an internship at Fortune Brands corporate headquarters in Lincolnshire, Illinois. Along with their application, they must submit a resume, 2 letters of recommendation, and official transcripts.

Financial data The program provides a paid internship and (based on successful internship performance) a $7,500 scholarship.

Duration 8 to 10 weeks for the internship; 1 year for the scholarship.

Additional information Eligible undergraduate institutions are Florida A&M University, Florida State University, Hampton University, Howard University, Morehouse College, North Carolina A&T State University, Northwestern University, Spelman College, University of Chicago, and University of Wisconsin. Participating law schools are those at Howard University, Northwestern University, University of Chicago, and University of Wisconsin.

Number awarded Varies each year.

Deadline February of each year.

[1066]
FRANKLIN WILLIAMS INTERNSHIP

Council on Foreign Relations
Attn: Human Resources Office
58 East 68th Street
New York, NY 10021
(212) 434-9489   Fax: (212) 434-9893
E-mail: humanresources@cfr.org
Web: www.cfr.org

Purpose To provide undergraduate and graduate students (particularly minorities) with an opportunity to gain work experience in international affairs at the Council on Foreign Relations in New York.

Eligibility Applicants should be currently enrolled in either their senior year of an undergraduate program or in a graduate program in the area of international relations or a related field. They should have a record of high academic achievement, proven leadership ability, and previous related internship or work experience. Minority students are strongly encouraged to apply.

Financial data The stipend is $10 per hour.

Duration 1 academic term (fall, spring, or summer). Fall and spring interns are required to make a commitment of at least 12 hours per week. Summer interns may choose to make a full-time commitment.

Additional information Interns work closely with a program director or fellow in either the studies or meetings program and are involved with program coordination, substantive and business writing, research, and budget management. In addition, they are encouraged to attend the council's extensive meetings programs and participate in informal training designed to enhance management and leadership skills.

Number awarded 3 each year: 1 each academic term.

Deadline Applications may be submitted at any time.

[1067]
FREDRIKSON & BYRON FOUNDATION MINORITY SCHOLARSHIPS

Fredrikson & Byron Foundation
4000 Pillsbury Center
200 South Sixth Street
Minneapolis, MN 55402-1425
(612) 492-7117   Fax: (612) 492-7077
Web: www.fredlaw.com/firm/scholarship.htm

Purpose To provide financial assistance and summer work experience to minority law students from any state who will be practicing in the Twin Cities area of Minnesota.

Eligibility This program is open to African American, Asian American, Pacific Islander, Hispanic, Native American, and Alaska Native students enrolled in their first year of law school. Applicants must be interested in practicing law in the Minneapolis-St. Paul area. Along with their application, they must submit 2 recommendations, a writing sample from their first-year legal writing course, transcripts from undergraduate and law school, and a resume. Financial need is not considered.

Financial data The fellowship stipend is $5,000. The internship portion of the program provides a $1,000 weekly stipend.

Duration 1 year.

Additional information The scholarship is jointly sponsored by Fredrikson & Byron, P.A. and the Fredrikson & Byron Foundation. Fellows are also eligible to participate in an internship at the firm's offices in Minneapolis.

Number awarded Up to 2 each year.

Deadline March of each year.

[1068]
G. RICHARD TUCKER FELLOWSHIP

Center for Applied Linguistics
4646 40th Street, N.W.
Washington, DC 20016-1859
(202) 362-0700　　　　　　　Fax: (202) 362-3740
E-mail: info@cal.org
Web: www.cal.org

Purpose To provide an opportunity for graduate students (particularly minority graduate students) to participate in a research project during the summer at the Center for Applied Linguistics (CAL) in Washington, D.C.

Eligibility This program at CAL is open to candidates for a master's or doctoral degree in any field that is concerned with the study of language. Applicants must be currently enrolled in a degree program in the United States or Canada and must have completed the equivalent of at least 1 year of full-time graduate study. Minorities are especially encouraged to apply. Applicants must be proposing to work with CAL senior staff members on 1 of the center's existing research projects or on a suitable project suggested by themselves; priority is given to proposals that focus on language education, language testing, or language issues related to minorities in the United States or Canada.

Financial data Fellows receive a stipend of $2,400 plus travel expenses up to $1,000.

Duration 4 weeks during the summer.

Number awarded 1 each year.

Deadline April of each year.

[1069]
GEM M.S. ENGINEERING FELLOWSHIP PROGRAM

National Consortium for Graduate Degrees for
　　Minorities in Engineering and Science (GEM)
P.O. Box 537
Notre Dame, IN 46556
(574) 631-7771　　　　　　　Fax: (574) 287-1486
E-mail: gem.1@nd.edu
Web: www.gemfellowship.org

Purpose To provide financial assistance and summer work experience to underrepresented minority graduate students in engineering.

Eligibility This program is open to U.S. citizens who are members of ethnic groups underrepresented in engineering: American Indians, African Americans, Mexican Americans, Puerto Ricans, and other Hispanic Americans. Applicants must be enrolled as at least a junior in an accredited engineering discipline with an academic record that indicates the ability to pursue graduate studies in engineering (including a GPA of 2.8 or higher). Recipients must attend 1 of the 88 GEM member universities that offer a master's degree.

Financial data The fellowship pays tuition, fees, and a stipend of $10,000 over its lifetime. In addition, each participant receives a salary during the summer work assignment as a GEM Summer Intern, making the value of the total award between $30,000 and $60,000. Employer members reimburse GEM participants for travel expenses to and from the summer work site.

Duration Up to 3 semesters or 4 quarters, plus a summer work internship lasting 10 to 14 weeks for up to 3 summers, depending on whether the student applies as a junior, senior, or college graduate; recipients begin their internship upon acceptance into the program and work each summer until completion of their master's degree.

Additional information During the summer internship, each fellow is assigned an engineering project in a research setting. Each project is based on the fellow's interest and background and is carried out under the supervision of an experienced engineer. At the conclusion of the internship, each fellow writes a project report. Recipients must work on a master's degree in the same engineering discipline as their baccalaureate degree.

Number awarded Varies each year; recently, 327 of these fellowships were awarded.

Deadline October of each year.

[1070]
GEM PH.D. ENGINEERING FELLOWSHIP PROGRAM

National Consortium for Graduate Degrees for
　　Minorities in Engineering and Science (GEM)
P.O. Box 537
Notre Dame, IN 46556
(574) 631-7771　　　　　　　Fax: (574) 287-1486
E-mail: gem.1@nd.edu
Web: www.gemfellowship.org

Purpose To provide financial assistance and summer work experience to underrepresented minority students interested in obtaining a Ph.D. degree in engineering.

Eligibility This program is open to U.S. citizens who are members of ethnic groups underrepresented in engineering: American Indians, African Americans, Mexican Americans, Puerto Ricans, and other Hispanic Americans. Applicants must have attained or be in the process of attaining a master's degree in engineering with an academic record that indicates the ability to work on a doctoral degree in engineering (including a GPA of 3.0 or higher).

Financial data The stipend is $14,000 per year, plus tuition and fees; the total value of the award is between $60,000 and $100,000.

Duration 3 to 5 years for the fellowship; 12 weeks during at least 1 summer for the internship.

Additional information This program is valid only at 1 of 88 participating GEM member universities; write to GEM for a list. The fellowship award is designed to support the student in the first year of the doctoral program without working. Subsequent years are subsidized by the respective universities and will usually include either a teaching or research assistantship. Recipients must participate in the GEM summer internship; failure to agree to accept the internship cancels the fellowship.

Number awarded Varies each year; recently, 49 of these fellowships were awarded.

Deadline October of each year.

[1071]
GEM PH.D. SCIENCE FELLOWSHIP PROGRAM

National Consortium for Graduate Degrees for
  Minorities in Engineering and Science (GEM)
P.O. Box 537
Notre Dame, IN 46556
(574) 631-7771   Fax: (574) 287-1486
E-mail: gem.1@nd.edu
Web: www.gemfellowship.org

Purpose To provide financial assistance and summer work experience to underrepresented minority students interested in obtaining a Ph.D. degree in the natural sciences.

Eligibility This program is open to U.S. citizens who are members of ethnic groups underrepresented in the natural sciences: American Indians, African Americans, Mexican Americans, Puerto Ricans, and other Hispanic Americans. Applicants must be juniors, seniors, or recent baccalaureate graduates in the natural sciences (biological sciences, chemistry, computer science, earth sciences, mathematics, and physics) with an academic record that indicates the ability to pursue doctoral studies in the natural sciences (including a GPA of 3.0 or higher).

Financial data The stipend is $14,000 per year, plus tuition and fees. In addition, there is a summer internship program that provides a salary and reimbursement for travel expenses to and from the summer work site. The total value of the award is between $60,000 and $100,000, depending upon academic status at the time of application, summer employer, and graduate school attended.

Duration 3 to 5 years for the fellowship; 12 weeks during at least 1 summer for the internship. Fellows selected as juniors or seniors intern each summer until entrance to graduate school; fellows selected after college graduation intern at least 1 summer.

Additional information This program is valid only at 1 of 88 participating GEM member universities; write to GEM for a list. The fellowship award is designed to support the student in the first year of the doctoral program without working. Subsequent years are subsidized by the respective university and will usually include either a teaching or research assistantship. Recipients must participate in the GEM summer internship; failure to agree to accept the internship cancels the fellowship. Recipients must enroll in the same scientific discipline as their undergraduate major.

Number awarded Varies each year; recently, 40 of these fellowships were awarded.

Deadline October of each year.

[1072]
GEORGE V. POWELL DIVERSITY SCHOLARSHIP

Lane Powell Spears Lubersky LLP
Attn: Administrator of Attorney Recruiting
1420 Fifth Avenue, Suite 4100
Seattle, WA 98101-2338
(206) 223-6123   Fax: (206) 223-7107
E-mail: rodenl@lanepowell.com
Web: www.lanepowell.com

Purpose To provide financial assistance and work experience to law students who will contribute to the diversity of the legal community

Eligibility This program is open to second-year students in good standing at an ABA-accredited law school. Applicants must be able to contribute meaningfully to the diversity of the legal community and have a demonstrated desire to work, live, and eventually practice law in Seattle or Portland. They must submit a cover letter including a statement indicating eligibility to participate in the program, resume, current copy of law school transcript, legal writing sample, and list of 2 or 3 professional or academic references. Selection is based on academic achievement and record of leadership abilities, community service, and involvement in community issues.

Financial data The program provides a stipend of $6,000 for the third year of law school and a paid summer associate clerkship.

Duration 1 year, including the summer.

Additional information This program was established in 2005. Clerkships are provided at the offices of the sponsor in Seattle or Portland.

Number awarded 1 each year.

Deadline October of each year.

[1073]
GERALDINE R. DODGE FOUNDATION FELLOWSHIP

College Art Association of America
Attn: Fellowship Program
275 Seventh Avenue
New York, NY 10001-6798
(212) 691-1051, ext. 242   Fax: (212) 627-2381
E-mail: fellowship@collegeart.org
Web: www.collegeart.org/caa/career/fellowship.html

Purpose To provide financial assistance and work experience to art historians from culturally diverse backgrounds who are completing graduate degrees and are interested in working in New Jersey.

Eligibility This program is open to art historians who have been underrepresented in the field because of their race, religion, gender, age, national origin, sexual orientation, disability, or history of economic disadvantage. Applicants must be U.S. citizens or permanent residents and able to demonstrate financial need. They must expect to receive the M.F.A. or Ph.D. degree in the year following application and then be interested in working at a cultural institution in New Jersey.

Financial data The stipend is $5,000.

Duration 1 year: the final year of the degree program.

Additional information In addition to providing a stipend for the terminal year of their degree program, the College Art Association (CAA) helps fellows search for employment at a museum, art center, college, or university in New Jersey. Upon securing a position, CAA provides a $10,000 subsidy to the employer as part of the fellow's salary. Participating organizations must match this 2:1. In addition to administrative and/or teaching responsibilities, all fellows' positions must include a curatorial or public service component. Salary or stipend, position description, and term of employment will vary and are determined in consultation with individual fellows and their potential employers. This program began in 1993. Funding is provided by the Milton & Sally Avery Arts Foundation, Geraldine R. Dodge Foundation, National Endowment for the Arts, National Endowment for the Humanities, and Terra Foundation for the Arts.

Number awarded 1 each year.

Deadline January of each year.

[1074]
GRADUATE FELLOWSHIP IN PHILANTHROPY AND HUMAN RIGHTS

Higher Education Consortium for Urban Affairs
Attn: Graduate Fellowship Coordinator
2233 University Avenue West, Suite 210
St. Paul, MN 55114-1698
(651) 646-8831   Toll-free: (800) 554-1089
E-mail: mshiozawa@hecua.org
Web: www.hecua.org

Purpose To provide financial assistance and work experience to graduate students of color in Minnesota who are interested in working in the fields of philanthropy and human rights.

Eligibility This program is open to graduate students at universities in Minnesota who are members of ethnic or cultural groups historically underrepresented in higher education. Applicants may be studying any academic discipline, but they must be interested in working part time at the Otto Bremer Foundation while they are engaged in study for their graduate degree. Their work for the foundation involves philanthropy and human rights, including social and economic justice, shelter and housing, civic engagement, health disparities and resources, civic engagement, or organizational effectiveness within nonprofits. They must be able to collaborate their academic work with research for nonprofit organizations in Minnesota, Wisconsin, North Dakota, or Montana. Along with their application, they must submit a resume or curriculum vitae, 3 letters of reference, official academic transcripts, and a 1,500-word essay about themselves, their interest and involvement in human rights and social change, and their current research interest in their academic program. Selection is based on how the applicants think, analyze, and write; their definition and commitment to human rights; experiences that predict their potential in human rights, nonprofits, and fulfilling the objectives of the fellowship; current research interest and program; academic merit; and evidence of support from their academic institution.

Financial data Fellows receive $12,000, either as a scholarship (paid directly to them) or as a stipend (paid to their university for tuition).

Duration 1 year.

Additional information This program, established in 2003, is funded by the Otto Bremer Foundation.

Number awarded 3 each year.

Deadline February of each year.

[1075]
HACU NATIONAL INTERNSHIP PROGRAM

Hispanic Association of Colleges and Universities
Attn: National Internship Program
One Dupont Circle, N.W., Suite 605
Washington, DC 20036
(202) 467-0893   Fax: (202) 496-9177
TTY: (800) 855-2880   E-mail: hnip@hacu.net
Web: www.hnip.net

Purpose To allow Hispanic and other college students to experience the diversity and scope of professional careers available in the federal government and private corporations.

Eligibility This program is open to Hispanic and other college students who are interested in interning at federal agencies in Washington, D.C., at field offices nationwide, or with selected corporate partners. Applicants must be currently-enrolled undergraduate or graduate students who have completed at least the freshman year of college with a GPA of 3.0 or higher. U.S. citizenship or permanent resident status is required. Students who attend colleges that are members of the Hispanic Association of Colleges and Universities (HACU) receive preference. Selection is based on a letter of recommendation from a faculty member or administrator and a 1-page letter by the student explaining why he or she wishes to participate in the internship.

Financial data The salary is $420 per week for sophomores and juniors, $450 per week for seniors, or $520 per week for graduate and law school students. Round-trip travel expenses are included.

Duration 10 weeks during the summer or 15 weeks during the fall or spring semester.

Additional information Assistance in locating housing is available. Recently, interns were placed with 26 federal agencies and corporations.

Number awarded Varies each year; recently, 613 interns were placed through this program, including 97 sophomores, 96 juniors, 266 seniors, and 154 graduate students.

Deadline February of each year for summer; June of each year for fall; November of each year for spring.

[1076]
HARRY A. BLACKMUN MEMORIAL PUBLIC INTEREST GRANT

California Women's Law Center
3460 Wilshire Boulevard, Suite 1102
Los Angeles, CA 90010
(213) 637-9900   Fax: (213) 637-9909
E-mail: amanda@cwlc.org
Web: www.cwlc.org

Purpose To provide summer work experience at the California Women's Law Center (CWLC) to law students (particularly students of color).

Eligibility This program is open to law students interested in advocating for and securing the civil rights of women and girls. Applicants must be interested in working full time at the CWLC under the supervision of a staff attorney. Men, persons with disabilities, and people of color are encouraged to apply.

Financial data The stipend is $4,000.
Duration 10 weeks during the summer.
Number awarded 1 each year.
Deadline January of each year.

[1077]
HARVARD SCHOOL OF PUBLIC HEALTH UNDERGRADUATE MINORITY SUMMER INTERNSHIP PROGRAM

Harvard School of Public Health
Division of Biological Sciences
Attn: Administrator
655 Huntington Avenue, Building 1-1312
Boston, MA 02115-6021
(617) 432-4470   Fax: (617) 432-0433
E-mail: dbs@hsph.harvard.edu
Web: www.hsph.harvard.edu/sip

Purpose To enable underrepresented minority college science students to participate in a summer research internship at Harvard School of Public Health.

Eligibility This program is open to members of ethnic groups underrepresented in the sciences (African Americans, Mexican Americans, Chicanos, American Indians, Aleuts, Eskimos, Polynesians, Micronesians, and Puerto Ricans) who are currently college sophomores or juniors majoring in science. Applicants must be interested in participating in a research project related to biological science questions that are important to the prevention of disease (especially such public health questions as cancer, cardiovascular disease, AIDS, malaria, parasites, other infections, lung disease, and nutrition).

Financial data The program provides a stipend of at least $3,200, a travel allowance of up to $475, and free dormitory housing.

Duration 9 weeks, beginning in mid-June.

Additional information Interns conduct research under the mentorship of Harvard faculty members who are specialists in cancer cell biology, immunology and infectious diseases, molecular and cellular toxicology, environmental health sciences, nutrition, and cardiovascular research. Funding for this program is provided by the National Institutes of Health.

Number awarded 16 each year.

Deadline February of each year.

[1078]
HAYWOOD BURNS MEMORIAL FELLOWSHIPS FOR SOCIAL AND ECONOMIC JUSTICE

National Lawyers Guild
132 Nassau Street, Suite 922
New York, NY 10038
(212) 679-5100   Fax: (212) 679-2811
E-mail: nlgno@nlg.org
Web: www.nlg.org

Purpose To provide law students and professionals (especially minorities and women) with summer work experience in progressive legal work.

Eligibility This program is open to law students, legal workers, and lawyers interested in working with civil rights and poverty law groups. Applicants must submit essays on their legal, political, educational, and work experience; their

reasons for applying; what they expect to gain from the fellowship; the types of legal and political work they hope to do in the future; how this internship will help them in their goals; the kind of work structure with which they are most comfortable; and how they plan to share their summer experience and skills with others. Women and ethnic minorities are particularly encouraged to apply.

Financial data Interns receive a $2,000 stipend. Recipients are encouraged to seek other funding sources, including law school work-study and fellowship programs.

Duration 10 weeks during the summer; renewable the following year.

Additional information Recently, fellowships were available at the following organizations: the Asian Law Caucus (San Francisco, California), Cleveland Works, Inc. (Cleveland, Ohio), Camden Regional Legal Services, Farmworker Division (Bridgeton, New Jersey), Defender Association of Philadelphia (Philadelphia, Pennsylvania), East Bay Community Law Center (Berkeley, California), Florence Immigrant and Refugee Rights Project, Inc. (Florence, Arizona), Georgia Resource Center (Atlanta, Georgia), Harm Reduction Law Project (New York, New York), Lesbian and Gay Community Services Center (New York, New York), Massachusetts Correctional Legal Services (Boston, Massachusetts), Maurice and Jane Sugar Law Center for Economic and Social Justice (Detroit, Michigan), Meiklejohn Civil Liberties Institute (Berkeley, California), National Housing Law Project (Oakland, California), National Whistleblower Center (Washington, D.C.), Northwest Immigrant Rights Project (Seattle, Washington), Protection and Advocacy, Inc. (Oakland, California), and Southern Arizona People's Law Center (Tucson, Arizona).

Number awarded Approximately 25 each year.

Deadline January of each year.

[1079]
HBA–DC FELLOWSHIPS

Hispanic Bar Association of D.C.
Attn: Foundation
P.O. Box 1011
Washington, DC 20013-1011
(202) 388-4990   E-mail: foundation@hbadc.org
Web: www.hbadc.org/found.htm

Purpose To provide funding to Hispanic law students in Washington, D.C. who wish to gain work experience in public interest law during the summer.

Eligibility This program is open to first- and second-year Hispanic students at law schools in Washington, D.C. Applicants must be interested in working in the area of public law at a nonprofit, non-governmental organization in Washington that provides legal services at little or no cost to clients. They must submit a letter from a sponsoring organization, indicating its willingness to host them as a law student intern.

Financial data The stipend is $3,500.

Duration Summer months.

Number awarded 1 or more each year.

Deadline April of each year.

[1080]
HEADQUARTERS PARALEGAL INTERNSHIPS
National Wildlife Federation
Attn: Campus Ecology Coordinator
11100 Wildlife Center Drive
Reston, VA 20190-5362
(703) 438-6000   E-mail: internopp@nwf.org
Web: www.nwf.org

Purpose To provide an opportunity for paralegal students (particularly minority students) to gain summer work experience at the headquarters of the National Wildlife Federation.

Eligibility This program is open to paralegal students who have completed enough classes to understand the basics of legal research, client confidentiality, and working with legal documents. Applicants must be able to use Word; proficiency in Excel is a plus. They must also be able to conduct basic legal research online or in a library and to write clear, comprehensive summaries of research in English. Applications are strongly encouraged from people of diverse backgrounds, women, people of color, people of all sexual identities, and people with disabilities.

Financial data The salary is $340 per week for full-time work. A needs-based relocation stipend may be available for those who have experience working within or advocating on behalf of communities traditionally underrepresented, including, but not limited to, Native American, Latino, African American, and Asian American communities.

Duration Summer months, from 20 to 40 hours per week.

Number awarded 1 or more each year.

[1081]
HELLER EHRMAN DIVERSITY FELLOWSHIPS
Heller Ehrman White & McAuliffe LLP
Attn: Ethnic Diversity Task Force
275 Middlefield Road
Menlo Park, CA 94025-3506
(650) 324-7171   Fax: (650) 324-0638
E-mail: lkite@hewm.com
Web: www.hewm.com

Purpose To provide financial assistance and work experience to law students who can contribute to the diversity of the legal community.

Eligibility This program is open to first-year law students who show promise of contributing to the diversity of the law student and legal community. Applicants must possess a record of academic, employment, community, and/or other achievement indicating potential for success in law school and in the legal profession. Along with their application, they must submit a statement, up to 500 words, on their interest in the fellowship and how they would contribute to the diversity of the legal profession.

Financial data The program provides a stipend of $7,500 for law school and a paid summer associate clerkship.

Duration 1 year, including the summer.

Additional information This program was established in 2004. Clerkships are provided at offices of the sponsor in each of its 4 regions: Bay Area (San Francisco and Silicon Valley), east coast (New York and Washington, D.C.), northwest (Seattle), and southern California (Los Angeles and San Diego).

Number awarded 4 each year: 1 in each of the firm's regions.

Deadline January of each year.

[1082]
HERBERT SCOVILLE JR. PEACE FELLOWSHIP
Herbert Scoville Jr. Peace Fellowship Program
Attn: Program Director
110 Maryland Avenue, N.E., Suite 409
Washington, DC 20002
(202) 543-4100   Fax: (202) 546-5142
E-mail: scoville@clw.org
Web: www.scoville.org

Purpose To provide an opportunity for college graduates (particularly minorities and women) to work with a peace, disarmament, or nuclear arms control organization in Washington, D.C.

Eligibility Applicants must be college graduates who can demonstrate excellent academic accomplishments and a strong interest in issues of peace and security. Prior experience with public-interest activism or advocacy is highly desirable. U.S. citizens receive preference, although foreign nationals residing in the United States are occasionally selected. Complete applications for the fellowship must include 2 letters of reference; a statement describing how the applicant first learned of the program; another essay discussing qualifications, interests, fellowship objectives, and career goals; an essay of up to 1,000 words taking a position on some contemporary, contentious issue; a full curriculum vitae; and transcripts. Preference is given to applicants who have not had substantial prior public interest or government experience in the Washington, D.C. area. Women and people of color are strongly encouraged to apply.

Financial data Fellows receive a stipend of $1,900 per month, health insurance, and travel expenses.

Duration 6 to 9 months, in spring or fall.

Additional information Fellows serve as special project assistants on the staff of 1 of the following 23 participating organizations: Alliance for Nuclear Accountability, Arms Control Association, British American Security Information Council, Center for Defense Information, Center for Nonproliferation Studies, Center for Strategic and Budgetary Assessments, Council for a Livable World Education Fund, Federation of American Scientists, Institute for Energy and Environmental Research, Institute for Science and International Security, Lawyers Alliance for World Security/Committee for National Security, National Security Archive, National Security News Service, Natural Resources Defense Council, Nuclear Control Institute, Peace Action, Physicians for Social Responsibility, Russian American Nuclear Security Advisory Council, Henry L. Stimson Center, 20/20 Vision National Project, Union of Concerned Scientists, Women's Action for New Directions, and World Federalist Association. The program does not provide grant money or scholarships for students.

Number awarded 2 to 4 each semester. To date, more than 100 fellows have been selected.

Deadline January of each year for the fall semester; October for the spring semester.

[1083]
H.I.S. PROGRAM

Hispanic College Fund
Attn: National Director
1717 Pennsylvania Avenue, N.W., Suite 460
Washington, D.C. 20006
(202) 296-5400   Toll-free: (800) 644-4223
Fax: (202) 296-3774
E-mail: hispaniccollegefund@earthlink.net
Web: www.hispanicfund.org

Purpose To provide financial assistance and summer work experience to Hispanic American undergraduate students who are interested in preparing for a career in telecommunications.

Eligibility This program is open to U.S. citizens of Hispanic background (at least 1 grandparent must be 100% Hispanic) who are entering their freshman, sophomore, junior, or senior year of college. Applicants must be working on a bachelor's degree in accounting, business administration, computer science, economics, engineering specialties, finance, information systems, management, or other relevant technology or business fields. They must have an interest in telecommunications, have a cumulative GPA of 3.0 or higher, and be available to complete at least 2 consecutive summer internships before graduating from college. Financial need is considered in the selection process.

Financial data Stipends range from $500 to $5,000, depending on need and academic achievement. Funds are paid directly to the recipient's college or university to help cover tuition and fees.

Duration 1 year; recipients may reapply.

Additional information This program is a joint venture of the Hispanic College Fund (which provides scholarships), INROADS (which provides monthly coaching, leadership development, community service, and mentorship), and Sprint (which provides 10- to 12-week paid summer internships). All applications must be submitted online; no paper applications are available.

Number awarded Varies each year.

Deadline April of each year.

[1084]
HISPANIC DIVISION FELLOWSHIP

Library of Congress
Attn: Hispanic Division
101 Independence Avenue, S.E.
Washington, DC 20540-4850
(202) 707-2003   Fax: (202) 707-5400
E-mail: gdor@loc.gov
Web: www.loc.gov

Purpose To provide summer work experience in the Hispanic Division of the Library of Congress to recent college graduates.

Eligibility Applicants must be currently enrolled or recently graduated from an undergraduate or graduate program in the humanities, social sciences, or library science. They must be interested in working in the Hispanic Division of the Library of Congress. Thorough knowledge of Spanish is required.

Financial data The stipend is $1,200 per month.

Duration Approximately 8 weeks during the summer.

Additional information The Hispanic Division of the Library of Congress determines the scope of the assignment, but it involves doing bibliographical research, producing finding aids and bibliographic records, assisting Hispanic Division patrons, and working closely with primary source materials and publications dealing with Hispanics.

Number awarded Varies each year.

Deadline April of each year.

[1085]
HISPANIC LINK JOURNALISM FOUNDATION FELLOWSHIPS

Hispanic Link Journalism Foundation
Attn: Executive Director
1420 N Street, N.W.
Washington, DC 20005
(202) 238-0705   Fax: (202) 238-0706
E-mail: Hector@hispaniclink.org
Web: www.hispaniclink.org

Purpose To provide work experience in Washington, D.C. to Hispanics who are interested in preparing for a career in journalism.

Eligibility Talented Hispanics interested in preparing for careers in the media are eligible to apply. There are no specific educational, age, or experience requirements. Candidates need not be working as journalists now. Selection is based on writing skills (with emphasis on English language), analytical skills, potential, and commitment to pursue journalism as a career.

Financial data The stipend is $20.800 plus some travel and other benefits.

Duration 12 months.

Additional information The internships include attendance at seminars covering major areas of public policy. Interns work at Hispanic Link News Service in Washington, D.C., covering issues that impact the Hispanic community nationwide.

Number awarded 1 each year.

Deadline June of each year.

[1086]
HP SCHOLAR PROGRAM

Hewlett-Packard Company
Attn: Scholar Program Manager
8000 Foothills Boulevard
MS 5214
Roseville, CA 95747
(916) 785-3809   E-mail: hpscholars@hp.com
Web: www.hp.com/go/hpscholars

Purpose To provide financial assistance and summer work experience to underrepresented minority high school seniors and community college transfer students who are interested in studying computer engineering, electrical engineering, or computer science at designated universities.

Eligibility This program is open to graduating high school seniors and community college students who are members of an underrepresented minority group (African American, Latino, or American Indian). Applicants must be planning to major in electrical engineering, computer engineering, or computer science at the University of California at Los Angeles, San Jose State University, North Carolina A&T University, the University of Washington, or Morgan State University. They must be interested in working during the summer at a major Hewlett-Packard (HP) location in California, Colorado, Idaho, Oregon, Texas, or Washington. Selection is based on academic achievement, financial need, family's educational history (priority is given to first-generation students), letters of recommendation, a personal statement (communication skills, personal and professional qualities, community involvement), connections to HP Philanthropy and Education Partnerships, and demonstrated interest in math, science, and engineering.

Financial data The stipend is $3,000 per year. In addition, students receive a salary when they work at HP facilities during the summer. They also receive an HP laptop, printer, and PDA. The total value of the award exceeds $40,000 per student.

Duration 4 years of university study plus 3 summers of internships.

Additional information Applications must be submitted to the school the student wishes to attend.

Number awarded Approximately 120 each year.

Deadline March of each year.

[1087]
HSF/PFIZER INC. FELLOWSHIP PROGRAM

Hispanic Scholarship Fund
Attn: Selection Committee
55 Second Street, Suite 1500
San Francisco, CA 94105
(415) 808-2350   Toll-free: (877) HSF-INFO
Fax: (415) 808-2302   E-mail: college1@hsf.net
Web: www.hsf.net/scholarship/programs/pfizer.php

Purpose To provide financial assistance and work experience to Hispanic students working on a graduate degree in selected science-related fields at designated universities.

Eligibility This program is open to U.S. citizens, permanent residents, and visitors with a passport stamped I-551 who are of Hispanic heritage. Applicants must be enrolled full time at Carnegie Mellon University, Columbia University, Cornell University, Harvard University, Massachusetts Institute of Technology, New York University, Northwestern University, Stanford University, University of California at Berkeley, University of California at Los Angeles, University of Chicago, University of Pennsylvania, University of Texas at Austin, or University of Virginia. They must have a GPA of 3.0 or higher in a degree program in biostatistics, business administration, computer engineering, computer information systems, economics, electrical engineering, epidemiology, health administration, medicine, or public health. Along with their application, they must submit 600-word essays on 1) how their Hispanic heritage, family upbringing, and/or role models have influenced their personal long-term goals; 2) how they contribute to their community and what they have learned from their experiences; and 3) an academic challenge they have faced and how they have overcome it. Selection is based on academic achievement, personal strengths, leadership, and financial need. A mandatory summer internship is included in the program.

Financial data The fellowship stipend is $10,000 per year. A salary is paid for the internship.

Duration 2 years (the second year is contingent on successful completion of the 12-week summer internship).

Additional information This program is jointly sponsored by the Hispanic Scholarship Fund (HSF) and Pfizer Inc.

Number awarded 1 or more each year.

Deadline June of each year.

[1088]
IBM PHD FELLOWSHIP PROGRAM

IBM Corporation
Attn: University Relations
1133 Westchester Avenue
White Plains, NY 10604
Toll-free: (800) IBM-4YOU   TTY: (800) IBM-3383
E-mail: phdfellow@us.ibm.com
Web: www-306.ibm.com

Purpose To provide financial assistance and work experience to students (particularly minorities and women) working on a Ph.D. in a research area of broad interest to IBM.

Eligibility Students nominated for this fellowship should be enrolled full time in an accredited U.S. or Canadian college or university and should have completed at least 1 year of graduate study in the following fields: business, chemistry, computer science, electrical engineering, materials sciences, mathematics, mechanical engineering, physics, or related disciplines. They should be planning a career in research. Nominations must be made by a faculty member and endorsed by the department head. IBM values diversity and encourages nominations of women, minorities, and others who contribute to that diversity. Selection is based on the applicants' potential for research excellence, the degree to which their technical interests align with those of IBM, and academic progress to date.

Financial data Fellows receive tuition, fees, and a stipend of $17,500 per year.

Duration 1 year; may be renewed up to 3 additional years, provided the recipient is renominated, interacts with IBM's technical community, and demonstrates continued progress and achievement.

Additional information Recipients are offered an internship at 1 of the IBM Research Division laboratories and are given an IBM ThinkPad.

Number awarded Varies each year.

Deadline December of each year.

[1089]
ILLINOIS BROADCASTERS ASSOCIATION MINORITY INTERNSHIPS

Illinois Broadcasters Association
300 North Pershing Street, Suite B
Energy, IL 62933
(618) 942-2139   Fax: (618) 988-9056
E-mail: ilbrdcst@neondsl.com
Web: www.ilba.org

Purpose To provide funding to minority college students in Illinois who are majoring in broadcasting and interested in interning at a radio or television station in the state.

Eligibility This program is open to currently-enrolled minority students majoring in broadcasting at a college or university in Illinois. Applicants must be interested in a fall, spring, or summer internship at a radio or television station that is a member of the Illinois Broadcasters Association.

Along with their application, they must submit 1) a 250-word essay on how they expect to benefit from a grant through this program, and 2) at least 2 letters of recommendation from a broadcasting faculty member or professional familiar with their career potential and 1 other letter. The president of the sponsoring organization selects those students nominated by their schools who have the best opportunity to make it in the world of broadcasting and matches them with internship opportunities that would otherwise be unpaid.

Financial data This program provides a grant to pay the living expenses for the interns in the Illinois communities where they are assigned. The amount of the grant depends on the length of the internship.

Duration 16 weeks in the fall and spring terms or 12 weeks in the summer.

Number awarded 12 each year: 4 in each of the 3 terms.

[1090]
INROADS NATIONAL COLLEGE INTERNSHIPS

INROADS, Inc.
10 South Broadway, Suite 700
St. Louis, MO 63102
(314) 241-7488   Fax: (314) 241-9325
E-mail: info@inroads.org
Web: www.inroads.org

Purpose To provide an opportunity for young people of color to gain work experience in business or industry.

Eligibility Eligible to apply are African Americans, Hispanics, and Native Americans who reside in the areas served by INROADS and wish to prepare for a career in business, computer science, engineering, science, or liberal arts. Applicants should be 1) seniors in high school with a GPA of 3.0 or higher, an ACT composite score of 20 or better (or the SAT equivalent), or a rank in the top 10% of their class; or 2) freshmen or sophomores in 4-year colleges and universities with a GPA of 2.8 or higher.

Financial data Salaries vary, depending upon the specific internship assigned; recently, the range was from $170 to $750 per week.

Duration Up to 4 years.

Additional information INROADS places interns in Fortune 1000 companies, where training focuses on preparing them for corporate and community leadership. The INROADS organization offers internship opportunities through 48 local affiliates in 32 states and the District of Columbia.

Number awarded Approximately 7,000 high school and college students are currently working for more than 900 corporate sponsors nationwide.

[1091]
INTERNSHIP IN EDUCATIONAL MEDIA

Metropolitan Museum of Art
Attn: Internship Programs
1000 Fifth Avenue
New York, NY 10028-0198
(212) 570-3710   Fax: (212) 570-3782
E-mail: mmainterns@metmuseum.org
Web: www.metmuseum.org

Purpose To provide work experience at the Metropolitan

Museum of Art to recent college graduates (particularly minorities) interested in educational media.

Eligibility This internship is available to recent college graduates in museum studies, design, instructional technology, or related fields. Applicants must be interested in planning, creating, and producing publications for families, teachers, students, and the general museum public. Strong computer skills are required. Applicants of diverse backgrounds are encouraged to apply.

Financial data The honorarium is $22,000.

Duration 12 months, beginning in June.

Additional information The intern will acquire skills in preparing materials for print, electronic, and video production.

Number awarded 1 each year.

Deadline January of each year.

[1092]
INTO THE FIELDS INTERNSHIPS

Student Action with Farmworkers
Attn: Internship Coordinator
1317 West Pettigrew Street
Durham, NC 27705
(919) 660-3652   Fax: (919) 681-7600
Web: cds.aas.duke.edu/saf/internship.htm

Purpose To provide rural work experience during the summer to students from farmworker families and those attending a college or university in the Carolinas.

Eligibility This program is open to 1) students from farmworker families anywhere in the United States, and 2) students currently attending a college or university in North or South Carolina. Students from outside the Carolinas who are not from farmworker families may apply, but they are not given preference. Spanish skills are required for most placements. Applicants must be interested in working for participating organizations in rural, agricultural areas of North or South Carolina (most placements are in North Carolina).

Financial data Interns receive a stipend of $1,200 to pay for food, gas, electricity, water, telephone and other miscellaneous expenses, but they are required to raise half of that themselves. The program provides either furnished housing in a family or group setting or (for interns who do not wish to live in such a setting) a partial rent subsidy. It also pays the airfare for students from farmworker families who fly to the Carolinas for the program. Interns who successfully complete the program receive a $1,500 post-service educational award.

Duration Summer months.

Additional information Interns participate in workshops during an orientation session at the beginning of the summer and during a mid-summer and final retreat. Those workshops prepare them for their specific placements and develop their leadership skills. Training sessions familiarize participants with such specific farmworker issues as demographics, legal rights, immigration, education, health, documentary studies, and community and labor organizing. As a final project, interns must either 1) complete a documentary project of the cultural and artistic traditions of farmworkers through direct interviews and photography of farmworkers, or 2) participate in the traveling Levante Theater Group that uses drama to initiate discussion among farmworker students, parents, and educators. Recipients are responsible for raising $650 of their living stipend.

Number awarded   Varies each year; recently, 28 of these internships were provided.

Deadline   February of each year.

[1093]
IWPR SUMMER INTERNSHIPS

Institute for Women's Policy Research
Attn: Internship Coordinator
1707 L Street, N.W., Suite 750
Washington, DC 20036
(202) 785-5100   Fax: (202) 833-4362
E-mail: iwpr@iwpr.org
Web: www.iwpr.org/employment_intern.html

Purpose   To provide work experience opportunities during the summer at the Institute for Women's Policy Research (IWPR) to minority and other students interested in women's policy issues.

Eligibility   This program is open to college students, graduate students, and recent graduates who are interested in economic justice for women. Applicants must have good computer skills, excellent writing and communication skills, and an interest in women's issues. Prior office experience is desirable and a background in the social sciences and/or statistics is preferred. People of all ethnic, cultural, economic, and sexual orientations are encouraged to apply.

Financial data   Interns receive a stipend of $100 per week and a local transportation subsidy.

Duration   At least 10 weeks; some flexibility can be arranged for starting and ending dates.

Additional information   Interns work in Washington D.C. for IWPR, a nonprofit research organization that works primarily on issues related to equal opportunity and economic and social justice for women. They work in 1 of 3 departments: research (reviewing literature, collecting data and resources, gathering information from public officials and organization representatives, and preparing reports and summaries), communications and outreach (handling special requests for public information materials, planning special events, editing and proofreading, and assisting in the maintenance of web activities), or development (grant-writing, nonprofit fundraising, and direct mail programs). The institute gives special emphasis to issues of race, ethnicity, and class in its projects.

Number awarded   Varies each year.

Deadline   February of each year.

[1094]
JACK AND LEWIS RUDIN INTERNSHIPS

Metropolitan Museum of Art
Attn: Internship Programs
1000 Fifth Avenue
New York, NY 10028-0198
(212) 570-3710   Fax: (212) 570-3782
E-mail: mmainterns@metmuseum.org
Web: www.metmuseum.org

Purpose   To provide work experience at the Metropolitan Museum of Art during the summer to minority and other students interested in a museum career.

Eligibility   This internship is available to college students who show a special interest in preparing for a museum career. Applicants of diverse backgrounds are especially encouraged to apply.

Financial data   The honorarium is $3,000.

Duration   10 weeks, beginning in June.

Additional information   Interns are assigned to departmental projects (curatorial, administration, or education) at the Metropolitan Museum of Art; other assignments may include giving gallery talks and working at the Visitor Information Center. The assignment is for 35 hours a week. The internships are funded by a grant from Jack and Susan Rudin.

Number awarded   3 each year.

Deadline   January of each year.

[1095]
JACKIE JOYNER-KERSEE MINORITY INTERNSHIP

Women's Sports Foundation
Attn: Award and Grant Programs Manager
Eisenhower Park
1899 Hempstead Turnpike, Suite 400
East Meadow, NY 11554-1000
(516) 542-4700   Toll-free: (800) 227-3988
Fax: (516) 542-4716   E-mail: wosport@aol.com
Web: www.womenssportsfoundation.org

Purpose   To provide work experience at the Women's Sports Foundation to women of color interested in a sports-related career.

Eligibility   This program is open to women of color who are undergraduate students, college graduates, graduate students, or women in career change. Applicants must be interested in working at the foundation offices on Long Island, New York. They must submit a personal statement that includes their sports background and current participation, issues and sports topics that interest them, their motivation for interning with the foundation, and what they hope to receive for themselves from the experience. An interview is required.

Financial data   The salary is $1,000 per month.

Duration   Sessions run from January through May, June through August, and September through December. Interns may complete 1, 2, or 3 sessions consecutively, but they must complete each session in its entirety.

Additional information   Assignments are available in the athlete services, development, education, program management, public relations and communications, publications, special events, and web editorial departments. Interns may receive academic credit for their work.

Number awarded   2 or 3 each year.

Deadline   Applications should be submitted no later than 120 days prior to the desired internship start date.

[1096]
JAMES E. WEBB INTERNSHIPS
Smithsonian Institution
Attn: Office of Fellowships
Victor Building, Suite 9300, MRC 902
P.O. Box 37012
Washington, DC 20013-7012
(202) 275-0655   Fax: (202) 275-0489
E-mail: siofg@si.edu
Web: http:

Purpose To provide summer internship opportunities throughout the Smithsonian Institution to minority students in business or public administration.

Eligibility This program is open to U.S. minority undergraduate seniors and graduate students majoring in areas of business or public administration (finance, human resource management, accounting, or general business administration). Applicants must have a GPA of 3.0 or higher. They must seek placement in offices, museums, and research institutes within the Smithsonian Institution.

Financial data Interns receive a stipend of $450 per week and a travel allowance.

Duration 10 weeks, starting in June.

Number awarded Varies each year.

Deadline January of each year.

[1097]
JAMES H. DUNN, JR. MEMORIAL FELLOWSHIP PROGRAM
Office of the Governor
Attn: Department of Central Management Services
503 William G. Stratton Building
Springfield, IL 62706
(217) 524-1381   Fax: (217) 785-7702
TDD: (217) 785-3979
Web: www.illinois.gov/gov/intopportunities.cfm

Purpose To provide recent college graduates (particularly minorities, women, and persons with disabilities) with work experience in the Illinois Governor's office.

Eligibility Applicants may be residents of any state who have completed a bachelor's degree and are interested in working in the Illinois Governor's office or in various agencies under the Governor's jurisdiction. They may have majored in any field, but they must be able to demonstrate a substantial commitment to excellence as evidenced by academic honors, leadership ability, extracurricular activities, and involvement in community or public service. Along with their application, they must submit 1) a 500-word personal statement on the qualities or attributes they will bring to the program, their career goals or plans, how their selection for this program would assist them in achieving those goals, and what they expect to gain from the program; and 2) a 1,000-word essay in which they identify and analyze a public issue that they feel has great impact on state government. A particular goal of the program is to achieve affirmative action through the nomination of qualified minorities, women, and persons with disabilities.

Financial data The stipend is $27,900 per year.

Duration 1 year, beginning in August.

Additional information Assignments are in Springfield and, to a limited extent, in Chicago.

Number awarded Varies each year.

Deadline January of each year.

[1098]
JEANNE SPURLOCK MINORITY MEDICAL STUDENT CLINICAL FELLOWSHIP IN CHILD AND ADOLESCENT PSYCHIATRY
American Academy of Child and Adolescent Psychiatry
Attn: Department of Research, Training, and Education
3615 Wisconsin Avenue, N.W.
Washington, DC 20016-3007
(202) 966-7300, ext. 105   Fax: (202) 966-2891
E-mail: emagee@aacap.org
Web: www.aacap.org/research/Spurlck2.htm

Purpose To provide funding to minority medical students who are interested in working with a child and adolescent psychiatrist during the summer.

Eligibility This program is open to African American, Asian American, Native American, Alaska Native, Mexican American, Hispanic, and Pacific Islander students in accredited U.S. medical schools. Applicants must present a plan for a clinical training experience that involves significant contact between the student and a mentor. The plan should include program planning discussions, instruction in treatment planning and implementation, regular meetings with the mentor and other treatment providers, and assigned readings. Clinical assignments may include responsibility for part of the observation or evaluation, conducting interviews or tests, using rating scales, and psychological or cognitive testing of patients. The training plan should also include discussion of ethical issues in treatment.

Financial data The stipend is $2,500. Fellows also receive reimbursement of travel expenses to attend the annual meeting of the American Academy of Child and Adolescent Psychiatry.

Duration 12 weeks during the summer.

Additional information Upon completion of the training program, the student is required to submit a brief paper summarizing the clinical experience. The fellowship pays expenses for the fellow to attend the academy's annual meeting and present this paper. This program is supported by the Center for Mental Health Services of the Substance Abuse and Mental Health Services Administration.

Number awarded Up to 14 each year.

Deadline March of each year.

[1099]
JEANNE SPURLOCK RESEARCH FELLOWSHIP IN DRUG ABUSE AND ADDICTION FOR MINORITY MEDICAL STUDENTS
American Academy of Child and Adolescent Psychiatry
Attn: Department of Research, Training, and Education
3615 Wisconsin Avenue, N.W.
Washington, DC 20016-3007
(202) 966-7300, ext. 105   Fax: (202) 966-2891
E-mail: emagee@aacap.org
Web: www.aacap.org/research/Spurlck1.htm

Purpose To provide funding to minority medical students who are interested in working with a child and adolescent psychiatrist researcher-mentor during the summer on drug abuse and addiction.

Eligibility This program is open to African American, Asian American, Native American, Alaska Native, Mexican American, Hispanic, and Pacific Islander students in accredited U.S. medical schools. Applicants must present a plan for a program of research training in drug abuse and addiction that involves significant contact with a mentor who is an experienced child and adolescent psychiatrist researcher. The plan should include program planning discussions; instruction in research planning and implementation; regular meetings with the mentor, laboratory director, and the research group; and assigned readings. Research assignments may include responsibility for part of the observation or evaluation, developing specific aspects of the research mechanisms, conducting interviews or tests, using rating scales, and psychological or cognitive testing of subjects. The training plan also should include discussion of ethical issues in research, including protocol development, informed consent, collection and storage of raw data, safeguarding data, bias in analyzing data, plagiarism, protection of patients, ethical treatment of animals. etc.

Financial data The stipend is $2,500. Fellows also receive reimbursement of travel expenses to attend the annual meeting of the American Academy of Child and Adolescent Psychiatry.

Duration 12 weeks during the summer.

Additional information Upon completion of the training program, the student is required to submit a brief paper summarizing the research experience. The fellowship pays expenses for the fellow to attend the academy's annual meeting and present this paper. This program is co-sponsored by the National Institute on Drug Abuse.

Number awarded Up to 5 each year.

Deadline March of each year.

[1100]
JERE W. THOMPSON, JR. SCHOLARSHIP

Dallas Foundation
Attn: Scholarship Administrator
900 Jackson Street, Suite 150
Dallas, TX 75202
(214) 741-9898   Fax: (214) 741-9848
E-mail: cmcnally@dallasfoundation.org
Web: www.dallasfoundation.org

Purpose To provide financial assistance and work experience to disadvantaged students who are majoring in civil engineering at public universities in Texas.

Eligibility This program is open to disadvantaged students in civil engineering or construction engineering at public colleges and universities in Texas; special consideration is given to residents of counties in the service area of the North Texas Tollway Authority: Collin, Dallas, Denton, or Tarrant. At the time of application, students must be full-time sophomores. Finalists may be interviewed. Financial need is considered in the selection process.

Financial data Stipends range up to $2,000 per semester, beginning in the recipient's junior year; the maximum award is $8,000 over 4 semesters.

Duration 1 semester; may be renewed for up to 3 additional semesters, provided the recipient remains a full-time student, maintains at least a 2.5 GPA, and submits a grade report within 45 days after the end of each semester.

Additional information Recipients of the Thompson Scholarship are given an opportunity for a paid internship in the Dallas area during the summer between their junior and senior year. Assignments are available at the scholarship's sponsors: North Texas Tollway Authority, Brown and Root Services, Carter & Burgess, Inc., and HNTB Companies.

Number awarded 1 each year.

Deadline March of each year.

[1101]
JOHN MCLENDON MEMORIAL MINORITY POSTGRADUATE SCHOLARSHIP AWARD

National Association of Collegiate Directors of Athletics
Attn: NACDA Foundation
24651 Detroit Road
P.O. Box 16428
Cleveland, OH 44116
(440) 892-4000   Fax: (440) 892-4007
E-mail: bhorning@nacda.com
Web: nacda.collegesports.com

Purpose To provide financial assistance and work experience to minority college seniors who are interested in working on a graduate degree in athletics administration.

Eligibility This program is open to minority college students who are seniors, are attending school on a full-time basis, have a GPA of 3.0 or higher, intend to attend graduate school to earn a degree in athletics administration, and are involved on the college or community level. Candidates are not required to be student athletes. Current graduate students are not eligible.

Financial data The stipend is $10,000. In addition, 1 recipient each year is offered the opportunity to serve a 9-month internship in the office of the National Association of Collegiate Directors of Athletics (NACDA).

Duration 1 year.

Additional information Recipients must maintain full-time status during the senior year to retain their eligibility. They must attend NACDA-member institutions.

Number awarded 5 each year.

Deadline January of each year.

[1102]
JUDITH L. WEIDMAN RACIAL ETHNIC MINORITY FELLOWSHIP

United Methodist Communications
Attn: Communications Resourcing Team
810 12th Avenue South
P.O. Box 320
Nashville, TN 37202-0320
(615) 742-5481   Toll-free: (888) CRT-4UMC
Fax: (615) 742-5485   E-mail: REM@umcom.org
Web: crt.umc.org/rem

Purpose To provide work experience to Methodists who are members of minority groups and interested in a communications career.

Eligibility This program is open to United Methodists of racial ethnic minority heritage who are interested in preparing for a career in communications with the United Methodist Church. Applicants must be recent college or seminary graduates who have broad communications training, including work in journalism, mass communications, marketing, public relations, and electronic media. They must be able to understand and speak English proficiently and to relocate for a year. Selection is based on Christian commitment and involvement in the life of the United Methodist Church; achievement as revealed by transcripts, GPA, letters of reference, and work samples; study, experience, and evidence of talent in the field of communications; clarity of purpose and goals for the future; desire to learn how to be a successful United Methodist conference communicator; and potential leadership ability as a professional religion communicators for the United Methodist Church.

Financial data The stipend is $30,000 per year. Benefits and expenses for moving and professional travel are also provided.

Duration 1 year, starting in July.

Additional information Recipients are assigned to 1 of the 65 United Methodist Annual Conferences, the headquarters of local churches within a geographic area. At the Annual Conference, the fellow will be assigned an experienced communicator as a mentor and will work closely with that mentor and with United Methodist Communications in Nashville, Tennessee. Following the successful completion of the fellowship, United Methodist Communications and the participating Annual Conference will assist in a search for permanent employment within the United Methodist Church but cannot guarantee a position.

Number awarded 1 each year.

Deadline March of each year.

[1103]
KAISER MEDIA INTERNSHIPS IN URBAN HEALTH REPORTING

Henry J. Kaiser Family Foundation
2400 Sand Hill Road
Menlo Park, CA 94025
(650) 234-9220   Fax: (650) 854-4800
E-mail: pduckham@kff.org
Web: www.kff.org/about/mediafellowships.cfm

Purpose To provide summer work experience to minority college or graduate students who want to specialize in urban public health issues and health reporting.

Eligibility Minority college or graduate students studying journalism or a related field may apply for this internship program if their career goal is to be a reporter on urban health matters. Strong writing skills and previous newsroom reporting experience are essential. Reporting experience and/or academic expertise in health, medical, or science-related issues (or urban affairs) is valuable but not required. Applicants must be U.S. citizens or permanent residents.

Financial data This program provides a stipend of at least $500 per week and all travel expenses.

Duration 12 weeks in the summer.

Additional information This program, sponsored by the Henry J. Kaiser Family Foundation, began in 1994. Each participating news organization selects its own intern; recently, those were the *Atlanta Journal-Constitution, Boston Globe, Los Angeles Times, Detroit Free Press, Mercury News* of San Jose, *The Oregonian* of Portland, *Plain Dealer* of Cleveland, *Sun-Sentinel* of Fort Lauderdale, *Milwaukee Journal Sentinel, Orlando Sentinel, Washington Post,* KXAS/5-TV of Dallas-Fort Worth, WAGA/5-TV of Atlanta,

and KTVU/2-TV of San Francisco-Oakland. The program begins with a 1-week orientation program in Washington, D.C. at the National Press Foundation in June and concludes with a 1-week wrap-up in Boston at the end of the summer. In between, interns report and write urban health stories at their host papers or television stations.

Number awarded 14 each year: 1 at each participating news organization.

Deadline Applicants to print organizations should submit their applications prior to the end of November; applicants to broadcast organizations should submit their applications in early January.

[1104]
KATU THOMAS R. DARGAN MINORITY SCHOLARSHIP

KATU-TV
Attn: Human Resources
2153 N.E. Sandy Boulevard
P.O. Box 2
Portland, OR 97207-0002
(503) 231-4222
Web: www.katu.com/insidekatu/scholarship.asp

Purpose To provide financial assistance and work experience to minority students from Oregon and Washington who are studying broadcasting or communications in college.

Eligibility This program is open to Native Americans, African Americans, Hispanic Americans, or Asian Americans who are U.S. citizens, currently enrolled in the first, second, or third year at a 4-year college or university or an accredited community college in Oregon or Washington, or, if a resident of Oregon or Washington, at a school in any state. Applicants must be majoring in broadcasting or communications and have a GPA of 3.0 or higher. Community college students must be enrolled in a broadcast curriculum that is transferable to a 4-year accredited university. Finalists will be interviewed. Selection is based on financial need, academic achievement, and an essay on personal and professional goals.

Financial data The stipend is $4,000. Funds are sent directly to the recipient's school.

Duration 1 year; recipients may reapply if they have maintained a GPA of 3.0 or higher.

Additional information Winners are also eligible for a paid internship in selected departments at Fisher Broadcasting/KATU in Portland, Oregon.

Number awarded 1 each year.

Deadline April of each year.

[1105]
KELL-MUNOZ EDUCATION FELLOWSHIP

Cooper-Hewitt, National Design Museum
Attn: Internship Coordinator, Education Department
2 East 91st Street
New York, NY 10128-0669
(212) 849-8380   Fax: (212) 849-8328
E-mail: edu@ch.si.edu
Web: ndm.si.edu/Education/internships.html

Purpose To provide work experience at the Smithsonian Institution's Cooper-Hewitt, National Design Museum in

New York City to Latino/Hispanic graduate students and recent graduates interested in a career in the museum profession.

Eligibility Applicants must be of Latino/Hispanic descent and either currently enrolled in a degree-granting graduate program or graduated from a graduate program in the 6 months prior to the start date. They should have a commitment to working in museums. Candidates with experience in arts administration, art history, education, communications, design, or architecture are eligible to apply. Familiarity with office procedures and computer skills are required. Along with their application, they must submit a resume, current transcripts, 2 letters of recommendation, and a 1- to 2-page essay describing their career goals as a museum professional and how the fellowship will help to achieve them.

Financial data The stipend is $10,000.

Duration 10 months, starting in September.

Additional information This program is funded by the Smithsonian Center for Latino Initiatives and Kell-Muñoz Architects.

Number awarded 1 each year.

Deadline July of each year.

[1106]
KNIGHT RIDDER MINORITY SCHOLARS PROGRAM

Knight Ridder, Inc.
Attn: Office of Diversity
50 West San Fernando Street, Suite 1200
San Jose, CA 95113
(408) 938-7734   Fax: (408) 938-7755
Web: www.knightridderscholars.com

Purpose To provide financial assistance and work experience to minority high school seniors who are interested in going to college to prepare for a career in journalism.

Eligibility This program is open to minority seniors graduating from high schools in areas served by Knight Ridder. Applicants must be interested in attending college to prepare for a career in the newspaper industry. They first apply to their local Knight Ridder newspaper and compete for local scholarships; selected winners are then nominated for this award. Both "news" and "business" students are eligible.

Financial data The stipend is $5,000 per year for the freshman and sophomore year and $15,000 per year for the junior and senior year.

Duration 1 year; may be renewed for up to 3 additional years, if the recipient maintains a GPA of 3.0 or higher and satisfactory performance on internships.

Additional information Recipients are offered an internship opportunity at a Knight Ridder newspaper during the summer. News scholars work in the newsroom, writing and editing stories, taking photographs, crafting illustrations, and designing news pages. Business scholars complete internships in advertising, marketing, information technology, circulation, and other areas essential to the industry. At the end of the sophomore year, recipients must agree to work at a Knight Ridder newspaper for 1 year after graduation.

Number awarded Up to 5 each year: 2 for news, 2 for business, and 1 for either.

[1107]
KNIGHT RIDDER MINORITY SPECIALTY DEVELOPMENT PROGRAM

Knight Ridder, Inc.
Attn: Office of Diversity
50 West San Fernando Street, Suite 1200
San Jose, CA 95113
(408) 938-7734   Fax: (408) 938-7755
Web: www.kri.com/working/interns.html

Purpose To offer a training program to young minority journalists who are interested in concentrating in a specialty beat or department.

Eligibility Minorities who recently graduated from college with a major in journalism are eligible to apply for internships at selected Knight Ridder newspapers if they are interested in working in an area of the newspaper industry in which minorities are underrepresented, such as high-profile beat assignments, computer-assisted reporting, photojournalism, and graphic arts.

Financial data Salaries are determined by the scale of the participating newspapers.

Duration 1 year.

Additional information Specialty interns are selected by and work at the following Knight Ridder newspapers: the *Detroit Free Press,* the *Philadelphia Inquirer,* or the *San Jose Mercury News.* Interns are not guaranteed employment following completion of this program.

Number awarded 1 or more each year.

Deadline December of each year.

[1108]
KNIGHT RIDDER ROTATING INTERN PROGRAM

Knight Ridder, Inc.
Attn: Office of Diversity
50 West San Fernando Street, Suite 1200
San Jose, CA 95113
(408) 938-7734   Fax: (408) 938-7755
Web: www.kri.com/working/interns.html

Purpose To offer a training program to young minority journalists who are interested in working at 3 or 4 Knight Ridder newspapers.

Eligibility Minorities who recently graduated from college with a major in journalism are eligible to apply if they are interested in working in a variety of newsrooms, news assignments, and markets.

Financial data Salaries are determined by the scale of the participating newspapers.

Duration 1 year.

Additional information Rotating interns are selected by and work at the following Knight Ridder newspapers: the *News-Democrat* in Belleville, Illinois; the *Contra Costa Times* in Walnut Creek, California; the *Fort Worth Star-Telegram;* or the *Kansas City Star.* Information is available from each of those newspapers and from Reginald Stuart, Coordinator, Knight Ridder Rotating Internship Program, 13102 Tamarack Road, Silver Spring, MD 20904, (301) 879-0085, E-mail: rstuart5@juno.com. Interns are not guaranteed employment following completion of this program.

Number awarded 1 or more each year.

Deadline December of each year.

[1109]
LABOR AND ADVOCACY INTERNS

Labor Council for Latin American Advancement
Attn: Policy and Communications Analyst
888 16th Street, N.W., Suite 640
Washington, DC 20006
(202) 347-4223   Fax: (202) 347-5095
E-mail: emoreno@lclaa.org
Web: www.lclaa.org/internship.html

Purpose To provide college students with work experience at the national headquarters of the Labor Council for Latin American Advancement (LCLAA).

Eligibility This program is open to students interested in working at the LCLAA national headquarters in Washington, D.C. Applicants must have basic computer skills, especially knowledge of Microsoft Office. Preference is given to applicants who are bilingual in English and Spanish. Other desirable qualifications include leadership abilities, good academic performance, strong interpersonal and communication skills, knowledge of unions, commitment to social justice, and knowledge of HMTL, Photoshop, Quark, and Adobe illustrator.

Financial data These are paid internships.

Additional information LCLAA is a national organization for Latino/a trade unionists throughout the United States and Puerto Rico. Internship projects may include (but are not limited to) assisting national staff and chapters with LCLAA organizing and political campaigns, working with communications coordinators to support events planning, assisting in the development of training and educational materials, attending meetings to discuss policies that affect Latino working families, translating LCLAA materials from English to Spanish, and writing, editing, and collecting articles and pictures for LCLAA's newsletter, *La Voz Latina.*

Number awarded 2 each year.

[1110]
LANDMARK SCHOLARS PROGRAM

Landmark Publishing Group
c/o Rich Martin, Managing Editor
The Roanoke Times
201 West Campbell Avenue
Roanoke, VA 24011
(540) 981-3211   Toll-free: (800) 346-1234
E-mail: rich.martin@roanoke.com
Web: www.landmarkcommunications.com

Purpose To provide work experience and financial aid to minority undergraduates who are interested in preparing for a career in journalism.

Eligibility This program is open to minority college sophomores, preferably those with ties to the mid-Atlantic states (Delaware, Maryland, North Carolina, South Carolina, Virginia, and Washington, D.C.). Applicants must be full-time students with a GPA of 2.5 or higher. They must be interested in preparing for a career in print journalism and in an internship as a reporter, photographer, graphic artist, sports writer, copy editor, or page designer.

Financial data The stipend is $5,000 per year. During the summers following their sophomore and junior years, recipients are provided with paid internships. Following graduation, they are offered a 1-year internship with full benefits and the possibility of continued employment.

Duration 2 years (the junior and senior years of college).

Additional information The internships are offered at the *News & Record* in Greensboro, North Carolina, the *Virginian-Pilot* in Norfolk, Virginia, or the *Roanoke Times* in Roanoke, Virginia.

Number awarded 1 or more each year.

Deadline November of each year.

[1111]
LASPACE UNDERGRADUATE RESEARCH ASSISTANTSHIPS

Louisiana Space Consortium
c/o Louisiana State University
Department of Physics and Astronomy
371 Nicholson Hall
Baton Rouge, LA 70803-4001
(225) 578-8697   Fax: (225) 578-1222
E-mail: laspace@lsu.edu
Web: laspace.lsu.edu

Purpose To provide undergraduate science and engineering students (particularly minorities, women, and persons with disabilities) in Louisiana with a mentored research experience in the space sciences.

Eligibility This program is open to U.S. citizens who are high school seniors, recent high school graduates, and students currently enrolled at 1 of the Louisiana Space Consortium (LaSPACE) member schools. The consortium is a component of the U.S. National Aeronautics and Space Administration (NASA) Space Grant program, which encourages participation by members of groups underrepresented in mathematics, science, and engineering (women, African Americans, Native Americans, Native Pacific Islanders, Mexican Americans, Puerto Ricans, Alaska Natives, and persons with disabilities). Applicants must be studying or planning to study a space- or aerospace-related field or program at an LaSPACE institution full time. They must coordinate with a faculty member at the institution who will file a joint application with the student and agree to serve as a mentor on a proposed research project. Selection is based on scholastic accomplishments, pertinent science experiences and accomplishments, leadership and recognitions, intellectual abilities, character, and relevance of the proposed research project to a future career in space or aerospace fields.

Financial data Grants are provided in blocks of $5,000. Funding may support 1 or 2 assistants. Funds may be used for wage support for the student(s), travel for a student research presentation, or research supplies.

Duration 12 months.

Additional information The LaSPACE member institutions are Baton Rouge Community College, Dillard University, Grambling State University, L.S.U. Agricultural Center, Louisiana State University and A&M College, Louisiana Tech University, Loyola University, McNeese State University, Nicholls State University, Northwestern State University of Louisiana, Southeastern Louisiana University, Southern University and A&M College, Southern University at New Orleans, Southern University at Shreveport-Bossier City, Tulane University, University of New Orleans, University of Louisiana at Lafayette, University of Louisiana at Monroe, and Xavier University of Louisiana. This program was established in 2000 as a replacement for the LaSPACE Undergraduate Scholars Program. Funding for this program is provided by NASA.

Number awarded 5 each year.

Deadline March of each year.

[1112]
LATINO ISSUES FORUM PUBLIC POLICY SUMMER FELLOWSHIP

Latino Issues Forum
785 Market Street, Suite 300
San Francisco, CA 94103
(415) 284-7220   Fax: (415) 284-7210
E-mail: lifcentral@lif.org
Web: www.lif.org

Purpose To provide summer work experience at the Latino Issues Forum to undergraduate and graduate students interested in public policy in California.

Eligibility This program is open to undergraduate juniors and seniors, graduate students, and professional students who are interested in working at the policy and advocacy institute's Fresno office. They must have strong writing, communication, and analytical skills and be interested in working on policy analysis, advocacy, and various aspects of California policy.

Financial data A stipend is paid (amount not specified).

Duration 3 months during the summer, beginning in June.

Additional information Interns assist the Institute's program staff in research, legislative/policy analysis, and advocacy campaigns. They work with public, private, and community organizations.

Number awarded 3 to 5 each summer.

[1113]
LAW FELLOWSHIPS

Congressional Hispanic Caucus Institute, Inc.
911 Second Street, N.E.
Washington, DC 20002
(202) 543-1771   Toll-free: (800) EXCEL-DC
Fax: (202) 546-2143   E-mail: chci@chci.org
Web: www.chciyouth.org

Purpose To provide Latino recent law school graduates with the opportunity to gain work experience in a public interest law organization or the office of a U.S. federal judge.

Eligibility This program is open to U.S. citizens and permanent residents of Latino background who graduated from law school within the past year. Applicants must be interested in gaining experience in a public interest law organization or the office of a U.S. federal judge. They must be able to demonstrate high academic achievement (preference is given to those with a GPA of 3.0 or higher), consistent active participation in public and/or community service activities, and superior analytical and communication skills (oral and written).

Financial data This program provides transportation to and from Washington, D.C., a monthly stipend of $2,500, and health insurance.

Duration 9 months, beginning in September.

Number awarded 1 or more each year.

Deadline February of each year.

[1114]
LEIGH COOK FELLOWSHIP

New Jersey Department of Health and Senior Services
Attn: Office of Minority and Multicultural Health
P.O. Box 360 Suite 501
Trenton, NJ 08625-0360
(609) 292-6962   E-mail: omh@doh.state.nj.us
Web: www.state.nj.us

Purpose To provide financial support for a summer research internship to law, public health, and medical students (particularly minority students) in New Jersey.

Eligibility This program is open to students in medical science, law, or master's of public health programs who are residents of New Jersey attending school in the state or elsewhere. Applicants must be interested in working on a supervised project at the New Jersey Department of Health and Senior Services in Trenton in the areas of minority health, senior services, HIV/AIDS, substance abuse, health insurance, environmental or occupational health, public health, or family health. Minority students are encouraged to apply. Selection is based on commitment to minority and/or public health, as demonstrated by community-based service, volunteer work, public health service advocacy, coalition building, and involvement in student organizations that address minority and public health issues.

Financial data The stipend is $5,000.

Duration 10 to 12 weeks during the summer.

Number awarded 1 each year.

Deadline April of each year.

[1115]
LENA CHANG INTERNSHIPS

Nuclear Age Peace Foundation
1187 Coast Village Road, Suite 1
PMB 121
Santa Barbara, CA 93108-2794
(805) 965-3443   Fax: (805) 568-0466
E-mail: youth@napf.org
Web: www.wagingpeace.org

Purpose To provide work experience at the Nuclear Age Peace Foundation in Santa Barbara, California to ethnic minority undergraduate and graduate students.

Eligibility This program is open to ethnic minority students currently enrolled in undergraduate or graduate course work who can demonstrate financial need and academic excellence. Students from the Santa Barbara (California) area may apply for academic year internships. Summer internships are open to students from anywhere in the United States. Applicants must submit their transcript; 2 letters of recommendation; a letter of intent describing their work experience, educational background, field of study, plans after graduation, and preference for fall, spring, or summer internship; and a copy of their resume or curriculum vitae.

Financial data The stipend is $2,500 for summer; interns are responsible for their own transportation and housing costs. Academic year interns receive $1,250.

Duration The summer internship is 10 weeks of full-time work. Academic year interns are expected to work at least 200 hours.

Number awarded 3 each year: 1 for the summer and 2 for the academic year.

Deadline March of each year for the summer internship; July of each year for fall; December of each year for winter/spring.

[1116]
LIBRARY OF CONGRESS JUNIOR FELLOWS PROGRAM

Library of Congress
Library Services
Attn: Junior Fellows Program Coordinator
101 Independence Avenue, S.E., Room LM-642
Washington, DC 20540-4600
(202) 707-5330   Fax: (202) 707-6269
E-mail: jrfell@loc.gov
Web: www.loc.gov/rr/jrfell

Purpose To provide summer work experience at the Library of Congress (LC) to upper-division and graduate students, particularly minorities, women, and students with disabilities.

Eligibility This program at the LC is open to applicants with subject expertise in the following areas: American history and literature; cataloging; history of graphic arts, architecture, design, and engineering; history of photography; film, television and radio; sound recordings; music; rare books and book arts; librarianship; and preservation. Applicants must 1) be juniors or seniors at an accredited college or university, 2) be at the graduate school level, or 3) have completed their degree in the past year. Applications from women, minorities, and persons with disabilities are particularly encouraged. Applications must include the following materials: cover letter, Application for Federal Employment (SF 171) or a resume, letter of recommendation, and official transcript. Telephone interviews are conducted with the most promising applicants.

Financial data Fellows are paid a taxable stipend of $300 per week.

Duration 3 months, beginning in either May or June. Fellows work a 40-hour week.

Additional information Fellows work with primary source materials and assist selected divisions at the Library of Congress in the organization and documentation of archival collections, production of finding aids and bibliographic records, preparation of materials for preservation and service, completion of bibliographical research, and digitization of the Library's historical collections.

Number awarded Varies each year; recently, 6 of these internships were awarded.

Deadline April of each year.

[1117]
LIBRARY OF CONGRESS SUMMER INTERNSHIPS

Library of Congress
Library Services
Attn: Affirmative Action and Special Programs Office
101 Independence Avenue, S.E., Room LM-612
Washington, DC 20540-4600
(202) 707-5479   Fax: (202) 707-6269
E-mail: letu@loc.gov
Web: www.loc.gov

Purpose To provide summer work experience at the Library of Congress (LC) to undergraduate and graduate students, particularly minorities, women, and students with disabilities.

Eligibility This program is open to U.S. citizens enrolled at an accredited college, university, or Tribal College at the undergraduate or graduate level. Relevant areas of study include accounting, anthropology, the arts, education, foreign languages, history, information technology, library science, management, photography, and sociology. Applicants must be interested in working during the summer at the Library of Congress. Women, minorities, and persons with disabilities are particularly encouraged to apply.

Financial data The stipend is $1,500.

Duration 10 weeks, beginning in June. Fellows work a 40-hour week.

Additional information Interns work on a number of high-priority projects of the Library of Congress, including digital preservation, audiovisual preservation, and the impact of technology on copyright protection.

Number awarded Varies each year.

Deadline May of each year.

[1118]
LIFCHEZ/STRONACH CURATORIAL INTERNSHIPS

Metropolitan Museum of Art
Attn: Internship Programs
1000 Fifth Avenue
New York, NY 10028-0198
(212) 570-3710   Fax: (212) 570-3782
E-mail: mmainterns@metmuseum.org
Web: www.metmuseum.org

Purpose To provide museum work experience at the Metropolitan Museum of Art to disadvantaged graduate students and recent graduates who wish to prepare for a career in art history.

Eligibility This program is open to recent college graduates and students enrolled in master's degree programs in art history. Applicants should come from a background of financial need or other disadvantage that will jeopardize their preparing for a career in art history without the support.

Financial data The honorarium is $15,000.

Duration 9 months, beginning in September.

Additional information Interns are assigned to 1 or more of the Metropolitan Museum of Art's departments, where they work on projects that match their academic background, professional skills, and career goals. This program was reestablished in 1998 with funding from Raymond Lifchez and Judith L. Stronach.

Number awarded 3 each year.

Deadline January of each year.

[1119]
MAB FOUNDATION MINORITY INTERNSHIP PROGRAM

Michigan Association of Broadcasters
Attn: MAB Foundation
819 North Washington Avenue
Lansing, MI 48906
(517) 484-7444   Toll-free: (800) YOUR-MAB
Fax: (517) 484-5810   E-mail: mabf@michmab.com
Web: www.michmab.com

Purpose To provide an opportunity for minority students at colleges and universities in Michigan to gain work experience at radio and television stations that are members of the Michigan Association of Broadcasters (MAB).

Eligibility This program is open to minority students enrolled at a Michigan college, university, or vocational school and working on a degree in broadcasting, telecommunications, media studies, engineering, or a related field. Applicants must be interested in an internship at a MAB station for which they will receive academic credit. They must be recommended by their school's faculty.

Financial data The stipend is $1,000.

Number awarded Varies each year.

[1120]
MARIA ELENA SALINAS SCHOLARSHIP PROGRAM

National Association of Hispanic Journalists
Attn: Scholarship Committee
1000 National Press Building
529 14th Street, N.W.
Washington, DC 20045-2001
(202) 662-7145   Toll-free: (888) 346-NAHJ
Fax: (202) 662-7144   E-mail: nahj@nahj.org
Web: www.nahj.org

Purpose To provide financial assistance and work experience to Hispanic American students interested in preparing for a career as a journalist in Spanish-language radio or television.

Eligibility This program is open to high school seniors, undergraduates, and first-year graduate students. Applicants must demonstrate a sincere desire to prepare for a career as a journalist in Spanish-language television or radio. They must submit 1) an essay in Spanish that explains why they are interested in a career as a Spanish-language journalist, and 2) work samples that are in Spanish. Selection is based on commitment to the field of journalism, academic achievement, awareness of the Latino community, and financial need.

Financial data The stipend is $5,000 per year; the program also provides funding for an internship during the summer

Duration 2 years.

Additional information This program, which began in 2002, is sponsored by the Univision network and administered by the National Association of Hispanic Journalists (NAHJ) as part of its Rubén Salazar Scholarship Fund. The recipient participates in a summer internship with either the news division of the Univision network or with a Univision affiliate near them.

Number awarded 2 each year.

Deadline January of each year.

[1121]
MARIAM K. CHAMBERLAIN FELLOWSHIPS

Institute for Women's Policy Research
Attn: Internship Coordinator
1707 L Street, N.W., Suite 750
Washington, DC 20036
(202) 785-5100   Fax: (202) 833-4362
E-mail: iwpr@iwpr.org
Web: www.iwpr.org/employment_fellow.html

Purpose To provide work experience at the Institute for Women's Policy Research (IWPR) to college graduates and graduate students (especially students or color) who are interested in economic justice for women.

Eligibility Applicants for this internship should have at least a bachelor's degree in social science, statistics, or women's studies. Graduate work is desirable but not required. They should have strong quantitative and library research skills and knowledge of women's issues. Familiarity with Microsoft Word and Excel is required; knowledge of STATA, SPSS, SAS, and graphics software is a plus. People of color are especially encouraged to apply.

Financial data The stipend is $1,600 per month and includes health insurance and a public transportation stipend.

Duration 9 months, beginning in September.

Additional information The institute is a nonprofit, scientific research organization that works primarily on issues related to equal opportunity and economic and social justice for women. Recent research topics for the fellow included women's wages, political participation, access to health care, and other indicators of the status of women on a state-by-state basis; the work and welfare experiences of low-income women on the state and national levels; reforming such income support policies for women as unemployment insurance, family leave, and Social Security; strategies for improving child care access, affordability, and quality; and older women's economic issues.

Number awarded 1 each year.

Deadline February of each year.

[1122]
MASS MEDIA SCIENCE AND ENGINEERING FELLOWS PROGRAM

American Association for the Advancement of Science
Attn: Directorate for Education and Human Resources
1200 New York Avenue, N.W.
Washington, DC 20005-3920
(202) 326-6441   Fax: (202) 371-9849
E-mail: spasco@aaas.org
Web: ehrweb.aaas.org/massmedia.htm

Purpose To provide internships during the summer to science and engineering students (especially underrepresented minorities and students with disabilities) who are interested in gaining experience in science journalism.

Eligibility The program is open to college juniors, seniors, graduates, and postgraduate students in the natural, physical, health, engineering, computer, and social sciences and mathematics. Students from underrepresented communities, including Black, Hispanic, Native American, and those with disabilities, are encouraged to apply. Applicants must be interested in working as reporters, researchers, and production assistants at radio and television stations, newspapers, online sites, and magazines. Students majoring in English, journalism, science journalism, or other nontechnical fields are ineligible.

Financial data Fellows receive a stipend of $450 per week and travel expenses to and from their sites.

Duration 10 weeks in the summer; may be extended, depending upon the interest of the media site.

Additional information Interns work as reporters, researchers, or production assistants in a variety of media. They may be assigned to work for newspapers, magazines, television, or radio. This program began in 1973. It is sponsored by the American Geophysical Union, the American Mathematical Society, the American Physical Society, the American Physiological Society, the American Society for Microbiology, the American Sociological Association, the Burroughs Wellcome Fund, the Foundation for Child Development, the Institute of Electrical and Electronics Engineers, and the Society for Industrial and Applied Mathematics. Recent assignments included *Chicago Tribune,* Dateline NBC, Environment Hawai'i, KUNC-FM, *Los Angeles Times, Milwaukee Journal-Sentinel,* National Public Radio, Portland *Oregonian, Popular Science, Richmond Times-Dispatch, Sacramento Bee, Scientific American, Seattle Times, St. Louis Post-Dispatch, U.S. News & World Report,* Voice of America, WNBC, and WOSU-AM.

Number awarded Varies; generally, 20 to 30 each year.

Deadline January of each year.

[1123]
METPRO/EDITING PROGRAM

Newsday
Attn: METPRO/Editing Director
235 Pinelawn Road
Melville, NY 11747-4250
(631) 843-2367   Toll-free: (888) 717-9817, ext. 2367
Fax: (631) 843-4719   E-mail: jobs@newsday.com
Web: www.metpronews.com

Purpose To provide an opportunity for minorities to obtain training for editing positions on daily metropolitan newspapers.

Eligibility Applicants for the Minority Editorial Training Program (METPRO) should be minority (African American, Asian American, Hispanic, American Indian) college graduates with excellent writing skills and an interest in a newspaper career. Selection is based on academic record and potential. Previous professional editing experience is not required.

Financial data Trainees receive a weekly stipend, a monthly housing allowance, and medical benefits for the first year. During the second year, trainees receive compensation and benefits applicable at the newspaper where they are working.

Duration 2 years.

Additional information Participants in this program receive intensive training in editing at *Newsday* during the first year, including a 2-week orientation, 3 weeks of reporting in Queens and on Long Island, 10 weeks of full-time classroom instruction, and 31 weeks of work as editors on *Newsday* copy desks. During the second year, they work for 1 of the 11 Tribune Company newspapers (in Allentown, Pennsylvania; Baltimore, Maryland; Chicago, Illinois; Fort Lauderdale, Florida; Greenwich, Connecticut; Hartford,

Connecticut; Los Angeles, California; Melville, New York; Newport News, Virginia; Orlando, Florida; or Stamford, Connecticut).

Number awarded Up to 10 each year.

Deadline January of each year.

[1124]
METROPOLITAN MUSEUM OF ART INTERNSHIPS FOR COLLEGE STUDENTS

Metropolitan Museum of Art
Attn: Internship Programs
1000 Fifth Avenue
New York, NY 10028-0198
(212) 570-3710   Fax: (212) 570-3782
E-mail: mmainterns@metmuseum.org
Web: www.metmuseum.org

Purpose To provide summer work experience at the Metropolitan Museum of Art to college students, particularly students with diverse backgrounds.

Eligibility These internships are available to college juniors, seniors, and recent graduates who have not yet entered graduate school. Applicants should have a broad background in art history. Freshmen and sophomores are not eligible. Applicants of diverse backgrounds are encouraged to apply.

Financial data The honorarium is $3,000.

Duration 10 weeks, beginning in June.

Additional information Interns are assigned to departmental projects (curatorial, administration, or education) at the Metropolitan Museum of Art; other assignments may include giving gallery talks and working at the Visitor Information Center. The assignment is for 35 hours a week. The internships are funded in part by the Lebensfeld Foundation, the Billy Rose Foundation, the Solow Art and Architecture Foundation, the Ittleson Foundation, and the Tianaderrah Foundation.

Number awarded 14 each year.

Deadline January of each year.

[1125]
METROPOLITAN MUSEUM OF ART INTERNSHIPS FOR GRADUATE STUDENTS

Metropolitan Museum of Art
Attn: Internship Programs
1000 Fifth Avenue
New York, NY 10028-0198
(212) 570-3710   Fax: (212) 570-3782
E-mail: mmainterns@metmuseum.org
Web: www.metmuseum.org

Purpose To provide summer work experience at the Metropolitan Museum of Art to graduate students, particularly students with diverse backgrounds.

Eligibility These internships are available to individuals who have completed at least 1 year of graduate work in art history or in an allied field. Applicants of diverse backgrounds are encouraged to apply.

Financial data The honorarium is $3,250.

Duration 10 weeks, beginning in June.

Additional information Interns are assigned to research or writing or to a special exhibition at the Metropolitan Museum of Art, depending upon the needs of the department. The assignment is for 35 hours a week. The internships are funded in part by the Lebensfeld Foundation, the Billy Rose Foundation, the Solow Art and Architecture Foundation, the Ittleson Foundation, and the Tianaderrah Foundation.

Number awarded 10 each year.

Deadline January of each year.

[1126]
METROPOLITAN MUSEUM OF ART 6-MONTH INTERNSHIPS

Metropolitan Museum of Art
Attn: Internship Programs
1000 Fifth Avenue
New York, NY 10028-0198
(212) 570-3710   Fax: (212) 570-3782
E-mail: mmainterns@metmuseum.org
Web: www.metmuseum.org

Purpose To provide work experience at the Metropolitan Museum of Art to candidates who can promote diversity in the profession.

Eligibility This program is open to graduating college seniors, recent graduates, and graduate students in art history or related fields. Selection is based on an essay in which applicants indicate how their selection will promote greater diversity in the national pool of future museum professionals and describe their financial need.

Financial data The stipend is $10,000.

Duration 6 months, beginning in June.

Additional information Interns work at the Metropolitan Museum for 35 hours a week.

Number awarded 2 each year.

Deadline January of each year.

[1127]
MIAMI UNIVERSITY MINORITY RESIDENT LIBRARIAN

Miami University
University Libraries
Attn: Dean and University Librarian
King Library, Room 271
Oxford, OH 45056-1878
(513) 529-2800   E-mail: hendribn@lib.muohio.edu
Web: www.lib.muohio.edu

Purpose To provide a residency for minority librarians at Miami University.

Eligibility This program is open to minorities who graduated from library school within the past 2 years and are interested in preparing for a career in academic librarianship. Applicants must have a master's degree from a library school accredited by the American Library Association. They should have a familiarity with and knowledge of advancing technologies, an ability to work collegially in a team environment, possess a knowledge of and interest in academic libraries, and demonstrate the ability to establish and maintain good working relationships with faculty, students, and other library users as well as library staff.

Financial data The stipend is $33,500. Benefits include the standard insurance package.

Duration 1 year; may be renewed for 1 additional year.

Additional information Interns are exposed to all areas of the university library's operations, including public, technical, and administrative services. Actual assignments are based on the interests of the intern and the needs of the library.

Number awarded 1 each year.

Deadline June of each year.

[1128]
MICKEY LELAND ENERGY FELLOWSHIPS

Academia Resource Management
Attn: Michey Leland Energy Fellowships
535 East 4500 South, Suite D120
Salt Lake City, UT 84107-2988
(801) 273-8911   Toll-free: (866) 863-3570
Fax: (801) 277-5632   E-mail: info@armanagement.org
Web: www.armanagement.org/mlef.htm

Purpose To provide summer work experience at fossil energy sites of the Department of Energy (DOE) to underrepresented minority undergraduate and graduate students.

Eligibility This program is open to students currently enrolled at an Historically Black College or University (HBCU), Hispanic-Serving Institution (HSI), or Tribal College or University (TCU). Applicants must be entering their junior year, senior year, or first year of a master's degree program with a major in mathematics, engineering, or science and a GPA of 2.8 or higher. They must be interested in a summer work experience at a DOE fossil energy research facility. U.S. citizenship is required.

Financial data Weekly stipends are $500 for undergraduates or $650 for graduate students. Travel costs for a round trip to and from the site and for a trip to a designated place for technical presentations are also paid.

Duration 10 weeks during the summer.

Additional information This program began as 3 separate activities: the Historically Black Colleges and Universities Internship Program established in 1995, the Hispanic Internship Program established in 1998, and the Tribal Colleges and Universities Internship Program, established in 2000. Those 3 programs were merged into the Fossil Energy Minority Education Initiative, renamed the Mickey Leland Energy Fellowship Program in 2000. Sites to which interns may be assigned include the Albany Research Center (Albany, Oregon), the National Energy Technology Laboratory (Morgantown, West Virginia and Pittsburgh, Pennsylvania), Lawrence Berkeley National Laboratory (Berkeley, California), Argonne National Laboratory (Argonne, Illinois), Pacific Northwest National Laboratory (Richland, Washington), Rocky Mountain Oilfield Testing Center (Casper, Wyoming), or Strategic Petroleum Reserve Project Management Office (New Orleans, Louisiana), Other possible locations include United States Geological Survey (Reston, Virginia), Marathon Oil Corporation (Houston, Texas), Schlumberger (Sugar Land, Texas), or U.S. Department of Energy Headquarters (Washington, D.C.). Information is also available from the Department of Energy, Office of Fossil Energy, 1000 Independence Avenue, S.W., Washington, DC 20585. The coordinator for the Historically Black Colleges and Universities program is Dorothy Fowlkes, (202) 586-7421, E-mail: dorothy.fowlkes@hq.doe.gov. The coordinator for the Hispanic and Tribal Colleges and Universities programs is Vanessa Dodson-Cunningham, (202) 586-0445, E-mail: vanessa.dodson@hq.doe.gov.

Number awarded Varies each year; recently, 39 students participated in this program.

Deadline February of each year.

[1129]
MICROSOFT NATIONAL SCHOLARSHIPS

Microsoft Corporation
Attn: National Minority Technical Scholarship
One Microsoft Way
Redmond, WA 98052-8303
(425) 882-8080   TTY: (800) 892-9811
E-mail: scholars@microsoft.com
Web: www.microsoft.com/college/ss_overview.mspx

Purpose To provide financial assistance and summer work experience to undergraduate students, especially underrepresented minorities and women, interested in preparing for a career in computer science or other related technical fields.

Eligibility This program is open to students who are enrolled full time and making satisfactory progress toward an undergraduate degree in computer science, computer engineering, or a related technical discipline (such as math or physics) with a demonstrated interest in computer science. Applicants must be enrolled in their sophomore or junior year and have earned a GPA of 3.0 or higher. Although all students who meet the eligibility criteria may apply, a large majority of scholarships are awarded to female and underrepresented minority (African American, Hispanic, and Native American) students. Along with their application, students must submit an essay that describes the following 4 items: 1) how they demonstrate their passion for technology outside the classroom; 2) the toughest technical problem they have worked on, how they addressed the problem, their role in reaching the outcome if it was team-based, and the final outcome; 3) a situation that demonstrates initiative and their willingness to go above and beyond; and 4) how they are currently funding their college education.

Financial data Scholarships cover 100% of the tuition as posted by the financial aid office of the university or college the recipient designates. Scholarships are made through that school and are not transferable to other academic institutions. Funds may be used for tuition only and may not be used for other costs on the recipient's bursar bill.

Duration 1 year.

Additional information Selected recipients are offered a paid summer internship where they will have a chance to develop Microsoft products.

Number awarded Varies. A total of $540,000 is available for this program each year.

Deadline January of each year.

[1130]
MILDRED COLODNY SCHOLARSHIP FOR GRADUATE STUDY IN HISTORIC PRESERVATION

National Trust for Historic Preservation
Attn: Scholarship Coordinator
1785 Massachusetts Avenue, N.W.
Washington, DC 20036-2117
(202) 588-6124   Toll-free: (800) 944-NTHP, ext. 6124
Fax: (202) 588-6059   E-mail: david_field@nthp.org
Web: www.nthp.org/help/colodny.html

Purpose To provide financial assistance and summer work experience to graduate students (particularly minority students) interested in working on a degree in a field related to historic preservation.

Eligibility Eligible to apply are students in their final year of undergraduate study intending to enroll in a graduate program in historic preservation and graduate students enrolled in or intending to enroll in historic preservation programs; these programs may be in a department of history, architecture, American studies, urban planning, museum studies, or a related field with a primary emphasis on historic preservation. Applicants must submit an essay in which they discuss their career goals and how their pursuit of a graduate preservation degree relates to those goals, including evidence of their interest in, commitment to, and/or potential for leadership in the field of preservation. Selection is based on the essay, a resume, 2 letters of recommendation, academic transcripts, and financial need. Applications are especially encouraged from people of diverse racial, ethnic, cultural, and economic backgrounds.

Financial data The program provides a stipend of up to $15,000 towards graduate school tuition, a stipend of $5,000 for a summer internship with the sponsor following the student's first year of study, and up to $1,500 towards the student's attendance at a National Preservation Conference.

Duration 1 year; nonrenewable.

Additional information Internships may be completed at 1) the sponsor's Washington, D.C. office; 2) a regional office or historic museum site; or 3) the offices of 1 of the sponsor's partner organizations.

Number awarded 1 each year.

Deadline February of each year.

[1131]
MINORITY ACCESS INTERNSHIP

Minority Access, Inc.
Attn: Directory of Internship Program
5214 Baltimore Avenue
Hyattsville, MD 20781
(301) 779-7100   Fax: (301) 779-9812
Web: www.minorityaccess.org

Purpose To provide work experience to minority and other undergraduate and graduate students interested in internships at participating entities in Washington, D.C. and throughout the United States.

Eligibility Applications are accepted from full-time undergraduate and graduate students with at least a 3.0 GPA. Students must be U.S. citizens for most positions. All academic majors are eligible. Interns are selected by participating federal government and other agencies. Most of these are located in Washington, D.C., but placements may be made anywhere in the United States.

Financial data All internships are paid. The weekly salary ranges from $390 for college sophomores to $520 for graduate and professional students. In addition, most internships include paid round-trip travel between home and the internship location.

Duration Spring internships are 5 months, starting in January; summer internships are 3 months, starting in August; fall internships are 4 months, starting in September.

Additional information Minority Access, Inc. is committed to the diversification of institutions, federal agencies and corporations of all kinds and to improving their recruitment, retention, and enhancement of minorities. The majority of interns are placed in the Washington, D.C. metropolitan area. Both full-time and part-time internships are awarded. Students may receive academic credit for full-time internships. Students are expected to pay all housing costs. They are required to attend a pre-employment session in Washington, D.C., all seminars and workshops hosted by Minority Access, and any mandatory activities sponsored by the host agency.

Number awarded Varies each year.

Deadline February of each year for summer internships; July of each year for fall internships; and December of each year for spring internships.

[1132]
MINORITY FELLOWSHIP IN ENVIRONMENTAL LAW

New York State Bar Association
Attn: Environmental Law Section
One Elk Street
Albany, NY 12207
(518) 463-3200   Fax: (518) 487-5517
E-mail: kplog@nysba.org
Web: www.nysba.org

Purpose To provide an opportunity for minority law students from New York to work during the summer on legal matters for a government environmental agency or public interest environmental organization in the state.

Eligibility This program is open to members of a minority group (African American, Latino, Native American, Alaskan Native, Asian, or Pacific Islander) who are 1) enrolled in a law school in New York, or 2) New York residents enrolled in a law school in the United States. Applicants must be interested in summer employment working on legal matters for a government environmental agency or public interest environmental organization in New York. They must submit a resume, transcripts, 2 letters of recommendation, and an essay describing their interest in environmental issues and reasons for wanting to participate in the fellowship.

Financial data The stipend is $6,000.

Duration At least 10 weeks during the summer.

Number awarded 1 each year.

Deadline December of each year.

[1133]
MINORITY MEDICAL STUDENT SUMMER EXTERNSHIP IN ADDICTION PSYCHIATRY

American Psychiatric Association
Attn: Department of Minority and National Affairs
1000 Wilson Boulevard, Suite 1825
Arlington, VA 22209-3901
(703) 907-8653   Toll-free: (888) 35-PSYCH
Fax: (703) 907-7852   E-mail: mking@psych.org
Web: www.psych.org

Purpose To provide funding to minority medical students who are interested in working on a research project during the summer with a mentor who specializes in addiction psychiatry.

Eligibility This program is open to minority medical students who have a specific interest in services related to substance abuse treatment and prevention. Minorities include American Indians, Alaska Natives, Native Hawaiians, Asian Americans, Hispanic/Latinos, and African Americans. Applicants must be interested in working with a mentor who specializes in addiction psychiatry. Work settings provide an emphasis on working clinically with or studying underserved minority populations and issues of co-occurring disorders, substance abuse treatment, and mental health disparity. Most of them are in inner-city or rural settings.

Financial data Externships provide $1,500 for travel expenses to go to the work setting of the mentor and up to another $1,500 for out-of-pocket expenses directly related to the conduct of the externship.

Duration 1 month during the summer.

Additional information Funding for this program is provided by the Substance Abuse and Mental Health Services Administration (SAMHSA).

Number awarded 10 each year.

Deadline April of each year.

[1134]
MINORITY-SERVING INSTITUTIONS INITIATIVE

University of Michigan
Attn: Population Fellows Program
1214 South University, Second Floor
Ann Arbor, MI 48104-2548
(734) 763-9456   Fax: (734) 647-0643
E-mail: msi.pop@umich.edu
Web: www.sph.umich.edu/pfps

Purpose To provide work experience to undergraduates and recent graduates of minority-serving institutions who are interested in preparing for a career in international family planning.

Eligibility This program is open to 1) upper-division undergraduate students enrolled at Historically Black Colleges and Universities (HBCUs), Hispanic-Serving Institutions (HSIs), and Tribal Colleges and Universities (TCUs); and 2) individuals who have received a graduate degree from an HBCU, HSI, or TCU. Applicants must be preparing for a career in international family planning/reproductive health or population-environment. They must be U.S. citizens or permanent residents with a GPA of 2.8 or higher. Fields of study may include anthropology, area studies, biology, business administration, communications, computer science, economics, education, environmental sciences, health sciences, human services, languages, management, marketing, nursing, political science, pre-medicine, psychology, public affairs, public policy, social work, sociology, or statistics.

Financial data Interns receive an entry-level professional stipend, transportation to and from the placement site, and modest summer housing.

Duration Summer months for undergraduates; 3 to 4 months for graduates.

Additional information Internships are based in a mix of domestic and international placement sites. Domestic placements are usually based in New York, Baltimore, or Washington, D.C. and may include brief periods of international travel. Overseas placements are generally in Africa or Latin America. Graduate interns also take supplementary course work to prepare for the program's Population and Population Environment Fellowships. This program, established in 1994, is administered through the University of Michigan and funded by the U.S. Agency for International Development.

Number awarded Varies each year.

Deadline January of each year.

[1135]
MISSOURI SPACE GRANT CONSORTIUM SUMMER HIGH SCHOOL INTERNSHIPS

Missouri Space Grant Consortium
c/o University of Missouri at Rolla
229 Mechanical Engineering Building
1870 Miner Circle
Rolla, MO 65409-0050
(573) 341-4699   Fax: (573) 341-4607
E-mail: finaish@umr.edu
Web: www.umr.edu/~spaceg

Purpose To provide work experience during the summer to high school students (particularly minorities and females) in Missouri interested in a career in an aerospace field.

Eligibility This program is open to Missouri high school students who have just completed their junior or senior year. Applicants must be proposing a specific research or education project in a research laboratory, a computing facility, or the galleries of the St. Louis Science Center. U.S. citizenship is required. The Missouri Space Grant Consortium is a component of the U.S. National Aeronautics and Space Administration (NASA), which encourages participation by women and underrepresented minorities.

Financial data The maximum award is $2,000.

Duration Summer months.

Additional information This program is funded by NASA.

Number awarded Approximately 10 each year.

[1136]
MISSOURI SPACE GRANT CONSORTIUM UNDERGRADUATE SCHOLARSHIPS AND INTERNSHIPS

Missouri Space Grant Consortium
c/o University of Missouri at Rolla
229 Mechanical Engineering Building
1870 Miner Circle
Rolla, MO 65409-0050
(573) 341-4699   Fax: (573) 341-4607
E-mail: finaish@umr.edu
Web: www.umr.edu/~spaceg

Purpose To provide research experience to undergraduate students (particularly minority and women students) in Missouri working on a degree in an aerospace field.

Eligibility This program is open to undergraduate students studying engineering, physics, astronomy, or planetary sciences at member institutions of the Missouri Space Grant Consortium. Applicants must be proposing a specific research or education project in a research laboratory, a computing facility, or the galleries of the St. Louis Science Center. U.S. citizenship is required. The Missouri Space Grant Consortium is a component of the U.S. National Aeronautics and Space Administration (NASA), which encourages participation by women and underrepresented minorities.

Financial data Awards are approximately $2,000 for the summer or $3,000 for the academic year.

Duration Both summer and academic year appointments are available.

Additional information The consortium members are Southwest Missouri State University, University of Missouri at Columbia, University of Missouri at Rolla, University of Missouri at St. Louis, and Washington University. This program is funded by NASA.

Number awarded Varies each year; recently, 25 students received approximately $60,000 in support.

[1137]
MONTGOMERY SUMMER RESEARCH FELLOWSHIPS IN LAW AND SOCIAL SCIENCE FOR MINORITY UNDERGRADUATE STUDENTS

American Bar Foundation
Attn: Assistant Director
750 North Lake Shore Drive
Chicago, IL 60611
(312) 988-6500   Fax: (312) 988-6579
E-mail: fellowships@abfn.org
Web: www.abf-sociolegal.org/Fellowship/mpost.html

Purpose To provide an opportunity for underrepresented minority undergraduates to work on a summer research project in the field of law and social science.

Eligibility This program is open to African Americans, Hispanic/Latinos, Puerto Ricans, and Native Americans who are sophomores or juniors in college, have a GPA of 3.0 or higher, are working on a major in the social sciences or humanities, and are willing to consider a research-oriented career. Applicants must submit a brief essay on their future plans and why this fellowship would contribute to them, official transcripts, and a letter of recommendation from a faculty member familiar with their work.

Financial data Participants receive a stipend of $3,600.

Duration   35 hours per week for 10 weeks during the summer.

Additional information   Students are assigned to an American Bar Foundation Research Fellow who involves the student in the design and conduct of the fellow's research project and who acts as mentor during the student's tenure.

Number awarded   4 each year.

Deadline   February of each year.

[1138]
MULTICULTURAL ADVERTISING INTERN PROGRAM

American Association of Advertising Agencies
Attn: Manager of Diversity Programs
405 Lexington Avenue, 18th Floor
New York, NY 10174-1801
(212) 850-0734   Toll-free: (800) 676-9333
Fax: (212) 573-8968   E-mail: naip@aaaa.org
Web: www.aaaa.org

Purpose   To provide racial minority students with summer work experience in advertising agencies and to present them with an overview of the advertising business.

Eligibility   This program is open to college juniors, seniors, and graduate students who are Black/African American, Asian/Asian American, Pacific Islander, Hispanic, North American Indian/Native American, or multiracial. Applicants may be majoring in any field, but they must be able to demonstrate a serious commitment to preparing for a career in advertising. They must have a GPA of 3.0 or higher. Students with a cumulative GPA of 2.7 to 2.9 are encouraged to apply, but they must complete an additional essay question. U.S. citizenship or permanent resident status is required.

Financial data   Interns are paid a salary of $350 to $400 per week. If they do not live in the area of their host agencies, they may stay in housing arranged by the sponsor. They are responsible for a percentage of the cost of housing and materials.

Duration   10 weeks during the summer.

Additional information   Interns may be assigned duties in the following departments: account management, broadcast production, media buying/planning, creative (art direction or copywriting), digital/interactive technologies, print production, strategic/account planning, or traffic.

Number awarded   Varies each year; recently, 56 interns were placed in 32 member advertising agency offices located in Boston, Chicago, Detroit, Warren (Michigan), Minneapolis, New York, San Francisco, and Seattle.

Deadline   January of each year.

[1139]
MURF FELLOWSHIPS PROGRAM

California Institute of Technology
Attn: Minority Undergraduate Research Fellowship
   Program
Student-Faculty Programs Office
Mail Code 139-74
Pasadena, CA 91125
(626) 395-2887   Fax: (626) 449-9649
E-mail: murf@its.caltech.edu
Web: www.its.caltech.edu/~murf

Purpose   To provide an opportunity for underrepresented college juniors to work in a research laboratory at California Institute of Technology (Caltech) or the Jet Propulsion Laboratory (JPL) during the summer under the guidance of scientists and engineers.

Eligibility   This program is open to African Americans, Hispanics, Native Americans, Puerto Ricans, and other students whose gender is underrepresented in a discipline. Applications are also encouraged from first generation college students and those attending an institution that presents challenges for success at an elite research university. Applicants must be undergraduate juniors or nongraduating seniors with a GPA of 3.0 or higher and majoring in astronomy, biology, chemistry and chemical engineering, engineering and applied science, geological and planetary sciences, mathematics, or physics. They must be interested in a program at either Caltech or JPL working on a research project under the supervision of a faculty member and a postdoctoral fellow and/or advanced graduate student. U.S. citizenship or permanent resident status is required.

Financial data   Students receive a fellowship stipend of $4,000 for the 8-week program, $4,500 for the 9-week program, or $5,000 for the 10-week program. Housing and travel allowances are also provided. Meals and other expenses are not covered.

Duration   8 to 10 weeks during the summer, beginning in June.

Additional information   Support for this program is provided by the NSF Center for Science and Engineering Materials and the Howard Hughes Medical Institute.

Number awarded   Up to 15 in biology and chemistry; up to 6 in astronomy, earth and space sciences, engineering, mathematics, and physics.

Deadline   December of each year.

[1140]
NASA ACADEMIES

National Aeronautics and Space Administration
Goddard Space Flight Center
Attn: Office of Higher Education
Building 28, Room N159
Greenbelt, MD 20771
(301) 286-0904   Fax: (301) 286-1610
E-mail: David.J.Rosage@nasa.gov
Web: www.nasa-academy.nasa.gov

Purpose   To provide opportunities to selected students (particularly underrepresented minority and female students) to work during the summer on research projects at specified field centers of the National Aeronautics and Space Administration (NASA).

Eligibility Applicants for this program must 1) be enrolled as juniors, seniors, or first- or second-year graduate students; 2) maintain a minimum GPA of 3.0; 3) major in engineering, science, mathematics, computer science, or other area of interest to the space program; 4) be U.S. citizens or permanent residents; and 5) be interested in a program in which they work at a NASA field center under the direction of NASA scientists and engineers. NASA is strongly committed to increasing cultural diversity among its pool of future leaders; underrepresented minority and female students are encouraged to apply.

Financial data Stipends range from $3,000 to $4,000; round-trip travel to the center, housing, meals, and local transportation are also provided.

Duration 10 weeks during the summer.

Additional information This program, which began in 1993, currently operates at 4 NASA centers: Goddard Space Flight Center in Greenbelt, Maryland; Glenn Research Center in Cleveland, Ohio; Marshall Space Flight Center in Huntsville, Alabama; and Ames Research Center in Moffett Field, California. Applications are also available from the Space Grant Consortium office in each state; for a list of those, contact NASA.

Number awarded Up to 20 students are selected for each of the participating NASA field centers.

Deadline January of each year.

[1141]
NASPA MINORITY UNDERGRADUATE FELLOWS PROGRAM

National Association of Student Personnel
   Administrators
Attn: MUFP
1875 Connecticut Avenue, N.W., Suite 418
Washington, DC 20009-5728
(202) 265-7500, ext. 3003   Fax: (202) 797-1157
E-mail: mufp@naspa.org
Web: www.naspa.org/resources/mufp

Purpose To provide summer work experience and leadership training to minorities and students with disabilities who are completing their second year in college.

Eligibility Eligible to be nominated for this program are 1) ethnic minority students (Native, African, Asian, or Hispanic Americans), and 2) students with disabilities. Applicants must be completing their sophomore year in a 4-year institution or their second year in a 2-year transfer program. They must be able to demonstrate academic promise and be interested in a future in higher education.

Financial data Participants are offered a paid summer internship and payment of all expenses to attend the leadership institutes.

Duration The internship lasts 8 weeks during the summer. Leadership institutes last 4 days.

Additional information The program, initiated in the 1989-90 academic year, offers 3 main components: 1) participation in a 1- or 2-year internship or field experience under the guidance of a mentor; 2) participation in a summer leadership institute designed to enhance skill building and career development; and 3) participation in an 8-week paid summer internship designed to encourage the development of future student affairs and higher education administrators. Information is also available from Brian O.

Hemphill, MUFP National Coordinator, University of Arkansas, Associate Vice Chancellor and Dean of Students, 325 Administration Building, Fayetteville, AR 72701, (501) 575-5004, E-mail: hemphill@uark.edu.

Number awarded Varies each year; recently, more than 170 undergraduates were participating in the program.

Deadline September of each year.

[1142]
NATIONAL MUSEUM FELLOWS PROGRAM FOR MINORITY STUDENTS

Atlanta History Center
Attn: Director, National Museum Fellows Program
130 West Paces Ferry Road, N.W.
Atlanta, GA 30305-1366
(404) 814-4024   Fax: (404) 814-2041
E-mail: bgaines@atlhist.org
Web: www.atlhist.org

Purpose To provide museum training to minority students who are attending designated colleges and universities in selected cities.

Eligibility This program is open to undergraduate students at 9 designated colleges and universities in metropolitan Atlanta and at other academic institutions that operate in conjunction with the Chicago Historical Society, Minnesota Historical Society, Maryland Historical Society, Kentucky Historical Society, and Conner Prairie Museum in Fishers, Indiana. Candidates must be interested in preparing for a museum career and must be nominated by their college or university; each participating institution may nominate 3 students. Nominees must be full-time juniors or seniors in the following academic year with a declared major in a liberal arts discipline. Minority students (African American, Asian American, Latino American, Native American, or any other ethnic group underrepresented in the museum profession) are encouraged to seek nomination from their major professors.

Financial data The stipend is $6,000. Fellows also receive a library of scholarly and professional museum texts and memberships in their home state historical society, the American Association of Museums, and the American Association of State and Local History. Their college or university is asked to provide 2 semesters of course credit at no additional tuition expense.

Duration 12 months.

Additional information This program began in 1994 at the Atlanta History Center, and was expanded in 1998 to include the Chicago Historical Society and the Minnesota Historical Society. In 2002 it expanded again to include the Maryland and Kentucky historical societies and the Conner Prairie Museum. Funding is provided by the Knight Foundation. During the academic year, fellows attend 24 weekly seminars at their home site, where they conduct research and receive hands-on experience in curation, collections care, exhibitions development, interpretive programming, education, development and fundraising, public relations and marketing, and library/archives management. During the summer, fellows perform a 12-week apprenticeship at their home site and travel to the Smithsonian Institution and other museums throughout the United States.

Number awarded Varies each year.

Deadline May of each year.

[1143]

NATIONAL MUSEUM OF NATURAL HISTORY RESEARCH TRAINING PROGRAM

National Museum of Natural History
Attn: RTP Program Coordinator
NHB, Room 59A, MRC 166
P.O. Box 37012
Washington, DC 20013-7012
(202) 633-4548   Fax: (202) 786-0153
E-mail: sangrey.mary@nmnh.si.edu
Web: www.nmnh.si.edu/rtp

Purpose To provide undergraduate students (particularly minorities, women, and undergraduates with disabilities) with a summer research training internship at the Smithsonian Institution's National Museum of Natural History in Washington, D.C.

Eligibility This program is open to currently-enrolled undergraduate students interested in preparing for a career in anthropology, botany, entomology, invertebrate zoology, mineral sciences and geology, paleobiology, or vertebrate zoology. Although foreign students may apply, all applicants must be proficient in reading and understanding English. Applications are especially encouraged from women, international and minority students, and persons with disabilities.

Financial data Interns receive a stipend of approximately $3,000, housing, an allowance for transportation to Washington, D.C. (generally $500), and a research allowance (up to $1,000).

Duration 10 weeks during the summer.

Additional information The heart of the program is a research project, designed by the intern in collaboration with a museum staff advisor. In addition, students participate in a laboratory experience and collection workshop; lectures, discussions, tours, and field trips; and other regular museum activities, such as seminars and special lectures. This program receives support from a number of funds within the Smithsonian and from the National Science Foundation through its Research Experiences for Undergraduates (REU) Program and Louis Stokes Alliances for Minority Participation Program.

Number awarded 20 to 24 each year.

Deadline January of each year.

[1144]

NATIONAL PHYSICAL SCIENCE CONSORTIUM GRADUATE FELLOWSHIPS

National Physical Science Consortium
c/o University of Southern California
3716 South Hope Street, Suite 348
Los Angeles, CA 90007-4344
(213) 743-2409   Toll-free: (800) 854-NPSC
Fax: (213) 743-2407   E-mail: npschq@npsc.org
Web: www.npsc.org

Purpose To provide financial assistance and summer work experience to underrepresented minorities and women interested in working on a Ph.D. in designated science and engineering fields.

Eligibility This program is open to U.S. citizens who are seniors graduating from college with a GPA of 3.0 or higher, enrolled in the first or second year of a doctoral program, completing a terminal master's degree, or returning from the work force and holding no more than a master's degree. Students currently in the third or subsequent year of a Ph.D. program or who already have a doctoral degree in any field (Ph.D., M.D., J.D., Ed.D.) are ineligible. Applicants must be interested in working on a Ph.D. in the physical sciences or related fields of science or engineering. The program welcomes applications from all qualified students and continues to emphasize the recruitment of underrepresented minority (African American, Hispanic, Native American Indian, Eskimo, Aleut, and Pacific Islander) and women physical science and engineering students. Fellowships are provided to students at the 117 universities that are members of the consortium. Selection is based on academic standing (GPA), course work taken in preparation for graduate school, university and/or industry research experience, letters of recommendation, and GRE scores.

Financial data The fellowship pays tuition and fees plus an annual stipend of $16,000. It also provides on-site paid summer employment to enhance technical experience. The exact value of the fellowship depends on academic standing, summer employment, and graduate school attended, but exceeds $200,000.

Duration Support is initially provided for 2 or 3 years, depending on the employer-sponsor. If the fellow makes satisfactory progress and continues to meet the conditions of the award, support may continue for a total of up to 6 years or completion of the Ph.D., whichever comes first.

Additional information This program began in 1989. Tuition and fees are provided by the participating universities. Stipends and summer internships are provided by sponsoring organizations. Students must submit separate applications for internships, which may have additional eligibility requirements. Internships are currently available at Amgen Inc. in Thousand Oaks, California (biochemistry, chemistry, organic chemistry, and life sciences); HRL Laboratories in Malibu, California (chemistry, computer science, materials science, and physics); Lawrence Livermore National Laboratory in Livermore, California (astronomy, chemistry, computer science, geology, materials science, mathematics, and physics); Los Alamos National Laboratory in Los Alamos, New Mexico (computer science, engineering, mathematics, and physics); National Security Agency in Fort Meade, Maryland (astronomy, chemistry, computer science, geology, materials science, mathematics, and physics); Sandia National Laboratory in Livermore, California (biology, chemistry, computer science, environmental science, geology, materials science, mathematics, and physics); and Sandia National Laboratory in Albuquerque, New Mexico (chemical engineering, chemistry, computer science, materials science, mathematics, mechanical engineering, and physics). Fellows must submit a separate application for dissertation support in the year prior to the beginning of their dissertation research program, but not until they can describe their intended research in general terms.

Number awarded Varies each year; recently, 13 of these fellowships were awarded.

Deadline November of each year.

[1145]
NATIONAL SECURITY INTERNSHIP PROGRAM

Pacific Northwest National Laboratory
Attn: Science Education Programs
902 Battelle Boulevard
P.O. Box 999, MS K8-15
Richland, WA 99352
(509) 375-2569   Toll-free: (888) 375-PNNL
E-mail: peg.jarretts@pnl.gov
Web: science-ed.pnl.gov/postings/nsip.stm

Purpose To provide undergraduate and graduate students (particularly minority and female students) with an opportunity to work on a national security-related science research project at Pacific Northwest National Laboratory (PNNL) during the summer.

Eligibility This program is open to undergraduate and graduate students who have a GPA of 3.0 or higher (preferably 3.4 or higher). Applicants should be majoring in chemistry, computer science, electrical engineering, nuclear science, or physics. They must be interested in working at PNNL on a summer science project related to national security. Women and minorities are encouraged to apply. Selection is based on academic achievement, prior experience, and technical interest.

Financial data Interns receive a stipend (amount not specified).

Duration 8 to 12 weeks during the summer; may be extended up to 1 year of part-time work during the academic year.

Additional information Tuition reimbursement is available to interns who agree to work as full-time employees at PNNL for a set period of time following graduation. Interns who accept tuition reimbursement and then fail to complete full-time employment for the specified period of time must repay a prorated portion of the educational expenses.

Number awarded 10 each year.

Deadline January of each year.

[1146]
NCAA ETHNIC MINORITY AND WOMEN'S INTERNSHIP PROGRAMS

National Collegiate Athletic Association
Attn: Director of Professional Development
700 West Washington Avenue
P.O. Box 6222
Indianapolis, IN 46206-6222
(317) 917-6222   Fax: (317) 917-6888
E-mail: dmoorman@ncaa.org
Web: www.ncaa.org

Purpose To provide work experience at the National Collegiate Athletic Association (NCAA) office to women or minority college graduates.

Eligibility This program is open to women and ethnic minorities who have completed the requirements for an undergraduate degree. They must have demonstrated a commitment to preparing for a career in intercollegiate athletics and the ability to succeed in such a career.

Financial data Interns receive up to $1,600 per month; this includes a $200 monthly housing allowance.

Duration 1 year, beginning in June.

Additional information Interns work at the NCAA national office in Indianapolis. Positions are available in administrative services, branding and communications, championships, education services, enforcement services, governance, membership services, and men's and women's basketball.

Number awarded Varies each year; recently, 11 of these internships were awarded.

Deadline February of each year.

[1147]
NEW JERSEY SPACE GRANT CONSORTIUM UNDERGRADUATE SUMMER FELLOWSHIPS

New Jersey Space Grant Consortium
c/o Stevens Institute of Technology
Edward A. Stevens Hall, Room 130-B
Hoboken, NJ 07030-5991
(201) 216-8964   Fax: (201) 216-8929
E-mail: sthangam@stevens-tech.edu
Web: www.njsgc.org

Purpose To provide financial assistance for summer research experiences in space-related fields to minority and other college students in New Jersey.

Eligibility This program is open to undergraduate students who have completed at least 2 years at member institutions of the New Jersey Space Grant Consortium (NJSGC). Applicants must be proposing a program of space-related research in industry or at universities and their affiliated research laboratories. Their field of study may be aerospace engineering, biological science, chemical engineering, computer science and engineering, electrical engineering, material science and engineering, mechanical engineering, natural science, or physical science. U.S. citizenship is required. The New Jersey Space Grant Consortium is a component of the U.S. National Aeronautics and Space Administration (NASA) Space Grant program, which encourages participation by women, underrepresented minorities, and people with disabilities. Selection is based on a biographical sketch, a brief statement of what they hope to accomplish as a space grant fellow, a statement of career goals (including their relationship to aerospace engineering and science), and a description of their plan for the immediate future.

Financial data The stipend is $600 per week, with an additional $600 per student available for laboratory supplies.

Duration 10 weeks during the summer.

Additional information Members of the NJSGC include New Jersey Institute of Technology, Princeton University, Rutgers University, Stevens Institute of Technology, and the University of Medicine and Dentistry of New Jersey. This program is funded by NASA.

Number awarded 10 to 12 each year. Approximately 60% of the fellows are placed in industries (or industry sponsored programs) and 40% go to universities and their affiliated research laboratories.

Deadline March of each year.

[1148]
NEWHOUSE SCHOLARSHIP PROGRAM

National Association of Hispanic Journalists
Attn: Scholarship Committee
1000 National Press Building
529 14th Street, N.W.
Washington, DC 20045-2001
(202) 662-7145   Toll-free: (888) 346-NAHJ
Fax: (202) 662-7144   E-mail: nahj@nahj.org
Web: www.nahj.org

Purpose To provide financial assistance and summer work experience to Hispanic American undergraduate students interested in preparing for careers in the media.

Eligibility This program is open to college juniors and seniors who are of Hispanic descent and interested in preparing for a career in English-language journalism as a reporter, editor, photographer, or graphic artist. Applicants must submit an official transcript; a 1-page resume with their educational background, work history, awards, internships, other scholarships, language proficiency, and any work done for their school newspaper, radio, and/or television station; samples of their work; 2 reference letters; a 500-word autobiography written as a news story; and documentation of financial need. Selection is based on commitment to the field of journalism, academic achievement, awareness of the Latino community, and financial need.

Financial data The stipend is $5,000 per year; the program also provides funding to attend the association's convention and an internship during the summer between the junior and senior year.

Duration 2 years.

Additional information This program, which began in 1994, is sponsored by the Newhouse Foundation and administered by the National Association of Hispanic Journalists (NAHJ) as part of its Rubén Salazar Scholarship Fund. The recipient participates in a summer internship at a Newhouse Newspaper.

Number awarded 2 each year.

Deadline January of each year.

[1149]
NONPROFIT SECTOR RESEARCH FUND WILLIAM RANDOLPH HEARST ENDOWED SCHOLARSHIP FOR MINORITY STUDENTS

Aspen Institute
Attn: Director, Nonprofit Sector Research Fund
One Dupont Circle, N.W., Suite 700
Washington, DC 20036
(202) 736-5838   Fax: (202) 293-0525
E-mail: nsrf@aspeninstitute.org
Web: www.nonprofitresearch.org

Purpose To provide an opportunity for minority students to learn more about nonprofit activities, including philanthropy and its underlying values, through a summer internship at the Aspen Institute in Washington, D.C.

Eligibility This program at the Aspen Institute is open to minority graduate and undergraduate students. Applicants must be interested in learning about nonprofit organizations by working at the institute, by assisting in preparations for its annual conference, and by engaging in general research and program support for its grantmaking and outreach efforts. They must be able to demonstrate outstanding research skills, background in the social sciences or humanities, writing and communication skills, financial need, and U.S. citizenship.

Financial data Stipends range from $2,500 to $5,000, depending on the recipient's educational level, financial need, and time commitment.

Duration 10 to 12 weeks during the summer.

Additional information This program, established in 1991, is funded by the William Randolph Hearst Foundation.

Number awarded Varies each year.

Deadline March of each year.

[1150]
NSBE/SHPE/SWE MEMBERS SCHOLARSHIP

Morgan Stanley
c/o Joyce Arencibia, IT College Recruiting
750 Seventh Avenue, 30th Floor
New York, NY 10019
(212) 762-4000
E-mail: diversityrecruiting@morganstanley.com
Web: www.morganstanley.com

Purpose To provide financial assistance and work experience to members of the National Society of Black Engineers (NSBE), Society of Hispanic Professional Engineers (SHPE), and Society of Women Engineers (SWE) who are working on an undergraduate degree in computer science or engineering.

Eligibility This program is open to active members of NSBE, SHPE, and SWE who are enrolled in their sophomore or junior year of college (or the third or fourth year of a 5-year program). Applicants must be enrolled full time and have a GPA of 3.0 or higher. They must be willing to commit to a paid summer internship in the Morgan Stanley Information Technology Division. All majors and disciplines are eligible, but preference is given to students preparing for a career in computer science or engineering. Along with their application, they must submit 1-page essays on 1) why they are applying for this scholarship and why they should be selected as a recipient; 2) a technical project on which they worked, either through a university course or previous work experience, their role in the project, and how they contributed to the end result; and 3) a software, hardware, or new innovative application of existing technology that they would create if they could and the impact it would have. Financial need is not considered in the selection process.

Financial data Students who receive a scholarship as juniors (or fourth-year students in a 5-year program) receive $10,000 for their final year of college. Students who receive a scholarship as sophomores (or third-year students in a 5-year program) receive $5,000 for their junior year (or fourth year of a 5-year program).

Duration 1 year; may be renewed for the final year for students who receive a scholarship as sophomores (or third-year students in a 5-year program).

Additional information The program includes a paid summer internship in the Morgan Stanley Information Technology Division in the summer following the time of application.

Number awarded 1 or more each year.

Deadline February of each year.

[1151]
ONEDOT MSI SUMMER INTERNSHIP PROGRAM

ADNET Systems, Inc.
11260 Roger Bacon Drive, Suite 403
Reston, VA 20190
(703) 709-7218　　　　　　Fax: (703) 709-7219
Web: www.adnet-sys.com

Purpose To provide work experience at offices of the U.S. Department of Transportation (DOT) to minority and disabled students.

Eligibility This program is open to students who are from Historically Black Colleges and Universities (HBCUs), Hispanic Service Institutions (HSIs), Tribal Colleges and Universities (TCUs), Asian American and Pacific Islander communities, and disability communities. Applicants must be U.S. citizens currently enrolled in a college or university as a sophomore or above (including graduate students) with a GPA of 3.0 or higher. They must be interested in an internship with a DOT agency, including the Office of the Secretary, Bureau of Transportation Statistics, Federal Aviation Administration, Federal Highway Administration, Federal Motor Carrier Safety Administration, Federal Railroad Administration, Federal Transit Administration, Maritime Administration, National Highway Traffic Safety Administration, Research and Special Programs Administration, and St. Lawrence Seaway Development Corporation. Jobs have included, but are not limited to, accounting, business, human resources, international affairs, operations, computer science, mathematics, engineering, journalism, and criminal justice. Along with their application, they must submit 200-word statements on 1) their community activities, hobbies, associations, publications, and other relevant experience; and 2) why they want to participate in this program.

Financial data Interns are paid a stipend and receive housing.

Duration 10 weeks in summer or 15 weeks in fall or spring.

Additional information Information on this program is also available from the U.S. Department of Transportation, Office of Civil Rights, Minority Serving Institutions and Educational Partnerships (S-30.10), 400 Seventh Street, S.W., Room 5414A, Washington, DC, (202) 366-8964, Fax: (202) 366-7717, TTY: (202) 366-9696, E-mail: roger.peralta@ost.dot.gov.

Number awarded Varies each year.

Deadline May of each year for summer; July of each year for fall; November of each year for spring.

[1152]
OREGON STATE BAR CLERKSHIP STIPENDS

Oregon State Bar
Attn: Affirmative Action Program
5200 S.W. Meadows Road
P.O. Box 1689
Lake Oswego, OR 97035-0889
(503) 431-6338
Toll-free: (800) 452-8260, ext. 338 (within OR)
Fax: (503) 598-6938　　　E-mail: dgigoux@osbar.org
Web: www.osbar.org

Purpose To provide job opportunities for minority law

students in Oregon and to provide an incentive to prospective employers to hire minority law students in the state.

Eligibility Applicants must be minority law students (African Americans, Asian Americans, Native Americans, or Hispanic Americans) with financial need. They are not required to be enrolled at a law school in Oregon, but they must demonstrate a commitment to practice in the state. Along with their application, they must submit 1) a personal statement on their history of disadvantage or barriers to educational advancement, personal experiences of discrimination, extraordinary financial obligations, composition of immediate family, extraordinary health or medical needs, and languages in which they are fluent; and 2) a state bar statement in which they describe their intention to practice law in Oregon and how they will improve the quality of legal service or increase access to justice in Oregon. Selection is based on financial need (30%), the personal statement (25%), the state bar statement (25%), community activities (10%), and employment history (10%).

Financial data This program pays a stipend of $5.00 per hour; the employer must then at least match that stipend.

Duration 1 academic year or summer months.

Additional information The selected student is responsible for finding work under this program. The job should be in Oregon, although exceptions will be made if the job offers the student special experience not available within the state.

Number awarded 20 each year.

Deadline January of each year.

[1153]
OREGON STATE BAR PUBLIC HONORS FELLOWSHIPS

Oregon State Bar
Attn: Affirmative Action Program
5200 S.W. Meadows Road
P.O. Box 1689
Lake Oswego, OR 97035-0889
(503) 431-6338
Toll-free: (800) 452-8260, ext. 338 (within OR)
Fax: (503) 598-6938　　　E-mail: dgigoux@osbar.org
Web: www.osbar.org

Purpose To provide minority law students in Oregon with summer work experience in public interest law.

Eligibility Qualified minority law students may be nominated by faculty selection committees at Oregon's 3 law schools (Willamette, University of Oregon, and Lewis and Clark) after the completion of their first year of law school. Nominees must have demonstrated a career goal in public interest or public sector law. Each school may nominate up to 5 students. Nominees must submit 1) a personal statement on their history of disadvantage or barriers to educational advancement, personal experiences of discrimination, extraordinary financial obligations, composition of immediate family, extraordinary health or medical needs, and languages in which they are fluent; and 2) a state bar statement in which they describe their intention to practice law in Oregon and how they will improve the quality of legal service or increase access to justice in Oregon. From the nominees of each school, 2 students are selected on the basis of financial need (30%), the personal statement (25%), the state bar statement (25%), and public service (20%).

The information on those students is forwarded to prospective employers in Oregon and they arrange to interview the selectees.

Financial data Fellows receive a stipend of $4,800.

Duration 3 months during the summer.

Additional information There is no guarantee that all students selected by the sponsoring organization will receive fellowships at Oregon law firms.

Number awarded 6 each year: 3 from each of the law schools.

Deadline January of each year.

[1154]
THE OREGONIAN MINORITY INTERNSHIP PROGRAM

The Oregonian
Attn: Director of Recruiting and Training
1320 S.W. Broadway
Portland, OR 97201
(503) 221-8039   Fax: (503) 294-5012
E-mail: jobs@news.oregonian.com
Web: www.oregonian.com/newsroom/jobspg1.htm

Purpose To provide work experience at *The Oregonian* in Portland to minority college graduates who are interested in a career in journalism.

Eligibility This program is open to recent college graduates who are African American, Asian American, Hispanic, American Indian, or Pacific Islander. Applicants must be committed to a career in newspapers and be interested in an internship at *The Oregonian* that combines practical experience with professional mentoring in 8 specialized areas: arts reporter/critic; business reporter; copy editor/news editor; graphic artist/page designer; local news reporter; medical/science reporter; sports reporter; or photographer/photo editor.

Financial data A competitive salary is paid.

Duration 2 years.

Additional information Midway through the second year, interns may apply for any position open on the staff of *The Oregonian;* if no opening is available, assistance is provided in finding another job.

Number awarded 3 each year.

Deadline February of each year.

[1155]
PAUL D. WHITE SCHOLARSHIP

Baker & Hostetler LLP
Attn: Kathleen Ferdico
3200 National City Center
1900 East Ninth Street
Cleveland, OH 44114-3485
(216) 861-7092   Fax: (216) 696-0740
Web: www.bakerlaw.com

Purpose To provide financial assistance and summer work experience to minority students at selected law schools.

Eligibility This program is open to first- and second-year law students of African American, Hispanic, Asian American, or American Indian descent. Applicants must be attending 1 of the following schools that currently participate in the program: Case Western Reserve School of Law,

Cleveland-Marshall School of Law, Howard University School of Law, Ohio State University Moritz School of Law, University of Michigan School of Law, the University of Texas School of Law, University of California at Los Angeles School of Law, University of Cincinnati College of Law, University of Denver College of Law, University of Florida Levin College of Law, and University of Colorado School of Law.

Financial data The program provides a stipend of $5,000 and a paid summer clerkship with the sponsoring firm.

Duration 1 year, including the following summer.

Number awarded 1 each year.

[1156]
PAULINE A. YOUNG RESIDENCY

University of Delaware
Library
Attn: Coordinator, Personnel and Staff Development
Newark, DE 19717-5267
(302) 831-1594   Fax: (302) 831-1046
E-mail: jbrewer@udel.edu
Web: www2.lib.udel.edu/personnel/brochure.htm

Purpose To provide full-time professional work experience at the University of Delaware Library to underrepresented minority and other graduates of accredited library schools.

Eligibility This program is open to recent graduates of library schools accredited by the American Library Association Applicants must be able to demonstrate strong written and oral communication skills, an interest in developing a career in academic librarianship, the ability to work independently as well as with colleagues and library users from diverse backgrounds, a willingness to learn, and a desire for professional growth. Members of underrepresented racial and ethnic groups are particularly encouraged to apply.

Financial data Compensation is at the level of assistant librarian; benefits include health coverage, dental insurance, course fee waiver, and relocation assistance.

Duration 2 years; nonrenewable.

Additional information In the first year, residents gain professional experience by rotating through several different areas of the University of Delaware Library. In the second year, they concentrate in 1 area to further specific professional goals. In addition, they are offered opportunities for committee service, specialized training, and professional workshops. Residents are eligible to apply for continuing positions at the library.

Number awarded 1 every other year.

Deadline April of each even-numbered year.

[1157]
PEDRO ZAMORA PUBLIC POLICY FELLOWSHIP

AIDS Action
1906 Sunderland Place, N.W.
Washington, DC 20036
(202) 530-8030   Fax: (202) 530-8031
E-mail: zamora@aidsaction.org
Web: www.aidsaction.org/fellowship_new.htm

Purpose To provide work experience at AIDS Action to minority and other undergraduate and graduate students interested in public policy.

Eligibility This program is open to undergraduate and graduate students who can demonstrate strong research, writing, and organizational skills and experience working in a professional office. Familiarity with HIV-related issues and the legislative process is preferred. Applicants must 1) describe their participation in school, work, or extracurricular activities related to HIV and AIDS (e.g., peer prevention programs, volunteer activities); 2) describe their participation in any school or extracurricular activities related to advocacy (e.g., lobbying, political campaigns); 3) explain why they would be the best candidate for this fellowship; and 4) explain how they would use the skills they acquire from the fellowship. People of color, women, gay, lesbian, bisexual, transgender, and HIV-positive individuals are encouraged to apply.

Financial data A stipend is provided (amount not specified).

Duration From 8 to 26 weeks.

Additional information Responsibilities include assisting in researching a variety of public health and civil rights issues related to HIV prevention, treatment, and care; attending Congressional hearings and coalition meetings; monitoring voting records; reviewing the Federal Register and Congressional Record; and preparing correspondence, mailings, and briefing materials. Fellows must commit to a minimum of 30 hours per week at AIDS Action in Washington, D.C.

Number awarded Varies each year.

Deadline March of each year for summer; July of each year for fall; October of each year for spring.

[1158]
PFIZER/UNCF CORPORATE SCHOLARS PROGRAM

United Negro College Fund
Attn: Corporate Scholars Program
P.O. Box 1435
Alexandria, VA 22313-9998
Toll-free: (866) 671-7237   E-mail: internship@uncf.org
Web: www.uncf.org/internships/index.asp

Purpose To provide financial assistance and work experience to minority undergraduate and graduate students majoring in designated fields and interested in an internship at a Pfizer facility.

Eligibility This program is open to sophomores, juniors, graduate students, and first-year law students who are African American, Hispanic American, Asian/Pacific Islander American, or American Indian/Alaskan Native. Applicants must have a GPA of 3.0 or higher and be enrolled at an institution that is a member of the United Negro College Fund (UNCF) or at another targeted college or university. They must be working on 1) a bachelor's degree in animal science, business, chemistry (organic or analytical), human resources, logistics, microbiology, organizational development, operations management, pre-veterinary medicine, or supply chain management; 2) a master's degree in chemistry (organic or analytical), finance, human resources, or organizational development; or 3) a law degree. Eligibility is limited to U.S. citizens, permanent residents, asylees, refugees, and lawful temporary residents. Along with their application, they must submit a 1-page essay about themselves and their career goals, including information about their interest in Pfizer (the program's sponsor), their personal background, and any particular challenges they have faced.

Financial data The program provides an internship stipend of up to $5,000, housing accommodations near Pfizer Corporate facilities, and (based on successful internship performance) a $15,000 scholarship.

Duration 8 to 10 weeks for the internship; 1 year for the scholarship.

Additional information Opportunities for first-year law students include the summer internship only.

Number awarded Varies each year.

Deadline January of each year.

[1159]
PGA TOUR DIVERSITY INTERNSHIP PROGRAM

PGA Tour, Inc.
Attn: Diversity Internship Program
100 PGA Tour Boulevard
Ponte Vedra Beach, FL 32082
Toll-free: (800) 556-5400, ext. 3520
E-mail: MIP@mail.pgatour.com
Web: www.pgatour.com

Purpose To provide summer work experience to minority undergraduate and graduate students interested in learning about the business side of golf.

Eligibility This program is open to full-time undergraduates who have completed their sophomore year and graduate students. Applicants must be men or women of African American, Asian American, Native American, or Hispanic descent. International students are eligible if they are legally permitted to work in the United States. Although all interns work in the business side of golf, the ability to play golf or knowledge of the game is not required for most positions.

Financial data Interns receive competitive wages, up to $500 for travel expenses, and (for some) subsidized housing and discounts on company merchandise.

Duration 9 to 13 weeks during the summer.

Additional information This program was established in 1992. Positions are available in communications, corporate marketing, human resources, information systems, international and domestic television, legal department, retail licensing, tournament operations, and professional services. Most assignments are in Ponte Vedra Beach, Florida.

Number awarded Varies each year; recently, 32 of these internships were provided.

Deadline February of each year.

[1160]
PHILADELPHIA INQUIRER MINORITY GRAPHIC ARTS INTERNSHIP

Philadelphia Inquirer
Attn: Oscar Miller, Director of Recruiting
400 North Broad Street
P.O. Box 8263
Philadelphia, PA 19101
(215) 854-5102   Fax: (215) 854-2578
E-mail: inkyjobs@phillynews.com
Web: www.philly.com/mld/philly

Purpose To provide graphic design experience during the summer at the *Philadelphia Inquirer* to minority college students interested in careers in journalism.

Eligibility Minority college students entering their sophomore, junior, or senior year in college are eligible to apply if they are interested in working in the art department at the *Philadelphia Inquirer*. Applicants should submit 5 to 7 samples of their work (published or unpublished), a resume, a cover letter, and references.

Financial data The salary is $573 per week.

Duration 10 weeks beginning in June.

Number awarded 1 each year.

Deadline November of each year.

[1161]
PHILADELPHIA INQUIRER MINORITY PHOTOJOURNALISM INTERNSHIP

Philadelphia Inquirer
Attn: Director of Photography
P.O. Box 8263
Philadelphia, PA 19101-8263
(215) 854-5045   E-mail: cmurray@phillynews.com
Web: www.philly.com/mld/philly

Purpose To provide summer work experience at the *Philadelphia Inquirer* to minority students who are interested in preparing for a career in photojournalism.

Eligibility Minorities who are fully matriculated undergraduate or graduate students with at least 1 prior internship are eligible to apply if they are interested in gaining work experience in photojournalism at the *Philadelphia Inquirer*. Applicants must submit a portfolio with up to 2 pages of slide duplicates showing creativity in news, general features, sports, and environmental portraiture. At least 1 photo essay should be included.

Financial data The salary is $647 per week.

Duration 10 weeks during the summer.

Additional information A complete set of Nikon equipment is available for use during the internship.

Number awarded 1 each year.

Deadline November of each year.

[1162]
PNNL STUDENT RESEARCH APPRENTICESHIP PROGRAM

Pacific Northwest National Laboratory
Attn: Science Education Programs
902 Battelle Boulevard
P.O. Box 999, MS K9-83
Richland, WA 99352
(509) 375-2569   Toll-free: (888) 375-PNNL
E-mail: kathy.feaster@pnl.gov
Web: science-ed.pnl.gov/precollege/srap.stm

Purpose To provide an opportunity for underrepresented minority students who live within commuting distance of Pacific Northwest National Laboratory (PNNL) to work on a research project at the laboratory during the summer.

Eligibility This program is open to high school students who live within daily commuting distance of the laboratory. Applicants must be at least 16 years of age and of Hispanic, African American, or Native American ethnic origin. They must have an expressed interest in and potential for educational opportunities and careers in science, engineering, mathematics, or computer technology.

Financial data The stipend is $300 per week. Students who commute more than 50 miles each way receive a travel allowance.

Duration 8 weeks, beginning in June. Participants may reapply for a maximum of 3 summer appointments while in high school.

Additional information This program was established in 1979. Students spend 4 days a week assigned to a scientist-mentor in a specific research area. The other day is devoted to educational, career, and leadership development activities involving laboratory demonstrations, field trips, self-esteem, team building, and communications workshops.

Number awarded Varies each year.

Deadline February of each year.

[1163]
PRLDEF CORPORATE LEGAL INTERNSHIPS

Puerto Rican Legal Defense and Education Fund
Attn: Education Division
99 Hudson Street, 14th Floor
New York, NY 10013-2815
(212) 739-7497   Toll-free: (800) 328-2322
Fax: (212) 431-4276   E-mail: sonji_patrick@prldef.org
Web: www.prldef.org/Internship.htm

Purpose To provide work experience to law students of color interested in a summer internship arranged by the Puerto Rican Legal Defense and Education Fund (PRLDEF).

Eligibility This program is open to law students of color who are interested in preparing for a career in a corporate legal department. Applicants should submit a current resume, cover letter, and legal writing sample.

Financial data Each corporation determines the stipend.

Duration 10 weeks in the summer.

Additional information Recently, internships were available at Allstate Insurance Company (Chicago, Illinois), Bristol-Myers Squibb (New York and New Jersey), IBM (White Plains, New York), Johnson & Johnson (New Jersey), Metropolitan Life Insurance Company (New York City), Pfizer Pharmaceuticals (New York City), and Verizon (New York City).

Number awarded Varies each year.

Deadline December of each year.

[1164]
PROCTER & GAMBLE RESEARCH AND PRODUCT DEVELOPMENT SUMMER INTERN PROGRAM

Procter & Gamble Company
Miami Valley Laboratories
Attn: Doctoral Recruiting Office, Box SI
11810 East Miami River Road
P.O. Box 538707
Cincinnati, OH 45253-8707
(513) 627-1035   Fax: (513) 627-2266
E-mail: doctoral.im@pg.com
Web: www.pg.com/science/research_tech.jhtml

Purpose To provide summer work experience to underrepresented minorities and other doctoral students who are interested in chemical or biological careers.

Eligibility Applicants must be currently enrolled in graduate school or in the senior year of undergraduate study planning to enter graduate school in the fall to work on a Ph.D. in chemical engineering, chemistry, most areas of the life sciences, statistics, and toxicology. U.S. citizenship or permanent resident status is required. Positions are also available to students currently studying or planning to study for a Pharm.D., M.D., D.V.M., or D.D.S. degree. These internships are intended for students who plan to prepare for a career as research associates in research and product development. Special consideration is given to applications from underrepresented minority (African American, Hispanic/Latino, Native American) students.

Financial data Interns receive competitive salaries, depending of their year in school and field of study. Procter & Gamble pays round-trip airfare between school or home and Cincinnati as well as local transportation between university housing and the work site.

Duration 10 to 12 weeks, beginning in June.

Additional information Interns engage in full-time research at 1 of Procter & Gamble's 4 corporate technical centers in Cincinnati.

Number awarded 15 to 20 each year.

Deadline February of each year.

[1165]
PROFESSIONAL ASSOCIATES PROGRAM FOR WOMEN AND MINORITIES AT BROOKHAVEN NATIONAL LABORATORY

Brookhaven National Laboratory
Attn: Diversity Office, Human Resources Division
Building 185A
P.O. Box 5000
Upton, New York 11973-5000
(631) 344-2703   Fax: (631) 344-5305
E-mail: rpalmore@bnl.gov
Web: www.bnl.gov/diversity/programs.asp

Purpose To provide professional experience in scientific areas at Brookhaven National Laboratory (BNL) to underrepresented minorities and women.

Eligibility This program is open to underrepresented minorities (African Americans, Hispanics, Native Americans, or Pacific Islanders) and women who have earned a bachelor's degree. Applicants must be seeking professional experience in such fields as biology, chemistry, computer science, engineering, health physics, medical research, and physics. They must plan to attend a graduate or professional school and express an interest in long-term employment at BNL.

Financial data Participants receive a competitive salary.

Duration 1 year.

Additional information Interns work in a goal-oriented on-the-job training program under the supervision of employees who are experienced in their areas of interest.

Number awarded Varies each year.

Deadline Applications may be submitted at any time.

[1166]
PUBLIC INTEREST LAW PROGRAM SUMMER FELLOWSHIP

Public Interest Clearinghouse
Attn: PILP Director
47 Kearney Street, Suite 705
San Francisco, CA 94108
(415) 834-0100, ext. 307   Fax: (415) 834-0202
E-mail: ahamill@pic.org
Web: www.pic.org

Purpose To provide funding to minority and other law students interested in a summer internship in public interest law in California.

Eligibility This program is open to students completing either their first or second year of law school who have a demonstrated commitment to public interest law. Applicants must be interested in a summer internship with a California nonprofit IOLTA-funded organization. Legal services programs in California are given preference. Government programs, including criminal defense or prosecution, are not eligible. The organization must agree to supervise the fellow's work on a substantive legal advocacy project. Students must submit, along with their application, a 2-page personal statement on how their experience (personal, educational, and/or work) demonstrates a commitment to the practice of public interest law, the nature and impact of the work they will perform as well as what they expect to achieve as a fellow, and why this work will help them to realize their post-law school career objectives. People of color, persons from low-income or working class backgrounds, and disabled persons are especially encouraged to apply.

Financial data This program provides a stipend of $2,000, and the sponsoring organization is expected to contribute another $500. Fellows may obtain other funding as long as the total amount earned does not exceed $5,000.

Duration 10 weeks during the summer.

Additional information This program began in 2001.

Number awarded 2 each year: 1 to a law student completing the first year and 1 to a law student completing the second year.

Deadline April of each year.

[1167]
PUERTO RICO LOUIS STOKES ALLIANCE FOR MINORITY PARTICIPATION UNDERGRADUATE RESEARCH STIPENDS

Puerto Rico Louis Stokes Alliance for Minority Participation
c/o University of Puerto Rico at Rio Piedras
Facundo Bueso Building, Office 304
P.O. Box 23334 University Station
San Juan, PR 00931-3334
(787) 764-0000, ext. 5801   Fax: (787) 766-1293
E-mail: a_feliciano@acupr1.upr.clu.edu
Web: www.prlsamp.org

Purpose To provide an opportunity to participate in research projects to students in Puerto Rico studying science, mathematics, engineering, and technology as part of the Puerto Rico Louis Stokes Alliance for Minority Participation (PR-LSAMP).

Eligibility This program is open to undergraduate students at universities in Puerto Rico that participate in the alliance. Applicants must be majoring in such fields as biology, chemistry, physics, engineering, geology, agricultural science, or environmental sciences. They must be interested in participating in a research project at a local or national university or laboratory. Selection is based on financial need and academic performance. Preference is given to students who are both low-income and first-generation college students.

Financial data Stipends range from $500 to $2,000 per year, depending on the need of the recipient.

Duration Recipients participate in research projects during the academic year or summer.

Additional information The PR-LSAMP was established in 1991 with funding from the National Science Foundation.

Number awarded Approximately 300 each year.

[1168]
RESEARCH AND ENGINEERING APPRENTICESHIP PROGRAM (REAP) FOR HIGH SCHOOL STUDENTS

Academy of Applied Science
1 Maple Street
Concord, NH 03301
(603) 228-0121   Fax: (603) 228-0210
Web: www.aas-world.org/youth_science/reap.html

Purpose To provide an opportunity for disadvantaged high school students to engage in a research apprenticeship in mathematics, science, or technology.

Eligibility Applicants must be economically and socially disadvantaged high school students who have an interest in mathematics, science, or technology. Recipients are selected on the basis of previously demonstrated abilities and interest in science, mathematics, and technology; potential for a successful career in the field as indicated from overall scholastic achievement, aptitude, and interest areas; recommendations of high school teachers and administrators; and an interview.

Financial data Interns receive a salary in accordance with student minimum wage guidelines.

Duration Summer months.

Additional information The program provides intensive summer training for high school students in the laboratories of scientists. The program, established in 1980, is funded by a grant from the U.S. Army Research Office. Students must live at home while they participate in the program and must live in the area where an approved professor lives. The program does not exist in every state.

Number awarded Varies; recently, approximately 120 students were funded at 52 colleges and universities nationwide.

Deadline February of each year.

[1169]
RESOURCES FOR THE FUTURE SUMMER INTERNSHIPS

Resources for the Future
Attn: Coordinator for Academic Programs
1616 P Street, N.W.
Washington, DC 20036-1400
(202) 328-5060   Fax: (202) 939-3460
E-mail: mankin@rff.org
Web: www.rff.org

Purpose To provide internships to minority and other undergraduate and graduate students interested in working on research projects in public policy during the summer.

Eligibility Candidates must be in their first or second year of graduate training, with skills in microeconomics, quantitative methods, or occasionally other social and natural sciences. Outstanding undergraduates may also be eligible. Applicants must be interested in an internship in Washington, D.C. in 1 of the divisions of Resources for the Future (RFF): the Center for Risk, Resource, and Environmental Management, the Energy and Natural Resources division, or the Quality of the Environment division. Applicants must be able to work without supervision in a careful and conscientious manner. Women and minority candidates are strongly encouraged to apply. Both U.S. and non-U.S. citizens are eligible, if the latter have proper work and residency documentation.

Financial data The stipend is $375 per week for graduate students or $350 per week for undergraduates.

Duration Summer months; beginning and ending dates can be adjusted to meet particular student needs.

Additional information Interns assist in research projects in complex public policy problems amenable to interdisciplinary analysis, often drawing heavily on economics. Further information on the Center for Risk, Resource, and Environmental Management is available from Marilyn Voigt at (202) 328-5077, Fax: (202) 939-3460, E-mail: voigt@rff.org; on Energy and Natural Resources and on Quality of the Environment from John Mankin at (202) 328-5060, Fax: (202) 939-3460, E-mail: mankin@rff.org.

Deadline March of each year.

[1170]
RETAIL MANAGEMENT INSTITUTE INTERNSHIPS

INROADS, Inc.
10 South Broadway, Suite 700
St. Louis, MO 63102
(314) 241-7488   Fax: (314) 241-9325
E-mail: info@inroads.org
Web: www.inroads.org

Purpose To provide an opportunity for young people of color to gain work experience in retailing.

Eligibility Eligible to apply are African Americans, Hispanics, and Native Americans who reside in the areas served by INROADS and wish to prepare for careers in department stores, mass merchant discount stores, specialty stores, consumer electronic stores, supermarkets, or ready-to-wear specialty stores. Applicants must be high school seniors or freshmen or sophomores in accredited 2- or 4-year colleges or universities with a GPA of 2.5 or higher. Students attending a 2-year college must intend to transfer to a 4-year college or university. Some applicants may be asked to take the Retail Readiness Assessment test and achieve a score within the 40 to 60 point range. All applicants must be permanent residents of the United States. Along with their application, they must submit official transcripts, a resume, SAT or ACT scores (for high school seniors and first-semester college students), and a 250-word essay on why this internship is right for them.

Financial data Salaries vary, depending upon the specific internship assigned.

Duration Up to 4 years.

Additional information INROADS places interns in companies where they receive the necessary pre-professional training and experience to launch a career as a manager of a department, store, district, or chain of stores. The INROADS organization offers internship opportunities through 48 local affiliates in 32 states and the District of Columbia.

Number awarded Varies each year.

[1171]
RICHARD B. FISHER SCHOLARSHIP

Morgan Stanley
c/o Joyce Arencibia, IT College Recruiting
750 Seventh Avenue, 30th Floor
New York, NY 10019
(212) 762-4000
E-mail: diversityrecruiting@morganstanley.com
Web: www.morganstanley.com

Purpose To provide financial assistance and work experience to members of minority groups who are preparing for a career in technology within the financial services industry.

Eligibility This program is open to members of minority groups who are enrolled in their sophomore or junior year of college (or the third or fourth year of a 5-year program). Applicants must be enrolled full time and have a GPA of 3.0 or higher. They must be willing to commit to a paid summer internship in the Morgan Stanley Information Technology Division. All majors and disciplines are eligible, but preference is given to students preparing for a career in technology within the financial services industry. Along with their application, they must submit 1-page essays on 1) why they are applying for this scholarship and why they should be selected as a recipient; 2) a technical project on which they worked, either through a university course or previous work experience, their role in the project, and how they contributed to the end result; and 3) a software, hardware, or new innovative application of existing technology that they would create if they could and the impact it would have. Financial need is not considered in the selection process.

Financial data The stipend is $5,000.

Duration 1 year.

Additional information The program includes a paid summer internship in the Morgan Stanley Information Technology Division in the summer following the time of application.

Number awarded 1 or more each year.

Deadline February of each year.

[1172]
ROSWELL L. GILPATRIC INTERNSHIP

Metropolitan Museum of Art
Attn: Internship Programs
1000 Fifth Avenue
New York, NY 10028-0198
(212) 570-3710   Fax: (212) 570-3782
E-mail: mmainterns@metmuseum.org
Web: www.metmuseum.org

Purpose To provide work experience at the Metropolitan Museum of Art during the summer to minority and other students interested in a museum career.

Eligibility This internship is available to college juniors, seniors, recent graduates, and graduate students who show a special interest in preparing for a museum career. Applicants of diverse backgrounds are especially encouraged to apply.

Financial data The honorarium is $3,000 for undergraduate students and recent graduates or $3,250 for graduate students.

Duration 10 weeks, beginning in June.

Additional information Interns are assigned to departmental projects (curatorial, administration, or education) at the Metropolitan Museum of Art; other assignments may include giving gallery talks and working at the Visitor Information Center. The assignment is for 35 hours a week. The internships are funded in part by the Thorne Foundation.

Number awarded 1 each year.

Deadline January of each year.

[1173]
RUTH CHANCE LAW FELLOWSHIP

Equal Rights Advocates, Inc.
1663 Mission Street, Suite 250
San Francisco, CA 94103
(415) 621-0672   Fax: (415) 621-6744
E-mail: sgersh@equalrights.org
Web: www.equalrights.org/about/jobs.asp

Purpose To provide work experience at Equal Rights Advocates (ERA) to recent law school graduates who are interested in working for the equal rights of women and minorities.

Eligibility This program is open to recent law school graduates who are licensed to practice law in California. Applicants must be able to demonstrate knowledge of and commitment to women's rights and legal issues affecting women; skill in legal research, analysis, and writing; knowledge of and commitment to civil rights and legal issues affecting people of color and other disadvantaged populations; ability to complete assignments and responsibilities accurately and in a timely manner; proficiency in computer applications; commitment to and involvement with community concerns; verbal and written communication skills; and ability to interact professionally and effectively with coworkers, board members, volunteers, outside counsel, court personnel, organization donors, and guests. Preference is given to applicants who are bilingual in English and Spanish, Cantonese, or Vietnamese.

Financial data The annual salary ranges from $35,000 to $37,500; benefits are also provided.

Duration 1 year, beginning in September.

Additional information Equal Rights Advocates is a nonprofit, public interest law firm that is dedicated to combating the disenfranchisement of women, particularly low-income and minority women. The responsibilities of the fellow include overseeing and coordinating an advice and counseling program, assisting staff attorneys with ongoing litigation, and participating in the firm's public policy and education activities.

Number awarded 1 each year.

Deadline January of each year.

[1174]
SCA GENERAL DIVERSITY INTERNSHIPS

Student Conservation Association, Inc.
Attn: Diversity Internships
1800 North Kent Street, Suite 102
Arlington, VA 22209
(703) 524-2441   Fax: (603) 543-1828
E-mail: diversity@thesca.org
Web: www.thesca.org/ci_diversity.cfm

Purpose To provide work experience during the summer to minority and disabled students at private, nonprofit, state, and federal agencies involved in conservation.

Eligibility This program provides summer internships through cooperating federal, state, private, and nonprofit agencies. It is open to currently-enrolled students who have completed at least the freshman year of college with a GPA of 2.5 or higher. U.S. citizenship or permanent resident status is required. Although all students may apply, the program is designed to allow students of color and students with disabilities, traditionally underrepresented in the conservation field, to experience the type of careers available to them. Possible placements include interpretation and environmental education; backcountry patrol; recreation management; archival and museum studies; archaeological surveys; cave studies; historical/cultural resource studies; landscape architecture and planning; biological research and monitoring; and wildlife, forestry, and fisheries management.

Financial data The stipend is $50 per week for internships of 12 weeks or $160 per week for positions of 6 to 12 months. Other benefits include payment of travel expenses, housing, worker's compensation, and accident insurance.

Duration 12-week, 6-month, 9-month, and 1-year positions are available.

Additional information While participating in the fellowship, students engage in ongoing career counseling, mentoring, personal and career development services, and additional training by the professional staff at each host site. Recently, available positions included Golden Gate National Recreation Area (California), Mammoth Cave National Park (Kentucky), Arlingtonians for a Clean Environment (Virginia), Dinosaur National Monument (Colorado), Lassen National Park (California), and Kenai Fjords National Park (Alaska).

Number awarded Approximately 40 each year.

Deadline February of each year.

[1175]
SCIENCE AND ENGINEERING APPRENTICE PROGRAM

George Washington University
Attn: Office of Science and Engineering Apprentice
   Program
1776 G Street, N.W., Suite 171
Washington, DC 20052
(202) 994-2234   E-mail: seap@gwu.edu
Web: www.gwseap.net

Purpose To provide an opportunity for high school students (especially women, African Americans, and Hispanics) to work during the summer on research projects at selected Department of Defense laboratories.

Eligibility This program is open to high school students interested in careers in science and engineering. A goal of the program is to encourage women, African Americans, and Hispanics to expand their interest in science and engineering careers. Applicants must submit a 1-page statement on their personal goals and why they want to participate in a research project at a Department of Defense laboratory, 1 or 2 letters of recommendation, and a transcript. Most laboratories require U.S. citizenship, although some accept permanent residents. In a few laboratories, security clearance is required. Selection is based on grades, science and mathematics courses taken, scores on national standardized tests, areas of interest, teacher recommendations, and the personal statement.

Financial data The stipend is at least $1,500. Students are responsible for transportation to and from the laboratory site.

Duration 8 weeks during the summer.

Additional information Funding for this program is provided by the U.S. Department of Defense. Participating laboratories include the Armed Forces Institute of Pathology (Washington, D.C.); Army Engineer Research and Development Center, Topographic Engineering Center (Alexandria, Virginia); Army Medical Research Institute of Chemical Defense (Edgewood, Maryland); Army Research Laboratory (Aberdeen Proving Ground, Maryland and Adelphi, Maryland); Army Research, Development and Engineering Command (Aberdeen Proving Ground, Maryland); Center for Health Promotion and Preventive Medicine (Aberdeen Proving Ground, Maryland); Defense Threat Reduction Agency (Fort Belvoir, Virginia); Night Vision and Electronic Sensors Directorate (Fort Belvoir, Virginia); Walter Reed Army Institute of Research (Silver Spring, Maryland); Aviation and Missile Command (Redstone Arsenal, Alabama); Army Communications-Electronics Command (Fort Monmouth, New Jersey); Army Forces Command (Fort McPherson, Georgia); Army Soldier and Biological Chemical Command (Natick, Massachusetts and Rock Island Arsenal, Illinois); and Anser Corporation (Arlington, Virginia).

Number awarded Varies each year.

Deadline February of each year.

[1176]
SCIENCE STUDENT INTERNSHIPS

Quality Education for Minorities (QEM) Network
1818 N Street, N.W., Suite 350
Washington, DC 20036
(202) 659-1818   Fax: (202) 659-5408
E-mail: qemnetwork@qem.org
Web: qemnetwork.qem.org

Purpose To provide underrepresented minority students with an opportunity to work during the summer with agencies and organizations involved in making science policy.

Eligibility This program is open to African Americans, Alaska Natives, American Indians, Mexican Americans, and Puerto Ricans who have successfully completed at least the sophomore year in an accredited, degree-granting institution. Applicants must be 1) working on a graduate or undergraduate degree in a mathematics, science (life or physical sciences, political science, or computer science), or engineering field; 2) interested in increasing and affecting the public's understanding of mathematics, science, and engineering issues; and 3) concerned about influencing science-oriented public policy at the national, state, and local levels. U.S. citizenship is required.

Financial data The stipend is $3,000 for undergraduates and $4,000 for graduate students. Other benefits include round-trip airfare between home or school and Washington, D.C. and housing for all interns who are not from the Washington, D.C. metropolitan area.

Duration 10 weeks during the summer.

Additional information Past assignments have included work in the National Science Foundation, the National Aeronautics and Space Administration, the Smithsonian Institution, the Environmental Protection Agency, and the mathematics, science, and engineering component of the Quality Education for Minorities (QEM) Network. Interns are also expected to become involved in an academic year project at their home institutions. Each intern must identify a faculty advisor and define a specific project that provides quality educational experiences for low-income minority students; interns prepare a written description of the follow-up project, an interim progress report, and a final report on the outcome of the project.

Number awarded Varies each year.

Deadline January of each year.

[1177]
SCMRE GRADUATE RESEARCH INTERNSHIPS

Smithsonian Center for Materials Research and
    Education
Attn: Coordinator of Research and Education
Museum Support Center
4210 Silver Hill Road
Suitland, MD 20746-2863
(301) 238-3700, ext. 121   Fax: (301) 238-3709
E-mail: bishopr@scmre.si.edu
Web: www.si.edu

Purpose To provide funding to minority and other graduate students interested in gaining research experience at the Smithsonian Center for Materials Research and Education (SCMRE).

Eligibility This program is open to graduate students interested in working in an area of SCMRE research pro-

gramming activity: biogeochemistry; characterizing and preserving natural history collections, photographic materials, and modern materials; preservation science; analysis and characterization of archaeological materials; and conservation treatment and development. Applicants must submit a resume (including transcripts), a statement of experience and intent, and references. Minorities are especially encouraged to apply.

Financial data The stipend is $14,000. Other benefits include a $2,000 travel allowance and health insurance.

Duration 1 year.

Number awarded Varies each year.

Deadline February of each year.

[1178]
SCOTTS COMPANY SCHOLARS PROGRAM

Golf Course Superintendents Association of America
Attn: Scholarship and Student Programs Manager
1421 Research Park Drive
Lawrence, KS 66049-3859
(785) 832-3678   Toll-free: (800) 472-7878, ext. 3678
E-mail: psmith@gcsaa.org
Web: www.gcsaa.org

Purpose To provide financial assistance and summer work experience to high school seniors and college students, particularly those from diverse backgrounds, who are preparing for a career in golf management.

Eligibility This program is open to high school seniors and college students (freshmen, sophomores, and juniors) who are interested in preparing for a career in golf management (the "green industry"). Applicants should come from diverse ethnic, cultural, and socioeconomic backgrounds, defined to include women, minorities, and people with disabilities. Selection is based on cultural diversity, academic achievement, extracurricular activities, leadership, employment potential, essay responses, and letters of recommendation. Financial need is not considered. Finalists are selected for summer internships and then compete for scholarships.

Financial data Each intern receives a $500 award. Scholarship stipends are $2,500.

Duration 1 year.

Additional information The program is funded by a permanent endowment established by Scotts Company. Finalists are responsible for securing their own internships.

Number awarded 5 interns and 2 scholarship winners are selected each year.

Deadline February of each year.

[1179]
SENATOR GREGORY LUNA MEMORIAL LEGISLATIVE SCHOLARS PROGRAM

Senate Hispanic Research Council, Inc.
815-A Brazos
PMB 147
Austin, TX 78701
(512) 499-8606   Fax: (512) 499-8607
E-mail: SHRC@sbcglobal.net
Web: www.tshrc.org/generalDetail.asp?ID=169

Purpose To provide Hispanic undergraduate and graduate students at colleges and universities in Texas with an opportunity to gain work experience at the Texas Senate.

Eligibility This program is open to undergraduate and graduate students who have completed at least 60 semester hours at an accredited 2- or 4-year educational institution in Texas; recent graduates are also eligible. Applicants must demonstrate leadership potential, academic achievement (preference is given to applicants with a GPA of 2.75 or higher), excellent writing and composition skills, and an interest in government, public policy, and Mexican American issues. They should be interested in a career in law, political science, public policy, or communications. Along with their application, they must submit a personal statement on the experiences or activities that led to their interest in government and this internship program, a sample of their best-written work completed for school, and a letter of recommendation.

Financial data Interns receive a stipend sufficient to cover the expense of living and working in Austin.

Duration Approximately 5 months, during the term of the Texas Senate, beginning in mid-January.

Additional information This program began in 2002. Interns are assigned to the office of a state senator to perform a variety of legislative tasks, including drafting legislation, floor statements, articles, press releases, legislative research summaries, and hearing agendas. The Senate Hispanic Research Council was established in 1993 to provide educational and leadership opportunities to all segments of the Hispanic community in Texas.

Number awarded Varies each year; recently, positions were available for 11 interns.

Deadline October of each year.

[1180]
SEO CAREER PROGRAM

Sponsors for Educational Opportunity
Attn: Career Program
30 West 21st Street, Suite 900
New York, NY 10010
(212) 979-2040   Fax: (212) 647-7010
E-mail: careerprogram@seo-usa.org
Web: www.seo-usa.org

Purpose To provide undergraduate students of color with an opportunity to gain summer work experience in selected fields in the United States or Hong Kong.

Eligibility This program is open to undergraduate students of color at colleges and universities in the United States. Applicants must be interested in a summer internship in 1 of the following fields: accounting, asset management, corporate law, global corporate financial leadership, information technology, investment banking, management consulting, or philanthropy. They should be able to demonstrate analytical and quantitative skills, interpersonal and community skills, maturity, and a cumulative GPA of 3.0 or higher. Along with their application, they must submit 1) information on their extracurricular and employment experience; 2) an essay of 75 to 100 words on how the program area to which they are applying related to their professional goals; and 3) an essay of 250 to 400 words on either an example of a time when they had to operate outside their "comfort zone" or their definition of success. Personal interviews are required.

Financial data Stipends range from $600 to $1,000 per week.

Duration 10 weeks during the summer.

Additional information This program was established in 1980. Most internships are available in the New York City metropolitan area (including Connecticut and New Jersey), although some asset management positions are available in San Francisco and investment banking internships are also open in San Francisco and (for students fluent in Mandarin or Korean) in Hong Kong.

Number awarded Varies each year; recently, more than 300 internships were available at more than 40 firms.

Deadline January of each year.

[1181]
SHELL LEGISLATIVE INTERNSHIP PROGRAM

National Association of Latino Elected and Appointed
     Officials
Attn: NALEO Educational Fund
1122 West Washington Boulevard, Third Floor
Los Angeles, CA 90015
(213) 747-7606, ext. 127   Fax: (213) 747-7664
E-mail: info@naleo.org
Web: www.naleo.org

Purpose To provide Latino college students from selected states with an opportunity to gain summer work experience with an elected or appointed official from their home state.

Eligibility Applicants must be residents of Arizona, California, Colorado, Florida, Illinois, New Mexico, New York, or Texas (but need not attend college in those states), be currently enrolled in an accredited 4-year institution as a junior or senior, be U.S. citizens or legal permanent residents, be of Latino origin, demonstrate leadership potential, and possess a sense of commitment to the Latino community.

Financial data Interns receive transportation, meals, and housing to participate in the annual conference; transportation and housing during their week in Washington, D.C.; and a stipend of $1,500 for the internship in their home state.

Duration 4 weeks during the summer, beginning in June.

Additional information Interns attend the annual conference of the National Association of Latino Elected and Appointed Officials (NALEO), where they meet and network with Latinos who are involved in leadership positions at the municipal, state, federal, and nonprofit levels; experience 1 week in Washington D.C. with federal elected and appointed officials, White House staff, and Congressional staffers; and spend the rest of the time working with a Latino elected or appointed official in their home state. Funding for this program is provided by the Shell Oil Company.

Number awarded Varies each year; recently, 11 of these internships were awarded.

Deadline March of each year.

[1182]
SMITHSONIAN MINORITY STUDENT INTERNSHIP
Smithsonian Institution
Attn: Office of Fellowships
Victor Building, Suite 9300, MRC 902
P.O. Box 37012
Washington, DC 20013-7012
(202) 275-0655   Fax: (202) 275-0489
E-mail: siofg@si.edu
Web: www.si.edu/ofg/Applications/MIP/MIPapp.htm

Purpose To provide minority undergraduate or graduate students with the opportunity to work on research or museum procedure projects in specific areas of history, art, or science at the Smithsonian Institution.

Eligibility Internships are offered to minority students who are actively engaged in graduate study at any level or in upper-division undergraduate study. An overall GPA of 3.0 or higher is generally expected. Applicants must be interested in conducting research or working on museum projects in history, art, or science at the institution.

Financial data The program provides a stipend of $400 per week; travel allowances may also be offered.

Duration 10 weeks during the summer or academic year.

Number awarded Varies each year.

Deadline January of each year for summer or fall; October of each year for spring.

[1183]
SODEXHO PUBLIC HEALTH FELLOWSHIP
Congressional Hispanic Caucus Institute, Inc.
911 Second Street, N.E.
Washington, DC 20002
(202) 543-1771   Toll-free: (800) EXCEL-DC
Fax: (202) 546-2143   E-mail: chci@chci.org
Web: www.chciyouth.org

Purpose To provide Latino graduate students and recent college graduates with the opportunity to apply their academic expertise in the area of public health policy during a work experience program in Washington, D.C.

Eligibility This program is open to U.S. citizens and permanent residents of Latino background who graduated from a college or university (with a bachelor's or graduate degree) within the past year or are currently-enrolled graduate students. Applicants must be interested in gaining experience in the area of public health policy. They must be able to demonstrate high academic achievement (preference is given to those with a GPA of 3.0 or higher), consistent active participation in public and/or community service activities, and superior analytical and communication skills (oral and written).

Financial data This program provides transportation to and from Washington, D.C., a monthly stipend of $2,061 (or $2,500 for fellows who already have a graduate degree), and health insurance.

Duration 9 months, beginning in September.

Additional information Placements are available in Congressional offices and federal agencies, advocacy groups, the media, and a broad range of policy-related organizations, but must focus on health issues. This program is sponsored by Sodexho, Inc.

Number awarded 1 each year.

Deadline February of each year.

[1184]
ST. PETERSBURG TIMES 1-YEAR INTERNSHIPS
St. Petersburg Times
Attn: Deputy Managing Editor
490 First Avenue South
P.O. Box 1121
St. Petersburg, FL 33731-1121
(727) 893-8869   Toll-free: (800) 333-7505, ext. 8869
Fax: (727) 892-2257   E-mail: hooker@sptimes.com
Web: www.sptimes.com/internship

Purpose To provide news reporting work experience at the *St. Petersburg Times* to minority and other recent college graduates.

Eligibility This program is open to graduated college seniors from any state who are interested in preparing for a career in the newspaper industry. Applicants should have experience at a college publication and at least 1 professional internship. They must submit a cover letter, resume, 3 references, and 10 or 12 clips that show the range of their work. Preference is given to applicants who will add diversity to the newsroom.

Financial data The salary is $625 per week. Full benefits are provided.

Duration 1 year, beginning in September.

Additional information Interns work in local news reporting at the *St. Petersburg Times.*

Number awarded 2 each year.

Deadline January of each year.

[1185]
STUDENT CANCER RESEARCH FELLOWSHIP
University of Colorado Cancer Center
Attn: Education Division
Biomedical Research Building, Room 523
4200 East Ninth Avenue
Campus Box B187
Denver, CO 80262
(303) 315-3967   E-mail: Connie.Bair@UCHSC.edu
Web: www.uchsc.edu/cancer/students/mainidea.html

Purpose To provide an opportunity for high school, college, dental, medical, and nursing students (particularly underrepresented minority students) to work during the summer on a cancer research project in Colorado.

Eligibility This program is open to high school juniors and seniors, college undergraduates, and dental, medical, and nursing students. Applicants must be interested in working on a cancer research project at the University of Colorado Health Sciences Center, the Boulder campus of the University of Colorado, or other institutions in the Denver area. Along with their application, they must submit a 2-page essay explaining why they wish to apply for this fellowship, school transcripts, and 2 letters of recommendation. Underrepresented minority students are particularly encouraged to apply.

Financial data A stipend is awarded (amount not specified).

Duration 6 to 8 weeks during the summer.

Additional information Funding for this program is provided by an education grant from the National Cancer Institute.

Number awarded Varies each year.

Deadline February of each year.

[1186]
SUMMER HONORS UNDERGRADUATE RESEARCH PROGRAM

Harvard Medical School
Division of Medical Sciences
Attn: Minority Programs Office
260 Longwood Avenue, Room 432
Boston, MA 02115-5720
(617) 432-1342   Toll-free: (800) 367-9019
Fax: (617) 432-2644
E-mail: SHURP@hms.harvard.edu
Web: www.hms.harvard.edu

Purpose To provide an opportunity for underrepresented minority students to engage in research at Harvard Medical School during the summer.

Eligibility This program at Harvard Medical School is open to underrepresented minority college students who have had at least 1 summer (or equivalent) of laboratory research. Applicants should be considering a career in biological or biomedical research.

Financial data The program provides a stipend of approximately $350 per week, dormitory housing, travel costs, a meal card, and health insurance if it is needed.

Duration 10 weeks during the summer.

Number awarded Varies each year.

Deadline January of each year.

[1187]
SUMMER RESEARCH OPPORTUNITIES PROGRAM (SROP)

Committee on Institutional Cooperation
1819 South Neil Street, Suite D
Champaign, IL 61820-7271
(217) 333-8475   Fax: (217) 244-7127
E-mail: cic@uiuc.edu
Web: www.cic.uiuc.edu/programs/SROP

Purpose To provide an opportunity for minority undergraduates to gain research experience at member institutions of the Committee on Institutional Cooperation (CIC) during the summer.

Eligibility This program is open to sophomore and junior African Americans, Mexican Americans, Native Americans, Puerto Ricans, and other Latinos. Applicants may be majoring in any field at any university in the United States, but they must be interested in conducting a summer research project under the supervision of a faculty mentor at a CIC member institution.

Financial data Participants are paid a stipend of $2,500 plus up to $1,100 toward room and board and travel to and from the host institution. Faculty mentors receive a $500 research allowance for the cost of materials.

Duration 8 to 10 weeks during the summer.

Additional information Participants work directly with faculty mentors at the institution of their choice and also engage in other enrichment activities, such as workshops and social gatherings. In July, all participants come together at 1 of the CIC campuses for the annual SROP conference. The CIC member institutions are University of Chicago, University of Illinois at Urbana-Champaign, University of Illinois at Chicago, University of Iowa, University of Michigan, University of Minnesota, University of Wisconsin at Madison, University of Wisconsin at Milwaukee, Indiana University, Michigan State University, Northwestern University, Ohio State University, Indiana University/Purdue University at Indianapolis, Pennsylvania State University, and Purdue University. Information is also available from Yolanda Zepeda, Assistant Director for Graduate Education and Diversity, 08K Bricker Hall, 190 North Oval Mall, Columbus, OH 43210-1366, (614) 247-5068, E-mail: zepeda@uiuc.edu Students are required to write a paper and an abstract describing their projects and to present the results of their work at a campus symposium.

Number awarded Varies each year; recently, 513 students participated in this program.

Deadline January of each year.

[1188]
SUMMER RESEARCH PROGRAM IN ECOLOGY

Harvard University
Harvard Forest
324 North Main Street
P.O. Box 68
Petersham, MA 01366-0068
(978) 724-3302   Fax: (978) 724-3595
E-mail: hfapps@fas.harvard.edu
Web: harvardforest.fas.harvard.edu

Purpose To provide an opportunity for minority and other undergraduate students and recent graduates to participate in a summer ecological research project at Harvard Forest in Petersham, Massachusetts.

Eligibility This program is open to undergraduate students and recent graduates interested in participating in a research project at the Forest in collaboration with an investigator from Harvard University, Marine Biological Laboratory Ecosystem Center, University of New Hampshire, or other institutions. The research focuses on the effects of natural and human disturbances on forest ecosystems, including atmospheric pollution, global warming, hurricanes, treefalls, and insect outbreaks. Investigators come from many disciplines, and specific projects center on population and community ecology, paleoecology, land-use history, wildlife biology, biochemistry, soil science, ecophysiology, and atmosphere-biosphere exchanges. Students from diverse backgrounds are strongly encouraged to apply.

Financial data The stipend is $3,600. Free housing and meals are also provided.

Duration 12 weeks during the summer.

Additional information Funding for this program is provided by the National Science Foundation (as part of its Research Experience for Undergraduates Program) and the Andrew W. Mellon Foundation (as part of its United Negro College Fund Summer Internship Program for Ecology Research).

Number awarded Up to 25 each year.

Deadline February of each year.

[1189]
SUMMER TRANSPORTATION INTERNSHIP PROGRAM FOR DIVERSE GROUPS

Department of Transportation
Federal Highway Administration
Attn: Office of Human Resources
HAHR-3, Room 4323
400 Seventh Street, S.W.
Washington, DC 20590
(202) 366-1159
Web: www.fhwa.dot.gov/education/stipdg.htm

Purpose To enable students from diverse groups to gain work experience during the summer at facilities of the U.S. Department of Transportation (DOT).

Eligibility This program is open to undergraduate students who are women, persons with disabilities, and members of diverse social and ethnic groups. Applicants must be U.S. citizens currently enrolled in a degree-granting program of study at an accredited institution of higher learning at the undergraduate (community or junior college, university, college, or Tribal College) or graduate level. They must be entering their junior or senior year (students attending a Tribal College must have completed their "first year" of school). Students who will graduate during the spring or summer are not eligible unless they have been accepted for enrollment in graduate school. Major fields of study include, but are not limited to, aviation, business, criminal justice, economics, engineering, environmental studies, hazardous materials, law, management information systems, marketing, planning, public administration, or transportation management. Applicants must be interested in a summer work experience at various DOT facilities. They must have a GPA of 3.0 or higher. Law students must be entering their second or third year and must be in the upper 30% of their class. Selection is based on an expressed interest in pursuing a transportation-related career, GPA or class standing, a reference from a professor or advisor, the endorsement of the department chair, an essay on transportation interests, areas of interest outside of school, and completeness of application package.

Financial data A stipend is paid (amount not specified).

Duration 10 weeks during the summer.

Additional information Assignments are at the DOT headquarters in Washington, D.C., a selected modal administration, or selected field offices around the country.

Number awarded Varies each year; recently, 17 interns participated in this program.

Deadline February of each year.

[1190]
TEACH FOR AMERICA FELLOWSHIPS

Teach for America
315 West 36th Street, Sixth Floor
New York, NY 10018
(212) 279-2080   Toll-free: (800) 832-1230
Fax: (212) 279-2081
E-mail: admissions@teachforamerica.org
Web: www.teachforamerica.org/program.html

Purpose To provide an opportunity for minority and other recent college graduates to serve as teachers in America's rural and urban public school classrooms.

Eligibility This program recruits students or college graduates for appointments in school districts with severe teacher shortages. A special effort is made to select corps members who are diverse in every respect, particularly with regard to ethnic, racial, and cultural background. All academic majors are eligible, but applicants with a mathematics, science, or engineering major are especially encouraged. No previous education course work is necessary, but a GPA of 2.5 or higher and U.S. citizenship or permanent resident status are required.

Financial data This program covers major expenses for the summer institute, including room and board and academic materials. It also covers room and board during a regional induction. Corps members are responsible for the cost of transportation to the summer institute, and from the summer institute to their placement site. They are also responsible for their own moving expenses, testing fees, and any necessary credits and district fees. During a transitional period before they begin working, they are eligible for grants and no-interest loans ranging from $1,000 to $5,000, depending on their financial need and cost of living in their assigned region. Teach for America then places recruits in jobs paying $25,000 to $43,000 per year. This program also has a relationship with AmeriCorps that makes participants eligible for forbearance on student loans during their period of service and to receive an AmeriCorps education award of $4,725 for each year of service.

Duration 2 years.

Additional information Once selected for this program, participants attend a 5-week summer institute where they receive additional professional development and support. They then travel to their assigned regions for a 1- to 2-week induction, which helps orient them to the schools, school districts, and communities where they will be teaching. Urban assignments are currently available in Atlanta, Baltimore, Chicago, Detroit, Houston, greater New Orleans, Los Angeles, New Jersey, New York City, Phoenix, the San Francisco Bay Area (especially the east bay), St. Louis, and Washington, D.C.; rural assignments are available in south Louisiana, the Mississippi delta (in Arkansas and Mississippi), an Indian reservation in New Mexico, eastern North Carolina, and the Rio Grande Valley of Texas. There is a $25 application fee.

Number awarded Nearly 2,000 each year.

Deadline February or October of each year.

[1191]
TELECOMMUNICATIONS FELLOWSHIPS

Congressional Hispanic Caucus Institute, Inc.
911 Second Street, N.E.
Washington, DC 20002
(202) 543-1771   Toll-free: (800) EXCEL-DC
Fax: (202) 546-2143   E-mail: chci@chci.org
Web: www.chciyouth.org

Purpose To provide Latino recent college graduates with the opportunity to apply their academic expertise in the area of public telecommunications policy during a work experience program in Washington, D.C.

Eligibility This program is open to U.S. citizens and permanent residents of Latino background who graduated from a college or university (with a bachelor's or graduate degree) within the past year. Applicants must be interested in gaining experience in the area of public telecommunications policy. They must be able to demonstrate high academic achievement (preference is given to those with a GPA of 3.0 or higher), consistent active participation in public and/or community service activities, and superior analytical and communication skills (oral and written).

Financial data This program provides transportation to and from Washington, D.C., a monthly stipend of $2,500, and health insurance.

Duration 9 months, beginning in September.

Additional information Placements are available in Congressional offices and federal agencies, advocacy groups, the media, and a broad range of policy-related organizations, but must focus on telecommunications issues.

Number awarded 1 or more each year.

Deadline February of each year.

[1192]
TRAINEESHIPS IN OCEANOGRAPHY FOR MINORITY UNDERGRADUATES

Woods Hole Oceanographic Institution
Attn: Education Office
Clark Laboratory 223, MS #31
360 Woods Hole Road
Woods Hole, MA 02543-1541
(508) 289-2219   Fax: (508) 457-2188
E-mail: education@whoi.edu
Web: www.whoi.edu

Purpose To provide work experience to minority group members who are interested in preparing for a career in the marine sciences, oceanographic engineering, or marine policy.

Eligibility This program is open to ethnic minority undergraduates enrolled in U.S. colleges or universities who have completed at least 2 semesters of study and who are interested in the marine sciences, oceanographic engineering, or marine policy. Applicants must be U.S. citizens or permanent residents and African American or Black; Asian American; Chicano, Mexican American, Puerto Rican or other Hispanic; or Native American.

Financial data The stipend is $396 per week; trainees may also receive additional support for travel to Woods Hole.

Duration 10 to 12 weeks during the summer or 1 semester during the academic year; renewable.

Additional information Trainees are assigned advisors who supervise their research programs and supplementary study activities. Some traineeships involve field work or research cruises. This program is sponsored by the Northeast Fisheries Science Center of the National Marine Fisheries Service (U.S. National Oceanic and Atmospheric Administration), the Center for Marine and Coastal Geology (U.S. Geological Survey), and the Office of Naval Research.

Number awarded 4 to 5 each year.

Deadline For a summer appointment, applications must be submitted in February of each year. For the remaining portion of the year, applications may be submitted at any time, but they must be received at least 2 months before the anticipated starting date.

[1193]
TRANSPORTATION SECURITY ADMINISTRATION MINORITY INTERNSHIP PROGRAM

ADNET Systems, Inc.
11260 Roger Bacon Drive, Suite 403
Reston, VA 20190
(703) 709-7218   Fax: (703) 709-7219
Web: www.adnet-sys.com

Purpose To provide work experience at facilities of the U.S. Transportation Security Administration (TSA) to minority and disabled students.

Eligibility This program is open to students who are from Historically Black Colleges and Universities (HBCUs), Hispanic Service Institutions (HSIs), Tribal Colleges and Universities (TCUs), Asian American and Pacific Islander communities, and disability communities. Applicants must be U.S. citizens currently enrolled in a college, university, or law school as a sophomore or above (including graduate students) with a GPA of 3.0 or higher; recent (within 6 months) graduates are also eligible. They must be interested in an internship at a TSA facility. Jobs have included, but are not limited to, accounting, business, human resources, law, computer science, mathematics, journalism, and criminal justice. Along with their application, they must submit 200-word statements on 1) their community activities, hobbies, associations, publications, and other relevant experience; and 2) why they want to participate in this program.

Financial data Interns are paid a stipend and receive housing.

Duration 10 weeks in summer or fall; 15 weeks in spring.

Additional information Recently, assignments were available at TSA facilities in Denver, Detroit, Honolulu, Houston, Miami, Newark, San Francisco, and Washington, D.C.

Number awarded Varies each year.

Deadline April of each year for summer; July of each year for fall; November of each year for spring.

[1194]
UNCF/HOUSEHOLD CORPORATE SCHOLARS PROGRAM

United Negro College Fund
Attn: Corporate Scholars Program
P.O. Box 1435
Alexandria, VA 22313-9998
Toll-free: (866) 671-7237 E-mail: internship@uncf.org
Web: www.uncf.org/internships/index.asp

Purpose To provide financial assistance and work experience to minority and other students majoring in fields related to business.

Eligibility This program is open to rising juniors majoring in accounting, business, computer science, finance, human resources, or marketing with a GPA of 3.0 or higher. Applicants must be interested in an internship with Household International, the program's sponsor, at 1 of the following sites: Bridgewater, New Jersey; Charlotte, North Carolina; Chesapeake, Virginia; Chicago, Illinois; Dallas, Texas; Indianapolis, Indiana; Jacksonville, Florida; Monterey, California; New Castle, Delaware; San Diego, California; or Tampa, Florida. Preference is given to applicants who reside in those areas, but students who live in other areas are also considered. African Americans, Hispanic Americans, American Indians, and Asian Americans are encouraged to apply. Along with their application, students must submit an essay on their personal and career goals and objectives, a letter of recommendation, and an official transcript.

Financial data This program provides a stipend of up to $10,000 per year and a paid internship.

Duration 8 to 10 weeks for the internships; 1 year for the scholarships, which may be renewed.

Number awarded Varies each year.

Deadline February of each year.

[1195]
UNCF/SPRINT SCHOLARS PROGRAM

United Negro College Fund
Attn: Corporate Scholars Program
P.O. Box 1435
Alexandria, VA 22313-9998
Toll-free: (866) 671-7237 E-mail: internship@uncf.org
Web: www.uncf.org/internships/index.asp

Purpose To provide financial assistance and work experience to minority students who are majoring in selected business and science fields.

Eligibility This program is open to members of minority groups who are enrolled full time as juniors or seniors at a 4-year college or university in the United States. Applicants must have a GPA of 3.0 or higher and be majoring in accounting, business, computer engineering, computer information systems, computer science, economics, electrical engineering, finance, industrial engineering, journalism, marketing, management information systems, public relations, or statistics. They must be interested in a summer internship at Sprint. Along with their application, they must submit a 1-page personal statement describing their career interests and goals, a current resume, a letter of recommendation, official transcripts, and a financial need statement.

Financial data This program provides a paid internship and (upon successful completion of the internship) a need-based stipend of up to $7,500.

Duration 10 to 12 weeks for the internships; 1 year for the scholarships.

Additional information This program is sponsored by Sprint. Recipients may attend any of the 39 member institutions of the United Negro College Fund (UNCF), other Historically Black Colleges and Universities (HBCUs), or an accredited majority 4-year college or university.

Number awarded Varies each year.

Deadline October of each year.

[1196]
UNION SUMMER INTERNSHIPS

AFL-CIO
Attn: Union Summer
815 16th Street, N.W.
Washington, DC 20006
(202) 639-6220 Toll-free: (800) 952-2550
Fax: (202) 639-6230 E-mail: unionsummer@aflcio.org
Web: www.aflcio.org/aboutunions/unionsummer

Purpose To provide minority and other college juniors and seniors with a summer opportunity to learn more about social justice through workplace and community organizing.

Eligibility This program is open to college students entering their senior year or planning to graduate. Applicants must be interested in participating in a summer activity to learn more about organizing unions to work for social justice. Desirable qualifications include "strong commitments to social and economic justice, as well as an openness to work with people of a different race, ethnicity, religion or sexual orientation." Applicants should be "people oriented, enthusiastic, energetic, flexible and willing to work long hours on an unpredictable schedule." Previous union experience is not required. Women and people of color are especially encouraged to apply.

Financial data The stipend is $300 per week. Transportation to the site and housing are also provided.

Duration 2 sessions are held each summer, each lasting 5 weeks; the first session begins in June and the second in July. Interns are assigned to 1 of those sessions.

Additional information Internships are conducted at selected sites throughout the country.

Number awarded Varies each year; since this program began in 1996, more than 2,500 students and other activists have participated.

Deadline April of each year.

[1197]
U.S. COAST GUARD MINORITY-SERVING INSTITUTIONS INTERNSHIP PROGRAM

ADNET Systems, Inc.
11260 Roger Bacon Drive, Suite 403
Reston, VA 20190
(703) 709-7218 Fax: (703) 709-7219
Web: www.adnet-sys.com

Purpose To provide summer work experience at facilities of the U.S. Coast Guard to minority and disabled students.

Eligibility This program is open to students who are from Historically Black Colleges and Universities (HBCUs), Hispanic Service Institutions (HSIs), Tribal Colleges and Universities (TCUs), Asian American and Pacific Islander communities, and disability communities. Applicants must be U.S. citizens currently enrolled as a sophomore or higher undergraduate, graduate, or law student with a GPA of 3.0 or higher. They must be interested in an internship at a Coast Guard facility. Jobs have included, but are not limited to, accounting, business, health management, human resources, international affairs, law, computer science, engineering, journalism, and criminal justice. Along with their application, they must submit 200-word statements on 1) their community activities, hobbies, associations, publications, and other relevant experience; and 2) why they want to participate in this program.

Financial data Interns are paid a stipend and receive housing.

Duration 10 weeks in the summer.

Additional information Most openings are at Coast Guard headquarters in Washington, D.C., other recent assignments included Coast Guard facilities in Honolulu (Hawaii), Massena (New York), New London (Connecticut), Norfolk (Virginia), and Topeka (Kansas). Information is also available from Karen Gillaspie, (202) 267-1866.

Number awarded Varies each year.

Deadline April of each year.

[1198]
VAID FELLOWSHIPS

National Gay and Lesbian Task Force
Attn: Policy Institute
214 West 29th Street, Fourth Floor
New York, NY 10001
(212) 604-9830   Fax: (212) 604-9831
E-mail: ngltf@ngltf.org
Web: www.thetaskforce.org/about/vaid.htm

Purpose   To provide work experience related to the leadership of people of color in the progressive movement for lesbian, gay, bisexual, and transgendered (LGBT) equality.
Eligibility   Applicants must be enrolled in a degree program at least half time as an undergraduate, graduate, or law student or have successfully completed an undergraduate, graduate, or law degree within the preceding 12 months. They should have 1) a desire to work in a multicultural environment where commitment to diversity based on race, ethnic origin, gender, age, sexual orientation, and physical ability is an important institutional value; 2) demonstrated leadership in progressive and/or LGBT communities; 3) extensive research, writing, and critical thinking skills; 4) knowledge of, and commitment to, LGBT issues; and 5) computer proficiency in word processing, database work, e-mail, and Internet research. The program supports and recognizes the leadership of people of color and other emerging leaders in public policy, legal, and social science research.
Financial data   The stipend is $400 per week. Fellows are responsible for their own housing and living expenses.
Duration   11 weeks, either in the winter or summer.
Additional information   The Policy Institute of the National Gay and Lesbian Task Force (NGLTF), founded in 1995, is the largest think tank in the United States engaged in research, policy analysis, and strategic action to advance equality and understanding of LGBT people. Its activities include the racial and economic justice initiative, family policy issues, aging and youth policy issues, voting behavior and political representation issues, public opinion, workplace benefit and discrimination issues, the impact of anti-LGBT ballot initiatives and the anti-LGBT movement, and documenting basic demographics of the LGBT community.
Number awarded   Normally, 1 winter and 3 summer fellows are selected.
Deadline   January of each year for winter; March of each year for summer.

[1199]
VILLAGE VOICE/MARY WRIGHT WRITING FELLOWSHIP

Village Voice
Attn: Editorial Department
36 Cooper Square
New York, NY 10003-7118
(212) 475-3300
Web: www.villagevoice.com

Purpose   To provide work experience to minority college students interested in interning at the *Village Voice*, a weekly newspaper published in New York City.
Eligibility   This program is open to minority college students interested in interning at the *Village Voice*. While journalism experience is not an absolute requirement, candi-

dates should possess research skills, an aptitude for critical thought, and a familiarity with the *Village Voice*. Interested students should submit samples of their written or editorial work, a resume, a letter of recommendation, an application form, and a self-addressed stamped envelope.
Financial data   The stipend is $150 per week.
Duration   4 months, usually beginning in January, May/June, or September.
Additional information   The *Village Voice* is known for its investigative journalism as well as coverage of cultural events (including reporting on film, art, theater, books, and dance). Interns have the opportunity to work with well-known journalists on the newspaper. College credit may be arranged.
Number awarded   Varies each session.
Deadline   December for the spring session; March for the summer session; July for the fall semester; November for the winter session.

[1200]
VIRGINIA PRESS ASSOCIATION MINORITY INTERNSHIPS

Virginia Press Association
Attn: Minority Internship Program
11529 Nuckols Road
Glen Allen, VA 23059
(804) 521-7570   Toll-free: (800) 849-8717
Fax: (804) 521-7590   E-mail: arleneh@vpa.net
Web: www.vpa.net

Purpose   To provide summer work experience in journalism to minority students in Virginia.
Eligibility   This program is open to minority students at the level of sophomore through graduate school who are residents of Virginia or attending a college or university in Virginia. Applicants must have at least a 2.0 GPA, be able to type and/or use a word processor, be willing to move to the location of the host newspaper, and have a driver's license and access to a car. They must be interested in a summer internship at a newspaper in Virginia. Along with their application, they must submit a college transcript, 3 references, a 1-page resume, 3 samples of published work, and a 500-word essay on why they want to work in the newspaper industry and how this internship will help them advance their career plans.
Financial data   These are paid internships.
Duration   10 weeks during the summer.
Number awarded   2 each year.
Deadline   March of each year.

[1201]
VITO MARZULLO INTERNSHIP PROGRAM

Office of the Governor
Attn: Department of Central Management Services
503 William G. Stratton Building
Springfield, IL 62706
(217) 524-1381   Fax: (217) 785-7702
TDD: (217) 785-3979
Web: www.illinois.gov/gov/intopportunities.cfm

Purpose   To provide minority and other recent college graduates with work experience in the Illinois Governor's office.

Eligibility Applicants must be residents of Illinois who have completed a bachelor's degree and are interested in working in the Illinois Governor's office or in various agencies under the Governor's jurisdiction. They may have majored in any field, but they must be able to demonstrate a substantial commitment to excellence as evidenced by academic honors, leadership ability, extracurricular activities, and involvement in community or public service. Along with their application, they must submit 1) a 500-word personal statement on the qualities or attributes they will bring to the program, their career goals or plans, how their selection for this program would assist them in achieving those goals, and what they expect to gain from the program; and 2) a 1,000-word essay in which they identify and analyze a public issue that they feel has great impact on state government. A particular goal of the program is to achieve affirmative action through the nomination of qualified minorities, women, and persons with disabilities.

Financial data The stipend is $27,900 per year.

Duration 1 year, beginning in August.

Additional information Assignments are in Springfield and, to a limited extent, in Chicago.

Number awarded Varies each year.

Deadline January of each year.

[1202]
VSA ARTS INTERNSHIPS

VSA Arts
Attn: Human Resource Manager
1300 Connecticut Avenue, N.W., Suite 700
Washington, DC 20036
(202) 628-2800   Toll-free: (800) 933-8721
Fax: (202) 737-0725   TTY: (202) 737-0645
E-mail: hr@vsarts.org
Web: www.vsarts.org/x214.xml

Purpose To provide work experience in arts education at the Very Special Arts (VSA) program of the John F. Kennedy Center for the Performing Arts.

Eligibility This program is open to upper-division undergraduate and graduate students in arts education, arts administration, museum education, and/or disability fields. Applicants must be interested in working in 1 of the following departments at the VSA office in Washington, D.C.: arts administration, communications, educational research, event planning, exhibition design and fabrication, or information technology. Along with their application, they must submit a cover letter describing their career goals, a resume, 2 letters of recommendation, and writing samples. Minorities and persons with disabilities are encouraged to apply.

Financial data A stipend of $650 per month may be paid.

Duration 3 months, in the fall (September through December), spring (January through April), or summer (June through August).

Additional information The sponsor, VSA Arts, was formerly known as Very Special Arts.

Number awarded 1 or more each year.

Deadline Applications may be submitted at any time.

[1203]
WALT DISNEY STUDIOS AND ABC ENTERTAINMENT WRITING FELLOWSHIP PROGRAM

Walt Disney Studios and ABC Entertainment
Attn: Writing Fellowship Program
500 South Buena Vista Street
Burbank, CA 91521-4389
(818) 560-6894   E-mail: abc.fellowships@abc.com
Web: www.abctalendevelopment.com

Purpose To provide support to minority and other writers interested in developing their craft at Walt Disney Studios and ABC Entertainment.

Eligibility This program is open to all writers, although a goal of the program is to seek out and employ culturally and ethnically diverse new writers. Applicants must submit a writing sample; for the feature films division, that should be a completed live-action motion picture screenplay (up to 120 pages) or a full-length 2-to-3 act play; for the television division, the sample should be a full-length script appropriate for a half-hour or 1-hour television series, based on a current prime time television or cable broadcast series.

Financial data The salary is $50,000.

Duration 1 year, beginning in January.

Additional information Fellows train with creative teams either at Walt Disney Studios or ABC Entertainment. This program began in 1990.

Number awarded Up to 11 each year.

Deadline June of each year.

[1204]
WALTER O. SPOFFORD, JR. MEMORIAL INTERNSHIP

Resources for the Future
Attn: Coordinator for Academic Programs
1616 P Street, N.W.
Washington, DC 20036-1400
(202) 328-5060   Fax: (202) 939-3460
E-mail: mankin@rff.org
Web: www.rff.org

Purpose To provide summer internships to minority and other graduate students interested in working on Chinese environmental issues at Resources for the Future (RFF).

Eligibility This program is open to first- or second-year graduate students with a special interest in Chinese environmental issues. Applicants must be interested in an internship in Washington, D.C. at RFF. They should have outstanding policy analysis and writing skills. Women and minority candidates are strongly encouraged to apply. Both U.S. and non-U.S. citizens (especially Chinese students) are eligible, if the latter have proper work and residency documentation.

Financial data The stipend depends on individual circumstances. Support for travel expenses and visa assistance are also available.

Duration The duration of the internship depends on the intern's situation.

Number awarded 1 each year.

Deadline February of each year.

[1205]
WCVB-TV SUMMER MINORITY INTERNSHIP PROGRAM

WCVB-TV
Attn: Human Resources Department
5 TV Place
Needham, MA 02494-2303
(781) 433-0461   Fax: (781) 449-6682
E-mail: lwalsh@hearstsc.com
Web: www.thebostonchannel.com

Purpose To provide work experience at WCVB-TV in Boston to minorities who are interested in broadcast journalism as a career.

Eligibility Applicants must have completed their freshman year, be majoring in some field of broadcasting, be U.S. citizens, and be minorities or others disadvantaged by economic or social conditions. They must be interested in interning at WCVB-TV in Boston.

Financial data Interns receive the minimum wage for 37.5 hours per week. They also receive funding for meals and transportation.

Duration 12 weeks during the summer.

Additional information This program at WCVB-TV provides an opportunity for participants to obtain an overview of the television broadcasting field in news, programming, public affairs, or sales. Interns must provide their own transportation.

Number awarded 5 each year.

Deadline April of each year.

[1206]
WILLIAM KELLY SIMPSON INTERNSHIP FOR EGYPTIAN ART

Metropolitan Museum of Art
Attn: Internship Programs
1000 Fifth Avenue
New York, NY 10028-0198
(212) 570-3710   Fax: (212) 570-3782
E-mail: mmainterns@metmuseum.org
Web: www.metmuseum.org

Purpose To provide summer work experience at the Metropolitan Museum of Art to minority and other graduate students interested in ancient Egyptian art.

Eligibility This internship is available to graduate students who have completed the course work for a master's degree in Egyptology or in art history with a main emphasis on ancient Egyptian art. Applicants of diverse backgrounds are encouraged to apply.

Financial data The honorarium is $3,250.

Duration 10 weeks, beginning in June.

Additional information The intern works with the curatorial staff at the Metropolitan Museum of Art on projects related to the museum's Egyptian collection or a special exhibition. This internship is funded by the Marilyn M. Simpson Charitable Trust

Number awarded 1 each year.

Deadline January of each year.

[1207]
WISE PROGRAM

Washington Internships for Students of Engineering
c/o IEEE-USA
1828 L Street, N.W., Suite 1202
Washington, DC 20036-5104
(202) 785-0017   Fax: (202) 785-0835
E-mail: e.wissolik@ieee.org
Web: www.wise-intern.org/apply.html

Purpose To provide summer work experience in the Washington D.C. area to minority and other engineering students.

Eligibility This program is open to third- and fourth-year undergraduate engineering students and recent graduates beginning study in an engineering policy-related master's program. Interns learn about the operation of government and the interaction between the engineering community and the government in matters of public policy, as well as the way in which engineers can and do contribute to public policy decisions in complex technological matters. Minority students are encouraged to apply. U.S. citizenship is required.

Financial data The stipend is $1,800; lodging and travel expenses are also covered.

Duration 10 weeks, in the summer.

Additional information This internship program is sponsored by a number of engineering and scientific societies, which select and sponsor the student participants. Sponsors include the American Institute of Chemical Engineers (AIChE), the American Nuclear Society (ANS), the American Society of Civil Engineers (ASCE), the American Society of Mechanical Engineers (ASME), the Institute of Electrical and Electronics Engineers (IEEE), the National Science Foundation (NSF), the National Society of Professional Engineers (NSPE), and the Society of Automotive Engineers (SAE). Interns are under the guidance of an engineering professor and receive academic credit. Applicants seeking sponsorship by ANS, ASCE, ASME, or IEEE must be members of those societies.

Number awarded Up to 16 each year.

Deadline December of each year.

[1208]
Y.E.S. TO JOBS COLLEGE PROGRAM

Y.E.S. to Jobs
P.O. Box 3390
Los Angeles, CA 90078-3390
(310) 358-4922   Fax: (310) 358-4330
E-mail: ytjcollegedir@aol.com
Web: www.yestojobs.org

Purpose To provide work experience to minority college students interested in a managerial career in the music industry.

Eligibility This program is open to minority (African American, Asian American, Hispanic American, and Native American) students from 18 to 25 years of age who are actively enrolled in a college or university in Los Angeles or New York. Applicants must have a GPA of 2.5 or higher and an interest in music, media, or business. They must be interested in employment during the fall, winter, or spring in entry level positions at record companies, retail stores, radio and television stations, cable networks, trade publications, film and production companies, public relations and entertainment law firms, or multi-media companies. There is no formal application; interested students must submit a cover letter and resume. The program manager invites selected students to an interview and offers assignments on a first-come, first-served basis.

Financial data Employers establish the salary they pay interns, but most are minimum wage.

Duration The length of the internship varies according to the needs and interests of the employer and the intern.

Additional information This program was established by A&M Records in 1987, and was expanded to include college students in 2003. Y.E.S. stands for Youth Entertainment Summer.

Number awarded Varies each year.

Deadline Applications may be submitted at any time.

[1209]
Y.E.S. TO JOBS HIGH SCHOOL PROGRAM

Y.E.S. to Jobs
P.O. Box 3390
Los Angeles, CA 90078-3390
(310) 358-4922   Fax: (310) 358-4330
E-mail: yestojobs@aol.com
Web: www.yestojobs.org

Purpose To provide summer work experience to minority high school students interested in a managerial career in the music industry.

Eligibility This program is open to minority (African American, Asian American, Hispanic American, and Native American) high school students from 16 to 18 years of age in the following cities: Atlanta, Los Angeles, Miami, Nashville, New York, and Washington, D.C. Applicants must have a GPA of 2.8 or higher, a 90% attendance record in school, and an interest in music, media, or business. They must be interested in full-time summer employment in entry level positions at record companies, retail stores, radio and television stations, cable networks, trade publications, film and production companies, public relations and entertainment law firms, or multi-media companies. Selection is based on self-motivation, dependability, and willingness to take initiative and work hard.

Financial data Employers establish the salary they pay interns, but most are minimum wage.

Duration 8 to 10 weeks during the summer.

Additional information This program was established by A&M Records in 1987, and became a nonprofit organization in 1994. Y.E.S. stands for Youth Entertainment Summer.

Number awarded Varies each year; recently, more than 250 internships were provided.

Deadline February of each year for positions in Los Angeles; March of each year for other cities.

[1210]
ZINA GARRISON MINORITY INTERNSHIP

Women's Sports Foundation
Attn: Award and Grant Programs Manager
Eisenhower Park
1899 Hempstead Turnpike, Suite 400
East Meadow, NY 11554-1000
(516) 542-4700   Toll-free: (800) 227-3988
Fax: (516) 542-4716   E-mail: wosport@aol.com
Web: www.womenssportsfoundation.org

Purpose To provide work experience at the Women's Sports Foundation to women of color interested in a sports-related career.

Eligibility This program is open to women of color who are undergraduate students, college graduates, graduate students, or women in career change. Applicants must be interested in working at the foundation offices on Long Island, New York. They must submit a personal statement that includes their sports background and current participation, issues and sports topics that interest them, their motivation for interning with the foundation, and what they hope to receive for themselves from the experience. An interview is required.

Financial data The salary is $1,000 per month.

Duration Sessions run from January through May, June through August, and September through December. Interns may complete 1, 2, or 3 sessions consecutively, but they must complete each session in its entirety.

Additional information Assignments are available in the athlete services, development, education, program management, public relations and communications, publications, special events, and web editorial departments. Interns may receive academic credit for their work.

Number awarded 2 or 3 each year.

Deadline Applications should be submitted no later than 120 days prior to the desired internship start date.

Indexes

Program Title Index

If you know the name of a particular funding program and want to find out where it is covered in the directory, use the Program Title Index. Here, program titles are arranged alphabetically, word by word. To assist you in your search, every program is listed by all its known names or abbreviations. In addition, we've used an alphabetical code (within parentheses) to help you determine if the program falls within your scope of interest: S = Scholarships; F = Fellowships; L = Loans; G = Grants; A = Awards; and I = Internships. Here's how the code works: if a program is followed (S) 141, the program is described in entry 141 in the Scholarships section. If the same program title is followed by another entry number—for example, (L) 680—the program is also described in entry 680 in the Loans section. Remember: the numbers cited here refer to program entry numbers, not to page numbers in the book.

Association of Research Libraries Leadership and Career Development Program. *See* MLA/ARL Leadership and Career Development Program, entry (F) 558

Association of Schools of Public Health/Centers for Disease Control and Prevention/Agency for Toxic Substances and Disease Registry Internships. *See* CDC/PRC Minority Fellowships, entry (G) 756

AstraZeneca Fellowship/Faculty Transition Awards, (F) 412, (G) 742

Atherton Scholarship. *See* Robert and Martha Atherton Scholarship, entry (F) 624

Atlanta Journal and Constitution Minority Internships, (I) 1014

AT&T Laboratories Fellowship Program, (F) 413, (I) 1015

AT&T Undergraduate Research Program, (I) 1016

Auzenne Fellowship for Graduate Study. *See* Delores A. Auzenne Fellowship for Graduate Study, entry (F) 447

Avon Grant Scholarships, (S) 41

AWIS Seattle Scholarships, (S) 42

Bahethi Scholarship. *See* American Meteorological Society Undergraduate Scholarships, entry (S) 25

Baker Award. *See* Worldstudio Foundation Scholarships, entries (S) 382, (F) 675

Baker Corporation Scholarship Program for Diversity in Engineering. *See* Air Products and Chemicals Scholarship for Diversity in Engineering, entry (S) 234

Baker Corporation Scholarship Program for Diversity in Engineering. *See* Michael Baker Corporation Scholarship Program for Diversity in Engineering, entry (S) 13

Baker Family Foundation Scholarship, (S) 43

Balfour Phi Delta Phi Minority Scholarship Program, (F) 414

Banks Memorial Undergraduate Scholarship. *See* Sharon D. Banks Memorial Undergraduate Scholarship, entry (S) 318

Bannerman Memorial Fellowships. *See* Sabbaticals for Long–Time Activists of Color, entry (F) 627

Barbara Dezmon Scholarship. *See* AIMMS Excellence Scholarships, entry (S) 10

Barbara Jordan Health Policy Scholars Program, (I) 1017

Barbara Jordan Memorial Scholarship, (S) 44, (F) 415

Barrows Minority Doctoral Student Scholarship. *See* Lionel C. Barrows Minority Doctoral Student Scholarship, entry (F) 530

BASF Agricultural Products Scholarships, (S) 45

Baum Endowed Scholarship. *See* American Meteorological Society Undergraduate Scholarships, entry (S) 25

Bay Area Community Service Scholarships, (G) 743, (I) 1018

Bay Area Minority Summer Clerkship Program, (I) 1019

Beck Fellowship. *See* Stan Beck Fellowship, entries (S) 325, (F) 645

Behavioral Sciences Postdoctoral Fellowships in Epilepsy, (F) 416, (G) 744

Behavioral Sciences Student Fellowships in Epilepsy, (G) 745

Bell Labs Graduate Research Fellowship Program, (F) 417, (I) 1020

Belpré Book Award. *See* Pura Belpré Book Award, entry (A) 986

Benton Scholarship. *See* American Meteorological Society Undergraduate Scholarships, entry (S) 25

Bernard L. Majewski Fellowship, (G) 746

Bernbach Minority Scholarship Fund. *See* Bill Bernbach Minority Scholarship Fund, entry (F) 418

Berrien Fragos Thorn Arts Scholarships for Migrant Farmworkers, (G) 747

Betty A. DeVries Memorial Fund. *See* Associated Colleges of Illinois Scholarship Program, entry (S) 36

Beyond Margins Award, (A) 961

Bienstock Fellowship. *See* N.S. Bienstock Fellowship, entry (G) 896

Bill Bernbach Minority Scholarship Fund, (F) 418

Biloxi Sun Herald Minority Scholarship Program, (S) 46

Biomedical Research Training Program for Underrepresented Groups, (I) 1021

Bistany Memorial Scholarship Program. *See* Joanna Bistany Memorial Scholarship Program, entry (S) 194

Blackmun Memorial Public Interest Grant. *See* Harry A. Blackmun Memorial Public Interest Grant, entry (I) 1076

Blake Memorial Scholarship. *See* Connecticut Association of Latinos in Higher Education Scholarships, entry (S) 85

Blaszcak Scholarship. *See* Fleming/Blaszcak Scholarship, entry (S) 135

Blechschmidt Award. *See* Geological Society of America General Research Grants Program, entry (G) 816

Blitman, P.E. Scholarship to Promote Diversity in Engineering. *See* Maureen L. and Howard N. Blitman, P.E. Scholarship to Promote Diversity in Engineering, entry (S) 228

Blue Cross Blue Shield of Wisconsin Nursing Scholarships, (S) 47

BNSF Scholarship Program, (S) 48

Board of Governors Medical Scholarship Program, (F) 419

Bob Glahn Scholarship in Statistical Meteorology, (S) 49

Bob Hagley Scholarship. *See* Cleveland Advertising Association Education Foundation Scholarships, entry (S) 77

Bob Stanley and Al Compton Minority and International Scholarship, (S) 50

Bobolink Foundation Award. *See* Worldstudio Foundation Scholarships, entries (S) 382, (F) 675

Bolin Fellowships for Minority Graduate Students. *See* Gaius Charles Bolin Fellowships for Minority Graduate Students, entry (G) 815

Bolivar Award. *See* Simon Bolivar Lecture Award, entry (A) 991

Bombay Sapphire Awards. *See* Worldstudio Foundation Scholarships, entries (S) 382, (F) 675

Booker T. Washington Scholarships, (S) 51

Boone Memorial Scholarships. *See* Ester Boone Memorial Scholarships, entry (S) 126

Booz–Allen & Hamilton Scholarship. *See* NNOA/Booz–Allen & Hamilton Scholarship, entry (S) 269

Boston Chapter Minority Scholarship, (F) 420

Bouchet Award. *See* Edward A. Bouchet Award, entry (A) 966

Bowen Foundation Internships. *See* Emma L. Bowen Foundation Internships, entry (I) 1055

Bradley Fellowship Program. *See* Dan Bradley Fellowship Program, entry (I) 1044

Bradley Scholarship. *See* Ed Bradley Scholarship, entry (S) 112

Breakthrough to Nursing Scholarships for Racial/Ethnic Minorities, (S) 52

Brennan Memorial Scholarship. *See* Cleveland Advertising Association Education Foundation Scholarships, entry (S) 77

Brock Memorial Scholarship. *See* Cathy L. Brock Memorial Scholarship, entry (F) 428

S–Scholarships   F–Fellowships   L–Loans   G–Grants   A–Awards   I–Internships

McCormick Tribune Minority Fellowship in Urban Journalism at the Chicago Reporter. *See* Robert R. McCormick Tribune Minority Fellowship in Urban Journalism at the Chicago Reporter, entry (G) 925

McGuire Memorial Fund. *See* Associated Colleges of Illinois Scholarship Program, entry (S) 36

McKelvey Award. *See* Worldstudio Foundation Scholarships, entries (S) 382, (F) 675

McLean Award. *See* Franklin C. McLean Award, entry (A) 968

McLendon Minority Postgraduate Scholarship Program. *See* John McLendon Memorial Minority Postgraduate Scholarship Award, entries (F) 518, (I) 1101

McNamara Family Creative Arts Project Grants, (G) 858

Medical Library Association Scholarship for Minority Students. *See* MLA Scholarship for Minority Students, entry (F) 557

Medical Library Association/Association of Research Libraries Leadership and Career Development Program. *See* MLA/ARL Leadership and Career Development Program, entry (F) 558

Medlin Scholarships. *See* Geological Society of America General Research Grants Program, entry (G) 816

MEFUSA Scholarships for Latino/as, (S) 229

Mellon Foundation Early Career Fellowship in Economic Studies. *See* Andrew W. Mellon Foundation Early Career Fellowship in Economic Studies, entry (G) 737

Mellon Foundation Junior Faculty Fellowships. *See* ACLS Fellowships, entry (G) 723

Mendenhall Fellowships for Minority Scholars. *See* Five College Fellowship Program for Minority Scholars, entry (G) 810

Mental Health and Substance Abuse Services Fellowship, (F) 537

Mental Health Dissertation Research Grants to Increase Diversity in the Mental Health Research Arena, (G) 859

Mental Health Research Fellowship, (F) 538

Mental Health Substance Abuse Clinical Fellowship Program, (L) 695

Mentor Graphics Scholarships, (S) 230

Mentored Clinical Scientist Award for Underrepresented Minorities, (G) 860

Mercedes–Benz Scholarships, (S) 231

METPRO/Editing Program, (I) 1123

Metropolitan Life Foundation Awards Program for Academic Excellence in Medicine, (F) 539

Metropolitan Museum of Art Internships for College Students, (I) 1124

Metropolitan Museum of Art Internships for Graduate Students, (I) 1125

Metropolitan Museum of Art 6–Month Internships, (I) 1126

Mexican American Bar Association Scholarships, (F) 540

Mexican American Engineers and Scientists General Scholarships. *See* MAES General Scholarships, entries (S) 220, (F) 532

Mexican American Engineers and Scientists Presidential Scholarship, (S) 232, (F) 541

Mexican American Legal Defense and Educational Fund Law School Scholarship Program. *See* MALDEF Law School Scholarship Program, entry (F) 533

Mexican Fiesta Scholarships, (S) 233, (F) 542

MFP Dissertation Support, (G) 861

MFT Minority Supervision Stipend Program, (F) 543

Miami University Minority Resident Librarian, (I) 1127

Michael Baker Corporation Scholarship Program for Diversity in Engineering, (S) 234

Michaels Scholarship Program. *See* Taylor Michaels Scholarship Program, entry (S) 333

Michele Clark Fellowship, (F) 544

Michigan Association of Broadcasters Foundation Minority Internship Program. *See* MAB Foundation Minority Internship Program, entry (I) 1119

Michigan Space Grant Consortium Fellowships, (G) 862

Michigan Space Grant Consortium Research Seed Grants, (G) 863

Mickey Leland Energy Fellowships, (I) 1128

Mickey Williams Minority Student Scholarship. *See* PDEF Mickey Williams Minority Student Scholarship, entry (S) 284

Microbiology Undergraduate Research Fellowship, (G) 864

Microsoft National Scholarships, (S) 235, (I) 1129

Migrant Farmworker Baccalaureate Scholarship, (S) 236

Mildred Colodny Scholarship for Graduate Study in Historic Preservation, (F) 545, (I) 1130

Millender Fellowship, (G) 865

Milly Woodward Memorial Scholarship. *See* Northwest Journalists of Color Scholarship Awards, entry (S) 272

Minnesota Association of Counselors of Color Student of Color Scholarship. *See* MnACC Student of Color Scholarship, entry (S) 245

Minnesota Space Grant Consortium Scholarships and Fellowships, (S) 237, (F) 546

Minorities in Clinical Oncology Program Grants. *See* Mentored Clinical Scientist Award for Underrepresented Minorities, entry (G) 860

Minorities in Government Finance Scholarship, (S) 238, (F) 547

Minority Access Internship, (I) 1131

Minority Access to Research Careers (MARC) Faculty Predoctoral Fellowships, (F) 548

Minority Access to Research Careers (MARC) Faculty Senior Fellowships, (G) 866

Minority Access to Research Careers Predoctoral Fellowships. *See* Ruth L. Kirschstein NRSA Program for NIGMS MARC Predoctoral Fellowships, entry (F) 626

Minority Affairs Committee Award for Outstanding Scholastic Achievement, (A) 976

Minority Community College Transfer Scholarships, (S) 239

Minority Dental Student Scholarship, (F) 549

Minority Dissertation Research Grants in Aging, (G) 867

Minority Editing Training Program/Editing. *See* METPRO/Editing Program, entry (I) 1123

Minority Educational Foundation of the United States of America Scholarships for Latino/as. *See* MEFUSA Scholarships for Latino/as, entry (S) 229

Minority Faculty Development Scholarship Award in Physical Therapy, (F) 550

Minority Faculty Fellowship Program, (G) 868

Minority Fellowship in Environmental Law, (I) 1132

Minority Fellowship Program Dissertation Support. *See* MFP Dissertation Support, entry (G) 861

Minority Fellowship Program in Mental Health, (F) 551

Minority Geoscience Student Scholarships, (S) 240, (F) 552

Minority Medical Faculty Development Program. *See* Harold Amos Medical Faculty Development Program, entries (F) 491, (G) 825

Minority Medical Student Clinical Fellowship in Child and Adolescent Psychiatry. *See* Jeanne Spurlock Minority

---

Richard and Helen Hagemeyer Scholarship. *See* American Meteorological Society Undergraduate Scholarships, entry (S) 25

Richard and Jean Coyne Family Foundation Awards. *See* Worldstudio Foundation Scholarships, entries (S) 382, (F) 675

Richard B. Fisher Scholarship, (S) 306, (I) 1171

Richard D. Hailey Law Student Scholarships, (F) 622

Richard Gast Fellowship. *See* EMAF Fellowship Program, entry (F) 459

Richard S. Smith Scholarship, (S) 307

Risk and Development Field Research Grants, (F) 623, (G) 923

Rivera Mexican American Children's Book Award. *See* Tomás Rivera Mexican American Children's Book Award, entry (A) 998

Robert and Martha Atherton Scholarship, (F) 624

Robert D. Watkins Minority Graduate Fellowship, (G) 924

Robert K. Fahnestock Memorial Award. *See* Geological Society of America General Research Grants Program, entry (G) 816

Robert R. McCormick Tribune Minority Fellowship in Urban Journalism at the Chicago Reporter, (G) 925

Robert Toigo Foundation Fellowships, (F) 625

Roberts, Sr. Scholarship. *See* Elliott C. Roberts, Sr. Scholarship, entry (F) 458

Robinson Memorial Prize in Surgery. *See* James H. Robinson Memorial Prize in Surgery, entry (A) 974

Robinson Scholarship. *See* Jackie Robinson Scholarships, entry (S) 187

Robles–Lopez/Pampers Parenting Institute and Procter & Gamble Scholarship. *See* Juanita Robles–Lopez/Pampers Parenting Institute and Procter & Gamble Scholarship, entry (F) 521

Roche Research Scholar Awards in Liver Diseases. *See* AGA Research Scholar Awards, entry (G) 728

Rockwell Automation Scholarships, (S) 308

Rodriguez Scholarship. *See* American Meteorological Society Undergraduate Scholarships, entry (S) 25

Ronald H. Brown Memorial Scholarship, (S) 309

Rooks Fellowship for Racial and Ethnic Theological Students. *See* Adrienne M. and Charles Shelby Rooks Fellowship for Racial and Ethnic Theological Students, entry (F) 394

Rosa Parks Visiting Professors Program. *See* Martin Luther King, Jr., Cesar Chavez, Rosa Parks Visiting Professors Program, entry (G) 856

Rosewood Family Scholarship Fund, (S) 310

Ross Research Fund Award. *See* Geological Society of America General Research Grants Program, entry (G) 816

Roswell L. Gilpatric Internship, (I) 1172

Roth Manufacturing Engineering Scholarship. *See* Edward S. Roth Manufacturing Engineering Scholarship, entries (S) 116, (F) 456

Roy J. Shlemon Scholarship Awards. *See* Geological Society of America General Research Grants Program, entry (G) 816

Roybal Public Health Fellowship. *See* Edward R. Roybal Public Health Fellowship, entry (I) 1053

Royce Osborn Minority Student Scholarships, (S) 311

Rudin Foundation Awards. *See* Worldstudio Foundation Scholarships, entries (S) 382, (F) 675

Rudin Internships. *See* Jack and Lewis Rudin Internships, entry (I) 1094

Russell, Jr. Memorial Scholarship. *See* Louis B. Russell, Jr. Memorial Scholarship, entry (S) 217

Ruth Chance Law Fellowship, (I) 1173

Ruth L. Kirschstein NRSA Program for NIGMS MARC Predoctoral Fellowships, (F) 626

Ryskamp Research Fellowships. *See* Charles A. Ryskamp Research Fellowships, entry (G) 760

Sabbaticals for Long–Time Activists of Color, (F) 627

SACNAS Genome Scholars Program, (F) 628

Sahli–Kathy Woodall Minority Student Scholarships. *See* Don Sahli–Kathy Woodall Minority Student Scholarships, entry (S) 102

Salinas Scholarship Program. *See* Maria Elena Salinas Scholarship Program, entries (S) 221, (I) 1120

Sallie Mae Fund First in My Family Scholarship Program, (S) 312

Sally D. Funderburg Research Scholar Award in Gastric Biology Related to Cancer. *See* R. Robert & Sally D. Funderburg Research Scholar Award in Gastric Biology Related to Cancer, entry (G) 919

Saraswati (Sara) Bahethi Scholarship. *See* American Meteorological Society Undergraduate Scholarships, entry (S) 25

SCA General Diversity Internships, (I) 1174

Scholarship for Minority Students in Memory of Edna Yelland. *See* CLA Scholarship for Minority Students in Memory of Edna Yelland, entry (F) 432

Scholarships for Dependents of ICIA Members, (S) 313

Scholarships for Minority Accounting Students, (S) 314, (F) 629

Schroeder Endowed Scholarship in Meteorology. *See* Mark J. Schroeder Endowed Scholarship in Meteorology, entry (S) 222

Science and Engineering Apprentice Program, (I) 1175

Science Policy and International Security Fellowship Program, (G) 926

Science Student Internships, (I) 1176

Science Teacher Preparation Program, (S) 315, (F) 630

Scientist Development Award for New Minority Faculty, (G) 927

SCMRE Graduate Research Internships, (I) 1177

Scott Award. *See* NASCAR/Wendell Scott Award, entries (S) 255, (F) 563

Scott Book Scholarships. *See* Carl A. Scott Book Scholarships, entries (S) 64, (F) 426

Scotts Company Scholars Program, (S) 316, (I) 1178

Scoville Jr. Peace Fellowship Program. *See* Herbert Scoville Jr. Peace Fellowship, entry (I) 1082

Scripps Fellowships in Environmental Journalism. *See* Ted Scripps Fellowships in Environmental Journalism, entry (F) 650

Selected Professions Fellowships for Women of Color, (F) 631

Semiconductor Research Corporation Master's Scholarship Program, (F) 632

Senator Gregory Luna Memorial Legislative Scholars Program, (I) 1179

SEO Career Program, (I) 1180

Service League Minority Nursing Scholarship, (S) 317

Sharon D. Banks Memorial Undergraduate Scholarship, (S) 318

Shaw Industries/HENAAC Scholars Program, (S) 319

Sheldon M. Wolff, M.D. Fellowship in International Health. *See* Diplomacy Fellowships, entry (G) 784

S–Scholarships   F–Fellowships   L–Loans   G–Grants   A–Awards   I–Internships

---

Tuberous Sclerosis Complex Research Program Idea Development Awards, (G) 937

Tuberous Sclerosis Complex Research Program Natural History Development Awards, (G) 938

Tucker Fellowship. *See* G. Richard Tucker Fellowship, entry (I) 1068

UNCF/Household Corporate Scholars Program, (S) 340, (I) 1194

UNCF/Pfizer Postdoctoral Fellowships, (G) 939

UNCF/Sprint Scholars Program, (S) 341, (I) 1195

Underrepresented Mental Health Minority Research Fellowship Program, (F) 659

Union Summer Internships, (I) 1196

Unitarian Universalist Association Incentive Grants, (F) 660

United Methodist Ethnic Minority Scholarships, (S) 342

United Methodist Scholarship Program, (S) 343, (F) 661

United Methodist Women of Color Scholars Program, (F) 662

United Negro College Fund/Household Corporate Scholars Program. *See* UNCF/Household Corporate Scholars Program, entries (S) 340, (I) 1194

United Negro College Fund/Sprint Scholars Program. *See* UNCF/Sprint Scholars Program, entries (S) 341, (I) 1195

United Parcel Service Scholarship for Minority Students, (S) 344

United States Department of State Student Intern Program. *See* Department of State Student Intern Program, entry (I) 1048

United States Institute of Peace Senior Fellowships, (G) 940

University of California President's Postdoctoral Fellowship Program, (G) 941

University of North Carolina Campus Scholarships–Part I, (S) 345

University of Wisconsin Visiting Minority Scholar Lecture Program, (G) 942

University Postdoctoral Fellowship Program, (G) 943

UPS Diversity Scholarships, (S) 346

Urban Scholars Postdoctoral Fellowship Program. *See* HUD Urban Scholars Postdoctoral Fellowship Program, entry (G) 834

U.S. Coast Guard Minority–Serving Institutions Internship Program, (I) 1197

U.S. Department of Housing and Urban Development Urban Scholars Postdoctoral Fellowship Program. *See* HUD Urban Scholars Postdoctoral Fellowship Program, entry (G) 834

U.S. Department of State Student Intern Program. *See* Department of State Student Intern Program, entry (I) 1048

USA Funds Access to Education Scholarships, (S) 347, (F) 663

USA Funds Hawaii Silver Anniversary Scholarships, (S) 348, (F) 664

Vaid Fellowships, (I) 1198

Vallin Memorial Scholarship. *See* Connecticut Association of Latinos in Higher Education Scholarships, entry (S) 85

VanDaveer Scholarship. *See* Gerry VanDaveer Scholarship, entry (S) 152

VATE Minority Scholarship Award, (S) 349

Verizon Workforce Response Scholarships, (S) 350

Vermont Loan Forgiveness for Culturally Diverse Education Students, (L) 712

Vermont Space Grant Undergraduate Scholarships, (S) 351

Vikki Carr Scholarship Awards, (S) 352

Village Voice/Mary Wright Writing Fellowship, (I) 1199

Villarreal–HDA Foundation Scholarships. *See* Dr. Juan D. Villarreal–HDA Foundation Scholarships, entries (S) 107, (F) 451

Vinson & Elkins L.L.P. Scholarship, (S) 353

Virgil Hawkins Fellowship Program, (F) 665

Virginia Association of Teachers of English Minority Scholarship Award. *See* VATE Minority Scholarship Award, entry (S) 349

Virginia Badger Scholarship. *See* AWIS Seattle Scholarships, entry (S) 42

Virginia Higher Education Teacher Assistance Program, (S) 354

Virginia Medical Scholarship Program, (L) 713

Virginia Nurse Practitioner/Nurse Midwife Scholarship Program, (L) 714

Virginia Press Association Minority Internships, (I) 1200

Virginia Society of Certified Public Accountants Minority Undergraduate Scholarship, (S) 355

Virginia Space Grant Aerospace Graduate Research Fellowships, (G) 944

Virginia Space Grant Aerospace Undergraduate Research Scholarships, (G) 945

Virginia Space Grant Community College Scholarship Program, (S) 356

Virginia Space Grant Teacher Education Scholarship Program, (S) 357, (F) 666

Virginia Teaching Scholarship Loan Program, (L) 715

Vito Marzullo Internship Program, (I) 1201

Vouras Dissertation Research Grant. *See* Paul P. Vouras Dissertation Research Grant, entry (G) 904

VSA Arts Internships, (I) 1202

Wal–Mart Achievers Award, (S) 358

Walt and Milly Woodward Memorial Scholarship. *See* Northwest Journalists of Color Scholarship Awards, entry (S) 272

Walt Disney Studios and ABC Entertainment Writing Fellowship Program, (G) 946, (I) 1203

Walter O. Spofford, Jr. Memorial Internship, (I) 1204

Wanek Fund Award. *See* Geological Society of America General Research Grants Program, entry (G) 816

Ward Scholarship. *See* Associated Colleges of Illinois Scholarship Program, entry (S) 36

Warner Norcross & Judd Law School Studies Scholarship, (F) 667

Warner Norcross & Judd Paralegal Assistant Studies Scholarship, (S) 359

Warner Norcross & Judd Secretarial Studies Scholarship, (S) 360

Warren G. Magnuson Educational Support Personnel Scholarship Grant, (S) 361

WASA/PEMCO 21st Century Educator Scholarship, (S) 362

Washington Association of School Administrators/PEMCO 21st Century Educator Scholarship. *See* WASA/PEMCO 21st Century Educator Scholarship, entry (S) 362

Washington Bureau Minority Scholarships, (S) 363

S–Scholarships　　　　**F–Fellowships**　　　　**L–Loans**　　　　**G–Grants**　　　　**A–Awards**　　　　**I–Internships**

Sponsoring Organization Index

The Sponsoring Organization Index makes it easy to identify agencies that offer financial aid primarily or exclusively to minorities. In this index, sponsoring organizations are listed alphabetically, word by word. In addition, we've used an alphabetical code (within parentheses) to help you identify which programs sponsored by these organizations fall within your scope of interest: S = Scholarships; F = Fellowships; L = Loans; G = Grants; A = Awards; and I = Internships. Here's how the code works: if the name of a sponsoring organization is followed by (S) 141, a program sponsored by that organization is described in the Scholarships section in entry 141. If the same sponsoring organization's name is followed by another entry number—for example, (L) 680—the same or a different program sponsored by that organization is described in the Loans chapter in entry 680. Remember: the numbers cited here refer to program entry numbers, not to page numbers in the book.

S–Scholarships   F–Fellowships   L–Loans   G–Grants   A–Awards   I–Internships

---

S–Scholarships   F–Fellowships   L–Loans   G–Grants   A–Awards   I–Internships

Hanley Wood LLC, (S) 118
Harry J. Bosworth Company, (F) 549
Hartford Foundation for Public Giving, (S) 85
Harvard University. Divinity School, (G) 956
Harvard University. Harvard Forest, (I) 1188
Harvard University. John F. Kennedy School of Government, (G) 807
Harvard University. Law School, (G) 920
Harvard University. Medical School, (I) 1186
Harvard University. School of Public Health, (I) 1077
Havanera Company, (S) 246, (A) 978
Health Professions Education Foundation, (L) 683
Heller Ehrman White & McAuliffe LLP, (F) 493, (I) 1081
Henry J. Kaiser Family Foundation, (I) 1017, 1103
Henry Luce Foundation, (G) 827, 852
Herbert Scoville Jr. Peace Fellowship Program, (I) 1082
Hewlett–Packard Company, (S) 6, 172, 208, (I) 1086
Higher Education Consortium for Urban Affairs, (F) 489, (I) 1074
Hispanic Alliance for Career Enhancement, (S) 158–159
Hispanic Association of Colleges and Universities, (S) 56, 91, 148, 255, 332, 338, 358, (F) 441, 482, 563, (I) 1075
Hispanic Bar Association of D.C., (I) 1079
Hispanic Chamber of Commerce–Wisconsin, (S) 287–288
Hispanic College Fund, (S) 48, 99, 118, 125, 163, 165, 175, 215, 251, 254, 312, (I) 1083
Hispanic Contractors of Colorado, (S) 166
Hispanic Dental Association, (S) 107, 296, 339, (F) 451, 606, 658
Hispanic Engineer National Achievement Awards Conference, (S) 4, 18, 20, 95, 138, 144, 146, 161, 250, 271, 274, 319, (F) 494
Hispanic Heritage Awards Foundation, (S) 167, (A) 970
Hispanic Lawyers Association of Illinois, (F) 499
Hispanic Link Journalism Foundation, (I) 1085
Hispanic Metropolitan Chamber, (S) 67, 168, (F) 427, 500
Hispanic Public Relations Association, (S) 169
Hispanic Scholarship Fund, (S) 40, 61, 78, 80, 83, 132, 147, 149, 162, 173, 197, 263, 321, (F) 411, 424, 435, 478, 507, 569, (G) 858, (I) 1087
Hispanic Scholarship Fund Institute, (S) 123, 267
Hispanic Theological Initiative, (F) 502, (G) 829–830, (A) 971
HNTB Companies, (S) 192, (I) 1100
Household International, (S) 340, (I) 1194
Howard Hughes Medical Institute, (F) 496, 505, (G) 828, 832, (I) 1139
Howard University, (I) 1017
HRL Laboratories, (F) 570, (I) 1144
Hudson River National Estuarine Research Reserve, (G) 888
Huntington Library, Art Collections, and Botanical Gardens, (G) 813
Hyatt Hotels & Resorts, (S) 174

IBM Corporation, (F) 509, (I) 1088, 1163
ICI Educational Foundation, (S) 175
Idaho Migrant Council, Inc., (S) 176
Idaho Space Grant Consortium, (S) 178, (G) 835–836
Idaho State Board of Education, (S) 177
Idaho State Broadcasters Association, (S) 179
Illinois Arts Council, (G) 837

Illinois Association of Realtors, (S) 181, (F) 510
Illinois Broadcasters Association, (I) 1089
Illinois Department of Public Health. Center for Rural Health, (L) 691
Illinois Migrant Council, (S) 180
Illinois. Office of the Governor, (I) 1097, 1201
Illinois Student Assistance Commission, (L) 690, 696
Image de Seattle, (S) 182, (F) 511
Independent Colleges of Washington, (S) 350, 365
Independent Press Association, (G) 818
Indiana Space Grant Consortium, (G) 838
Indiana State Teachers Association, (S) 96, 217
Indiana University. Minority Faculty Fellowship Program, (G) 868
Infectious Diseases Society of America, (G) 770
INROADS, Inc., (S) 163, (I) 1083, 1090, 1170
Institute for Civil Society, (G) 839
Institute for Diversity in Health Management, (F) 428, 458
Institute for Women's Policy Research, (I) 1093, 1121
Institute of Electrical and Electronics Engineers, (I) 1122, 1207
Institute of Electrical and Electronics Engineers. Circuits and Systems Society, (S) 293
Institute of Food Technologists, (S) 226–227
Institute of Industrial Engineers, (S) 344
Institute of International Education, (G) 764
Institute of Real Estate Management Foundation, (S) 150, (F) 484
Intel Corporation, (S) 6
International Communications Industries Association, Inc., (S) 185–186, 313, (F) 513
International Conference of Symphony and Opera Musicians, (A) 993
Iota Sigma Pi, (S) 42
ITS Washington, (S) 386, (F) 677
Ittleson Foundation, (I) 1124–1125

J. Robert Gladden Society, (F) 515, (G) 844, 958
Jackie Robinson Foundation, (S) 187, 268
Janssen Pharmaceutica Products, L.P., (G) 728
January, (G) 876
Japan Foundation. Center for Global Partnership, (G) 720
JCPenney Company, Inc., (S) 246, (A) 978
Jerome Foundation, (G) 855
John D. and Catherine T. MacArthur Foundation, (F) 623, (G) 923
John F. Kennedy Center for the Performing Arts. American College Theater Festival, (A) 990
John O. Butler Company, (F) 549
John S. and James L. Knight Foundation, (I) 1142
Johnson & Johnson Medical, Inc., (I) 1163
Johnson & Johnson/Merck Consumer Pharmaceuticals, (G) 728
JPMorganChase, (S) 197
Justice Allen E. Broussard Scholarship Foundation, (F) 522

Kaiser Permanente, (F) 466
Kansas Association of Migrant Directors, (S) 152, 198
Kansas Board of Regents, (S) 199, (L) 693
KATU–TV, (S) 200, (I) 1104

S–Scholarships   F–Fellowships   L–Loans   G–Grants   A–Awards   I–Internships

Residency Index

Some programs listed in this book are restricted to residents of a particular city, county, state, or region. Others are open to applicants wherever they may live. The Residency Index will help you pinpoint programs available only to residents in your area as well as programs that have no residency restrictions at all (these are listed under the term "United States"). To use this index, look up the geographic areas that apply to you (always check the listings under "United States"), jot down the entry numbers listed after the program types that interest you (scholarships, fellowships, etc.), and use those numbers to find the program descriptions in the directory. To help you in your search, we've provided some "see also" references in each index entry. Remember: the numbers cited here refer to program entry numbers, not to page numbers in the book.

Tenability Index

Some programs listed in this book can be used only in specific cities, counties, states, or regions. Others may be used anywhere in the United States (or even abroad). The Tenability Index will help you locate funding that is restricted to a specific area as well as funding that has no tenability restrictions (these are listed under the term "United States"). To use this index, look up the geographic areas where you'd like to go (always check the listings under "United States"), jot down the entry numbers listed after the program types (scholarships, fellowships, etc.) that interest you, and use those numbers to find the program descriptions in the directory. To help you in your search, we've provided some "see also" references in each index entry. Remember: the numbers cited here refer to program entry numbers, not to page numbers in the book.

Subject Index

There are hundreds of different subject areas covered in this directory. You can use the Subject Index to identify both the subject focus and the type (scholarships, fellowships, etc.) of available funding programs. To help you pinpoint your search, we've included hundreds of "see" and "see also" references. In addition to looking for terms that represent your specific subject interest, be sure to check the "General programs" entry; hundreds of funding opportunities are listed there that can be used to support study, research, or other activities in *any* subject area (although the programs may be restricted in other ways). Remember: the numbers cited in this index refer to program entry numbers, not to page numbers in the book.

Calendar Index

Since most funding programs have specific deadline dates, some may have already closed by the time you begin to look for money. You can use the Calendar Index to identify which programs are still open. To do that, go to the type of program (scholarships, fellowships, etc.) that interests you, think about when you'll be able to complete your application forms, go to the appropriate months, jot down the entry numbers listed there, and use those numbers to find the program descriptions in the directory. Keep in mind that the numbers cited here refer to program entry numbers, not to page numbers in the book. Note: not all sponsoring organizations supplied deadline information to us, so not all programs are listed in this index.

Scholarships:

January: 31, 34, 46, 50, 52, 68, 78, 83, 98, 105, 116, 124, 129, 135, 143, 147, 154, 194, 204, 221, 224, 226, 235, 249, 253, 265, 270, 286, 293, 299, 308, 311, 326–328, 334, 363, 384

February: 8, 15, 19, 21–22, 24–26, 45, 49, 51, 53, 62, 66–67, 69, 71, 81–82, 96, 100–102, 117, 120, 127, 132–133, 140, 153, 158–159, 167–168, 171, 178, 183–184, 188, 205, 208–209, 211, 216–217, 222, 228, 230, 238, 263, 267, 273, 277, 297, 301, 306, 316–317, 331, 340, 351, 356–357, 361, 367, 371, 374–375, 377, 379, 388

March: 5–6, 37, 42, 54, 60, 63, 74, 97, 111, 113, 123, 126, 136, 141, 150, 152, 160, 166, 170, 172, 174, 179, 187, 192, 195–196, 198, 206, 210, 214, 223, 233, 237, 240, 245, 248, 258–259, 262, 266, 269, 275, 283, 287–288, 290–291, 310, 335–337, 347–348, 352–353, 362, 382–383, 389

April: 4, 13, 18, 20, 23, 30, 40, 48, 55, 58, 65, 73, 79, 84–87, 92, 95, 99, 104, 112, 114, 118, 121, 125, 134, 138, 144, 146, 161, 163, 165, 173, 175–176, 185–186, 199–202, 215, 229, 234, 247, 250–252, 254, 257, 261, 264, 268, 271–272, 274, 282, 298, 300, 303–305, 312–313, 319–320, 323, 329, 342, 355, 359–360, 365, 376, 381

May: 1–2, 28, 35, 38, 41, 44, 56, 64, 72, 90–91, 103, 108, 133, 139, 148, 169, 182, 190, 213, 219, 227, 231, 239, 243–244, 246, 255–256, 292, 294, 307, 314, 322, 332, 338, 358

June: 93, 107, 122, 128, 145, 149, 156, 193, 212, 236, 241, 279, 281, 296, 302, 321, 325, 339

July: 10, 47, 107, 180, 296, 339

August: 89, 225, 349

September: 32, 88, 106, 109, 119, 331, 336, 364, 387

October: 33, 57, 75–77, 80, 142, 157, 205, 220, 232, 260, 284, 289, 341, 350, 370, 385–386

November: 2, 39, 70, 115, 133, 191, 197, 207, 218, 242, 278, 318, 330, 344, 346

December: 9, 29, 61, 94, 110, 162, 189, 295

Any time: 11–12, 43, 155, 164, 181

Fellowships:

January: 413, 417, 430, 439, 445–446, 449, 456, 459, 462, 465, 469–470, 478, 487, 493, 496, 503–506, 518, 534, 537–538, 543, 551, 560–561, 564, 566–567, 595, 598–599, 603, 608–609, 616, 623, 628, 631–632, 641, 646, 662, 668, 672, 674

February: 394, 399, 401, 403, 405, 416, 427, 434, 457, 474, 489, 500, 512, 515–516, 525, 527, 529, 531, 536, 545, 547, 562, 572–573, 581, 584–585, 590, 594, 612, 625, 635, 640, 643, 649–650, 654, 659, 666

March: 393, 395, 397–398, 425, 431, 440, 444, 448, 455, 461, 476, 483–484, 488, 490–491, 495, 499, 520, 522, 535, 542, 546, 552–553, 559, 575, 582, 610, 618, 644, 656, 663–664, 669, 675

April: 402, 407, 411, 419–420, 429, 436, 442, 450, 452, 464, 494, 498, 501, 513, 519, 521, 524, 544, 548, 565, 571, 574, 593, 601, 607, 615, 617, 619, 624, 626, 633–634, 642, 660, 667, 671

May: 391–392, 415, 426, 432, 441, 468, 473, 482, 511, 514, 563, 568, 588, 622, 629, 638

June: 406, 443, 451, 460, 466, 477, 507, 523, 528, 530, 569, 580, 589, 606, 645, 658, 672–673

July: 408, 451, 467, 549, 606, 657–658

August: 400, 438, 461, 553–554, 576, 600

September: 412, 453–454, 472, 508, 533, 614, 648–649, 656, 678

October: 404, 409, 414, 423, 428, 435, 458, 471, 475, 479–481, 485, 525–526, 532, 541, 579, 596, 613, 620, 636, 639, 655, 676–677

November: 392, 410, 439, 463, 492, 502, 514, 539, 550, 555, 557, 570, 583, 601, 604–605, 610, 627, 647

December: 390, 424, 502, 509, 517, 548, 553, 583, 626, 651

Any time: 497, 510, 597, 602, 610

Loans:

January: 704

February: 681, 686, 690, 695–697, 699, 711

March: 693, 700, 712

April: 702–703, 710

May: 679–680, 683, 687, 691

June: 698, 708, 714

July: 701

October: 682–683, 705, 712

November: 684, 688, 707, 709